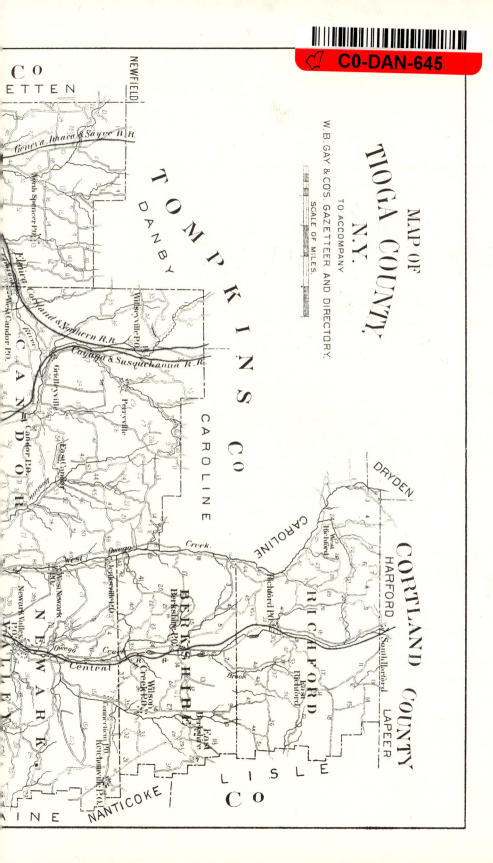

MAP OF
TIOGA COUNTY.
N.Y.

TO ACCOMPANY
W. B. GAY & COS. GAZETTEER AND DIRECTORY.
SCALE OF MILES.

HISTORICAL
GAZETTEER

—OF—

Tioga County, New York,

1785–1888.

Followed By

A Directory of
Tioga County, New York
1887—1888

All having been published previously by

W. B. GAY & CO.

Syracuse, New York — 1887

With added Index to Historical Gazetteer

Tioga County Historical Society
Owego, New York 13827
1985

Reprinted by the
Tioga County Historical Society
110-112 Front Street
Owego, New York 13827

ISBN: 0-932334-73-3
Manufactured in the United States of America

A *quality* product of
HEART OF THE LAKES PUBLISHING
Interlaken, New York 14847
1985

PART FIRST.

HISTORICAL

GAZETTEER

—OF—

Tioga County, New York,

1785–1888.

COMPILED AND EDITED

—BY—

W. B. GAY,

EDITOR OF SIMILAR WORKS FOR RUTLAND, ADDISON, CHITTENDEN, FRANKLIN,. GRAND ISLE, LAMOILLE, ORLEANS, WINDSOR, ESSEX, CALEDONIA, AND WINDHAM COUNTIES, IN VERMONT, BERKSHIRE AND HAMPSHIRE COUNTIES, IN MASSACHUSETTS, AND CHESHIRE, AND GRAFTON COUN- TIES, IN NEW HAMPSHIRE.

PERMANENT OFFICE   -   -   -   SYRACUSE, N. Y.

" He that hath much to do, will do something wrong, and of that wrong must suffer the consequences ; and if it were possible that he should always act rightly, yet when such num- bers are to judge of his conduct. the bad will censure and obstruct him by malevolence, and. the good sometimes by mistake."—SAMUEL JOHNSON.

PUBLISHED BY

W. B. GAY & CO.,

SYRACUSE, N. Y.

ERRATA.

PART FIRST.

In seventh line, second paragraph, page 192, read 1851, for "1857."
In eighth line from bottom, page 192, read Hull for "Hall."
In tenth line from bottom, page 383, read 1876, for "1776."
In ninth line, second paragraph, page 387, read Mrs. Lovejoy for "Mr. Lovejoy."
In second line, second paragraph, page 388, read comprise for "confine."
In fifth line, second paragraph, page 391, read Wheeler H. for "George W."
With reference to Mr. LeRoy W. Kingman's history of the town of Owego, we wish to make an explanation, fearing that we have left some points ambiguous. On page 361, we say: "This completes the biographical sketches furnished by Mr. Kingman," etc., and, "We add the following additional sketches." The latter sketches end with the heading, "Business Centers," on page 383, and Mr. Kingman's sketch continues, the remainder of the history being his matter, except an interpolation of a brief sketch of the "present business interests," page 391, and "physicians," page 393, by the Publishers. We make this explanation to justly relieve Mr. Kingman from the responsibility of authorship of any facts we may have inserted in his sketch.

PART SECOND.

In the town of Spencer, page 185, should have been inserted the following : Brock Thomas, president Farmers' and Merchants' Bank. stock dealer, farmer 50, in Chemung county 450, and in Tompkins county 50. h VanEtten.

GENERAL CONTENTS.

INDEX TO ILLUSTRATIONS.

INTRODUCTION.

In presenting to the public the "Historical Gazetteer and Directory" of Tioga county, we desire to return our sincere thanks to *all* who have kindly aided in obtaining the information it contains, and rendered it possible to present it in the brief space of time in which it is essential such works should be completed. Especially are our thanks due to the editors and managers of the county papers for the uniform kindness they have evinced in calling public attention to our efforts, and for essential aid in furnishing material for the work. We have also found valuable aid in the following: Judge Avery's "Susquehanna Valley" papers; Everts' "History of Four Counties;" French's "Gazetteer of New York;" Child's "Gazetteer of Broome and Tioga Counties;" Wilkinson's "Annals of Binghamton;" Hon. W. F. Warner's "Centennial History;" and in various pamphlets and manuscripts, while those who have aided us by extended personal effort we have credited in the pages where their work occurs.

That errors have occurred in so great a number of names is probable, and that names have been omitted which should have been inserted is quite certain. We can only say that we have exercised more than ordinary diligence and care in this difficult and complicated feature of book-making. Of such as feel aggrieved in consequence of errors or omissions, we beg pardon, and ask the indulgence of the reader in noting such as have been observed in the subsequent reading of the proofs and which are found corrected in the *Errata.*

It was designed to give a brief account of all the church and other societies in the county, but owing in some cases to the negligence of those who were able to give the necessary information, and in others to the inability of any one to do so, we have been obliged to omit special notices of a few.

We would suggest that our patrons observe and become familiar with the explanations at the commencement of the Directory on page 3, Part Second. The names it embraces, and the information connected therewith, were obtained by actual canvass, and are as correct and reliable as the judgment of those from whom they were solicited renders possible. Each agent is furnished with a map of the town he is expected to canvass, and he is required to pass over every road and call at every dwelling and place of business in the town in order to obtain the facts from the individuals concerned, whenever possible.

The margins have been left broad to enable anyone to note changes opposite the names.

While thanking our patrons and friends generally for the cordiality with which our efforts have been seconded, we leave the work to secure that favor which earnest endeavor ever wins from a discriminating public, hoping tney will bear in mind, should errors be noted, that "he who expects a perfect work to see, expects what ne'er was, is, nor yet shall be."

W. B. GAY.
M. F. ROBERTS.

GAZETTEER

OF

TIOGA COUNTY, NEW YORK.

*CHAPTER I.

"Tribes of the solemn League! from ancient seats
Swept by the whites like autumn leaves away,
Faint are your records of heroic feats
And few the traces of your former sway."—HOSMER.†

ABORIGINES, ORIGIN AND ANTIQUITY OF—THE CARANTOUANNAIS—THE
ONNON-TIOGAS—THE IROQUOIS—INDIAN WARS—LAND TITLES—INDIAN
VILLAGE AT OWEGO—TIOGA POINT—SIR WILLIAM JOHNSON'S EXPEDI-
TION—THE REVOLUTION—SULLIVAN'S EXPEDITION—CLOSE OF INDIAN
DOMINION.

ETHNOLOGY has no more inviting and yet more difficult
field of inquiry than that pertaining to the origin and history of those aboriginal races, which for unknown ages
prior to the advent of the European, had occupied, and swayed
the destinies of the American continent. A puzzle to the scholar
and antiquary for nearly four centuries, and giving rise to various
theories which have generally proved far more ingenious than
convincing; nevertheless it has been by no means a fruitless

---

*Prepared by Prof. James Riker, of Waverly, member of the historical societies of
New York, Long Island, Massachusetts, Pennsylvania and Wisconsin, the N. E. Hist. and
Gen. Soc., and N. Y. Gen. and Biog. Soc.; and author of *Annals of Newtown, History of
Harlem, St. Bartholomew, 1572, Capt. Van Arsdale and Evacuation Day, 1783,* etc.

†These lines, which head a chapter of the late Judge Charles P. Avery's, *The Susquehanna Valley,* (page 244, *St. Nicholas* magazine), are from a poem by Col. William Howe
Cuyler Hosmer, who married a sister of Judge Avery. He was born at Avon, N. Y., in
1815, and was well known as the "Bard of Avon."

2*

study. By the reflex light of Indian tradition and history, and the concurrent testimony of the mounds, defensive works, war weapons, domestic utensils, tumuli, and other surviving relics of those races, we read, in faint but pathetic outline, the strange story of nations once numerous and powerful, but long since dispossessed or exterminated.

A statement of some general conclusions arrived at by eminent students of Indian archeology will be found to have a bearing upon the special inquiry before us. Wilson, in his work entitled *Prehistoric Man*, concurring in an opinion advanced long before his time, observes: "Some analogies confirm the probability of a portion of the North American stock having entered the continent from Asia by Behring's straits or the Aleutian islands, and more probably by the latter than the former." But Morgan, in his *Indian Migrations*, emphasizes this opinion, by cogent arguments, which tend to prove that the aboriginal peopling of North America began at the northwest coast and spread by degrees southward and eastward, till, in process of time, the remotest portions of the continent were occupied. That this race was of Tartar origin, many analogies and evidences seem to prove,— "physical considerations, and the types of man in northeastern Asia point to this section of Asia as the source, and to the Aleutian islands as the probable avenue, of this antecedent migration." But again, "the systems of consanguinity and affinity of several Asiatic stocks agree with that of the American aborigines." This remarkable fact bears with equal force upon the original identity of the North American tribes, affording, says Morgan, " the strongest evidence yet obtained of the unity of origin of the Indian nations within the region we have defined." And this is further strengthened by the uniform agreement in the structure of their languages, and their stage of development,—though the languages themselves form many dialects, of which the Algonquin and the Iroquois are taken as the two principal representative groups.

The multiplication of tribes, the differences of dialect and location, the division and subdivision into the roving Indians, who subsisted by fishing, hunting and war, and the village tribes, whose maintenance was chiefly from agriculture, were but the results of time, and the struggle for supremacy inseparable from the barbaric state. The former of these two classes were necessarily the more numerous and warlike, the latter more advanced in the knowledge of useful arts. From a variety of considerations we may conclude that for ages before its discovery by Columbus, the American continent was the scene of sanguinary wars, a perpetual and fierce struggle for the mastery, which could only result in the subjugation, expulsion, or extinction of the weaker, and in the temporary elevation of the stronger race. A natural result was to render these nations unstable in their possessions, which were theirs only so long as they could hold them per force of numbers and arms. It has been argued with much probability, that the Indians found in central New York, when first known to Europeans, were only the successors of other peoples of more ancient date, and farther advanced than they in the arts of civilized life. But at what era, or by what agency, the more cultured race had been made to succumb to the ruder tribes subsequently found here, is unknown to history.

It is this reign of barbarism, and deadly strife for supremacy, which at once confronts us upon our earliest introduction to this immediate locality, whose history we are now considering. At the dawn of the sixteenth century, it was within the domain of a tribe of savages, whom Champlain, * with his imperfect knowledge of this people, denominates the *Carantouannais*, and which, from its French suffix, would mean, the people of Carantouan; but we strongly suspect the term to be nothing else than an attempt at the name *Susquehanna*.

They were reputed to be a very warlike clan, and able to keep at bay the numerous foes who dwelt around them, though, according to Champlain, they composed but three villages. These were quite distant from each other, along the Susquehanna and Chemung rivers, but were all fortified towns. The principal one, their chief stronghold, occupied that singular eminence near Waverly, familiarly known as "Spanish Hill." Another of these towns was located, according to a reliable authority, † at the northern angle of the junction of Sugar creek with the Susquehanna river, in the borough of North Towanda; the third town, probably, being the well known work on the south side of the Chemung river, near Elmira. They thus commanded the stretch of country now comprising the three adjoining counties,—Tioga and Chemung, and Bradford, in Pennsylvania. Their principal seat, before mentioned, bore the Indian name of *Onnon-tioga*, sig-

---

* *Les Voyages de la Nouvelle France*, Paris, 1632. See extracts, translated, in *Documentary History of New York*, vol. 3, p. 1.

† Gen. John S. Clark, of Auburn, N. Y., to whom we are indebted for having first indicated the sites occupied by these Indian villages. See *Waverly Advocate*, May 17, 1878.

nifying *the village on the hill between the rivers;* the intervale below, where Athens is now situated, being simply called Tioga,— pronounced *te-yoge-gah,*—and meaning *between the rivers,* or *at the forks.* These three villages, says Champlain, lay in the midst of more than twenty others, against which they waged war. Among these he no doubt includes the Iroquois, who were hostile to the Onnon-tiogas, from whom their nearest castles were only about thirty miles distant.

To the northward of the Onnon-tiogas was a large country, then famous for " the deer and beaver hunting,"—its limits the shores of Lake Ontario, but reaching westward to the Genesee river, and eastward down the Mohawk. Here lay the scattered castles and settlements of the Iroquois, otherwise called the Five Nations, who at no remote period anterior to this date, had been driven from the northern side of the lake and the north bank of the St. Lawrence, by the then more warlike Adirondacks, of Canada, a branch of the Algonquin race.

The Iroquois, with their congeners, the Hurons, Eries, Susque-hannas, etc., were marked by language and personal traits suffi-cient to distinguish them from the numerous other tribes classed under the generic term of Algonquins ; but it has been ably argued that they too were of Tartar or Asiatic extraction. The rough handling they had received from the Adirondacks produced a mortal enmity, and wrought a marvelous change in the Iroquois, who by giving themselves to a regular course of training, from being simple cornplanters, became brave and ex-pert wariors. Supplied with firearms, through their traffic with the Dutch traders on the Hudson, the skill they acquired in the use of this new weapon, soon made them more than a match for their enemies, and wholly diverted them to war and conquest. Among the first to feel the weight of their arms were the adja-cent Shaouonons (whom Schoolcraft makes the same as the Shawnees), within whose limits, as would appear, they had tres-passed when they fled thither from the Adirondacks. These were no insignificant foe,—so warlike, haughty and cruel, that the Dutch called them *Satanas!* Victory, however, turned in favor of the invincible Iroquois, who drove the Satanas from their lands, and forced them to retire westward, save a portion of the tribe which submitted to the conquerors and became tributary. This conquest, which dated about the year 1620, extended the area of the Iroquois country (beginning with the Onondagas), to a dis-tance of " sixty miles" southward from Lake Ontario, and west-

ward to Niagara.* Fired by success, the Iroquois, and especially the Mohawks, thirsted to avenge themselves upon the Adirondacks, and in a series of encounters the latter were finally van-
quished and almost annihilated. The Mohawks also subdued
the Mohicans, on the upper Hudson, subsequently completing
their subjugation by pursuing them down that river nearly to
Manhattan, and destroying their castles at Wickquaskeek, in Westchester. Meanwhile the other four tribes,—the Onondaga,
Oneida, Cayuga and Seneca,—turned their arms, in 1653, against
a tribe occupying the southeastern boader of Lake Erie, and
hence called the Eries, or otherwise (from Erie which signifies
cat), the Cat Indians. This name is given by the Canadians to
the Shawnees, and which favors the belief that the Eries were no
other than the expelled Satanas, still unsubdued, and whom the
relentless Iroquois were bound to extirpate. Two years completed this conquest ; and it would appear that it was immediately
followed by the final war upon, and overthrow of the Onnon-
tiogas, seated as before stated, upon the Susquehanna and Chemung rivers.

If the Onnon-tiogas were of Algonquin stock, it would account
for the enmity the Iroquois had shown toward this tribe for at
least a half century ; but if they were Susquehannas, as we think
they were, and who, according to Morgan, were congener to
the Iroquois, then we probably find the reason for this hostility
in a family feud ; and what wars have been more bitter and
more deadly than those waged between kindred ? However, it
happened that Champlain, governor of Canada, unwisely took up
the quarrel of the Adirondacks with the Iroquois, as early as 1609.
Entering the Mohawk country, by way of the Sorel river, he met
and defeated a party of Mohawks, on the bank of Lake Champlain, who fled in dismay at the discharge of muskets, it being
their first introduction to this deadly weapon, afterwards made
so efficient in their hands. Six years later (1615), Champlain,
with a force of French, Adirondacks and Hurons, made a descent
by way of Lake Ontario, upon the castle of the Onondagas. The
invaders had an offer from the Onnon-tiogas to assist them with
five hundred of their wariors, and when Champlain was ready,
he dispatched messengers to inform that distant tribe that he had

---

*By referring to a map of the state, it will be seen that this conquest must have reached
a line nearly identical with the northern limits of the southern tier of counties. At that
date, therefore, Tioga county was not yet a part of the Iroquois country. See a deed in
Doc. Hist. of N. Y., I : 773.

begun his march, so they might meet at the same time before the enemy's fort. The party, consisting of twelve of the most resolute Indians and a French interpeter named Stephen Brule, proceeded in canoes across the lake and reached Onnon-tioga by a circuitous route, which they took for fear of being intercepted by the Chouatouarouon, or otherwise the Cayugas. The Onnon-tiogas gave them a warm greeting, entertaining them with feasting and dancing, as was their custom. But so much time was thus wasted, that the reinforcement did not reach the fort until two days after Champlain had abandoned the siege. The party therefore returned to Onnon-tioga, accompanied by Brule, who spent the winter with them, and in visiting neighboring tribes; during which he descended the Susquehanna to the sea, returning again to his new-made friends, the Onnon-tiogas, and of all which he afterwards gave Champlain a full account. He described the castle at Onnon-tioga as situated in a beautiful and rich country, in a commanding position, well fortified by earthworks and pallisades, after the manner of the Hurons, and containing more than eight hundred warriors.

This attempt of the Onnon-tiogas to aid the Adirondacks against the Iroquois only aroused the latter to new acts of hostility, and the former were soon after assailed by a party of Mohawks and their Mohican allies, who had descended the north branch of the Susquehanna, and with whom were several adventurous Dutchmen from the trading post on the Hudson. But the assailants were repulsed, and three Dutchmen were taken prisoners. The Onnon-tiogas, never having seen any of this nation, took them for Frenchmen, and therefore spared their lives, and conveyed them to the coast, by the Susquehanna and Delaware rivers, where falling in with a Dutch explorer, Capt. Hendricksen, he procured their ransom.

It only remained for the Iroquois to effectually arm himself with the resistless musket, in order to deal the final blow to the hated Onnon-tiogas. Of the details of this tragic event, history is silent. It is only intimated that they " were conquered and incorporated with the Five Nations." Doubtless they were driven from their position with slaughter, and their strong works demolished, of which some of the *debris* was visible long after this section was settled by the whites, and parts of the earthworks being even yet plainly traceable.* It may be inferred that the

---

*SPANISH HILL.—The earliest mention of this name I have found, is in Gordon's *Gazetteer*, 1836, though his predecessor Stafford, in 1813, speaks of the hill, as from 100 to

Onondagas and Cayugas were the chief instruments in their sub-jugation, as these two tribes, a little later, claim the land along the Susquehanna; saying that it belongs to them alone, and that "the other three nations, viz: the Senecas, Oneidas and Maquaas, have nothing to do with it."

Flushed with victory, the Iroquois led their devastating war parties down the Susquehanna, scattering the nations on its banks, till in 1676, their conquests here culminated in the overthrow of the Andastes, a part of the Susquehannas, and then "the sole enemies remaining on their hands," and by the destruction of their castles. The neighboring Delawares had also submitted to the conquerors, being stripped of all rights in their lands, forbid-den to use arms, and reduced to the condition of "women." Subsequently, however, their "uncles," the Six Nations, assigned them a home at Tioga, "and lighted a council fire there."

But we have no need longer to follow the fierce Iroquois in the bloody war-path, which was kept well trodden till their insatiate greed of conquest had subjugated the most distant tribes; it is enough for our purpose to have shown in what manner this sec-tion of country whose history we are reviewing, came to pass under their iron domination.

Another contest now opened, bloodless but obstinate, waged to settle the question, which of the English colonies should reap

---

110 feet high, "and which correspondents describe as apparently a work of art." But in neither of his two editions does Stafford give its name; an omission calculated to cast doubt upon its supposed antiquity. Yet with a knowledge of the fact that Spanish adven-turers, in the sixteenth century, explored many parts of our country in search of gold, and actually pushed their search to the shores o Lake Ontario, one can scarcely resist the conviction that the name of Spanish Hill has some association with those old gold seekers. Gordon states that at that date (1836), on the summit of the hill were "vestiges of fortifica-tions, displaying much skill in the art of defense, having regular intrenchments, which per-fectly commanded the bend of the river." And, says Hon. W. F. Warner, "this breastwork is still easily and distinctly traceable around the entire brow of the hill, even now, after fifty years of cultivation of the surface. It was of considerable height before the plateau was denuded of its trees, and must have been a formidable work. Well defined remains of an inner fortifica-tion may also be seen at the center of the hill, extending from the steeper part on the east side, to the steeper part on the west side." General Clark finds by actual survey "that the area enclosed by the embankment contains abont ten acres." At the west side of the hill, upon a plateau near its base, are also remains of an Indian burying ground. "That a frightful contest took place at or near Spanish Hill," says Mr. Warner, "is more than prob-able; * * it is also a well established fact, that the Indians had a superstitious fear about the hill, so strong that they would not go upon it. So sanguinary a contest, while it would have added to the glory and courage of the Iroquois, still would have left in the savage mind a horror of the spot where so many of their braves had fallen." Mr. Warner here refers to a supposed battle between the savages and Spaniards, and whence the hill may have taken its name. But leaving the derivation of the name out of the question, as too uncer-tain; would not the slaughter by the Iroquois of their own kinsmen, the Onnon-tiogas, better account for that peculiar dread, which, we are told, the sight of the hill always inspired in the Indians? We suggest this with much deference to our esteemed townsman, whose views upon our local antiquities are not to be lightly set aside.

the most advantage from the Iroquois conquests; New York and
Pennsylvania were the chief contestants. It was argued that if
the latter province got control of the Susquehanna river, she would
also control the trade with the Iroquois, and divert it from
Albany to Philadelphia. As the fur trade was a mine of wealth
to the Albanians, and told upon the prosperity of the whole
province, it was of great consequence to secure it. New York
had greatly the advantage from the length of time she had
enjoyed this trade; and from having kept unbroken the "cove-
nants of friendship" made with the Iroquois tribes as early as
1623, when Albany was first colonized. The Cayugas, who with
the Onondagas claimed the conquered lands on the Susquehanna,
were at first willing and urgent to have some white men settle
upon that river, for their greater convenience in trading; but
the Albanians, for obvious reasons, brought every influence to
bear to prevent it, and were successful. In the year 1679, the
Cayugas and Onondagas, in virtue of their sole ownership, proceeded to make over these conquered lands to the government
of New York; and four years later, while William Haig, agent
for Penn, was at Albany, trying to effect a purchase of those
lands, these tribes formally ratified "the gift and conveyance"
to New York, by an instrument dated September 26, 1683. It
included all the conquered country upon the Susquehanna, as
far down as the *Washinta*, or Falls, and therefore covered the
present Tioga county.* The Indians "accepted in full satisfaction : a half piece of duffels cloth ; two blankets ; two guns; three
kettles : four coats ; fifty pounds of lead ; twenty-five pounds of
powder." To which was added the promise: "the Governor
will compensate you therefor, when occasion permits."

The effect of this transfer was to exclude white settlers from
this region of country, and to extend over it, for another full
century, the long dismal night of aboriginal barbarism. Very
little is known of the Indian history of Tioga county during
this period. On the Susquehanna, which skirts or intersects its
southern tier of townships, and at that time served as a great
highway for Indian travel, was the only known Indian town and
planting grounds within the county limits,—*Owegy*, or Owego ;

---

* Morgan, in the *League of the Iroquois*, a high authority, places this county within the
territority of the Cayugas and Onondagas. Next eastward of the latter were the Tuscaroras, a tribe expelled from South Carolina in 1712, and received by the Iroquois, who
thence became the Six Nations. The Onondagas gave the Tuscaroras a part of their
country.

while the interior was a primeval wild of stately forest, and reserved as hunting grounds, where the ingenious beaver built his dam thwart purling stream, and the bear, wolf and panther, the timid elk and deer, roamed freely at will. In the nature of the case, its history, what there was of it, could deal only in exploits of the hunter, the march and counter-march of savage hordes, and in deeds of carnage and cruelty, which, if known, would be only too painful to recite.

Tioga Point, occupied by Delawares, was a famous stopping-place for the Indians when on their expeditions; from it radiated their well-beaten trails, east, west, north and south, to the remotest tribes and localities. The occupation of the Point by the Delawares, dated from 1742. There lived and ruled their king, Tiedescung, a shrewd and influential chief, who in 1755, during the French war, incited his Indians to bloody raids upon the English settlements. After two years he made peace, when he removed his seat to Wyoming. The same year other bands of hostiles, formed about Tioga, fell upon the frontier settlements of Orange and Ulster counties. In 1763, war was renewed by a fearful massacre, committed by the Delawares at Wyoming. Early the next year, Sir William Johnson, Indian agent on the Mohawk, sent two hundred Oneidas and Tuscaroras to chastise them, and who, on February 26th, surprised a large party on their way to attack our settlements, led by a son of King Tiedescung, the noted Captain Bull, whose hatred of the whites was intense, and had led him to do them great injury. Bull and forty of his men were taken prisoners. Thereupon the Delawares fled from the Susquehanna and its vicinity, escaping up the Chemung to the country of the Genesees, a sub-tribe of the Senecas, by whom they had been encouraged to take up the hatchet. Another party sent out by Johnson, followed in the wake of the fugitives, and destroyed the villages Coshocton and Canisteo. They also burnt three towns and four villages on and near the Susquehanna river, with quantities of corn. Peace again followed.

But the first notes of the Revolution was a signal for the uprising of the Six Nations, whose tribes, save only the Oneidas and Tuscaroras, espoused the British cause. In the spring of 1777, a large body of these, numbering about seven hundred warriors, assembled in camp near Owego,* ready to strike a blow at the

---

* At this date Owego was a large Indian village of about twenty houses. It was burnt August 19, 1779, with its fields of standing corn, by order of General Clinton, on his way

unprotected settlements, on the advance of an expected British force up the Hudson; but upon the approach of St. Leger from the north, these Indians went to his assistance, which was followed by a repulse at Oriskany, and at Fort Schuyler, by an inglorious flight. These hostile tribes now found it safe to retreat westward to the Seneca country and the British post at Niagara. From this quarter came all the aggressive movements of the Indians against our frontier settlements during that war. It was by way of the Chemung and Susquehanna that the infamous John Butler, with his Indians and Tories (embarking on floats and rafts at Tioga Point), proceeded in 1778 to the fearful massacre at Wyoming. The noted chief, Joseph Brant, to whom many of the horrors of that period are justly attributed, did not participate in the Wyoming tragedy, being then on an expedition to burn Springfield at the head of Otsego lake; but he took part, the same season, in the ruthless massacre at Cherry Valley. In the interim since the affair at Wyoming, Colonel Hartley, of the Continental forces, ascended the Susquehanna, as far as Tioga Point, where he burnt the Indian village of about twenty houses, having also destroyed Queen Esther's castle, which stood a little below, on the west side of the Susquehanna, and was the seat of that noted squaw chieftain.

By the same route, the Chemung and Susquehanna, the Indians and rangers, under Brant and Butler, proceeded in 1779, to the bloody battle of Minisink. Brant met and joined this expedition as he was returning from the ravage of Fantin-kill, in Ulster county. The speedy retribution visited upon these murderous bands, by General Sullivan's forces, the same year, when they were signally defeated at Newtown, and their country devastated, is too well known to require any further notice here. It was a blow from which the Indians never recovered, though petty depredations, by small parties from Niagara, who passed this way to reach the white settlements, were kept up till the close of the war. The very next year Brant came through here, with some sixty of his warriors, destined for Schoharie. Crossing the Susquehanna at Tioga Point, on rafts, he detached eleven Indians on the trail to Minisink, to secure prisoners or scalps, which latter, at Niagara, would bring them eight dollars apiece.

---

down the river to join Sullivan. The Indians had deserted it on his approach. " This is the Indian town that Sergeant Hunter was carried to, who was taken 10th November last [1778] below Cherry Valley, on this same river, as he was returning with his Scout." *Sullivan's Indian Expedition*, p. 202.

Brant, when within thirty miles of the fort at Schoharie, surprised a party who had gone out under Captain Alex. Harper, to scout, and also to make maple sugar. Three of these were killed in the first onslaught, and the rest taken prisoners ; their lives being spared only through the *finesse* of Captain Harper, who was personally known to Brant. With his captives Brant returned to Tioga Point and had gone a little way up the Chemung, when the whooping of his Indians was suddenly answered by the startling *death yell!* It proceeded from some of the party who had gone to Minisink. They had succeeded in taking five white men, and had brought them as far as the east side of the Susquehanna, opposite Tioga Point, when, during the night, the anxious prisoners managed to loosen their bands, and to dispatch nine of the sleeping Indians, with their own tomahawks. The other two, one of whom was badly wounded, fled, crossed the river, and were resting near Chemung, when Brant's party came up. On hearing what had happened, the infuriated Indians were for killing their prisoners at once ; when strangely enough, the unhurt survivor of the Minisink party, who was a chief, and had known the prisoners at Schoharie, interposed and saved their lives. They were then taken on to Niagara.

With the close of the war, in 1783, which put an end, not only to these atrocities, but to Indian dominion in this fair region, and opened it to civilization, we must conclude this summary of its aboriginal history.

Much has been said laudatory of the Iroquois; writers have been fascinated with the genius of their confederacy, the wisdom and eloquence of their counsellors, and the extent of their dominion. But let calm reason prevail. They are worthy of as much admiration as an Alexander, or a Napoleon, ambitious, rapacious conquerors, who waded through seas of blood to the acquisition of spoils, territory, power and glory. An occasional instance of justice or humanity will not suffice to hide from view the savage butcheries which mainly fill up the Indian annals. That, as human, they were not devoid of generous instincts, none will deny, and a consideration of their better characteristics, curious customs and home life, might have relieved in some degree the dark picture here presented ; but as the Indian tribes differed but little in these respects, it has been deemed unnecessary to repeat, in this brief essay, details already familiar to most readers.

CHAPTER II.

THE BOSTON PURCHASE*—COXE'S MANOR—TOWNSHIP OF HAMBDEN
FORMED—GOSPEL TRACTS—NEW TOWN ERECTED IN MONTGOMERY
COUNTY—WATKINS AND FLINT PURCHASE.

NO MAN of the present generation had a better opportunity
to study the history of this region than the late Judge
Charles P. Avery, of Owego, and no man was better quali-
fied to write it. In 1853 he published a series of articles, under the
general title of *The Susquehanna Valley*, in the *St. Nicholas*, a literary magazine published monthly at Owego. So few copies of
this magazine are now known to exist, and so few of our readers
can have access to them, that for their benefit we quote a few para-
graphs from the number for December, 1853, pages 297–303.

"Soon after the close of the revolutionary war, Massachusetts
claimed, under her original charter from the crown, a large body
of land lying within the limits of the State of New York. In the
final disposition of this claim, by award of arbitrators in 1786,
that state became the owner, subject, of course to the Indian title,
of several millions of acres lying in the western part of our state,
and also 230,400 acres upon the Susquehanna river, lying between
the Chenango river and the Owego creek, then called a river,
and embracing in extent, very nearly the westerly half of the
county of Broome, and the easterly half of the county of Tioga,
as the boundaries of these two counties now are.

"That claim of Massachusetts forms a link, not an unimportant
one, in the chain of interesting events which mark the early history of our state. By reason of its general interest a brief space
may therefore be devoted profitably to a statement of the grounds
upon which it was based; and inasmuch as its history will serve
to elucidate some important facts directly connected with the
pioneer opening of this portion of the Susquehanna valley, a cur-
sory examination of its historical features seems peculiarly
adapted to our 'Gleanings.'

"In the year 1606 a grant of land lying chiefly within the present limits of the United States was made by James I., king of
England. It comprised in width upon the Atlantic sea-board, all
the land between the fortieth and forty-eighth degrees, north latitude, and extending in a belt of that width, westerly from sea to

---

* Prepared by D. Williams Patterson, genealogist, of Newark Valley, whose extensive
researches into the history of the settlement and growth of this section have brought him a
knowledge of the subject equalled by that of none other.

sea. It was known as the Plymouth Grant, for the reason that it was made to persons many of whom lived in Plymouth, England.

"The Crown gave to the great Plymouth council, as it was called, which was incorporated in the year 1620, the right to transfer any portions of this land, comprised within those degrees of latitude, in such parcels or quantities as the council might deem best. Accordingly, in the year 1628, the Massachusetts Bay grant was made in due form, the boundaries of which were the Merrimac on the north, the Charles river on the south, 'and in that width running west from the Atlantic ocean to the South sea on the west part.' This was confirmed as a charter by Charles I., in the year 1629.

"Next in order came the Connecticut grant of 1630, which was like the preceding one, part and parcel of the Plymouth grant, and, like it, its easterly and westerly limits were 'the two seas.' This was renewed and confirmed by Charles II., in 1662, with the usual charter to establish a government, make laws, etc. The southeast corner of the State of New York, lying within the north and south lines of this grant was never claimed to have been included within it ; for that portion of our state at the time it was originally made by the Plymouth council, as well as at the time when it was confirmed, was possessed and owned by the Dutch.

"It may be mentioned in this connection, that the grant made afterward, (in 1681), by Charles II. to William Penn, of the territory included within the limits of Pennsylvania conflicted with this previously granted and confirmed Connecticut charter, out of which conflicting claims that long train of troublesome and bloody affairs eminated at Wyoming, known as the Yankee and Pennamite feud, commencing before and resumed after the revolutionary war, between the settlers holding under those respective titles.

"Our New York charter dates in 1664, having been given by Charles II. to his brother the Duke of York and Albany, in honor of whom, after the surrender of the island of Manhattan by the Dutch, to the English, the city of New York, before that called New Amsterdam, took its present name. Soon afterward, upon the reduction of Fort Orange, where Albany is now situated, that place received its present name, also in honor of the Duke.

"At the close of the revolutionary struggle Massachusetts formally interposed her claim, under her royal charter of 1628, which was dated, as will be observed, prior to the one confirmed to the Duke of York, and insisted upon her legal right to a belt of land lying in the state of New York, comprised within the northern and southern bounds of her original grant, extending across the State of New York, and, by its terms from 'sea to sea.'

"The state of New York resisted the claim, but both parties were too patriotic to make it the cause of civil strife. The blood of their sons had scarcely yet grown cold which had been profusely shed upon a common altar. They peaceably petitioned con-gress for the appointment of commissioners to examine the res-pective claims and make a final arbitrament which, it was agreed, should be binding upon both.

" Ten commissioners* were appointed, pursuant to the petition, in whom the parties in difference had the utmost confidence, for they were men of established integrity, and known ability, and the two states appeared before them, by their agents and counsel, at Hartford, in November, 1786. Their award was, in substance, that New York should cede to Massachusets the right of pre-emption of the soil from the native Indians, and all other estate, except government, sovereignty, and jurisdiction, to a large body of land lying in the western part of our state, containing more than three millions of acres, and also to 230,400 acres lying, as before stated, upon the Susquehanna, and particularly described in the award as follows: ' To be located to the northward of and adjoining to the lands granted respectively to Daniel Coxe and Robert Lettice Hooper, and their respective associates, and between the rivers Owego, and Chenango.'

" Confining our attention to the body of land embraced within these two streams, as more intimately connected with the general object of this series of articles, it is seen that, over it, the award secured to New York exclusive jurisdictional rights, incident to sovereignty, while it gave to Massachusetts the right of negotia-tion with, and purchase from our Indian predecessors—the origi-nal lords of the soil.

" It was also provided by the award that Massachusetts should have the right to hold treaties with the Indians on the lands, and with such *armed force*, as might be deemed necessary for the more effectual holding of any treaty or conference ; also that a copy of the proceedings of every treaty and of every grant from Massachusetts to any individual should be recorded in the office of the Secretary of the State of New York, within six months after such treaty or grant.

" The Indians having been always viewed and treated as an independent power, although living within our borders, and, after the revolutionary war, as helpless as tenants at sufferance, still no negotiation or agreement with them, as a nation, would have been deemed valid, unless approved by the President and Senate of the United States—the treaty making power. Their approval was an indispensable pre-requisite, and, as a power, delegated by the states under the National Constitution, paramount to all claims on the part of the states of Massachusetts or New York, under their colonial charters or otherwise.

" The body of land lying between the Owego creek and the Chenango river, being the 230,400 acres awarded to Massachus-

---

" * They were John Lowell, James Sullivan, Theophilus Parsons, Rufus King, James Duane, Robert R. Livingston, Robert Yates, John Haring, Melancthon Smith, and Egbert Benson."

etts and since known and designated as the Boston Purchase or Ten Townships, was granted by that state to Samuel Brown, of Stockbridge, Berkshire county, Massachusetts, and his associates. Nearly all of the grantees resided at the time of the purchase in that county, and many of them in that town. The title was conveyed by resolution of the legislature of that state, and approved by the Governor, November 7, 1787. Among other things it states the purchase price to have been 3,333 Spanish milled dollars, payable in two years and subject to a deduction of the sum necessarily paid by the grantees to the natives in extinguishment of their claim. It recites also that Samuel Brown and three other grantees, viz.: Elijah Brown, Orringh Stoddard, and Joseph Raymond, on behalf of the company had purchased, on the 22d day of June preceding, the right of the natives, and fully extinguished their claims.

"Another fact is gleaned from this documentary evidence of historical interest to those now living upon the McMaster Half-Township, on which the village and a portion of the town of Owego is situated. The resolution recites that James McMaster was found in possession of a part of the tract, by the four gentlemen above named, at the time of their negotiation and treaty with the Indians, and that to quiet his claims Samuel Brown had entered into a contract to convey to him that half-township, the bounds of which, as set forth in the legislative resolve, will be hereafter given. It is scarcely necessary to say that it was part and parcel of the body of land to which the Massachusetts purchasers were then seeking to get the title. McMaster, by the help of Amos Draper, an enterprising trader and a man of great influence with the natives, had already ingratiated himself to such an extent with them that he was found at this time, as it appears, in actual possession, and unless conciliated by Brown and his friends, those two gentlemen, by their already great and increasing influence might at the least embarrass, if they did not interpose an effectual barrier to the consummation of any treaty with or cession of land from the Indians. Their claims to a portion of the land were certainly equitable on the score of priority, and feeling this they were not backward in using the superior advantage which their familiar footing with the natives gave them. The other party, it is true, could offer more gold, and the strong arm of government was on their side, but Indian fidelity was equal to the test, and the covenant-chain with McMaster and Draper was kept bright.

"A fact substantiating this good faith on the part of the natives and tallying well with the provision in favor of McMaster in the legislative resolve has been handed down by tradition. Having received it from two independent sources, the writer thinks it authentic and of sufficient interest to be repeated. The account is that four gentlemen, acting on behalf of the Massachusetts purchasers, met the Indians in council at the mouth of the O-le-out, near Unadilla, where, for reasons not satisfactorily

known, nothing final took place. They next met them at Nanticoke, at which place negotiations were started with them from
day to day, but were as often broken off, and sometimes abruptly
concluded. This occurred for several days in succession, until the
fact became known that the want of success was attributable to
the opposition of McMaster and Draper, who had brought to
bear their powerful influence with the natives and who, but for
an ultimate compliance with their terms by Brown and others,
would thus have effectually prevented an extinguishment at this
time of the Indian title. Another council was called at a place
a short distance above Binghamton, the Massachusetts purchasers hoping by the removal to escape the embarrassment experienced at Nanticoke, which was more immediately within the
sphere of the influence of their rivals; but the new council was
opened with no better prospect of success, until a compromise
of the conflicting interests was effected by a contract entered
into by Samuel Brown, for himself, and on behalf of his associates, with McMaster, which provided that in case the authorities
of Massachusetts should make a grant of the land in question to
their company, there should be assured to James McMaster
eighteen square miles of land, now known as the McMaster
Half-Township, on which Owego stands, to be bounded as follows: ' South by the north line of a patent made to Daniel R. Coxe
and associates; west on Owego river [now Owego creek] to
extend up said river [creek] from said line six miles and eastward from said river [creek] three miles; the east line to be
straight, and to be so run as to make the above mentioned
quantity of land, and to be as nearly parallel as may be to the
general course of said river [creek].'

"After the execution of this contract, negotiations were
renewed under more favorable auspices. A treaty was concluded and a formal cession of the 230,400 acres was then made,
and the Indian title extinguished; James Dean superintending
throughout the whole of the negotiation as the representative
and agent of Massachusetts.

"Evidence of the treaty having been duly adduced, that state
formally granted to Brown and his associates that body of land,
with the exception of the McMaster Half-Township, which was
conveyed to Brown alone, in order that he might perform his
contract with James McMaster more conveniently, and convey
the title directly to him in pursuance of its terms. This was
accordingly done, and the latter has been since known as the
patentee of that half-township, although he received his title
from Samuel Brown, to whom the letters patent were directly
issued, and who was, in strictness, the sole original patentee of
that, as he and his associates were of the whole body of land
since known as the Boston Purchase, or Ten Townships."

The first step toward the division of the lands held in common
by the sixty proprietors, was the survey of three townships on

the south part of the tract—the Chenango on the east, in which the lots were numbered as high as 222; the Nanticoke township next, in which were 181 lots; and the Owego township on the west.

In the Chenango township were two men already in possession, who were not members of the company, and who did not participate in the drawing. An amicable arrangement was made with them by which each had a good farm. These were Joshua Whitney, who had lot No. 37, containing about four hundred acres, at the southeast corner of the tract next to the Chenango river, and Thomas Reichardt, (commonly pronounced Record, now anglicised into Richards) who had lot No. 207, containing about two hundred acres, lying partly on the south side of the Susquehanna river. The west line of the Chenango township crossed the Susquehanna river, just west of Stoddard's Island. The Nanticoke township extended west from that line to within about seven and a half miles of the west line of the Ten Townships, and nineteen of its lots are now included in the town of Owego.

After the townships of Chenango and Nanticoke were surveyed into lots, the sixty associates partitioned the land among themselves, and the legislature of the state of New York by an act passed 3d March, 1789, confirmed to the associates, in severalty, the land as they had divided it. The list as given in that act, is, perhaps, the only complete list extant of the original sixty associates. The following alphabetical list has a number prefixed to each name to indicate its place in the original list:

8. Ashley Moses,
5. Bement Asa,
6. Bement Asa, Jr.,
25. Bingham Anna,
7. Bishop Elkanah,
36. Bishop Nathanial,
9. Blin Elisha,
53. Bradley Asahel,
52. Bradley Elisha,
54. Bradley Josiah,
45. Brown Beulah,
2. Brown Elijah,
35. Brown John,
1. Brown Samuel,
44. Brown Samuel, Jr.,

41. Brown Stephen,
18. Brown William,
48. Chapman John,
46. Coleman Dudley,
27. Cone Ashbel,
58. Cook Ebenezer,
26. Cook Philip,
10. Crocker Ezekiel,
47. Curtis Elnathan,
37. Curtis Isaac,
14. Dwight Henry Williams,
39. Eagleston Azariah,
49. Edwards Jonathan,
43. Ingersol Jonathan,
30. Jenks Isaac,

3*

20. Larnard Simon,
12. Lusk Elizabeth,
31. Mason Ebenezer,
60. Morell John,
42. Nash Stephen,
38. Newhall Allen,
33. Parks Warham,
50. Parsons Elihu,
51. Parsons Eliphalet,
24. Parsons Jacob,
57. Partridge Oliver, Jr.,
22. Patterson Amos,
13. Pepoon Silas,
15. Pierson Benjamin,
16. Pierson Jeremiah H.,

17. Pierson Joseph,
32. Pierson Josiah G.,
21. Pierson Nathan,
23. Pixley David,
4. Raymond Joseph,
59. Rockwell Abner,
56. Sergeant Erastus,
11. Seymour Ira,
3. Stoddard Orringh,
19. Strong Ashbel,
40. Thompson Thaddeus,
29. Walker Caleb,
28. Walker William,
34. Williams Ebenezer,
55. Woodbridge Jonathan.

The Owego township was surveyed in two parts, the East Half-Township, and the West Half-Township, which last according to an agreement made, was deeded by Samuel Brown, of Stockbridge, 17 Dec., 1787, to James McMaster, of Mohawk. The deed, for 11,520 acres, was witnessed by Walter Sabin, and proved by his testimony in Tioga county, 3 July, 1792, and recorded. Since this deed was given the West Half-Township has been properly known as "McMasters Half-Township;" but through ignorance his name has also been quite commonly applied to the "East Half-Township of the Boston Purchase."

James McMaster, of Mohawk District. Montgomery county, N. Y., by a deed of 4 Feb., 1788, conveyed to Amos Draper, of Choconut, lots 16 and 19 of 100 acres each, and lots 30, 32, 52 and 56, of 143 acres each, of his Half-Township, and describes them as surveyed by Walter Sabin.

The East Half-Township was divided into sixty lots, and was partitioned among the proprietors by deed, with map, 12 May, 1790, at the same time as the Grand Division.

Six hundred lots were then laid out, in thirty courses of twenty lots each, for a great division, or, as it has always since been called, "The Grand Division of the Boston Purchase." These lots, and the sixty in the East Half-Township, were distributed among the proprietors, by a deed, accompanied by a map, dated 12 May, 1790. The list of proprietors who signed this deed of partition differs very much from the list who shared in the first two townships, from two causes: first, some of the associates had sold their rights in the undivided lands ; and secondly, a considerable

number had authorized Samuel Brown to act for them in drawing the lots, which he did, and afterward conveyed their share
by deed.   As a result of these causes, only thirty-seven names
are in this deed; and of this number, at least twelve are not named
in the former list.   So that seventy-two names appear as proprietors, in the two lists.   The parties to this deed were as follows :

1. Samuel Brown, Esq.,   Stockbridge, Mass.
2. Charles Stone, yeoman,   "   "
3. Asa Bement, Jr., blacksmith.   "   "
4. Josiah Ball, cordwainer,   "   "
5. Elkanah Bishop, husbandman,   "   "
6. Timothy Jearoms [Jerome], carpenter, "   "
7. Moses Ashley, Esq.,   "   "
8. Henry Williams Dwight, Esq.,   "   "
9. David Pixley, gentleman,   "   "
10. Anna Bingham, widow,   "   "
11. Isaac Curtis, miller,   "   "
12. Timothy Edwards, Esq.,   "   "
13. Theodore Sedgwick, Esq.,   "   "
14. Elisha Blin, inn keeper,   Great Barrington, Mass.
15. Ezekiel Crocker, gentleman,   Richmond, Mass.
16. Benjamin Pierson, gentleman,   "   "
17. Nathan Pierson, gentleman,   "   "
18. Josiah G. Pierson, gentleman,   "   "
19. Ebenezer Williams, gentleman,   "   "
20. William Bartlett, blacksmith,   "   "
21. Nathaniel Bishop, Esq.,   "   "
22. Joseph Pierson, joiner,   New York City.
23. Ashbel Strong, Esq.,   Pittsfield, Mass.
24. Francis Plumer, gentleman,   "   "
25. Israel Williams, gentleman,   Hatfield, Mass.
26. William Billings, Esq.,   Conway, Mass.
27. Ashbel Cone, blacksmith,   West Stockbridge, Mass.
28. William Walker, Esq.,   Lenox, Mass.
29. Caleb Walker, gentleman,   "   "
30. Azariah Egleston, gentleman,   "   "
31. Theodore Thompson, physician,   "   "
32. Job Northrop, yeoman,   "   "
33. Levi Tumbling,* yeoman,   Lee, Mass.

* In other records "Thomling" and "Tomling."

34. Samuel Arnold, yeoman,   Canaan, N. Y.
35. Ebenezer Mason, gentleman,   Spencer, Mass.
36. Allen Newhall, gentleman,   New Haven, Conn.
37. Jonathan Edwards, clerk,   "   "

Of the six hundred lots in the Grand Division, one hundred and fifteen are in Newark Valley; sixty-eight in Berkshire; ninety-three in Richford; two in the southeast corner of Dryden, Tompkins county; eighteen in Cortland county; and the remainder in Broome county.

North of the Grand Division the proprietors surveyed a tier of seventy lots, known as the "long lots," the title to which was never confirmed by the state, and the proprietors lost the land, although the state acknowledged their right by giving to the soldiers an equivalent for the deficiency, in the military tract; and the Surveyor General, in his published map, calls it "North Tier Boston Ten-Townships." The first eight of these "long lots" are in Dryden, and the other sixty-two are in Cortland county.

There was but one royal grant of lands to individuals direct (other than the Massachusetts charter) in the territory of the county, and that was for a tract of 29,812 acres, lying in the present southerly half of the town of Owego and a portion of Nichols. This tract was patented to Daniel, William, and Rebecca Coxe, and John Tabor Kemp and Grace (Coxe), his wife, January 15, 1775, and has since been known as Coxe's Manor, or Patent. It was a portion of 100,000 acres patented to them in consideration of the surrender of their rights in a "province called Carolana, consisting of a territory on the coast of Georgia and the Carolinas, together with the islands of Veanis and Bahama, and all other islands off that coast, between the 31st and 36th degrees of north latitude, as granted by Charles I., October 30, 1629, to Sir Robert Heath, and from him devised to the present grantees through their father." To these grantors 47,000 acres were granted in Oneida and 23,000 acres elsewhere (in Otsego or Delaware counties). The petition for this grant was filed October 31, 1774, and described the tract as being in the county of Tryon, and as "beginning at a place called Owegg, on the Susquehanna river, and runs along the northern boundary of Pennsylvania." On January 4, 1775, a return of survey was made for the parties named in the patent, which described the tract as beginning "opposite the mouth of Owegy creek."

The portion of the present town of Owego south of the Susquehanna, and the town of Nichols, was called the township of Hambden. The lands in the township, aside from Coxe's Manor, were sold as follows: to Robert Morris, several tracts in Owego; Alexander Macomb, 6,930 acres in Owego and Vestal, February 15, 1785, vol. xliii., p. 123, Land Papers, New York; Nicholas Fish, 7,040 acres in Owego, and 6,400 acres in township seven of the tract purchased of the *Oneidas and Tuscaroras*, in Owego and Nichols, vol. xliii, pp. 84 and 85, Land Papers; William Butler, return of survey for 3,000 acres in Nichols, adjoining Coxe's Patent on the west, January 12, 1775, vol. xxxv., p. 14; John Reid, similar return for 3,000 acres adjoining Butler on the west, January 12, 1775, vol. xxxv., p. 15; Richard Robert Crowe, similar return January 20, 1775, for 2,000 lying between Reid's tract and the Susquehanna, which bounds it on the west, vol. xxxv., p. 23, Land Papers.

On the 10th of November, 1784, Rebecca, John D., and Tench Coxe filed a caveat in the land-office protesting against the granting by the state of any certificates of location, warrents of survey, or letters patent for lands west of the Delaware river, bounded south by Pennsylvania, until the claim of said protestors, or their assigns, to a tract of 29,812 acres of land, on the east bank of the Susquehanna, was lawfully and fully recognized. The claims of the Coxe heirs were confirmed subsequently, and the tract, as surveyed in 1806–7, was found to contain 30,900 acres.

Gospel and literature tracts were also set off in Owego township, comprising about three square miles, adjoining Coxe's Manor on the north. Colonel Nichols subsequently acquired a large tract of land in the towns of Owego and Nichols.

In 1788, on March 22, the legislature erected a new town* in Montgomery county, the boundary line beginning at the intersection of the pre-emption line of Massachusetts with the Pennsylvania State line, and running due north from the point of intersection along the pre-emption line to the distance of two miles north of Tioga river; thence in a direct line at right angles to the pre-emption line east to the Owego river (West Owego), to intersect said river at a distance of four miles on a straight line from the confluence thereof with the Susquehanna; then down the Owego and Susquehanna to the Pennsylvania line; and

---

* Chemung.

thence along said line to the place of beginning. This tract,
which covers the present town of Barton and the greater portion of Tioga, in Tioga county, and the towns of Southport,
Elmira, Ashland, Baldwin, and Chemung, and a portion of Big
Flats, Horseheads, Erin and Van Etten, in Chemung county, had
been settled by a number of persons, who could not agree upon
a proper division of their locations, and the act creating the town
appointed John Cantine, James Clinton, and John Hathorn commissioners to inquire into and settle the disputes which had arisen
among the settlers concerning their possessions, and to assign
and allot lands to the claimants who were actually settled on the
lands, or who had made improvements, intending to settle. The
allotments were to be not less than 100, nor more than 1,000 acres
each, and also provided that the lands were to be settled within
three months after the state acquired the Indian title. The
lands were bought at one shilling and sixpence per acre. These
commissioners proceeded under their authority to survey and
plot the town, and February 28, 1789, the legislature confirmed
their report, and authorized the commissioner of the land-office
to patent the lands to the parties named on the map submitted
by the commissioners of the town, and extended the time of settlement to one year after the state had acquired the Indian title.
Certificates of location were issued by the commissioners, which
were assignable, and thus parties acquired large tracts, which
were patented to them under one patent.

On August 4, 1791, John W. Watkins, a lawyer in New York
city, and Royal W. Flint, and certain associates, applied to the
Commissioners of the Land-Office for the ungranted lands lying
east of the Massachusetts pre-emption, west of the Owego creek,
south of the Military Tract, and north of the town of Chemung,
as then laid out,—estimated to contain 363,000 acres,—for which
they agreed to pay the price of three shillings and fourpence per
acre. (Vol. xi., Land Papers, p. 141.) The proposition was
accepted, and the tract surveyed, and a return made April 7,
1794, and a patent issued June 25, 1794, to John W. Watkins,
who subsequently conveyed to his associates, as their interests
indicated. The lands were described in the patent as follows:

" Beginning at the northwest corner of the township of Chemung, as originally surveyed and laid out, on the east bounds of
the lands ceded by this State to the Commonwealth of Massachusetts, and running along the line run for the north bounds of
said township of Chemung south 87° 40' east, 2,857 chains to

Owego creek, being the west bounds of a tract of 230,400 acres, also ceded by this State to the Commonwealth of Massachusetts; thence up along same bounds northerly to the township of Dryden, being one of the townships of the tract set apart for the troops of this state lately serving in the army of the United States; thence along the south bounds of the townships of Dryden, Ulysses, and Hector, and the same continued west 2,786 chains to the line run for the east bounds of the said first above-mentioned ceded lands, which line is commonly called the pre-emption line; then along the same a true south course 1,220 chains to place of beginning."

This tract includes the present towns of Spencer and Candor.

---

*CHAPTER III.

First Settlement—Character of the Settlers—Growth of Population—Organization—Original Boundaries—Curtailment of Territory—Present Boundaries—Topography—Geology—Streams—Soil
—Agricultural Statistics—Agricultural Societies.

IN the previous chapter we have stated the manner in which the original titles to the land within the present limits of the county were obtained. Upon the "Boston Purchase," where the village of Owego now is, the first white settlement was made; but as this fact is set forth in detail in connection with our history of that town, it is not necessary to repeat the story here.

Several causes operated to bring settlers to the County of Tioga from several localities. The army of Gen. James Sullivan, which passed through the valley in the summer of 1779, was composed of officers and soldiers from New Jersey, Connecticut, Massachu-setts and New York. The officers of the expedition were astonished at the advance the Iroquois had made in agriculture. A letter of Gen. James Clinton states that the corn was "the finest he had ever seen." Another officer states that there were ears of corn that measured twenty-two inches in length. The broad valleys of the Susquehanna, Chenango and Chemung, with their rich fields of corn, and orchards of apple trees, must have presented to the soldiers an inviting and attractive appearance,

---

*In this chapter, and in some others, we quote extensively from the writings of Hon.
William F. Warner, of Waverly. We hereby acknowledge our obligation to him for all.

as contrasted with the sandy soil of New Jersey, and the rocks and harder soil of Connecticut and Massachusetts. Upon returning to their homes at the close of the war, in 1783, these soldiers carried their reports of the territory they had traversed to friends and neighbors in their several states. We have seen that Massachusetts claimed the territory which forms the County of Tioga, and, as early as 1787, made a grant which, not being disputed as was the case with grants of the territory of Wyoming, many settlers in the Wyoming valley abandoned their possessions, and came to this county to find new homes; and Tioga thus gained some of her very best citizens among the early settlers from that locality. These coming mainly from Massachusetts and Connecticut, brought with them the general characteristics of the people of those states. Among them were men and women of culture and refinement, who exerted a powerful influence in restraining others who might have been inclined to acts of lawlessness. In general, this body of pioneers was composed of entire families; and the good order maintained was greatly owing to the presence of the noble wives, mothers and sisters of the pioneers, and who, while sharing in the hardships and privations incident to a pioneer life, presented examples of piety, virtue and true womanly heroism. Scantily furnished with domestic utensils and implements of husbandry, a spirit of liberality and mutual assistance was fostered. Many had for years suffered the fatigues and hardships of service in the army, and came empty handed, but with stout hearts, to carve for themselves a home in the new settlement. The exigencies of a pioneer life are always severe, but frugal means lead to frugal habits; common necessities unite a community in a common brotherhood. Doubtless there were many incidents in the lives of these early settlers of generosity and bravery, but where all were brave and generous so little notice was taken of such deeds that no record of them was thought to be necessary, nor is there record of a single act of violence.

The record of these settlements, their growth and progress, is given in the histories of the several towns, further on in this work; the growth of the county as a whole may be seen by the following, showing the population for several periods since 1800, viz: 1800, 6,862; 1810, 7,899; 1820, 14,716; 1825, 19,951; 1830, 27,690; 1835, 33,999; 1840, 20,527; 1845, 22,456; 1850, 24,880; 1855, 26,962; 1860, 28,748; 1865, 30,572; 1870, 33,178; 1875, 32,915; 1880, 32,673.

The county was legally organized under its present name* by an act of the legislature passed February 16, 1791. It was carved out of territory previously embraced within the limits of Montgomery county, which had been called before and during the revolutionary war, down to the year 1784, Tryon county, in honor of one of the late colonial governors, who, unfortunately, proved himself throughout the national struggle an uncompromising enemy to the American cause. By reason of this his name had become so unpalatable to the people of the state that it was no longer applied to the county; and by legislative enactment in that year (1784) the name of Montgomery was substituted, in honor of the Irish soldier, General Montgomery, who fell during his gallent attack on Quebec at an early period of the war.

At the date of its organization, Tioga county embraced not only its present limits, but also the counties of Chemung, Broome and Chenango. Its boundaries were Otsego county on the east; the Military Tract and Herkimer county on the north; Ontario on the west—out of which Steuben was erected in 1796; and the Pennsylvania line on the south. Its towns, commencing at its westerly limit, were Newtown, Chemung, Owego, none of whose territory was then where it now is, but all of it lay west of the Owego creek, and then embraced what are now Tioga, Candor, Spencer, Barton and Nichols, in Tioga county, and Caroline, Danby and Newfield, in Tompkins county; next easterly to Owego creek was Union, which included within its limits what are now Owego, Newark, Berkshire and Richford, in Tioga county, Union, Vestal, Lisle, etc., in Broome county, and the westerly portion of what is now Chenango county; next easterly was Chenango; and next easterly and northerly was Jericho, which covered territory then lying in the easterly part of what is now Chenango county. Thus it is seen that the six old towns, Newtown, Chemung, Owego, Union, Chenango and Jericho, then covered territory which the fifty-two towns of Chemung, Tioga, Broome and Chenango counties, and three towns, Caroline,

*The name of the county is derived from that of the river that once flowed through its western portion, now the county of Chemung. Morgan, is his "League of the Iroquois," gives the derivation and signification of the word as follows: "The various tribes of the Confederacy had a different pronunciation for the word. In the *Oneida* dialect it was Te-ah-o-ge; in the *Mohawk*, Te-yo-ge-ga; in the *Cayuga*, Da-a-o-ga; and in the *Seneca*, Da-ya-o-geh; but all meant 'at the forks.' In the text of the work quoted it is written Ta-ya-o-ga. On Guy Johnson's map of 1771 it is written Ti-a-o-ga. The eloquent Red Jacket pronounced it Tah-hiho-gah, discarding the suffix 'Point,' which has been universally added when applied to the locality known now as Athens, Pa. He said the Indian word carried the full meaning,—'the point of land at the confluence of the two streams,' or 'the meeting of the waters.'"

Danby and Newfield, in Tompkins county now cover, fifty-five in all.

The first loss sustained by Tioga in the organization of other counties was in 1798, when the northeasterly corner of her ancient domain, and a strip from the westerly part of Herkimer, were taken to make up the then county of Chenango, which, in its turn was found large enough, in 1806, to admit of the erection of Madison county out of its northern half. Next in the order of time, 1806, was the organization of Broome county, taken from Tioga, and named in honor of the then Lieutenant Governor. It embraced, originally, the old towns of Chenango, etc., and territory forming Owego, Newark, Berkshire and Richford. The next change was in 1822, when the territory now included within the towns of Owego, Newark, Berkshire and Richford was taken from Broome and re-annexed to Tioga, and the towns of Caroline, Danby and Newfield were taken from Tioga and added to Tompkins. By the same legislature Tioga county was divided into two jury districts, Owego and Elmira becoming half-shire towns. This latter act proved to be but a preliminary step to the subsequent establishment of Chemung county, resulting, in 1836, in a complete severance of the connection and mutuality of interests.

This leaves the county of which we write as it is to-day, with an area of about 542 square miles, bounded north by Tompkins and Cortland counties, east by Broome county, south by the Pennsylvania line, and west by Chemung county. It is divided into nine towns, as follows: Barton, Berkshire, Candor, Newark Valley, Nichols, Owego, Richford, Spencer and Tioga.

The surface of the country is broken by the prolongation of the Alleghany mountains, which enter in a series of ridges northerly through the territory, and attain a nearly uniform elevation of 1,200 to 1,400 feet above tide. These ridges are severed diagonally by the valley of the Susquehanna, and are separated by numerous lateral valleys, which extend in a north and south direction, and give a great variety of feature to the surface. The width of these valleys varies from a few rods to a mile, and sometimes more. They are frequently defined by steep acclivities, which rise from 250 to 400 feet, the summits of which are broad and rolling, and afford excellent land for dairy purposes.

The rocks of the county belong to the Chemung and Catskill groups. All the rocks cropping out on the surface north of the Susquehanna, and those underlying the south of it, may be classed with the Chemung group, and those crossing the hills south of the river with the Catskill group. There are no important minerals; a deep drift consisting of sand, gravel and clay lies in the valleys and covers the adjoining hills. This deposit near East Waverly is eighty feet deep, and a wide belt of it seems to extend north in an almost unbroken line from that place to Cayuga lake.

The principal streams are Susquehanna river and Owego, Catatonk, Cayuta, Pipe, Wapasening and Apalachin creeks, with their branches. These streams have generally rapid currents, and furnish valuable water-power. Their valleys, in their upper courses, are generally narrow, but expand as they approach the Susquehanna into broad and beautiful level intervals.

The soil in the valleys is a deep, rich, gravelly loam, with an occasional intermixture of clay and sand. The land in the Susquehanna valley is especially noted for its fertility. The uplands are gravelly and sandy, and produce an abundance of grass, which renders the land valuable for grazing and dairy purposes. Since the removal of the most valuable timber, the inhabitants are mainly occupied in agricultural pursuits. The dairies of the county are becoming noted for their excellence in the principal markets, and are rapidly increasing in their productiveness. The county's agricultural resources may be estimated from the following figures, taken from the census report of 1880:

The county then had 3,401 farms, representing 243,175 acres of improved land, and were valued at $10,949,806.00. Upon these farms were raised 8,397 bushels of barley; 129,131 bushels of buckwheat; 313,087 bushels of Indian corn; 652,918 bushels of oats; 9,236 bushels of rye; 83,367 bushels of wheat; 436,317 bushels of potatoes; 2,200 pounds of hops, and orchard products to the value of $25,342.00. Its live stock enumerated 7,482 horses; 77 mules; 534 working oxen; 17,794 milch cows, and 11,620 other cattle; 21,914 sheep and 8,253 swine. From this stock was produced 89,780 pounds of wool; 310,133 gallons of milk; 2,150,885 pounds of butter, and 24,712 pounds of cheese.

The Tioga County Agricultural Society was organized in 1819. The only account of it extant is in the *American Journal*, a newspaper published at Ithaca by Ebnezer Mack, and now known as the Ithaca *Journal*. That paper gives an account of a meeting of the society at the house of Andrew Purdy, in Spencer, on Wednesday, November 10, 1819, together with the by-laws, which were signed by Thomas Maxwell, secretary.

On March 28, 1837, the society was reincorporated by act of the legislature. James Pumpelly, Anson Camp, Ezra Canfield, Francis Armstrong, Stephen Strong, Henry McCormick, Ira Clizbe, John Coryell, Erastus Goodrich, Asa Wolverton, Ira Woodford, Russell Gridley, Henry Miller, George Fisher, Stephen Wells, Jr., Ezekiel Rich, David Williams, Horatio Collins, Joseph T. Waldo, Abram Hotchkiss, Otis Lincoln, Nicholas Schoonover, Samuel Mills, Isaac Shepard and William Platt, "and such persons as might thereafter be associated with them," were made a body corporate by the name of the Tioga County Agricultural Society. The act was to continue in force twenty years, and the society was empowered to hold and convey real estate not exceeding in value $5,000.00. Thomas Farrington was chosen president of the society. The first fair was held in October, 1841, on land owned by James Pumpelly, at the northwest corner of Main and McMaster streets, in Owego. Annual fairs were held for six successive years. The last one, in 1846, was a failure, owing to some dissatisfaction because one exhibitor who owned some very fine horses had received all the best premiums.

The society was re-organized July 21, 1855, at a meeting held in the old village hall, in Owego, and articles of incorporation were subsequently filed in the office of the Secretary of State. Harvey Coryell, of Nichols, was chosen president, William Smyth, secretary, and Thomas I. Chatfield, treasurer. The first fair of the re-organized society was held October 23 and 24. The live stock and farming machinery were exhibited on the lot at the southeast corner of Main and William streets, and the fruits, domestic articles, etc., in the village hall. The next year the fair was held in the same places, but in 1857, a piece of ground owned by George W. Hollenback, corner of Division and Front streets, in the eastern part of the village, was leased for five years, at a yearly rental of $100.00. The ground was surrounded by a high board fence, a race-track was constructed, and fairs were held there until 1864. In 1862, there was some dissatisfaction because all premiums amounting to $3.00 and over were paid in silver-plated ware. In 1864, the location of the grounds was changed. The society leased and fenced in thirteen acres of land on the J. J. Beers farm, just north of the village line, located on the north side of the highway leading from the old Ithaca and Owego turnpike to Leach's Mills. In 1865, horse racing was made a prominent feature of the fair. This, together with the the paying of premiums to farmers in silver-plated ware, increased the dissatisfaction to such an extent that the fairs of the two following years were failures.

An attempt to re-organize the society was made in 1871. A public meeting was held at the court-house on the 18th of October. Thomas I. Chatfield was elected president of the society, William Smyth, corresponding secretary, George Worthington, recording secretary, and Stephen S. Truman, treasurer. Nothing further was done, and no attempt was made to hold a fair.

Another and more successful attempt to re-organize the society was made August 10, 1872, when another meeting was held at the court-house. At a subsequent meeting, held on the 24th of the same month, the society was re-organized by the election of Herbert Richardson, of Newark Valley, president, William Smyth, of Owego, secretary, and George Truman, of Owego, treasurer. The first fair of the re-organized society was held on the Owego Driving Park, September 16, 17, and 18, 1873, and successful annual fairs have been held on the same grounds ever since. The following is a list of the presidents of the society since its organization:—Thomas Farrington, Owego, 1841–42; Charles F. Johnson, Tioga, 1843–46; Harvey Coryell, Nichols, 1855; Louis P. Legg, Berkshire, 1856; Chester Randall, Richford, 1857; W. R. Shoemaker, Nichols, 1858; William Ellis, Barton, 1859; John McQuigg, Spencer, 1860; David Taylor, Tioga, 1861–62; George Woodford, Candor, 1863; Louis P. Legg, Berkshire, 1864; Samuel B. Smith, Nichols, 1865; John L. Taylor, Owego, 1866–68; Thomas I. Chatfield, Owego, 1871; Herbert Richardson, Newark Valley, 1872–73; Frederick W. Richardson, Newark Valley, 1874–75; John S. Giles, Owego, 1876; William H. Armstrong, Newark Valley, 1877–80; George J. Nelson, Tioga, 1881; Frederic C. Lowman, Nichols, 1882; John Smith, Jr., Owego, 1883; W. Hulse Shaw, Tioga, 1884–87.

From 1855 to 1861, inclusive, William Smyth was secretary of the society. John L. Taylor was secretary in 1862 and 1863; Thomas I. Chatfield, in 1864 and 1865, and William H. Corey, in 1866, 1867 and 1868. Mr. Smyth was again secretary in 1871 and 1872, and his son, William A. Smyth, succeeded him, holding the office from 1873 to 1876, inclusive. Since the latter year, LeRoy W. Kingman has been secretary of the society.

Thomas I. Chatfield was treasurer from 1855 to 1861, inclusive. Dwight I. Bloodgood was treasurer from 1862 to 1868, inclusive.

Stephen S. Truman held the office in 1872, and George Truman
in 1873. Mr. Chatfield was again treasurer from 1873 to 1876,
inclusive. A. Chase Thompson was treasurer from 1877 to 1880,
inclusive. His successor, James M. Hastings, is the present
treasurer.

The Northern Tioga Agricultural Society was not organized,
as might be supposed, in opposition to the county society whose
fairs are held at Owego, but rather to occupy territory which did
not seem to be reached by the county organization.

In the summer of 1880, the Newark Valley Farmer's Club
decided to take the initiatory steps towards holding a local fair or
farmer's exhibition ; and a temporary organization was formed
for that purpose, with the following officers : D. M. Sturtevant,
president; D. H. Miller, James Borthwick, vice-presidents;
Charles L. Noble, secretary ; Egbert Bement, treasurer; F. W.
Richardson, general superintendent; L. S. Burch, marshal.

The exhibition was held on the grounds now occupied by the
society, at Newark Valley, September 15 and 16, 1880. No
admission fee was charged and no premiums paid; but so great
was the enthusiasm shown and so large was the exhibit made,
that it was at once apparent that ample material was at hand for
a successful society. A few weeks later the Farmer's Club issued
a call to the farmers and business men of Northern Tioga, and a
meeting was held in Elwell Hall, Newark Valley, November 23,
1880, which resulted in the organizing of a society to be known
as the Northern Tioga Agricultural Society, and a few days
later the articles of incorporation were filed in the clerk's office
of Tioga county and in the office of the secretary of state, and
the society entered upon its legal existence. The officers for the
first year were as follows: L. S. Burch, president; Theodore
Mayor, C. F. Curtis, vice-presidents ; Charles L. Noble, secretary;
J. R. Hankins, treasurer; J. R. Ford, E. F. Johnson, C. H.
Randall, F. G. Bushnell, D. M. Sturtevant, W. T. Shaw, William
Elwell, L. D. McCullough and F. W. Richardson, directors. The
grounds now occupied by the society, taken from the farms of
Ichabod Ford and Edwin P. Smith, were at once leased, and the
following summer a half-mile track was graded, suitable buildings were erected, and on the 4th, 5th and 6th of October, 1881,
the first annual fair of the society was held. The result was all
that could have been desired, both in point of attendance and
exhibits, and from that time to the present, each annual exhibition
has shown a marked improvement over its predecessors, the

entries rising gradually from 1,068 in 1881, to 2,012 in 1887, while the cash receipts show a corresponding increase. Constant improvements have been made both in the grounds and the premium list, until the Northern Tioga Agricultural Society fairly ranks as one of the best managed and most prosperous organizations of its kind in Southern New York.

---

*CHAPTER IV.

ADMINISTRATION OF THE LAW—EARLY COURTS—CHANGES AND ESTAB-
LISHMENT OF NEW COURTS—COUNTY BUILDINGS—JUDICIARY AND CIVIL
LIST.

AT the time of the organization of the county (1791), the various courts of law, from those of a general jurisdiction to those of a specific and limited jurisdiction, had already been instituted and organized throughout the state, either by derivation from the common law, or by the constitution and the various enactments of the legislature. With a very few except-ions of courts since abolished, the courts of law of that time have continued until the present writing with powers and jurisdictions of so kindred a nature that they are easily identified. There has been very little change in the essential nature of those powers and jurisdictions, or even in the number and grades of the various courts since. There have been made, however, great changes in the executive scheme and machinery of these courts. These changes are simply those of the natural growth and develop-ment of the administration of law, equity and justice; and they may be easily traced through the history of the constitutional and statute laws of the state.

The paramount court of the state was the court for the trial of impeachments and for the correction of errors. It was pro-vided for by the first constitution of the state, 1777, and was established by an act of legislature in 1784. It was composed of the president of the state senate, senators, chancellor, and judges of the supreme court, or the major part of them. As a court for the trial of impeachments, it had power to impeach all

---

*Prepared by S. Jay Ohart, of Owego.

public officers of the state " for mal and corrupt conduct in their respective offices." Two-third majority of the members present was necessary in order to successfully impeach. This court still continues, with some modifications. It is now composed of the president of the state senate, senators or the major part of them, and the judges of the court of appeals, or the major part of them. Since it was first established, in 1784, this court has been deprived of much of the jurisdiction orginally conferred upon it, by the adoption of new state constitutions and by the various amendments thereto, and by numerous enactments of the state legislature.

As a court for the correction of errors, this was a species of appellate court of last resort, and had power to redress and correct all errors happening in the court of chancery, the supreme court, the court of probates and the court of admiralty. This branch of the court continued until the adoption of the new state constitution, which went into effect January 1, 1847. It was supplanted under provisions of the constitution of 1847, by the court of appeals, although it is a noteworthy feature that the new constitution of 1847 made no direct abolition of this court; but it was practically disposed of by that instrument by abolishing the offices of chancellor and justices of the supreme court, who in part made up the court for the trial of impeachments and for the correction of errors.

The new state constitution of 1847 provided for the institution of the court of appeals, consisting of eight judges, and the court was subsequently organized under provisions of enactment of the legislature, and is still in existence. The judges thereof are elected by popular vote, and since the adoption of the judiciary article to the state constitution, November 2, 1869, the court has been composed of a chief justice and six associate justices and the tenure of office is for a term of fourteen years. Its sessions are held in the city of Albany. It is an appellate court of last resort in the state, having general jurisdiction in law, equity and justice.

There was another court already organized at the time of the erection of the county, known as the court of exchequer. It was a court having jurisdiction of fines, forfeitures and amerciaments. It was abolished by the repealing acts of 1828, in anticipation of the revised statutes of the state which went into effect January 1, 1830.

The court of chancery was another court already in existence and fully organized, to the jurisdiction of which the county of Tioga was subject upon its erection. This court had jurisdiction of general equity jurisprudence. The executive officer of the court, originally under the provisions of the constitution of 1777, was a sole chancellor, appointed by the governor of the state with the advice and consent of the council of appointment. His tenure of office was during good behavior, or until he arrived at the age of sixty years. Subsequently, when the revised statutes went into effect, January 1, 1830, provision was made for the appointment of vice-chancellors, one for each of the eight judicial circuits. The duties of the vice-chancellors were analagous to those of the circuit justices of the supreme court. The court of chancery continued until the first Monday of July, 1847, when it was abolished under the provisions of the new state constitution, which went into effect January 1, 1847. This constitution provided for a supreme court, with general jurisdiction in law and equity; and since its adoption the history of equity jurisprudence is identical with that of the supreme court.

The supreme court of judicature was also already fully organized, having general jurisdiction of civil matters. Originally it consisted of three members, a chief justice and two associates, who were appointed by the governor of the state with the advice and consent of the council of appointment. Their tenure of office was during good behavior, or until each should attain the age of sixty years. Afterward the number of associate judges was increased to three, and subsequently to four. The terms of the court were held at the state capitol, and the justices of the court continued to be appointed until June 7, 1847, when, under the provisions of the new constitution, they became elective by popular vote, and they have since continued to be so chosen. An act of the state legislature of 1786, however, authorized the trial of issues in the supreme court to be held in the county where the causes arise, and established circuit courts to be held in the vacations of the court at least once a year in each county of the state, by the justices or some one of them. The act of 1791, creating Tioga county, however, provided that it should not be the duty of the justices of the supreme court to hold a circuit court once in every year in Tioga county, unless in their judgment they should deem it proper and necessary. An act of February 10, 1797, nevertheless, appointed the circuit of Tioga county to be held on the tenth day after the second Tuesday in May, yearly. The state was at this time

4*

divided into four judicial districts, and the county of Tioga was included in the "western district," so-called. April 17, 1823, an act was passed dividing the state into eight circuit districts, corresponding with the eight senatorial districts in extent of territory. Under this arrangement Tioga county was in the sixth circuit district.

February 22, 1788, the state legislature by enactment established courts of oyer and terminer, having general criminal jurisdiction, and directed that the justices of the supreme court, or either of them, together with the judges and assistant judges of the courts of common pleas of each county of the state, or any three or more of them, should constitute the court. The terms of oyer and terminer were also authorized to be held in the respective counties at the times when the justices of the supreme court should be holding the circuit court in such county.

The supreme court, the circuit court thereof, and the court of oyer and terminer having been thus established throughout the state prior to the erection of Tioga county, the county became subject to the jurisdictions thereof from the time of its organization. These courts have continued in existence until the present time. It will be interesting, nevertheless, to notice some changes which were made in the executive arrangement of these courts from time to time.

The revised statutes of the state which went into effect January 1, 1830, provided for the construction of the supreme court to consist of a chief justice and two associates, and divided the state into eight circuit court districts, also made provision for eight additional circuit court justices, one for each district. These circuit court districts were made to correspond to the eight senatorial districts. The county of Tioga was annexed to the sixth judicial district, and has remained in that district down to date. This scheme was continued, with some modifications, until the adoption of the new state constitution, which went into effect January 1, 1847. Out of this new constitution, the amendments thereto, and the subsequent acts of the state legislature, has grown our present elaborate arrangement of the supreme court, circuit courts thereof, and courts of oyer and terminer, the systematic executive arrangement of which elicits the admiration of the world of jurisprudence. They consist of so-called "departments," of which there are five in the state. Terms of circuit courts and courts of oyer and terminer are held in the various counties by a sole circuit justice. Under the present arrangement the office of justice of the supreme court is elective,. and the tenure thereof has been, since the adoption of the judiciary article to the state constitution, November 2, 1869, for a term of fourteen years. The county of Tioga, under the present judicial arrangement, is in the fourth department and in the sixth judicial district, which has five justices, two of them general term justices and three of them circuit justices.

Courts of common pleas, having limited civil jurisdiction, and courts of general sessions or general sessions of the peace, having limited criminal jurisdiction within the respective counties of the state, had also been provided for by the state constitution and by various acts of the state legislature before the erection of the county; but they were especially provided for by the act of February, 1791, creating the county. This act provided that there should be two terms of said courts held in the county each year. The first terms thereof were directed to be held on the fourth Tuesdays of June and January of every year, at the house of George Hornwell, in Chemung (now in Chemung county). These courts originally were composed of a first judge, three associate judges and four assistant judges. Three of these were necessary to be *en banc* to constitute the court, one of which three was required to be either the first judge or one of the associate justices. In 1818, the offices of assistant judges were abolished by an act of legislature, and the revised statutes of 1830 provided for a first judge and four judges of the county courts of each county. These species of courts continued with some modifications until the adoption of the new state constitution of 1847. That instrument provided for one county judge in each county, except the county of New York, who alone held the county court, which was thus made to supplant the court of common pleas. He also, together with two justices of the peace, called justices for sessions, holds the court of sessions, having limited criminal jurisdiction within the county which in turn, since January 1, 1847, has supplanted the court of general sessions or general sessions of the peace. Under the original system the first judge, the three associate judges and the four assistant judges were appointed by the governor of the state with the advice and consent of the council of appointment. The tenure of office of the first judge was during good behavior, or until he attained the age of sixty years; and commissions of appointment to the judges of the county courts (other than the first judge), etc., were required to be made, by the constitution of 1777, once at least in every three years. With this exception the duration of the term of said officers was during the pleasure of the council of appointment. In 1830, the revised statutes authorized the nomination and appointment of the judges (a first judge and four assistant judges) of county courts by the governor of the state, with the consent of the state senate, and their tenure of office was for a term of five years, subject to removal for cause; and by the new state constitution of 1847, the office of sole county judge was made elective by popular vote and the tenure of office was for a term of four years. This term was by the adoption of the judiciary article to the state constitution November 2, 1869, changed to six years' duration, which is the present tenure of the office. Justices for sessions, sitting with the county judge, constituting the court of sessions, are elected annually by popular vote and are required to be acting justices of the peace.

Courts of probate, or what are now known as surrogate's courts, had also already been instituted throughout the various counties of the state, prior to 1791, by common law jurisdiction and by an act of legislature passed February 20, 1787, and by legislative acts subsequent thereto. These courts had original general jurisdiction of the probate of wills, administration of decedents' estates, and of all controversies relating thereto. The original statute of 1787, provided for the appointment of a sole surrogate in and for each county by the governor of the state and the council of appointment, to serve during the pleasure of said council. The revised statutes of 1830 authorized the nomination and appointment of surrogates by the governor of the state, with the consent of the state senate, and fixed the tenure of their office at a term of four years. Surrogates in and for each respective county continued to be appointed, with some subsequent modifications and conditions, until the new state constitution of 1847; and by that instrument the office of surrogate was consolidated with that of county judge, and since that time the office of surrogate in Tioga county is identical with that of county judge, as to manner of election and as to tenure of office. It is needless to add that this species of court is still extant in Tioga county, having the same general jurisdiction.

Courts of justice's of the peace, having specific and limited jurisdiction of petty civil controversies, and courts of general sessions of the peace, held by justices of the peace, having jurisdiction of petty crimes and misdemeanors, were also inaugurated throughout the various counties of the state at the time of the organization of the county; and they are still continued, having nearly the same general jurisdiction as they had when the county was first created. Courts held by justices of the peace, exercising jurisdiction of petty crimes and misdemeanors, are now denominated as courts of special sessions. Justices of the peace were originally appointed by the governor of the state and the council of appointment under provision of the constitution of 1777; and their tenure of office was during the pleasure of the council of appointment, except that it was required that commissions of appointment should be issued at least once in three years. Justices of the peace continued to be appointed until the amendment to the state constitution, ratified in November, 1826, and since that time they have been chosen by the electors within the various towns of the state. The tenure of office is now for a term of four years.

The act of the state legislature of 1791, creating the county of Tioga, provided that, until other provisions be made in the premises, the courts of said county should be held at the house of George Hornwell, in Chemung, and directed that a court-house and jail in the county should be erected at such place as the judges and justices and supervisors, or the major part of them, should direct and appoint. July 12, 1791, the justices and supervisors of the county met and selected a site for the new court-house and jail. The site selected was east of the Nanti-coke creek, now in the village of Chenango, a small settlement on the west side of the Chenango river in the town of Union. A petition was made to the state legislature by the judges, justices and supervisors of the county, for authority to raise a sum of money sufficient to build such buildings. In pursuance thereof, an act was passed by the legislature on February 18, 1792, authorizing the levying and collection of three hundred pounds, with an additional sum of nine pence on the pound for collecting the same, for building a court-house and jail, and authorizing the appointment of three commissioners by the supervisors and judges of the court of common pleas on the first Tuesday in May, 1792, to superintend the building of the new court-house and jail upon the site selected July 12, 1791. The same act authorized the courts of said county to be held at the house of Nehemiah Spalding, situate near Nanticoke creek aforesaid, after the end of the term of said court to be held on the fourth Tuesday of June, 1792, until the new court-house should be built and fit for the reception of the court. In conformity with the provisions of this act the court-house and jail were erected in 1793.

There sprung up at once intense local jealousies and strifes among the inhabitants of the county, as to the permanent location of the new county buildings. There appears to have been a numerous sprinkling of inhabitants in the vicinity of what are now the cities of Elmira and Binghamton, and the chief struggle as to the location of the county seat of the new county was between those two localities. And thus early in our history was engendered a strife for local dominancy, which has continued unabating until the present day. The Chemung inhabitants secured a temporary dominancy by the act of February, 1791; and the Nanticoke inhabitants wrested it from them by the act of February, 1792. But their victory was not an exclusive one, for the inhabitants of Chemung immediately set to work and constructed a building for a jail, at Newtown Point, so-called, in the town of Chemung, and January 14, 1793, secured the passage of an act of legislature recognizing the same as the jail of the county, "until further legislative provisions in the premises;" and also authorizing the holding of the courts of common pleas and general sessions of the place, in said county from and after April 1, 1793, on the first Tuesday in May, October and February, of every year, alternately at the house of Joshua Whitney, at Chenango, in the town of Union, and at the said new jail building at Newtown Point, in the town of Chemung, and directed the adjournment of said courts at the end of the January term of 1793, to the first Tuesday of May, 1793, to be held in this new jail building at Newtown Point. This dual arrangement threw some confusion into other official departments of the county, and there appears to have been a struggle to have the dual arrangement carried throughout all of those official departments, and doubts at once arose as to the power and authority to do this, particularly among the new loan officers. Once more the legislature was appealed to, and March 25, 1794, an act with a preamble reciting this state of affairs was passed, authorizing and requiring the new loan officers to hold the new loan office in the towns of Union and Newtown, alternately, at or near the places of holding said courts, and directing that the next meeting of the said new loan officers be held in the town of Union, aforesaid.

March 17, 1795, the good people of the Nanticoke vicinity secured the passage of an act directing that the sheriff of Tioga county, from and after May 1, 1795, compute and receive mileage fees from Nanticoke bridge, in the town of Union, and from no other place.

The location of Chenango Village, in which the new court-house and jail had been erected, in 1793, was changed to Chenango Point (now city of Binghamton) in 1799, but the citizens of that vicinity were still persistent to maintain local supremacy, and the contention seems to have continued until 1801. March 31, 1801, the state legislature enacted that the judges and assistant justices in the County of Tioga, at the next term of their court, commencing on the first Tuesday in May, 1801, divide the county into two jury districts, "as nearly equal as may be convenient;" and authorized the holding of the courts of common pleas and general sessions of the peace at the court-house "about to be erected at Chenango Point, in the town of Chenango, instead of the house of Joshua Whitney, in the town of Union, and at the court-house at Newtown alternately."

March 5, 1794, Onondaga county was formed, March 15, 1798, Chenango county was formed and March 28, 1806, Broome county was formed, all taken from Tioga county and embracing all of the territory east of Owego creek. The act of March 28, 1806, directed the holding of the courts for Broome county in the court-house then erected in Chenango, and for the county of Tioga at the court-house in the town of Newtown, and the provisions for two jury districts in the county of Tioga was abolished.

Meantime a large settlement had grown up at Spencer. The court-house at Newtown was a rude affair, constructed of logs and covered with clap-boards, situate approximately, upon the present corner of Church and Sullivan streets, in the city of Elmira. That new county buildings would soon have to be constructed in Tioga county was manifest. What is now the town of Owego was known as the town of Tioga, and had been set off into the new county of Broome in 1806. Directly upon the formation of this new county of Broome, Spencer began to contest with the Newtown community for the location of the anticipated new county buildings, and for local supremacy. The name of the town Newtown was changed to Elmira, by act of legislature April 6, 1808, so it will be proper hereafter to speak of the locality as Elmira. Spencer was then sometimes known as "Pumpkin Hook;" but nothing daunted, she wrested from Elmira the sway of local dominancy and secured the location of the new county buildings there. February 17, 1810, an act was passed by the legislature appointing Nathaniel Locke, Anson Carey and Samuel Campbell, "commissioners to locate a new court-house site." In the winter of 1811, these commissioners removed the county seat from Elmira to Spencer. By the same act, Joshua Ferris, Isaac Swartout and Samuel Westbrook were appointed to superintend the erection of the new building. September 28, 1810, two acres of land, situate in Spencer, were purchased of Andrew Purdy out of his farm, for the price of $20.00. The new building was situate upon the corner where Messrs. Emmons Bros' store now is. This new court-house was built by Mr. Purdy, on contract, under the personal superintendence of Samuel Westbrook, and cost $5,595.60. It was a wooden building, two stories high. On the ground floor were four appartments, one of which was used for a prison for criminals, another for the imprisonment of debtors, the other two for the jailers apartments. The second story contained the court-room proper and two jury-rooms.

The strife was still rife between the Elmira and Spencer localities for dominancy, and the Elmira community still persisted in maintaining a species of independence. Accordingly, June 8, 1812, Tioga county was again divided into jury districts, the eastern and the western; and the courts of the county were held at Elmira and Spencer alternately. In January, 1821, the court-house in Spencer was destroyed by fire. It was occupied at the time by the jailor, John J. French, a revolutionary soldier. He was the father of three daughters, who occupied the jury-rooms in the second story for their appartments. The fire which destroyed the building broke out at mid-night, in these rooms. They claimed that it originated in the chimney, but many were uncharitable enough to assert their belief that the jailor's girls set the building on fire at the instigation of certain persons who were desirous of having the county seat removed to Elmira.

The legislature, March 31, 1821, passed an act directing the next courts to be held where the sheriff of the county should designate, and the first court of common pleas so held was to designate where the next term should be held, and so on from term to term, till a new court-house should be erected. It was also made lawful to confine the prisoners in the Tompkins county jail, or in the jail at Elmira.

A temporary court-house, one story high, was erected about twenty or thirty rods west of the old one. It adjoined a school-house, the latter being used during sessions of the court, a door having been cut between the buildings in order to give access from one to the other. The buildings were used for court purposes until the spring of 1822. The temporary court-house was removed fifteen or twenty rods west of its original location, to where it now stands, between George Rosecrance's wagon shop and Seth O. Sabin's blacksmith shop, where it is used to store lumber in.

In the meantime, the legislature, by act of April 12, 1813, revised the division of the state into towns, and exchanged the names of the towns of Owego and Tioga one for the other, as they are now denominated. And by an act passed March 22, 1822, the towns of Berkshire, and Owego, then including the new towns of Richford and Newark Valley also in the county of Broome, were annexed to the county of Tioga; the county as reconstructed was divided into two jury districts; and the act authorized the construction of new court-houses and jails in both Elmira and Owego. The two jury districts were designated the eastern and western. The eastern district comprised the towns of Tioga, Spencer, Danby, Caroline, Candor, Berkshire and Owego. The western district comprised the towns of Cayuta, Catharine, Chenango and Elmira. This act made it the duty of the board of supervisors at their annual meeting in October, 1822, to levy a tax of $4,000.00 and, in 1823, an additional tax of $2,000.00, to pay for the construction of new buildings, on condition that $2,000.00 additional be raised by voluntary subscriptions and paid in, and that lots for building sites should be conveyed free of expense to the county. Three commissioners were appointed to take charge of the construction of each of the court-houses. John R. Drake, Gen. Anson Camp and Charles Pumpelly were nominated the commissioners to build the one in Owego.

This act dividing the county into two jury districts also directed the courts for the eastern district to be held at the hotel of Erastus S. Marsh, which was situate upon the site of the present Ah-wa-ga House in Owego, until the new court-house should be erected. And the courts for the western jury district continued to be held at Elmira, until March 29, 1836, when it was made into an independent county and denominated Chemung county, by an act of the legislature.

February 28, 1799, the trustees of the Owego settlement acquired a considerable tract of land of James McMaster for a village park. In pursuance of the act of March 22, 1822, requiring that a lot for a building site for the new court-house and jail in Owego should be conveyed free of expense to the county, a further legislative act was passed April 17, 1822, authorizing the trustees of the village of Owego with the consent of the inhabitants of said village, to convey to the supervisors such parts of the lands originally conveyed by James McMaster and Rachel, his wife, to the trustees of the inhabitants of the Owego settlement as may be necessary to be occupied for the use of a court-house and jail to be erected in said village. Thereupon a meeting of the free holders and inhabitants of the village of Owego was held at Marsh's tavern, on the 12th day of October, and assent and authority given to the trustees of the public grounds in said village to deed to the supervisors of the county so much of the public grounds as they might "deem necessary to erect a court-house, and other necessary buildings upon as appendages to the court-house." The trustees of Owego settlement accordingly, on October 29, 1822, deeded to the supervisors of the county the ground on the corner of Main and Court streets, in Owego village, upon which are now situate the new sheriff's residence and jail, the old county clerk's office and the old jail building. The court-house was built by contract, Ralph Manning of Berkshire, constructing the cellar and Seth Bacon, of Candor, the structure. The work was completed in 1823. It fronted on Court street and had a hall running through its centre from east to west. On the north side of the hall were a sheriff's living room and an office. On the south side were two jail rooms and a kitchen. The stairs leading to the court-room proper, occupying the whole upper floor, were at the east end of the building.

At a special meeting of the board of supervisors, held March 3, 1851, it was decided to build a new sheriff's residence and jail. It was first proposed to build the new jail between the court-house and the old county clerk's office. The ground was then occupied by a fire engine house, which had been built there by the village in 1843, by permission of the supervisors. The plan was afterward changed, and it was decided to build east of the court-house. The village trustees were requested to remove the engine house, as the rear part occupied a portion of the ground needed for the jail. But they did not feel authorized to remove it or relinquish the right of the village to the ground without first obtaining an expression of the inhabitants. The matter was decided at a public meeting of the citizens of the village held on the 20th of March, 1851, when the trustees were directed to

remove the building before the first of April. On the day following that of the citizens' meeting, the supervisors directed the
county treasurer to loan $6,000.00 to be expended in building the
new sheriff's residence and jail. The jail was to be built of brick,
lined with two-inch oak planks, with one-half inch iron spiked to
the bond timbers and confined at the top and bottom by bars of
iron two and one-half by three and one-half inches, placed
horizontally, bolted to the bond timbers. It was built by J.
Conklin, of Elmira. The sheriff's residence still stands, being the
small brick structure on Main street east of the new sheriff's
residence and jail, and occupied by the telephone company and
others for offices. The old jail portion of the building was sold
in 1884 to A. H. Keeler for $125.00 and torn down by him.

In the summer of 1852 the court-house was repaired and re-
modeld by John Gorman and Chauncey Hungerford, at an expense
of $1,500.00. The judges bench and bar, which had been at the
west end of the court-room, were removed to the east end, and
additional stairs were built at the west end of the building. A
cupola, in which was afterwards, in 1855, placed a bell, was
built upon the roof at the west end of the court-house, and
various other changes were made. This court-house was sold to
A. H. Keeler and torn down by him, in 1877, after the brick
court-house in the park had been completed.

September 2, 1868, at the Tioga county oyer and terminer, the
grand jury of the county indicted the court-house and jail of the
county and " presented the Tioga county court-house as unsuitable
and inconvenient for the transaction of the legal business of the
county, and presented the Tioga county jail as insecure and inconvenient for the confinement of persons charged with crime;"
and " recommended that immediate action be taken by the proper
authorities for the building of a new court-house and jail as soon
as practical."

November 23, 1869, the board of supervisors passed a resolution to appoint a committee of three to procure plans, specifications and estimates for a new court-house, and to report at the
next annual meeting of the board; and Messrs. John A. Nichols,
of Spencer, John H. Deming, of Richford, and Frederick O.
Cable, of Owego, were appointed such committee, and made
their report to the board November 17, 1870. On December 1,
1870, a resolution was passed by the board of supervisors to pro-
ceed with as little delay as practical to erect a new court-house
and a new jail for the county, and a committee of three, consist-

ing of Messrs. John. H. Deming, of Richford, John J. Taylor and Daniel M. Pitcher, of Owego, was appointed to obtain plans and estimates of builders or architects of the expense thereof. This committee reported at a special meeting of the board of supervisors held on December 28, 1870, and recommended the public square in the village of Owego for a site. On the 9th of January, 1871, a meeting of the citizens of Owego Village was held and consent given to convey the public square to the supervisors for a court-house site, which site was adopted by the supervisors at a special meeting held January 12, 1871, but no other building except the court-house was to be erected thereon. The state legislature passed an act authorizing the board of trustees of Owego village to convey the public park to the supervisors for a court-house site, January 20, 1871, which was done by deed bearing date February 14, 1871. The present elaborate court-house was thereupon constructed, in 1871–73, in pursuance of the plans and specifications of Miles F. Howes, a resident architect of Owego village, by Messrs. A. H. Keeler and Jonathan S. Houk, contractors at the contract price of $55,700.00. The plans were altered, however, subsequently, to the letting of the contract and important changes made. The structure was completed in 1873, and on November 26, 1873, accepted by the board of supervisors at a total cost of constructing and fitting of $65,318.90.

The building of a new jail was for the time being abandoned, but the board of supervisors in annual session, November 23, 1881, resolved to build a new jail, either on the bank of the river or on the site of the jail above referred to; and on December 6, the site on the corner of Main and Court streets, upon which the old court-house of 1823 had been built, was selected. At a special meeting of the board, held April 17, 1882, the plans for a new jail and sheriff's residence were finally adopted, and the contract for constructing the same was awarded to John F. Corchran, of Owego, and the contract for the iron work was awarded to the Owego Iron Works, and the finishing and the plumbing to E. H. Cook & Co., of Elmira, and May 18, 1882, the board passed an act authorizing the borrowing of $20,000.00 on the bonds of the county of Tioga for the purpose of building a new sheriff's residence and jail. The new structure was erected in 1882–83, in pursuance of the foregoing plans and specifications. The sheriff's residence is built of brick and joined to it is the jail proper, built of solid stone masonery. The completed structure was accepted at a special meeting of the board of supervisors, held March 30, 1883, at a total cost of erecting, fitting with steam-heating, water and gas fixtures, grading grounds, etc., of $22,-739.13.

An act of the state legislature, passed April 3, 1798, provided for the recording of deeds and conveyances made and executed after the first day of February, 1799, in Tioga county, among others, in the clerk's office of the county, in books to be provided by the clerk of the county for that purpose. The county clerk's office was kept in Newtown from the time of the erection of the county, in 1791, until 1804. There was no specific county building used for a clerk's office at this era. The office was usually kept at the residence of the incumbent. March 20, 1804, the legislature, reciting a preamble that "sundry inhabitants of the county of Tioga had by their petition represented to the legislature that many inconveniences arise," enacted that from and after July 1, 1804, "the office of clerk of Tioga county should be kept in a central situation in said county, not more than three miles from the village of Owego, on the north side of the river Susquehanna." The clerk of the county at that time was Matthew Carpenter, of Newtown. Accordingly, in pursuance of the provisions of the enactment, Mr. Carpenter, in July, 1804, opened an office in Owego (then Tioga) and placed the same in charge of Samuel Avery, whom he appointed deputy county clerk, July 4, 1804. The exact place where Mr. Avery kept his office it is now impossible to determine, after an exhaustive effort we have been unable to identify it for surety. It is conjectured that he probably had desk room in the law office of his brother, John H. Avery, who was a lawyer, and had his office in a building on the bank of the Susquehanna river, on Front street, near the present residence of Dr. C. L. Stiles. Subsequently, Samuel Avery removed from Owego to Nanticoke, and thereupon, August 3, 1805, Mr. Carpenter appointed James Pumpelly, of Tioga (now Owego), as deputy county clerk of the county. Mr. Pumpelly moved the office to his land office, on Front street, where the building stood until a few years ago when it was moved back from the street, where it is still standing. Dr. William Jones, who was a cousin of Mrs. James Pumpelly, was also appointed deputy county clerk of the county, to act in the absence of James Pumpelly, January 11, 1806*. The clerk's office re-

*The official appointments of Samuel Avery, James Pumpelly, and William Jones, as deputy county clerks of Tioga county, by Matthew Carpenter, are to be found recorded in

mained in the old Pumpelly land office building until the town of Owego (then Tioga) was set off into Broome county, March 28, 1806. Upon the foot of this, the office of the clerk of the county was removed back to Newtown, in pursuance of an act of the legislature of April 7, 1806, requiring that the "clerk of Tioga county should keep his office in the Village of Newtown, any law to the contrary notwithstanding," where it remained until removed to Spencer, in pursuance of an act of the legislature passed March 12, 1813, which required that the clerk's office of the county should be kept " within two miles of the new court-house in the town of Spencer."

The first distinctive county clerk's office building was built in Spencer, in 1818. It was constructed of brick, at a cost of $1,139.00 and stood a short distance south of the court-house. The builder was Andrew Purdy, of whom the land upon which it stood had been purchased, and the commissioners appointed to superintend its construction were Abel Hart, of Candor, and Judge Henry Miller and Joshua Ferris, of Spencer. After the building was completed the supervisors refused to pay Mr. Purdy the entire amount of his claim, which subsequent proceedings showed to be a fair and just one. An application was made to the legislature, which passed an act April 12, 1822, appointing Richard Townley, Richard Smith and Luther Gere commissioners to audit Mr. Purdy's claims, which were subsequently allowed by them in full. After the destruction of the court-house in Spencer, in January, 1821, an act was passed by the legislature, April 15, 1823, repealing the act requiring the Tioga county clerk's office to be kept in Spencer. The same act appointed Parlee E. Howe, of the County of Onondaga, Henry Towar, of Ontario county, and Charles Kellogg, of Cayuga county, " a committee to determine a proper site for a county clerk's office in Tioga county, said site to be within one mile of one of the court-houses in the county," and the clerk was required to remove his office to the place so designated within thirty days. The office was removed to Owego from Spencer in July, 1823, in conformity to the decision of these commissioners. The building in which it was kept was a small one-story structure on the bank of the Susquehanna river, on the south side of Front street, about twenty feet east of the present residence of Mr. William A. King. The basement of the building was occupied by the late Stephen

the Tioga county clerk's office, in Deed Book No. 6, at pages 25 and 328, and Deed Book No. 7, page 72, respectively.

B. Leonard, deceased, as a printing office, where he published the *Owego Gazette*. The clerk of Tioga county at this time was Thomas Maxwell, who resided in Elmira. Upon the removal of the office to Owego, it was placed in charge of Major Horatio Ross, whom Maxwell appointed deputy county clerk.

April 10, 1824, the legislature of the state passed an act authorizing the supervisors to dispose of the old clerk's office in Spencer, built in 1818, and April 21, 1825, the legislature passed another act which appointed Joseph Berry, Elizur Talcott and John Ripley, all of Owego, commissioners " to cause to be erected a suitable and sufficient fire-proof building for a clerk's office in the village of Owego," and authorized them•to receive the monies realized from the sale of the clerk's office in Spencer, pursuant to the act of April 10, 1824. It also directed the supervisors at their next annual meeting to cause a tax to be levied not exceeding $1,000.00 nor less than $800.00 including the amount received from the sale of the Spencer clerk's office, to be expended in building the new clerk's office. The Spencer clerk's office was sold to Andrew Purdy, April 23, 1825, for $210.00, and the board of supervisors at their annual meeting in November, 1825, directed that it be applied to the use of the commissioners for building a fire-proof clerk's office at Owego, and that an additional sum of $600.00 be levied and raised by tax on the towns of the eastern jury district for the purpose of erecting a fire-proof clerk's office in the village of Owego, making in all $810.00.

The office was built by Abner Beers, near the south-west corner of the court-house lot, on Court street, in 1825, and cost $792.00. A committee of three; Messrs. Samuel Barager, of Candor, William H. Moore, of Berkshire, and William A. Ely, of Owego, appointed to settle the accounts of the commissioners, reported to the board of supervisors that the new clerk's office was completed and that there remained unexpended the sum of $18.00, at the annual meeting of the board in November, 1826. The new building was one story high, with brick floors, and 18x28 feet insize. Its height was twelve feet. It contained two rooms with four windows and the shutters were of wood, cased with sheet iron. It was as near fire-proof as could be made.

This clerk's office, as the county grew in population and its business increased, became too small for the purposes intended, and, in 1854, it was deemed necessary to build a new one. In the fall of that year the supervisors resolved to build a new one at an expense of $2,000.00 and appointed Harvey Coryell, of Nichols,

Samuel Mills, of Barton, and Josiah Rich, of Candor, to procure plans, etc. In April, 1855, the old clerk's office was torn down, and during the same year the brick one now occupied by the Owego Free Library, on Court street, was erected on its site. The mason work was done under the supervision of Thomas Ireland, and the carpenter work by Almerin S. Waring. The cost was $2,200.00. Mr. Waring made a poor job of it, in order to make his contract as profitable as possible to himself, and was consequently obliged to make several alterations to the interior before the supervisors would accept and pay for it. While the building was being constructed, the grand-jury room, in the northwest corner of the old court-house, was occupied as the clerk's office, the documents and records of the county being removed thereto.

The clerk's office was kept in the brick structure on Court street, from 1855 until the completion and acceptance of the new court-house, in 1873. Rooms for a clerk's office had been constructed and fitted up in the southeast corner of the new court-house, into which the clerks office was moved in the winter and spring of 1874, where it has since been kept.*

JUDICIARY AND CIVIL LIST.

Justice of the Supreme Court.

John M. Parker,..1859–67†

Surrogates.

John Mersereau,	1791	Robert Lawrence,	1821
Balthazar De Haert,	1798	Charles Baker,	1825
William Woodruff,	1802	William Maxwell,	1829
William Jenkins,	1805	Thomas Farrington,	1835
Caleb Baker,	1806	Nathaniel W. Davis,	1840
Robert Lawrence,	1808	Alansan Munger,	1844
Isaac S. Boardman,	1820		

First Judges.

Abram Miller,	1791	Latham A. Burrows,	1825
John Patterson,	1798	Grant B. Baldwin,	1828
John Miller,	1807	John R. Drake,	1833
Emanuel Coryell,	1810	Stephen Strong,	1838
Gamaliel H. Barstow,	1818	Alanson Munger,	1843
Silas Hopkins,	1823		

*The compiler of this chapter desires to express his acknowledgements to Mr. LeRoy W. Kingman for valuable assistance rendered him; and also for the liberty of selecting material from historial sketches prepared by Mr. Kingman and published in the *Owego Gazette*, of August 2, 9, and 16, 1883.

†Date of Elections.

County Judges and Surrogates.

Charles P. Avery,..... 1847–55
Stephen Strong,....... 1856–59
Thomas Farrington,.... 1860–71
Charles A. Clark, ... 1872–83
Charles E. Parker,..... 1884–89

Special Judges and Surrogates.

Charles A. Munger, ... 1853–55
Alanson Munger, ... 1856–58
William F. Warner,.... 1859–61
Alanson Munger,....... 1862–64
Charles A. Munger,.... 1865–67
Adolphus G. Allen,.... 1868–70
James B. Caryl,........ 1871
J. Newton Dexter, ... 1872–74
Jacob B. Floyd,.... ... 1875–77
J. Newton Dexter, ... 1878–80
D. Wellington Allen,... 1881–83
Adolphus G. Allen,.... 1884–86
Judge F. Shoemaker,.. 1887–89

Judges of Common Pleas and Sessions.

Joshua Mersereau,
John Miller,
Elijah Buck,
Emanuel Coryell, } 1798

Caleb Baker,
Phineas Catlin,
Lewis Beers,
Joseph Speed,
Henry Wells, } 1810

August Boyer,
John Cantine, } 1814

Joshua Ferris,
Noah Goodrich,
Stephen Beers, } 1816

Thomas Floyd, 1820

William Jenkins,
Jacob Willsey,
Henry Miller.
Benjamin Jennings, } 1821

Latham Burrows,
David Williams,
John H. Knapp, } 1823

John McConnell, 1825

Darius Bently,
J. Talcott Waldo, } 1827

John G. McDowell,
John R. Drake, } 1828

Joseph L. Darling,
Elijah Shoemaker, } 1832

George Fisher, 1833

J. Westlake,
Ira Clizbee,
Samuel Barager, } 1836

Elisha P. Higbee,
Arthur Yates, } 1838

Clark Hyatt, 1844

Assistant Justices.

John Konkle,
Thomas Floyd,
John Robinson,
Joel Smith, } 1810

John Cantine,
Benjamin Wynkoop,
Elijah S. Hinman, } 1816

Justices of Sessions.

J. Talcott Waldo,
Thomas Yates, } 1848–49

Gamaliel H. Barstow,
Samuel Barager, } 1850

*5

J. Talcott Waldo, Israel S. Hoyt,	1851	Samuel C. Bidwell, John H. Yontz,	1870
J. Talcott Waldo, Sylvester Knapp,	1852	Luther B. West, H. H. Bidwell,	1871
Oliver A. Barstow, Samuel Barager,	1853	Luther B. West, George Cooper,	1872
Gaylord Willsey, Aug. T. Garey,	1854	Luther B. West, Daniel B. Nash,	1873
Robert B. Miller, Samuel Barager,	1855–56	Anson M. Kimball, John C. Parmelee,	1874
Nathaniel F. Moore, John L. Howell,	1857	Daniel B. Nash, John C. Parmelee,	1875
Nathaniel F. Moore, Thomas Yates,	1858	Gershom A. Clark, Robert B Miller,	1876
Edwin H. Schoonover, Aug. T. Garey,	1859	Chas. F. Curtis, Robert B. Miller.	1877
Robert B. Miller, Lorain Curtis,	1860	Daniel B. Nash, Junius Collins,	1878
Robert B. Miller, Samuel Barager,	1861	Gershom A. Clark, Charles F. Curtis,	1879
Samuel C. Bidwell, Samuel Barager,	1862	John C. Parmelee, Daniel B. Nash,	1880
Horace C. Hubbard, Samuel Barager,	1863	Ira Hoyt, George H. Grafft,	1881
William E Gee, Luther B. West,	1864	William B. Georgia, Noah Goodrich,	1882
Lorain Curtis, Samuel Barager,	1865	John C. Parmelee, Ira Hoyt,	1883
Oscar Glezen, John H. Yontz,	1866	Ira Hoyt, Noah Goodrich,	1884
Samuel C. Bidwell, William F. Belden,	1867	Ira M. Howell, Ira Hoyt,	1885–86
Herbert Richardson, John H. Yontz,	1868	Junius Collins, Ira M. Howell.	1887
Herbert Richardson, William F. Belden,	1869		

District Attorneys.

William Stuart,	1796	Stephen Strong,	1844
Vincent Matthews,	1813	Ezra S. Sweet,	1847
John L. Tillinghast,	1818	Alanson Munger,	1850
William Maxwell,	1822	Benjamin F. Tracy,	1853
Eleazar Dana,	1823	Delos O. Hancock,	1859
Aaron Konkle,	1826	Isaac S. Catlin,	1865
Andrew K. Gregg.	1835	Delos O. Hancock,	1867
Stephen Strong,	1836	Eugene B. Gere,	1870
Ezra S. Sweet,	1838	Lyman Settle,	1873
John J. Taylor,	1841	Howard J. Mead,	1880
George S. Camp,	1843	John G. Sears,	1886

County Clerks.

Thomas Nicholson,.....	1791-92	LeRoy W. Kingman,...	1853-58
Matthew Carpenter,	.1792-1817	Thomas C. Platt,.......	1859-61
Thomas Maxwell,......	1817-28	Horace A. Brooks,.....	1862-73
Green M. Tuthill,......	1829-34	John J. VanKleek,.....	1874-76
David Wallis,..........	1835-43	John C. Gray,...	1877-82
Moses Stevens,........	1844-52	John J. VanKleeck.....	1883-88

Sheriffs.

James McMaster,..........	1791	Robert L. Fleming,........	1840
Joseph Hinchman,........	1795	Charles R. Barstow, ...	1843
Edward Edwards,..... ...	1799	John J. Sackett,.....	1846
Guy Maxwell, ...	1800	Nathan H, Woodford,.....	1849
John Cantine,.............	1804	Robbins D. Willard,......	1852
William Woodruff,........	1805	Samuel Mills,.............	1855
William Jenkins,..........	1806	Daniel L. Jenks,..........	1858
Jonathan Platt,...........	1810	Frank L. Jones,...........	1860
Miles Forman,...........	1811	Barney M. Stebbins,.......	1860
Jonathan Platt,...........	1813	Hiram W. Shoemaker,....	1861
Miles Forman, ...	1815	Joseph B. Upham,.........	1864
Elijah S. Hinman,.	1819	Barney M. Stebbins,......	1864
Henry Wells,......... ..	1819	Lewis W. Truesdell,......	1866
Miles Forman,...........	1821	Thomas F. Pearl,..... -	1869
William Jenkins,..........	1822	Charles C. Brooks,........	1872
E. Shoemaker,............	1825	William H. Rightmire, ...	1875
Henry McCormick,.......	1828	Timothy Robertson,.......	1878
Lyman Covell,...........	1831	Burr J. Davis,............	1881
John Jackson,......... ...	1834	Charles Rodman,.........	1884
Prentice Ransom,........	1837		

County Treasurers.

Jonathan Fitch,...........	1793	William P. Stone,.........	1847
Orringh Stoddart, ...	1795	Charles Platt,.............	1848
David Pixley,.............	1798	Franklin Slosson,.........	1851
Samuel Tinkham,........	1803	Ezra S. Buckbee,.........	1854
Joshua Ferris, ...	1804-36	Gordon G. Manning,......	1860
John Carmichael,........	1837	John B. Brush,............	1863
Daniel Armstrong,........	1843	Eli W. Stone, ...	1872
Franklin Slosson,........	1846	Charles F. Parmele,.......	1881

CHAPTER V.

THE internal improvements of our state were commenced at the close of the last century, and were a stupendous undertaking. More than half of the state was in forest. To make passable roads through an almost unbroken wilderness, over rugged mountains, and to bridge swift and broad streams, required indomitable energy and an unshaken faith in the future growth and prosperity of the state. We cannot withhold our admiration of the wisdom of those men upon whom devolved the duty of shaping legislation upon this subject. The plan adopted was that of granting charters to companies for the construction of turnpikes in all parts of the state. The first act affecting the county of Tioga was the appointment of commissioners, in 1797, to lay out a turnpike from "Kaatskill Landing," on the Hudson, to the town of Catharines, in Tioga (now Tompkins) county. The completion of this work led subsequently to the construction, by citizens of Owego and Ithaca, of the Owego and Ithaca Turnpike, and, as early as 1816, Tioga county appears to have had connection with all the great thoroughfares of the state.

The next step in the matter of internal improvements was the construction of canals. The Hudson and Erie was opened for traffic in 1825, to the great advantage of the state at large, but with very little direct benefit to the people of Tioga county, indeed it rather retarded the growth and prosperity of the county. We return for a moment to the period of the construction of the Ithaca and Owego Turnpike. The opening of this avenue gave an outlet from the north, through the county, to Owego upon the Susquehanna, and a very considerable traffic in salt, plaster, flour and grain was carried on to supply the markets in Pennsylvania and Maryland. A circumstance connected with the construction of this turnpike is perhaps of sufficient interest to be noticed. A contest arose between the owners of the two rival taverns on Front street, the Bates tavern and the Franklin, as to the terminus of the road at Owego. The present McMaster street was the original highway leading northward from the village. Each of the owners of these public houses strove to secure the terminus at his inn. The contest was sharp and even bitter. The proprietors of the turnpike finally compromised the matter by fixing the terminus of the road at the intersection of North avenue with Main street, about midway between the rival taverns.

Large store-houses were built at Owego, and for many years this was the principal source of supply of the above mentioned articles for a large territory. The traffic became so large, in fact, that in 1824 an effort was made to navigate the Susquehanna by steamboat, but which was not only a failure but caused a serious disaster by the explosion of its boiler. The river furnished means of transportation by canoes and the Durham boat, propelled by the use of setting-poles, and later, by a modern "ark," which, like the ephemeron, had but a brief existence, terminating with a single voyage down the Susquehanna. By means of these Durham boats and arks an extensive traffic was maintained. The citizens of the county, not willing to be left behind in the growing prosperity of the state, with commendable energy obtained a charter, in 1828, for a railroad from Ithaca to Owego, which was opened for use in 1834, the cars being propelled by horse-power, making a line of communication with Cayuga lake and the Erie canal. Direct communication with the city of New York was accomplished by the extension of the Erie railroad to Owego in the month of June, 1849.

A second effort was made, about 1835, to navigate the Susquehanna by steam-power. The Susquehanna Steamboat and Navigation company was formed, which procured the construction of a stern-wheel boat. This novel attempt at river navigation also proved unsuccessful. It served to illustrate, however, the enterprise of the commercial men of that period, and their desire to keep abreast with the internal improvements going forward in other portions of the state.

At the first session of the VIth Congress of the United States, 1799–1800, a mail-route was established from the Hudson, by way of Kaatskill, Harpersfield, Oleout, Unadilla and Windsor, in New York, to Tioga Point (Athens), Pa. The same act provided for a mail-route from Wilkesbarre, by way of Wyalusing, Tioga

Point, Newtown (Elmira),Painted Post and Bath, to Canandaigua. It is difficult to conceive how a mail could have been conveyed over these routes, where there were neither roads nor bridges. For fifteen years, however, the pioneer had been dependent upon private hands, and chance ways and means for receiving by letter or verbal communication, intelligence from distant friends. A postoffice was established at Owego, with Stephen Mack as post-master, about 1803. In 1814 the mail was carried between Chenango Point and Tioga Point in a one-horse wagon. This was continued until 1816, when Conrad Peter commenced carry-ing the mail between Owego and Newburg, on the Hudson, in a wagon drawn by four horses. Nine years later (1825), Stephen B. Leonard established a line of coaches running twice a week between Owego and Bath, Steuben county. Subsequently Lewis Manning and his son, Chester J. Manning, of Owego, Major Morgan, of Chenango Point, Cooley and Maxwell, of Newtown (Elmira), and John McGee, of Bath, became the proprietors of the great Southern Tier Mail and Passenger Coach Line, between Newburgh and Bath, which became a daily line and was con-tinued until the opening of the New York and Erie railroad, in 1849. Thus the first fifty years of this century were a period in which were made three marked advances in the mail service: first, from the irregular and chance service, to one at intervals of two weeks; second, a mail twice each week, and improving to a daily delivery; third, the present mail service by railroad, beginning in 1849.

The changes wrought in the facilities for travel, commerce, transportation of the mails, and by the invention of the telegraph, all within the past forty-five years, are as marvelous as any of the thousand-and-one tales of the "Arabian Nights" Entertainment." As an illustration of the magnitude of these changes let it be noted that towns distant from each other twenty miles by coach have practically been rendered but two miles apart by the intro-duction of the railroad.

The Cayuga and Susquehanna Railroad was the second rail-road chartered in this state. It was incorporated January 28, 1828, with a capital stock of $150,000.00 and authorized to con-struct a road from Ithaca to Owego. No attempt, however, was made to construct the road until the building of the Chemung canal from Elmira to Watkins. The successful accomplishment of this project was regarded by the citizens of Ithaca and Owego as detrimental to the interests of their towns, and a movement was started by Simeon DeWitt, then a resident of Ithaca, and others to build the road. In March 1832, the capital stock was increased to $300,000.00 and the road was opened in April, 1834. In the following month the capital stock was increased to $450,-000.00 and in April, 1838, the legislature authorized a loan to the company of $250,000.00 taking a lien upon the road and its appurtenances. The "panic" of 1837 crippled the company; it failed to pay the interest to the state, and on May 20, 1842, the comptroller sold it at auction to Archibald McIntire and others. The road as originally constructed was twenty-nine miles in length, with two inclined planes ascending from Ithaca. The first of these was 1,733⅓ feet long, with 405 feet rise, and the second was 2,125 feet in length, with a rise of one foot in twenty-one. The total elevation in eight miles was 602 feet above its southern terminus at Ithaca. It was operated on the first plane by a stationary steam-engine, while horses were used as the motive-power on the balance of the road. After passing into the hands of Mr. McIntire, the inclined planes were replaced by others of lesser grade, traversing the mountain in a zigzag manner, and locomotives superseded the horse-power and stationary engine. The main line of the road is now 34.61 miles in length, and the total track mileage is 40 61. The road is leased to the Delaware, Lackawanna and Western Railroad company, and is operated by them as the Cayuga division.

The New York, Lake Erie and Western Railroad company was incorporated as the New York and Erie Railroad company, April 24, 1832. In 1861 it was re-organized as the Erie Railway company, which organization was continued until 1878, when it was again re-organized, this time as the New York, Lake Erie and Western. The first section of this road was opened for traffic from Piermont to Goshen, in 1841; from Goshen to Middletown in June, 1843; to Port Jervis in January, 1848; to Binghamton in December, 1848; to Elmira in October, 1849; to Corning in January 1850; and through to Dunkirk, the then western terminus, May 14, 1851. The opening of the road brought a wealthy and comparatively isolated section of the state in communication with the sea-board, and soon became the outlet for a large Western traffic. Although the "Erie," as it is familiarly known, has had a checkered career, it has ever been regarded as one of the representative railways of the United States. The road crosses the towns of Owego, Tioga, and Barton, in Tioga county.

The Southern Central Railroad company was incorporated in September, 1865, as the Lake Ontario, Auburn & New York railroad, but subsequently its present corporate title was substituted. The company as originally organized was authorized to construct a road from Fair Haven, on Lake Ontario, to Athens, near the Pennsylvania state line. Twenty-five miles of the road were opened in 1869; forty-three in 1870; twenty-seven in 1871; and the remaining twenty-two miles in the winter of 1871–72. The Southern Central railway is 117 miles in length. It crosses the towns of Richford, Berkshire, Newark Valley, Owego, Tioga and Barton, in Tioga county. On January 1, 1887, the road was leased to the L. V. R. R. Co. for a period of 975 years.

The Geneva, Ithaca and Sayre Railroad Company is successor to the Geneva, Ithaca and Athens Railroad Company, which was formed by a consolidation, May 25, 1874, of the Ithaca and Athens and the Geneva and Ithaca Railroad Companies. The former was opened in 1871, the latter in 1874. Having defaulted in payment of interest, the G. I. & A. R. R. was placed in the hands of a receiver, March 24, 1875, and re-organized under its present name, October 2, 1876. On April 5, 1879, the Cayuga Southern Railroad, by an act of the legislature, was consolidated with the G. I. & S. R. R. Co., and now forms a part of its line. The former road was organized as the Cayuga Lake Railroad in 1867; opened May 1, 1873; sold under foreclosure July 26, 1877, and re-organized. The G. I. & S. R. R. enters the southwestern part of the county, and after passing through a part of Barton, enters Chemung county, to appear in Tioga county again, passing through the town of Spencer.

The Elmira, Cortland and Northern Railroad Company is a re-organization, March 7, 1884, of the Utica, Ithaca and Elmira Railroad Company. That company was constituted by a con_solidation of the Ithaca and Cortland, and Utica, Horseheads and Elmira Railroad Companies, the former of which was organized July 31, 1869, and the latter April 2, 1870. It traverses the towns of Spencer and Candor, in Tioga county.

The Delaware, Lackawanna and Western Railroad, as it passes through Tioga county, traversing the towns of Owego and Nichols, was originally built as the New York, Lackawanna and Western Railroad. In October, 1882, it was leased to the Delaware, Lackawanna and Western Railroad Company, thus extending that company's line through to Buffalo.

CHAPTER VI.

NEWSPAPERS OF OWEGO—OF WAVERLY— OF NEWARK VALLEY—OF SPENCER —OF CANDOR.

THE first newspaper published in this part of the State of New York was *The American Constellation.* It was established November 23, 1800, and was dated at " Union, Tioga County, N. Y.," although it was really printed at Chenango village. a small settlement on the Chenango river, about one mile above the present city of Binghamton. Mr. Cruger afterward removed his printing office to Owego. The name of the paper was changed in August, 1803, to *The American Farmer,* and some time afterward Stephen Mack became its publisher. In the winter of 1813, Stephen B. Leonard purchased a one half interest in the paper. June 15, 1814, after the death of Judge Mack, Mr. Leonard changed the name of the paper to *The Owego Gazette,* which name it still bears. In October, 1827, Jonas B. Shurtleff became Mr. Leonard's partner. This partnership continued two years, when Mr. Shurtleff withdrew from the firm. John J. C. Cantine was Mr. Leonard's partner from 1833 to 1835. In the fall of the latter year the establishment was sold to Shurtleff & Bull. In July 1836, Mr. Shurtleff purchased his partner's interest and continued the publication of the paper until February, 1839, when Edward P. Marble became the proprietor. In December, 1841, the paper passed into the hands of Charles C. Thomas, and Alanson Munger became its editor. July 15, 1842, Thomas Woods succeeded Mr. Thomas as proprietor of the paper, and Gideon O. Chase became the editor. In January, 1843, Hiram A. Beebe purchased the paper, subject to a chattle mortgage of $400, which had been given by Mr. Marble. At this time the division of the Democratic party into "Hunkers" and "Barnburners" occurred. The leaders of the "Barnburners" induced Mr. Woods to foreclose the mortgage, and the establishment was sold to Mr. Woods. Mr. Beebe at once secured a new press and material and opened a new office. The result was that two papers called *The Owego Gazette* were published at the same time. A suit brought to collect payment for certain legal advertising, resulted in a decision in favor of Mr. Beebe, the court holding that the sale of the *Gazette* printing office on a mortgage foreclosure did not include the good will or the name of the paper. Mr. Woods was accordingly compelled to discontinue the publication of his paper. Mr. Beebe sold the *Gazette* to Thomas Pearsall, in July, 1845, who sold it to David Wallis & Son, in March, 1846. The next year Mr. Beebe repurchased the paper. In August, 1871, he sold a one-half interest in the establishment to LeRoy W. Kingman. In September, 1880, the latter became sole proprietor. The *Gazette* has always been Democratic in politics.

On the 2d of September, 1828, Stephen S. Chatterton commenced the publication of the *Owego Free Press,* and supported John Quincy Adams, the Republican (or Whig) candidate for President. Gen. Jackson, the Democratic candidate, was elected and after the election the publication of the paper was discontinued.

The organ of the old Whig party, the *Owego Advertiser,* was established in Owego, in 1836, and its first number was issued March 25th. In June, 1853, the establishment was sold to a stock company, composed of William Smyth and eleven other persons, and the office was leased for one year to Powell & Barnes. At the same time the name of the paper was changed to the *Southern Tier Times.* Mr. Smyth purchased the interests of the other stockholders, in June, 1854. June 7, 1855, he changed the name to *Owego Times.* In 1872, Mr. Smyth took his son, Wm. A. Smyth, into partnership, and the paper has since been published by Wm. Smyth & Son. Since the formation of the Republican party the *Times* has been its organ.

The division of the Democratic party in this state into two factions, one of which was known as the "Free Soil" Democrats, resulted in the establishment of a "Free Soil" newspaper in Owego. It was called *The Tioga Freeman.* Its editor was Gideon O. Chase, it was owned by a stock company, and John Dow was the publisher. Its first number was issued May 2, 1848. In September, 1849, the office was destroyed by fire and its publication was discontinued.

In April, 1853, Chas. P. Avery, Thomas C. Platt, Chas. A. Munger, and others, issued the first number of a monthly magazine called *St. Nicholas.* It was published one year. It contained among other things a series of papers entitled " The Susquehanna Valley,'' written by Judge Avery, and which have been the foundation of all early history of Tioga county.

August 23, 1855, Andrew H. Calhoun issued the first number of the *Owego American*, the organ of the American, or " Know-Nothing " party. Its business office was in Owego, but the paper was printed on the press of *The American Citizen* at Ithaca. Mr. Calhoun was the "Know-Nothing" candidate for State Senator and was defeated. At the conclusion of the campaign the publication of the paper was discontinued.

In 1870, Charles H. Keeler, the proprietor of a job printing office, commenced the publication of a small advertising sheet, for free circulation, known as the *Trade Reporter.* It was enlarged and called the *Tioga County Record*, March 18, 1871. August 3, 1885, the paper was sold to C. S. Scott and is now published as a daily and weekly, by Messrs. Scott & Watros.

The defection of a large number of the prominent men of the Republican party, known as Liberal Republicans, resulted in the establishment of an organ in Owego. It was called *The Ahwaga Chief*, and its first number was issued February 23, 1872. Its last number was published November 1, 1872, with the close of the Presidential campaign.

The publication of *The Workingman*, the organ of the Greenbackers, was commenced in Owego, November 1, 1877, by two printers, Webster & Graves. It died a natural death with its issue of February 28, 1879.

Benjamin B. F. Graves commenced the publication of a newspaper in the interest of Temperance on the 18th of January, 1879. It was entitled *The Family Journal and Temperance Advocate*, and was published but five weeks.

Another Temperance organ, *The Resolute*, was published the same year. Its first number was dated April 12, 1879. Its editors were G. M. Jordan and G. W. Tyson. It expired with its thirty-fourth issue, November 8, 1879.

The *Owego Blade*, a Republican newspaper was established January 1, 1880, by McCormick & Young. It afterward became the property of Eugene B. Gere, who published it until April, 1887, when it was discontinued.

The first number of the *Owego Press*, a monthly newspaper devoted to educational matters, was issued by C. R. Burnette, in September, 1886, and expired with its twelfth issue, August, 1887.

Daily Journalism in Owego.—The first attempt to establish a daily newspaper in Owego was made in 1838, by Mr. Calhoun, publisher of the Owego *Advertiser*. Its first number was issued October 18th, in that year. It was published but a few weeks.

The next attempt to establish a daily journal was made by Mr. Beebe, in 1855, the first number appearing on the 18th day of October. It was discontinued on the 6th of the following December.

The *Daily Gazette* was revived May 27, 1861, at the commencement of the civil war. It was not properly sustained by the public and its publication was discontinued in the following October.

Backed by neither capital nor brains, the first number of the *Daily Owegoan* appeared October 7, 1879. It was published by Dorsey B. Gibson. It struggled along until the 4th of the following August, when it ceased to exist.

The Owego *Daily Blade* was established by E. B. Gere, and its first number was issued November 4, 1882. With its issue dated April 23, 1887, its publication was discontinued.

The daily edition of the *Record*, previously mentioned, was started December 20, 1886, by Messrs. Scott & Watros, its present publishers.

Waverly Newspapers.—The *Waverly Luminary* was established by Thomas Messenger, October 3, 1851. The office of the paper was on the second floor of the Spalding block, and here under Messenger, " Brick " Pomeroy took his first lessons in " the art preservative of arts," and, it is said, at an early age developed those traits of character which have since made him so well known. The *Luminary* had a brief existence of about ten months. F. H. Baldwin soon after purchased the office and material, and, September 17, 1852, published the initial number of the *Waverly Advocate*. M. H. Bailey succeeded him in 1853, publishing the paper for a few months, when, in 1854, F. H. Baldwin and William Polleys purchased the paper, and continued the publication until 1860, when O. H. P. Kinney succeeded to Mr. Baldwin's interest. Polleys & Kinney continued as publishers till 1883, during which year both died, the former in June and the latter in September. G. D. Genung, who for about a year previous to Mr. Kinney's death had edited the *Advocate*, continued its publication, for the administrators of the estates, G. F. Wellar and J. G. Kinney, until the following April, when legal questions regarding the settlement of the estates of the deceased publishers arose that resulted in the closing of the office. Soon after this, J. C. Shear purchased the Kinney interest in the business ; and, July 15, 1884,

E. M. Fenner purchased the paper and resumed its publication. January 1, 1885, Mr. Fenner's father became nominally associated with him in the publication of the *Advocate*, under the firm name of E. M. Fenner & Co., and G. D. Genung was again engaged as manager and editor of the paper, a position which he has filled to the present time. February 1st., E. M. Fenner retired from the concern, and June 15th it was sold to Messrs. Wellar & Shear, who continued the publication until November 1, 1885, when they sold to its present proprietor, E. L. Vincent, a talented newspaper man. The paper has been increased to a nine-column folio, new type, presses, etc., have been added, and it is now the leading paper published in the place, and ranks with the foremost country newspapers of the day. It is Republican in politics, liberal and enterprising, and under the present management more prosperous than ever before in its history.

The Waverly Enterprise, was established October 15, 1867, by Frank T. Scudder, a young man of much ability. It first appeared as a four-column monthly folio, 12x18 inches, then as a semi-monthly of 18x24 inches, and thus continued for about three years, when it was changed to a five-column folio, and published as a weekly. It was enlarged from time to time until, in 1873, it was an eight-column folio, and one of the most prosperous newspapers in the county. Mr. Scudder's health failing, he sold a half interest, in 1874, to P. C. Van Gelder. The partnership continued about six months, when Mr. Van Gelder purchased Mr. Scudder's remaining interest, and then sold a half interest to Amos Roberts. Shortly after, Mr. Van Gelder leased his interest to J. A. Fraser, and the business was continued until October 7, 1876, by Roberts & Fraser, at which date the office was entirely destroyed by fire. The subscription list and good-will of the office were then purchased by James B. Bray, who was formerly foreman of the office, but was at that time conducting a job office of his own, and the paper was revived under its present title, *The Waverly Free Press*. Mr. Bray, who had been in failing health for many years, soon found that the added responsibility was undermining his remaining strength, and in December, 1877, he sold the office to Cyrus Marsh, who continued in the office but two weeks, when Mr. Bray assumed control again, and has since continued as editor and proprietor. The office has always been prosperous, especially so under the management of its founder and the present proprietor. The paper is especially devoted to local news and home interests, and is fearless in all

matters pertaining to the public interests. It has always been
Independent Republican in politics, but never extremely partisan.

The *Waverly and Athens Democrat*, a seven-column folio, was
established by David P. Shutts, in the winter of 1867–68, and was
continued by him about one year, when he formed a partnership
with S. C. Clizbe; but the partnership existed but a few months,
when Mr. Clizbe retired, and Mr. Shutts continued the paper
until 1870, when it suspended. The material was purchased by
Polleys & Kinney, then proprietors of the *Waverly Advocate*. Mr.
Charles Rogers was the political editor of the *Democrat*.

The *Waverly Review* was established by Ira L. Wales, during
the summer of 1875. It was a seven column folio, Democratic in
politics, and from the first had a precarious existence. Two
attempts were made to establish a daily paper, but neither succeeded beyond a few months, and in April, 1882, Mr. Wales
closed his office here, and moved the material to Binghamton.

The *Waverly Tribune*, an eight page weekly, was established in
1882, by W. H. Noble and A. G. Reynolds, under the firm name
of Noble & Reynolds. The first number appeared April 27, and
three numbers were issued by this firm, when Mr. Reynolds sold
his interest to A. C. Noble, a brother of the senior partner. Since
that time the paper has been conducted by these brothers, under
the firm name of Noble & Noble. From the outset the *Tribune*
has met with success, the office having grown from a small job
office to one of the best equipped in the county. The paper is
non partisan.

Newark Valley Newspaper. — The *Tioga County Herald* was established March 4, 1876, by G. M. Jordan, now a resident of San
Antonia, Florida, and George Riley, Jr., now one of the proprietors of the *Press*, at Ottumwa, Iowa. In May of the same year
Mr. Riley disposed of his interest in the business to H. A.
LeBarron. Messrs. Jordan and LeBarron conducted the paper
until August 25, 1877, when Charles L. Noble purchased the
interest of Mr. LeBarron. On January 1, 1878, Mr. Noble became sole proprietor, and conducted the paper until January 1,
1884, when G. E. Purple became a member of the firm, and since
that time the paper has been published by Noble and Purple.

Spencer Newspapers. — The first attempt at publishing a newspaper in Spencer was made in 1874. In the spring of that year,
Otho Hedges, a young man who probably possessed more enterprise than capital, took up his residence in the village and began
the publication of the *Spencer News*. The first number had four

pages, about 9x12 inches. In a few weeks the paper assumed somewhat larger proportions ; but struggled along with a small circulation. Toward the close of the summer, an enlargement was made to four six-column pages, with a "patent" outside, and the *News* made quite a pretentious appearance ; but this sudden expansion seemed to be in excess of the elasticity of the editorial funds, and a financial explosion took place in the fall of that year. No further effort at journalism was made in Spencer until the summer of 1878, when the *Spencer Herald* was started by Pride &Foote, on the 22d of August, an independent journal which is maintained to the present. In the fall of 1878 Mr. Pride retired from the concern, and Foote continued the publication to the summer of 1880, when it was purchased by J. LeRoy Nixon, who enlarged the paper from seven columns to eight, and soon thereafter to nine; but finding this size too expensive for profit, dropped back to eight columns, its present size. On January 1, 1887, the office was purchased by its present owners, P. C. Van Gelder & Son, who put in steam-power, and other facilities, dressed the paper in new type, and changed its form from four to eight pages. The paper has a large local circulation, and a liberal local advertising patronage.

Candor Newspapers.—The first venture in journalism in Candor was made in 1867, by Clizbe & Mandeville, who issued the *Candor Press* for a time, and sold it to Benjamin Graves, who continued its publication under the name of the *Candor Free Press* for some time, and then discontinued it. In 1872, Wales & Cameron issued the *Candor Review*, Ira S. Wales succeeding; and in 1873 the office was burned, and the publication of the paper discontinued. *The Independent*, the next in order, was established by T. H. Pride, October 14, 1876, and was continued until a recent date, since which time the village has been without a paper.

CHAPTER VII.

WAR OF THE REBELLION—FIRST MEETING OF COUNTY COMMISSIONERS— SUBSEQUENT MEETINGS—APPROPRIATIONS—STATEMENT OF TOTAL EX- PENDITURES.

IN a work so brief in its scope as this *Gazetteer*, it would be folly to attempt a detailed history of the various regiments and companies made up wholly or in part by Tioga county men, who served in the late rebellion. In our remarks on this subject, then, we will confine ourselves to the action of the county supervisors during the war period.

The first meeting of the board for war purposes was held April 27, 1861. It was called by the clerk, by request of seven supervisors, and Watson L. Hoskins was chosen chairman and Franklin Slosson, clerk. Six thousand dollars were appropriated for relief of soldiers' families, and a committee appointed to negotiate a loan for that amount on the faith of the county. The disbursement of the funds was placed in the hands of the supervisors of the respective towns, with authority to draw on the treasurer for such amounts as were needed. The resolution passed unanimously. At the annual meeting in November an additional sum was appropriated to the volunteer aid fund. At a special meeting held July 29, 1862, Charles C. Thomas, chairman, and Watson L. Hoskins, clerk, the board voted to raise $3,920.00 to pay a bounty of $10.00 each to 392 men to fill the quota of the county, and also $1,500.00 to pay the expenses of procuring the enlistment of the same. On August 20, the same year, $4,840.00 were appropriated to pay the same bounty to 484 men, then required to fill the quota of the county under the call of the president. Supervisors Pratt, of Barton, Deming, of Richford, and Thomas, of Owego, were the disbursing committee. The clerk having enlisted, Thomas C. Platt was elected to fill the vacancy. The treasurer reported in November, 1862, the payment of $7,317.00 for relief of soldiers' families, of which $817.00 were refunded by the state, and for bounties $7,420.00, expenses $1,134.00, and interest $298.34—total, under bounty resolutions, $8,852.34.

On December 17, 1863, at a special meeting, a bounty of $300.00 was offered to volunteers under the call of November, 1863, requiring 427 men to fill the quota of the county. Bonds to the amount of $130,000.00 were authorized to be issued, payable $40,000.00 on the first day of February, 1865 and 1866, and $25,000.00 on the same day in 1867 and 1868, provided so much funds were needed. The amount paid for each town was to be charged against the same, and collected of the town by tax.

On February 5, 1864, the board voted to continue the bounty of $300.00 for men enlisting under the call of January, 1864, and changed the time of payment of the bonds to $20,000.00 February 1, 1866 and 1867, and the balance in 1868. On February 25 the bounty was voted to be paid to 286 men already enlisted and credited.

On July 26, 1864, the treasurer had paid 702 volunteers, and had issued bonds to the amount of $210,600.00. A bounty was then voted of $300.00 per man for volunteers, under the call for 500,000 men, and a vote was had making the bonds already issued a general county charge, to be assessed at large upon the county. Other bonds were voted, $40,000.00 to be paid February 1, 1869, and the balance February 1, 1870, with interest at seven per cent., and for an amount sufficient to pay for men to fill the quota, which was subsequently found to be 327, and $98,100.00 of bonds were issued. At the annual meeting of November, 1864, the sum of $2,660.00 was voted to pay recruiting agents $10.00 per man for recruits. $63,564.00 were raised, by tax on the several towns, for bounties paid this same year.

On December 30, 1864, the bounty of $300.00 was continued to volunteers enlisting to fill the quotas, and on January 24, 1865, a bounty of $300.00 for one year and $600.00 for three years was offered to volunteers enlisting for the respective terms, and bonds voted to be paid. one-half in one year and the balance in two years. On March 1, 1865, the bounty to one-year volunteers was increased to $450.00 and bonds for same made payable February 1, 1866. On May 10, bonds for $5,100.00 for expenses were issued, payable February 1, 1866. At the annual meeting, the county treasurer was authorized to re-issue bonds falling due February 1, 1866, to the amount of $125,000.00 and to pay the towns $3,355.00 for bounties paid by them respectively. A claim made by Broome county for volunteers furnished, and credited to Tioga, was compromised by the payment of $3,000.00.

The total amount of appropriations for war purposes by the county authorities was as follows:

Under the orders of 1861 for relief of volunteers and their families	$ 13,079.00
Under calls of 1863 and 1864 for 700,000 men, 702 volunteers at $300.	210,600.00
Under the call for 500,000 men 1864, 362 men	97,800.00
Under the call of 1865	128,550.00
Total bounties and relief	$450,029.00
Expenses	13,978.00
Interest paid on bonds	102,302.00
Total payments by the county	$566,309.00

From this amount is to be deducted the amount refunded by

the state under the general bounty law, viz., cash	$ 49,100.00
Revenue 7 per cent. bonds	210,000.00
Interest paid to the county on the latter	18,076.00
Total from state	$277,176.00
Net amount paid by county	$289,133.00

Besides this, the towns paid heavy amounts for bounties, in addition to the county bounty. The last county bond for war purposes was paid in 1870.

*6

GAZETTEER OF TOWNS.

———

B ARTON* lies in the southwestern corner of the county, and is bounded north by Spencer and a small portion of the county line, east by Tioga and Nichols, south by the state line, and west by the county of Chemung. It has an area of 32,686 acres, of which about 28,000 acres are improved land. It was taken from Tioga and formed into a separate township by an act of the legislature passed March 23, 1824. It has been the scene of tragic events—its early record rises to the romance of history, and is traced by a competent hand in the first chapter of this work. The original titles to the soil, how obtained, etc., is detailed in chapter two. To these chapters we refer the reader.

Topography.—The surface of the town is generally hilly, though a small portion of level land lies along the southern border. The highlands on the west rise abruptly from the valley of Cayuta creek,† and are divided into two ridges by the valley of Ellis creek. Their summits are broad and rolling, and to some extent covered with forests. The principal water-courses are the Cayuta, Ellis, and Buttson creeks. They flow in a southerly direction, and empty into the Susquehanna, which forms the south part of the east border, dividing the town from Nichols. The Chemung river forms a very small portion of the west border of the south part. The soil is a rich alluvium in the valleys, and a sandy and gravelly loam upon the hills. A sulphur spring is found on Ellis creek, near the center of the town. The inhabitants are chiefly engaged in agricultural pursuits, stock-raising and dairying being the specialties.

Origin of the Name of Barton.—In 1849, Prof. Chauncey A. Goodrich published what he styled *A Revised and Enlarged*

———

* For this sketch we are largely indebted to Hon. William Fiske Warner, and city editor George D. Genung, of Waverly.

† Locally, this stream is known as Shepard's creek.

Edition of Noah Webster's Unabridged Dictionary. In this work the word " Barton " is defined as follows : " Saxon, (bere-ton, Barley town.) The demain lands of a manor; the manor itself, and sometimes the out-houses." He gives as authorities, Johnson and Blount. In 1656, Thomas Blount, of England, published a *Dictionary of Hard Words.* In 1754, about a century later, Samuel Johnson published his celebrated dictionary, in which he follows Blount as to the origin and meaning of this word. As we see, about a century later, Noah Webster publishes his dictionary, giving the same origin and meaning of the word, and Johnson and Blount as authorities.

The first constitution of the state of New York was adopted April 20, 1777. Up to this period, and until the year 1813, the law pertaining to personal and real property was the same as it was in England, and many of the original owners of land granted by patent by the state, made arrangement for the formation of " manors," whereby, as in England, large landed property might be held and perpetuated in families. Some of the well-known families of this state owned large manors upon the Hudson river, such as the Livingston Manor, Radcliff Manor, and others.

Upon a map of the county of Tioga, published by the Surveyor-General of the state of New York, in 1829, showing the original survey and numbers of lots, there appear two large lots in the plot of Coxe's Patent. These large lots appear, by this old map, to be reserved, and the word " manor " is printed upon them. Upon the same map appears lot No. 175, in the town of Barton, bounded on the west by Cayuta creek, and extending eastward about four miles, and one and one-half miles in width. Undoubtedly this large lot was intended by the original patentee to be reserved as a manor, and we will suppose that being familiar with the quaint old Saxon word, he placed the word " Barton " upon the survey of the land that was filed in the proper office in Albany.

A town frequently derives its name from that of some prominent individual resident, or the owner of a large amount of its territory. For example, the town of Nichols derived its name from Nichols, the patentee of a large portion of the land in that town, but who never resided there. No prominent person by the name of Barton ever lived or owned property in Barton. It is a reasonable conjecture, therefore, that when the project of forming a new town from Tioga was conceived, surveys and original maps were consulted for proper boundaries. Upon making such examination, probably, this word "Barton" was found upon one of the maps, and hence the name of the town became Barton.

In this connection it should be stated that the ambitious projects of the original patentees for reserving large landed estates for their families, and perpetuating them, were forever defeated by the legislature of the state, in 1813, by a law forbidding the creation of such estates, and providing that land could only be devised for the benefit of two lives in being, and twenty-one years beyond two such lives.

It would appear that the word "barton" is used by modern writers in a much more restricted sense than formerly attached. For example, Thomas Hardy, one of the most careful writers of England, in a recent work, revives this almost obsolete word in the following sentence: "Now his nearest way led him through the dairy barton,"—a yard or appurtenance of a dairy farm, as is evident from the context. But this is only one of many instances in which words have lost their original meaning.

Spanish Hill.—This interesting elevation, though just without the town's limits, must be noticed in the history of Barton. Spanish hill is situated in the immediate vicinity of Waverly, in the township of Athens, Pa. This hill is one of the notable features of the valley. A range of hills stretches from the Chemung river along the north side of Waverly for the distance of a mile and more, to Cayuta creek; Spanish hill lies south of the west end of this range, and is about five hundred yards east of the Chemung river. Its east, south and west sides are quite abrupt and form nearly three-fourths of a circle, rising to the height of one hundred and twenty-five feet above the river. The top is nearly level, and embraces about twelve acres. The broken hillocks lying adjacant to the north suggest the idea that at some period they formed a part of this hill, and that Spanish hill had then the form of a cone, and that by some titanic labor the cone had been cut away and the earth carelessly thrown in uneven masses to the north side, leaving a level plane one hundred and twenty-five feet in elevation above the surrounding plane below. An examination of the stones upon the top of the hill quickly dispells this supposition, as it is at once observed that these stones contain shells, and that the surface of this hill once formed the bed of the sea, and the hill therefore was formed by natural causes and not by the hand of man. Spanish hill is a beautiful object, and visable from all parts of the triangular valley. But why is it called *Spanish* hill? Like the origin of the name of the town of Barton, the answer to this question is only speculative, and yet the following theory is so plausable as almost to force conviction as to the genuine origin of the name; and being so plausable it is deemed of sufficient importance to entitle it to a place in a work of this character.

The discovery of this continent by Columbus, in 1492, necessarily created a great excitement in Spain, then one of the most powerful nations of the world. Her naval power was superior to all others, and England had trembled by reason of the powerful naval force that had been sent by Spain threatening to crush the kingdom. After the discovery, the Spanish government sent many expeditions to make further discoveries and conquests. Cortez, Pizzaro and other Spanish leaders carried the Spanish flag to Central America, Mexico and Peru, bringing back rich spoils from these conquered lands. De Soto, in 1541, conducted one of these notable expeditions through Florida and made the discovery of the Mississippi. These were expeditions sent by the government of Spain. But the intense interest caused by these regular expeditions sent out for legitimate purposes, led to the organization of private and irregular expeditions, organized for the purpose of plunder and the search for gold and silver, that in their character were not unlike pirates. It is supposed that a band of this character, composed of about two hundred, sailed from Spain about the time De Soto landed in Florida, in the year 1541. This band made their way further north and entered the bay of Chesapeake. They were armed to the teeth, and were provided with all implements needful for mining purposes. The idea prevailed that all the rivers of the new continent led to rich mines of gold and silver. The discovery of gold along the streams of California, in 1849, gives a fair illustration of the wild excitement that prevailed in Spain in the year 1540, about three centuries earlier. This band of two hundred anchored their vessel in the Chesapeake Bay, and leaving it in the care of a portion of the crew, made their way up the Susquehanna. Above the rapids, below Harrisburgh, they made suitable boats for the conveyance of their provisions, camp and mining tools. At this period the Five Nations of Indians occupying the territory that now forms the State of New York, had been formed as a confederacy, and dominated all the tribes as far south as the gulf of Mexico. They had become enraged by reason of the Spanish treatment of their tributary tribes inhabiting Florida, and kept a watchful eye upon all the movements of the Spanish expeditions, large and small, regular and irregular. Of this powerful confederacy the Spaniards appear to have been wholly ignorant. The moment, however, this marauding band of 200 Spaniards landed in Chesapeake Bay, a fast runner carried the information to the chiefs of the Five Nations at the head waters of the Susquehanna. The southern border of these five tribes was at Tioga Point (Athens), four miles south from Spanish hill, and at the confluence of the Susquehanna and Tioga (Chemung) rivers. The confederate Indians watching the approaching Spaniards, prepared to meet them somewhere in the vicinity of Spanish hill. The pirates, finding that an armed force was assembled to contest their invasion, sought this prominent hill for shelter.

It is supposed that the Five Nations were able to oppose this marauding band by not less than five thousand warriors, poorly armed with bow and hatchet, formidable weapons in warfare against Indians, but of small account against the weapons used by Spaniards. Ignorance, of course, existed upon both sides as to the arms to be used. The Spanish band could not remain long in their fortified position. Food and water would soon become exhausted, and they resolved to cut their way out. The multitude of Indians assembled knew these marauders as "Espanas," at this time a name hateful to them by reason of the cruelties practiced upon their tributary tribes in Florida and Georgia. Armed as this band was, with weapons of warfare unknown and superior to those of the Indians, it was not unreasonable to suppose they might cut their way through, but the vast superiority of the Indian force more than balanced the inequality of arms, and not a Spaniard was spared. The slaughter of the Indians, however, was frightful. Probably not less than one, or perhaps two thousand fell. So frightful was the slaughter that the hill was called the "Espana," and the early pioneer reports that the Indians found remaining in the locality had a dread of the hill, and could never be induced to ascend it, a tradition existing among them that a powerful spirit inhabited the hill, fatal to any Indian who should venture to ascend it. Confirming this theory is the fact that in the year 1865, a flood in the Susquehanna, greater than had been known by any one living upon its banks, tore away a bank on the border of a meadow that had been undisturbed from the earliest period—then nearly a century—and exposed a rude boat, thirty feet in length by four feet in breadth, and three feet in height, formed by crude planks cut by broad-axes, and fastened by wooden pins. In short, exactly such a boat as would have been constructed by a marauding band for transportation of necessaries, such as indicated by this Spanish force. The writer* was informed by James Hanna, a pioneer of the valley, in 1816, and a notable hunter, that he found a bayonet with Spanish inscriptions, at the base of Spanish hill, but that his sons caused the bayonet to be made into a spear for fishing, and so the valuable testimonial was lost.

The intelligent reader will receive the foregoing theory at its just value, and until a better theory is found, this must remain unquestioned.

Settlement and Growth.—The first to settle in the town of Barton and make for themselves and their posterity homes among the giant pines that thickly covered its valleys, were Ebenezer Ellis and Stephen Mills, who, in 1791, settled near the mouth of Ellis creek.

Ebenezer Ellis came from Forty Fort, near Wyoming, in 1787, making his way up the Susquehanna in a canoe. He first located in the present town of Nichols, upon what is known as the old "Samuel Walker" farm. He remained there until 1791, when he came into Barton. His cause for the move and again making a clearing in the forest, we are unable to explain. Here he first settled upon the farm afterwards owned by John Hanna, with whom he subsequently traded for a farm at the mouth of Ellis creek, making the exchange for the purpose of gaining control of the water privilege and building a saw-mill. This exchange was made not long after the settlement, and most historic accounts have erroneously stated that upon this latter farm he made the first settlement. He had thirteen children, among whom were Samuel, Jesse, Cornie, Abigail, William and Alexander. The latter was the first white male child born in the town. He married Betsey Saunders. by whom he had twelve children, viz.: Ira D., Charles B., Zeno W., who died in infancy, Solon S., who died at the age of four years, Nancy, Sarah, wife of Robert Fitzgerald, Christopher S., Nelson A., Lewis B., Cyrus, Charlotte M., wife of Nathan Saunders, and Hiram. William married Lydia, daughter of Israel Seeley, of Orange county, N, Y., by whom he had thirteen children, viz.: William, Fanny, who died in infancy, John, of Geneva, Ill., Sela, of Ellistown, Amanda, wife of Charles Pemberton, Sally, wife of Henry Swartwood, of Kansas, Ransom, Lydia, Charlotte, wife of James Parker, and Elizabeth. Two others died in infancy. Charles B. married

---

*Hon. W. F. Warner, of Waverly.

Elizabeth Maria, daughter of Robert Curtis, by whom he has two
children, viz.: J. Addison, and F. Leontine. J. Addison married
Alice, daughter of George Edgcomb. Gilbert S., son of Sela,
married Amanda, daughter of Robert Curtis, by whom he has
had three children, viz.: Harvey W., who died in infancy, Arthur
C., and Eddie M., who died in infancy.

Stephen Mills, originally from Connecticut, also first located in
Nichols, moving to Barton about the same time as Mr. Ellis. He
was a revolutionary soldier, and became a pensioner under the
act of 1832. His son Lewis married Elizabeth, daughter of John
Hanna, by whom he had three children : Miama, widow of Syl-
vanus Wright, William G., of this town, and John, of Athens,
Pa. William G., married Susan, daughter of John O. Shakelton,
by whom he has had eight children, viz.: Charles, Elizabeth
(Mrs. Cornelius Case), Charlotte (Mrs. Spencer Brougham),
Augusta (Mrs. Thurlow Gale), Wilson, Theodore, Adolphus and
Anna.

About this time also (1791) Benjamin Aikens settled where the
village of Barton now is. He owned a tract of 900 acres, of which
Gilbert Smith afterwards became the purchaser. These pioneers
were joined by John Hanna, Ezekiel Williams, Luke Saunders,
Samuel Ellis, and James Swartwood, all of whom were here
previous to 1795.

John Hanna was born in Scotland, and when a boy came to
this country, working his passage as a servant to the captain of
the vessel in which he sailed. He landed at Philadelphia, and
soon made his way up to Nescopeck Falls, Pa. Here he subsequently engaged in the distillery business, losing heavily owing to the
depreciation in value of Continental money. Here also he married
Margaret McCulloch, who came from the same town in Scotland
as himself, though they were not acquainted with each other there.
After his business failure at Nescopeck Falls, he came to this
town, and purchased a farm at the mouth of Ellis creek. He subsequently purchased of Peter C. Lorillard, of New York city, a
thousand acres of land in the locality known as "Ellistown," the
original deed of which is now in the possession of Mr. J. E. Hallet, of Waverly. It is told that at stated periods he used to go
on horseback to New York with gold in a saddle-bag to make pay-
ments on his land. Their first habitation here was a log house,
which had only an earth floor, and there being no saw-mill he was
obliged to split planks from pine logs and hew them smooth for
flooring. He had no threshing floor, so was obliged to keep his

grain until winter and thresh it on the ice of a little pond on his premises. For salt he had to travel to Horseheads, following an Indian trail and returning with only half a bushel at a time, which he was expected to share with his neighbors. During the cold summer of 1816, people were for months without bread, and subsisted chiefly on "greens," made from various herbs and plants. Mr. Hanna cut rye while it was yet in the milk, dried it on sticks laid across a kettle of live coals, and in this way succeeded in preparing for mill half a bushel of grain. When it returned to them and they had made their first bread from it, their neighbors were invited in to feast on the "luxury." Mr. Hanna's first location he did not occupy long, as he had an opportunity to exchange with Ebenezer Ellis as we have stated, who owned the farm just north of the one now owned and occupied by John G. Hill. Mr. Hanna's barn was the first frame building ever raised in the town, and in it convened the first Methodist quarterly meeting held here. His sturdy Scotch qualities made him invaluable in those early times, and the noble qualities of his heart were evinced in the acts of his daily life. His home for many years was the stopping place of itinerant preachers, and, until a more convenient place was provided, people for many miles round met at his house for public worship. Mr. Hanna was also a veteran of the revolution. He died at the great age of 102 years. Mr. and Mrs. Hanna were the parents of nine children, as follows: John, Nancy, wife of John Swartwood, and afterward the wife of John Shoemaker, Jane, wife of Joseph Swain, of Chemung, William, Margaret, wife of Elisha Hill, Betsey, wife of Lewis Mills, George, Sally, wife of Squire Whitaker, and Martha wife of Joseph G. Wilkinson. William married first a Miss Saunders. His second wife was Jane, daughter of Isaac Raymond, by whom he had eight children, viz.: William, Edward, Stella, wife of Thaddeus Ellis, George, Adelbert, Frederick, Maud, wife of Arthur Fitch, of Arkansas, and Emmet, who died at the age of nine years. George married Stella, daughter of Jonathan Catlin, of Tioga, by whom he has one child, Earl, born September 13, 1882. John, Jr., married Deborah, daughter of John Hyatt, by whom he had four children, viz.: Mary, wife of William T. Ellis, Sally, wife of David C. Lyons, of Wisconsin, Julia, wife of D. B. Horton, of Owego, and Ira, of this town. The latter married Martha A., daughter of Daniel Park, of Nichols, by whom he had four children, viz.: Charles F., of Barton, Sarah, Leonora and Ida L. Leonora married J. E. Merritt, of Athens, Pa., and has four children,—Lena, Orrin, Ray and Ralph. Charles F. married Hattie, daughter of Lewis Crotsley, of Barton, by whom he has four children, born as follows: Celia, November 18, 1873; Louis, July 20, 1876; Homer, June 12, 1879; and Myra, May 7, 1885.

Luke Saunders came from Connecticut. He married Sarah Dewey, by whom he had eight children, viz.: Sarah, wife of Beriah Lewis, Parish, Jabez, Nathan, Betsey, wife of Alexander Ellis, Christopher, Nancy, wife of William Hanna, and Robert. Parish married Barbara, daughter of Ebenezer Ellis, by whom he had five children, viz.: Lucinda, widow of Thomas F. Johnson, Hiram, deceased, John, Benjamin and William.

James Swartwood came from Delaware. He had a family of nine children, viz.: Mary, wife of Isaac Shoemaker, Martha, wife of Benjamin Smith, Sarah, wife of Joseph Langford, Katie, wife of Baskia Jones, Benjamin, James, Jacob, John and Ebenezer. Benjamin married Catherine, daughter of Ezekiel Williams, by whom he had nine children, namely, James, Ezekiel, Martha, wife of Luther Goodenow, John, Benjamin, Harriet, wife of Robert Light, Lydia, wife of Adam VanAtta, William and Mary. Ezekiel married Margaret A. VanAtta, by whom he has had two children, Nancy, widow of John Harding, and John M., who died in his twenty-second year.

In 1796 John Shepard purchased of General Thomas, of Westchester county, one thousand acres of land, at five dollars per acre, extending along the state line, from Shepard's creek at Factoryville, near the fifty-ninth mile-stone, to the sixtieth milestone; thence across the north end of Spanish hill, to the Chemung river, and from the "narrows" across the mountain beyond Shepard's creek; thence down the state line again. This embraced the present villages of Waverly and Factoryville, and many fine localities back of these villages. Large portions of this territory are still retained in the possession of the Shepard family.

Among the early settlers on Cayuta creek were Charles Bingham, Layton Newell, Lyon C. Hedges, Philip Crans, Justus Lyons, John Manhart, and Moses and Elisha Leonard. These families were principally from New England, and were among the most industrious and worthy people of the town, and many of their descendants now reside in that valley, particularly at "Lockwood," which long bore the name of "Bingham's Mills," in honor of this pioneer family.

Among the early settlers of Barton village, other than those already mentioned, were William Bensley, George W. Buttson, who early built a saw-mill upon the stream which bears his name, John Hyatt, Eliphalet Barden, Benajah Mundy, Samuel Mundy, Peter Barnes, Peter Hoffman and Selah Payne.

William Bensley came, originally, from Smithfield, Wayne (now Pike) county, Pa. He removed to this town May 10, 1803, and settled on the farm now owned by John Park, on the river road, about one mile west of Barton village. This place was retained in the Bensley family for upwards of eighty years, it having first been owned by John Bensley, brother of William. William Bensley married Mary, daughter of Isaac Bunnell, by whom he had nine children, viz.: Gershom, John, Daniel, Henry, Eleanor (Mrs. Richard Shoemaker), Elizabeth (Mrs. Charles B. Smith), Anna, who died in infancy, Mary A. (Mrs. James Brink), and Sarah (Mrs. Daniel Van Gorder). Mr. Bensley was a weaver by trade, but followed, to a considerable extent, lumbering and farming. Henry married Betsey Brink, by whom he had six children, three of whom arrived at maturity, viz.: Mary, wife of Frank Kelley, of Athens, Pa., John, of Nichols, and Archibald, deceased. John married Lucy Wrigley, by whom he has had six children, viz.: Henry, deceased, Leora, wife of James Davison, Frederick, Arthur and John, Jr. Daniel married Lucina P. Felt, of Potter county, Pa., by whom he had four children, viz.: Elliott L., who lives on the homestead, Charles and Daniel, who died in infancy, and Bertha L. Elliott L. married Mary E., daughter of John Westfall, of Chemung, by whom he has two children, Gertie, born October 8, 1880, and Nellie, born December 1, 1884.

Charles Bingham left the Wyoming Valley at the time of the Indian massacre there, and with his family was obliged to steal his way by night, in Durham boats, in order to escape the savages. In their first settlement they were so troubled by Indians that he returned to Wilkesbarre. The year following, he came again and settled near Spanish hill. Here they were afflicted with small-pox and lost one or two children. They then removed north, up Shepard's creek about six miles, and settled on the farm now owned by E. Van Buren. The great inducement for him to settle there was the growth of maple trees in that vicinity, maple sugar being about the only thing then marketable. His sons were John, Ebenezer, Jonathan and Charles, Jr. His daughters were Anna, who married a Mr. Drake, Margurite, who married a Mr. Hedges, and Sarah, who married a Mr. Sanford. Charles, Jr., built a mill at Lockwood, upon the site where the Bingham

Brothers mills now are, and it was among the first in this section built on Shepard's creek. He married Anna M., daughter of David Davis, by whom he had six children, viz.: Mary J., wife of Bernard Campbell, of St. Croix county Wis., Jefferson, of Waverly, Ann E., wife of Rev. La Fayette Ketchum, of Owego, George W. and Edmund J., of Lockwood, and David T., deceased. George W. married Mary A. Inhoff, of Marietta, Pa., by whom he has had ten children, viz.: Jessie D., Fred, Helen and Mary (twins) who died in infancy, Clara, Joseph, Robert, deceased, Mary A., George and Harry. Edmund J. married Libbie K. Baldwin, of Chemung, by whom he has five children, Addie L., James B., Marion, Arthur and Laura A.

David Davis settled first in the Catskill region, afterward in Greene, Chenango county. His son Samuel H. married Minerva Barnes, of this town, by whom he had two children, viz.: Mary M. and Hannah A., the latter the wife of Eugene Van Buren, who resides on the homestead. Their children are Lena T. and Pearl. Samuel Davis was a blacksmith by trade, but was also engaged in lumbering and farming.

Sutherland Tallmadge came from Schaghticoke, Schoharie county, N. Y., very early in the history of this county and settled on the farm now owned by Mr. Elliot, and occupied by Tallmadge Hulett. His brother Franklin settled on the farm now owned by James Sliter. The locality is still known as Tallmadge hill.

Charles B. Smith, son of Jonas, was born in Sheshequin, Pa., in 1814. His mother died when he was but four years of age, and he came to this town to live with the Bensley family. He married Elizabeth, daughter of William Bensley, by whom he had one son, Rushton. The latter married first, Ellen Bunnell, by whom he has one child, Ione, wife of Lewis Mills, of Sayre. His present wife is Katie, daughter of H. V. Kinner, of South Waverly.

Elisha Hill was born in Connecticut, May 4, 1793. About 1818 he came from Plainfield, or Hartford, Conn., to Bradford county, Pa., with all his possessions tied in a pack which he carried across his shoulder. He remained there two years, when he returned to Connecticut, and brought back with him his brother Caleb. In 1821 he removed to this town and located on the farm now owned and occupied by his son, John G. He was a soldier in the war of 1812, and served at Black Rock and other points. He married Margaret, daughter of John Hanna, who was born December 16, 1798, and by whom he had five children, born as follows: John

Griffin, September 17, 1821; Philomela, wife of Alanson Welton, of Factoryville, May 7, 1823; Sarah, February 26, 1826; Hannah, July 28, 1828; Elizabeth, wife of Joseph Park, of Nichols, September, 26, 1831; and Tabitha J., wife of Montgomery Mead, of Waverly, August 26, 1837. John G. married Elizabeth, daughter of David Boardman Cure of this town. Elisha Hill died September 20, 1864, and Mrs. Hill died September 4, 1880. Caleb Hill married Eunice Durphy, of Smithfield, Pa., by whom he had five children, viz.: Erastus, a member of the legislature of the state of Missouri; Polly, wife of —— Davis, deceased; Alonzo, a physician of Malden, Mo., Hon. David B., the present governor of the state of New York, and Sarah, deceased.

Salmon Johnson was born in Vermont, near Lake Champlain, and at an early day came to this town, locating at " Ellistown." His son, Thomas Floyd, married Lucinda, daughter of Parish and Barbara (Ellis) Saunders, by whom he had five children who arrived at maturity, viz.: Barbara (Mrs. William Weller), D. Jane (Mrs. Edward Tozer), Sarah (Mrs. Oscar F. Burke), Cyrus, and Emma L., (Mrs. Charles Parker). Salmon Johnson moved to the state of Ohio, where he died.

Peter Bogart, or " Van de Bogart," as the name was originally written, came from Princetown, now in Schenectady county, N. Y., about the beginning of the present century, and settled in Tompkins county, between Ithaca and Newfield, on the farm now known as the Crawford farm, and in 1825 removed to this town, and located on the farm now owned by Cornelius Harding. He married, first, Betsey Hunter, and they had children as follows: Michael, Catherine (Mrs. Joseph Joyce), John, Eva (Mrs. Jesse Bailey), Joseph, Mindred, Betsey (Mrs. Casper Lampman), Polly (Mrs. Samuel Ford), Jane (Mrs. Edward Sherwood), Fanny (Mrs. David Johnson) James, and two or three who died in infancy. He married second, Maria, daughter of Samuel Gray, of Tompkins county, by whom he had thirteen children, viz.: Sarah (Mrs. E. Foster), Jeremiah, Peter, Caroline (Mrs. Henry Lounsberry), Charles, who died at the age of twenty-five, William, Samuel, Loury, David, who died in infancy, George W., and Emma (Mrs. Andrew Nevin), of Boston, Mass. George W., married Amelia, daughter of Daniel Rogers, of Barton, by whom he has one son, G. Frederick. James married Lucinda, daughter of Robert Curtis, by whom he has had three children, viz.: Leonora (Mrs. John W. Morgan), Henry M., of Waverly, and Robert C., who died in October, 1878. John married Ruth, daughter of Nathaniel

Bailey, of Tompkins county, by whom he had nine children, viz.:
Peter V., Charlotte (Mrs. Alanson Williams), Nathaniel, Elijah,
who died at the age of four years, James, Joseph, John, and Ira
J., who died at the age of five years. Peter V., married first,
Matilda Williams, by whom he had one child, Merritt Delos. His
present wife was Sarah A. Dailey, by whom he has had two children, Olive, who died at the age of nine years, and Orpha Eveline, wife of Guy V. Spear, who has two children, born as follows: Anna, February 18, 1882, and Clyde, December 28, 1883.
Mr. P. V. Bogart has dealt largely in real estate, having owned
at one time eight hundred acres. He has been engaged principally in lumbering and farming. Peter Bogart, Sr., died November 16, 1857, aged ninety-three years.

Abial F. Hill came from Deer Park, Orange county, N. Y., in
1814, and located on the farm now owned by Ira Hill, on the
Shepard's creek road. He married Francis Burns, by whom he
had seven children, viz.: Anna Jane, (Mrs. Thomas Shelp), S.
Maria (Mrs. Freeman Shelp), deceased, Mary A., (Mrs. Ira G.
Hill), Mahala, second wife of Freeman Shelp, Charles M., de-
ceased, Adaline, wife of Joseph Quackenbush, deceased, and
Arminda, widow of Stephen Clearwater.

Freeman Shelp came from Montrose, Pa., very early in the
history of Tioga county, and was engaged in driving stage from
Towanda, Pa., to Ithaca. By his second wife, S. Mahala, daugh-
ter of Abial Hill, he had three children, viz.: Charles F., of
Waverly, Francis M. (Mrs. Charles Hill), deceased, and Belle A.
The latter married A. T. Andre, of Lockwood, and has one son,
Freeman J.

Joseph Bartron came from Meshoppen, Pa., and settled in
Nichols, on the bank of the Susquehanna, at a place called Smith's
Mills, where he worked, being by trade a mill-wright. He re-
moved to this town in 1821, and cleared the farm now owned by
his son Joseph. He built the first saw-mill on Buttson creek, for
Gilbert Smith. The mill was located about where the Erie rail-
road now crosses the creek. He married Betsey Place, who bore
him eight children, viz.: James, Eliza (Mrs. Morris Walker),
Anna (Mrs. Jonathan Rolf), Moses, Delila, widow of Daniel
Graves, Chloe (Mrs. Elijah Van Gorder), Joseph, and John P.
Joseph married Harriet, daughter of George W. Johnson, who
bore him nine children.

George W. Johnson came from Ithaca, N. Y., and located in
this town. He married Betsey Severn, by whom he had thirteen

children, viz : Abram, John, Charles, Amyette, Jane, Matilda, Elvira, Julius, Harriet, Washington, Josiah, James, and Cynthia. John married Jane, daughter of James Garrett, of Tioga.

Eliphalet Barden was born in Connecticut, and after his marriage came to Greene, Chenango county, N. Y., and in 1821 removed to this town, and settled on the farm now owned by Francis Giltner. He married Miriam Priest, by whom he had eight children, two only of whom are living, Freelove, wife of N. W. Schoonover, and Zalmon, who resides on road 39. The latter married Mary A., daughter of William Todd, of Tioga, and they have had four children, viz.: Charles E., of Tonawanda, N. Y., Freelove L., wife of William Holt, of Tioga, William M., who died at the age of eight years, and Mary E., wife of Frank Harding, of this town.

John Parker settled in Ellistown, at an early date. He married Lizzie Ellis, by whom he had seven children, viz.: Frederick, Henry, Clark, James, Hiram, Caroline, and Abby. James married Charlotte, daughter of William Ellis, who bore him eight children—Frances, Albenia, Genervy, Charles, Mattie, Christina, Mack, and Hermeone.

John W. Van Atta was born November 1, 1782, and came from Rockburg, Warren county, N. J., about 1827, and located on the farm now owned by A. J. Van Atta, on road 52. He married Elizabeth Albright, who was born August 16, 1787, and by whom he had eleven children, born as follows: Peter, July 28, 1810; Margaret, November 21, 1811; Adam, November 18, 1813; William, February 1, 1816; Benjamin, June 6, 1818; Caroline, June 19, 1821; Sarah, July 15, 1823; Isaac, July 22, 1826; Azariah J., December 15, 1827; and Rebecca M., December 11, 1832. Peter married Fanny J., daughter of Reuben Harding, by whom he had two sons, Oscar H., and Clarence, of this town. Peter and Benjamin were musicians in the old state militia.

Shaler Shipman was born in Connecticut, April 21, 1800, and came to this town in 1829, settling first on the farm now owned by P. G. Schuyler, and then removed to the one now occupied by Adam Albright, where he resided until his death. He built two saw-mills, and was engaged in lumbering and farming during most of his life. That section of the town, about the geographical center, is commonly called Shipman Hollow. He married first, Melinda Speer, by whom he had ten children, born as follows : Prosper, March 2, 1829; Lucy A., October 11, 1830; Abram, September 27, 1832 ; Rachel, June 10, 1834; Philip H.,

March 5, 1836; Stephen, April 27, 1838; Susan M., March 25, 1840; Rufus T., October 23, 1841; George W., September 25, 1844; and Harvey D., August 21, 1847. His second wife, Barbara (Bowman) Hunt, bore him four children, viz.: Perlie E., January 24, 1868; Shaler B., January 26, 1869; Orrilla M., January 4, 1871; Ada M., August 8, 1876. Mr. Shipman died December 24, 1878. Rufus T. Shipman enlisted October 1, 1861, in Co. H, 10th N. Y. Cavalry, and served until August 14, 1862. when he re-enlisted in Co. B, 6th N. Y. Heavy Artillery, and served until September 14, 1865. He married Frances, daughter of Asa Doty, who has borne him three children—Ella A., born November 2, 1866, died August 5, 1874; Isaac D., born March 29, 1873; and Cleveland, born March 8, 1885, died March 24, 1885.

James N. Harding, son of Charles, was born near Montgomery, Orange county, N. Y., and in 1833 came to this town and located on Tallmadge Hill, upon the farm now occupied by his son, C. N. Harding. He married Susan Tenney, and reared five children, viz.: Gilbert, Horace T., Clara, Charles E., and Cornelius N. Horace T. married Elizabeth, daughter of Jacob Swain, of Chemung, by whom he has had eight children, viz.: C. Willis, Theodore M., Fred, Charley, Bert, Mamie, Arthur, and Ella, who was born October 7, 1878. C. Willis married Nellie, daughter of H. Burt, and has two daughters, Grace and Ethel. Theodore M., married Nettie, daughter of George Edgcomb, and has one child, Marion. Charles E. married Julia E., daughter of Galaliel Bowdish, of Montgomery county, N. Y., and has had four children, viz.: James O., Robert E., Charles L., and George A.

John Harding, son of Reuben, came with his parents from the town of Minisink, Orange county, N. Y., when he was about six years of age. He married Nancy, daughter of Ezekiel Swartwood, rearing two children, Amelia H., wife of Rev. F. P. Doty, of Thompson, Pa., and Frank, who resides on the homestead. The latter married M. Ella, daughter of Zalmon Barden, of this town. Reuben Harding settled on Tallmadge Hill, on the farm now occupied by Elliott Harding.

James Madison Sliter, son of Peter, was born in Coeymans, Albany county, N. Y., September 11, 1815. When three years of age his parents removed to Guilford, Chenango county, where they remained two years, and then removed to Bainbridge, N. Y., where he resided until November 1, 1834, when he came to this town and has since resided here. He purchased first some timber property and afterward the farm now owned by Orson Dickerson. On April 30, 1839, he married Elizabeth A., daughter of Rev. Henry Ball, a Baptist minister of this town. In 1842 he removed to his present home. They had born to them nine children,—S. Emily, Jefferson B., of Athens, Pa., inventer of the Bonner scroll wagon-spring, Clarissa, Alice, wife of Harrison Lewis, Anna, wife of Frank W. Phillips, of Waverly, Estell, Julia, Katie, wife of Marshall Brown, and Eveline G., wife of Amos Harding. Mrs. Sliter died June 10, 1886.

David Boardman Cure came from Hector, Schuyler county, N. Y., about 1835, and located on Hector Hill, upon the farm now owned by John Brewster, where he purchased one hundred and fifty acres of land. He married, first, Achsa Hubbell, by whom he had three children, Jackson, Adliza and Phidelia. His second wife was Maria Shipman, by whom he had seven children, viz.: Elizabeth, David E., Sarah, Amos, James, Franklin E. and Delphine.

Sheldon Morgan, son of Theodore, a Quaker, of Horseheads, N.Y., married Abigail, daughter of Samuel and Abigail (Stephens) Warner. They had ten children born to them, viz.: Francis, November 22, 1833, died December 6, 1835 ; Charles H., of Wellsborough, Pa.; George B., of Waverly; William W., who was killed at the battle of Lookout Mountain, May 1, 1864 ; Frances A., born October 17, 1843, and died April 27, 1866; Theodore T., August 7, 1846, served four years in the Union army, was for nine months a prisoner in Andersonville, died February 3, 1874; John W., a member of Co. I, 109th N. Y. Vols.,now of Waverly, born January 27, 1849 ; Joseph S., February 11, 1852, of East Waverly, and Calvin P., May 15, 1855, now of Parsons, Kas. John W. married Nora W., daughter of James Bogart of the town of Barton. Frederick S. Morgan, a member of Co. H., 109th N. Y. Vols., enlisted August 3, 1863, and was mustered out July 21, 1865 ; was wounded in the battle of Spottsylvania, May 12, 1864. He married Emma R., daughter of Enos Genung, March 23, 1871, and by whom he has three children, Bertha D., Howard and Harry G.

Daniel J. Lum, son of Lyman, was born in New Berlin, N. Y., May 26, 1821, and in 1840 came to Factoryville, where he remained about six months and then removed to Tioga Center, where he engaged in lumbering and farming for about twenty years. He returned to Factoryville in 1874, and from thence removed to Waverly, where he has since resided. He married

7*

Orpha W., daughter of Rev. Henry Primrose, September 3, 1845. Four children were born to them: William Durella, October 19, 1846, died in Harewood Hospital, Washington, D. C., June 13, 1864; Mary T., October 14, 1848; Henry E., September 25, 1853, died June 15, 1878; and Mattie Captola, June 27, 1860. Mr. Lum enlisted December 21, 1863, in Co. A, 14th Heavy Artillery, N. Y. Vols., and also on the same date his son William Durella enlisted in the same regiment and company, but was afterward transferred to the 6th N. Y. Heavy Reserves. Mary T. married Melvin J. Baker, February 4, 1871, and there have been born to them three children,—Ola Corrinne, April 21, 1875, died April 13, 1879; Myron Elmer, February 6, 1877, died April 18, 1879; and Edwin Durella, born September 29, 1880.

John Solomon came from Orange county, N. Y., about 1840, and located on West Hill, upon the farm owned by Mr. Kennedy. He married Phœbe Valentine, by whom he had six children—Maria, John V., George, Sarah, William, and Catherine Louise. John V. married Ann Amelia, daughter of B. O. Van Cleft, by whom he has one daughter, Carrie, wife of Horace Steward.

Jacob Andre, son of George, came from Sussexshire, England, when he was eighteen years of age, and settled first in Delaware county, where he married Deborah, daughter of Sterling Hubbell, of Delhi. In 1844 he came to this town and settled on the farm now owned by George Georgia, which he cleared. His children were Isaac, of Factoryville; Jacob N., of Montrose, Pa.; William, deceased; A. T., of Lockwood; George, of Factoryville; John H., of this town; Newton, deceased; and Angeline, wife of Charles Smith, of Waverly.

Lewis Mulock, son of William and Rebecca (Seybolt) Mulock, was born in Mount Hope, N. Y., November 11, 1808. He married Mary, daughter of Peter Corwin, in 1832. About 1850 he came into this county and located on Tallmadge Hill, where he engaged in farming for several years. His children are Theodore, now of Athens, Pa.; Albert; Angeline, wife of Jacob Coleman; Gabriel, of Waverly; Mary A., wife of Rev. A. B. Scutt Coe, of Lancaster, Pa.; and Corwin, of Waverly. For the purpose of securing for his children superior educational advantages, Mr. Mulock removed to Waverly when his family was young, and has since resided there. He has been a justice of the peace here two terms of four years each.

Thomas B. Hunt was born in Cooperstown, N. Y., October 23, 1830, came to this town in 1851, and afterward purchased a farm

in Smithboro. He married Barbara, daughter of Absalom Bowman, by whom he had two children: Sanford E., born September 13, 1857, died in 1859, and William W., of this town, born
December 17, 1860.

Allen LaMont, son of David, was born in Schoharie county,
N. Y., June 22, 1825, and at an early age came to Tioga Center,
where he was engaged in lumbering during his early years. In
1860 he came to Waverly and purchased a farm on the Shepard's
creek road, engaging also in the produce business in Waverly
village, during the latter years of his life in partnership with
S. D. Barnum. He married Mary, daughter of Amos Canfield,
of Tioga, by whom he had two daughters, Grace and Ellen. He
died February 28, 1884.

Jacob D. Besemer, son of James, was born in Caroline, N. Y.,
in 1820. He married Harriet, daughter of Daniel Vorrhis, by
whom he had five children, viz.: Kate, wife of William Frisbie;
Daniel V.; James, and George of this town; and Annie, wife of
S. Hubbell, deceased. Mr. Besemer came to this town and
located on the farm now owned by his son Daniel V. The latter
married Delphine A. Hubbell, by whom he has two children—
Gracie J., born December 11, 1878, and Reed V., born August
11, 1881.

Dr. Ezra Canfield, son of Amos, was born on the homestead in
Smithboro, February 13, 1854. He received his early education
there and at Waverly and Binghamton. He entered the office
of Dr. O. A. Jakway, of Breesport, N. Y., and that of his brother,
Dr. Enos Canfield, of VanEttenville. He graduated from the
Medical University of New York City in 1879. His first location
was at VanEttenville, where he remained until 1882, when he
came to Lockwood, where he has since practiced. He married
Emma, daughter of Bishop Kline, of Allentown, Pa., in 1874.

The comparative growth of the town may be seen by the following citation of the census reports for the several enumerations
since its organization: 1825, 585 ; 1830, 972 ; 1835, 1,496 ; 1845,
2,847 ; 1850, 3,522 ; 1855, 3,842 ; 1860, 4,234 ; 1865, 4,077 ; 1870,
5,087 : 1875, 5,944 ; 1880, 5,825.

Initial Events.—Ebenezer Ellis built the first house, harvested
the first crops, and his son Alexander was the first white child
born here. The old brick church in Factoryville, now occupied
by the Old School Baptist Society, was the first brick building
erected. Elias Walker built the first tavern. The first postoffice
was established at Factoryville, in 1812, and Isaac Shepard was

the first postmaster. Deacon Ephraim Strong was the first
teacher. He was a gentleman of culture, and, in addition to
teaching his own large family taught the children of his neighbors in his own house. The Emery Chapel (Methodist Episcopal)
at Ellistown was the first church edifice erected. Ebenezer and
Samuel Ellis built the first saw-mill, on Ellis creek. George
Walker, Sr., erected the first grist-mill, in 1800, on Cayuta creek,
at Factoryville. Josiah Crocker and John Shepard built a fulling-mill on Cayuta creek, near the state line, in 1808, and Isaac
and Job Shepard erected a woolen-mill near it, in 1810. Dr.
Prentice, from Connecticut, was the first physician, William
Giles the first lawyer, and Rev. Valentine Cook the first preacher.

Organization.—The first town meeting was held at the house
of Gilbert Smith, April 27, 1824, when the following officers were
elected: Gilbert Smith, supervisor; John Crotsley, town clerk;
Jonathan Barnes, A. H. Schuyler, and William Hanna, assessors;
William Crans, Frederick Parker, and John Giltner, commission-
ers of highways; John Parker, constable and collector; John
Hanna, jr., and Seeley Finch, overseers of the poor; Gilbert
Smith, Eliphalet Barden, and Nathaniel Potter, commissioners
of common schools; James Birch, Ely Foster, Joseph Tallmadge,
Samuel Mills, and Jonathan Barnes, inspectors of schools; George
W. Johnson, Abraham Smith, and Joseph Tallmadge, fence-view-
ers; John Hyatt and Joel Sawyer, poundmasters.

BUSINESS CENTERS.

WAVERLY VILLAGE.—This village, one of the most important
business centers in this section, and, next to Owego, the largest
village in the county, has had a phenomenally rapid growth and
prosperous business career; for it is practically only since the
completion of the Erie railroad, in 1849, that it has sprung into
importance.

Situated upon the east bank of the Chemung river, in the extreme southeastern corner of the county, surrounded by a delightful region of hill and valley, Waverly's location is extremely
pleasant. While viewing its busy streets, its rows of business
blocks, its manufactories, fine residences, and pleasantly shaded
avenues, it is difficult to conceive that its site only a few years
since was a cultivated farming region. But such is in reality the
case.

Among the early settlers and principal owners of what is now the village site, was Isaac Shepard, whose father, in 1796, as previously stated, bought 1,000 acres of land, at $5.00 per acre, embracing the sites of both Waverly and East Waverly, and much valuable territory north and south of these villages. In 1819 Deacon Ephraim Strong purchased 153 acres of this tract, a strip nearly 100 rods wide, extending northward nearly through the center of the present village. The first house here was built by Mr. Strong, probably in that year, although it has been stated that it was built in 1810. It was located near the site of Dr. Frederick M. Snook's residence, and apple trees now standing on Mr. Snook's place were planted by the deacon in those early days.

In 1821 the Chemung turnpike (Chemung street) was laid out, and in 1825 Isaac Shepard built the pioneer hotel of the place. It stood on the site of the present Charles Shepard residence, on West Chemung street. In the following decade the number of settlers was greatly augmented. Owen Spalding, with his brother Amos, came in 1831. The latter occupied a small log house near the site of the present residence of Mrs. Harriet Tannery, until 1833, when he built what now constitutes the rear part of J. Dubois' house, opposite C. E. Merriam's residence, and moved into it. Owen Spalding occupied a plank-house on the present site of Dr. Snook's residence. This was probably the house built by Deacon Strong. In 1833 Mr. Spalding built a house on the site now occupied by Hon. R. A. Elmer's residence. This house was afterward removed to the southwest corner of Chemung street and Pennsylvania avenue, where it now stands, and where Mr. Spalding died.

In March, 1833, Joseph Hallet, Sr., came up from Orange county, and purchased of Valentine Hill, 100 acres of land near the present residence of J. E. Hallet, and extending northward from Chemung street, for which he paid $1,100.00. He was accompanied by his sons Gilbert H. and Joseph E. The latter settled upon the above mentioned farm, his house standing upon what is now Fulton street, between the present residences of Mrs. Fritcher and E. G. Tracy. At that time there were but fifteen buildings in the place, namely: one hotel, one distillery, one blacksmith shop, one log dwelling, one plank dwelling, six small frame dwellings, and four barns. These were Isaac Shepard's hotel, Jacob Newkirk's distillery and dwelling, Thomas Hill's house, and another small house, all near the Shepard residence ; the dwelling of Elder Jackson, a Baptist minister, whose house

stood just west of the present residence of W. F. Inman, and the
Elder's blacksmith shop, which stood where now stands the
Slaughter residence ; Amos Spalding's house, and Owen Spalding's plank house, and the log house into which Gilbert Hallet
moved, and O. Spalding's, Jackson's, Newkirk's, and Shepard's
barns, the latter the large red barn now standing on Pine street,
the only remaining land-mark of those early days.

Gilbert Hallet moved into the log house vacated by Amos Spalding, and the following year built and removed into a house that
stood where now stands H. L. Stowell's brick house. In the next
year, 1835, he purchased Elder Jackson's house above referred to,
together with forty-five acres of land, paying therefor $1,000,00.
This place and the one hundred acres bought by Joseph Hallet
were purchased by Jackson and Hill, respectively, of Isaac Shepard. Three years prior to this time, Elder Jackson, who was very
anxious to return to Orange county, had offerered the place to
Jesse Kirk for $500.00. The land lay south of Chemung street,
the east line passing near E. J. Campbell's residence, southward
through Slaughter & Van Atta's and E. G. Tracy's drug stores
to the 60th mile stone, thence west along the state line to the
center of Dry brook, thence north, following the center of Dry
brook to Chemung street, and west along Chemung street to the
place of beginning, comprising what is now the business portion of
the village.

At this time Harris Murray lived in a small wooden house where
" Murray's stone house " now stands, in South Waverly, and
Mr. Murray offered to sell to Mr. Hallet one hundred acres there
for $1,000.00. These sales illustrate how lightly the land in this
valley was valued at that time.

While these settlments were being made along the Chemung
road, other pioneers were pushing on beyond and locating on the
hill northwest of the village, now called " West Hill."

This portion of the Susquehanna valley had been the scene of
many forest fires, lighted either intentionally or carelessly by
hunters, and had been so frequently burned over that but little
save second growth pines remained, and this is said to have been
the reason why many of the early pioneers refused to locate here,
they thinking that land that would produce naught but "scrub
pines " was of little value, and accordingly pushed on to the highlands beyond, believing that the heavy growth of timber there
indicated a fertile and productive soil.

Among those who settled there first, probably during the years

1830-35, Piere Hyatt, Paris and Robert Sanders, David Carmichael, Jonathan Robins, G. W. Plummer, Jacob Swain, Nathan Slawson, and Steven Van Derlip ; after these came Daniel Blizard, David Mandeville, Sr., Peter and Lewis Quick, S. T. Van Derlip, W. A. Lane, Jesse Kirk and others. Of these we believe none are now living and but few of their decendants remain on the old homesteads.

Between the years 1837 and 1850 the number of settlers in the village increased rapidly, among the new comers being Captain Benjamin H. Davis, F. H. Baldwin, H. M. and W. E. Moore, Richard A. Elmer, Sr., and his sons Howard and Richard A., Jr., Jacob Reel, E. J. Brooks, J. A. Corwin, Sylvester Gibbons, R. O. Crandall, the first physician, Peter Wentz, the first justice, George Beebe, the first lawyer, and many others.

The street running from Charles Sawyer's residence on Chemung street to the hotel at East Waverly, was laid out in 1835, and in 1843 Pennsylvania avenue was laid out south as far as the present residence of Levi Curtis, and in the same year Waverly street was opened down as far as the present Aplin residence. On the avenue Charles Howard built a house where Levi Curtis' residence now stands, Isaac Drake built one on the site of the Mrs. Bucklin residence, Milo Hulet built one where H. S. Butts' residence now stands, and Frank Sutton one on the corner of Pennsylvania avenue and Park Place. The latter was torn down by Mr. Elmer, a few years since.

In 1842 G. H. Hallet and Andrew Price built a foundry on the northwest corner of Chemung and Waverly streets, where A. I. Decker's residence now stands. A short time afterwards Daniel Moore opened a cabinet shop in the second floor of this building. Later the foundry was changed into a hotel and bore the name of the Clarmont House.

In 1843 J. E. Hallet built a house on Waverly street, for one of the employes of the foundry. This was the first house on the street. In the same year Edward Brigham built a hotel on the present site of the M. E. church, and Robert Shackelton built a store and dwelling house combined where now stands the Methodist parsonage.

The first store was kept by Alva Jarvis, or " Squire Jarvis " as he was called, in the spring of 1841, in a wooden building between the sites of the present residences of Mrs. Fritcher and A. I. Decker. In the following fall G. H. Hallet opened a store just west of H. L. Stowell's present residence.

In 1843 was begun the construction of the the Erie railroad, an event that proved a great impetus to the growth of the hamlet, an impetus whose force is not yet expended. There were then here probly two or three hundred inhabitants. Poor management and other causes combined to retard the progress of work on the new railroad, and it was was not until 1849 that the road was completed. In the mean time Waverly Village was steadily growing.

About the time the railroad was completed, Broad street was laid out, and cross-streets connecting Broad and Chemung streets quickly followed. Houses sprang up like magic on every side, and on Broad street there was a strife to see who should erect the first buildings and be the earliest to embark in business.

The railroad passed through lands owned by Owen Spalding, Captain Davis and Isaac Shepard, and each gave the right of way. A part of the land given by Captain Davis was that on which the Erie buildings are now situated. The depot was built and opened about the time of the completion of the road, and was the first building in that part of the village. Mr. Ely was the first station agent, but was soon succeeded by J. S. Smith. While the depot was in process of erection, William Peck erected a small building on the bank, a little west of where now stands the Warford House, and opened a saloon. Afterwards the building was enlarged, a basement built, to which the saloon was removed, and a general store opened on the ground floor. In 1855 or 1856, the building was again enlarged and converted into a hotel. It was first known as the Waverly House, and later as the Courtney House. During the year 1849, a little after Peck opened his saloon, Captain Davis built and opened a saloon and boarding-house between the Waverly House and the present site of the Warford House. A year or so later this building was enlarged to nearly double its original size, and opened as a hotel. It was afterward sold to Stephen Bennet, who for several years prior 'to this time, had been engaged in blacksmithing on West Chemung street. In the fall of 1856, Cyrus Warford bought the house, and in 1857 it was burnt down. The property was uninsured, and was a total loss to Mr. Warford.

While the hotels were being built, several stores were in course of construction on Broad street, and in November William Gibbons opened a store. Amos Spalding had erected a large wooden block on the site of the present brick block, and in this Hiram Moore opened a store about Christmas, and nearly the same time

T. J. Brooks opened the third store, and John A. Corbin the fourth store, the last three being in the Spalding Block. Following these, others were opened in quick succession. Isaac Shepard erected the Shepard Block, corner of Clark and Broad streets, and in the store now occupied by G. B. Witter, opened a dry goods store, while in the room now occupied by Gerould & Co., Charles Shepard and J. I. Reeve opened a hardware store and tin shop. In 1850 Hiram Moore built a foundry near the present site of Slawson's furniture store. This was afterwards changed into a saloon, and later into a hotel, and bore the name of the Central House. In this year John Hard opened a jewelry store, the first in the place. It was located where now stands Rowland's liquor store.

With these buildings springing up so rapidly on Broad street, the parties who had opened stores on Chemung street discovered that they must get " down town " if they would secure a share of the business, and accordingly moved, not their goods alone, but their buildings also. Chamber's furniture store, that stood near the present site of W. F. Inman's residence, was moved to the corner of Broad and Clark streets, and is now occupied by J. H. Hern as a grocery. George Hanna purchased G. H. Hallet's store, and moved it down near the present site of the Van Velsor Block, where it was occupied by Hiram Payne as a furniture store. Cyrus Warford had a store on the present site of Mrs. Orange's residence, and this he moved down and it is now occupied by Nelson's harness store.

In 1852, B. P. Snyder built the hotel for many years afterward known as the Snyder House, now called the Hotel Warford. In 1855 Cyrus Warford purchased the house, and still owns it, although he retired from its management in 1873.

The name Waverly was not officially applied to the village until the year 1854. Until about 1840 or 1845, the little settlement on Chemung street was called " Villemont," a name given it by Isaac Shepard. After this the village was called by this name, " Waverley," " Loder," etc., to distinguish it from Factoryville, until the final organization, in 1854. For several years after this even, the name was spelled " Waverley." Application for incorporation was made December 12, 1853, and the question was put to a vote of the citizens on the 18th of January following, which resulted in 114 votes for and forty-four against. The name Waverly was given at the suggestion of Mr. J. E. Hallet, by whom it was borrowed from the immortal works of Sir

Walter Scott. Several other names were proposed, among which were "Shepardsville," "Davisville," and "Loder," the latter being in honor of Benjamin Loder, vice-president of the then recently completed railway. The first election of village officers was held March 27, 1854, at which the following officers were elected, viz: Francis H. Baldwin, William Gibson, Hiram M. Moore, Peter Dunning, and Alva Jarvis, trustees; Squire Whitaker, John L. Sawyer, and B. H. Davis, assessors; William P. Owen, collector; Owen Spalding, treasurer; P. V. Bennett, clerk; Morris B. Royall, Absalom Bowman, and W. A. Brooks, street commissioners; David E. Howell, poundmaster.

Captain Davis was the first postmaster, and received his appointment in 1849, from President Fillmore. He kept the office for a short time in Cyrus Warford's store, and afterwards in a small building adjoining "Squire" Jarvis' store on the west. This building he afterward moved down to near the present site of the Commercial Hotel. In 1852 the Captain built the "Davis Block," the brick building now known as the Exchange Block, and removed the postoffice into it, in the store now occupied by H. M. Ferguson & Co. In 1852 the Democrats elected their first President, Franklin Pierce, and on the principle that "to the victors belong the spoils," he appointed Squire Jarvis, a Democrat, to the position of postmaster, an office he held until 1861, when Abraham Lincoln appointed William Polleys to succeed him.

BIOGRAPAICAL.

Dr. William E. Johnson was born near Port Jervis, N. Y., October 17, 1837; was educated in the common schools, prepared for college at Neversink academy, and graduated at the Albany Medical college, December 31, 1859. In 1862 he was made examining surgeon of the twenty-sixth senatorial district, at Binghamton, to examine recruits, and soon after received a commission as first assistant surgeon of the 109th N. Y. Vols.; was subsequently promoted to surgeon of the same, then to brigade surgeon 3d Division 9th Corps, and then became one of the chiefs of the operating staff of the 3d Division. After the close of the war, in 1865, the Doctor came to Waverly and established himself in practice here, where he has since resided, being prominently identified with the growth and business progress of the place, serving it in many ways. The Doctor married Mattie M. Fuller, of Scranton, Pa., May 1, 1873, and has no children. The Doctor is surgeon-in-chief of the Robert Packer Hospital.

Richard Allison Elmer was born in Sussex county, New Jersey, August 28, 1808. He was the eldest son of Micah Allison Elmer. and grandson of Dr. William Elmer, of Goshen, and Richard Allison, of Wawayanda, Orange county, N. Y., and great grandson of Dr. Nathaniel Elmer, of Florida, and General William Allison, of Goshen, N. Y. He was a descendant of Edward Elmer, who came to America with the company of persons comprising the church of the Rev. Thomas Hooker, in 1632, and settled with the rest of Hooker's company, in Hartford, Conn., in 1636, and was one of the original proprietors of the city. At an early age he was thrown upon his own resources, and there was added to his responsibilities the care and education of his younger brothers and sisters. While engaged in farming and kindred pursuits, under his guidance, one brother entered college, and subsequently became a clergyman ; the other was engaged in business. His attention was early called Westward, and he became interested in Western lands. In November, 1850, he settled in Waverly, having been induced by his brother, the Rev. Nathaniel Elmer, then Presbyterian clergyman at Waverly, to give up his intention to locate in the West. He was largely interested in matters pertaining to the growth of the town, and while he was a person of unobtrusive manners and quiet force, he was always identified with its schools and churches, and matters pertaining to the advancement of the morals, and the government of its citizens. He died comparatively young, August 8, 1867. He was married September 11, 1832, to Charlotte Bailey (daughter of Colonel Jonathan Bailey, of Wawayanda). She died September 6, 1883, leaving four children : Howard, Mary, Richard A., and Antoinette Elmer.

Rev. Nathaniel Elmer, brother of Richard Allison Elmer, mentioned above, was born in Sussex county, New Jersey, January 31, 1816. He was graduated at Union College, New York, in 1840, and was ordained a minister of the Presbyterian church, October 24, 1844. He established the first Presbyterian church at Waverly, and was its first pastor, which position he held nine years. He wa married to Mary Post, in May, 1849, and died at Middletown, July 11, 1884, leaving one daughter, Elizabeth.

Howard Elmer was born in Wawayanda, Orange county, N. Y., August 2, 1833, the eldest son of Richard Allison and Charlotte (Bailey) Elmer He was prepared for college at the Ridgebury and Goshen academies, but delicate health prevented the continuance of his course. Soon after coming to Waverly with his father, in 1850, a lad of seventeen, he entered the Waverly Bank, after which he was engaged by the Chemung Canal Bank and the First National Bank of Elmira. In 1864 he organized the First National Bank of Waverly, and was until 1868 its cashier, after which he became its president, which position he has continued to hold. Having great faith in the value of the geographical advantages of the valley in which Waverly is situated, in 1870 he associated with himself the late Charles L. Anthony, of New York, and the late James Fritcher, and Richard A. Elmer, his brother, of Waverly, and purchased the several tracts of land, nearly one thousand acres, now embraced by Sayre and its surroundings. The panic of 1873 and consequent depreciation of values, for a time checked the growth of the proposed town considerably, but he did not swerve from his course, and with an absolute faith in its future prosperity he built the town of Sayre, which to-day has a population of three thousand, and monthly pays off over eight hundred men. Upon the death of Mr. Anthony, he induced the Packer family, E. P. Wilbur, and Robert Lockhart, of South Bethlehem, Pa., to assume the Anthony interest, and it resulted in centering at Sayre the great shops of the Pennsylvania & New York, and the Lehigh Valley railroads, which are prominent factors in the prosperity of Waverly and Athens. Through his encouragement the Cayuta Wheel and Foundry, and the Sayre Pipe Foundry were built. He also built the Sayre and Athens waterworks. He is president and active manager of the Sayre Land Company, the Sayre Water Company, the Sayre Pipe Foundry Company, the Cayuta Wheel & Foundry Company, and the Sayre Steam Forge Company. Mr. Elmer is also a director of the Pennsylvania & New York Railroad Company, the Geneva, Ithaca & Sayre Railroad Company, and treasurer of the Buffalo & Geneva Railroad Company. During the years 1875 and 1876 he was receiver of the Ithaca & Athens, and Geneva & Ithaca railroads. He has always refrained from holding any public office. He married, in October, 1865, Miss Sarah P. Perkins, daughter of the late George A. Perkins, of Athens, Pa.

Richard Allison Elmer* is a son of the late Richard Allison Elmer, of Waverly, and Charlotte (Bailey) Elmer. He was born in Wawayando, Orange county, N. Y., June 16, 1842, and is the

*This sketch of Mr. Elmer was contributed, at our solicitation, by Mr. Charles Nordhoff, of the New York *Herald*.

second in a family of four, Howard Elmer being his elder brother.

His family removed to Waverly in 1850, and have remained established there ever since. He was educated at the Waverly High School, and subsequently at Hamilton College, from which he was graduated in 1864. He intended to practice law, and pursued his studies for that purpose, and was admitted to the bar, but in 1867 the death of his father led him to abandon this plan of life, and he joined his brother, Howard Elmer, who was then president of the First National Bank of Waverly, became cashier of that bank, and the two succeeded to their father's business. He remained cashier of the First National Bank for twelve years, during which time, by his energy and business ability, he so developed the position about him that his firm became one of the largest investors of private trusts in the state of New York.

In 1870, he joined his brother Howard, Mr. Charles L. Anthony, of New York city, and Mr. James Fritcher, in the purchase of a tract of land in Pennsylvania, near Waverly, which now bears the name of Sayre, and has become a great manufacturing and railroad center, where large bodies of men are employed.

He still retains his original interest at Sayre, and besides being a director of the First National Bank, is director of the Sayre Land Company, the Sayre Water Company, the Cayuta Wheel Foundry Company, the Sayre Pipe Foundry Company, and the Sayre Steam Forge Company. Busied with these and other enterprises, which gave full occupation to his energies, Mr Elmer, though he took always a prominent part in political as well as local and charitable movements, never sought political office. His name was prominently mentioned in the Republican state convention, in 1879, for the place of state treasurer, as being in consonance with his business pursuits.

In 1881, on the accession of President Garfield, the urgent public demand for trenchant and long needed reform in the post-office department led General Garfield to look around for a citizen of more than common courage, energy and business capacity to fill the place of second assistant postmaster general, in which bureau of the department the required reforms were to be made. Without Mr. Elmer's knowledge, several gentlemen, prominent and influential with the President and the new administration, recommended him as the fittest man within their knowledge for this place, and able to do the required and very difficult work of reform. The President determined to nominate him, and it was only when this was decided upon that Mr. Elmer was told of what was proposed. He had but a day to consider the question of accepting the position, and with his reluctant consent his name was sent to the senate. He was confirmed May 5, 1881, and soon after removed to Washington, and assumed his new duties.

The affairs of the postoffice department, particularly of that part under the control of the second assistant postmaster general, known as the star route and steamboat service, had fallen into such disorder under the previous administration as to become one of the gravest public scandals in the history of the government; attracting the attention of the whole country, and being exposed and denounced by the journals of both parties, as well as in congressional committees and debates. All demands for efforts at reform had been successfully resisted, and President Garfield on entering the presidency, felt that a thorough extirpation of the gross maladministration and waste in this part of the public service was absolutely necessary to the success and good fame of his administration. He promised his unfaltering support to Mr. Elmer, and thus encouraged, the work was begun. Mr. Elmer found himself strongly opposed by those who had in various ways profited by the corruption and maladministration, many of them men of influence, and supported by others prominent in the country.

Almost entirely unknown to the circle of political leaders in Washington, and unfamiliar with the Department and with the Capitol, Mr. Elmer steadfastly pursued the work of reform he had undertaken. Overcoming all obstacles placed in his way, and the very great difficulties which necessarily met him at every step of an extremely intricate business, he, in three years of arduous and unceasing labor, completed the reform he had undertaken.

This done, he resigned his place in February, 1884, to attend to his neglected private interests. On resigning, he received the well merited thanks of President Arthur, and of the head of the Post Office Department. His course and his success had already won the approval of the country, which saw with surprise and satisfaction the substitution of economy, honesty and efficiency in that branch of the service which had long been notorious for the most scandalous abuses.

A brief statement of the results he achieved shows their value and importance. In the first year of his service he saved the Treasury $1,778,000. In the second and following years these savings amounted to over $2,000,000 per annum. Against the efforts of one of the most powerful combinations the country has known, he restored order and economy to the carrying of the Star Route and other mails, and without stinting the service the savings he enforced and brought about were so great as to make the Post Office Department self-supporting for the first time in thirty years. This encouraged Congress to agree to his recommendation to lower the letter rate from three cents to two cents.

The press of the country freely expressed its satisfaction with Mr. Elmer's conspicuous success in one of the most difficult works of administrative reform ever undertaken. The New York *Herald* said editorially of him, in July, 1882, in a comparison of his work with that of his predecessor:

"The saving Mr. Elmer has effected on the Star Route service alone, is more than enough to make the whole postal service self-supporting. That is what the public gains by the labors of an honest man, and it enables the Postmaster General to say, that for the year ending July 1, 1883, the Post Office Department will not only be self-supporting, but will have a surplus of one and a half million dollars. Such reductions in the cost of the service, without impairing its efficiency, tell their own story. They reflect the greatest credit on Mr. Elmer, as also on Postmaster General Howe, without whose strong and constant support Mr. Elmer would not have been able to carry out the reforms he has made in a service which had become corrupt, demoralized, and inefficient."

In June of the following year, the New York *Herald*, discussing the condition of the postal service, praised "Mr. Elmer's extraordinary administrative capacity, courage and honesty," and said, "As to Mr. Elmer, the Second Assistant General, it was his task when he came into office to reform the Star Route service, and weed out of it the extravagance and corruption which had filled it under his predecessor. Mr. Elmer did this, and he deserves the thanks of the country for doing it admirably. In the first year of his service he made a saving of over one-half of the amount spent the previous year; in the second year he effected still greater savings, and he did this in such a manner that no complaints were made of insufficient service."

Shortly after retiring to private life, Mr. Elmer organized in the City of New York the American Surety Company, of which he became and remains president. Soon after he had established this organization, he fell ill from long-continued and severe labor, and suffered for nearly two years from the results of too great and prolonged a strain. He did not, however, give up work, and his care and skill have made his corporation the largest and most successful of its kind in the world.

In the spring of 1887, on the application of the Surrogate of New York, Judge Noah Davis, acting as appointed referee, took testimony, at great length, to examine into the soundness of the plan on which the American Surety Company carried on its business, and the responsibility of its guarantees, both in regard to individuals and trusts. In his official report to the Surrogate, Judge Davis went at length into the manner in which the Company does its work, and his conclusions were:

"The capital of the Company remains wholly unimpaired. The reserved fund and the net surplus show that the business of the Company has been, during its short term of existence, both prosperous and profitable.

"The business of the Company is strictly confined to Fidelity Insurance, and the evidence shows that it engages in no other business. It divides this business into two classes, which it calls Judicial and Fidelity. The former embraces all the business pertaining to Courts of every kind, and includes undertakings or bonds in appeals, on attachments and other process in suit, bonds of guardians, of administrators, executors, trustees, receivers, and all other obligations of sureties in courts of law, equity and probate, which involve the fidelity of appointees, except public officers. The second class includes bonds and guarantees of the fidelity of employees of corporations and persons whose relations to their employers are fiduciary in any pecuniary sense, except also public officers. The judicial business has been conducted in eleven different States of the United States, but chiefly in New York and Pennsylvania."

As to the Fidelity branch of the business, Judge Davis said:

"Thus far the business has proved itself to be a safe and profitable form of insurance, and the experience of this Company has justified the policy of the statute which authorizes the organization of such corporations. The conclusions which the Referee has reached from the examination of this case are, that the American Surety Company has not only satisfactorily justified in respect of its qualifications to become surety in this particular matter, but has shown that as surety in judicial proceedings, it presents a system of security worthy of the confidence of the Court, and of the public, and largely superior to that which can be offered by individual sureties.

"The management of the affairs of the Company by its officers has been most creditable to their capacity and integrity."

On this report the Surrogate made an order June 1, 1887, that, "The American Surety Company be accepted as surety on the bond of Ana de Rivas Herques given in the above entitled matter, or upon any new bond that she may be required to give in this proceedings."

Mr. Elmer is a director of the Wabash railroad, the Atlantic & Danville railroad, the Phoenix Fire Insurance Company, and several New York and New England corporations.

In 1883 he became interested in several Mexican properties, and out of this relation grew the International Company of Mexico, of which he was one of the founders and the treasurer, and to whose success he has largely contributed.

Mr. Elmer married June 16, 1870, Miss Sarah Foster France, daughter of the late J. Foster France, of Middletown, New York, and has three sons, Robert France Elmer, Richard Allison Elmer Jr., the third of his name, and Charles Howard Elmer.

John L. Sawyer, born in Orange county, N. Y., in 1811, came to Barton in 1833, engaging in farming and lumbering. After the construction of the Erie railroad, in 1849, he removed to Waverly village, where he was long and prominently identified with the village's growth and prosperity, and where he resided until his death, in 1871. For many years he represented the town in the board of supervisors. Mr. Sawyer married Julia Smith, of Orange county, who bore him two children, Henry M. and J. Theodore. The former, born in 1832, married Maria, daughter of Senator Nathan Bristol, of Waverly, in 1856, and died two years later without issue. J. Theodore was born in Barton in 1834. He was educated at the district schools and Goshen Academy, and engaged with his father in the lumber business in Waverly and Canada. For a time he conducted a private bank, and in 1874 organized the Citizens Bank of Waverly, of which he is president. He represented his town two years in the board of supervisors, and in 1878 and 1879 the county of Tioga in the state legislature. In 1872 Mr. Sawyer married Alice Lyman, of Goshen, Conn., and has one child, Ellen, born in 1874.

Moses Lyman who was born in Goshen, Conn., a son of Moses and Mary A. (Hadley) Lyman, August 20, 1836; was educated at Goshen Academy and Brown University; began the lumber business at Windsor Locks, Conn., and McIndoes Falls, Vt., in 1859, where he remained till 1862. He then enlisted in the 15th Vt. Vols., as 1st Lieutenant of Co. F. In 1865, he came to Waverly and established a lumber business here under the firm name of Jennings & Lyman, and has since been a resident of the village. In 1872 he built the car-wheel foundry at the present village of Sayre, acting as treasurer of the company till he sold out his interest in 1884. Mr. Lyman is now identified with the Salisbury Iron interests of Connecticut, and is Eastern sales agent for the Shelby Iron Co., of Alabama, owns the Waverly Toy Works, and is president of the Lyman Bank, of Sanford, Fla., established in 1882. Mr. Lyman married Miss Ellen A. Douglass, of Mauch Chunk, Pa., who bore him two children, Moses and Isabel, and died in August, 1871. In March, 1883, he married Miss Sarah H. Beebe, daughter of P. S. Beebe, of Litchfield, Conn.

Henry G. Merriam, of the firm of Merriam Bros., was born in Goshen, N. Y., March 5, 1837. He was educated at the Farmer's Hall Academy, of Goshen, and graduated at Brown (R. I.) University,' in 1857, and from 1861 to 1865 was principal of Leicester Academy, Mass. He then came to Waverly and established the hardware business which he has since conducted as senior partner. Mr. Merriam married Fanny W. White, of Worcester, Mass., in 1867, and has two children, Harry E. and Grace M. Mr. Merriam was the first president of the board of education here, and has held the office eleven years.

Judge Ferris Shoemaker is the fifth son of Richard Shoemaker, who was a son of Benjamin, a son of Daniel, the original settler of that name in the town of Nichols, and was born June 22, 1838, in Athens township, Pa. Later in the same year his parents moved to Susquehanna county, Pa. Here he grew to manhood and made it his home until he moved to Waverly, in 1873. He was educated at Wyoming Seminary, Kingston, Pa., and at the Normal School, Montrose, Pa. Prior to 1861 he engaged in teaching for several years, but soon after the war broke out he enlisted in the U. S. Marine Corps, and served four years and three months, returning home in the spring of 1866. The following fall he was elected register of wills, etc., of Susquehanna county. This office he filled three years, and in February, 1870, was appointed prothonotary by Governor John W. Geary, to fill vacancy caused by the death of W. F. Simrell. While performing the duties of these offices he found time to pursue the study of law in the office of Hon. W. H. Jessup, of Montrose, and in the spring of 1871 was admitted to practice in all the courts of the county. He was afterwards admitted to the bar in Bradford and Wyoming counties, and after coming to Waverly, in 1873, was admitted to practice in the supreme court of New York. For the past fourteen years he has been in constant practice in both states. At the general election of 1886 Mr. Shoemaker was elected special county judge, on the Republican ticket. He married Gertrude S. Sweet, of Montrose, Pa., September 1, 1869, and has had five children, all of whom except one are living, viz.: Richard S., Tila N., Mabel and Max Albrecht, residing with their parents.

Jacob B. Floyd was born in Chemung, N. Y., April 26, 1839. He was educated in the public schools of his native town, in the Genesee Wesleyan Seminary, of Lima, N. Y., and the Wyoming Seminary, of Kingston, Pa., taking a college preparatory course. He began the study of law at the Albany Law school, graduating in 1871. He immediately began practice at Waverly, and has been in practice here ever since. He has held the office of special county judge, was a member of the state assembly in 1882, and held other minor offices. Mr. Floyd married Matilda H. Snyder, of Scranton, Pa., August 14, 1861, and has had three children, only one of whom, a daughter, Florence, a graduate of Wellesly college, is living.

Adolphus G. Allen, son of Samuel and Miranda (Sheffield) Allen, was born at Troy, Pa., November 30, 1830. His studies were begun in the common schools, and he prepared for college in the Troy academy ; but left off ideas of the classics for law, beginning study with General James Nye, at Hamilton, N. Y., and completed them with Goodwin & Mitchel, of the same place, and was admitted to the bar at the general term at Binghamton, January, 1853. The next spring he was admitted to the Brad-ford county bar, and immediately moved to Factoryville, and in the spring of 1854 located in Waverly, where he now is. He has held the office of town clerk, trustee of the village, been special county judge two terms, and was a member of the state legislature in 1886. Judge Allen married Sarah S. Walker, of Factoryville, in March, 1853, and has two children, D. Welling-ton, a practicing attorney of Waverly, born June 18, 1854, and Kate, wife of Clarence C. Campbell, born January 1, 1860.

William Polleys was born in Malden, Mass., August 18, 1816, and when about ten years of age removed with his parents to Bradford county, Pa. When about eighteen years of age, he entered the office of the Elmira *Republican*, as an apprentice. After mastering the trade, he remained in the office until 1840, when he and Alva S. Carter purchased the paper, and continued the publication until 1845, when they sold their interest, and the name was changed to the *Elmira Advertiser*. In 1854 Mr. Polleys removed to Waverly, and entered into partnership with F. H. Baldwin, in the publication of the *Advocate*, then but recently changed in name from the *Waverly Luminary*, and continued one of its publishers up to the time of his death. July 17, 1861, Mr. Polleys was appointed postmaster by President Lincoln, and for fourteen years following held that position, when he voluntarily retired. From early manhood Mr. Polleys took an active interest in politics, and until the demise of the Whig party, belonged to that organization, but on its dissolution, he united with the Re-publicans, and much of the strength and success of their party in Tioga county can be traced to his energy, perseverance and untiring work. For his friends and the success of his party, no sacrifice was too great. He took an active interest in all public enterprises, and in everything that was calculated to advance the interests of the village. He died suddenly June 26, 1883.

Richard D. Van Deuzer came from Orange county, N. Y., to Waverly, in 1852, when there were but four or five hundred inhabitants in the village, and has been connected with public enterprises here ever since. He built the Waverly steam flouring-mill, and conducted it until it was destroyed by fire. He built also, a planing-mill in Waverly, and a steam saw-mill on Shepard's creek. The former was twice destroyed by fire. Previous to his connection with manufacturing projects, he was engaged in mercantile pursuits, and conducted the first coal-yard in Waverly. He was one of the incorporators of the old Waverly Bank, also of the First National Bank, and was the first president of the latter institution, which office he held seven years. He was one of the first stock-holders, and helped organize the G. I. & S. R. R. company, and in connection with John Sawyer, secured the right of way from the village to Dean's creek, a distance of seven miles, for one dollar. Mr. Van Deuzer was president of the village corporation at the opening of the Lehigh Valley R. R., and in honor of the occasion a banquet was given at the Snyder House, at which he presided. Mr. Van Deuzer married Harriet Everson, by whom he had five children, viz.: Fanny, wife of W. H. W. Jones, Howard C., Mamie C., Annie L., and Richard D., Jr. Howard C. married Kittie Towne, of Rockford, Ill.

Gurdon G. Manning was born in Berkshire, N. Y., December 30, 1825. He was educated in the common schools, and attended the Owego academy. He then taught school several years, went to Owego as a clerk for Truman, Stone & Buckbee, where he remained six years. In 1856 he went into the dry goods business with C. E. Schoonmaker. In the latter part of 1860 he was elected county treasurer, and sold his interest to his partner, and in 1861 removed to Factoryville, where he entered the mercantile trade again, in company with Silas Fordham. In 1876 he removed to Waverly village, and since January, 1886, has held the office of justice of the peace. Mr. Manning married Sarah A. Adams, October 23, 1851, and has had born to him three children, viz.: Lucius R., a banker of Tacoma, W. T., Charles E., an assistant engineer in the U. S. Navy, and Jennie S., wife of James P. Nevins, of this town.

Ambrose P. Eaton was born in the old town of Union, now Chenango, Broome county, N. Y., June 4, 1826. He was educated in the public schools of his native town, studied law with

Hon. Charles E. Parker, of Owego, was admitted to practice at Binghamton, in 1868, and has been in practice in Tioga county since. Mr. Eaton married Mary H., daughter of Calvin Johnson, March 13, 1851, and has one child, Mary E., wife of James A. Roberts, of Tioga. Mr. Eaton's home is in Smithboro, though his office is located in Waverly.

William Fiske Warner, one of Waverly's lawyers, has been prominently identified with the later growth of the village, and is widely known as a writer and student of local history. In Owego, his former home, we print a biographical sketch of this gentleman.

Benjamin Genung was an early settler in this vicinity. Jean Guenon, one of the exiled Hugenots who took refuge in Holland, set sail from Amsterdam, April 2, 1657, in the ship "Draetvat," Captain John Bestevaer, and came directly to New Amsterdam (New York). The next year he settled at Flushing, L. I., where he acquired some land, and remained until his death, in 1714. His wife was Grietie, or Margaret Sneden, of Harlem, whom he married August 30, 1660, and who survived him about thirteen years. They left besides daughters, two sons, John, born in 1669, and Jeremiah, born in 1671. From these it is believed, have decended the entire, and now widely scattered family of Genung, in this country. Benjamin Genung, a soldier of the revolution, settled in New Jersey, and at an early day came to Dryden, Tompkins county, when that county formed a part of Tioga. He had six children,—Barnabas, Aaron, Rachel, Philo, Peron and Timothy. Barnabas married Susan Johnson, by whom he had twelve children who arrived at maturity—Lydia, Nathaniel, Abram, Harrison, Ann, Rebecca, Sally, Enos, George, Merilda and Barnabas. Abram married Martha, daughter, of James R. Dye, by whom he has two sons, John Franklin and George Frederick (twins), the former professor of rhetoric in Amherst college, the latter professor of Greek, Latin and political economy in Benedict Institute, Columbia, S. C. Enos H. was born February 26, 1825, and has lived principally in Tioga county since 1852. He married Sarepta, daughter of George Earsley, of Caroline, N. Y., April 7, 1850, and by whom he has six children, viz.: Emma (Mrs. Fred Morgan), George D., the well known journalist of this village, Dell (Mrs. George Gardner), Priscilla (Mrs. George Stevens), Luella (Mrs. William Ewen) and Reuben E. Mrs. Genung died September 18, 1882. Salmon A., son of Nathaniel, was born January 27, 1841, married Mary E., daughter of Asa Doty, of Towanda, Pa., September 21, 1861, and is now a resident of Waverly. George D. Genung married Mary A. VanDerlip, a daughter of S. T. VanDerlip, of Waverly, June 16, 1876. Three children have been born to them, Arthur, deceased, G. Leyl and M. Lucille.

Squire Whitaker was born in Deckertown, N. J., June 1, 1808, and came with his parents to this town in 1816. He walked the entire distance, which in those days was not considered a remarkable feat, and assisted in driving a cow. In 1832 he married Sally, daughter of John Hanna, and for about two years resided in Ellistown. They afterward moved to the farm on Tallmadge Hill now owned by his son Lewis, then an unbroken forest. He set up a temporary house on crotched sticks, which the family occupied while his log-house was building. He subsequently built a framed house, which was burned, and his neighbors kindly aided him to re build, and in nine days had his house ready for occupancy. Their children were Horace, Jane (Mrs. D. D. Knapp), Pheobe (Mrs. Hatfield Hallett), Lewis, James, William and Frank (Mrs. Wilbur Finch). Lewis married Frances, daughter of James Parker. In 1849, the family removed to Waverly and took up their home at the homestead in Chemung street, where Mr. and Mrs. Whitaker continued to reside to the time of their death. Mrs. Whitaker died about fifteen years ago, and Mr. Whitaker on May 15, 1887. He was appointed captain of the state militia by Governor Marcy. In 1844 Tioga county offered a banner to the town that would bring to Owego the largest delegation in favor of Polk and Dallas. Mr. Whitaker was at the head of the greatest number, and took the prize.

Banking Institutions.—The Waverly Bank was organized in 1855, with John C. Adams, president, and George H. Fairchild, cashier. The business was at first opened in the northwest room of the Snyder House, and a year or two later, upon the completion of the bank building corner of Broad and Loder street, removed into it. In about 1865 it was changed to a National bank, and in 1871 was moved into the building now occupied by the Citizens Bank.

About the first of April, 1872, a private bank was opened in the same building, H. T. Herrick, president ; George Herrick, cashier; H. T. Sawyer, teller. They also held the same positions in the National Bank, and within a month after the organization of the private bank, the National went into the hands of a receiver. J. S. Thurston, of Elmira, was the first receiver appointed, and at the end of a month he resigned and was succeeded by J. T. Sawyer, who served for about three months and resigned. J. B. Floyd was then appointed and closed up the business. In May of the following year, 1873, the HerrickBank also suspended, and J. T. Sawyer and R. A, Elmer were elected assignees and effected a settlement of the business.

The First National Bank was organized February 13, 1864, with a capital of $50,000.00. Its first officers were R. D. Van Deuzer, president; R. A. Elmer, vice-president; H. Elmer, cashier. In February, 1884, their charter was extended twenty years. The present officers are Howard Elmer, president; N. S. Johnson, vice-president; F. E. Lyford, cashier.

The Citizens Bank was incorporated under the banking laws of the state of New York, June 18, 1874, and commenced business on the first of July following, with a capital of $50,000.00. The first officers were J. T. Sawyer, president; M. Lyman, cashier. The present officers are J. T. Sawyer, president; S. W. Slaughter, vice-president; F. A. Sawyer, cashier.

Gas Light Company:—The Waverly Gas Light Company was organized January 7, 1873, with a capital of $50,000.00, and the works were completed August 15th of the same year. They were constructed by Deily & Fowler, engineers of Philadelphia, and cost the company $50,000.00. The village was first lighted with gas July 24, 1873. The first officers of the company were William F. Warner, president; Frederick W. Warner, secretary; E. W. Warner, treasurer. William F. Warner is still president, and Henry G. Merriam, secretary and treasurer.

Waverly Library and Museum.—A library and museum was opened on Park avenue, June 10, 1885, due mainly to the efforts of Prof. Riker, seconded by the generous co-operation of the citizens. The library contains some 2,500 volumes and 1,000 pamphlets, and has a circulating and a reference department, the latter embracing many rare and valuable works. It is made free to the public, excepting the circulating department, for the use and increase of which an annual fee is charged. It has worked well and given great satisfaction in the short period of its existence.

FACTORYVILLE.—The name "Factoryville" was originally applied to all the territory now included in both Waverly and East Waverly, and took its origin from the number of factories and mills erected along Shepard's creek in the early part of the century. The village is pleasantly located, but its prosperity de-

8*

parted when, in 1849, the completion of the Erie railroad caused Waverly to spring up on its western border, and while the latter has advanced rapidly in population and in commercial and manufacturing interests, the former has made but very slight progress. The village now contains one church (Old School Baptist), three stores, two hotels, one tannery, one steam saw-mill, wagon shops, blacksmith shops, etc., a fine school building, belonging to the graded school system of Waverly and East Waverly, and has about 500 inhabitants. Waverly in her growth has pushed out in all directions, but particularly towards Factoryville, until now the two unite and practically constitute one village, the name Factoryville even locally having given way to " East Waverly," and doubtless within a few years both will be comprised within the corporate limits of Waverly, and " Factoryville " will exist only in memory and in history.

A survey of Factoryville was made in 1819, by Major Flower. John Shepard owned the land on which the village is now located, and he divided it into large lots, and sold them to Thomas Wilcox and Moses and Elisha Larnard, who divided them into village lots, which were sold, and neat and comfortable buildings were erected upon them, some of which are now standing. The post-office was established here in 1812, with Isaac Shepard as postmaster. The office was first located in the woolen mill, and later in Mr. Shepard's store on the Owego road (Chemung street). The establishment of mail and stage lines over the newly constructed turnpike, made the "tavern" a necessity, and in 1824 one was erected by Isaac Shepard, on the lot where now stands the C. H. Shepard residence, and a few years later John Shackelton, Sr., built a tavern and stage-house at East Waverly.

At a very early date in the history of the town, mills and factories were erected here. In the year 1800 George Walker built a grist-mill, and in 1808–09 John Shepard, of Milltown, and Josiah Crocker, then recently removed from Lee, Mass., erected a fulling-mill, carding-machines and saw-mill. Later, Isaac and Job Shepard, sons of John Shepard, the former the father of Charles and William Shepard, erected a woolen factory, which was afterwards bought and enlarged by Alexander Brooks, an uncle of C. C. Brooks. This building was destroyed by fire in 1853. It was rebuilt by Mr. Brooks' sons, William and Gilbert, as an agricultural implement factory. It was afterwards again destroyed by fire, and rebuilt in part by William Brooks. In 1863 C. C. Brooks bought a half interest in the concern of William Brooks, and they enlarged the buildings, added a foundry, machine-shops, etc. In 1870 Messrs. Brooks sold the establishment to A. B. Phillips, who again converted it into a tannery. In 1879 A. I. Decker purchased the property, and in August, 1882, the buildings were again destroyed by fire. Mr. Decker at once commenced rebuilding, and in January, 1883, was again ready for business.

About the year 1824 Jerry Adams built a tannery near the state line, and later he sold the industry to one Norris, who in 1834 sold to Luther Stone, father of William and James Stone. In 1842 Mr. Stone removed the building and put up a much larger and better one. In 1860 this was burned down, but was rebuilt the same year. In 1866 Luther Stone died and his sons continued the business until 1868, when James sold his interest to J. A. Perkins, and two years later William also sold to Mr. Perkins, and the latter continued the business for several years. In 1883 the Sayre Butter Package Co. leased the building, which for a few years preceding this time had been unused, and now it is the scene of this important industry.

BARTON is a post village situated near the southeast corner of the town of Barton, on the north bank of the Susquehanna river, and is a way-station on the N. Y. L. E. & W. railroad. It contains one church (M. E.), one school-house, one hotel, two general stores, one feed and saw-mill, and about two hundred inhabitants. Of the early settlers in this vicinity we have already spoken. The village is about five miles from Waverly.

RENIFF is a post village situated near the northwest corner of the town. The postoffice was established here in March, 1881, with Willis E. Gillett postmaster, who has continued in office to the present time. The village contains a school-house, saw, planing, shingle, and feed-mills, creamery, general store, blacksmith-shop, and about a dozen dwellings. The patrons of the postoffice are about 200. The mills are owned by W. E. Gillett, as is also the store and blacksmith-shop, and he owns a half interest in the creamery. Mr. Gillett is largely engaged in farming, and employs upwards of thirty men. Although comparatively a young man, he has shown remarkable enterprise and energy in establishing and maintaining most of the business interests of the place, and Reniff owes almost its entire existence to him.

LOCKWOOD is a post village situated on the western border of the town, about seven miles north of Waverly, on Shepard's creek, and is a station on the G. I. & S. R. R. The postoffice was

established in 1869, as Bingham's Mills, with G. W. Bingham
postmaster. The name was afterwards changed to Lockwood.
The population is about 200. The village has one church (M. E.),
a school house, custom and flouring-mill, two saw and planing-
mills, two blacksmith-shops, two turning, scroll-sawing, and
wagon-shops, one hotel, two general stores, and one grocery and
meat market. It is exceedingly bright for a place of its size, and
is remarkable for its industry and thrift.

NORTH BARTON postoffice is located in the northern part of
the town, near the head-waters of Ellis creek.

HALSEY VALLEY is a post village extending from the town of
Tioga partially over into the northeastern corner of Barton township. A description of it may be found in the history of Tioga.

MANUFACTURING INDUSTRIES.

The Novelty Furniture Works of Waverly were established by
Hall & Cummings, in 1873, in South Waverly. In 1876 the
works were removed to Athens, Pa., where, under the present
firm of Hall & Lyon, the business prospered and grew until it
ranked among the largest and most successful in the state of
Pennsylvania. In June, 1884, the works were completely destroyed by fire. The people of Waverly, wisely realizing the importance of manufacturing as an element of growth and prosperity, made a very liberal proposition to Messrs. Hall & Lyon to
re-build their works in their beautiful and thriving village. The
proffer being accepted, the works were re-built, on a much
enlarged basis, and were ready for operation in the autumn of
1884. At the present time the works consist of three main brick
buildings, besides a brick boiler and furnace house, and a large
dry-kiln capable of thoroughly kiln-drying three million feet of
lumber annually. For convenience of arrangement, thorough
equipment and facility for receiving the raw materials and shipping the finished product, these works are not surpassed by
any similar institution in the whole country. Now more than
72,000 feet of floor space is utilized, and constant employment is
afforded to 125 workmen, with a promise of constant growth and
expansion in the near future. Messrs. Hall & Lyon now maintain
a large sales room in Philadelphia, and their product finds market
also throughout New England, New York, and Pennsylvania.

*D. H. Eaton & Son's Refrigerator, Butter and Oyster Pail Manu-
factory* was established in July, 1885, by the above firm who are

the patentees. The pail is made of tin, with a jacket of sheet or galvanized iron so fitted as to allow a free circulation of air between the pail and jacket; the latter being perforated at the top and bottom. There are sizes for holding five, ten, fifteen, twenty and fifty pounds of butter. By thorough tests it has been proved of surpassing coldness for the transmission of butter, and they may be returned to the shipper and re-used many times. The works are situated in East Waverly, on Main street, under the supervision of the firm.

The Sayre Butter Package Company was established by Richard D. Van Deuzer, who secured the patent in July, 1882, and who erected the buildings and put in the machinery necessary for their manufacture. In October of the same year he entered into partnership with James A. Clark, which partnership was continued until 1884. The factory is situated on Main street, in East Waverly, and is run by both steam and water-power. They make the first tin butter package with wooden jackets and covers ever manufactured in this section, and Mr. Van Deuzer was the first to introduce them into New York, Pennsylvania, New Jersey and the New England states. The tub is made of tin with an elm jacket, bottom and top hoops and wooden cover. There are three sizes made, holding twenty, thirty and fifty pounds. There are thirty-five hands employed, and the capacity is 1,000 packages in ten hours. The present proprietors are R. D. & H. C. Van Deuzer, of Waverly, and F. T. Page, of Athens, Pa. This firm has recently added the manufacture of baskets of all varieties, made of staves and splints, and the entire management is under the supervision of R. D. Van Deuzer.

The Decker Tannery, located at Factoryville, has already been spoken of in connection with the sketch of that village. The tannery gives employment to twenty-five hands, and has the capacity for turning out 50,000 sides of leather per annum.

C. M. Crandall's Toy Manufactory, on Broad street, was established here by him in 1885. He came from Montrose, Pa., where he had carried on the business a number of years. He manufactures about $40,000.00 worth of toys per year, employing fifty hands. His goods consist of a vast number of ingenious mechanical toys, all of which are invented and manufactured by himself. The production is disposed of entirely to New York jobbers, orders for a single style of toy often amounting to several thousand dollars.

John C. Shear's Grist and Flouring-Mill, on Broad street, was built by Weaver & Shear, in 1878. Since 1882 the mill has been owned and operated by Mr. Shear. It is operated by steam-power, has four runs of stones, one set of rolls, four brakes, and other modern machinery to correspond. Mr. Shear employs four men, and grinds about 200 bushels of grain per day, with the capacity for turning out 450. He does principally custom work.

James Lemon's Foundry and Machine Shop, on Broad street, was originally established by him in 1850. He located on Broad street then, about where Clark's hardware store now is, his being the third building erected on the street. Mr. Lemon continued in business at this point until 1856, when he sold to H. M. Moore, and moved to about what is now No. 150 Broad street. About twenty years ago he located at the site he now occupies. He manufactures plows, stoves, plow and agricultural fixtures, etc.

The Reniff Mills were built by Isaac Barnes and George Newell, upwards of fifty years ago. The present mill was built about forty years ago, but has been enlarged and extensively improved by the present owner, Willis E. Gillett. Its capacity for saw-ing and planing is 2,000,000 feet per annum. There is also a feed and shingle-mill in connection.

The Gillett & Decker Creamery was established in the spring of 1887, by W. E. Gillett and A. I. Decker. It is situated at Reniff, is run by a six horse-power engine, and is equipped with all the most improved machinery known to the manufacture of butter. It runs this year about 175 gallons of milk per day.

The Cayuta Creamery was established in 1883, at Barton Center, and was known as the "Barton Center Creamery." In the win-ter of 1887 it was removed to East Waverly, near the Geneva & Sayre R. R. depot. Its capacity is for 1,000 cows, employs five men, and runs delivery wagons for supplying private families with milk products. It was established by F. A. Schuyler, and was run by him until the spring of 1887, when H. T. Harding entered into partnership with him, and it is now run under the firm name of Schuyler & Harding.

The Lockwood Flour and Custom Feed-Mill was established in 1853, by Charles Bingham, and is now run by Bingham Brothers. It is situated in the village of Lockwood, on Shepard's creek. It is run by steam and water-power, has four runs of stones, and good facilities for grinding buckwheat. Its capacity is about 200 bushels in ten hours.

The Lockwood Saw, Planing, and Lath Mills, are run by the Bing-ham Brothers. The present mills were built by Bingham, Lyons

& Co., in 1879. They are situated on Shepard's creek, are run by a forty horse-power engine, and have the capacity for 10,000 feet of lumber per day. The head sawyer is J. A. Stever.

A. V. C. Vail & Co.'s Steam Saw and Planing-Mill is situated at Lockwood village, near the G. I. & S. R. R. It was removed there from road 2, in 1880. Its capacity is 5,000 feet per day.

A. Brook's Turning ond Scroll-Sawing Works, at Lockwood, are fitted with a four horse-power engine, a variety of circular and scroll saws and lathes, and all equipments necessary to do the finest work in that line. A specialty is made of the manufacture of church seats, where a variety of styles and patterns may be seen. The business was established in 1880.

C. H. Coleman's Turning, Scroll-Sawing, Wagon and Blacksmith Shops are situated near Bingham's mills, in Lockwood. The works are run by an eight horse-power engine, have a planer, various saws, etc., also facilities for doing all kinds of repairing at short notice.

C. F. Hanna's Circular Saw-Mill is situated on Ellis creek, about one mile from the River road, and is run by steam-power. It was built by the present proprietor in November, 1884. Its capacity is from 5,000 to 8,000 feet in ten hours. The first mill on this site was built by Foster, Newland & Smith, about 1859.

CHURCHES.

The Tioga and Barton Baptist Church.—After the Revolution, when immigration began to set in from the Eastern states, the Congregational denomination of Connecticut sent out the Rev. Seth Williston as a missionary, and we find him holding religious services in different places in the county as early as 1795. The earliest religious organization formed in the county was on February 20, 1796. Several families from Bedford, Mass., settled along the river between Tioga Center and Smithboro, calling their settlement "New Bedford." Among them was a Baptist minister, the Rev. David Jayne. Assisted by a deputation from the Baptist church at Chemung (now Wellsburg), a church was organized, comprising nine members, and styled the "Baptist Church at New Bedford," Rev. D. Jayne being the first minister, and so continued for fourteen years. Subsequently, as the settlement extended further north, a portion of the society formed a new organization at Tioga center, and the old society became established near Halsey Valley, and took a new name, calling itself " The Tioga and Barton Baptist Church." In 1848 they constructed a new church edifice, at a cost of $800.00, which will seat 300 persons. The society now has fifty members, with Rev. Franklin J. Salmon, pastor.

The First Presbyterian Church of Waverly, located on Pennsylvania avenue, was organized with twenty-two members, June 8, 1847, by the Revs. Thurston, Carr and Bacchus, a committee from the Chemung presbytery. They erected a church edifice in 1849, enlarged it in 1860, and in 1886 the society erected at a cost of $30,000 a handsome brick church of a modern style of architecture. It will seat 600 persons, has large parlors, pastors study, etc., in the rear of the anditorium, over which is the large Sunday school room. Rev. Nathaniel Elmer was the first pastor. Rev. John L. Taylor is the present pastor.

The Methodist Episcopal Church of Waverly, located on Waverly street corner Chemung, was first organized as a class at Factory-ville, in 1828, with five members, namely : Elisha Tozer (leader), Rachel Tozer, Philena Tozer, Joshua Wilcox, and King Elwell. The first church edifice was erected in Factoryville in 1840, and dedicated the same year by Rev. Horace Agard, pastor. The trustees were Jacob H. Russell, Alpheus H. Tozer, and Gilbert H. Hallett; presiding elder, George Harmon. The society sold the church building to the Baptist society of Waverly, who took it down and erected their present commodious house of worship. The Methodist society removed to Waverly and built a frame church edifice, which was dedicated in March, 1864, by Bishop Janes. It was destroyed by fire in 1865. The present substantial and attractive brick building was erected, and dedicated in 1867, by Rev. Hiram Mattison, D. D. Rev. James O. Woodruff is the present pastor.

The First Baptist Church, located on Park avenue, corner of Tioga street, was originally organized at Ulster, Bradford county, Pa., June 24, 1824, at the house of Joseph Smith. Elder Levi Baldwin, from Smithfield, Dea. Asa Hacket, F. Perkins, Eliphalet Barden, and Selah Finch, from Chemung Baptist church, Tioga county, N. Y., and Isaac Cooley, formed the council. Deacon Asa Hacket was chosen moderater, and Levi Baldwin, clerk. The following named persons, sixteen in number, composed the original organization: Elder Thomas Bebe and Betsey Bebe, his wife, Joseph Smith and his wife, Euphenia Smith, Lockwood D. Smith, Alexander Hibbard and his wife Polly Hibbard, Abel J. Gerold and Nancy Gerold, his wife, Cornelius Quick and his wife.

Margaret, Sisters Simons, Holcomb, Weriot and Lucretia Norton. It was first styled the " Athens and Ulster Baptist Church," and meetings were held at Athens, Ulster and Milltown. The name was changed March 10, 1832, to the " Athens and Chemung Baptist Church," and again, on May 14, 1836, to " Factoryville Baptist Church." Finally, in 1865, it was established at Waverly. The society have a neat and commodious church edifice, which will comfortably seat 500 persons. The present pastor is Rev. Daniel H. Cooper.

The Chemung Old School Baptist Church, located at Factoryville, was organized January 7, 1846, with nine members, as follows: Moses Slawson, David Proudfoot, Henry Rowland, Nathan Carey, Mary Carey, Fanny Carey, Betsey A. Slawson, Mary Slawson and Sarah Rowland. They met for worship in the houses of members and in the school-house until 1864, when the brick church erected by the New School Society, about 1830, was purchased by them at a cost of $1,100.00. The building will seat about 250 persons. Elder M. W. Vail is the present pastor.

The Grace Episcopal Church, located on Park avenue corner of Tioga street, was organized December 28, 1853. The certificate of organization is signed by Rev. George Watson, the rector of St. Paul's church, of Owego, Levi Gardner, Arthur Yates, Thomas Yates and A. P. Spalding. The society has a very tasty church building, erected about 1855. The first rector was Rev. Horatio Gray. The present rector is Rev. George Bowen.

The Church of Christ, located on Providence street, was organized July 8, 1877, with seven members, and a Sabbath school with twenty-one teachers and scholars was established at the same time.

St. James Roman Catholic Church is located on Chemung street corner of Clark. The first Roman Catholic church erected in Waverly was built in 1852. The lot whereon the building stood on Erie street, was deeded gratis to the Rt. Rev. John Timon, first bishop of Buffalo, by the late Owen Spalding, who also gave the lots for all the protestant churches first erected in Waverly. The affairs of the parish were attended to by Rt. Rev. James T. Mc Manus, the present Vicar General of the diocese of Rochester. The pastor's residence was in Owego, as there were not enough Catholics in Waverly to support a pastor. The parish priest of Owego was the only one in Tioga county. The money to build the first church was collected by the late John Sliney. The seating capacity was about three hundred, but at the time the church was built and for several years after, the building was too large for all the Catholics of Smithboro, Barton, Chemung and Waverly. The present house of worship is a handsome, comodious edifice, with elegant memorial windows of stained glass, given by the members of the congregation. The lot is finely laid out. The pastoral residence, an elegant house, stands on the northwest corner of the lot. This building was erected about twenty years after the first church was built. The lot was purchased by the late John Sliney, and held in trust for the congregation for years, until they were able to build thereon. The first resident pastor was Rev. James Brady, now located at Arcade, Wyoming county. The present pastor is Rev. Edward McShane.

The North Barton Methodist Episcopal Church was organized in 1869, with eighteen members. The church was erected in 1870, at a cost of $1,500.00. The first pastor was Rev. William H. Gavitt. The present pastor is Rev. Ziba Evans.

The Methodist Episcopal Church of Barton Village was organized about 1805, at the house of Peter Barnes. Benjamin Aikens, Peter Barnes and his wife, Gilbert Smith, his sister Betsey Smith, and Samuel Mundy were among the earliest members. Peter Hoffman, Selah Payne, and Daniel Bensley joined soon after. For many years the society was supplied by circuit preachers, who, traveling long distances, were able to hold meetings but once in four weeks. Rev. Timothy Lee and Rev. Horace Agard are mentioned as among the earliest circuit preachers. Benjamin Aikens was the first local preacher. The society held the first camp-meeting in the county, at Smithboro, in 1807, and their regular meetings were held in private houses, the woods, and the school-house, until 1836, when the present church edifice was completed, costing $1,100.00. It has sittings for about 400 persons. Rev. William H. Pearne was the first resident pastor, and Rev. Luther Peck is the present one.

The Methodist Episcopal Church of Lockwood was organized at an early date, the society first holding services in private houses, often at Charles Bingham's residence. In 1854 a church building was erected, which gave place to the present structure in 1886. It will seat 250 persons and is valued at $4,000.00. The society now has sixty members, with Rev. Ziba Evans, pastor.

The Methodist Episcopal Church at Ellistown is an old building, but we have been unable to collect any reliable data from which to compile a sketch. The society has now no organization there.

BERKSHIRE lies in the northeastern part of the county, and is bounded on the north by Richford, east by the county line, south by Newark Valley, and west by Caroline and Candor, containing an area of about 17,443 acres, 12,474 acres of which is improved land. The surface of the town is pleasingly diversified by lofty hills and fertile valleys, the former attaining a mean elevation of rom 1,200 to 1,400 feet. East and West Owego creeks, with their tributaries, form the water courses of the township, the former entering on the north, near the center, flowing a southerly direction through the town; the latter forms the dividing line on the west between Berkshire and the towns of Caroline and Candor. The soil of this territory is principally clay—in the valley of East creek yellow loam, with clay underlying; on the east, gravelly loam. The valleys and west hills were timbered with beech, maple, and iron-wood, the east hills with pine and hemlock.

Settlement.—The story of the " Boston Purchase," or " Boston Ten Townships," we have already detailed in chapter two. It devolved upon some of the proprietors therein named to found the township of Berkshire, a town that takes its name from the region of the famous Berkshire Hills of Massachusetts, and which it, indeed, in physical contour, greatly resembles. From these pioneers of the Puritan East, also, seems to have fallen upon their descendants of to-day, and to them is due, much of the prosperity, the integrity, character and intelligence for which the citizens of Berkshire are so justly celebrated. Nowhere have the manners of a people, their customs, their high sense of duty, their strict observance of the Sabbath, their love for the church and the school followed the line of descent more closely than in the township of Berkshire. These pioneers came not empty-handed nor empty-headed, for aside from their native New England thrift they were possessed of some means and had availed themselves of a fair opportunity in the school-room.

Until 1808 the locality was known as " Brown's Settlement," after the pioneer family of that name. Brown's Settlement, then, was begun on the first day of April, 1791, by five men who left Stockbridge, Mass., on February 23d, spending thirty-seven days on the way, and bringing their tools and provisions on two sleds, drawn by ox-teams. These pioneers were Isaac and Abraham Brown, brothers, Daniel Ball, Elisha Wilson, and John Carpenter, the latter coming as the hired man of the Browns. Two other men, Messrs. Dean and Norton, came in the party as far as Choconut, now Union, where they remained.

Thus in brief is the story of the pioneer settlement of the town of which we write. Of these early ones and many who followed them we will speak, under the head of

EARLY HOUSEHOLDS OF BERKSHIRE.*

Isaac Brown, b at Stockbridge, Mass., 25 Oct., 1766, second son of Capt. Abraham and Beulah (Patterson) Brown, came to Brown's Settlement with the pioneer party in 1791, leaving Stockbridge, 23 Feb. and reaching their destination 1 April. He probably worked with his brother, Abraham, till 1793, when he began to make a clearing for his own home. He married with Clarissa Ball, who was born in Stockbridge, 14 Nov., 1775, daughter of Josiah and Esther (Ward) Ball, and settled in a log house on the east side of the road on the south half of lot 305, a little south of where the railway crosses the road. Here he had just fairly started a pleasant home, when he died, 10 April, 1797, the first adult to die in the settlement. His widow died 12 Feb., 1844. Their children were:

I. —— Brown, a daughter, died in infancy.

II. Isaac Brown, b 4 Oct., 1797, six months after his father's death, was brought up by his grandmother, Beulah Brown, and married, 5 July, 1820, with Eleanor Branch, daughter of Levi and Electa (Lyman) Branch. She was born in Richmond, Mass., 29 Nov., 1796, and died 4 July, 1867. He died at Newark Valley. They had a family of ten children, several of whom are yet living.

Josiah Ball, b at Watertown, Mass., 16 Dec., 1742, son of John and Lydia (Perry) Ball, a shoemaker, m 26 Feb., 1768, with Esther Ward, who was born in Worcester, Mass., 7 March, 1750-51, daughter of Major Daniel and Mary (Coggin) Ward. They settled in Stockbridge, Mass., and of their thirteen children all were born there but the youngest. In June, 1794, they came to Berkshire, and settled on lot 337, where their son-in-law, Luke B. Winship, dwelt for many years after them. He died 26 July, 1810. She died 9 March, 1836. For some years he had an extra log house, which, in the season for moving, he kept to accommodate those settlers who needed a temporary shelter while pre-

---

* Extracts from an unfinished work, in manuscript, entitled, *Folk Book of the Boston Purchase*, by D. Williams Patterson, of Newark Valley.

paring their houses. At other times it was used for a school-house, or for his shoe shop. Children :

I. William, died when two years old.

II. Daniel, b 27 Dec., 1769.

III. William, b 18 Oct., 1771.

IV. Stephen, b 29 Jan., 1774.

V. Clarissa, b 14 Nov., 1775, m Isaac Brown.

VI. Samuel, b 13 Nov. 1777.

VII. Henry, b 21 Nov., 1779.

VIII. Josiah, b 28 Jan., 1782.

IX. Isaac, b 27 Dec., 1783.

X. Electa, b 9 June, 1788, d 6 Sept., 1869.

XI. Charles, b 4 Sept., 1790, d 9 Jan., 1814.

XII. Cynthia, b 24 April, 1793, m with Luke Bates Winship.

YIII. Mary, b in July, 1801, and died when eighteen months old, about 11 or 12 Jan., 1803. The mother was over fifty years old when this child was born.

Daniel Ball, b at Stockbridge, Mass., 27 Dec., 1769, son of Josiah and Esther (Ward) Ball, has been called one of the pioneers of Berkshire. He came here as one of the pioneer party of five who began the work in Brown's Settlement, 1 April, 1791, but did not work in the present limits of Berkshire toward clearing a home for himself or his father. He returned to Stockbridge in the fall, probably before his comrades did, and married at Lenox, Mass., 31 Oct., 1791, with Lucia Wells, daughter of Col. William Wells, of Lenox. In June, 1794, he returned to Berkshire with his father's family, bringing his wife and daughter, and settled in a log house on lot 336, near the present home of Charles S. Manning. They moved, about 1820, to Victor, N. Y., and thence to Michigan, where they died ; he about 1833 ; she about 1840. They had ten children :

I. Ann, b at Stockbridge, in 1792.

II. William Wells, b in Berkshire, 8 Sept., 1794, the first white child born within the limits of the town, married in February, 1820, with Harriet Cook, daughter of Ebenezer Cook, Esq., and was living in Dec., 1820, where James Cross now lives. He afterward bought the farm of Abraham Brown, where his son Rodney A. Ball now lives, in Newark Valley, and died there 15 Jan., 1880.

III. Horatio. IV. Henry. V. Hester. VI. Sophia.

VII. Chester. VIII. Calvin. IX. Davis. X. Myron.

William Ball, b at Stockbridge, Mass., 18 Oct., 1771, a cloth-dresser, m with Phebe Bement, daughter of Asa and Ruth (Neal) Bement, and settled in Berkshire about 1794. They afterward moved to Tioga. and thence to Victor, N. Y., where they died; she about 23 April, 1847; he some years earlier. It is supposed that he built the first cloth-dressing works in Berkshire. He left there before Dec., 1820. Their children were:

I. George. II. William, a physician, settled in Victor, N. Y. III. Asa. IV. James. V. Albert. VI. Mary.

VII. Charles, a physician, b in Tioga, N. Y., 19 July, 1824, settled in Victor. VIII. Phebe.

Stephen Ball, born in Stockbridge, Mass., 29 Jan., 1774, son of Josiah and Esther (Ward) Ball, is entitled to rank among the leaders in the settlement of Berkshire. He came in 1793, when nineteen years old, to prepare a home for his father's family, on lot 336, on which he cut the first tree. Here he made a clearing, built a log house, raised a little corn, and perhaps a few potatoes, turnips and beans, made some provision for keeping a cow, and, in the fall, sowed a piece of wheat, and returned to Stockbridge. In February, 1794, he came again, bringing with him a cow, and lived alone till his father's family came, in June, 1794, and only on Sundays meeting his nearest neighbors, Isaac Brown and Daniel Gleazen. He married, in 1801, with Polly Leonard, daughter of Capt. Asa and Olive (Churchill) Leonard, and settled on the northeast corner of lot 337, where the hotel is now kept. Here they spent most of the remainder of their lives. She died 3 Oct., 1850, and he died 19 Feb., 1857. Their children were:

I. Olive Leonard, b 2 Nov., 1801, m with Robert Akins.

II. Mary, b 12 May, 1803, died 21 March, 1815.

III. Harriet, b 19 July, 1805, m with Aaron P. Belcher.

IV. Eliza Ann, b 7 Oct., 1807, m with Charles Brown.

V. Richard Leonard, b 9 June, 1809, died 21 May, 1848.

VI. James Ward, b 24 May, 1811, m with Sypha Matson, and settled at Ottawa, Ill.

VII. Caroline, b 14 May, 1813, m with Carlisle P. Johnson.

VIII. Levi, b 26 March, 1815, m 28 Oct., 1841, with Betsey Ann Royce, and lives on the line between lots 385 and 416.

IX. Anson, b 19 March, 1817, m 5 Jan., 1848, with Caroline Moore, and died at Berkshire, 27 April, 1884.

X. Asa, b 26 April, 1819, m 15 Oct., 1845, with Esther Maria Manning, who died 15 May, 1887. He resides in Berkshire, a deacon of the Congregational church.

XI. Mary Sophia, b 2 Feb., 1821, m with Dr. Edward H. Eldredge.

XII. Robert Henry, b 5 Feb., 1823, m 19 Dec., 1850, with Maria Henrietta Conklin, and lives in Berkshire.

XIII. Frances Calista, b 2 Jan., 1825, m with George Clark Royce, and d 21 Oct., 1853.

Samuel Ball, b at Stockbridge, Mass., 13 Nov., 1777, son of Josiah and Esther (Ward) Ball, came to Berkshire in 1794, m about 1803, with Jerusha Slosson. They dwelt at one time on lot 103, in Newark Valley, but in 1818 sold to Ezekiel Rich, returned to Berkshire village, and thence to the west border of the town, and settled on the east side of the road, opposite the house of Phineas Case, on southwest quarter of lot 380, and was living there in Dec., 1820. Afterward they went to Lawrenceville, Pa., where they died ; he, 12 Sept., 1841; she, 5 February, 1870, aged ninety-six years. Children were :

I. Nancy, b 18 May, 1805, m with Joseph Weaver.

II. Lodema Farnham, b 6 May, 1806, m with Charles Frederick Akins.

III. Frederick William, b 6 June, 1808, d 9 April, 1835.

IV. Adeline, b 1 April, 1811, m with her cousin Clark Slosson.

V. Ball, b 7 Dec., 1813, died young.

VI. Cynthia Winship, b 10 March, 1818, m with Amasa Daily, and second with her cousin, Ezbon Slosson.

Henry Ball, b 21 Nov. 1779, married with Sarah Judd Moore, daughter of Henry Moore, and settled in Berkshire. He bought for fifty dollars, the old house of Dr. Joseph Waldo, 23 May, 1808, and moved it up to the place where his sons afterward lived, on the west side of the road, near the northeast corner of lot 337, second house below the hotel. He died 22 Sept., 1837 : she died 7 June, 1856 Their children were :

I. Henrietta, b 14 Oct., 1811, died 16 Sept., 1862, according to her gravestone, "aged 49 years and 11 months," which is a year too little, if the date is correct.

II. Gilson, b 29 Dec., 1812, married with Rhoda Ann Johnson, and was killed by a falling tree, 4 March, 1871.

III. Sophronia, b 1814, died 14 April, 1824, aged nine years.

IV. Franklin, b 25 Sept., 1816, m 29 March, 1859, with Margaret Meagher, and died at Newark Valley.

V. Eliza, b 7 June, 1819, died 19 Nov., 1840.

VI. Martin Henry, died unmarried, 28 July, 1875.

VII. Susan Sophronia, died in Berkshire, unmarried.

VIII. Alvah Moore, resides in Berkshire on his father's homestead.

Josiah Ball, b 28 Jan., 1782, was an excellent school-teacher, and a maker of wooden pumps. He married with Lucy Leonard, and settled in Berkshire village, where they died; she 5 Oct., 1856; he 23 Oct., 1862. Children:

I. Emily, b 12 Aug., 1804, m with Horatio Collins.

II. Sabrina, b 18 Dec., 1806, m with Addison Collins.

III. Julia, m with Dwight Waldo, and died 20 Jan., 1843.

IV. Mary, m with John Waldo, and settled at Portage, N. Y., where she died 13 May, 1887.

Isaac Ball, son of Josiah, came to Berkshire with his parents in June, 1794; m 20 Oct., 1808, with Cassandra Johnson. They settled on the east side of the road, on lot 336, where Charles O. Lynch now lives, and died there; he 20 Nov., 1856; she, 19 Sept., 1858. Their children were:

I. Francis Augustus, b 17 Aug., 1809, d 14 April, 1819.

II. Abigail, b 15 Jan., 1811, m with Nathaniel Bishop Collins.

III. Plandon Halsey, b 20 May, 1813.

IV. Eunice, b 17 Nov., 1815.

V. Margery, b 23 June, 1818, m with Theodore Leonard.

VI. John, b 31 July, 1820, married with Mary Ann Ralyea, daughter of Dene and Mercy (Bradley) Ralyea, of Union, N. Y.

VII. Francis, b 14 April, 1824.

IX. Jay, b 10 May, 1827.

Joseph Gleazen lived in Stockbridge, Mass., till after his sons came to Brown's Settlement, after which he and his wife came to live with them, but never had a separate household in Berkshire. He died 9 March, 1816, aged seventy-five years. During the last years of her life she was not of sound mind. They had children, perhaps not in the following order:

I. Daniel, m with Rebecca Barnes.

II. Jesse, m with Mercy Adsel.

III. Caleb, had three wives, and lived at Richford.

IV. Sarah, m with —— Doud, and second, 21 Oct., 1802, with Nathan Ide.

V. Joseph, b about 1772, m with Lovice Bailey.

VI. Ebenezer Ede, a tailor, m with Susanna Scott, who came to Berkshire with the family of Noah Lyman, and in Dec., 1820, they dwelt in Berkshire, on the west side of the way, a little below where Nathaniel Bishop Collins afterward built his brick house, and after that he moved to Newark Valley, and died there in the old Lincoln tavern house. His wife, born 25 July, 1784, married (2d) 5 March, 1832, with Samuel Gleazen, his brother, and died in Richford, 5 Feb., 1853.

VII. Samuel, b in Stockbridge, Mass., 4 April, 1783, was brought up by Silas Pepoon, Esq. He came to Berkshire later than his brothers, and settled in Richford.

Daniel Gleazen came to Brown's Settlement, probably, in the spring of 1794. He was a son of Joseph Gleazen, of Stockbridge, Mass. Tradition says that he first settled on the southeast quarter of lot 377, on the hill road, but afterward built a brick house on the road that lies in the hollow. He married at Berkshire, 26 Jan., 1805, with Miss Rebecca Barnes. They had seven children:

I. Luke. II. Eli, b perhaps about 2 June, 1808. III. Ruth.

IV. Rebecca, b perhaps about 3 Dec., 1813. V. Joseph.

VI. William, b perhaps about 15 March, 1820.

VII. Barnes, b perhaps about 12 Feb., 1822.

Jesse Gleazen, brother of Daniel, probably came at the same time. He joined the church in Stockbridge, Mass., in 1790, was dismissed 2 Oct., 1803, to the church about to be formed at Tioga, N. Y., of which he was a constituent member, and continued a member till 3 Oct., 1813. He married at Berkshire, 29 Oct., 18—, with "Miss Mercy Adzdil," as John Brown, Esq., recorded it; but the name may have been Adsel, or Hadsel. Their children were:

I. Sarah, bap 20 Nov., 1803.

II. James Adsel, bap 20 Nov., 1803.

III. Mercy, bap 4 April, 1805.

IV. Betsey Ruth, b 22 May, 1810, bap 2 Sept., 1810.

V. Huldah Ann, b 2 March, 1813.

Joseph Gleazen, Jr., was born in Stockbridge, Mass., about 1772, son of Joseph Gleazen. The date of his advent to Berkshire is not known, but he probably came with his brothers. He was taxed for highway work three days in 1798, and married 16 May, 1803, with Lovice Bailey, (or "Vicey," as John Brown recorded the name) sister of Levi Bailey. He first settled on West Owego creek, west of the road, on the southwest quarter of lot 380, where Eleazer Lyman and his son, Daniel Lyman, afterward lived, just north of where the towns of Candor and Caroline corner together on the creek. In April, 1820, he left this place and settled in a log house on the southeast quarter of lot 342, on Berkshire Hill. Afterward they moved to Newark

9*

Valley, and died there; he 21 Sept., 1849, in his 77th year; she 15 Oct., 1850, in her 65th year.   Their children were:

I. Silas Pepoon.   II. Emeline, d 3 July, 1863, aged 54. III. Sabrina.

IV. George Densmore, b 27 Feb., 1814, resides in Newark Valley; m with Mary Ann Benton.

V. Lavina.   VI. Julia.

VII. Semantha, m with Amasa Day Durfee.

Consider Lawrence was born at Canaan, Conn., 8 Feb., 1777; m 11 Sept., 1796, with Wealthy Peck. who was born 27 Oct., 1775.   His name appears in John Brown's book 24 May, 1797, and he was taxed for work on highways, three days in 1798, and his name was in the tax list of 1802.   He dwelt on the southwest quarter of lot 338, where Charles Backus Ford has since lived. He died 20 Feb., 1857, and his obituary notice said that he " came to Berkshire sixty-one years ago," which indicates 1796 as the year in which he came.   He probably spent the summer before his marriage in preparing his home.   Their children were:

I. Maria, b 30 Aug., 1797, m with Thomas Langdon, of Berkshire.

II. Isaac Peck, b 8 Feb., 1799, m 20 Jan., 1821, with Catharine Cole.

III. Miles Lewis, b 6 Nov., 1800, m 26 March, 1834, with Sylvia C. Foote and settled in Berkshire.

IV. William, b 14 Feb., 1803, m 14 Sept., 1840, with Laura Woodruff.

V. Betsey, b 27 Aug., 1804, m 25 Dec. 1821, with Gamaliel Whiting.

VI. Josiah, b 14 Sept., 1806, m with Martha Baird.

John Brown, b at Stockbridge, 18 July, 1765, eldest son of Captain Abraham and Beulah (Patterson) Brown, came to Brown's Settlement in Feb. 1796.   He settled on lot 296, and built a saw-mill there.   He married 20 Feb., 1800, with Mehitable Wilson, daughter of Elijah and Mary (Curtis) Wilson, of Stockbridge, where she was born, 19 Dec., 1768.   He was one of of the first justices of the peace in the town of Tioga, and was supervisor of that town for four years.   He was also supervisor of the new town of Berkshire, in 1808 and 1809, and in Oct., 1809, was appointed a judge of Broome county court of common pleas, which office he held at his death, 14 Oct., 1813.   She survived till 3 Aug., 1857.   Their children were:

I. John, b 14 Feb., 1801, a surveyor, mill-wright, and farmer, died unmarried 12 Nov., 1869.

II. Mary Wilson, b 1 Aug., 1802, unmarried.

III. Francis Henry, b 6 March 1804, died unmarried.

IV. Charles, b 11 Oct., 1805, married 6 Oct., 1835, with Eliza Ann Ball, daughter of Stephen and Polly (Leonard) Ball, and died 28 March, 1869.

V. Juliana, b 5 July, 1807, died 19 Nov., 1869.

VI. Frances Cornelia, b 19 March, 1809, unmarried.

Asa Leonard, b 30, Jan., 1759, son of Abiel Leonard, of Connecticut, married 11 Oct., 1781, with Olive Churchill, who was born in Stockbridge, Mass., 20 Feb., 1764, daughter of Samuel and Elizabeth (Curtis) Churchill. They dwelt in Stockbridge, and afterward in West Stockbridge, and started in Feb., 1793, with the Slossons, to settle in Berkshire; but on reaching Choconut, now Union, N. Y., they stopped on account of her health, and stayed with her brother, Asahel Churchill, till the next winter, and then retuned to Massachusetts. Early in the year 1797, they made another trial, and reached Berkshire, where they spent the rest of their lives. He died 24 March, 1836; she died 21 Aug., 1844. Their children were:

I. Polly, b 11 Feb., 1783, married with Stephen Ball.

II. Solomon, b 23 Nov. 1784.

III. Lucy, b 3 Jan., 1787, m with Josiah Ball, Jr.

IV. Anna, b 16 Sept., 1788, m with Henry Griffin.

V. Levi, b 5 July 1790, m with Lucia Avery, and d 16 July, 1862.

VI. Nancy, b 26 April, 1792, m with Isaac Hitchcock.

VII. Louis Gigette, b 30 July, 1794, m 28 Feb., 1821, with Hannah Royce, and died at Berkshire, 1 Nov. 1830. She was still living there in 1887.

VIII. Henry, b 14 Aug., 1797, at Berkshire, m with Julia White, and settled at Ithaca, N. Y., where he died 7 March, 1863.

IX. George W., b 5 April, 1799, d 23 April, 1799.

X. Sabrina, b 28 Aug., 1800, d 22 Nov. 1809.

XI. Amanda, b 6 Aug., 1802, m with John Brush Royce.

XII. Chester, b 9 Oct., 1805, m 12 Oct. 1826, with Susan Maria Wilson; settled at Newark Valley, where he died 25 Nov., 1841, and she died at Owego.

XIII. Leonard, a son, b 5 June, 1807, d 29 June, 1807.

Solomon Leonard, son of Asa Leonard, came to Berkshire with his father, and on reaching his majority became a partner with him in the business of tanning and currying. He married 30

Jan., 1813, with Nancy Ann Waldo, and settled on the south side of Leonard street, where their son, Joseph Waldo Leonard, now lives. She died 18 Sept., 1865 ; he died 24 March, 1866. Their children were :

I. Jane, b 1 Nov., 1813, m 23 July, 1839, with Wm. C. Churchill, and died 23 May, 1851.

II. Theodore, b 13 Feb., 1815, m 15 June, 1842, with Margery Ball.

III. Frederick William, b 8 Oct., 1816.

IV. Mary Elizabeth, b 14 July, 1818, m 6 Oct., 1845, with Charles Mills, of Little Falls, N. Y., who died 3 May, 1849; and she m (2nd) 11 Nov., 1850, with Melancthon Rogers.

V. Joseph Waldo, b 27 May, 1820, m 12 Oct., 1852, with Mary Ann Campfield, and resides on his father's homestead.

VI. Henry Griffin, b 27 March, 1822, m 12 Feb., 1850, with Catharine Campfield.

VII. Edwin Dwight, b 25 Feb., 1824.

VIII. Frances, b 25 July, 1826, m with Dr. Frederick A. Waldo, of Cincinatti, Ohio.

IX. Nancy Bliss, b 11 April, 1828, m with George Clark Royce.

X. George Franklin, b 15 Nov., 1829, m 17 Nov., 1850, with Eunice Patch.

XI. Jerome, b 17 Aug., 1830, m 1 Oct., 1862, with Araminta Boyer.

Ebenezer Cook, b at Stockbridge, Mass., about 1772, married there 3 April, 1793, with Elizabeth Churchill, who was born there 8 Sept., 1774, daughter of Samuel and Elizabeth (Curtis) Churchill. He came to Berkshire early in 1797, in company with his brother-in-law, Asa Leonard, and they began business as tanners and curriers under the name of Leonard & Cook, and according to the custom of that day made shoes also. He settled first in a small log house which stood near where Joseph Waldo Leonard dwelt in 1881, then built a shop on the corner opposite the brick meeting-house, where the brick house now stands ; and just north of that, a small framed house, into which he moved his family 25 April, 1804. In this house he died 17 March, 1812. He served for several terms as justice of the peace, was always dignified with the title " 'Squire," and was universally respected, although he followed too diligently the fashion of the times. His widow was named in the census of Dec., 1820, and died 23 June, 1825. Their children were:

I. Harriet, b 22 Oct., 1793, m with William Wells Ball.

II. Aurilla, b about Oct., 1795, m with Denis Corsaw ; Clarissa, b about June 1798, d 1 March, 1815.

III. Charles West, b 1 Feb., 1800, m 7 Oct., 1823, with Amy Royce, settled in Richford, and moved in 1834 to Chicago, Ill., where she died 24 Aug., 1835; and he married a second wife, and died 19 May, 1845.

IV. Abigail West, b about 1802, d when eighteen months old.

V. Abigail West, b 26 April, 1804, m with James Hobart Ford.

VI. Henry William, b in 1806, d 3 Aug., 1825, aged 19 years.

VII. George West, b 9 Dec., 1808, drowned 15 June, 1810.

VIII. George Churchill, b 10 March, 1811, m 10 Nov., 1834, with Lucy Maria Williams, and settled at Newark Valley ; removed about 1844 to Chicago, Ill., where he died.

Azel Hovey was born 13 Aug., 1741, old style, perhaps, at Lebanon, Conn., m with Jemima Phelps, who was born at Leba·non 4 April, 1745. It is said that they dwelt in New London, Conn., for many years, but their records have not been found there. They came to Berkshire, either with or soon after their son Azel, and lived with him while he dwelt in Berkshire. They afterward went to Newark Valley and were cared for by their son David Hovey. He died 17 June, 1818, in an old log house that stood on the west side of the road nearly opposite the house in which George Dohs now lives. His death was from pleurisy, occasioned by working in the water during a freshet. She died at the house of her son-in-law, John Harmon, 14 July, 1829. Tradition says: "They had eleven children." We have the names of nine, viz.:

I. Azel. II. Abigail, m with William Dudley.

III. Jemima, b about 1775, m with John Harmon.

IV. Eunice, m with Asahel Hatch, of Richmond, Mass.

V. Jedediah, settled in Hartford, Conn. VI. Abel.

VII. Nathan, was living in Berkshire in 1812.

VIII. Zeruiah, died unmarried. IX. David.

Azel Hovey, b at New London, Conn., about 1763, eldest child of Azel and Jemima (Phelps) Hovey, married with Lucy Rockwell, daughter of Abner and Deborah Rockwell, and came to Berkshire as early as the beginning of 1798, and in that year was assessed to work five and a half days on the highway. He settled on the east side of the creek, on the north half of lot 385, near where the old road crossed the creek. He sold this place to Capt. Henry Griffin, and then lived on the place previously owned by his brother-in-law, William Dudley, and this he sold to

Barnabas Manning.   They afterward lived in Union, now Maine,
N. Y., and then in Newark Valley, where he died 14 Sept., 1838,
in his seventy-fifth year, on the place now owned by Clark Walworth.   Their children were:

I. Julia Rockwell, m with Harlow King.

II. Eliza, b at Berkshire, 11 April, 1798, m with David Councilman.

III. George, settled at Belvidere, Ill.

IV. Azel, died at Rochester, N. Y., unmarried.

V. Hannah, b at Berkshire, 8 Aug., 1802, m with Allen Watkins,
and died 9 May, 1886, at Belvidere, Ill.

VI. Clarinda, m with Newell Watkins.

VII. Jedediah, died young.

VIII. Calvin, m with Mary Wheeler, and settled at Belvidere, Ill.

IX. Lucy Ann, m with Leander King, of Belvidere, Ill.

X. Sabrina, went to Belvidere, Ill.

XI. Henry, went to Belvidere, Ill.

XII. William, was sheriff at Belvidere, Ill.

XIII. Amanda, went to Belvidere, Ill.

Jeremiah Campbell, a blacksmith, lived on the east side of the
road, in the north part of lot 416, close to the present north line
of Berkshire.   He married at Stockbridge, Mass., 2 Jan., 1792,
with Elizabeth Rockwell.   He was taxed to work on the highways, in 1793, three days, and was also in the tax-list of 1802. He
still lived in the same place when the census of Dec., 1820, was
taken, and moved, a few years later, to Binghamton, N. Y.
Among his children was Rachel Campbell, who married with
Silas Warren Bradley.

Ephraim Cook was taxed to work three and a half days on the
highways, in 1798, and his name was on the tax-list of 1802. His
dwelling place at that time has not been ascertained, but later he
lived within the present bounds of Richford, on the south part
of lot 460, at the angle of the road where Lyman Jewett now
lives.   He was living as lately as October, 1813, but the date
of his death, which was caused by the bite of a rabid dog, has
not been found.   He was a farmer, and came, it is said, from
Preston, Conn.   His children were:

I. Polly. II. Althea. III. Harvey, m with Clarissa Smith.
IV. Phila, (perhaps Philena).

Josiah Howe was assessed to work three days on the highways,
in 1798, and his name was on the tax-list of 1802.   He had a child
born 8 July, 1808, and another 17 August, 1813, names unknown.

Benjamin Olney was assessed to work three days on the high-ways, in Berkshire, in 1798.

Josiah Seeley was assessed to work three days on the highways in 1798.

David Williams, b at Richmond, Mass., 3 May, 1775, m there 1 July, 1798, with Jerusha Pierson, who was born at Sag Harbor, L. I., daughter of Zachariah and Sarah (Sanford) Pierson, who afterward settled in Richmond. They came to Berkshire in June, 1800, and settled on the northwest quarter of lot 345, where his son George now lives. He built a saw-mill and a grist-mill, and the sites are still occupied in the village. His wife died of con-sumption 2 April, 1807, aged thirty-two years and six months. He married (2d) 25 Dec., 1811, with Samantha Collins. He died 17 April, 1867, aged nearly ninety-two years. Judge Avery, in 1854, said of him:

" The discharge of many important official duties and trusts has devolved upon Judge Williams in the course of his long and use-ful career. He served upon the Bench of the Court of Common Pleas of Broome county, as one of the Associate Judges, from the year 1815 down to the time when his town was given back to Tioga, in 1822, and with the exception of one year, he held the position continuously, from the first date of his service until 1826; having been transferred to the Bench of the Tioga Com-mon Pleas, by appointment, after the change of boundaries. For three years, while his town was within the limits of Broome, and for six years after it had been surrendered to Tioga, he was its Supervisor, and for many years, commencing at an early date, he discharged the duties of many minor offices, with exactness, good judgment, and ability.

" In 1827 and 1831, Judge Williams represented his county in the Legislature, and from the various posts which he has been called upon to fill, he has always retired with the increased re-gard and respect of his constituents.

" Methodical in his habit of thought, firm in his adherence to what he has deemed rules of right, and of uncompromising integ-rity, he will leave to those who are to follow him, an example of moral worth, and an impressive illustration of what may be achieved by fixed purpose, steady effort and well regulated life."

His children were:

I. Lucinda, b 3 May, 1805, m 22 July, 1829, with Alfred John Piggatt Evans, of Binghamton.

II. John Chamberlin, b 16 March, 1818, m with Emily Win-ship, who died 1 March, 1853, and (2d) 30 Oct., 1855, with Susan Elizabeth Goodrich, and now lives at Farmerville, in Covert N. Y.

III. George, b 31 May, 1829, m 27 Feb., 1851, with Louisa Janette Barnes, and resides on his father's homestead.

Ransom Williams, born in Richmond, 9 March, 1778, brother of David Williams, came to Berkshire about the same time. He married 13 Dec., 1801, with Olive Collins, of Richmond, who was b 29 Feb., 1780, daughter of Dan and Amy (Bristol) Collins. They settled on the south half of lot 345, on the west side of the road, nearly opposite the street which leads to the railway station. He was a very worthy, useful, and intelligent man, much interested in the cultivation of vocal music, and his home was always the seat of a generous hospitality. They died without children; he 17 June, 1839; she 31 Jan., 1845.

Heman Williams, b at Richmond, Mass., 9 Jan., 1788, (brother of David and Ransom) came to Berkshire, perhaps some years later than they, and was accidentally killed 17 Sept., 1816, while raising a bridge, near the residence of Col. John B. Royce. Judge Nathaniel Bishop, of Richmond, wrote to his daughter, Mrs. Lucy Bement, on Sunday 6 Oct., 1816: " I have felt unable, since the news of Heman Williams's terrible death, to visit his father, but shall improve the first time that I can prudently do it, for I feel a painful sympathy for him."

Miss Wealthy Collins should be named in connection with the household of Ransom Williams, of which she was an honored member for many years. She was a sister of Mrs. Olive Williams. She left Richmond 15 Nov., 1803, and was two weeks on the road to Berkshire. She married, 25 June, 1835, with Judge Calvin McKnight, of Watertown, N. Y. He died at Guilford, Conn., 25 Nov., 1855, aged seventy-two years and three months. She died at Newark Valley, 12 Jan., 1869, aged eighty-two years and nine months. Her retentive memory yielded many interesting traditions of the early settlers. She was born at Richmond, Mass., 3 April, 1786.

The second marriage recorded by the Hon. John Brown was of " Mr. George Vicory to Miss Susana Paine," in Dec., 1800. If at any time they dwelt in Berkshire they soon removed to Caroline N. Y., and settled on the N. M. Toby farm. He wrote his name Vickery.

Edward Paine lived in Berkshire, or its vicinity, as early as Sept., 1802, and had a brother here who, it is supposed was Thomas Paine, who, with his wife bought goods of Joseph Waldo, 2d, as early as 16 June, to be paid for in " cash or tow cloth." Their home has not been ascertained.

Artemas Ward, b at Charlton, Mass., 23 April, 1757, son of Benjamin and Mary (Oaks) Ward, m with Hannah Perry, of

Sturbridge, Mass., and dwelt at Charlton till after two of their children, and possibly more, were born, "then removed to the state of New York." (See the Ward Genealogy, pp. 53 and 96). He was a hatter, and before the 4th of July, 1800, had settled on the east side of the road, opposite where Dea. Asa Ball now lives, on seventy-five acres of land, in the west part of lot 336, which he soon afterward sold, with a log house thereon, to William Dudley. He then moved to the northwest quarter of lot 265, now in Newark Valley, and built a small house just where the railway now lies, as the road then was nearly twenty rods further east than it is now, and his house was on the west side of the road. This place he sold, as early as 1808, to the Rev. Jeremiah Osborn, who added to the small house then on it, the house of two stories which James Williams afterward moved to its present site, west of the present road, where Dwight Waldo afterward lived. He then lived for a time in Bement and Wilson's mill-house, after which he returned to Massachusetts with his family, and settled near Spencer, perhaps at Charlton. It has been impossible to find a full account of his children, as follows:

I. Lydia, b at Charlton, Mass., 4 Nov., 1789.

II. Ruth, b at Charlton, Mass., 24 March, 1791.

III. Daniel. IV. Delia.

V. —— Ward, who was deformed by spinal disease; and this may have been the child who died 20 Aug., 1807.

VI. —— Ward, b 31 Aug., 1808.

Elijah H. Saltmarsh began to board with John Brown, 15 April, 1800. He kept a little store just below the Isaac Brown house, and made potash on the bank of the creek just west of where Mr. Brown's widow and children have lived. Among Mr. Brown's charges was one, 10 June, 1800, for boarding Mr. Moore, Ball, and others. As he was not in the tax-list for 1802, he probably made a short stay in town, and probably was never a householder there.

John Saltmarsh appears in John Brown's book, 4 Dec., 1800, and brought a suit against "Jincks Angell, and B. Andrus," in Aug., 1801.

William Gardner came from Connecticut about 1800. At one time he attended the grist-mill of Bement & Wilson, in Newark Valley, and he sometimes extracted teeth. He m with Polly Gaston, and settled on the north side of the road, on the northeast quarter of lot 419, where he died in June, 1816. She joined the church at Newark Valley, 6 July, 1817, was dismissed 12 Jan.,

1823, with several others, and two days later, was one of the constituent members of the church at Richford. She died at the house of her son William, 11 Sept., 1848. Their children were:

I. William. II. Polly, m with Jacob Burghardt.

III. Achsah, m with John Rees Burghardt.

IV. Miriam, m with Ransom Rich, and second with Edward Newton Chapman.

V. John Gaston, VI. Lucy Butler.

Joseph Waldo was born at Windham, Conn., 5 Oct., 1755, son of Zacheus and Talitha (Kingsbury) Waldo; was a physician and surgeon, served in that capacity for some time in the revolutionary war; married 17 July, 1788, with Ann Bliss, who was born in Springfield, Mass., in April, 1769. She was familiarly known as Nancy. They dwelt for a few years in West Stockbridge, Mass., then moved to Richmond, Mass., where he joined the Congregational church, in Aug., 1794. He afterward moved to Lisle, N. Y., and thence, in October, 1800, to Berkshire, where he settled on the south 173 acres of lot 304, which he bought 8 Nov., 1802, and built thereon, in 1806, an elegant house for the time, in which he spent the remainder of his life. He dwelt previously on the west side of the road, a little south of where the school-house now stands, in a small framed house, which he sold for fifty dollars, 23 May, 1808, to Henry Ball, who moved it up to Berkshire village. He was, for many years, the only physician in the valley, north of Owego, and had a very large practice. He was one of the founders of the "First Church in Tioga," 17 Nov., 1803, and was dismissed 5 July, 1833, to become one of the constituent members of the Congregational church in Berkshire. He enjoyed in a remarkable degree, the esteem and confidence of the community. She died 14 Sept., 1836. He died 13 Feb., 1840. Their children were:

I. Mary, b 10 March, 1790, m with Joseph Waldo, 2d.

II. Nancy Ann, b at West Stockbridge, Mass., 10 Dec., 1791, m with Solomon Leonard.

III. Joseph Talcott, b at Richmond, Mass., 28 Aug., 1794, a physician and surgeon, m in Jan., 1827, with Maria Belcher, who died 23 Feb., 1830, and he m (2d), 19 Sept., 1833, with Hannah B. Belcher, and d in Berkshire, 4 March, 1857.

Nathaniel Ford, b 30 March, 1768, son of James and Rachel (Backus) Ford, married 23 April, 1795, with Caroline Rees, who was born 24 Jan., 1777. They settled in Richmond, Mass., and joined the church there in Jan., 1796. They came to Berkshire in February, 1801, and settled on the north half of lot 304, on the same spot now occupied by Mr. Ball. They were constituent members of the First Church of Tioga 17 Nov., 1803, and he was elected its first deacon 4 April, 1805. They were dismissed 21 June, 1833, and were among the founders of the Congregational Church of Berkshire. He died 22 March, 1858, aged ninety years; she died 23 June, 1859. "Their lives and examples are their best eulogies." Their children were:

I. Caroline, b at Richmond, Mass., 1 May, 1796, m with William Henry Moore.

II. Nancy, b at Richmond, Mass., 21 Aug., 1797, m with Eldad Post.

III. Maria, b at Richmond, Mass., 23 July, 1800, died at Catatonk, N. Y., unmarried, 10 June, 1861.

IV. Rachel, b at Berkshire, 5 June, 1803, died in Lenox, Mass.

V. Lucinda, b at Berkshire, 27 Aug., 1805, m with Harris Jewett, and died at Catatonk, N. Y., in July, 1868.

VI. James Hobart, b at Berkshire, 26 Sept., 1807, m 29 April, 1835, with Abigail Weeks Cook. He died 29 May, 1854, without children, and she died at Chicago, Ill., 24 Nov., 1874, and was buried in Berkshire.

VII. Nathaniel, b at Berkshire, 11 Sept., 1809, died 4 Dec., 1809.

VIII. Katharine, b at Berkshire, 30 March, 1812, m with Dr. Levi Farr, of Greene, N. Y., and m (2nd) with William Anner, of Harlem, and afterward lived at Binghamton, N. Y.

Col. Absalom Ford, b 8 Dec., 1760, elder brother of Dea. Nathaniel Ford, dwelt also in Berkshire. He died 11 Feb., 1845, aged eighty-four years. His wife, Zeriah, died 19 March, 1826, aged sixty-nine years. They were probably not here earlier than 1820.

William Dudley was probably in Berkshire as early as 1801. His name is in the tax list for 1802. He bought of Artemas Ward seventy-five acres of land in the south third of lot 336, and settled in a log house, near the west end of the lot, on the west bank of the creek, directly east of where Dea. Asa Ball now lives. He afterward built a small framed house opposite where Dea. Asa Ball now lives. His first wife was Abigail Hovey, daughter of Azel and Jemima (Phelps) Hovey. Some people have thought that she died in Connecticut, but Mrs. Jerusha (Harmon) Watson, who was her niece, testified that she died in Berkshire, and was the first woman who was buried in the

Brown cemetery. He went back to Connecticut, and married a second wife, whose name has not been found. His name appears in John Brown's account book 13 Dec., 1805, and about that time he left home with a drove of mules, and died away from home. The council that ordained the Rev. Jeremiah Osborn, the first pastor of the First Church in Tioga, now Newark Valley, met at the house of the Widow Dudley 18 Feb., 1806, and she returned to Connecticut between that time and April, 1806. The children of William and Abigail (Hovey) Dudley were:

I. Ruth, who kept her father's house after the death of her mother, till his second marriage, after which she taught school.

II. Doddridge, settled in the Genesee county. III. Alanson.

IV. Chester, went South with his father to drive mules, and died away from home, about the same time that his father died.

Joseph Freeman was brought up in Richmond, Mass., by Vine Branch, his father having died before his birth. He married with Eunice Gaston, daughter of John and Miriam (Northrop) Gaston, of Richmond, and came to Berkshire early in 1802, but owned no land till 1814, when he bought a small place west of where Joseph Talcott Leonard lived in 1881. He had, in the meantime, spent one year in Sullivan, Madison Co., N. Y. He hung himself in July, 1832, while in a delirious state. She died at Covert, N. Y. Their children were:

I. Eunice Maria, died unmarried.

II. Rufus Branch, died in Illinois about 1847.

III. Gilbert Gaston, b 23 Aug., 1808, and lives at Berkshire with his daughter, Mrs. William T. Shaw.

IV. Lucy Ann, baptized at Newark Valley, 24 Dec., 1828, m with Elmon Daniels, and died at Trumansburgh, N. Y.

V. Henry Barnes, b at Sullivan, N. Y., about 1812, was living at Galt, Ill., in 1877.

VI. Harriet Elizabeth, b at Berkshire, m with Willis D. Horton, of Covert, N. Y., and died there.

VII. Ruth Matilda, b at Berkshire, died there when about two years old.

Nathan Ide married at Berkshire, 21 Oct., 1802, with Mrs. Sally Doud. She was a daughter of Joseph Gleazen. One of their children was born 4 Feb., 1810. Mr. Ide died before Dec., 1820, at which time his widow was living on lot 380, just south of the house of Eleazer Lyman.

Daniel Carpenter was born at Stockbridge, Mass., 7 Jan., 1778, son of Abner and Lydia, (Brown) Carpenter; was in Berkshire as early as April, 1803, and possibly a year earlier, and settled near the centre of lot 302, which his deceased brother, John Carpenter, had selected for his home. He went back to Massachusetts, and married at Becket, 10 March, 1807, with Ruth Snow, daughter of Levi and Lydia (Rudd) Snow. He came again to Berkshire that spring alone, and she joined him in October, 1807. He died on this farm 2 June, 1855. His children were:

I. Lydia, b 22 Dec., 1807, m with Alexander Maples.

II. Mary, b 21 Sept., 1810, m with Fowler Haight.

III. Sylvia, b 6 Aug., 1812, m with Thomas Goldsmith Haight.

IV. Martha, b 9 March, 1815, m with Gideon Sipley.

V. John, b 5 Jan., 1818, m with Amanda Masten, and settled at East Maine, N. Y.

VI. Abner Dewey, b 18 Aug., 1820, went to St. Louis, Mo., in 1844, and has not been heard from since 1847.

VII. Caroline, b 1 Feb., 1823, m with Edward Herrick, of Candor, N. Y.

VIII. Daniel D., b 20 Nov., 1825, died 9 Dec., 1846.

IX. Andrew Jackson, b 5 Nov., 1828, m with Jerusha Cortright, and settled in Michigan.

X. Edward Snow, b 15 Aug., 1831, m with Climena Ann Hawley, and lives in Ithaca. N. Y.

XI. George, b 19 May, 1834, m with Louisa Freeman; and m (2d) Frances Scott. He settled on his father's homestead.

Samuel Collins, b at Guilford, Conn., 11 Aug., 1768, son of Samuel and —— (Cook) Collins, m 22 Oct., 1793, with Betsey Bishop, who was born at Guilford, 4 Sept., 1774, daughter of Nathaniel and Ruth (Bartlett) Bishop. They came to Berkshire in 1805, and settled on the north part of lot 376, where Mrs. Albert Collins now lives. He built his new home in 1808. He died 4 July, 1840, of consumption, after having repeatedly foretold that he should die on that day. She died 1 Aug., 1864, aged nearly ninety years. Children:

I. Semanthe, b at the old Collins homestead in North Guilford, Conn., 7 Sept., 1794, m with Hon. David Williams.

II. Addison, b at Lenox, Mass., 29 March 1796, m with Sabrina Ball, moved to Rochester, N. Y., where he practiced law; went thence to Hadley, Will Co., Ill., where he died 27 March, 1867.

III. Horatio, b at Lenox, Mass., 2 July, 1799, m with Emily Ball.

IV. Eliza, b at Lenox, Mass., 25 Jan. 1804, m with Theodore Hart, a merchant of Virgil, N. Y., and removed to Canandaigua.

V. Nathaniel Bishop, b at Berkshire, 8 July, 1806, m with Abby Ball, and (2d) with Candace Harrington, and died in Berkshire.

VI. Frederick, b 29 June, 1812, m with Nancy Mason White, and settled in Hadley, Ill.

VII. Albert, b 16 July, 1816, m with Mary Ann Rightmire, daughter of James Rightmire, and died in Berkshire, on the homestead of his father.

Noah Lyman, b at Durham, Conn., about Dec., 1773, son of Noah and Eleanor Lyman, married 12 Nov., 1795, with Lucy Bishop, daughter of Nathaniel and Ruth (Bartlett) Bishop, of Richmond. She was born at Guilford, Conn., 4 Sept., 1774. They dwelt in Richmond till the beginning of 1805, when they came to Berkshire, and settled in a log house on the south part of lot 416, of which he owned one hundred acres. This house stood about two rods west of the site afterward occupied by the Brookside Seminary. The following letter, which she wrote in this house, gives such a lively description of the pleasures of her humble home in the wilderness, and such a feeling account of the interest which the settlers felt in the welfare and pleasure of each other, as to make it exceedingly valuable to the reader of the present time:

TIOGA, Feb. 14th, 1807.

" *Dear Parents :*

I have this minute put my three children to bed, and you would suppose they were in good health, if you knew how merry they are. Nancy acts like a dunce, and the other two laugh at it—anything if they are but pleasant. I wish you could see the inside of my cottage this evening, it looks quite agreeable, a charming fire, the corners full of wood, a clean hearth, and, to complete the picture, the great Black Dog that Den loves so well is asleep on the floor. We have had a good visit from Brother Nat. and Major Hyde, with their wives; they staid three days and we were all together most of the time, and I do not know when we have spent our time more agreeably. We have also had a visit from Judge Patterson and his wife. You know our manner of visiting, when a friend comes the whole circle is formed, the news soon spread, invitations were sent and in a short time the whole band were at Mr. W's, [Ransom Williams.]

" Esqr. Patterson came himself and carry'd us down in his sleigh. Betsey [her twin sister, Mrs. Collins] is complaining of the Rheumatism this winter and is quite lame part of the time, but not so as to prevent her doing more than a well woman should. Susa [Susanna Scott] is still with her. My own health has been better and I began to think that I should soon be well, but the last week has convinced me that it is the same crazy frame yet, it is no disappointment, I have not the promise of good health a moment, nor do I wish it, unless it is His will, who has the power to give it, if best for me. I hope however that I am not wholly unthankful, that I am for the most of the time pretty comfortable and able to take care of my family.

"Our friend Jerusha [the wife of David Williams, who died 2 April, 1807,] is descending the hill. She is evidently in a confirmed consumption. I do not know what she thinks herself. Her husband is not willing any person should tell her the danger she is in for fear of depressing her spirits—mistaken tenderness I think, and unfriendly kindness tho' well meant; how is it possible that any person can see so near a friend going down to the Grave without warning them of the great change that awaits them? Will the shock be greater now than at the hour of death? We should not be surprised if she should not live a month, and yet nobody has ever said one word to her with regard to her future state. I asked her husband if he knew her thots respecting her situation, he said he did not, but that he evaded the question when she enquired of him whether he thot she would ever get well. I told him I knew it was a painful task, but it might be the source of great consolation hereafter—he made no reply, and I said no more, but my mind was not at ease. What if poor Beriah [the writer's brother, Beriah Bishop, who died 17 Aug. 1805, of consumption] had been neglected, how should we have felt? I cannot think but Mr. Williams will soon alter his sentiments, I hope he will.

"It is likely Mrs. Griffing is released from her sufferings and at rest, poor woman, she has lived a life of sorrow. Give our love to our good friends at Richmond, and believe us your affectionate children   LUCY LYMAN."

"Mother Hovey sends her best Love with many thanks for the fruit."

Superscribed, "Nathaniel Bishop, Esqr., Richmond."

He sold his farm in Berkshire about 1814, to Asahel Royce, and moved to Rawson Hollow, where he died 18 Feb., 1815. His last work had been to make a coffin for one of his neighbors, who had died of the same disease, pleurisy, which seemed then to be epidemic in that place. She married (2d) with Asa Bement. The children of Noah and Lucy (Bishop) Lyman were:

I. Dennis, b at Richmond, Mass., 2 Feb., 1797, died 4 Aug., 1824, unmarried.

II. Ruth Bartlett, b at Richmond, Mass., 26 July, 1799, m with William B. Bement.

III. Nancy Bishop, b at Richmond, Mass., 23 Jan., 1802, m with Sylvester Blair, of Cortland Village, N. Y.; and (2d) with John Judson, of Columbus, Warren Co., Penn., where she died.

IV. Lavina, b at Richmond, Mass., 25 Oct., 1804, died at Berkshire, 2 Aug., 1806.

V. Henry, b at Berkshire, 23 or 25 Feb., 1811, m 11 Jan., 1837, with Laura Thurston, who still lives in Newark Valley; and died at Harford, N. Y., 17 Sept., 1843.

VI. George, b at Berkshire, 14 Oct., 1813, resides at New Albany, Ind., a hearty, genial, pleasant man who is admired by all.

Capt. Heman Smith lived in Berkshire county, Mass., at one time in Stockbridge, at another in Lenox. He probably came to Berkshire in 1805, as it is known that he was here in January, 1806, where his name appears on John Brown's account book. He settled on the farm now occupied by his great-grandson, Arthur E. Smith, on lot 418, and died there about July, 1812. His first wife was Miriam Moody, who died in Massachusetts. His second wife was Lucy Taylor, who also died in Massachusetts. He married (3d) with Almira Messenger, daughter of Martin and Margaret (Woodruff) Messenger. Capt. Smith's children were :

I. Miriam, (by first marriage) m with —— Clothier, of Saratoga, N. Y.

II. Samuel (by second marriage).

III. Lucy, m Nathaniel Johnson.

IV. Mercy, m with Daniel Clark, of Danby, N. Y.

V. Sarah. VI. Polly, m with Alden Baker, of Berkshire.

VII. Heman, m with Clarissa Goodale.

VIII. Lydia, m with —— Clothier, a brother of Miriam Smith's husband.

IX. Clarissa, (by third marriage) m with Harry Cook, of Berkshire, son of Ephraim Cook.

X. Eunice, b at Lenox, Mass., 16 April, 1800, came to Berkshire, with her parents, about 1805, and in 1806 was taken into the family of Dr. Joseph Waldo, of Berkshire, and dwelt there till her marriage with Ezekiel Dewey, and still lives in Berkshire, her good memory having furnished the evidence of many historical facts.

XI. Horace, went South.

XII. Dolly, m with Thomas Curran, and settled in Caroline, near Slaterville, N. Y.

Henry Griffin, born at Guilford, Conn., about 1780, son of Joseph and Jemima (Vaill) Griffin, a master mariner, came to Berkshire about 1804, or 1805, and settled on the north half of lot 385, which he bought of Azel Hovey. He built on it a small framed house, which Deodatus Royce moved across the road to make room for his brick house, and afterward made a wagon house of it. He m about 1808, with Anna Leonard, and after the war of 1812, finding his life in the woods distasteful, he moved his family to New York city, and resumed seafaring. He died on a voyage between San Domingo and Porto Rico, under circumstances which led his friends to believe that he was murdered. Her father brought her and her children back to his own house. She afterward went to dwell with her son, at Woodstock, Ill., where she died 23 Nov., 1850. Their children were :

I. Julia Ann Colt, b 2 May, 1809, m with Elijah Wilson, of Newark Valley.

II. George Henry, b 23 March, 1812, m with Mary Butler, of Manlius, N. Y., and settled at Woodstock, Ill., where he died in 1872.

III. Franklin, b 20 Sept., 1814, m Miss —— Thompson, of Crystal Lane, Ill., went to Colorado, and died there in 1879.

IV. Amanda Leonard, b in New York city, 20 Sept., 1817, m with —— Dwight.

Osmyn Griffin, brother of Henry, came to Berkshire with him, and afterward went to Canada, where he died.

John Griffin, brother of Henry and Osmyn, came with them to Berkshire, and remained two or three years, then returned to Richmond, Mass., became a Methodist, and married 1 Oct., 1808, with Lydia Redfield. He afterwards preached for many years in the M. E. church. He returned to Berkshire after his marriage, and the first three of his twelve children were born here.

Peleg Randall was in Berkshire, as early as April, 1803. Peleg Randal " of Tioga," bought 120 acres of the south part of lot 418, in 1805, for $360.00, of Levi Chapin and Jerusha, his wife, of Wethersfield, Conn. He settled on the west part of his farm, on the southwest side of the road to Rawson Hollow, opposite the road which now leads north into the town of Richford. He was born 9 May, 1775, and married with Eunice Kimball, who was born in April, 1771, and and died 22 March, 1856, aged eighty-four years, and eleven months. He died 26 March, 1856. Their children were:

I. Eunice, m with Nathaniel Boyer, and moved to Ovid, N. Y.

II. Chester, m with Ann Eliza Whitaker, who was born about 7 July, 1810, and died 30 Dec., 1843, at the birth of her first child, who was buried with her ; and he married (2d) with Hannah Smith, daughter of Samuel and Theodosia (Dewey) Smith.

10*

III. Nathan Peleg, settled at East Troy, Wis.

IV. David Kimball, died 2 Oct., 1839, aged 29 years and nine months.

Joseph Belcher, b at Preston, Conn., 25 June, 1764, m 2 March, 1786, with Lucy Hall, who was born in 1767, daughter of Capt. John and Jemima (Bell) Hall. Her father, then of Castleton, Vt., was killed by the British, 6 July, 1777, the day before the battle of Hubbardton. They dwelt on his father's homestead in Preston, till the latter part of June, 1805, then moved, passing through Albany 4 July, 1805, reaching Berkshire a few days later, and settled on the north half of lot 297, where they died ; she 9 Sept., 1812, aged forty-five years ; he, 5 Jan., 1819. Their children were :

I. Lydia, b 2 Aug., 1786, m with Alexander Gaston.

II. Jonathan, b 8 Feb., 1788, m in 1808, with Betsey Bement, and settled in Newark Valley, where they died ; she, 12 June, 1845 ; he, 7 Jan., 1853.

III. Abigail, b 31 Jan., 1790, m with Daniel Gilbert.

IV. Lucy, b 28 Dec., 1891, m with John W. Bessac.

V. Joseph, b 10 Jan., 1794.

VI. Frederick, b 2 or 21 May, 1798, m 3 Jan., 1821, with Rebecca Short Brown. They dwelt in Richford till 1844, then moved to Woodstock, Ill.

VII. Elijah, b 5 June, 1800, settled in Newark Valley, where he died 11 Dec., 1879, having survived three wives.

VIII. Maria, b 15 July, 1802, m with Dr. Joseph Talcott Waldo.

IX. Esther, b 8 Aug., 1804, died at Berkshire, 26 July, 1820.

X. Betsey, b 10 Oct., 1806, m with Orlando Warren, of New York, and still living, July, 1887.

XI. Susan, b 13 June, 1808, d 10 Feb., 1829.

XII. Harriet, b 2 Sept., 1812, m with Clark Waldo.

Elijah Belcher, b at Preston, Conn., 18 March, 1772, son of Moses and Esther (Rudd) Belcher, m with Lydia Clark, daughter of Pharez and Olive (Jewett) Clark, of Preston. They dwelt for some years at Cherry Valley, N. Y., and she died there. He m (2d) with Eliza Putnam, daughter of the Rev. Aaron Putnam, of Pomfret, Conn. In July, 1805, they settled in Berkshire, on lot 297, about fifty rods west of the road, and midway between his brother, Joseph Belcher, and his brother-in-law, John W. Bessac. She died suddenly, 31 Oct., 1807, in her forty-third year. He married 3d with Lydia Burbank, daughter of Timothy and Hannah (Ripley) Burbank, and sister of Col. Christopher Burbank, of Newark Valley. He died 20 Sept., 1849, aged 77 years. His widow died 28 Sept., 1850, aged sixty-seven years. There is no doubt that his name should have been in the census of Dec., 1820, instead of Jonathan Belcher, which was a clerical error. His children were two by the first wife, two by the second, and one by the third, viz :

I. Olive, married with Dr. David N. Richards, and m (2d) with John Fish, of Augusta, N. Y.

II. Lydia Clark, m 25 Feb., 1821, with Daniel Phillips.

III. Moses, settled and died at Cherry Valley, N. Y.

IV. Aaron Putnam, m with Harriet Ball.

V. Hannah Burbank, b 19 March, 1813, m with Dr. Joseph Talcott Waldo.

Samuel Hutchinson, b in Hebron, Conn., 8 Nov., 1769, m 4 Nov., 1795, with Abigail Brainerd, and dwelt in Canaan, N. Y., till 1805 or 1806, then moved to Berkshire, where he built a log house on the west side of the road, just above the bridge, opposite the brick house which Col. John B. Royce has occupied for nearly sixty years. After a few years he moved over the East hills, and settled in the valley of the Wilson creek, near the home of his wife's father and brother, and both died there ; she, 18 April, 1843, he, 17 Sept., 1854. Their children were :

I. Harvey, b 13 Oct., 1797, m in 1830 with Sarah Torry.

II. Irena, b 24 Aug., 1799, m with John Clark.

III. Orlando, b 25 July, 1801, d in Berkshire 5 May, 1831.

IV. Polly, b 18 Dec., 1803, m 10 Jan., 1838, with Jedediah Leathe Robinson, who died in Richford, N. Y., 28 Aug., 1842, and she m (2nd) 8 Oct., 1843, with his brother, Thomas Amsdell Robinson.

V. Williams, b in Berkshire, 17 April, 1806, m 24 Dec., 1835, with Rhoda Maria Benton, who was b in Lenox, Mass., 7 Feb., 1810, daughter of Erastus and Elizabeth (Paul) Benton.

VI. Orrin, b 20 Oct., 1808, d 5 March, 1828.

VII. Lavinia, b 21 Nov., 1810, m with John Hobart Pringle.

VIII. John, b 8 Aug., 1814, m with Alzina Heath, and settled at Richford.

Samuel Johnson, b at Preston, Conn., 27 Oct., 1757, son of Joseph and Abigail (Belcher) Johnson, m there 25 Oct., 1781, with Eunice Park, who was born there 20 Aug., 1763, daughter of Moses and Sarah (Brewster) Park. They dwelt at Preston till after the birth of their eldest child, then at New Marlborough,

Mass., till 1803, and at West Stockbridge, Mass., till April, 1806, when, with three of his children, Cassandra, Sally and Elijah, he came to Brown's Settlement. His wife and other children left West Stockbridge on Wednesday, 13 June, 1806, two days after "the great eclipse." They dwelt one year in the small framed house which William Dudley's widow had just vacated. In the spring of 1807 he moved to Newark Valley, having bought of Isaac Rawson the place where Egbert Bement now lives, in which he dwelt till 1815, when he bought of Jonas Muzzy a farm of fifty-five acres, on the south part of lot 58, on which they died; she, 2 Jan., 1833; he, 1 Sept., 1845, in his eighty-eighth year. Their children were:

I. Abigail, b 5 Jan., 1784, died 2 Jan., 1785.

II. Cassandra, b 17 Nov., 1885, m with Isaac Ball.

III. Abigail, b 17 May, 1788, m with Spencer Spaulding.

IV. Sally, b 29 July, 1790, m with Chester Goodale.

V. Eunice, b 12 June, 1792, m with Moses Spaulding.

VI. Elijah, b 15 June, 1794, m 10 Jan., 1818, with Lucina Hooper, who was born at West Stockbridge, 17 May, 1798, daughter of Capt. Elisha and Ruth (Newell) Hooper. They dwelt for many years at Flemingville, then moved to Flint, Mich., where he died 6 Sept., 1847. She married (2nd) with Dea. William B. Bement, and returned to Newark Valley.

VII. Cinderella, b 1 Sept., 1796, married 24 Dec., 1817, with Solomon Jones.

VIII. Nancy, b 31 July, 1798, m with Harvey Rich.

IX. Moses Park, b 6 Aug., 1802, died unmarried at the homestead of his father probably 1 June, 1875, as he was found dead in his bed the next morning.

John Gregory, b at Danbury, Conn., about 1765, m with Rachel Benedict, daughter of Josiah and Sarah Benedict, of Danbury, where she was born about 1767. They settled in Lenox, Mass., as early as 1791, and moved to Berkshire in the spring of 1806, arriving there on Friday, 9 May, 1806. They settled on the south half of lot 385, and built the house which has since been occupied by Horatio Collins and his son, Junius Collins. Here they died; she, 30 Dec., 1838, aged seventy-one years; he, 14 Dec., 1849, aged eighty-four years. They were buried at Richford, and his grave-stone calls him "John Gregory the 4th," which probably indicates that his father, grandfather and great-grandfather each bore the name of John. [See the Benedict Genealogy, p. 287.] Their children were:

I. Henry, b at Lenox, Mass., 15 July, 1791, a salesman, married 10 Feb., 1818, with Abigail Huntington, and settled in Ithaca, N. Y., where they died; he, in May, 1824, aged thirty-three years, she, 26 April, 1880, after a widowhood of nearly fifty-six years.

II. Electa, b at Lenox, Mass., 21 March, 1793.

III. Lucy, b at Lenox, Mass., in 1795, died at Berkshire in February, 1865, aged seventy-one years, buried at Richford.

IV. Eli Benedict, b at Lenox, Mass., 20 Oct., 1797, a trader, died at Berkshire, unmarried, in March, 1845, aged forty-eight years, and was buried in Richford.

V. Eliza Ann, b at Lenox, Mass., dwelt in Berkshire till the death of her brother, Eli B., and after that with her sister-in-law, and nephew, in Ithaca, N. Y.

Ichabod Brainard was born in Haddam, Conn., 19 Aug., 1749; m in Richmond, Mass., in 1770, with Susanna Williams, who was born in Colchester, Conn., 28 Sept., (old style), 1751, daughter of John and Abigail (Crocker) Williams. He served in the war of the revolution. They settled in Canaan, N. Y., and on a Sunday in the latter part of June, 1773, they went to church, and returning, found their house and all it contained entirely consumed by fire. In 1807 they came to Berkshire, and settled on lot 348–373, in the valley of Wilson creek, arriving at their new home on the eighteenth of June. She died there 8 April, 1813. He died at Cortlandville, N. Y., 20 Aug., 1833. Their children were:

I. Abigail, b 8 June, 1771, m with Samuel Hutchinson.

II. Alice, b 26 April, 1773, d 26 Sept., 1797.

III. Susanna, b 15 April, 1775, d 16 Aug., 1797.

IV. James, b 5 June, 1777, m 26 Jan.,1803, with Abigail Welch, and died in Caroline, N. Y., 17 Oct., 1856, and she d at Wellsborough, Pa., 25 July, 1861.

V. Clarissa, b 21 March, 1780, died in Berkshire.

VI. Williams, b in 1783, died in 1787.

VII. Ichabod, b 4 Feb., 1785, m 4 Feb., 1805, with Orpha Cook, who was born in Colebrook, Conn., and they dwelt in Berkshire, in the same place with his father, settling there at the same time, and afterward moved to Cooperstown, N. Y., and he had children, 1. Edward, b 13 Sept., 1807. 2. Jared, b 23 June, 1809. 3. Lewis Nash, b 11 Jan.,1812. 4. William Henry, b 30 Jan., 1816, all in Berkshire.

VIII. David Williams, b 28 May, 1787, m 10 Aug., 1811, at

Lisle, N. Y., with Laura Parsons, and they dwelt for five years at Lisle, then settled at Cortlandville, N. Y., where they died, she 26 Dec., 1836, he 9 Oct., 1848.

IX. Lydia, b 20 Aug., 1789, died in Berkshire, unmarried.

X. Jireh, b 10 Aug., 1792, died 15 Nov., 1793.

Isaac Goodale, b in Amherst, Mass., 16 Nov., 1755, son of Isaac and Ellen Goodale, m at Northampton, Mass,, 26 Aug., 1779, with Jemima Warner. They dwelt in Northampton and Westhampton till about 1797, and at Pittsfield, Mass., till 1808, then settled on Berkshire hill, on lot 378, at the angle of the road on the place now owned by Henry Payne, where she died 29 April, 1819, aged 62 years. He m (2d) with Sally (Whitney) Cobb, widow of Elijah William Cobb, and daughter of Asa Whitney. She was b about 1770, and died at Berkshire 13 June, 1825, aged 60 years, according to her grave-stone; but her age was probably four or five years less than that. He m (3d) with Electa Andrews, who died in Richford, at the house of Joseph Belcher. He died on his farm at Berkshire, 23 Nov., 1834, aged 79 years. His children were:

I. Isaac, b at Northampton, Mass., 1 Oct., 1780, was living in Richford in Dec., 1820, and afterward settled in Michigan.

II. Huldah, born at Westhampton, Mass., 26 March, 1782, m with Samuel Smith, of Berkshire, and died there 5 July, 1811.

III. Susanna, b 26 July, 1784, m with Moses Stanley.

IV. Eli, b 17 April, 1786, died in Ohio.

V. Chester, b 7 Dec., 1787, m with Sally, daughter of Samuel Johnson, settled on his father's homestead, and moved about 1842 to Genesee, Mich.

VI. Electa, b 22 Jan., 1790, m with John Ayres.

VII. Clarissa, b 19 April, 1792, m with Heman Smith, and, after his death, with Nathaniel Johnson.

VIII. Spencer, b 20 July, 1794, m with Mary Gorsline, and dwelt for some years in Newark Valley, afterward near Buffalo, N. Y., where he died.

IX. Moses, b 2 Aug., 1796, settled in Michigan.

X. Naomi, b 4 Aug., 1793, at Pittsfield, Mass., and two years later, on the death of her aunt, her name was changed to Abigail Goodale. She m with Asa Curtis, of Maine, N. Y., and (2d) with Stephen Butler.

XI. Maria, name changed to Sally, b 8 Jan., 1801, m with Eber Johnson, of Richford, and settled in Michigan.

XII. William Warner, b 1 Dec., 1801, settled in Missouri. He m with Rachel Goodale.

Capt. Bill Torry and his household came from Durham, Greene county, N. Y. It is said that he was a soldier of the revolutionary war. He dwelt for some years in the log house which Noah Lyman built, about two rods west of where the Brookside Seminary afterward stood. In 1820 he lived on lot 224, where Capt. Edward N. Chapman afterward lived, in Newark Valley. He went back to Berkshire and lived where Dr. J. Talcott Waldo built his new house. It is remembered that the neighbors "made a bee" one winter and drew about forty loads of green wood for him. At night he said, "Well, now! you have brought me a great lot of green wood, and I wish you would go to the creek and catch a load of suckers for me to kindle it with;" and after that he bought his wood. He was born in Durham, Conn., 6 Oct., 1761, baptized there, 28 Feb., 1762, son of Sarah Torry, who owned the covenant at Durham, 6 Aug., 1758, and afterward married with Samuel Wilkinson. She moved, with her son, to Durham, N. Y., and died there. He married with Mehitabel Baldwin, of Durham, Conn. They came to Berkshire 13 May, 1808, and for a few months dwelt in a log house just above where Samuel Collins was then building his new house, then moved to the large log house (where Nathaniel Bishop Collins afterward built his brick house) which Samuel Collins had first occupied on coming to town. He died in Berkshire, 15 April, 1852, in his 91st year. Their children were:

I. Samuel, b in Durham, Conn., 15 Aug., 1787, m 11 Dec., 1816, with Sarah Durfee, who died 25 Aug., 1870.

II. Delie, b about 1789, died 1 May, 1830, aged 40 years.

III. Rhoda, b about 1791, died 3 Jan., 1854, in her 63d year.

IV. William, b about 1793, died at Romulus, N. Y., 7 June, 1852, and his wife, Lois, died 10 June, 1838, in her 37th year.

V. John, b about 1795, m with Sophia Ann Collins, who was born 23 July, 1797, built the house opposite the M. E. church, and died there 28 Aug., 1880, in his 86th year, without children.

VI. Sarah Wilkinson, b 5 June, 1797, m with Harvey Hutchinson, and died 8 June, 1886, aged 89 years and 3 days.

VII. Seth Baldwin, died in Michigan.

VIII. Patty Brown, b about 1801, died in Berkshire, 31 May, 1810, aged 9 years.

IX. Betsey Baldwin, b at Durham, N. Y., 4 Aug., 1804, now resides in Berkshire.

Samuel Torry lived on a farm on Strong brook, directly west of that of Luke B. Winship and Henry M. Ball. His wife joined the church in Stockbridge, Mass., in 1807, and at Newark Valley, 6 July, 1817. He joined the church at Newark Valley, 3 April, 1831, and they were dismissed 5 July, 1833, to the new church at Berkshire. Their children were:

I. Julia, bap. 11 March, 1818.

II. Delia, bap. 2 Jan., 1820, m with Asa Witter.

III. Elizabeth Baldwin, b 20 Dec., 1820, bap. 1 July, 1821.

IV. John, bap. 6 Oct., 1822.

V. David Baldwin, bap. 3 Aug., 1828.

Seth Akins, b at Durham, Conn., 25 July, 1762, and baptized the same day, son of Robert and Sarah Akins, was a mariner, served in the war of the revolution, was wounded and captured on a vessel, confined for some time in a prison-ship in New York harbor, and carried to his grave the scars made by the bayonets of the enemy. For his services he received a pension in the latter years of his life. A fracture of the leg, unskillfully treated, left it an inch shorter than the other. He married 8 May, 1786, with Content Rossiter, who died 17 May, 1789. He married (2d) 26 Sept., 1790, with Sarah Griswold, who died in Berkshire, 15 Aug., 1843. He dwelt for a time in Berkshire county, Mass., afterwards in Durham, Greene county, N. Y., and early in the present century came to the west part of Berkshire, and finally settled in a log house east of the road, a little north of where the cheese factory now stands, on the north half of lot 380, where Stephen H. Boyer now owns. In 1812 he built a framed house near the southwest corner of Mr. Boyer's orchard, and dwelt there till about 1833, when they went to live on a part of the same farm, with his son, Lyman P. Akins, at whose house he died 6 Sept., 1837. His sea-chest, more than a hundred years old, is carefully kept by one of his grandsons. His children were:

I. Sarah, b 13 Dec., 1786, died 9 Jan., 1787.

II. Seth Warner, b 7 July, 1791, died at Berkshire, 15 Aug., 1825, unmarried.

III. Content, b 29 March, 1793, was commonly called Tenty, married with Aaron Livermore, and died in Michigan, about 1868.

IV. Lyman Parmalee, b 3 March, 1795, married in 1821, with Betsey, daughter of Eleazer Lyman. He was several times supervisor of Berkshire, and twenty-four years in succession justice of the peace. He died without children, 15 Dec., 1884, sixty-three years after marriage. His widow still lives on the Akins homestead. They provided a good home for several children of other people.

V. Sally, b 19 March, 1797, d 6 Oct., 1798.

VI. Robert, b 19 June, 1799, married about 1827, with Olive Leonard Ball, who died at Berkshire, 29 March, 1867, in her 66th year. He died at Sheldrake, N. Y., in March, 1885.

VII. William Henry, b in Berkshire county, Mass., 1 March, 1804, married in May, 1827, with Eliza, daughter of Daniel Surdam, of Richford. She died at Berkshire, 18 Jan., 1839. He married (2d) with Catharine House, of Dryden, N. Y., who is still living. He was a wheelwright, having learned his trade of Enoch S. Williams, of Newark Valley, and became a prolific inventor, some of his devices proving to be of importance and value, as the table and feeding devices for sewing machines, now in universal use, and the permutation lock for safes and bank vaults. He died at Ovid, N. Y., 3 Jan., 1877.

VIII. Charles Frederick, b 26 March, 1807, married 10 Dec., 1830, with Lodema Farnham Ball, who died 12 June, 1838, at Berkshire. He married (2d) with Lucy Semantha Dewey. He died in Berkshire, 17 June, 1842, and his widow married (2d) with John Rightmire, of Caroline, N. Y., and died 18 Jan., 1854.

Elijah William Cobb, b at Canaan, Conn., 24 Sept., 1765, son of Elijah and Amy (Lawrence) Cobb, m at Salisbury, Conn., 17 or 27 Feb , 1786, with Sally Whitney, who was born in Cannan, Conn., about 1770, daughter of Asa Whitney, by his first wife. They dwelt in Canaan till 1802, then moved to Lenox, Mass., and thence, a few years later to Berkshire, settling on the farm now owned by Erasmus Legg, a mile east of Speedsville, where he died 12 Aug., 1815, aged 53 years, according to his grave stone, which makes the age two years too great. She m (2d) with Isaac Goodale. Elijah Cobb's children were:

I. Joshua Whitney, b Nov., 1786, m in June, 1816, with Susan Doty, and died at Elsie, Mich., 2 May, 1851.

II. Permelia, b 18 or 20 Jan., 1791, m with Isaiah Gridley Barker, and died at Henrietta, N. Y., 11 Feb., 1830.

III. Charilla Matilda, b 5 Nov., by town record, or 6 Dec., 1793, by family record, m with John Burnett, of Hampton, Conn., and died in Utica, N. Y., in Feb., 1864.

IV. Daniel Johns, b 18 Oct., (or Nov.) 1793, m with Charles Hoyt, and died in Dansville, Mich., 13 Nov., 1857.

V. Lydia Edmunds, b 19 March, 1798, m with Thomas Davis, in 1815, and died at Dryden, N. Y., 22 Oct., 1860.

VI. Lyman, b 18 Sept., 1800, a teacher, m 7 April, 1822, with Harriet Chambers, of Caroline, N. Y., and died at Colesburgh, Penn., 20 Oct., 1864 ; was author of several school-books, which had a short run, as they were in opposition to the innovations which Noah Webster was making in the English language.

VII. Nancy, b at Lenox, Mass., 19 Oct., 1802, m at the house of Dea. Elijah Curtis, in Newark Valley, 19 Jan., 1826, with Asahel Jewett, and died at Richford, 27 June, 1836.

VIII. Sarah Whitney, b at Lenox, Mass., 13 Nov., 1804, m with Thomas Preshow, and died at Colesburgh, Penn., in Feb., 1869.

Barnabas Manning, b at Scotland, in Windham, Conn., 14 Sept., 1769, son of Andrew and —— (Seabury) Manning, married 20 Dec., 1792, with Esther Belcher, who was born at Preston, Conn., 31 March, 1770, daughter of Moses and Esther (Rudd) Belcher. They came to Brown's Settlement about 1810 or 1811, and he bought seventy-five acres of land east of the road on the south side of lot 336, which had been owned by William Dudley ; and of Daniel Ball, seventy-five acres west of the road on the south side of lot 337 ; and of James Robbins, one hundred acres on the south part of lot 335, so that his farm of 250 acres extended the whole length of the three lots. He built the house on the west side of the road, where his son-in-law, Asa Ball, now dwells. His wife died 30 June, 1819, without children. He married (2d) 17 Feb., 1820, with Phebe Lincoln, who was born at Western, now Warren, Mass., 7 Aug., 1791, daughter of Thomas and Lucy (Holbrook) Lincoln. He died 11 Feb., 1856, in his 87th year. She died 4 Dec. 1872. Their children were :

I. Esther Maria, b 11 March, 1821, m with Asa Ball, and died 15 May, 1887.

II. Charles Seabury, b 25 Sept., 1822, m at Union, N. Y., 11 Oct., 1848, with Mary Jane Gray, who was born at Binghamton, N. Y., 21 April, 1826, daughter of Arthur and Ann (Van Nanre) Gray. She died 26 March, 1887.

III. Jane, b 17 Feb., 1824, m with Luther Andrews. He died 7 Jan,, 1887.

IV. Eliza, b 7 May, 1828, m 23 June, 1852, with George Henry Akins, and lives at Ovid, N. Y.

V. Catharine Lincoln, b 2 Feb., 1831, m with George Andrews, who died 19 March, 1876. She died 8 Jan., 1881, without children.

Asahel Royce, b at Lanesborough, Mass., 7 May, 1771, son of

Adonijah and Amy (Brush) Royce, m 22 Jan., 1792, with Sally Betsey Clark, who was born at Lanesborough, 29 June, 1772. About 1801 they moved to Richmond, Mass., where she joined the church, in April, 1808. They left Richmond 5 Feb., 1814, for Berkshire, and settled on the north half of lot 385, where his son Deodatus afterward built his brick house. He also bought one hundred acres of Noah Lyman, on the south half of lot 416, on which he built the house now occupied by his grandson, J. Talcott Leonard, it having been moved to its present site, when he sold the grounds, in 1846, to the Rev. William Bradford, as a site for Brookside Seminary. In this house they settled about 1818, and died there; he, 18 March, 1847; she, 25 April, 1848. Their children were:

I. Deodatus, b at Lanesborough, Mass., 28 Jan., 1793, m 25 Dec., 1817, with Emily Bement, daughter of Asa Bement, of Newark Valley, was for many years a deacon of the Congregational church in Berkshire, built the brick house where his father first settled; and in that house they died; she, 5 Sept., 1875.

II. John Brush, b at Lanesborough, Mass., 9 June, 1795, a wool-carder and cloth-dresser, taught school in Richmond, Mass., the winter that his father left there, took care of his father's cattle during the winter, and in May, 1814, drove them to Berkshire, where he married, 1 Jan., 1823, with Amanda Leonard, daughter of Asa and Olive (Churchill) Leonard, began house-keeping on the morning after their marriage, in the log house on the west side of the way, above the bridge, and lived there till 1829, when he built the brick house in which he is yet living, at the age of ninety-two years.

III. Almon, b 15 April, 1797, died 8 Feb., 1799.

IV. Haanah, b 21 Dec., 1799, m with Louis Gigette Leonard.

V. Amy, b 10 Jan., 1803, m with Charles West Cook.

VI. —— Royce, a son, b 1 March, 1805, died 2 March, 1805.

VII. Harriet Laminta, b 27 March, 1807, m with William Russell Starr, of Ithaca, N. Y.

VIII. Betsey Ann, b 9 April, 1810, m with Levi Ball.

IX. Phebe Permelia, b 5 Nov., 1813, died 22 May, 1825.

Notes to Census Table.—The names in the following table marked with a star have already been mentioned; the others are referred to in the following notes, by corresponding numbers. It may be well to state, also, that there were no unnaturalized foreigners, no blacks, and no one engaged in commerce in the town. The total population was 586.

CENSUS OF BERKSHIRE, DECEMBER, 1820.

NAMES.	Under 10 years.	10 to 16 years.	16 to 18 years.	16 to 26 years.	26 to 45 years.	45 and upwards.	Under 10 years.	10 to 16 years.	16 to 26 years.	26 to 45 years.	45 and upwards.	Agriculturists.	Manufacturers.
1. Roswell H. Brown					2		3			1		2	
2. Jed Chapman	5	1	1	2	1			1		1			3
3. *Daniel Gleazen	3	2				1	2	1		1		1	
4. Jonathan Belcher	1	1		1	1	1	1		3	1	1	2	2
5. John W. Bessac	1				1		3			1		1	
6. Elisha Jenks		2		1	1			2	1		1	3	
7. Calvin Jenks				1					1			1	
8. Luther Hamilton	1	1		1			1			1		1	
9. Joel Smith and Jesse Smith				1	1								2
10. Ephraim Reniff	3	2						1	1	1		1	
11. Samuel Osborn			1	2	1			2		1	1	3	
12. Schuyler Legg					1		4	1		1		1	
13. Amos Peck	1				1				2				1
14. Daniel Jenks	1			1			3	1					
15. Reuben Legg				1	1				2		1	1	
16. Larned Legg				1					1			1	
17. *Daniel Carpenter	1			1	1		3	1	1	1		2	
18. Isaac Bunnel	1			1					1			1	
19. Samuel Haight	3	1	1	1	1			2	1		1	3	
20. Eleazer Lyman, Jr	1			1					1			1	
21. Thomas Keeny		1	2	3		1	1	2	3		1	5	
22. *Joseph Gleazen	1	1	1			1	3	1		1		2	
23. Thomas Bunting	1			1		1	3	1	1			2	
24. Joseph Belcher	1				1		2	1		1		1	
25. William Whiting		1		1	1	1			2	1	1	3	
26. Eleazer Valentine	3	2	1	2	1		2			1		4	
27. William S. Smith	2		1	1	1		2			1		2	
28. *Isaac Goodale			1	1		1			1		1	2	
29. Stephen Butler				1	1		1			1		1	
30. Alden Baker	2				1		1			1		1	
31. *Asa Leonard	1	1		2		1		1	1		1	3	
32. *Solomon Leonard	3			2			2	1	1	1			3
33. John S. Thorp	1			1			2			1		1	
34. Isaac Hitchcock	2			1			2		1	1		1	
35. *Anna Griffin	1			1			1	1					1
36. Selick Paine	2			1						1			1
37. William Moore	2			1			1		2			1	
38. Andrew Rees	3			1			1			1		1	
39. Anna Collins	1						1			1		1	
40. John Ayres	2			1			3	1	1			1	
41. Lyman Hull				1			1	1	1			1	
42. *Jesse Gleazen			1	1		1	1	1	2		1	2	
43. *Peleg Randal	1	2				1		1			1	1	
44. *Polly Gardner	1				1		1	2			1		
45. Moses Stanley	2	1			1		2			1			1
46. Clarissa Smith	2			1				1	1			1	
47. Samuel Smith	1		1	1	1		3			1	1	2	
48. Hooker Bishop	2			1	1		2			1		1	
49. Cicero Barker	1				2		1			1			2
50. Aaron Livermore	1				1		3			1		1	
51. Eleazer Lyman	1	1			1		2		1	1		2	
52. *Sarah Ide			1	1			2		1		1		
53. *Seth Akins		1		1		1					1	3	
54. Elias Walker	2				1		3			1		1	
55. Phinehas Case	2	1			1		1			1	1	1	
56. Leman Case				1			1		1				1
57. *Samuel Ball		1			1		2	2		1		1	
58. Levi E. Barker	2	2			1		2	2	1	1		1	
59. Isaiah G. Barker					1		4	1		1			1

CENSUS OF BERKSHIRE, DECEMBER, 1820.—CONTINUED.

NAMES.	No. Males and Ages.						No. Females and Ages.					Agriculturists.	Manufacturers.
	Under 10 years.	10 to 16 years.	16 to 18 years.	16 to 26 years.	26 to 45 years.	45 and upwards.	Under 10 years.	10 to 16 years.	16 to 26 years.	26 to 45 years.	45 and upwards.		
60. Edmund Barker					1		1		1			1	
61. Erastus Benton	1						2	2	1			1	
62. *Consider Lawrence		1	2	4	1				1		1	5	
63. Lyman Durfee	2			1	1				1				2
64. John Durfee		1		1		1		1		1		2	
65. *Samuel Torry					1		2			1		1	
66. Ezra Landon				1	1				1			1	
67. Abraham Hotchkin		1					1		1			1	
68. *Jeremiah Campbell	2	1					1	1	3		1	1	
69. *Asahel Royce		1					1	2	2	1	1	1	
70. *Deodatus Royce	1				1		1		2			1	
71. *John Gregory			1		1		1	1	2		1	2	
72. Thomas Langdon	1				1		1		1			1	
73. *Samuel Collins	2	1		2	1				2		1	1	
74. *Ebenezer E. Gleazen					2				1				1
75. Joseph Cook				1					1				1
76. *Henry Ball	2				1		3			1		1	
77. *Stephen Ball	4	1			1		1	2	1			1	
78. *William Ball	1		1						1			1	
79. *Elizabeth Cook	1	1		1			1		1		1		
80. *Ransom Williams	1				1		1			2		1	
81. *David Williams	1			2		1			1			2	1
82. *Ichabod Brainerd, Jr	2	2			1				1			1	
83. *Ichabod Brainerd							1			2		1	
84. *Samuel Hutchinson	1	2		2		1	1		2		1	2	
85. Marcus Ford				2					1				2
86. Luke B. Winship	1		2	3	2		3			2	1	1	3
87. John Rounseville	1	1	1	1		1					1	1	
88. *Mehitable Brown		1	1	3					2	1	1	1	3
89. *Joseph Waldo		1		1	1		1	1	1	2		1	
90. *Nathaniel Ford		2					1	1	1	1	2	1	
91. *Barnabas Manning					1		1	1	1			2	
92. Ralph Manning					2		1		1			1	1
93. *Isaac Ball	2				1		3	1	1			1	
Totals	94	41	15	65	58	30	102	43	65	57	31	113	29

1. Roswell H. Brown lived on lot 417, in the first house south of the present town of Richford ; but little has been remembered of him beyond the fact that when slightly elevated in tone, he wished to be addressed as "Mr. Roswell H. Brown, Esq., Sir." One of his children was born 29 Dec., 1821. Afterward he lived on lot 303, on the west bank of Strong brook, south of the road, near the corner where a road branches off to the north. Among his children were William and Hannah.

2. Capt. Jed Chapman, a carpenter and joiner, lived below Mr. Brown, on the east side of the same road, in the second house above Mr. Leonard's tannery. He was born at Saybrook, Conn., 14 Dec., 1781, m 28 Sept., 1803, with Content Canfield, and settled at Durham, N Y. In the spring of 1811 they moved to

Berkshire, and thence, in Dec., 1831, to Newark Valley, where they died ; he, 28 Dec., 1852 ; she, 14 Feb., 1861. His mother, Amanda Denison, married with Eleazer Hodges, by whom she had several children. Capt. Chapman's children were as follows:

I. Edward Newton, b 25 July, 1804.

II. Elizur Brown, b 6 Oct., 1806, m with Julia Blackman, and resides at Jackson, Mich.

III. Mary Amanda, b 10 Dec., 1808, m 1 April, 1834, with Isaac Van Alstein.

IV. William Henry, b 25 Dec., 1810, m 14 Jan., 1835, with Electa Ayres.

V. George Miller, b 24 March, 1813, m 16 Sept., 1835, with Esther Miranda Williams, and now lives at Newark Valley.

VI. Richard Mulford, b 7 Aug., 1815, died at Napierville, Ill., 4 May, 1842.

VII. Aaron Canfield, b 29 April, 1818, resides in Newark Valley.

VIII. Noyes Palmer, b 25 Aug., 1820, now lives in Newark Valley.

IX. Lyman Furry, b 14 Aug., 1822, resides in Newark Valley.

X. Charles Denison, b 15 Oct., 1824, lives in Michigan.

XI. Lucy Elvira, b 12 Feb., 1827, died 16 Sept., 1829.

4. Jonathan Belcher, is undoubtedly a clerical error for Elijah Belcher, already mentioned.

5. John William Bessac lived on lot 297, west of the road which goes over the hill, and west of the creek. He was born in Hudson, N. Y., 26 April, 1790, a son of Jean Guilliaume and Anah (Nichols) Bessac. He married in January, 1813, with Lucy Belcher, daughter of Joseph and Lucy (Hall) Belcher. He died 9 Dec., 1868. She died 23 May, 1868. " Mr. Bessac was no ordinary man. With a mind of singular brilliancy and power, he combined a temper of unusual sweetness, the keenest wit, and a playful humor that rendered him a most genial and instructive companion." His father was born 4 Feb., 1760, in Mon Valant, France. The children of John William and Lucy (Belcher) Bessac were as follows:

I. Joann Frances, b 7 Feb., 1814.

II. Calista Maria, b 18 March, 1816.

III. Henry William, b 6 April, 1818, m with Emily Hull.

IV. Esther B., b 6 March, 1820.

V. John Bertrand, b 28 July, 1822, d 30 Sept., 1824.

VI. Fayette B., b 12 July, 1824.

VII. Catharine E., b 7 Dec., 1827.

VIII. Susan, b 13 Nov., 1829.

IX. Frederick Oriel, b 12 March, 1831.

X. Mary Elizabeth, b in Aug., 1834.

6. Elisha Jenks lived on lot 300, east of the creek road, and north of the hill road. It is said that he was a cousin of Michael Jenks, the first settler there. Laban Jenks was his brother. Elisha Jenks was born about 27 June, 1774, and died 13 Nov., 1840. His wife, Anna, was born about 27 Sept., 1771, and died 15 June, 1854.

7. Calvin Jenks lived on the east end of lot 300. He was a son of Elisha Jenks. He married with Anna Brown, daughter of Capt. Brown, and died on the same place, about 1886,

8. Luther Hamilton lived in the first house southwest of Daniel Carpenter, on lot 302. He m at Stockbridge, Mass., 2 Nov., 1815, with Sylvia Carpenter, who was born there 14 March, 1782. She died 10 June, 1832.

9. Joel Smith and Jesse Smith had no settled residence in 1820. They were carpenters and not married. Joel Smith was killed in Owego, as early as 1866, by the fall of a building which he was moving. Jesse Smith, b at Lee, Mass., 5 May, 1792, served as a soldier in the war of 1812. He married with Betsey Legg, and settled on the north half of lot 419, where Newell Robinson now lives. They had four children, viz.:

I. Deborah Williams, b about 1826. II. Daniel B., b about 1828. III. Miranda M., b about 1830. IV. James R., b about 1832.

Their house was burned on 21 Dec., 1840, after the family had gone to bed, and all were consumed in the fire except the eldest daughter, who was away from home attending school. She married with Russel W. Freeland, and now resides at Ouaquaga, N. Y. It was long supposed that the fire was accidental; but years after it a story was in the papers that a murderer, under sentance of death, confessed that he saw Mr. Smith receive some money at Richford, followed him home, asked to be kept over night, and when the family were sleeping rose to get the money, and Smith and his wife being roused by the noise, he killed them in their bed with an axe, set the house on fire, and escaped with seventeen dollars, his whole booty.

10. Ephraim Reniff's residence has not been ascertained.

11. Samuel Osborn lived on the west side of the road, next above Elisha Jenks, and about a quarter of a mile from him. He had eight or nine children, one of whom, Betsey, m with Lyman Legg. Samuel Osborn was born about 3 Sept., 1762, and died

19 April, 1840. Mary, his wife, was born about 11 Nov., 1770, and died 18 March, 1832.

12. Schuyler Legg lived on the hill, on the southeast quarter of lot 301, where his son, Layton J. Legg, has since lived. His farm joined on the west end of Luther Hamilton's farm. He was a son of Reuben Legg, and grandson of David. He had children b 19 July, 1811; 24 Oct., 1812; and 28 Aug., 1820. His wife, Hannah, died 11 Oct., 1860, aged 74 years.

13. Amos Peck, a shoemaker, lived on the road above Samuel Osborn. At a later time he lived on the hill, half a mile west of Schuyler Legg. His child, probably the second, was born 20 Feb., 1822.

14. Daniel Jenks lived above Amos Peck. He had previously lived on the east end of lot 300, which he sold to Calvin Jenks. He was the eldest son of Elisha Jenks. He married with ——, a daughter of Thomas Keeny.

15. Reuben Legg's residence has not been ascertained.

16. Larned Legg, youngest son of Reuben Legg, m with —— Whiteley.

18. Isaac Bunnel lived north of Carpenter, where Charles Scott now lives, on the southeast quarter of lot 339. He was son of Dea. John and Hannah Bunnel. His wife, Rachel, died 5 Sept., 1842, aged 43 years, 1 month and 11 days. Their daughter, Eliza, died 14 Aug., 1841, aged 5 years, 7 months and 14 days.

19. Samuel Haight lived in the hollow, away from the road, west of Isaac Bunnel,

20. Eleazer Lyman, Jr., lived on Berkshire East Hill, near Samuel Haight, and was then a farmer and teacher. He was born at Peru, Mass., 18 August, 1802, (see Note 51), married there 18 Sept., 1819, and in the following month came to Berkshire; and after five or six years moved to Belfast, Allegany Co., N. Y., and thence, in October, 1829, to Friendship, N. Y., where he began the study of medicine, and received his diploma in 1832, while living at Bolivar, N. Y., to which place he moved in March, 1832. He returned to Berkshire in April, 1834, and moved again in April, 1835, to Great Bend, Pa., where his wife died 13 Oct., 1838. He married (2d) about 1842, with Sally Clark, of Great Bend, and was killed there by a vicious horse, 6 January, 1845. His children were:

I. Chauncey Almeron, b at Berkshire, 19 July, 1820, a lawyer, served in the war of 1861, reaching the rank of Lieut.-Colonel, and resides at Lock Haven, Pa.

II. Charles Eleazer, b at Richford, 27 Nov., 1824, a lawyer; served in the war of 1861, reaching the rank of Captain; and resides at Great Bend, Pa.

III. Betsey Jane, b at Belfast, N. Y., 21 Dec., 1828, died in infancy.

IV. James Wellman, b at Friendship, N. Y., 6 March, 1830; served as a surgeon in the war of 1861, and finally as Lieut.-Col. of 203d Pa. Volunteers, and was killed at Fort Fisher, 15 January, 1865.

V. Betsey Keziah, b at Bolivar, N. Y., 24 May, 1832; m with J. F. Nice, and lives at Williamsport, Pa.

VI. Alice Elvira, b at Berkshire, 9 June, 1834; m with Elijah Cobb, and lives at Little Sioux, Iowa.

VII. Vincent Page, b at Great Bend, Pa., 15 June, 1836,; resides at Portland, Oregon.

VIII. Clara Janet, b at Great Bend, Pa., 10 Feb., 1844; m with J. C. Scott, and lives at Waverly, N. Y.

21. Thomas Keeny lived near the center of lot 339, where Alfred Hyde Ford lived at a later time.

23. Thomas Bunting lived in a log house east of the road, above Joseph Gleazen, near the corner of the roads. He had moved to that place in April, 1820, when he sold his former home to Mr. Gleazen. Tradition says that he soon went back to New Jersey, from whence he came.

24. Joseph Belcher lived on the northwest quarter of lot 343, at the angle of the roads. He was a son of Joseph and Lucy (Hall) Belcher, and m about 1815 with Wealthy Whiting, widow of —— Judd, and daughter of William Whiting. They removed to Richford, where she died 6 Oct., 1859, aged 70 years. He married (2d) with Laura A. Appleton. He died at Richford, 16 March, 1868, aged 74 years. His children were:

I. Lucy, m with Whiting Valentine, and m (2d) with Rev. Timothy Dwight Walker. She died broken hearted, 13 March, 1868, three days before her father's death.

II. Horatio, m with Amanda Hungerford, of Caroline, and was killed while sitting on his horse before Petersburgh, Va., seven balls having entered his body.

III. Galitzin, died in California.

IV. Flavel, served in the rebel army in the war of 1861.

V. Marietta, m with John Deming.

VI. Joseph, b 7 Jan., 1828, died young.

VII. Useria, b 5 April, 1829; died 27 Jan., 1830.

11*

25. William Whiting, lived on the east side of the road on the crown of the hill, on the south half of lot 343, south of Joseph Belcher, and east of Joseph Gleazen.

26. Eleazer Valentine lived near the south line of the southeast quarter of lot 379, on the south side of the road, where George Rich Ford afterward lived. He had a child born 5 Nov., 1820.

27. William Sterry Smith, a shoemaker, lived a little north-west from Eleazer Valentine, near the middle of the south half of lot 379, afterward the Charles Nixon place.

29. Stephen Butler lived next north or northwest of Isaac Goodale, on the old road, long since discontinued, which led from Isaac Goodale's to the Berkshire and Rawson Hollow road. He married 18 Aug., 1815, with Olive Baker, who d 18 Jan., 1851. She was born at Cheshire, Mass., 10 Nov., 1788, eldest child of Waterman and Mercy (Bowen) Baker. He married (2d) with Abigail Goodale, widow of Asa Curtis, of Maine, N. Y. She was born at Pittsfield, Mass., 4 Aug., 1799, tenth child of Isaac and Jemima (Warner) Goodale. He died at Newark Valley. He had a child born 8 March, 1822

30. Alden Baker lived on the same old road, north of Stephen Butler, and probably on the southwest quarter of lot 383. He was born in Cheshire, Mass., 10 Sept., 1790, second child of Water-man and Mercy (Bowen) Baker, and m 19 Dec., 1816, with Polly Smith, daughter of Heman and Miriam (Moody) Smith.

33. John S. Thorpe, probably, lived above Solomon Leonard, on the same side of the way, just south of the little stream.

34. Isaac Hitchcock, b at Bethlehem, Conn., 8 Feb., 1786, son of Jared and Irena (Bartholomew) Hitchcock, m with Nancy Leonard, daughter of Asa and Olive (Churchill) Leonard. They joined the church at Newark Valley, 2 Jan., 1820, and were dismissed to the church at Berkshire, 5 July, 1833. He died 20 Feb., 1867. She died 6 Dec., 1872. Their home was on the west side of the road, on the northwest quarter of lot 377; afterward on the north side of Leonard street, where his daughters now live. Their children were:

I. Chauncey B., b 1 July, 1812, m at Franklin, N. Y., 22 Nov., 1838, with Sarah Maria Lovelace, and lives at Geneva Lake, Wis.

II. Horatio, b 8 Sept., 1814, m at McLean, N. Y., 16 Feb., 1841, with Louisa Susan Brown. He was a physician, and died at Chicago, Ill.

III. Juliette, b 18 Dec., 1816, m 1 Jan., 1845, at Berkshire, with Dwight Waldo. She resides on her father's homestead, a widow.

IV. Charlotte, b 23 Dec., 1818, m 7 Sept., 1843, at Berkshire, with Charles Lull.

V. Susan, b 1 March, 1824, d 3 Sept., 1825.

VI. Caroline, b 19 March, 1826, and resides on her father's homestead.

VII. Dwight, b 25 Nov., 1828, died 10 Oct., 1847.

36. Sellick Payne, a carpenter and joiner, came from Richmond, Mass., without his family, in 1816, to build the new meeting house, which was dedicated 4 July, 1817. In 1820 he moved his family from Richmond to Geneseo, N. Y., and thence, in the same year, to Berkshire. He dwelt, the first winter, in the old log house of David Williams, on the west side of the way, just north of the school-house. During several years he moved from place to place, as he had contracts for building ; at one time in Richford, at another in Newark Valley, and finally built the house where his son, Henry Payne, now lives, opposite the Congregational meeting-house, in Berkshire.

37. William H. Moore, a trader, lived on the east side of the road, where Dr. Gay now lives, and had a store (since burned), on the corner, just north of his house. Within a few years, after 1820, he bought the next place south of his house, and built a new store opposite the school-house, and then built the front part of the house where Mrs. Betsey Bidwell now lives, a little south of the store.

38. Andrew Rees, a farmer, is remembered as always driving a fine team of horses, but his place of residence has not been ascertained. It is probable that he was at Mr. Moore's store when he gave the particulars of his family.

39. Anna Collins was widow of Dan Collins, a cooper, who died 27 June, 1820, in the kitchen part of the house now occupied by Mrs. Betsey Bidwell. Her maiden name was Anna Lisk, and she was born 6 July, 1780. She had three children. Bristol Lisk Collins b 26 May 1809; died at Berkshire, 17 July, 1814; Orra Ann Collins, b 3 Dec. 1811 ; and George Bristol Lisk Collins, b 19 Dec. 1815. She moved to one of the Western states with her children, a few years later.

40. John Ayres, in Dec., 1820, was living in the house of Isaac Hitchcock.

41. Lyman Hull, lived where Nathan Rightmire now lives, east of the road, on the northeast quarter of lot 383. He died 23 March, 1823, aged 34 years and 4 months.

42. Jesse Gleazen lived on the west side of the way, near the north line of lot 383, in Dec., 1820.

45. Moses Stanley lived "in a blackberry patch," on the old road which has long been out of use, and probably on the northwest quarter of lot 383. He was a joiner, and married with Susanna Goodale. They moved to Veteran, N. Y., where she died 1 March, 1826. He is known to have been in Berkshire as early as October, 1807. His wife joined the church 7 Feb., 1813, and was dismissed 22 June, 1823. Their children were:

I. Lucy, b (probably) 26 Aug., 1808, bap. 17 March, 1813.

II. Lovina, b (probably) 29 Oct., 1810, bap. 17 March, 1813.

III. ——, a daughter, bap 12 Oct., 1813.

IV. Mary, bap 8 Jan., 1815. V. Chauncey, bap 2 Aug., 1818.

46. Clarissa Smith lived down in the valley, on a little stream, on lot 418. She was a daughter of Isaac Goodale, and was born at Westhampton, Mass., 19 April, 1792. She was the widow of Heman Smith, Jr., who had his leg crushed while clearing his land, about 21 June, 1820, and died from the injury, about 7 July, 1820. Her youngest child, by Mr. Smith, was born after his death, 20 Nov., 1820. Her second husband was Nathaniel Johnson, of Richford.

47. Samuel Smith lived on the road to Rawson Hollow, and probably on the northwest quarter of lot 419.

48. Hooker Bishop lived on the south side of the hill road, on the western slope of the hill, near the centre of lot 420, about thirty rods east of the Keith Blackman house, and about three-eighths of a mile east of the creek road at Rawson Hollow. He was born at Richmond, Mass., 30 March, 1781, son of the Hon. Nathaniel and Ruth (Bartlett) Bishop, and married in Berkshire, 20 August, 1812, with Sabra Clark. Soon after the census was taken they moved to a small house on the farm of Samuel Collins, west of the Richford road, and very near where the railway crosses the road ; and in this house she died 9 March, 1821. He died 28 June, 1821, at the house of Samuel Collins, to which he was taken so that his sister, Mrs. Collins, could more easily care for him. Their children were:

I. Mary, b 28 May, 1813.

II. John Bartlett, b 23 May, 1815 ; m 24 June 1846, with Sarah Jane Merchant, and had one daughter, who m with William Elwell.

III. Betsey, b 17 April, 1817; m with David M. Sturtevant, and lives in Newark Valley.

IV. Nathaniel, b 21 Oct., 1819; died 26 April 1822.

49. Cicero Barker, a wool-carder and cloth-dresser, lived on the corner, east of the creek road, and south of the hill road, at Rawson Hollow on the west end of lot 420. His twin brother, Cephas Barker, lived with him, and had a share of the business. Their shop was on the east bank of the creek, where the firkin factory now stands, and they took the water from the pond of Lyman Rawson's grist-mill, which stood at the west end of the dam in the town of Caroline.

50. Aaron Livermore lived on lot 420, a few rods south of Cicero Barker, and about ten rods east of the creek road, at Rawson Hallow. A few years later he moved farther south and lived west of the road, on lot 380. He was born at Spencer, Mass., March, 1782, and married with Content Akins. After his death she moved to Michigan with her children, about 1856, and settled at Dexter or Ingham. He and six of his twelve children are buried at Speedsville, N. Y., and the other six settled in Michigan.

51. Eleazer Lyman lived in a log house on the bank of the creek, on the northwest corner of lot 381, about twenty rods west of the present road. A year or two later he built a new house near the north line of the lot, on the east side of the road. His farm is now occupied by S. D. Freeland, who lives on the west side of the road. He was born 28 May, 1780, a son of Major Ozias and Sally (Parker) Lyman; married at Peru, Mass., in Feb., 1802, with Betsey Raymond, who was born 1 Oct., 1783, daughter of Amos and Alice (Joslin) Raymond, of Peru. They dwelt in Peru till October, 1819, then settled as above stated in Berkshire, where she died of cancer, 1 Sept., 1851. He died there of consumption 5 Feb., 1853. Their children were:

I. Eleazer, b at Peru, Mass., 18 Aug., 1802; m at Hinsdale, Mass., 18 Sept., 1819, with Sally Payne, daughter of Ebenezer Payne. He died at Great Bend, Pa., 6 Jan., 1845.

II. Betsey, b at Peru, Mass., 4 Aug., 1804; married 10 Sept., 1821, with Lyman P. Akins.

III. Alice Raymond, b at Peru, Mass., 27 July, 1806, died there 27 July, 1806.

IV. Raymond, b at Peru, Mass., 13 April, 1808, and died there 29 Dec., 1814.

V. Alice, b at Peru, Mass., 3 April, 1810, died 16 Feb., 1814.

VI. David, b at Peru, Mass., 25 Nov., 1812; died 20 Feb., 1814

VII. Obias, b at Peru, Mass., 15 Sept., 1814; died 15 Sept., 1814.

VIII. Alice, b at Peru, Mass., 23 Feb., 1816, married with John Harper Heggie, and lives at Colesburgh, Potter Co., Pa.

IX. Daniel Raymond, b at Peru, Mass., 27 Feb., 1818, m with Sarah Jane Blair, daughter of George and Rhoda (Blackman) Blair. He died 19 Sept., 1880, at Jackson, Mich., where she still resides.

X. Persis, b in Berkshire 18 Feb., 1820; married there, 18 Feb., 1841, with Austin Blair, son of George and Rhoda (Blackman) Blair. They settled at Eaton Rapids, Mich., where she died 30 Jan., 1844. He was elected Governor of Michigan in November, 1860, served during several terms, and was known as the "War Governor of Michigan."

XI. Nancy, b at Berkshire 16 Feb., 1822; married there Nov., 1842, with Daniel Brown Jenks, and resides at Speedsville, N. Y.

XII. Mary, b at Berkshire 27 Feb., 1824; married there with Levi J. Osborn, and lives at Big Rapids, Mich.

XIII. David Ballou, b at Berkshire, 21 Dec., 1826; married with Caroline Douglas, and died in Silver Township, Cherokee Co., Iowa, 24 Nov., 1886.

XIV. Sarah, b at Berkshire 2 April, 1829: married Feb., 1844, with George Landers Haynes, and resides in Owego, N. Y.

54. Elias Walker lived on the southwest quarter of lot 341, east of the road, just north of the orchard now owned by the Whiting family, and directly east of the village of Speedsville. The house no longer stands there. He removed to Moravia, N. Y.

55. Phineas Case, a blacksmith, came with his wife from Litchfield County, Conn., settled on lot 380, and built the house west of the road and directly opposite the cheese factory, now owned by E. D. Legg. His shop was on the same side of the way, and about fifteen rods south of his house. He moved to the west part of Candor, on the Spencer road, and died there.

56. Leman Case was a carpenter, came from Litchfield county, Conn., and married with Polly Jenks, daughter of Laban Jenks, an early settler at Speedsville. He settled in a house that was built by Job Hall, on lot 380, west of the road, some thirty or forty rods south of his brother, Phineas Case. He moved to Michigan not far from 1824.

58. Levi E. Barker lived on the hill, on the northeast quarter of lot 341.

59. Isaiah Gridley Barker, a silversmith and repairer of watches, lived about twenty rods south of the road and northeast of Levi E. Barker, on the same lot, 341. He m in 1811, with Permelia Cobb, who was b in Canaan, Conn., 20 Jan., 1791, daughter of Elijah William and Sally (Whitney) Cobb. She died 11 Feb., 1830, at Henrietta, N. Y., aged 39 years. Their children were:

I. Rhoda, d in Feb., 1830.

II. Mary Ann, b 1 Jan., 1814, m with Mr. Birdsall, and d before 1851.

III. Eliza, died in 1826. IV. Beda.

V. Permelia, was born 6 Oct., 1820, m in 1835, with Sidney Waite, who died at Appleton, Wis., in 1869, and she was living there in 1875.

VI. and VII. Twin sisters, died. VIII. Lyman Cobb.

IX. William Whitney, m with Eliza D. Lincoln, of Pike, N. Y., in 1851.

60. Edmund Barker lived on the same lot, 341, very near its north line, and just west of the angle where the road turns east on the lot lines.

61. Erastus Benton, a school teacher, lived south of the road, on the north border of lot 342. He came from Lenox, Mass. His wife was Elizabeth Paul, and their children were:

I. Harriet, b at Lenox, Mass., m with Henry Johnson.

II. Rhoda Maria, b at Lenox, Mass., 7 Feb., 1810, m with Williams Hutchinson.

III. Mary Ann, b at Lenox, Mass., m with G. D. Gleazen.

IV. Lucretia, b at Berkshire, died when a year old.

V. Charlotte, m with John Haddock, and lives in Candor, near Speedsville.

VI. Charles, b about 14 Jan., 1820, lives on the homestead.

VII. Lyman Cobb, b 21 Aug., 1821, lives at Jenksville.

VIII. A son, died young. IX. A son, died young.

X. Martin, died when 17 years old.

63. Lyman Durfee, a carpenter and joiner, lived on the southeast quarter of lot 338, where S. B. Aikens has since lived. He was born at Richmond, Mass., 14 March, 1792, m 19 Oct., 1815, with Hannah Hatch, of Richmond. He died in Wisconsin, 2 March, 18—. She died 12 Nov., 1844, aged 51 years, 9 months and 2 days, and was buried in West Newark.

64. John Durfee lived on the same place with his son, Lyman Durfee.

66. Ezra Landon lived in the north part of Berkshire, on top

of the hill, a mile east of where Col. Royce lives. He married with Ruby Chapin, a niece of Samuel Lucas, who had formerly lived on the same place, and died without children. Mrs. Landon inherited his property. Landon and his wife were Methodists, but finally went off and joined the Mormons. He had a child b 10 May, 1821.

67. Abraham Hotchkin lived in a log house on the west side of the road, opposite the site of the brick house since built by Col. John B. Royce. He had already sold the house and land to Col. Royce, but continued for several years to dwell there. He was born in Guilford, Conn., 16 July, 1779, married in 1805, with Parthenia Bement, eldest daughter of Asa Bement. They afterward settled on lot 218, in Newark Valley, and died there; he, 28 Feb., 1842; she 2 June, 1847. They had two children:

I. Marshal, b in Newark Valley, 18 May, 1806, died 24 May, 1874. He had three wives—Juliaette Williams, Abigail (Harmon) Branch, and Mary Edwards Muzzy, who still lives in Newark Valley. His daughter, by his first wife, is yet living on the homestead of her father and grandfather.

II. Abby Lavinia, b at Newark Valley, 26 Aug., 1808.

72. Thomas Langdon, in December 1820, lived in a small house just north of the house of Samuel Collins. He married in April 1816, with Maria Lawrence, daughter of Consider Lawrence. Their children were.

I. Wealthy, b 27 July 1817, m in Dec. 1838, with Stanley Sheffield Hinman, and settled at Monroeton, Penn.

II. Benjamin, b 6 June, 1819, m in Sept. 1846, with Eveline Perry, of Owego, and settled in Monroeton, Penn.

III. ———, b 25 Feb. 1821.

IV. Eliza, b 1 Sept. 1822, m in Sept. 1846, with William Wiltse, and settled at Speedsville, N. Y.

75. Joseph Cook, a distiller, lived in the village of Berkshire. His wife was ——— Livermore, and they moved to Lisle, N. Y.

85. Marcus Ford, a blacksmith, b at Lenox, Mass., 13 Feb. 1796, lived just north of the corner opposite the Congregational church. He never married. His sister, Margaret Ford, who was born at Lenox, 29 April, 1798, kept his house during his life. He died 17 June, 1838. In 1820 when the census was taken, their brother, Charles Backus Ford, b at Lenox, 28 Aug., 1791, a shoemaker, lived in the house with them. They came to Berkshire about 1814. Margaret Ford m 7 July, 1846, with David Smith, of China, N. Y.

86. Luke Bates Winship lived on the west side of the road, on the homestead of Josiah Ball, on lot 33. He was born at Union, N. Y., 31 March, 1794, a clothier, tanner, inn-keeper and farmer. He m 22 Feb., 1816, with Cynthia Ball. They had ten children, and died there.

87. John Rounseville lived on the east side of the road, below the Isaac Brown place, in a small framed house which was built by Elijah H. Saltmarsh, for a store.

92. Ralph Manning, a nephew of Barnabas Manning, lived in 1820, where Charles S. Manning now lives. He married with Betsey Cobb, who was born about 16 June, 1794, and died 6 June, 1848, aged 53 years, 11 months and 20 days. He married (2d) with Maria Archibald, sister of Samuel Archibald, of Owego, and she is still living, at Alden, McHenry Co., Ill. He had two children, Sophia Manning, b 2 Oct., 1819; and Gurdon G. Manning, b 30 Dec., 1825, now resides at Waverly.

This completes the matter furnished by Mr. Patterson, and we add the following :

The comparative growth of the town may be seen by reference to the following figures, showing the population for the several years cited : 1810, 1,105 ; 1820, 1,502 ;* 1825, 1,404; 1830, 1,711 ; 1835, 964 ; 1845, 878 ; 1850, 1,049 ; 1855, 1,068 ; 1860, 1,151 ; 1865, 1,073 ; 1870, 1,240 ; 1875, 1,304 ; 1880, 1,304.

Additional Sketches.—Ezekial Dewey was born in Westfield, Mass., in 1797, and came here about 1816, locating first in that part of Berkshire which is now Richford. He married for his first wife, Lucy, daughter of Nathaniel Johnson, of Richford, who bore him five children, Lucy, Samantha, Jane E., David W., Charles J., and Ezekiel H. Of these only two are living, Charles J., of Berkshire, and Ezekiel H., of Rochester, Mich. He married Eunice, daughter of Heman Smith, for his second wife, and had born to him one child, Amanda, wife of John Rightmire, of Caroline, N. Y. Mr. Dewey died February 11, 1887, aged eighty-nine years.

Ichabod Ford was born in Norwich, Conn., and came to this town with his family in 1822. He married twice, first, Rebecca Thomas, of Barnstable, Mass., and reared eight children, viz : Charles B., Susan T., Marcus, Margaret, Elijah T., Caroline,

---

* The apparent discrepancy between this number and that given by the census table on page 146, is due to the fact that the table only includes those that lived within the *present* limits of Berkshire.

Lebbeus and Alfred. His wife died in 1813, and he married for his second wife Theda Abby, and reared four children, Calvin, Susan, Ichabod and Philena. Alfred H., who was born in Lenox, Mass., December 30, 1808, came here in 1822, married first, Betsey Rich, who bore him one child, George R., and second, Eunice, daughter of John Rewey, of Newark Valley. Two children were born to them, John R., of this town, and Phœbe, who married Theodore Dykeman. Lebbeus Ford also came here from Lenox, in 1822, engaged as a blacksmith, and was for a long time the only blacksmith in town. He married Sarah W. Witler, and had born to him four children, namely, Marcus, Harriet H., William W., and one who died in infancy. William W. married Florence J., daughter of Sylvester Simmons, and has had born to him four children, as follows: Sarah W., Annie L., Harriet H. and Mary J.

Daniel P. Witler, son of Josiah, was born in Windham, Conn., moved to Homer, N. Y., in 1812, and came to Berkshire in 1833. He married Elizabeth, daughter of Samuel Humphrey, and reared nine children, viz: Asa, Betsey, Mary, John, Lester, Lucretia, Jasper, Daniel and Sarah. Of these only two are living, Jasper, of Dundaff, Penn., and Sarah, widow of Lebbeus Ford. Asa married Louisa, daughter of Ralph Collins, for his first wife, who bore him nine children, and for his second wife he married Delia, daughter of Samuel Torrey, and had born to him five children.

John F. Kimball was born in Scotland, Conn., in 1811, and came to Berkshire in 1835, locating on the farm where he now resides. He married Ruth, daughter of Maj. Peleg Ellis, of Dryden, and has three children, namely, James P., surgeon and major at West Point, Olive, and Grace (Mrs. Lorenzo J. Stannard).

John Bunnell came to this county, from Pike county, Pa. Henry J., one of his fourteen children, was born in December, 1803, married Eliza A. Livermore in 1828, and in 1830 he purchased and made the first settlement on the farm where he now resides. He has had born to him six children, viz.: John G., Charles A., deceased, William H., Mary E., Sarah, and James H., who died in infancy.

Erastus E. Humphrey, son of Roswell, was born in Canton, Conn., and moved to Speedsville, which was then a part of Tioga county, in 1812.

Frederick Shaff was born in Duchess county, in 1752, and came to this town to live with his son, who had been here since

1841. Mr. Shaff was 105 years of age when James Buchanan was elected president, and that was his last vote. He died in 1859, aged 107 years.

Joseph Walter, son of Elijah, moved to Newark Valley, from New Marlboro, Mass., in 1830. He married twice, first, Abigail Manley, and second, Hannah Schoonover. His son George was born in New Marlboro, and came to this county when only eight years of age. He married Martha, daughter of Joel Allen, of Caroline, N. Y., and in 1851 purchased and made the first clearing on the farm where he now resides.

Charles L. Mayor came here, from Switzerland, in 1849, and purchased the farm where his son Theodore now resides. He was a graduate of a medical college in Paris, practiced medicine a while in Switzerland, and also for eight years in Berkshire. In 1857 he returned to his native land for a visit, but was detained there by sickness, and died in 1863. He left four children, namely: Theodore, Dr. Edward A., of Owego, and Julia and Paul, who live in Switzerland. Theodore married Emma, daughter of Daniel Root, of Richford, and has two children, Jennie, wife of G. O. Steele, of Owego, and Charles D. The latter married Harriet, daughter of William Patch, and resides on the farm with his father.

Peter Youngs, son of Abram, was born in Marathon, August 28, 1827, and lived there until he was twenty eight years of age. He purchased and made the first settlement on the farm where he now lives, in March, 1857. He married for his first wife, Mary J., daughter of Reuben Smith, who bore him five children, viz.: Morris, Orson R., Annie, deceased, Frank W., and Jessie C. His wife died July 10, 1877, and he married for his second wife, Mary A. Higgins, of Caroline Center, N. Y., December 26, 1877.

William Shaw, son of Henry, was born in Charlton, N. Y., and came to this town in 1820, locating on the place where his son William T. now lives. He married Betsey Talmage, and reared five children, viz.: Lucy M., Elizabeth, William T., Henry B. and Hannah M.

George W. Northrop, son of Ebenezer G., was born in South Kingston, R. I., April 30, 1831, moved to Tioga county in 1842, and practiced medicine in Nichols where he lived six years. He lived in Richford some years. and came to Berkshire, where he now lives, in 1874. He served in the late war in Co. E, 76th N. Y. Vols., and in Co. F, 50th N. Y. Vols., and received an injury of the spine near Yellow Tavern, Va. For seven years he has not been able to stand.

Ezra Simmons was born in Little Compton, R. I., moved to Moravia, N. Y., in 1829, living there until March 17, 1834, when he moved to Newark Valley, and located on the farm now owned by T. S. Councilman, where he died. He married Anna Luther, and reared five children, viz.: Eliza, deceased, Joseph, of Newark Valley, Sylvester, of this town, Mary (Mrs. T. S. Councilman), and Abbie, widow of Seth Watson. Sylvester was born in Warren, R. I., October 9, 1818, married Mary J., daughter of Calvin Jenks, of Berkshire, and has five children, namely: Florence I., wife of William W. Ford, Emory A., of Owego, Sarah, wife of Anson W. Pake, William E., of this town, and Anna E., wife of V. W. Schooley, of Warwick, N. Y.

Organization.—Berkshire was known as "Brown Settlement" until 1808, when the territory comprising Richford, Berkshire and Newark Valley was formed from Owego (then called Tioga), and given the name it now bears, from Berkshire county, Mass. Newark Valley was formed from Berkshire April 12, 1823, under the name of Westville; and Richford was taken off, under the name of Arlington, April 13, 1831. These encroachments have left the town the smallest in the county. At the first town meeting, held Tuesday, March 1, 1808, Ebenezer Cook was moderator, and the following officers were chosen: John Brown, supervisor; Artemus Ward, town clerk; Esbon Slosson and Ebenezer Cook, assessors; Henry Moore and Elijah Belcher, poormasters; Noah Lyman, Hart Newell and Samuel Haight, commissioners; Peter Wilson, collector and poundmaster; Jesse Gleazen and Adolphus Dwight, constables; Asa Bement, Nathaniel Ford, Asa Leonard, John Bement, Lyman Rawson and Elisha Jenks, fence-viewers; Elisha Jenks, poundmaster.

BUSINESS CENTERS.

BERKSHIRE VILLAGE.—This neat, quiet little village, with its air of eminent respectability, is located upon the east branch of Owego creek, on the Southern Central railroad and near the center of the town. It consists of three general stores, one drug store, one hardware and furniture store, one harness-shop, one tailor-shop, one barber-shop, one shoe-shop, three blacksmith shops, two wagon-shops, one billiard room, one grist-mill, two saw-mills, one novelty works, one manufactory of wagon hubs and brewery shavings, two manufactories of beam-house knives, and one sole-leather tannery, and about 300 inhabitants.

The people of Berkshire and vicinity are justly proud of its beautiful and well-kept cemetery. Money and labor have not been spared in its care, and so impressed are the people of the northern part of the county that the cemetery organization is a permanent one, and that the grounds will ever be cared for, that the cemetery is being filled rapidly with dead of the northern part of this, and the adjacent portions of the three adjoining counties. Many of the soldier dead lie in this beautiful spot, and the Grand Army posts of this place, and also the one of Richford, strew these graves of their comrades with flowers, and hold appropriate exercises the 30th of each May. The Cemetery Association was organized iu 1867.

The first school was taught by David McMaster, in the shoeshop of Josiah Ball, and the shanty of Josiah Wilson. This early interest in educational matters has never flagged. The schools of Berkshire have enjoyed more or less celebrity. The district schools have received the support of the citizens generally, and select schools were popular and well patronized until the passage of the free school act. In 1845 Rev. William Bradford founded the Brookside Seminary, which soon passed into the hands of Rev. Frederick Judd, and became noted as a training school for boys, Nor was the school a local one. The students came from adjoining towns and counties, and not a few have attained prominence in fields of politics, literature, and the arts and sciences. One mile south of the village existed at one time, a boarding-school for young ladies, but its existence was short. There is at present in process of erection, a handsome two-story school building.

WILSON CREEK postoffice is located in the southern part of the town.

The Berkshire Tannery was built by S. & J. W. Leonard & Sons, in 1849. It was operated by water-power, and made upper-leather. On May 12, 1865, it was purchased by the present proprietors, Davidge, Horton & Co., who enlarged its capacity, and added steam-power. The tannery gives employment to forty hands, and turns out 40,000 sides of sole leather per annum.

John Ball's Saw-Mill was built by Deodatus Royce, in 1849, and purchased by Mr. Ball in 1851. It is operated by water-power, and cuts 300,000 feet of lumber per annum.

The Berkshire Flouring Mills, Leet & Hollenbeck, proprietors, was originally built by Judge David Williams, in 1818. The present building was erected by Mr. Williams, in 1839. It is operated by water-power, has three runs of stones, and grinds annually about 40,000 bushels of grain.

The Speedsville Creamery and Cheese Factory, located on road 18, was built by a stock company in 1868. The stock was subsequently bought in by John Higgins and Lyman Kingman, and in 1886 a half interest was bought by George R. Rounsevell. The milk of 400 cows is manufactured into butter and cheese annually.

M. A. Owen & Brother's Cooperage, on road 1, employs seven hands and turns out 10,000 butter tubs per year.

Sherwood & Horton's Hub Factory was established by Sherwood & Lamson, in 1882, and on the 10th of the following January the firm was changed to its present title. They employ thirty hands and turn out about 25,000 wagon hubs annually. In March, 1883, the manufacture of beer shavings was added, in which quite an extensive business is done.

Milo G. Japhet's Saw-Mill was built by C. B. Hemingway, in 1883, and was purchased by the present proprietors in 1885. He manufactures 500,000 feet of lumber, 400,000 chair rounds, 500,000 toy broom-handles, and 10,000 platforms for platform rocking-chairs per year, employing eight hands.

Military History.—Frederick Shaff, a soldier of the revolution, died here in 1860, at the advanced age of 107 years. Demas Orton a pensioner of the Mexican war died here in 1884, aged about 100 years.

Although the vicinity of Berkshire was not without its slave-holders at an early day, there existed a general and widespread opposition to this " peculiar institution " of the South for years preceding the rebellion, and the town was not without its members of the "underground railroad." Frederick Douglas and other slaves received substantial aid from this organization on their journey to Canada, Douglas having been a guest of the Hon. C. P. Johnson, an old abolitionist. Consequently, at the several calls for troops the town responded in men and money, the ladies assisting with hospital supplies. Charles R. Eastman and Earnest deVallier were the first to enlist, with Gen. Isaac Catlin, then Captain of Co. H., 3d N. Y. Infy.

The total call during the war was for 115 men from the town of Berkshire, which was filled by thirteen drafted, all of whom paid $300.00 each, by the enlistment of forty one men from abroad, and the balance enlisted from the town. Of this number, three deserted ; only nineteen are known to be living ; eighteen, or nearly twenty-eight per cent. were killed or died during their term of enlistment ; eighteen came home broken in health and died during the few succeeding years; the fate of sixteen is unknown ; and the balance are men whose health has suffered from exposure and hardships, whose best years were spent in the service of their country,—years which to most men decide their success in after life.

Church History.—The first church building, a barn-like structure, was located upon the farm of Dr. E. Mayor, and was then the only house of worship within the present limits of the county. Services were held morning and afternoon, with Sabbath-school in the interim. The congregation was composed of residents scattered over a large territory. The roads new and almost impassable. No little devotion was evinced by these pioneers who remained in this well-ventilated structure four or five hours with no fire except that afforded by the "foot-stove," an almost obsolete word to the present generation.

In 1817 a more pretentious church was built near the site of the former. The erection of the frame was the occasion of a demonstration, the like of which the valley had never seen. People came from a distance and remained three days, until the last timber was in place.

There are now three churches in the town,—the Congregational, the Methodist, at the village, and a Baptist church situated in the northwest corner of the town. The Congregational society has existed since the beginning of the present century. They worshiped in a building three miles below the village until the completion of the one now occupied, in December, 1834.

The society is a strong one and is in a prosperous condition, under the pastoral guidance of Rev. J. J. Hough. The Methodist church was organized in 1825, and in 1827 the present church building was erected, and the society, which has grown in strength and numbers, has in contemplation a handsome place of worship to be erected in the near future. Its present pastor is Rev. Mr. Beers.

———

CANDOR* the largest township in the county, lies in the central part of the same, and is bounded north by the county line, east by Berkshire, Newark Valley and a small part of

* Prepared by Rev. Charles C. Johnson, late of Candor, now of Sherburne, N. Y.

Owego, south by Tioga and west by Spencer and a small part of the county line. It originally formed a part of the Boston and Flint Purchase, the history of which has been detailed in the opening chapters of this work. Of this location there were taken to make the present town the whole of Township 12, the northeast and southeast section of Township 9, southeast section of Township 10, and south half of Township 11. Prior to the completion of this arrangement, certificates of location and certificates of survey had been granted in this town to John W. Ford, 350 acres, January 23, 1794, known as Ford Location; John Cantine, 800 acres, where Willseyville now is, and known as the Big Flatt, and another plat of 1,200 acres; to James Clinton 200 acres; Nathan Parshall, 200 acres, these latter having been granted March 7, 1792, and all located on the road leading from the mouth of the Owego river to the head of Cayuga lake. The town was set off from Spencer, February 22, 1811, and has an area of 51,334 acres, of which 33,572 acres is improved land.

The surface of Candor consists of high, broad, rolling uplands, separated into ridges by the valleys of streams flowing southerly. Its streams are the Catatonk, Doolittle, and Shendaken creeks. The Catatonk creek heads in a small marsh in the town of Spencer, and takes a southeasterly course of twenty miles, uniting with the Owego creek a short distance above its mouth. The valley along this creek varies from 2,000 to 3,000 yards in width. Shendaken creek enters the Catatonk at Booth Settlement. Doolittle creek is a small stream that joins the West Owego creek at Weltonville. The soil in the valleys consists generally of gravelly loam, and yields fine crops of wheat, corn, etc. The uplands are better adapted for grass than grain. The hills were originally mostly covered with hemlock and pine, and the valleys with heavy growths of pine, oak, beech and maple. In instances the pines have reached 175 feet in height and five feet in diameter, and immense quantities of lumber of fine quality have been manufactured and sent to market at an early day from this valley. The streams furnish abundant water privileges for manufacturing purposes, and saw-mills, grist-mills and tanneries have long been in active and extensive operation. The farms are largely used for dairying purposes, and the connections by the two railroads which cross the town, a history of which we have given in an earlier chapter, furnish ample opportunities for shipping.

Settlement and Growth.—That part of the Watkins and Flint

Purchase lying in the territory now designated as the town of Candor, was surveyed in 1793, by two men from Farmington, Conn. They were Capt. Joel Smith and Isaac Judd. Those who were thinking to settle here, selected lots of 104 acres each, for which they paid seven shillings per acre.

The deeds were made out in June of that year, after which four men with their families came on from Connecticut, following from Owego an Indian trail leading up the Cattatong (now Catatonk) valley. They were Elijah Smith, Collins Luddington, Thomas Hollister, and Job Judd, Sr. They halted at a spot near the present cemetery. Here the first trees were felled for actual settlement.

Indians of the Onondaga tribe had a fort on the bank of the the Catatonk creek, and also wigwams in the western part of the town. They were then friendly to the white settlers, though in previous years white captives were imprisoned in the fort. Some of these captives were ransomed and sent back to Wyoming, Pa., by Amos Draper, an Indian agent living where Owego now is.

These first settlers began at once to fell the forest trees and erect for themselves habitations. Thomas Hollister built his log cabin on the lot now occupied by the cemetery. Elijah Smith settled near by. Collins Luddington began clearing the forest adjacent to Elijah Smith; then moved down the trail, and cleared and built on the spot now marked by the home of Harvey Ward. Job Judd went farther down the stream, and began clearing on the farm which has since for many years been the homestead of John Kelsey. Mr. Judd had been a soldier in the revolutionary army. He moved in 1820 to Indiana.

Joseph Booth, of Farmington, Conn., purchased a lot for his son, Orange F. Booth, in 1793, and had it deeded to him. The boy was then twelve years of age. In 1801 he came on and settled on the farm, where he spent the remainder of his days. His six sons settled in Candor, three of whom, Dennis, Orange and Edwin A., are now living.

Another revolutionary soldier, Israel Mead, came in March, 1795, from Bennington, Vt., bringing his wife and five children with an ox-team and sled. He settled in the west part of the town, on the farm now owned by Mr. Schofield. His son, William Mead, was the first white child born in what is now the town of Candor.

Joel Smith, Jr., another soldier from the patriot army,

12*

brought his family of wife and five children from Connecticut in the spring of 1795. He was a captain in the 3d Connecticut regiment, served through the war of the revolution, being present at the surrender of Lord Cornwallis, in 1781. He surveyed a portion of this territory in 1793. So accurate was he as a surveyor, that his surveys are referred to even at this day, to settle landmarks and titles. He taught school in Candor and Owego, and is spoken of as an active, energetic man, methodical in all his business, and living to the advanced age of eighty seven years.

Elijah Hart and David Whittlesey came to the settlement here in the winter of 1794–95. They built a small grist-mill and a sawmill where the tannery and saw-mill of John Ryan recently stood. This first mill was burned in 1813. Abel Hart and his son, Capt. Abel Hart, Jr., came from Stockbridge, Mass., to Choconut, now Union, Broome county, in 1792 ; four years later Capt. Hart settled in Candor, building a plank house, which he enlarged by additions as need required. In this house religious meetings were held, and Capt. Hart having obtained a license to keep a public house, also opened it as an inn for travelers. His wife was Rachel Smeden, of Union, N. Y., by whom he had nine children. His son Abel, born September 23, 1814, married Louisa, daughter of Leonard Hall, of Danby, N. Y., by whom she has three children, viz.: George H., Adelaide A., wife of Amos Hixon, of Ithaca, and Lewis A., of Candor. George married Mary Carter, of Greene, N. Y., and has one son, Albert C. Lewis A., married Carrie, daughter of William Young, of Binghamton, N. Y., by whom he has two sons, A. Ralph and Harold Lester.

Thomas Hollister kept the first public house, in 1795. He also built the first log barn, and the first framed house. Bringing the seeds from Connecticut, he raised young apple trees, and set out the first orchard in the new settlement.

Settlements were made on the Big Flats in 1797, by Jacobus Shonich, and at Park Settlement by Capt. Daniel Park. Elisha Forsyth and Thomas Park. William Bates came from Owego in 1796 and settled on the road to Wilseyville. His wife died in Spencer, at the advanced age of 102 years. Capt. Eli Bacon and Seth Bacon settled here in 1798.

In 1802 Russel Gridley settled in the west part of the town, on the farm now owned by his grandson, William C. Gridley, on the old road to Spencer, north side of the creek. He built the first framed house on that road. The next year Selah Gridley, his father, came on from Farmington, Conn., and, with his son, purchased 1,900 acres of land. He was an ex-soldier of the revolution, serving on Washingtons's body-guard. He appeared always well dressed, in the mode of the day; long stockings and knee-breeches, shining shoe buckles, and three cornered hat. Equally precise in his speech, he won the name of " Deacon Slick." Russel Gridley moved over to the new road to Spencer, where he built a log house, leaving for several years the tree tops on the first course of logs.

In 1805 Jacob Clark came from Orange county and bought in the east part of the town the first farm sold from the Isaac Bronson purchase of 10,000 acres. His family came to the settlement with a team of horses. His brother, Samuel Clark, came a little before. The next summer he bought the farm now owned by his nephew, Hiram Clark. Their nearest neighbor to the north was in Caroline, and on the south at Owego creek. Three years later Elisha Johnson settled two miles south, and John Brown just north of them, while Walter Hamilton located near.

In 1806 a number of settlers with large families located at Crine's Corners, in the north part of the town. Among these were Elias Williams, John and Joseph White, Pearson Phillips and Daniel Bacon. At the age of eleven years Harvey Potter came to Candor, with Dea. Asa North. He became a prominent townsman, and for many years was an excellent leader of sacred music.

In 1810 Capt. Hart built a framed house, in which he lived and kept a public house for many years He augmented his business with a blacksmith shop, and being a public spirited man he erected and run a distillery—then supposed to be a necessity in any civilized community, as no family wished to be without ardent spirits. In those days women had practical acquaintance with the loom, so Capt. Hart built a house for weaving. In the looms of this " weave house" three grades of woolen cloth were manufactured, and linen cloth woven for bedding and for frocks. In 1806 Capt. Hart and Thomas Gridley built a saw-mill, farther up the creek, and lumber was soon plenty enough to give every log house a floor. Previous to sawed lumber, split logs were put down for flooring. These primitive log cabins were covered with a bark roof, supported by poles. Not unfrequently a large section of bark served as a door, and oiled paper admitted some light at the window. A few stones served as a fire-place, and an opening in the roof above them let out the smoke, and let in the daylight. Until fodder could be raised on the clearings, the cattle

subsisted on rations browsed from fallen tree tops. A few potatoes were early raised, and abundant deer in the forest furnished
venison. Bears disputed with men the possession of the few
swine they brought with them, and wolves made sheep hus
bandry a precarious industry. Aleck Graham proved himself a
mighty hunter, killing the bears and trapping the wolves. Grain
was carried a long distance to mill, or bruised in a hard-wood
stump, hollowed out for a mortar. A yard of calico print sold
for one dollar, and a bushel of oats sufficed to pay for a pound of
nails.

In 1805 the sons of Bissel Woodford came from Farmington,
Conn. Chauncey and Ira settled at West Candor, and Cyrus in
Spencer. Their cousins, Truman, Ozias and Sylvester Woodford also settled in town. Ebenezer Lake came in 1813, and Elijah
Blinn, Beri Strong and other neighbors formed the Blinn settlement, in 1814. Hon. Jacob Willsey from Fairfield, Herkimer
county, gave his name to Willseyville, in 1815. The Woodbridge
families settled in the southern part, and John Kelsey in 1818.

Mr. Lewis, the father of Thomas N. Lewis, bought 1,000 acres
of the Watkins and Flint Purchase, but never lived in this region.
In 1825 Jonathan B. Hart his nephew, came here from Connecticut as his agent. For many years he was the undertaker of the
town, and was prominently identified with the earlier Sunday
school interest in the community.

At an early date there were twenty two taverns on the road
from Ithaca to Owego. This turnpike was established on an Indian
trail in 1808. In 1797 a turnpike from Catskill Landing on the
Hudson river, was opened as far as the town of Catharine. Over
this for many years were drawn supplies of iron, tin, dry goods
and implements. The first store was kept by Philip Case, near
the location of the North Candor station of the E., C. & N. R. R.
Daniel Olivet taught the first school, in 1797. Joel Smith also
taught school, and was the first justice of the peace. Dr. Horatio
Worcester was the first physician. Horatio Durkee, came from
Meredith, N. H., and built the first tannery, on the site now
occupied by the woolen factory of Capt. Barager. Another
tannery was afterward built, by John Ryan and Hiram Smith;
the Estey tannery much later. After the disastrous fire which
swept the settlement in 1813, Caleb Sackett erected a grist-mill,
which was succeeded by a better one built by John Kirk and Mr.
Tryon. A woolen-mill was erected in 1824, by the brothers Artemus and Isaac V. Locey. This mill was sold to Joseph Mathews

in 1838. Isaac V. Locey manufactured wool-carding machinery for a series of years.

Charles Frederick Barager was the youngest of eleven children, and the seventh son born to Samuel Barager and Ruhamah Sears. His father, Samuel Barager, descended from the Holland Dutch, and was born in Albany County, N. Y., in 1793. He served in the war of 1812, and for his services in said war received a land warrant for 160 acres of government land, and before he died he was placed upon the U. S. pension rolls, and after his death the pension was continued to his widow during her life. At the close of the war, in 1814, he married Ruhamah Sears, and the year following, 1815, they came into the wilderness of Tioga county, and settled in the town of Candor. The name of Samuel Barager is inseparably connected with the history of Tioga county and the town of Candor. On his arrival at his new home he taught school, and as the sparse population learned his worth they placed him in offices of trust. For many years he was supervisor of his town, and in 1829 was sent to the legislature as a member of assembly, and was the colleague of Millard Fillmore. On his return home from Albany, he was elected justice of the peace, and many times was elected associate judge. As the population increased, he grew in its esteem, and from far and near " Judge Barager " was referred to as the arbitrator of nearly every difficulty, the judge of nearly every dispute. In his official capacity he always advised friendly settlement. and when litigation could not be avoided the confidence of his neighbors in him and his judgment was such that an appeal therefrom was seldom taken, and when it was taken never reversed. He held office for over half a century consecutively, and died in the harness of public service, in April, 1871, full of years and good deeds, and the large concourse of truly mourning friends who followed his remains to the grave, attested his usefulness by asking the question " Where can we find one to fill his place?"

Mr. Barager's mother, Ruhamah Sears, was directly descended from Richard Sears, who came from England in 1620. Her father was Daniel Sears, who came to Albany county in 1793, from near Danbury, Conn. Her father, Daniel, and her grandfather, Knowles Sears, served in the war of the revolution, the former as private, and the latter as captain. The mother of Ruhamah Sears was Catharine Warren, at whose home General Washington and staff often stopped, near Danbury, Conn. Ruhamah was born in Albany county, in 1796. She inherited the devoted, industrious and frugal nature so proverbial of her New England ancestry, so much so that her home duties and devotion to her family, and services and charity to her neighbors absorbed her life. Mentally she was remarkably clear and comprehensive. Religiously she was the embodiment of true piety. She was the true wife and the devoted mother, and no more expressive words can be said of her than her appreciative children had chiseled upon her monument in the cemetery in Candor, where she was buried in April, 1878, "Dear Mother, we still look up to thee."

Charles Frederick Barager was born in Candor, December 5, 1838. His boyhood was devided between the district school, the old homestead farm, and the "sports of the village green." Ambitious to know more of the world than could be learned in the quiet village of his birth, he started in the fall of 1859 for a trip through the South. He spent nearly a year in St. Tammany Parish, La., and returned home in the fall of 1860, satisfied, for the time being, with travel. He entered a select school and with renewed energy applied himself to the task of completing his education. But in the spring of 1861 the alarm of war filled the land, and fresh from witnessing the crime of slavery, and filled with indignation, because it existed in our country boasting of its wonderful freedom, he dropped his books and enlisted under the first call for troops, May 21, 1861. He was chosen first lieutenant by his company, which was Co. K., and it was assigned to the 26th N. Y. Vols. With this regiment he only served a few months, and returned home and raised another company, which was Co. H., 137th regiment. Of this company he was chosen captain, and with it he served during the war. At Gettysburg, on the evening of July 2, 1863, he was ordered by General Green to take his command and advance from Culps Hill and engage the advancing skirmish line of the enemy. The rebels were in such force that he was driven back to the light line of earth works from which he started, but in the engagement he was wounded and carried from the field. He was also wounded in the battle of Peach Tree Creek, Ga. He was engaged in the battles of Chancellorsville, Va., Gettysburg, Pa., Peach Tree Creek, Ga., Wauhatchie, Tenn., Lookout Mountain and seige of Atlanta, besides many minor engagements and skirmishes. With impaired health he was mustered out of the service at the close of the war and returned to his home, and as soon as his health would permit he again turned his attention to the acquirement of knowledge, and in 1867 he entered the Albany Law University,

Charles F. Barager

from which he graduated and was admitted to the bar in 1868. While in search of an inviting place to practice his profession in the Southwest, he became interested in the blackwalnut lumber business in Missouri and Illinois, and from that he engaged in other business enterprises, and finally abandoned his profession altogether. He grew oranges in Florida, was a merchant in the Red river valley of the north, and a lumberman on the shores of Lake Superior. In 1876 he returned to the old homestead, in his native village, to be with his aged mother and to give her that supreme satisfaction of spending her last days under the old roof which had sheltered her in joy and sorrow for so many years. Not wishing to be idle he purchased the Candor Woolen Mills, and operated them with such vigor and success that in 1880 and 1881 he built a new mill, all of which he is now running. He was always an active Republican, but it was not until 1879 that he became a candidate for office, in which year he was elected supervisor of his town, redeeming it from Democratic rule. He declined to become a candidate the second time; he also declined the use of his name for office again, until 1883 he was persuaded to become the candidate for member of assembly, in his native county of Tioga. In 1882, and for the first time in more than twenty years, the Democrats elected the member in Tioga county, and to recover the lost ground Captain Barager was unanimously placed in the field and was elected by nearly four hundred majority. He was re-elected in 1884. In the assembly of 1884 and '85 he served upon many important committees, and also served upon the special committee to investigate the armories and arsenals of the State. He was appointed one of the committee of the legislature to accompany the remains of General Grant from Albany to New York, and to attend his funeral in that city August 8, 1885. In 1885 he was elected senator of the 26th senatorial district, by over 3,000 majority. During his term as senator he was chairman of the committee on poor laws and state prisons, and served upon other important committees. The convention of his county, July 15, 1887, unanimously recommended him for re-nomination, and allowed him to select the delegates to the senatorial convention.

In the year 1867 Captain Barager married Mary Markell, who is directly descended from the French Captain Markell, who was with M. De Montcalm at the seige of Quebec. And Major Andrew Fincke, who was assigned by General Washington aid-de-camp to General La Fayette, on his arrival in this country, was her great-uncle. Among her nearer ancestry are the Markells, who early settled in the Mohawk Valley, some of whom were John, Jacob and Henry Markell, who served as judges, members of the legislature, and of Congress. They have had born to them four children. The eldest, Charles F., Jr., died in 1879. The living ones are Ruhamah Sears, Samuel Frank, and Vida Mary.

Elijah Smith, one of the early settlers of Candor, came to this town about 1790, and made the first settlement on the farm now owned by Amzi Smith, where he built the first framed house in the town. The building is still standing, though not now occupied as a dwelling. He purchased 200 acres, a portion of which is still owned by his grandchildren. He reared a family of six children, four of whom were sons, namely: Selah, Jesse, James, and Amzi. The last mentioned married Julia Potter, whose people were also early settlers of the town, and had born to him five children, as follows: Lucius, John, Philemon, Caroline, and Harriet, all of whom are living.

Ezra Smith came from Westchester county, and was one of the early settlers at Willseyville. He located upon the farm now owned by Morgan White, where he resided until his death, in 1818. He married Anna Cooley, who bore him four children, Waterbury, Jesse D., Hiram, and Ogden, all of whom located in that vicinity, and reared families. The eldest, Waterbury, and father of Wakeman B., of Candor village, was born in 1793, married twice—Abigail Bradley, who bore him one son, Wakeman, and second, Polly Coburn, who died without issue. Waterbury died in 1848, aged fifty-five years. Wakeman B., born in 1817, married Emeline Barager, in 1841, and has four children, Mary C., Delphine, Fred B., and William B.

Jared, son of Joel and Lydia Smith, came with his parents from Connecticut, in 1795, and settled on the farm now occupied by Henry Smith, which farm they cleared. He married Sarah Ward, December 31, 1822. There were born to them four children, viz.: Angeline E., wife of David Burleigh, of Ithaca, Mary S., wife of D, H. Coon, of Montrose, Pa., Charles O., of Waverly, and Henry G., who now resides on the homestead. The latter married Rosa, daughter of Merritt N. Way, of Candor, in 1862, and has three children, Harry L., Sadie and Eva.

Abel Galpin came from Stockbridge, Mass., about 1790, and made the first settlement on the place now owned by Asa Phelps. He married Mary Wright and reared thirteen children. Simeon, son of Abel, was five years of age when they came to Candor.

He married Jane Taylor, and had born to him five children, as follows ; Samuel, Jasper, James, Abel F. and Jane, wife of Alexander Henderson. Benjamin Galpin was born in 1790, married Martha, daughter of Levi Williams, an early settler, and reared seven children, six of whom grew to maturity, viz.: Jerusha, Franklin, Mary, William, Fanny M. and Ann E. Caleb Galpin married Fannie, daughter of James Brink, and reared the following children: Elisha, James, Martha, Polly, John, Ameck, Calvin and Caleb W. Elisha married Jerusha, daughter of Benjamin Galpin, and eleven children were born to them, namely, Martha A., Ezra, Mary L., Susan, Wealthy, Cordelia, Francis, Stephen D., Franklin P., Myron E. and Mary E

Hiram Williams came from Connecticut in 1795, and made the first settlement on the farm now owned by his grandson, William I. Williams. This place is known as Ford's Location, Mr. Ford having received 350 acres for his services as surveyor. Mr. Williams married Abigail Ford, who bore him six children, as follows: Betsey, Sally, Nancy, Eunice, Alfred and Ira. Alfred married Esther Lane, and reared six children, viz. : Susan, Mary, Pluma, Tracy, William I. and Edgar. Of these William I., who is the only one living, resides on the homestead. He married a daughter of Stephen Gaskill, and has two children, Frank, of Clay Center, Kan., and Carrie, wife of Philander G. White, of Hoboken, N. J.

Levi Williams, an early settler, married Jerusha, daughter of Zephaniah White, and reared six children—Joel, Martha, Stephen, Lewis, Anna and Uzal.

Daniel Bacon was one of the first to make a clearing in the town, locating with Thomas Hollister on the ground where the Candor cemetery now is, as we have shown. They spent the summer here, and returned to Connecticut, where they remained a year. The following year Daniel, Seth, Eli and John F. Bacon, brothers, came here, the first three locating on road 97. John F. first settled in what is now Danby, but remained there only a few years, when he came back to Candor, locating on the same road as his brothers. He married Sarah Galusha, of Salisbury, Conn., and reared six children, viz. : Abigail, Sarah, Alma, Mary, John G., and Cynthia D., only one of whom, John G., is living. The latter was born in Danby, December 29, 1805, married Mary, daughter of Samuel Hull, and has had born to him four children —George, John J., Cynthia, and one who died in infancy. Of these George G. is the only one living. He married Flavia L., daughter of Sterling J Barbour, and has one child, Mary Belle. Daniel Bacon, son of Seth, was born in Woodbury, Conn., and came to Candor in 1805. He was for a long time colonel of state militia, was a millwright and a civil engineer. He married Susan, daughter of Capt. Jesse Smith, of Candor, and reared five children—Esther, Seth, Theodore, Harvey and Eloise. Of these, three are living, Seth, of New London, Ia., and Harvey and Eloise, of Candor.

Jasper Taylor, one of the early settlers in the eastern part of the town, came about 1795, locating in Weltonville. He had served in the revolution. He married Maria Edmunds, and reared eleven children, viz.: Samuel, Jane, Levi, Jared, James, Calvin, Jasper, Luther, Robert, Maria and Catherine, all deceased. Jasper was born in Candor, in 1806, married Catherine, daughter of Charles Blewer, and had born to him three children, Mary, Samuel E. and William. The first saw-mill in Weltonville was built by this family.

Joseph Schoonover, son of Benjamin, first located on the farm now owned by Samuel Barrett. He was elected one of the first officers of the town, in 1811. He married Elizabeth Decker, and ten children were born to them, viz.: David, Ira, Daniel, Fayette, Franklin, Lydia, Hannah, Simeon, Jacob and Elias. The last mentioned was born in Candor, January 5, 1812, married Mary, daughter of Reuben Chittenden, of Newark Valley, and reared nine children, as follows: Eudora, Oscar, Corolyn, Sarah, Olive, Mary, Lola, Joseph and Chloe. Of these, only four are living, Eudora, wife of James Miller, of Kirkwood, N. Y., Oscar, of Woodstock, Ia., Corolyn, wife of S. J. Northrup, of Montrose, Pa., publisher of the *Montrose Sentinel*, and Sarah, wife of B. R. Van Scoy.

Caleb Hubbard was an early settler, first locating on the farm now owned by William H. and John F. Hubbard, in 1805. He was a carpenter by trade and built many of the early houses in the town. He married Mary Hull, and seven children were born to them, namely, George, Achilles, Editha, Joseph, Mary, Caleb, and Phœbe. Editha, wife of Pinkey Clark, of Green Springs, and Phœbe, wife of Luther B. Wright, of Portage, O., are the only ones living. George Hubbard married Sophronia, daughter of Isaac Judd, and had born to him four children,—William H., John F., Sarah and Eliza S., wife of Z. R. Easton. William H. married three times, first, Maria R., daughter of Daniel Hart, who bore him two children, Frances M. and Ella H., both deceased; second, Mary E. Hart, a sister of his first wife, who also bore him two children, Frances, wife of T. S. Booth, and Mary S., deceased; and third, Elibbie N., daughter of Joel H. Strong, and has had born to him two children, George W. and Mertie E., both residing at home. John F. married Maria, daughter of Rev. Gaylord Judd, and resides in Denver, Col. Sarah married Rev. Charles W. Judd, and together spent eighteen years as missionaries in India. Eliza S., daughter of George Hubbard, married Zenas R. Easton, of Delphi, and has five children, namely, Sarah F., George H., Charles J., Frederick R. and Wilbert A. Achilles married Marilla Hubbard, by whom he had four children, viz.: Albert C., of Candor, Asa A., deceased, Harriet, (Mrs. George Nelson, of Caroline) deceased, Mariette, wife of Gran Tier, of Potter county, Pa. Albert C. married Mary, daughter of William Shroop, of Candor, by whom he has four children,— Addie, wife of Henry M. Jewett, of Catatonk; George W., of Candor; William W., of Fairport, N. Y.; and Frank, who resides with his father. Mary, daughter of Caleb, married Northrup Edmunds, and had one child, Caleb W., who now resides in Candor. The latter married Laura E., daughter of Orton Johnson, of Candor, and has one child, Cora J.

Charles Henderson was born in Onondaga county, married Lydia Ray, and made the first settlement on the farm now owned by Nelson J. Galpin.

Ahira Anderson, a native of Connecticut, came to Candor, from Vermont, about 1810, and located on the farm now owned by Philander Anderson, on Anderson Hill. He was a tanner by trade, married Martha, daughter of Daniel Andrews, and had born to him ten children, eight of whom grew to maturity, viz.: Chester, Johnson, Marshall, Almira, who married Lewis Pultz, Daniel, Mary, who married Andrew Carman, Amarilla, and Charlotte, who married Amzi Prichard. Of these, Amarilla, widow of John Wolverton, is the only one living. Daniel married Fidelia Frisbee, and reared six children—Mary, Chester, Charlotte, Ezra, Frederick, and Edwin S. Johnson married Annice Preston, of Wallingford, Vt., and reared six children, as follows: Charles, LeRoy, Sylvenus, Emily, Fidelia, Joel and Philander. The last mentioned was born in this town, married Rebecca Andrews, and has had born to him four children, Eva A., wife of Fred A. Blewer, of Weltonville, Carrie L., Mary B., deceased, and Frank L,, deceased. Mr. Anderson resides on the homestead where he was born. Marshall Anderson married

Hannah Harris, and had born to him eight children, viz.: James, Stephen, Mariette, Eliza, John, and three who died young. Charles LeRoy, son of Johnson Anderson, was born in Candor, June 13, 1820, married twice; first, Mary A., daughter of Jacob Shaw, and second, Cordelia, daughter of Elisha Galpin. Three children were born to him, Charles A., deceased, Ezra L., and one who died in infancy.

Miles Andrews, son of Jesse, came to this town from Wallingford, Vt., in 1810, making the first settlement on the farm now owned by Philander Anderson. He was a soldier of the war of 1812, married Electa, daughter of Asa Warner, and reared five children, namely: Levi R., Philetus, David W., George W. and Electa. Levi was born in Candor, January 16, 1821, married Julia, daughter of Thomas Barden, and five children were born to them, viz.: Asa, Mary A., wife of Thomas Gaige, Thomas, Romeo, and Franklin. David, son of Miles, married Theresa, daughter of Charles C. Howard, and the following children have been born to him: George F., Charles, Elmer, and Laura. Jonathan Andrews, brother of Jesse, came here from Wallingford, Vt, in 1810, and made the first settlement on the farm now owned by Joel Anderson. After living here several years, he moved to Newark Valley. He married Betsey Aldrich, and had born to him twelve children. His son Daniel married Lucinda, daughter of Lewis Pult, and reared seven children, viz.: Eliza, Lewis, Rebecca, wife of Philander Anderson, Johnson, of Newark Valley, Betsey, deceased, Heman and Ezra, of Newark Valley.

Dr. Elias Briggs came from Massachusetts about 1810, and settled in Weltonville, where he practiced medicine for thirty-five years. He married Ruby Stebbins, by whom he had three children who arrived at maturity, viz.: Lyman, Ursula, and Mary L., who now resides in the village of Candor. Dr. Briggs died in 1850.

Lewis J. Mead, son of Lewis, was born in New Jersey, married Jane Ellston, and came to this town about 1827, locating on West Owego creek, upon the farm now owned by Russell J. He reared six children, viz.: Elizabeth, Russell J., Asa E., Alanson, Sarah J., deceased, and William.

Ezekiel Mead moved to Wayne county, Pa., from New Jersey, married Abigail Owen, and located in Owego in 1802, on the farm now owned by John B. Brownell. He had born to him six children, viz.: Benjamin, Joshua, George, Lewis, Aseneth, and Sarah. Joshua, who was two years of age when he came to Owego, has been engaged in farming and lumbering, married Abigail, daughter of Henry Lewis, of Colchester, N. Y., and has seven children, Abel, Halloway, Edward, William H., Charles, Riley, and Ezekiel.

David P. Mead was born in Groton Hollow, August 28, 1815, and came to Tioga county in 1867, locating in Candor village, where he has carried on the business of wagon making. He married Mary P. Green, September 25, 1843, who has borne him three children, Howard J., John G., and Emma K. (Mrs. Martin Willsey). The eldest, Howard J., studied law with Lyons & Donelly, of Ithaca, and graduated at the Albany Law School in 1873, and is now of the law firm of Mead & Darrow, of Owego. He has served as district attorney six years.

Cornelius Cortright was one of the first settlers in the eastern part of the town, came from Delaware county, and in 1805 made the first settlement on the farm now owned by Samuel Cortright. He married Phœbe Decker in Delaware county, and both made the journey here on horseback, Mrs. Cortright holding their son, Simeon, who was then only five years of age, in her arms. Ten children were born to them, viz.: Simeon, Jacob, Eleanor, James, Levi, Lyman, Edward, Phœbe, Margaret and Samuel. Simeon married Mary, daughter of George Lane, and reared twelve children, as follows: George, Henry, deceased, James F., Eliza A., wife of Levi Blewer, Margaret, deceased, Phœbe A., wife of William G. Blackman, Jane, widow of Hollister Wright, Sarah A., wife of Van Debar Baker, of Owego, Maria, wife of George Burt, Elsie, wife of Henry Davison, of Newark, Lucy B., wife of D. O. Manning, of Dryden, and Mary G., wife of John Van Demark. James, son of Cornelius, was born January 18, 1809, married Esther, daughter of Henry Jacobs, and nine children were born to him, six of whom are living, viz.: Charles, John, Hulda M., Augusta, Augustus and Alvah.

Walter Herrick, born in Duchess county, March 9, 1781, was one of the early settlers in the eastern part of this town, locating in Weltonville, on the farm now owned by his son Walter, in 1806. He married Minerva, daughter of Dr. Stephen Hopkins, of Athens, and reared nine children, viz.: Edward, Charles, Celestia, wife of E. P. Miller, of Tunkhannock, Pa., Harriet, Maria, Stephen, Eliza, Minerva, wife of Jesse Phelps, of Flemingville, and Walter.

Nathaniel Ketchum came from North Hebron, Washington county, N. Y., about 1815, and located near Flemingville, in

the town of Owego, where he engaged in farming. He married
Aseneth, daughter of Lewis Mead, of Owego, by whom he had
seven children, viz.: Ezekiel, Eleanor, wife of Israel Johnson, of
Candor, Joseph B., Henry, of Spencer, Sarah, wife of James C.
Hannible, of Washington county, William P., of Candor, and
Julia, wife of Henry Woodard, of Michigan. William P. married
Lany S. Ivory, of Jacksonville, Tompkins county, N. Y , Jan-
uary 7, 1863, by whom he has had six children, viz.: Emma, wife of
Dey Rhodes, of Moravia, N. Y., Willie A. and Mary A. (twins),
Daniel J., Charles H., and Jessey, who died at the age of two
years and seven months.

Sylvester Woodford came to this town, from Farmington,
Conn., in 1805, and made the first settlement on the farm now
owned by his son Sylvester. He married Diana Tillotson, and
reared five children, namely, George, Luther, Chauncey T., Eliza,
widow of Elbert Judson, of Danby, and Sylvester. Ozias, brother
of Sylvester, came here at the same time, and settled where H.
W. Loring now lives. They made the journey with an ox-team,
arriving here about the middle of March. Church service was
held for a long time in Sylvester's barn. Sylvester, Jr., was
married twice; first, Jane, daughter of John Dykeman, of New
Milford, Pa.,who bore him two children, Frank S. and Jennie (Mrs.
Charles Fiebig); and second, Martha J. Barto. His son Frank
S. married Jennie Deyo, and has two children, Fred and Charles.
Luther married Rhoda Potter, and reared four children, namely,
Mary, wife of O. L. Ross, of Owego, Louise M., Diana and
Florence.

Chauncey Woodford, son of Bissel, was born in Farmington,
Conn., October 14, 1782, married Nancy, daughter of Asa North
November 21, 1803, and came to this town in 1805. He made
the first settlement on the farm now owned by his sons, Elbert
and George. He came first in 1804 and built a rude log house,
into which he moved his family. They were troubled by wild
animals, which were very numerous at this time, and all were
obliged to keep their sheep in pens. Truman Woodford, Ira
Woodford, James North and Manna Hart also came from Farmington, and at about the same time. Bissel Woodford came about
1825, and spent his last days with his children. He was a revolutionary soldier, and died September 3, 1835, aged eighty-one
years. Six children were born to Chauncey Woodford, namely,
Asahel, Emily, widow of Hiram Smith, of Lansing, Mich., Diana,
who married Ogden Smith, Loisa, widow of Joseph Mathews, of

Binghamton, Elbert C. and George. Elbert C. was born January 8, 1823, married Sarah, daughter of Wright Dunham, of Nichols, and has two children, E Jerome and Emma T. (Mrs. C. N. Day), of Spencer. George Woodford was born April 3, 1826, married Mary, daughter of William Loring, and has three children, Asahel H., Adelaid M. (Mrs. Charles F. Andrews), of Newark Valley, and Charles G., who is engaged in the First National Bank, at Owego.

Timothy C. Reed was born February 14, 1814, near Penobscot, Me., and came with his parents to Candor when but two years of age. For thirty two years Candor village was his home. He was engaged in farming twenty-five years in West Newark, where he had a farm of one hundred and fifty acres. Here on May 3, 1836, he married Sarah J., daughter of William Richardson. She was born June 8, 1817, and now resides in Ross street, Owego, to which she came with her husband when he retired from farm life in 1874. Mr. Reed died April 1, 1882. Their children are Frances D., born June 25, 1837, married S. O. Hayward, of Buffalo ; Herbert B., born July 27, 1839, now living in Mount Morris, N.Y.; Sarah J., born December 16, 1845, married John L. Taylor, of Owego ; and Mary T. born May 20, 1849, married J. A. Willey, of Freeville, N. Y.

Henry Hover was born in Delaware, Pa., October 8, 1791, and came to Candor at the age of fifteen years. He married Hannah Van Gorder, and reared ten children. He died at Weltonville, June 10, 1877, aged about ninety six years.

Solomon Hover came to this town, from Delaware county, in 1807, and made the first settlement on the farm now owned by Benjamin Hover. He married Peggy Bolton, and reared ten children,viz.: Joseph, Elijah, Eleanor, Benjamin, Lodwick,Gilbert, Solomon, Katy, Henry and Sally. Of these Solomon and Henry are the only ones now living.

Solomon Vergason came here from Standing Stone, near Towanda, Pa., in 1808, and made the first settlement on the farm now owned by Seth Hammond. His son David, who was only seven years of age when they came, married Susan, daughter of Iddo Cass, and six children were born to them, namely, Stephen, Solomon, George, Iddo, Adelaide, and one who died in infancy.

Samuel Hull, son of George Hull, Jr , and a lineal descendant of George Hull, who came from England in 1630 and settled in Dorchester, Mass., was born June 15, 1755, married Freelove Kelsey, June 20, 1781, and reared twelve children, viz.: Jonas,

James, Samuel, Lebbeus, Russell, Electa, Hubbard, Pheobe, Curtis, Catharine, Alanson and Hannah. Mr. Hull came to Candor in 1809, and made the first settlement on the farm now owned by his grandson, Nathan T. Hull. Samuel, Jr., was born July 9, 1785, married Sabrina Teall, and had born to him nine children, as follows: James B., Clarissa R., Mary, Lydia M., Samuel, Catharine A., Henry H., Nathan T., and Elizabeth S. Nathan T. was born October 14, 1824, married Ada M., daughter of Daniel Oakley, and six children were born to them, only three of whom are living, namely, Elizabeth G. (Mrs. Hiram Henderson), Mary J. (Mrs. Charles Perkins), of Bradford, Pa., and Daniel O.

George Douglass, came from Ireland, and made the first settlement on the farm now owned by William Douglass, in 1812. He reared three children, John, Charles and Jane. John married Emerancy, daughter of Caleb Cass, and had born to him six children, viz: Caleb, George, John, Mary, Emma J. and Olin. Charles married Julia, daughter of Sylvester White, and reared four children, Mary, Maria, Roxy and William. Jane married Robert Duff, and two children were born to them, George and Sarah.

Reuben Fletcher was one of the early settlers in the western part of the town. He came from Moravia, and made the first settlement on the farm now owned by Laura Crum.

Osgood Ward was born in New Hampshire, married Hannah Huggins, and came to Candor, from Kingston, Ont., in 1812. He lived several years on the place where Harvey Cowles now lives, and was the father of ten children, viz: Sarah, Nelson, Cynthia, Mary, Charles, Warren, Harvey, Adeline, Eliza and Hiram. Hiram was born at Kingston, January 16, 1802, came here with his father, married Adaline, daughter of William Stanley, and ten children were born to him, viz: Elmina, Susan, Stanley, Charles, deceased, Adelaide, Oscar, Cynthia, Mary, Helen and Sarah. Susan lives in Berlin, Wis., Stanley lives in South Danby, and the others reside in Candor.

John J. McIntyre, son of Samuel, was born in Washington, Vt., September 5, 1795, and came to Candor in October, 1813, with a yoke of cattle and a span of horses for his uncle, Ephraim Jones. He made the first settlement on the farm now owned by Theron Kyle. He went back to Vermont, and returned to this town the following winter with his father and family, and has lived here since that time. He married Betsey Williams, in

February, 1817, and has had born to him seven children, six of whom are living.

James Ross came to this town from Barkhamsted, Conn., in 1814. He married Sally Case, and the following children were born to him, Ralph, Ratus, Flavel, Alvira, Lester, Harry, Lydia, Edmund and Agnes.

Daniel Cowles and his son Rufus came to Candor, from Farmington, Conn., in 1809, and made the first settlement on the farm now owned by Mr. Ross. They were both brick and plaster masons. Daniel and Eunice (North) Cowles had five children born to them, namely, Rufus, Romeo, Shubael, George and Horace. Mr. Cowles died in 1870, aged seventy-nine years. Rufus married Rebecca, daughter of James Curran, of Spencer, and had eight children born to him, viz : Eunice, Emeline, Melinda, Daniel, James, Horace, and two who died young. Daniel and James are the only ones now living. James C. married Helen, daughter of Hiram Ward, and has two children, Wallace J. and Nellie L. Romeo married Sally, daughter of Hiram Williams, and reared nine children, five of whom are living, viz.: Angeline, wife of Jesse H. Smith, Sarah, wife of Morris Humiston, Mary, wife of Jesse N. Sackett, of Great Bend, J. Harvey and Harriet (Mrs. Charles F. Jewett).

Isaac Comstock, came to Candor, from Smithfield, R. I. He purchased a tract of land, consisting of 400 acres, on West Owego Creek, in 1820.

Captain William Scott came to this town, from Adams, Mass., in 1820. He made the first settlement on the farm now owned by Jonas S. Foster, his adopted son.

Joel C. Strong located in this town about 1825 or 1830, coming here from Duanesburg, and made the first settlement on the farm now owned by his son Charles S. He married twice, first, Ann Lake, who bore him one child, Martha A., widow of Hezekiah Whitmore, of Newark Valley, and second, Olive Lake, who bore him five children, viz : Mary, wife of Julian Clinton, of Newark Valley, Josiah, Munson, Charles S. and Olive J., deceased.

Beri Strong came to Candor, from Duanesburg, in the spring of 1816, and made the first settlement on the farm now owned by Robert Barden. He married Elizabeth Hatch, and had born to him eight children, viz.: Lewis, Hebron, Solomon T., Isaac B., Curtis B., Hannah A., Silas H., and Orrin. Hebron Strong married Irene, daughter of Benjamin Patch, and four children were

13*

born to him, of whom only two are living, Anson B., and Wesley H.

Daniel Lounsbury, son of Timothy, was born in Bethany, Conn., and located in Tioga in 1816, on the farm opposite the old cemetery near Tioga Center. He lived there about ten years, years, then moved to Candor, and settled on the farm owned by George and E. C. Woodford. He married Sarah, daughter of Alanson Wooding, of Bethany, and reared five children, viz.: Janet, Laura, David W., Daniel and Lucy. Of these, three are living, Janet, widow of John J. Harlen, David W., who is engaged in lumbering at Ettenville, and Daniel, of this town. The latter married Philinda, daughter of George Tuttle, and has one child, Lois E. Mr. Tuttle came here in 1833, and located on the farm now owned by Warren H. Tuttle. Lois E. married Frank E. Dewey, and they have one child, Homer.

Abel Owen came here from Trumansburg, in 1821, and made the first settlement on the farm now owned by Abel C. Owen. He married Millesent Robinson, and had born to him four children, Sarah M., Daniel R., Emeline Corson, and Abel C.

Jonathan Hart, son of William, was born in New Briton, Conn., August 25, 1800, married Elvira Humiston, of Plymouth, Conn., and came to Candor in 1825, locating on the place where he now lives. He was engaged in the furniture and undertaking business here for forty-eight years. When he was twenty years of age he joined the Congregational church of New Haven, since which time he has been an active member of both church and Sunday school. In 1822 he joined the order of Free Masons, and was an active member in Mount Olive Lodge. He organized Candor Lodge, No. 411, June 18, 1856, and worked under a dispensation until July 22, 1857, when they received a charter from the Grand Lodge, and he was elected the first master.

Charles Dennis came to Candor, from Otsego county, in March, 1826, and located on the farm now owned by Daniel Knapp. He married Emma Hoyt, and reared seven children, only two of whom are living, Edmund and Alfred.

Josiah Hatch came here from Duanesburg, in March, 1823, and made the first settlement on the farm now owned by Charles Strong. He married Polly, daughter of Solomon Doty, and had born to him five children, only two of whom grew to maturity, Elsie B., wife of Russel Mead, and Parker.

Stoughton S. Downing, son of John, was born in Lincoln, Vt., June 20, 1818, came to Candor in 1837, and married Jane, daughter of Daniel Searles. He has four children, namely, Jay S., Lincoln L., Ray M. and Della A.

Mansfield Bunnell, son of Solomon, was born in Plymouth, Conn., where he married Sophronia Miller, and moved to Owego in 1834. He lived there two years, then came to Candor, and, with Sidney Hayden, purchased a farm of Rev. Jeremiah Osborn, where they began the manufacture of brick. Mr. Bunnell had one child born to him, Florilla S., who married John Whitley, Jr., and has one child, Noel B. The latter is engaged in the insurance business, at Tavares, Fla.

Charles C. Howard, son of Stephen, was born in Schuyler county, in June, 1805, and came to Candor in 1830, locating on road 36. He married Laura O., daughter of Jonathan Phelps, and nine children were born to him, viz.: Warren, Minerva A., wife of Samuel Benjamin, Theresa J. (Mrs. D. W. Andrews), Charles, of Alpine, N. Y., Rhoda M. (Mrs. Morgan Eastman), Margaret E., wife of S. F. Kyle, Hiram O., Loring P., pastor of the Methodist Episcopal church at Spencer, and Laura E., wife of L. E. Baker, of Spencer.

Rowland Van Scoy, son of Samuel, married Rachel, daughter of Isaac Drew, and reared three children, namely, Isaac D., Rowland S., a banker at Maple Rapids, Mich., and Sally. Isaac D. was born in Kent, N. Y., and came to Tioga county in 1837. He lived fourteen years near Weltonville, and then purchased and made the first settlement on the farm where he now lives. He married Julia A., daughter of Josephus Barrett, and has four children, as follows: Knowlton, Burt R., Josephus and Ann B. Josephus is engaged in fruit growing in Smithville, Md. Burt R. was born in this town, December 16, 1837, and married Sarah E., daughter of Elias Schoonover. He served in the late war, in Co. B, 21st N. Y. Cav. In 1865, he purchased the farm where he now lives. He has five children, namely, Ada D., Lulu, Bertha, Drew and Mabel.

Rodaker Fuller, son of David, was born in Colchester, June 5, 1809, married Fernunda, daughter of David Brown, and has one child, Samuel G. He made the first settlement on the farm where he now resides.

VanNess Barrott, son of Josephus, was born in Kent, N. Y., married Deborah Wixom, and came to Candor with his family in 1834. He purchased the farm where Elliott Barrott now lives, which he subsequently sold, and purchased the farm and saw mill owned by his son, Samuel R. He was one of the first to engage in the dairy business, and many people used to come to his house to see him make butter, and learn how it was done. He made and used the first churn power used in this section, it being the tread wheel, similar to that used at the present time. He was also at one time engaged in lumbering. He reared seven children, viz.: Samuel R., Simeon W., of Candor, Josephus, of Newark Valley, Amial W., Betsey, Phœbe, wife of Nathaniel Sherwood, of Apalachin, and Marilla, wife of George Thomas.

John E. Robbins purchased and made the first clearing on the farm where he now lives, in 1847.

William L. Fessenden, son of Henry, was born at Montrose, Pa., September 10, 1816, and at an early age learned the trade of a cabinet-maker. After living in various places, he located at Peruville, where he carried on the furniture and undertaking business for twenty-one years. While here he joined the Methodist Episcopal church, and became a local preacher. Later he joined the Wesleyan Methodist society, and was ordained as a minister in April, 1858. He married Adaline, daughter of David George, and has six children, viz.: Mary A., wife of George T. Brooks, Harvey G., of Waverly, Charles H., of New York City, Geograny, David S., and William N., of New York city.

John M. VanKleeck, son of Laurence, and grandson of John L., was born in Clinton, February 9, 1805. His father and grandfather moved to Danby, in 1806. John M. married Amy, daughter of William Brock, and came to Candor in 1834, locating on the farm where he now resides. He has had born to him three children—Phebe A., deceased, Charles H., and John J., of Owego.

William Richardson moved to Newark Valley, from Attleboro, in 1818, and located on West Owego creek, on the farm now owned by Munroe Barrett. He married Millie Capron, and reared eight children, as follows: William, deceased, Elias, of McGrawville, Millie, deceased, Horace, of Candor, Fanny, Hannah, wife of George Waldo, of Waverly, Jane, widow of Timothy Reed, and Nancy.

Samuel Miller moved to Newark Valley, from Sennett, about 1836, purchased 500 acres of land in the western part of the town, and built the first saw-mill on the place now owned by William Custard. He married Eunice, daughter of Daniel Storke, of Sennett, and reared thirteen children, viz: Emeline, wife of Peter Sitzer, of Auburn, Julia, Cyrus, who resides in Tunkhannock, and is president of the bank there, Nancy, Daniel, a physician in this town, John, of Horseheads, William, also of Horseheads, Lucinda, wife of Alanson White, of Sennett, Augustine, of Candor, Ellen A., wife of Walter Herrick, of this town, Frank G., of Iowa, Peter, of Tunkhannock, Pa., and Emmett, of Horseheads. The children were all living when the youngest was thirty years of age, yet the father and mother had never seen all their children at one time. Augustine married Charlotte A., daughter of Collins Maine, of DeRuyter, N. Y., and has one child, Fred. The latter resides at home, and is engaged in stock dealing. He married Mary F., daughter of Edwin and Polly Webster, and has two children, Burt W. and Edwin A. Dr. Daniel S. Miller was born in Sennett, N. Y., June 1, 1823. He studied in the public schools and at the Berkshire Medical College, of Pittsfield, Mass., in 1847. He began practice at Martville, N. Y., and came to Candor in 1851, and has practiced here since. He married Helen J. Caruth, in 1848, and has had one child, Ada, who became the wife of William R. Wardwell and died in 1876. Mr. Miller has held the office of supervisor.

Dr. John C. Dixon was born in Gilbertsville, Otsego county, November 12, 1831, and in 1839 went to Owego to reside with an uncle, his parents having died. In 1845 his uncle, Rev. John Bayley, located in Candor, and Dr. Dixon came with him. He studied with Dr. L. Sullivan, and graduated at the Albany Medical College in December, 1854, began practice here, but shortly removed to Minnesota, where he resided until after the war broke out, when he entered the service and remained two years, or till the close of the war. After this he returned to Candor and has been in practice here since. Dr. Dixon married Sarah Frances, daughter of Daniel Hart, in December, 1856.

Dr. William E. Roper was born in Danby, N. Y., February 18, 1853, studied in the common schools, at the Ithaca Academy, and graduated at the Homeopathic Hospital College, of Cleveland, Ohio, in March, 1881, and immediately began practice in Candor, where he has since resided. He married Eliza Holmes, December 29, 1880, and has one child, a son.

William J. Cole was born in New Jersey, October 5, 1815, and came to Tioga county in 1850, locating on a farm in the town of Tioga. In 1868 he was appointed steward of the county house in Owego, where he remained four years, and in 1872 came to Candor village, where he has resided since. He married Susan Elston, who bore him five children, four of whom are living, viz.: Chauncey A., Sarah E., (Mrs. Frank Finch, of Alfred Center),

Kate (Mrs. C. J. Dodge, of Binghamton), and Arminda (Mrs. Eugene Hollenbeck). Mrs. Cole died in May, 1886, and in November, 1886, he married Mrs. Maggie S. Clowes, of Watkins, N. Y.

Elbert O. Scott was born in Franklin, Delaware Co., N. Y., March 6, 1839, studied in the public schools of his native town, studied law with Hon. W. C. Lamont, of Richmondville, and was admitted to the bar in May, 1860, and has been in practice here since 1866.

Dr. Algernon J. Harris was born in Candor, July 31, 1859, a son of Dr. James J. Harris, who died here in 1863, after several years practice in the village. Dr. Harris studied in the public schools of Candor, graduated at Eastman's Business College, Poughkeepsie, N. Y , in 1876, studied medicine with Dr. L. D. Farnham, now of Binghamton, N. Y., and graduated at the College of Physicians and Surgeons in New York City, in May, 1882, practiced in Wayne county, Pa., one year, and then came to Candor village, where he has since resided. He married Miss Josie C. Williams, June 25, 1884, and has one child, a son.

Henry Hull came from Vermont and located on Anderson Hill very early in the history of the county. He married Nancy, daughter of Clark Delano, by whom he had seven children, viz.: Susan, Oren and Oscar, deceased, Leonard, of Candor, Mary A., widow of the late Leonard White, Alfred, of Owego, and Calvin, of Phelps, N. Y. Leonard, who was a member of Co. K, 179th N. Y. Vols., married Adeline, daughter of William White, of Candor, by whom he has three children, viz.: Mina, wife of Alonzo Harding, of Catatonk, who has one child, Eugene; Frederick E. and William Franklin. Alfred married Permelia, daughter of Augustus Clark, September 17, 1862, by whom he has two children, Byron O., born April 2, 1867, and Rosetta, born May 21, 1870.

Augustus Holmes came from Albany county, N. Y., to this town in 1821, where he engaged in farming. He married Waty Tanner, of Duchess county, by whom he had eight children, viz.: Susan, Ebenezer, deceased, Samuel, of Candor, Cinderella, wife of William Doolittle, deceased, Caroline, the present wife of William Doolittle, John T., Job, deceased, and Rufus, of Newark Valley.

Osgood Ward came from New Hampshire to Canada where he remained about one year, and then removed to Montrose, Pa., and thence to Candor, where he located on the farm now owned in part by Mr. Seaman, about the year 1813. He married Hannah Huckins, of Portsmouth, N. H., by whom he had twelve children, viz: Sarah, wife of Jared Smith, deceased, Hiram, of Candor, Eliza, wife of Ansel Hubbard, Mary A., wife of Almon Woodruff, of Dakota, J. Nelson, deceased, Cynthia, widow of J. B. Bacon, of Candor, Charles, deceased, Warren A., who died at the age of seventeen years, Harvey H., of Candor, Adeline C., wife of A. A. McGill, of Missouri, and two who died in infancy. Harvey H. married Phœbe B , daughter of Nathaniel Spaulding, of Ithaca, by whom he has had two children, Alla, who died in Manistee, Mich., in October, 1882, leaving a widow and one child, Harold ; and Luella Spaulding Ward, wife of W. J. Terry, of Ithaca, N. Y., and who has one child, Jerome Ward Terry.

William White came from Vermont many years ago, and located in Spencer. He married Phœbe Rundle, by whom he had twelve children, eleven of whom arrived at maturity. Their names are John, Lucinda, wife of Charles Frisbie, of Halsey Valley, Maria, wife of William Ross, of Wisconsin, Azubah, wife of William Brown, of Iowa, Elnathan, Lavinna, wife of Peter Cinnamon, of Hudson, N. Y., Eveline, wife of George Campbell, of New Albany, Pa., Lewis, deceased, Sewell, who died in the army, Leonard and Adeline, wife of Leonard Hull, of Candor. Leonard married Mary A., daughter of Henry Hull, by whom he had two children, Alice Isabel, wife of Jerome Van Zile, and Emily O., wife of Frederick Hover, of Candor. Leonard White was a member of Co. H., 137th N. Y. Vols., and was killed in the battle of Lookout Mountain, November 28, 1863.

Aaron Lovejoy, son of Nathan, was born March 17, 1817, and came to Candor in December, 1834. On December 25, 1839, he married Mary Curtiss, by whom he had four children, born as follows: Horace A., October 5, 1840; Mary E., December 14, 1841; Lyman B., February 26, 1843; and Emeline, December 13, 1844. Mrs. Lovejoy died December 27, 1844, and on June 8, 1845, Mr. Lovejoy married Sarah J. Bundy, by whom he had eight children, viz.: Elam, born July 27, 1846; Caroline, March 3, 1847 ; Lucy A., October 9, 1849; Willard A., July 27, 1851 ; Orpha March 16, 1853; Silas, April 14, 1855 ; Sarah, January 30, 1858 ; and Frank, April 12, 1861. The second Mrs. Lovejoy died April 9, 1881, and Mr. Lovejoy, January 30, 1885. Lyman B. married Phœbe A. Jordan, of Candor, June 21, 1875. Their children are Aaron L., born August 15, 1866, Frank S. and Fred W. (twins), born January 30, 1868, Thomas S., June 8, 1870. Mrs. Lovejoy died November 14, 1874, aged twenty-eight years. His second wife is Mandana A. Gillivaray, whom he married June 30, 1875, and their children are Nettie M., born July 10, 1876, Almond B., February 18, 1879, and Mary E., March 26, 1882. Fred W. died January 1, 1868. Willard A. married Nellie, daughter of William H. Decker, of Candor, October 24, 1874, by whom he has had five children, born as follows: Evalenia, March 17, 1876, Minnie M., May 21, 1878, Myrtie May, October 3, 1880, Freddie Leroy, December 23, 1882, died June 28, 1883, Bessie, born May 8, 1884, and Clyde L., March 20, 1887.

Richard Field came from Swaford, Oxfordshire, England, in November, 1854, and located in Spencer, where he engaged in farming and in which occupation he continued for five years. He then engaged in mason-work, and in 1868 came to Candor, where he built the first house on Mountain avenue. He married first, Sarah Smith, by whom he had eight children. His present wife is Malvina (Jackson) Hooper, by whom he has one child.

Cyrenus Elmendorf was born in Hopewell, Orange county, N. Y., in February, 1826. At the age of ten or twelve years he obtained work at Homowack, Sullivan county, N. Y., and afterward learned the carpenter and joiner trade in that place. He removed from there to Candor village in 1855, where he engaged in building operations, principally that of bridges. In partnership with John J. Sackett he built the Hulmboldt Tannery, in 1859, and carried on the business of tanning in connection with others under the firm name of C. Elmendorf & Co., until 1865. He then disposed of his interest to Hoyt Brothers, of New York. In 1858 he bought the foundry here and in the name of S. Horton & Co. conducted the manufacture of stoves and agricultural machinery. He married, first, Hannah, daughter of William Lewis, of Ulsterville, Ulster county, N. Y., by whom he had seven children, viz.: Perthena A., wife of L. D. Willard, of Candor, William C., of New Jersey, Esther, wife of John Coglan, of Candor, Charles, who died at the age of eight years, Lucas, of Candor, Eloise, wife of Edward Blynn, of McLean, N. Y., and Clarence, who is engaged with his father. During the greater part of Mr. Elmendorf's residence in Candor he has been actively and prominently identified with its business interests. His present wife is Nancy (Wells) Leet.

J. W. Henderson was born in Starrucca, Pa., in 1834, and came to Candor in 1859, where he was employed in the Hulmboldt Tannery for about eight months. He then went to Berkshire, where he entered the employ of Davidge & Horton, where he remained for seven years. He then returned to Candor, and from there went to Etna, N. Y., where he managed a large dairy farm for E. S. Estey, until 1871, when he returned to Candor a second time, and took charge of the Hulmboldt Tannery, as superintendent. Mr. Henderson married Caroline, daughter of Isaac Baker, of this town, by whom he has two children, Nellie E., and Fred D.

Frederick Parmele was born in Guilford, Conn., March 28, 1814, and in 1840 came to Owego, where he lived until 1855, when he went to Kentucky, and remained about five years. He then returned to this county, and located in Candor, where he engaged in the wheel-wright business, which he conducted here for twenty years. He married Harriet, daughter of Stephen Dexter, in 1841. Their children are C. Frederick, of Hastings, Neb., Stephen R., of Brooklyn, N. Y., Ella, who died at the age of five years, and George D., of Rochester, Minn.

William L. Carpenter, son of Eli and Sarah (Van Renselaer) Carpenter was born in Greenbush, N. Y., August 16, 1799 In 1813 he went to Salina, now a part of the city of Syracuse, where he remained more or less for five years, assisting in the work of boring for salt water. At that time there was nothing where the city of Syracuse now stands, but a tavern, a small store, and a few houses, all surrounded by a dense alder swamp. In the fal of 1819 he went to Watertown, N. Y., where he remained about four years, engaged as a machinist with William Smith, who owned a large machine shop on an island in the Black river, and which was within the corporate limits of the village. Here he married Sarah, daughter of William Smith, by whom he had two children, Matthew, late of Wisconsin, and Sarah, wife of William Pell, of New Bedford, Mass. Mr. Carpenter lost his wife in 1831. He then went to New Orleans, and after eight years returned to Binghamton, N. Y., where he married Lauretta Towsley, January 9, 1839, and by whom he has had six children, viz.: Mary J., wife of William Hunt, Lewis S., deceased, William J., of Binghamton, Lucy, wife of Burton Sherwood, of Varna, N. Y., Sarah L., wife of Fred Hoag, of Binghamton, and Orly V., of Candor. About 1867 Mr. Carpenter came to Candor, where he has been conducting the business of machinist and wagon worker. He joined the order of Free Masons in Chittenango Lodge, No. 128, Chittenango, N. Y., January 14, 1821, and is probably one of the oldest living masons in the state.

Anthony M. Tyler, a soldier of 1812, was one of the early settlers in the town of Newark Valley, and was an early and earnest supporter of Methodism in this section. He married Harriet W., daughter of William S. Packer, of Albany county, N. Y., and sister of William S., Jr., who instituted and endowed the Parker Institute of Brooklyn. Their children were Harriet, who married Silas Tappan, Nancy A., who married Ezekiel Noble, of Newark Valley, William S., who died in the army, Joseph A., who married Morgiana Forsyth, Eunice A., wife of Eldredge Forsyth, of Owego, Oscar, who removed to Ilinois, where he died, John J. and Sanford A., now of DeKalb, Ill.

Reuben Allen came with his father, when quite young, to Newark Valley, and settled three miles from the village between East creek and West creek. He married Myrinda, daughter of John Watkins, of Newark Valley. There were eleven children born to them, namely : Lucy, George, Lydia, M. Sarah, Charles, P. Maria, Grace A., John R., Amasa, Mary and Martha. P. Maria married Louis F. Durussel, of Owego, July 4. 1857. They have three children, Mary Ella, born August 27, 1854; George Alfred, born December 11, 1856, and Anna Martha, born March 29, 1858.

Augustus Clark, son of Austin, came with his parents from Massachusetts when he was about seventeen years of age, and settled on what is known as Anderson hill, in Candor, where they cleared a farm and built a log house. Mr. Clark assisted in the construction of some of the first roads, and having learned the carpenter's trade, aided in erecting some of the earlier houses of this section. He married first, Betsey Darling, by whom he had four children—Polly (Mrs. Charles Farnham), Alvin, Clarissa (Mrs. James Stewart), and Horace. His second wife was Mary Decker, by whom he had two children, James and Mary. His third wife was Sarah Gould, by whom he had six children, namely, Almira (Mrs. Ransom Pultz), Elizabeth, (Mrs. Herman Berry), Jane, Emily (Mrs. John Young), Sarah (Mrs. Joseph Decker), and Permelia (Mrs. Alfred Hall). Mr. Clark was aflicted with blindness for thirty-three years of his life. He died in July, 1862, and Mrs. Clark died in 1868. Jane married William Gould and has two children, Amanda (Mrs. John Bingham), and Ephraim C.

John Kelsey was born in Kensington, Conn., May 2, 1796, the youngest of the six children of William and Dorothy (Goodrich) Kelsey. In 1818 they removed to Candor, John being then twenty-two years of age. He settled on the farm where he spent the remainder of his days, living in one place nearly sixty-nine years. He married first Rachel Potter, of Candor, with whom he lived seven years. There were no children by this marriage. After her death he married Mary Ann Woodbridge, of Salem, Pa., in 1837, who bore him six children, of whom five still survive, one dying in infancy. Those living are Mary E., who married Norman Hart, September 7, 1865 ; Laura Ann, unmarried; John Woodbridge, who married Matilda Simms in September, 1864, served in the late civil war nine months ; and the other two children are Sarah A., and Dora G., who are at present living in the old home   The mother of these children died January 17, 1875, sixty-four years of age.   John Kelsey survived the last wife eleven years, and at his death, March 7, 1886, lacked but eight weeks of ninety years.

The comparative growth of the town may be seen by the following citation from the census reports for the several enumerations since its organization :   1820, 1,655 ; 1825, 2,021 ; 1830, 2,656; 1835, 2,710 ; 1845, 3,422 ; 1850, 3,433 ; 1855, 3,894 ; 1860, 3,840 ; 1865, 4,103 ; 1870, 4,250 ; 1875, 4,208 ; 1880, 4,323.

Organization.—At a town-meeting of the town of Candor, holden March 5, 1811, at the house of Captain Abel Hart, the meeting proceeded to the choice of town officers. The following persons were chosen : Joel Smith, supervisor ; Asa North, town clerk ; William Scott, Orange F. Booth, Samuel Smith, assessors ; Nathaniel Sackett, Seth Bacon, Charles Taylor, commissioners of highways ; Truman Woodford, constable and collector ; Abel Hart, Asa North, overseers of the poor ; Eldad Picket, Daniel Parks, constables ; Joseph Delind, Charles Taylor, Eli Bacon, Job Judd, fence-viewers and damage-prizers ; Thomas Parks, James McMaster, Ezra Smith, poundmasters ; Jacob Harrington, Seth Bacon, Ozias Woodford, Joseph Kelsey, Daniel Cowles, George Allen, Reuben Hatch, William Taylor, Joseph Schoonover, Thomas Baird, Daniel H. Bacon, Jacob Clark, Alexander Scott, overseers of highways of thirteen districts.

Thomas Gridley, familiarly known as " Squire Hemlock," had delegated to him the privilege of naming the new town. Why the name of Candor was chosen is a matter of conjecture.

BUSINESS CENTERS.

CANDOR VILLAGE.—For many years this place was in two settlements, known as Candor Corners and Candor Centre, but the gradual growth of both have united them, and they are now known as the village of Candor It is situated on the Catatonk creek, nearly in the centre of the town, and is a station on the Cayuga and Susquehana division of the Delaware, Lackawanna and Wesern Railroad. The first settlement in the town was made upon this site, and many of the descendants of the early settlers are now living here. It has a population of about 1,100 inhabitants, and is a thriving manufacturing village.

WILLSEYVILLE, a post village, is situated on what was known as the Big Flat or Cantine location, and is on the north branch of the Catatonk creek, in the northwest part of the town. A map of the lands about 1817 shows that Christian Hart had settled fifty acres on the south side, Jack Chambers on one hundred acres next north, Jacobus Shenich two hundred acres, where the depot now is, and on this place he kept tavern as early as 1798. November 1, 1809, he sold to Ezra Smith, who kept the tavern until 1812 or 1813, when it burned down.

WELTONVILLE is a small post village, located on the east line of the town, on West Owego creek. It contains a postoffice, backsmith-shop, wagon-shop, and school-house. It was named in honor of Rev. A. J. Welton. Jasper Taylor, Cornelius Cortwright, and others came in here at an early day. They built their first houses at the base of the hill, fearful that the flats would be covered with water.

WEST CANDOR, a post village, was commenced by Israel Mead, in 1796. Selah Gridley and Captain Ira Woodford were early settlers, and their descendants are yet living here. It is a station on the Utica, Ithaca and Elmira Railroad, and contains a depot post office, hotel, school-house, steam and water-power saw-mill, and is about three and a half miles west of Candor village.

CATATONK, a post village, is situated on Catatonk creek, near the south line of the town, and is a station on the Delaware, Lackawanna and Western Railroad, and contains a depot, postoffice, church, blacksmith shop, two saw-mills, and tannery. The latter was built by Sackett & Forman, in 1852, purchased by G. Truman & Co, in 1864, and bought by E. S. Esty & Co., May 24, 1875, and is now known as Catatonk Humboldt Tannery.

The First National Bank of Candor, was incorporated March 3, 1864, with a cash capital of $50,000.00 and began business right after The officers were Norman L. Carpenter, president; Jerome Thompson, vice-president; and J. J. Bush, cashier. Mr. Carpenter died in the spring of 1865, and Mr. Booth, the present incumbent, succeeded him as president. In January, 1865, John W. McCarty succeeded Mr. Thompsom as vice-president, and the following month Mr. Bush resigned as cashier and was succeeded by Jerome Thompson. In 1868, the bank was robbed of a large amount of money, the details of which may be seen from the following entry in the bank's books under date of December 18, 1868, viz.:

" Last night this bank was entered by burglars and robbed of about $13,000.00 in currency and $5,000.00 in 5 per cent. U. S. bonds, besides about $1,200.00 in bonds belonging to other parties, left here for safe keeping. The above named property was in a burglar-proof safe, purchased of Herring & Co. in the year 1864. The burglars after tearing down the vault door laid the safe down on the bottom of the vault, door-side up, and sprung the sides with steel wedges sufficiently to admit powder, and blew the door open, abstracted the contents and made their escape."

None of the property was ever recovered, and no trace of the burglars obtained. The bank now has, however, a Herring's six-step, burglar-proof safe, with an additional burglar-proof chest inside.

Candor Lodge, Free and Accepted Masons, was organized June 18, 1856, under a dispensation from the Grand Lodge of the State of New York, by the following members, who were its first officers, viz.: Jonathan B. Hart, worshipful master; Samuel Barager, senior warden; Stephen Dyer, junior warden; James L. Thomas, secretary; Solomon Mead, treasurer; William Van Vleck, senior deacon; Walter Hunt, junior deacon; and Morris W. Holley, tyler. Only one of these survives, Jonathan B. Hart, who is in his eighty-seventh year, and although unable to participate in the active duties of the lodge, his interest in and his zeal for the institution is as great as ever. Brother Hart was initiated in Federal Lodge, No. 17, Watertown, Conn., in 1822, and is therefore one of the oldest masons now living, having been a mason sixty-five years. The first seeker after masonic light under the dispensation was M. B. Weaver, who was initiated July 16, and made a master mason September 13, 1856. At a meeting of the Grand Lodge, held in June, 1857, a charter was granted, and at a meeting of the lodge held July 22, Candor Lodge, No. 411, Free and Accepted Masons was duly instituted, and the following named brethren installed as its officers, by representatives of the grand officers of the Grand Lodge of the State of New York, viz.: Jonathan B. Hart, worshipful master; Morris W. Holley, senior warden; Edward C. Coryell, junior warden; James L. Thomas, secretary; Jerome Thompson, treasurer; John W. McCarty, senior deacon; M. B. Weaver, junior deacon; and Solomon Mead, tyler. The first application for membership under the charter was H. Frank Booth, under date of August 5, 1857, who was raised to the sublime degree of master mason, September 16, 1857. Since the organization of the lodge to the present time, July 1, 1887, 199 members have been received by initiation, and thirty-six by affiliation, of whom forty-seven have withdrawn, thirty-nine have died, and fifty-eight have allowed themselves to be dropped from the roll. The following named brethren have served the lodge as worshipful master for one or more terms, viz.: Jonathan B. Hart, four terms; Jerome Thompson, three terms; Thomas B. Little, five terms; Thomas Eighmey, five terms; H. Frank Booth, seven terms; George H. Hart, three terms; W. L. Little, one term; and Charles F. Baylor, two terms. Lodge meetings from its organization until January 1, 1875, were held in a room located in the attic of what was then known as the Candor Center Hotel, which was fitted up and furnished by Brothers James L. Thomas and Jonathan B. Hart, whose zeal for the institution induced them to advance several hundred dollars for that purpose. In January, 1875, large and commodious rooms more centrally located were secured, in the Youngs block, and fitted up and furnished by the fraternity in modern style, and with all the paraphernalia usual to the order. Ten members of the lodge have been exalted to the Royal Arch degree, and became members of New Jerusalem Chapter, No. 47, of Royal Arch Masons, Owego, N. Y., one of whom, H. F. Booth, was elected and served as High Priest of the Chapter for one term. Six have received the degree of Knighthood, and became members of St. Augustine Commandary, No. 38, Ithaca, N. Y., and two, H. F. Booth and J. F. Booth, are thirty-second degree members of Corning Consistory, Ancient and Accepted Scotish Rite, Corning, N. Y. The lodge also enjoys the distinction given it by the appointment of one of its members, H. F. Booth, to the position of District Deputy Grand Master of the Twentieth Masonic District. Candor lodge is in a prosperous condition, and is said to be one of the best posted and most correct working lodges in the state.

Candor Woolen Mills, owned by Hon. Charles F. Barager, have already been mentioned. Mr. Barager began the manufacture of horse-blankets here in 1879. He employs fifty hands and turns out 50,000 blankets per year.

The .Humboldt tannery was built by Cyrenus Elmendorf and John J. Sackett, in 1859, and the business was conducted by them and by Mr. Elmendorf and others for several years. In 1865, the establishment passed into the hands of Messrs. E. S. Estey & Sons, who are the present proprietors. It is built on Catatonk creek, and has a capacity for tanning 40,000 sides, and employs twenty five men. It is under the supervision of J. W. Henderson, who has been in charge since October, 1871. The buildings were destroyed by fire in June, 1868, and immediately rebuilt by the Messrs. Estey.

The Candor grist-mill, Abram Beebe, prop., was built at an early date in the history of the town, by Jesse and Ogden Smith, brothers, who were prominent in the early enterprises of the town. It is operated by both steam and water-power, has four runs of stones, and the usual equipment of modern machinery, grinding about 400 bushels of grain per week. The property is owned by the Foster Hixon estate, of Ithaca, and leased by Mr. Beebe.

Lewis R. Hoff's grist-mill, on Main street, was purchased of the Sackett estate by his father, Lewis Hoff, in 1875. Lewis R. bacame part owner in December, 1886, and has run it alone since the 1st of April. It has four runs of stones, is operated by both steam and water-power, and grinds about 400 bushels of grain per week.

S. E. Gridley's Planing Mill, on Mill street, was built by George H. Hart, about 1879, and has been owned by Mr. Gridley since March, 1885. The mill has a planer and matcher, jig-saw, rip-saw, lathe, moulder, etc., and is operated by both steam and water-power.

White Brothers Chair Factory, located at Willseyville, was established in February, 1886, for the manufacture of White's patent bent chairs and folding tables. They have an extensive factory three stories high, eighty-five feet long, thirty-five feet wide. It is operated by a sixty horse-power engine, and employs thirty hands, and manufactures 30,000 chairs and 10,000 tables annually.

Barrott's Saw-Mill, located on West Owego creek, was built by —— Schoonover. It is operated by water-power, has lumber saw, lath saws, planer and matcher, turning lathes, shingle machine, etc. The mill employs four men and cuts 300,000 feet of lumber and a large quantity of lath, shingles, etc. annually. In 1880 Mr. Barrott built a grist-mill to run in connection with the saw-mill. It was two runs of stones, and grinds annually 10,000 bushels of grain.

William A. and John F. Hubbard's Saw-Mill, on road 96, was originally built by Jesse Smith, about 1818. It was rebuilt by John A. Chidsey, and in 1862 was purchased by the present proprietors, who in 1875 added a custom grist-mill. The mill cuts about 500,000 feet of lumber per year.

George B. Pumpelly's Saw and Feed-Mill, near Gridleyville was built by him in 1884, upon the site of one destroyed by fire. It is operated by steam-power, has a circular-saw, feed-mill and shingle machine, and turns out about 35,000 feet of lumber per week, and 60,000 shingles.

H. and M. Van Deuser's Saw-Mill, located at Catatonk, is operated by water-power. It was built by R. H. Sackett, in 1831, and in 1884 sold it to the present proprietors. It employs four hands and cuts annually 1,000,000 feet of lumber.

CHURCHES.

Congregational Church of Candor.—Religious meetings were held in Candor, then a part of Owego, as early as 1796. These were continued, being held sometimes in the dwelling of Captain Abel Hart, sometimes in his " weave house," and sometimes in a barn belonging to Sylvester Woodford. At a meeting held in the latter place June 29, 1808, having invited Reverends Seth Williston and Jeremiah Osborn to assist in the organization, Ebenezer Sanford, Rhoda Sanford, Asa North, Laura North, Eli Bacon, Sarah Bacon, Job Judd, Ozias Woodford and Theda Woodford agreed to walk together as a church of Christ: thus forming the first church organization in Candor. Following the tradition of the Pilgrim Fathers they organized it after the polity called Congregational, and having emigrated from Farmington, Conn., they incorporated the ecclesiastical society as " The Farmington Society." Rev. Daniel Loring was the first pastor. Previous to 1811 the church was designated as " The Second Congregational Church of Spencer ;" as the town of Spencer was formed from Owego in 1806, and the town of Candor from Spencer in 1811. From 1833 to 1850 the church was connected with the Presbytery of Geneva, then, by vote of the church, returning to Congregational usage. In 1852 it became connected with the Susquehanna Conference of Congregational churches, called Susquehanna Association since 1865. The church and society built a small house of worship in 1818, on ground adjacent to the store now owned by McCarty & Thompson. A second and more commodious house of worship was built in 1825 on the north side of the creek on the site of the house now owned by Spencer McCapes. In 1837 the first parsonage was built, west of the church, and is now owned by Lewis Griffin. The present brick church edifice was dedicated August 25, 1868, without debt or collection. The parsonage adjacent to the church was built in 1870.

St. Marks Protestant Episcopal Church of Candor was organized April 23, 1832, and Rev. Lucius Carter was the first rector. In January, 1835, the society decided to purchase the lot they now occupy, and build a church, which they did, and were occupying the building in December, 1837. The cost was $5,000.00. The building was generally repaired in 1868.

Methodist Episcopal Church of Candor.—Rev. John Griffin, Geo. Densmore, and others of the circuit preachers, held services several years before the little gathering met in the house of Jared Smith, in 1827, to worship according to their doctrinal views, and to organize a Methodist Episcopal church. They were fifteen in number,—Judge Samuel Barager and wife, Mr. and Mrs. James Smith, Mrs. Hannah Gilbert, Mr. and Mrs. Thomas Hewett, Mr. and Mrs. George Hubbard, Mr. and Mrs. A. Hubbard, Mrs. Asaph Colburn, and Mr. and Mrs. Jared Smith forming a class, with Thomas Hewett as leader. The first public services were held at a school-house. The first meeting-house was erected on the site of the present church, at a cost of about $2,000.00. In 1865 the present church was built, costing about $10,000.00.

Baptist Church of Candor.—A meeting of members of different Baptist churches met at the house of Hiram Allen, March 11, 1852, to take into consideration the propriety of forming a Baptist church to be known as the Candor Village Baptist Church. A council was invited from the sister churches of Owego, Montrose, Tioga Center, Owego Creek, Willseyville, Spencer, West Danby, Caroline, and Barton. Delegates responded to the invitation, and services were held in the school-house. Elder E. Kimball was called to the chair, and H. D. Pinney chosen clerk.

The council, after hearing a statement from the committee of the Candor Baptist brethren, unanimously "*Resolved*, that the council fellowship these brethren, and that public services be held at the Methodist chapel in the afternoon." Hiram Allen was elected deacon, and B. H. Mills, clerk. J. W. Emery was called

14*

to be the first pastor. The house of worship was built in 1855, at a cost of $5,000.00, and was generally repaired a few years ago.

Baptist Church of West Owego Creek.—This church was the second Baptist church, as the Tioga and Barton Baptist Church was the first one. Fifteen persons met together on the first day of May, 1802, and entered into a covenant, which was signed by Louis Mead, Lovina Mead, Jasper Taylor, Catharine Taylor, John Bunnell, Hannah Bunnell, George Lane, Sarah Lane, Peter Gorbet, Sarah Gorbet, Abram Everett, Deborah Everett, Samuel Steward, Alvin Steward, and Elizabeth Jacobs. Services were held in dwelling-houses and school-houses for some years. Rev. Levi Baldwin was the first pastor. A church edifice was built in 1844.

Fairfield Baptist Church was built in 1871, its members withdrawing from the mother-church, on Owego Creek.

Willseyville Baptist Church.—This church was organized in 1839, with fifteen members, among whom were Jacob Willsey and wife, William and Martin Willsey, and Warren Willsey and wife. The first pastor was Elder E. Kimball. The meeting-house was built in 1840.

The Baptist Church of Pipe Creek was organized in 1842, with thirty-eight members. Their first pastor was Rev. Mark Dearborn.

The Methodist Church at Anderson Hill was organized in 1860, with twenty members. Rev. Thomas Burgess was first pastor.

Union Church at East Candor was organized in 1858, with eighty members, composed mostly of Methodists, under the charge of the Caroline Church, Rev. ——Van Valkenburg, first pastor.

Union Church at Catatonk was organized 1861.

Methodist Episcopal Church of Pipe Creek was organized in 1830. Rev. Gaylord Judd was the first pastor.

A Free-Will Baptist Church was organized about 1816. Their meetings were held in the school-house near Jared Smith's, and the one near Daniel Bacon's. Rev. John Gould was the first pastor, and about 1830 went West and joined the Mormons. This church was disorganized about 1831. A Free-Will Baptist church was organized on West Owego creek about 1820, but soon disbanded.

NEWARK VALLEY* lies in the eastern part of the county, and is bounded north by Berkshire, east by the county line, south by Owego and a small part of the county line, and west by Candor.

The territory within this town has changed its name so often as to perplex the person who attempts to write its history. From 16 Feb., 1791, till 14 March, 1800, a part of the town of Union, in the county of Tioga, and bearing the local name of Brown's Settlement during that time. From 14 March, 1800, till 12 Feb., 1808, a part of the town of Tioga, at first in the county of Tioga, but after 28 March, 1806, a part of the county of Broome, taking also, during that time, as its ecclesiastical name, "the Society of Western." From 12 Feb., 1808, till 12 April, 1823, a part of the town of Berkshire, remaining in Broome county till 21 March, 1822, then restored to Tioga county. Separately organized, as Westville, 12 April, 1823 ; becoming Newark by change of name, 24 March, 1824 ; and again Newark Valley, 17 April, 1862 ; but retaining till 5 July, 1833, an ecclesiastical connection with Berkshire.

Always a quiet farming community, remote from the bustle and enterprise of cities, with little chance for acquiring mental culture from great schools and libraries; with no great manufacturing interests in her borders, her history has little of interest beyond the personal history of those who have dwelt in the town ; and that for the first third of the time since the settlement was made, is also a part of the history of other towns.

Brown's Settlement was begun on the first day of April, 1791, by five men who left Stockbridge, Mass., on the twenty-third day of February, and spent thirty-seven days on the way, bringing their tools and provisions on two sleds, drawn by ox-teams. These pioneers were Isaac Brown and Abraham Brown, brothers, Daniel Ball, Elisha Wilson, and John Carpenter, who came as the hired man of the Browns. Two other men, —— Dean, and —— Norton, came in their company as far as Choconut, now Union, where they remained.

The valley of the East Owego creek, with its natural beauty, and its advantages for the immediate support of human life, made it seem an earthly paradise in the estimation of the natives of the rocky hills of New England ; and as the venerable and honorable David Williams, of Berkshire, feelingly said, on the ninetieth

*Prepared by D. Williams Patterson.

anniversary of his birth: "Every blow that has been struck by man in the valley has diminished its beauty, and every farm in the town, if restored to its primitive state, would be worth more to-day than with all the improvements that man has made here." Through the valley, from the south line of Newark Valley to the north line of Berkshire, the timber was mostly hard wood, as beech, birch and maple, with white pines of great size scattered singly and in groups, with so little undergrowth that very little preparation was needed to enable a team and sled or cart to pass from one end to the other, with a moderate load.

Pioneer Items.—The very first work done by Elisha Wilson, while his pioneer comrades went back to bring on the remainder of their goods, was to make a stock of maple sugar for their use during the summer; and though he had to cut his wood, make his troughs, tap the trees, and gather the sap by hand and boil it down without help, he had made one hundred and fifty pounds during their absence of eleven days.

Every pioneer was a hunter, and deer were so plenty that no one felt a lack of meat, while the streams were so full of trout and other fish that enough could be taken for a meal in a few minutes. Even shad were abundant in the Susquehanna river in May and June, till about 1830 (when the dams built by the State of Pennsylvania, at Shamokin and Nanticoke, barred their further passage and destroyed the fisheries), the only drawback to taking them being the clearness of the water, which enabled the fish to see and avoid the nets, unless the fishing were done in the night. Often a bear would be found and killed, so that the settlers could enjoy a change in their bill of fare.

Almost every early settler understood and practiced the art of tanning deer-skins, from which they made their own gloves, mittens and leather breeches, and for more than sixty year the manufacture was continued in a small way for export to other towns, and every woman became expert in the art of sewing leather goods.

Wolves were the great enemy of the settlers, who had hard work to protect their sheep and lambs, and a lady who has but lately died, incidentaly mentioned the fact that she remembered when the wolves came into the barn-yard of Enoch Slosson, on the present village green, and killed his lambs; and persons are yet living who remember seeing wolves brought into the valley by hunters who had shot them on the hills.

Many of the early settlers here had been the neighbors and

friends of the Stockbridge Indians, some of whom, as well as the Oneidas and Onondagas, occasionally visited the settlement, but no trouble ever arose between them, as the settlers knew the character and feelings of the Indians, and having in good faith bought and paid for their lands, and made with them a treaty of friendship; they knew that they could implicitly trust them, and confide in them, unless the whites should first break the compact ; and they never hesitated to admit the roving natives to the hospitalities of their log houses whenever they passed the settlement. One instance is remembered and told, where two Indians called at the house of Asa Bement, and asked for a meal which Mrs. Bement provided for them. One being satisfied, rose from the table saying : " Me tank you," while the other said : " Me no tank yet," meaning that he had not yet finished his meal.

Every house was a work shop, or domestic manufactory ; every chimney corner held a blue dye tub ; a delightful generator of ammonia, which did not prevent its use as a warm seat for one of the younger children, whose position was often admirably adapted for star-gazing through the top of the broad chimney. In this tub was dyed the wool or woolen yarn to be used for the winter stockings of the family, and for the filling of the linsey woolsey cloth, the favorite material for the every day gowns, petticoats, and aprons of the wives and daughters of that day, and the linen yarn to be used in making the striped or checked linen cloth for handkerchiefs and aprons. Every girl was taught to spin wool and tow on the great weeel during the warm weather of summer; and liner on the little wheel, in the winter ; and nearly every woman knew how to weave plain cloth ; while the fine linen goods for table cloths, and the woolen blankets or coverlets for beds, which were to be nicely figured, had to go into the hands of the professional weaver. Some very nice articles of this domestic spining and weaving are yet to be seen in the valley.

The tow cloth was used for working-clothes for the men, as trousers, shirts, and frocks, and the linen for finer wear for men and women, and for summer sheets, as well as towels, strainers, etc. When the fulling mills were built so that every girl could have a nice pressed flannel dress every winter, she had little more to ask in the way of dress ; and when the women could have the wool carded by machines, and avoid the task of carding by hand, it was considered a great help in the labor of the summer.

When cotton cloth began to be brought in from the eastern factories, it was not known, as now, by its various grades or uses, as sheeting, shirting, etc., but by the name "factory," which distinguished it from the domestic, or home-made cloth. The women were careful not to wear out their good gowns, with their long, narrow, gored skirts, when about their domestic work, but thought a good petticoat and short gown sufficient to meet all the requirements of fashion and good taste.

Among the household industries which flourished in Berkshire and Newark Valley for many years, was the braiding and sewing of grass bonnets, commonly called Leghorn bonnets. This began soon after the war of 1812 ended, but whether it grew out of the economy which was then necessary, or was the result of the new meeting-house, which was dedicated 4 July, 1817, would be hard to decide. Some families became so noted for this work that young women came to them from other towns to learn the art. Miss Ruby Leach, of Corbettsville, in Conklin, N. Y., and Miss Roxania Trowbridge, daughter of Noble Trowbridge, of Great Bend, Pa., came about 1825 to the family of Joseph Belcher, on Berkshire Hill, and spent several months, during which Miss Leach made a quantity of braid of such unusual fineness and beauty that Miss Betsey Belcher made from it a bonnet for exhibition at a fair in Albany, and received the first premium, a set of silver spoons, and the bonnet was sold for sixty dollars. This industry declined with the change of fashions, but as late as 1850, many mens' fine hats were made in the two towns.

Early Settlers.—Elisha Wilson, eldest child of Elijah and Mary (Curtis) Wilson, was born at Stockbridge, Mass., 13 Aug., 1767, went over the Boston Purchase with the surveying party in 1790, selected lot 184 for his future home, and bought it of Elisha Blin, on his return to Mass. Starting again from Stockbridge, 23 Feb., 1791. with several companions, they reached their destination 1 April, 1791, and he spent the summer in preparing his land for culture, and raising a crop of corn and vegetables. He built a log house, with a single roof of bark, near the bank of the creek, west of the road and nearly opposite the site of his home in after years, where Levi B. Hammond now lives; and this house, which some years later had a better roof, was standing, and sometimes occupied as a dwelling till 1830. After spending two winters at his old home in Stockbridge, this became his permanent home. He married 9 Dec., 1799, with Electa Slosson, who died 19 Nov., 1862, aged more than ninety years. He died 11 Nov., 1857, aged over ninety years. Their children were:

I. Elijah, b 11 Oct., 1800, died at Detroit, Mich.

II. Mary, b 17 Jan., 1802; d 21 April, 1819.

III. Susan Maria, b 16 July, 1807; m with Chester Leonard, who died 25 Nov., 1841.

IV. Charles Frederick, b 10 Sept., 1810; m 22 Sept., 1833, with Elnora Woodford, daughter of Giles and Eunice (Wilcox) Woodford, of Burlington, Conn., where she was born 13 June, 1815. He died at Prescott, Wis., 17 Feb., 1881, in his 71st year, without children, and she returned to Newark Valley, where she still resides.

Abraham Brown, b at Stockbridge, Mass., 28 June, 1768, was a farmer and surveyor. He visited the Boston Purchase in 1790, with a party of surveyors, and had probably been with them as an assistant in the previous year of their labor, and it is said that on one occasion he was detached from the party to verify some work, lost his way, and was out four days before he found his comrades. He came in the pioneer party, in 1791, and began his settlement on lot 257, which had fallen to his mother, in the division, about on the same spot where the Congregational meeting-house was built a few years later, and where John Harmon, after buying the south half of the lot, built his brick house, which still stands there. After his mother came to Brown's Settlement he lived with her, where Rodney Ball now lives, on the north half of the lot, and died there, 19 September, 1828, unmarried.

John Carpenter, born at Stockbridge, Mass., 24 Oct., 1772, eldest child of Abner and Lydia (Brown) Carpenter, was employed as an assistant to Isaac and Abraham Brown, and was one of the pioneers in Brown's Settlement, in 1791. He was probably here every year till his marriage, at Stockbridge, about the first of January, 1797. He had bought land on lot 302, in Berkshire (where his brother Daniel Carpenter afterward lived) and intended to settle upon it. Six weeks after his marriage he started again for Brown's Settlement to prepare a home for his wife, and the first news which she had from him was of his death and burial. He was the second adult person who died in the colony, and the first in the limits of Newark Valley. He was boarding with Ezbon Slosson's family in the log house where the lecture room of the Congregational church now stands, and was apparently, in as good health as ever, when he heard of the death of Isaac Brown, 10 April, 1797, and said: "Now I will go and take Brown's farm to work," but three days later, 13 April, 1797, he died, and was ready to join his neighbor Brown in the new cemetery.

Ezbon Slosson, b at Stockbridge, Mass., 28 Jan., 1769, (son of Enoch Slosson) married there 26 Aug., 1790, with Electa Williams, daughter of Azariah and Beulah (Brown) Williams of Stockbridge, where she was born 20 Sept., 1772. He came to Brown's Settlement early in 1792, with the returning pioneers, and began his new home on lot 138, building a cabin of logs with a bark roof, about where the mill-house stands, in which Philander M. Moses now lives. In Feb. 1793, he again left Stockbridge, bringing with him his wife and daughter, and his parents with some of the younger members of their family, arriving at their new home 4 March, 1793. In the fall of 1795, a heavy storm raised the water so as to float the puncheon floor of their house, and the bark roof slid off, compelling them to go in the night, through the water to his father's log house, where they dwelt till could build a new one on the spot where the lecture-room of the Congregational church now stands. In 1806 he built the first framed house in Newark Valley, which, as the south end of the old hotel, was torn down in April 1887. Later, he built a house on the spot where Mrs. John Davidge now lives. He died 2 June, 1838. She died at the house of Otis Lincoln, 12 Feb., 1853. Those who followed them to the settlement were made welcome to a part of their log house, while getting their own ready for use, and it sometimes sheltered two families at once, besides their own. After building this framed house he kept an inn, a small store, and also built a distillery about where Mr. Caldwell now lives. Their children were:

I. Caroline, b at Stockbridge, Mass., 23 Feb., 1791; married in 1812, with Ezekiel Rich.

II. Sarah, b 2 Aug., 1796; m with Otis Lincoln.

III. William, b 3 July, 1800; m 1 July, 1824, with Maria Benjamin, and two of their children, George W. Slosson, and Mrs. Phebe Elizabeth Todd still live in Newark Valley.

IV. Franklin, b 20 Feb., 1805; m 19 Jan., 1832, with Nancy Rich, and settled in Owego.

V. Semantha, b 20 Sept., 1808; m with Simeon Rich Griffin.

Enoch Slosson, b at Wilton, Conn., 13 Aug., 1733, son of Nathaniel and Margaret (Belden) Slosson, married at Sharon, Conn., 9 Aug., 1757, with Sarah St. John, daughter of Mark and Hannah St. John, of Wilton, where she was born in 1738. They settled at Kent, Conn., where they joined the church; she, 4 June, 1759, by letter from Sharon; he, by profession, 29 March, 1761;

but soon moved to Stockbridge, Mass., where they joined the church, 7 Nov., 1762, by letter from Kent.

In February, 1793, they left Stockbridge with part of their children, in company with their son, Ezbon Slosson, and his family, and came to Brown's settlement, arriving 4 March, 1793, and dwelt in the house with their son till 1794, then built a log house where Dr. R. B. Root afterward lived and died. She and her daughter in-law saw no other woman till September, when Dr. Tinkham's wife came from Owego, on horseback, to visit them. She was dismissed from the church at Stockbridge, 2 Oct., 1803, and became a member of the new church, 20 Nov., 1803, the first Sunday after its organization, her name standing first on the list of admissions. She died 10 March, 1819, in her 81st year. There is no record of his admission to the church of Newark Valley, but tradition says that he became a member in 1820. He died 21 Feb., 1827, in his 94th year. Many years of his life were clouded by mental derangement. Their children were:

I. Mabel, b at Kent, Conn., 5 Oct., 1758; married with Abraham W. Johnson.

II. Lucinda, b at Kent, Conn., 8 Jan., 1761; m 26 Nov., 1778, at Stockbridge, Mass., with Abijah Williams, son of Joshua Williams. She died at Stockbridge about June, 1782, leaving an only child, Enoch Slosson Williams, who was born at Stockbridge, 13 Dec., 1781, who was brought up by his grandparents, and came with them to Brown's settlement in 1793.

III. Sarah, b at Stockbridge, Mass., 4 March, 1764; m there 4 April, 1782, with William Holley, and died there about 1783, without children.

IV. Electa, b at Stockbridge, Mass., 7 Sept., 1766; died young.

V. Ezbon, b 28 Jan., 1769; see under 1791.

VI. Electa, b at Stockbridge, Mass., 3 March, 1772; came to Brown's Settlement in 1794, and married with Elisha Wilson, the pioneer settler.

VII. Jerusha, b at Stockbridge, Mass., in Nov., 1774; came to Brown's Settlement in 1794, and m with Samuel Ball.

VIII. Ruth, b at Stockbridge, Mass., 24 Aug., 1777; came to Brown's Settlement in 1794, and married with Joel Farnham.

IX. Enos, b at Stockbridge, Mass., 24 May, 1780, came to Brown's Settlement with his parents in 1793; m 8 Aug., 1803, with Rebecca Culver, and moved, about 1816, to Lawrenceville, Penn.

Asa Bement, b at Stockbridge, Mass.,10 June, 1764, son of Asa and Ruth (Neal) Bement, was a blacksmith and farmer. He married 19 Jan., 1786. with Abigail Brown, daughter of Samuel and Abigail (Burr) Brown, of Stockbridge, where she was born 31 July, 1762. He was one of the sixty associates who bought the ten townships, and in the grand division he drew lot 177. In the summer of 1792 he began to fit it up for a home, by clearing some land, building a log house, and sowing some wheat. John Brown, of Stockbridge, charged him, 5 Sept., 1792, with " six bushels of seed wheat delivered at Union, at 4s. 6d.—£1. 7s." This wheat, without doubt, was part of the first crop raised in the valley by Brown's brothers, Isaac and Abraham, yet it was sold to him at the very low price of seventy-five cents a bushel, or just what it was then worth in Stockbridge. Having sown his wheat, he went back to Stockbridge to spend the winter with his family. He bought boards for a sled-box at Stockbridge, 12 Feb., 1793, and started a day or two later, in company with Enoch and Ezbon Slosson, and their families, to come again to the land of promise, and arrived 4 March, 1793. John Brown again charged him with " Sundries paid by Isaac at Owego, viz.:

" 1793, March 13. To one bushel of ears of corn,   1s. 0d.
                 To two bushels & ½ of ears of corn, 2s. 6d.
      April 13. To eight bushels of wheat, a 4s. 6d. 36s. 0d.
      May   10. To five bushels of oats,   9s. 4½d.
                 To three bushels of potatoes,   4s. 6d.
                 To keeping a swine ten weeks,   3s. 9d.
                                                   ――――――――――
                                                  £2. 17s. 1½d.

At the end of this second summer he returned to Stockbridge, feeling that his new home was ready for his family, so after spending most of the winter enjoying the privileges of settled society, he bought of John Brown another lot of " boards for a Sleigh box, 2s.," 4 Feb., 1794. He soon started with his wife and four children for this sylvan paradise. The place on which he settled had natural beauties and advantages equal to any in the valley, and two of its beautiful maple groves yet grace the landscape. His wife died 14 Nov., 1814. He married (2d), 18 Oct., 1815, with Lucy Bishop, widow of Noah Lyman, and daughter of Judge Nathaniel and Ruth (Bartlett) Bishop, of Richmond, Mass., previously of Guilford, Conn., where she was born 4 Sept., 1774. He died 21 April, 1847. She died 19 July, 1852. He had by his first wife, eight children, and by the second, one.

I. Parthenia, b at Stockbridge, 9 Feb., 1787, m with Abraham Hotchkin.

II. Betsey, b at Stockbridge, 28 Nov., 1788, m with Jonathan Belcher.

III. Frances, b at Stockbridge, 18 Dec., 1790, m with Zina Bushnell.

IV. Abigail, b at Stockbridge, 18 June, 1793, m with Henry S. Granger.

V. William Brown, b at Newark Valley, 29 May, 1796, a very enterprising, capable man, long a deacon of the church at Newark Valley, where he died 21 March, 1870.

VI. Emily, b 23 Sept., 1798, m with Deodatus Royce.

VII. Mary, b 8 March, 1801, m with George Williams.

VIII. Frederick Burr, b 14 Nov., 1804, m with Mary Ann Armstrong, and m (2d) with Mary Elizabeth Williams.

IX. Jane, b 14 Aug., 1816, m with Major Frederick Theodore Wells, and still lives in Newark Valley.

Peter Wilson, (a brother of Elisha Wilson) was born at Stockbridge, Mass., 29 Nov., 1770 ; came to Brown's Settlement in the spring of 1793, and made his home on lot 217, west of the creek where Daniel Chamberlain now lives. He married 28 Feb., 1802, Lydia Saltmarsh, daughter of William and Elizabeth (Patterson) Saltmarsh, formerly of Watertown, afterwards of Richmond, Mass., where she was born 26 Nov., 1775. At the first town meeting of Berkshire, 1 March 1808, he was elected collector and poundmaster. He and his wife joined the church 7 Jan. 1816, he receiving baptism the same day ; and he was elected one of its deacons, 16 Oct., 1817, serving till his death, 23 April, 1845, " universally respected and beloved, and his death as generally and deeply lamented." She died 9 March 1846. Their children were :

I. Phebe b 3 Feb., 1803, m with Joseph Westfall, and had three children, of whom the eldest, Dea. Joseph Frederick Westfall now lives on her part of her father's homestead.

II. Eliza Abby, b 5 Oct., 1805 ; d 3 March 1807.

III. Eliza Abby, b 22 Oct., 1807 ; m with Derick Ralyea.

IV. Laura, b. 11 May, 1810.

V. William, b 30 July, 1812 ; m with Clarissa Cook Corsaw, and both are dead.

VI. Mary Elizabeth b 31 March, 1816 ; died 24 April 1839.

Abraham W. Johnson, a laborer said to have come from Cheshire, Mass., married with Mabel Slosson, and came to Brown's Settlement in 1794. His name first appeared on the account book of

John Brown, Esq., 3 April 1798, and it was on the highway tax-list for that year. He probably worked for Mr. Brown, who charged him with a cow, at sixteen dollars, 13 Nov., 1798; and "Feb. 26, 1799, to the use of a house 15 months, 16s." They dwelt at one time on the bank of Spring brook, not far from the head of Waring's trout pond, and down to a late date, their old tansy bed could still be found there. At one time they owned a house and some land, but her mental infirmity, a heritage from her father, increased, perhaps by the opium habit, and his unfortunate appetite confirmed by many years of labor in a distillery, brought them to poverty, and their last home in Newark Valley was in a log house built by the poor-master for them, in the hollow north of the road, between the house of Hiram Griffing, and the brook that comes down from Glen Echo. Later one or both of them were taken to the poor-house, and probably died there, but the dates have not been ascertained. They had two children Lyman Johnson and Lucinda Johnson.

Levi Bailey, a hatter, was here in 1795; went back to Stockbridge, Mass., where, as of Union, N. Y., he married 19 Nov., 1795, with Pamelia Brown, daughter of Isaac and Elizabeth (Warren) Brown, of Stockbridge. He brought his wife to Brown's Settlement early in 1796, and in the winter of 1796–97 he lived in the log house which stood on the west side of the way, between Bement & Wilson's mill house and Wilson creek, and just below where Beriah Wells afterward built his house and chair factory. Possibly he dwelt, in 1798, near the home of John Brown, Esq., and it is said that he once lived on the West Owego creek. Afterward he owned and lived on the place now occupied by Egbert Bement, living at one time, according to Judge Williams, on the east side of Whig street. He was one of the constituent members of the church, 17 Nov., 1803. She joined it in August, 1804, having been dismissed from the church at Stockbridge, 5 June, 1803, "to the church about to be formed at Tioga." They were dismissed, in Feb., 1816, and moved to Greene, Trumbull Co., Ohio. Their children were :

I. Isaac Brown. II. Lewis. III. Eliza, m in Ohio.

IV. Pamelia, m in Ohio. V. Edwin, bap. in Aug., 1804

VI. ——, an infant, d between 14 May and 29 June, 1807 ; name not recorded.

VII. Orin Martin, b 24 Sept., 1808 ; bap. 27 Nov., 1808.

VIII. Abby, b 18 June, 1810.

Beulah Brown, widow, one of the sixty associates in the purchase of the ten townships, came to Brown's Settlement, in February, 1796, with her sons, John, Joseph and Lemuel, and settled on lot 257, where Rodney Ball now lives. She was born at Watertown, Mass., 20 Jan., 1741 or 1742, daughter of Joseph and Lydia (Marean) Patterson, and married about 1764, with her cousin, Abraham Brown, who was born at Watertown, in 1740, youngest child of Dea. Samuel and Mercy (Patterson) Brown, afterward of Stockbridge. He served in the early part of the revolutionary war as a captain of militia, and died 8 Jan., 1777, of small-pox, which was communicated to him by a letter. She was dismissed from the church at Stockbridge, 5 June, 1803, and became one of the constituent members of the first church in Tioga, (now Newark Valley) 17 Nov., 1803, her name being fifth on the list. She was a woman of good mental powers, with a kind heart and benevolent disposition. She died 6 July, 1820, and a trustworthy tradition says that in the last year of her life she had made eighty cheeses and taken care of them with her own hands. Her children were:

I. John, b at Stockbridge, 18 July, 1765; settled in Berkshire.

II. Isaac, b at Stockbridge, 25 Oct., 1766; settled in Berkshire.

III. Abraham, b at Stockbridge, 28 June, 1768; settled in Newark Valley.

IV. Joseph, b at Stockbridge, 16 March, 1771; settled in Newark Valley.

V. Lemuel, b at Stockbridge, 1 Feb., 1775; settled in Owego.

Joseph Brown came to Brown's Settlement with his mother, Beulah Brown, in February, 1796. He married early in 1797, with Experience Stafford, who was born in Vermont. 8 Feb., 1778, daughter of Abel and Rebecca (Short) Stafford, afterward of the town of Owego, now Tioga, N. Y. His name is not on the highway tax-list of 1798, which seems to indicate that he was not then a separate householder. He owned the north half of lot 98, and built his house on the gravelly knoll, just north of Hope Cemetery, and between that and the residence of David W. Noble. His blacksmith shop was on the opposite side of the way, in the corner of the old orchard, a few feet south of William T. Noble's old store. He died 20 Jan., 1808, and was buried in the Brown cemetery, at Berkshire. His widow married with Daniel Churchill, and died 26 June, 1864, though her gravestone erroneously says 6 June. Their children were:

I. Laurinda, b 23 Oct., 1797; m with Nathan Slosson.

II. Rebecca Short, b 4 April, 1799; m with Frederick Belcher.

III. Beulah Patterson, b 22 Jan., 1801; m with Lester H. Fuller.

IV. Experience, b 26 Sept., 1803; m with Ephraim Munson Clark.

V. Joseph Patterson, b 15 June, 1805; m with Lura Matilda Russell, and his descendants live at Little Rock, Ark.

VI. Amos Patterson, b 8 April, 1808; died on his father's homestead, 10 Sept., 1865, and his widow and daughter still live in Newark Valley.

William Solomon Lawrence, b at Canaan, Conn., about 1757, son of Jonas and Tryphena (Lawrence) Lawrence, married 12 Oct., 1780, with Esther Dutton, and they dwelt in Canaan till 1796, and in the early part of that year came to Brown's Settlement, and settled in a log house on the east side of the way, on the south half of lot 63, where Hart Newell built the framed house that was burned in November, 1856, while owned by Lyman Barber, whose daughter, Mrs. W. T. Loring, has more recently occupied the same spot with her new dwelling. In the latter part of the summer of 1797, he went to buy wheat at Sheshequin, Penn., and on his way home, at Tioga Center, his horses, frightened by the violent barking of a dog, became unmanageable, overturned the wagon and threw him out, crushing his head against some heavy drags of wood that had been drawn together by the roadside, and killed him at once. His widow married 20 Sept., 1801, with Abel Stafford, and afterward moved to Canada, where she drowned herself in a trough of water. Their children, all born in Canaan, were:

I. Experience, b 28 July, 1781; m with Joel Gaylord.

II. Jonas, b 25 Nov., 1782, d in 1785.

III. Rebecca, m with David Hammond.

IV. Erastus, d unmarried at Natchez, Miss.

V. Cyrus, m with Olive Dewey.

VI. Sophia Lawrence, m with Russell Fowler.

VII. Charlotte, m with John P. House.

VIII. Betsey, m with Austin Fowler.

IX. Orange, b 23 Feb., 1796; m with Sarah House, and settled at Orangeville, Canada West (now Ontario), which was named for him.

Three of these children, Cyrus, Betsey and Orange, took their own lives.

Abel Lawrence, b at Canaan, Conn., 22 Sept., 1763; son of Jonas and Tryphena (Lawrence) Lawrence; married 6 Oct., 1783, with Abigail Rockwell. He married (2d) in 1790, with

Lucina Granger, daughter of Joel Granger, who was born 19 Dec., 1770.. They came to Brown's Settlement in April, 1796, soon after his brother, William Solomon Lawrence, and settled on the east side of the way, on lot 58, next north of that piece on which John Freeman settled. The two pieces had been owned together, and in the division it is said that an advantage of five acres had been given to that which Freeman had, because of the broken land along the little stream which came down through it. Their log house sheltered them here till the winter or spring of 1822, when they moved into the framed house, still standing (between that of Lucius W. Spaulding and that of William Floyd Monell), which was raised 12 Oct., 1821. He died 26 July, 1835. She died 8 Feb., 1837. His children were (by first wife):

I. Jonas, b at Canaan, Conn., died young.

II. Tryphena, b at Canaan, Conn., died young.

III. Abigail, b at Canaan, Conn.

(By second wife).

IV. Tryphena, b at Canaan, Conn., 22 April, 1793; died 31 July, 1871, unmarried.

V. Jonas, b at Canaan, Conn., 14 Sept., 1794; married with Ann Thomas.

VI. and VII. Twins, b in the spring of 1796, soon after the family came to Brown's Settlement; died very young.

VIII. William Solomon, b 19 Oct., 1797.

IX. Bersheba Lucina, b 16 Jan., 1800; married with Anson Miner Howard. She d 3 June, 1887.

X. Joel Granger, b 2 Jan., 1801.

XI. Charlotte, b 26 Dec., 1804; married with Pomeroy Gorsline.

XII. Susan, b 26 Aug., 1806; married with James L. Gorsline.

XIII. Wealthy L., b 30 Sept., 1808; married with Elisha Forsyth, of Owego.

XIV. Abigail Salome, b 7 Feb., 1810; died at Mrs. Forsyth's, in Owego, Feb., 1876.

Solomon Williams, b at Stockbridge Mass., 21 or 23 July, 1763, son of Azariah and Beulah (Brown) Williams; married there, 24 Nov., 1794, with Hephzibah Hart, who was born 28 March, 1772, youngest daughter of Job and Eunice (Beckley) Hart. They came to Brown's Settlement in February, 1796, and lived in the log house with his brother-in-law, Ezbon Slosson, till their own plank house was ready for use. This was built on the Knoll, or hillside, directly east of the first bark-covered cabin. A few years later he built a house on Whig street, (where Fred W. Richardson now lives) in which they died; she, 17 Aug., 1831: he, 10 or 12 June, 1838. They both joined the church, 3 April, 1831, and he was then baptized. Their children were.

I. Elisha Williams, b in 1798; died when eight years old.

II. George, b 2 May, 1801; a printer, author, bookseller, and later, a lumber merchant; m with Mary Bement; dwelt in Hamilton, N. Y., till 1839, at Owego, till May 1844, then at Belvidere, Ill., where he d 9 Jan., 1856.

III. James, b 23 June, 1803; moved to Belvidere, Ill., in 1844; m in June 1852, with Emily Royce, and died in Belvidere.

IV. Nancy, b 11 April, 1807; died at Hamilton, N. Y., 13 Feb., 1845, unmarried.

V. Sabrina, b 3 Sept., 1809.

VI. William Hart, b 10 or 11 Dec., 1811; a jeweler; resides now in Albany, N. Y,

VII. Robert, b 8 Oct., 1813 ; m 9 May 1844, with Jane Elizabeth Royce, and settled at Belvidere, Ill.

VIII. Sarah, b 28 Feb., 1816; m with Warren Pierce.

IX. Mary Elizabeth, b 2 Dec., 1818; m with Frederick B. Bement.

Joseph Hosford, son of Joseph, was a soldier in the war of the revolution. The date and place of his birth have not been found. He married at Stockbridge, Mass., 1 Aug., 1793, with Mary Williams, (often called Polly) daughter of Azariah and Beulah (Brown) Williams, and grand-daughter of Dea. Samuel and Mercy (Patterson) Brown, of Stockbridge, where she was born about 1772, baptized 1 Aug., 1773, and joined the church in 1783. They came to Brown's Settlement in the spring of 1796, arriving before Solomon Williams had his house ready for use, and for some weeks they also lived in the log house with Ezbon Slosson's family while he was building one for himself. Probably the name recorded " Joseph Hufford," in the highway tax list of 1798, for three days of work, was intended for his name. The clerk may have mistaken the long s, then in common use for an f. The Hon. Amos Patterson of Union, who then owned lot 103, gave him twenty-two acres of the southwest corner of the lot, lying west of the creek, as a token of regard for his fellow-soldier. On this land he settled. His log house stood west of Spring brook, and a few rods southwest of the wheel factory, or turning shop, successively occupied by Enoch S. Williams, Jesse Truesdell, Samuel Moses, and at present by Aaron C. Stevens. The street which lies about twenty rods south of his little farm was named Hosford street, as a memorial of him. This land he sold to Enoch S. Williams. His wife was dismissed with several others, 5 June, 1803, from the church at Stockbridge, to that about to be formed at Tioga, now Newark Valley, which she joined 20 Nov., 1803, the first Sunday after its organization, her name being the eighth on the list of members. She was dismissed in 1809, remained here till after the middle of Feb. 1810, and then with her husband and children went to Hunts Hollow, Livingston County, N. Y., where she died in 1841. He died there in 1843, of apoplexy. There children were :

I. Electa, bap at Stockbridge, Mass., 18 Oct., 1795.

II. Charles, bap at Newark Valley, 14 Feb., 1810.

III. Eunice Williams, bap at Newark Valley, 14 Feb., 1810, died at Bloomfield, N. Y.

IV. Mary, bap at Newark Valley, 14 Feb., 1810 ; m with —— Parker, and settled in Hebron, Ill.

V. Abigail, bap at Newark Valley, 14 Feb., 1810.

VI. ——, an infant, died at Newark Valley, 14 May, 1807.

VII. Franklin, b at Newark Valley, 22 Feb., 1809, bap there 14 Feb., 1810 ; dwelt at Hunts Hollow, N. Y., on his father's homestead.

Joseph Hosford, aged 84 years, died in Newark Valley, 1 May, 1806. He was the father of the preceding, and probably lived with him. There is no evidence that he had a separate household, after he came here, nor is the time of his coming known.

Michael Jenks was taxed in 1798 to work four and a half days on the highway. He came to the Boston Purchase, 12 Aug., 1796, in company with Jonas Muzzy and two others from Spencer, Mass., and settled on lot 261, now the N. W. corner lot in the town of Newark Valley. Perhaps Laban Jenks and Elisha Jenks mentioned below were those two companions. The postoffice and hamlet of Jenksville were named for him. He was born 16 Aug., 1773, eldest son of Isaac and Ruth Jenks, of Spencer, Mass., and married there 2 March, 1797, with Sarah Hunt, who was born in Spencer, Mass., 31 Oct., 1774, daughter of Aaron and Lavina Hunt, of Spencer, and previous to 1770, of Paxton, Mass. The father of Mr. Jenks was one of the sixty associates in the purchase of the ten townships.

In connection with the name of Michael Jenks Judge Avery gave the names of Laban Jenks, Elisha Jenks, Captain Scott, and Thomas Baird, as " early pioneers, well known and much re-

15*

spected," but their names do not appear in the early tax list. Michael Jenks built the first saw-mill at Jenksville, and a few years later went down the Susquehanna river, sold his lumber, received his pay for it, and since that day no tidings of him have ever reached his family and friends. They had two sons:

I. Otis, b at Jenksville, in the latter part of the year 1797; lived to be over fifty years old, and died unmarried.

II. Michael.

Jonas Muzzy, b at Spencer, Mass., 2 April, 1775, at noon, son of Jonas and Sarah (Draper) Muzzy, came to the Boston Purchase 12 Aug., 1796; stopping first on the West Owego creek, with his old acquaintance, Michael Jenks. Afterwards he came over to Brown's Settlement and worked for Elisha Wilson, as a farm hand and miller. As he was not a householder, nor an owner of land, his name does not appear in the highway tax-list of 1798. He married 27 Aug., 1801, with Thersey Moore, daughter of Henry and Lucy (Churchill) Moore, and began housekeeping the next winter on a farm of fifty-five acres on the south part of lot 58, which he bought of John Freeman, 5 Dec., 1801, for four hundred dollars. From the spring of 1806 till the spring of 1810, they dwelt in a small house just north of her father's house, then returned to his farm, which they finally left 10 Sept., 1812. He then dwelt for some years on the place with her father, after which he bought a farm on the north part of lot 218, on which he lived till the spring of 1824. He then lived in Wilson's mill-house, and attended the grist-mill till April, 1826, when he moved again to the farm on which her father had died, remaining there till 20 April, 1830, when he settled on the farm on Muzzy brook, on the south half of lot 183, where they died, she, 31 Aug., 1861; he, 17 Dec., 1864. He never forgot the fact that he was born at noon, for his father required his service till noon of the day on which he attained his majority; and he often told of that last half day, spent in building rail fence in a snow storm, without mittens. Their children were:

I. Lucy, b 17 July, 1802; m with Frederick Bean.

II. Sarah, b 13 May, 1804; m with Giles Slosson.

III. Henry Moore, b 20 Dec., 1805; m 25 Feb., 1829, with Mary Ann Farrand, who died 14 May, 1843. He died 22 Sept., 1886.

IV. Gilbert, b 11 or 12 May, 1808.

V. Sabrina Leonard, b 2 Jan., 1810; m with Henry B. Slosson, and died 6 Jan., 1867.

VI. Mary Edwards, b 30 July, 1812; married with Marshal Hotchkin, and still lives in Newark Valley.

VII. William Henry, b 28 Feb., 1814.

VIII. Alvah, died 18 March, 1816, aged four weeks.

IX. John, b 20 May, 1817; died 5 Dec., 1817.

X. Emily, b 5 Nov., 1818; resides in Newark Valley.

XI. Charles, b 25 Nov., 1820; m 30 Dec., 1860, with Helen T. North, and now lives on the homestead of his father. Two other children died when a few days old.

Uriah Simons, (or Simonds as the name was sometimes written), was the son of Francis and Zipporah (Cleveland) Simons, of Brooklyn, Conn., where he was b 2 April, 1768, according to his family record. He married 1 Aug., 1793, with Olive Tucker, daughter of John and Thankful (Eggleston) Tucker, of Stockbridge, Mass., where she was born 10 Feb., 1770. They dwelt in Stockbridge till the early months of 1797, then came to Brown's Settlement and dwelt, for a few years, on the west bank of the creek, on lot 224 (now called the Branch lot), then moved to lot 218, on the Muzzy brook, (now owned by Riley Tappan), where they died; he 26 Sept., 1844; she, 26 Jan., 1860. Their children were:

I. Ebenezer Francis, b 21 March, 1794, settled in Cortlandville, N. Y.

II. John Tucker, b 15 Jan., 1796; d 22 Sept., 1796.

III. Thankful Eggleston, b 30 Sept., 1797; went to Stockbridge and dwelt with her grandparents.

IV. Joseph, b 25 June, 1799; d 13 Jan., 1800.

V. Emeline, b 11 Oct., 1800; d 6 Oct., 1847, unmarried.

VI. Catharine Huff, b 10 April, 1802; m with Alfred Belcher Prentice.

VII. Frederick, b 16 Sept., 1804; a genial, pleasant, happy man; captain of a military company; d 23 Jan., 1863, unmarried.

VIII. Lucy Newell, b 20 Oct., 1806; d 2 April, 1839, unmarried.

IX. Mary, b 16 Jan., 1808; d 19 Oct., 1880, unmarried.

Thomas Thayer is not remembered in the local traditions, and probably soon left Brown's Settlement. His name is in the first highway tax-list, 1798, between the Wilsons and Asa Bement, which position leads to the supposition that he lived in their mill-house, on the west side of the road, and that he came here about 1797, as a millwright, to assist in building their grist-mill, in that year, yet there is a possibility that he dwelt on lot 185, where John Hedges afterward settled, as his tax was as large as many of those who owned farms.

John Freeman, whose origin has not been learned, was living, in 1797, on the east side of the way, in a log house on a long narrow farm of fifty-five and a half acres, on the south side of lot 58, and was taxed in that year to work three and a half days on the highway. In 1800 he was one of the nine postmasters in the new town of Tioga, and was elected one of the commissioners of highways, 1 April, 1801, and on the sixteenth of that month, he and Henry Moore laid the highway now known as Whig street. He sold his farm for $400 to Jonas Muzzy, 5 Dec., 1801, his wife, Ame Freeman, signing the deed, which was witnessed by Peter Wilson and John Freeman, Jr., who was probably their son. He moved to Spencer (now Caroline, in Tompkins Co.), and settled on the north half of lot 11, in the northwest quarter of township number 11, of Watkin's and Flint's "Twelve Townships," which he mortgaged 24 April, 1806, to Oliver Huntington, to secure him from any claims for dower which might be made by Freeman's daughter, Sally Steward, the widow of Henry Steward, upon certain land which Steward had sold to Huntington. The farm which he sold in Newark Valley has since been occupied by Jonas Muzzy, Samuel Addis, Samuel Johnson, Mrs. Nancy(Johnson) Rich, George E. Rich, and lastly by William Floyd Monell.

John and Amy Freeman had children:

I. John. II. Barney. III. Sally, m Henry Steward.

IV. Amy, m with Aaron Legg.

Barney Freeman, a son of John and Ame Freeman, lived with his parents or near them, probably on the same lot, in 1797, and was taxed to work three days on the highway in 1798. He was baptized and joined the "First Church in Tioga," now Newark Valley, 20 Nov., 1803, on the first Sunday after its organization; he being its tenth member, and the first to join it "on profession of faith." He died in November, 1808, according to the church record, perhaps at his father's house, in Caroline. He was long remembered as having unusual ability in vocal music, and as being "quite a singing-master." No record of wife or children has been found.

"About this time (1797) a Mr. Fellows, of Spencer, Mass., came here with his son to locate a lot for him. They selected the lot Jonas Muzzy afterwards purchased, now owned by George Rich, of Owego, and in the town of Newark Valley. After completing his arrangements, Mr. Fellows started for Massachusetts, and the son commenced chopping, feeling that now he was commencing life in good earnest, and that every stroke was for his own future good. Some time during the day a limb fell from a tree he was chopping, by which he was killed. That night Jonas Muzzy, who worked for Elisha Wilson, taking one of his horses, started to overtake Mr. Fellows. After a long and terrible ride he arrived, about daybreak, at a tavern where Colesville now is, just as Mr. Fellows was preparing for breakfast. After getting some refreshment and rest, they returned to the settlement, and the son was buried in the Brown Cemetery."

The foregoing account, quoted from page 126, of the history of four counties, is based wholly on the memories of the children of Jonas Muzzy, who often recited the particulars to them. There is reason to doubt its truth, as to the names of the persons, for on that point their memories differed, some calling the name Fellows, while others thought another was the true name.

Mrs. Daniel James Borthwick, a granddaughter of Abel Lawrence who lived on the next farm, has many times heard the tradition as handed down in that family; which says that John Freeman lived on the farm at the time the accident occurred; that the young man was about seventeen years old and was the son of Mrs Freeman's brother, who had just made her a visit, and left the lad there hoping that a few weeks of life in the woods would benefit his health which was not good. He was not at work, but feeling homesick, had gone out to see Mr. Freeman at this work, and, when as a tree was about to fall, and he was told where to go, took a contrary course and was caught by the tree which crushed him to death. She thinks the name was Lavett or Leavett. Perhaps the real name may never be fully decided.

The year 1797 must have been one of peculiar sadness to the early settlers; Isaac Brown and John Carpenter having died suddenly, in April, and William Solomon Lawrence and this young man having been accidently killed in the summer.

David Sherman Farrand, b at Canaan, Conn., 9 Jan., 1769; son of the Rev. Daniel and Jerusha (Boardman) Farrand, and grand son of Rev. Daniel and Jerusha (Sherman) Boardman of New Milford, Conn., married at Stockbridge, Mass., 5 May, 1796, with Mary Bacon, daughter of the Hon. John and Gertrude (Rousby) Bacon, who was born on her mother's plantation on the Pacomoke river, in Somerset county, Md., 11 Dec. 1769. Her father, at her marriage, lived in Stockbridge, and gave her lot 265, on which they settled, as early as the spring of 1798, (see first highway district) though the family chronicle makes it two years later, and possibly Mr. Farrand did not bring his wife and children till

the later date. She died 25 Feb. 1844. He died 1 April, 1849.
Their children were:

I. Lucia, b at Stockbridge, in Jan., 1798 ; changed her name
to Jerusha, and married with William Pierson, who still lives on
the homestead. She died 15 June 1880, without children.

II. Elizabeth Bacon, b at Newark Valley, 1 Sept., 1800, and
died there, unmarried, 17 April, 1856.

III. Esther, b at Newark Valley, 18 Jan., 1803 ; and still resides
there with her husband Daniel Chamberlain.

IV. Mary Ann, b at Newark Valley, 15 April 1805, married
with Henry Moore Muzzy.

V. Francis Henry, b at Newark Valley, 12 Dec., 1809 ; d 25 Jan.,
1835, unmarried.

Benjamin Sparrow was born at East Haddam, Conn., 9
Nov., 1762, was baptized at Millington, Conn., 9 Jan., 1763,
son of John and Anna Sparrow, from Eastham, Mass. He
was in Brown's Settlement as early as 1798, (see first highway
district,) and in 1804 lived in the north part of Owego, where
George Southwick afterward lived, and it was at his house that
Dr. Tinkham, of Owego, died, while on his way home from a professional visit to Dea. Peter Wilson. Nothing is known of his
family, except from Dr. Waldo's accounts for attendance on some
of them. His place of residence in Brown's Settlement has not
been identified.

William Stow was taxed in 1802. He died 14 Sept., 1808, aged
sixty years. He lived where Philander M. Moses built the house
in which Henry Sprague now lives, on the east side of Owego
street. He choked to death at table, if tradition says truly.

In 1798, according to the town records of Union, vol. I, p. 5,
Abraham Brown was pathmaster of the " 16th District from S. W.
cor. of Lot 432 to North line of Js McMasters half township."
This included the whole of the present towns of Berkshire and
Newark Valley, and the list which follows probably includes the
name of every man who was settled in the two towns in the
spring of 1798. A few of the names can not now be located, and
some of them do not otherwise appear. In Newark Valley, all
of the settlers, at that time were probably in the valley, while in
Berkshire some dwelt on the West hill, and some on the West
Owego creek. The number opposite each name represents the
number of days which each man was to work:

Joseph Gleason, Jr	3	*Thomas Thayer	3
Josiah How	3½	Josiah Ball	8½
Ephraim Cook	3½	Stephen Ball	3
Jesse Gleason	5	William Ball	3
Daniel Gleason	4	Daniel Ball	4½
Josiah Seeley	3	Josiah Harris	3
Caleb Gleason	5½	Benjamin Oney	3
Azel Hovey	5½	Zelotes Oney	3
Asa Leonard	4½	*Abraham Brown	4½
Ebenezer Cook	3½	Jeremiah Cammel	3
Consider Lawrence	3	*Asa Bement	6½
Abraham Johnson	3	*Enoch Slosson	6½
John Brown	5	*Ezbon Slosson	3½
*Levi Bailey	3	*Solomon Williams	4
Benjamin Sparrow	3	*Joseph Hufford	3
*David Sherman Farrand	5½	*John Freeman	3½
*Uriah Simons	3	*Barney Freeman	3
*Elijah Wilson	4½	*Abel Lawrence	3½
*Peter Wilson	3½	*Michael Jenks	4½

These names which have the * before them were probably all in what is now Newark Valley, and possibly one or two more. There is evidence that two of the names are incorrect: Josiah Harris should be Elisha Harris, and Joseph Hufford should be Joseph Hosford.

Henry Moore, b at Simsbury, Conn., 30 Jan., 1755, son of Henry and Elizabeth (——) Moore, settled in Stockbridge, Mass., where he married 21 Nov., 1782, with Lucy Churchill, daughter of Samuel and Elizabeth (Curtis) Churchill of Stockbridge, where she was born, 22 Nov., 1762. In the begining of 1799, they came to the Boston Purchase and settled on lot 178, in a log house which stood a little south of where Mr. Loveland now lives. Afterwards he built a small framed house, and later a larger one, which, after being remodeled is now owned by Mr. Loveland. In the later years of their lives they lived on the corner, named from him, in the house now occupied by Mrs. Asher C. Tappan, and there they died; he, 5 July, 1824; she, 22 June, 1846. Their children were:

I. Thersey, b at Stockbridge, 14 Oct., 1783; taught school in Asa Bement's barn in the summer of 1799; m with Jonas Muzzy.

II. William Henry, b at Stockbridge, Mass., 23 May, 1785; m 8 Dec., 1814, with Caroline Ford. He built the house now occupied by George Dohs, on the east side of Whig street, and moved in 1816, to Berkshire, where he died 11 Dec., 1845.

III. Sarah Judd, b at Stockbridge, 22 March, 1787; m with Henry Ball, of Berkshire.

IV. Peter, b at West Stockbridge, 15 Jan., 1789; m 1 Jan., 1824, with Eliza Harper Hyde, who was born in Virginia, 13 Jan., 1798, daughter of Henry and Elizabeth (Harper) Hyde. They settled on the east side of Whig street in the first house above Moore's corner. She died 3 May, 1858. He m (2d) 27 Sept., 1860, with Mary Almira (Smith) Copley, who it still living. He died 23 May, 1861.

V. Alvah Churchill, b at West Stockbridge, 2 Feb., 1791; died 10 Oct., 1813.

VI. Olive Leonard, b at Stockbridge, 21 March, 1794: died 6 Aug., 1862.

VII. Daniel, b at Stockbridge, 18 Nov., 1796; a farmer and teacher; m at Lenox, Mass., 7 Oct., 1821, with Electa Porter, who was born at Colebrook, Conn., 18 Sept., 1797, daughter of James and Jerusha (Lucas) Porter. They settled on the north side of the road at Moore's Corner. He died 6 July, 1859. She died at Williamsburgh, L. I., (Brooklyn, E. D.) 23 April, 1868.

VIII. Elizabeth, b at Newark Valley, 20 Oct., 1801; died.

IX. Sophronia, b at Newark Valley, 14 June, 1808; died.

Timothy Williams, son of Stephen Williams, came to Brown's Settlement, as the pioneer of his father's family, in the early part of 1800. bringing with him his younger brother, Stephen Williams, Jr., and settled on lot 103, which his father had bought of Hon. Amos Patterson. They boarded with Ezbon Slosson, in the log house where the Congregational lecture-room now stands, while building their own log house, which stood on the site of the first house south of the Methodist parsonage. He married 12 Dec., 1803, with Phebe Hedges, and settled in the original log house, with his father. In 1809, they moved to Victor, N. Y., where she died about 1815, or 1816. He married (2d) with a widow Keyes of Royalton, N. Y. He died at Grass Lake, Mich., about 1860, aged nearly eighty years. His children were:

I. Prudence, b in 1804; died at Victor, N. Y., about 1810, from an accidental injury to the head. She was commonly called "Dency."

II. Nathan, b 9 Sept., 1806; settled at Grimsby, Canada West, where he m 15 Jan., 1827, with Rachel Wilcox, and died there, 29 Oct., 1881.

III. Elisha, b 3 Aug., 1808; was brought up by Ezekiel Rich. He was at New Berlin, N. Y., about 1835, and his friends have never heard from him since that time.

IV. Nancy, b at Victor, N. Y.; a very energetic and useful teacher, spent most of her active life in Newark Valley, and now lives at Ontario. She was brought up by her grand-father, Jonathan Hedges.

V. Lydia Selina, b at Victor, N. Y.; was brought up by Dea. William B. Bement. She m with John McGregor, of Grimsby, Canada West, where she d about 1860.

VI. Emeline, b at Victor, N. Y., m with Henry Robinson, of Grimsby, C. W., and died there about 1865.

VII. Maria, b at Victor, N. Y., m with John Raynor, and m (2d) with Ezra Parney, and is still living at Townsend, Norfolk Co., Ont.

Children by second wife.

VIII. Sally, b at Grass Lake, Mich, m with Jackson Simpson.

IX. Eunice, b at Grass Lake, Mich., married, and she and her husband died in Iowa.

Lyman Rawson was in Newark Valley as early as 1800, and was taxed there in 1802. He lived on the farm, since owned for many years by Dea. Elijah Curtis, and his brother-in-law Lemuel Blackman, dwelt there with him. He owned a distillery, in the hollow, west of Whig street, just below the place where Jules Fivaz now lives, and the well at that place was dug to supply it with water, and was referred to in the survey of Whig street, 16 April, 1801, as "Lyman Rawson's well." He married with Deborah Keith, daughter of Eleazer Keith.* After leaving Newark Valley, they settled in the valley of the West Owego creek, in Caroline, and the place is now known as Rawson Hollow. He died 25 July, 1826, aged 51 years. She died 16 March, 1851, aged 75 years and 11 days.

Isaac Rawson, was also an early settler of Newark Valley, living at the place where Egbert Bement now lives, and was taxed in 1802. He sold the place, probably to Levi Bailey, about 1807.

Nathaniel Blackman and wife, Sarah, lived and died in Peru, Mass. They had ten children:

---

*Eleazer Keith, m with Mary Green; they dwelt in Marlborough, Conn., where he died during the revolution. She died at Lyman Rawson's, aged 99 years. Children: I. Eleazer, settled in Peru, Mass. II. Deborah, b 5 March, 1776; m with Lyman Rawson, see text. III. Eunice, m with Lemuel Blackman. IV. Rhoda, m with Abraham Blackman. V. Luther, m with Mary Hooker, of Geneseo, N. Y., and settled at Rawson Hollow, in Caroline, where he died 11 April, 1812, aged 36 years.

I. Eleazer, remained in Peru.

II. Nathaniel, remained in Peru.

III. Abraham, b about 8 Oct., 1766; married with Rhoda Keith, and settled in Caroline, where his grandson, Henry Blackman, has since lived. She died 9 July, 1839, aged 67 years. He died 19 July, 1853, aged 86 years, 9 months and 11 days.

IV. Martha, married with James Tracy.

V. Leonard, married at Peru, Mass., with Eunice Keith; they came early to Lisle, and thence, soon after, to Newark Valley, and settled on the north half of lot 143, in company with his brother-in-law, Lyman Rawson. They sold the farm to Edward Edwards, and moved to Caroline. In 1812 they returned to Newark Valley and dwelt till 1824, on the southwest quarter of lot 261, about forty rods east of the West creek road, and on the south side of the hill road. In 1820, he managed the saw-mill there, which was rated at thirty thousand feet per year. In 1824, he moved to a place on Berkshire hill, which he afterward sold to Marble Cushman.

VI. Sarah, m Ezekiel Jewett, of Caroline.

VII. Lydia, m with ——Blanchard, of Marathon, and died at the house of her sister, Mrs. Tracy, about a year after her marriage, without children.

VIII. Levi, lived with Eli, and died unmarried.

IX. Esther.

X. Eli, m with Susan Jenks, daughter of Elisha Jenks, of Jenksville.

The children of Lemuel and Eunice (Keith) Blackman were:

I. Russell, b before 1800. II. Horace. III. Mary.

IV. Silence, m with —— Durand, and lives at Jackson, Mich., a widow.

V. Julia Ann, b 10 Jan., 1808; m with Elizur B. Chapman, and in May, 1830, removed to Jackson, Mich.

VI. ——, b 20 July, 1810, a daughter.

Stephen Williams, b at Hartford, Conn., about 1743; married with Rachel Halliday, and settled in Stockbridge, Mass., where he made wooden plows, wagons, carts, and did some carpenter's work. In the beginning of 1801, in the very early days of the present century, they came to the "promised land," and settled in the log house which their sons had prepared for them in the preceding year. After a few years he built a small framed house, which has been rebuilt, and has been for fifteen years the home of the Rev. Jay Clizbe. She joined the church at Stockbridge, in 1792; was dismissed 5 June, 1803; became a member of the new church in Tioga, now Newark Valley, 20 Nov., 1803, the first Sunday after it was organized, and died 20 June, 1826. He died 15 Oct., 1823, aged eighty years. Their children were:

I. Nathan, b at Stockbridge, Mass., and died there when sixteen years old.

II. Roxa, b at Stockbridge, 7 July, 1776; m 4 July, 1804, with Pynchon Dwight. See Dwight genealogy, p. 726.

III. Timothy, b about 1778.

IV. Lydia, b about 1782; died in 1811, aged 29 years.

V. Stephen, b at West Stockbridge, Mass., 19 Aug., 1783.

VI. Henry, b at West Stockbridge, Mass., in 1786.

VII. Oliver, b at West Stockbridge, Mass., 12 Oct, 1788.

VIII. Eliza, b at West Stockbridge, Mass., about 1792; she was commonly called Betsey, and perhaps her full name was Elizabeth. She taught school in 1818, opposite the east end of Silk street, the first school in that district. She married with Leander Hooper. and settled in Royalton, N. Y.

Jonathan Hedges was born about 1749, probably at East Hampton, Long Island. It is probable that he moved first to New Jersey, where he married with a Miss —— Russell, who may have died before he left New Jersey. He settled on lot 183, as early as 1801. He was a weaver. The road from Berkshire street to his house, two hundred and twenty-eight rods long, was laid in 1805. He m (2d) with Catharine Bowen. She was born at Newport, R. I., and dwelt there till after the war of the revolution, and died at Newark Valley, 18 Jan. 1833, aged 72 years. He died 10 April, 1835, aged 86 years. His children were:

I. Jason, a mason, no records of him have been found, except the birth of one of his children, 9 Dec., 1808, and another, 24 July, 1810. He seems, in 1820, to have lived on the farm with his father, and to have had four children. In 1827 he lived in a small framed house that stood till 1840, where Philander P. Moses built the house in which Henry Sprague now lives; and not long after that he moved to Flamborough, Wentworth Co., Canada West, where he died.

II. Phebe, m with Timothy Williams.

The following were by the second wife:

III. Daniel, settled in Candor, N. Y., and had several children, one of whom was Daniel Miller Hedges. He bought for $519, 23 Nov., 1805, 173 acres of lot 380, of Pierpont Edwards, of New York city, and probably lived for a time on that in Berkshire.

IV. John, b about 1790; m with Seressa Maria Snow, and settled on the homestead of his father, where she died 16 Aug., 1847, aged 37 years. He died 22 Sept., 1859, aged 69 years, and leaving a widow, Angeline, who died at Candor, N. Y., 24 Jan., 1886. She was born about April, 1805.

V. Esther, m with Isaac Miller, of Caroline, N. Y.

VI Catharine, m with Harvey Wilkinson, and went west.

Joseph Waldo, b at Coventry, Conn., 7 April, 1780, fourth son of John and Lucy (Lyman) Waldo, came to Brown's Settlement about 1801, soon after his uncle Dr. Joseph Waldo came, and to distinguish them he was called Joseph Waldo, 2d. He bought some land on the north part of lot 217, and in March, 1802, began to trade there, in a small building. According to his account-book, nails were then one shilling and six pence per pound; 7x9 glass, ten cents per pane; and six yards of purple calico, at 6s. 6d. per yard, or $4.88 for the whole, was enough to make a dress for Josiah Balls's wife; while Elisha Wilson bought seven and a half yards of chintz, at 6s. 6d. per yard; but whiskey was one dollar per gallon, and lump sugar thirty-nine cents per pound. He married in Jan., 1808, with Mary Waldo, daughter of Dr. Joseph Waldo, and about that time built his house, which has since been occupied by the Rev. Marcus Ford, Lewis Smith, Harvey B. Smith, and owned in 1887 by Mrs. Ann Eliza Lawrence. He and his wife joined the church 3 Oct., 1819, and were dismissed 2 July, 1824. She died 8 Oct., 1830. Their children were:

I. Margaret, b 17 Sept., 1810, bap 3 Oct.. 1819, joined the church on the same day, and was dismissed 8 May, 1831.

II. Martin Bliss, b 9 Aug , 1811; bap 3 Oct., 1819.

Mial Dean, b at Adams, Mass., 14 Feb., 1768, son of Perez and Sibyl (Pearce) Dean, m Sarah Stafford, who was born 23 Nov., 1771, daughter of Abel and Rebecca (Short) Stafford. They came to Owego, in 1793, (with her father's family), and settled first at the head of the Narrows, where Joel Talcott afterward dwelt. After the death of William Solomon Lawrence, Mr. Dean bought his place on the north part of lot 63. Here he built a saw-mill, where the Knapp family now live, and that is said to be the first dam which was built across the creek in this town, as the dam to the Wilson mill only crossed a branch of it. He was named in the tax-list of 1802. She died 7 March, 1822. He married (2d) with Philotha Rude, widow of —— Hefford, and she died 26 Aug., 1849. He died 22 June, 1849. Their children were:

I. Alanson, b 28 Dec., 1789; m with Laura Dewey. He died, without children, 8 Feb., 1851; she died 23 Aug., 1866.

II. Perez Dean, b 17 Dec., 1791; m with Betsey Sterling, of Candor, N. Y., and went to Oxford, Upper Canada.

III. Sibyl Dean, b at Owego, 15 Aug., 1794; m with Richard Perkins.

IV. Stafford Abel, b at Owego, 16 Jan., 1797; m 14 Sept., 1820, with Abigail Warren, who died 16 Feb., 1859. He m (2d) with Harriet (Tiffany) Udell, and died 21 April, 1868.

V. Mial, b at Newark Valley, 20 Sept., 1799; m 11 May, 1819, with Bethia Lane. He died in Michigan.

VI. Frederick S., b 20 Feb., 1802; Married with Caroline Jayne, who died 13 April, 1827. He m (2d) with Harriet Clark, of Owego, and moved to Michigan.

VII. Lyman, b 20, March, 1804; m with Esther Scott.

VIII. Sarah, b 15 Sept., 1807, m with Joseph E. Russell.

IX. Deidamia, b 28 Feb., 1810; m with Alonzo Brundage.

X. Leroy, b 17 or 20 May, 1812; m with Betsey Tapper.

XI. Clarissa, b 20 June, 1814; m with —— — Wood.

Joel Gaylord, a shoemaker, came from Connecticut as early as 1801, and in July of that year he was living in a log house just where stands the piggery at the south end of the wing of Scott Smith's house. His name was on the tax-list of 1802. He m with Experience Lawrence. He bought of John Rewey the farm now owned by Dea. Eben Griswold, on lot 23, and dwelt there till 23 May, 1822, then moved to Oak Hill, in Union, N. Y., having sold his place to Phineas Spaulding. A few years later he moved to Springville, Erie Co., N. Y. It has been impossible to get a full record of his children, all of whom were born in Newark Valley.

I. William, b about 1803; m 8 Jan., 1829, with Eliza Ann Williams. They moved to Union, N. Y., and near where the school-house now stands, in the hamlet of Hooper, he had a shop in which he made wagons and fanning-mills.

II. Alvena, b about 1805, and died before Dec., 1820.

III, Horace, b 17 March, 1806; went to Union, in 1822, and there married with Rebecca Ann Powers, daughter of James Powers, of Union. He moved to Springville, N. Y., and his son George Hamilton Gaylord was living there a few years ago.

IV. Joel was probably the one who was born 26 May, 1808. He became blind, and went to Pennsylvania, where he died.

V. Joseph, b about 1815, was only seven years old when his father left town, since which no account of him has been found. Several people have remembered him as the youngest of four boys.

VI. ——, name not found, b 3 March, 1822, probably died young.

Linus Gaylord, a brother of Horace Gaylord, and probably several years younger, had a wife Sarah, and they settled on the west side of the creek, on lot 59; in a log house which stood just northwest of the bridge which crosses the race of Sidney Belcher's saw mill. The new road up the west side of the creek covers the ground on which it stood, and a very handsome elm tree, which grew up in the southeast corner of the house still marks the spot. On the twenty-ninth day of June 1820, he went out after supper to cut a few more trees, to make his work for the day look a little better; after a while his wife failed to hear his ax, and on going out to look for him found him senseless and bleeding with his skull broken by a falling limb. She made an alarm, and soon the neighbors came and carried him into the house. Dr. Waldo was called, and trepanned the skull but he did not rally from the shock, and died the next morning. Mrs. Gaylord returned fo Connecticut after a few years, with her children, three sons and two daughters, all of whom were less than ten years old at the father's death, and the youngest was born 6 Jan., 1820. Their children were:

I. Eson. II. Araminta. III. Cephas. IV. Polly. V. Linus, b 6 Jan. 1820.

Enoch Slosson Williams, lived where his grandson Royal Root Williams now lives, a little north of Hosford street, on the northwest corner of lot 98. He was a wheelwright and cabinet-maker. He was born at Stockbridge, Mass., 13 Dec., 1781, son of Abijah and Lucinda (Slosson) Williams, and, as his mother died when he was only six months old, was brought up in the family of his grandfather, Enocn Slosson, and came with them to Newark Valley. He learned his trade with Joel Farnham, of Tioga, N. Y. He m 26 Dec. 1802, with Rachel Wood, of Owego, who was born 19 May 1787; died 22 Aug., 1820, and was the first person buried in Hope Cemetery, on Thursday, 24 August, 1820, except two who were removed from other graves, on the same day. He m (2d) 1 March, 1821, with Betsey Hull, daughter of Silas and Eunice Hull of Berkshire. She was born 19 Aug., 1793, and died 17 Dec., 1853. He died at Reynoldsville, N. Y., 8 Sept., 1855, and was buried near his wives in Hope Cemetery. He built the first saw-mill where Hunt's old mill now stands, on the east side of the creek; and afterward built on the brook which comes out of Glen Echo, a few rods above where Charles Baldwin now lives, and near the place where Stephen Williams's sons, Stephen, Henry and Oliver Williams had formerly built one. Children:

I. Emeline, b 22 Feb., 1804; m with Charles Farnham.

II. Eliza Ann, b 13 April, 1806; m with William Gaylord.

III. Almerin, b 30 Aug., 1808; m with Margaret Van Wormer.

IV. Juliet, b 8 Sept., 1811; m with Marshal Hotchkin.

V. William Thomas, b 11 Aug., 1814; m with Lucia Ann Legg, and m (2d) with Mrs. Doney. He resides in Newark Valley.

VI. Marquis de la Fayette, b 14 March, 1817; m with Almira Allen, and (2d) with Margaret Eugenia Farley, and now lives at Trumansburgh, N. Y.

VII. Horatio Nelson, b 8 Feb., 1820; m with Emily Brown, and m (2d) with Anna S. Naramore; settled at Painted Post, N. Y.

VIII. Franklin, b 4 Nov., 1821; resides at Palmyra, N. Y.

IX. Theodore, b 12 March, 1824; resides at Newark Valley.

X. Elizabeth Rachel, b 23 Oct., 1826.

XI. Sarah Jane, b 15 Jan. 1829; m with Washington A. Noble.

XII. Enoch Slosson, b 16 Jan,, 1831; resides in Candor, N. Y.

XIII. Eunice Augusta, b 3 Aug., 1835; m with Riley T. Dean.

Pynchon Dwight was born in Lenox, Mass., 24 June, 1780, son of Joseph and Lydia (Dewey) Dwight. "In 1795 he went to Cooperstown, and from there in 1801, to Cincinnatus, and thence in 1802, to Berkshire, N. Y., where he spent the next fifteen years. He then removed to Royalton, N. Y., where he spent the next twenty-three years of his life, and in 1840 went to Jackson, Mich., to live, where he d Aug. 3, 1855, aged 75." See the Dwight Genealogy, p 726. He married 4 July, 1804, with Roxa Williams, daughter of Stephen Williams. She died at Royalton, 9 Jan., 1832. He m (2d) 10 July, 1836, with Mrs. Betsey Bascom. His home in Newark Valley was the south part of the north half of lot 58. He built his first log house about where Ephraim Nixon now lives, supposing it to be on his land, but it proved to be north of the line, on that of his brother, Adolphus Dwight. He sold this farm, about 1816, to Moses Spaulding, whose son, Lucius Wells Spaulding, still lives on it. "He is said to have been a man of noble parts, pleasing and intelligent, and commanding in his personal appearance. He was in early life a teacher, but his chief employment in life was that of farming. He was never rich, but always honest and upright in all his dealings, and was a kind father and benevolent friend." His children were:

I. Henry, b 25 June, 1805, died 24 March, 1806.

II. Henry Williams, b 30 June, 1807; m with Eliza Columbia Chaplin, of Hartland, N. Y., and settled at Royalton, N. Y., where he died in 1843.

III. Harriet Eliza, b 12 Jan., 1809; m with Warren Green

IV. Lydia Williams, b 2 Nov., 1811; m with John H. Bennett.

V. Emily, b 4 Jan., 1814, d 3 Sept., 1837; "an accomplished young lady, and of a very lovely character."

VI. Roxa Semantha, b 23 Sept., 1820; m with Hiram Stevens, and died 19 Aug., 1854.

Adolphus Dwight, b at Lenox, Mass., 15 July, 1782, son of Joseph and Lydia (Dewey) Dwight, came to Newark Valley about the same time that his brother, Pynchon Dwight, came. He settled on the north part of lot 58, in a small framed house about where William T. Loring built his brick house, on the west side of the road. He married 26 Nov., 1807, with Mercy Dean, who was born 22 Oct. 1787, daughter of Perez and Sibyl (Pearce) Dean. He sold his place about 1817, to Spencer Spaulding, and moved to Cincinnatus, N. Y., and, after 1838, to Pike, Wyoming Co., N. Y., where he died 31 Dec., 1858, aged 77. His children were:

I. Titus Harrison, b 14 Aug., 1808; settled at Pike, N. Y.

II. Lydia Dewey, b 11 Feb., 1810; m with Alvah Gregory.

III. Laura, b 6 Oct., 1812; m with Noyes Wheeler Brown.

IV. Amanda, b 28 Jan., 1815; m with George L. Bosworth.

V. Chauncey, b 23 March, 1817; m with Charlotte Morrison, and settled at Milan, Ohio.

VI. Nancy, b 24 Dec., 1819; m with Rufus Wilkinson.

VII. Polly, b 23 March, 1822; m with John Wilkinson.

VIII. Adeline, b 23 July, 1824; m with Calvin Cone.

IX. Jane Louisa, b 17 Feb., 1827; m with Curtis L. Barnes. See the Dwight Genealogy, pp. 729, 730.

Parley Simons, born at Brooklyn, Conn., son of Francis and Zipporah (Cleveland) Simons, married with Hopeful Bement, who was born at Stockbridge, Mass., 22 June, 1774, daughter of Asa and Ruth (Neal) Bement. Her father gave her the south half of lot No. 19, next to the south line of the town, and about 1803 they settled on the east end of it, building their house east of the road. It has been said that they dwelt there as early as 1801, but November, 1803, is the earliest date for which there is positive evidence of his residence here. She died 1 May, 1837. He went, about 1849, with his son, to Wisconsin, and died there. Their children were:

I. Francis Bement, b about 1804; married with Sarah Rewey, who was born at Stockbridge, Mass., in September, 1801, daughter of John and Lucy (Taylor) Rewey, and settled in the house with his parents. She died 23 Jan., 1847, aged 45 years and 4 months. He married (2d), 10 Nov., 1847, with his cousin, Abby Lavinia Hotchkin.

II. Nancy, b about 6 May, 1806; married with Lewis Rewey, and after his death, with Mr. Heath, of Speedsville, N. Y.

III. Hopeful Maria, b 13 July, 1808; and died 28 Feb., 1828.

Richard Ely Colt, whose birthplace and parentage have not been ascertained, was in Brown's Settlement as early as September, 1803. He settled on lot 224, and built on the north border of it, the small framed house in which Capt. Levi Branch and his son-in-law, Ansel H. Hammond, lived so long, and which was finally moved by Daniel H. Miller, to make room for his present house. His wife, Elizabeth, died 22 Nov., 1809. He sold his farm about 1814, to Capt. Branch, and returned to Pittsfield, Mass. Of his children: Laura P. Colt, b about 6 Jan., 1804, died 21 July, 1805, aged 18 months and 15 days; and another was born 20 Aug., 1808. There are indications that the maiden name of Mrs. Colt was Parsons.

John Harmon, b in New Marlborough, Mass., 17 Sept., 1778, son of David and Jerusha (Wilcox) Harmon, came to Brown's Settlement as early as November 1803. He married about 1805, with Jemima Hovey, and settled on the northeast quarter of lot 258, where his house was burned in April 1821, and in that fire his family record was burned. In 1831 he moved to the south half of lot 257, where he built a brick house on the site of the first and second meeting-houses, and some people thought he showed some extravagance in going to Stockbridge, Mass., for marble caps for the doors and windows. His wife died 28 March, 1838. He married (2d) with Mrs. Phebe (Spaulding) Dix. He died 17 Feb., 1853. His children were:

I. Abigail, b 15 Sept., 1806; married with Levi Branch, and after his death, with Marshal Hotchkin.

II. Jerusha, b 18 July, 1808; married with Samuel Smith Watson.

III. ——, b 23 Sept., 1811; died on the same day.

Gaylord Harmon, b at New Marlborough, Mass., 4 Feb., 1785,
16*

came to Brown's Settlement not long after the arrival of his brother, John Harmon, and lived in the same part of the town for several years. In 1820 he dwelt in a log house on the west side of Owego street, where Edward Joslin has lately built a house, just north of Dea. Eben Griswolds' house. A few years later he lived on the north side of the Wilson creek, west of Berkshire street, in the log house which Elisha Wilson first built. He married with Anice Warren, who died at Hector, N. Y., 4 Jan., 1831. He died at Mansfield, Penn., 28 Sept., 1850. It has been impossible to find a full list of their children. Some of their names follow : Frederick, b 10 Oct., 1807. Anna, b 13 Aug., 1809. Wealthy, b 26 Jan., 1816; died at Corning, N. Y., 13 Jan., 1879. Washington, b 9 April, 1818. George, b 2 April, 1820. ——, b about 1822 ; died aged one day. Gabriella, b 27 Oct., 1824. ——, b in Jan., 1831, and was buried with the mother.

David Hovey, b in Connecticut, about 1781, youngest child of Azel and Jemima (Phelps) Hovey ; m about 1806 with Lucinda Harmon, whom he first met about a year before at the marriage of his sister, Jemima, with John Harmon, the brother of Lucinda. They settled on the farm now owned by Stephen W. Ames, on lot 223, and on selling that to Dea. Ebenezer Pierce, in 1817, removed to the house now owned by George Dohs, on the east side of Whig street, and thence in the spring of 1822, to the house which he had just built, on the south part of lot 183, which is now occupied by Charles Muzzy. He had cut away just enough of the woods to make room for the house. In this house she died on Saturday, 30 July (though the church record says 29) 1825, aged about 42 years. He became ill the next week, with typhoid fever, and died 19 Sept., 1825, aged about 44 years. Their children were :

I. Nathan, b in Nov. 1807 ; was brought up by Peter Moore, m with Euretta Townsend of Great Barrington, Mass.; traded for several years in Newark Valley, and moved to Clyde, N. Y.

II. David, b 15 Jan., 1810 ; a teacher, settled in Texas. He was brought up by Beriah Wells.

III. Charlotte, b 3 May, 1812; was brought up by Elijah Belcher of Berkshire ; and died 5 July, 1869, unmarried.

IV. Chester, b 9 Feb., 1814 ; was brought up by Dea. Nathaniel Ford of Berkshire, and died 9 Feb., 1847, unmarried.

V. Henry, b 2 June, 1817; was brought up by Ezbon Slosson ; settled in Jackson, Mich. He was wounded in the eye at the battle of the Wilderness, and typhoid fever supervened, causing his death 19 June, 1864. He was buried at Arlington Heights.

VI. Mary, b 25 Jan., 1820; was brought up by John Harmon.

VII. John, b 25 Jan,, 1823; was brought up by John Harmon; m 1 Jan., 1845, with Sarah Ann Dix, and was killed by the cars at Union, N. Y., 19 Feb., 1863.

Samuel Addis, married with Submit Bartlett, who was born at Durham, Conn., 10 April, 1764, and baptized there, 15 April, 1764, daughter of Abraham and Submit Bartlett. After living at West Stockbridge, Mass., they moved in the spring of 1806, in company with Samuel Johnson, and settled on the south part of lot 58, previously owned by John Freeman and Jonas Muzzy, and built thereon a small framed house. In 1810 they went to live in the family of Hart Newell (whose wife was a younger sister of Mrs. Addis) and moved with them in 1824 to Sempronius, now Moravia, N. Y., where she died, without children, 19 Sept., 1825, having been wholly blind for thirteen years. He went to Canada, and died there, date and place not known.

Daniel Churchill, b at Stockbridge, Mass., 16 Dec., 1777; son of Jacob and Lyllis (Reed) Churchill; a mason; came to Brown's Settlement in 1800, with the two sons of Stephen Williams. He may not have bought land here at once, as he was not taxed in 1802; but soon after that he bought the farm now occupied by Mrs. Wells and her children, on the south part of lot 103, and built thereon the south front part of the house now in use there. About 1806 he married with Achsah Gaston, who was then visiting with her sister, William Gardner's wife. She died 30 Aug., 1808, leaving him with three children, the eldest only seventeen months old. He then moved into the house with Mrs. Experience (Stafford) Brown, widow of Joseph Brown, and a few months later married with her. Their home was east of Owego street, on the gravelly knoll just north of Hope cemetery. He died 2 March, 1847. She died on Sunday, 25 June, 1854, though her headstone gives the date 6 June. His children were:

I. Emeline, b 15 March, 1807; m with James W. Hammond.

II. Achsah, twin, b 15 Aug., 1808; m with Peter Rutherford, of Union, N. Y.

III. Annis, twin, b 15 Aug., 1808; m with Sylvester Howard.

IV. Seymour, b 22 Dec., 1810; a physician; m 4 July, 1830, with Catharine·Day, and died 9 July, 1864.

V. George, b 25 Feb., 1813.

VI. Amanda, b 18 May, 1816; died in July, 1837.

VII. Mary Belinda, b 2 April, 1820; m with Dr. Carlton Monroe Noble, and now lives at Waverly, N. Y., a widow.

Alanson Dewey, son of Abner Dewey, and brother of John Bement's wife. was born about 1780. He married at Stockbridge, Mass., 29 Nov., 1802, with Annis Churchill, daughter of Jacob and Lyllis (Reed) Churchill, of Stockbridge, where she was born 20 Sept., 1782. In March, 1806, they moved from Stockbridge to Newark Valley, and were living here as lately as the latter part of 1810. John Bement brought his family and goods, and his charge was made 31 March, 1806.

" To Journey to Chenango, seven days 8s. per day...$ 9.34
    " Six days coming home, at $1................. 6.00
    " Expenses on the road...................... 10.00"

and the account was settled 13 Aug., 1810. No one has been found who could tell where Mr. Dewey dwelt, when he left town, to what place he went, nor the number or names of his children, of whom it is only known that one received medical treatment 8 June, 1808, and died 10 June, 1808; one was born 13 Jan., 1810, and probably died very early, and another was born 22 Oct., 1810; since which nothing has been learned of any member of the family.

John Waldo, b at Scotland, Conn., 27 Jan., 1776, second son of John and Lucy (Lyman) Waldo, married 18 March, 1798, with Polly Rich, of Cherry Valley, N. Y., who was born at Worcester, Mass., in 1781, daughter of Luther and ———— (Jones) Rich; she died 6 Feb., 1799. He married (2d) 17 Sept., 1800, with Betsey Clark, daughter of Pharez and Olive (Jewett) Clark, of Preston, now Jewett City, Conn. They came to Brown's Settlement in 1806, and he built and settled in a small framed house near that of his brother, Joseph Waldo, 2nd. He afterward moved this house to the farm of David S. Farrand, which he worked for several years. About 1810 they went over the east hill and began the settlement on the Wilson creek, where Dea. William B. Bushnell has since lived. She died 29 Jan., according to the grave-stone in Hope cemetery, or 30 Jan., 1836, aged 67 years, according to the family record. He died 18 March, 1867, and was buried in the little cemetery which he set apart for the public to use as a burial-place, on the west bank of the Wilson creek, on his farm, at what should have been called Waldo, instead of New Connecticut, or Connecticut, as the postoffice there was named. His children were:

I. Rensselaer John, b at Cherry Valley, N. Y., 26 Jan., 1799, m 13 June, 1822, with Eunice Parsons Branch and settled in Berkshire, where they died; he, 28 March, 1870; she, 24 Jan., 1875.

II. Orson, b 17 March, 1802, m in Sept., 1825, with Lydia Waldo, daughter of Lyman Waldo, and died at Moravia, N. Y., 23 Dec., 1871.

III. Polly, b 2 Jan., 1804, m with Elijah Belcher.

IV. Emma, b 6 Feb., 1806, m with Julius Hopkins Spaulding.

V. Lucy, b 29 Feb., 1808, died 19 Feb., 1831.

VI. Clark, b 19 May, 1810, m 1 Dec., 1831, with Harriet Belcher, and died 18 May, 1853.

VII. Lyman Llewellin, b 6 Feb., 1812, m in June, 1836, with Grace Ann Andrews.

VIII. Joseph, b 31 July, 1814, died 7 Aug., 1814.

IX. Albert Gallatin, b 2 Aug., 1815, married in June, 1846, with Sarah Kennedy.

X. Betsey Clark, b 23 Jan., 1818, resides in Newark Valley.

XI. Charles, b 16 Dec., 1819, married 20 Jan., 1848, with Antoinette Phelps.

XII. Milton, b 28 Aug., 1822, a clergyman of the Presbyterian church, graduated at Hamilton College, in first division, 1848; A.M., 1851; D.D., 1868; and at the Auburn Theological Seminary in 1852. He has been a very active, useful man as a teacher and as pastor of several churches. He married in Auburn, N. Y., 6 Sept., 1855, with Maria Leonard Hardenbergh, daughter of John Haring and Hester Van der Heyden (Allen) Hardenbergh, of Auburn, where she was born 29 Dec., 1829. They reside at Amherst, Mass., but on account of his health he spends most of his time in Florida.

John Bement, b at Stockbridge, Mass., 3 Sept., 1776, son of Asa and Ruth (Neal) Bement; married with Amy Dewey, who was born 23 March, 1778, daughter of Abner Dewey. They dwelt in Stockbridge till April, 1807, then moved to Newark Valley, and settled on the north half of lot 19, which was given to him by his father. This place he sold to William Jayne, and moved, in March 1820, to Victor, N. Y., where they died; she, 30 March, 1826; he, 31 March, 1843. Their children were:

I. Phebe, b 26 March, 1798; m with John C. Lincoln.

II. Heman Dewey, b 18 March, 1799.

III. Sewell, died when two years old.

IV. Esther, b 19 Sept., 1802.

V. John Sewell, b 9 June, 1804; d 13 Nov., 1813.

VI. Mary Amy, b 13 Nov., 1806; m with Silas Boughton, and after his death, with De Forest Boughton, sons of Abraham Boughton, and dwelt in Victor, N. Y.

VII. Asa Marshall, b 8 Oct., 1809.

VIII. John Charles, b 31 Aug., 1811; settled at Waverly, Bremer Co., Iowa.

IX. Hopeful, b 21 Nov., 1813; d 4 April, 1814.

X. ——, a son, b in 1814; died aged six weeks, between 14 Nov. and 9 Dec., 1814.

XI. Hopeful, b 24 Oct., 1817.

XII. Jane, b at Victor, 22 Feb., 1823.

Hart Newell, b at Farmington, Conn., 25 June, 1776, son of John and Ruth (Merriam) Newell; married with Mindwell Bartlett, who was born at Durham, Conn., 6 July, 1770, and baptized there 8 July, 1770, daughter of Abraham and Submit Bartlett. They dwelt for a time in West Stockbridge, Mass., then moved to Union, N. Y., and thence, about 1807 or 1808, to Newark Valley, and settled in a log house which had been built by William Solomon Lawrence, on the south half of lot 63. Here he built the framed house which was afterward burned. Oliver Williams was married at his house in 1809. In 1824, having sold his farm to Lyman Barber, he moved to Sempronius, now Moravia, N. Y., and after some years, to Wales, Erie Co.. N. Y , where they died. The date of her death was 28 Jan., 1849; that of his death has not been learned. Their children were:

I. Dennis, b at West Stockbridge, Mass., 12 Dec., 1801, by family record, while the town record says 1802; married 16 Dec., 1824, with Catharine M. Curtis, who was born 9 March, 1806, and died 20 Feb., 1851. They settled in Aurora, Erie Co., N. Y., where he was living as late as 1870.

II. Mindwell, b at Union, N. Y., 16 Nov.. 1804; married 9 April, 1830, with Joseph Munsell Merrow, who died 9 Dec., 1859, at Moravia, N. Y., where she still resides.

John Rewey, born at Stockbridge, Mass., 28 Feb., 1778, son of John and Hannah (Neal) Rewey, was apprenticed to his cousin Asa Bement, to learn the trade of blacksmith, and came with him, in 1794, to Brown's Settlement. When of full age he returned to Stockbridge, where he married with Lucy Taylor, daughter of Ephraim and Sarah (Dewey) Taylor, of Stockbridge, where she was born 12 June, 1779. In October, 1807, they came from Stockbridge to Newark Valley, and built a log house where Edward Joslin has lately built a house; and near this place he killed a bear. They moved 23 March, 1808, to a log house which stood where Dr. W. J. Burr now lives, and thence to a small framed house which now forms a part of the house occupied by Mrs. Polly Smith and her sister. He built a framed shop in 1812, with a tenement in the south end of it, where Samuel Markram afterward built his house. In 1818 he built where A. C. Chapman now lives, a small framed house, which was afterward moved and became the beginning of John Butler's house. In this house he dwelt till about 1821 or 1822, when he moved to the farm on the north half of lot 144, and lived at first in a small house which stood near Bement's mill, and his new house was built a year or two later. She died 22 Sept., 1831. He married (2d) with her sister, Ann Taylor, widow of Adam Waters, of Stockbridge. He died 26 May, 1845. His children were:

I. Lewis, b at Stockbridge, 25 Jan , 1800 ; m 15 Oct., 1823, with Nancy Simons. They settled at Speedsville, where he and his brother, Henry Rewey, had a wool-carding and cloth-dressing shop. He died there 2 March, 1841.

II. Sarah, b at Stockbridge, in Sept., 1801 ; married with Francis B. Simons.

III. Oliver, b at Stockbridge, 16 July, 1804; married 1 Jan., 1826, with Mary Ann Sears, who died 18 March, 1839, in the house now occupied by Mrs. Mary E. Hotchkin. He married (2d) 8 Nov., 1839, with Emeline Allen, who still lives in Newark Valley. He died 19 Jan., 1883.

IV. Henry, b at Stockbridge, 9 July, 1806; married with Mary Wiltse, daughter of James and Nancy Wiltse, of Caroline, N. Y. They dwelt in Speedsville till the latter part of May, 1844, when they moved to one of the western states, and he was still living at Plattsville, Grant Co., Wis., as lately as 1884.

V. Eunice, born at Newark Valley, 1 Sept., 1808; married with Alfred Hyde Ford, of Berkshire.

VI. Elbridge Gerry, b 4 Dec., 1809, according to Dr. Waldo's account-book, or 8 Sept., 1810, according to the guess-work on his head-stone ; dwelt on the homestead of his father, unmarried, and was cruelly murdered on the evening of 25 June, 1879.

VII. Hannah, b 4 March, 1812; died 30 April, 1840.

VIII. Emily, b about 1814 ; married with Charles Cook Corsaw.

IX. Phebe, b 6 Oct., 1816; died 24 Sept., 1877.

Edward Edwards, b at Elizabeth, N. J., 20 Jan., 1763, second child of the Hon. Timothy and Rhoda (Ogden) Edwards, bought of Lemuel Blackman and Lyman Rawson, a farm on the north half of lot 143, on which he dwelt for several years, beginning perhaps about 1807 or 1808. He then moved to Union, and settled near the mouth of the Nanticoke creek. He joined the church 14 June, 1812, and was dismissed to Ithaca 12 Jan., 1823. He left Newark Valley in April, 1817. His wife was Mary. Edward Edwards had children as follows:

I. John K., a merchant, lived at Union, N. Y., became demented, and was tenderly cared for at his own cost, in the Broome County Home, until his death.

II. Robert Ogden, m with Caroline Keeler, and lived and died at Chenango Forks, N. Y.

III. Mary, bap 2 Aug., 1812; married when about forty years old with John McKinney, of Binghamton, N. Y., and after his death with Rev. Mr. Ercambrough.

IV. Timothy Edward, bap 2 Aug., 1812; married and had one daughter.

V. Edwin, bap 2 Aug., 1812.

VI. Henry, bap 2 Aug., 1812; settled at Warrensburgh, N. Y.

VII. Alexander Hamilton, bap 2 Aug., 1812; died at Ithaca, N. Y., when about twenty or twenty-one years old.

VIII. Charles, bap 2 Aug., 1812; a merchant, lived in Union, N. Y., and married with Jane Morse, daughter of Elias Morse, of Vestal, N. Y.

Jonathan Edwards, b at Elizabeth, N. J., 16 Oct., 1764, third child of the Hon. Timothy and Rhoda (Ogden) Edwards, married at Stockbridge, Mass., with his cousin, Lucy Woodbridge, daughter of Jahleel and Lucy (Edwards) Woodbridge, of Stockbridge, where she was born 14 April, 1769. They came to Brown's Settlement about the same time that his brother, Edward Edwards came. They dwelt in a log house at what is now called Moore's Corners, where Daniel Moore afterwards lived, and where Martin Mead now lives. They went from there to Binghamton, N. Y. He joined the church 23 Dec., 1810, and had nine infant children baptized 19 May, 1811, to wit.: Matthias Ogden, Lucy, Cornelia, Jonathan, Timothy, Richard, Rhoda Ogden, Sarah Elizabeth, and Joseph Woodbridge.

Jesse Truesdell, wheelwright, lived on lot 103, a few rods south of where Ransom Gleazen now lives. The house stood just south of the old well which is still in use on that place. He was a witty and companionable little man, fond of the good things of this life, and would work industriously in his little shop on Spring brook (which is now owned by Aaron C. Stevens) till he had a wagon load of spinning wheels, reels, etc., and then enjoy the pleasures of travel, till they were sold. He was born at North Salem, N. Y., 23 Dec., 1787, son of Jabish and Bethia (Paddock) Truesdell; married 5 March, 1812, Dolly Talcott, who was born in Marlborough, Conn., 23 April, 1789, daughter of Elizur and Dorothy (Lord) Talcott. She died 17 April, 1856. He died 9 March, 1865. Their children were:

I. Eunice Bethia, b at Owego, 9 Nov., 1812, her mother being there on a visit; m with —— Platt.

II. Charles Augustus, b 21 April, 1815; died at Kingsbury, Laporte Co., Ind., 5 Sept., 1838, unmarried.

III. Lucy Ann, b 23 March, 1818; d 10 April, 1818.

IV. Abial, b 17 March, 1819; died 29 March, 1819.

V. Lucy Ann, b 24 April, 1820; m with Lyman F. Chapman, and still lives in Newark Valley.

VI. Mary Elizabeth, b 17 Aug., 1824; died 30 Oct., 1876, unmarried.

VII. Sarah Sophia, b 13 July, 1827; m 29 Jan., 1860, with Loring Hewen. She m (2d) with Joseph Simmons, and lives in Newark Valley.

VIII. George Lord, b 9 March, 1830; died at Candor, N. Y., 18 Feb., 1881.

IX. Lucius Ambrose, b 13 or 14 Feb., 1833, died.

The Rev. Jeremiah Osborn, first pastor of the first church in Berkshire and Newark Valley, was born in Lenox, Mass., 29 Aug., 1778, son of Josiah and Hephzibah Osborn. The church and society voted to call him, 24 Dec., 1805; he accepted the call, 11 Jan., 1806; the council called to assist, met 18 Feb., 1806, at the house of widow Dudley, (now in Berkshire) and examined him. They then adjourned to the meeting-house, (now in Newark Valley) 19 Feb., 1806, and he was then ordained. He was dismissed at his own request, 27 Jan., 1819. He removed to Candor, N. Y., where he was installed 15 Sept., 1819, and dismissed 21 Sept., 1831. He afterward preached in Ohio, till 1839, when he started to visit his mother, at Lenox, and on the way, he fell dead, 20 July, 1839, at the house of his brother, in Fabius, N. Y., and was buried there. His wife was Susanna S. Woodruff, daughter of the Rev. Hezekiah North Woodruff, of Scipio, N. Y. She died, at Girard, Erie Co., Penn., 24 March, 1863, aged seventy-five years. Their children were:

I. Hezekiah Woodruff, b 8 Oct., 1808; m 30 May, 1839, with

Evelina Lydia Smith ; was installed pastor of the Congregational church at Mesopotamia, Ohio, in Jan., 1840, and died 29 Oct., 1854, leaving three children.

II. Chauncey, b 1 Aug., 1811 ; m in 1840, with Susanna Nutting; was installed pastor of the Congregational church as Farmington, Ohio, in 1842, and died at Dearborn, Mich., 30 Nov., 1856, without children.

III. Susanna, b 30 May, 1813 ; m in 1832 with the Rev. J. Alden Woodruff, and died in Hartford, Trumbull Co., Ohio, 11 April, 1845. She had eight children.

IV. Sarah Alden, b 27 Jan., 1816 ; m in Monroe, Ohio, 16 Sept., 1834, with Jedediah Chapman, and now resides at South Bend, Indiana. She has three children.

V. Maria Elizabeth, b 12 Sept., 1818 ; was a teacher for many years m 15 Oct., 1873, with Deacon Gervase Spring, and now resides at Claridon, Ohio.

VI. Clarinda, b at Candor, N. Y., 17 June, 1821 ; m 8 June, 1859, with Orson Warrener, of Claridon, Ohio, where she now lives.

VII, Josiah Olmstead, b at Candor N. Y., 17 Oct., 1823 ; m in April 1846, with Mary Ann Hanchet, and has three children. He has been a preacher in the Methodist church from 1853, till the fall of 1885, when his voice failed. He resides at McKean, Erie Co., Penn.

Notes to Census Table.—The names in the following table which are marked by a star, have already been noticed or located; the others are referred to in the following notes by corresponding numbers. We would also add that, there were no unnaturalized foreigners in the town, nor any blacks. The total population was 655, living within the *present* limits of the town.

James Wheeler, and Thankful, his wife, joined the church by letter 6 July, 1817, and were dismissed 5 July, 1833, to the new church at Berkshire. It is remembered that they were the first settlers at Ketchumville. The name does not appear in the census, and possibly their residence was east of the town line.

1. George Sykes, a native of Suffield, Conn. lived on the east side of the road, on the west bank of the creek, on the south half of lot 264. He died 26 Oct., 1825, in his 38th year.

2. Moses Spaulding dwelt on the east side of the way, on the north half of lot 58, where his son Lucius Wells Spaulding now lives.

CENSUS OF NEWARK VALLEY, DECEMBER, 1820.

NAMES.	No. Males and Ages.						No. Females and Ages.					Agriculturists.	Manufacturers.
	Under 10 years.	10 to 16 years.	16 to 18 years.	16 to 26 years.	26 to 45 years.	45 and upwards.	Under 10 years.	10 to 16 years.	16 to 26 years.	26 to 45 years.	45 and upwards.		
1. George Sykes	3				1		1	1	1			1	
2. Moses Spaulding	1				2		1	1	1			1	
3. *Abel Lawrence	1		1	3		1	1	2	3	1	1	4	
4. Samuel Johnson				1		1			1		1	2	
5. *Gaylord Harmon	2	1			1		2	1		1		1	
6. Elijah Johnson					1		1		1	1			1
7. *Joel Gaylord	1	2	1	1	1				1	1		2	
8. *Sarah Gaylord	3						2			1			
9. Jonathan Belcher	1	1			1		3			1		1	
10. David Bebee	1				1		4			1		1	
11. Jacob Conklin	1			1	1		1		1				1
12. William Janes	3	1			1		1	1	1	1		1	
13. *Parley Simons				1		1		1	1		1	2	
14. Alexander McDaniel	1		1			1	1		2		1	2	
15. Elihu McDaniel	3	1			1		1			1		1	
16. Simeon Galpin	2	1			1					1		1	
17. George Lane	2				1		2			1		1	
18. Nathan A. Gates		1		2	1		1			1		3	
19. Daniel Mead	3				1		1	1				1	
20. Jabez Stevens	1			1		1			2		1	2	
21. Seth Stevens	1			1					1			1	
22. John Belden	1	2	1	1		1	1		1			1	
23. Jacob Remele	2				1		3		1				1
24. *Jesse Truesdell	1			1	1		2		1				2
25. *Enoch S. Williams	3	1	1	1	1		1	1	2				3
26. Charles Brown	1	2			1		1		1	1		1	
27. Elijah Walter				1		1		2	2		1	2	
28. Benjamin Walter	1			1					1			1	
29. Ethan Brown	2				1		1		1	1		1	
30. John Brown		3				1			1		1	1	
31. Luke McMaster					1				1	1		1	
32. Teunis Decker	1	1			1	1			1		1	1	2
33. Alexander F. Wilmarth					1				1			1	
34. William Richardson	1	1			1		3	1	1	1		3	
35. John Millen							1		1		1	1	
36. William Millen					1		1		1			1	
37. John Bunnel	1		1	2		1				1		3	
38. John Bunnel, Jr				1					1			1	
39. *Lemuel Blackman	1	1		2		1		3	1	1		4	1
40. Zelotes Robinson	1					1	1	1		1		1	
41. Lyman Legg	3				1					1		1	
42. Ebenezer Robbins	1	2		1		1	3				1	2	
43. Loring Ferguson	2					1	1			2		1	
44. *John Harmon		2			2			2			1	2	
45. Joseph Freeman	1	2			1		3		1	1		1'	
46. *John Waldo	3	1		1	1		1	2	1			2	
47. Lyman Waldo	2	3	1	1		1	2		2	1	1	3	
48. Ebenezer Pierce	2		1	2	1		1			1		3	
49. *Abraham Brown		1			1		1			2	1	2	
50. *David S. Farrand		1					1		1	2	1		
51. Lyman Barber	1				1					1		1	
52. Levi Branch	2	1					1	2	2		1	1	
53. Bill Torry							1		2	2	1	1	
54. *Joseph Waldo, 2nd	1				1		1		1				
55. *Peter Wilson	1		1				2	1	2	1		2	
56. Roswell Livermore	1				1		1		1	1	1	4	1
57. *Elisha Wilson	1			3			1		1	1	1	4	
58. Marcus Ford					1					1			
59. Stephen Wells							1			1			

CENSUS OF NEWARK VALLEY, DECEMBER, 1820.—CONTINUED.

NAMES.	No. MALES AND AGES.						No. FEMALES AND AGES.					Agriculturists.	Manufacturers.
	Under 10 years.	10 to 16 years.	16 to 18 years.	16 to 26 years.	26 to 45 years.	45 and upwards.	Under 10 years.	10 to 16 years.	16 to 26 years.	26 to 45 years.	45 and upwards.		
60. Lucius Wells............		1			1		2			1			1
61. *Asa Bement.............	2	1		2		1	1		2	1	1	3	
62. *Jason Hedges...........	2				1			2		1		1	
63. *Jonathan Hedges.......					1	1	1	1	1			1	2
64. Absalom Baird..........							1					1	1
65. Joseph Prentice.........	2				1				2			1	1
66. *Uriah Simons...........		1			1	1		2	2			1	2
67. Duick Whipple..........				1				1	1	1		1	1
68. Joseph Allen		1				1		1	1		1	1	
69. John Watkins...........	2	1	1	1		1	2	1		1		2	
70. Mial Dean, Jr...........	1			1					1			1	
71. Luke Baird..............	1	2		1		1			2		1	2	
72. Silas Allen..............				1			2		1			1	
73. Adolphus Pierce.........	1				1					1		1	
74. William Baird...........							1		1			1	
75. John Allen............	3				1		1			1		1	
76. Harvey Marshall........				1					1			1	
77. *Jonas Muzzy...........	1	2				1	3	1	2	1		1	
78. *Henry Moore...........		1	1	2	1	1		1	1	1	1	3	
79. Elijah Curtis............	2				1		1		1	1		1	
80. *David Hovey...	2	2			1		2			1		1	1
81. Elijah Higbe............					1	1		1	1			1	1
82. *Solomon Williams	2		1	2		1	2	2				1	3
83. *Ezbon Slosson..........		1		1		2		1	1			1	3
84. Otis Lincoln............	1	1		4	1		2	1	2	1		2	2
85. *Abraham Johnson.......					1	1		1			1		
86. *John Rewey...........		1	1	2	1		3	1	1			3	
87. Horace Jones............	1	1		1	1				1		1		3
88. Oliver Williams..........	2				1	1	1	1	1	1	1	1	
89. John Gould..............	1	2			1		2			1			
90. Stephen Williams, Jr.	3	1			1		2			1	1	1	
91. Henry Williams..........		1			1		4			1		1	
92. Ezekiel Rich............	2	1		2	1		2		2	1			4
93. William Gardner.........					1		1		1				1
94. John Stedman...........		1			1		4	1	1	1		1	
95. Dexter Parmenter.......	4	1			1	1	1		1	1		1	
96. Daniel Churchill.........	2	1			1		1	1	1	1		1	
97. Chester Goodale.........	1				1		1		1	1		1	
98. Spencer Spaulding.......					2					1		1	1
99. Hart Newell.............				1	1		1	1	1		1	2	
100. William Wilbur........ .						1				1		1	
101. Richard Perkins.........	2				1				1				
102. *Mial Dean..............	1		1	2		1	1	2			1	3	
103. Alanson Dean...........					1					1			1
104. Anson Higbe...........	1			1	1		2		1			2	
105. Hosea Eldredge..........	1	1			1		1			1			
Totals...........	110	57	14	57	67	43	96	48	80	59	38	131	25

4. Samuel Johnson, dwelt on the east side of the way, on the south half of lot 58, in the second house below that of Moses Spaulding. [See Early Households of Berkshire, for an account of his household.]

6. Elijah Johnson, son of Samuel Johnson, lived in a log house, in the same yard with his father. [See Early Households of Berkshire.]

9. Jonathan Belcher, son of Joseph Belcher, dwelt on the west end of lot 23, where Hiram Holden now lives. [See Early Households of Berkshire.]

10. David Beebe, had lately sold his farm to Jonathan Belcher, and was temporarily staying in a small house, which stood west of the road near the north line of the Wade farm.

11 Jacob Conklin, had lately come from Orange county, and lived on the hill-side east of the road, on the south part of lot 23, where no house remains. In 1822 he built the house now occupied by William Wade.

12. William T. Jayne. [See later families of Richford.]

14. Alexander McDaniel, lived on the west end of lot 20, the S. W. corner of Newark Valley, and had built a saw-mill there on the West Owego creek, which then cut about seventy thousand feet of lumber each year. Soon after that time he moved to Candor, settling on lot 19, where Henry Richardson now lives; where he died 6 Jan., 1840, aged 70 years, 8 months, and 21 days, according to his grave stone at West Newark, which has his name as "McDonel."

15. Elihu McDaniel lived also on lot 20.

16. Simeon Galpin, lived on the N. W. quarter of lot 60, east side of the creek road, just north of that road which crosses the creek to Weltonville, where Henry Blewer now lives. He owned no land, but had abundance of pine timber. He crossed the creek on a foot bridge, near the site of Blewer's mill. In 1812 a Mr. Sullivan, also a squatter, lived in the next house below him.

17. George Lane, lived north of Simeon Galpin, probably on lot 61.

18. Nathan A. Gates, lived east of the road, on the S. W. quarter of lot 60, where Charles Blewer now lives. He was son of Nathan Gates who settled in Candor. He probably settled here in 1817, "the year after the cold summer." He afterwards moved to Penn Yan, N. Y., where he died about Feb., 1860. His only child is the wife of Cornelius Hover.

19. Daniel Mead, lived on the east side of the road, on lot 100.

20. Jabez Stevens and wife, each over forty-five years old, were living on the southeast quarter of lot 65, where Henry Zimmer afterward dwelt for many years. He probably came from Knox, N. Y., in 1819, with his son, Seth Stevens. He was not of sound mind, and after the death of his son Seth, he went west with his wife and other children. His son Elisha married with Lucretia Higbe, youngest child of Elijah Higbe.

21. Seth Stevens, son of Jabez Stevens, above, was the first one of the settlers from Albany and Schoharie counties to come into the "east settlement" in Newark Valley. He left Knox, N. Y., in a sleigh, 19 March, 1819, the day on which Van Alstine was hung at Schoharie, and settled in the house at the corner of the roads on lot 56, which was built and occupied by Capt. Elisha Hooper, and was afterward kept as a public house for many years, by Joseph Cookson. His land was the south part of lot 65, and on this, at the top of the hill, he had cleared a few acres, had a cellar dug and partly stoned, and timber for the frame of a house, when, about the first of October, 1820, he became ill, and died about the 15th of October, 1821. His wife and two young children went back to live with her parents, and his clearing was covered with a thick growth of thrifty young white pine trees, which were not cleared off till after 1840. Stevens and his father were the only householders living, in 1820, on the road that leads east from G. B. Sutton's, within the present town of Newark Valley.

22. John Belden lived in a log house on the southeast corner of lot 102, very near the remains of a small house in which Joel Shaw once lived. He left town in a few years, and little is known of his family. One of his children was born 28 April, 1820.

23. Jacob Remele, a shoemaker, lived on the east bank of the creek, south of Silk street, in the plank house which Solomon Williams built, east of the site of the grist-mill, and which was burned 5 Jan., 1871, then the home of Sarah Jones and her sister, Susanna Jones. He was son of Jacob Remele, of Stockbridge, Mass., where he was baptized 6 July, 1785. It is not known when he left town, nor to what place he went. One of his children was born 25 Jan., 1814; one was drowned 10 May, 1815, (a young girl having tried to cross the creek on a single pole with the child on her back); two were pupils, in the summer of 1818, in the school at the head of Silk street; another was born 10 Nov., 1820; while the census seems to show two sons and three daughters, all under ten years of age, in Dec., 1820, yet no one has yet been found to remember any name of wife or child.

26. Charles Brown lived on the west side of the road, on the northwest quarter of lot 140, a little north of the end of the hill road. He died there, 23 July, 1827, aged 46 years. His wife, Sally S. Brown, died there 22 May, 1826, aged 43 years. It is said that he was not akin to the Browns who dwelt further up

the creek. They had two sons and a daughter, who went west after their parents died.

27. Elijah Walter lived on the east side of the road, on lot 140, northwest quarter, where Elton Cortright now dwells. He had formerly lived in Norfolk, Conn. He married with Mary Scranton Field. He was a deacon of the Congregational church of West Newark. He died 10 Nov., 1836, aged 79. She died 29 Dec., 1841, aged 78 years.

28. Benjamin Walter lived on the west side of the road, a little above his father, Elijah Walter, on the same lot. He married with Almira Brown, daughter of John Brown. She died 4 Ian., 1844, in her 47th year. He married (2d) with Repina Rich, daughter of David Rich, of Caroline. She died 22 March, 1849, aged 54 years. He married (3d) 17 July, 1851, with Nancy Seymour, who was born at Whitney's Point, N. Y., 7 April, 1803, daughter of John and Sarah (Stoddard) Seymour. Previous to his third marriage he removed to the village of Newark Valley; and in 1866, went to Pulkton. Ottawa Co., Mich., where he died 22 Feb., 1868, in his 73d year. He was a man of more than ordinary intelligence, with piety of such a high order that no church could be found sufficiently sound on the questions of slavery and temperance, to warrant him in becoming one of its members. He had by his first wife one daughter, Mary.

29. Ethan Brown lived on lot 141, on the west side of the road, where Joshua Carpenter now lives. He was born about 1791, son of John Brown. He married with Nancy M. Wilmarth, daughter of Benjamin and Susanna (Capron) Wilmarth. She died 1 May, 1868, aged 79 years; he died 30 May, 1873, aged 82 years. Their children were: John, George, Maria, Susan, Caroline.

30. John Brown lived on the west side of the road a little above his son John Brown, and on the same lot. He came there from Stockbridge about 1818, with his wife Esther and a few of his fourteen children. His wife died on that place. He was a stone-cutter, and in the latter part of his life, not always quite sound mentally, spent much of his time away from home. He is said to have died at Palmyra, N. Y., where he was cutting stone to be used in building locks on the Erie canal, and was buried there by the Free Masons, of which order he was an enthusiastic member; and it is further said that they protected his grave by an iron railing. Several of his children died in New England; some married and remained there; among others were:

Ethan, mentioned above, No. 29. John.

Almira, m with Benjamin Walter, No. 28.

Henrietta, the youngest, b 25 June, 1806, m with Horace Richardson, and died in Candor, 22 May, 1881.

31. Luke McMaster, a laborer, married with Lucinda Williams, a half-sister of Enoch Slosson Williams, and had several children. There is no evidence yet found that he ever owned a home; and his house at this time has not been identified, though he probably worked for one of the Browns, and lived in one of their log houses. A few years later he lived in the old house of Enoch S. Williams, on top of the hill, south of the present home of Franklin G. Dean. Some of his children were born, ——, 8 Aug., 1820, which probably died young; ——, 15 Sept., 1821, and this may have been Miriam, who is said to have died of whooping-cough, about 1828 or 1829.

32. Teunis Decker lived on the east side of the road, on lot 180, about twenty rods north of where William Watkins now lives. He was a blacksmith, and probably came there about 1818. He married with Susanna (Capron) Wilmarth, widow of Benjamin Wilmarth, and daughter of Joseph and Sarah (Foster) Capron, of Attleborough, Mass., where she was born 29 June, 1765. He died 18 Dec., 1839, in his 74th year. She died 6 Oct., 1852.

33. Alexander Foster Wilmarth lived in the same framed house with his mother and step-father, Teunis Decker, on lot 180. They had built this house since they settled on the lot in 1816, which had then no building except a log cabin which had been built for a shop for " shingle-weaving." He was born at Stockbridge, Mass., 4 Sept., 1793, son of Benjamin and Susanna (Capron) Wilmarth, and married with Electa Tracy. He died 5 May, 1822. His children were:

I. James Otis, b 2 Nov., 1820, died 1 July, 1821.

II. Nancy M., b 31 Dec., 1821, m with William Watkins, and still lives on her father's homestead. Mr. Wilmarth had two sisters, Susanna, who m with Charles DeLand, a clergyman of the Baptist church, and settled at Lodi, N. Y., and Nancy M., who married with Ethan Brown, and his elder half-brother, Benjamin, afterward lived in Newark Valley.

34. William Richardson lived on the west side of the road, on lot 181, where Monroe Barrett now lives. He was born in Attleborough, Mass., 6 April, 1770, son of Vinton and Abigail (White) Richardson; not as stated in the Richardson memorial, p. 294.

He married 23 March, 1797, with Milla Capron, who was born in Attleborough, 23 April, 1779, daughter of Joseph and Sarah (Foster) Capron. See the Capron Genealogy, p. 135. Her name was, perhaps, a contraction of Melicent. She died 1 Nov., 1848, in her 70th year. He died 17 Sept., 1861, aged 91 years and 5 months. Their children were all born in Attleborough, except the youngest.

I. William, b 4 June, 1798, ; died 13 July, 1854.

II. Milla Capron, b 29 Nov., 1799, m with William Solomon Lawrence, and died 25 Jan., 1835. One of her daughters, Mrs. D. J. Borthwick, still resides in West Newark.

III. Elias, b 3 March, 1802 ; is still living.

IV. Horace. b 22 Nov., 1803 ; m with Henrietta Brown, daughter of John Brown, and still lives in the east border of Candor, in sight of his father's homestead. His wife died 22 May, 1881.

V. Fanny, b 22 May, 1807.

VI. Herbert, b 20 March, 1811 ; m 13 Feb., 1838, with Esther Waldo. He died 28 Dec., 1882. His son, Fred Waldo Richardson, now lives in the village of Newark Valley.

VII. Hannah Maria, b 13 Sept., 1813 ; m with George Frederick Waldo, of Waverly, N. Y.

VIII. Sarah Jane, b 8 June, 1817.

IX. Nancy Capron, b 6 Oct., 1820 ; m with Theodore Jenks, and died 8 Oct., 1865.

35. John Millen lived on the east side of the road, on the northwest quarter of lot 221, about ten rods south of where Elisha Millen now lives. It is said that he came from Stockbridge, Mass. He died 11 March, 1830, aged 77 years. He married with Sarah ——, who died 30 Dec., 1838, aged 72 years. They had children :

I. William, b about 1791. See below. II. James.

III. Cynthia, m with Levi Cortright.

IV. Rachel, m with Lodawick Hover.

36. William Millen lived on the east side of the road, on lot 221, where Elisha Millen now lives. He was a son of John Millen, above. He died 28 Aug., 1862, aged 71 years. His wife died 25 July, 1865, aged 66 years.

40. Zelotes Robinson, attended the grist-mill, and lived east of it, on the north side of the road which led to the mill. His only child was a daughter who married and went west.

41. Lyman Legg lived on the west side of the road, on lot 261,

17*

very near the northwest corner of the lot and of the town. The water for the mill was taken out of the creek on his land. His house was very near the bank of the creek. He was a son of Reuben Legg, and a grandson of David Legg. He m with Betsey Osborn, daughter of Samuel Osborn. He died there and was buried in the cemetery on the next farm above. One of his children, probably the third son was born 3 July, 1820.

37. John Bunnel lived on the west side of the way, on the southwest quarter of lot 260, where Cornelius Ackerman now lives. He had first settled in the Park Settlement, in the southeast corner of Candor, and remained there till after the birth of his oldest son. He and his wife, Hannah, were constituent members of the "Baptist church of West Owego Creek," 1 May 1802, now in Candor, and he was elected its first deacon. He was a shoemaker, farmer, and a very successful hunter and trapper of wolves and bears. He caught one bear and several wolves after 1820. He died 15 Jan., 1840, in his 68th year. She died 7 Nov., 1837, in her 60th year. The following list of their children may not be complete.

I. Isaac, b at Park Settlement, in Candor, N. Y. See census of Berkshire, note 18.

II. John. See below, note 38.

III. Henry, still living in Berkshire.

IV. Anna, had medicine from Dr. Waldo, 5 Aug., 1812.

V. James, b 11 Sept. 1808 ; died 22 May 1809.

VI. Gershom, b 9 May, 1810 ; died, date not stated.

VII. Jesse, b 17 Feb., 1811 ; died 17 April, 1811.

VIII. David, may have been born 4 Aug., 1812.

IX. Cornelia, b 22 March, 1817 ; died 1 July, 1817.

X. William, b about 1818.

XI. Benajah, b about 1820.

38. John Bunnell, Jr., lived on the same lot with his father, on the hill-side about eighty rods east of the road where no house stands now. One of his children was born 21, March, 1821.

42. Ebenezer Robins, came from Peru, Mass., in Nov., 1812, and, in Dec., 1812, settled on lot 182, where his son Harlow Robbins succeeded him, and his granddaughter, Mrs. Hinsdale now lives.

43. Loring Ferguson, came from Peru, Mass., as early as the spring of 1812, and began to work for John Bement, 6 March, 1812. He settled in a log house which he built near the centre of fifty acres on the northeast corner of lot 179. A few years later

he moved to Berkshire, and lived on the west end of Dr. Waldo's farm, on Strong brook, where he dwelt for six years, then moved to the west side of Wilson creek, in the south part of Berkshire. He was born in Blandford, Mass., 15 Feb., 1787, son of John and Sarah (Knox) Ferguson. His parents came with him to Newark Valley, and his mother died here 19 April, 1817. Same year later his father returned to Blandford, and died there. After getting his parents well settled he returned to Peru, and there married 13 Oct., 1813, with Laura Cone, whom he brought to Newark Valley. He died in Berkshire, 20 Nov., 1838. His widow returned to New England in 1840, and died 2 June, 1860, at the house of her youngest daughter, in Columbia, Conn. His children, all born in Newark Valley were:

I. Chauncey Ackley, b 12 June, 1815; moved to Wisconsin, where he enlisted, but taking the measles, he died 20 Jan., 1862, without having left the state for active service.

II. Selden Knox, b 8 May, 1817; died of consumption at Hinsdale, Mass., 14 June, 1857.

III. Olive Melissa, b 1 June, 1820; died of gangrene, at Peru, Mass., 22 May, 1866.

IV. Lansing Spencer, b 3 June, 1822; resides at Middlefield, Mass.

V. Asenath Caroline, b 21 Aug., 1826.

45. Joseph Freeman. His home in Dec., 1820 has not been ascertained. See Berkshire, 1802.

47. Lyman Waldo, brother of John Waldo, lived in the same neighborhood, and built the first house east of the Wilson creek, on the south side of the Ketchumville road. He came from Burlington, N. Y., about 1817, and finally moved to Portage, N. Y., where he died 23 July, 1865, aged 91 years and 15 days.

48. Ebenezer Pierce lived on lot 223, where S. W. Ames now dwells.

51. Lyman Barber lived east of the present road, and west of the old road, in the house which had been lately vacated by the Rev. Jeremiah Osborn, on lot 264, near the north line of the town.

52. Levi Branch lived on lot 224, on the west side of the way, where D. H. Miller now dwells.

53. Bill Torry lived in a small house on the same lot, east of the way, where Capt. E. N. Chapman afterward built his house. [See Early Families of Berkshire.]

56. Roswell Livermore lived in a log house, on lot 217, on the

east bank of the creek, north of the road where it turns to cross the creek.

58. Marcus Ford lived in the house with Elisha Wilson. He was born 29 March, 1793 ; was ordained 13 Dec, 1820, and on that day a portion of the census of Newark Valley was taken.

59. Stephen Wells lived south of Wilson creek, and west of the road, in the house which his son, Beriah Wells, had built a few years before.

60. Lucius Wells lived in the same house with his father, Stephen Wells.

64. Absalom Baird lived on the north side of the east and west road, at Moore's Corner, where Martin Mead now lives.

65. Joseph Prentice lived on lot 183, east side of the way, where —— Henderson now lives.

67. Duick Whipple lived on the south part of lot 223, on the old road, since discontinued, on top of the hill, north of where William Reeves now lives. The old barn still stands near his dwelling-place, but the house was long since moved away.

68. Joseph Allen lived on the first road that leads to the north, above where William Reeves lives, and about a quarter of a mile from the parting of the roads.

69. John Watkins lived on lot 219, within the corner of the road where it bends to the northwest, leading to the West Owego creek.

70. Mial Dean, Jr., lived in the same house with John Watkins, and was improving a place on the southwest side of the road, at or near the place where Lyman Freeland now dwells.

71. Luke Baird lived on the hill, on a private road, north of the place lately owed by Elbridge Barber, and his son, Darius Barber.

72. Silas Allen lived in a log house, a little above the place lately owned by the Barbers, and on the south side of the road.

73. Adolphus Pierce lived in the field, about forty rods northwest from Luke Baird's, and between his place and that of Mial Dean, Jr.

74. William Baird lived on the road above Joseph Allen, and not far from where Jireh Councilman now lives.

75. John Allen lived on the north side of the road where now stands the Barber house, which was built by Elder Snyder.

76. Harvey Marshall lived in a log house on the farm of John Watkins, and northwest of where Watkins lived. He soon

moved to Spencer with his wife and only child, which was not born till after the census was taken.

79. Elijah Curtis lived on the north half of lot 143, on the west side of Whig street.

81. Elijah Higbe lived on the west side of Whig street where Egbert Bement now lives. His grave-stone in Hope cemetery shows the date of his death as 13 Sept., 1820, but the census proves that he was alive in Dec., 1820, and he probably died 13 Sept., 1821.

84. Otis Lincoln lived in the "Old Tavern," which he kept nearly 20 years, where the new brick school-house is now taking form.

87. Horace Jones lived in a small framed house, which stood on the west side of the way, and now, on its original site, forms part of the dwelling house of Mrs. Polly Smith.

88. Oliver Williams, probably lived in the house with his father, where the Rev. Jay Clizbe has since lived, and his parents were counted as of his family.

89. John Gould lived on the west side of the way, about where E. G. Tibbitts now lives. The house was a small one built for a mitten shop by the Williams Brothers.

90. Stephen Williams, Jr., lived on the west side of the way, in the first house north of Silk street.

91. Henry Williams lived on the south side of Silk street, where N. P. Chapman now lives.

92. Ezekiel Rich lived in the south or old part of the house now occupied by Mrs. Jane Wells and her children. See later families of Richford.

93. William Gardner lived on the east side of the road, where P. P. Moses built the house now occupied by Henry Sprague.

94. John Stedman lived on the east side of the road, where W. A. Noble and J. T. Noble now dwell. See later families of Richford.

95. Dexter Parmenter (otherwise written Palmeter) lived in a small house which stood on the west side of the way, about mid-way between Stedman's house and that of Daniel Churchill.

96. Daniel Churchill lived on the east side of the way, on the gravelly knoll, a few rods north of the cemetery.

97. Chester Goodale lived in a log house where Ephraim Nixon now dwells, on the west side of the way.

98. Spencer Spaulding lived on the west side of the way, where William T. Loring afterwards built his brick house.

99. Hart Newell lived on the east side of the way, on the south half of lot 63, where Lyman Barber afterward lived.

100. William Wilbur lived in a log house with a framed lean-to which stood where the south end of the wing of W. S. Smith's farm house now stands, on the north half of lot 63, east of the way.

101. Richard Perkins lived on the south border of lot 98, west of Owego street, and north of the road that leads to Knapp's.

103. Alanson Dean lived on the east side of the road, just on the line of lots 63 and 98, in the same house with his father.

104. Anson Higbe lived on the west side of the way, opposite the road to Union, on the south half of lot 98, where his grandson, George Byron Sutton, now dwells.

105. Hosea Eldredge lived in a log house, on the north side of the Ketchumville road, east of the Wilson creek road, where George Andrews once lived, and later his brother, Luther Andrews, on lot 266. He was born at Ashford, Conn., 4 June, 1783, son of Hezekiah and Elizabeth (Whiton) Eldredge; removed when sixteen years old to Salisbury, Conn., where he m 6 Oct., 1805, with Cyrene Collins, who was born there 2 Feb., 1783. They left Salisbury about the beginning of 1811, and dwelt at Edmeston or the adjoining town of Plainfield, N. Y., till early in 1818, when they settled on the place described above. They joined the church by letter, 3 Oct., 1819, and were dismissed to Ithaca, N. Y., 16 Oct. 1835. He died 31 March, 1837. She died 5 May, 1838. They had three children :

I. Edward Hezekiah, b 11 Sept., 1806; a physician; m with Marcia Belinda Orven, and m (2d) 19 Oct , 1857, with Mary Sophia Ball.

II. Mary Abigail, b 9 Oct., 1809.

III. Horace Newton, b in Plainfield, N. Y., 4 June, 1812.

Early Highways.—No record has been found of the formal or official laying out of the first highway through the valley, on the east side of the creek from the place now owned by G. B. Sutton, to the north line of Berkshire, now known as Owego street, south of the Green; and Berkshire street, north of it. For several years this road was used on the east side of the creek, across lots 217, 224, and the south half of 257, between the creek and where the railway now runs, but after good bridges were made across the creek the road on the west side took the whole travel, and the other was discontinued. Another change has been made above the village of Newark Valley, where the road till after 1846 crossed the low swampy land between the hill and the creek.

It was then worked along the base of the hill, by cutting out and throwing down enough of the rock to form the roadbed. This improved road was begun on the first day of June, and finished on the third day of July. The year is not positively remembered, but it was about 1848. It was made by Otis Lincoln. Charles Baldwin, who then worked for him, claims to have been the first man to jump into the water where it was three feet deep, to begin the work, and his courage was sharpened by a silver dollar and an extra drink of whiskey.

Soon after Wilson's mill was built, a road was laid from the place now owned by Edwin Smith, across the creek to "Moore's corner," thence up the Muzzy brook, and over the hill to the Jenks Settlement, so that the people there might have a road to the grist-mill. Of this road no survey has been found. This road went nearly northwest to the top of the hill, at the place now owned by Fred W. Richardson, then down the hill to the west creek.

Of Whig street, the following tells the story:
"1801, April 16th.

The survey of a road ascertained as the following manner, viz.:

Beginning on the road leading from the village of Owego to Brown's Settlement at a stake an stones standing in the west line of said road near Enoch Slosson's barn, from thence north-west 36 rods to a stake and stones on the west bank of the creek, thence north 45' east to a maple staddle near Lyman Rawson's well, thence the same course to a stake and stones, near the house of Henry Moor, thence the same direction until it intersects the road leading to Jenks Settlement. Certified by

JOHN FREEMAN,
HENRY MOOR.

On the seventh of July, 1803, a road measuring 1,138 rods, or eighteen rods more than three miles and a half long, with twenty-four different courses, was laid from "a marked tree south of Daniel Carpenter's house," near the center of lot 302, in Berkshire, "to intersect the road laid from Jenks Settlement to Wilson's Mills." This road ended near the school-house, east of the Hotchkin house, now occupied by Mr. Reeves, but instead of coming down along the brook where the road now runs, by the farm of Stephen W. Ames, it came over the top of the hill far to the west of his house.

"Survey of a road laid by the commissioners, in and for the town of Tioga, Feb. 18th, 1804.

"Beginning on the division line between Joseph Brown and Dan'l Churchill, 3d line being the centre of the road; thence W.

67 chains ; thence N. 22° W., 10 chains ; thence N. 65° W., 6½ chains ; thence N. 80° W., 16½ chains ; thence N. 37° W., 15 chains ; thence N. 70° W., 12 chains ; thence S. 87° W., 4½ chains ; thence—40° W., 5 chains ; thence N. 66° W., 15 chains ; thence N. 78° W., 5 chains ; thence S. 85° W., 5 chains ; thence S. 70° W., 10 chains ; thence N. 70° W., 5 chains ; thence N. 81° W., 10 chains ; thence S. 75° W.. 12½ chains to the West Owego Creek.

Certified by ABRAHAM BROWN,
LEMUEL BROWN."

This road was probably never opened. Its starting point was at the south line of the farm now owned by the family of the late Frederick T. Wells, and passed directly over the hill on which Royal R. Williams lives, on the line between lots 98 and 103. The principal work to be done on it for many years, was in hauling logs and wood, all of which naturally passed twenty rods further south through the woods, and went around the hill on level ground, where the road was afterward laid. The record of the present road, known as Hosford street, went out of existence when the town records of Newark Valley were burned.

"A description of Roads laid by the Commissioners in and for the town of Tioga, 1805.

"Also a road Beginning at a stake and stones standing North of Asa Bement's house, on the east side of the road leading through Brown's Settlement, thence North 88 degrees east 12 chains ; thence North 72 degrees east, 29 chains & 75 links ; thence North 82 degrees east, 15 chains and twenty links, to a Beach tree marked E. H., standing on the farm of Jonathan Hedges."

Certified by ASA LEONARD, } Comm'rs
SAMUEL BROWN, } of
} Highway."

Many years passed before any settlement was made in that part of the town, east of Mr. Hedges, and not till after 1820 was the road opened from that road north, up the Wilson creek.

In the same certificate with the foregoing, was the survey of a road measuring a trifle over five and six-tenths miles, " beginning at a Birch tree standing in the east line of lot No. 160, in the Nanticoke township," and running " to the Road leading through Brown's Settlement," opposite the place now owned by G. B. Sutton.

"Survey of a road leading from Henry Williams' to Daniel Cortwrect's, on West Owego creek, laid and surveyed April 11, 1814. Beginning on the Creek road, one rod north of Henry Williams' north line, runing west 18 chains in such manner as will take three rods wide on Stephen Williams' land, and one rod wide on said Henry Williams' land, thence north 69 degrees west, 4 chains and 30 links, thence north 74°, west 7 chains and 75 links," etc. This measurement brings the road upon the west bank of the Spring brook, and the survey continues through twenty-two additional courses, a distance of seven hundred and twenty rods, "to intersect the road on the West Owego." This makes the whole distance, as then measured, a few feet more than two and five-eighths miles. The east end of this road received the name of Silk street, about 1840, from the fact that Sylvanus Merchant, who lived on it, kept silk worms for several years. This road was laid by John Waldo and Abraham Brown, the highway commissioners of the town of Berkshire, and it seems to have been the last road laid before the town of Westville, now Newark Valley, was set off from Berkshire.

Organization.—The town of Westville, authorized by the legislature, 12 April, 1823, was organized by a meeting of the inhabitants at the house of Otis Lincoln, 2 March, 1824, and the election of a full board of town officers, whose names, except the minor officers, have already been printed in the History of Four Counties, p. 147. The name of the town was changed by act of the legislature, 24 March, 1824, to Newark. The destruction of all town records by fire, 16 Oct., 1879, gives a special importance, historically, to anything that may be recovered, in relation to the early history of the town. The early custom was to adjourn the town meeting to the regular day for holding it in the next year, which led the clerk to call it an adjourned meeting, rather than the annual meeting. The following is a copy of the record made by the clerk at the second town meeting, it being the first held after the town took the name of Newark. The spelling of two or three names only has been changed to conform to the family usage:

"At an adjourned meeting of the inhabitants of the town of Newark, held March 1, 1825, at the house of Otis Lincoln in said town, Anson Higbe in the chair—The following officers were elected to office:

Solomon Williams, Supervisor.
Beriah Wells, Town Clerk.
John Waldo, Francis Armstrong, Peter Moore, Assessors.
Benjamin Wilmarth, Abraham Brown, Jonathan Belcher, Commissioners of Highways.
Ebenezer Pierce, Peter Wilson, Overseers of the Poor.
William Slosson, Collector; William Slosson, Constable.

Francis Armstrong, William Richardson, Lyman Waldo, Commissioners of Common Schools.

George Williams, Elijah Wilson, Benjamin Walter, Inspectors of Common Schools.

Overseers of Highways, District No. 1, Francis Armstrong; No. 2, John Rewey; No. 3, Levi Smith; No. 4, John Harmon; No. 5, Ebenezer Robbins; No. 6, John Waldo; No. 7, James Wheeler; No. 8, Reuben Chittenden; No. 9, Simeon Galpin.

Fence Viewers—Voted that there be six fence viewers, Moses Spaulding, Alanson Dean, Charles Brown, Lyman Legg, Abraham Hotchkin, Denick Whipple.

Josiah Benjamin, sealer of weights and measures.

Voted that the commissioners and inspectors of common schools for the year 1824, and the present year be allowed the compensation which the law prescribes for their services.

Voted that the sum of seven dollars and twenty-five cents be paid Anson Higbe out of the funds belonging to the town for money expended on the highways some years past.

Voted, double the sum of school money which we receive from the state, be raised by the town.

Voted, that this town raise twelve dollars for the purpose of procuring the standard weights and measures.

Voted, that this meeting adjourn to the first Tuesday of March next at ten o'clock A. M., at this place."

The name of the town, changed 17 April, 1862, to Newark Valley, should once more be changed to Arkley, that it might be distinctive, and never again be confounded with Newark, N. J., Newark in Wayne Co., N. Y., or with Cherry Valley, N. Y.

BUSINESS CENTERS

NEWARK VALLEY.—While the population of Brown's Settlement was confined to the valley, the social center was naturally the business center. The church was built on lot 257, near the home of Mrs. Beulah Brown; and the first store was not far away, near the north part of lot 217, little more than the width of a single lot intervening. The first road made to accommodate the early settlers on the Wilson creek, in the New Connecticut district, came down the steep east hill-side, from northeast to southwest, coming out at the east end of the road which crosses the creek in front of the house of Rodney Ball. Another road, almost as hard to travel, came down the west hill, connecting with the valley road near the center of lot 224, and this is still open, but very little used.

When the hills on each side began to be settled, the roads of necessity followed the lateral streams or valleys, and business began to increase near the points where they entered the valley, and soon separate business centers were formed where the villages of Berkshire and Newark Valley now stand, and began to force social life and interest to form about the same centers, and led to the division of the town ; but possibly the conservative powers of Calvinism might have kept the church united at the old center till the present day, if some teachers of a new faith and practice had not begun to occupy the new fields and grow up with the villages, thereby stimulating the " standing order," as they were formerly called in Connecticut, to arouse themselves to meet the new condition of affairs.

Here ends the historical matter for Newark Valley furnished by D. Williams Patterson ; and we add the following additional facts:

The village is a neat, thriving, even handsome community of about 800 souls. It has some dozen or more stores of various kinds, a large tannery, two steam saw-mills, grist-mill, and the usual complement of mechanics' shops.

KETCHUMVILLE is a small post-village located in the northeastern corner of the town.

JENKSVILLE is a small post-village located in the northwestern part of the town, on the west branch of Owego creek. This village was settled as early as 1797. Michael Jenks built a saw-mill in 1803, and a grist-mill in 1814.

WEST NEWARK, a small settlement about two miles south of Jenksville, containing a postoffice.

NEW CONNECTICUT is a small settlement in the northern part of the town.

Davidge, Landfield & Co.'s Tannery.—From an early date the site of this firm's building has been used for tanning purposes ; first for tanning deerskins, etc., and their manufacture into gloves, mittens and articles of clothing. The property passed through several hands, and the buildings have been twice destroyed by fire. In 1865 George H. Allison, John Davidge and Jerome B. Landfield purchased the property, and commenced business under the firm name of Allison, Davidge & Co. They continued the business till 1867, when Allison became sole owner. In 1868, however, Davidge, Landfield & Co. bought the property, and no change has since been made, except to transfer Mr. Davidge's interest to his heirs after his death. The tannery has 132 vats, and turns out about 50,000 sides of sole leather per year, giving employment to about forty hands. George F. Sherwood is superintendent.

Lucius E. Williams' Saw-mill was built by Moore, Cargill & Co. in the autumn of 1867, and Mr. Williams became sole owner in August, 1886. The mill is operated by steam-power, is supplied with a circular saw, planer, matcher, etc., and has the capacity for cutting 3,000,000 feet of lumber per year.

The Jenksville Steam Mills were built in 1879, by Daniel L. Jenks, for sawing lumber and threshing grain. In the fall of 1882 the steam grist-mill was built by Jenks & Nixon. In 1884 Charles D. Nixon bought of Jenks his interest in the mills and the the farm property connected with them, and remodeled and improved the saw-mill, added a planing-mill, and a hay-press and cider-mill, all of which are run by steam-power. The grist-mill has three runs of stones, and a specialty is made of feed and buckwheat grinding. The saw mill has a capacity for 10,000 feet in twelve hours. The management of the mills and the supervision of the farm is under the personal direction of Mr. Nixon, who carries on the latter according to the most advanced and scientific methods, and it is known as a model farm for productiveness.

Jenksville Custom Grist-Mill was built in 1814, by Michael Jenks, for James Pumpelly, and was deeded by the latter to Daniel Boughton. The next proprietor was Chester Johnson, who sold to Alfred Smith, in February, 1856. Mr. Smith disposed of the property to Egbert Crans, in the spring of 1860, but in the fall of 1861, Crans deeded the property back to Mr. Smith, who then rebuilt the saw-mill on a larger and more improved plan. In the fall of 1866, Mr. Smith again disposed of the property ; this time to Peter S. Dunning, who lost it by mortgage foreclosure. It was bid off by Hiram Payne, who deeded it to the present owner, George W. White. The mills are run by water-power. The grist-mill has three runs of stones, and a capacity of 300 bushels per day. The specialty is feed and buckwheat grinding. The first saw-mill on West creek, was built by Michael Jenks, in 1803, the present one being the third that has been built on this site. Its capacity is about 4,000 feet in twelve hours.

Franklin Davis's Saw-Mill, on road 25, was built by him in the spring of 1870, upon the site of one then destroyed by fire, and which had been in use about 20 years. The mill has a circular saw, bench saw, etc., and turns out about 500,000 feet of lumber per year.

BIOGRAPHICAL.

Royal W. Clinton was born in Colebrook, Conn., March 1, 1823, the eldest child of a family of thirteen children. His father, Lyman Clinton, Jr., and his grandfather, Lyman Clinton, Sr., the latter a native of Connecticut, born April 3, 1771, died April 30, 1855, much respected in the community in which he lived. The wife of Lyman Clinton, Jr., and mother of Royal W., was Miranda, daughter of Wells Stone, of Sharon, Conn. In 1831 they removed to Newark Valley, arriving in the month of May, after a tedious journey of two weeks. Lyman Clinton, Sr , had visited this section in 1830, and had selected six hundred acres of land for the purpose of dividing it among his children, reserving a portion thereof for himself. Lyman Clinton, Jr., not being satisfied with the location of his allotment, chose a different one a mile and a half east of the present village of Newark Valley, where he remained until the winter of 1871, when he removed to the village; and three years later, July 4, 1874, he passed away, aged seventy-five years. His widow died January 17, 1882.

Royal W. Clinton received a common-school education, and attended a select school two years. He lived with his father until he was nineteen years of age, and two years later married Anna C., eldest daughter of William and Rosanna Knapp, of Newark Valley. Immediately subsequent to his marriage, he became proprietor of his father-in-law's wool-carding and cloth-dressing establishment, which business he conducted summers, and during the winter months got out lumber, for about five years. About this time he purchased a lot of timber-land, one and one half miles east of the village, from which he commenced cutting the lumber, erecting a steam saw-mill on the property, which was the first one operated successfully in the town. He cleared a farm of one hundred and fifty acres in the vicinity of the mill, making improvements from time to time, until it became a valuable property.

In 1861 he sold the mill, and in company with his brother-in-law, H. W. Clinton, built another mill, and from that time until the present, has engaged extensively in the lumber trade, purchasing, in addition to what he sawed himself, all that sawed by three or four other mills in the surrounding country. In 1867 he found it necessary, in order to facilitate his rapidly increasing business, to remove to a more central point; hence he erected a fine residence in the village, where he now resides. In 1866 he engaged in the mercantile business with his son-in-law, Morris Elwell and brother, at Newark Valley, which is at present conducted by William Elwell. During the year 1866 he was appointed one of the railroad commissioners for the bonding of the town for the construction of the Southern Central Railroad, and in 1873 he was made one of the directors of the company in recognition of his valuable services in procuring this necessary improvement. He has held various town offices in the gift of his fellow citizens of the Republican party, to which political organization he belongs. At the age of nineteen he experienced religion, and united with the Methodist Episcopal church of Newark Valley, of which he has ever since been an active and efficient member. He contributed one-fourth of the entire cost of the present beautiful structure of the society, and for nearly forty years consecutively he has been superintendent of the Methodist Episcopal Sunday-school of Newark Valley, and has been classleader for forty-two years. In February, 1887, Mr. Clinton proposed to school districts Nos. 2 and 14, that they unite in a union graded school district, and thus afford good school facilities at the village. In event of this proposition being accepted, he promised to build, at his own expense, a fine school building, the districts to purchase a site therefor. This they did, choosing the old Lincoln hotel property, paying therefor $1,700.00. Plans were made, and the present fine brick school building is the result, erected at a cost of $10,000.00. The building is 60x68 feet, two stories, slate roof, iron cornices, etc., and forms a lasting monument to its munificent donor. Mr. Clinton is supervisor of the town, which office he has held for three consecutive terms. The family of Mr. and Mrs. Clinton consists of three children, namely : Ella J., born April 20, 1845 ; Austin W., born March 11, 1850; Arthur G., born March 3, 1856. Austin W. was graduated with honors from Cornell University, in the class of 1872, and he and his brother are now engaged in the mercantile and lumber business at Harford Mills, Cortland Co., N. Y. The daughter, Ella W., is the wife of Morris Elwell, of Newark Valley. Mrs. Clinton died June 13, 1882, and January 3, 1883, he married Mrs. Caroline Burroughs, daughter of Sherwood Sterling, and widow of Stephen Burroughs, of Bridgeport, Conn.

The Rev. Jay Clizbe, fifth pastor of the church in Newark Valley, was born at Amsterdam, N. Y., 16 June, 1836 ; son of

R.W. Clinton,

Ellis and Ruth (Gillet) Clizbe. He was graduated at Union college, in 1861, and at Andover Theological Seminary, in 1864, taking the valedictory in each. He was ordained 5 April, 1865, at Amherst, Mass., where he was pastor till 5 April, 1867 ; traveled in Europe from July, 1868, till September, 1869, and was pastor at Marshall, Michigan, for one year. He began his ministry in Newark Valley, 14 January, 1872 ; was installed as pastor, 25 September, 1872, and so continued till 1 January, 1887, when, on account of illness, the relation was terminated at his own request. During the last years of his pastorate he spent about a year and a half in Europe, for the benefit of his health. He married, at Amherst, 28 Feb., 1866, with Mary Eliza Hills, daughter of Leonard Mariner and Amelia (Gay) Hills, of Amherst.

Rev. Marc Fivas, a resident of Newark Valley, where he died in July, 1876, at the age of eighty-four years, was a noted man in the literary world, and especially so in the world of science. He was born in Vevay, Switzerland, in 1792 : was a clergyman in the National church, and professor of natural sciences in the Academy of Lausanne, and one of the first teachers of Prof. Louis Agassiz. By reason of political trouble in his native land, he came with Prof. Matile and others to Newark Valley in 1849. He was a member of historical and scientific societies in Europe, and lectured before the scientific societies of New York and Philadelphia. He was a man of fine culture and ripe scholarship.

Hon. Jerome B. Landfield, of the firm of Davidge, Landfield & Co., has been a resident of Newark Valley since 1865, when his firm succeeded that of Howe & Lincoln in the tanning business. Mr. Landfield was born at Harvard, Delaware Co., N. Y., November 6, 1827, eldest son of Clark and Hannah (Thomas) Landfield, of that place. He began business life in the mercantile trade, and in 1858 commenced the tanning business, becoming associated with John Davidge, when they purchased the tannery at Newark Valley. though he continued in trade here until a comparatively recent date. In 1873 and '74, Mr. Landfield served his district in the legislature, having also been elected from Delaware county to the legislature of 1864. In 1867 he was elected county superintendent of the poor, an office he held till January, 1871. He has also served as supervisor, railroad commissioner, etc., in the Republican ranks. Mr. Landfield married, for his first wife, Elizabeth Canouse, in 1853, who bore him

four children, none of whom are living. Mrs. Landfield died in
May, 1865, and in September, 1866, Mr. Landfield married Helen
Rogers, of Chenango Forks, Broome Co., who has borne him
three children, two of whom are living, Jerome B., Jr., born
May 6, 1872, and Grace H., born in 1874.

William Cargill was born in Tyringham, Mass., July 13, 1831,
the second son of Heman and Olive (Sears) Cargill. Mr. Cargill
came to Tioga county with his brother John, in 1852, locating in
Berkshire, to begin the manufacture of hand-rakes, a business he
remained in till 1856, when he came to Newark Valley and located
upon the so-called Randall farm. After eleven years of farm life
he sold this property and in company with L. E. Williams began
the manufacture of wagons at Newark Village. Soon after in
1867, the firm name was changed to Moore, Cargill & Co., and they
then built the present L. E. William's steam-mill. With this institution Mr. Cargill was identified till August, 1886. In the mean
time Messrs. Williams and Cargill added the furniture and undertaking business, and at the latter date they divided, Mr. Williams
taking the lumber-mill and Mr. Cargill the latter business, which
he still continues. Mr. Cargill married Adaline A. Graves, of
Southboro, Mass., August 16, 1853, who has borne him seven
children; Wilbur G., of Southfield, Mass., Eliza G. (Mrs. William
Ryan), Frank H., of Rochester, N. Y., Olive S. (Mrs. Cornelius
S. Burroughs), Minnie E., Rennie B. and Nellie.

Dr. William J. Burr, son of Andrew, was born in Homer, Cortland county, N. Y., March 28, 1818. He received his early education in that place and his preparatory professional education there and in Ithaca. He graduated from the medical department of Hobart College, Geneva, N. Y., in the class of '45.
He commenced practice in Tompkins county, where he remained
for five years and a half, and afterward practiced in Allegany
county for eleven years. In the fall of 1861, from patriotic
motives, he entered the Union army as private, and was at once
made assistant surgeon of the 59th Regt. N. Y. Vols., and afterward promoted to the office of surgeon of the 42d N. Y. Regt.,
and was again promoted to staff surgeon. For nearly three years
he was a member of the operating staff of his division. He continued in the service until the close of the war. He then came to
Newark Valley and began the practice of his profession, in which
he still continues. In August, 1845 he married Jane C., daughter of Otis Lincoln. They have had born to tnem four children,
viz.: William H., a veterinary surgeon, Sarah, wife of E. H.

Becker, president of the Buffalo fertilizer company, George L., who has recently been appointed instructor in the school of History in Cornell University, and Ella wife of C. O. Upton, of Colorado. Dr. Burr was a member of the Medical associations of this and Allegany counties, and has been presiding officer in each. He was also a member of the American Medical association.

Dr. Cornelius R. Rogers, was born in Windham, Pa., June 20, 1837, a son of Daniel and Huldah (Farmer) Rogers. He came to Owego with his parents when two years of age, and was educated in the common schools, at Owego academy, and at Binghamton academy. From the age of eighteen to twenty-five he was a successful school teacher. In 1861 he married Miss H. H. Tracy, of Newark Valley, and has two children, M. Anna Rogers, the accomplished organist of the Methodist Episcopal church, Owego, and James T. Rogers, assistant postmaster at Owego. In 1862 he was appointed keeper of the Tioga county poor-house, which position he held five years. During this time he studied medicine under the late Dr. H. Arnold, of Owego, and attended Bellevue Hospital Medical College in 1864-5, and Geneva Medical College in 1866-7. where he graduated. He also has a diploma from the medical department of Syracuse University, dated June, 1877. In 1868 he located at Whitney's Point, and became a very successful practitioner. In 1876 he removed to Newark Valley, and from thence to Owego in 1879, and in 1884 returned to Newark Valley. He held the office of coroner of Tioga county from 1877 to 1883. In 1880 he was elected president of the board of school commissioners of Owego, and served very efficiently for three years, during which time the elegant new high school building was erected. He is a member of the Broome and Tioga county medical socities, both of which he has served as president. He is at present health officer of the town of Newark Valley. He is a member of the Methodist Episcopal church, and an active Sunday school worker.

Dr. Francis M. Bishop, son of Lewis D. and Samatha J. (Livermore) Bishop, was born at Castle Creek, N. Y., Dec. 16, 1839. The doctor studied in the common school of his native town, and graduated at Hahneman Medical College, at Philadelphia, Pa. He began practice at Newark Valley, in 1874, and has been in practice here since. Dr. Bishop married Olive L. Matthews, of LeRaysville, Pa., May 1, 1864, and has one child, an infant daughter, two having died.

Romaine F. Bieber was born in Newark Valley, Oct. 23, 1853,

18*

son of Henry and Catharine (Sebastion) Bieber. He studied in
his native town, graduated at the Wyoming Seminary, of Kingston, Pa., in 1879, and commenced the study of law with E. H.
Ryan, now of Syracuse, N. Y., and was admitted to the bar in
November, 1882. Mr. Bieber, married Alma Settle, November
2, 1881, and has two children, a son and a daughter.

Alfred Smith, son of Ezra, was born in Scipio, Cayuga county,
N. Y., January 1, 1816. The year following, his father removed
to Springwater, Livingston county, N. Y., where the family remained a few years and then removed to Richmond—in that part
of the town afterward set off and called Canadice—Ontario
county, N. Y. In 1840 Mr. Smith removed to the town of Candor where he engaged in farming, and also worked at the trade
of carpenter and joiner. In February, 1856, he purchased the
mill property at Jenksville, and conducted the business of the
mills until the spring of 1860, when he sold to Egbert Crans. In
the fall of that year he went to Leavenworth, Kan., where he engaged under contract with William S. Rayburn, of Philadelphia,
Pa., to cut and deliver at the steamboat landing, in the winter of
1860-61, four hundred cords of wood for use upon the river steam-
ers. The following summer he engaged in freighting in the
Rocky mountains. In the fall of 1861 he returned to Jenksville
and Crans deeded the mills back to him. In the winter of 1865–
66 he rebuilt the saw-mill upon a more improved plan, with
greater facilities. In the fall of 1866 he disposed of the mills and
water privilege to Peter S. Dunning, who took possession January 1, 1867, and Mr. Smith engaged in farming. On September
13, 1843, he married Mary, daughter of Harry and Betsey (Cady)
Armstrong, by whom he had two children, Charles B., born June
2, 1844, a locomotive engineer, who was killed at his post of duty
on the Atlantic and Great Western R. R., September 30, 1867;
and a daughter who died in infancy. Mrs. Smith died June 2,
1857. His present wife is Susan A., daughter of the late Calvin
and Annis (Brown) Jenks, of Berkshire, by whom he has one
daughter, Mary L.

Russell Mead was born on the Minisink river in N. J., and at
an early age removed with his father's family to Carmel, Putnam
county, N. Y. At the age of twenty-five years he came to Weltonville and located on a farm, a portion of which is now owned
by Walter Herrick. He afterwards moved into this town, on
the farm now occupied by Willis Hover. He married Sally Ann,
daughter of Josephus Barrott, of Putnam county, by whom he

had ten children, the eldest of whom was Rogers D., now residing on road 1, in this town. He married Martha, daughter of Mrs. Jemima Hover, of Candor, and has ten children, viz.: Milden, S. Amy, Priscilla, Milton, Russell B., Clyde V., Arletta, Hattie, John A. R., and Maggie J. Mr. Mead has been engaged principally in farming. Was postmaster at West Newark after the death of his father, who was postmaster at that place for many years.

Michael Van Wormer came from Guilderland, Albany county, about 1825, and located in East Newark, on the farm now owned by Ira Shoultes. He married Hannah Sturgess, by whom he had ten children, their oldest being Margaret, who married Almeron Williams, December 12, 1829. Their children were: Adalinda, Juliet, Cammilla, Stella, Ada A., Royal R., Wright B., of South Owego, Angeline, Eliza, and Adelma.

George Hoff came from Kinderhook to Albany county when a young man, and from there to Tioga county, where he settled in the town of Tioga. He bought a farm and cleared a place for a home for his family, and during most of his life continued farming in different localities in this county. He married Catherine Dubois, of Columbia county, by whom he had nine children, who arrived at maturity. Next to the youngest of these was Erastus, who came to this town in 1859, where he has since been engaged in farming. Previous to that date he was engaged in mercantile pursuits. He married Mary E. Harlin, of Candor, and has five children, viz.: Stella E., John H., Carrie E., Jennie, and Alice M.

Timothy S., son of Jacob Councilman, of Lisle, N. Y., was born in that town February 19, 1823. He married first Rebecca Braman, of Lisle, December 25. 1845, and by whom he had one son, Jira F. He came to this town in 1856 and located on the farm now occupied by his son on road 19. His second wife was Mary G. Simmonds. Jira F. married Calista J., daughter of Samuel S. Rodman, of Union.

John, son of John Borthwick, was born in Monogan, Monogan Co., Ireland, whither his father had moved from the Highlands of Scotland, and at the age of nine years came with his father's family to this country and settled in the town of Montgomery, Orange Co., N. Y. He married Sarah Porter, of Bloomingburgh, N. Y., by whom he had twelve children, viz.: William, a soldier, who died at Fortress Monroe, Joseph, of Berkshire, Mary J., who married Abram Hover, now deceased, D. James, of this town, Edward, who died in Illinois in 1854, Almira, who died in infancy, George, of Sierra Nevada, Cal., where he has lived since 1851, Alexander, of Candor, Sarah, wife of Charles W. Allen, Dorcas, wife of Charles Guyon, Esther, wife of Lucius Keith, and Delphine. Mr. Borthwick came to this town in 1823, and located on the farm now owned by Charles Hill. D. James married Milla M., daughter of William S. and Milla (Richardson) Lawrence, December 11, 1845, and have had born to them four children, viz.: Lucina J., wife of C. R. Ackerman, Milla, wife of Sheridan Hall, George H., and Edward, who died at the age of six years.

Noyce Chapman, son of Jed, was born August 25, 1820. He married Mary A., daughter of Moses and Bridget (Robinson) Livermore, January 20, 1847, by whom he had two children, Wealthy M. and Frederick H., of this place. Wealthy M. married Wright B. Williams, and has four children, viz.: George A., Emma L., Lyman F. and Bennie C. Frederick H. married Chloe Shaw, and has one child, Ida L.

Abel Merrill was born October 9, 1798, and married Lucinda Bullock, who was born September 3, 1803. Their children are Louisa S., born May 12, 1831, Norman L., born October 28, 1832, Mary B., born July 26, 1840, and Mattie A., born May 1, 1845.

Edwin P. Smith, son of Henry and Meribah (Collins) Smith, was born in Milford, Otsego Co., in 1828. When twelve years of age he came with his father's family to Nanticoke, N. Y., and from there he removed to this town where he has been engaged chiefly in farming. He married Mary, daughter of Consider Howland, of Lisle, N. Y., in 1852, and has two children, viz.: Jabez and Mary. Jabez married Belle Donley, of Newark Valley, and has one child, Thur, aged three years.

Henry B. Guyon, son of James, born December 10, 1807, came from Union, Broome county, in 1841, and located on the farm now owned by his son, Charles S. He married Rebecca M. Thorn, October 8, 1833, by whom he had eight children, born as follows: Charles S., October 28, 1834; Theodore, October 22, 1836; Esther, December 29, 1838; Ruth A., August 9, 1841; Mahala, November 23, 1844; Josiah J., June 14, 1850; Henry T., November 12, 1852; and John W., December 30, 1856. Ruth A. died June 27, 1842; Mahala, April 18, 1846; Theodore, April 9, 1863; Esther, August 25, 1877. Mrs. Guyon was born June 13, 1814, and died February 27, 1869. Mr. Guyon married for his second wife Mary Schoonover, January 20, 1870. His death occurred March 15, 1876. Charles S. married Dorcas, daughter of John Borthwick, December 8, 1860.

Anthony Tappan came from Middleburg, Schoharie Co., N. Y., and located on the farm now occupied by Henry Loveland. He married Anna Cook, by whom he had seven children, viz.: William, Hellena, wife of David Taylor, Asher, Nancy, Silas, Riley A. and John C. Riley A. married Jane E. Watson, by whom he has two sons, viz.: Watson and Charles A.

CHURCHES.

Congregational Church—Religious services had been held prior to the organization of this church, in barns and dwelling-houses, and conducted by Rev. Seth Williston, a missionary from Connecticut. This church was formed as the first Congregational church in the town of Tioga, Thursday, November 17, 1803. The constituent members were Dr. Joseph Waldo, Nathaniel Ford, Jesse Gleazen, Levi Bailey, Beulah Brown, and Caroline Ford. The church was organized by Rev. Seth Williston and Rev. James Woodward, missionaries from Connecticut. Mrs. Sarah Slosson, wife of Enoch Slosson, Mrs. Mary Hosford, wife of Joseph Hosford, and Mrs. Rachel Williams, wife of Stephen Williams, Sr., joined the church on Sunday, November 20, 1803, three days after its organization. They probably had letters of dismission from churches in the east, as Barney Truman joined the church on profession of faith the same day and the first Sunday of its existence, making the number of its members at that time ten. It had no officers until April 4, 1805, when Nathaniel Ford was elected deacon, and no preaching except by the Connecticut missionaries.

The society of Western was organized October 23, 1805, and fifty-eight of the inhabitants signed an agreement, November 11, 1805, fixing a rate of from two to eight per cent. which each should annually pay upon his property for the support of the gospel. December 24, 1805, the church and society voted to call Rev. Jeremiah Osborn to settle with them, at a salary of $275 annually, with an annual increase of $25 until it reached $350. This call was accepted January 11, 1806, and the church and pastor elect called a council to assist in his ordination. The council met at the house of Widow Dudley. March 3, 1811, the church applied for a union with the Presbytery of Cayuga, and was admitted as a constituent member, September

11, 1811, and remained in that connection until July 2, 1869. Since that time it has been associated with Congregational churches. Rev. Mr Osborn remained with them until 1818, when he resigned; was succeeded by Rev. Marcus Ford, who was ordained December 3, 1820, filled the position acceptably, and resigned on account of ill health April 27, 1859. Samuel F. Bacon became their pastor in 1866; Samuel Johnson in 1871. Jay Clisbe, January 14, 1872, commenced his labors. At present they have no pastor.

During the winter of 1830-31 a revival occurred, and in the April communion 107 joined the church by profession of faith, and six by letter; in July following twenty-two more, thus more than doubling the membership. January 12, 1823, eight members were dismissed to form the North church, in Berkshire, now the Congregational church of Richford. Three were dismissed, September 14, 1823, to form a church on West Owego creek. In June and July, 1833, seventy-two members were dismissed to be embodied in a church at Berkshire, which was organized July 24, 1833, with sixty eight members, of whom fifty-four were from this church. The first house of worship was built north of the village of Newark Valley, where now stands the brick house owned by Samuel Watson. It was erected as early as 1803 or 1804, and was a plain framed house, twenty-four by thirty-six feet in size, with posts eleven feet high and a steep roof. It was never finished, but was left open from floor to rafter. This is the style of meeting-houses that for fourteen years the ancient worthies of this church worshiped in, without a fire, except the few coals the good old mothers carried in their foot-stoves. This building was moved across the way, a little below its original site, in the corner of the sugar-maple grove, afterwards used by Rev Mr. Ford for a barn.

The second house was built on the old site and dedicated July 4, 1817. It was forty-five by fifty-five feet, with a spacious gallery and the old fashioned high pulpit. For fourteen years more the congregation worshiped here, when the gradual growth of the two centers of business, Berkshire and Newark Valley, each three miles from the meeting-house, made it inconvenient for the people. September 1, 1831, the society instructed the trustees to consult the several individuals belonging to the society relative to a change of place of worship, and report it next meeting. The trustees reported in favor of moving, and the report was accepted, the north part of the society giving their consent.

$1,944.86 was subscribed for a new church, and the contractor bought the old house, took it down, and used it in the new house, built on the site where the present church stands (Otis Lincoln presenting half an acre for that purpose), and substantially like the old one. In 1849 it was moved back from the street and rebuilt in modern style, dedicated, and used seven years. In 1867 it took its third journey, about 100 feet to the north, to make way for its successor. In 1868 the present building was erected at a cost of $12,725, and was dedicated January 14, 1869. After the completion of the new church the old "traveling sanctuary" was again removed, and is now used and known as the "Allison Opera House."

Methodist Episcopal Church.—As early as 1822, Rev. George W. Densmore, stationed at Chenango, visited and preached through here, by way of Lisle, making a circuit. He was one of the first ministers in Oneida Conference. Admitted on trial in 1810, full communion in 1811, ordained in 1812. In 1826 Rev. Herota P. Barnes and Fitch Reed preached occasionally, there being no Methodist organization here. During the years 1831-32, David A. Shepard, located at Berkshire, preached here, and held quarterly meetings in the old town-house in 1831, and organized the first society, composed of seven members, Minerva Collins, Mary Ann Ruey, Munson and Experience Clark, Miel Dean and wife, and Selecta Williams. In 1833, this place was recognized by the Oneida Conference as Newark Station, and Moses Adams was the first stationed minister, the church being built under his pastorate. The society now has a fine brick edifice, erected in 1883. There is a branch society at East Newark, about three miles east. At this place they erected a fine church in 1859.

A Free-Will Baptist Church was located at this place prior to 1820, with a meeting-house on the corner of Main and Silk streets ; Rev. John Gould as pastor. It was in a weak condition, and the most of the members united with the Methodist church after their organization.

The Baptist Church of Newark Valley was organized October 27, 1857, by a council composed of delegates from other churches; among them Revs. L. Ranstead, J. W. Emory, —— Smith, of Candor, and W. H. King, of Owego. There were twenty-six constituent members at the formation of the church. The first baptism in the church was Stephen Platt, April 11, 1858. Rev. D. T. Leach preached here as a missionary from the Home Missionary Society, and was settled as a pastor June 9, 1860. Services were held for a short time in the Congregational church, and about 1858 a church was erected. In 1869 a large and commodious brick edifice was erected at a cost of $10.000.

A Congregational Church was organized at West Newark, in 1823, with twelve members. The first services were held in William Richardson's barn. In the winter of 1823–24 they built a school house sufficiently large for church purposes also, and worshiped there until 1848, when the present one was built. Rev. Zenus Riggs was the first pastor.

The Alpha Methodist Episcopal Church was organized at Jenksville in 1852, with twenty-five members. The first pastor was Rev. —— Salisbury.

A Reformed Methodist Church was organized at Ketchumville, with nine members, in 1837, and a church erected in 1852.

———

NICHOLS* is that part of the county lying in an angle formed by the western boundary of the town of Owego, and the Pennsylvania line, and is bounded on the north and west by the Susquehanna river. Owing to the peculiar course of the river, the town is of an irregular shape, having a breadth at the eastern end of some five or six miles, which diminishes towards the western part to scarcely more than one mile, the extreme length on the southern line being between ten and eleven miles. This territory was formerly a part of the town of Owego, from which it was separated and added to Tioga, in 1813. In 1824 it was taken from Tioga and organized into a separate township. The western part of the town thus organized was included in a considerable tract of land known as Hooper's Patent, which embraced lands in other parts of the state. The eastern part was known as Coxe's Manor, or Patent, concerning which we have spoken in subsequent pages of this work.

The surface of the town is mostly upland, terminating in steep declivities upon the river, and broken by the narrow valleys of small streams. The summits of the hills are broad, and attain an altitude of from three hundred to five hundred feet above the river. A productive gravelly loam forms the soil of the valleys, and a moderately fertile, gravelly, and clayey loam, underlaid by red sandstone, the hills. The principal stream in the town is the

———

*Prepared by Miss Mary L. Barstow, of Nichols Village.

Wappasening creek, which enters the town from Bradford county, Pa., at the hamlet of the same name, and flows north into the Susquehanna. That river forms the north and western boundaries of the town. As an agricultural town Nichols has always been prosperous. Every year has seen the area of her cleared land increased, and her general condition improved. Fine farms and good farm houses are to be seen in every part of the town. There is no finer agricultural town in the Susquehanna Valley, nor one which, to the passing traveler, presents a more agreeable succession of hill and valley, woodland, meadow and running stream. It has an area of 19,850 acres, of which 14,200 acres is improved land.

Early Settlement. --The first permanent settler in the town was probably Emanuel Coryell, who came to the Susquehanna Valley as agent for Colonel Hooper, for the sale of his lands. He found there however, several of these irregular settlers that are commonly found on new lands. Among them we find the name of Mills, Ellis, Pierce and Walker. The children of Ellis and Pierce were said to be the first white children born in the town. Only George Walker became a permanent resident. He was the father of Samuel Walker, afterwards well known in the town. Among other early settlers honorable mention should be made of Isaac Sharp, a settler of mixed blood, who was a soldier in the army of General Gates, and was present at the " taking of Burgoyne." He raised a large family of sons, who were afterwards well known among the lumbermen and laborers of the country. There were also two families of the name of Jones, one of whom was said to have raised the first crop of wheat grown in the town.

Emanuel Coryell, a patriot of the revolution, was the son of the proprietor of Coryell's Ferry, on the Delaware, where Washington and his army were ferried over before the battle of Trenton. An accident which happened to him in infancy, prevented him through life, from walking without the aid of a cane. Owing to this circumstance, his father felt it necessary to give him as liberal an education as was to be had at the time, in order to his taking up one of the learned professions. He chose that of medicine, and had become a student in the office of a Dr. Ingham, at Coryell's Ferry, at the beginning of the war, when he at once threw aside his books and entered the army, where, as he was prevented by his infirmity from entering the ranks, he went into the commissary department, where he did good service, ranking as captain, during the entire war. He, with the rest of his father's family, and the American people generally, came out of the conflict rich in hope and the consciousness of duty well performed, but with very little of the means wherewith to support their families. A year or two before the close of the war he had married a lady of Bucks county, Pa., and at its close, having no profession, he took up his residence on his father's farm. He soon, however, became engaged with Colonel Hooper in exploring and surveying lands of which the latter was patentee, and at length became his agent for the sale of those on the Susquehanna.

These lands, as we are told by the Hon. C. P. Avery, in his *Susquehanna Valley*, to which the writer is indebted for many facts relating to the settlement of the town, were held at reasonable prices, and liberal means were adopted to induce immigration from the Eastern States. Judge Avery adds: "The liberal promptness with which valuable territory in Nichols was placed in the market, caused that portion of the county to fill up more rapidly at an early day, than any other section within its limits." Having, at a visit made to the county during the previous summer, in company with Colonel Hooper, selected a spot whereon to pitch his tent, Mr. Coryell left his home at Coryell's Ferry some time during the summer of 1791, and started for the "Susquehanna Country," a journey much more formidable to the emigrant of that day than one beyond the Mississippi would be at present. They traveled in an emigrant wagon, which carried the family, consisting of himself, his wife and five children, and a young girl living with them, named Isabel Mac Adams. We are told that a cow was driven along with them for the benefit of the children. They must necessarily have had another man with them, as Mr. Coryell, with his infirmity, would scarce have been able to undertake such a journey without assistance. They crossed the country from the Delaware to the Susquehanna, which they reached at Wilksbarre. Here they were detained for a time while making arrangements to ascend the river. At the end of a week a craft was procured which Judge Avery calls a "Durham boat," but which we have heard spoken of simply as a flat boat. It was probably not unlike one of our large ferry-boats, but, of course, must have contained a cabin. This was manned by two boatmen, who propelled it up the river by means of setting-poles. Placing his wife and family on board of this primitive conveyance, together with such articles of furniture and household stuff as they had been able to bring with them, they set out on the remainder of the journey. This, we may easily believe, it took them two weeks to accomplish, as the river was low and they frequently had to lie by to wait for a rise of water. They finally landed at a place known afterwards as Coryell's Eddy. It was at the foot of a high bank, on the top of which stood the log cottage which was to afford them temporary shelter. This was occupied by an old man named James Cole, who lived there with his wife and daughter and a grandson, Elijah Cole, and cultivated some fields along the river. This man was from Wyoming Valley, and, with his family, was familiar with many of the tragic events connected with its history. In this house Mr. Coryell and his family found a home until another log dwelling in the vicinity could be made ready for their reception. In this they lived for some years, until they were able to procure materials for the erection of a better one. This, too, was built of logs, "weather-boarded," that is, covered with siding to give it the appearance of a framed house. It stood near a fine "Indian clearing" of some ten or twelve acres, about a mile above the first one, and here grew up Mr. Coryell's large family of sons and daughters.

With the exception of the lands lying contiguous to the river, the country at that time was covered with forests, principally of white pine, a tree always indicating a fine soil wherever it grows, but mingled with ash, maple, hickory and beech, and other valuable hard woods. These woods abounded with game and the rivers with fish. The shad, that best of all river fish, came up in immense numbers every spring, and were caught by the settlers in nets, the owners of the land along the river being entitled to a certain quantity for the "land right." These fish, salted down, formed an important and very acceptable addition to the stores of the settlers. The climate was mild, though the winters were cold and invariably snowy, and there were no prevailing diseases except those caused by the malaria commonly found where forests are being cleared up. Mr. Coryell, who, as he was appointed a few years later first Judge of the county court, is commonly spoken of as Judge Coryell, took up for himself a tract of land along the river, which must have comprised an area of nearly a square mile, or 640 acres; extending from what is now the Asbury church lot, on the west, to a point above, where the public road and the river approach each other; besides three or four hundred acres of wild land lying on both sides of the Wappasening, a mile above its mouth.

The next settler on the river, in point of time, was General

John Smyth, who wrote his name as it is here spelled. He came to town in the year 1794. He, too, was a soldier of the revolution, from Monroe county, Pa. He was accompanied by his three sons, only one of whom, however, finally made it his home in Nichols. Mr. Nathan Smith inherited his father's farm, which lay between that afterwards owned by Edmund Palmer and the lands purchased soon after by Mr. Shoemaker, who was the next person to settle on that fine tract of land known then and since as the Maughantowano Flats.

Daniel Shoemaker, a revolutionary soldier and pensioner, was of that Shoemaker family whose name occurs with such tragic significance in the history of Wyoming. He emigrated directly from Monroe county, Pa. He must also have taken up nearly or quite a square mile of land. The Maughantowano Flats since corrupted to Montontowango—comprised some of the choicest lands not only in the county, but in the state. They had been, as Judge Avery tells us, the favorite corn ground of the Indians, who had not yet disappeared from the country, some families living, we are told, at the mouth of the Wappasening creek. The county has afforded some valuable Indian relics.

Edmund Palmer came to Nichols not far from the year 1800. He purchased a farm below, and immediately adjoining the Shoemaker property. In 1804 he married a daughter of Judge Coryell, and built a house on this farm, where he lived many years. He subsequently purchased the farm lying between the property of Judge Coryell and that of the Smiths, of a man named Barnes, who was perhaps the original purchaser. In 1827 he built the house so long the home of the Palmer family. Meantime, settlers came into other parts of the town. Colonel Richard Sacket came from Long Island. The date of arrival is not known. He purchased a square mile of land, the lower line of which must have been just above the present village of Hooper's Valley. He built his house near a stream called the Little Wappasening creek, which divided his land into two nearly equal parts. The Colonel was said to have been, at home, a gentleman of wealth ; but the pleasures of the turf, for which Long Island has been famous, together with generous housekeeping, and a general carelessness about business matters, gradually reduced his fortune till at length finding that he had a family growing up about him, while his means for maintaining them were diminishing, he abandoned the race ground and other kindred delights, and turned his thoughts toward emigration. Having been in the county of Tioga before, where he was hospitably entertained at the house of Judge Coryell, he decided to take up his residence in the same town. His family consisted of a wife and several daughters, and having brought and established them in their new home, he settled down to get his living by farming. But it was late in the day to take up a new business. and the Colonel lacked the energy that had impelled him in the pursuit of pleasure. He was a charming man in society; an excellent man in community; a genial host, an agreeable neighbor; but all this did not prevent his constantly growing poorer, until at the time of his death he was utterly reduced; while in possession of property that ought to have made him one of the wealthy men of the county. He died in 1827. Soon after his death his family received a large property from the death of one of his brothers, who died in Syracuse, to which city they finally removed; and his widow, after having experienced the extremes of fortune, finally died in affluence. The property at Nichols was left encumbered with a law-suit, which was finally decided in favor of his heirs, and it gradually came into the market. The part that was occupied by the family as a home is now owned by Mr. Sherwood.

In 1793 Jonathan Platt and his son, who bore the same name, with their families, came into the county from Westchester county, N. Y. They purchased land up the river, a mile above the village of Nichols, and built a house known as the Platt homestead for many years. Miles Forman, a son in-law of the elder Platt, came two or three years later. and settled near the same spot, building the house known as the Forman homestead, which remained in the family until the decease of his grandson, the late Stephen Forman, who died in 1884. The elder Platt died within two or three years after his arrival. His son, Major Platt, and his son-in-law, Major Forman, both afterwards filled the office of sheriff of the county, the one for two years and the other for three. The office at that time was an appointive one, and held but for a term of one year at a time. Benjamin Lounsberry another son-in-law of Mr. Platt, settled a few miles farther up the river.

Four brothers named Hunt, three of whom took up farms on the river, must have come into that part of the town not far from the same time. We hear also the names of Laning, Dunham, Smith and Evans, among the earlier settlers on Coxe's Patent. Ezra Canfield probably came somewhat later. He built the brick house, the first in the town, standing at the corner of the river and the hill roads; which gave the name of Canfield Corners to the postoffice afterwards established there. Although this was perhaps a part of the territory of Nichols somewhat harder to reduce and cultivate than the western part, yet its inhabitants formed a community of most prosperous farmers. Their lands have constantly improved from year to year, and there are more names of the original settlers to be found there than in any other part of the town. Mr. Lounsberry raised a family of seven sons, all of whom at one time owned farms which still remain in their families. The house built by Mr. Canfield is at present the property of Samuel Smith.

Caleb Wright came to Nichols at an early day, and took up land a mile in extent along the river, lying on both sides of the Wappasening creek and including that where the village of Nichols now stands. He was a millwright by trade, and must have been possessed of some means. He built a dam across the creek, with a race nearly half a mile in length, and erected above the mouth of the stream the first grist mills and saw-mills in the town. He had a family of sons, who did not, however, inherit his habits of sobriety and industry. Most of them parted with their rights to their father's estate before his death, some went west, which at that time meant the state of Ohio, where their descendants became prosperous and even wealthy. Thomas Wright, one of his sons, settled on a farm on the river, probably deeded to him by his father, where he built a framed house which stood about half way between the road and the river, in the rear of property now owned and occupied by Mr. Ross, in the village of Nichols. His farm was immediately above that of Stephen Dodd, who also built a framed house on the upper edge of his farm, which is still in existence though little more than a heap of ruins. Thomas Wright was for some years a prosperous farmer, but finally fell into difficulties and sold his farm to Jacob Middaugh, a settler from the Delaware, and moved to some distant part of the town. His family all did well and two of his sons were at one time, and perhaps still are, among the wealthy men of Tunkhannock, Pa.

Among the poorer settlers in the town, Stephen Reynolds deserves mention. He came from eastern New York, and settled on the bank of the creek, on land belonging to Judge Coryell, where there was a "sugar bush," that is, a collection of maple trees, from which the maple sugar was made, which is now regarded as such an article of luxury. Mr. Reynolds was a cooper, and worked during the year from place to place at his trade, except a few weeks in the spring, when he and his family made sugar.

He was very poor, and could neither read nor write, the same being true of many of the emigrants, but he brought up his family of sons to be what he himself was, honest and industrious. These all accumulated property, and became the owners of good farms, and their descendants are some of them among the substantial men of the county. The manufacture of sugar was, at that time, an industry of considerable importance in the country, the settlers depending on it almost entirely for their supply of that article. Parties of men would leave their homes, at the proper time in the spring, and go sometimes considerable distances into the woods, till they found a place for a "sugar camp," where they would stay during the sugar season, returning often with some hundreds of pounds of sugar, which they made a profitable article of merchandise.

Judge Coryell, soon after his arrival in the county, was called to fill various public offices. After being supervisor of the town he represented the county in the assembly of the state six different times during the twelve years subsequent to 1796, and was then appointed first judge of the court of common pleas for the then widely extended county of Tioga. This office he held until disqualified by age, according to the old constitution of the state. His death in 1835 was the severing of another of those links already becoming few, which bound together the two great periods of our national history. Until his twenty-third year he was a subject of the King of England. From his thirty-first, he was a citizen of our great republic. He had lived at a historic time. He was familiar with the men and the events of the revolution, and with those of succeeding times, when the republic was on trial, and its success or failure trembled in the balance. He was an ardent politician as he had been an ardent patriot, and he scarcely outlived the feelings engendered by the conflicts of that period. He was a man of fine manners, with that quick sense of honor and courtesy that we are apt to attribute exclusively to gentlemen of the old school. He filled the numerous offices to which he was called in the town and county of Tioga, with credit and ability. His hospitable mansion was ever open to entertain strangers, and to receive the large circle of relatives and friends that delighted to do him honor. He was a generous host, an easy landlord to his many tenants, and a steady friend to the poor. He reached the venerable age of eighty-one years. He outlived none of his children, nine of whom, with numerous grandchildren, followed him to his grave in the Coryell cemetery, where they are now nearly all gathered to his side. His wife, who outlived him several years, was one of the most interesting women of her time. There are some yet living who remember her conversation attractive alike to young and old, and her num- erous anecdotes of persons and things, not only in the remote, but in the nearer past, which if they could have been preserved, would have made valuable additions to the chronicles of the county. She was the last among us who had seen Washington. Judge Coryell's large landed estate on the river was divided among three of his five sons. The homestead farm was occupied by his youngest son, Harvey Coryell. The Coryell mansion, so long known as the residence successively of father and son, was built by Judge Coryell in 1811 or 1812, near the spot where the old one stood, which was pulled down when the new one was finished.

The two farms below were those of John and Emanuel Coryell, the house of the latter standing on the spot where stood the log dwelling of James Cole, who had once entertained Colonel Hooper and his friends, and afterwards made a temporary home for Judge Coryell and his family. When this old man died, we do not know. His grandson, Elijah Cole, married Isabel Mac Adams, while she was yet a young girl, and was for many years a tenant of Judge Coryell. He raised a large family of sons, who were afterwards well known in the county. This lower farm of Judge Coryell was originally designed for his eldest son Charles Coryell, who married a daughter of Judge Patterson, of Union, Broome county. He lived on the place for a while but grew discontented with farm life and left it and went away. He finally studied medicine with Dr. Stout of Bethlehem, Pa., and practiced successfully during the remainder of his life, both in Pennsylvania and New York. He died in Ithaca, Tompkins county, N. Y., in 1873. He left three sons by his first wife. His second wife was a Miss Smith whom he married in Philadelphia. The other son of Judge Coryell who was the youngest but one of his family, after receiving his education at Union College, studied law in Elmira with the Hon. Vincent Mathews, after whom he was named. He was admitted to the bar and settled in Bath, Steuben county, where he married a daughter of Dugald Cameron, Esq., of that town. This lady died after a brief married life of three or four years, after which, her husband abandoned the profession of law, and became a minister of the Gospel, and was for many years a laborious and successful preacher in the

Methodist Episcopal church. He was stationed in the years 1834–35 in Syracuse, N. Y., where he built the first Methodist church in that city where there is now a Methodist University. He retired from active service some years since, and now lives in Waverly, N. Y., at the advanced age of eighty-seven years, the last survivor of the eleven children of Judge Coryell. His only surviving son the issue of his first marriage, is a farmer in Nichols. Of the children of the second wife who was a Miss Lounsbury, of Onondaga county, only daughters survive, two of whom, with their families, compose his household in Waverly.

The landed property of Mr. Shoemaker was also divided among three sons, Daniel, who occupied the upper farm, Elijah, the one now owned by Mr. Jacob Stuart, and Nicholas, the one below. On the upper farm the old gentleman had built a very good house where, in the family of his son, he died in 1845. This house was destroyed by fire in 1849, and replaced by Mr. Shoemaker by the one now standing there, at present owned and occupied by Mr. Bensley. Elijah Shoemaker in 1825 filled the office of sheriff of the county, and was afterward one of the county judges. He was for many years a prosperous farmer, but at length meeting with reverses, he, in 1844 sold his farm and with his family went to Illinois, where he died in 1845.

These six farms belonging to these two families have now with two exceptions passed into the hands of strangers. That of Nicholas Shoemaker is still owned by his two sons, William and Edgar. The first occupying his father's house, and Robert Coryell still occupies the house of his grandfather Emanuel Coryell.

Mr. Nathan Smith, who inherited the farm of his father, was never married, but with a sister, also unmarried, kept house in the paternal mansion, for many years. The late Hon. Washington Smith, and his sister, the late Mrs. Aaron Chubbuck, grew up in their house. Besides these they took into their family during their period of housekeeping, not less than eleven indentured children, both boys and girls, who were carefully and conscientiously brought up in habits of honesty and industry and of whom it was said that they all "went out and did well in the world." The practice of bringing up indentured children was a common one at that day, among the farmers, who in that way, not only assisted the children and their parents, but secured valuable help, on their farms and in their families.

Mr. Smith's property was left to his relatives who still retain possession of it. Mr. Washington Smith in 1841 was elected

19*

member of assembly and some time during the years of the war occupied the position of state auditor. He died in 1874, and his family still occupy the farm inherited from their uncle.

The Palmer family have all passed away. The father and mother and the eight children with one exception all lie in the Coryell cemetery in sight of the house where they all lived so long. That house is now occupied by tenants.

John Smith, or Smyth, as the name was formerly spelled, while living in Sussex county, N. J., in the years of the revolution, was an acting magistrate and a major of militia. He was called into service four different seasons during the war, and was ordered by letter from General Washington to take certain stores of wheat and other provisions, which had been gathered by the Tories for the use of the British, and distribute it among the families of the militia, which order he executed; and as long after as the year 1794, after he had settled in the Susquehanna Valley, he was prosecuted by one individual for grain which was included in said stores; but being so fortunate as to have preserved the order of General Washington, he presented it and defeated the claim. While Washington's army was retreating before the British from New York toward Philadelphia, Major Smith was ordered to take charge of the artillery, and in crossing the bridge at New Brunswick, as soon as the troops were over, to cut away the bridge, which order he carried out, the night being exceedingly dark. After settling in this town, he acted as magistrate and as a supervisor of his town. He owned the tract known as the Maughantowano Flats. His wife was Elizabeth Ogden, by whom he had five children, viz.: Elizabeth, Nathan, Gilbert, David and John. The latter was engaged on the Canadian frontier during the war of 1812, where he did valient service. He married, first, Nancy A. Goodwin, by whom he had seven children, viz.: Mary A., Julia A., Madison, Amanda, Eliza A., Sarah A., and Washington. His second wife was Margaret (McCarty) Miller, by whom he had one child, Theron O. Mary A. married John S. Dean, by whom she had three children, viz.: Julia A., Jefferson B., deceased, and Nathan S., of this town. Sarah A. is the widow of the late Rev. Jacob Allington, a minister of the M. E. denomination, by whom she has one daughter, Emily J., who resides with her mother in this town. Washington married Jane B., daughter of the late Hon. Elijah Shoemaker, who for several years was a judge of the county. Their children are Catharine E. and Phebe J., who reside with their mother on the homestead. Mr. Washington Smith died November 13, 1874, aged sixty-three years. Nathan S. Dean married Frank, daughter of Daniel Shoemaker, of Windham, Pa., by whom he has two sons, Daniel J. and John S

James and Elijah Cole came from Delaware and located on the Wappasening creek, near where the Howell property lies. The exact date of their coming into the county is not known, but they were located on the farm where Emanuel Coryell subsequently resided, as early as 1787, and when Judge Coryell and Robert Lettice Hooper visited the valley on their exploring and surveying tour they were entertained at their house. They claimed but a possessory interest in the land they occupied, having as yet received no title from the patentees. Elijah had seven sons, viz.: James, Joseph, John, George, Daniel, Charles and Edward, all deceased. James married Betsey, daughter of John Hoover, by whom he had seven children, the only surviving one being Horace, of Nichols.

Daniel married Julia A. Holcomb, of Ulster, Bradford Co., Pa., by whom she had four children, Truman, Alfred, Sidney and Myra. Truman married Alice Van Dermark, by whom he had two children, Clayton D. and Charles. Alfred married Helen Waterman.

In 1786, Miles Forman came from Peekskill, Westchester Co., N. Y., and located one and one-half miles from the present site of Nichols village, on the farm now owned by George A. Ingersoll. He married Ann Platt and reared a large family. His father came from England. Miles Forman was the ninth sheriff of Tioga county, when that county included four counties.

The eldest son, Smith, married Martha Miller, of Southport, Chemung Co., N. Y., in 1818, and reared a large family. He built and lived on the part of the farm nearest Nichols. His eldest son, John, is the present owner. He married Ann Osterhout, of La Grange, Wyoming Co., Pa., in 1862. They have three children living, Mary, Smith and John.

Benjamin Shoemaker came to America, from Holland, in the decade of 1620-30, and settled near Philadelphia. His son Benjamin, who is buried, and whose will is on record at Easton, Pa., was the father of Daniel Shoemaker, who settled just west of the Water-gap in Pennsylvania--now called Broadheads -where he owned a custom and flouring mill. About the year 1797, he visited Big Flats, in Chemung county, and Painted Post, in Steuben county with the intention of settling there where large tracts of land were offered him for ninety cents an acre. But there being nothing but an Indian trail from Athens, Pa., to that territory, he returned and purchased about 1,000 acres of land in this town, mostly squatter claims. He had but one brother, Elijah, who settled in the Wyoming valley, and who was tomahawked by Windecker at the massacre of Wyoming. Daniel married Anna McDowell, by whom he had seven children, born as follows : Hannah, February 7, 1777, who married Isaac S. Swartwood ; Elizabeth, January 22, 1779, wife of George Nyce ; Benjamin, February 8, 1781 ; John, March 22, 1783 ; Robert, May 20, 1785 ; Sarah, May 26, 1787 ; Elijah, July 28, 1789, once sheriff, and afterward associate justice of Tioga county; Nicholas, January 27, 1792, who settled where his son William R. now lives ; Daniel McD., February 24, 1795 ; who occupied the homestead of his father, where the cottage of John Bensley now stands ; Anna, July 8, 1797, wife of William Ross. Benjamin, who settled on Wappasening creek, in Pennsylvania, married Eunice Shaw, by whom he had seven children, viz.: Richard, Mary, Elijah, Samuel, Daniel, Anna, and John. Elijah, son of Daniel Shoemaker, married first, Phebe, daughter of Laban and Jane (McDowell) Blanchard, by whom he had seven children, viz.: Jane, widow of Washington Smith ; George N., Nicholas, Charles McD., and Elijah B., deceased ; Jonathan Platt, and Phebe, also deceased. He married second, Catharine Floyd, of Chemung, N. Y., by whom he had two children, Hannah Shoemaker, A. M., who is preceptress of Hamlin University, Minn., and Capt. Thomas Floyd Shoemaker, of California. Nicholas married Hannah Blanchard, by whom he had five children : James and Anna, deceased ; William R., and Edgar, of Nichols ; and Caroline, wife of Col. Fred M. Shoemaker, of Wilkesbarre, Pa., now deceased. Daniel McD. married Maria Thurston, who was born in New Marlboro, N. H., May 19, 1797, and by whom he had five children, viz.: Hiram W , Elizabeth N., Horace A., who died in infancy ; Horace A., 2d, and Lyman T. Edgar, son of Nicholas Shoemaker, born February 23, 1837, married Laura A., daughter of Zina Goodsell, of this town, by whom he has had seven children, viz.: Caroline, Edgar, Stella, Zina, Mary A., who died at the age of two years ; May, and Fannie Maud. Horace A., son of Daniel McD. Shoemaker, received his early education at Kingston, Pa., and at Little Falls, N. Y. He studied for the profession of civil engineer, which profession he followed for nine years, during which time he was engaged on the N. Y. L. E. & W. R. R.; on the Blue Ridge &

Pendleton R. R., and on the West Branch canal. He married Hester L., daughter of James Comfort, of Lanesboro, Pa., by whom he has three children, viz.: Rev. Hiram R., now located at Naverino, N. Y., George Winthrop, a physician and druggist at Billings, Mont., and Martha E., preceptress of the Middleburgh academy, Schoharie county, N. Y.

Jonathan Hunt came from Bedford, Westchester county, N. Y., in 1802, and located first on what is known as the Sackett farm, one mile below Nichols village on the river road. He was a soldier of the revolution under Gen. Warren, was in the engagement at Bunker Hill and served until the close of the war. He was born in Boston, Mass., about the year 1760. His wife Millisant Brown, was born about the same year, though the exact date of the birth of either is not known. They had nine children born as follows : Ehenezer, May 6, 1783 ; Mary wife of Peter Turner, April 24, 1786 ; Willard, January 22, 1789; John, December 22, 1791 ; Adonijah, August 10, 1793 ; Jonathan, Jr., March 4, 1795 ; Irena, wife of James Brown, April 30, 1797 ; Seth, February 15, 1799, and Harvey, February 15, 1801. Ebenezer married Abigail (Dodd) White, who had by her first husband three children, viz.: Clarissa, Seymour and Ruth ; and by Mr. Hunt, Williston of this town, Henderson of Wisconsin, Phebe, wife of Jeremiah Armstrong, Abigail, Eliza J., and Ebenezer, Jr. Williston married first Alida (Van Alstyne) Vorhis who died in 1860. His present wife is Emily (Russell) Orcott. Jonathan Hunt, Jr., married Martha Brown, December 5, 1820, by whom he had nine children born as follows: Benjamin, April 8, 1823 ; Ezra C., October 27, 1824 ; Permelia, October 14, 1826 ; Susan J., October 16, 1828, wife of Thomas Kyle ; Ananius W., June 4, 1831 ; Andrew C., May 21, 1834 ; Thomas, June 23, 1836; Adonijah, September 5, 1838 ; Martha E., April 23, 1842 ; Jonathan, Jr., died August 17, 1884, and Martha, his wife January 30, 1885. Harvey Hunt married Mary Brown of Orange county, N. Y., by whom he had six children viz.: Jonathan, who died in July, 1886 ; Elizabeth, George F., a physician of West Bend, Wis.; Samuel, a lawyer of Menomonee, Wis.; Lewis, of Newark Valley, and Marcella, who, with her sister Elizabeth occupies the homestead. Mrs. Hunt died in September, 1865, and Mr. Hunt in August, 1886. Dr. George F., married Anna Salisbury by whom he has one son, Frederick. Samuel married Gelila Campbell of Owego, and Lewis married Lucy Buttles by whom he has two daughters, Lillian M. and Alice. Willard, son of Jonathan Hunt, married Mary, daughter of George Walker, the latter came from near Sunsbury, Pa., and located at Factoryville. He bought five hundred acres of land at that place, and then came on the river and purchased a tract a mile square. The homestead is the Kiff farm on the river road one mile from the state line. Mrs. Hunt had nine children viz.: Sally, Brown, Mary, Charlotte, James, Samuel, George, Fannie, who died at the age of three years, and Delos. Samuel married first Eliza Slawson of Nichols, by whom he had one son Julius, who died in infancy. His present wife is Cynthia (Loveland) Wright. James B., son of Willard Hunt married Catherine Sims of Sheshequin, Pa., by whom he had ten children viz.: Helen, Emily, Alonzo, Mary, John W., Sarah, Nora, Ida, Dora, and James, Jr. John W. married Maud, daughter of Gideon P. Holman of Illinois, by whom he had two children viz.: Clara and Ethel. Ezra C. son of Jonathan Hunt, Jr., married Mary, daughter of John W. Laning, March 26, 1851, and by whom he had two children; H. Dell, born January 2, 1852, wife of Frank H. Roper, and Charles F. born August 10, 1854. Mrs. Hunt died Febuary 4, 1881, aged 55 years, and Charles F., September 21. 1862. Adonijah, son of Jonathan Hunt, Jr., married Lucinda, daughter of Peter Brown of Litchfield, Pa. Mr. Hunt has been engaged chiefly in lumbering and farming and is the proprietor of a grist and saw-mill, located on road 37.

Benjamin Lounsberry was born April 11, 1767, in Stamford, Conn. He lost his father at the age of four years, and his mother married Jonathan Platt and removed to Bedford, Westchester county, N. Y., where he remained until 1793, when he came to this town and selected a farm to which he brought his family the following year. He married Elizabeth, daughter of Jonathan and —— (Smith) Platt, born February 7, 1772, and by whom he had nine children, born as follows: Harriet, June 7, 1793, wife of John W. Laning; Hannah, May 23, 1795, wife of Samuel H. Dunham, now deceased; Platt, September 18, 1797; Charles, July 19, 1800; Horace, December 12, 1804; Benjamin, May 4, 1807; James, October 2, 1809; William, December 6, 1812; and Norman, May 7, 1815. Benjamin, Sr., died May 31, 1857.

Platt Lounsberry married Sarah Laning, by whom he had eleven children, viz.: Sarah, wife of Robert Howell, Platt, Jr., of Windham, Pa., Mary, Amos, of Tioga, Horace, of Nichols, Prudence, wife of James Morey, of Windham, Pa., Betsey, wife of Andrew Hunt, of Litchfield, Pa., Benjamin, of Tioga, Harriet and George, of Nichols, and Enoch, who died at the age of twenty years. Mrs. Lounsberry died January 7, 1877. On April 25, 1824, Charles, son of Benjamin Lounsberry, Sr., married Rachel, daughter of Thomas and Sarah (Chatterton) White, who was born December 8, 1800, and by whom he had five children, viz.: Benjamin, who died in infancy, Charles, Mary A., wife of Harvey W. Dunham, John, and Harriet, who resides on the homestead, about three miles above Nichols village, on the river road. Mr. Lounsberry was a much respected citizen, and his life to the end was an exemplary one. He died March 21, 1872, and Mrs. Lounsberry April 10, 1870. William Lounsberry married Sarah Raymond, of Bedford, Westchester county. N. Y., by whom he had three children, viz.: William R , Edward W., deceased, and Jennie. He married, second, Julia (Knapp) Husted, now also deceased. Mr. Lounsberry died July 12, 1887. William R. married Mary, daughter of William McKerlie, of Townsend, Ont., November 3, 1875, and resides on a portion of the homestead, on the river road three miles above Nichols.

Thomas White came from Clinton county in 1814, and located on the farm now occupied by Albert Robertson. He married Sarah Chatterton, by whom he had nine children, viz.: Nancy, wife of Nathaniel Moore, William, John, Rachel, who married Charles Lounsberry, Catharine, who married Beniah Schoonover, Joseph, Mary, who married Daniel Granger, Ann (Mrs. Thomas Whyte), of Tioga, and Richard, of Illinois, who is the only surviving member of the family. Joseph married Fannie, daughter of John Smith, Sr., by whom he had four children, viz.: William W., Almira E., widow of Daniel Sackett, Joseph F., of Binghamton, and Frank A., wife of David B. Thomas. William W. married Emeline E., daughter of Andrew D. Kimber, of Waverly, N. Y., by whom he has one son, Louis B.

Henry P. Coryell, son of Emanuel and Sarah (Potter) Coryell, married Augusta, daughter of Stephen Mills, of Barton, by whom he had three children, viz.: Mary, Robert P , and Charlotte. Robert P. married Catherine H. E. Wheelhouse, by whom he has one child, Henry Wheelhouse Coryell, born September 29, 1886.

Ursula, widow of Sylvanus Dunham, came from East Town, N. Y., about 1808 or 1810, and located on the river road about half a mile above Nichols, where Stephen Dunham now lives. She had ten children, viz.: Polly, Henry, Isaac, Betsey, Wright, Sylvanus, Daily, Nelson, Ebenezer, and Sidney. Wright,—who was elected to the assembly in 1829, also in 1859,—married Harriet Brown, by whom he had seven children, viz.: William, Amelia, Frances, Maria, Mary, Eben and Sarah. Eben was born on the old homestead, which he now owns, situated at the end of the bridge across the Wappasening creek, in the south part of the town. in 1825. He has been engaged in mercantile business in Nichols for twenty-two years, and is the oldest resident merchant now actively engaged in business in the town. He married Amelia, daughter of Charles R. Brown, of Towanda, Pa., by whom he has had three children, viz.: Louise D., wife of Prof. L. O. Wiswell; Charles D., who died in infancy, and Willie B., who died at the age of seventeen years.

David Briggs came from Washington county, about 1808, and settled in that section of the town known as Briggs's Hollow. There are many of his descendants in the town, especially in the locality settled by him.

John Smith was born in Heidelburg, Pa., in 1769, and came to this county in 1798, and located on the river in Tioga on the farm now owned by James Steele. He married Sally, daughter of Richard Tilbury, by whom he had three children, viz.: Richard, John and Henry. Richard married Katie Decker, by whom he had thirteen children. John married Almira, daughter of Joseph and Sally (Roach) Granger, of Tioga Center, by whom he had twelve children, viz.: Lucinda, widow of Amos Lane, Cornelia, widow of Abijah Ketcham, Fannie, who married Joseph White, George, and Adaline, who married James Howell, Charles, of Nichols, Emily, wife of John Leonard. of Owego, John Jr., of Nichols, Almira, widow of Thomas F. Goodnough, Joseph, Anna, wife of Alburn S. Parmelee, of Owego, and Harvey R., of Nichols. John, Jr., married Jane R., daughter of Cyril Pearl, in 1852, by whom he has five children, viz.: Edna J., wife of Platt Dunham, Jr., Clara R., wife of Frederick Pearl, Charles F., John Pearl and Katie. Harvey married Fannie, daughter of Ferris Howes, by whom he has three daughters, Lottie, Gennie and Mary. Mr. Harvey Smith is a violinist and has led an orchestra and engaged in musical entertainments since he was sixteen years old, covering a period of thirty years, and from which he has realized sufficient to make him proprietor of " Meadowside Farm," which lies on the river road about half way between Owego and Nichols, having new buildings with all the modern conveniences, and is withal one of the most complete in its appurtenances in this section.

Thomas Park, who was a soldier in Washington's army, was engaged with his regiment at the time of the Wyoming massacre, when his wife, who had a child but three days old, was carried away captive in a canoe to Forty Fort. Mr. Park was sent home on a furlough by an order of the General to look after his family, and he joined Sullivan's expedition and pursued the savages to Canada. The following spring, while he was making sugar on his farm in Wyoming, the valley was visited by Indian scouts who shot him twice in the thigh, and he carried the balls with him to the grave. Previous to the war of the revolution, and when but sixteen years of age, he was engaged as a sailor in the English navy during the French and English war. About two years after the close of the revolution, he purchased 400 acres of land on the state line on the east side of the Susquehanna river. His son Daniel married Patty, daughter of Luke Saunders, of Barton, by whom he had ten children. His second wife was Nancy Ellis, by whom he had three children. Joseph, his sixth son, married Elizabeth, daughter of Elisha E. Hill, of Barton, and resides on a portion of the estate of Thomas Park.

Stephen Reynolds came from Greenwich, Washington Co., N. Y., about ninety years ago, and located near the site of the mills at Hooper's Valley. He married Sarah Babcock, by whom he had thirteen children, the sixth of whom was Joseph, who is now seventy-nine years of age, and resides on his farm in this town. His life has been spent principally in lumbering and farming. His wife was Amanda, daughter of Reynolds Babcock, by whom he had eight children, viz.: Stephen, of Chemung; Elizabeth, who died in infancy; John S., of Nichols; George and Curtis, deceased; Mary A., wife of Schuyler Bixby; Caroline, wife of Francis Mills, and Alvy, both deceased. Stephen married, first, Sarah A. Buttolph, of Nichols, by whom he had six children, viz.: Joseph J., who died in infancy; Angeline, deceased; Albert, of South Owego; Isum I., of this town; Ella and Isaac S., deceased. Isum I. married Carrie, daughter of Levi Baker, of Nichols, by whom he has two children, Eben and Charles Levi.

John S., son of Joseph, married Deliverance A. Bixby, by whom he had four children, Amos, Enoch, Alvy and Lottie. Mrs. Reynolds died in 1876. His present wife is Roxany Sipperly, daughter of Robert Fleming, of Flemingville.

Wait Smith was born April 4, 1779, and in 1802 came from Tunkhannock, Pa., in a canoe, and settled in Smithboro, where —— Platt and George F. Eckert now live. He built a shop and conducted the blacksmithing business there, and for many years his was the only blacksmith shop between Owego and Athens. He married Rachel, daughter of Ezekiel Newman, by whom he had eleven children, the oldest of whom, Lucinda, married James Waterman. Wait Smith settled above the present village of Smithboro; Ward Smith and James Smith settled there also, the former near the corner and the latter just below. A Benjamin Smith came in and settled on a farm above Wait Smith, and a Joshua Smith, a millwright, came in there from Vermont; Jared Smith, a stone-mason; Gabriel Smith, a preacher, and a Daniel Smith also settled in there. None of these Smiths were related except Ward and James, who were brothers. In consequence of all these Smiths locating there the place was called Smithboro.

John Waterman, of English descent, came from Peekskill, N. Y., in the year 1800, and settled first on the place known as the Wright farm, in Smithboro. His son, James, married Lucinda, daughter of Wait Smith, of Smithboro, by whom he had thirteen children, born as follows: William, Aug. 22, 1819; Mellissa J., Sept 23, 1821; Alonzo C., Nov. 23, 1821; Wait S., April 23, 1826; James O., March 25, 1828; John G., June 20, 1830; Mary A., July 21, 1832; Ezekiel N., Oct. 9, 1834; Martha J., Oct. 22, 1836; Samuel C., July 24, 1839; Sarah M., Nov. 29, 1840; Benjamin M., Aug. 2, 1842, and Helen, April 26, 1845. Alonzo C. married Sarah J. Parks, of Nichols, by whom he has seven children, viz.: Walter S., Martha J., Mary, Harriet, James, Elma A. and Margaret. John G. married Margaret, daughter of Job Wolverton, of Barton, March 27, 1859. and by whom he has had three children, born as follows: Eliza G., Jan. 2, 1860. died Feb. 8, 1879; Charles H., born Sept. 19, 1861, and Katie D., Sept. 25, 1871. Benjamin M. married Helen L. Sears, by whom he has two sons, Fred and Jed.

Sampson Howell, of Sussex—now Warren—county New Jersey, was born in 1718 and died there February 3, 1803. His children were Sampson, Elizabeth, Isaac, James, Levina, Levi, Nathan, Garrett, John, Aaron, Achsa, Lucretia, and Usual O. James came to this town in 1806 and located first on the river road where Thaddeus Steward now lives. He next removed to the farm now occupied by Emanuel Coryell which property he traded with Elijah Cole for the property on Wappasening creek, recently occupied by John L. Howell, his son. He subsequently purchased other parcels of land until his estate amounted to several hundred acres. He married Amelia, daughter of Robert Laning, of New Jersey, by whom he had six children who arrived at maturity, viz.: Elizabeth, William, Frances, wife of Stephen Morey, John L., Mary A. wife of William Morey, and Robert. Robert Howell was born on Wappasening creek September 4, 1815, and at an early age evinced a curiosity and taste for Geology. His mind first awoke to the wonders of this science as he strolled, a child, along the creek which exposed to view a variety of curious stones, drift and fossils; but the disadvantages under which the youth of those early days labored, forbade him to know anything of the secrets which lie hidden in them all. Finally, as if by the direction of Providence, a yankee doctor brought into the country a work on Geology, the first ever seen in this section. The book was bought by a neighbor—an Englishman who had retired from the British army—and of him young Howell purchased the work, paying him therefor one hundred young apple-trees from his father's nursery. This was his elementary text-book and the nucleus of a scientific library now containing several hundred volumns. Though his education was limited to a few quarters in the district schools, he ranks high among the scientists of his day. He has lectured on geology, mineralogy, paleontology and the animal kingdom; and has contributed much that is valuable on the subject of agriculture, ornithology and on native forest trees. For forty years he has kept a record of the weather, for twenty-one years for the weather bureau at Washington. He was a member of the American society for the Advancement of Science for twenty years; his name having been presented by Prof. Aggisiz. He has also been a faithful collector for the Smithsonian Institute at Washington, D. C. Though in his seventy-third year he manages his farm and is still a most diligent student, devoting the time not given to his farm work to scientific studies. He has recently been appointed by the U. S. geological survey, commissioner for Tioga county, to look up the forest resources of the county. He married first Rhoda, daughter of Joseph Morey, by whom he has one son Arthur M. His present wife is Sarah, daughter of Platt Lounsberry, of this town.

Oscar E. Farnham, son of Joel Farnham, of Tioga, was born in that town Sept. 17, 1839. He received his early education there and at the Owego Academy. At the breaking out of the war he was employed on his father's farm and at the turner's trade. On April 19, 1861, he enlisted in Co. H, 3rd N. Y. Inf., and served until June, 1863, when he re-enlisted in the 5th N. Y. Cavalry, in which regiment he served until mustered out in July,

1865. About one year of this time was spent in rebel prisons, where he suffered untold hardships and privations. While being transferred in cattle cars with several hundreds other prisoners, he, with twenty-five of his comrades in misery, escaped by jumping from the train at Millen, Ga. All were retaken but five, four of whom kept together, but Mr. Farnham was separated from them and traveled alone three hundred miles through marshes, woods and swamps, subsisting on nuts, roots and berries, and on food stolen for him by colored people whom he met in his journey. He traveled thirty-four days before he reached the Union lines, where he joined Sherman's army in front of Atlanta, a few days before that city was taken. He was detailed an orderly at Gen. Sheridan's headquarters, in the winter of 1864-65. Mr. Farnham was at the battle of Big Bethel—the first real battle of the war—and was also present at Appomatox when Lee surrendered. He married Jane Wilson, by whom he has three children, viz.: Minnie, wife of Charles White; Lillian and Philip Sheridan. His grandfather, Joel Farnham, came from Wyoming, Pa., to the town of Tioga when there was but one house where the village of Owego now stands. He settled on the farm owned by the late Frederick A. Farnham, where he built a carding-mill, wheelwright-shop and cider-mill. He married Ruth, daughter of Enoch Slawson, of Newark Valley, by whom he had ten children.

Henry Washburn came from Flat Brook, N. J., about the year 1808, and located on the farm now occupied by the widow of Absalom Adams, on the river road at Hooper's Valley. He then bought a farm of something over a hundred acres, and the first clearing he made was on the farm now owned by Henry Neal. He married Sarah Harris, by whom he had eight children, viz.: Noah, Nicholas, Rachel, wife of Conwell Ellis; Hiram, Benjamin, Henry, Betsey, wife of Henry Riddle; Reuben, Hannah, and Esther, wife of Andrew Raising. Nicholas settled where John H. Washburn now lives. He married Mercy Hoover, by whom he had eight children: Sarah, who died at the age of three years; Elizabeth, wife of Hiram Ellis; Reuben, of Illinois; Joshua, John H., a member of Co. K, 109th Regt., N. Y. Vols.; Abiah, wife of John Barr, Jr.; William, of Nichols, and Mercy J., wife of Chester Ellis. George H., son of Noah Washburn, married Nettie, daughter of John Adams of Cameron county, Pa.

Anna, the widow of Luther Hale, came from Bennington, Vt.,

in 1814, having one child, Ruth, now the wife of Daniel White, of this town. Mrs. Hale married Dr. William Wood, and after his decease, Jacob Totten. Her daughter, Ruth, married first, Hiram Rogers, by whom she had one child who died in infancy. Her second husband was Peter Goss.

Joshua White came from Duanesburg, N. Y., in the spring of 1819, and located on the farm now occupied by Bretton Briggs. He married Rhoda Duel, by whom he had nine children, born as follows: Wilbur, February 15, 1787; Doris, December 22, 1789; William, January, 20, 1791; Phœbe, April 13, 1793; Charlotte, September 4, 1796; Silas, September 6, 1798; Daniel, August, 10, 1801; Stephen, April 14, 1806; Mahala, widow of Abraham B. Ward, October 23, 1808. Daniel, married Maria Morey, by whom he had ten children, viz.: Benjamin, who died in infancy; Joseph W. and Henry, of Nichols; Charles, of Owego; Diantha, wife of Elihu Briggs; Platt, of Nichols; Laura, wife of Aaron VanDyke; George, Perry, deceased; and Susan, wife of Dr. Gordon, of Sandusky, O. His present wife is Ruth (Hale) Goss; Joseph W., married Permelia, daughter of Jonathan Hunt, December 25, 1845, and by whom he has four children, viz.: Martha J., wife of John H. Wait, Benjamin F., a physician of Wellsboro, N. Y., Samuel H., and Maria, wife of Fred Bostwick. Platt married Fannie M., daughter of Elbridge Russell, of Owego, by whom he has one son, Frank P.

Nathaniel Moore was born in New Hampshire, and when he was but three years of age, his parents moved to Plattsburg, in this state. In 1816 he removed to this town and located on what is known as the Moore homestead. He married Nancy, daughter of Thomas White, by whom he had eight children. When he settled here there was no land cleared between the river school house and his place, except a piece where J. Lounsberry's saw-mill now stands, and a piece near where Benjamin Dunham's house now stands. This piece was sowed with Canada thistles for sheep pasture, the seed having been brought from Canada for this purpose by Joseph Densmore, who resided on the place.

Absalom Adams, son of Rev. George Adams, who was also a corporal in the war of the revolution, was born in Wilkesbarre, Pa., March 3, 1797. He located in Barton in 1830, where he remained until April, 1846, when he removed to this town and settled on the farm now occupied by his widow and his daughter, and which is under the management of his grandson, S. B. Adams. He married Maria Moss, by whom he had six children,

viz.:   Elizabeth S. and George Q., deceased ; Louisa M., wife of
Henry Light, of Tioga, and Eliza (twins); Maria, wife of William
H. Manning, of Owego ; and Horace G., of Norwich, N. Y. Mr.
Adams died December 8, 1884.   Mrs. Adams still resides on the
homestead.

Eben W. Whipple came from Palmer, Mass., in 1822, and
located first in Windham, Pa., where he resided until 1829, when
he came to this town and settled on the farm now owned by his
son, Andrew G. Whipple, on road 33.   He married Nancy,
daughter of Gideon Graves, a soldier of the revolution, by whom
he had eleven children, viz.; D. Adams, of Owego ; Andrew G.
of Nichols ; Martha, who died at the age of thirteen years ; Harriet, widow of Anson Dunham ; Adeline, widow of Frank Roper;
David L., deceased; Mary P., wife of Levi Terbush ; Nancy, who
died at the age of ten years ; Eben, who died in infancy ; Willett,
also deceased, and Marcia, wife of James Lounsberry, Jr. Mrs.
Dunham married first, Robert Laning, by whom she had three
children, viz.:   Judd, who died at the age of eight years ; Willett
S., of Chicago, Ill.; and Robert F., of St. Paul, Neb.

Joseph Ketcham came from Rensselaer county, N. Y., very
early in the history of this section, and settled on the farm now
owned by Loring C. Pearl.   His second son, Abijah, married
Cornelia, daughter of John Smith, Sr., of this town, by whom
he had seven children, viz.: T. Jefferson, deceased ; Charlotte,
wife of La Fayette Williams, of Candor ; Charles, of Owego ; Eli
G., of Nichols ; Adelbert, of Owego ; Emma, wife of Stephen
Evans, and George, of Williamsport, Pa.   Eli G. married Harriet E., daughter of Anson Dunham, by whom he has three sons,
Clarence, George and Clark.

Peter, son of Nathaniel Brown, was born in Bedford, Westchester county, N. Y., Sept. 10, 1795, and when five years of age
his father removed with his family to Orange county, N. Y.
Here Peter married, and after several years his wife died, leaving him with a family of six children.   He was a soldier of the
war of 1812, and served at Harlem Heights.   After the death of
his wife, he removed with his family to Litchfield, Pa., where he
married Elizabeth, daughter of Aaron Van Gorder, Aug. 1, 1840,
by whom he had five children, viz.: Levina, wife of Henry
Morse, of Litchfield ; Lucinda, wife of Adonijah Hunt, of Nichols ; Martha, wife of Abram Bennett ; Nancy, wife of Oren Park,
of Litchfield, and S. Otis Brown, of Nichols.   The latter married

Lemira, daughter of Alanson Munn, of Litchfield, Pa., by whom he has two children: Hanlan Reed and Archie.

Aaron Van Gorder came from Sussex county, N. J., in 1819, and settled in Tioga, near Smithboro. He married Sarah Warner, by whom he had thirteen children, viz.: Jacob, Elijah, Daniel, Elizabeth, widow of Peter Brown; Ellen, Israel, Clara, Adam, Margaret, Mary, Horace, Charles and Allen.

Cranston V. S., son of Isaac Bliven, was born in Windham, Conn., Oct. 3, 1808. He came with his father's family to the town of De Ruyter, Madison county, N. Y., when about three years of age, and from there to Cortland county, and from thence to Tompkins county, after he had served an apprenticeship at wagon-making. He married Caroline R., daughter of Joshua Gager, of Binghamton, by whom he had three children, Cranston, a merchant of Nichols; Caroline R. and Eugene. Mr. Bliven came to this town in 1834, and established the wagon-making business at Hooper's Valley. He now lives retired, after having spent fifty years in active business here. Cranston married Adell, daughter of Jonathan Platt, by whom he has two children, Frank C., aged fourteen years, and Bessie, aged twelve.

Zina Goodsell was born in Catskill, N. Y., August 22, 1815, and when sixteen years of age came with his father's family and settled in Smithfield, Pa. In 1842 he married Lydia, daughter of Ebenezer Slawson, by whom he has had five children, viz.: Sarah A., deceased, William, Laura, wife of Edgar Shoemaker, Joshua, Jane J., wife of Charles Bostwick, of Rome, Pa. In 1844 Mr. Goodsell settled near the state line, on the farm now occupied by Eben Stanton.

Dr. George P. Cady was born in Windsor, Berkshire county, Mass., January 1, 1833. He received his early education at Hinsdale Academy; and his degree from Berkshire Medical College, at Pittsfield, in 1855. Soon after, he removed to Nichols, N. Y., and entered into partnership with his uncle, Dr. G. M. Cady, which partnership lasted until 1874. Here he married Susan, daughter of Hon. Nehemiah Platt, by whom he has two children, Margaret J. and George M.

Dr. George M., son of Dr. George P. and Susan (Platt) Cady, was born in Nichols in 1865. He received his education here and at Binghamton, and graduated from the New York Medical University in 1887. He is in partnership with his father and is junior member of the firm of Latham & Cady, druggists.

Dr. Edward, son of Levi Pease, was born in Windham, Pa., in

October, 1851. He was educated there and at Rome, Pa. He studied medicine with Dr. Warner, of Le Raysville, Pa., and with Dr. Cady, of this place. He graduated from the Medical College of Ann Arbor, Mich., in 1873. He has practiced here since September 1, 1874.

Early Items.—The settlers, whether poor or otherwise, had to undergo all the hardships and privations incident to the life of the emigrant. They had to make their way from wilderness to civilized country with very little help. They lived very much upon their own resources. Nearly all the clothing for their families, as well as the supply of articles necessary to support life, were produced at home. For many years there was no store nearer than Athens, Pa., or Owego, where articles of general merchandise were sold, and an expedition to either of these places, which could only be undertaken in the winter when there was sleighing, was an arduous undertaking for the house-wife, and not to be entered upon more than once or twice a year. And everything, too, had to be done by hand—there was no machinery. Carding, spinning, weaving and sewing in-doors, and sowing, reaping, mowing and threshing, on the farm. There were no fanning-mills, even the winnowing of the grain had to be done by a hand fan. This was an implement made of basket work about three feet in diameter; about one-half its circumference flat, and the remainder turned up like a basket, and holding perhaps half a bushel of grain. The person using it took it between his hands, by the two handles on either side, like those of a corn basket, and shaking it up and down separated the chaff towards the flat part of the fan, where it could be brushed off or carried away with the wind. This must, one would think, have been a somewhat slow process, and it must have taken a man some time to "thoroughly purge his floor" of any quantity of grain. The nearest gristmill was for a long time several miles away, up the Chemung river. Whenever a grist was wanted, a messenger, generally a boy, was put on horse-back with a bag of wheat behind him and sent to mill. When he arrived there, as the mill was small, he had to wait his turn among other customers. If the water was low, he frequently had to come home without his grist, and thus the mistress of the house was often days together without bread, having to supply its place with potatoes or other vegetables, or rice, of which edible some of the good house-wives with a view to such exigencies, sometimes contrived to keep a store on hand. Crab apples and wild plums grew in the fields, and berries of all kinds, including strawberries, were plentiful. These made the delicacies of the table.

Facilities for education could scarcely be said to exist at all. The state had as yet made no provision for the instruction of its children, and the settlers had to take up with such teachers and such schools as they were able to procure. These schools could only be taught during the summer, in some barn or other out-of-door building fitted up temporarily for the purpose, the teacher being some transitory person who had found his way into the country, and had no other employment, or some one of the inhabitants who could sometimes be induced by the necessities of the time, to devote a few weeks or months to the instruction of the children. Occasionally we hear of a lady being engaged in some of the families as private instructress. At one time, for several successive summers, the children of Judge Coryell, and probably others, were sent across the river to a school near Smithboro. The first school-house in the town, we are told by one of our local histories, was a log school-house which stood on what is now the farm of Samuel Smith, up the river. The first one that we hear of elsewhere stood at a turn in the road about half a mile below the residence of Judge Coryell. This however, must before long have disappeared, as we next hear of the children walking two or three miles to a school on what is now the farm of Harvey Dunham. This also must have been removed, and the next we have any knowledge of was in the village of Nichols. We do not know exactly at what time the first public school law of the state was passed, but as we find mention made in 1812, of a superintendent of public instruction, it probably dates not far from that time. The town must then first have been divided into districts. The one which comprised the village of Nichols originally included those immediately above and below it, on the river. The one below was set off first, and a school-house was built which, after being removed once or twice, was finally fixed at Hooper's Valley, where there is a very good school building. The one above was, after a time, set off into a district by itself, but was finally made a part of it again at a later period. We have no record of the building of the school-houses in the other districts of the town, but the one in Dist. No. 1, the extreme western district on the river must have been built early ; and the old "line school-house," which is so called from its position near the state line, in the district up the Wappasening, has probably stood more than half a century. These schools throughout the

20*

town must have been of an inferior character in very many
instances. They were supplemented by occasional select schools
of more or less merit; but these finally disappeared with the
establishment of the graded school in the village of Nichols.

The comparative growth of the town is shown by the following figures, giving the census enumeration for the years mentioned: 1825, 951; 1830, 1,284; 1835, 1,641; 1845, 1,924; 1850,
1,905; 1855, 1,871; 1860, 1,932; 1865, 1,778; 1870, 1,663; 1875,
1,687; 1880, 1,709.

Organization.—Nichols was set off from Tioga and organized
as a separate township, March 23, 1824. Owing to the destruction by fire of the town records, we are debarred from giving the
customary proceedings of the first town-meeting. The burning
of the building in which the records were kept, together with
its contents, occurred in 1864, during the clerkship of Luther
Conant.

BUSINESS CENTERS.

NICHOLS VILLAGE is situated near the Susquehanna, at the
point where the highway running parellel to that river, is joined
by the one running north from the Pennsylvania line. At the
time of the arrival of Dr. Barstow, in 1812, the lumber trade
which afterwards became one of the prominent industries of the
county, had made little more than a beginning. But southern
New York and northern Pennsylvania were rapidly filling up
with a hardy race of pioneers before whom the forests were soon
to disappear. Besides the mills of Caleb Wright, mentioned
before, at the mouth of the Wappasening, James Howell an
emigrant from New Jersey, whose sons J. L. Howell and Robert
Howell are still living among us, built or purchased one up the
stream about a mile distant from the river. Mills were also built
at various points along the creek both in Nichols and in the
adjoining County of Bradford, Pa. All the lumber manufactured
at these mills had to find its way down the creek to the river to
the various landings where it was to be rafted; that is, made into
floats or "arks" to be sent down the river. The junction of
these two great highways of the country nearly midway between
the eastern and western extremities of the town, seemed to present a central point where a village might grow up. The dwellers on the hills as well as those in the valley, began to feel the
want of some nearer place than the neighboring towns, where

they could obtain the articles necessary for the convenience and comfort of their families. They wanted stores and shops ; they wanted a resident physician. They wanted mechanics, and they wanted schools. The place was ready ; there was only lacking some person of sufficient energy to take advantage of the situation, and the right man finally came. The ground on which the village was built was at this time pretty well cleared up, though the woods approached it on the south and west.

Gamaliel H. Barstow, so long and prominently known both in the town and in the county, was an emigrant from Connecticut. He was born on one of the hardest and rockiest farms in the town of Sharon, Litchfield county, in 1784. He lived and worked on his father's farm until past his majority, when he left it and went to Great Barrington, Mass., to the house of his brother, Dr. Samuel Barstow, where he applied himself to the study of medicine. He had had at the age of seventeen a great desire to study law, but his father objected so strongly, having a prejudice against lawyers,—by no means peculiar to himself at that time— who, he thought, were men who got their living without work, and, therefore, could not be honest, that he was obliged to give up the idea. This was much to be regretted, as the peculiar bent of his mind rendered him much more capable of attaining success in this profession than the one he finally adopted. He, however, went so far as to procure a copy of Blackstone's Commentaries, of the contents of which he made himself master. This knowledge proved of the greatest possiblle value to him in subsequent years. He was accustomed to say that he would never have been able to fill the places in the Legislature and on the Bench, to which he was afterward called, without it. Having remained with his brother until he obtained his degree in 1811, he turned his thoughts towards the West, that being then, as now, the great field where young men sought fame and fortune. He first came to Wysox, Bradford county, in northern Pennsylvania, where his brother, Dr. S. T. Barstow, settled some years before. Here he remained some months while making his observations and looking about for some eligible place where he could finally pitch his tent; and hearing at length of the settlement on the Susquehanna in the adjoining county of Tioga, where there seemed to be a good opening for a physician and a man of enterprise, he determined, without seeing the country, to try his fortune there. Having made this decision, with characteristic energy he returned at once to Connecticut to make his preparations for emigration to this new scene of action. These were few, as the journey was made in a one-horse wagon, which carried beside himself, such articles as he deemed necessary to the practice of his profession in a new country, and also certain articles of merchandise with which he proposed to add to his resources in a country where shops were not. With this modest equipment he left his father's house in November, in the year 1811, to make a journey of more than two hundred miles, over bad roads in severe weather, to an unknown country. He crossed the Hudson at Coxsackie; we are not told his route, but it brought him to Owego and thence to the Wappasening. He passed through the country and went directly to the house of his brother, on the Wysox. Here he remained a few weeks to rest, and then adding a few hundred dollars' worth of goods from his brother's store to those he had brought with him, he returned to his place of destination and took up his quarters at the house of Jacob Middaugh, where he arrived the 7th of January, 1812. Here he hired a couple of rooms, one for an office and store and the other for a bedroom, and Mr. Middaugh having agreed to board him, he there began his long career in the valley of the Susquehanna. His accommodations were limited, and his board by no means luxurious, but he has often been heard to say, that blessed with health and hope and indomitable courage, the months that he spent there were among the happiest of his life.

The ground where the village now stands was, as we have said, a part of that purchase by Caleb Wright. It was now, at least a part of it, in the possession of Robert Williams, a son-in-law of Mr. Wright. He owned the land on the east side of the street running south to the foot of the rising. ground which for some years seemed to form the boundary to the village in that direction. This was sold in acre lots to the emigrants as they came in, there being eight between the corner and the foot of the hill. Dr. Barstow purchased the corner lot, for which he paid the sum of one hundred dollars. Opposite this corner on the river side stood a log house, occupied by Simmons Clapp, while a few rods farther up stood another, belonging to Mr. Williams himself. There had, until this time, been no resident physician south of the river, and Dr. Barstow's presence in the town becoming known, he was soon in the enjoyment of considerable practice, which constantly increased. The prospect of ultimate success soon became so encouraging that he very soon built a house, and about a year after his arrival he married a daughter of Judge

Coryell and commenced house-keeping. He soon after put up another building for a store and office.

The next arrival that we hear of was George Kirby, who had been an acquaintance and intimate friend of Dr. Barstow in Great Barrington. One day, in the summer of 1814, he surprised his friend by driving up to his door with very much such a horse and wagon as had brought him into the country, and laden, too, with materials for his business. He purchased land nearly opposite that of Dr. Barstow, on the river street, where he built a house. The next summer he returned to Massachusetts for his wife and child. Mr. Kirby was by trade a shoemaker, which proved a most lucrative business, and he was soon able to build a tannery, and afterwards a large building for the manufacture and sale of shoes. To these he added other industries and was soon one of Nichols' most prosperous men. He built the first steam mill in the town, a few years after.

Other emigrants came in, and the lots belonging to Mr. Williams were soon sold. The land on the opposite side of the street, which probably still belonged to Mr. Wright, extending south from the river street some twenty or thirty rods, was for a long time unsold and unenclosed. This strip, with the exception of the upper part, or church lot, eventually came into the possession of the heirs of Major Platt, and was enclosed for building purposes. Among those who purchased lots of Mr. Williams previous to 1820 were Captain Peter Joslin, Dr. John Petts, Dr. John Everitt, James Thurston, Isaac Raymond, Joshua Brown, and many others whose names are yet heard in the town.

Henry and Wright Dunham, two of a numerous family of brothers who came into the town at different times from Madison county, purchased farms up the Wappasening, where Henry Dunham, who was a son-in-law of Caleb Wright, built a gristmill, in 1822, which is still owned by his son-in-law, Samuel Dunham. Silvenus Dunham, who came later, built a carding machine and fulling-mill, which were for years the only ones in the town.

Not far from 1820, Major Platt left his farm up the river, and came down to "The Corners," by which euphonious appellation the village was long known by those living out of it, and built a very good house where he kept a hotel up to the time of his death, in 1825. This house, which must now be the oldest in the village, and is still one of the best, is at present occupied for the same purpose by a grandson of Major Platt, who bears his name.

A store and house were also built directly opposite, which were occupied soon after by Nehemiah Platt, who was a prosperous merchant and business man for a good many years.

In 1819 Dr. Barstow purchased the homestead farm of Caleb Wright, then recently deceased, of his grandson, James Wright. This is believed to have been nearly the last piece remaining of the old man's originally large property. This added farming to Dr. Barstow's already varied business. He not long after this built a distillery, which probably did not pay, as it was soon abandoned. He also erected a small building on the Wright farm for the manufacture of potash, which he carried on for some years, sending a considerable quantity every year to New York. This, too, finally became unprofitable, and was given up. In 1833 he purchased the mills at the mouth of the creek, of John Cassell.

Although the town was fast becoming agricultural, yet a large lumber trade from a considerable part of the country round about centered there for many years, and its purchase and sale necessarily made a large part of the businesss of the merchant, and sometimes of the farmer, as it constituted an important and frequently the only medium of exchange between them and poor settlers, while he was trying to turn his own land into a farm. The production of lumber, taking it from the felling of trees in the woods, to its sale in the markets of Southern Pennsylvania, was a most laborious pursuit, involving not only hard work, but often a good deal of risk to life and limb. The trade helped to develop the resources of the country, and many of those engaged in it, made it very profitable, though few made fortunes; and when it finally gave place to the cultivation of the soil, the coun try was more prosperous. It yet has its place among the industries of the country, but the manner of carrying it on has entirely changed. Previous to 1825, all the goods purchased in New York by the merchants of our town had to be brought by teams from Catskill on the Hudson. In that year the completion of the Erie canal brought them to Ithaca, which was within a two days journey, one going and one coming. In 1833 the Ithaca and Owego railroad brought them to Owego, which was very near home. In 1852 the Erie railroad brought them to Smithboro, and now the D., L. & W. road brings them to our doors. So much for the march of modern improvement.

Dr. Barstow not long after becoming a house holder, was appointed justice of the peace, his first commission being for the town of Owego. It was during the same year that the territory south of the river was made a part of Tioga. In the year 1815, and the two succeeding years, he was elected to the assembly of the state, and soon after that to the senate, the members of which body then held their places for four years. In 1818 he succeeded Judge Coryell as first judge of the county, and was in 1825, and again in 1838, elected by the legislature treasurer of the state. During the frequent absences from home which these positions required, it became necessary to find some person who could attend to his affairs at home, and at his solicitation, Dr. John Everitt, a young man just commencing the practice of medicine in his native town of Sharon, Conn., came to Nichols, and was taken in by him as partner, and became a member of his family. This gentleman, two years after, married a daughter of Judge Coryell, and settled in Nichols. Becoming discontented, however, after a while, for some reason, he went back with his wife and family to the East, and lived for some years in Duchess county, N. Y. He returned eventually to Nichols, where his descendants still live. Dr. Barstow, who was never fond of his profession, gave it up entirely before the departure of Dr. Everitt, and Dr. Petts, who was by this time settled in the village with a wife, had the monopoly of the profession until the arrival of Dr. John Chubbuck, who came in to the village about 1830 or 1831.

In 1824, as we have shown, the town was set off from Tioga and received an organization of its own. The village had been called Rushville by Dr. Barstow, in honor of Dr. Rush, of Philadelphia, the founder of the system of medical practice most in vogue at that day. The town would probably have received this name, but when it came to the establishment of the postoffice, it was discovered that there was already a town of that name in the state, in Yates county; a new name therefore had to be found. It was finally called Nichols, in honor of Colonel Nichols, who was then in possession of the rights as patentee, which formerly vested in Colonel Hooper. In return for this compliment, Col. Nichols directed Judge Coryell to give $200.00 to the town to be used as it pleased in the erection of some public building. This was finally used towards the building of the church. The first postmaster in the new town was Charles R. Barstow. Until this time there was no postoffice south of the river, the mails for the town all being brought from Smithboro. There was probably at that time a new mail line established from Owego through Nichols to Towanda, the county seat of Bradford. There was certainly such a one in operation in 1830, bringing us a mail about

three times a week.   About that time a passenger coach and four
horses was put on it, but probably did not prove a success and
before long was taken off.   There was for a time a postoffice established at Canfield Corners, about four miles up the river on this
same line, but it was removed before many years.   There is now
another office in the southeastern part of the town called East
Nichols.

The clearing up of the forests had left the country covered
with pine stumps.   To get rid of these unsightly objects became
a problem of no small magnitude.   The stumps of other trees
would soon decay and were easily removed, but the roots of the
pine which extended to an immense distance from the trunk and
were filled with turpentine, it used to be said would last forever.
Various attempts were made at a somewhat early period in the
history of the village to invent some machine for pulling them ;
but without success.   The science of mechanics was not perhaps
well understood, as no one seemed able to hit upon any method
by which sufficient power could be obtained to dislodge these
"old settlers."   It was finally reserved for Mr. Briggs, a blacksmith in the village of Nichols, about the year 1832, to invent such
a machine.   It consisted of a number of cogged wheels of iron of
graduated sizes working into each other, the power being obtained
by what is known in mechanics as the "decrease of motion."   In
this way he constructed a machine of immense power which,
worked by a single yoke of oxen, not only pulled up the stumps
with their tremendous roots, but was also applied to the moving
of houses.   By the aid of this machine, which has since then been
simplified and improved, but which, it is believed, was the first
successful invention of the kind, the face of the country improved
rapidly, and the value of the farms very much increased.   The
stumps being drawn, it then became a question as to what was to
be done with them.   It was almost an endless task to burn them,
though that often had to be done.   A few were thrown into the
river, but the freshets instead of carrying them down to the sea,
floated them up on the flats. At length some shrewd genius conceived the idea of making them into fences, which proved a great
success.   They were placed side by side, the roots all the same
way, and when placed along the highway these roots towering
into the air sometimes ten or twelve feet presented a not unpic-
turesque appearance, and constituted a barrier which might
amost have turned an invading army.   This machine ought to
have brought its inventor a fortune, but he left the town not long

after its completion, and the writer has no knowledg of his subsequent history.

The village after 1825 improved rapidly, until then it contained but few houses of much size or pretention. In the year 1827, Mr. Kirby built the house on River street now in possession of his son-in-law Mr. Smith. Soon after, Nehemiah Platt, a son of Major Platt, and the only one of his sons who made Nichols his home, built the large brick house occupied by his family so long, and now in possession of his son-in-law, Dr. G. P. Cady. These were followed within a few years by Doctor Petts, C. R. Barstow, and George Coryell, who erected houses which are still among the best in the village; others were enlarged and improved and trees began to be planted. To Doctor Petts must be given the credit of having set out the first of the maples which now shade our streets. They were placed in front of his own house, now owned and occupied by Mr. De Groat. The house now belonging to Eben Dunham was long occupied as a hotel by Isaac Raymond, and afterwards by Peter Joslin, where good quarters and excellent entertainment were always to be had. Dr. Barstow built his house on River street in-line with those of Mr. Kirby and Mr. Platt, in 1835. His old house, every vestige of which has disappeared, is worth a description as having been the beginning of the village. It extended from east to west with three front doors looking towards the north. Over the two toward the west was a low veranda surrounded by banisters except a space where three or four steps led down to a small door yard in which stood several large locusts. The eastern part which was built after the other, had over the door a small two storied portico, the upper part surrounded by a railing with a door opening into the chamber above. One like it, probably could not now be found in the country. A wing extended towards the south opening on the other street. It was used some years after Dr. Barstow left it as a hotel; the yard was thrown open and the trees having some time before been destroyed by the locust worm it became a part of the public street which in this way acquired a greater width in that direction than it has below the opposite corner. George Wilson, a son-in-law of Mr. Kirby, about the same time fitted up a residence just above that of Dr. Petts. He finally became the owner of the property of Dr. Petts, which he occupied till the time of his death, in 1850. Harvey Coryell built the house on the hill now in possession of Mrs. Elsbree. He occupied this house until the death of his

father, Judge Coryell, in 1835, when he removed to the homestead farm, and the widow and unmarried daughters of Judge
Coryell took possession of the house he had left. The hotel on
the corner was built in 1838 by Mr. Platt. These men were
then, and for some years afterwards the principal business men
of the village and their names are identified with much of its
history.

Our business men since then have been O. A. Barstow, P. H.
Joslin, Selim Kirby, J. L. Howell, Eben Dunham, Harris
Brothers, C. Bliven, Edward Joslin, C. I. Sherwood, John R.
Edsall, general merchants; Joslin & Alden, A. A. Swinton, and
Colman & Horton, dealers in stoves and hardware; Cady &
Latham, druggists; L. Conant, dealer in shoes, besides several
dealers in groceries.

C. R. Barstow was a son of Dr. Samuel Barstow, of Great
Barrington, Mass. He came to Nichols while a boy, and grew
up in the family of Dr. Barstow, his father's brother. He was a
partner of his uncle in the mercantile business for a while before
going into business for himself. In 1844, he was elected sheriff
of the county, and removed to Owego. At the end of his term
as sheriff he was elected member of the assembly, after which he
was made postmaster at Owego, and after his removal from that
office occupied for a time the post of harbor-master in New
York. He finally returned to Owego. He married a grand-
daughter of Major Platt, by whom he had a large family of
children, all of whom he outlived, except a son and daughter.
He sent three sons into the army, two of whom never returned.
The survivor, Capt. Sumner Barstow, finally settled at Big
Rapids, Mich., where his father died in 188—. The daughter is
the wife of Hon. Thomas C. Platt.

Oliver A. Barstow, a brother of C. R. Barstow, came to Nichols, too, while yet little more than a boy, and lived some years in
the family of his uncle. He was also for a time his uncle's partner. He at length married a daughter of Edmund Palmer and
commenced business for himself as a merchant, and has been one
of our most enterprising and successful men. He was a member
of assembly in 1866, and was previous to 1884, for forty years, a
member of the board of justices of the county of Tioga. A man
who has been elected by the popular vote so many times, to fill
such an office, may be said to have possessed the confidence of
the community in which he lives. He has for some time retired

from active business and makes his home with his daughter at Hooper's Valley.

The exact period at which the first school-house was built in the village is uncertain, but it was probably as early as 1817. It stood on the lower corner of the unoccupied ground before referred to, directly opposite the spot now occupied by the Barstow house. This vacant ground—a green, as it was called—served for many years as a charming place of recreation for the school children and young people of the village. The house consisted of but one moderate-sized room, with a single row of desks built against the wall, with a row of benches in front which were without backs, so that the scholars who practiced writing could sit with their faces either way, and another row in front for the smaller children. It was warmed in winter by a large fireplace at one end, and was entered by a door having a wooden latch, which was raised by a leather string. This primitive temple of learning must have stood some ten or fifteen years when the fire-place gave place to a stove, and the interior was altered so as to accommodate a greater number of scholars, and the house was painted red. The "old red school-house" stood until the growth of the village seemed to demand its removal and the erection of a new one. The exact year is not remembered, but it must have been about 1844 or 1845. This new one was built on the west side of the street, about half way between the corner and the foot of the hill, at the cost of two hundred dollars. A building of this kind was very soon entirely inadequate to the wants of the village. It was occupied, however, until 1871. A lot on Cady avenue was then purchased of Dr. G. M. Cady for the sum of five hundred dollars, and the present school building erected at a cost of four thousand, where a graded school has been maintained since 1874.

The town in 1856 contained 13 school districts, and the entire amount of public money that year was $807.78, and the allotment to District No. 2, which comprised the village of Nichols, was $82.70. There are at present, 1887, 12 districts, No. 2 and No. 3 extending a mile up the river having been consolidated. This year the public money for the village district alone is $440.73. The gross amount of salaries for the three teachers in the graded school is $960.00

The Susquehanna river though a beautiful stream, renowned in poetry and song, has yet been found by the dwellers on its banks, very often a troublesome neighbor. For many years its waters during the spring freshets though often overflowing its banks did no very great damage. But with the receding of the forests these became more sudden and violent, and frequently came into the streets in the lower part of the village. In 1865 it reached the point of inundation, invading the houses and causing general consternation and a good deal of damage. Since then it has twice been in the streets, the last time in seventy-two—since which a long succession of dry seasons has given us a rest from these inflictions. The Wappasening creek was, we are told at the first settlement of the country a narrow stream that was crossed by a fallen tree. The clearing up of the country has transformed it into a raging torrent coming down in the spring time with a fury that sweeps everything before it. The first bridge, which was nearly as long again as the present one, must have been built not long after the settlement of the village. The force of the stream made constant repairs necessary, and it was at least entirely rebuilt before 1865. The inundation of that year swept it entirely away. It was then rebuilt and shortened, the upper half being replaced by a causeway. The ends of this bridge being, like the others, insecure and needing constant repair, it was finally in 1882 replaced by the fine iron bridge which at present spans the stream. An iron bridge was built the same year across the same stream a mile above the village. The New York and Erie railroad which reached Smithboro in 1851, did a great deal for Nichols although the nearest station was two miles distant. There being no capitalists at Smithboro to take advantage of its position, the grain trade from a considerable extent of country centred at Nichols where our merchants, principally Barstow and Kirby, operated for a time so largely as to control the market on the Central Division of the road. This furnished employment to a great many persons, brought a good many new inhabitants into the town and gave an impetus to trade beneficial alike to town and country. Some of our best business establishments date from about this time.

In 1852, the old Owego and Towanda Mail line was discontinued and a daily mail established between Smithboro and Nichols. The mails are now carried from Nichols by a tri-weekly line to some of the towns in Bradford county. There is no direct line at present between Nichols and Towanda.

In 1868 the main street of the village was well built up from the corner to the foot of the hill, a distance of rather more than a hundred rods. The lower ground on the creek, on the east of the village, prevented its being built up much farther on the river street, in that direction. Beyond the bridge it has, however, been a good deal built up since that time. That part of the street extending toward the west was gradually being occupied, and more room for building lots seemed to be called for; and during this year several new streets were laid out. Cady avenue, which runs from the upper end of River street toward the south, till it is joined by Platt street, which connects it with the main street at the foot of the hill. West avenue leaves the river street about sixty rods west from the corner, and running south joins Howell street, which connects it with the main street. Walnut street runs from Howell street towards the south into one of the old streets commonly called the back street, which runs from the main street towards the hill on the west of the town. The two older streets have never been formally named, but are commonly called the Main and the River streets. Other names have been suggested, but these will probably remain. A short street connects the main street with Cady avenue about midway between the corner and the foot of the hill, and two short streets have since been laid out between the river street and the depot. The new streets were well laid out, planted with trees, and very soon built up, and now offer some of the most attractive residences in the village.

Dr. George M. Cady came to Nichols in 1847. His nephew George P. Cady came a few years later. He studied medicine in the office of his uncle and elsewhere and after taking his degree became his uncle's partner. These gentlemen both became sons-in-law to the Hon. Nehemiah Platt. In 1884 Dr. G. P. Cady purchased the property on the corner formerly owned by Dr. Barstow, and erected the brick block which bears his name. This block contains, on the ground floor, Cady & Latham's drug store, the dry goods store of Edward Joslin, and the Doctor's office. The second story contains three suits of living rooms, while the third consists of a fine hall for public meetings and public gatherings of all kinds; something the village had long wanted. The two adjoining stores, the grocery store of Mr. Westbrook, and the large hardware store containing the post-office, which were built soon after, with the broad plank walk extending in front of the entire line of stores at that end of the street, which was built at the same time, has greatly improved the appearance of the town. On the death of Mr. Kirby, which occurred in 1864, the two large buildings on the street below his house, which he built for the convenience of his business, were removed, leaving an unbroken line of residences on that street, and a continuous line of view up the street. The D. L. & W. railroad, which was built in 1882, passed through the village between the street and the river, destroying the succession of fine orchards which formed the background of the village in that direction. In their place we have the railroad depot with its usual adjuncts. Mr. John Fenderson has built a steam-mill near the depot, and a creamery has also been established by a Mr. Baker, from New York city. Immense quantities of lumber, bark, and pressed hay, and other produce, are constantly shipped to New York, and the business done here is probably greater than at any other station between Binghamton and Elmira. But with all its benefits it has not been altogether advantageous. It has cut up some of our farms very much to their injury, and its frequent crossings of the highway has nearly spoiled the fine drive up and down the river.

HOOPER'S VALLEY.—In 1828, Thomas Pearsall, with two brothers, Gilbert and Nathaniel Pearsall, came to Nichols from Chenango county, and purchased landed estate along the river, a mile and a half below the village. He built mills on the river, opened a store and invested largely in the lumber trade, and at the same time became instrumental in getting up the Nichols and Smithboro Bridge Company. These various enterprises involved the employment of a great many hands, and brought together a great many persons, mechanics and laboring men, and a little village soon sprang up along the street facing the river— the handsome house of Mr. Pearsall standing at the lower extremity. This village, which was supposed to be the beginning of a much larger one, which might in time rival its neighbor at the corner, received the name of Hooper's Valley, in honor of the original patentee. But Mr. Pearsall failed in business; the store was closed and the mill changed hands. Many persons who had purchased village lots gave them up and went elsewhere, and the growth of the village ceased. Gilbert Pearsall, however, retained possession of the real estate, and the village, in the midst of a rich farming country, maintained its existence. The mills were purchased by Mr. Higley who, in their place, established a fulling-mill and carding machine. These were a few years after destroyed by fire. The almost total cessation of the domestic manufacture of woolens in the town, rendered fulling-mills no longer profitable or even necessary. Mr. Dunham's had some time before ceased work, and Mr. Higley's were never re-built. In 1854, a postoffice was established at Hooper's Valley for the benefit of the lower part of the town, which has, from that circumstance, come to be known by the name of the village, in the neighboring towns. In 1875, Mr. L. Burr Pearsall, a son of Gilbert Pearsall, built the steam saw and planing-mill now in operation there. He also built, some years before, a handsome dwelling house at the upper end of the village. Hooper's Valley is now a busy little village, with a public school and several shops and some pretty houses, although it does not promise ever to become much larger than at present. Mr. Thomas Pearsall was the principal agent in the formation of the Nichols and Smithboro Bridge Company, which built the first bridge over the Susquehanna, in 1831. It was destroyed by a freshet the ensuing winter. It was rebuilt, to be again swept away in 1837. It was again rebuilt, but remained standing only until 1865, when the excessive floods of that year again swept it away a third time. Being of the utmost importance to the town and village of Nichols, especially after the building of the Erie railway, it was immediately rebuilt. It was, however, doomed to final destruction by the waters. In 1880, the northern half of it was carried away. The building of the D. L. & W. railroad the next spring, on the Nichols side of the river, made the bridge to Smithboro no longer a necessity, and it was not again rebuilt. As the mails, however, still continued to be brought on the Erie road, a rope ferry was established near the place where the bridge had stood.

Mr. Nehemiah Platt died in 1850. He had been a politician of some note, and was at one time a member of the State Senate from the sixth senatorial district. He had a large family, to whom he left a considerable estate. His eldest son is a citizen of Nichols, occupying the house of his grandfather. His own house is occupied by his son-in-law, Dr. G. P. Cady.

Dr. Barstow died in 1865 at the age of eighty years. He was well known in both state and county political circles, and his career at home is identified with the history of the village, and for a considerable period with that of the town. In all things done for its improvement he had an interest and took a pride in its development. During his fifty years' residence here he had seen many and great changes, and many of them he had helped to bring about. But he outlived most of his contemporaries, and was wont to complain somewhat sadly of the loneliness of his old

age. He had the misfortune to outlive both his sons. His eldest,
Samuel Barstow, was educated as a lawyer, and going west settled in the city of Detroit, Mich. Here he acquired considerable
eminence as a lawyer, and was for some years a man of influence
in that city, but died in 1854. He left a son who outlived his
grandfather, but died unmarried at the age of twenty-six years.
The second son, John C. Barstow, who was at one time the village postmaster, died unmarried at his father's house in 1862.
His life was saddened by these domestic losses, and also by the
war of the rebellion which swept away many young relatives in
whom, in the absence of sons of his own, he took a pride. The
Coryell and Barstow families that from their numbers and long
residence in the town exercised, at one time, a controlling influence in its affairs, have now nearly disappeared. The few that
remain of the first seem destined to become fewer, while of the
second but two of the name now survive in the town where there
were once large families. The same, however, may be said of
other large families in the town. Dr. Barstow did not leave a
large property. His house was left as a life possession to his
second daughter, who still occupies it with a tenant.

The town of Nichols has sent fifteen members to the assembly,
seven of her citizens having filled that position. Besides those
already mentioned, Ezra Canfield was elected in 1837, Wright
Dunham in 1829 and '39, John Coryell in 1838. Five of her citizens have filled the office of sheriff, three of them by the popular
vote. She has also sent two members to the state senate, one to
congress, and one of her citizens was twice elected treasurer of
the state, and four have occupied a place on the bench of judges.
The town was well represented in the late war, a large number
of young men having enlisted, many of whom were among the
"unreturning brave." Two died at Andersonville. Two of its
citizens held slaves: Judge Coryell, one man, and Major Platt, a
man and his wife and daughter. The men left their masters as
soon as the law made them free. The females remained, and the
old woman was cared for by the Platt family as long as she lived.

Although the absence of manufactures at the village has prevented it from growing rapidly, it has constantly increased in
extent, in population, material wealth and in beauty of appearance.
It has changed from a hamlet, to a beautiful and well-kept
village. Its streets are well laid out, clean and shaded throughout with fine trees. Old and unsightly buildings have been
removed and in their places we have neat and handsome dwell-

ings with pleasant yards and gardens. No disaster either of nature or fortune has ever checked its progress. Its citizens have been singularly fortunate with regard to fires. No dwelling has ever been burned within the limits of the village. With the exception of the late Mr. Kirby's store, which was burned in 1882, three or four shops are all that have been destroyed by fire. One of these, however, involved the loss of the records as we have stated. The business of the town continued to increase, and our citizens even looked forward to a time when the railroad might bring manufactures to them that would change our village to a flourishing town. The disastrous failure of a private bank in a neighboring town, in which most of the business men were interested, has, however, brought a cloud over its horizon, and interposed what we can only hope will be a temporary check to its prosperity. The population of the village at present is about 400. The want of accuracy in dates in the foregoing sketch is owing partly to the destruction of the town records as mentioned, and partly to the passing away of the entire generation of those whose recollections might have assisted those of the writer.

MANUFACTURES.

L. Burr Pearsall's Circular Saw, Planing and Shingle-Mill was built by Gilbert Pearsall in 1876. It is situated just off the River road at Hoopers Valley, is run by steam power and has a capacity of 10,000 feet in ten hours. It has also a feed run; employs seven men, and is under the supervision of the proprietor who is also largely engaged in farming.

Dunham's Grist-Mill on Wappasening creek was built by Henry, Wright and Ebenezer Dunham, brothers, about 1822–23. It is run by water power, with two runs of stones, doing mostly custom work. It has facilities for manufacturing flour. It is now owned and rnn by Caleb Wright.

Hunt's Saw and Grist-Mills on road 37, were built by Adonijah Hunt in 1884. The first mills on this site were built by his father, Jonathan Hunt, Jr., and were carried away by high water in 1883. The circular saw-mill has a capacity of 5,000 feet in ten hours. The custom mill has three runs of stones, and facilities for grinding buckwheat.

The Nichols Steam Flour, Saw and Planing-Mills were built by John Fenderson in 1885. They are located near the D. L. & W. R. R. depot, off River street and adjacent to the railroad tracks.

21*

The flour mill has two runs of stones and roller capacity for fifty barrels a day, a specialty is made of buckwheat grinding in its season. The circular saw and planing-mill has a capacity of 10,000 feet per day.

The Nichols Creamery was established in the spring of 1887, and was first in operation on May 5th, of that year. It was built and is conducted by W. and R. B. Baker, and has a capacity for 20,000 lbs. of milk per day. It is situated near the river and convenient to the D. L. & W. R. R. depot. It has an engine of ten horse-power, a Danish-Weston seperator and all the modern equipments.

CHURCHES.

The few clergymen that found their way into the country at an early day were Methodist ministers from the Baltimore conference. They were always made welcome and the houses of the people thrown open to them to preach in. But their visits were few and far between, and the inhabitants of the country commonly devoted their Sundays to visiting, which, as they had little leisure during the week and nothing else to do on Sunday, was not perhaps, surprising. Books were scarce in most families, newspapers in many, probably nearly unknown. In 1817 one of the Methodist conferences extended its boundaries so as to take in a part of the State of New York, and the entire town of Tioga was included in a circuit. *A church was organized in the lower part of the town, south of the river with five members. They had no pastor over them in the modern sense of the term, but two ministers "rode the circuit," preaching two successive Sundays alternately in the same place. The Rev. John Griffing was one of the first preachers. They preached in school-houses, private houses, or barns, or in the open air ; whenever they could bring the people together to hear them. The first church in the town was the old Asbury Methodist church. It was built in 1822, on land given by Judge Coryell on the lower border of his estate ; a plot of ground above the church being set off and reserved by him as a burial ground for himself and family.

The ground below was given by Mr. Palmer for a common burial ground. This church was filled for many years every Sunday with a good congregation, but it gradually diminished with

*It is maintained and on good authority, that a Methodist class was formed several years prior to this date by Benjamin Lounsberry, Sr., Thomas White and Adonijah Westcott, all young men, and that their first meetings were held in a school-house which stood on the north side of the River road just below the Riverside Cemetery.

the disappearance of some of the old families, till it became a question as to whether the services there should not be discontinued. It has, however, increased again, and there is now a congregation, and a Sunday-school is kept up a part of the year. In 1824 the Rev. Horace Agard was sent on to the circuit. He was a preacher of some talent, and was much liked by the people. He finally purchased a few acres of land and built a modest cottage just below what is now Hooper's Valley, and located his family there permanently. His health failed and he was obliged to abandon active work some years before his death, which occurred in 1850. As a citizen of our town he was much respected. After his death his widow and family went to the State of Iowa. Nichols was made a station with a resident minister in 1835.

The first church in the village of Nichols, now known as the Methodist church, was built in 1829. The ground which it occupies, which seemed to afford a more eligible site for the purpose than any other in the village, was secured to the town by the liberality of Major Platt. It had been in possession of Squire Joseph Webster, of Windham, Pa., by whom it was conveyed to the town in accordance with an arrangement made by Major Platt with him and Mr. Sylvenus Dunham. This latter gentleman had made a contract with Major Platt for the purchase of a piece of ground on which to build a house. Major Platt made a deed of this land to Mr. Dunham, in consideration of which Mr. Dunham conveyed to Squire Webster a piece of land which he owned in Windham, near or adjacent to that gentleman's farm, who in his turn, deeded the lot in Nichols to the trustees of the church. Whether this arrangement was made before the death of Major Platt, or by some provision of his will, cannot now be told; probably, however, it was by the latter, as Major Platt died in 1824, and the final deed was not signed until just before the death of Squire Webster, in 1831. The church was built by contributions from the inhabitants of the town generally, who gave on the express condition that the church should be free for all denominations of Christians to preach in. It was built by contract, by Mr. Hezekiah Dunham, of Windham, Pa., for two thousand dollars, excepting the foundation, which was a separate affair, and built by the men of the town coming together, bringing stone and employing the proper mechanics and rendering general help. In this way a foundation was laid as strong as brick and mortar could make it. A box was enclosed in the corner-stone containing a list of the trustees of the church, of the town officers for

the year, the names of the governor and lieut-governor of the
state, and the president and vice-president of the nation, and perhaps some other documents.   There were also copies of the cur-
rent numbers of the county papers, whatever they may have been.
The names of the trustees were Emanuel Coryell, Nehemiah
Platt, Gamaliel H. Barstow, Ezra Canfield, John Cassel, Peter
Joslin, Jonathan Hunt, Edwin Ripley, Wright Dunham, John
Petts, Sylvester Knapp, Cyrus Field, Daniel Ferguson, Justus
Brown and James Thurston.   These men, who represented
nearly every part of the town, have all passed away.   One of
them, Sylvester Knapp, was from Smithboro, from which we infer
that Smithboro helped to build the church.

On this foundation Mr. Dunham erected a superstructure
which has now stood fifty-eight years without showing any sign
of weakness or decay.   Lumber was then plenty and cheap, and
the frame was constructed of large and solid pine timbers of
great strength, the beams of the front of the tower extending
from the foundation up.   It was built after the fashion of the
times, with a high pulpit at the end of the auditorium towards
the entrance, and galleries that would seat nearly as many persons
as the floor below.   It was dedicated the next winter, although
there was no means of warming it then, nor for some time after.
The dedicatory sermon was preached by the Rev. Mr. Platt,
pastor of the Presbyterian church at Athens, Pa.   The Methodists
presently removed their preaching place from the old school-
house to the church, which they have continued to occupy from
that time, preaching for many years but once a day, and that in
the afternoon, while any others desiring to use it, had the morning hours.   The house being free was used not only by all denominations of Christians, orthodox and others, but for almost
every other purpose for which a public building was necessary,
exhibitions, concerts, public meetings of all kinds, including
political.   A Mormon even, on one occasion, found his way into
the pulpit.   As a consequence the church was ill kept, ill cared
for, and often neglected.   There were, from time to time, some
alterations made in the interior to render it more comfortable for
ministers and people, and in 1858 it was put in very good repair
with some farther alterations, and the trustees grew rather more
careful about allowing such indiscriminate use of it as had been
the custom.   In 1871 the interior was entirely remodeled in accordance with the modern style of church building.   The galleries were removed, the seats reversed, stained glass windows

put in, and twenty feet added in the rear to make room for a pipe organ, in front of which a simple desk supplied the place of a pulpit. The bell was purchased in 1867, during the pastorate of the Rev. Asa Brooks. At this time also, the time of preaching was changed from afternoon to morning.

During the pastorate of the Rev. George Comfort, in 1873, the church was regularly incorporated as the First Methodist church of Nichols, although it is still a free church, open to any who may wish to preach there at any hour not already occupied. The Presbyterians we shall have occasion immediately to speak of. Other denominations have, at different times, made some attempts to establish themselves here, but without success.

In 1843, died Miss Sidney Coryell, an umarried daughter of Judge Coryell, who, with a sister, also unmarried, and her mother had been inhabitants of our village since 1835. This lady left no will, but requested before her death that a portion, at least, of her property should be given to the Methodist church at Nichols, of which she was a member. Her friends consenting, her wish was carried out by her sister, the next summer, by the purchase of the Methodist parsonage lot of Mr. Nehemiah Platt, for the sum of nine hundred dollars. There was then but one house standing on it, which was occupied as a parsonage until 1871, when the present parsonage was built. Two or three years later the lot was divided and the town half sold to Mr. Babcock.

The Presbyterians had no church in Nichols until after the erection of the church building in 1829. A church was then organized with thirteen members. Their first pastor was the Rev. Mr. Ripley, an old gentleman with no family, who found a home with some one of his members. He remained but one year, and was succeeded by the Rev. Ira Smith, who, with a large family, served the church two years on the very moderate salary of two hundred dollars, with the addition, probably, of the rent of a house. After his departure the church was for many years without a regular pastor. The pulpit was occasionally filled by ministers from the neighboring towns, and for a few years subsequent to 1844, for the period is not precisely remembered, the Rev. John Gibbs, a retired minister, who came into the town as a resident, officiated as pastor. In 1859, the Rev. Henry Carpenter was hired and remained two years, and was succeeded by the Rev. George M. Life. This gentleman was a native of Virginia, but being loyal to the Union, he left the state on the breaking out of the war, and came to the residence of his brother, who was also a clergyman, in Muncey, Pa. Hearing, while at this place, of their want of a pastor at the church at Nichols, he came here and was hired by the trustees of the church, and remained here eight years. He had no great talents as a preacher, but made himself very acceptable as a pastor and as a financier in church matters. It was during his pastorate that the Presbyterian church edifice was built. It was done, too, just after the close of the war, when the hard times rendered the accomplishment of such an enterprise almost hopeless. It was built and finished, however, and dedicated in the fall of 1867. He married a lady of some wealth, in Muncey, and just after the completion of the church, built himself a very handsome private residence, which, at his departure from the town, in 1870, was purchased by the church for a parsonage. Since that time the pulpit has been occupied by a succession of preachers. Mr. Life may be said to have built up the church by giving it a " local habitation" and standing in the town, which it had not had before. The River Valley Methodist church was built in 1873, on ground given by Jonathan Hunt, during the pastorate of the Rev. Mr. Comfort, a few miles up the river.

The first graves in Nichols were made on a knoll on the river not far from the house of the late Henry Coryell. These graves have long since disappeared. Major Platt had a private cemetery on his farm up the river, where for many years those of the Platt family who deceased were buried. Caleb Wright also buried his dead on his own farm. The first village cemetery, or " burying-ground" as it was called, was the gift of Mr. Wright to the town. It was a piece of ground comprising less than an acre, at the upper end of his farm. It was a few years ago enlarged by the purchase of a small piece of ground from Daily Dunham. The private cemetery of the Dunham family, which was laid out some time afterward, joins it on the upper end. This ground served as a place of interment for our village for many years, and it is still sometimes used. The Riverside Cemetery association was regularly incorporated, June 1, 1861, by the inhabitants of the upper part of the town. The cemetery consists of one acre lying on that part of the public road that runs along the river bank, about three or four miles above the village. The Nichols cemetery, lying rather more than a mile below the village was established by an association incorporated February 10, 1876. These cemeteries are well laid and well kept and supply a want that had long been felt in the town.

OWEGO,* the shire town of Tioga county, is situated in the southeast corner of the same, and is bounded north by Newark Valley, east and south by the county line, and west by Nichols, Tioga, and a small part of Candor. At the time the county was organized, February 16, 1791, the territory comprised in the present town of Owego was a part of the town of Union, which then included within its limits the present towns of Berkshire, Newark Valley, Owego, and Richford, in Tioga county, and also territory in the present counties of Broome and Chenango. The original town of Owego at that time lay west of the Owego creek, and included the present towns of Candor, Nichols, Tioga, and Spencer, and all of Barton except that portion lying west of Cayuta creek, together with the towns of Caroline, Danby, and Newfield, (then called Cayuta), in Tompkins county.

On the 14th of March, 1800, the present town of Owego was organized from Union and named Tioga, and when Broome county was organized on March 22, 1806, the town became a part of her territory. The disadvantages of having a town of Owego on the west side of the Owego creek, and a village of Owego in the town of Tioga on the east side of the creek were such that in the revision of the statutes, in 1813, the names of the towns of Owego and Tioga were exchanged, the one for the other, as they now exist.

The town of Owego again became a part of Tioga county, March 22, 1822, when all the territory that had been taken with Broome county in 1806, was restored to Tioga.

Old Indian Boundary Lines.—An undeniably correct account of the early land grants and of the first occupation of the territory included within the limits of the present town of Owego, together with the acquisition of the tract of eighteen square miles of land by James McMaster, now known as the McMaster Half Township, on which Owego stands, has been already given in this work. The abandonment of the hunting grounds on the Susquehanna river and the gradual occupancy of the land by white settlers from the Eastern States followed.

The original league of the Iroquois consisted of five nations of Indians, the Onondagas, Oneidas, Mohawks, Cayugas, and Senecas. The Six Nations were constituted, in 1712, by uniting with the Tuscaroras.

The dividing line between the Cayugas and Onondagas com-

*Prepared by LeRoy W. Kingman, of Owego.

menced on Lake Ontario, near the mouth of the Oswego river and
on its west side, and, passing between the Cross and Otter lakes,
continued south into Pennsylvania, crossing the Susquehanna
river west of Owego   The Cayugas were west of the line.

The boundary line between the Senecas and Cayugas commenced at the head of Sodus bay on Lake Ontario, and running
south nearly on the longitude of Washington, crossed the Clyde
river, near the village of that name, and the Seneca river, about
four miles east of its outlet from the Seneca lake. Continuing south
and inclining a little to the east, the line ran nearly to the lake at
its head, and having crossed the Chemung river east of Elmira, it
passed into Pennsylvania. The territory of the Cayugas lay upon
both sides of Cayuga lake, and extended to the eastward so as to
include the Owasco.

The line between the Onondagas and Oneidas ran from the
Deep Spring, near Manlius, south into Pennsylvania, crossing
the Susquehanna river, near its confluence with the Chenango.

In brief, the Senecas were west of the Cayugas, the dividing
line crossing into Pennsylvania, east of Elmira. The Cayugas
were east of this line and were divided from the Onondagas by
the line which crossed into Pennsylvania, west of Owego. The
Onondagas occupied the present town of Owego and the western
part of Broome county, and were divided from the Oneidas by
the line which crossed the Susquehanna near its confluence with
the Chenango.

Another tribe, the Nanticokes, had undisputed possession of this
portion of the valley of the Susquehanna. Their headquarters
were about fourteen miles above Owego, near the mouth of the
Choconut creek, and across the river at Union. The Nanticokes
had been driven from the south and were identical with Indians
of the eastern shore of Virginia, who were known as the Nantaquaks. They were admitted into the confederacy of the Iroquois
but were then tributaries and acted in concert with them, enjoying the protection of the league.

After the white people began to settle here the Indians gradually left the country. The late William Pumpelly informed the
writer that when he came here, in 1805, Indians were frequently
seen about the streets, but most of them had removed to Oneida
county. They were accustomed to hold their councils and dan-
ces at the Indian spring, in Tioga. As late as 1812, there were
Indians scattered all about the county, and on the island below
Leach's mills there were half a dozen slab huts occupied by

Indians, who spent their time in fishing and hunting, while their squaws made bead work and baskets, which they sold to the white people on general training and other public days.

Indian Nomenclature.—Owego was known in the Indian dialect as Ah-wah-gah, and it was pronounced as thus spelled by the Indian captors of Mrs. Jane Whitaker, the white girl, who escaped the massacre of Wyoming and was taken with other prisoners to Tioga Point (Athens) and thence to Owego, while on their way to Unadilla.* In Lewis H. Morgan's " Ho-de-no-sau-nee, or League of the Iroquois," it is spelled in the Onondaga dialect " Ah-wa ga;" the " a " in the second syllable being pronounced as in the word " fate."

In the " Documents Relative to the Colonial History of the State of New York " it is variously spelled, " Owegy," " Oweigy," and " Oswegy." In early maps it is spelled " Owegy " and " Owega." The early settlers pronounced the name O-wa-go; " a " pronounced as in " fate." It was also so written in the town records of the town of Union, and in the journals of officers of Clinton's and Sullivan's armies, and also in early letters and documents.

The word " Ah-wa-ga " signifies, according to Wilkinson's " Annals of Binghamton," swift, or swift river. Judge Avery, who is undoubtedly correct, says its signification is " where the valley widens."

That part of the village of Owego nearest the mouth of the Owego creek, known as Canawana, was " Ca-ne-wa-nah." In the Seneca dialect it was " Ne-wa-na Canoeush," meaning, literally, " little living water." It was so named from the spring, known as the Indian spring, situated a little west of the Owego creek, at the northern base of the cliff, north of the Main street bridge. The present name is obtained by the arbitrary transposition of syllables.

Susquehanna is written in Smith's history of Virginia, " Sas-que-han-nough," and by Morgan, in his " League of the Iroquois," in the Indian dialect, " Ga-wa-no-wa-na-neh," meaning " Great Island River." Wilkinson's " Annals of Binghamton " says that the word signifies " long and crooked river." In a list of Indian names of rivers and settlements in Pennsylvania it is given as " Winding water."

Heckwelder, in his " Indian Names of Rivers, Creeks, and

---

*See " The Susquehanna Valley," by Judge Avery in *St. Nicholas*, 1853, page 123.

Noted Places in Pennsylvania," says the word Susquehanna (properly "Sisquehanne," from " Sisku," for mud, and " hanne," a stream) was, probably, at an early time of the settling of this country, overheard by some white person, while the Indians were at the time of a flood or freshet remarking, "Juh! Achsi quehanne," or "Sisquehanne," which is: "How muddy the stream is," and, therefore, taken as the proper name of the river. Any stream that has become muddy will at the time it is so be called " Sisquehanna."

At the meeting of the Presbytery at Newport, in October, 1885, a young Indian whom the Presbytery had taken under its care, said that the river received its name in this way: An Indian standing on one side of the banks called across to the other, "Susque," which interpreted means, " Are you there?" His friend replied, " Hanna,' which means, "I am here." A white man standing near heard it and named the river accordingly. This derivation appears to be rather far-fetched.

The word " Anna " appears to be a general Indian term meaning " river." The word " Susque " is said to have meant in the aboriginal dialect, "long and crooked." Thus we have the Susqueh-anna, the Lackaw-anna, and in Virginia, the North Anna, South Anna, Rix-anna, and Flav-anna.

Early Settlers.—The first white men to visit this town of whom we have any account, were a portion of General Sullivan's army, in 1779. On the 17th of August, in that year, Captain Daniel Livermore, of the 3d New Hampshire regiment of General Poor's brigade, with a detachment of nine hundred men from General Sullivan's army, marched up the Susquehanna river from Tioga Point (Athens, Pa.,) to meet General Clinton's expedition of 1,500 men, which was coming down from Otsego lake.

At Owego, Captain Livermore destroyed the Indian village, which was on the river's bank at and below William street, and which consisted of about twenty wigwams, the natives having fled on the approach of the troops. Two days afterward they effected a union with Clinton's army of 1,500 men at Charamuk (Choconut, about one and one-half miles above Union) and the entire body then marched to Owego, arriving August 19th, and remaining encamped here two days, on account of rainy weather.

One of the soldiers in General Clinton's army in this expedition was James McMaster, of Florida, Montgomery county. Pleased with the appearance of the valley and the apparent advantages of the land for farming purposes, he returned four years later, in 1784, on a prospecting visit. The only white man in these parts then was Amos Draper, an Indian trader, who resided at Choconut, and who was engaged in trafficking with the natives at various points. Through Draper's influence, McMaster conciliated the Indians, so that when he returned here the next year he was unmolested.

In April, 1785, McMaster, accompanied by his brother, Robert McMaster, William Taylor, a bound boy, John Nealy and William Woods, left Florida for Owego. They came down Otsego lake to the Susquehanna river, and on down to Owego. Their farming implements and cooking utensils were conveyed in a boat, while some of the party went with four horses by land. Having arrived here, they constructed a cabin of pitch-pine logs upon the flat, about fifty rods above where the flouring mill in Canawana now stands. They planted ten acres with corn on the homestead farm of George Talcott, after which they built a more substantial log house on the ground now occupied by George L. Rich's residence, near the lower end of Front street. The latter house stood facing the river, near its bank. After the corn had been hoed, the party returned to Montgomery county. After finishing their harvesting upon the Mohawk, they came back to Owego in the fall and gathered their crop, which had not been molested by the Indians.

Amos Draper came to Owego to reside in the spring of 1787, and his was the first white family to settle here. Draper had resided at Kingston, Pa., from which point his family removed, in the fall of 1786, to Nanticoke, where he had been engaged in trafficking with the Indians for several years. They commenced living in the house that McMaster and his party had built two years previous.

Amos Draper and his brother, Joseph Draper, who was a surveyor, and who was also afterward a resident of Owego, were sons of Major Simeon Draper, who was one of the forty settlers or proprietors of the township of Kingston, under the old Connecticut claim, in 1768. "Amos Draper," says an old document in possession of the writer, "deceased on the 24th of May, 1808, at about 2 o'clock P. M., in the town of Owego, in the county of Tioga, N. Y., with a cancer on the left cheek—after passing through the most excruciating pain for nearly one year—and was buried in the burial ground in the village of Owego, in the town of Tioga, and county of Broome, and State of New York. The stone at the head is marked A. D. The grave to the north is his daughter, which deceased with small pox."

The first white child born within the present limits of Tioga county was Selecta Draper, daughter of Amos Draper. She was born in Owego, June 19, 1788, and married Stephen Williams, Jr., of Newark Valley, in 1809. She died at the residence of her son, L. E. Williams, in Newark Valley, April 2, 1865.

The family of James McMaster removed to Owego in the spring of 1788, and settled in a house near the river, opposite the foot of the street now known as Academy street. In the same year the family of John McQuigg came from New Hampshire and settled in a house situated where Camp's furnace now stands, a short distance below Park street. McQuigg was a revolutionary soldier. He died in Owego, in 1813.

These houses were all on the line of the old Indian trail and fronted upon the river. This was washed away long ago by the freshets of successive years. There were trails on both banks up and down the Susquehanna. The one on the north side followed the bank closely from the eastern part of the town all the way to the Owego creek at its mouth. On the west side of the creek it continued along close to the river bank to the narrows, near Tioga Center. This trail was wide enough for the passage of horses with packs, cattle, etc., and in some places it was wide enough for wagons. It was widened after the coming of the white people and became the main highway through southern New York from the east to the west. Another Indian trail was the " Cayuga Lake trail," running north and south. It entered the north part of the village of Owego, and ran direct to the river. It was nearly identical in its course with the streets now known as McMaster and Academy streets.

When the early settlers came into this country, these trails were the only roads opened through the forest, and were for many years the only route of travel. Along their line the early settlers built their houses. All of the Indian trails along the banks of the Chemung and Susquehanna rivers and their tributaries converged upon Tioga Point (Athens, Pa.), at the junction of these two rivers. They became gathered into one, which, descending the Susquehanna, formed the great southern trail into Pennsylvania and Virginia.

Although James McMaster was the owner of such a vast amount of land, he died poor. He sold it piece by piece, much of it for a mere song, and in his later days went to live in Candor, where his daughter, Mrs. Caleb Sackett, resided. His death was caused by being thrown from a horse, in 1818. McMaster was the first sheriff of Tioga county, elected in 1791.

The old town of Union, in the county of Tioga, as formed by an act of the legislature, February 16, 1791, extended from the Chenango river to the West Owego creek, and from the Pennsylvania state line to the south side of the military tract. This, of course, included the whole of the present town of Owego. The town was organized April 5, in the same year, by the election of town officers, and three months later (July 12, 1791), it was divided into road districts by the commissioners of highways. From the lists of persons assigned to work on the highways, we obtain the names of the settlers at that early day, residing between the Owego creek and the head of the Big Island. The list is as follows:

James McMaster,	John Carmon,	Amos Mead,
Phineas Thompson,	Elias Williams,	James Barnes,
Emmanuel Deuel,	Timothy Sibley,	Benjamin Selden,
John Caster,	Daniel Ferguson,	Thomas Jordan,
Jehu Barney,	Daniel Ferguson, Jr.,	Elisha Bates,
Robert McMaster,	Reuben Harrington,	Stephen Dean,
Amos Draper,	Jacob Harrington,	Benjamin Marsh,
John McQuigg,	Jeremiah Harrington,	Stephen Aylsworth
John Nealy,	William Bates,	Benjamin Bates.

The names of those residing between the head of the Big Island and the present line between Tioga and Broome counties, were as follows:

Silas Gaskill,	Matthew Hammond,	Amariah Yates,
Uriah Gaskill,	Daniel Thurston,	Isaac Harris,
Wilder Gaskill,	Benjamin Lewis,	Thomas Tracy,
Samuel Smith,	Daniel Hilton,	Cohoon Runnals,
Charles Dodge,	Nathan Hammond,	Roswell Smith,
Jonathan Hammond,	David Hammond,	John Kelly,
Seth Jakeway,	Moses Reed,	William Roe,
John Taylor,	Levi Wheeler,	John Rowley,
James Sarner,	Samuel Atkins,	Zimri Barney,
Moses Ingersoll,	David Barney,	Richard ——,
Reuben Holbook,	Frances Norwood,	Jeremiah Taylor,
Gideon Thayer,	William Read,	Daniel Read.

Some of the persons named above may have resided east of

the present Tioga county line. Many of them were squatters, too poor to buy land, and subsisting by fishing and hunting, and they remained here only until driven from the land by the owners. Others were owners of land by purchase, and remained permanent residents. Many of their descendants are still residents of the town.

Organization.—The first town meeting in the old town of Tioga (Owego), was held at Capt. Luke Bates's tavern, in Owego village, on the 3d day of April, 1800. Col. David Pixley was chosen moderator, and the following town officers were elected: Supervisor, John Brown; town clerk, Lemuel Brown; assessors, Asa Bement, Asa Camp, Henry Steward; collector, Jesse Gleazen; overseers of the poor, Vine Kingsley, Lemuel Brown; commissioner of highways, Stephen Mack; constables, Henry Steward, Stephen Ball, Stephen Mack; fence viewers, Vine Kingsley, Stephen Bates; pound-master, Vine Kingsley; pathmasters, Silas Gaskill, John McQuigg, Edward Pain, John Freeman, Asa Leonard, Laban Jenks, John Barney, Wilder Gaskill, David Buriel.

Town meetings were held in April each year until 1813, when the day was changed to the first Tuesday in March. In 1831, the day was again changed to the first Tuesday in February. The last change was made to accommodate the river raftsmen, who were usually absent down the river during the spring freshets, and who comprised a large proportion of the voting population.

The first record of votes cast in the town was that of April 29, 1802, for congressman, senators and assemblymen. The highest total vote cast was eighty-four. At the last election, in November, 1886, the total vote cast in the town for member of assembly was 2,342.

BIOGRAPHICAL.

Capt. Lemuel Brown was born in Berkshire county, Mass., in 1775, and came to Owego in 1790. In 1795, he built the first tannery erected in Tioga county. It stood on the west side of the Southern Central railroad track, north of Talcott street, in the village of Owego. He was an overseer of the poor eighteen years, and held other town offices. He died in Owego, December 5, 1815.

Capt. Mason Wattles was the first man to engage in the mercantile business in Owego. He came here, in 1792, from

Franklin, Otsego Co., N. Y. He was very wealthy and became owner of much of the land now occupied by the business portion of the village. He failed in business, in 1799. He afterward, for several years, held the office of justice of the peace. He was associate judge of Broome county* from 1807 to 1812, and also clerk of Broome county from February 18, 1811, to November 9, 1812. He subsequently removed from Owego to New York, where he died.

Dr. Samuel Tinkham was born in one of the New England States about the year 1767, and came to the town of Tioga about the year 1792. Besides practicing his profession he kept a store in Owego. He died in the town of Newark Valley, while on a professional visit to a patient, September 30, 1804. His sons were Samuel S., and David P. Tinkham.

Dr. James H. Tinkham, the only son of Samuel S. Tinkham, was born in Owego, March 16, 1836. In July, 1861, he entered the United States navy as a surgeon. During a visit to Owego in 1879, he was attacked with quick consumption and died June 2d in that year. He was a physician of great promise, and during his illness he was ordered as fleet-surgeon to the West Indies squadron.

Dr. Elisha Ely came to Owego from Saybrook, Conn., in the fall of 1798. He died here three years afterward of consumption, contracted by exposure while he was surgeon in the federal army during the revolutionary war. His sons were William A., Daniel, Gilbert, Elisha, Edward and James Ely.

William A. Ely was born at Saybrook, October 16, 1788. He was for fifty years a prominent merchant and business man in Owego. He was a member of the first board of trustees of Owego village, and supervisor of the town of Owego from 1825 to 1830, inclusive, and also in 1832 and 1833. He died in Owego, November 27, 1863. His sons are Alfred G., Charles E., and Frederick Ely, of New York city, and Edward O. Ely, of Boston, Mass.

Daniel Ely was born at Saybrook, in 1796. He was for many years an active business man, and a merchant. He was postmaster of Owego from February 4, 1842, to November 25, 1844. He died in Owego, November 25, 1844.

James Ely was born in Owego, in 1809, and was engaged in the mercantile business with his brothers, William and Daniel. He

* From March 28, 1806, to March 22, 1822, the present towns of Berkshire, Newark Valley, Owego and Richford were a part of Broome county.

was supervisor of the town of Owego in 1834, and 1852, and represented Tioga county in the assembly of 1851. He removed to Grand Rapids, Mich., where he died on the 20th of December, 1862.

Stephen Mack was born in Massachusetts, May 20, 1765. In 1799 he kept a country store at Cooperstown, N. Y., and had a contract with the government to furnish about 100,000 spars, to be delivered at Baltimore. In March of that year, a freshet in the Susquehanna river carried away all the timber, which he had purchased and paid for in goods at his store, and made him a bankrupt. He came down the river to Owego in search of his timber, but found it would cost as much to hunt it up and get it together again as it was worth, so he made no further effort to secure it. He was so highly pleased with Owego, that he removed here the same spring. In 1805, he purchased *The American Farmer* printing office, and published the newspaper until his death. He lived in Owego only fifteen years, but during that time he was one of the most prominent and influential citizens. He held the offices of commissioner of highways, excise commissioner, and constable. He was for several years a justice of the peace, and served as supervisor of the town of Tioga (now Owego) in 1807, 1808, 1811, and 1812. He was appointed first judge of Broome (now Tioga) county, November 9, 1812, and served three years. He died in Owego, April 14, 1814. After his death his widow and his son Horace, who was then fifteen years of age, set the type and worked the edition of *The American Farmer* until Stephen B. Leonard took possession, in the following June.

Gen. John Laning was born at Lambertsville, N. J., in October, 1779. He came to Owego in August, 1801. He engaged in lumbering and the mercantile business, and brought plaster from Cayuga lake for shipment down the river in arks to a market. He was killed by falling through a hatchway in his storehouse on Front street, on the 12th of February, 1820. One of his sons, John C. Laning, is still a resident of Owego.

Eleazer Dana, the first practicing lawyer in Owego, was born at Ashford, Conn., August 12, 1772. His father, Anderson Dana, was killed in the massacre of Wyoming. He studied law at Newtown (Elmira), and was admitted to the bar, in 1800. Immediately thereafter he removed to Owego. He was the second postmaster of Owego, from 1802 to 1816. He was appointed surrogate of Broome county, in 1806, and also represented the county in the assembly of 1808—9. He was district attorney of Tioga county from 1823 to 1826. He was a member of the first board of trustees of Owego village, in 1827, and one of the original trustees of the Owego academy, which office he held until his death, which occurred May 1, 1845. He was also one of the original trustees of the Presbyterian church, organized in 1810, which office he also held during his life.

John H. Avery, the second resident lawyer in Owego, was born in 1783. He came to Owego, in 1801. He was a member of assembly, in 1814. He died in Owego, September 1, 1837. His sons were Charles P. and Guy H. Avery. The latter resides in New York.

Charles P. Avery, a son of John H. Avery, was born in Owego, in 1818. He studied law in the office of his brother-in-law, Thomas Farrington, and was admitted to the bar, in 1840. He was chosen judge of Tioga county, in 1847, being the first judge elected by the people in the county under the change of the judicial system by the constitution of 1846. At the expiration of his term of office he was re-elected. Judge Avery was greatly interested in the Indian and pioneer history of this part of the state, at a time when many of the early settlers of Tioga county were still alive, and from them he obtained much information regarding the early history of the valley of the Susquehanna, which otherwise would have been lost. Much of this has been preserved in a series of papers, entitled "The Susquehanna Valley," which were printed in a magazine, called *St. Nicholas*, which was published in Owego, in 1853-4. This is the only work of any particular historical value that has been heretofore published in Tioga county. He also took a deep interest in the aborigines of the country. When the Indian missionary, Sa-sa-na Loft, was killed at Deposit, in 1852, he caused a monument to be erected to her memory, on the hill in the eastern part of Evergreen cemetery, in Owego. Judge Avery possessed a rare collection of Indian relics, a list of which was published in the "Susquehanna Valley" papers, and which, after his death, were sold to a gentleman in Rochester. In 1856, Judge Avery removed to Flint, Mich., where he practiced law until the spring of 1872, when, on account of his health having become impaired by the climate of that state, he returned to Owego. He died here on the 31st of August, in that year.

John Hollenback was born near Wilkesbarre, Pa., November 2, 1780. He came to Owego in 1801 or 1802, and commenced a general mercantile business. He died, childless, June 13, 1847,

22*

and bequeathed the greater portion of his large property to to his nephew, George W. Hollenback.

George W. Hollenback was born at Wyalusing, Pa., August 25, 1806. He entered the store of his uncle, John Hollenback, as a clerk, in 1831. He was engaged for many years in the mercantile and lumbering business. He died in Owego, December 30, 1878. Mr. Hollenback was supervisor of the town of Owego in 1850, 1851 and 1855; trustee of the village in 1852, 1854 and 1862, and president of the village in 1854 His sons were William H., Frederick, John G., and Charles E Hollenback.

James Pumpelly was the eldest son of John Pumpelly, who served with distinction in the early Indian and French wars, and who was present at the siege of Louisburg, and was at the side of Gen. Wolfe when he fell mortally wounded on the Heights of Abraham, in 1759. John Pumpelly, his wife, and five of their children, James, Harmon, William, Harriet, (afterward Mrs. David McQuigg), and Maria, (afterward Mrs. Abner Beers), removed from Salisbury, Conn., to Beers's Settlement, in Tompkins county, N. Y., in May, 1802. He died in 1820, at the advanced age of 93 years. James Pumpelly was a surveyor. He commenced by surveying the Owego village plot and laying it out into two acre lots. He then surveyed the West Half Township, and laid it out into 143 acre lots. In this work he was assisted by his younger brothers. He became agent for large tracts of land, owned by friends in the east. He opened a land office, and engaged extensively in real estate transactions on his own account, soon becoming one of the largest land-owners in this part of the state. He died in Owego, October 4, 1845, leaving two sons, George J. and Frederick H. Pumpelly. James Pumpelly did more for the advancement of Owego as a village than any other one of her early citizens. He was the first president of the village after its incorporation, in 1827, and held that office five successive years. He also represented Broome (now Tioga) county in the assembly of 1810. He was actively interested in educational matters, and it was mainly through his influence and efforts that the first Academy building was erected in Owego, in 1827. He was the first president of the board of trustees of that institution, and held that office several years.

Charles Pumpelly, the second son of John Pumpelly, was born at Salisbury, Conn., in 1780. He came to Owego in the winter of 1802-3 and engaged in the mercantile and lumber business. He was successful in his business enterprises and for many years was one of the prominent and influential men of the county. He was supervisor of the town of Owego, in 1809, 1810, and from 1821 to 1824, inclusive. He represented Tioga county in the Assembly of 1825, and was a member of the constitutional convention, in 1821. He died in Owego on the 6th of January, 1855.

William Pumpelly, the third son of John Pumpelly, was born at Salisbury, Conn., June 17, 1789. He came to Owego, in 1805, and entered the service of his elder brother as a surveyor. In 1812, he commenced a mercantile business, and continued until 1844, when he retired. He died in Owego, November 17, 1876. His second wife, Mary H. (Welles) Pumpelly, was a lady of fine accomplishments, an artist, and the author of a volume of poems. His sons are John Pumpelly, of Albany, and Professor Raphael Pumpelly, distinguished as a geologist and mineralogist, of Newport, R. I.

Harmon Pumpelly, the fourth son of John Pumpelly, was born at Salisbury, Conn., August 1, 1795. He was in early life employed for several years in surveying lands for his brother, James. He afterward engaged in lumbering and became wealthy. In 1841, he removed to Albany, of which city he became one of the most prominent men in financial circles. He died in that city September 29, 1882. He was a member of the first Board of Trustees of Owego village and was re-elected four times. In 1835, he was president of the village.

Daniel Cruger, Jr., who was the first printer and newspaper publisher in Owego, entered the printing office of a Mr. Webster, in Albany, in 1794, at the age of fourteen years. After he had served his time he established a paper called *The American Constellation* at Union (then in Tioga county) November 23, 1800. In August, 1803, he removed his establishment to Owego, and changed the name of the paper to *The American Farmer*. Two years afterward he sold the paper to Judge Stephen Mack. From Owego he removed to Bath, where he edited a newspaper for some time. He studied law and was admitted to the bar, in 1809. In 1814, 1815, 1816, and 1826, he represented Allegany and Steuben counties in the assembly, and was speaker of that body in 1816. He was district attorney of the seventh New York district from March 17, 1815, to June 11, 1818, and from the latter date continued as district attorney of Steuben county until February 19, 1821. He represented the 20th congressional district in the 15th congress, in 1817–19. While in congress he became acquainted with Mrs. Lydia Shepard, of Ohio county,

Va., who was in Washington trying to collect a claim of her deceased husband against the government. He subsequently married her. He afterward gave himself up entirely to agricultural pursuits and the management of his wife's property. He was a director of the Northwestern Bank of Virginia, and it was while attending to the duties of that position he was stricken with the disease from which he died nine days afterward. His death occurred at Elm Grove, Va., July 12, 1843.

Capt. Sylvenus Fox, a carpenter by trade, was born at North Glastonbury, Conn., May 6, 1797, and came to Owego with the Talcotts, in 1803, when but six years of age. He acquired his title of captain from having been in command of an independent military company, about the year 1831. He was a public spirited citizen and rendered important service in laying out streets and forwarding various public improvements. He was elected a village trustee, in 1832, and served eleven years. He was president of the village, in 1840. He died in Owego, August 24, 1871.

William, Nathan, Anson, and Hermon Camp came to Owego from New Preston, Conn., in 1804 or 1805. William, the eldest, was born in 1777, and Nathan in February, 1782. They opened a general country store in Owego. Nathan was a man of literary tastes and founded the village library. He died May 19, 1819. His sons were Frederick, George, and Nathan Camp.

William Camp was killed by the bursting of the boiler of the steamboat *Susquehanna* at Nescopeck Falls, opposite Berwick, Pa., May 5, 1826. In 1812, Mr. Camp was appointed an associate judge of Tioga county, and was reappointed in 1817.

Gen. Anson Camp was born October 17, 1784. He was engaged in the hat manufacturing business and kept a hat store. He was brigadier general of the 41st Brigade of Infantry. He represented Tioga county in the assembly, in 1825. He was president of the village, in 1832 and 1833, and supervisor of the town five years. He died in Owego, March 22, 1838. Gen. Camp was unmarried.

Hermon Camp was born in 1777. He went from Owego to Trumansburg, Tompkins county, in December, 1805, as clerk in a store, which his brothers, William and Nathan, had established there. He became a prominent man in that county. He held the offices of sheriff and member of assembly, and was for several years president of the Tompkins County Bank at Ithaca. He died at Trumansburg, June 8, 1878.

George Sidney Camp, the second son of William and Abigail (Whittlesey) Camp, was born at Owego, February 5, 1816. Hav-

ing made his preparatory studies at the Owego academy, he entered, in February, 1832, the last term of freshman year, Yale College, from which at the close of sophomore year he removed to the University of the City of New York. He was a winner at Yale, as a member of the sophomore class, of the first prize for English composition. Leaving the university at the close of his junior year he studied law, first in the office of Hon. Stephen Strong, at Owego, and subsequently in the office of Hon. Gerardus Clark, at the City of New York, and was admitted to the bar as an attorney, May 18, 1838. He practiced law the first two or three years of his professional life, in the City of New York, a portion of the time, that is from November, 1839, as a partner of Hon. Thomas W. Clerke, who was afterward elected a justice of the supreme court. December 16, 1841, he returned to Owego, where he has ever since resided. He was compelled to seek a country residence by the breaking down of his health from an attack of laryngitis, which became chronic, and of which he has never since been entirely cured ; so that all of his subsequent professional life has been that of one more or less an invalid, subject, as he has thus been, from the slightest cause, to contract a cold that rendered all professional labor absolutely impracticable, and having been, for periods of four or five years at a time, wholly unable to try or argue a cause. The effects of this chronic evil yet tell upon his health and life.

During the early residence of Mr. Camp in the City of New York, and in the year 1841, he contributed to the then popular *Harper's Family Library*, a volume on " Democracy ; " subsequently, in 1852, translated into Spanish, and published in Bogota, by Lorenza Maria Lleras, secretary of state of New Granada.

On returning to Owego he entered into partnership with Mr. Strong. That copartnership continued, with the exception of the two years of 1846 and 1847, that the latter was in congress, until the year 1856, when Mr. Strong was elected judge of Tioga county. During this period Mr. Camp held the only public office he ever filled, which was that of district attorney of Tioga county, to which he was appointed in 1845.

In 1851, he had the sole charge, as the attorney of Metcalf Thurston, to mark out the line of defence and make the necessary preparation to defend him (as was successfully done), from an indictment for the murder of his brother-in-law, Anson Garrison, Governor Daniel S. Dickerson being the leading, and Hon. John J. Taylor, the associate counsel.

The only case of any general public interest of which he has lately had the principal charge, is the McGraw–Fiske will case, against the Cornell University, which was argued before the general term of the supreme court of the fourth judicial department of New York, at Utica, in April, 1887; and in the argument of which for the family of the testatrix, he was associated with Judge George F. Comstock, of Syracuse, and Hon. Esek Cowen, of Troy. The amount of property at stake in the controversy is a million and a half of dollars, and four days' time were allowed by the court for the argument of the case on both sides.

The only literary labor, aside from the volume of *Harper's Family Library*, above mentioned, that he has ever ventured upon, was undertaken at the suggestion of his then pastor, Rev. Dr. Samuel H. Hall, and was published in two numbers of the *American Presbyterian Theological Quarterly Review* for April and July, 1865, on the subject of "The Government of the Primitive Church."

During the past fourteen years he has devoted himself, at intervals of professional labor, to the cultivation of his farm of 135 acres, that forms the eastern limit of the village of Owego, and to the rearing of thoroughbred Jersey cattle. To these the methods of modern and scientific agriculture have been studiously and liberally applied.

Mr. Camp is one of the oldest, if not the oldest lawyer, engaged in the active practice of the law in the New York southern tier of counties, and he can hardly look forward to the much longer continuance of a laborious professional career which already covers the period of half a century.

General Isaac B. Ogden was born in New Jersey, in 1805. His mother died when he was a child, and he was brought up by his grandmother, Mrs. Canfield, of Smithboro. He learned the trade of a cabinet maker, in Owego, and then spent several years in New York city. He subsequently returned here and engaged extensively in cabinet making, in company with Messrs. Dana and Kingsbury. He was greatly interested in the welfare and improvement of Owego. He held various offices of trust, chief of which was president of the village, from 1846 to 1849, inclusive. He was a member of the board of trustees eleven years. General Ogden died in Owego, April 14, 1868.

General Oliver Huntington was born December 22, 1771, and came to Owego in 1804, settling on the Huntington creek (so named in honor of him), about a mile north of the Court House.

He opened the first drug-store in Owego, and was also engaged in shipping produce down the river. In 1812 he was commissioned Brigadier-General of the 41st Brigade of New York Infantry. In 1814, he was commissioned sheriff of Broome county, which then comprised, in addition to its present territory, four of the towns of Tioga county. He died in Owego, November 13, 1823. One of his sons, Wait T. Huntington, was a merchant at Ithaca, and was elected clerk of Tompkins county in 1837. He was an ingenious man, and was the inventor of the calendar attachment now in use on clocks, and other valuable patents.

Major Horatio Ross was one of Owego's earliest merchants and a gentleman of wealth. He was born about the year 1755, and came here from Frederick, Md., in 1805, and opened a general country store. He was a slaveholder and brought his slaves with him. He failed in business, in 1818, and did not resume business. He was deputy clerk of Tioga county from 1823 to 1828. He died in Owego in November, 1828. Major Ross was unmarried.

Jonathan Platt, Jr., was a son of Major Jonathan Platt, Sr., who was one of the earliest settlers of Nichols, to which town he came from Bedford, Westchester county, N. Y., in 1793. He was born at Bedford, October 18, 1783. In 1805, he came to Owego and entered Gen. John Laning's store as a clerk. Five years later he commenced the mercantile business for himself, which he continued with various parties until 1849, when he retired from business. Mr. Platt was one of Owego's most public-spirited citizens. He was president of the village, in 1834, and a trustee from the incorporation of the village, in 1827, for many years. He was also for many years president of the Bank of Owego. Mr. Platt and David Turner built the "red mills," two miles north of Owego, in 1820. His sons were Charles and Edward J. Platt.

William Platt, another son of Major Jonathan Platt, Sr., was born at Bedford, N. Y., October 29, 1791. He studied law in Owego with John H. Avery, and was the third practicing lawyer to locate in the village. He died in Owego January 12, 1855. Mr. Platt was for many years agent for the tract of land known as Coxe's Patent. His sons were Thomas C., Frederick E., and William H. Platt.

Hon. Thomas Collier Platt was the son of William Platt, Esq., for many years a prominent and highly esteemed member of the bar of Tioga county, and of Lesbia (Hinchman) Platt. He was born at Owego, Tioga county, N. Y., July 15, 1833. His grand-

father, Major Jonathan Platt, was one of the earliest settlers of
Tioga county, having emigrated with his father, Jonathan Platt,
senior, from Bedford, Westchester county, N. Y., and settled
upon what was for many years known as "the Platt Homestead,"
in the town of Nichols. One of Mr. Platt's uncles, the Hon.
Nehemiah Platt, was a former member of the senate of the state
of New York.

Mr. Platt, after pursuing his preliminary studies at the Owego
Academy, entered the class of 1853, at Yale College, the commencement of the freshman year. He was compelled to leave
college, on account of ill-health, in December, 1850; but received
from the college, in 1876, the honorary degree of M. A.

On the 12th December, 1852, he was married to Miss Ellen
Lucy, daughter of Charles R. Barstow. Three sons, now living,
are the fruit of this marriage: Edward T., Frank H., a graduate
of Yale College, of the class of 1877, and a member of the New
York law firm of McFarland, Boardman & Platt, and Henry B.,
a graduate of Yale, of the class of 1882.

Mr. Platt engaged, very early in life, in mercantile pursuits at
Owego, and this part of his business career, which terminated
in 1873, was attended with remarkable success. During this
period, he was elected, at the early age of twenty-six years, (A.
D. 1859,) county clerk, and clerk of the courts of the county of
Tioga, and officiated during three years in that capacity, to the
universal satisfaction of the public.

At the commencement of the civil war of the rebellion, no citizen of the county was more active, or efficient, in stimulating the
enlistment of volunteers; or, during the whole continuance of
the strife, in organizing and promoting the measures necessary
to secure enlistments and recruits, and in providing for the sub-
sistence and comfort of the families of soldiers who were at the
front.

From this time forward, he took a leading and very controlling position in the politics of Tioga county; but he exhibited a
marked self control, and great political sagacity, in patiently
waiting to serve and promote the advancement of others, before
aspiring to any other personal preferment, instead of impatiently
and selfishly grasping, as so many other politicians commonly
do, at every object, great or small, that comes within their reach.

It was not, therefore, until the contest arose for the membership of the 42d congress, that he was nominated, in 1871, as the
Republican candidate, by the Republican convention of the 28th

district of the state of New York. This nomination he declined. But he was again nominated, and was elected, to represent the same district, in the 43d congress, (A. D. 1873;) and, again renominated and elected to represent the same district, in the 44th congress, (A. D. 1875;) when, having thus served two terms, (4 years,) he declined any further renomination. During these congressional terms, he was a prominent and influential member of the committee on postoffices and post roads; and, also, of the committee on the Pacific railroad. As a member of congress, he acquired the unlimited confidence of the Republican administration, and was honored with, and ever afterwards retained, the warm personal friendship of the president, Gen. Grant. The personal popularity of Mr. Platt, which these repeated evidences of public favor sufficiently attest, was faithfully earned, not only by a laborious and conscientious discharge of his public duties, as a congressman, but by a prompt, uniform, and orderly attention to any matters of private interest, or business confided to him by his constituents of whatever party.

In 1879, he became connected with the United States Express company, as its general manager and president, and has ever since discharged the duties of those offices, at the City of New York, where he now lives.

In the exciting campaign of of 1877, Mr. Platt was chosen permanent chairman of the Republican state convention which was held at the city of Rochester, N. Y.; and, on taking his seat, delivered an address which must be still fresh in the memory of all, as one of singular appropriateness, and exhibiting very marked ability.

In the year 1880, he was appointed by Gov. Cornell a commissioner of quarantine for the term of three years, and became president of the board. This office he still holds.

Prior to this period, he had become largely interested in a very extensive enterprise for the manufacture and sale of lumber, in the state of Michigan, which was followed by the success which has, so far, universally attended all of Mr. Platt's business undertakings, and which was advantageously and profitably closed out in 1881.

Mr. Platt was elected, by both houses of the state legislature, a member of the senate of the United States from the state of New York, to succeed Hon. Francis Kernan, whose term expired March 4, 1881. It was known to some of Mr. Platt's most intimate friends that he did not find the position, though so gratifying to his utmost personal ambition, absolutely free from all countervailing elements; and he never obtained, with the general public, the credit to which he was, in fact, justly entitled, of being the first to form, and impart to his more distinguished colleague, his private purpose of resigning; a purpose which he carried into effect, May 16, 1881.

Mr. Platt was for several years a very efficient member of the Republican New York state committee; and afterwards a member, and one of the executive committee, of the Republican national committee. He was also a delegate from the state of New York to the last three Republican national conventions.

Mr. Platt has been, for many years, president of the Tioga National Bank of Owego, president of the Southern Central railroad, and a director of several other railroads. He is also one of the principal proprietors of the very extensive and successful agricultural works at Owego, where the Champion grain drill and Champion wagon are manufactured; the business name of the copartnership being "Gere, Truman, Platt & Co."

It cannot be denied that, in all the vicissitudes of party politics, Mr. Platt has invariably maintained a position of commanding influence. This position has been due to his very just perception and estimation of the characters of men, his personal knowledge of the individual relations and political histories of so many influential politicians, his accurate appreciation of the motives that control human actions, and his sound practical sense and judgment in applying those means and resources to practice. Results have too often borne testimony to his great executive talent and ability to admit of their being questioned by the most jealous and envious critic. Aside from these elements, however, one must have known but very little of Mr. Platt, personally, to have not discovered that his methods of dealing with men are eminently satisfactory, because singularly outspoken, frank and honorable, and exempt from all tergiversation and treachery. One soon learns from him, very distinctly, whether or not he can have his political support; and if he gets an assurance of it, that support is given with remarkable and unreserved heartiness.

Mr. Platt never forgets a kindness rendered, and is unstinted in his effort to more than repay the obligation. Perhaps it is his greatest defect as a politician, that he is but too apt to be equally mindful of any demonstrations of a contrary character. His old neighbors in Tioga county need not be reminded with what a generous hand he has found positions for, and bestowed personal favors upon, so many, that probably to no other man living in that locality are so many thus indebted. And yet, these have all been most quietly and unostentatiously bestowed; without reclamation for the favor rendered, and without invidious reproaches, if that favor has been ungenerously and ungratefully forgotten.

John R. Drake, for many years one of the most public-spirited citizens of Owego, was a son of Rev. Reuben Drake, and born at Pleasant Valley, Orange Co., N. Y., November 28, 1782. He came to Owego in October, 1809. Judge Drake was for many years engaged in the mercantile business and in the manufacture of lumber. He was first judge of Broome county from 1815 to 1823, and of Tioga county from 1833 to 1838. He was a member of congress from 1817 to 1819; member of assembly in 1834; and president of the village of Owego from 1841 to 1845, inclusive. He died in Owego, March 21, 1857. He had but one son, Theodore Drake, who resides at Fredericksburg, Va. Judge Drake was a public-spirited citizen, and prominent in all measures for the benefit of the village.

Dr. Godfrey Waldo came to Owego from Plymouth, N, H., in the summer of 1810, and practiced medicine here until 1839, when he removed to Birmingham, Mich.; thence he removed, in 1845, to Pontiac, in the same state, where he died, September 16, 1848.

Dr. Jedediah Fay was born at Hardwick, Mass., January 30, 1786. He came to Owego, in 1811, and commenced the practice of medicine in company with Dr. Samuel Barclay. He afterward engaged in the mercantile business. From 1830 to the time of his death he conducted a drug store. In 1815 he was commissioned captain of a troop of the 8th regiment of cavalry. In 1820 he became surgeon of the 53d regiment of infantry, which position he resigned three years later. He was postmaster of Owego from 1820 to 1842. He died in Owego, April 23, 1848. His sons are George W. Fay, of Owego, and Frederick J. Fay, of Columbus, Ohio.

Isaac Lillie was a school-teacher and land surveyor. He was born at Scotland, Windham Co., Conn., in 1789, and came to Owego in 1814. He died here September 23, 1864.

John Ripley was born at Coventry, Polland Co., Conn., in 1792, and removed to Owego in 1814. He was under-sheriff of Tioga county from 1823 to 1832, and justice of the peace from 1853 to

1857. He was re-elected in 1858, and continued in office until his death, which occurred January 22, 1860.

Col. Henry McCormick was born at Painted Post, N.Y., March 5, 1791, and died at St. Peter, Minn., May 22, 1874. In 1812, he went to Newtown (now Elmira) and enlisted as a volunteer in the army. He came to Owego to reside in 1814. He was the first gunsmith in Owego. In the latter years of his life he was engaged in farming. He was sheriff of Tioga county from 1828 to 1831, and also a member of the Board of Trustees of Owego village, in 1832 and 1833.

Stephen Strong was born in Connecticut, October 11, 1791, and removed with his parents to Jefferson county, N.Y., when very young. In 1814 or 1815, he came to Owego, where he at first taught school and afterward studied law. He was district attorney of Tioga county from July, 1836, to July, 1838, and was reappointed in 1844. He was appointed first judge of Tioga county April 18, 1838, and held that office until February 2, 1843. He was elected to the office of county judge, in November, 1855, and served four years. He was also the representative of the 22nd district in the congress of 1845-7. He died at Waterloo, N.Y., April 5, 1866, to which place he had removed the year previous.

Stephen B. Leonard was born in New York city, April 15, 1793, and came to Owego in his youth with his father, Silas Leonard. He learned the printer's trade in the office of the *American Farmer*. He purchased the office, and in 1814, changed the name of the paper to *The Owego Gazette*, which he continued to publish until 1835, when he was elected to congress. He was re-elected in 1839. Mr. Leonard was postmaster of the village of Owego from 1816 to 1820, and from 1844 to 1849. He was a village trustee, in 1822 and 1823, and supervisor of the town in 1854 and 1856. During the administration of President Buchanan, he was a deputy United States marshal. In 1816, he established the first stage route from Owego to Bath. He had previously carried the first mail through Tioga county on horseback, in order to deliver his newspaper. He died in Owego, May 8, 1876. His sons are William B. Leonard, of Brooklyn; Hermon C. Leonard, of Portland, Oregon, and George S. Leonard, of Owego.

Latham A. Burrows was born at Groton, Conn., in 1793, and was admitted to the bar of Tioga county, in 1816. From February 14, 1821, to January 1, 1822, he was county clerk of Broome county, and from 1824 to 1827, inclusive, an associate judge of Tioga county. In 1827, he was elected first judge of Tioga county, being the first professional lawyer who sat upon the bench of the common pleas in this county. He was also state senator from 1824 to 1828. He commenced a general mercantile business in Owego in 1828. During his mercantile career he was president of the village from 1836 to 1839, inclusive. He subsequently removed to Buffalo, where he died on the 25th of September, 1855.

Colonel Amos Martin was born at Salisbury, Conn., in 1775, and removed, in 1815, to Candor, in this county, where he opened a country store. Two years later he removed to Owego, where he continued the mercantile business until his death, which occurred May 14, 1835. While engaged in the mercantile business, he was also proprietor of the hotel known as the Goodman Coffee House, from 1819 to 1823. Colonel Martin's sons are John H. Martin, of Kansas City, Mo., and Jay H. Martin, of Tioga Center.

David Turner was a son of Abner Turner, one of the earliest settlers on the Owego creek, in the town of Tioga, three miles north of Owego village, and was born in 1800. He was engaged in the mercantile business in Owego from 1818 to 1835, most of the time with Jonathan Platt, Jr. His son, Edward Turner, resides at Flint, Mich.

John Carmichael was born at Johnstown, Montgomery (now Fulton) county, N. Y., August 12, 1795. He learned the trade of a jeweler and watchmaker, in Albany. He came to Owego in October, 1819, and opened a jewelery store, continuing in business until September, 1849. He was the first collector of the village of Owego, at the time of its incorporation, in 1827, and was re-elected every year thereafter until 1834, inclusive. He was village assessor four years, and was elected treasurer of Tioga county, in 1837. He died in Owego, April 24, 1878. His sons were Charles S. and Horace Carmichael. The former is still a resident of Owego.

Ziba A. Leland was one of the early lawyers of Owego, and was born in Vermont. He came to this village and formed a law partnership with John H. Avery May 1, 1820. In April, 1822, he was appointed justice of the peace. From Owego he removed to Bath, where he was first judge of Steuben county from 1838 to 1843. He also represented that county in the assembly, in 1842 and 1843. Later in life he removed to Auburn, and thence to Saratoga, where he died.

Gurdon Hewitt was born at New London, Conn., May 5, 1790.

He came with his parents to Oxford, N. Y., in 1796, and afterward removed to Towanda, Pa., where he engaged in the mercantile business. He became a resident of Owego in 1823. He was the first president of the Bank of Owego, and subsequently for a number of years its cashier. Upon coming to Owego he commenced a general mercantile business in company with his brother-in-law, Jonathan Platt, Jr. A year afterward he purchased Mr. Platt's interest and continued the business alone until 1837, when he formed a partnership with John M. Greenleaf. The firm of Greenleaf & Hewitt existed until September, 1849. There after Mr. Hewitt devoted his entire attention to the banking business and the management of his large property. He died in Owego, December 24, 1871. His sons are Gurdon and Frederick C. Hewitt.

Dr. Ezekiel B. Phelps was born at Hebron, Conn., in 1800. After graduating at the New Haven Medical College, in 1824, he practiced medicine at Manchester, Conn. In September of the same year he removed to Owego, where he has since resided.

John M. Greenleaf was born at Granville, Washington county, N. Y., May 19, 1806. He came to Owego in the fall of 1826. In 1833 he entered into the mercantile business with Lyman Truman, which partnership continued three years. From 1837 to 1849 he was engaged in the same business with Gurdon Hewitt. He died in Owego, August 23, 1881. His son, Dr. J. T. Greenleaf, resides in Owego.

Ezra S. Sweet was born at New Bedford, Mass., June 3, 1796. He came to Owego in December, 1825, and commenced the practice of law. He was for several years a justice of the peace, and was district attorney of Tioga county from 1838 to 1841, and from 1847 to 1851. He also represented the county in the assembly, in 1849. He died in Owego, October 16, 1869. He has one surviving son, Charles H. Sweet, who resides in Elmira.

Aaron P. Storrs was born at Mansfield, Conn., in 1811, and came to Owego with his uncle, Rev. Aaron Putnam, in December, 1827. In September, 1835, he engaged in the general mercantile business, and has continued in that and the hardware business, with various partners, until the present time. He is at present a member of the hardware firm of Storrs, Chatfield & Co.

Thomas Farrington was born at Delhi, Delaware county, N. Y., February 12, 1799. At the age of thirteen years he was an orderly upon the staff of his father, Gen. Putnam Farrington, in the war of 1812. He graduated at Union College, in 1826, and came to practice law in Owego in 1828. He represented Tioga county in the assembly in 1833 and 1840, and was appointed surrogate of the county April 30, 1835. He was a member of the board of trustees of the village of Owego in 1839 and 1857, and president of the village in 1850. He was appointed treasurer of the state of New York on February 7, 1842, and served until February 3, 1845. In the latter year he was appointed adjutant-general of the state. He was re-appointed state treasurer February 2, 1846, and served until November 2, 1847. He was elected judge of Tioga county in 1859, and was twice re-elected, serving three terms of four years each. He died in Owego, December 2, 1872. His wife was a daughter of John H. Avery. His sons are Edward A., of New York, and Frank J., of St. Paul, Minn.

Dr. Ezekiel Lovejoy was born at Stratford, Conn., July 6, 1803. He studied medicine in New York city, and, after taking his degree of Doctor of Medicine, was for a time surgeon in the navy of the republic at Buenos Ayres. He came to Owego, in 1829, and was the first physician to practice Homeopathy in Owego. Dr. Lovejoy never held but one public office, that of supervisor of the town of Owego, in 1854. He died in Owego August 15, 1871.

Aaron, Lyman, and Asa H. Truman, sons of Shem Truman, of Old Canaan, Conn., were early settlers of Park Settlement, in the town of Candor—Aaron, in 1804; Lyman, in 1805; and Asa H., in 1810.

Aaron was born at Granville, Mass., July 27, 1785, and died January 13, 1823. He married Experience Park, of Connecticut, in 1805. She died in 1844. His sons were Lyman, Orin, Charles, Francis W., and George Truman.

Lyman Park Truman was born at Park Settlement, March 2, 1806. In 1830, he came to Owego and entered Asa H. Truman's store as a clerk. Three years afterward he commenced the mercantile business on his own account. In May, 1836, the firm of L. Truman & Brothers was formed and they conducted a successful lumber and mercantile business for nearly thirty years. In this firm Mr. Truman was associated with three of his brothers, Orin, Frank, and George. In 1856, Mr. Truman became president of the Bank of Owego, and continued at the head of that institution and its successor, the First National Bank of Owego, until a short time prior to his death. During his active life Mr. Truman filled various town offices, from constable to supervisor. In 1857, he was chosen state senator from the 24th district, and was re-elected in 1859 and 1861. He died in Owego, March 24, 1881, leaving a large fortune as the result of his active life.

Orin Truman was born at Park Settlement, February 17, 1811, and died in Owego, September 30, 1885. He was unmarried.

Charles Truman resides at Flemingville, where he has held the office of justice of the peace for nearly thirty years. He was born November 11, 1807. His sons are Aaron, Lyman B., Elias W. and Charles F. Truman.

George Truman was born June 16, 1816, and resides in the village of Owego. He is the head of the firm of George Truman, Son & Co., and president of the First National Bank. His sons are Gilbert F., William S., and George Truman, Jr., all residents of Owego.

Francis W. Truman was born December 13, 1812, and was until recently at the head of the manufacturing firm of Gere, Truman, Platt & Co., in Owego.

Lyman Truman was born at Granville, Mass., in 1783, and died at Park Settlement, November 2, 1822. His sons were Levi B., Stephen S., James and Benjamin L. Truman. Levi B. died May 21, 1879, at Park Settlement. Stephen S. and Benjamin L. Truman are residents of the village of Owego.

Asa H. Truman was born at Sparta, N. Y., February 26, 1793. He taught school at Park Settlement, and afterward, from 1816 to 1825, kept a tavern and country store at Flemingville. In the latter year he came to Owego village, where he conducted a general mercantile business until his death, which occurred February 6, 1848. His sons were Lucius Truman, who resides at Wellsboro, Pa., William H. Truman, who lives in New York, Charles Truman and Edward D. Truman. The latter died in Dixon, Ill., June 6, 1862. Charles was lieutenant of a company of infantry during the rebellion, and was killed in battle in 1862.

William H. Bell was born six miles north of Owego village, on the West Owego creek, November 18, 1811. His father, William Bell, was a farmer. He was engaged in the lumber and mercantile business in Owego twenty years. He retired from active business in 1867. In 1870 he was stricken with paralysis, from the effects of which he died on the 20th of April, 1876.

Gideon O. Chase was born at Cambridge, Washington Co., N. Y., March 29, 1808, and in early life was a cabinetmaker. He came to Owego in 1832. He represented Tioga county in the assembly in 1844 and 1845. From 1846 to 1849 he was under-sheriff of the county. In May, 1848, he established the *Tioga*

Engraved by Samuel Sartain Phil^a

Lyman Trumbull

Freeman, which he edited until its publication was discontinued, in September, 1850. He was in the employ of the Erie Railway Company from 1855 to 1867, most of the time as station-agent at Smithboro, at which place he died, March 26, 1887.

Col. Nathaniel W. Davis was born at Weston, Fairfield Co., Conn., May 10, 1807. He studied law at Ithaca, and came to Owego to practice, in 1832. He was surrogate of Tioga county from 1840 to 1844, and member of assembly in 1844 and 1863. He was also a village trustee in 1839 1842, and 1847, and president of the village in 1859 and 1860. He was much interested in military affairs, and was for several years colonel of the 53d and 54th regiments of New York State militia. He died in Owego, July 31, 1874. His only son, Nathaniel W. Davis, Jr., is a resident of the town of Tioga.

John Mason Parker was among the earliest as well as the foremost lawyers of the county. He was the son of John C. Parker, a prominent lawyer of Washington county, N. Y., and was born in Granville, in that county, June 14, 1805. He obtained his preliminary education at Granville Academy, of which institution the distinguished teacher, Salem Town, L. L. D., was then preceptor, and he graduated with the highest honors at Middlebury College, in 1828. He pursued the study of law in the office of Hon. John P. Cushman, in the city of Troy, was admitted to the bar in 1833, and soon after settled at Owego, in the practice of his profession. His thorough scholarship, his well trained and logical mind, his industry and uncompromising integrity soon won for him a foremost place at the bar, as well as the entire confidence and admiration of the people of the county. Marked deference was at once universally accorded to his legal opinions by all his rivals in the profession. They were characterized by great thoroughness of research, and the preparation of his causes by an absolute completeness that left no point unprovided for.

At all times he bore a personal character not only exempt from reproach, but entirely above suspicion. His conversation and personal demeanor were always cultivated and refined, universally free from anything that would have offended the most delicate and fastidious.

He was elected to represent the 27th (now 28th) congressional district of the State of New York in the U. S. House of Representatives two consecutive terms, from 1855 to 1859. In 1859 he was elected a justice of the supreme court of the state, and was continued in that exalted position until his death. During the

23*

last six years of that period he was a justice of the general term
of the third department, having been so designated by Governor
Hoffman. During part of his judicial service he sat as a member
of the court of appeals.

In his earlier life Judge Parker was in politics a Whig, but
upon the formation of the Republican party he became and thereafter remained a steadfast and prominent member of that party.

As a judge he was invariably courteous to all. He heard with
the utmost patience and equanimity, everything that suitors had
to urge. He never impatiently interrupted or captiously criti-
cised counsel. He never availed himself of his position on the
bench to demonstrate his own superiority to those who were
before him. He never consciously allowed any extraneous considerations to bias his opinions, nor tolerated officious and
irregular attempts to influence him. A temperament naturally
and constitutionally nervous was subdued to equanimity by
severe self control. And suitors uniformly went from the
tribunal over which he presided with the conviction that their
cases had been thoroughly examined and considered and fairly
and honestly decided. The numerous opinions delivered by him
and spread through the volumes of reports from 1859 to 1873 are,
after all, his best memorial as a judge.

The degree of LL.D. was conferred upon him by Middlebury
College, in 1865. He was an active member of St. Paul's church,
Owego, and at the time of his death its junior warden.

Judge Parker married for his first wife, Catherine Ann, daughter
of Charles Pumpelly, of Owego, in September, 1835. She died
in December, 1845, leaving four children, of whom two only now
survive, Charles Edward, a prominent lawyer and now County
Judge of Tioga county, and Francis Henry, who is Lieut.-
Colonel of Ordnance, U. S. army. On March 1, 1854, he married
for his second wife Stella A. Pumpelly, who still survives him.

On the evening of December 6, 1873, Judge Parker died of
apoplexy, at his residence in Owego. He was thus called away
by death in the midst of his activity and usefulness, universally
esteemed and regretted.

Few men have lived to old age whose public and private
course and character would bear the brightest and most search-
ing light of investigation as well as that of Judge Parker. He
seems to have been born with high principles and aims, with a
humane and kindly nature, with refined tastes and a strong in-
tellect, qualities which would have won him the confidence,

respect and affection of any community. He will be remembered as the able and upright public man and the beloved Christian gentleman.

Hon. Charles E. Parker, the present county judge and surrogate of Tioga county, eldest son of John M. Parker, was born in Owego, August 25, 1836. He was educated at the Owego academy, and graduated at Hobart college, in Geneva, N. Y., in the class of 1857. Upon leaving college he studied law with his father, and was admitted to the bar in the fall of 1859. He was elected to the convention of 1867, held at Albany, to amend the constitution of the state of New York, and with one exception was the youngest member of that body. In the fall of 1883 he was elected to the office which he now holds. As this work is being published, he is a candidate for election to the office of justice of the supreme court of the sixth judicial district. With these exceptions he has held no political office, but has been steadily engaged in the practice of his profession in his native village.

In 1865, Judge Parker married Mary, daughter of Judge Thomas Farrington, of Owego. He has always been a Republican in politics, and is a member of St. Paul's church.

As a lawyer, Judge Parker ranks among the leading members of the profession, and enjoys the thorough confidence and respect of the people of the county.

Timothy P. Patch was born at Ashburnham, Mass., December 3, 1809. He came to Owego in February, 1834, and opened a meat market. He continued in that and the grocery business until 1855. In 1860, he removed to Towanda, Pa., where he resided until his removal to Corning, N. Y., a few months previous to his death, which occurred June 30, 1882. In 1850, Mr. Patch built a three-story brick block in Lake street, in which was Patch's Hall, which at the time was the largest public hall in the village.

Joshua L. Pinney was born at Armenia, Duchess Co., N. Y., October 17, 1783. He came to Owego in June, 1835, and commenced a drug business, which he continued in company with his sons, until his death, which occurred October 15, 1855. One of his five sons, Hammon D. Pinney, is still a resident of Owego.

Robert Cameron was born, in 1817, in Chanceford township, York Co., Pa., and came to Owego with his brother, John Cameron, in 1831, and entered the store of another brother, James Cameron, as a clerk. In 1840, he opened a grocery store, and continued in business until 1869, when he retired from active business.

George B. Goodrich was born in the town of Tioga, December 1, 1816, and came to Owego to reside, in 1831. He was, from 1837 until his death, at the head of the dry goods store of G. B. Goodrich & Co. He was also president of the Owego National Bank from the time of its establishment, until his death, which occurred Jaunary 8, 1886.

Dr. Lucius H. Allen was born in Lunenburg (now Athens), Greene county, N. Y., January 31, 1796. He studied medicine in Connecticut, and graduated at Brown University, in Providence, R. I., in 1820. Thereafter he resided eleven years in Buffalo and Cherry Valley, N. Y. He removed to Berkshire, in this county, in 1830, and two years later he came to Owego, where he has ever since resided.

Andrew H. Calhoun was born in Boston, Mass., April 1, 1798. He came to Owego, in 1836, and commenced the publication of the *Owego Advertiser*, which he continued until April, 1853. He was clerk of the state senate, in 1848-9, and canal appraiser, in 1851-2. In 1863, he was appointed to a clerkship in the New York custom house, which position he held at the time of his death, which occurred in Brooklyn, December 17, 1874.

William F. Warner was born at Hardwick, Vt., January 18, 1819, and came to Owego, in 1834. He practiced law with Col. N. W. Davis, and was afterward a member of the law firm of Warner, Tracy & Walker. Mr. Warner was a public-spirited citizen, and was conspicuous in all movements for the advancement and improvement of Owego. He was clerk of the village from 1848 to 1854. He was the first president of the village elected by the people, in 1855, and was re-elected, in 1856 and 1857. He organized the Owego Gas Light Company, in 1856, of which he was president, superintendent and treasurer many years. Since September, 1871, he has been a resident of Waverly. At present he holds the office of special county judge of Tioga county. Mr. Warner wrote the Centennial History of Tioga County, in 1876, and was the leading spirit in organizing the centennial celebration of the battle of New Town, and the erection of a monument in commemoration of that event, in 1879.

William P. Stone was born in Stillwater, Saratoga Co., N. Y., in 1810, and came with his parents to Tioga county, in 1817, and settled near Flemingville. In 1834, he came to Owego and en-

J. M. Parker

gaged in the mercantile business, which he continued, with various partners, until February, 1874, when he retired from active business.

Hon. John J. Taylor, for many years the most prominent Democratic politician, and one of the most prominent members of the bar of Tioga county, was born in the town of Leominster, Worcester county, Mass., April 27, 1808. His parents, John Taylor and Anne Taylor, came from Oldham, near Manchester, England.

Leaving the common school when about fourteen years of age, and pursuing the studies preparatory to entering college, at the New Ipswich academy, in New Hampshire, and the Groton academy, in Massachusetts, he entered Harvard university, Cambridge, from the latter academy, in 1825, at the age of seventeen. He graduated therefrom in August, 1829, in a class of over sixty members, in which were included Benjamin Curtis, afterwards justice of the supreme court of the United States, George W. Bigelow, afterwards chief justice of the supreme judicial court of the commonwealth of Massachusetts. Oliver Wendell Holmes, Samuel F. Smith, author of " My country, 'tis of thee," Benjamin F. Pierce, afterwards superintendent of the coast survey, James Freeman Clarke, William H. Channing, and others whom the people, not only of this but of other countries, have delighted to honor.

After graduating, he spent a few months in teaching, a part of the time in the high school of the Franklin Institute of Philadelphia.

In 1830, he came to the city of Troy, N. Y., and passed two years as a law student in the office of Judge David Buel, and, after that, some months in the office of Hon. John A. Collier, at Binghamton, N. Y. From Binghamton he went to Greene, Chenango county, where he spent two years, part of the time in the study, and a part of the time in the practice of the law.

On the last day of December, 1834, he removed to Owego, where he has ever since resided, and entered into a law partnership, on the 1st day of January, 1835, with the late Judge Stephen Strong, which continued until August, 1838, when it was dissolved by mutual consent.

On the 18th day of May, A. D., 1837, he married Miss Emily Laning, daughter of Mrs. Mary Anne Laning, of Owego, and the sister of Mrs. Ellen H. Bicking and Mary Anne Rosette, of Philadelphia, and of Augustus C., Matthias H., and John C. Laning.

By her he had only one son, John L. Taylor, who was born June 24, 1839, and who, having espoused Miss Sarah J. Reed, is now the father of a family of four children, to wit, Robert J., Emile G., Mary L., and Emily. Mr. John J. Taylor's only daughter, Sarah, was born June 27, 1841, and having married Mr. L. Burr Pearsall, died early, leaving no issue now surviving her.

Mr. Taylor, on his arrival at Owego, speedily won his way to the first rank in the profession, among members of a numerous bar of universally conceded ability; so that his employment on one side or the other of every important case became a matter of course.

He took a leading part, as a Democrat, in the politics of the county, and was appointed by the Court of Common Pleas, in the year 1838, its district attorney. He discharged the duties of that office for five years successively, when he was compelled to resign it by the pressure of other business.

In 1846, he was elected to represent the county of Tioga, in the convention of that year, to revise the constitution of the State of New York; and, in 1850, was the Democratic candidate for congress in the 26th district of the State of New York, composed of the counties of Chenango, Broome and Tioga, but was defeated by Henry Bennett, of Chenango county.

In 1852, having been again selected as the Democratic candidate for congress in the congressional district composed of the counties of Tioga, Tompkins, and Chemung, he was elected over his opponent, the Hon. Charles Cook, of Havana. He served as a member of the committees on foreign affairs, and on the District of Columbia. He stood very high in favor with the Democratic administration. He was tendered by President Pierce, but declined, the appointment of commissioner to settle the northwestern boundary of the United States, and his name was widely canvassed for collector of the port of New York.

In 1858 he was selected as the Democratic candidate for lieutenant-governor of the state of New York, and was run on the ticket with Hon. Amasa J. Parker, as the Democratic candidate for governor. Both were defeated, the Democratic party being then largely in the minority in the state.

During all this period Mr. Taylor actively and successfully continued the practice of his legal profession. A studious and laborious life had made him a master of the learning of that profession, and great natural acuteness of discernment and thoroughly sound practical common sense gave him unusual accu-

John J. Taylor—

racy in the application of its principles to cases as they arose. A character of unimpeachable integrity, and a habit of candid statement always inspired those he addressed with confidence, and his lucid and exhaustive arguments uniformly left but little remaining to be said after he had finished what he had to say; so that he was always a sound, effective and successful speaker, whether in his political addresses, or his forensic efforts.

He assisted in the organization of the Bank of Tioga, which was afterwards changed to the National Union Bank, and was for many years its president. He was elected and officiated for many years as the vice-president, and afterwards as the president of the Southern Central Railroad Company.

Mrs. Taylor died November 25, 1879; since which time Mr. Taylor's own health has been so infirm as to preclude all attention to any other business than such as the management of her estate and his own private property has made necessary.

Frank L. Jones was born at Lisle, Broome county, N. Y., October 29, 1822, and came to Owego, in 1837. He was in the mercantile business, and afterwards in insurance. In February, 1868, he was appointed sheriff of Tioga county, to fill a vacancy. He was president of the village of Owego, in 1869, and postmaster from 1871 to 1879. In July, 1880, he was appointed agent and warden of Auburn State Prison, which position he held at the time of his death, which occurred at Coudersport, Pa., November 8, 1883. While a resident of Pennsylvania, in 1852, he was elected sheriff of Potter county.

Thomas I. Chatfield was born at Great Barrington, Mass., September 16, 1818. He was by trade a baker, and when he came to Owego, in March, 1839, he worked as a journeyman until the following October, when he commenced business on his own account. He afterward engaged in the grocery business, which he continued until a short time previous to his death, which occurred May 2, 1884. Mr. Chatfield was a prominent and public-spirited citizen. He served four years as village trustee, and three years as village supervisor. He was also president of the village, in 1868. In 1853, he represented Tioga county in the assembly, and was a candidate for state treasurer, in 1869. He was a member of the state senate, in 1871 and 1872. He was also treasurer of the Tioga County Agricultural Society, for many years. He has one son, T. I. Chatfield, Jr., who resides in Owego.

Alanson Munger was born at Ludlow, Mass., February 5, 1801.

In 1827, he removed to Hamilton, N. Y., and thence to Owego, in 1840. He formed a law partnership with Stephen Strong, which continued two years. He practiced law during the remainder of his life with no partner. He was appointed judge of Tioga county, in February, 1843, and surrogate, in January, 1844. He was elected district attorney, in 1850, and special county judge, in 1861. He died in Owego December 31, 1877.

Charles A. Munger, a son of Alanson Munger, was born at Hamilton, N. Y., July 13, 1830. He commenced the practice of law when he was twenty-one years of age. He held the office of justice of the peace, and was special county judge of Tioga county from 1853 to 1855, and from 1865 to 1867. He was a gentleman of fine culture, a contributor to the magazines, and a poet of no ordinary genius. A volume of his poems was published, in 1874, subsequent to his death, which occurred September 3, 1873.

Dr. Hiram N. Eastman was born in Herkimer county, N. Y., August 17, 1810. He graduated as a physician at Fairfield Medical College, in 1838, and commenced practice at Candor, in this county. In January, 1840, he removed to Owego, where he resided until December, 1861, when he removed to Geneva, where two years previously he had been appointed Professor of Materia Medica and Theory and Practice of Medicine, in Geneva Medical College. In August, 1870, he was appointed lecturer on Materia Medica and Hygiene at the University of Buffalo. He subsequently removed to Waverly, Iowa, where he remained until October, 1874, when he returned to Owego, where he died on the 14th day of October, 1879. His sons are Dr. C. C. Eastman, of the Binghamton Insane Asylum; Dr. R. W. Eastman, of Owego; Rev. Rush Eastman, of Torresdale, Pa.; and Rev. George N. Eastman, of New York city.

Henry N. Hubbard was born at Middle Haddam, Mass, January 18, 1809. He came to Owego in September, 1841, as a clerk for Greenly & Shapley, merchants. In May, 1843, he became a member of the firm, one of the partners retiring, and he continued in business until his death, which occurred on the 8th of May, 1883. He has one son, Henry D., who resides at Torrington, Conn.

Arba Campbell was born in Lebanon, Madison county, N. Y., March 3, 1809. When but two years of age his parents removed to Susquehanna county, Pa. When grown to manhood, he spent the summer months in buying and selling wool, and the winter in teaching school. He subsequently went to New York city,

Charles E. Parker

where he remained until 1842, when he removed to Owego and engaged in the wool trade, in which he was successful. To this business he added that of pulling and tanning sheep skins. At about forty years of age he became interested in farming, particularly in agricultural chemistry, making many scientific experiments and giving much of his time and thought to it. The results of his experiments have been frequently published, and are remarkably instructive. During a sojourn abroad, Mr. Campbell visited the farms of France and England, obtaining much information from observation, which was subsequently applied to experiments here. Mr. Campbell owns four farms—two in Tioga county, one in Chemung county, and one in Pennsylvania, in Bradford county.

Gen. Benjamin F. Tracy was born at Apalachin, in 1829, and is the son of Benjamin Tracy, of whom mention is made in the history of the settlement of Apalachin. In early life he taught school in Owego, and afterward studied and practiced law. In November, 1853, when but twenty-four years of age, he was elected district attorney of Tioga county, and in 1856, he was re-elected over Gilbert C. Walker, who was subsequently his law partner and afterward governor of Virginia. The law firm of Warner, Tracy & Walker was dissolved a short time previous to the breaking out of the rebellion. In 1862, General Tracy was elected to the assembly, and in the same year he organized the 109th regiment, N.Y. vols., of which he was the colonel. He served with distinction in the battles of the Wilderness and Spottsylvania Court-house, and after returning from the front was placed in command of the rebel prison camp and headquarters for drafted men, in Elmira. At the close of the war he went to Brooklyn, where he resumed the practice of law. October 1, 1866, he was appointed United States district attorney for the eastern district of New York by President Johnson, and again January 23, 1871, by President Grant. At the end of his second term he declined reappointment and renewed his law practice, in company with his brother-in-law, General Catlin. He was a member of Plymouth church, and in the celebrated Beecher–Tilton trial was prominent among the counsel for the defence. General Tracy was appointed an associate judge of the court of appeals of this state, December 9, 1881, in place of Judge Andrews, promoted to chief judge. At the close of his term of office he declined a renomination. He is now out of active politics and devoting his attention to his law practice in Brooklyn.

Hiram A. Beebe was born in the town of Bridgewater, Pa., March 11, 1817, and learned the printer's trade in the office of the Montrose *Volunteer*. In January, 1843, he came to Owego and became editor of the *Gazette*, continuing his connection with that newspaper until September 1, 1880, with the exception of about a year, in 1846, when he resided at Westfield, Mass., where he edited the Westfield *Standard*. During his residence at Westfield he was elected a member of the Massachusetts legislature. Mr. Beebe was president of the village of Owego, in 1852 and 1871, and postmaster nine years from May, 1853.

Ezra S. Buckbee was born, in March, 1827, three miles north of the village of Owego. He came to Owego when sixteen years of age. He was engaged in the mercantile business until his death, which occured August 10, 1883. He was supervisor of the town of Owego, in 1861, and was twice elected treasurer of Tioga county, serving from 1854 to 1860.

Charles R. Barstow was born at Great Barrington, Mass., in March, 1804, and came to the town of Nichols, in 1816. He was loan commissioner of Tioga county from 1840 to 1842. He was elected sheriff, in 1843, and member of assembly, in 1846. From 1849 to 1853, he was postmaster of Owego. In April, 1865, he was appointed a port warden of New York city, and held that office until August, 1868. He died at Big Rapids, Mich., December 10, 1880.

Hon. William Smyth was born in County Derry, Ireland, June 19, 1819. His ancestry, both on his father's and mother's side, were among the defenders of Londonderry, strongly supporting King William, Prince of Orange, in the struggle for Protestant ascendency, which at that time caused such intense bitterness in Ireland.

The subject of this memoir, having received a thorough classical education, entered the Royal Academic Institute, Belfast, from which he was graduated, in 1842, having taken second honors in the Greek and moral philosophy classes. He also spent two years in Edinburgh University. For the next three years he was engaged as a private tutor in a gentleman's family, and prepared three young men for entering Glasgow University. He was afterward employed as principal of a classical school in County Derry.

In 1847, he married Martha, eldest daughter of Daniel Stewart

Mackay, of Moss Side, County Antrim. The same year he emigrated to America, landing in New York the 27th of November. For a few months his time was employed in writing contributions to the New York *Sun* and New York *Observer*. March 4, 1848, he visited Owego, and was engaged by the trustees of the Owego Academy as principal, entering upon his duties the 12th of April following, which position he retained until June, 1854, when he resigned on account of ill health. The most successful period in the history of the Owego Academy was during his administration. The management found it necessary to add three departments, and he had engaged six assistants, having an average attendance of 250 pupils.

In 1854 he purchased the Owego *Advertiser*, and soon thereafter changed the name to the Owego *Times*, which name it has since retained. As a journalist Mr. Smyth occupies quite a prominent position.

In 1857, Mr. Smyth was elected school commissioner of Tioga county, and re-elected, in 1860, this time by the very large majority of 1,012 votes. The same year he was appointed village clerk; in 1863-64 he served as trustee of the village, and in 1865-67 was its president; in 1867, was appointed justice of the peace; in 1872, he represented Tioga county in the assembly; in 1873, was appointed deputy superintendent of the state insurance department, which office he held for three years, and at the resignation of the Hon. O. W. Chapman, he became acting superintendent, and held the office for one year, until his successor was appointed. It was during his incumbency that a rigid examination of insurance companies commenced, which resulted in the indictment of the officers of the Security Life Insurance company, of New York. Pending this examination, frauds were discovered, and Acting Superintendent Smyth energetically pressed the case, and secured the indictment and conviction of its president and vice-president, being the first instance in the history of life insurance in this state where the president of a life company was convicted.

Mr. Smyth has always taken a commendable interest in the material development of the village. During the time he was its president many desirable improvements were consummated. Among other items, the first steam fire-engine was purchased during his administration. In 1862, '63, and '64, he was chief engineer of the fire department, which organization owes much of its present success to the energy and enterprise of Mr. Smyth.

In 1881, he was for the fourth time elected president of Owego village. During his presidency he secured a free bridge across the Susquehanna river. On the last day of his term that year, he, ably assisted by many of the most progressive citizens, succeeded in raising $25,000 in cash or equivolent securities and paid that amount over to the president of the Bridge company, taking therefor a warranty-deed from the Bridge company to the Town of Owego. This removed one of the greatest obstructions to the material and numerical progress of the village. This toll bridge had existed for 50 years. The increase in travel across this bridge since it became free is at least ten fold.

William Smyth is now and he has been since its organization an active and efficient member of the Republican party. He was chairman of the Whig delegation sent to the Syracuse convention, in 1856, from Tioga county, and with Hon. John A. King, president, marched from Corinthian hall to Weiting hall where the Free Soil Democrats and anti-Slavery Whigs united, forming the Republican party whose glorious record in the State of New York need not be mentioned in this connection.

Rev. William H. King, D. D., was born in the town of Otsego, Otsego Co., N. Y., October 8, 1820. His father, William King, was a farmer. He attended school at Franklin, Delaware county, and at Madison University, from which institution he graduated as Master of Arts, in 1857. Ten years afterward the degree of Doctor of Divinity was conferred upon him by the same institution. In 1843, he commenced teaching in the academy at Waverly, and continued five years. While thus engaged he commenced preaching. In 1849, he was ordained as a clergyman at Athens, Pa., and commenced his labors as pastor of the Baptist church of that place. In March, 1854, Doctor King accepted a call to Owego, and was pastor of the Baptist church of this village twenty-seven years. In 1881, he resigned the pastorate on account of poor health and declining years, and retired from active labor.

Rev. James Holwell Kidder was born and educated at Portland, Me., and graduated at the General Theological seminary, in New York city, in the class of 1860. He was ordained deacon by Bishop George Burgess, in St. Luke's church, Portland, July 11, 1860, and priest, also by Bishop Burgess, in Christ's church, Eastport, Me., June 19, 1861. Mr. Kidder was in charge of St. Thomas's church, Camden, Me., until November, 1860; then of Christ's church, Eastport, Me., about three years, until entering

W. Smythe

on the rectorship of St. Matthew's church at Unadilla, N. Y., July 1, 1863. Five years afterward, August 1, 1868, Mr. Kidder came to Owego, and has since that time been rector of St. Paul's church.

Gilbert C. Walker was born at Cuba, N. Y., August 1, 1833. He came to Owego in August, 1855, and in 1858 became a member of the law firm of Warner, Tracy & Walker. He removed to Chicago, in 1859, and thence to Norfolk, Va., in 1864, where he was president of the Exchange Bank of Norfolk, until 1867. In 1869 he was elected governor of Virginia. In July, 1874, he was elected to congress from the third (Richmond) district, and re-elected, in 1876. He died at Binghamton, N. Y., May 11, 1885.

General Isaac S. Catlin was born at Apalachin, in this county, July 8, 1833. He studied law in New York city, was admitted to the bar, and commenced practice in Owego. Soon afterward, in 1859, he became a member of the law firm of Warner, Tracy & Catlin. In January, 1861, he was elected president of the village, and served until June, when he entered the volunteer service of the United States, as captain of a company in the Third New York Volunteers. In the summer of 1862, upon the organization of the 109th regiment, he became its lieutenant-colonel, and was promoted to colonel upon the resignation of Colonel Tracy. In 1864, while leading the charge at Petersburg, Va., he lost his leg by the explosion of a mine. After the war General Catlin was elected district attorney of Tioga county, serving from 1865 to 1868. He was appointed a colonel in the regular army, and was stationed two years at Louisville, Ky. He was promoted to Brigadier-general during this period. He afterward commenced the practice of law in Brooklyn, where he has been twice elected district attorney of Kings county.

Charles Austin Clark was born at Guilford Center, Chenango county, N. Y., on the 28th day of May, 1833. He was the eldest son of Austin Clark, who was born at Tolland, Conn., October 15, 1799, and grandson of Gershom Clark, who was born September 5, 1755, and who removed from Connecticut with a large family and settled at Guilford Center in October, 1814, where he died in March, 1840. Austin Clark removed with his family to the vicinity of South New Berlin, in the spring of 1835, where he resided until the spring of 1856, when he removed to the town of Berkshire, Tioga county, N. Y., where he resided until he died, April 2, 1882, having reared to manhood and womanhood five sons and six daughters, of whom four sons and four daughters survive him.   At an early age Charles not only manifested a desire to obtain an education, but very many scholarly and manly characteristics.   He was endowed with an excellent memory and in many respects gave evidence of possessing a fine order of mind. His parents desired to give him a liberal education, but unfortunately they were poor.   With them their son had to share all the labors and disadvantages of poverty.   This he did cheerfully. Not discouraged by adverse circumstances he pursued his studies zealously, and became well-known throughout the community as the brightest scholar and clearest and most independent thinker of his years.   Throughout his boyhood days he attended the schools in his native county during the winter months, but during the summer it was necessary for him to work with his father on the farm.

When seventeen years of age he entered upon the labors of a teacher in a common school near Gilbertsville, Otsego county. He soon after entered the office of Dr. S. C. Gibson, of South New Berlin, and commenced the study of medicine.   He was for some time a student in the University of Michigan, at Ann Arbor, and graduated from the medical department of that institution, in the spring of 1853.

He commenced the practice of medicine as a regular physician, at Berkshire, Tioga Co., N. Y., in April, 1853.   On the 30th of May following, he was married to Evelyn Amelia Hodges, of Oneonta, whose family had then recently removed from Morris, Otsego Co., N. Y., where she had been reared.   Having spent the summer in Berkshire, Dr. Clark was induced to move to Bainbridge, Chenango county.   Here he practiced his profession for a short time, but in the spring of 1854 he was induced to take charge of a large and flourishing select school.   In this enterprise he was very successful, and at the next annual town meeting he was elected superintendent of common schools, which office he continued to hold as long as he remained in Bainbridge, at the same time keeping up his select school, which remained in a flourishing condition.   While residing at Bainbridge his only son, Henry Austin, was born, March 31, 1855.   He is now an attorney, having been admitted to the bar at the general term at Binghamton, May 5, 1876.   He practices his profession in company with his father at Owego, where he holds a very prominent position as a member of the bar, and is conceded to have no superior in Tioga county in scholarly knowledge of the law, or ability to make application of it.   In the spring of 1856, Mr.

Clark made an engagement to teach in New Jersey. After remaining a year in New Jersey, he returned, in the spring of 1857, to Berkshire, to which town his father had removed, in the spring of 1856. Here he engaged for three years in the mercantile business; then he tried, successively, Richford, Marathon, and Oneonta. While residing in Berkshire, his only daughter, Emily Lucretia, was born, April 16, 1859.

Having purchased a farm near Ketchumville, in the town of Newark Valley, he decided to retire from mercantile life. Accordingly he went to his farm and lived upon it during the years 1864 and 1865. In early life it was his ambition to become a lawyer. Many obstacles, however, stood in his way. At length there seemed an opportunity for him to gratify his long cherished desire. Accordingly he devoted himself to the study of law for years while carrying on his business. He moved from his farm to Oneonta, early in 1866, entered the law office of General S. S. Burnside, overcoming all obstacles, was admitted at the general term in Binghamton, May 15, 1867, to practice in all the courts of the state of New York, and was subsequently admitted to practice in the United States courts.

In the spring of 1867 he returned to the town of Newark Valley, and his energy soon secured for him a prominent position at the bar. While he resided at Newark Valley his practice extended into the neighboring counties of Broome and Cortland. In 1869 he was elected supervisor of Newark Valley, and was re-elected the next year, and the year following, without opposition. In the fall of 1871, he was nominated as the candidate of the Republican party, for the office of county judge, and after an exciting canvass, was elected by a majority of 822. He entered upon the duties of the office January 1, 1872, and on the 29th of August, following, removed his family to Owego, where he still resides. In the fall of 1877 he was unanimously re-nominated for the same office, and re-elected by a majority of 1,256. At the close of his second term, in the fall of 1883, Judge Clark declined to be a candidate for re-nomination, and beyond any question he had proved one of the most courteous, able, correct and popular county judges and surrogates Tioga county has ever had. In the fall of 1883, Judge Clark was a prominent candidate for the nomination for justice of the supreme court, and after a convention which held for five days, was barely defeated.

In 1876 Judge Clark was elected an elder in the First Presbyterian church of Owego, in which church for several years he had been an active member, and which position he still holds. On March 17, 1878, his wife died, a lady of force of character and amiable disposition, full of charity and good works.

On December 28, 1880, Judge Clark was again married, to Mrs. Celestia D. Arnold, widow of Captain Thomas S. Arnold who was killed in battle in the war of the rebellion, and a daughter of H. Nelson Dean, late of Owego, deceased, and formerly of Adams, Massachusetts, where she was born and reared. January 1, 1884, when Judge Clark retired from the office of county judge, he and his son formed a co-partnership, under the firm name of C. A. & H. A. Clark, and since that time have enjoyed and at the present time continue to have a large and remunerative law practice.

Judge Clark is now in company with his son, busily engaged in the pursuit of professional duties, hoping for years of success and enjoyment in his home and with his family, having concluded to shake the dust of politics from his garments and devote his life to his professional and personal duties.

John J. Van Kleeck comes from Holland ancestry, whose family tree is readily traced back to the year 1630, when Baltus Van Kleeck emigrated from Holland to New Amsterdam, and whose descendants afterward settled in what is now the city of Poughkeepsie, Duchess county, New York, where they built the first dwelling, which was known as the "Van Kleeck House." General Washington made it his headquarters when in that vicinity, during the revolutionary war, and it long remained a very interesting landmark. The Van Kleecks took a prominent part in the government of the colony, and Duchess county was represented in the colonial assembly by Baltus Van Kleeck, Jr., in 1715–16; by Johannes Van Kleeck in 1726–27; and by Leonard Van Kleeck in 1768–75.

John J. Van Kleeck is the son of John Manning and Amy Jane (Brock) Van Kleeck, and was born in the town of Candor, September 21, 1848. His early years were passed upon his father's farm in Candor, and in attending the district school of the neighborhood. And with the advantages for an education afforded by the common schools of the state, including attendance for two winters at the village schools in Candor and Spencer, supplemented by his reading and self-instruction, he laid the foundation of his mental acquirements. Determined to embark for himself in life, alone and unaided, in the fall of 1867, he sought and obtained employment as a clerk in the grocery store of Jerry S.

J Van Kleeck.

Kinney, of Candor, who was also at the time a justice of the peace. Young Van Kleeck gave to the duties of his new position great care, showing much aptitude therefor, and paying close attention to the business of the justice's office; thus evincing a predilection at that early age, for clerical work. His fine penmanship was much admired and gained him quite a notoriety; so much so that in February, 1868, he secured a position as a copyist in the county clerk's office, through the recommendation of Delos O. Hancock, Esq., then a prominent lawyer of the county, with whom Mr. Van Kleeck had previously considered the advisability of pursuing the study of law.

It was in the county clerk's office, under the training of Horace A. Brooks, Esq., and his sister Miss Chloe, that he became conversant with the duties of a position, he was destined to fill so acceptably. Industrious and self-reliant, he applied himself not only to the immediate, but to the future or contingent needs of the office, by examining questions in advance of the actual requirement, and thus made himself of great value therein. And moreover, by the time he had attained his majority, he had become, through his own sterling worth, a recognized factor in the politics of the county. Mr. Brooks, his senior, having served nearly twelve years as county clerk, was not a candidate for re-election, in 1873, and the Republican party nominated Daniel M. Pitcher, one of the party veterans, and since postmaster at Owego. The Greeley canvass of 1872 had divided the Republicans, and Mr. Van Kleeck was tendered a unanimous nomination for the office of county clerk by the Democrats and Liberal Republicans, which he accepted. The contest was very spirited, and the youth of Mr. Van Kleeck was urged by his opponents as an argument against his election; but owing to his strong following and personal popularity in the county, he succeeded in overcoming the usual overwhelming Republican majority, and was elected, thus becoming the first Democratic official elected in Tioga county in over a quarter of a century.

His administration of the clerk's office was most excellent, and he naturally became a candidate for re-election in 1876. He was defeated, however, by a small majority, party-lines being closely drawn in presidential years. He then engaged in the fire insurance business and the negotiation of western farm loans, which business he still carries on, and it is a well known fact that not one dollar has ever been lost by any of his clients in any loan negotiated through him. In 1881, he was elected a justice of the peace

24*

of the town of Owego, for a full term, by a handsome majority. In 1882, he was again a candidate for county clerk against the incumbent, John C. Gray, whom he defeated by a majority of two hundred and thirty. In 1885, he was re-elected over Henry W. Childs, the Republican candidate, by a majority of two-hundred and eighty, and is now serving his third term.

While attending carefully to his public duties, Mr. Van Kleeck has nevertheless found time to engage in various outside enterprises, and much of the business prosperity of his adopted village is owing to his public spirit. Among the corporations which he has originated and promoted are the Owego Mutual Benefit Association, a popular life insurance company of which he is secretary and a director ; the Owego Cruciform Casket Company, of which he is secretary, a director and acting treasurer, and the Owego Electric Light and Motor Company, of which he is also a director and secretary. The secret of Mr. Van Kleeck's success lies in his urbanity, his kindness of heart, his industry, his integrity and self-reliance, joined with superior ability and capacity for accomplishing whatever he undertakes. Just in his dealings, faithful to his friends, and loyal to his high standard of manhood, he is to-day, through his own merit, one of the foremost men in the county.

On January 6, 1875, he was married to Frances Josephine Byington, the accomplished and youngest daughter of the late Lawyer Byington, of Newark Valley. The union has proved a very pleasant and happy one.

Nicholas Rodman, son of John and Hannah (Gorse) Rodman, was born in Middleburg, Schoharie county, N. Y., September 23, 1809, and came to Owego in 1830. He located on the farm now occupied by him about three and one-half miles from Apalachin, on the river road. He married Phœbe (La Monte) Clark, by whom he had six children, viz.: Mary J., wife of Henry Hayes, Clarissa, wife of Isaac L. Potter, of Owego, Marilla, wife of Henry Coffin, now deceased, Charles, at present sheriff of Tioga county, George, of California, and Callie, wife of James Risen, of Gaskill's Corners. Mrs. Rodman died in 1854.

Samuel Abbey, born January 18, 1755, married Miriam Hall (born March 15, 1757), April 11, 1775. They had fourteen children, born as follows: Rachel, February 10, 1776 ; Sheubel, February 20, 1778 ; Hannah, February 22, 1780 ; Polly, January 3, 1782 ; Jerusha, January 16, 1784 ; Miriam, January 27, 1786 ; Jes-

Charles A. Clark

sie, July 1, 1788 ; Anna, May 2, 1790; Olive, September 25, 1792 ; Ruth, June 27, 1794; Phœbe, January 13, 1796 ; Lydia, March 11, 1798; Reuben, July 13, 1800; Jemima, April 8, 1803. Reuben Abbey came from Schoharie county, N. Y., in 1831. His daughter Sabrina married John, son of Thomas Baird, May 21, 1848. They had five children, born as follows : James Lewis and Lewis James (twins) March 4, 1849; Thomas, July 2, 1851 ; William R., July 23, 1853 : and Tryphena H., July 13, 1856. Lewis J. married Georgiana (born April 10, 1850), daughter of Abner Merrick, July 27, 1881. Their children are John A., born March 20, and died May 26, 1883 ; Bessie R., born September 10, 1884, and Jessie S., born November 18, 1886.

Clarence A. Thompson was born in Owego, February 1, 1848. He was educated at the Owego academy, and the Oneida Conference Seminary at Cazenovia. On the 18th day of July, 1864, he entered the First National Bank of Waverly, as book-keeper, and was subsequently assistant cashier, and afterwards cashier of the bank. In April, 1870, he became teller of the First National Bank of Owego, and, in 1881, was made assistant cashier. He held that position till August 6, 1883, when the Owego National Bank was opened, of which institution he has ever since been cashier. Mr. Thompson is one of the progressive young men of the village. He was instrumental in having the telephone exchange established here, and was one of the prominent men in building the various steamboats plying between Owego and Big Island. He was treasurer of the village in 1876 and 1880, and as a member of the board of school commissioners, was one of the committee who had charge of the construction of the Free Academy.

This completes the biographical sketches furnished by Mr. Kingman, and by the friends of the subjects of the longer ones accompany the portraits, and we add the following :

Additional Sketches.—Moses Ingersoll, a soldier of the revolution, and who served under his father, Captain Peter Ingersoll, came from Half Moon Point, Mass., to the town of Owego, in 1791, where he bought five hundred acres of land, and settled on the farm now owned by E. F. Searles. He married Lavina Lee, by whom he had five children : Mary (Mrs. Simeon Decker), Winthrop, Sarah (Mrs. Ephraim Wood), Nancy (Mrs. Thomas Day), and John. Winthrop married Anna Hall, by whom he had five children, who arrived at maturity : Moses, Stephen H.,

William, James, and Mary (Mrs. Merritt Ireland). William married Caroline, daughter of Elijah Walter, by whom he had five children: Mary, wife of John Miller, Delphine, wife of Gilbert Webster, George A., of Nichols, Clinton, and Carrie, wife of Garry Hunt. George A. married Huldah Cornell, by whom he has five children: Fred, Fannie, Lena, Willie, and Louie.

Hugh Fiddis was a descendant of Scotch refugees, who settled in the town of Enniskillen, in the northern part of Ireland. He came to this country in about the year 1762, and was afterwards married to Hannah Eldridge, of Groton, New London county, Conn. They had two children, Katy and Hugh Eldridge. Katy was born at Groton, in 1764. She married and died there. Hugh Eldridge was born at Groton, August 5, 1766. When he was about two years of age, his father, who was captain of a merchantman, was lost at sea. In 1795, he came from Connecticut to Owego, where, in 1798, April 15th, he married Anna Brown, who was born at Brookfield, Fairfield county, Conn., February 11, 1777. Their children were all born at Owego, viz.:—Hugh Eldridge, June 15, 1793; Polly July 11, 1801; Robert November 17, 1808; James Edwin, May 22, 1819. The youngest son, James Edwin, married Emeline Rensom, at Owego, May 28, 1845. Emeline Ransom was born April 7, 1822, at Tioga Center. Kate, daughter of James and Emeline Fiddis, was born at Owego, March 11, 1851. She was married May 30, 1867, to William Head, of Owego. Cora Head, their daughter, was born at Owego February 14, 1868.

Colonel Asa Camp, born in Rhode Island in 1760, served in the revolutionary war, and though young, he was assigned the task of commanding the party that buried Major Andre, the spy. Sometime after the close of the war he came to this town and settled not far from the present eastern boundary line, on the north bank of the river, where a considerable settlement afterward sprang up, and was named Campville, for him. At the time he located here, the country was a dense wilderness inhabited by wild beasts, and he was obliged to shut up his stock at night to protect them from the ravages of the wolves and panthers. He had to go down the river forty miles in a canoe, to mill; and once when recovering from a fever and his physician prescribed oysters, he was obliged to send a man with a team to Albany, that being the nearest point at which they could be procured. He was justice of the peace for a long period, and had the reputation of a loyal, conscientious citizen, and very benevolent in his conduct towards the sparse inhabitants in that section, who were struggling for a living. For many years he kept a public house for the accommodation of mail carriers and stock-men. The thoroughfares of those days were marked only by blazed trees, and travelers were not numerous. His family con-sisted of five sons and one daughter. Four of his sons settled on farms in close proximity to him. Colonel Camp died in 1848. His youngest son, John, born in November, 1788, settled on a farm near Campville in 1819, and resided there until his death in 1870. Of his children remaining in Tioga county are Mrs. R. W. Hines, and John Jr. The latter has been in the employ of the Erie railroad since 1848, and has traveled upwards of 2,720,016 miles.

David Taylor, son of Cornelius, was born in the town of Owego, August 20, 1802. He married Helena Tappan, January 8, 1827. Nine children were born to them: Nancy A., October 13, 1827; Lucy M., April 20, 1829; Cornelius, December 31, 1831; Charles H., April 13, 1834; Tappan A., December 16, 1836; Catharine, December 23, 1838; David C., April 15, 1841; Sarah, October 11, 1843; and Mary D., October 17, 1847.

Richard Sykes was born early in the seventeenth century, and emigrated from London in 1630–33 with George Winthrop and others, and settled in Roxbury, Mass. He had three sons, namely, Increase, Samuel, and Victory. The latter had three sons, Jona-than, Samuel and Victory. Samuel had one son, Victory, who had two sons, viz.: Samuel and Victory. The latter had eight sons, the second of whom was George, who, in 1811, came to that portion of Berkshire now included in the town of Newark Valley. He married Ruth Gaylord, of Connecticut, January 15, 1811, by whom he had six children, as follows: Ambrose B., Edward F., George M., Theodore P., of Owego, Horatio W., and Lucy J. Theodore P. married Electa B. Chapman, of New-ark Valley. Richard Sykes died in March, 1676, and Phœbe, his wife, in 1683. George Sykes died October 26, 1825, aged thirty-seven years, and his wife, September 3, 1869, in her eighty-first year.

Nathaniel Catlin, son of Nathaniel, born September 24, 1796, came from New Jersey with his parents when very young. The family settled in Nichols about three miles below Owego on the farm now owned by O. W. Young. Nathaniel, Jr., married Jane D. Broadhead, and reared six children, namely, Delinda, wife of Gen. B. F. Tracy, Maria (Mrs. Avery Olmstead), Avery B., a customs officer of New York city, Isaac S., a lawyer of Brooklyn, George, of Apalachin, and Hannah, deceased. He was one of the first Abolitionists of this section, and still lives on the farm which he has occupied for sixty years. Mrs. Catlin died in 1875.

Rev. John Griffing, of Guilford, Conn., married Lydia Redfield of that place, and came to the town of Berkshire [See Berkshire], and was one of the first preachers in this section. They had twelve children born to them—Henry, September 17, 1809; Clarissa, December 29, 1810; Lydia, February 13, 1813; John, March 26, 1815; Daniel S., January 7, 1817; Beriah R., March 27, 1819; Artemesia, March 5, 1821; James S., October 28, 1822; Samuel B., August 1, 1825; Osmyn, September 22, 1828; Permelia, February 8, 1831; and Mary M., August 13, 1834. Samuel B., son of Rev. John Griffing, married Lucy M., daughter of David Taylor, of Owego, April 17, 1848. Three children were born to them, viz.: Helena A., July 9, 1849; Lydia Permelia, who died in infancy; and David T., March 31, 1853, now of Iowa.

Dr. Samuel Standish Tinkham, a descendent of Miles Standish, was a graduate of Dartmouth College, and came to Owego in 1793, where he engaged in the practice of medicine. He married Mary, daughter of Col. David Pixley, one of the original proprietors of the Boston Purchase, by whom he had three children, Sarah E., who was the first wife of William Pumpelly, Samuel Standish, who married Lois Willoughly, and David Pixley, who married Harriet G. Drake. Dr. Tinkham lived on Front street, where Mrs. Wall's house and W. C. Renwick's garden are located.

Elisha Forsyth, of English descent, was among the very early settlers in this county, having come from Connecticut to Marietta, Pa., thence up the Susquehanna in a canoe, to Union, from whence he subsequently removed to this town and located at Park settlement on Owego creek. He married Freelove, daughter of Capt. Thomas Park, a privateersman of the revolution. Mr. Forsyth spent the greater portion of his life in this town engaged in lumbering and farming. Their children were George, Catherine who married Nathaniel Webster, Azor, Elisha, Experience, who married Martin Smith, Gilbert, and Eldridge, born August 5, 1812. The latter during his early years was engaged with his father in the lumber business, and subsequently in painting which has been his occupation for nearly forty years. He married first, Mary Fisher, of Ontario county, N. Y. His present wife is Eunice, daughter of the late Anthony M. Tyler, of Newark

Valley. Gilbert and Azor were artists, the former having acquired considerable ruputation as a portrait painter. Among his students was Thomas LaClear a noted painter of New York city. George, born July 2, 1798, married first, Mary Chapman. His second wife was Rachel Puffer, by whom he had four children, namely: Ira, born August 6, 1831, now of Los Angeles, Cal., William S., born November 7, 1833, Adelaide E., born May 19, 1836, married George H. Woughter, and Augusta, born December 31, 1838, married George Sawyer. Mr. Forsyth died October 5, 1876. William S., married first, Maria, daughter of Charles Corbin, October 23, 1854. His present wife is Margaret, daughter of Edward Howard whom he married June 12, 1882. His children born as follows, are Ettie M., August 6, 1855, George Roosa, May 8, 1872, and Clarence Augusto, November 1, 1886. Elisha, Jr., was born in Owego, February 14, 1801. He married Wealthy L., daughter of Abel Lawrence, of Newark Valley, February 1, 1827. Their children were Julia A., widow of John D. Baker, Morgiana (Mrs. Joseph Tyler) Charles, H. Truman, Gilbert T., George F., William L., Mary Lucina, and Edward A. H. Truman, born August 3, 1834, married N. Adaline, daughter of Robert Williams of Greensburg, Pa., September 6, 1863. Their children are Florence, born June 20, 1864, died August 3, 1865, George F., born August 12, 1866, Charles E., November 11, 1868, Fannie, February 24, 1871, Zenora T., June 10, 1873, and Mary W., November 7, 1875. H. Truman was a member of Co. K., 76th Regt. Pa. Vol's., having enlisted July 14, 1863, and was mustered out at the close of the war. Gilbert T., born August 29, 1839, married Susan E., daughter of John Lord, January 16, 1860. Their children are Charles F., born October 13, 1860, William M., September 9, 1862, and Minnie G. and Mettie M., (twins) July 15, 1864. Charles F., married Anna Worth of Freeport, Ill., and has one child, Lillian E., born December 3, 1884. William M., married Emma Taylor. Mary Lucina, married W. Harrison Camp, who served in Co. C. 23d Regt. N. Y. Infantry, and who re-enlisted in 1863 in the 5th N. Y. Cavalry. He served in many battles and skirmishes, and was mustered out at the close of the war. Elisha Forsyth, Jr., was fife-major in the 50th N. Y. Regt., and his son George was drum major of the same regiment.

Francis M. Baker, son of John D. and Julia (Forsyth) Baker was born March 26, 1846. He married Mary, daughter of Jesse McQuigg, of Flint, Mich., February 16, 1869. They have one

child, George H., born August 28, 1871.   Mr. Baker was president of the New York State Firemen's Association, and is general superintendent of the Addison & Northern Pennsylvania
railroad.   His home is in Owego.

John R. Drake, son of Rev. Reuben Drake, of Pleasant Valley,—now Plattekill—Orange Co., N. Y., came to Owego in 1809,
and located on Front street, about where the bridge now crosses.
He was elected county judge, represented this district in the
assembly, and in congress.   He was actively engaged in mercantile business here for many years, being a large dealer in lumber.
He built the first dock in Owego, and the first piece of sidewalk
laid in the town was laid by him, in front of his store.   It is also
said that he was the first to possess a two-horse carriage and
covered sleigh here.   Being of a progressive nature, he was very
active, and evinced great interest in getting the railroad here,
donating nine acres of his farm to the company.   He married
Jerusha, daughter of Rev. Joseph Roberts, by whom he had five
children, viz: Harriet, Adaline, widow of Bradford Gere, Delphine, first wife of Harmon Pumpelly, Theodore, of Fredericksburg, Va., and Charlotte M., widow of Edward Raynsford, of
Washington, D. C.   Judge Drake died in 1857.   Harriet married
David Pixley Tinkham, by whom she had three children, Sarah,
Arianna, who married Gen. William P. Innes, of Grand Rapids,
Mich., and John F.   Sarah married Edward G. Gibson, by whom
she has one son, Dr. Edward T. Gibson, of Minneapolis, Minn.
David P. Tinkham was a merchant in Owego, but died in 1836,
at the early age of thirty-two years.   In 1817 Mrs. Tinkham,
accompanied by her father, left home to attend the Moravian
boarding-school at Bethlehem, Pa.   They went down the river
on a raft as far as Berwick, and from there across the mountains
in a four-horse covered wagon, called a stage.   Her piano was
the first in this section, having been brought here from New
York in 1821.

Benjamin Bates came from Massachusetts and settled on the
large island about three miles east of Owego.   They had seven
children—Elisha, William, Benjamin, Prudence, Abigail, Lucinda and Rachel.   Lucinda was born August 16, 1800, and in
1816 married Jared Lillie, by whom she had twelve children,
Mary, Sarah, William, served in Co. A, 109th Regt.; Benjamin,
George W., served in the 9th N. Y. Cavalry ; Jared, Abbie J.,
Charles, was a member of Co. H, 109th Regt.; James, was a mem-

ber of the same company and regiment; Darius, served in Co. G, 44th Regt., and Frederick, in Co. H, 109th Regt.

Erastus Meacham, son of Silas, was born in Cornwall, Litchfield county, Conn., February 9, 1798, and came with his father's family to the town of Danby when but seven years of age, and remained there until he arrived at the age of fourteen, when he was apprenticed to a blacksmith. Having served his time, he came to Owego, in December, 1822, and engaged to work for a blacksmith named Taylor, and remained with him until the following March, when he hired the shop which stood where the Central House now stands, and conducted the business himself. He afterward sold out and bought a farm of 150 acres in the town of Tioga, which he conducted for fifteen years. With this exception Owego has been his home since 1822. He married Betsey, daughter of Truman Lake, of Spencer, November 9, 1820. Five children have been born to them, viz: Myron E., Mary A. (Mrs. Henry Shipman), deceased; Maria, who died in infancy; Melinda and Milton H.. who also died in infancy. Mrs. Meacham was born in Greenville, Greene county, N. Y., January 3, 1803, and removed with her parents to the town of Spencer when but twelve years of age. Mr. and Mrs. Meacham are in the sixty-seventh year of their married life, and he, despite his ninety years, still attends to the business of blacksmithing and horse-shoeing. Melinda married John M. Head, October 3, 1849, and has had nine children, born as follows: Lottie A., October 9, 1851; Anna M., October 20, 1853; Sarah, September 9, 1856; John J., March 12, 1859; Ida M. and Eddie B. (twins), August 23, 1862; Frederick L. and Frank L. (twins), March 16, 1866—died in September of the same year—and Linnie B., born September 14, 1868. John M. Head was born February 13, 1822, was a member of Co. C, 137th Regt., Infy.; enlisted August 20, 1862; taken prisoner at Chancellorsville May 2, 1863; was mustered out in June, 1865, and died April 14, 1869. Lottie A. married Charles D. Meacham, by whom she has 'had five children, born as follows: Ella M., April 30, 1876; Fred R., November 29, 1879; Leon, July 14, 1881, died August 9, of the same year; Clarence L., born August 16, 1883, and Merle L., born July 16, 1885, died March 7, 1887. Anna married Royal B. Ferguson, April 13, 1871.

James Grimes, son of James, was born at the foot of the Green Mountains, in Vermont, in 1793, and when but nineteen years of age enlisted in the war of 1812. His uncle, Moses Grimes, having located in Owego sometime previous to the war, James Jr., came

on here after its close and engaged first as a farmer with his
uncle, afterward as builder.   He married first Margaret Whitney.
by whom he had eleven children.   His second wife was Sarah
Dennis by whom he had five children, viz. : George and Frederick,
now of Michigan, James A., and Carrie, wife of John H. Bunzy
of Owego ; and one who died in infancy.   When Mr. Grimes
came to Owego there was but one building, and that a log tavern
that stood on the northwest' corner of Main street and North
avenue.   The children of John H., and Carrie (Grimes) Bunzy,
are Adelbert and Minnie E.

Capt. David Nutt came from Vermont to the town of Owego
in 1816, and settled on Apalachin creek, where he cleared the
farm now owned by Norman Billings   He built a saw-mill and
engaged in lumbering and farming until 1844.   He married
Susan Bell, of Massachusetts, about 1817.   There were six children
born to them, viz.: Sally, wife of Elijah Sherwood, of Apalachin,
Romanzo, now of Iowa, Fidelia wife of Don Carlos Farwell, of
Portland, Oregon, Lorenzo, deceased, Maurice, of Alexandria,
Dakota, and Mary J., wife of A. Lindsley Lane, of Apalachin,
born May 2, 1832.   Mr. Nutt died in 1877, aged eighty-one,
and Mrs. Nutt in 1882, aged ninety-four.

John Jewett, a soldier of the revolution, came from Putnam
county in the fall of 1817, and located on the river road a mile
east of Apalachin.   His son Asa married Bathsheba Wooden, by
whom he had four children, viz.: Maurice, of Apalachin, Harry,
of Owego, Emily, now deceased, and Matilda, wife of Daniel
Dodge, of Owego.   Mr. Jewett died in 1819.   Mrs. Jewett afterward married Benjamin F. Tracy, and had four children, namely,
George, now deceased, Harrison and Harvey, of Apalachin, and
Benjamin F., of Brooklyn.

Josiah Morton came from Plymouth, Chenango county, to the
town of Owego in 1818, and located on a farm on what was
known as Chapman Hill.   He married Lucinda Sholes, by
whom he had seven children.   His son Levi was eleven years
old when his father came to Owego, and has since resided here.
He was engaged in shoemaking in Owego for twenty-five years,
and then moved to Apalachin, where he has since resided, about
forty-three years.   He married Margaret Freeland, by whom he
had three children—Ellen, wife of George Tracy ; Emily, wife
of Roswell Camp, of Wisconsin ; Elizabeth, wife of David LaMont,
of Owego.   Mr. Morton has been married twice since, and is

now in his eightieth year. The present Mrs. Morton was Maria, widow of James T. Smith.

James Lane, son of James, came from Delaware previous to 1812, and enlisted in the war of that year. Upon his arrival in this county, he located at Weltonville. In 1817 he married Jane, daughter of Rev. Charles Taylor, a Presbyterian minister, who came from the North of Ireland about 1804. Their children were Samuel, a minister of the United Brethren denomination ; Nancy, who married John VanDemark; Eliza (Mrs. Albert Barton); Charlotte (Mrs. Noah Goodrich); Charles ; Catherine (Mrs. Johnson Barton); and A. Lindsley, born April 6, 1831. The latter married Mary J., daughter of Captain David Nutt, January 31, 1856, and by whom he has two children, Don Carlos, born July 31, 1858, and Edgar S., born June 6, 1864. Don Carlos married Frederica, daughter of Augustus Olmstead, in June, 1881, and has one child, Floyd L., born June 24, 1883. Charles Lane, son of James, Jr., married Mary, daughter of Samuel Brownell, by whom he had ten children, viz.: Egbert, Frank, Frederick, Libbie, Fannie (Mrs. Charles McNeil), Winnie, Eloise, wife of Herbert Johnson, of Barton, Alice (Mrs. D. G. Underwood), Annie and Lewis.

John Livingston, son of Jacob Livingston, of Livingston Manor, Sullivan county, N. Y., was born April 23, 1768. He came very early to Campville, where he settled. He married Magdalena Palmetier, who was born November 14, 1777, and by whom he had thirteen children. Their second son, Peter, married Christiana Becker, by whom he had eleven children, viz.: Catherine (Mrs. William Whittemore), Peter, John, Margaret, Hannah (Mrs. Platt Jewett), Elizabeth, Chancelor, George, William, and Anna (Mrs. Fred Boynt). Margaret married Alonzo DeGroat, by whom she has three children, Charles, James, and Eva May. James married Maud Blewer, by whom he has one child, James, Jr.

Thomas Baird, son of Daniel, was one of the pioneers of this county, he having come very early to the town of Candor, where he located about one mile from Speedsville. He married Sally Putnam, of Worcester, Mass., who bore him five children, viz.: John, Aaron, Martha, Thomas, Jr., Mary, and William. Mary was born in Candor, August 10, 1813, and married Luther T. Keith, September 27, 1836. They had three children, one who died in infancy, S. Elizabeth, who married E. M. Blodgett, May 31, 1863, and whose second husband is W. Van Over, whom she married June 23, 1869 ; and George W., who married Anna Court, of Speedsville, N. Y., May 31, 1863. The latter have had four children, born as follows, viz.: Avery T., March 23, 1864, Mary E., May 7, 1865, Rose A., December 23, 1868, and Willie H., born July 17, 1885, died March 17, 1886. Mr. Luther Keith died May 18, 1884.

Henry Wait came from Half Moon, Saratoga county, N. Y., about the year 1818, and located near the southwestern part of the town, where he had purchased about nine hundred acres of land. His sons, William and Henry, live on portions of the land purchased by him. He is represented as having been a liberal and benevolent man, who did much to improve the roads, and to help the poor settlers who located about him. He married Eunice Shepard, by whom he had twelve children. Mrs. Wait died in 1854, and Mr. Wait died in 1858. George A., son of Henry and Mary (Russell) Wait, married Anna, daughter of George O. and Sarah (McKee) Kile, September 30, 1878, and has one child, Floyd A., born December 21, 1882.

William Williamson, son of Marcus and Mary (McLean) Williamson came from Westchester county and settled in Scipio, Cayuga county, N. Y. From thence he came to the town of Owego and settled three miles from Flemingville, and made the first settlement in that locality in 1820. At the time of his settlement there the country was a wilderness and his nearest neighbor was three miles distant. They often found it necessary when going out at night, to carry a pine torch, and also to build fires about their buildings to keep the wolves away. He married mary R., daughter of William and Abigail (Park) Ferguson. Eight children were born to them and all arrived at maturity. They were, Abigail (Mrs. Hulburt Bates), Mary (Mrs. Reuben B. Locke) Loesa, William H., who was the second to enlist from the town of Owego, served in Co. H., 3d Regt. N. Y. Vols., under Captain Catlin, as corporal, was promoted surgeon and afterward captain; while home on a furlough, which he spent in recruiting, he was taken sick and died, so never served as captain—Augusta (Mrs. Isaac Smith), Anna, Hannah, second wife of Hulbert Bates, and Theodore. Mrs. Williamson died February 16, 1880, and Mr. Williamson died February 22, the same year.

Oliver Pearl came from Connecticut, about 1820, and located first about one mile west of Wait's church. His children were Hannah (Mrs. Philip Baker), and Mercy (Mrs. Loren Fuller), Daniel, Oliver, Walter and Cyril. Cyril married Rosanna, daughter of Thomas Farmer, May 29, 1820. Six of their children arrived at maturity, viz.: Walter, of Nichols, Loring C., of Owego, John F. and Austin, now deceased, Thomas F., of Hastings, Neb., and Jane R. Walter, married Catharine Rapplegee, by whom he had eight children, viz.: Mary M., who died in infancy, Cyril, Emma J., Marcella, George, Myram and Hattie, who died at the age of eighteen months. Loring C. married Clementina, daughter of Stephen Capwell in 1845, and has four children, viz.: Frances E., wife of Warren A. Lane, of Nichols, Helen R., wife of Emmet Barton, of Schoharie, N. Y., Charles C. and Frederick J., of Owego. Austin married Diana B., daughter of Ebenezer Warner, of Sanford, N. Y., and had one child, Freddie who died in 1854, aged four years.

Myram W. Pearl, son of Walter H. Pearl, married Emma, daughter of George Merrick, December 5, 1878, and has two children, Ada, born April 13, 1880, and Marcella, born August 16, 1883.

Adam Gould came to this town from Washington, Duchess county, N. Y., February 28, 1822, locating south of the river and engaged in farming, having bought 540 acres of wild land there. His wife was Judith, daughter of Paul Coffin, of Nantucket.

William Sherwood came from Duchess county to Trumansburg early in the present century, and from thence to this county, where he located on the lower one hundred acres now comprised in the farm of John Holmes, about the year 1824. He married Polly Wicksom, by whom he had eight children who arrived at maturity, viz.: Elijah, John, Betsey, widow of Cornelius Goesbeck, William H., Nathaniel and Mary J., (twins) all of Owego, Hanna, wife of Alfred Van Wagoner of Duchess county, and Deborah. Elijah married Sally, daughter of Capt. David Nutt of Owego and had eight children, viz.: David W., of Belmont, N. Y., Ursula, wife of Dr. J. M. Barrett, and George J., of Owego, Henry W., a Baptist clergyman now of Syracuse, N. Y., John, who died in infancy, Susie, wife of Dr. Judson Beach, of Etna, N. Y., Edgar, who died at the age of six years, and Deliah, wife of Dr. H. Champlin of Chelsea, Mich. Mr. Sherwood died in October, 1873. William H., married Olive, daughter of Willard Foster in 1855. Their children are Elsworth, Grace, and Charles. Elsworth married Flora Abbey and has one child, Roy. Nathaniel Sherwood married Phoebe, daughter of Van Ness Barrett of West Newark, in 1861, and they have had born to them three sons, Van Ness, Samuel and J. Ross.

Matthew La Mont came from Schoharie county about 1825 and located on the farm now owned by Humphrey C. Slocum, where he controlled the La Mont ferry. He married Ruth McNeil, by whom he had twelve children. His eldest son, Marcus, married Hannah Hoagland by whom he had four children, namely : Abram H., superintendent of the Orphan's Home at Binghamton, Susan J., wife of Rev. William Life, preceptress of Rye Seminary, Cyrenus M., of this town, and Isabelle, who died at the age of sixteen years.

Ralph Hibbard, son of Ebenezer, was born in Norwich, Ct., and was a soldier at New London in the war of 1812–15. He married Jemima, daughter of Zebadiah Maynard of Norwich, and came to Owego in 1825. They had three children, namely : Ralph, A. Maria, and Charles, now of Granville, Mich. Ralph, married Elizabeth, daughter of John Sweet of Owego, by whom he had two children, Frances, and George R., a merchant of Owego. Frances married James E. Jones of Owego, November 4, 1874, and has one child, Flora A., born December 29, 1879. A. Maria is the widow of —— Curtis. Mrs. Jemima Hibbard is now in her ninety-first year.

Ezra Tallmadge, the son of John, was born in the town of Malta, Saratoga county, N. Y., February 18, 1797. He was united in marriage with Zilpha Gould, in the year 1821. He remained in Malta until 1826, when, at the age of twenty-nine, with his wife and two children, he removed to this county. The journey was made with an ox-team, and as the roads were bad and the weather unpleasant, they reached their destination under many difficulties. The land which he had purchased being covered with a dense forest, he first took quarters with his family in a log house on a lot located by Anson Camp, since known as the Camp farm, and about two and a half miles from his own place. He then cleared a spot, built him a log house, and cut through the woods a road of nearly two miles in length. About this time he lost a little son, whose death was the first one which occurred in the settlement for twenty-six years. At this period there were but three voters in that part of the county. He was a man of strong Christian character and for fifty years was in enjoyment of church membership. A Methodist society was formed near his home, and he was class-leader for many years. Mr. Tallmadge was eminently a good man, faithful in all the sacred relations of domestic life, and faithful as a father in Israel. He died on Sunday evening, May 5, 1872, aged seventy-five years. Ezra W.

Tallmadge married Angeline, daughter of Henry and Mary (Russell) Waite, June 5, 1864, and by whom he has had five children, viz.: Ida M., wife of Lowell E. Kyle, Philip Albert, who died September 5, 1868, Mary P., Frutilla J., and Gurdon Ezra W., who died September 16, 1886, aged eleven years.

James Blow came from East Winfield. N. Y., in 1827, and cleared the farm now owned by his son Henry. He married Margaret Brown, who. like himself was a native of the North of Ireland. They had twelve children. Of these Henry married Catharine, daughter of John McNeil, by whom he had eleven children, James, Harmon, Minard, Arthur, Elizabeth, Henry, Diana, Margaret, George, Almeda, and Frank L. The latter married Mary Franklin of Pennsylvania, and has two children, namely, Alice and Henry. Francis, son of James Blow, married Amanda, daughter of Sylvester Fox of Owego, January 15, 1841, by whom he had six children, viz.: Harriet, Hiram, Sarah, Francis, Jr., all of Titusville, Pa., Ella, and William, of Owego. William married Emma, daughter of Miner Russell. Mr. Blow died in March, 1885.

Sylvester Fox came from Connecticut to Windown, Pa., and thence to Owego in 1826, and located on the farm now occupied in part by Spencer Bostwick. He married Olive Smith, and eight of their children arrived at maturity, namely, Pernine, Allen, Amanda, widow of Francis Blow, Sylvester, Sarah, wife of Jacob Mericle, Ira, William, deceased, and Merinda, wife of Edward Briggs of Nichols.

George W. Hollenback, for nearly fifty years a prominent business man of Owego, was born in Wyalusing, Pa., August 25, 1806. He was the eldest son of John Hollenback of Martinsburg, Va., who left his birth-place and settled in Pennsylvania in 1795. He was for many years engaged in business and was on intimate terms with the old time merchants of Philadelphia. A gentleman of the old school, he was distinguished for an ease of manner and a generous hospitality which attracted many friends. His son, George, first came to Owego in 1816, for the purpose of attending school. On the fifth of December, 1828, he returned again to Owego and entered the store of John Hollenback as clerk, where he remained until 1831, when he entered into business for himself, near Towanda, Pa. After his marriage with Miss Jane Gordon, a lady of Scotch-Irish parentage whose ancestors on the father's side were distinguished in Scottish history, he acceded to the earnest wish of his childless relative, and with his

wife removed to Owego, in 1838, and again entered the store of
John Hollenback, who was widely known as one of the most
active and energetic business men of his day.   In the fall of 1847
Mr. Hollenback, with Jacob Hand, entered into a partnership
with Mr. William H. Bell, who had also been a clerk for John
Hollenback, under the firm-title of Wm. H. Bell & Co., which
parnership continued twenty years.   They conducted an extensive general mercantile business, and engaged largely in the
manufacture and traffic in lumber.   On January 16, 1867, the
firm, from which Mr. Hand had previously withdrawn, was
dissolved by mutual consent, and the property owned by them
was divided.   Mr. Hollenback retained the store and Mr. Bell
took the saw-mill and lumber tract in the south part of the town
of Owego, and after the dissolution of the firm of William H.
Bell & Co., Mr. Hollenback took two of his sons, George F. &
John G., into partnership with him, and continued the general
mercantile business until the fall of 1871, when they disposed of
their stock and commenced a wholesale and retail crockery business.   This business they continued until October, 1873, when
they sold their stock to D. C. Tuthill.   Mr. Hollenback took a
great interest in public affairs.   He died at his home in Owego,
December 30, 1878, aged seventy-two years.   His wife, who had
been an invalid, suffering from consumption for several years,
survived him a little more than two years, passing peacefully
away on the morning of April 14, 1881.   Of the four sons and
three daughters born to them, the youngest daughter died
October 28, 1874.   Two daughters remain at the homestead,
which was bequeathed to them and their brother Charles E.,
by their father.

William Henry Hollenback married Mary McLain, of Owego, in July, 1868, and by whom he has seven children.   He
resides on his farm, in the town of Owego.   George Frederick,
or " Fred," as he was familiarly called, was born in Owego.   He
received his education here and at the Brookside school, presided over by the Messrs. Judd, at Berkshire, and finally at a
private school.   In April, 1861, he enlisted in the 3d Regt., N. Y.
Vols., and served two years under Gen. I. S. Catlin.   In 1878, he
married his cousin, Augusta, daughter of George Gordan, of
Frenchtown, Pa., by whom he had one child, George Frederick.
He died May 11, 1882.   John Gordan early evinced a predilection for a mercantile career.   After finishing his studies he entered the store of W. H. Bell & Co., as clerk.   He afterward

Arba Campbell

spent some time in Rochester, N. Y. He returned and entered into business with his father and brother. After two or three years, they disposed of the business, and he accompanied his brother to California, where he remained a year. On his return he entered into partnership with C. A. Link, in the clothing business. In October, 1875, he married Miss Lizzie Dean, of New York. They have one daughter, Florence, and reside at Los Angeles, Cal., where Mr. Hollenback conducts a real estate business.

Charles Edward Hollenback was born in Owego, Feb. 3, 1849. He prepared for college at the Owego academy, under the tutorship of Prof. Prindle. He entered Union college at Schenectady, N. Y., in 1868, and was graduated therefrom in the classical course in 1871, taking the first prize in oratory. In September, 1871, he commenced the study of law, in the office of Hon. John J. Taylor, and was admitted to the bar in 1874, when he formed a partnership with C. D. Nixon, known as the firm of Nixon & Hollenback, which continued for a year. In 1876 and 1877, he had charge of the law office of Hon. E. B. Gere, who was then member of assembly. He afterward opened an office on his own account, with a large and constantly increasing practice. Mr. Hollenback, or " Dick," as he was called by his friends, was one of the most active of Owego s young Democrats. He was chosen chairman of the Democratic county committee, in 1881, and continued at the head of that committee until he was taken sick. He was the Democratic candidate for district attorney, in 1876 and 1882, and for supervisor of the town of Owego, in the latter year. He died November 9, 1884.

James Kenyon, of English descent, was born in Pittsfield, Berkshire county, Mass., November 1, 1813. When twenty-two years of age he came to Owego, and engaged as a journeyman machinist to Henry Camp, in whose service he remained thirty-five years. He married Amanda, daughter of Chauncey Hill, of Tioga, June 30, 1839. Four children were born to them, namely: Albert J., born September 22, 1841, now chief engineer of the U. S. Navy, in which service he has been since the fall of 1861; Lesbia A., born June 21, 1844, the wife of William Peck; Anna L., born August 8, 1850, the widow of Charles R. Strang; and Calvin F., born March 5, 1854, and who died September 8, 1875. Mrs Strang has two children, namely: Samuel P., born March 6, 1872, and Annette Kenyon, born June 7, 1874.

Moses Knight was born February 10, 1808, in Crawford, Orange
25*

Co. N. Y. He married Mary J. Middaugh, of Sullivan Co., N. Y., November 1, 1832. In 1835 he came to Owego and engaged in the clothing business, in which he continued until his death, which occurred June 10, 1862. Their children were Thomas H., deceased, Elizabeth, Mary L., deceased, and William, of Austin, Texas.

Daniel Stanton, born December 14, 1794, came from Norwich, Mass., and located in the town of Nichols in 1830, and in 1836 moved onto the farm now occupied by his son Asa. He married Almira Johnson April 14, 1820, by whom he had eight children, viz.: Maria, who died March 14, 1849, Asa, born August 15, 1822, Elizabeth, widow of Oliver P. Chaffee, Lucinda, widow of Hiram Shays, of Owego, Clarissa, wife of A. J. Stanton, and Levi, of Bradford county, Pa., Jonas, who was drowned September 4, 1853, and Almira, wife of David Smead, of Owego.

William S. Pearsall, son of Thomas, was born October 14, 1796, in Bainbridge, N. Y., where his father located very early, and with his brothers inherited large tracts of land which their father had owned. The latter was a native of Long Island. William, Nathaniel, Gilbert and Thomas came to this town from Chenango county, and settled in and near Apalachin, where they engaged in building mills and in lumbering, shipping large quantities in rafts down the river. In 1837, they had established a lumber business in the city of Baltimore, Md. In 1840, William built a grist and saw-mill at Apalachin, which was the only grist-mill in this section at that time, and which did the mill business of farmers for many miles. When they first came here there was but little of the village of Apalachin. Gilbert built and kept a store there. William purchased two hundred acres there, and the larger part of the village is on a portion of this tract. One hundred acres of it he afterward sold to Ransom Steele. William Pearsall married Eliza, daughter of Col. Samuel Balcom, of Oxford, N. Y., a sister of Judge Ransom Balcom and Judge Lyman Balcom, of Steuben county. Seven of the children that were born to them arrived at maturity—George, of Fort Scott, Kas.; Jane, who died at the age of seventeen; Martha, wife of F. C. Coryell; Cornelia, (Mrs. John King); Ransom S., of Apalachin; Col. Uri B., of Fort Scott, who entered the army as a private before he was twenty-one years of age, and upon the close of the war was brevetted Brigadier-General; Mary, of Owego; and Charles W., of Syracuse. Ransom S. married Adaline, daughter of Clinton and

Ann Billings, and has four children, Grace L., William C., Anna L. and Emily.

Stephen Dexter, a civil engineer, was born in Cranston, R. I., May 16, 1792. He lived in Windham, Conn., but many years ago came by invitation to Ithaca, N. Y., to stake out lots and make a map of the village. In 1838 he removed to Owego, where he spent the remainder of his life. He was engaged on the survey for the Erie railroad, and among other works laid out Evergreen Cemetery, Owego. Early in life he married Deborah Thurston, of Exeter, R. I. Mr. Dexter died July 5, 1876.

Anthony D. Thompson, son of Henry, was born in Goshen, Orange county, N. Y., June 4, 1822, and came with his father's family when but three years of age, to the town of Owego. His father conducted a farm and a hotel at Campville for twelve or fifteen years, and then removed to this village and engaged in blacksmithing. With the exception of two years spent in Towanda, Pa., Anthony D. has since made Owego his home. For six years he was engaged with his father in the shop, but failing health compelled him to abandon his trade and he entered the stage office of the Owego Hotel, which stood on the site of the present Ah-wa-ga House. That position he resigned and removed to Towanda, and ran a line of stages for three years between Towanda and Waverly, and at the same time conducted a livery stable at each of those places. Selling his interests there, he engaged in the service of the Erie railroad in 1850, and has continued with them until this time, covering a period of thirty-seven years. His first wife was Sabrina, daughter of Chauncey Hill, by whom he had five children, namely: Clarence A., of the Owego National Bank, Charles S., deceased, A. Lizzie, wife of Walter Curtis, Sadie and Harry G. Mrs. Thompson died January 14, 1873.

Dr. Elias W. Seymour, son of William, who was a cousin of the late Governor Seymour, was born in Windsor, N. Y., February 7, 1823. When he was eight years old his parents removed to Binghamton, his father having been elected a representative in congress from that district. He was subsequently appointed judge of Broome county, which office he filled for several years with ability, and which he held at the time of his death, in 1849. The Doctor came to Owego when eighteen years of age. In 1850, he married Louisa L., daughter of John Dodd. He commenced the study of medicine in 1866, attending lectures in Philadelphia, Pa., and in 1870, entered upon the practice of his profession.

In 1866, he was elected master of Friendship lodge, F. & A. M., and again in 1870, serving, both terms, with great satisfaction. He died June 26, 1881.

Luman Wood, son of David Wood, came from Duchess county, in 1839, and located in Tompkins county, where he remained three years, when he came to this town where he resided until his death, in 1872. He married Catharine, daughter of Nathan Bullard, by whom he had seven children, George H., Enos V., a member of the New York city police force, Harriet (Mrs. Joseph Nichols), Franklin T., Nathan D., Emma, wife of Frank Bullard, and Edward B.

Jacob Bunzy came from Knox, Albany county, N. Y., many years ago, and located in Broome county, and afterward removed to the town of Owego and located at Gaskill's Corners. He married Sophia, daughter of John O'Brian by whom he had eight children, viz : John, Mary (Mrs. John A. Kens), Charles, George, Emma (Mrs. Charles Card), Nelson, Alice (Mrs. William Crum) and Lill (Mrs. Job Williams). Charles, married Lizzie, daughter of Artemas Walters, and has two children, Susie and Archie.

Samuel Hauver came from Lee, Mass., in 1848, and located near Smithboro where he engaged in farming. He married Lois Buttles of Lee, by whom he had six children, viz.: Margaret, Charles, of Elmira, E. Jane, Lucy, George, of Nichols, and Frank, of Owego. Mr. Hauver died October 30, 1874. Margaret married Robert Snell, by whom she has one son, Samuel B. Charles married Martha Smith and has five children. E. Jane married Nelson Codner, and has eight children. Lucy married Charles Prince of Orwell, Pa., and has one son. George married Clara, daughter of George Seager, January 1, 1881, by whom he had one child, Delmer G., born June 30, 1884, who died August 22, 1884. Frank married Mary, daughter of James S. Maine, of Windham, Pa., and has one child, F. Earl, born July 13, 1886.

Jesse Thomas came from Chester, Mass., to the town of Nichols in 1824, and purchased the farm on which Horace Lounsberry now resides. In 1854 he disposed of that property and bought a farm near the large island on the south side of the river where R. A. Barnes now resides. He married Jemima, daughter of Joseph Clark, of Windsor, Conn. His son, Charles C. Thomas, learned the printing business and worked at it until 1844, when he engaged in mercantile business in Westfield, Mass., where he continued nine years. He then returned to Owego and establised a book and newspaper business on the site now occupied by

Coburn & Strait. He afterward engaged in the boot and shoe business with Isaac Hall. He married Sylvinea Wentz, of Binghamton, February 28, 1843, by whom he has two children, Charles F., now chief clerk of the R. G. Dunn Commercial Agency at Detroit, and Emma A.

Levi Slater came from Connecticut to Delaware county, where he engaged in teaching. General Cantine, who owned a military tract in the northern part of this county and in Tompkins county, which was then a part of Tioga county, induced Mr. Slater, by the offer of a grant of land, to migrate to that section. From him Slaterville takes its name. David, son of Levi, came to Owego village, some thirty years since, and engaged in teaching and in surveying. For twelve years he was street commissioner of the village of Owego. He married Phœbe, daughter of Lewis Howes, of Putnam county. Four children were born to them, namely, Frank B., Sarah A., who married LeRoy A. James, and who died in 1870, Dorus M., now of Elmira, and Miles O., now of New York city. David Slater died in his eighty-second year. Frank B. married Gertrude Connor, of New York city, May 30, 1871.

J. B. G. Babcock came from Pennsylvania to Owego, and during the years of the war was prominent in business here, being engaged in the wool business with D. M. Pitcher. He married Lovisa Douglass, by whom he had seven children, viz.: Annie, Lottie, Emily, Mattie, Joseph, Zachary T., and John B. G. The latter married Emma J., daughter of J. Parker Vose, by whom he has one child, Georgiana.

Charles M. Haywood was born at Ludlow, Vt., August 16, 1833, and passed his early life on a farm. At the age of sixteen he began the trade of marble and granite finishing. In 1856, at Littleton, N. H., he first embarked in business for himself, and in 1860 he came to Owego, where he has since resided. Mr. Haywood's business success encouraged him to build, in 1875, upon the east side of North avenue, one of the best brick blocks in the village, where he is extensively engaged in the marble and granite business, having also a branch business at Waverly. His residence, on the corner of Temple and Liberty streets, is attractive and imposing. While Mr. Haywood has never been a politician, in the common acceptation of the term, he has long possessed much local influence in the Republican party, and has often been called to positions of trust and responsibility, the discharge of the varied duties of which has invariably been characterized by ability, fidelity and integrity. It is characteristic of Mr. Haywood that he is never idle, and never in a hurry, but steadily pursues whatever work he may have in hand,—that he is upright, honorable, unobtrusive, generous, public-spirited, self-sacrificing, and a most estimable and respected citizen.

The following are some of the positions he is holding at the present time: supervisor of the village, and ex-officio chairman of the board of supervisor of the county; treasurer of the State Grand Lodge of Knights of Honor, since 1875; representative to the Supreme Lodge of Profection, for six years past; treasurer of the Owego Mutual Benefit Association, since its organization; treasurer of Tioga Lodge, No. 335, I. O. O. F., for many years; treasurer and trustee of the First M. E. Church of Owego, and member since 1852; presiding officer of Owego Chapter, No. 510, R. A. M., having taken all the degrees in masonry, including the 95th; director of the Masonic Relief Association, of Elmira, for seventeen years; and president of the Owego District Camp Meeting Association during the past fifteen years. The following are some of the positions Mr. Haywood has heretofore occupied: Supervisor of the town of Owego in the year 1877; supervisor of Owego village in 1844–5; village trustee of the Third ward in 1871; president of Owego village in 1872, being re-elected for the three succeeding years without opposition; chief of the Owego fire department in 1876, and a delegate to the National Board, at Philadelphia; a charter member of the Supreme Lodge, Knights of Honor, and a representative to that body in 1875–76, 77 and 78, being now a Past Grand Director of this state; and charter member of the State Grand Lodge, Knights and Ladies of Honor, and its grand protector in 1880–81. Being, in 1883, a leading spirit in building a steamboat, and fitting up Hiawatha Island, he was president of the Owego Steamboat Company during the first two years of its existence. He was one of the principal movers in causing to be erected, in 1885, the Tioga county insane asylum. Mr. Haywood married Hannah Kneeland, of Proctorsville, Vt., in 1854.

James N. Hill, son of Chauncey and Lucy (Sexton) Hill, was born in the town of Tioga, December 14, 1816. His early education was received in the public schools, and at an early age he was apprenticed to the carpenter and joiners trade. He married Harriet Emily, daughter of Edward S. and Lydia (Curry) Madan, April 4, 1839. Their children were Sarah E., Lydia L., Charles O., and Ida E. (Mrs. G. A. Morton). For many years Mr. Hill

C. M. HAYWOOD.

was prominently engaged in business in Owego, as a manufacturer and as a contractor and builder. Mr. Hill died January 5, 1887. Sarah E. married A. H. Keeler, June 17, 1858, and has three children,—James B., Minnie, and Julia A. Minnie married J. A. Mabee, and has one child, John A., born August 20, 1879. Lydia L. married Ernest de Valliere, in April, 1864, and has five children, Lena, Nina, Herman, Louie, and Allie. Edward S. Madan, father of Mrs. Hill, and son of Thomas D. and Charity (Odell) Madan, or de Madan, as the name formerly was written, was born in Sing Sing, N. Y., in 1786. His father was a soldier of the revolutionary war, and a French Virginian by birth. Edward lived in New York city during his early years, and there learned the cabinet-maker's trade. He married, September 20, 1810, Lydia, daughter of Benjamin Curry, of Florida, Orange county, N. Y. Eight children were born to them, as follows: Anna Eliza, January 6, 1812 ; Sarah J., May 9, 1814 ; Mary L., February 27, 1816; Harriet E., September 2, 1819 ; Caroline A., October 29, 1821 ; Andrew, April 15, 1824; Frances M., April 30, 1827; and Benjamin C., April 24, 1829. Mr. Madan and four brothers served in the war of 1812. In 1822 he removed to Newark Valley, where he remained only two years, when he came to Owego, where he engaged as contractor and builder. He was a member of the order of Free Masons, for sixty-two years, and both he and Mrs. Madan were, for many years, members of the First Presbyterian church of Owego. In politics he was a Democrat of the Jacksonian school. His life, from 1824, was spent in Owego. He died October 11, 1868. Andrew Madan married first, Phœbe Sears, April 4, 1857. His present wife is Sarah Searls, whom he married January 16, 1877.

Harry Jewett was born in Putnam county, N. Y., October 22, 1813. He came to Tioga county in the winter of 1816–17, with his parents, who located at Apalachin. In 1858, Mr. Jewett came to Owego village. In 1864 he began the grocery business on Front street, continuing the same till 1876. In 1860, he was elected justice of the peace, resigned in 1865, was again elected in 1876, and held the office till 1883. In 1884, he was appointed assessor, and held the office till 1887. Mr. Jewett married Loraine Goodsell, September 11, 1837, who died November 18, 1865. He again married, Esther Finley, June 17, 1867. He has three children, Emily (Mrs. T. E. Royall), Henry L., of Brooklyn, and Frederick G., of Cambridge, Ohio.

Laban M. Jenks was born at Jenksville, in Berkshire, February 28, 1810, where he resided all his life, dying August 28, 1865. He married, November 17, 1836, Eliza J. Armstrong. Their children were Mary E., born January 26, 1837; Byron J., September 25, 1842; Robert B., a physician of Elmira, born March 17, 1845, and William W., a lawyer of New York city, born October 22, 1850.

Caleb J. Chaffee was born in Providence, R. I., February 11, 1814. In 1832, he removed with his parents to Warren, Pa., and in the spring of 1835, he came to Owego and engaged in the lumber business, and has resided here since. Mr. Chaffee married Angeline N. Bowen, who has borne him four children, only one of whom, Elizabeth (Mrs. George H. Pratt), of Cincinnati, Ohio, is living.

Benjamin W. Brownell, who resides near Flemingville, has lived upon the farm he now occupies since 1826. He was born at Foster, R. I., September 21, 1813, and came here with his father, Gideon, in 1826. Gideon purchased what is known as the Furguson farm, named from William Furguson, the first settler thereon. Mr. Furguson sold to John Parmenter, he to John Lincoln, and he in turn to Mr. Brownell. The latter died in 1828. Benjamin married Sarah C. Tucker, of Vestal, N. Y., who bore him ten children, and died in 1885. The children now living are, John C., Sarah C., Julia (Mrs. Elliot Barrett), Charles, George and Emma (Mrs. Luther Harris).

Edmund Wood, from Middleboro, Mass., came to Owego in 1817, locating upon the farm now occupied by his son Royal P. Mr. Wood married Laura A. Dean, February 14, 1833, who bore him three children, Royal P., born April 6, 1834; Eliza D., born March 27, 1836, and Tillson, born June 23, 1838. Mr. Wood died May 28, 1877. Of the children, Royal P. and Eliza (Mrs. E. D. Brink) are now living. Royal, who occupies the homestead, married Sarah E. Keeler, December 2, 1858, and has four children.

Elizur Talcott was a direct descendant of John Talcott, who came from England in 1632 and settled in Newton, Mass. He came to Owego, with his family in 1802. He married Dorothy Lord and reared several children, among whom was Elizur, Jr. The latter was born February 1, 1780, married a Miss Bliss and had born to him five children. Of these, Joel, born March 20, 1807, married Eunice Benton, September 5, 1830, and reared two children, George B. and Charles, both of whom now reside on on road 40. The former married Margaret Mason, December 25, 1868, and the latter Sarah Van Atta, January 1, 1865.

Edward P. Herrick was born February 24, 1808, and has lived in Tioga county all his life. He has been twice married, and has four children, Perlee, of Newark, Charlotte M. (Mrs. George Lake), Jennie (Mrs. John C. Brownell), and Edward W., of Binghamton, N. Y.,

Simeon L. Barrett was born in Kent, N. Y., March 13, 1810, and came to Tioga county in 1836, locating in Candor till 1875, when he removed to Flemingville, where he now resides. Mr. Barrett married Margaret Hover, in 1845, and has ten children now living—Jemima (Mrs. Franklin Cortwright), Minerva (Mrs. John W. Taylor), Elliott, Vanness, Monroe, Eugene, Adelia (Mrs. Charles E. Wood), Edith (Mrs. Frederick Smith). Ida (Mrs. Edwin Rowe), and John F.

Amzi Stedman was born in Connecticut in 1783, and came to Tioga county with his sister's family, Mrs. Polly Pritchard, in 1790, and settled upon the farm now owned by Asa Pritchard. He married Anna Canfield, who bore him thirteen children, three of whom,—Amos C., Rachel (Mrs. Rachel Cogswell), and Lyman T., are living. The latter still occupies the old homestead farm. He married Polly Joslyn, September 15, 1846, and has one child, Wheeler, who is in business at Flemingville.

Isaac Whittemore, the first settler in the Whittemore Hill neighborhood, was born in Vermont, in 1798, and located on the old homestead about 1830. He married Jane Ditmorse, and reared twelve children, of whom seven are now living, viz.: Mary A. (Mrs. Daniel Cornell), Isaac V., Alvin, Virgil, Alonzo W., Egbert, and Harriet (Mrs. Fred Rounds).

BUSINESS CENTERS.

OWEGO VILLAGE.—In his centennial history, entitled, "Tioga County from 1784 to 1776," William F. Warner describes the situation of Owego village as follows:

"It is situated at the confluence of Owego creek and the Susquehanna river. The corporate limits of the village are, on their south and west lines, about one and a half miles in extent; the north and east lines are of less extent. To the north of the village, and about half a mile from the river, there is a bold 'headland' that rises to the height of four or five hundred feet, jutting into the valley, its slopes facing the south and west, upon the latter of which is situated Evergreen Cemetery. This headland forms the northern and northeastern boundaries of the village. The river, flowing from the east, makes a beautiful curve at the eastern border of the village. By a road along the south face of the headland, as well as by the road to the cemetery, easy access is had to the top; and standing upon this bold elevation, there is to be had a view extending for miles up and down the river, and over the valley extending northward, of remarkable beauty and diversity."

Early Settlers of the Village.—In 1791, there were but six families residing on the site of the present village of Owego. Seven years later, by an assessment made by Guy Maxwell, of New Town (Elmira), dated October 1, 1798, it is shown that there were at that time, nineteen houses in the village, most of which were built of logs. Land was then worth only from three to eight dollars per acre.

Many of the early settlers were revolutionary soldiers. One of them was Emmanuel Deuel, who settled in the northern part of the village, in 1790. The same year Captain Lemuel Brown came from Berkshire county, Mass., and erected the first tannery in the village. Mason Webster settled here, in 1791. He came from Lenox, Mass. He died December 26, 1854. Dr. Samuel Tinkham, the first practicing physician, came in 1792, and Capt. Mason Wattles, the first merchant, the same year. Dr. Elisha Ely came, in 1798, and Stephen Mack, in 1799. Ephraim Wood also came in the latter year, from Rutland, Vt. He died February 8, 1855.

Elizur Talcott, and his sons, George L., and Elizur Talcott, Jr., removed, in 1802, from Glastonbury, Conn., to Elmira, where they were employed in building a dwelling house. The next year they came to Owego and settled in the northwestern part of the village. The former died November 28, 1831; the second, November 30, 1873, aged ninety years, and the latter, January 28, 1867.

Prominent among the early settlers was Captain Luke Bates. He was the first white settler between Union and Campville. At an early day he purchased of James McMaster, various tracts of land in the town of Owego, and became owner of much of the land on which the village was subsequently built. In 1795 he built the first tavern in Owego village. It occupied a portion of the ground where the Ah-wa-ga House now stands, and was destroyed by fire in 1829. Captain Bates was an old sea captain. He died in 1813, near the Little Nanticoke creek, where he conducted a distillery.

James Hill

Owego as an Early Business Point.—Owego was the earliest settlement in this part of the state of New York, and, owing to its situation, became an important business point. The early settlers engaged in lumbering and shipping their product down the Susquehanna river in rafts, to a market. In 1808, the Owego and Ithaca turnpike was opened to travel. Then Owego became the outlet to a large section of the country. All the flour, grain, salt, plaster, etc., for the southern and eastern market, was brought down Cayuga lake by boat to Ithaca, and then to Owego by teams. The traffic was so great that from five hundred to eight hundred loaded wagons usually passed over the turnpike in a single day. From here it was sent in arks down the river. The cost of transporting a barrel of salt or flour from Ithaca to Baltimore, was one dollar and seventy-five cents. An ark cost seventy-five dollars, and would carry two hundred and fifty barrels. The trip from Owego to Baltimore occupied from eight to twelve days. At Baltimore the lumber in an ark would sell for about forty dollars.

The transportation business was so great that, in the summer of 1825, three steamboats were built, as an experiment. The *Cadorus* was built at Lock Haven, Pa., and was run up to Owego the next year. After an absence of four months, the captain returned and reported that the navigation of the river was entirely impracticable. The second boat, the *Susquehanna*, was built at Baltimore. She was destroyed by the explosion of her boiler at Nescopeck Falls, while ascending the river, May 5, 1826, and several of her passengers were killed. The third boat, the *Pioneer*, was run as an experiment on the West Branch of the Susquehanna river, and proved a failure. In 1835, another boat called the *Susquehanna*, was built in Owego, by Wilkesbarre and Owego capitalists. This boat made several trips up and down the river, but proved useless for the purpose intended.

The business of transporting merchandise from Ithaca to Owego attained such great proportions that, in 1828, a number of capitalists, residing in Ithaca and Owego, chief among whom was James Pumpelly, obtained a charter from the legislature to build a railroad between the two villages. This was the second railroad chartered in the state of New York, and it was opened to the public in April, 1834. It entered the village at the north and extended down through the village park, and up Front street. The cars were run by a switch under the stores. on the river's bank, where their contents were readily unloaded into arks.

In the fall of 1849, the New York and Erie railroad was completed to Owego, and all traffic by river, with the exception of lumber, potatoes, etc., ceased.

In the morning of September 27, 1849, a fire destroyed all except three of the stores on Front and Lake streets. One hundred and four buildings, exclusive of barns, were burned, entailing a loss of about $300,000. Nearly all the buildings were of wood. This great calamity checked, but did not permanently impair the prosperity of the village. The business men, without delay, caused the erection of the present substantial brick blocks in the place, and progress was thereafter continuous.

The centre of trade at the time of the early settlement of the village of Owego was that portion of Front street, nearest to Church street. Where the Ahwaga House now stands, Capt. Luke Bates built a tavern (in a portion of which was a store) as early as 1795. Eight years afterward, Charles Pumpelly bought the property.

The first merchant in Owego was Mason Wattles, who came here in 1792. Bates and Wattles bought land of James McMaster, and were owners of many of the lots which are now the most valuable in the village. The merchants doing business in Owego previous to 1810 were Mason Wattles, Thomas Duane, William and Nathan Camp, Gen. John Laning, Maj. Horatio Ross, John Hollenback, Charles Pumpelly, Gen. Oliver Huntington, and Gen. Anson Camp.

Owego to-day, has a population of about 6,000 people, and contains one agricultural works, three foundries and machine shops, one piano manufactory, one boot and shoe manufactory, one harness manufactory, one brewery, one marble works, two bottling works, one coffin manufactory, two carriage manufactories, three planing mills, two flouring mills, one saw mill, two soap manufactories, seventeen groceries, eleven dry and fancy goods, and variety stores, five millinery stores, four clothing stores, three hat stores, five boot and shoe stores, five drug stores, two furniture stores, three fruit stores, three book and news stores, three bakeries, four hardware stores, three livery stables, two laundries, four cigar manufactories, three coal yards, ten hotels, thirteen saloons, five liquor stores, thirteen physicians, five dentists, eighteen lawyers, six churches, four insurance offices, five barber shops, three banks, four newspapers, four job printing offices, three jewelry stores, four telegraph offices, one telephone office, three photograph galleries, three railroad depots, two express offices, four meat markets, one tea store, one milk depot, one sewing machine store, two musical instrument stores, three harness shops, one fishing-tacle store, one cooper's shop, one silver spoon manufactory, two public halls, and various tailor, blacksmith and other shops.

Village Improvements.—Soon after the coming of the first white people, the settlement was regularly surveyed and laid out as a village. The survey was made by Amaziah Hutchinson, in 1788 and 1789, and completed by David Pixley, Jr., in 1789 and 1790. The village territory comprised all of lot No. 23 in the original survey of McMaster's Half Township, and was known as the " Town Plot." It was bounded on the south by the Susquehanna river. The western boundary line ran from a point on the river bank near where Mr. Lovejoy's residence stands on Front street, north, diagonally across the village park, to near the corner of Church and Temple streets, continuing thence in a straight line past the corner of Fox street and Spencer avenue to a point about where the gate to Evergreen Cemetery now is. The north line ran from the latter point to Main street, a little west of the N. Y., L. E. & W. railroad. The east line extended from the latter point south past the corner of Ross and Front streets to the river.

The first highway through Owego was regularly laid out November 7, 1791, by Amos Draper, William Bates, and William Whitney, the first commissioners of highways of the town of Union. It commenced at the fording place in the Owego creek, near where Main street now crosses the creek and extended east on the present course of the street to the Kiuga (Cayuga) road, now McMaster street, and down to Front street, then known as the " Main river road." Thence the highway followed the present course of Front street east out of and beyond the present limits of the village. At the same time the Cayuga road was regularly laid out as a public highway, extending from " Robert McMaster's landing " at the foot of the street now known as Academy street, to near John Nealey's home on the Owego creek.

On Hutchinson's map there were two streets running east and west which were identical with the present Main and Front streets, but much narrower than at present. There was a road where Lake street now is and it extended in a direct line from the river out of the village. A lane extended from the river north along the west line of the old Avery property north to where Temple street now runs. Another lane extended north from the river where Paige street now is, to Temple street. Another lane was extended from Main street north, along the line of W. L. Hoskins's residence to a point about where East Temple street now runs. These were all the streets in the village at that time.

Village Incorporation.—The village of Owego was incorporated by an act of the legislature, dated April 4, 1827. The population of the town of Owego, at that time was about 3,000 and of the village 750. The first election was held in June, 1827, at the court-house. The first trustees elected were James Pumpelly, Eleazer Dana, Harmon Pumpelly, William A. Ely, and Jonathan Platt, Jr. The board organized by choosing Mr. Pumpelly president of the village, and Ezra S. Sweet, clerk. In 1854, an amendment to tne charter provided for the division of the village into five wards, and the election of the president by the people direct. William F. Warner was the first president elected under the amendment, in 1855.

The charter of 1827 provided that the village limits should confine all that part of the town of Owego then included within the jail limits of the eastern jury district, or as such jail limits should be established at the Court of Common Pleas at its next session, in the following May, and should contain not to exceed three hundred acres of land. The territory under this charter comprised all the land bounded south by the river, north by Temple street, west by William street, and east by Ross street. The village boundaries were again enlarged by act of the Legislature, April 9, 1851, and were subsequently enlarged by acts dated April 15, 1854, April 15, 1857, and April 3, 1872.

Village Park.—On the 28th of February, 1797, James McMaster sold to the people of the settlement of Owego, for the sum of ten pounds sterling, a little more than three acres of land for a village park. The piece comprised all the ground now occupied by the village park and Court street, and the land on which the county jail, the old county clerk's office, and the old academy building stand. To hold this land, McMaster, in the deed conveying it, named Capt. Mason Wattles, John McQuigg, and Capt. Luke Bates as "Trustees of Owego Settlement." On the 4th of September, 1813, Eleazer Dana and John H. Avery, were chosen to succeed Bates and McQuigg, who had died a short time previous. Gen. Anson Camp was chosen to succeed Captain Wattles upon the latter's removal from Owego soon afterward, and Messrs. Dana, Avery, and Camp continued to act as trustees until the incorporation of the village, in 1827. That portion of the park occupied by the jail and old clerk's office was sold by the trustees to the supervisors of Tioga county, October 29, 1822. The old academy lot was sold to the trustees of the Owego academy, April 8, 1828.

First Village School.—The first school in Owego was taught by a man named Quincy. And I here make correction of a blunder, founded in misinformation and made permanent through the gross stupidity of a superanuated and incompetent manufacturer of catch-penny history.

French's "Gazetteer of the State of New York" is remarkable particularly for its many blunders. Among others, in a foot note on page 652 (edition of 1860), it says that "the first school was taught by —— Kelly, in 1792."

In 1872, one Hamilton Child published a "Gazetteer and Business Directory of Broome and Tioga Counties," in which the blunder of French's Gazetteer was reproduced, Mr. Child, as a matter of course, repeating the statement that "—— Kelly" was the first teacher.

In 1879, what purports to be a "History of Tioga, Chemung, Tompkins, and Schuyler Counties," was printed in Philadelphia. In compiling this remarkable aggregation of blunders, a genial and fossiliferous old gentleman named Dr. Everhart, was sent here to write the history of Owego. He soon accumulated a vast fund of rich and varied misinformation. The writer of this sketch, in casual conversation, incidentally informed Dr. Everhart that Quincy was the first school teacher and that if he would go to Mrs John Carmichael (at that time the oldest living resident of the village, and the only survivor of Quincy's pupils), he could learn all the particulars he might desire. He did so. A few days afterward he came to the writer, in high glee, saying that in looking over some papers in the old Pumpelly land office he had come across the name, "John Kelly," and that as there were few settlers here at that early period he was sure that he had discovered the full name of the teacher. So, assuming that Mrs. Carmichael was mistaken in regard to the teacher's name, the statement that John Kelly was the first teacher went into the "History," and Mrs. Carmichael was quoted as authority. The truth is, that John Kelly was not a school teacher at all, but a farmer, who lived in the neighborhood ot Campville, six miles distant from Owego. His name will be found among those ordered to do highway duty, in 1791.

Quincy taught school in the small log house, which stood on

the east side of Court street, where the old Academy building
now stands. He had a scar on his face, which disfigured him
badly. It was said that he had been disappointed in love, and had
shot himself in the mouth in an attempt to commit suicide, the
ball breaking the jaw and causing his mouth to be twisted to one
side.

At a late period there was an old log school-house on the south
side of Main street, a little west of where St. Paul's Episcopal
church now stands. This was torn down and a frame building
erected in its place. The latter was two stories high, and the
second floor was occupied as a lodge room by the Masonic fraternity. Isaac Lillie and Erastus Evans were at different periods teachers of the school. The latter was the teacher when the
building caught fire, one day, in the summer of 1835, while
school was in session, and burned to the ground.

The question of building an academy in Owego, was agitated
as early as 1817. Nine years later, by act of the legislature,
James Pumpelly, William Camp and John H. Avery were appointed commissioners to sell the "gospel lot" and apply the
proceeds to such school purposes as should be directed by a vote
of the inhabitants of the town. On the 19th of December, 1826,
at a special town meeting, it was unanimously voted to appropriate the yearly income of the interest arising from the sale of the
"gospel lot" to the endowment of an academy. On the 8th of
April, 1828, the trustees of Owego Settlement, deeded the old
academy lot, on Court street, to the trustees of the Owego Academy. The academy was built in 1827, on a contract, by Col.
Amos Martin, and Abner Beers had charge of its construction.

James Pumpelly was president of the first board of trustees
of the academy, which was composed of Rev. Aaron Putnam,
Col. Amos Martin, Dr. Joel S. Paige, Latham A. Burrows, Eleazer Dana, Gurdon Hewitt, Rev. Joseph Castle, Charles Pumpelly, Jonathan Platt, Anson Camp, and Stephen B. Leonard.
Rev. Edward Fairchild was the first principal of the academy.
Sixty male, and sixty-one female pupils attended the first term.

The several school districts in the village were consolidated
by act of the legislature, dated April 23, 1864, and the academy
was merged into the "Union Schools of the Village of Owego,"
as a free school, under control of a board of school commissioners, elected by a vote of the people.

The present academy, at the southwest corner of Main and
Academy streets, was built in 1883, at a cost of $25,000.

First Mills—The first saw-mill in Owego was built by James McMaster and Amos Draper some time previous to the year 1791. It stood on the east side of the Owego creek, a little above the present Main street bridge. The first flouring-mill was built by Col. David Pixley, in 1793. It stood on the west side of the Owego creek, in the town of Tioga, opposite the Indian spring. Colonel Pixley was one of the earliest settlers of the present town of Tioga. He was one of the proprietors of the Boston Purchase, and came from Stockbridge, Mass , in 1791, at the age of fifty-one years. He was a colonel in the Colonial army, and fought in the battle of Quebec, under General Montgomery. He was treasurer of Tioga county from 1798 to 1803. Some time previous to the year 1800, he removed to Owego village. He owned a large tract of land on the west side of the Owego creek, which he sold to Eliakim and Judge Noah Goodrich, Jr., in 1802. He died in Owego, August 25, 1807.

Of the present mills and manufactories of the village, that of Gere, Truman, Platt & Co., is the most extensive. This factory, known as the "Drill Works," is conducted in the old Bristol Iron Works property, and the business is the continuation of that established by George W. Bristol and others, in 1866. The present firm employs a large force of men in the manufacture of "Champion" farm wagons, grain and fertilizer drills, harrows, etc.

Dorwin, Rich & Stone, at Canawana, are extensively engaged in the manufacture of flour.

Shaw & Dean, whose mills are located on Central avenue, are also extensive merchant millers.

Sporer, Carlson & Berry, on North avenue, are well-known manufacturers of pianos, and dealers in musical merchandise. This business was started in May, 1857, by E. Hosford, dealer in pianos. In the fall of 1861, a firm was organized, consisting of H. Norton, F. Sporer, and O. M. Carlson. They subsequently associated with them Mr. J. Berry, and again the firm became as it exists at present. In 1867, they were burned out, but started again in 1868.

Moore & Ross, extensively engaged in the manufacture of carriages, wagons, and sleighs, began business here April 1, 1859.

The Owego Cruciform Casket Company conducts a large business in the manufacture of burial caskets.

Arba Campbell, extensively engaged in tanning sheep skins, built his tannery here in 1871, and began business under the firm

26*

name of A. Campbell & Co., January 1, 1872. The tannery has
twenty-four vats, and the capacity for turning out five hundred
sheep skins per day, and employs about eighteen hands.

H. N. Dean & Son's tannery had its beginning in a small way,
many years ago, when Elihu Parmenter built a small tannery in
connection with his shoeshop, on the opposite side of the street
from the present site. He increased its capacity from time to
time, and moved the tannery to the site now occupied. In 1860
he disposed of the property to Alanson P. Dean, of Berkshire
county, Mass., who in turn increased the capacity. His brother,
H. Nelson Dean, became interested with him, and finally, with his
son, Ransom B., bought the whole property. H. Nelson died in
August, 1872, and the whole property reverted to Ransom B. and
his brother, Isaac N. The latter soon after disposed of his interest
to Ransom, who still owns the tannery, retaining the firm title of
H. N. Dean & Son. The tannery has sixty double vats, ten
liquor vats, seven lime vats, five "soaks," three "baits," and two
"pools," making in all, eighty-seven vats; gives employment to
twenty-five men, and turns out about 25,000 sides per year, principally of card and russet leather, using about a thousand cords
of bark. Albert H. Upton is superintendent.

L. & G. Brown's apiarist's supply manufactory, located off
North avenue, was established by them in 1881, where they manufacture hives, boxes, foundations, &c. The factory is run by
a six horse-power engine.

Alexander J. Thomas's green-houses, on Main street, were
erected by him in 1885. He has several hundred square feet
under glass, and does a large business in cut flowers and plants.

Banks.—The First National Bank of Tioga, located on Front
street, was organized January 6, 1865, to supercede the old Bank
of Owego, a state institution, organized with $200,000.00 capital.
The First National Bank's capital is $100,000.00. The charter
was renewed in 1885, for twenty years. The first officers were
Lyman Truman, president; John B. Brush, cashier. The present officers are George Truman, president; Arba Campbell,
vice-president; William S. Truman, cashier; Francis E. Brockway, teller.

The Tioga National Bank, located on Front street, was organized in January, and began business April 1, 1865, with a capital of
$100,000.00. In January, 1865, the charter was renewed for
twenty years. The first officers were T. C. Platt, president;
W. S. Lincoln, vice-president; F. E. Platt, cashier. The present

officers are T. C. Platt, president; L. B. West, vice-president; F. E. Platt, cashier; E. W. Stone, assistant-cashier.

The Owego National Bank, located on Lake street, was organized May 10, 1883, with a cash capital of $50,000.00. On May 29th the first meeting of stock-holders was held, when the following officers were elected, G. B. Goodrich, president; C. E. Parker, vice-president; A. J. Kenyon, 2d vice-president; Clarence A. Thompson, cashier. On August 6th the bank was opened for business. The present officers are Charles E. Parker, president; R. B. Dean and A. J. Kenyon, vice-presidents; C A. Thompson, cashier; and James A. Bassett, teller. The capital has not been changed since organization, and the bank has a surplus fund of $7,000.00.

Physicians.—Dr. John Frank was born in Virgil, Cortland county, N. Y., September 3, 1797. He received his early education there, studied medicine, and for nine years was a practitioner in that place. He received diplomas from the Eclectic Medical Colleges of Albany and Syracuse. He came to Owego in 1837, where he has been in active practice ever since. He married Sally, daughter of Jacob Price, of Virgil, by whom he had two daughters, viz.: Catherine and Diantha, both deceased. Catherine married Albert Thomas, by whom she had one child, Kate, wife of Joseph B. Ball, of Cleveland, O. Diantha married Isaac Hall, and had one child, Emma, wife of S. B. Wellington, of New York city. Although in his ninetieth year, the Doctor still has a large and successful practice.

Dr. John T. Greenleaf was born in Owego, January 26, 1847, and received his education in the schools of this place. He graduated from the New York Homeopathic Medical College in 1867. After six months spent in Candor, he removed to Owego, where he has since continued to practice. He has been three times married, his present wife being Hattie, daughter of P. W. Meeker, of this village.

Dr. Warren L. Ayer was born at Little Meadows, Pa., June 6, 1843, a son of Isaac and Mary A. (Thurber) Ayer. He studied in the district schools, and when ten years of age his parents moved to Apalachin, and he there studied in the private school taught by John E. Barnaby, and subsequently by A. N. Alvord, preparing for college, expecting to enter during the autumn of 1862; but instead he enlisted in Co. H, 109th N. Y. Vols., remaining in this regiment till July, 1864, when he was commissioned captain of Co. G, 127th U. S. C. Vols., and was finally mustered out in December, 1865. Immediately on his return, the Doctor began the study of medicine with Dr. E. Daniels, of Owego, and graduated from the Long Island College Hospital, in June, 1868, served a year in the Hartford City Hospital, became assistant to Dr. John G. Orton, of Binghamton, for three years, and in June, 1872, began practice in Owego, where he has since resided. Doctor Ayer married Sarah A. Dwight, of Binghamton, December 21, 1871, and has three children, daughters.

Dr. Merritt T. Dutcher was born in Somerset, Niagara county, N. Y., December 17, 1843. He was educated in the graded schools of his native village, and on September 6, 1862, enlisted in Co. K, 151st Regt., N. Y. Vols., Infantry. He served until June 1, 1865, when he was mustered out. November 12, 1873, he married Mary Stoutenburg, of Duchess county, N. Y. The Doctor is a graduate of the New York Homeopathic Medical College.

Dr. C. R. Heaton is a native of Newark Valley, born in 1842. He graduated at Geneva Medical College, in 1864, and began practice at Newark Valley, and soon moved to Maine. He afterward returned to Newark Valley, and in 1876 permanently located in Owego. Doctor Heaton belongs to Friendship Lodge, No. 153, and is Past Master of Newark Valley Lodge, No 614, Past High Priest of New Jerusalem Chapter, No. 47. He has been a member of Malta Commandary, of Binghamton, for twenty-one years. Dr. Heaton is known as one deeply interested in the advancement of the place. He is treasurer of the Cruciform Casket Company, and director in the Owego National bank. He holds the position of medical director in the Owego Mutual Benefit Association, and that of director of the Mutual Relief Society of Rochester. He is a member of the County and State Medical Societies, and his professional and business duties make his life a very active one.

Dr. Charles L. Stiles was born in Sussex county, N. J., October 24, 1837; studied medicine with Dr. S. M. Hand, now of Norwich, N. Y., and graduated at the Geneva Medical College, in February, 1865, began practice at Gibson, Pa.; came to Owego in May, 1868, and has been in practice here since. Dr. Stiles married Marietta Archibald, May 18, 1864, and has three children, a son and two daughters.

Dr. A. F. Crans was born in Dwaar's Kill, Ulster county, N. Y., July 24, 1841. He received his education at the Middletown Academy, in Orange county, N. Y., and when fifteen years of age he removed with his parents to Candor, and subsequently to Owego. He studied medicine with Drs. Armstrong and Daniels, of Owego, attended the University of Michigan, at Ann Arbor, and subsequently the Eclectic College, of New York city, from which institution he graduated. He practiced for a short time in Halsey Valley, and at Carbondale, Pa., for seven years. From there he removed to New York, where he remained in practice six years, and in March, 1877, came to Owego, where he has since resided. He married Martha Embodee, by whom he has one child, Mattie.

Dr. Andrew T. Pearsall was born in Florence, Lauderdale county, Ala., April 22, 1839. When he was four years of age his father returned to Tioga county, which had previously been the home of the family, and the doctor received his education here, and at Hobert College, Geneva, N. Y. He entered the College of Physicians and Surgeons in New York city, from which institution he graduated in 1861. He was brigade surgeon in the Confederate service three years during the war; after which he settled in Montgomery, Ala., where he practiced medicine until 1876, when he returned to Owego, where he has since continued in practice.

Dr. James M. Barrett was born September 1, 1841, in Duchess county, N. Y. With his parents he moved to Tioga county, when nine years old. His mother died when he was twelve years old, at which time he left home to find one for himself. May 21, 1861, he enlisted in Company K., 26th N. Y. Vols., and served in the army of Virginia until his discharge, in December, 1862, on account of wounds received at the second battle of Bull Run, on August 30, 1862. He attended the Owego Academy for the four years following his discharge, then taught school until 1871, when he entered the medical department of the University of Michigan, from which he graduated, in the class of 1874. He practiced medicine, in Pennsylvania, for the first eight years after his graduation. In the fall of 1881 he moved to Owego, where he now resides. He held the office of U. S. Examining Surgeon for pensions, under President Arthur. He is now serving his second term as coroner of the county, and is secretary of the Tioga County Medical Society.

Dr. George B. Lewis was born at Apalachin, December 9, 1865, a son of Dr. Isaac W. and Ellen (Sutton) Lewis. He studied in the high school of his native village and at the Owego Academy, beginning the study of his profession with his father, and afterward attending lectures at the University of Vermont, graduating at the medical department of the University of the City of New York, in 1884, after which he was in Bellevue Hospital about a year and a half, and immediately began practice in Owego, where he has since been located.

FLEMINGVILLE is situated at the junction of the east and west branches of the Owego creek, five miles north of Owego, and derives its name from one of the early settlers, Captain David Fleming, who was also the first postmaster. Captain Fleming came from Newton, Sussex county, N. J., to the town of Nichols, in this county, in 1806, removing thence, two years afterward, to Flemingville. He served in the war of 1812 as captain in the third company of the third regiment, heavy artillery, and fought in the battles of Sackett's Harbor, Lake George, Erie, etc. He died at Flemingville, February 4, 1862, aged eighty-two years.

His son, General Robert L. Fleming, was seven years of age when the family settled at Flemingville. At the age of twelve he accompanied his father with the Federal army, as his waiter, and was a witness of the battles in which his father was engaged. After the war he organized a company of state militia, of which he was chosen captain. About the year 1835, he was elected, by a vote of the field officers, a brigadier-general, in command of the Ninth Brigade of New York State Artillery. In the war of the rebellion he assisted Colonel Kane in organizing his "Bucktail regiment," in Elk county, Pa. He was elected sheriff of Tioga county in 1840, and served four years. He died on the 26th of February, 1877.

The earliest settler of Flemingville was, probably, Asahel Pritchard. He was born in Connecticut, May 28, 1763. He came into the Wyoming valley with his step-father, and after the massacre, in July, 1778, he came to Nichols, in this county. Soon afterward he came to Flemingville, where he settled on the East Owego creek, and engaged in deer hunting. He bought the farm on which his grandson, Asa Pritchard, now resides, about a mile north of the Flemingville church, and paid for it in the game he shot, and without doing a day's work on his farm himself, he hired others to clear it, and paid them from the proceeds of his hunting. Soon after coming to Flemingville, he returned to Connecticut, where he married Polly Stedman, on the 22d day of August, 1790, returning at once, accompanied by his wife, who rode all the way on horseback. He died at Flemingville, September 24, 1840.

Mrs. Stedman's brother, Amzi Stedman, was born in Connecticut, January 14, 1783. He was seven years of age when his sister was married, and he accompanied her to Flemingville. He became the owner of the farm next above the Pritchard farm, on which his son, Lyman Stedman, now resides. He died at Flemingville, February 21, 1854.

Daniel Ferguson and Daniel Ferguson, Jr. came to Flemingville sometime previous to 1791. The elder Ferguson was a soldier in the revolutionary war. Judge Avery, in his "Susquehanna Valley" papers, (*St. Nicholas*, p. 361) says:

"During the early progress of the war, then a young man, he was taken captive upon the Delaware, by the Indians, and brought by them to the present site of the village of Owego, where he was detained as a captive through the winter, and for a larger proportion of the year. The Indian family by whom he had been adopted, and with whom he lived, occupied their bark lodge near where Paige street intersects River [Front] street. Upon his subsequent settlement in this town he was able to designate its precise locality, by its proximity to the Indian burial mound, near or upon the homestead premises of the late Eleazar Dana, Esq., which retained its peculiar shape long after the village was settled. The summer next after his capture, he accompanied his foster-father upon an expedition to the Delaware, and by an ingenious stratagem escaped in the night, and made his way to a white settlement at Port Jervis, in Orange county, where his friends resided previous to his capture. In relating the incidents of his captivity, he uniformly made mention of the considerate kindness, exhibited by the Indian family toward him at all times."

Jeremiah Brown and his son, Benjamin Brown, were early settlers near the present village of Union, Broome county, some time previous to 1791. They removed to Flemingville, in 1796. None of their descendants reside here, but Solomon Brown, a son of Benjamin, lives at Union.

Another early settler was Richard Searles, who was born in 1753, and who came from Bedford, Mass., to Nichols, in 1791, removing thence to Flemingville, in 1795, where he built a sawmill. He died September 9, 1849.

Charles E. Truman, of Flemingville, was born in Candor, November 1, 1807, and located upon the farm now owned by his son, Charles F., in 1816. He married Harriet Webster, May 26, 1836, who has borne him nine children, all of whom are living, and in 1886 they celebrated their golden wedding. The children are Aaron B., Adelaide (Mrs. Henry W. Blewer), Adeline (Mrs. Frank J. Blewer), Helen, Lyman B., Elias W., Charles F., Lucy

(Mrs. William Mead), Lydia (Mrs. Adelbert Hammond). Mr. Truman has held most of the minor town offices, has been a justice of the peace for the past twenty-four years, and postmaster about the same period.

APALACHIN is situated on the south side of the Susquehanna river, eight miles east of Owego village. It derives its name from the town of Apalacon, Susquehanna Co., Pa., where the Apalachin creek rises. Apalacon and Apalachin are, apparently, corruptions of the name Appallachian, the general appellation of the great mountain system, stretching from Maine to Alabama.

There was no village at Apalachin until about the year 1836, when William S. Pearsall came here from Chenango county. Ransom Steele came soon afterward from Owego, to open and manage a branch store for John Hollenback. He afterward engaged in the mercantile business on his own account, and was for many years also engaged in lumbering.

Four brothers, Nathaniel, Thomas, William S. and Gilbert Pearsall, came together to Tioga county, or at about the same time. They built saw-mills, and owned them in partnership, at Apalachin, Hooper's Valley, and Pea Island, near the Pennsylvania line, and also owned a large lumber yard near Baltimore. In the financial depression of 1837, they failed in business. Gilbert and William Pearsall obtained an extension of time, and afterward resumed business. The brothers at the same time dissolved their partnership and divided their property. About the year 1840, Gilbert and William Pearsall built grist-mills at Hooper's Valley and Apalachin, at a cost of from $5,000.00 to $6,000.00 each.

William S. Pearsall and Ransom Steele were the active business men of Apalachin, and were the chief stockholders of the bridge, which was built across the Susquehanna river at Apalachin, in 1849, at a cost of $75,000.00, and which was afterward carried away by a freshet.

The earliest settler of Apalachin was Isaac Harris, a Quaker, who came, in 1786, from Providence, R. I. The next year he returned, and removed his wife (*nee* Nancy Reed, whom he married in 1786), and household goods, coming down the river from Cooperstown in a rough boat, which he built for that purpose. Mr. Harris and a partner had made a contract for the purchase of the land known as Coxe's Patent, paying part down. His partner started for Philadelphia to pay the balance, and was never heard from afterward. Mr. Harris settled on the Apalachin creek, on the river road, on what has since been known as the Glann farm and the Pardon Yates farm. The first white child born at Apalachin was their daughter, Phebe, who married Willard Thayer, and settled on the Holland Purchase. Isaac Harris died about the year 1835, aged seventy-four years.

Amariah Yates came from Massachusetts, in 1791, and settled at the mouth of the Apalachin creek. One of his sons, Paul Yates, settled about two miles east of Owego, on the west side of the Little Nanticoke creek.

Caleb Nichols and his son, Simeon Nichols, both revolutionary soldiers, came from Rhode Island, in the latter part of the year 1791. The former died in 1804, and the latter May 16, 1856, aged ninety-three years.

John Bills and his nephew, Abel Bills, came from New Lebanon, N. Y., in 1792.

Major David Barney, a revolutionary soldier, came down the river from Cooperstown, with a large family of children, and was one of the first settlers of the town of Vestal, Broome county. He removed to Apalachin, in 1802, and built the first house on Apalachin creek.

John Hicks Horton came from Rhode Island, soon after Caleb Nichols came, and settled two miles below Apalachin, opposite Campville.

Thomas Tracy came to this vicinity with his wife and infant son, Benjamin Tracy, and settled near the mouth of Tracy creek Broome county, in 1790. The creek received its name from Mr. Tracy. In 1801, he removed with his family to Caroline, Tompkins county, and thence to the Holland Purchase, near Buffalo. His son Benjamin, several years afterward, returned and settled on the Apalachin creek, where he raised a large family of children, one of whom is Gen. Benjamin F. Tracy, of Brooklyn. Benjamin Tracy died January 31, 1883.

John Jewett, with his sons Asa and John Jewett, Jr., came from Putnam county, in the winter of 1816-17, and settled one mile west of Apalachin. He was the grandfather of Harry Jewett, Esq., of Owego. While residing in Putnam county, he had held the offices of county clerk and member of assembly. He died in April, 1849.

Henry Billings settled at Apalachin, about the year 1822, and kept the first tavern here.

Dr. Isaac W. Lewis, of Apalachin, was born in Owego, January 2, 1821. His parents soon after removed to Glenville, N. Y., where they resided till he was fourteen years of age, when they returned to Owego. The doctor attended the common schools there, and after coming here graduated from the Manninton Academy, at Silver Lake, Pa., began the study of medicine with Dr. Ezekill Daniels, and graduated at the Castleton, Vt., Medical College, in 1848. He commenced practice in Silver Lake, Pa., and in 1852 came to Apolachin, where he has practiced since. Dr. Lewis married Ellen Sutton, in 1844, who bore him five children, three of whom are living, viz.: James A., a physician, of Ithaca, N. Y., Hattie E. (Mrs. William Inderlid), and George B., a practicing physician, of Owego. Mrs. Lewis died in 1874, and in 1876 the doctor married Mrs. Susan A. Catlin, of Tioga, N. Y.

B. F. Tracy & Son's Marshland stock farms here, consist of six hundred acres, on the river road, where they carry on very extensively the business of breeding and raising the best blooded trotting horses. They have been engaged in this business since 1878, and have constantly on hand from one hundred to one hundred and twenty-five head of horses, and employ about twenty-five men. As breeders of superior trotters, the Messrs. Tracy have a wide spread reputation, and their system and equipments for raising and breaking trotters are second to none in the country.

CAMPVILLE is situated on the north bank of the Susquehanna river, seven miles east of Owego. The first settler was Col. Asa Camp. He came from Columbia county, N. Y., to the town now called Vestal, in Broome county, in the spring of 1789, removing thence to Apalachin, in 1792, and subsequently to Campville, in 1800. He was a sergeant in the revolutionary war.* He was a witness of Major Andre's execution, and assisted in digging his grave. He built the first tavern at Campville, in 1800. He held the offices of poundmaster, assessor, commissioner of highways, and overseer of the poor, and was supervisor of the town of Owego, in 1817 and 1818. He was eighty-eight years of age at the time of his death, which occurred July 17, 1848. His sons, Roswell and Silvester Camp, were both equally prominent men in that part of the town.

Campville was early known as East Owego, but when Stephen

---

* Wilkinson's "Annals of Binghamton" (page 88) says of Colonel Camp: "He served in the revolutionary war, in the capacity of sergeant, four years; commanded at Fort Frederick, on the Mohawk; and with fifteen men in the fort effectually repelled two hundred Indians and Tories. When a flag was sent in for them to surrender, Sergeant Camp sent word back, 'that Yankees lived there; and if they got the fort they must get it by the hardest.' He was in the battle of White Plains; was in one battle on the sea, near the banks of Newfoundland, and was also at Valley Forge."

Yours truly

B. F. Tracy

B. Leonard was in congress he caused the name to be changed to Campville, in honor of Colonel Camp.

GASKILL CORNERS is a hamlet situated on the Little Nanticoke creek, about five miles northeast of Owego. It derives its name from Joseph Gaskill, who was born at Richmond, N. H., April 22, 1780, and removed to the town of Owego with his father, Silas Gaskill, March 20, 1789, and to Gaskill Corners, in 1822. He married Mariam Wilcox, January 1, 1803, and became the father of six children. Of these, only Paul and Samuel are living. Mr. Gaskill died here June 19, 1866.

Elijah Walter was one of the first settlers at Gaskill Corners, about 1810. He came from Great Barrington, Mass., and located upon what is now known as the Walter farm. He married Abigail Gifford and had five children who attained an adult age, only three of whom, Alonzo, Artemas, and Sarah (Mrs G. R. Curtis) are living. Artemas who still lives at the Corners, was born February 14, 1822, married Frances Hagan, August 21, 1841, and has eight children now living.

The postoffice was established here in July, 1866, and Clark Green was the first postmaster. The present postmaster is Harmon Curtis.

SOUTH OWEGO is situated about seven and one-half miles southeast of Owego, near the Pennsylvania line.

GIBSON CORNERS, situated about four miles south of Owego, was so named from Eli Gibson, who settled there in the spring of 1835. He was born at Stowe, Middlesex county, Mass., June 17, 1795, and died March 12, 1864.

WAIT SETTLEMENT, situated in the southwest corner of the town, was so named from Henry Wait, who purchased 900 acres of land and removed thereon from Saratoga county, in 1819.

The County Poor Farm, on road 40, consists of one hundred acres, upon which is located the County Alms House and Insane Asylum. The indigent ones here are supported at the expense of the town from which they have gained a residence, while transient ones, or those having no permanent place of residence, are supported at the expense of the county at large. The alms house is a large stone structure, built in 1839-40. The insane asylum, located opposite the latter, is a wooden structure, built in 1885–86. It is very commodious and complete, having accommodations for, and does accommodate, others than indigent unfortunates. It is said to be the finest county asylum in the state. The property was purchased and devoted to the purposes of a poor farm, in 1836. The institution now has about fifty inmates at the alms house, and thirty-six in the asylum. The institution and farm are now under the charge of Daniel Johnson, who was appointed to the position in 1879.

Nathan H. Ellis's Grist Mill, on road 40, was built about 1826. The present proprietor purchased the property July 1, 1885. The mill was purchased by John Pettigrove, about 1854, who owned the property till purchased by Mr. Ellis. In connection with the mill Mr. Pettigrove operated a distillery for many years. The mill has three runs of stones, and one set of rolls. He does custom work.

Homer Searles's Steam Saw-Mill was built by him about 1880. It has a circular-saw, and cuts about 500,000 feet of lumber per year, giving employment to six men. In connection with the mill he has a threshing-machine, and shingle and lath-mill.

Mrs. Margaret Walter's Saw-Mill was built about 1874. It is operated by steam-power, has a circular-saw, and does custom work.

Harmon Curtis's Saw and Feed Mill, at Gaskill Corners, was built by him in 1883. It is operated by steam-power, has a circular saw, and also a threshing-machine in connection. The saw-mill turns out about 200,000 feet of lumber per year.

Campbell & Lamphere's saw and planing mill, at Apalachin, was built by Charles Baker, in 1884, and was bought by the present firm in the spring of 1887. The mill has a circular-saw, bench-saws, planer and matcher, turning lathe, etc., being fully equipped throughout, and operated by steam-power.

Leonard Foster's saw and feed-mill, on road 27, was built by him in 1870, upon the site of the old Foster mill, built by his father, Daniel R. Foster, in 1836. The present mill is run by steam-power, has a circular-saw, lath-mill, planer, etc., and turns out about 500,000 feet of lumber per year, employing about eight men during the winter season. The feed mill is for custom work.

CHURCHES.

First Presbyterian Church of Owego.—On the 7th day of August, 1810, the society with which the First Presbyterian Church of Owego is now connected, was formed, and Solomon Jones, Caleb Leach, Abraham Hoagland, William Camp, James Pumpelly, and Eleazer Dana were elected trustees. No church was organized until July 24, 1817. On that day a congregational church, consisting of eleven members, was organized. The church was taken under the care of the presbytery of Cayuga, in August, 1817, and was transferred to the presbytery of Tioga on the organization of that body. In July, 1831, the church abandoned the Congregational form of government and adopted the Presbyterian form of government in full, electing Solomon Jones, William Platt, Eleazer Dana, and William Pumpelly, ruling elders. The first pastor of the church was Rev. Daniel Loring. The present pastor is Rev. Alexander C. McKenzie. Services were held in the school-house on Main street, near McMaster street, until 1819, when a church was built of wood at the northeast corner of Temple street and North avenue. This church was torn down, in 1854, and the present brick edifice erected on its site.

The Methodist Episcopal Church of Owego was regularly organized in 1817, at which time it was taken from the Tioga circuit. At that time Rev. Mr. Payne was the pastor. Through his efforts their first church edifice was built, in 1822, at the southeast corner of Main and Academy streets. Previous to this time meetings had been held in the Main street school-house. The present brick church on Main street was built, in 1870. The present pastor is Rev. W. M. Hiller.

The first Baptist Church of Owego was organized on the 20th of September, 1831, by a society of thirty persons, at a meeting held in Daniel Chamberlain's wagon shop, which stood at the southwest corner of Park and Main streets. The meetings were held for a few weeks in the wagon shop, a box placed on the front bench serving as a pulpit. In November, the society obtained the use of Masonic Hall on Front street, where services were held until 1836, when the wooden church at the southeast corner of Church and Main streets, which had been built the year previous, was dedicated. This church was removed, in 1857, and the present brick edifice erected upon its site. The first regular pastor was James R. Burdick, who assumed charge, in June, 1833. The present pastor is Rev. Reuben E. Burton.

The African Methodist Episcopal Church was organized about the year 1843. The first preacher was Rev. Joshua Johnson. Their church, on Fox street, was formerly the lecture-room of the First Presbyterian church, and was removed from Temple street to its present location. The present pastor is Rev. R. H. Shirley.

St. Paul's Episcopal Church was organized February 10, 1834. Services were held in the old Presbyterian lecture-room, which

stood on the east side of Court street, adjoining the old academy ground, until 1839, when the present church was built on
the south side of Main street. Rev. John Bailey was the first
rector of the church. The present rector is Rev. James H.
Kidder.

Congregational Church of Owego.—In February, 1850, forty-six
members of the First Presbyterian Church withdrew by certificate, and formed the Congregational Church of Owego. Rev.
Samuel C. Wilcox was engaged as pastor. Services were held at
the court-house until February, 1852, when a wooden church
was completed on the west side of Park street. This church was
destroyed by fire, in December, 1877, and the present brick
church was built on its site in the following year. The present
pastor of the church is Rev. Oliver R. Howe.

St. Patrick's Roman Catholic Church of Owego was organized
about the year 1840. Rev. Father John Sheridan was the first
priest. The church was built in 1847. The present pastor is
Rev. Father Thomas D. Johnson. St. Patrick's school-house
was built in 1860. The Convent of the Sisters of Mercy was
instituted, in 1865, and changed into St. Joseph's Orphan Asylum, in 1871.

The Flemingville Methodist Episcopal Church was organized in
1811, with fifteen members. The church building, a wooden
structure erected in 1834, will comfortably seat 300 persons, and
is valued, including grounds, etc., at $3,600.00. The society now
has 260 members, with Rev. C. D. Shepard, pastor.

The Free Will Baptist Church of South Apalachin was organized
in October, 1816, with fourteen members, and Rev. John Gould
was the first pastor. A church building was erected in 1844, and
gave place to the present structure in 1859. The society now
has fifty members, with Rev. William Fuller, pastor.

The South Owego Methodist Episcopal Church was organized
about 1830, and Rev. John Griffing was its first pastor. The
church building was erected in 1857. The society now has fifty
members, with Dr. L. W. Peck, pastor.

The Free Will Baptist Church of Apalachin was organized by its
first pastor, Rev. H. S. Ball, in 1869. The church building was
erected in 1872. The society has at present no regular pastor.

The Whittemore Hill Methodist Episcopal Church was built in
1850-51. The society was then organized. It belongs with the
Union, Broome county, charge, and Rev. George T. Price is

pastor. It is a neat wooden structure, and the land for its site was leased to the society by Isaac Whittemore, for $1.00, "so long as it is used for church purposes," then to revert to the farm.

———

RICHFORD* is located in the northeast corner of the county. Its surface is mostly up-land, broken by narrow valleys. The West Owego creek forms the western boundary, and the east branch of the creek forms the principal valley, which runs through the middle of the town, north and south. The northern boundary is the division line between Tioga and Cortland counties, and the south boundary is five miles south of the north line, the lines running parallel, due east and west. The east line of the town is quite irregular, though it is the dividing line between the counties of Broome and Tioga, having been fixed on original lines of certain lots which were numbered in the original survey of the "Boston Purchase," and the lines running north and south, only extended between, running from either parallel to another, so that the north and south lines of lots did not range one with the other, hence there is seven right angles in the east line of the town, some of which turn east and others west. In area, the town comprises ninety-two original lots, averaging about two-hundred and seventy-five acres each, and numbering from lot No. 421, in the south-east corner, to lot No. 431, on the south side; and on the north side from lot 569, in the north-east corner, to lot 580. The town is from seven to ten miles wide, in an air line across from the east to the west line. On the north border is the highest lands in the county, indeed, the border is on the ridge of the great watershed that forms two sides of the vast lake basin that is drained through the Gulf of St. Lawrence. This summit divides the drainage, the water flowing northward into the basin, and onward into the St. Lawrence, to mingle with the waters that flow southward, through Chesapeake Bay, in the Atlantic. The summits are 2,000 feet above tide. In the creek valley, where the depot is located, the altitude is 1,090 feet above sea level, 271 feet higher than Owego. This difference in altitude occasions more variation in climate than does the difference in latitude. The highest point in the aforementioned valley is in

*For much of the matter relative to the history of this town, we are indebted to Mr. C. J. Robinson, of Richford.

Dryden, four miles north of the town of Richford, the elevation being 1,208 feet above tide. Near the northeast corner of the town, on lot 530, and farm of James Sears, is an elevated point of arable land, from which may be seen, by the aid of a telescope, the waters of Lake Ontario, and eastward, the landscape stretch-ing across the north part of Broome and south part of Chenango and south corner of Otsego counties, into Delaware county, the view extending into eight counties. This high point is the sum-mit of the angle in the watershed, running northward and west-ward, stretching along some six miles south of lake Erie, onward around the south basin. All along on the watershed ridge, on either slope, the land is arable, and the most elevated lands are equally productive with the valleys, indeed, the best farms in the town lie on the high ranges.

Origin of Name.—The village of Richford first took its name, in 1821, at the time the "public square" was surveyed and granted by deed, for public purposes. The grantors were Ezekiel Rich, who donated the north half, and Stephen Wells, the south half. Both deeds set forth that: "Said land is to be used for a public square, and for no other purpose, reserving to all persons owning or possessing the land around said square the privilege of twelve feet in front of the line of square for piazzas, flagging, shade-trees, and railing ; but no person to set the front of his building over in front of the square." The deeds bear date October 9, 1821, and they were duly executed on October 13, 1821, by being acknowl-edged in due form before David Williams, who was then a judge of the court of common pleas, in and for the county of Broome, and the deeds were recorded in the Broome county clerk's office, in book of deeds No. 8, page 20, on the 24th day of October, 1821. From Mr. Rich, the village was called "Richford," which ulti-mately became the name of the town. It should be remembered, in this connection, that Broome county was formed from Tioga, March 28, 1806, and that Owego and Berkshire, formerly adjoin-ing towns, were re-annexed to Tioga county, March 21, 1822, which made the territory of the town of Richford a part of Tioga county.

Until as late as 1812, the territorial limits of the town of Rich-ford was, practically, an unbroken wilderness of primitive forest. The aborigines had located their camps and hunted here, long before, and some lingered after the settlement began. An open-ing of a few acres in the southwest corner of the town, on lot 423, near the present residence of Widow Jewett, had been made by the Indians, leaving traces of cultivation. From no records can the exact date when the first white settlement was begun, nor can it be said definitely to whom belonged such honor. One well versed in the pioneer history of this section, however, has placed in our hands the following article, entitled the

EARLY HOUSEHOLDS OF RICHFORD.[*]

Evan Harris, if tradition is correct, was the first settler where the village of Richford now stands. He was a weaver, and came from Berkshire county, Mass., but how early, is not known. He was certainly here before 6 Jan., 1808, on which day he earned half a dollar by chopping for Joseph Waldo, of Berkshire. He dwelt in the log house where Nathaniel Johnson afterward lived, north of the spring where Philip Lacy now lives. His wife died 19 Feb., 1812, and was buried in the Brown cemetery, below the village of Berkshire. It is said that she died of consumption, and there is evidence that her passage to the grave was made as easy as possible by the use of paregoric. The names of his children are not known, with the exception of one son, Evan Harris, Jr., who was badly burned, according to tradition, by falling backward into a kettle of hot maple sugar, 10 April, 1812. This was nearly two months after the mother's death, the father was away from home, and the lad helped himself out of the kettle, and did not stop till he reached the house of Jeremiah Campbell, over a mile down the valley, where Mrs. Campbell kindly cared for him till his burns were healed. Another child was born 17 Aug., 1811.

Elisha Harris was in the same region as early as March, 1808, and perhaps was a relative of Evan Harris. He had children:

I. ——, b 24 Dec., 1808. II. ——, b 28 Dec., 1811.

It is thought that Elisha Harris lived in what is now called Caroline, N. Y. His name occurrs in John Brown's account book, in December, 1798, and he was taxed, in 1802, in Tioga.

Paul Stevens was an early settler of Richford, on lot 424, one of the south tier of lots in the town. He built a log house, on the side of the way, but the road when properly laid passed directly over the site of it. This place he sold in the spring of 1821, to Gad Worthington, and left the place with all of his family. He is remembered as a worthy, pious man, and Mrs. Caroline Rich

---

[*] From an unfinished work, in manuscript, entitled the " Folk Book of the Boston Purchase," by D. Williams Patterson, of Newark Valley.

27*

thought he was a member of the First Church of Tioga, etc. But
the records do not reveal his name. He used to go up the valley
to lot 533, about three miles above the village, to make his maple
sugar.

Only an imperfect list of his children has been found :

I. Paul, probably the eldest son, born as early as 1797 ; was
drafted as a soldier in the war of 1812. He remained in Richford after his father moved away, and was evidently of full age
in April, 1818, able to buy whiskey, tobacco, and clothing on credit,
and 17 July, 1818, he prepared for haying, by purchasing a scythe
at one dollar and fifty cents. He is remembered as the drummer
of the Berkshire company of militia, and able to play his part in
all the military customs of that time.

II. Seth, was about Richford in March 1818; and probably
went away with his father, soon after that.

III. David, is also remembered as one of the family.

IV. ——, b 14 May 1809, name unknown.

John Watson lived on the N. E. quarter of 421, the S. W. corner lot of Richford, where Daniel P. Witter now lives. He married
with Susanna Smith, and dwelt in Rutland, Mass., tell after their
first child was born ; then moved to Hinsdale, Mass., and, April,
1810, came to the Boston Purchase. He finally had another
attack of Western fever, went to Unadilla, Michigan, and there
died. Their children after the first, were born in Hinsdale, Mass.:

I. Susan, m with James Livermore, of Caroline Centre.

II. Rebecca, m in 1810, with Ira Richards of Hinsdale, Mass.,
and settled in Riga, N. Y.

III. Mary, m with Abraham Burghardt, Jr.

IV. Sally, died in childhood at Hinsdale, Mass.

V. Samuel Smith, b 13 May, 1800: m 4 March, 1829, with
Betsey Rounseville, who died at Caroline, N. Y., 18 July, 1833,
aged 29 years. He m (2d) 3 September, 1834, with Jerusha
Harmon. In 1838 they moved to Newark Valley, and died there.

VI. John, settled at Unadilla, Michigan, and was living there
in 1881.

VII. James Lockhart, m with Mary Gilbert, and settled on the
West Owego creek in the N. W. corner of Berkshire, and died
there.

VIII. Jane, died in Richford, when about sixteen years old.

Artemas Watkins, born in Peru, Mass., 25 Aug., 1786, son of
John Watkins, married with Phebe Gilbert, who was born at
Peru, about 1790, daughter of Benson Gilbert. They left Peru,

about 1812, and settled in Richford, west of the turnpike, on the southwest quarter of lot 461, which place is now owned by Richard Moore. His brother, John Watkins, settled in Newark Valley, about the same time. She died 30 May, 1840, of erysipelas, aged 51 years, 3 months and 10 days. He died 20 May, 1865, of apoplexy, aged 78 years. They were buried at Speedsville. Their children were:

I. Betsey, b at Peru, Mass., 8 April, 1809, ; m with Levi Gilbert; died 15 Jan., 1855.

II. Anna, b at Peru, Mass., 12 Dec., 1811; m with Erastus E. Humphrey, and they reside at Speedsville, N. Y.

III. Semantha, b at Richford, about 1812 ; m with John B. Leonard. She m (2d) with Daniel Rowley, of Richford, and died 24 Jan., 1887, aged 75 years.

IV. Benson Gilbert, m with Elizabeth Parsons, and resides at Montrose, Penn.

V. Reuben, died at Richford, when two years old.

VI. Lyman, m with Lucia Hastings, daughter of Joel Hastings, and died at Owego, aged 63 years.

VII. Polly, m with Leroy Krum, and resides at Elmira, N. Y., a widow.

VIII. Ira W., b at Richford, 4 April, 1822 ; m with Lydia Hubbard, and resides at Cortland village, N. Y.

IX. Amanda M., b in 1824 ; m with John B. Crandall, and they reside at Cortland, Ill.

X. Amos Greenleaf, b 24 June, 1826, at Richford ; m there, 13 March, 1850, with Catharine Elliott, who died 27 July, 1866. He m (2d) at New York, 9 Feb., 1870, with Sait Hover, daughter of Cornelius and Eunice (Squires) Hover. He resides at Richford, a justice of the peace.

XI. Cynthia A., b in 1828; m with William A. Hines, and lives at Manchester, Iowa.

XII. Harriet, b 25 Aug., 1831 ; m with Squire D. Freeland, son of Joseph Freeland, and they reside in the southwest corner of Richford.

Samuel Smith, son of Heman and Lucy (Taylor) Smith, was born at ——, Mass., about 1784; m with Huldah Goodale, daughter of Isaac and Jemima (Warner) Goodale, of Berkshire, N. Y., formerly of Westhampton, Mass., where she was born on Tuesday, 26 March, 1782. They settled on Berkshire West hill, where she died 5 July, 1811. He m (2d) with Theodosia Dewey, who was born at Pittsfield, Mass., 28 Nov., 1791, daughter of

Ezekiel and Hannah (Barker) Dewey. They were among the earliest settlers at the village of Richford, where he built a small house, about 1813, east of the valley road, and north of the turnpike, in which he kept a tavern, till about 1817, when he sold it, probably to Beriah Wells, and moved to lot 384, on the northeast quarter, east of the road, where he died 3 May, 1846, aged sixty-two years. She died at Berkshire, 24 May, 1864, aged seventy-two years and six months. Tradition says that one of his children died at Richford, and was buried in the ground now occupied as the garden of the hotel. Their other children were:

I. Hannah, b at Richford, 29 Nov., 1813.

II. Miriam, b at Berkshire, 3 Dec., 1819.

III. Ezekiel Dewey, b at Berkshire, 16 Feb., 1822; m at Berkshire, N. Y., 5 March, 1845, with Jane Ford, who died there, 29 May, 1852. He m (2d) with Mary Scott, and died at Owego, of consumption.

IV. Lucy T., b at Berkshire, N. Y., 13 Jan., 1825, and died there, 18 Jan., 1850.

V. Charlotte, unmarried.

Nathaniel Johnson lived on the west side of the road in the village of Richford, and was one of the early settlers in that part of the town, if some traditions are trustworthy. He married with Lucy Smith, a sister of Samuel Smith, and daughter of Heman and Lucy (Taylor) Smith, of Berkshire. She died, and he m (2d) with Clarissa Goodale, widow of his first wife's brother, Heman Smith, Jr., and daughter of Isaac and Jemima (Warner) Goodale. Mr. C. J. Robinson calls him "the third settler within the domain of Richford," and says: "He moved into the house vacated by Mr. Evan Harris in 1814. He remained on the lands he first purchased during sixteen years, and then migrated west. Mr. Johnson's home was the home of tramping missionary and circuit preachers. These Christian devotees were ever kindly welcomed by the new settler and his family, and as Mr. Johnson was not a professor or church member, those callers used to call their host ' Brother-in-law Johnson,' and sometimes ' The good sinner.'" Other people, who had the advantage of knowing him personally, say that he was a very worthy, zealous and consistent member of the Methodist church. He dwelt where Mr. Hotchkiss S. Finch now lives, on the west side of the way. They had children:

I. Lucy, b at Fairfield, Vt., 15 Jan., 1800, m with Ezekiel Dewey. II. Smith.

III. Eber, m with Sally Goodale, and after living in Richford for several years, moved to Michigan. They had a child born 18 Aug., 1821.

IV. Rachel, m with William Warner Goodale.

V. Norman. It has been said that he became a Mormon.

VI. Zilpha, b about the latter part of March, 1810, m with Daniel Farnham, who died in Ithaca, N. Y. She afterward settled in Syracuse.

Heman Daniels came with his father, Nathan Daniels, from Brandon, Vt., to Paris, Oneida Co., N. Y. He married with Elvira Walker, from Conn., and settled in Susquehanna county, Penn., and, after a few years, returned to Sangersfield, Oneida Co., N. Y. In the spring of 1816, they came into Richford, via Cortlandville, and settled where Alfred Davis now lives, on the west side of the road, on lot 574, the middle lot of the north tier, in the present town of Richford, and this was the first household in the east valley, north of the village, and dwelt there in Dec., 1820. He was born in 1787, and died 6 March, 1883, aged nearly ninety-six years. He was a soldier of the war of 1812. She died 28 April, 1836. They were buried at Harford. Their children were:

I. Heman, b in Susquehanna Co., Penn., 16 Nov., 1809, m March, 1836, with Nancy Gleazen, and they still live in Richford, on lot 548.

II. Elmon Walker.

III. Elvira, m with Henry Blackman.

IV. Calvin Walker.

V. Betsey Maria, m with Ezekiel Brerly, and m (2d) with Erastus Sheldon, and they now dwell in Owego.

VI. ——, a son, died when a few days old.

VII. Jason, b at Richford, settled at Montello, Wis., and in 1886, moved a few miles from there.

Samuel Gleazen, b at Stockbridge, Mass., 4 April, 1783, son of Joseph Gleazen, was a mason. He m 1 January, 1804, with Nancy Rathbone, of Stockbridge, who was born 22 July, 1784, and died at Richford, 1 July, 1831. He married (2d) 5 March, 1832, with Susanna (Scott) Gleazen, widow of his brother, Ebenezer Ede Gleazen. He dwelt in Stockbridge, till 1808; then settled in the west border of Berkshire, afterward at Berkshire village, and moved in the spring of 1817 to the village of Richford, in which he then built the fourth house, near where the Congregational church stands. For this house he cut a place in the woods just large enough so that the remaining trees should not reach the house in falling. In the spring of 1826 he returned to Stockbridge, and remained till the fall of 1828, when he returned via the Erie canal and Cayuga Lake to Richford, where he died August, 1865, aged eighty-two years. Mr. Gleazen was brought up by——Pepoon of Stockbridge, which accounts for his remaining there after the rest of the family came to Berkshire. His children were :

I. Horatio Jones, b at Stockbridge, Mass., 9 November, 1804 ; m 2 February, 1835, with Marietta Chaplin, and died in Cortlandville N. Y., in May, 1860.

II. Abigail Pepoon, b at Stockbridge, Mass., 28 November, 1806 ; m with her cousin, Absalom Gleazen, son of Caleb Gleazen.

III. Nancy, b at Berkshire, 18 July, 1809 ; m March, 1836, with Heman Daniels, and they still reside in Richford, and the accuracy of this history depends essentially upon their excellent memories.

IV. Lorain Grant, b at Berkshire, 17 September, 1811 ; m with Jane A. Wentworth, and settled in Iowa, where he died 27 December, 1855.

V. Mary, b at Berkshire, 4 June, 1813 ; died 8 November, 1813.

VI. Mary, b at Berkshire, 12 December, 1814 ; m March, 1836, with Ransom Sexton. She died. He still resides in Richford.

VII. Hannah, b at Richford, 9 January, 1818 ; died 4 March, 1851, unmarried.

VIII. Caroline, b at Richford, 3 July, 1820 ; died 29 August, 1824.

IX. Samuel, b at Richford, 19 April, 1823 ; died 10 December, 1823.

X. Samuel, b at Richford, 29 September, 1824 ; died 10 December, 1825.

XI. Caroline E., b at Stockbridge, Mass., 4 March, 1828 ; m 25 December, 1848, with Simeon Bryant, and died at Harford, in June, 1854.

"Mr. Stove" is remembered by Mrs. Daniels, as one of the men who lived at the site of Richford village, when her father moved there, in 1817, but he soon moved away.

Beriah Wells kept a tavern north of the turnpike, and east of the present village green, in two small houses which had been drawn together and fitted up by him. One of these houses had been built for a tavern, about 1813, by Samuel Smith. The other was built a year or two later, by his brother-in-law, Nathan Johnson. Mr. Wells was born in Richmond, Mass., 1 Feb., 1782, in a house which stood on the state line, between Massachusetts and New York; married in Hopkinton, Rhode Island, 22 Oct., 1806, with Lois Wells, daughter of Thompson Wells, of Wellstown, in that town. He was a painter and chairmaker, and settled at Lenox, Mass. In the spring of 1813, he came to Berkshire, now Newark Valley, and, about the first of June, began the manufacture of chairs, as told to his wife in his letter of 21 June, 1813. His family arrived here shortly before 21 Nov., 1813, and lived in the house with Elisha Wilson one year, while he was building his house and shop, on the west side of Berkshire street, the first building south of the Wilson creek. In Aug., 1817, he moved to Richford, and kept the tavern, as above stated, till 3 April, 1821, when he returned to Newark Valley, having exchanged his Richford property with Ezekiel Rich, for a farm on the south side of lot 103, where his daughter-in law and grandchildren now live. He was a prudent, thrifty, careful man, contented with small gains, not disposed to waste either time or money, but always taking time to do his work in the most thorough manner; so deaf as to make it hard to take a part in social converse, and possessing a more kind and generous heart than those who were not intimate with him were aware of. His wife died 23 June, 1854, aged 71 years. He died 30 June, 1861. Their children were:

I. Frederick Theodore, b at Lenox, Mass., 26 Oct., 1807; married at Newark Valley, 22 Feb., 1837, with Jane Bement. He died on his father's homestead, 11 Nov., 1866, and his widow and children still live there.

II. Palmer, b at Richford, 27 June, 1817, and died there 6 Feb., 1818.

III. Edwin Lucius, b at Richford, 3 Aug., 1820; married 14 Feb., 1855, with Harriet E. Schoonover, and settled in Lisle, N. Y., where he died 18 April, 1873.

Stephen Wells, b about 1754, m with Love Ford, who was born 9 Oct., 1758, daughter of James and Rachel (Backus) Ford. She died at Lenox, Mass., 12 Oct., 1786. He married (2d) at East Windsor, Conn., 14 Sept., 1788, with Caroline King, who was born 6 March, 1752, daughter of Zebulon and Keziah (Loomis) King. They moved to Newark Valley about 1815, and thence, about 1821, with his son, Lucius Wells, to Richford, where he died 18 Feb.,

1824. He m (3d) with Mrs. Elizabeth (Butler) Griffith, who died at Richford, 2 June, 1838, aged 77 years. He died 14 June, 1838, aged 84. Children:

I. Stephen. [See below.]   II. Beriah.   [See above.]

III. Betsey, b at Lenox, Mass., 12 Dec., 1784, died there, 12 Aug., 1790.

IV. Love, b at Lenox, Mass., 6 Oct., 1786, m there 16 Dec., 1810, with Rodolphus Cotton, of Lenox.

V. Lucius, b at Lenox, Mass., 11 Sept., 1789, m there 21 Nov., 1811, with Mary Porter. They dwelt in Albany, N. Y., Newark Valley, N. Y., and finally in Ithaca, N. Y., where they died; he, 28 Aug., 1831, she, 31 July, 1865.

Stephen Wells, Jr., a painter and chair maker lived south of the turnpike and east of the Valley road. He built the house in which Levi Owen now lives, and dwelt therein. He was born at Lenox, Mass., 20 June, 1777, eldest child of Stephen and Love (Ford) Wells; joined the church there, 20 October, 1799; m there 4 Jan., 1801, with Lois Hubbard, of Lenox. They were dismissed 21 Jan., 1810, to Dr. Neill's church at Albany, and returned 24 Sept., 1815, to that at Lenox, of which he had already been elected a deacon, 1 Sept., 1815. They probably settled at Richford, about 1818; and, after a few years removed to Steuben county, N. Y. Their children were:

I. Hubbard Ford, b at Lenox, 11 Dec., 1801.

II. Eliza, b at Lenox, 11 May, 1803; m 27 June, 1826, with Col. Smith, of Sherburne, N. Y.

III. George, b at Lenox, 14 June, 1805.

IV. Mary, b at Lenox, 25 Jan., 1807; m with Chauncey Hubbard.

V. Luke, b at Albany, N. Y., about 1812; baptized at Lenox, 19 March, 1815; was crippled with a disease of the hip; and died at Richford, of dropsy of the head, 12 Aug., 1821, aged nine years.

VI. Henry, b at Richford, in 1821; bap. at Newark Valley, 12 Aug., 1821; and was drowned in the mill-pond at Richford, 20 July 1824, aged three years.

Ezekiel Dewey lived in the village of Richford. He was born in Westfield, Mass., 9 May, 1797, son of Ezekiel and Hannah (Barker) Dewey, came to Richford, in the fall of 1816, and married there "3 July, 1817," with Lucy Johnson, daughter of Nathaniel and Lucy (Smith) Johnson, of Richford. At one time he lived a mile west of Richford village. His wife died 27

December, 1828 ; and he married (2d) with Eunice Smith, daughter of Heman and Almira (Messenger) Smith. She is still living in Berkshire. He died in Berkshire. His children, as follows, were all by the first wife, except the youngest.

I. ——, a daughter, b at Richford, died at birth, July, 1818.

II. Lucy Semantha, b 18 Oct., 1819, at Richford, m with Charles Frederick Akins, and married (2d) with John Rightmire, of Caroline, and she died 18 Jan., 1854.

III. Jane Elizabeth, b 21 April, 1821, at Richford ; m with Nathan Rightmire.

IV. David Wesley, b at Berkshire, 18 Feb., 1823; m with —— Delavan, of Freetown, N. Y., and died about 1873.

V. Charles Johnson, b at Richford, 10 May, 1826, resides in Berkshire.

VI. Ezekiel Hannum, b at Richford, 8 Oct., 1827 ; resides at Rochester, Mich.

VII. Amanda, b at Richford, 3 Aug., 1831, m with John Rightmire, of Caroline, as his second wife, 29 May, 1854.

William Belden lived west of the road on the north half of lot 424, where his son William F. Belden now lives. He was born in Lenox, Mass., 1 April, 1786, son of Oliver and Anna (Steel) Belden ; m there 4 April, 1809, with Phebe Wright, who was born at East Hartford, Conn., 16 October, 1788, daughter of Aaron and Phebe (Schalenger) Wright. They dwelt in Lennox, till 1818, then settled in Berkshire, now Richford, living first in a log house from which Paul Stevens had lately moved, while building a new house, into which they moved in October, 1818. On his first trip he reached Richford 31 March, 1818, with a wagon load of goods drawn by a yoke of oxen and a horse. He went back for his family, and reached Richford with them on Friday, 17 July, 1818. It is said that he taught the first school there, in his own house. She died 13 May, 1855. He died 2 April, 1859. Their children were :

I. Fanny Maria, b at Lenox, Mass., 8 April, 1810, and is still living in Richford.

II. William Franklin, b at Lenox, Mass., 1 June, 1813.

III. Frederick Carlos, b at Richford, 6 March, 1820.

Gad Worthington lived east of the road, on the south half of lot 424, where Charles F. Curtis now lives. He was born at Colchester, Conn., 28 May, 1786, son of Dan and Louis (Foote) Worthington, of Colchester. He m at Lenox, Mass., 27 August, 1812, with Fanny Belden, who was born there 26 February, 1793, daughter of Oliver and Anna (Steel) Belden. They dwelt in Lenox, till the fall of 1818, then moved to Richford, where he died 10 March, 1861. He built in 1819, the first saw-mill, and two or three years later, the first grist-mill, at the village of Richford. Their children were:

I. Dan Leander, b 14 August, 1813; m 6 January, 1836, with Indiana Louise Pierson.

II. Gad Belden, b 2 October, 1815; m 22 June, 1840, with Anna Maria Dixon, who died 20 May 1854. He m (2d) 8 Sept., 1856, with Susan Towner.

III. Fanny, b 17 July 1817; m 20 Nov., 1845, with Oscar Packard.

IV. Samuel Kellogg, b 16 July 1822; m at Hamilton, Ohio, 13 Sept., 1855, with Rachel Woods.

V. John, b 29 Jan., 1824; m 21 Sept., 1852, with Mary Kimberly.

VI. Mary Ann, b 16 June, 1828; m 5 Oct., 1848, with Hon. Wheeler H. Bristol, of Owego.

VII. Robert, b 25 Jan. 1830; m Dec., 1859, with Jane Bristol. He died at Oakland, Cal., 13 Aug., 1862.

George T. Pierce bought the north half of lot 548, which he visited in the fall of 1817, and made arrangements to have a log house built on it, east of the road, but by a miscalculation the house was built on the south half of the lot, just below the middle. In the spring of 1818, he brought his family from Paris, Oneida Co., N. Y., and settled in this house. His wife was —— Simmons, a cousin of George P. Simmons, and a sister of Mrs. Simmons. They must have brought with them as many as five or six children, none of whom remain in Richford. This was the second household in the east valley of Richford, north of the turnpike.

George P. Simmons, from Paris, N. Y., bought the south half of lot 548, and in the fall of 1818, made a settlement on it, east of the road, where Mrs. Vincent now lives. He married with —— Simmons, his own cousin, and a sister of Mrs. Pierce, above named. They must have brought with them as many as five or six children, none of whom remain in Richford.

Augustus VanBuren, a very worthy negro, came to Richford, in 1818, and settled on twenty-two acres of land on lot 424, which he bought of Gad Worthington. His house still stands east of the road, a short distance below the bridge. He brought a letter of dismission from the church at Lenox, Mass., and he and his wife, Sibyl, were constituent members of the church at Richford, 14 Jan., 1823. He had been a slave in the VanBuren family, at

Kinderhook, and often said that he had many times carried in his arms the infant, Martin VanBuren, who in return, sent him money, in his old age, to buy tobacco with. Mr. W. F. Belden says "he bought his freedom by working seven years for Judge Walker, in Lenox, Mass., who paid his master 115 pounds sterling for him. He died, aged 102 years, respected by all." Sibyl VanBuren died 27 Feb., 1846. She was his second wife, and was not the mother of his children. They were:

I. ——, a daughter. m at Kinderhook, and remained there.

II. Hetty, who m with Augustus VanDyke. They joined the church at Richford, 12 Aug., 1829, by letter from the P. R. Dutch church, of Kinderhook, N. Y., and she died, 30 Jan., 1841, aged 48 years.

III. Sarah, was admitted a member of the church at Richford, by profession of faith, 14 Jan., 1823, the day of its organization, and died 23 May, 1838, aged about 40 years.

IV. Joseph, died in Richford.

Notes to Census Table.—In December, 1820, the Hon. Chester Patterson, of Union, N. Y., who was then enumerating the inhabitants of Broome county, passed through the town of Berkshire, which then included the town of Richford. His list shows, forty-five householders within that part of the town which is now included in Richford, only six of whom then lived east of the valley of the East Owego creek. The following is his list of names, with such notes as have been gathered in relation to them, and it is believed to be substantially correct, though not so full as could be wished. The names in this list preceded by a star, have already been mentioned; the others are referred to in the following notes, by corresponding numbers. It may be well to add, also, that there were no unnaturalized foreigners in the town, only three blacks, and no one engaged in commerce. The enumeration makes the total population 263.

2. Henry Krum, lived in or near Richford village, perhaps on the turnpike west of there. He married with Harriet Rounseville, who was born at Caroline, N. Y., 25 Jan., 1801, daughter of John and Rebecca (Chamberlain) Rounseville. In Dec., 1820, when the census was taken they had only one daughter. They have since had another daughter and two sons. They afterward moved to Caroline, and he died at Slaterville, N. Y., in October, 1886. She was living in June, 1887, with her daughter, Mrs. Harrison Banfield, on Snyder Hill, near Varna, N, Y. It is said that Mrs Krum was the first white child born in the town of Caroline, N.Y.

CENSUS OF RICHFORD, DECEMBER, 1820.

NAMES.	No. Males and Ages.						No. Females and Ages.					Agriculturists.	Manufacturers.
	Under 10 years.	10 to 16 years.	16 to 18 years.	16 to 26 years.	26 to 45 years.	45 and upwards.	Under 10 years.	10 to 16 years.	16 to 26 years.	26 to 45 years.	45 and upwards.		
1. *Beriah Wells	1	1		1	1			1		2		2	
2. Henry Krum					1		1		1			1	
3. Benjamin Rathbun	1				1		2			1		1	
4. *Samuel Gleazen	1	1			1		4	1		1			1
5. *George P. Simmons	3	3			1		1			1		1	
6. *George T. Pierce	1	1			1		5			1		1	
7. *Heman Daniels	3				1		2			1		1	
8. Isaac Goodale	4				1		1			1		1	
9. John Newton	1				1					1		1	
10. Henry Morgan						1	3				1	1	
11. Zelotes Olney	1		1	1			1	2	1	1		2	
12. Elisha Briggs		1		1			1	2	1	1		1	
13. Caleb Arnold	2		1		1			1		1			1
14. Jacob Roads					1					1			1
15. *Artemas Watkins	2				1		3	1		1		1	
16. Wheeler Wood	1				1		3	1		1		1	
17. Elijah Gilbert		1	1	1	1		2		1	1		3	
18. Amos Raymond						1					1	1	
19. Daniel Raymond		1			1		1		1			1	
20. William G. Raymond	2			1	1		3	1	1	1		1	
21. Russell Freeland					2		7			2	1	2	
22. *John Watson		1	1	2		1	1				1	4	
23. David Draper	2				2		2		2			2	
24. Daniel Harrington	1	1			1		1		1		1	1	
25. William Lynch		2		1			3		1			1	
26. Jesse Gleazen, 2d					1		1		1			1	
27. Thomas P. Brown		1			1		3	2		1		2	
28. Jacob Burghardt	1		1	1	1					1		2	
29. Isaac Burghardt	4				1					1		1	
30. Abraham Burghardt				1	1						1	2	
31. Samuel Olney	1				1		1		1			1	
32. Abraham Burghardt, Jr	1				1		2			1		1	
33. Martha Tracy				1			4	1	3		1	1	
34. *William Belden	2				1		1	1		1		1	
35. *Gad Worthington	1			1	1		1			1		2	
36. *Augustus VanBuren						1			1		1		
37. *Ezekiel Dewey					1		1		1			1	
38. *Nathaniel Johnson		1		1	1			1	1		1	2	1
39. *Stephen Wells, Jr	2			1	1			1	1	1		2	
40. Thomas Tracy		1			1		1		2			1	
41. Ezra Howland				2			1		1			2	
42. Abraham Dudley		1		3		1		1	2		1	4	
43. Solomon Russel					1		1		2			1	
44. Thomas Robinson	1				1	1	3		1	1		1	1
45. Alexander S. Lamb												1	
Totals	39	17	4	23	30	11	67	17	26	25	11	60	5

3. Benjamin Rathbun, lived at Richford village. His history has not been found. He is remembered as a teamster, working about the mill, and in the woods, with his own oxen.

8. Isaac Goodale, lived, it is thought, on lot 580, the north-west corner lot in the town, near where George Baker has since lived. He was a farmer. He was born in Northampton, Mass., on Sunday, 1 Oct., 1780, son of Isaac and Jemima (Warner)

Goodale. He afterward moved to Michigan, and died there. His father lived on Berkshire West Hill, in 1820.

9. John Newton, lived it is thought, on the same lot with Isaac Goodale, but it has been found difficult to get a trustworthy account of them.

10. Henry Morgan, lived on the south side of the turnpike, between that and the creek, on the S. W. quarter of lot 501. He built the saw-mill N. W. of his house, on the little stream that comes down the hill there; and turned the water of Trout run into it to help drive the mill, which was not built till after 1820. He was engaged in agriculture, in 1820. His house was near the Willow bridge.

11. Zelotes Olney lived near the center of lot 501, north of the turnpike, and east of the road that leads up Trout run. He was taxed in the Brown's Settlement road district in 1798 to work three days, but probably he then lived below the south line of Richford. His name was also in the tax list of 1802. He had children—Oman, John, Samuel, No. 31 and others.

Benjamin Olney was assessed in the Brown's Settlement highway district in 1798, to work three days, but he probably left soon after, as his name is not in the tax list for 1802. His relation to Zelotes Olney is not known.

12. Elisha Briggs, a physician, lived north of the turnpike on the east end of lot 501, where the name of S. B. Allen is on the atlas.

13. Caleb Arnold lived on the turnpike, on lot 500. He was a blacksmith, and built there the first mills in Richford. His saw-mill, in 1820, was rated at forty thousand feet per year. His grist-mill does not appear in the census, and possibly had already gone out of use, for it is said that it required so much power that he fitted a crank to the bolt so as to turn that by hand. His mills were on the West Owego creek, and have since been known as the Robinson mills. Mr. C. J. Robinson says: "He erected a shop and machinery for the manufacture of cut nails, about the first of nail manufacturing in this country." He was recorded as engaged in manufacturing. He sometimes framed his own buildings, using a post-axe for beating out the mortises.

14. Jacob Roads lived on the turnpike northeast of Padlock, and on the southwest quarter of lot 498, where the atlas bears the name of J. Brooks. He was an Englishman. a mason, a quarryman, and is noted as engaged in manufactures.

16. Wheeler Wood, a farmer, lived in one of the five log houses

which composed the hamlet of Padlock; so named from the fact
that a padlock hung at each of the doors, and it is said that the
were so careful, that if a woman went to the spring for a pail of
water, she would lock the door, even if her husband was chopping wood in front of it; but some stories are too good to be
true. It is said that Henry Branch, of Newark Valley, was driving along this road about 1870, when his horse broke through the
covering of an old well, near the middle of the road, and had
hard work to get out. The well was about twenty feet deep, and
had gone wholly out of the memory of the people of that region.

17. Elijah Gilbert kept a tavern on the corner west of the
creek road, on lot 461, where the county atlas bears the name of
J. T. Osborn. He also made rakes, bedsteads, etc. He probably married with Betsey Watkins, and his sister, Sally Gilbert,
married with John Watkins, of Newark Valley. They came from
Partridgefield, now Peru, Mass., about 1812. Among their children:

Levi, m with Betsey Watkins, and settled at Waverly, N. Y.
Mary, m with James Lockhart Watson.
Melinda, moved to one of the Western States.

18. Amos Raymond; 19. Daniel Raymond; 20. William G.
Raymond; farmers, and perhaps brothers, all dwelt at or near
the hamlet of Padlock. Their history has not been obtained.

21. Russell Freeland lived on the hill road, on the south part
of lot 421, near the southwest corner of the present town of
Richford, and a short distance above the old Baptist meeting
house, now in ruins, in the northwest corner of Berkshire. He
was born in Blandford, Mass., about 1786, m about 1807, with
Emily Cushman, who was born at Becket, Mass., about 1787,
daughter of Jonah and Rachel (Whiting) Cushman, and sister of
Marble Cushman, of Berkshire. After living in Blandford for
twelve years, they moved to Berkshire, now Richford, where he
died as early as 1837, of typhus fever In the house with him
dwelt his widowed mother, one of his sisters, and his brother,
Joseph Freeland. Their children were:

I. Emerilla, b in Blandford, Mass.
II. Lydia, married with Julius Smith, of Richford.
III. Clarissa, b in Blandford, Mass.
IV. Mary, b in Blandford, Mass., resides at Port Dickinson,
N. Y.
V. Russell, b at Richford in 1821; married 30 Jan., 1845, with
Deborah Williams Smith, and they reside at Ouaquaga, N. Y.

VI. Vesta A., b at Richford, in 1826; married 6 May, 1850, with Deloss Tefft, of Edmeston, N. Y., and resides at Guilford, N. Y., three miles east of Oxford.

VII. Orin M., b at Richford, in 1829; married 11 Feb., 1857, with Jane A. Wilcox, daughter of Erastus and Laura Wilcox, of Tully, N. Y., and resides in Colesville, N. Y.

Joseph Freeland, who lived in the same house, and owned the north part of the same lot, was born about 1790, and had wife, Lydia, who died 7 April, 1875, aged 88 years. He died 1 Aug., 1879, aged 89 years. They were buried in the cemetery in the northwest corner of Berkshire. Among their children were two daughters, born before Dec., 1820. Lyman Freeland, of Newark Valley, and Squire D. Freeland, of Richford.

23. David Draper was a laborer, did not own a home, was often at the tavern, and sometimes did a day's work there, as early as December, 1817. Perhaps he hunted occasionally, as there is evidence that he bought a pint of whiskey and a canister of powder, 8 Sept., 1818. Another Draper, named Timothy, had the same habits, as early as 1817, but was not named in the census, though the number of persons enumerated in David's household, would indicate that Timothy, and his wife, too, may also have been members of it. Their house has not been identified.

24. Daniel Harrington lived on lot 460, east of the road, where Daniel Leach now lives. Reuben "Herinton," who may have been his father, was named in the Tioga tax-list of 1802.

25. William Lynch lived on lot 460, where Lyman Jewett now lives.

26. Jesse Gleazen, 2d, lived in a log home, northeast of the road, on lot 422, where the heirs of W. J. Patch now own. He was son of Caleb Gleazen, and grandson of Joseph Gleazen.

Caleb Gleazen, the father of Jesse Gleazen (2d), is said to have died on the hill west of where Mr. Heman Daniels now lives, but the date has not been found. He lived at different times, in various parts of the town, and sometimes out of the town. He had, in the course of his life, three wives, and twenty-one children. He was a soldier of the Revolution. He was assessed to work five and a half days on the highways, in Brown's Settlement, in 1798. One of his children was born 23 Dec., 1808.

27. Thomas P. Brown lived on the same road, on the N. E. quarter of lot 422, where the atlas bears the letters W. J. P. He was born 13 Nov., 1784. He married with Polly Burghardt,

daughter of Abraham and Lovisa (Rees) Burghardt. They
joined the church at Berkshire, now Newark Valley, by letter, 2
April, 1820, and were dismissed 12 Jan., 1823, to become constituent members of the church at Richford, which was formed 14
Jan., 1823. He was elected a deacon of the new church. He
afterward moved to Maine, N. Y., and probably died there 21
Feb., 1841, by church record, while his grave stone says 22 Feb.,
1841. His family went to Wisconsin. They may have had more
than the following children :

I. Azubah, b 21 March, 1807; d 17 Aug., 1835.

II. Betsey, b 11 June, 1809; d 24 April, 1809.

III. Betsey, bap 2 April, 1820.   IV. Sally, bap 2 April, 1820.
V. Mary, bap 2 April, 1820. VI. Semantha, bap 30 Sept., 1821.

28. Jacob Burghardt, (son of Abraham, No. 30) lived on the
same road, west side, on lot 423. He married with Polly Gardner, daughter of William and Polly (Gaston) Gardner, of Berkshire. They had a child born 22 June, 1821.

29. Isaac Burghardt (son of Abraham No. 30) lived on the east
side of same road, a short distance from his brother Jacob Burghardt. He had a child born 8 Jan., 1821.

30. Abraham Burghardt, Sen., lived on the east side of the
same road, on lot 223, (and with him dwelt his son John Burghardt, who died in 1886, having lived with his wife sixty years
lacking two months). He married with Lovisa Rees, (who was
a sister of Caroline Rees, the wife of Deacon Nathaniel Ford, of
Berkshire). She joined the church at Berkshire, now Newark
Valley, by letter, 6 June, 1813, and was dismissed with eight
others, 12 Jan., 1823, to form the church at Richford. Their children were :

Abraham, No. 32. Isaac, No. 29. Jacob, No. 28.

John Rees, m with Achsah Gardner.

Polly, wife of No. 27. Caroline, wife of No. 31.

31. Samuel Olney lived near the same road, out in the lot
between Isaac Burghardt and Abraham Burghardt, Sen. Soon
after 1820 he moved to Richford village, and afterward went West.
He m with Caroline Burghardt, daughter of Abraham and Polly
(Rees) Burghardt. Before her marriage she joined the church
of Berkshire, now Newark Valley, by letter, 6 June, 1813, and
was dismissed 12 Jan., 1823, with eight others, to organize a new
church at Richford. Samuel Olney was a son of Zelotes Olney,
No. 11. His children were :

I. Sally Lovisa, bap 6 July, 1817.

II. Franklin, bap 1 Nov., 1820. III. ——, born 8 Jan., 1822.

32. Abraham Burghardt, Jr., a son of Abraham and Lovisa (Rees) Burghardt, lived on the south part of lot 423, near the south line of the town, where E. T. Walker now owns. He married with Mary Watson, daughter of John and Susanna (Smith) Watson, and moved to Unadilla, Michigan. One of their children was born 3 Oct., 1821, and they had two at least before that.

33. Martha Tracy lived east of the road, on lot 421, the southwest corner lot in the town. She was the widow of James Tracy, and the daughter of Nathaniel and Sarah Blackman. Afterward she lived where Dea. Green Raymond has lived, in Caroline.

The six names which follow, were taken in connection with the census of Lisle, and were, of course in the eastern part of the town, on the border of Lisle.

40. Thomas Tracy, lived on the south side of the turnpike, near the north line of lot 470, where Ralph P. Smith now lives. He was, probably a son of Ebenezer and Electa Tracy, of Lisle, N. Y. He was in the neighborhood of Brown's settlement as early as 1803.

41. Ezra Howland. His place of residence has not been ascertained.

42. Abraham Dudley was probably the same who was a constituent member of the Richford Church, as Abraham N. Dudley. His residence has not been ascertained.

43. Solomon Russel. His dwelling place has not been ascertained.

44. Thomas Robinson, a maker of buckskin gloves and mittens, who afterward lived in Richford, and Newark Valley. He kept a public house on the turnpike, where Timothy Holcomb now lives. His full name was Thomas Amsdell Robinson. He was born at Concord, Mass., 26 Feb., 1787, son of Keen and Achsah (Leathe) Robinson. He m 15 March, 1812, with Juliet Cole, who died at Moravia, N. Y., 5 April, 1843. He m (2d) with Polly Hutchinson, widow of his brother Jedediah Leathe Robinson. He died at Newark Valley, 17 Oct., 1874. His widow died there, 18 Feb., 1879. He had nine children.

45. Alexander S. Lamb, seems to have had no family in 1820; and his place of residence has not been ascertained.

21. Thomas Keeny lived near the centre of lot 339, where A. H. Ford has since lived.

Ezekiel Rich was born at Cherry Valley, N. Y., 14 Aug., 1783;

28*

son of Simeon and Lucy (Lincoln) Rich ; m with Caroline Slosson, who was born at Stockbridge, Mass., 23 Feb., 1791, daughter
of Ezbon and Electa (Williams) Slosson.   They dwelt on lot 103,
in Newark Valley, till 3 April, 1821, when, having traded places
with Beriah Wells, he moved to the present site of Richford village, and continued there his business of manufacturing buckskin
goods, trading and farming, to which he added that of tavern
keeping.   He built the hotel building, and by his enterprise did
much to build up that part of the town of Berkshire, which, finally, on becoming a separate town was named in his honor.   He
died 18 April, 1854.   She joined the Congregational church of
Newark Valley, 2 April, 1820, was dismissed 12 Jan., 1823, to
become one of the constituent members of the Congregational
church of Richford, 21 Jan., 1823 ; and died.   Children :

I. Mary Ann, b 14 April, 1813 ; died 26 Dec., 1847.

II. Chauncey Leroy, b 29 Jan., 1815 ; a merchant ; still lives at
Richford, having been a director and trasurer of the Southern
Central Railroad Company from its formation to the permanent
lease of its road in 1887.

III. Angeline Eliza, b 23 Nov., 1816; m with Lewis Halsey
Kellogg, a physician, who died at Owatonna, Minn., 9 Oct., 1873.
She died at Rochester, Minn., 10 Nov., 1857.

IV. Lucien Densmore, b 21 Sept., 1818; and still lives at
Richford.   .

V. William Dunham, b 25 Dec., 1820; died 3 Jan., 1821.

VI. Maria Louisa, b 2 Sept., 1828 ; m with John More Benjamin, and settled at Painesville, Ohio.   He has been sheriff of
Lake county for two terms.

William Dunham was born 20 March, 1787, son of Isaac and
Charlotte (Lawrence) Dunham, and grandson of Jonas and Try-
phena(Lawrence) Lawrence.   He began life as a "commercial
traveler," or peddler, employed by Ezekiel Rich.   Coming home
in April, 1821, from one of his journeys, and finding that his
employer had moved ten miles further up the valley, he followed
the trail, and spent his life in Richford, passed in trade and manufacturing.   He moved to New York with his sons, and died 16
July, 1855.   He married, in Oct., 1822, with Matilda Slosson,
who was born 30 May, 1804, daughter of Enos and Rebecca
(Culver) Slosson.   She died in New York city, about 1873.   Children :

I. William S., b 22 Aug., 1825.

II. Matilda Orcelia, b 19 July, 1828. III. Robert H., (twin) b 29 June, 1832.

IV. Isaac S., (twin) b 29 June, 1832, died the same day.

John Stedman, married with Sylvia Catlin. They moved from Durham, Greene Co., N. Y., to Newark Valley, where she joined the church, 3 Aug., 1820, having had all of her eight children, except the eldest, baptized 3 July, 1820. At the census of 1820, they dwelt where Washington A. and James T. Noble now live, and moved in June, 1821, to Richford, where she was a constituent member of the church, 1823, having been dismissed from Newark Valley, 12 Jan., 1823. Their children were:

I. Sophronia, m with Aaron Jacobs.

II. Almira, m with Obadiah Livermore.

III. Eliza, m with Seth Torry.

IV. John Catlin, b at Durham, N. Y., 23 Jan., 1806; m with Julia Ann Slosson, daughter of Enos and Rebecca (Culver) Slosson. She died at Unadilla, Mich., 1 Aug., 1866.

V. Sarah, m with Simeon Rich Griffin.

VI. Mary, m with Reuben Watson.

VII. Sylvia, m 3 July, 1836, with Nelson Norton.

VIII. Anna, m with —— Hemingway.

Children of John Catlin and Julia Ann (Slosson) Stedman:

I. Susan Rebecca, b 2 March, 1829; died at Unadilla, Mich., 15 Oct., 1851.

II. Sylvia Maria, b 25 Oct., 1830; m with A. B. Wood, and settled at Owosso, Mich.

III. Enos Slosson, b 20 March, 1834; a lawyer; was first-sergeant in 26th Reg. Mich. Vol. Infantry, was captured at Petersburgh, Va., 16 Aug., 1864; and died in prison at Salisbury, N. C., 12 Dec., 1864, and was buried there.

IV. Ulysses, b 11 April, 1836, settled at Chattanooga, Tenn.

V. John Obadiah, b 17 Jan., 1838; settled at Unadilla, Mich.

William Tremble Jayne, b at Florida, in Warwick, Orange Co., N. Y., 21 Oct., 1782; son of Samuel and Lydia (Karscadden) Jayne; m there 16 Oct., 1802, with Jane Armstrong, who was born there 27 Feb., 1784, daughter of Francis and Patience (Rowley) Armstrong. In Nov., 1819, they moved to Newark Valley, and settled on the north half of lot 19, previously owned by John Bement. This place he sold in Feb., 1821, to his brother-in-law Francis Armstrong, and lived in the small house on the hill side, east of the road till, 1825, when they moved to Richford, where he died 24 Nov., 1850.   His widow married (2d) with Dea. Joseph Abbott Beecher.   His children were:

I. Caroline, b 6 July, 1803 ; m with Frederick S. Dean, and died at her father's house, 13 April, 1827.

II. Frances, b 14 Jan., 1806 ; m with Jacob Conklin, 20 Jan., 1831, as his second wife.

III. Mary Ann, b 3 Aug., 1809, and died the 19 Aug., 1811.

IV. Amzi Lewis, b 29 Oct., 1811 , m 12 March, 1833, with Charlotte Clark Robinson, daughter of Thomas Amsdell Robinson.

V. Samuel Armstrong, b 6 Nov., 1814 ; m 31 Oct., 1838, with Laura Rich, who died without children.   He married again.

VI. William Tremble, b 20 Nov., 1816 ; went West about 1837, was at Mobile, Ala., two years later, about to go to Vicksburgh, Miss., since which his friends have not heard from him.

VII. Mary Pitney, b at Newark Valley, 6 April, 1820 ; died at Richford, 11 Nov., 1835.

This completes the history furnished by Mr. Patterson, and we add the following pages of matter gleaned from Mr. Robinson, and other sources.

Additional Settlements.—Dr. Elijah Powell came from Chenango county, N. Y., and took up his residence in the embryo village in 1823, beginning practice as a physician and also acting as surgeon in the new settlement.   The young doctor, twenty-three years of age, soon acquired an extensive practice and rose to eminence in his profession, which he adorned until old age exempted him from duties he had assiduously performed.   On the 4th of July, 1826, the Doctor delivered the address at the first Fourth of July celebration held in Richford.   In 1824, he erected the brick building, now occupied as a store by H. Rowley, for his office and drug-store.   Two years later, he built the large brick building on the corner, connected with the office building, the larger one being designed for a dwelling, store and offices.   Socially, Doctor Powell was a kind, affable, sympathetic man, generous to a fault, ever ready to respond when called to visit the sick, whatever were the circumstances or conditions of those who needed medical treatment.   As a Christian, he was a devoted follower of Him who gave Himself a sacrifice for mankind.   He ever took a zealous interest in schools and educational matters, and he was the first county school commissioner in and for the county of Tioga.   Originally, these commissioners were appointed, but the law was changed so that they were and are elected, and the Doctor was elected the first after serving the appointed term. He was unmarried when he became a resident of Richford, and took for his wife a belle of the place, Miss Lydia Wells, who died of consumption, July 18, 1833. A few years later he married his second wife, Miss Jane Anderson, of New York city, by whom he had two sons and five daughters. At length he became worn out by hard service, for a large amount of which he received no pecuniary reward. He seldom dunned, never distressed his debtors, whose numbers exceeded, perhaps, one half the population of the town. After a lingering sickness, he died, January 12, 1876, aged seventy-three years, and was buried in accordance with the rites of Free Masons, to which order he had been a worthy member during nearly, if not all, of his majority.

Peter Perry, one of the early settlers in the western part of Richford, came here, from Massachusetts, and made the first settlement on the farm now owned by Edwin A. Perry. He married Jane Surdam, and reared five children, Norman, Eleanor, Luther, Jane, and Guerdon. Luther came here with his father, married Maria, daughter of Joseph Quimby, and reared nine children, four of whom are living, namely, Alonzo, Frank, Daniel M. and Edwin A. He was a distiller by trade, and for a long time run a distillery, the first in town, on the farm now owned by Orrin Walker. Mr. Perry died in July, 1866, aged sixty-one years.

Elijah Gilbert was also an early settler in this part of the town. Mr. Gilbert had some trouble with his neighbors, and locked his water-trough with a padlock, according to one version, since which time this locality has been known as Padlock.

Isaac C. Smith came from Hamden, in 1823. He married Sally Pryor, and reared eight children, viz.: Julius C., Jonas P., Franklin H., Polly M., Estella C., Ralph P., William W. and Sarah. Of these only two are living, Julius C. and Ralph P. The latter has married three times, first, Fidelia Smith, second, Lucy A., daughter of William Cross, who bore him three children, Edward, deceased, May E. and Maud W., deceased, and third, Mrs. Elizabeth Speed, of Caroline.

Horace Goodrich was born in Durham, Conn., May 6, 1787, married Eleanor, daughter of Ichabod Scranton, of Durham, and located here about 1820. He made the first settlement on the farm now owned by Daniel Leach, but after living there a few years, he found that he was not upon the tract of land that his title called for, and he was obliged to leave it. He moved to

Newark Valley, where he died in 1829. He reared six children, namely: Dwight, Horace B., Guernsey S., Jerusha C., William S. and Emeline M. Of these, only three are living, William S., Jerusha, widow of Benjamin Krum, and Emeline M. (Mrs. Bostwick Brigham).

Lemuel D. Polley was born in Massachusetts, and moved to Dryden when a small boy. He married Polly Smith, of that town, and came to Richford in the spring of 1825. He made the first settlement on the farm now owned by Solomon Polley.

Jabez Ayres was born in Sussex county, N. J., and made the first settlement on the farm owned by William Wright, about 1825.

James Brigham was born in Brookfield, Mass., married Marcia Hastings, and made the first settlement on land now owned by Benjamin Thomas. He reared a family of nine children, five of whom are living, namely, Lucia, widow of Henry Branch, of Berkshire, Laura and Bostwick, both of this town, Alfred, of Schuyler, Neb., and Elizabeth, wife of Edward Gilbert, of Brookfield, Mass. Bostwick married Emeline, daughter of Horace Goodrich, and has three children, Marcia, wife of George Barber, of Newark Valley, Emma, wife of Charles Dickerson, of Cardiff, and Charles, who lives at home.

John Hamilton, son of Eliakim, came from West Stockbridge, Mass., in 1835, and made the first settlement on the farm where Mrs. Catherine Decker now lives.

Dioclesian Sears was born in Lenox, Mass., and came here in 1832, locating on the place where his son, James M., now lives. Philip Sears came at the same time, and settled on the next place east.

Hotchkiss T. Finch was born in Windham, N. Y., May 12, 1831, and came here with his father, in 1841. In 1850, he purchased the saw-mill on the farm now owned by Delia Vincent, which he run until 1862, when he went to Lisle, and bought the Lisle flouring and saw-mills. He sold them the same year, came back to Richford in 1866, and in 1870, the firm of H. S. & J. W. Finch was organized. He married Charlotte E., daughter of Robert Ketchum, of Lisle, and has one son, Charles R. In 1875, he, with Ketchum & Co., purchased the store of C. D. & G. L. Rich, and the firm of Finch, Ketchum & Co., was organized. Charles R. was born in this town, November 22, 1866, married Katie, daughter of W. Dwight Hull, of Owego, and is engaged in farming.

Much of the eastern part of the town has been settled only a few years. Among those who made the first settlements were Ithiel Burleigh, who located on the place where G. C. Tubbs now lives, Anson Stanley, on the place where he now resides, Robert Tubbs, Augustus Hill, James Satterly and William B. Satterly. Mr. Burleigh remained on his place only three years, when the place was abandoned, and G. C. Tubbs purchased the property, in 1846, and began clearing the land.

What may serve to give readers an idea of the town's progress in growth is a knowledge of the dates of the formation of the school districts. There are fourteen districts, five of which are joint districts, and there are eleven school-houses in the town. Prior to 1819, no district was defined by metes or bounds, but a school had been kept at " Padlock" several terms, which was attended by the few children whose homes were situated on or near the turnpike, at points between the Owego creeks, and up as far as Willow bridge. Down to 1832, all of the territory lying east of the East Owego creek in the town of Berkshire, and north of the subsequent line between Berkshire and Richford, comprised one district, in area about one-half of the town. Just prior to the time Richford was set off from Berkshire, school district No. 10, of Lisle, was altered so as to take in six lots lying in Richford. When the town was divided, there were seven districts, including the joint ones.

The comparative growth of the town may be seen by the following citation from the several census enumerations since the town was organized : 1835, 882 ; 1845, 1,093 ; 1850, 1,208 ; 1855, 1,182 ; 1860, 1,404 ; 1865, 1,283 ; 1870, 1,434; 1875, 1,451 ; 1880, 1,477.

Organization.—The town of Richford was formed from Berkshire, first as the town of Arlington, April 9, 1831 ; its name being changed by act of legislature April 9, 1832. The town was duly organized, at the first town meeting, held at the Rich hotel, on Tuesday, March 6, 1832, when civil officers were duly elected, as follows : William Dunham, supervisor ; John C. Steadman, town clerk; William Belden, Hubbard F. Wells, and Heman Daniels, commissioners of highways ; Jacob Burget, Elijah Powell, and Tower Whiting, commissioners of common schools ; Simeon R. Griffin, Israel Wells, and Edward W. Surdam, school inspectors ; Nathaniel Johnson and William Raymond, overseers of the poor ; Obadiah Livermore, collector ; Hiram W. Tyler and Henry Talmage, constables ; Seth B. Torrey, sealer of weights and measures; Platt F. Grow, Eri Osburn, and David C. Garrison, justices of the peace. The said meeting took further action, to wit :

"Voted, The town raise a sum of money equal to that drawn from the treasury.

"Voted, That we pay the Inspectors of Common Schools seventy-five cents per day, as compensation for their services.

"Voted, That hogs may be commoners by being rung sufficiently and yoked with a sufficient yoke ; the yoke is to be twice the width of the neck above, and thirdth below.

"Voted, That no cattle nor hogs be commoners at any season of the year within one-half mile of the village of Richford.

"Voted, That O. L. Livermore be Poundmaster, and his yard be the Pound for the ensuing year.

"Voted, This meeting be adjourned to the house now kept by S. M. Crandal, on the 1st Tuesday in March, 1833."

Material and Mercantile Interests.—The prominent industrial interest of the town is agriculture in its various branches, particularly the dairy. The principal exports have been of live stock, hay, wool, pork and butter, chiefly the latter. No cereals are sent from the town, but recently the growing of potatoes for shipping has become a special industry. At present the resources of the farming community consists in potatoes, calves, and butter. Heretofore, lumbering in its various branches has been the most prominent pursuit in the eastern part of the town, a business that has died a natural death. The money paid for the lumber and bark has not materially enriched the town, not stopped therein, but been paid for merchandise brought from other parts, the locality serving simply as a camp.

Ezekiel Rich was the first to open a store in Richford. He commenced trade in 1821, and turned over the business to William Dunham, in 1823, who continued trade in the "Old Abby" until the corner brick building was completed, when he moved therein, about 1827. A few years later, Dunham vacated the brick store and opened a new store, situated on his experimental city plot, half-mile below, which went up with his visionary castle. While Mr. Dunham was yet trading in the Abbey, Gad Worthington erected a store about mid-way between C. L. Rich's residence and the public square. This was the first building erected in Richford to be used exclusively as a store, and he put in a stock of goods and commenced trade in 1825. Later Mr. Cook purchased the store of Worthington, and continued trade a few years.

About 1829, James Robins opened a store in the brick building vacated by Dunham, and his stock was of a greater variety and more complete than any store yet in the place. Robins continued business in the brick store until the present Rich's store was erected, in 1834, when he removed and occupied the new store, until 1844, when he sold to C. L. Rich and William Pierson. During the period of Robins's trading, there was not much competition, but while Rich & Pierson were trading, S. R. Griffin opened a store in the building now standing near t he corner of the street leading to the depot. Later, he sold to Enoch Glezen, who occupied the store a few years, after which C. A. Clark, of Owego, opened the store, and later still Nathaniel Moore, of Berkshire, opened it and after trading a while sold to W. H. Powell and M. Westcott, who wound up the competition, leaving the field to C. L. Rich and sons with J. H. Deming. Before Mr. Robins opened his store, Doctor Seaman erected the building now occupied by W. F. Miller and by C. H. Swift, for use as a store, and he put therein a stock of goods and continued trade several years ; and he run the only distillery ever put in operation here. In 1869, H. B. Rowley opened a store in the brick store, where he is still trading. About 1880, James S. Smith opened a store in the Rich block, and in 18— he sold his stock to W. C. Smith & Co.

In 1870, H. Tane and T. Brainard opened the old Seaman store a hardware and house furnishing store, with stoves and articles used about the house, together with the manufacture of tin, copper and ironware. The firm did business about three years, then made a general assignment to C. J. Robinson, who continued the business about three years and then closed it out.

In 1880, C. H. Swift opened a store and shop like that last mentioned, and in the same building, where he is still doing business.

One of the most popular stores is that owned and conducted by Mrs. Delos Yaple, in the Rich block. She has been in trade twelve or more years, carrying on millinery business in connection with her store.

At an early day Joseph Bayette (a Frenchman) came in the eastern portion of the town, settled and built a log house and manufactured cigars, then removed to Ithaca, returned in 1850, and, in the large building fronting the square, again commenced the manufacture of cigars. He was succeeded by his sons, who increased the business and employed twenty-five hands. They were succeeded by George and Edward Rich, sons of Chauncey

Rich, and the business was continued until the spring of 1877, when it was discontinued.

C. L. Rich, who commenced clerking for Mr. Robins, in 1834, has been chief of the mercantile trade in Richford. He retired from trade, to accept the office of treasurer of the Southern Central Railroad, of which he has been not only treasurer but also one of the leading directors and stockholders. He conducted the financial business of the road with so much ability that it remained in first hands much longer than any other road in the state or elsewhere. Mr. Rich, his sons and brother-in-law, are bankers, the sons being at the head of a bank in Fort Dodge, Iowa, C. L. having retired from active business on the road and now lives at his home in Richford.

BUSINESS CENTERS.

RICHFORD VILLAGE is located in the southern-central part of the town, where the railroad crosses the old Catskill turnpike. It has one church, one hotel, two general stores, hardware store, furniture store, millinery and grocery store, a saw-mill and novelty works, grist-mill, two blacksmith shops, and about 250 inhabitants.

EAST RICHFORD is a small settlement in the eastern part of the town.

WEST RICHFORD is a small settlement in the western part of the town.

Prior to the establishment of a postoffice in Berkshire village, about 1824, the office nearest to Richford was at a point on the Creek road one and one half miles south of the boundary, between Berkshire and Newark, eight miles distant from Richford. The Richford postoffice was established in 1830, with William Dunham postmaster. He kept the office in his dwelling, the "Old Abby," the first house erected in the village; afterward the office was removed into the brick store on the corner, and O. L. Livermore, officiated as deputy postmaster. Later, Simeon Crandal was appointed postmaster, and he removed the postoffice from the brick store into the Rich hotel, of which he was innkeeper. Later still, C. L. Rich was appointed postmaster, and he removed the office from the hotel into the store where, excepting a few years (1862 to '66) the office has been kept to the present time. Mr. Rich was succeeded by J. H. Deming, and at the next change in the administration, Mr. Rich was re-appointed. Matthew Westcott was appointed later. In 1866, C. D. Rich was appointed, and later he resigned in favor of C. W. Finch. In 1886 C. A. Clark was appointed, and is the present incumbent.

During a long period, the mails were carried by stages running on the turnpike, leading from Catskill to Ithaca, also on the road from Homer to Owego. As the mail going east reached Catskill, it was transferred to steamboats plying on the Hudson, and would make the round trip via New York city in five days. The two-horse stage line from Homer to Richford was discontinued in 183-, and the four-horse stage line on the pike was discontinued at the time the New York and Erie railroad was opened as far as Owego, June 1, 1849. A two-horse stage continued to carry the mail from Lisle through Richford to Ithaca, during a few years, up to 1852. And a two-horse stage transmitted the mail daily from Richford to Owego and return, up to the opening of the Southern Central railroad.

In 1852 a postoffice was established in the town, under the title of " West Richford Postoffice," Erie Osborn, postmaster. In 1860, this office was discontinued.

MANUFACTORIES.

The history of mills in the town begins with the ones erected by Caleb Arnold; but the exact date cannot be ascertained, though it was probably 1813. He had a saw and grist-mill also wool-carding works, located on the West Owego creek, on lot 500. The saw-mill was rebuilt in 1835; the other mill run down long before, and Mr. Arnold had left. The next saw and grist-mill was erected by Gad Worthington, on the East creek, at a point not far south of the depot, in 1823–24. A few years later, William Dunham bought the mills, and allowed them to run down later. In 1831, Simeon R. Griffin erected a grist-mill some forty rods northwest of the junction of Aurora street with the old pike road. The motor power was water taken from the brook, led onto a thirty foot over-shot wheel. The mill did a good business until 1840. After Griffin ran it a few years, he sold to Enoch Gleazen, who sold to Mr. Torrey, who let the mill go down. About 1830, a Mr. Wells erected a saw-mill just north of the village. Later, Abram Deming became owner of, and rebuilt the mill, and after sawing millions of feet of pine lumber, sold to Elisha Hart, who sold in turn to William Cross; and afterward Henry

Geer owned and repaired the mill, and later William Allen became owner, allowing it to go down.

About 1830, William Pumpelly, of Owego, erected a saw-mill on his lands, two miles north of Richford village. Afterward the mill was owned by Milton Holcomb, John Gee, and finally got into Clinton Cleveland's hands, who rebuilt it, with a large circular-saw, in place of the up-and-down saw. The mill is still in running order.

In 1850, Belden Brothers erected a saw-mill on their premises, some forty rods north of the highway bridge across the creek. The mill cut a vast quantity of lumber, and recently the supply of stock became exhausted, and the mill was abandoned.

In 1850, a saw-mill was erected on the creek a little south of Harford Mills, in this town. Subsequently, a factory for manufacturing sash, blinds and doors was erected beside the mill. The property is now owned by Mr. Granger.

In 1853, William Andrews built a steam saw-mill on lot 493, two and one-half miles east of the village, on the old pike road. It was the first steam motor used in the town. The mill was a costly structure, and ample in its capacity, had it been fittingly arranged ; but only one sash-saw was put in operation. The manufacture of lumber, under the circumstances, could not be made a success, financially, and Mr. Andrews was forced to sacrifice and return to Connecticut, his former home. The mill was not put to much use, and some three years after its completion, it burned. A few years later, Jones & Hubbard erected a new steam-mill on this site, with a circular-saw ; but the business still met with poor success, and after a few years the mill burned.

In the fall of 1870, Messrs. C. W. and H. S. Finch erected a steam saw-mill not far from the depot. A branch track is one of the appurtenances of the mill. The mill did an extensive business until September 12, 1871, when it took fire at midnight and burned, with all therein and about it. The owners at once rebuilt the mill, and again, October 31, 1879, at noon, the mill took fire, making a clean sweep of all therein and adjacent. Again the same owners promptly rebuilt, and the mill is now in operation. This mill is an institution very elaborate in machinery, whereby huge forest trees are wrought into articles for use, from a railroad bridge-beam one hundred feet in length, down to a clothspin ; and all kinds of lumber required for building is dressed complete in finish, ready to be nailed in place. The mill is of a capacity equal to sawing 25,000 feet of lumber per day, and has been run nearly all the time since it started. This mill has been a success, financially. C. W. Finch runs the mill, and H. S. Finch, with J. Allen, are the lumber merchants.

In 1876, Franklin Bliss erected a steam mill for grinding feed and threshing grain, about one-fourth mile west of the village. The same year H. S. Finch put in a mill for grinding feed, attached to his provision store, near the depot. In 1884, Mr. Bliss shut down his mill, and purchased the mill owned by Finch, and added one more run of stones, and other first-class machinery for manufacturing best quality of buckwheat flour. In the fall of 1886, the mill took fire at noon, and burned. Nothing was saved pertaining to the mill, and a large stock of grain was lost. The mill was very promptly rebuilt and put in operation, and Mr. Bliss is doing a good business, manufacturing buckwheat flour, and ships large quantities to Philadelphia and other markets, besides grinding many car-loads of grain each year for the home market.

The saw-mill of J. W. Allen, located, on road 18, is operated by water-power and has the capacity for cutting 1,000,000 feet of lumber annually. The first mill built on this site was about 1830, by Milton Holcomb; but has from time to time been rebuilt, and for a short time steam was used in the mill. It is equipped with lumber-saw, double lath-saw, planing and matching machines, and employs six men.

CHURCHES.

There are but three meeting-houses in the town, one of which is not utilized, or only opened occasionally. Of the three churches formed within the town, but one seems to hold out prosperously, the original first church, the nucleus of which were Puritans of the Mayflower lineage, from Massachusetts. The church record fails, by reason of the imperfect manner it has been kept, to give a full or comprehensive history of the church from the first. Fortunately, there is one survivor, Deacon W. F. Belden, whose parents were of the few originators, and he has himself been a member during nearly three-score years, during which time he has kept a private record, to which we are indebted for much of the ecclesiastical history of the town.

The first settlers in Richford were mostly families from Lenox, Mass., among whom was Stephen Wells, a deacon of the Presbyterian church in Lenox, who commenced holding meetings in the new (first) school-house, in 1821. On December 4, 1821, the few inhabitants of Richford assembled in the school-house, in the evening, for the purpose of considering the subject of organizing a church society and the building of a meeting-house. At this meeting a society was duly formed, to be known as " The North Society of the Town of Berkshire." The meeting was adjourned, to meet at the house (hotel) of Ezekiel Rich, one week later, and from week to week to meet at said house. Finally, the meeting took action by passing a resolution to build a meeting-house in the summer of 1822, at an expense of five hundred dollars, " and, if a steeple is put on, the cost of the structure not to exceed seven hundred dollars." The house was erected as per resolution, and soon after, the Rev. Seth Burt, a missionary sent out by the Berkshire and Columbia (Mass). Missionary Society, becamee the pastor. On December 23, 1822, thirty-one of the inhabitants of Richford and vicinity banded themselves together as a society, entitled " The Society of Columbia," which title it still retains. On January 14, 1823, a Christian Church was duly organized, according to the order of Presbyterian faith, with forty-one charter members, of which twenty-two presented letters, and nineteen made confession of faith. One of the most devoted of the charter members, Mrs. Ezekiel Rich, united with the old church of Berkshire (prior to the formation of Newark), the first Sabbath in April, 1820, and in 1821, she removed from Newark Valley to Richford, where she presented a letter of membership. She was one who aided the organizing of the church, and the last of the forty-one to die—ever zealous, she was the last to leave the Richford church militant and join the church triumphant, on the 2d day of June, 1883, aged ninety-two years.

The church was connected with the Cayuga presbytery. The first delegation of elders sent from Richford were Dea. S. Wells, Thomas P. Brown, and Deodatus Royce. The church continued as a Presbyterian order until 1827, when the members unanimously resolved to change and adopt the Congregational form of discipline, and duly appointed delegates to go and inquire into the standing of the " Union Association ;" also constituted delegates to attend a meeting of the presbytery for instructions, resolving to remain in the fold of the Presbytery on " the accommodation plan." November 2, 1827, the elders tendered their resignation, and the church became Congregational in form, but remained connected with the Presbytery until 1868, at which date, in October, the church connected itself with the Susquehanna Association, there being no change since.

In 1833, a church was formed in the town of Berkshire, as now bounded, and twelve of the members of the Richford church took letters to unite with the new organization at Berkshire village.

The first church edifice was erected on the site now occupied. The building was smaller in size than the last one built. Its style of architecture was Eastern, a steeple and bell, the latter still used. The front half of the steeple projected from the main edifice and rested on four large turned columns, having ornamental base and capitals. Internally, a gallery extended around on two sides and the rear end, forming a semi-circle, the central portion of which was occupied by the choir and a pulpit, the back of which was the inner wall of the vestibule. On the main floor were two aisles, between which were two tiers of seats, and on one side of either aisle was a row of seats in square sections, or "pews." The best of pine lumber was used in constructing the meeting-house; because the Lord had placed the material near at hand, His servants took it as His own, wherever found, without regard to the will of land-owners. In 1854, the old house was taken down and a new one of larger dimensions erected, and which has been rearranged internally and ornamented with a different style of steeple. The church-going people of early times here allude to the advent of "fire in meeting-houses." Furnaces and stoves were not then in use, and worshipers had to endure a severe ordeal when they attended meeting in winter; so after the stove came as a new blessing, warmth was a very grateful part of the meeting in cold weather.

The whole number in communion with the church up to February, 1875, was 278; the number at that date was, present and absent, seventy-three. In 1874, twelve took letters and joined other churches. At times there have been handsome accessions to the church; but death and emigration depleted the ranks to such an extent that augmentation permanently was scarcely possible.

Referring to the several pastors, Rev. Mr. Burt closed his term in 1825, leaving the church without a visable shepherd until 1827, when Rev. Henry Ford ministered one year. Rev. Mr. Cary occupied the pulpit a portion of the time up to 1829, at which date the Rev. David S. Morse became pastor, and continued such until April, 1833. Rev. Mr. Graves succeeded Mr. Morse, for a short period. In December, 1833, Rev. Mr. Ripley commenced

preaching in the Richford church each alternate Sabbath, continuing up to April, 1835, when Mr. Morse returned and continued
until 1840.   During 1841, Rev. Mr. McEwen occupied the pulpit,
and Rev. Mr. Babbitt during 1842, who was not succeeded until
1844, when Mr. Morse returned again, and continued pastor up to
1849.   Then Mr. Page served from 1850 to 1851, when Rev.
Jeremiah Woodruff officiated during a term of four years. In 1856,
Rev. Mr. Worden, who was pastor of the Methodist church at
Berkshire, occupied the pulpit here each alternate Sabbath   In
April, 1857, Rev. Richard Woodruff became pastor and served
six years, less one month, when, after preaching three sermons one
Sabbath, he died before morning, March 9, 1863, and was buried
beside his wife in the cemetery at Richford.   His age was sixty-
two. In July, 1863, Rev. J. S. Hanna commenced a term of pas-
toral service, continued one year, and the year following Rev.
David Gibbs served as pastor.   In the winter of 1866, Mr. Morse
served six months, also a six months' term in the winter of 1867.
His whole term of service was about eighteen years. He was
born in 1793, died in 1871, and lies buried in Richford cemetery.
Mr. Morse was a man of superior understanding.   In July 1868,
Rev. George Porter, from England, became pastor, and served
two years, less six weeks.   In July, 1870, Rev. Mr. Green took
charge, and served until May, 1873.   Another vacancy then
occurred, extending to November, 1874, when Rev. Mr. Thomas
commenced and served two years. Rev. E. W. Fisher commenced
April 1, 1878. The next pastor was A. D. Stowell, who commenced in June, 1880, and who was succeeded by Rev. E. P.
Dada, in May, 1882; Rev. George Miller, in September 1884, and
Charles Burgen, the incumbent pastor, commenced service May
1, 1887. The largest salary paid per year to any of the pastors
employed was one thousand dollars, to Mr. Porter, for the first
year. The Missionary Society has liberally contributed toward
paying the salaries.

In 1823 a Sabbath-school was established in which there were
sixty-five attendants, who resided within a territory stretching
nine miles east and west and seven miles from point to point, north
and south. Many who attended, found their way through the forest
by blazed trees. Here it is worthy of mention, in paying honor
due to faithful Christians, that a certain widow, Mrs. Gardner,
and her two daughters, who resided on lot 418, on the border of
the town of Berkshire, over two miles distant, were sure to be in
attendance each Sabbath regardless of inclement weather. Their

pathway to and from the meetings was over rugged, hilly ground, their course all the way marked only by blazed trees. The Sabbath-school has been well maintained to the present.

Of the early settlers in the town, a few were Episcopalians, who organized a church, and erected a small house on the site where now stands C. L. Rich's barn. It was built about 1832, and was removed to Speedsville, in 1843. No record of the proceedings of the Episcopalians in the town is obtainable ; but memories relate some incidents.

In 1857, a society was formed which was styled '' The Rich-ford Hill Christian Church," and in 1860 they erected a house, in which to worship according to their creed. They have a clear title to a desirable rural site of ample dimensions, including a cemetery, in which are erected monuments, some of which are elaborate and costly. At one time the church numbered thirty or more members, but later it fell to zero ; yet later still, a rally occurred and it recuperated, and now they have a shepherd who occupies the pulpit regularly, in connection with a neighboring society. Rev. Mr. Tyler officiates as pastor.

In 1864, a church society was duly organized in the eastern part of the town. Their creed was Baptist, and in 1870 they completed a church edifice. The number of members have not exceeded twenty-three. A portion of the time of their existence the vital spark seemed to wane to a low ebb. At present they have a joint interest in a minister who resides at a distance.

———

SPENCER* lies in the extreme north-western corner of the county, and is bounded north by the county line, east by Candor, south by Barton, and west by the county line. The town was formed by an act of the legislature passed February 28, 1806, receiving its name in honor of Judge Ambrose Spencer. At this time, however, it was a town of great extent, set off from Owego (now Tioga). From this large territory have been formed the towns of Candor, Caroline, Danby and Newfield, the latter three in Tompkins county, set off February 22, 1811 ; and Cayuta, in Schuyler county, organized March 20, 1824. Thus Spencer may truly be said to be a "mother of towns;" but these large

*For much of this sketch we are indebted to Mr. J. H. Palmer, of Spencer.

29*

concessions have shorn the parent town's territory to an area of only about 29,136 acres, 20,000 acres of which is improved land.

Topography.—The north-eastern portion of the town forms the water-shed between the Susquehanna river and Cayuga lake. The ridges have a general north and south direction, their declivities steep, and their summits broad and broken. Catatonk creek, flowing east, breaks through these ridges at nearly right angles, forming a deep and narrow valley. This is the principal stream, though there are numerous small tributaries to it. The soil is a gravelly loam in the valleys, and a hard, shaly loam upon the hills. Dairying, stock-raising, and lumbering are the chief pursuits of the people.

SETTLEMENT AND GROWTH.

Benjamin Drake, in connection with Joseph Barker, made the first settlement in the town of Spencer, in the year 1794. The place of his nativity is not known, and as none of his descendants are now living here, nothing of his early life, previous to settlement here, can be ascertained. He settled on the site of Spencer village, or what was for many years the village, the lower corners, as the north and west portions of the village have mostly been built up in comparatively a few years. Mr. Drake's first cabin was built of logs, poles and bark, near the bank of Catatonk creek, half, or three-quarters of a mile east of the village. His time was occupied in clearing his land, and when, after the labors of the day were over, and the shades of night had gathered around the humble home of the settlers, and they had retired to rest, their sleep was often disturbed by the howling and snarling of the wild beasts that inhabited the wilderness around them. Tradition says that Mr. Drake built the first frame dwelling-house in town, a part of which is standing on the spot where Andrew Purdy formerly resided, and known for many years as the " Purdy tavern," and now owned by the estate of Hon. Abram H. Miller. He also built the first grist-mill. How long he resided here, and the time or place of his death, is not known. His daughter, Deborah, was the first white child born within the present town limits.

Joseph Barker, as stated above, came to Spencer in the year 1794, from Wyoming, Pa. He settled on the place now owned by C. W. Bradley, a little north of the center of the village of Spencer, his land extending south of and including the old cemetery, which he partially cleared off and gave to the town as a public burial-place. At that early day there was no town organization, and consequently no town officers, common interests prompting the settlers to friendliness and a general effort to build up good society, and also to extend a cordial greeting and welcome to those who came to settle and make a home among them. But as their numbers increased, the necessity of forming such an organization became apparent, and it was effected in 1806, and the first town meeting was held April 1st, of that year, Mr. Barker being elected justice of the peace, an office he held till the election of Israel Hardy, in 1830. The first school was organized in Mr. Barker's house, but the date is not known. Many of his descendants are still living in this and adjoining towns. He was a man of strict integrity, and was respected and honored by all around him.

Edmond and Rodney Hobart, brothers, came from Canaan, Litchfield county, Conn., in the year 1795. Edmond settled on the farm now owned and occupied by James B. Hull, his brother Rodney going about a mile farther north, where he resided for many years, the place now being owned by Benjamin F. Lewis, excepting about four acres where the house stands, that is now owned by Mr. E. Signor. Edmond Hobart is said to have put in and harvested the first crop of wheat, and he also built the first saw-mill. His family consisted of seven children, five boys and two girls, and their conveyance from Yankee land to Spencer was a wagon drawn by oxen, and they were seventeen days on the road, making the third family in the town. Their oldest son, Prescott, while using the axe—the principal and most useful tool the settlers had—received a slight cut which terminated in lockjaw, the first year they were here, his death being the first one in town. Charlotte, the oldest daughter, married Daniel McQuigg, of Owego, who purchased the homestead of the heirs, in 1815, (Mr. Hobart died in 1808) and it was kept in the family many years, his son Daniel occupying it till about the year 1844, when it was sold to Deacon James B. Hull, who now lives on it. Esther, the youngest daughter, married Horace Giles, of Owego, in 1814, and in a few months moved to Spencer, where the widow lived till her death, in 1832. Mr. and Mrs. Giles lived on the same farm for fifty-five years. He died December 16, and she, December 18, 1870, aged eighty and seventy-seven years, respectively. Two daughters and one son are now living, one, Charlotte Giles Converse, occupying the homestead.

Others came soon after the settlement was begun, but the exact date cannot now be ascertained. John and George K. Hall, from Westchester county, N. Y., came about 1798, and settled on a part of what for many years has been known as the John McQuigg farm. Soon after the year 1800, the arrivals became more frequent. Among them may be named the following: Joshua Ferris, from Westchester, Doctor Holmes, from Connecticut, and Stephen Bidlack, from Wyoming, in 1800; Henry Miller, Andrew Purdy, Thomas Mosher, C. Valentine, John and Leonard Jones, David and Richard Ferris, from Westchester county, N. Y., and George Watson, from Canaan, Conn., between that date and 1805; Truman, Joshua, Abram and Benjamin Cowell, brothers, came from Connecticut about 1807 or 1808; George Fisher and family, from Albany, N. Y., in 1810; Thomas Fisher and family came soon after, and settled in what has long been known as Fisher's Settlement, his wife being the first person to drive a horse from the settlement (now the village), through the woods to their home ; Solomon Mead, Joseph Cowles, Alvin Benton, Thomas Andrews, H. Lotze, Joel Smith, Benjamin Jennings, Moses Reed, Levi Slater, Ezekiel Palmer and his son, Urban Palmer, came prior to 1815 ; Shubael Palmer and wife, with a family of six children, came in February, 1817, bringing both family and goods by oxen through woods and over hills, with roads such as is usually found at that time of the year. The next few years arrivals were numerous, and among them may be found the names of Dodd, Lake, Lott, Dean, Garey, French, Sackett, Riker, Vose, Harris, Bradley, Wells, Benton, Nichols, Adams, Casterline, Scofield, Swartwood and Butts.

Isaac, William and Daniel Hugg, brothers, came from Canaan, Conn., the first two in 1800, and Daniel four years later, and settled in that part of the town known for many years as Hugg Town, now called North Spencer. Isaac settled at the head of the pond, his land extending to the road leading from Spencer to Ithaca ; but built his house and resided till his death, in 1837, where Horace Furman now lives. This family consisted of eleven children, six girls and five boys. The youngest daughter, Sophia, is still living, and is in good health for one who has seen eighty-four years.

William Hugg settled on the farm afterwards occupied by his brother, Daniel. His family consisted of twelve children, eight daughters and four sons, none of whom are now living. He only resided here three or four years, moving to West Danby, where he and his wife were both buried.

Daniel Hugg arrived in Spencer, in 1804, and settled on the farm previously occupied by his brother, William, where Frank Adams now lives, and resided there till the death of his wife, in 1849, after which he lived with his children till his death, in 1855, having been a resident of Spencer for fifty one years. His family of six daughters and one son are all dead. At the organization of the First Congregational church, Daniel Hugg and Achsah Hugg, his wife, were two of the original members, and he was one of the first deacons, a title he retained till his death. The descendants of these three brothers can be counted by the score, and are not only to be found in Spencer and surrounding towns, but in several different States of the Union, and as far as known are honored and respected members of the communities in which they reside.

Rev. Phineas Spalding was born in Woodstock, Vermont, in 1759. While a mere boy he enlisted in the revolution, was present at the surrender of Burgoyne, saw him deliver his sword to his captors, and was one of the guard placed over the prisoners taken at that time. Afterwards, in the darkest hours of that terrible struggle, he joined that portion of the army with Washington, late in the autumn of 1777, and when the inclemency of the weather rendered it necessary to go into permanent winter quarters they marched for eight days, leaving marks from their bleeding feet upon the frozen ground, till they came to Valley Forge, where they spent the winter. Their cabins were made with the boughs of trees hung on sticks or poles, under which they would build their fires, and gather around them, poorly clothed, and many without blankets, coats or shoes, and often obliged to feed on horse meat, which, in consequence of their extreme hunger, seemed to taste sweeter than any meat they had ever eaten before. After leaving the army he married a Miss Rebecca Jacques, by whom he had three children, Rebecca, Phineas, and Polly, the latter of whom was only a few weeks old when Mrs. Spaulding died. After marrying again (Miss Susanna Hotchkiss), he removed to Whitehall, N. Y., where Nancy, Amy, and William were born. About 1796, he came to what was then called Tioga Point, and lived for one year on a place called the Shepard farm, during which time his son James was born. While living here, he came to Spencer and selected the place upon which he afterward settled his family, in the year 1798. The place has been known for many years as the John McQuigg place. Here, in the woods, the sturdy pioneer erected his log cabin, cleared his land, and made him elf and family a home, and soon had the satisfaction of seeing the growing crops, and also neighbors settling around him. Here three more children were added to Mr. Spalding's family, viz.: Susanna, Jesse, and Joseph. As neighbors increased,and he being the only male professor of religion in the town,he was impressed that duty called him to preach the gospel to those around him, and yielding to these convictions, he preached, in his own house, the first gospel sermon in the town,in 1799. At the organization of the Baptist church, in 1810, he was chosen deacon, licensed to preach, and in 1813, was ordained, and was for many years pastor of the church. Previous to this he removed to a farm about two miles south of West Danby, where he lived several years, and here Ebenezer and Betsey were born. Mrs. Spalding died there in 1832, after which he lived with his children. He died in 1838, aged seventy-nine years, at the residence of his daughter Amy (Mrs. Barker), at West Danby, and his remains repose in the old cemetery in Spencer. Three of his children are still living, Mrs. Amy Barker, at West Danby, N. Y., aged ninety-four years; Ebenezer, in Wisconsin, aged seventy-nine years; and Mrs. Betsey Cowell, at North Spencer, aged seventy-seven years. Those who have died lived most of them to be old, and were useful and honored citizens. Phineas died at Havanna, aged eighty-six years. Polly, the next oldest child, was married to John Underwood, and this was the first marriage in town. She died in Spencer, aged seventy-five years. Nancy moved to Ohio at an early day, and died in 1838. James died at West Danby. Joseph died in Washington, and William, where he had lived for many years, at Mottville, aged eighty-two years.

Stephen Bidlack, son of James, came to Spencer, from Athens in 1800, and made the first settlement on the farm now owned by Ransom Bidlack. He married Lois, daughter of Capt. Samuel Ransom, and reared eight children, only one of whom, Ransom, is living.

Richard Ferris came from Peekskill, in 1805, and located on land now owned by Elmer Garrott. He reared a family of nine children, only one of whom, Mary, is living. The latter was born March 22, 1787, and has lived here since she was eighteen years of age. She is the widow of John Forsyth, who was a pensioner of the war of 1812.

Truman Cowell, one of the early settlers, came from Coxsackie, about 1806, and made the first settlement on the farm now owned by Edward Cowell. He had born to him two sons and eight daughters, viz.: Nathan, James, Naomi, Eunice, Anna, Roxy, Polly, Rhoda, Della, and Harriet.

Nathaniel Scofield, an early settler, located on the farm now owned by Luther Blivin, about 1806. His son Horace married Naomi Cowell, and six children were born to them, as follows: Betsey M., Nathaniel, Mary A., Truman, Roxanna and Horace.

William Loring, son of Abel, was born in Barre, Mass., November 18, 1780, and moved from there to Granville, N. Y., when quite young. He married Hannah, daughter of Theophilus Tracy, of Norwich, Conn., October 8, 1808, and nine children were born to them, viz.: Horace, William T., Lucena, Wealthy, Susan, Sarah, Louisa, Mary, and Harriet. Mr. Loring located in this town in February, 1811. Lucena Loring married James B. Hull, and has one son, Loring W.

Arthur Frink was one of the early settlers here, and located on the farm now owned by William Ransom.

Peter Signor came from Greenville, N. Y., in March, 1812, and purchased the farm which was settled by Bartley Roots, in 1810, and which is now owned by Albert Signor. He married Lorena, daughter of Adonijah Roots, and had born to him three children, Albert, Adonijah, and Anna, widow of Jehiel House, of Danby. Albert was born in Greenville, May 12, 1803, married Anna, daughter of Levi English, and has two children, Adonijah and Mary A. (Mrs. Ira Patchen), of Danby. In 1834 he purchased the farm where he now lives, which was then a wilderness, with no building except an old saw-mill, built a few years previous, and which he has re-built, and has cut from 100,000 to 400,000 feet of lumber annually.

One of the first settlers of what is known as the Dean Settlement, was Nicholas Dean, who came from Westchester county, in June, 1816, and built the first house on the place now owned by Mary Deyo, in October, 1817. Among other early settlers who came to this location were Elisha Sackett, from Peekskill, in 1820, locating where Jasper Patty now lives, John Williams, who settled on the farm now owned by George Pearson, and Eli Howell, who settled on the farm now owned by W. H. Fleming.

Maj. Tunis Riker came from New York city, in 1817, and located on the farms now owned by O. P. Riker and Antoinette Riker. He served as a major in the war of 1812. He was a carpenter by trade, which occupation he followed here. He married Eleanor Moore, of New York, and reared a family of twelve children.

Edward Bingham came from Jay, Vt., about 1819, and located on the farm now owned by his grandson, I. A. Bingham. He served in the war of 1812. Ira, one of his twelve children, married Sally, daughter of Elisha Holdridge, and five children were born to him, viz.: Eliza, deceased, Sarah, Mary, I. Augustus, and Seth H.

Edward Hobart, an early settler, made the first settlement on the place now owned by James B. Hull. It is said that the first piece of wheat raised in the town was grown on this farm.

Elisha Holdridge came from Bridgewater, Pa., in the spring of 1822, and purchased a farm, now owned by Dr. Norris, where he lived until 1837 or 1838, when he removed to Genoa. He married Mary Shaff, and reared nine children, only two of whom, Amos, of Spencer, and Samuel, of Hillsdale, Mich., are now living. Amos was born in Bridgewater, Pa., July 13, 1813, and was nine years of age when he came here. He married Wealthy, daughter of William Loring, of Spencer, and has two children, Edgar P., of Cortland, and William A., who lives here.

Lewis VanWoert, son of Jacob, was born in Cambridge, N. Y., December 5, 1794; married Tabitha Gould, and settled here on the farm now owned by Lewis J. VanWoert, in 1827. He reared five children, namely, William G., Lewis J., Eleanor M., Lydia E., and Mehitable, deceased.

John Brock came here in 1830, and purchased the farm now owned by William Lang. He was a farmer, and was also engaged in droving until within two years of his death, which occurred in 1872. He married Mary, daughter of A. Whitney, of Maryland, N. Y., and seven children were born to them, viz.: William, deceased, Ethiel, Ann E., wife of Seth Bingham, of Danby, John, Adaline, widow of Stockholm Barber, Thomas, and Dewitt C.

Benjamin Coggin located here, on the farm now owned by his grandson, George E. Coggin, in 1832. He married Phebe Vose, and six children were born to him, as follows: John, Loama T., Albert, Rachel V., Mary V., and Eveline C.

Solomon Davenport, son of Martin, was born at Port Jervis; lived in Caroline, N. Y., several years, and located here, on the farm now owned by Mrs. Valentine, in 1836. He married Ann, daughter of Samuel Snyder, of Caroline, and eight children were born to him, viz.: Henry, Sherman, Mary C., Jane A., Charlotte, Emma E., Sarah and Harriet A.

James Hagadorn came from Cherry Valley, in 1840, and settled on the farm now owned by his son David B. He married Lockey Genung, and five children were the fruits of this marriage, namely, Horace, who served as major in the late war, in Co. H, 3d N. Y. Infantry, and was killed in front of Petersburg, June 15, 1865, Rebecca, wife of Henry C. Shaw, Emma, wife of William Stone, of Curtis, Neb., Aaron, also of Curtis, and David B.

Jacob T. Shaw was an early settler of Flemingville, and located here, in 1840, on the farm now owned by William A. Shaw.

Alonzo Norris, son of Matthew N., who was an early settler of Erin, Chemung county, was born in Erin, October 2, 1833, studied medicine with E. Howard Davis, of Horseheads, for three years, and graduated from Jefferson Medical College, of Philadelphia, Pa., March 12, 1860. He began practice at Halsey Valley, where he remained about a year, and then located in this town. He has two children, John N. and Olive K., both residing at home.

Dr. Ezra W. Homiston was born in Brooklyn, N. Y., June 10, 1859. He studied in the public schools, and with his father, Joseph M., and graduated at the Bellevue Hospital College in March, 1883, and began practice in Brooklyn. In August, 1885, he came to Spencer, and has practiced here since. He married Adele Bumsted, of Jersey City, in 1882.

Rev. Luther Bascom Pert, son of Thomas Pert, was born in this town October 12, 1819. When fifteen years of age, he left home to prepare for college, at Cortland academy. He entered Hamilton College, and graduated, in the class of 1843. From 1849 to 1869 he practiced law in New York city, and in April, 1870, he was licensed to preach by the third New York Presbytery and continued a faithful minister to the time of his death. He was pastor of the Presbyterian church at Raisin, Mich., from 1870 to '74, at Londonderry, N. H., from 1874 to '79. In 1843 he married Miss Ellen P. Smith, of Spencer, by whom he had one daughter, Helen M., wife of Rev. W. W. Newman, Jr., who are now living abroad. Mrs. Newman has three sons, viz.: George Kennedy, a student in Williams College, William Whiting, now of Colorado, and Oliver Shaw, who is traveling with his parents. Rev. Mr. Pert died at Bergen Point, N. J., May 29, 1881, and his remains were brought to the home of his boyhood for interment.

Stephen Vorhis, son of Jotham Vorhis, was born in this town

in 1812. His preparatory education was received in Owego; he entered Hamilton College and graduated in 1836, and from Auburn Theological Seminary in '38. He was pastor of the Presbyterian church at Akron, O., for two years, at Danby, N. Y., fourteen years, Phoenix, N. Y., five years, Hammondsport, N. Y., eight years, and at Spencer fifteen years before his retirement. He married A. Louisa Ward, of Allegany county, N. Y., by whom he had three children, viz.: Mary H., Lillian, who died at the age of six years, and Harry S. Mr. Vorhis died July 17, 1885.

Dr. J. H. Tanner was born in Virgil, Cortland county, N. Y., October 17, 1834, and lived in that town some thirty years. He studied medicine with Dr. Knapp, in Harford, and graduated at Buffalo, N. Y., in 1862, when he returned home and formed a partnership with Dr. J.H. Knapp, which continued only for a short time. In October, 1863, he moved to Nineveh, Broome county, N. Y. In May, 1864, he married Cornelia G., eldest daughter of James Heath, of Harford. He continued his practice in Nineveh until January, 1865. He bought out Dr. Knapp, of Harford, and late in January, he removed to that place, where he continued his practice until the summer of 1866, when he sold out to Dr. Knapp, and moved to Weltonville, Tioga county, where he continued to practice until October, 1877. Here he buried his wife. In the fall of 1878, he married his second wife, and settled in Spencer, Tioga county, N. Y., where he now resides. He has one son, J. Henry.

Samuel Bliven, of Westerly, R. I., was a soldier of the revolution, and married Mary Green, by whom he had eight children. Among them was Luther, who married Rebecca Cook, by whom he had nine children. Of these, Samuel G., was born in Hartford, N. Y., January 1, 1799, lived there until he was a year old, when his people removed to Fort Ann, N. Y. When twenty-four years of age he came to Spencer, and has since resided here,—a period of over sixty-two years. He married Rebecca, daughter of Phineas Spalding, by whom he has had six children. He has been engaged principally in farming, and now lives retired in the village of Spencer. Mrs. Bliven died September 8, 1885, aged seventy-five years.

Capt. John Fields was another of the very early settlers of this town, and who in his early years was a member of the Queen's Rangers, a regiment of the British army. When his time of enlistment expired he asked for his discharge, but it was denied him.

He awaited his opportunity, and deserted, coming to this country, and in the war of 1812 took arms against the British, and served the American cause faithfully. He was taken prisoner at the battle of Lundy's Lane, and after a period of confinement was discharged. When the war closed he retired to his farm, in the eastern part of the town of Spencer, where he spent the remainder of his life. His wife was Lydia Bates, who died, leaving no children.

Joshua Tompkins was born in Oxford, England, September 22, 1815. On April 30, 1836, he left Liverpool in the packet "Napoleon," and arrived in New York the following month. He came direct to Spencer, where he located on the farm now owned by his brother James, and this town has been his only home in America. He married Susan, daughter of William and Hannah Lorring. He is now engaged in farming, and in building operations within the corporation of Spencer village. Mr. Tompkins is probably one of the oldest foreign born citizens of the town.

James Silke was born in Cork, Ireland, and for thirteen years after his arrival in this country he was in the employ of Halsey Brothers, of Ithaca, who were running one of the largest flouring mills at that time in Central New York. In 1874, he came to Spencer to take the management of A. Seely's mill, which position he still holds. He married Mary Wasson, of Ithaca, and has four children.

Dr. G. W. Davis was born in Trenton, Dodge county, Wis., May 29, 1851. When he was only seven years old his parents removed to Ithaca, N. Y., where he received his education. He entered the office of Dr. John Winslow, of Ithaca, and also the office of Dr. M. M. Brown, and Dr. P. C. Gilbert. He graduated from the University of Buffalo, in 1882. He located first in Newfield, Tompkins county, where he remained one year, and since then he has been located in Spencer village. He married Eva, daughter of Holmes Shepard, of Van Ettenville, by whom he has one child.

Truman Lake came to this town from Greenville, Green county, N. Y., in 1815, and settled on the farm now owned and occupied by Fred W. Lake. He married Clarissa, daughter of Rufus Brown, of New Malbury, N. Y., by whom he had six children, viz.: Betsey, wife of Erastus Meacham, of Owego, Maria (Mrs. Jacob Vorhis), Harvey, Rachel (Mrs. Joshua Philo), Hiram and Rufus, all deceased except Mrs. Meacham, who is now in her eighty-fifth year, and resides in Owego.

J. Parker Vose, son of John Vose of this town, married Nancy B., daughter of Isaac Buckley, of Danby, N. Y., in June, 1853. Their children are Emma J., wife of J. B. G. Babcock, of Owego, and Charles E.

S. Alfred Seely is a son of Seymour A. and Polly Seely, and was born in Newfield, Tompkins county, in 1842. Till the age of sixteen he attended the district school near his home, finishing his school days by several terms in Spencer and then in Ithaca. He taught school several terms, and at the age of twenty-one went to Elmira, N. Y., and in company with his brother, Seymour, commenced the manufacture of lumber, under the firm name of A. Seely & Bro. After eleven years in Elmira, they transferred their business to Spencer, purchased several acres of land near the G., I. & S. R. R. station, put up a large steam saw-mill, and went to work, employing at times two hundred men. In 1875 they erected a steam flouring-mill near their saw-mill, and this is now the only mill of its kind doing business in the town. Within a year or two, an addition has been made to it, in which the grinding is done by the roller process, and large quantities of the best flour are almost daily shipped to different parts of the country. In 1877, they commenced, in a small way, the mercantile business, which has enlarged till at present they occupy a large brick block, their stock including nearly everything needed or used in a farming or manufacturing community. In 1880, they built near their mills a large creamery, and it is now receiving the milk or cream from about 700 cows, brought from four or five towns and from three different counties. January 1, 1887, the partnership was dissolved, Seymour retiring and Alfred continuing the business alone. Mr. Seely married Emily LaRow, of Newfield, October 20, 1863, who bore him one child, a girl, who died at the age of four years. Mrs. Seely died in September, 1879; and in November, 1880, he married Mary E. Williams, of Romulus, N. Y., and has three children.

Silvenes Shepard was born in the town and county of Otsego, January 23, 1823. His parents moved to Virgil, Cortland county, in 1826, where he lived until the fall of 1839, at which time they moved on to a farm near the white school-house, at East Spencer. He worked on a farm summers and taught school winters, until the spring after he was of age, when he commenced the manufacture of tomb-stones, at East Spencer. He removed to the village in 1847, and continued in the business till his health gave out, in 1849. He, with his brother-in-law, commenced manufacturing tin-ware and selling stoves, in 1852, continuing in the business a few years, when he went to farming, working as he was able, until 1862, when he found employment in the store of Lucius Emmons, father of the Emmons Bros. He remained in their store five years, when he commenced business for himself, at the same place he now occupies. In April, 1867, without application or solicitation on his part, he received the appointment of postmaster, which office he held till October 17, 1885. He has been the recipient of many favors from the citizens of Spencer, having held the office of overseer of the poor, assessor, and supervisor. To the latter office he has been elected six times. He has been interested in the educational interests of the town nearly half a century, an advocate for free schools long before the enactment of our grand "free school law." While positive and decided in his views on all public questions, and free to express them in proper times and places, he is willing to concede the same right to others. He has always taken a decided stand against intemperance.

Charles J. Fisher's grandfather came from Frankfort-on-the-Main, Germany, to this country, in 1754, and, it is believed, settled in New York city. His son, George, came to Spencer, in 1810, his family consisting of nine children—five girls and four boys. Charles J., the third son, was born in Spencer, in 1817. He attended the common schools till the age of eighteen, when he entered his father's store as clerk, which business he followed for different merchants till 1850, when he commenced business for himself, carrying a stock of dry goods and groceries, and continued till some time during the rebellion, when he sold his stock of goods and opened a drug store, the first one in town, which business he still continues. He now lives on the place formerly occupied by his father, has always lived and done business on, or very near, the spot where his father settled, in 1810.

Dr. William Henry Fisher, son of Charles J. Fisher, was born January 31, 1854. He studied in the Spencer Academy, and studied medicine with Dr. T. F. Bliss, of Spencer, and entered Bellevue Hospital Medical College in 1874, graduated in 1876, and immediately began practice in Spencer village, where he has since resided. The Doctor married Alice Knight, daughter of Harding A. Knight, of Spencer, November 14, 1877, and has two children, a son and a daughter.

Roger Vose was born in Bedford, N. H., February 26, 1770. He married Anne Bassett, of Sharon, Mass., February 14, 1793, and moved with his family from Bedford, N. H., to Spencer, in the fall of 1826, and purchased the farm on which he lived until his death, which occurred November 24, 1843. His wife, Anne Vose, died March 2, 1834. Their children were: Samuel Vose, born at Bedford, N. H., December 27, 1793. He came to Spencer from Bedford, about the year 1818, and died here, August 3, 1854. John Vose was born at Bedford, N. H., October 20, 1796. He came to this country with his brother, Samuel, about 1818, and died March 5, 1871. Jesse Vose was born at Bedford, N. H., May 23, 1801, and died in 1845. Charles Otis Vose was born at Bedford, N. H., May 1, 1807, and died May 31, 1829. Alfred Vose was born in Bedford, N. H., August 10, 1812. He moved to this town from Bedford, at the same time of his father; was reared and continued to live on the place purchased by his father, up to the time of his death, which occurred September 20, 1883.

Lucius Emmons was born in Hartland, Hartford county, Conn., April 31, 1810. In early life he worked on a farm, later did office work, and then started out as a peddler, to what was then called the West (New York state). He came to Spencer to live in the spring of 1839, and married Nancy, daughter of Roger Vose, July 4, 1839. They removed to Candor, thence to Simsbury, Conn., in the fall of 1841, and thence back to Spencer, in the spring of 1844, where he remained until his death. He immediately started in the mercantile business on a small scale, and being a peddler himself, he soon formed the idea of sending out peddlers, which he did on a large scale, and for many years carried on a large business in general merchandise. He was taken sick in 1856 with a complication of diseases, from which he had nearly recovered at the time of his death, which occurred March 19, 1864.

Lucius Edward Emmons, son of Lucius and Nancy Emmons, was born at Spencer, August 23, 1846. He attended school at the Spencer academy, and at the age of nineteen years commenced work on his father's farm. At the age of twenty-one years, August 23, 1867, he became a partner with his elder brother, A. S. Emmons, as dealers in general merchandise, under the firm name of Emmons Brothers, succeeding the firm of Mrs. L. Emmons & Son. September 15, 1872, he was married to Cornelia M. Hull, daughter of Eben Hull, of Spencer. On a spot made vacant by a large fire, and owned by said firm, they erected, in the fall of 1876 and succeeding winter, a three-story brick drug store, and after the loss of their wooden structure (general store), on the opposite corner, they erected, in 1878, a large store of brick to carry on the same business. On April 23, 1880, the firm purchased of Dr. William H. Gregg, of Elmira, the formulas for and exclusive right to manufacture Electro-Silicon liniment, also Dr. Shorey's Investigator remedies, which medicine business they conducted under the name of the Electro-Silicon Liniment Co. On September 1, 1886, the firm of Emmons Brothers was dissolved by mutual consent, and by the expiration of the contract; L. E. Emmons continuing the drug business in the same store before used for that purpose. His children are Charlie Hull Emmons, aged eleven years; Freddie Earl Emmons, aged seven years, and Jessie Nell Emmons, aged six years.

Myron B. Ferris was born in Spencer, April 22, 1835, son of Joshua H. and Louisa (Fisher) Ferris. He studied in the Spencer Academy, and graduated from the Ithaca High School in 1849. He soon after began the mercantile business in Spencer, and continued in the same about twenty years, and upon the establishment of the bank here he became its assistant cashier, a position he still holds. Mr. Ferris has represented the town in the board of supervisors four years in succession, and represented his county in the legislature of 1873. Mr. Ferris married Hannah M. Cooper, daughter of Jessie B. Cooper, in 1853, and has three children, Nathan B., Stella L., and F. Harry.

The comparative growth of the town may be seen by the following citation from the several census enumerations since its organization: 1810, 3,128; 1820, 1,252; 1825, 975; 1830, 1,278; 1835, 1,407; 1845, 1,682; 1850, 1782; 1855, 1,805; 1860, 1,881; 1865, 1,757; 1870, 1,863; 1875, 1,884; 1880, 2,382.

Organization.—At a town-meeting held at the inn of Jacobus Schenichs, Tuesday, April 1, 1806, the following named officers were elected: Joel Smith, supervisor; Joshua Ferris, town clerk; Edmond Hobart, Daniel H. Bacon, Levi Slater, assessors; Moses Read, Benjamin Jennings, Joseph Barker, commissioners of highways; Lewis Beers, Samuel Westbrook, overseers of the poor; Isaiah Chambers, collector; John Shoemaker, Nathan Beers, William Cunan, John Murphy, and Isaiah Chambers, constables; John F. Bacon, John McQuigg, John Mulks, Jacob Swartwood, poundmasters; John I. Speed, John English, Joseph L. Horton, Jacob Herinton, Alexander Ennes, and Lewis Beardslee, fenceviewers.

The history of Spencer as the county-seat, the history of its railroads and newspaper, has already been given, in the general history of the county, in the earlier pages of this work.

BUSINESS CENTERS.

SPENCER VILLAGE is located on Catatonk creek, west of the center of the town, and on the G. I. & S. and the E. C. & N. railroads. From 1812 to 1821, it was the county-seat of Tioga county. It contains three churches, the old camping-ground of the Wyoming Conference, one union school or academy, six dry-goods and grocery-stores, two hardware-stores, two drug-stores, one agricultural store, two hotels, one livery-stable, one steam saw and grist-mill, one planing-mill, one plaster-mill, one marble-factory, eight blacksmith-shops, three wagon shops, two cabinet-shops, three millinery-shops, three shoe-shops, two tailor-shops, one paint-shop. two harness-shops, one dental office, three doctors' offices, two undertaking establishments, one photograph parlor, one meat-market, one job printing office, about one hundred and thirty-five dwelling-houses, and seven hundred inhabitants. The busy mills, the large number of neat and commodious private residences, with well-kept grounds attached, and the highly-cultivated fields surrounding the village, attest that the inhabitants have not forgotten the thrift, habits of industry, and economy which characterized their forefathers from Connecticut and Eastern New York.

SPENCER SPRINGS, lying three miles northeast of Spencer village, has valuable springs of sulphur and chalybeate mineral waters. The surroundings are picturesque, and it has been quite popular as a resort during the summer months.

NORTH SPENCER, about three and one-half miles north of Spencer, contains one church (Union), one school-house, a store, about twenty dwelling-houses, and one hundred inhabitants.

COWELL'S CORNERS, a hamlet on Catatonk creek, about one and one-fourth miles east of Spencer, contains a school-house, a shoe-shop, two cooper-shops, and about forty inhabitants.

The Farmers' and Merchants' Bank of Spencer was incorporated in March, 1884, with a paid-up capital of $25,000.00. The first officers were M. D. Fisher, president; O. P. Dimon, vice-president; C. P. Masterson, cashier. The present officers are Thomas Brock, president; O. P. Dimon, vice-president; M. D. Fisher, cashier; and M. B. Ferris, assistant cashier.

Spencer Creamery, S. Alfred Seely Proprietor.—The Spencer Creamery was established in 1880, by Hoke & Seely, and is located in the western part of the village, on Liberty street. At present they are manufacturing from the product of 700 cows, and are doubling their capacity yearly. All their equipments are of the latest and most improved patents. They run two DeLaval cream separaters, a steam butter-worker, and all the improved steam-power machinery, which is used in the manufacture of butter. They also manufacture cheese from skimmed milk. There are one hundred hogs and thirty calves fed at the creamery. Beside supplying families with the choicest butter, they ship to New York twice and three times a week. Last year they manufactured over 60,000 pounds. The creamery is under the superintendence of Mr. D. LaMont Georgia.

S. A. Seely's Flour and Custom Mill is situated on Mill street, near the G., I. & S. R. R. depot, and was built in October, 1873, by A. Seely & Bro. It was started with three runs of stones, and did at that time custom work, principally. In 1879, it was renovated and enlarged, another run of stones added, and also machinery necessary for making the new process flour. In the spring of 1886, it was again enlarged, and machinery added, making it a full-fledged roller-mill. The capacity of the roller department is seventy-five barrels in twenty-four hours. A specialty is made of buckwheat grinding, according to the new process, manufacturing flour from 45,000 to 50,000 bushels annually. Three men are employed, with James Silke, superintendent. Mr. Seely's large steam saw-mill, the largest in the state, has already been spoken of in detail.

Brundage's Carriage and Wagon Works.—De Witt C. Brundage came to Spencer when about eighteen years of age, and learned the trade of carriage and wagon making, serving an apprenticeship of three years with George Rosekrans. He bought the business of Rosekrans and has since run it almost continuously, at the same stand, in Van Etten street. He manufactures wagons, sleighs, and carriages, of the most approved styles, and does all kinds of repairing in the neatest and most workmanlike manner.

J. T. McMaster's Steam Saw-Mill, located on road 53, is operated by a fifty horse-power engine. It has a lumber-saw, lath-mill, wood-saw, and edger, and also a feed-mill, run by the same power. He employs twelve men, and cuts annually 800,000 feet of lumber and 500,000 lath.

Samuel Eastham's Saw-Mill, located on road 36, is operated by

30*

water-power, employs twelve men, and cuts from 800,000 to 1,000,-
000 feet of lumber annually. He has also a hay-barn where he
presses hay, and ships 1,000 tons annually.

Richardson & Campbell's Brick Yard, located on road 43, was
established in 1882. The clay is first-class. The firm employs
thirty-five hands, and have capacity for the manufacture of
3,000,000 brick annually.

CHURCHES.

The First Congregational Church was organized November 23,
1815, with seven members, as follows: Daniel Hugg, Achsah Hugg,
Urban Palmer, Lucy Palmer, Stephen Dodd, Mary Dodd, and
Clarissa Lake. Until the year 1828, the society met in dwelling-
houses, school-houses, and the court-house, the pulpit being supplied by missionaries. Rev. Seth Williston was the first missionary,
he having been sent out by the Congregationalists of Connecticut.
Rev. Gardner K. Clark was the first regularly installed pastor.
The church edifice was commenced July 3, 1826, and completed
two years later. It is of the style usually erected for houses of
worship in the country fifty years ago. It cost $2,500, and has
sittings for about 400 people. Recently the building, through the
munificence of Mr. Kennedy, has been extensively repaired and
embellished.

The Methodist Episcopal Church was organized in 1809, by Peter
Lott and his wife, Jeremiah Andrews, Esther Dean, Abraham
Garey, and Hester Ann Purdy. For many years the society was
supplied by circuit preachers of the Oneida Conference, who
came once in four weeks. They held meetings in private houses,
barns, and school-houses until 1828, when the present church was
completed. It cost $2,800, and will seat 450 people. Rev. Morgan
Rugar was the first resident pastor. Rev. Loring P. Howard
is the present one. This church, too, has recently been extensively repaired.

The Baptist Church.—Phineas Spalding was the founder of this
society, and preached to his brethren as early as 1799. The
society was more formally organized by Elder David Jayne,
February 11, 1810, and consisted of fifteen members, as follows:
Phineas Spalding, Susannah Spalding, John Cowell, Deborah
Cowell, Thomas Andrews, Jemima Andrews, Joseph Barker,
Phebe Barker, Mehitable Hubbard, William Hugg, Lydia Hugg,
Polly Underwood, Benjamin Cowell, Benjamin Castalin, and

Ruth Castalin. Its first church was erected about 1830, and located one mile east of the village. The present one was completed in 1853, costing, with the alterations since made, about $4,000. It is the largest church in the village of Spencer, seats 700 in the audience-room, and 300 in the Sunday-school room.

The Union Church at North Spencer was organized, with thirty members, in 1870, and its church edifice, which will seat 275 people, was erected the same year, at a cost of about $1,500.

TIOGA originally embraced the boundaries of what is now denominated as the town of Tioga, together with much other territory, and was distinctively organized into a township by an act of the legislature passed March 22, 1788, erecting the so-called "Old Town of Chemung," which was bounded as follows :

"Beginning at the intersection of the partition line between New York State and the Commonwealth of Massachusetts, and the Pennsylvania State line, (west of Elmira); and running from said point of intersection due north along said partition line to the distance of two miles north of the Tioga [now Chemung] river; thence with a straight line to the Owego river [creek], at the distance of four miles on a straight line from the confluence thereof with the Susquehanna river; thence down the Owego [creek] and Susquehanna to the Pennsylvania line; thence along the same to the place of beginning."

It will be seen then, that the northern, eastern and southern boundaries of the Old Town of Chemung were identical with the present like boundaries of the town of Tioga. This territory remained a part of the Old Town of Chemung, until the act of the legislature was passed, February 16, 1791, creating the county of Tioga. By that act, about one-half of this Old Town of Chemung, comprising the easterly half, with some other territory on the north, was erected into a new town, called Owego, which name it continued to bear until the act of the legislature of April 12, 1813, dividing the counties of the state into towns. Prior to the act of 1813, the territory next immediately east of the Owego creek, or the present town of Owego, was known as the town of Union, until April 1, 1800, when, by virtue of an act of the legislature passed March 14, 1800, a new and separate town was formed from the territory next east of the Owego creek, and called the Town of Tioga, which name it also bore until the act of 1813. By the act of April 12, 1813, the names of

these two towns, Owego on the west of the Owego creek, Tioga
on the east thereof, were exchanged one for the other, as they
now are. Each of these towns, however, originally included
much other territory than that embraced within their present
limits, other towns having been subsequently erected from them.

This town (Owego, from 1791–1813; Tioga, from 1813 to the
present), originally was bounded on the east by the Owego creek,
and a line running from the mouth thereof to the Pennsylvania
state line; on the south, by the Pennsylvania state line; on the
west, by the Cayuta creek; and on the north by the north bounds
of the original Tioga county. The town of Spencer, then including the present town of Candor, was erected out of this town,
February 28, 1806, and embraced all of that part of the town
lying north of the Old Chemung Township line. So that, as
respects the northern boundary of the town, it again became
identical with that which it was when the town formed a part of
the Old Town of Chemung, and it still is so. The town was
again divided, by an act of the legislature passed March 23, 1824,
and the towns of Nichols and Barton were erected from it, and
the town was territorially reduced to its present limits. The southern boundary thereof was restored to the Susquehanna river, and
in this respect also was again made identical with that which it
was when a part of the Old Town of Chemung.

The present boundaries of the town are as follows: Easterly,
by the Owego creek, which separates it from the town of Owego;
southerly, by the Susquehanna river, which separates it from the
town of Nichols; westerly, by a line drawn from the mouth of
Mundy's creek, northerly to the southwest corner of great lot
number 171, in the old Chemung township; thence along the line
of said lot to the north bounds of the town, or by the town of
Barton; and northerly, by the old Chemung township line, or by
the towns of Candor and Spencer. It is the only interior town
of the county, that is, the only one which is not bounded by territory lying without the county.

Surface.—Topographically considered, the town of Tioga includes 35,805 acres. Its surface is principally uplands, with
small areas of river-bed flats. The soil in the valleys and on the
river-beds is a dark loam, and on the uplands a gravel loam. Its
chief water-courses are Pipe and Catatonk creeks. There are,
however, several other smaller streams, which empty either into
these creeks, or into the Susquehanna river. Pipe creek is made
up of two branches, the northern and the western; the northern

branch rising in the town of Candor, and flowing nearly due south, and the western branch, rising in the town of Barton, and flowing nearly due east, meet in junction at Beaver Meadows, and flowing thence in a southeasterly course, empty into the Susquehanna at Tioga Center, near the center of the southern boundary. It is the real great water-course of the town. The Catatonk creek, entering from the town of Candor, flows in a southeasterly course across the northeast portion of the town, and empties into the Owego creek, midway of the eastern boundary of the town, and about two miles from the Susquehanna river.

The chief pursuit of the inhabitants of the town now is agriculture. In former times lumbering was one of the great avocations; but the timber has been so nearly cut down and the lands so thoroughly cleared, that there remains at this day, only a vestige of the former extensive industry.

Settlement and Growth.—The territory occupied by the old town of Chemung, was surveyed and platted by Clinton, Cantine, and Hathorn. Certificates of location and survey were granted in the present town of Tioga, as follows: To Isaac D. Fowler, Jacob Ford, Peter W. Yates, Josiah Richardson, and Thomas Klump, June 23, 1789, 8,000 acres on the river bank, and forming nearly a square now known as "Yates Location," Tioga Centre being in that tract; Archibald Campbell, same date, 3,000 acres, two islands included, lying north of "Yates Location" on the river-bank, and on Owego creek to confluence of the Catatonk creek; Thomas Palmer, same date, 3,000 acres, and 418 acres in the south part of the town, west of Smithboro; Jonas Poirs and Benjamin Koles, November 12, 1788, 540 acres where Smithboro now is, and this was assigned to Jesse Smith, February, 1789; Abraham Bancker, November 6, 1788, lot 188, 1,000 acres, assigned to John Ransom, February 28, 1792; James and Robert R. Burnett, January 15, 1789, lot 204, of 1,360 acres; Amos Draper and Jonas Williams, November 12, 1788, lot 160, 330 acres; Jesse Miller, Thomas Thomas, and Enos Canfield, same date, 2,765 acres; Samuel Ransom, same date, lot 162, 410 acres; Nathaniel Goodspeed, same date, lot 163, 430 acres; Silas Taylor, same date, lot 164, 230 acres; Samuel Ransom, Ebenezer Taylor, Jr., Prince Alden, Jr., Andrew Alden, Christopher Schoonover, and Benjamin Bidlack, same date, lot 165, 1,980 acres, assigned October, 1790, to Samuel Ransom; Ebenezer Taylor, Jr., William Ransom, Abijah Marks, Samuel Van Gorden, Benoni Taylor, and John Cortright, November 13, 1788, lot 166, 2,400 acres ; James Clinton, George Denniston, Alexander Denniston, and others, November 6, 1788, lot 167, 3,000 acres, with all islands in Owego river opposite said lot ; and to James Clinton, James Humphrey, William Scott, and James Denniston, lot 168, 4,000 acres; Brinton Paine, November 13, 1788, lot 169, 800 acres ; Peter A. Cuddeback, Peter Cantine, Peter Jansen, and Elisha Barber, November 6, 1788, lot 172, 4,000 acres; William and Egbert De Witt, March 4 1791, a lot of land containing 1,600 acres.

It seems to be conceded, generally, that among the earliest pioneers within the limits of the present town of Tioga, were Samuel and William Ransom and Prince and Andrew Alden. Samuel and William Ransom were sons of Samuel Ransom and Esther, his wife. This elder Samuel Ransom was a captain in the Continental army, and was killed July 3, 1778, at the historical massacre of Wyoming. These four persons came up the Susquehanna river, from Wyoming Valley, and made a settlement in the town about the year 1785. William Ransom and Andrew Alden settled a short distance south of the mouth of Pipe creek, upon the westerly bank of the river, where they built a log house, supposed to have been the first structure of the kind erected in the town.

In his "Centennial History," Hon. W. F. Warner, however, inclines to the opinion that there were transient settlers here earlier, remarking as follows:

"The late Judge Avery was clearly in error in stating that there was no settlement of the white race in the county earlier than 1783 or '84. In a journal kept by Lieut. Van Hovenburg, who accompanied Gen. James Clinton in the expedition down the Susquehanna to join Sullivan in 1779, mentions that 'the division marched ten miles from Owego down the river and encamped at Fitz Gerrel's farm.' This establishes the fact that as early as 1779, there was a settler either in the town of Tioga or Nichols.

"In the journal of Daniel Livermore, another officer, is the following entry: 'Saturday, August 21. This morning the troops march early, make but few halts during the day: at 5 p. m. encamp on the banks of the —— river, opposite —— farm, about seventeen miles from Owego.' Another journal described it as 'an abandoned plantation.'

"These are sufficient, however, to prove that at a much earlier period than has heretofore been claimed, there were settlers along the river. A settlement was made in the Wyoming Valley in 1769, and doubtless about the same time there were a few in this county, though they may have been forced to leave by reason of the disturbed state of the country during the revolution."

Samuel Ransom and Prince Alden settled about two miles further down the river, nearly opposite of Spendley's high bridge over the New York, Lake Erie & Western, and the Southern Central railway tracks. Of the ancestral history of the Alden brothers, nothing is known. Andrew Alden removed to the State of Ohio, about the year 1808, and Prince Alden died about the same year. Samuel Ransom was born September 28, 1759, at Canaan, now Norfolk, Ct.; married, in 1783 or 1784, to Mary Nesbitt, near Plymouth, Pa., and was drowned in the Susquehanna river, near Tioga Center, by the upsetting of a skiff, about the year 1807. His widow and seven children subsequently moved West, where they died. During his life-time, Samuel Ransom built on his land the first tavern, and the first school-house in the town. The tavern was situate a very few rods east of Spendley's high bridge, upon the highway. It was a log structure, but afterward a framed addition was built on to it. A few years before he died, he became involved financially, and dying, left but little property to his family. William Ransom was born May 26, 1770, at Canaan, now Norfolk, Ct.; married, in 1792, Rachel Brooks, daughter of James and Mary Brooks, at Tioga Center. This was the first marriage in the town of Tioga. William Ransom died in Tioga Center, January 8, 1822, leaving a widow and ten children, another child of theirs having died in infancy. Nine of the ten children have descendants living. These children of Major William Ransom make up the Tioga branch of the Ransom family, and the following is their genealogical record: Ira, born December 4, 1792; married, January 22, 1814, Sarah Forman, at Nichols, N. Y., and died June 1, 1848, at Wysox, Pa. Sybil, born August 14, 1794; married, February 1, 1816, Henry Light, at Smithboro, and died there April 15, 1877. David, born October 14, 1796; died unmarried, May 9, 1827, at Philadelphia, Pa. Benjamin, born September 26, 1799; married, July 7, 1821, Lucy Frost, at Tioga Center, and died there, January 18, 1830. William, born April 9, 1801; married, September 14, 1831, Angeline Martin, at Owego, and died at Tioga Center, February 7, 1883. Rachel, born August 23, 1803; married, January 23, 1823, David Wallis, at Tioga Center, and is still living upon the Wallis homestead, in the town of Tioga. Charles, born September 19, 1805; married, October 2, 1832, Hope Maria Talcott, at Owego, and died August 12, 1860, at Tioga Center. Printice, born Sep-

tember 17, 1807; married, October 19, 1830, Fanny Thurston, at
Owego, and is still living, at Iowa City, Ia. Harriet, born
August 15, 1809; married, May 19, 1840, Asa Guildersleeve Jack-
son, at Tioga Center, and died there, June 4, 1847. Charlotte,
born April 13, 1811; died, June 26, 1811, at Tioga Center. Mary
Johnson, born November 24, 1812; married, January 29, 1833,
Gilbert Strang, at Tioga Center, and died there, June 9, 1872.

The next advent of settlers appears to have been Lodowyck
Light, Jesse Miller, the elder, and Enos Canfield, who came
from the vicinity of Bedford, Westchester county, and located
upon a tract of five hundred acres, known as the "Light &
Miller Location," next west of where Samuel Ransom located,
extending southwesterly well toward the village of Smithboro.
They came on, made clearings and built their houses in about the
year 1787, and brought on their families about the year
1790. Lodowyck Light first built a small cabin, upon a small
knoll nearly directly across the road from the residence of the
late Henry G. Light, and soon afterwards built his log house
near the site of the latter, near the old well thereon, where he
lived until his death, August 26, 1830, being a month and four
days past seventy-eight years of age. His wife, Martha, died
September 28, 1842, four months and four days past eighty-six
years of age. The remains of these venerable pioneers lie buried
in the old burying-ground, upon the top of the hill, about one
mile east of Smithboro village. This old burying-ground is now
in a sorry state of dilapidation, and its condition ought to be improved at once for the sake of its preservation. This is also the
site of the first meeting-house in the town of Tioga, built in 1812,
by the Methodist and Baptist denominations. It was destroyed
by lightning in the summer of 1826; and there are those who are
so irreverent as to say that, it was the meet judgment of the
wrath of God, because of the intensity of the denominational
jealousies and unchristian differences between the two church
organizations. Lodowyck Light was a prominent citizen, and
took an active part in the political affairs of his day.

Jesse Miller, the elder, built his log cabin upon the site of the
old Miller homestead, very near where Thomas Watkins now
lives, a few rods east of the residence of Amos Canfield. His
wife's name was Kesiah, and they had four sons—Jesse, Jr.,
Ezra, Ziba and Amos; and several daughters, among whom were
Jerusha, Lucy and Polly. Jesse Miller, Sr., died April 9, 1812,
at the age of sixty-four years. Jesse Miller, Jr., removed West,

and died there.   Ezra, Ziba and Amos spent their lives in the town of Tioga, where they died, all of them leaving descendants, among the most venerable of whom is Mrs. Lucy Brooks, daughter of Amos Miller, and widow of Benjamin V. Brooks. She now lives with her children in Owego village, and has passed the very ripe age of eighty four years.   The wife of Amos Miller was Polly Jayne, daughter of the Rev. David Jayne, who was the first preacher of the town, and who is said to have begun his ministerial work here as early at least as 1795.

Enos Canfield settled and built a log house near the present residence of Amos Canfield, his son, and lived there until he died, December 14, 1822, aged fifty five years, ten months and seventeen days.   His wife was Polly (Robinson) Canfield, and she died May 7, 1849, at the ripe age of eighty-three years, ten months and nine days.   Enos Canfield was a promient citizen, and took an active part in the church affairs of his day, being a staunch adherent of the Baptist orthodox faith.   There were fourteen children born to this couple, of whom Amos Canfield still survives, and was eighty-eight years of age in March, 1887.   The latter married Ellen Knapp, and the fruit of their marriage has been nine children, now living.

Ezra Smith also immigrated into this town from Westchester county, about the year 1791, and settled at the point where the village of Smithboro is.   The land in that vicinity had been granted by the state to Poirs & Koles prior to that time, and by them assigned to Jesse Smith, a brother of Ezra.   Ezra Smith kept the tavern situate near where the store building of Walter C. Randall now stands.   He removed to the town of Candor, about the year 1809, and was succeeded by Isaac Boardman.

Colonel David Pixley was a pioneer, who had made exploring and surveying expeditions through this country, in the interest of the proprietors of the Boston Purchase, and finally settled in this town, just south of the Owego creek, on what is called the Campbell location.   He built his log house near where Ephraim Goodrich now resides, and a portion of the old structure is still standing.   In 1802, he sold his property in this town to Noah and Eliakim Goodrich, and removed to Owego.   A more extended sketch of Colonel Pixley will be found in the history of the town of Owego.

Dr. Samuel Tinkham settled in the town about the same time as Colonel Pixley, on the place now owned by A. J. Goodrich. He was a physician, and married Colonel Pixley's sister, Polly.

Abner Turner, of New Hampshire, who also accompanied Col.
Pixley upon his exploring expeditions in the interest of the proprietors of the Boston Purchase, settled near the east line of the
town, and opened a tavern. He died upon his homestead in this
town.

Another notable family of early settlers was the Brooks family.
Three brothers, James, John, and Cornelius, it is stated, their
father having died in the old country, emmigrated from Dublin to
this country. Their widowed mother died upon the voyage, and
was buried at sea. John and Cornelius settled, one in Massachusetts, the other in New Jersey. James Brooks married Polly
Johnson, in New Jersey, and settled in this town in 1791, on the
old Brooks homestead, upon the corner opposite where the Independent Order of Good Templers' lodge building now is, in
Tioga Center, near the house owned by Jerome Schoonover. The
exact locality is marked by the old Brook's well, at that point.
James Brooks died in 1810, and had five sons,—Cornelius, David,
John, Benjamin, and James, Jr. Cornelius took up his location
and built a log house in the orchard between the Susquehanna
river and the railways, opposite the blackwalnut tree, just west
of the present residence of Theodore Horton. He subsequently
moved West, and died at Olean, N. Y. David Brooks married
Susan Allen, and lived in a log house upon the bank of the Susquehanna river, opposite the present residence of James Higbee,
near the DuBois hay barn. He subsequently removed to Michigan, where he died. John Brooks built a tavern near the well,
by the present residence of Samuel Kuykendall, which he kept
for a few years, and then removed to Cincinnati, O. James
Brooks married Amy, daughter of Lodowyck Light, and for a
while lived in a house near the residence of Judson Gardner,
at Tioga Center, having taken up twenty-five acres of land there.
He afterward enlisted in the war of 1812, and was killed while
in the service. His widow, Amy, subsequently built a framed
house upon the top of the hill, immediately west of the residence
of the late Henry G. Light, and lived there. Three children
were born of this marriage, Chloe, Benjamin Van Campen, and
Patty.

In 1820, Chloe Brooks married John H. Yontz, who came into
this vicinity from Virginia, about 1818, and for a long time was a
prominent citizen of Smithboro and Tioga Centre. He died in
1875. His widow is still living at Smithboro, and is now eighty-
six years of age, with mental vigor unimpaired.

Benjamin V. Brooks married Lucy, daughter of Amos Miller, as has been stated before, and was for a long time a leading and prominent citizen of Smithboro, engaged in the industrial pursuits of farming and lumbering. He died December 27, 1873, at Owego, leaving his widow, and the following children : Horace Agard, Mrs. E. A. B. Mitchell, Chester, Mandana, and Chloe M.

Benjamin Brooks, son of James, married Patty Stowe, and lived in a double log house on the original Brooks homestead, at the old well, near the house now owned by Jerome Schoonover, as aforesaid. Four children survived him, of whom Ira and James are dead, and Mary Ives, living in Illinois, and Conelius Brooks, living at Tioga Centre, at the ripe old age of seventy-seven years.

Francis Gragg also immigrated into this town at a date uncertain, but supposed to be prior to 1800. He came originally from Schomokin Creek, Pa. His wife, Margaret, came with him. They moved into the old tavern built by John Brooks, upon the site of the residence of Samuel Kuykendall, and lived there until 1819, when they moved into an old house which stood almost exactly upon the site of the present house of Charles C. Van Norstran, where he lived the rest of his live. Margaret Gragg died July 26, 1824, and Francis died April 15, 1854. They are buried in the Van Norstran vault, about one mile west of Tioga Centre. They had only one child, Sally, who married John Van Norstran. Mr. Van Norstran also originally came from Shamokin Creek, Pa., and July 20, 1819, he moved into the Brooks-Gragg tavern, and was the proprietor of it until he died, June 6, 1837. Sally, his wife. died December 30, 1873. Eight children were born of this union, of whom John, Silas, Frank, Margaret, and William, are dead; and James, Charles C., and Mrs. Eliza Coburn (widow of Charles R. Coburn), are living.

Joel Farnham, who was a native of Wyoming and there at the time of the famous Indian massacre, located upon the old Farnham homestead, off road 12, about the year 1794, and died here August 15, 1858, aged over eighty-four years. His wife, Ruth, died August 30, 1862, aged eighty-five years. None of their ten children are now living. His son, Frederick A., born February 26, 1818, married Agnes L. Barclay, who bore him five children, Joel S., Alice L. (Mrs. George H. Day), Elisha W., Herbert A. and May E. Mr. Farnham died February 21, 1887, and his widow still occupies the old homestead.

George A. Farnham, the eldest grandson of Joel, Sr., and son of Sylvester, now resides on road 12.

Jeremiah White settled about 1794, on the place afterwards owned by Elizur Wright, Abel Stafford, and subsequently by John Dubois. He was a good mechanic, and was the first husband of Mrs. Whitaker, who was taken captive at Wyoming in 1778, when twelve years of age, carried to Canada, kept two years, then released and sent home. He removed to Catatonk Creek, and died suddenly, in 1805, from injuries received in a mill.

William Taylor accompanied James McMaster to Owego, in 1785, as a bound boy. After planting and securing a crop of corn, they returned to their headquarters on the Mohawk. Jacob Catlin, son of Nathaniel Catlin, said he used to hear Amos Draper tell of McMaster's raising corn and the Indians watching and caring for it in his absence, and who, at the harvesting of the same, received from him a share of the crop. He cut dead pines on the bank of the creek, felled them into the water, bound them together with withes, forming a raft, on which he put his corn and floated it down the river to Wilkesbarre to mill. Mr. Taylor did not return to Owego until 1793, and soon after came to this town and occupied the Henry Young farm. In 1800, he made arrangements to sell his property, and in 1801, removed to Candor, and died in 1849, aged eighty-two years. Nathaniel came from Orange county in 1800, and decided to purchase the farm of William Taylor, and in 1801 brought his family and completed the purchase.

Daniel Mersereau emigrated from Staten Island, in 1794, and settled where Brindley Wallace now lives. He was impressed by the English, taken on board a vessel, and kept several days, but by interference of friends was released. He died in 1848, aged eighty-six years.

Cornelius Taylor settled here in 1794, and was from Plymouth, Wyoming—sold part of his farm to Mersereau. He died in 1848, aged seventy-seven years.

Jonathan Catlin was an early settler at what is known as Goodrich Settlement. Five of his six sons located, in 1820, at what is still known as Catlin Hill, viz.: Stephen, Jonathan, Joseph, James and Nathaniel. Nathaniel, born September 4, 1787, married Elleanor Van Riper, March 22, 1829, who bore him ten children. Mrs. Catlin died September 16, 1856, and Mr. Catlin married for his second wife Mrs. Mary J. Wolverton, who bore him two children, and still survives him. Mr. Catlin died October 31, 1866. Ten of the children are living, viz.: George,

Sarah (Mrs. Herman N. Goodrich), Charles M., Frederick H., Frank K., Andrew R., Nathaniel R., Chauncey R , William and Lavern. Joseph married three times and had born to him fifteen children. He died February 17, 1885. Stephen married twice, Chloe Higgins and Betsey Decker, respectively, had a family of seven children. Jonathan married Patty Spencer, and had a family of six children. James married Mary Heacock, who bore him eight children.

Noah Goodrich, from Connecticut, with his family, in 1802, located in what is known as Goodrich Settlement. He was born August 30, 1764, and died July 19, 1834. He married twice, and reared a family of five children. All his four sons, Erastus, Aner, Norman and Ephraim, located in this vicinity, spending their lives here, and of whom Ephraim is still living. Aner was born September 30, 1789, and married, January 19, 1815, Ruth Stratton, who bore him four children, two of whom, Andrew J. and Emily N. (Mrs. L. Truman), are living. The former was born October 18, 1827. Aner's children were John, born December 5, 1830, and died July 20, 1876; one, who died in infancy ; Emily N., born December 30, 1817.

Norman Goodrich, son of Noah, was born December 30, 1792. He married Eliza True, in 1822, who bore him eight children, viz.: Noah, born April 5, 1823; Herman N., born October 11, 1824, married Sarah E. Catlin, had one son, Charles T., and died in November, 1874; Mary L., born August 20, 1826; Rhoda A. (Mrs. B. C. Stiles), born May 29, 1828, married October 23, 1849, and her children are Fred H., Mary E. (Mrs. Stephen Goodrich), Sarah A., Helen G. (Mrs. William Millrea), and George B. (Mr. Stiles died February 27, 1882); Mortimer N. and Malvina, twins, died in infancy; Abner T., born March 23, 1830, died September 12, 1853 ; and Jairus T., born November 18, 1838, married Alice Smith, May 8, 1884. Noah, son of Norman, married Charlotte R. Lane, May 15, 1845, who has borne him five children, three of whom are living,—Hiram E., born December 31, 1847, Jennie E. (Mrs. F. C. Steele), born August 29, 1849, and Ella J. (Mrs. W. Luce), born December 30, 1859.

Ephraim Goodrich, son of Noah, Sr., was born October 31, 1815 ; married Hannah B., daughter of George C. Horton, who has borne him two children, Ruth A., born May 22, 1844, died December 26, 1878, and Charles E., born October 7, 1850, married Mary E. Raymond, June 10, 1874, and died March 3, 1882.

Eliakim Goodrich came to Tioga with his cousin Noah, in 1802.

He married Sarah Leland, in 1781, and had a family of twelve children, as follows :   Ansel, born in 1782, married Mary Strickland, and died in 1819 ; Ira, born in 1785, married Fear Potter, and died in 1825 ; Cyprion, born in 1786, married Abigail Giles, and died in 1850 ; Lucy, born in 1788, married Joseph Berry, and died in ——; Alanson, born in 1790 ; Silas, born in 1793, married Mary A. Goodrich, and died in 1863 ; Sarah, born in 1795 ; Betsey, born in 1797, married Jonathan Platt ; Fanny, born in 1799, died young ; Jasper, born in 1801, married Betsey Thorn ; William, born in 1804, married Mary Fox, and died in 1872 ; and Fanny, born in 1806.

Alanson Goodrich, son of Eliakim, was born December 26, 1790, married Mary A Pixley, March 1, 1815, who bore him seven children,—Charles P., born September 27, 1816 ; Frederick, born October 1, 1818 ; Harriet D. (Mrs. Sherman Mosher), born June 22, 1821, died November 9, 1877 ; Eunice (Mrs. Horatio Brown), born March 11, 1826, died June 6, 1852 ; Elizabeth (Mrs. John C. Searls), born March 11, 1826, died January 8, 1856 ; Frances (Mrs. George O. Stroup), born September 24, 1830 : George L., born August 22, 1836, married Harriet S. French, April 9, 1863, and resides on the old homestead.

Silas Goodrich's children were Augusta J., born in 1829, married James S. Griffing ; Sarah A., born in 1831 ; James J., born in 1833, died in 1868 ; Ralph, born in 1836, married Jennie Connet, and second Dora Beebe ; Rachel, born in 1836, died in 1852 ; Mary C., born in 1839, married Gurdon Horton, March 26, 1863 ; Stephen S., born in 1842, married Mary Stiles, and resides on the old homestead, their children being Helen L., Mary F., Ralph H., and an infant.

Charles P. Goodrich, son of Alanson, married Harriet Stiles, October 1, 1840, who has borne him two children, Edgar and Mary.

Jonathan C. Latimer is the great-grandson of Colonel Jonathan Latimer, who, soon after the revolutionary war closed, in which he served as a colonel, moved from New London, Conn., his ancestral home for over a century, to the now state of Tennesee. Jonathan Latimer, the father of Jonathan C. Latimer, in 1831, when twenty-eight years of age, moved to Illinois and settled at Abingdon, Knox county, where he became a prominent and successful business man, accumulating a large estate, and commanding the love and respect of the entire community. Jonathan C. Latimer was born at Abingdon, Knox county, the young-

Jonathan C. Latimer

est child of a family of ten. His early years were spent on his father's farm, and he was trained to take part in the manual labor incident to a farmer's life ; enjoying however all the advantages of a liberal education. In 1862, while a student at Knox College, he enlisted for a short term of service as a private in Co. E., 71st Regiment Illinois Volunteers, and was in service until his regiment was honorably discharged. In 1864, he finished the regular classical course in Knox College, Galesburg, Ill., and graduated with the degree of A. B., and in 1867, received from the same institution the honorary degree of A. M. During the year of 1865 and 1866, he completed the course of study in the law department of Harvard University, at Cambridge, Mass., and secured from that University the degree of LL.B.

Mr. Latimer was admitted to the practice of law in the Supreme court of Illinois, in 1866, and practiced law successfully in Chicago until 1877, when, on account of the illness of his father-in-law, Col. William Ransom, he moved to Tioga Centre, his present place of residence. In 1871, he was married to Angie D. Ransom, daughter of Ira Ransom, and adopted daughter of Col. William Ransom. They have had three daughters, of whom Angie and Clara are now living, the second daughter, Sally, having died in infancy.

The Ransom family are well and favorably known along the Susquehanna valley, and noted for strong characteristics, and marked ability. Capt. Samuel Ransom, the great grandfather of Mrs. Latimer, and head of the family, as we have shown, was originally from Connecticut, but early settled in the Wyoming Valley. Col. Ransom was born at Tioga Centre, in 1801, and died there in 1883. He was a man of great executive power, and has left a lasting impress upon his town, being its leading business man, and citizen for many years. He was the promoter of several business enterprises, and at his death, left a large property to his adopted daughter.

Since moving to Tioga Centre, in 1877, Mr. Latimer has thoroughly identified himself with the interests of the people of Tioga county, and is actively interested in the moral and business problems coming before the people. He is largly engaged in farming, and lumbering, giving employment to a large number of men. In politics, he is a Republican, and has been three times in succession elected supervisor for his town, which is strongly Democratic. He has served one term as member of the legislature, and has received the unanimous nomination from his party, for a second term. Mr. Latimer is a member of the Methodist church, and has been superintendent of the church Sunday school of his place for many years.

John DuBois came shortly subsequent to 1800, and built the house which is still standing, a short distance east of the residence of Jesse Carpenter, one mile west of Tioga Centre. He owned a large tract of land, consisting of several hundred acres, where he settled. He was a prominent business man and left a large family of children, among whom were: John, Jr., Joseph, Ezekiel, and Abel. John DuBois, Jr., was the wealthiest man Tioga county has produced. He was born at Tioga Centre, and remained there until some time after he had attained his majority, when he removed to Pennsylvania, to engage in the lumber business. He owned large tracts of timber land in the neighborhood of DuBois city, Pa., which he founded, and where he had a large number of saw-mills. He had a large lumber yard at Williamsport, Pa. He was one of the largest and wealthiest dealers in lumber in the State of Pennsylvania. He died in 1886, leaving a fortune estimated at several million dollars to his nephew and namesake, John DuBois, son of Ezekiel DuBoise, of Tioga Centre.

Frederick Castle, and his nephew, John Castle, came shortly subsequent to 1800, and settled midway between Tioga Centre and Smithboro, where they owned a large tract of land. One of them built a tavern, which stood until 1878, when it was burned. It was known for many years as Spendley's broom shop.

A family named Saltmarsh came about the same time and settled in the same neighborhood.

Henry Primrose came shortly subsequent to 1800, and settled a few miles north of Smithboro, near the Barton line.

Jacob Crator came about the same time and settled in the same neighborhood, building the small red house, still standing, across the road from Peter Johnson's house.

Dr. David Earll was educated as a physician and practiced medicine a number of years. He has since resided upon his farm at Tioga Centre. He was also a merchant a short time. He has been for many years one of the prominent Democrats in the town. Has been justice of the peace, supervisor, county superintendent of the poor, 1882–85, member of assembly, 1859 and 1860. He married a daughter of Benjamin Ransom. Children: Lucy, Alice, Nellie, Edna, David.

John Gilbert Smith was for many years a prominent business man of the town. He operated an extensive saw-mill at Tioga

Centre. He was a prominent and active Democrat. He died in 1885. His only child, a daughter, married John E. Pembleton.

Josiah Stowell came to Smithboro about 1835, and erected a saw-mill which he operated several years. He also erected a hotel and a store, and was a prominent business man. Children: Delos, Calvin, and Cornell S.

Hon. Charles Rittenhouse Coburn, LL.D., was a son of Sarah, daughter of the celebrated Rev. Enoch Pond. He was born in Bradford county, Pa.; commenced teaching school at a very early age ; was principal of the Owego Academy, and afterward of the Susquehanna Collegiate Institute, at Towanda, Pa. He was president of the New York State Teachers' Association, county superintendent of schools of Bradford county, Pa., state superintendent of the common schools of Pennsylvania, 1863-66. He married Eliza VanNostrand. He died about 1870, at Nichols. His widow is still living, at Tioga Centre. Children : Frank, a lawyer, Sarah, who married Capt. James Hillyer, and Charles Sidney, of Tioga Centre.

Ambrose P. Eaton, one of the oldest residents of Smithboro, was born in the town of Union, Broome county, June 4, 1826, and came to Smithboro in the spring of 1849. He studied law in the office of Judge Charles E. Parker, of Owego, was admitted to the bar in December, 1868, at Binghamton, and since that time he has acquired quite an extensive practice, and has always been considered as a careful, trusty lawyer, a man of good judgment, and in the trial of cases has been very successful. In the fall of 1885, he formed a partnership with Hon. A. G. Allen, and moved his office to Waverly. He continued in partnership with Judge Allen until the summer of 1886, when the co-partnership was dissolved by mutual consent, Mr. Eaton opening an office and continuing the business in Waverly, where he has a large and growing practice. Mr. Eaton was postmaster of this village for several years, a member of the school board, and an active, earnest worker in the same, rendering valuable assistance in the erection of the school building, etc. Mr. Eaton is a man of strong convictions, will uphold what he thinks right, and condemn what he considers wrong, regardless of what others may say about it. For many years he has been a member of the Episcopal church here, and was for several years warden of Emmanuel church, of this place. He was an active, earnest worker in the church, contributing liberally to its support, and rendering it valuable ser-

31*

vices. Mr. Eaton married March 13, 1851, and has one daughter, wife of James A. Roberts, of Smithboro.

William E. Dorwin is one whose life-record affords a striking illustration of what earnest enterprise may accomplish in producing "a self-made man." He was born at Marathon, Cortland county, N. Y., March 18, 1837, where his boyhood and youth were passed, and where he obtained his only educational advantages, afforded by the district school. In 1857, when twenty years of age, he left for the West to begin the trials and struggles of manhood alone, as a switchman on the T. P. & W. R. R. in Illinois. In railroad work his time has ever since been passed. From the bottom round he gradually climed the ladder till made superintendent of the same road, a position he held eight years, and the same successively of the Mt. Claire & Greenwood Lakes railroad of New Jersey two years, and of the Brighton Beach railroad, of Long Island, four years. In 1880, he engaged with the firm of Smith & Ripley, of New York city, to build the Lacawanna railroad, from Binghamton to Buffalo, and since that time has been extensively engaged in railroad building, being now engaged in building the Chicago, Madison & Northern railroad.

In 1883, Mr. Dorwin purchased the famous "Glen Mary" farm, which he has since made his home. Mr. Dorwin is a veteran of the late war, having served in Co. B, 3d Ills. Cav., enlisting August 16, 1861, as a private, and was mustered out as 1st lieutenant. Aside from his railroad work and farm, Mr. Dorwin is also extensively engaged in milling here, as a member of the firm of Dorwin, Rich & Stone. Although a strong Republican worker, Mr. Dorwin has accepted no political honors. He married Miss Sarah Longley, of Jacksonville, Ills., in 1867, and has three children.

John Hill came to the town of Tioga, from Pittsfield, Mass., in March, 1793, accompanied by one of his sons. On October 9, the same year, his wife arrived, bringing the remainder of their children, eight in number. The latter party came down the river, a distance of forty miles, in two canoes, and landed opposite where the Ah-wa-ga House now stands, in Owego. Chauncey, a son of John Hill, was born in Pittsfield, Mass., November 19, 1791. For many years he was a pilot on the river, being engaged in that capacity first, when but eighteen years of age. On May 12, 1813, he married Lucy, daughter of Benjamin Sexton, of Granville, Pa. Mrs. Hill was born in Enfield, N. H,, May 3, 1796,

and is now living in Owego. They had born to them twelve children, namely, Susan, January 13, 1815, married Edward Lathrop; James N., December 14, 1816; Amanda M., August 5, 1819, wife of James Kenyon; Lucy, June 12, 1821, married Hiram Ireland, and died January 14, 1853; Sabrina, May 14, 1825; Maryann S., August 25, 1827; Sarah, December 4, 1829, died in infancy; Charles F., March 14, 1832; Emily, March 2, 1834; Sir William Wallace, May 14, 1836, and Frances A., the two later dying in infancy. Maryann, married Elijah Morehouse, by whom she had six children, viz.: Edward, deceased; James, of St. Paul, Minn.; Alice, Etta, wife of Irving Diamond; Hattie, wife of John Gray, of Apalachin, and Charles H. Mr. Morehouse died February 14, 1887, and Mrs. Morehouse died May 1, 1887. Emily married John B. Jones, March 14, 1850, by whom she has one daughter, Clara M., who married Edward J. Stout, now of Denver Col.

James Garrett was born in 1781. In 1812 he, with his wife Elizabeth, sailed from Belfast, Ireland, and first settled near the High Lands on the Hudson. In 1818 they started for the Wyoming Valley, but while passing down the Susquehanna, in the town of Tioga, one of his horses became lame and he settled about three miles north of Smithboro, on the farm now owned by his grandson William H. Johnson, where he lived until his death, which occured in 1871. They had two daughters, Eliza, who married John Y. Smith, and Maria Jane, who married John S. Johnson.

Abijah Russell came from Kent, Putnam county, to Tioga, in 1853, and located on the farm now owned by Rev. Ziba Evans. He married Eliza, daughter of Josephas Barrott, of West Newark, by whom he had six children—Van Ness, of Owego, Holmes, of Tioga, Emily, wife of Williston Hunt, of Nichols, Rosalia, wife of Charles Scott, Howard, deceased, and Hetty A., wife of Charles Catlin, of Owego. Emily married first John S. Orcott and has one child, Ella M.

Henry Primrose, son of Jacob and Martha (Runyon) Primrose, was born February 4, 1794, and married Mary, daughter of Peter and Eleanor Johnson, October 4, 1815. They had ten children, viz.: William, born May 5, 1817, died June 10, 1840; James, now of Barton, January, 21, 1819; Betsey J., of Tioga Centre, January 6, 1821; Nellie A., October 4, 1822, died October 21, 1822; Orpha W., August 28, 1823; Peter J., July 1, 1828, now of Washington Territory; Jacob, October 1, 1830, now of Menoinee, Mich.; Martha, wife of Thomas Johnson, of Tioga Center, December 7,

1833; Mary E., wife of James Williams, of Valejo, Cal., March 4, 1839; and Clarissa, wife of Edward McDonald, of Tioga Center, April 13, 1841. Mr. Primrose was a founder of Methodism in the town of Tioga, and a preacher and leader of the people of that denomination.

Joseph Winters, the late postmaster at Tioga Center, was born in Orange county, N. Y., April 2, 1820, and came to Tioga in 1860, where he remained until his death, recently. Mr. Winters married Julia A. Carpenter, for his for first wife, and for his second wife her sister, Elizabeth. Of his ten children, Judson B., is of the firm of Hyde & Winters, of Owego: Joseph E., is a practicing physician of New York city; Edgar, is of the firm of Starkey & Winters, of Owego, and Byron L., a law student in New York city.

Oren Waterman was born at Smithboro, March 25, 1828, and has always been a resident of the town, except a few years spent in Nichols. His father, James, came to Smithboro with his parents, John and Lucretia Waterman, in 1800. Oren married Sarah Wolverton and has five children.

Jared Foote, son of Ichabod, was born in Connecticut, January 22, 1789, married Sally Scott, April 2, 1810, and located in Delaware county, N. Y., where all of his seven children were born. In 1837 he removed with his family to Tioga, locating at what is known as Goodrich Settlement. His children were as follows: Alfred, born, October 22, 1811, married Margaret Grout, and died in May, 1885; Rebecca, born April 16, 1814, died March 24, 1843; Jared A., born May 11, 1817; Sally A., born July 26, 1819, died in 1871; Lyman B., born March 24, 1822; Elmira, born May 21, 1825; John, born October 11, 1826. Mrs. Jared Foote, Sr., died June 6, 1852, and for his second wife Mr. Foote married Sally A. Stiles, May 3, 1854, who died in the winter of 1886–87. Mr. Foote died May 6, 1875.

Stephen W. Jones, from Stockbridge, Mass., came to Tioga in 1807, locating upon the farm now owned by his grandson, Horace, on road 28. He had a family of six children, only one of whom, Mrs. Sarah Payne, of Waverly, N. Y., is living. Stephen P., the only one of the three sons who located permanently in the vicinity, married Fidelia Farnham, who bore him three children, Stephen W., Horace and Charles E. Horace married Rachel Anthony, November 24, 1857, who bore him four children, and died March 14, 1886. The children are Carrie (Mrs. N. B. Whitley), of Tavares, Fla.; George E. of the same place; Minnie, and Grace G.

John Whitley, from Vermont, located in the north part of Candor, in 1816. He had a family of thirteen children, only one of whom, Mrs. Lydia Brearly, of Caroline Centre, is living. His son, Joel S., who was six years old when his father came to Candor, located in Tioga in 1850, on road thirteen, where he died March 20, 1886. He married for his first wife Miss Hoffman, who died in 1843. For his second wife he married Emily Anderson, in 1844, who survives him. His two children are Arthusa P. (Mrs. Andrew Jewett), of Elmira, and Judson M., of Tioga.

Ira Anderson came with his family, from Warren, Rutland county, Vt., in 1810, and located in Candor, upon the farm now occupied by his grandson, Philander. He married Susan Andrews, who bore him seven children, Almira, Polly, Charlotte, Amarilla (Mrs. John Wolverton), of Candor, Johnson, Marshall, and Daniel, Amarilla being the only one now living. Daniel, born March 18, 1800, married Fidelia Frisbie, who bore him six children, Chester, Mary, Charlotte, Ezra, Frederick and Edwin. Ezra moved to Tioga in 1866, and now resides on road 12. He married Laura Gould, in January, 1866, and has three children. Marshall married Hannah Harris, who bore him eight children, James M., Stephen, Mariette, Albert, Amos, John, Eliza and Enos. James M. came to Tioga, in 1880, from Candor, and resides on road 12. He married Mary H. Easton and has two children living, Willis D. and John J.

Harris Jewett, born at Chenango Forks, N. Y., October 18, 1804, and located in Berkshire in 1830, upon the farm now owned by Walter Jewett. In 1854, he moved to Tioga, locating upon the farm he now occupies, on road 9. Mr. Jewett married Lucinda Ford, September 11, 1832, who bore him five children, three of whom are living, viz.: Charles F., born October 2, 1834; William A., born June 20, 1842; and Henry M., born October 24, 1850. Mrs. Jewett died July 21, 1868.

Lewis Lounsbury, from Connecticut, born February 21, 1794, was the first settler upon the farm now occupied by Mrs. Mary Lounsbury, in 1815. He married Charry Clark, December 12, 1816, who bore him eight children, five of whom are living, two in this town, Clark and Sheldon. Clark married Mary J. Howland, February, 6, 1849, and has two children, Cornelia and Harriet A., teachers. Lewis died January 11, 1861. Lewis, Jr., born December 10, 1820, married Mary Casterline, June 14, 1853, who bore him three children, Anson, John and Amy. Lewis, Jr., died April 24, 1887, and Mrs. Lounsbury occupies the homestead, with her children. Sheldon, son of Lewis, was born November 6, 1837, married Sarah J. Moe, May 8, 1878, and has three children. He resides on road 61.

Jonathan Emerson, from Albany county, N. Y., was the first settler upon the farm now owned by his son David B., about 1822. He married Mary Harlin, who bore him four children, Samuel H., Chester, Mary (Mrs. Alexander Duff), and David B. The eldest son, Samuel H., married Sarah Duncan and has three children. Jonathan died October 1, 1885, and his widow still survives him.

W. Hulse Shaw is one of the prominent farmers in the town. He came here from Orange county, N. Y., a few years ago. He was a soldier in the war of the rebellion, is president of the Tioga County Agricultural Society, was Democratic candidate for member of assembly, in 1885. He is interested in raising valuable live-stock.

Maj. Richard Spendley was for many years a prominent and wealthy resident of the town. He was one of the active Republicans of the town and county, and was often a delegate to state and other conventions. He was at one time supervisor. He removed to Salamanca a few years ago.

Henry Bogart was born in Ulster county, April 13, 1830, and came to Tioga in 1865. He married Sarah E. Cook, July 14, 1856, and has four children, Eugene D., Elmer E., Arthur and Earl.

We quote the following interesting matter from Judge Avery's "Susquehanna Valley" papers, published in 1853–54:

"This town, also, has the honor of having been the place of residence, for many of the later years of his life, of the distinguished patriot, Josiah Cleaveland, who gained his first laurels in the memorable battle of Bunker Hill. In June, 1843, he returned to the scene of his early heroism, and joined in the celebration of the completion of the monument which his grateful countrymen had reared: and there, within a few days after the commemoration of that event, surrounded by all the hallowing associations of the time and place, he resigned his soul into the hands of Him who gave it, by a remarkable and impressive providence, at the foot of the storied hill upon which his fame so proudly rested. His remains repose, in honorable burial, at Mount Auburn.

"An Indian burying-ground extended along the brow of the cliff, on the westerly bank of the Owego creek, in this town, upon the homestead premises of Messrs. J. Platt, and C. F. Johnson. It was a favorite burial place. Mrs. Whitaker narrates that upon the death of Ka-nau-kwis, whose name appears upon the Indian document, somewhat varied from the one given by her, he was brought to this place. Where he died she does not state, but Mrs. Williams recollects to have heard her father say that he received his death-wound at Tioga Point. His remains must therefore have been transported from that place to this favorite spot of interment, a distance of twenty-one miles. Although many Indian graves have been found upon the site of Owego, no indications have been there exhibited of an appropriation so exclusive for Indian burial in its ordinary mode, as the extended brow of this cliff. The rounded Indian burial mound, near the intersection of Paige and River streets, was formed either by its having been made the place of deposit for a large collection of remains upon their removal from original places of interment, or perhaps by the burial of a number of warriors who may have fallen in battle. It was not an ordinary Indian burial place.

" Many Indian graves were also found near the bank of the river, a short distance below Cassel's cove. The remains were found, here, in the usual posture, surrounded by the customary implements of the chase, and ornaments such as were usually deposited along with the body which they had contributed to support and adorn in life. But for this custom of our Indian predecessors very few of those articles, or of those of their domestic use, would have been now within our reach. The key which they have furnished to a store of Iroquois usages and antiquities, but for that national funeral rite, would have been kept from our hands.

" At the time of the pioneer settlement of this town, the evenly-wooded hill, sloping southerly upon the homestead of Mr. John Dubois, was found entirely stripped of timber, bearing the appearance of having been burned over and thoroughly cleared. It was shrubless as well as denuded of its trees. The even and remarkably uniform 'second growth' which now covers it, clearly shows this to be a fact, and corroborates the account.

" About twenty-two years since, in the easterly part of this town, upon the premises known in the olden time as the residence and home property of David Pixley, Jr., situated upon the westerly side of the Owego creek, something less than half a mile below the homestead of Mr. Ephraim Leach, a singular discovery was made. A large brass kettle was disclosed by the plough, literally filled with articles of various kinds, of ancient appearance and manufacture, and doubtless of no little value to the person who had taken the pains to bury them there. At the time of their deposit that immediate vicinity was thickly wooded, and well selected to avoid observation and escape discovery. Among other contents was a copper tea kettle, inside of which was found a pewter vessel, filled with untrimmed rifle balls, just as they came from the moulds. The other articles were an old-fashioned and peculiarly shaped hammer, a parcel of pewter plates of two sizes, the smaller ones showing no marks of use, bright, and undimmed by corrosion, and upon them the word ' LONDON' plainly impressed; a peculiarly-shaped iron or steel instrument, about six or eight inches in length, pointed, and like the head of an arrow or spear, except that it had a single barb about two inches long, on one side only; at its other extremity was a socket, apparently intended for a handle.

" This is an enumeration of a part only of the articles there found, but sufficiently complete to start many a conjecture as to their history, the time when they were secreted, whether in the revolutionary era, or anterior or subsequent to it. But, whatever may be our suppositions upon the subject, they can never take any more satisfactory form than that of mere conjecture. It may be mentioned, that at many of the earlier councils and treaties held by the Iroquois with the agents of the English government, during our colonial history, presents, similar to the major part of these, were distributed profusely among the natives, for the purpose of conciliating them, individually, and to keep bright the ' covenant-chain' with the confederacy. It would not be at all strange, if some of the Indian occupants of our valley, previous to their fleeing to the frontier upon the approach of Gens. Clinton and Sullivan, adopted this as a mode of secreting these articles from their white invaders, hoping to resume possession of them after their enemies had retired from the Susquehanna. Death or the fortunes of war might have prevented a realization of their hopes; or, if they returned, the precise spot where they were secreted, might have been forgotten : and thus these mementos of the past were left to slumber on until accident disclosed them to view."

The comparative growth of the town is shown by the following figures, from the census enumerations for the several enumerations since the town was organized: 1810, 500; 1820, 1,810; 1825, 991;

1830, 1,411 ; 1835, 1,987 ; 1845, 2,778 ; 1850, 2,839; 1855, 3,027 ; 1860, 3,202 ; 1865, 3,094 ; 1870, 3,272 ; 1875, 3,162 ; 1880, 3,192.

Initial Events.—The first log house was built by Major Wm. Ransom, who also built the first saw-mill, about 1792.

Major Ransom set out the first apple-tree, bringing it with him in a boat from Wyoming. He set out the first orchard on the west bank of the creek, and had the first nursery. George Tallcott, when on an exploring tour through the country, in 1790, says this was the first orchard he had seen between here and Albany.

Colonel David Pixley built the first grist-mill on Owego creek, in what is called to this day Pixley's Channel, in or before 1793. Previous to this and until the erection of Fitch's mill, four miles above Binghamton, in 1790, the settlers in this locality were obliged to go to Wilkesbarre with their grain by means of canoes, on the Susquehanna, which usually occupied about two weeks. The Mattesons very soon after 1793 built a mill at Canewana.

The first tavern was built of logs, and was kept by Samuel Ransom. The first framed house was built by Prince Alden.

A Mr. Denio was the first blacksmith, and had a shop at Tioga Centre. John Hill was the first carpenter.

Lodowyck Light built the first tannery, using dug-outs for vats, which was afterwards enlarged as a tannery and shoe-shop by his son, Henry Light.

Major William Ransom and Rachel Brooks, in 1792, took upon themselves matrimonial vows, and no record can be found earlier of marriages in the town.

The first recorded death is that of David Pixley, who died June 6, 1799, aged thirty-five years, and who was a son of Colonel Pixley. He was buried in the wilderness, and the Tioga cemetery occupies the same locality.

The first cemetery was the one called the Canfield cemetery, and is situated near the residence of Amos Canfield.

Rev. David Jayne was preaching here before 1796. The first camp-meeting was held on the hill on Lodowyck Light's farm, in 1807, and this hill was afterwards called by the irreverent ones of Pipe Creek, " Holy Hill." The first church was built on this place in 1812, and was a Union church.

The first school-house was built on Samuel Ransom's farm, before 1800.

The first store was kept by John Light and John Crise, at Smithboro.

A postoffice was first kept at Smithboro, by Isaac Boardman, in 1812, and by John DuBois, very soon after, at Tioga Centre. Stephen Leonard, of Owego, had the first mail contract through from Owego to Elmira, and a mail was delivered once a week. Ebenezer Meckin drove the first mail-coach through for Leonard.

The first ferry that crossed the Susquehanna river in this town was owned by John Decker and Gideon Cortright, who lived on Coxe's Patent as early as 1800.

Organization.—It is impossible to give the exact date of the first town meeting, nor a list of the officers there chosen. The records of the town were taken to Owego in 1834, to be used there to settle some point in a law-suit, and were destroyed by a fire that occurred in that village. For this reason we print the following list of officers. The list of supervisors was obtained from the county clerk's office, from 1795 to 1813, as from the town of Owego, and from 1813 to 1828 from the town of Tioga. No record can be found from that time until 1835, since which these officers are given complete:

Supervisors.

1795. Emmanuel Coryell,
1796. Lodowyck Light,
1797. Samuel Tinkham,
1798. John Smyth,
1799-1800. Jesse Miller,
1801-3. Joshua Ferris,
1804-9. Emmanuel Coryell,
1810-12. Noah Goodrich,
1813-17. Gamaliel H. Barstow,
1818-20. Emmanuel Coryell,
1821-23. Wright Dunham,
1824. Ziba Miller,
1825. George Matson,
1826-27. Ephraim Leach,
1828. Erastus Goodrich,
1835-40. Jesse Turner,
1841-43. Erastus Goodrich,
1844. Jesse Turner,
1845. Israel S. Hoyt.

1846-47. Jesse Turner,
1848. David Taylor,
1849-52. Gilbert Strang,
1853. William Ransom,
1854. David Taylor,
1855. David Earle,
1856. Gilbert Strang,
1857-58. Richard Spendley,
1859. Harris Jewett,
1860. Richard Spendley,
1861. Abel Dubois,
1862-64. Gilbert Strang,
1865. L. B. West,
1866-70. W. H. Bristol,
1871-73. Josiah Pickering,
1874-83. Stephen W. Leach,
1884-86. Jonathan C. Latimer,
1887. Stephen W. Leach.

Town Clerks.

1835. Charles Ransom,
1836-39. Gilbert Strang,
1840. Robert C. Cole,

1841. Orin Dubois,
1842-47. Gilbert Strang,
1848. Lott P. Luce,

1849. Nicholas Schoonover, Jr.,
1850–51. Cornelius D. Hoff,
1852. Erastus Hoff.
1853. Forman S. Higbe,
1854. Lott P. Luce,
1855. Elisha D. Ransom,

1856–57. Thos. F. Goodenough,
1858. Gilbert Strang,
1859–77. Moses Ohart,
1878. Chauncey J. Goodenough,
1879–87. Moses Ohart.

Justices of the Peace.

David Jayne,
Solomon Jones,
David Jayne,
Erastus Goodrich,
Robert C. Cole,
Sylvester Knapp,
Israel S. Hoyt,
Robert C. Cole,
Jared Foot,
Amos Canfield,
Cutler Woodruff,
Elijah Cleveland,
David Earle,
Sylvester Knapp,
Stephen W. Leach,
Israel S. Hoyt,
George L. Light,
Stephen W. Leach,
David Earle,
Joel S. Whitley,
Israel S. Hoyt,
Edwin H. Schoonover,
Joel S Whitley,
Francis F. Miller,
Israel S. Hoyt,
Thomas F. Goodenough,
Stephen J. Rider,
Cornelius C. Yontz.

Luther B. West,
John H. Yontz,
Noah Goodrich,
William C. Randall,
John H. Yontz,
Noah Goodrich,
Walter C. Randall,
Luther B. West,
Charles E. Ransom,
Noah Goodrich,
William J. Drake,
William W. Giles,
Charles Bonham,
Noah Goodrich,
William J. Drake,
Edgar Taylor,
Walter C. Randall,
David Earle,
Noah Goodrich,
Ira Hoyt,
Walter C. Randall,
Ira Hoyt,
David Earle,
Noah Goodrich,
Deloss Goodenough,
Peter Turner,
Abner G. Hill.

Internal Improvements.—A ferry was used across the river before 1800, by Decker & Cortright, near where Avery Horton lives. One was started by Caleb Lyons, in 1811, the landing being on the Eli Light farm. A wire ferry was constructed by Col. William Ransom, in 1842. Smithboro & Nichols Bridge Company was incorporated April 18, 1829, and Isaac Boardman, Nehemiah Platt, and John Coryell were appointed commissioners. The bridge was soon after built, and in the spring following its erection was washed away. The second was erected March 17, 1865. Three spans were carried away by the Whitneyville mill in a freshet, and it was repaired the same season.   On October 20, 1865, the new part was entirely blown down by a heavy gale, and was rebuilt in forty days.   March 17, 1868, at eight o'clock, A. M., two spans of the south end were carried away by a span of the Owego bridge coming down against it.   In 1880, it was again destroyed, and has not been rebuilt.

The Erie and the Southern Central railroads run through the town, following the Susquehanna river, having depots at Tioga Centre and Smithboro.

VILLAGES.

TIOGA CENTER is a small village of, approximately, four hundred inhabitants, situated about mid-way of the southern boundary of the town, at the mouth of Pipe creek.   It is a station on the New York, Lake Erie & Western and the Southern Central railways.   It has two churches, two hotels, a handsome union school building, a tannery, four stores, a postoffice, two blacksmith shops, a steam flouring mill, three steam saw-mills, two shoe shops, a resident physician and a drug store.

Tanning has been a thriving industry in Tioga Center since 1869.   A tannery was built in 1868, by Ransom, Maxwell & Co. for a sole leather tannery.   The firm was dissolved a short time thereafter, Col. William Ransom becoming the owner of the property.   In June, 1869, he sold the tannery to J. & P. Quirin, who came from Boston and entirely overhauled it and converted it into an upper-leather tannery, and began the tanning of calf-skins.   January 3, 1871, it was destroyed by fire; but through the progressiveness of the citizens of Tioga Center, the structure was again erected by subscription, and by the first of March, 1871, the tannery was again in full operation.   October 31, 1871, one of the boilers in the tannery exploded.   The explosion occurred in the morning, immediately after the blowing of the seven o'clock whistle.   The boiler was hurled through the beam-house, which is 150 feet long, and through the lime-house, into an open area, where it fell, upwards of 300 feet from the arch upon which it was resting.   A German, Thersal Van Order, was killed outright.   Philip Quirin, one of the proprietors, was so badly injured that he died in a few days, and S. Edware Mills was injured so that he is maimed for life.   Several others were injured, more or less seriously.   The tannery has a capacity for tanning 300,000 calf skins annually.   They are tanned here and transported to Boston and finished and marketed. The firm now consists of J. G. Quirin & Co. Owing to commercial depression during the past few years, the tannery has not been operated to anything like its fullest capacity as formerly, and during the last year (1887) very little, if any tanning has been attempted by the proprietors.

The steam flouring-mill is situate upon Pipe creek, on the site where the first saw-mill was erected, by Major William Ransom, in 1792. It was changed to a grist-mill in 1840, and in 1884 it was changed to a steam flouring-mill.

J. C. Latimer's steam saw-mill is located in Tioga Centre, upon the east side of the creek. It was built in 1820, and was a water-power mill until 1873, when it was equipped with steam. It was burned in October, 1879, but was immediately rebuilt. It also contains a feed-run and a shingle-machine. It has the capacity for sawing 2,000,000 feet of lumber annually.

The steam saw-mill of John E. Pembleton is also situate in Tioga Centre, about a half a mile up Pipe creek. It was built in 1834, by J. Schoonover and Andrew Todd, and sold in 1838 to Nealy & Smith, and was subsequently purchased by John G. Smith. It was a water-power mill until 1872, when it was changed to steam. It has connected with it lath and shingle machines, and is one of the best equipped mills along Pipe creek.

In 1879, Charles H. Tribe erected a steam planing-mill near the Southern Central railway depot, and afterward added to it a sawing department, so that now it is a complete and fully equipped steam saw and planing-mill.

The standing timber in the town of Tioga, however, has been so depleted that the lumbering industry of the town is rapidly waning, and beyond doubt a few short years hence saw-mills in Tioga will be among the things of the past.

HALSEY VALLEY.—In about 1790, Thomas, Nicholson, a surveyor, was employed to make the first partition survey of lands, belonging to the state, lying back from the Susquehanna. He bought 2,000 acres, including what is now known as Halsey Valley. He died in 1792, and a daughter was born to Mrs. Nicholson a short time after his decease, who was the lawful heir to this land. She died at eighteen years of age, and during her life this land became known as "Girl's Flat," a name it held for many years. Mrs. Nicholson became the wife of Zephaniah Halsey, whose children inherited the land by title through their mother; hence the name "Halsey Valley." It was not until about 1825 that these lands began to be sold and settled upon; then six hundred acres were sold to Seely Brothers, afterwards to Joseph West and Brother; four hundred to Presher Skillings, Van Nortunk, and others. The village is situated in the north-west part of the town, and partly in the town of Barton, and contains two churches,—Christian and Methodist; the latter being in Barton,—a school-house, a postoffice, three stores, two blacksmith-shops, two cooper-shops, and two physicians.

Luther B. West has long been a merchant here, and one of the most prominent of the section. It must ever be a pleasure to con-template the life of a self-made man,—one who, by strict adher-ence to a well defined plan of action, converts adverse circum-stances into successful and honorable results. Such, in brief, is that of Mr. West.

His parents, Joseph and Sally (Bliven) West, whose ancestors were active participants in the revolutionary war, emigrated from Fort Ann, Washington county, N. Y., to Spencer, bringing their effects in a large covered wagon, which was drawn by two yoke of oxen and one horse, at a speed of about fifteen miles each day, through the then wilderness country, camping out and sleeping at night in their wagon.

Arriving at Spencer in the fall of 1818, they began housekeep-ing in rented rooms, in the court-house, but soon after, a home was made south of the village, upon lands purchased by Mr. West, while he worked at his trade, that of carpenter and joiner. In 1826, he rented of Andrew Purdy, and occupied his tavern and farm in Spencer for ten years, and conducted the business until April, 1836, when he removed to Halsey Valley (then called Girl's Flats), on a tract of land purchased in 1832, of Isaac and Enos Briggs and John D. Seeley, upon which he had made some im-provements while living in Spencer. Here he resided, clearing land, lumbering and farming until March, 1857, when he died, leaving a widow who died in March, 1880, and four children, viz.: Charles, Luther B., Sarah J., who was the wife of Nicholas Schoonmaker, and Warren B.

Luther Bliven West, the subject of this sketch, was born at Spencer, April 13, 1823, and attended the district school until thir-teen years of age, when, by accompanying his father who at this time moved to Girl's Flats—then mostly a wilderness—his educa-tional advantages were ended, excepting a few weeks attendance during the following winter.

The pupils of the common schools of to-day may profitably

L. B. West.

contrast the educational advantages and collateral accompaniments they enjoy, with those furnished by the " People's College " of a half century ago. To assist in making the comparison, it may be stated that the architectural features of the Girl's Flats school-house were those common to structures of that class throughout the country, viz.: the building was constructed of rough logs, the spaces between which being filled with mud and sticks, a single section of window sash in each of three sides of the build-ing admitting the light, door, swinging on wooden hinges and was opened by pulling a string attached to a wooden latch. A single slab set upon wooden pegs inserted in two-inch holes, con-stituted a seat—no support being given to the pupil's back. Abundant warmth and ventilation were secured by burning logs four to six feet in length, in a large stone fire place and chim-ney, which logs were usually cut by the boys on Saturday afternoons, for use during the following week. The principal text books in use were Cobb's spelling-book and Daboll's Arith-metic. That nature and the school-master were in league was painfully evident to all, for, from the surrounding forest was obtained a never-ending supply of tough young beeches, which, under the skillful guidance of the latter, demonstrated his superiority, inculcated feelings of awe if not reverence, main-tained discipline and were practical definitions of thoroughness and liberality.

Remaining with his father and actively assisting in clearing land and lumbering until the spring of 1844. when, being of legal age, he commenced business for himself by farming land for a share.

On June 9, 1844, he married Martha L., daughter of William and Laura Presher, who were among the first settlers in the Valley, and had to contend for possession with bears, wolves, and panthers that then infested the forest. They raised a large family of children, of whom Mrs. West, the youngest daughter, was born in the town of Barton, June 1, 1824.

Not satisfied with the results obtained by farming, in the spring of 1846, without other capital than energy, and without practical knowledge of the business, he purchased a small stock of goods and opened a store at Halsey Valley. The country being new and money scarce, trade was conducted mostly for barter in staves, shingles and lumber, the outlet to market being either by canal at Ithaca, a distance of twenty-five miles, or by rafting on the Susquehanna river—eight miles distant—to Port Deposit and

Baltimore, Md. After many hard struggles, a fair business was established. In 1849, he purchased, and in connection with Eliakim D. Hoyt, put steam-power in a grist and flouring mill, and manufactured flour and sawed shingles in large quantities for market; also had a saw-mill, and by purchase placed upon the market lumber made by other mills. In 1854, as the country became better settled and improved, the mercantile branch of the business was enlarged, a new store opened, and his two brothers, Charles and Warren B., admitted to a partnership that was soon afterward dissolved. For many years after, he conducted alone a large and successful business, which was gradually closed out as more important matters claimed his attention.

In 1862, he was elected justice of the peace, and continued in office by re-election for twelve consecutive years, when he declined to serve longer. During this period, he was for several terms elected justice of the county sessions.

By special order, No. 528, dated August 15, 1863, issued by the Commander-in-chief, Horatio Seymour, Governor of New York, he was authorized to raise a regiment of infantry of the National Guard in the county of Tioga, and be commissioned colonel thereof, and immediately began the work. After partly organizing several companies he was obliged to abandon it and resign, by reason of the severe and protracted illness of his wife.

In 1864, he was appointed one of a committee to procure volunteers, and financial agent to fill the quota assigned to the town of Tioga, under the call of the President for troops. To carry out the work necessitated the issuance of bonds amounting to $10,000.00, which debt was paid the following year, leaving the town free from any bonded debt, such as most adjoining towns were loaded with for years thereafter, and a continual source of annoyance to the tax-payers. The prompt payment of this war debt was largely due to his persistent efforts and advocacy of the principle, that the payment of a debt made when the currency was inflated should not be deferred until the currency became contracted. In this instance, as is too often the case, where individual effort is exerted for the public good, the scheme was for a time bitterly denounced; but its merits were soon recognized and generally acknowledged. He regards this as his masterpiece in financiering.

In 1865, he was elected supervisor of the town of Tioga, and on January 18, 1865, he, with others, organized the Tioga National Bank, at Owego. Being one of the principal stockholders, he was elected to a directorship, and in February, 1869, to the vice-presidency—to both of which positions he has been annually re-elected to the present time.

Besides the enterprises before mentioned, he has been for the past twenty-five years extensively engaged in farming and dairying, and latterly is giving much attention to investments in improved farms in Kansas and Nebraska. To promoting the school and other interests of his neighborhood he has given much of his time and attention. Has always been identified with the principles of Democracy, and is a practical temperance man. In 1864, he embraced the cause of religion and united with the Methodist Episcopal church at Halsey Valley.

Upwards of forty-two years of uninterrupted enjoyment of married life had elapsed, when, on November 6, 1886, Death claimed the wife who had witnessed and assisted him in his early struggles, and had shared, but too briefly, the fruits of their triumphs over obstacles that would have discouraged others less persevering. She was a typical wife, a womanly woman and a mother whose greatest pride was her children, of whom there were five— three daughters and two sons—their births, etc., occurring as follows: Olive, July 20, 1847, married Charles O. Wood, November 2, 1870, and died August 20, 1872; Alice, July 20, 1850, married Dr. Charles E. Hollenbeck, December 29, 1875; Ida, December 31, 1858; Grant M., April 19, 1864; and Norman L., February 16, 1867.

Personally, Mr. West is a man of fine physique, somewhat military in his bearing, easily approached, an entertaining convarsationalist well informed on all general subjects, and an acknowledged authority on all matters with which he has business relations. Trained in the rugged school of self-education, his judgment of events and men seldom misleads him. Self-reliant, sagacious, bold yet cautious, practical, methodical, always using experience to sharpen foresight and over all a marked individualism easier recognized than described, are among his prominent traits of character, the judicious exercise of which has brought the abundant prosperity he now enjoys. Life to him seems most enjoyable, and he is seen at his best when absorbed in a business problem.

Ira Hoyt was of English descent, his ancestors settling at Danbury, Mass., at an early day. His grandfather, Nathaniel Hoyt, was an officer in the revolutionary army, and settled after the war at Winchester, Conn. He was a farmer, and reared a

32*

large family. He died at the advanced age of eighty-eight years. Ira Hoyt, 2d, was born in Danbury, in 1797. He was twice married ; and by his first wife were born to him five, by his second wife four, children. He died at the age of seventy-seven, in 1864. Ira, the eldest child of Ira and Anna Hoyt, was born in Litchfield, Conn., September 9, 1821. His boyhood days were passed in attending the common school, and in laboring upon the farms of his neighborhood, until he was twenty-one years of age, when he married Miss Helen M. Roberts. The issue of this union was two children : Charles, who died at the age of five years, and Josephine, who married John Hutchins. Helen Hoyt died in 1862, aged thirty-five years. In 1864, Mr. Hoyt filled the vacancy in his home by introducing therein as his wife Mrs. Hollenbeck, of Barton. In the year 1850, he removed to Tioga county, settling at Halsey Valley, which he has since made his home. Although by occupation a cooper, he owns a small farm, and engages himself mainly in its care, and in the propagation of fish. In the latter enterprise he has been very successful, and owns a very fine pond, of which he is justly proud. For many years he has also been engaged in the manufacture of butter packages, his factory being operated by both steam and water-power, and employing a number of men.

Dr. Charles Hollenbeck was born in the town of Barton, a son of Richard and Lydia A. (Hyatt) Hollenbeck, June 4, 1850. He studied in the district schools, at Waverly Institute, at Eastman's Business College at Poughkeepsie, beginning the study of medicine at Bellevue Hospital Medical College, graduating in March, 1874. He immediately began practice at Halsey Valley, where he has since been located. The Doctor married Alice West, daughter of Luther B. West, December 29, 1875.

SMITHBORO is a small post village located in the southwestern part of the town on the Susquehanna river, and on the N. Y. L. E. & W. and the S. C. railroads. It has a church, a fine school building, several stores, two hotels, mechanic's shops, etc.

Ezra Smith, after whom Smithboro was named, and who held letters patent, covering a large tract of land in this vicinity, came from Bedford, Westchester county, N. Y., in 1791, and settled at Smithboro, in the house on the corner where Walter C. Randall now resides. He afterward sold his property and kept the Half-Way House, a well known tavern, mid-way between Ithaca and Owego. Isaac S. Broadman bought the property of Ezra

Smith, at Smithboro, enlarged the house into a tavern; this was the first tavern at Smithboro, and he the first tavern keeper.

A family named Lyon settled at the ferry a short distance east of Smithboro; Lyon was the first keeper of the ferry; his house is still standing, on the west bank of the creek, just back of the house where Mrs. Eli Light resides, to which place it was moved from the middle of the present orchard. A family named Fountain settled in the same neighborhood. The Lyon house and the old Broadman tavern, the latter now much altered and improved, are the oldest buildings now standing in the vicinity of Smithboro. At a later period Wait Smith came from Wyoming, about 1800, and built the house which stood until 1865, where Houston Platt's house now stands; Ezekiel Newman came and built the house where Mrs. Zebulon Bowman now resides; Benjamin Smith came and built the house where Benjamin Lounsbury, Jr., now resides; James Schoonover, Jr., came and built the house which Amos Lounsbury resided in for several years, and which was recently moved away and mostly torn down to make a place for his new residence; Mrs. James Brooks, whose husband was a son of James Brooks, of Tioga Centre, who died in the war of 1812, built the house which is still standing on Meeting-House Hill, a short distance east of Smithboro.

Beriah Mundy came about 1787, and settled where Mundy Schoonover now resides; his house stood near the present house, but was afterward moved westward, across the creek, into the town of Barton, where it still stands, painted a brown color, and has been occupied for many years by the Barden family.

Edward V. Poole, son of Daniel, whose ancestors were the founders of Weymouth, Mass., in 1635, was born April 3, 1826, at Manyunk, a suburb of Philadelphia, Pa. He attended Wyoming Seminary, Kingston, Pa., 1849–50. He has been a merchant and business man nearly all his life; commenced in the lumber business at Beaumont, Pa., but afterward removed to Center Moreland, Pa. He then removed to Mt. Carmel, Ill., where he did a large mercantile and lumbering business. He then returned to Center Moreland, but soon after removed to Smithboro, in 1865, where he transacted a large mercantile business. He built a large, three-story, double store, which he occupied at Smithboro, and which was burned. He has been for many years one of the most successful business men of Tioga county. He married, September 11, 1850, Susan Carey, daughter of Samuel Carey, Esq., of Centre Moreland, Pa. Their children are Charles

F., of Tioga Center; Emily A., deceased; Murry E., a law student and graduate of Cornell University, to whom we are indebted for many facts in this sketch of Tioga; Clara I. (Mrs.
Titus Baker); and Laura F. (Mrs. Thomas B. Campbell).

Walter Crowley Randall was born October 15, 1828, in the
town of Owego. He learned the shoemaker's trade, which he
followed a great many years, 1835-65. He married, March 1,
1850, Amelia Carnochan. He settled first at Vestal, but soon
removed to Campville, where he remained only a short time, and
then moved to Smithboro, in 1852, when he was appointed bridge-
keeper, a position he held until 1883, a period of thirty-one years.
He commenced farming in 1865, which he followed three years.
He then commenced the mercantile business, which he followed
eight years, then commenced farming again, in 1880, which he
still follows. He was chiefly instrumental in founding the masonic lodge, at Smithboro, and was its first master, holding that
office several years, and being frequently sent as representative
to the Grand Lodge. He has also been a justice of the peace, at
different periods, for sixteen years.

STRAIT'S CORNERS is located on a branch of Pipe creek, on the
north line of the town, lying partly in Candor. David Strait,
from whom the place derives its name, settled here in 1825. The
village contains two churches,—Christian and Baptist; the latter
being in the town of Candor,—postoffice, school-house, store and
blacksmith-shop. Its postoffice was established in 1853.

GOODRICH SETTLEMENT is located just across Owego creek, the
corporation boundary of Owego on the west. Near by is the
famous "Glenmary" place, now owned by Colonel Dorwin.
This settlement has been the home for longer or shorter periods
of N. P. Willis, the poet; Hon. Wheeler H. Bristol, state treasurer; D. C. McCallum, formerly general superintendent of the
Erie railroad; Dr. Galloway, of the Electropathic Institute, of
Philadelphia, Pa.; and Charles F. Johnson.

GERMAN SETTLEMENT is a little hamlet east from Strait's Corners, mostly in the town of Tioga, and was settled by Germans
in 1830.

Leach's Grist Mill, on road 28, was built by Caleb Leach, in
1806. Mr. Leach was a native of Plymouth, Mass.; early learned
the trade of watch-maker; made the first twisted auger in the
United States; built the Fairmount water-works, at Philadelphia,
and had charge of the Manhattan water-works. When he came
here, in 1806, he established a carding-mill and grist-mill. He

spent his later years in Utica, where he died. The mill descended to Ephraim Leach, father of Stephen W., the present proprietor. It has four runs of stones, and has the capacity for grinding 25,000 bushels per year.

Stephen W. Jones' Saw-mill, on road 1, was built by James Pumpelly, in 1827, and came into Mr. Jones' possession in 1872. The saw-mill has a circular-saw, and the capacity for sawing 1,000,000 feet per year. The grist-mill has one run of stones, and does custom work. He also does planing, turning, etc. Employs two hands.

James R. Willmott's Saw-mill is located on road 28, where he also has a plaster-mill and ice-house.

CHURCHES.

At a very early day religious services were held in dwelling-houses, barns, and school-houses, mostly by circuit preachers of the Methodist denomination, and Baptist ministers. In 1796 the Baptist church of New Bedford was organized with nine members, partly from this town. Tioga was afterwards substituted for New Bedford, and in 1847 it was again changed to the Tioga and Barton Baptist church, the history of which will be found in the town of Barton. The Methodists were numerous, and held services in the Light neighborhood. Between April 14, 1805, and the 1st of May, the eccentric Lorenzo Dow preached at Pipe Creek, in the house of Andrew Alden, with whom he stopped. In the summer of 1807, Bishop Asbury presided at a camp-meeting on the hill, where the Union church was afterwards built. In his " Life " is this statement: "After attending the General Conference at Boston, on the 1st of June, 1807, he started for the West by a new route,—that of the Mohawk, the Geneva, the Chemung, and the Susquehanna. Turning south, he passed along the shores of Seneca lake, and down the lovely valley of the Chemung to the Susquehanna, near Owego. He then descended that river to Wyoming." While here he stopped at the house of Lodowyck Light. The Asbury camp-meeting grounds of Barton, Tioga, and Nichols charge were located on the same farm.

The Union church was built on this hill by both Methodists and Baptists, and used jointly by them until the lines of denominational differences became so tightly drawn they could not agree; which differences were finally settled, as far as the church was concerned, in the summer of 1827, when it was struck by lightning and entirely destroyed. This house was thirty by forty feet, with galleries round the entire building, and never finished ; the lower portion, however, being lathed and plastered.

Methodist Episcopal Church at Smithboro.—November 19, 1832, a meeting was held at the school-house in District No. 4, town of Tioga, to incorporate a society to be called the Methodist Episcopal Society of Smithboro, John Light, Andrew Bonham, and Benjamin V. Brooks as trustees. It was voted that the seal to be used by the trustees be the triangle, and a committee was appointed to build a church. This committee entered into a contract with C. C. Yontz and Willard Cratsley to erect a church for $1,500. January 7, 1835, " It was resolved, that all orthodox societies of any denomination shall have the privilege of preaching at any time in the Smithboro church, when unoccupied, but none other, at any time." Its church edifice was erected in 1833. The building was burned May 24, 1887. Rev. Luther Peck is the present pastor.

The Methodist Episcopal Church on Ross Hill was organized with thirty-six members in November, 1870, and its church edifice erected in the same year. Rev. A. B. Eckert was the first pastor ; Rev. Luther Peck, the present one.

Emmanuel Protestant Episcopal Church of Smithboro was organized in 1866, and its church edifice erected in 1874. The first vestry was composed of the following : wardens, John C. Gray and L. Burr Pearsall ; vestrymen, Gilbert Pearsall, G. O. Chase, John C. Pearsall, Frederick C. Coryell, W. C. Randall and O. A. Barstow. The first rector was Rev. J. F. Esch ; the first resident rector was Rev. John Scott, who was succeeded by Rev. Mr. Rodgers, for a short time, when he was succeeded by Rev. John A. Bowman, the present rector.

Baptist Church of Tioga Centre.—A number of Baptist brethren, members of the Owego Baptist church, living in this section, made application to that church to be allowed to act as a branch and receive members, which was granted, and January 13, 1838, they organized as a branch society at Canfield Corners, in the town of Nichols. October 13, 1838, they resolved to become a separate body. A council was called, and they were received as a church, with twenty-three members.

January 25, 1840, it was resolved to change the location to Nichols village. April 11, 1840, eleven members, residents mostly of this town, united by letter from what is now the Tioga and Barton church. December 12, 1840, Rev. Charles F. Fox was called to the pastorate. October 12, 1844, it was resolved to change the name to the Baptist Church of Tioga Centre, and services were held in the school-house in that place. In 1849, the present church was built, at a cost of $2,000. Rev. Mr. Tilden is the present pastor.

The Methodist Episcopal Church of Tioga Centre.—The Methodists of this section had been supplied with ministers from Barton for several years, but were regularly organized October 20, 1870, as a church. In 1872 a house was built, combining elegance and utility, at a cost of $8,000, and dedicated December 12, 1873. Rev. Mr. Todd is the present pastor.

The Christian Church, was organized at Strait's Corners, in 1850, with seventeen members, Rev. B. B. Hurd as pastor ; erected a house in 1855.

The Christian Church, at Halsey Valley, was organized in 1847 ; erected a meeting-house in 1856, Rev. A. J. Welton being the first pastor.

The Methodist Episcopal Church, at German Settlement, was organized by its first pastor, Rev A. W. Loomis, in 1856. The church building was erected in 1870. The society now has forty members, with Rev. A. Osborne, pastor.

PART SECOND.

DIRECTORY

—OF—

TIOGA COUNTY, NEW YORK.

1887--'88.

COMPILED AND PUBLISHED

—BY—

W. B. GAY & CO.

PERMANENT OFFICE   -   -   -   SYRACUSE, N. Y.

"He that hath much to do, will do something wrong, and of that wrong must suffer the consequences ; and if it were possible that he should always act rightly, yet when such numbers are to judge of his conduct, the bad will censure and obstruct him by malevolence, and the good sometimes by mistake."—SAMUEL JOHNSON.

SYRACUSE, N. Y.:
THE SYRACUSE JOURNAL COMPANY, PRINTERS AND BINDERS.
1887.

Owego Cruciform Casket Company.

Manufacturers of and dealers in all kinds of Lumber and Building Material. Planing and Matching, Re-sawing, Scroll Sawing, Bracket Sawing, Shaping and Turning of every description.

Doors, Sash and Blinds on hand and extra and odd sizes furnished at short notice.

French Glass of all sizes kept in stock, and Sash Doors and Windows glazed.

Flooring, Ceiling, Siding and Mouldings furnished in any quantity, large or small.

SHINGLES AND LATH.

All kinds of lumber in the rough or dressed kept constantly on hand.

Bee-hive and Honey-box material furnished to order.

Lumber taken in exchange for work.

Manufacturers of Hall's Celebrated Combined Sheathing and Lath, send for circulars and sample. Also manufacturers of all kinds of fine Cloth Covered Caskets, and dealers in fine finished wood Caskets and Coffins, and all kinds of

UNDERTAKER'S SUPPLIES.

Agents for Utopia, the "Triumph" Embalming Fluid of the age, and all kinds of Embalmer's Supplies.

All orders filled with accuracy and dispatch.

Send for illustrated album of styles and price list, and give us a trial.

OWEGO CRUCIFORM CASKET CO.,

OWEGO, TIOGA CO., N. Y.

Factory and Office, 42, 44 and 46 Delphine St.

DIRECTORY

—OF—

TIOGA COUNTY, NEW YORK.

EXPLANATIONS.

Directory is arranged as follows :—

1—Name of individual or firm.

2—Postoffice address in parenthesis if different from the name of town.

3—The figures following the letter r indicate the number of the road on which the party resides, and will be found by reference to the map in the back part of this work. Where no road number is given the party is suppossd to reside in the village.

4—Business or occupation.

5—A star (*) placed before a name indicates an advertiser in this work.

6—Figures placed after the occupation of a farmer indicate the number of acres owned or leased

7—Names in CAPITALS are those who have kindly given their patronage to the work, and without whose aid its publication would have been impossible.

☞ **For additional names, changes and corrections, see Errata.**

ABBREVIATIONS.--Ab., above; ave., avenue; bds., boards; bet., between; cor., corner; E., east; emp., employee; fac. op., factory operative; h., house; manuf., manufacturer; Mfg., manufacturing; N., north; n., near; opp., opposite; prop., proprietor; reg., registered as applied to live stock; regt., regiment; S., south; supt., superintendent; W., west.

The word *street* is implied.

BARTON.

WAVERLY VILLAGE.*

(Postoffice address is Waverly, unless otherwise designated in parenthesis.)

Ackerly Nathaniel. clerk L. V. R. R. freight office, h 47 Waverly.

ACKLEY & BAILEY, (P. R. A. and J. B. B.) props. Tioga Hotel, Fulton cor. Elizabeth.

ACKLEY PERRIN R., (Ackley & Bailey) h S. Waverly.

---

* For the sake of convenience we print the directory of the incorporated village of Waverly separate from the balance of the town of Barton.

STARKEY & WINTERS, promptly fill Mail and Telephone Orders.

Akins Jane, dressmaker, 118 Clark, bds. do.
Albertson Charles, milk depot and creamery, h 5 Orange.
Albertson Clarence, milk dealer, bds. 5 Orange.
Albertson Daniel, retired, h 11 Orange.
Aldrich Samuel, emp. Novelty Works, h 344 Broad.
Aldrich Vernie, emp. Novelty Works, h 344 Broad.
ALLEN ADOLPHUS G., (Allen & Campbell) also att'y at law, over 203 Broad, h 8 Park Place.
Allen D. Wellington, att'y at law, bds. 8 Park Place.
Allen Elizabeth G., widow Peleg, h 33 Waverly.
Allen Louis S., clerk, bds. 33 Waverly.
Allen William H., resident, h 321 Broad.
American House, (A. P. Head, prop.) 260 Broad.
Andre Jacob, retired, bds. 19 Chemung.
Angell Edward J., market gardener, h 472 Chemung.
Angell James E., market gardener 470 Chemung, h do.
Angell Mary L., green-house, 472 Chemung.
Aplin Eliza, widow James, h 29 Waverly.
Atkins William, retired, h 120 Clark.
Atwater Dewitt C., livery and boarding stable, Clark, and farmer 200, h 139 Clark.
Atwater Lewis D., teller, First National Bank, bds. 139 Clark.
Atwood Mary S., widow Rev. William, bds. Pennsylvania ave.
Atwood William W., station agent D. L. & W. R. R., h 50 Fulton.
BAILEY JOHN B., (Ackley & Bailey) bds. Tioga Hotel.
Baker Mary T. Mrs., millinery, 143 Waverly, h do.
Baker Melvin J., carpenter, h 143 Waverly.
Baldwin Albert B., boots and shoes, 6 Fulton, h 300 Chemung cor. Fulton.
Baldwin Francis H., retired, h 300 Chemung.
BALDWIN HUGH J., lumber, also builder and jobber, Broad n. Pennsylvania ave., h 320 Pennsylvania ave.
Ball John M. Rev., retired Baptist clergyman, h. 8 Pine.
Barber Clara A., preceptress academy, bds. 11 Broad.
BARNES & MILLER, (B. D. B. and L. C. M.) groceries and provisions, 277 Broad.
BARNES BENJAMIN D., (Barnes & Miller) bds. Seely's Hotel.
Barnes John C., mason, h 10 Elm.
Barnum & Personius, (S. D. B. and D. V. P.) seed, hay and grain, 264 Broad.
Barnum Hervey J., printer, bds. 166 Clark.
Barnum John W., book-keeper, h 166 Clark.
Barnum Lillian, book-keeper, 264 Broad, bds. Bradford.
Barnum Smith D., (Barnum & Personius) h Bradford.
Barr John, upholsterer, h over 251 Broad.
Barr John C., cabinet maker, Elizabeth, h Chemung.
Barrington Michael, laborer, h Erie.
BARROWS ABRAM H., (Wilcox & Barrows) h 120 Waverly.
Barton Alfred, clerk, h Clark.
Barton Charles, emp. pipe foundry, h 102 Waverly.
Bassett Henry, carpenter, h Orange.
Bassett James, clerk, bds. over 226 Broad.
Bauer Andrew M., painter, h 30 Broad.
Baxter Robert J., machinist, h 12 Providence.
Beach Arthur N., telegraph operator, bds. Christie House.

Beach Eliza J., physician, 208 Pennsylvania ave., h do.
Beams Horace E., emp. Swift & Co., h 28 Clark.
Beardslee Edson E., drayman, h 2 Ithaca.
Beardslee Mary Mrs., dressmaker, 2 Ithaca, h do.
Beekman Emma, dressmaker, 127 Chemung, bds. do.
Beekman Sarah A., widow Isaac, h 127 Chemung.
Bell Minor, emp. Novelty Works, h 25 Providence.
Belles William, emp. Thatcher & Co., h 427 Chemung.
Bellis Jacob, emp. Novelty Works, bds. 111 Howard.
Beman John, hack stable, and prop. transfer line, Clark, bds. Tioga Hotel.
Beman Merritt, h Loder, refused to give information.
Bennet Stephen, druggist, and sporting goods, Broad, h 5 Clark.
Bennett Alanson, night watch, h off Lincoln.
Bennett Alfred, retired, h 128 Chemung.
Bennett Frank, teamster, bds. 17 Providence.
Bennett Sophia, widow Amos, h rear 32 Fulton.
Bentley Abram W., livery, Broad, h 23 do.
Bentley John L., liveryman, Broad, bds. 23 do.
Berry Ira L., traveling salesman, h 106 Fulton.
Betowski W. Leon, merchant tailor, 123 Broad, h 10 Johnson.
Bill Mary, widow, h 343 Broad.
Bingham Jefferson, grocer, h 337 Broad.
Bissett William H., laborer, bds. Lyman ave.
Bixby Fred, telegraph operator, bds. 47 Fulton.
Bixby Harrison, h 446 Chemung.
Blizzard Edward, messenger, bds. 131 Fulton.
Blizzard George S., drayman, h 131 Fulton.
Blossom Amanda, dressmaker, bds. 16 Chemung.
Blossom Jason B., contractor and builder, 16 Chemung, h do.
Boda & Dimmock, (W. H. B. and C. S. D.) meat market, 231 Broad.
Boda William H., (Boda & Dimmock) h 32 Pine.
Bodle John D., carpenter, bds. 411 Chemung.
BOGART HENRY, engineer, h 8 Tioga.
Boggs Charles, porter, Hotel Warford, bds. do.
Boggs George, laborer, bds. 401 Chemung.
Bonfoey Hubert R., clerk L. V. R. R. freight office, h over 237 Broad.
Bonnell Benjamin W., clerk Erie freight office, h 122 Clark.
Boorom Chauncey D., carpenter, h Chemung.
Borland William, laborer, h 43 Orange.
Bostwick Silas W., painter and paper-hanger, Waverly, h do.
Botrand Sylvester, brakeman, h 139 Howard.
Bowen George Rev., rector Grace Church, h 400 Chemung.
Bowen George H., cutter, bds. 400 Chemung.
Bowen James, clerk postoffice, bds. 400 Chemung.
Bowen Mary I., clerk, bds. 400 Chemung cor. Waverly.
Boyd Harry C., cigar packer, h Fulton.
Bradley Julian A., machinist, h 22 Johnson.
Bradley William H., resident, h Loder.
*BRAY JAMES B., editor and prop. *Free Press*, also job printing, 15 Fulton, h 17 do.
Brewster Curtis, variety store, Broad, h 308 Pennsylvania ave.
Brewster Elliot S., carpenter, h Fulton.
Brewster Harvey C., emp. Erie depot, h 180 Clark.

Brewster M. Lewis, emp. Erie R. R., h 10 Pine.
Brewster Newton C., teacher of penmanship, h E. Waverly.
Brewster Rosanna, widow George, h 180 Clark.
Briley ——, widow ——. milliner over 151 Broad, h do.
Bristol Nathan S., clerk L. V. R. R. freight office, h 108 Waverly.
Brockitt George H., brakeman, h Spring.
BROOKS CHARLES C., insurance, over 201 Broad, h 106 Pennsylvania.
Brooks Charles E., chief of police, bds. 106 Pennsylvania ave.
Brooks Charles W., clerk, h 13 Orange.
Brooks Lizzie D., dress and cloak maker, 12 Waverly, h do.
Brougham Mary C., resident, h 501 Chemung.
BROWN CHARLES E., pianos, organs and sewing machines, 267 Broad, h 125 Lincoln cor. Hickory.
Brown Charles E., emp R. R. shops, Sayre, h Lyman ave.
BROWN DOWLINGTON J., tea store, 261 Broad, h 29 Orange.
Brown Ella, teacher, bds. 11 Broad.
Brown Jacob M., clerk, bds. 29 Orange.
Brown Merle A. J., clerk, bds. Lincoln cor. Hickory.
Brown Orilla, widow Jesse, h 39 Broad.
BRUSTER GEORGE C., art and ladies furnishing goods, 232 Broad, h Pennsylvania ave.
Buck Abbie B., widow Josiah T., h 206 Chemung.
Buck George, resident, h 130 Howard.
Buck Michael B., brakeman, bds. Loder.
Buckbee Augusta, widow Enos, h 119 Clark.
Buckley Nellie, widow Bradford, h 466 Chemung.
Buley James D., retired, h 35 Fulton.
Buley Joseph M., town collector, and sexton Presbyterian Church, h 112 Chemung.
Buley Joseph M., Jr., messenger, W. U. Tel. office, bds. 112 Chemung.
Buley Judd E., book-keeper for H. J. Baldwin, bds. 35 Fulton.
Buley Lewis J. Q., clerk, bds. 112 Chemung.
BUNN ALBERT R., boots and shoes, 219 Broad, h 121 Waverly.
Bunnell D. Ann, widow William, bds. 43 Waverly.
Burgess Lizzie T., teacher, bds. 505 Chemung.
Burke Mrs., widow ——, h Erie.
Bush Abram, passenger conductor, G. I. & S. R. R, room over 265 Broad.
Bush Laura S., (H. M. Wilcox & Co.) widow J. G., h 25 Waverly.
Butts Henry S., manuf. patent medicines, h 204 Pennsylvania ave.
Cadwell Lorenzo, retired, h 123 Chemung.
Cahill Michael, foreman repair shop, Erie R. R., h 57 Broad.
Cahill Michael J., clerk, bds. 57 Broad.
Cain Daniel W., laborer, h 33 Waverly.
Callahan John, laborer, h 121 Erie.
Camp Carrie Mrs., resident, h Clark.
Campbell Abram F., carpenter, h Clark.
Campbell Clarence C., coal dealer at East Waverly, h 8 Park Place.
Campbell Emery J., resident, h 420 Chemung.
Campbell Frank J., clerk, L. V. R. R. freight office, h 48 Fulton.
Campbell William, car inspector, h 111 Lincoln.
Canall Charles W., cigarmaker, bds. 135 Chemung.
Caney Phœbe A., laundress, h Hickory.
Careau Frances, dressmaker, bds. 43 Orange.

Carey Daniel G., patent medicine manuf., Broad, h 421 Chemung.
Carey Erastus, laborer, h Hickory.
Carey Rebecca C., widow William J., bds. 45 Orange.
Carey Samuel C., traveling salesman, bds. 421 Chemung.
Carmody Thomas F., saloon, Fulton h do.
Carmoody Simon, assistant train dispatcher, Erie R. R., bds. Warford House.
Carpenter Harrison W., laborer, h. 109 Lincoln.
Carpenter Lou A., widow Stephen, resident, bds. 33 Fulton.
Carr & Teachman, (C. S. C. & I. P. T.,) meat market 119 Broad.
Carr Clark S., (Carr & Teachman) h 34 Broad.
Carr Robert, brakeman, h 236 Broad.
Carroll John, station agent Erie depot, h 110 Fulton.
Case Angeline E., widow John, h 111 Howard.
Case Cornelius, carpenter, h 125 Howard.
Case George W., carpenter, h 47 Orange.
Case Irving, painter, bds. 125 Howard.
Case James, foreman Novelty works, h 24 Loder.
Chaffee Charles F., drug clerk, h 113 Park ave.
Chaffee Daniel, switchman, h 12 Loder.
Chaffee Ellen A., widow William A., h 5 Lincoln.
Chaffee Myrtie M., dressmaker, bds. 5 Lincoln.
Chall John, building mover, h 29 Broad.
Chamberlain Edward, drayman, h Pine.
Chambers Catharine, widow Thomas, bds. 15 Loder.
Chatam Myron, clerk, bds. Waverly.
Christie House, W. H. Goldsmith, prop., Fulton, opp. Erie depot.
Christie John M., retired, h. 27 Fulton.
Clark Benjaman B., retired, h 200 Penn. ave.
CLARK CHARLES H., bakery and confectionery, 121 Broad, h Pleasant.
CLARK JAMES A., hardware, stoves, etc., 217 Broad, h 316 Penn. ave.
Clark Lyman W., painter, h over 234 Broad.
Clark Warren M., foreman Sayre Butter Package Company, h 116 Waverly.
Clarke & Ralyea, (F. H. C. & W. H. R.) cigars and tobacco, 275 Broad.
Clarke Floyd H., (Clarke & Ralyea) h Chemung.
Clawsey James, laborer, h Erie.
Clemens Charles H., emp. pipe foundry, h 330 Broad.
Clohessy Michael J., clerk, h Pitney.
Cobb Adolphus, locomotive engineer, bds. Warford House.
Cochran Frisby M., engineer, h 123 Ciark.
Coffee John, laborer, h 112 Howard.
Cole Archie, cigarmaker, bds 104 Waverly.
Cole Charles, porter Commercial Hotel, bds. do.
Cole Mary, widow James, h 135 Howard.
Cole Minnie E., widow Edmond C., h 104 Waverly.
Coleman Gabriel, farmer, h 24 Park Place.
Colemam Jacob S., carpenter, h 24 Park Place.
Coleman Samuel, blacksmith, bds. 437 Chemung.
Collins Michael, switchman, h Broad.
Commercial Hotel, D. S. Kennedy, prop., Fulton cor. Elizabeth.
Compton Eugene, harness maker, h over 151 Broad.
Compton James E., miller, h 140 Waverly.
Compton Richard W., shoemaker, Erie, h do.
Comstock A. B. Mrs., art teacher, 126 Waverly.

Comstock Alphonso B., photographer over 208 Broad, h 126 Waverly.
Cone Betsey, widow John, h 3 Tioga.
Congdon Lynn, emp. Novelty works, h 337 Broad.
Conklin Levi K., emp. wheel foundry, h. 318 Broad.
Conley Michael, brakeman, bds. 381 Broad.
Cooper Daniel H. Rev., pastor Baptist church, h 13 Tioga.
Cooper Seymour R., sewing machines, 18 Johnson, h. do.
Corby Allen W., emp. Toy shop.
Corby Ezekiel, teamster, h 17 Providence.
Corey William A., carpenter, h 310 Penn. ave.
Cortright Lewis, switchman, h 131 Chemung.
Cortright Mrs., h 16 Loder.
Corwin Lewis, shoemaker, Broad, h Pine.
Corwin Oliver B., butter, salt, and grass seed, 270 Broad, h Fulton.
Coryell Vincent M., retired, h 20 Park ave.
Costello John, blacksmith, bds. 147 Howard.
Courtwright William H., emp. S. A. Genung, h Fulton.
Cowen William C., conductor, h 105 Clark.
Cramer John, locomotive engineer, h 202 Howard.
Crandall Charles M., manuf. Crandall's building blocks, toys and games, Broad n Spaulding, h. Howard.
Crandall Jesse M., book-keeper for C. M. Crandall, bds. Howard.
Criddle James, resident, h 8 Providence.
Crispin Charles E., photographer, bds. over 241 Broad.
Crogger George, barber, h over 283 Broad.
Crowley Jerry, laborer, h 219 Howard.
Cummings Edward, retired, h 33 Orange.
Curran Andrew, laborer, h 223 Erie.
Curran Catharine M., widow Thaddeus, bds. 159 Clark.
Curran Floyd, clerk, h 110 Howard.
Curran Merritt D., brakeman, h 2 Ithaca.
Curran Thomas, resident, h 121 Erie.
Curran William, emp. Erie R. R., h 18 Broad.
Curtis Frederick, barkeeper, h 416 Chemung.
Curtis Levi, miller, h 100 Penn. ave.
DAILEY WILLIAM E., mason, 1 Spring, h do.
Daily Harriet B., widow Peter, h 118 Clark.
Daily John, musician, h 14 Johnson.
Dalton Thomas, laborer, h 39 Broad.
Dalton William, brakeman, h 413 Chemung.
Darling Dexter H., clerk 202 Front, rooms do.
Davenport Frank L., laborer, bds. Chemung cor. Orchard.
Davenport Jacob, teamster, h 413 Chemung.
Davis Samuel S., emp. Novelty Works, h 26 Elm.
Dearborn Charles, conductor Lehigh Valley R. R., h Chemung.
Dearborn Mack, conductor, h 118 Clark.
Debabery Augustus, peanut vender, Broad n Loder.
DECKER ABRAM I., supervisor, also prop. Decker tannery, h Chemung.
Decker Andrew J., carpenter, h 18 Orange.
Decker Jefferson, laborer, h 45 Orange.
Decker John, emp. Decker's tannery, h 19 Clark.
Decker Seely, laborer, h 135 Howard.
DeForest Charles, supt. poor, h 114 Waverly.

Deitrich Lewis, watchman, bds. 381 Broad.
Delaney David C., emp. Erie Ex. Co., bds. 16 Providence.
Delaney Dewitt C., sewing machines, bds. Spaulding.
Delaney John, brakeman, h 113 Erie.
Delany Daisy, clerk, h Fulton.
Delany John, night watch Lehigh Valley R. R. office, h Fulton.
Delany Josie E., millinery, 211 Broad, h 47 Fulton.
Delany William E., freight agent D., L. & W. depot, h 47 Fulton.
Demorest Clarence L., boots and shoes, 247 Broad, h 7 Tioga.
Demorest Elmer, traveling salesman, h 44 Waverly.
Demorest Polly B., widow Leonard, h 7 Tioga.
Denn Alfred W., resident, bds. 22 Elm.
Denn Almira, resident, h 20 Elm.
Denn Angeline, widow Alfred, h 22 Elm.
Denton Mary, resident, bds. 6 Park Place.
Deuel Amos E., harness maker, 250 Broad, h Lincoln.
Deuel Amos E., Jr., postal clerk, h 108 Lincoln.
Deuel John T., manager for A. E. Deuel, bds. 108 Lincoln.
Devine Michael J., clerk, h 244 Broad.
Deyo William S., emp. Mills & O'Brien, h Broad.
Dick Andrew, carpenter, h Elm.
Dickson Jane, widow Charles, h 337 Broad.
Dilamarter John, laborer, h Chemung cor. Tioga.
Dimmick Franklin, retired, h 107 Chemung.
Dimmock Charles S., (Boda & Dimmock) h 192 Clark.
Dingee John T., florist, 116 Lincoln, h do.
Dingman Edward, mason, bds. Hotel Warford.
Dinmore Joseph V., resident, h 128 Clark.
Doane Emmett A., carpenter, bds. 138 Chemung.
Doane Gabriel P., contractor and builder, 138 Chemung, h do.
Dobell William, emp. Novelty Works, h over 151 Broad.
Dodge Ira G., lumber dealer, bds. 9 Providence.
Donnelly Owen, shoemaker, 218 Erie, h do.
Donovan Frank, brakeman, bds. 22 Park Place.
Dorsett & Faulkner, (S. C. D. and J. E. F.) meat market, 215 Broad.
Dorsett Samuel C., (Dorsett & Faulkner) h 105 Waverly.
Dorsey Albert B., emp. pipe foundry, h 232 Erie.
Douglass John, night clerk Tioga Hotel, bds. do.
Dove Burr, emp. Novelty Works, bds. 18 Chemung.
Dove Fred, cigarmaker, bds. 18 Chemung.
Dove Maria, widow Samuel, h 18 Chemung.
Downs Thomas, blacksmith, h Broad.
Draper Eli S., emp. Bottling Works, h 24 Clark.
Driscoll Mary, widow Jeremiah, bds. 105 Chemung.
Drobnyk Joseph F., cutter, h 125 Fulton.
DuBois Joseph, retired, h 22 Waverly.
Dunham James J., wagonmaker, Broad n Pennsylvania ave., h do.
Dunn Charles A., emp. pipe foundry, bds. Christie House.
Dunn Peter F., porter, bds. Broad n Loder.
Dunning Charity, widow William, h 138 Waverly.
Dunning Jacob P., retired, bds. Warford House.
Dunning Julia C., widow Jacob, bds. 47 Waverly.
Durfey Almira, widow Lyman, bds. 301 Chemung.

Durfey Edson B., miller, h Broad n Johnson.
Durfey Riton, resident. bds. 301 Chemung.
EATON AMBROSE P., att'y at law, Exchange blk., Main, h at Smithboro.
Edgcomb Leroy, resident, h 13 Lincoln.
Edmiston Thomas P., car inspector, h 48 Waverly.
Eichenberg Edward J., baker and confectioner, Athens, Pa., h Cadwell.
Eichenberg James, laborer, h 18 Chemung.
Eisenhart George H., cigarmaker, h 38 Pine.
Ellis Dell C., widow Fred F., h over 263 Broad.
Ellis Elizabeth, widow Joseph, h 313 Broad.
Ellis Henrietta, widow Joseph H., bds. 108 Waverly.
Ellis Lodesca, widow Cyrus J., h 229 Broad.
Ellis Hiram, clerk, h 117 Fulton.
ELLIS J. ADDISON, carpenter, h 23 Lincoln.
ELLIS SEELE H., art goods, 229 Broad, h do.
Ellis Sidney E., manager clothing store. 230 Broad, h over do.
ELMER HOWARD, prest. First Nat. Bank, h Pennsylvania ave.
Elsbree Eugene C., watchman, h 20 Providence.
Emery Bartholomew W., emp. Novelty Works, h 330 Broad.
Emmerson William E., clerk, h Center.
Englebreck John, harness maker and boarding-house, 21 Waverly.
ENGLEMAN GUS, variety store, 131 Broad, h 118 Chemung.
English David W., barber, 127 1-2 Broad.
Enos Truman E., book-keeper Citizens Bank, bds. 10 Park Place.
Enwright John, machinist, h 17 Johnson.
Evans Henry L., laborer, h Clinton ave., cor. Pine.
Everett Elijah H., clerk, h 338 Broad.
Excelsior Mutual Benefit Association, (C. C. Brooks, prest.; C. E. Pendle-
    ton treas.; L. C. Corey, secy.) over 201 Broad.
FAIRCHILD & THOMAS, (Murray F. & Holly W. T.) fire, life and ac-
    cident insurance, over First National Bank.
Fairchild Anna, clerk, bds. Bradford.
Fairchild Mary E., book-keeper Fairchild & Thomas, bds Bradford,
FAIRCHILD MURRAY, (Fairchild & Thomas) bds. Tioga House.
Falsey Margarett C., teacher, bds. Clark.
Falsey Mary, clerk, bds. Clark.
Falsey Michael, furniture finisher, h Clark.
Falsey Sarah A., dressmaker, Clark, bds. do.
FARLEY & SANDERS, (W. C. F. & C. H. S.) groceries, crockery, and
    provisions, 231 Broad.
FARLEY WILLIAM C., (Farley & Sanders) h 10 Broad.
Farrel John, emp. toy factory, bds. 329 Broad.
Farrell Mary A., widow Daniel, bds. 130 Lincoln.
Farricy Mary, widow Dennis, h Chemung cor. Erie R. R.
Faulkner John E., (Dorsett & Faulkner) h 4 Chemung.
Ferguson Hartwell M. & Co., (Edwin W. Horton) tobacco and cigars, 200
    Broad.
Furguson Hartwell M., (H. M. Furguson & Co.) h 133 Chemung.
Fern Julius E., candy maker, h over 249 Broad.
Fessenden Harvey C., clerk, h Clark.
Fessenden Harvey G., undertaker, h 121 Clark.
Floyd Elizabeth, widow Harvey, M., bds. 42 Waverly.

FLOYD JACOB B., att'y at law, Exchange bldg., Broad, h 42 Waverly cor. Tioga.

Flynn John, laborer, Chemung.

Flynn Michael, blacksmith. bds. 381 Broad.

FIRST NATIONAL BANK OF WAVERLY, (Howard Elmer, prest.; N. S. Johnson, vice-prest.; F. E. Lyford, cashier ; P. L. Lang, asst. cashier.) Broad cor. Fulton.

Fish George W., retired, h 295 Chemung.

Fish John B., telegraph operator, h Providence.

Fisher Alton A., clerk, bds. 100 Chemung.

Fisher George O., emp. Novelty Works, h 100 Chemung.

Fitzgeral Michael, laborer, h 378 Broad.

Follett Phoebe A., widow Sluman, h 50 Waverly.

Follett Sophia H., Mrs., resident, 32 Park ave.

Fosburg Ellen A., widow James, laundress, h 170 Clark.

Fralick Abram, machinist, h 113 Waverly.

Fralick Ransom, machinist, bds. 113 Waverly.

Frauenthal Isedore E., fruits and oysters, 244 Broad, bds. Tioga.

French George H., station baggage agent, Erie R. R., h 12 Tioga.

French Carrie, dressmaker, 314 Broad, h do.

French Hiram G., clerk, h 12 Tioga.

French Rachel, resident, bds. 12 Tioga.

French William T., clerk, h 4 Lincoln.

*FREE PRESS, James B. Bray, prop., 15 Fulton.

Freestone George S., (Parsons & Freestone) bds. 47 Fulton.

Frink Frederick, supt., Toy works, bds. Tioga Hotel.

Frisbie Chauncey M., book-keeper, 203 Broad, h. Chemung.

Fritcher Elsa M., widow James, h 301 Chemung.

Frost Minnie, clerk, bds. Erie.

Frost Thomas, laborer, h 211 Erie.

Fuller Mrs., widow, h 107 Howard.

Gallagher Patrick, car inspector, h 57 Broad.

Galloway Emory H., emp. L. V. R. R., h 21 Johnson.

Ganther Jacob, emp. L. V. R. R., h 25 Providence.

Gardner Elizabeth B., widow Levi, h 446 Chemung.

Gardner William H., resident, bds. 446 Chemung.

Gas Light Co. of Waverly, (William F. Warner, prest.; Henry G. Merriam, secy. and treas.) office Waverly, over Merriam Bros.

Gee Lucy, widow William, bds. 14 Broad.

GENUNG GEORGE D., editor *The Waverly Advocate*, h 105 Pine.

Genung Reuben H., emp. Novelty Works, bds. 155 Waverly.

GENUNG SALMON A., wood dealer, h Fulton.

GENUNG SHERMAN A., contractor and builder, sash, doors, blinds, etc., Fulton, h 12 Pleasant.

Gerould B. & Co., (J. H. Shoemaker) groceries and provisions, 111 Broad.

Gerould Beebe, (B. Gerould & Co.) h 41 Fulton.

Gibbons Hannah, widow Sylvester, h 246 Broad.

Gibbons James S., groceries and provisions, 546 Broad, h do.

Gibson Robert W., barber, over 213 Broad, h do.

Gilbert Elliot R., switchman, h 142 Clark.

GLEASON WILLIAM H., switchman, h 19 Elm.

Goade Richard J., machinist, h 27 Clark.

Goble Abner, carpenter, h 411 Chemung.

Goble Mary E., widow Smith, h 16 Providence.
Goff G. Halsey, manager Swift's Chicago dressed beef icing station, h 315 Broad.
Golden John, laborer, bds. Broad.
Golden Patrick, laborer, h Broad.
Goldsmith William H., prop. Christie House, Fulton, h do.
Gore Harry W., drug clerk, h 7 Athens.
Gorman Edward, emp. Erie R. R., h 10 Clark.
Gorman John, brakeman, h 345 Broad.
Gorman Michael, fireman, h 233 Erie.
Gormon Patrick, laborer, h 233 Erie.
Gorski Samuel, tailor, h 21 Chemung.
Goulden Charles F., law student, bds. Bradford.
Grace Bertha, teacher, bds. Blizard.
Grace Joseph, lumberman, h Blizard.
Grace Patrick J., carpenter, h 15 Loder.
Grafft George H., justice of the peace, over 214 Broad, h Main.
Gray Ann, widow Arthur, bds 22 Waverly.
Gray Dewitt C., coal, wood, lime and cement, Erie, h 124 Clark.
Green Edward, resident, h 28 Waverly.
Green Frederick C., clerk Christie House, bds. do.
Green Jesse, clerk, bds. 28 Waverly.
Green John P., retired, h 28 Broad.
Greer Fred, brakeman, bds. 127 Chemung.
Greer Henry C., fireman, h 314 Broad.
Gregory Charles W., painter, h 12 Broad.
Gridley Henry N., engineer, h 6 Tioga.
Griswold Frank, emp. Novelty Works, bds. 111 Howard.
Groesbeck Cornelius V., emp. U. S. express company, h 5 Broad.
Guyer James E., coal, lime and cement, also carriages, sleighs and farming implements, Clark, h 115 Waverly.
Hagadorn Henry, teaming and livery, 2 Broad, h do.
Hagadorn James C., liveryman, bds. 2 Broad.
Haight Guy C., bar-keeper 12 Fulton, h Broad.
Hair Daniel, emp. gas works, bds. Erie.
Hair John, emp. gas works, h Erie.
HALL & LYON, (S. C. H. & G. F. L.) novelty furniture works, 356 Broad.
Hall Eli R., tin-smith, h 13 Broad.
Hall Eugene A., baker, h Chemung.
Hall G. Munson, brakeman, rear 110 Chemung.
HALL STEPHEN C., (Hall & Lyon) h 33 Park ave.
Hallet & Son, (H. & H. W.) groceries, crockery and provisions, 245 Broad.
Hallet Harry W., (Hallet & Son) bds. 4 Tioga.
Hallet Hatfield, (Hallet & Son) h 4 Tioga.
Hallett Clarence W., painter, h 72 Fulton.
Hallett DeKalb, painter, bds. 72 Fulton.
Hallett Joseph E., insurance, 409 Chemung, h do.
Hamilton Simeon V., retired, h 120 Lincoln.
Hammond Charles, laborer, h 401 Chemung.
Hancock Irving, barber, over 225 Broad, h do.
Hancock Mary, widow Jeremiah, nurse, h Moore cor. Fulton.
HANFORD & LORD, (M. F. H. & L. F. L.) groceries, provisions and bakers, 222 Broad.

Hanford Edward S., asst. postmaster and town clerk, bds. Warford House.
HANFORD MAURICE F., (Hanford & Lord) h 14 Main.
Hanford Noah, emp. Novelty Works, h Lincoln.
Hanley Matthew, resident, h 235 Erie.
Hanna Charles G., emp. Erie express, h 129 Waverly.
Hanna James A., carpenter, h 139 Howard.
Hanrehan Michael, switchman, bds. 147 Howard.
Harden Oscar, clerk, bds. 29 Providence cor. Spaulding.
Harding Adney, carpenter, h 5 Providence.
Harding Jabez B., train dispatcher, L. V. R. R., h 14 Waverly.
Harding John, car inspector, h 216 Howard.
Harnden Daniel D., physician and surgeon, 7 Waverly, h do.
Harnden Rufus S., physician and surgeon, 31 Fulton, h 33 do.
Harrigan John J., engineer, h 103 Chemung.
Harris Elisha T., resident, bds. 31 Broad.
Harris Emeline E., widow Daniel N., resident, h. 31 Broad.
Harris George R., jeweler, 2 Fulton, bds. 31 Broad.
Harris Thomas, laborer, h 216 Erie.
Harsh Andrew, mason, bds. 333 Broad.
Harsh Cornelius, mason, h 333 Broad.
Harsh Harriet, widow Charles M., h 442 Chemung.
Hart Brothers, (Willard K , & Irving S.) groceries and provisions, 205 Broad.
Hart Irving S., (Hart Bros.) h 18 Maple.
Hart Willard K., (Hart Bros.) h 18 Maple.
Havens John, painter, h over 224 Broad.
Hawley Chauncey, emp. Toy factory, bds. 329 Broad.
Haworth John C., lamp lighter, h Moore.
Haworth Thomas W., printer, bds. Moore.
Hayes Fred B., (H. H. Hayes & Son) bds. 107 Fulton.
Hayes H. H. & Son, (Fred B.) drugs and medicines, 236 Broad.
Hayes Henry H., (H. H. Hayes & Son) h 107 Fulton.
Hayes John, emp. Novelty Works, bds. Broad.
Hayes Mary Mrs., resident, h Broad.
Hayes William, emp. Novelty Works, h Broad.
HAYWOOD CHARLES M., marble and granite cemetery works, 107 Broad, residence at Owego.
Head Anson P., prop. American House.
Head Richard, saloon and restaurant, 252 Broad, h do.
Hemstreet Anthony, resident, h 469 Chemung.
Hemstreet Gertrude, h 501 Chemung.
Hemstreet Ida M., clerk, bds. Chemung.
Henessy William, car inspector, h 27 Orange.
Henry Edward, barber, over 219 Broad, h do.
Hern Bert J., clerk, bds. 159 clark.
Hern John, groceries and provisions, 117 Broad, h 159 Clark.
Herrick Hugh T., book-keeper over 201 Broad, h 411 Chemung.
Hess Charles, carpenter, h 75 Fulton.
Hess Nirum J., contractor and builder, Fulton, h do.
Hesser Abram, emp. L. V. R. R., h 26 Lincoln.
Hewitt Henry, carpenter, h 32 Fulton.
Hickey John, resident, h 381 Broad.
Higbee Allison B., clerk, h over 218 Broad.
Higgins Edward M., tanner, h 23 Orange.

Higgins Edward W., brakeman, bds. 23 Orange.
Higgins Gilbert C., conductor, bds 23 Orange.
Higgins John J., engeneer, bds 23 Orange.
Higgins Mary, book-keeper, bds. 23 Orange.
Higgins Theresa, dressmaker, bds. 23 Orange.
Higgins William P., fireman, bds. 23 Orange.
Hildebrand Andrew, boots and shoes, 225 Broad, h 112 Clark.
Hill Erastus, carpenter and builder, h 10 Park Place.
Hill George W., shoemaker under 127 Broad, h 22 Loder.
Hill Henry, shoemaker Broad, h 22 Loder.
Hine Lucy A., widow Harrison, h 318 Broad.
Hinman Eliza A., widow Henry, boarding-house, 114 Chemung.
Hinman Helen, widow James, bds. 329 Broad.
Hinman Helen M., clerk, h 114 Chemung.
Hinman Sarah W., widow Charles, bds. 11 Providence.
Hinman Truman, retired, h 36 Broad.
Hinman William E , painter and paper-hanger, bds. 114 Chemung.
Hilton Willard M., physician and surgeon, Pennsylvania ave., h do.
Hoadley Miles S., conductor, h 104 Fulton.
Hoban John W., 255 Broad, h do.
Hoban William, clerk, bds. over 255 Broad.
Hoff I. P. & C., (William D. Hoff) jewelers, 202 Broad.
Hoff Ives P., (I. P. Hoff & Co.) h Fulton.
Hoff William D., (I. P. Hoff & Co.) h Pennsylvania ave.
Hogan Hugh, track walker, h Erie.
Holbert Emmet J., retired, h 9 Park ave.
Holland Phebe, widow Henry, h 229 Erie.
Holmes John A., traveling salesman, h Moore cor. Fulton.
Hoover John F., painter, h Fulton.
Hopkins James J., engineer, h 101 Chemung.
Hopkins William, emp. Novelty Works, bds. 16 Providence.
Horton Edwin W., (H. M. Ferguson & Co.) bds. 135 Chemung.
Horton Emma E. Mrs., fruit and confectionery, 210 Broad, h do.
Horton George, emp. Axel Works, bds. 330 Broad.
Horton James F., manager for Mrs. Emma Horton, h 210 Broad.
Horton Mary E., widow Daniel D., bds. Chemung cor. Orchard.
Horton Sarah, resident, bds. 3 Athens.
Horton William H., gardener, h 135 Chemung.
Hotalen Mordecai, carpenter, h 30 Orange.
Hotalen Peter, carpenter, h 6 Lincoln.
Hotalen Randall, drayman, h 139 Lincoln.
HOTEL WARFORD, (Wadsworth & Kelsey, prop's.) Broad cor. Fulton.
House Frank B., emp. Novelty Works, h Clark.
Hovey J. Fred, train dispatcher, L. V. R. R., h 128 Lincoln.
Hoyt Adeline, widow John L , resident, h 8 Orchard.
Hoyt C. Chester, switchman, h 8 Broad.
Hoyt Jehiel G., teamster, h 142 Clark.
Hoyt John H., employed in Sayre, bds. 8 Orchard.
Hubbell Nelson, station agent, h off Lincoln.
Hubbell William, teamster, bds. 17 Providence.
Hugg Lyman D., traveling salesman, h 106 Chemung.
Hugg Willis P., clerk, bds. 106 Chemung.
Huggins Carrie C., teacher, bds 2 Athens.

Huggins Elizabeth H., widow James A., h 2 Athens.
Hull Phillip M., teacher, h 18 Elm.
Hulse William H., butcher, h Ulster.
Hyatt Jonah G., inventor and patentee Hyatt's door carrier, h Waverly.
Ichenberg John, retired, bds. 129 Clark.
Inman William F., resident, h 400 Chemung.
ISLEY & SONS, stone cutters, and masons, dealars in curbing and flagging, 36 Waverly.
ISLEY JAMES, (Isley & Sons) 36 Waverly, h do.
ISLEY WALTER, (Isley & Sons) bds. 36 Waverly.
ISLEY WILLIAM R., (Isley & Sons) bds. 36 Waverly.
Jarvis Mary, widow Alva, h 6 Elm.
Jenkins Celia Mrs., resident, h 310 Pennsylvania ave.
Johnson Benjamin F., traveling salesman, h Pine.
Johnson Nathan S., vice-prest. First Nat. Bank, h Chemung.
Johnson Parmenas A., physician, 14 Pennsylvania ave., h do.
Johnson Solomon C., retired, bds. Pine.
JOHNSON WILLIAM E., physician and surgeon, 8 Waverly, h 44 Park ave.
Jones Charles W., book-keeper, h Chemung.
Jones James, bartender, bds. 125 Broad.
Jones John R., butter dealer, 268 Broad, h 19 Park ave.
Jones William H. W., book-keeper, 268 Broad, bds. 19 Park ave.
Jordan Charles S., saloon, 259 Broad, h do.
Kane John, laborer, h 225 Erie.
Kane John, butcher, h 132 Lincoln.
Kane Michael, brakeman, bds. Warford House.
Kaneir John, laborer, bds. Chemung cor. Broad.
Kaneir Patrick, laborer, h Chemung cor. Broad.
Kase John E., furniture finisher, h 39 Fulton.
Keefe John, emp. Erie R. R., bds. 19 Loder.
Keeler Faank W., foreman *Waverly Advocate*, h Pennsylvania ave.
Keeler George L., clerk, h Athens cor. Tioga.
Keeler Thomas, painter and paper-hanger, Broad, h Lyman ave.
Keller Charles, laborer, bds. 381 Broad.
Kelly Thomas, mason, h Erie.
Kelly Viola D., music teacher, bds. Elizabeth.
KELSEY CHARLES D., (Wadsworth & Kelsey) bds. Hotel Warford.
Kelsey William H., clerk, Hotel Warford, bds. do.
Kemp Milner, clerk, h 51 Waverly.
Kennedy Daniel A., clerk, h 12 Johnson.
Kennedy Duncan S., propr. Commercial Hotel, h do.
Kennedy Edward, turner, bds, 329 Broad.
Kennedy James, retired, h 12 Johnson.
Kennedy James H., clerk, bds. 12 Johnson.
Kennedy Michael W., cashier Erie freight office, bds. 12 Johnson.
Kenney Michael J., machinist, h 147 Howard.
Kenney William E., conductor, h 101 Spalding.
Kenrick James, emp. L. V. R. R., h 134 Howard.
Kenyon James A., retired, h 314 Pennsylvania ave.
Kilmer Clarence, emp. Novelty Works, bds. 25 Orange.
Kilmer John, clerk, h 25 Orange.
Kingsbury Frank A., clerk, h Lincoln.
Kinney Anna, widow Henry C., h 3 Providence.

Kinney F. Eloise, telephone operator, h 114 Clark.
Kinney Greeley, resident, h 322 Broad.
Kinney Horace, book-keeper Citizens Bank, bds. Howard.
Kinney H. Wall, clerk L. V. R. R. Ft. office, bds. Tioga House.
Kinney Juliet T., widow Newton, h 114 Clark.
Kinney Margaret, widow Daniel, h 113 Erie.
Kinney Michael, laborer, h 218 Howard.
Kinney Miles L., clerk, bds. 114 Clark.
Kinney Perley H., retired, h 134 Waverly.
Kinney Simon, depot police, h 40 Fulton.
Kinsman & Young, (J. E. K. & J. F. Y.) blacksmiths, 3 Pennsylvania ave.
Kinsman Fred, clerk, h Waverly.
Kinsman John E., (Kinsman & Young) h 10 Lincoln.
KLINE ALBERT, clerk, h over 253 Broad.
Knapp Charles, teamster, bds. 10 Park ave.
Knapp Charles S., watchmaker, bds. Waverly.
Knapp David D., jeweler, optician and engraver, 211 Broad, h 49 Waverly.
Knapp Harry W., clerk, bds. Read.
KNAPP JOSEPH W., dry goods, 203 Broad, h Read.
Kniffin Daniel R., clerk, h over 235 Broad.
Knight Henry C., resident, h 125 Waverly.
Krist Frederick, emp. Novelty Works, bds. 22 Park Place.
Krist Joseph, emp. Novelty Works, h 22 Park Place.
La Barre Jehiel T., carpenter, h 329 Broad.
Laine Henry T., emp. L. V. R. R., h 325 Broad.
Lambkin Russell, emp. Novelty Works, h 33 Fulton.
La Mont Phebe, resident, h 44 Broad.
Lane Irene A., widow Lewis, h Pine.
Lang Percy L., asst. cashier First Nat. Bank, h. 105 Chemung.
Langheed John H., emp. Atwater's Livery, h 127 Chemung.
Lantz George W., clerk, 138 Clark.
Lappla Philip H., wood carver, h 16 Park Place.
Lariew H. Porter, agent Elmira oil company, h Loder.
Larnard Asoeph S., confectionery and cigars, 3 Elizabeth, h do.
LARNARD A. WARREN, contractor and builder, Lyman ave. h do.
Larnard George H., clerk, bds. 3 Elizabeth.
Larnard Theo R., carpenter, h 129 Lincoln.
LASSLY ELIJAH M., livery and feed stable, Clark n Broad, h 141 Waverly.
Lathrop Frederick M., emp. L. V. R. R., h 8 Athens.
Lathrop Helen, widow Simon, h 8 Athens.
Lawrence Charles, stationery engineer, bds. 330 Broad.
Layman J. Lewellyn, emp. R. R. shop, Sayre, h 19 Clark.
Leavitt Clara W., widow Harry, bds. Lincoln.
Lehigh Valley R. R. Freight Office, Bert Hayden, agent, Fulton cor. Erie.
Lemon Israel G., fire and life insurance, over 245 Broad, h 17 Orange.
LEMON JAMES, foundry and machine shop and manuf. land rollers, Broad,
    h 8 Park ave.
Lenox Frank B., brakeman, bds. 263 Broad.
Lenox George F., baggageman, h 101 Broad.
LENT CLARENCE A., contractor and builder, Lincoln cor. Spring.
Lent W. Nelson, apiarist, bds. Lincoln.
Lester Albert J., clerk L. V. R. R. Ft. office, h 6 Athens.
Lewis John H., resident, h Pine.

Lewis Walter H., resident, h 17 Park Place.
Linden Hugh, emp. pipe foundry, bds. Christie House.
Lindsey Frances A. Mrs., laundress, h Pine.
Lindsey Grant W., cigar maker h over 336 Broad.
Lindsey William, carpenter, h 31 Clark.
Lindsley Parks, steward Tioga Hotel, bds. do.
Lockerby George, brakeman, h Elm.
Lockerby Wallace H., barber 12 Fulton, h Broad cor. Pine.
Lockwood George, tinner, bds. Warford House.
LORD LOUIS F., (Hanford & Lord) h 16 Main.
Lott John, car inspector, h Lyman ave.
Lowman Everette H., postal clerk, bds. 473 Chemung.
Lowman Harriet C., widow Hovey E., resident, h 473 Chemung.
Lowman Nathan B., clerk L. V. R. R. Ft. office, h 473 Chemung.
Lubars Anna D., widow John F., bds. 11 Lincoln.
Luce John G., book-keeper First Nat. Bank, h 22 E. Main.
Luce Joseph D., machinist, h Loder.
LUM DANIEL J., insurance, Waverly, h do.
Lum Mattie C., teacher, bds. Waverly.
LYFORD FREDERICK E., cashire First Nat. Bank, h 21 Park Place.
LYMAN MOSES, resident, h Waverly.
Lynch James, clerk, bds. Loder.
Lynch Rose A., millinery over 232 Broad, h do.
Lyon ——, farmer, h 111 Park ave.
LYON GEORGE F., (Hall & Lyon) h Fulton.
Lyons Charles T., physician and surgeon, retired, h 204 Chemung.
Lyons Smith E., clerk, h 29 Waverly.
Mack Mary Mrs., resident, h Broad.
Mahoney John, shoemaker, Broad, h 105 Chemung.
Mandeville Emmet. painter, bds. 16 Providence.
Mandeville Henry D., fireman, h Pine.
Mandeville Mahlon H., jeweler over 228 Broad, h 111 Fulton.
Manners Vincent C., clerk, bds. 11 Broad.
MANNING ELWIN W., manager for Mrs. E. W. Manning, 249 Broad, h 103 Waverly.
MANNING E. W. MRS., millinery of all kinds, 249 Broad, h 103 Waverly.
Manning Gurdon G., justice of the peace, over 206 Broad, h 37 Clark.
Maroney Daniel, railroad conductor, h 140 Howard.
Moseley George E., laborer. h 210 Howard.
Masonic Hall, Thomas Salisbury, janitor, Manners Block, Broad.
Masterson Julius C., retired, bds. 21 Johnson.
Maxwell Emily A., widow Albert P., h 18 Providence.
Maxwell Frank B., conductor, h Clark.
McArdle Bernard, blacksmith, 302 Broad, h Clinton ave.
McCarthy Daniel, engineer, h 19 Loder.
McCarthy James, laborer. h Erie.
McDonald Amanda, widow Alexander. h 422 Chemung.
McDonald David, baggageman, h 41 Waverly.
McDonald Duncan, retired, h 40 Waverly.
McDONALD DUNCAN, locomotive engineer, h Chemung.
McDONALD DUNCAN J., news and variety store, 247 Broad, h 422 Chemung.
McDonald Eliza, widow Morris, h 14 Clark.

2

McDonald Nellie, book-keeper Mills & O'Brian, h Howard cor. Spaulding.
McDonald Owen, laborer, h 201 Howard.
McDonald Owen, Jr., laborer, h 201 Howard.
McDonald Patrick, bar-tender Tioga House, bds. do.
McDONALD SARAH A. MRS., tailoring and gents' furnishing goods, 265 Broad, h Chemung.
McDonald Wellington, clerk, bds. Warford House.
McDonough Patrick, bds. 345 Broad.
McElwain Alexander, shoemaker, h 5 Chemung.
McElwain Margarett, widow Robert, h 5 Chemung.
McEwen William, emp. Novelty Works, h 155 Waverly.
McGuffie Matthew, clerk U. S. Ex. Co., h Loder.
McHale Patrick J., emp. L. V. R. R., h 19 Johnson.
McINTYRE ALBERT J., mason, Lincoln, h do.
McKerrow William, car inspector, h 111 Lincoln.
McKibbin Henry, emp. Novelty Works, bds. 18 Orange.
McMahon John, brakeman, bds. Commercial Hotel.
McNanara George, cigarmaker, h over 219 Broad.
McNeirney John, laborer, h 376 Broad.
McPherson Nancy, widow, Alexander, bds. 34 Broad.
McShane Edward Rev., pastor St. James church, h 103 Clark.
Mead Charles A., carpenter, h Spring.
Mead Eadie W., photographer, bds. 10 Providence.
Mead Joseph, traveling salesman, h 12 Pine.
Mead Montgomery, photographer, h 10 Providence.
Mead Tabitha J. Mrs., photographer over 204 Broad, h 10 Providence.
Meeker Mrs., widow John, h 24 Providence.
Melvin Emma Miss, laundress, h 2 Pennsylvania ave.
Mercereau & Co., (John and Henry) cigar manuf. Broad cor. Penn. ave.
Mercereau Henry C., (Mercereau & Co.) h 4 Park Place.
Mercereau Henry, (Mercereau & Co.) h Maple.
Mercereau John, (Mercereau & Co.) h Maple.
Mercereau John D., (Mercereau & Co.) h 15 Park Place.
MERRIAM BROS., (H. G. & C. E.) hardware, 235 Broad and 3 Waverly.
MERRIAM CHARLES E., (Merriam Bros.) Broad, h 414 Chemung.
Merriam Frank W., book-keeper 356 Broad, bds. 414 Chemung.
MERRIAM HENRY G., (Merriam Bros.) h 13 Park ave.
Merrill Arthur T., emp. R. R. shops Sayre, h 10 Tioga.
Merrill Elisha B., retired, h 22 Lincoln.
Merrill Lena E., emp. Toy Shop, bds. 10 Tioga.
Merrill Luke T., retired, h 109 Clark.
Miller Cassandra B., dressmaker 482 Chemung, h do.
Miller Charles, drayman, h 15 Johnson.
Miller Charles W., tinsmith, h 108 Howard.
Miller Edmund, retired, h 23 Fulton.
Miller Emma Mrs., resident, h 26 Waverly.
MILLER LOUIS C., (Barnes & Miller) h 15 Johnson.
Miller Samuel W., meat market, 248 Broad, h 482 Chemung.
MILLS & O'BRIAN, (T. M. & M. D. O'B.) bottling works, Elizabeth.
Mills Charles L., farmer 30, h 113 Chemung.
MILLS THEODORE, (Mills & O'Brian) h 25 Clark.
Mills Thomas, cabinet maker, h 103 Spaulding.

STARKEY & WINTERS, Wholesale and Retail Druggists, Owego.

Millspaugh Paul, clerk, bds. 109 Waverly.
Mink George R., cigarmaker, h 10 Athens.
Minick Benjamin F., retired, bds. 2 Orchard.
Minnick I. H. Mrs., dressmaker 28 Loder, h do.
Minnick Isaac H., machinist, h 28 Loder.
Minnick Robert F., clerk, bds 28 Loder.
Mitchell Thomas S., machinist, h 3 Athens.
MIX JAMES F., carpenter, R. R. shops Sayre, h 159 Waverly.
Moelich Julius, machinist, h 217 Howard.
Monyhan Johanna, widow John, h 138 Howard.
Monyhan John, blacksmith, h 138 Howard.
Monyhan Patrick, blacksmith, bds. 138 Howard.
Morgan William, fireman, h 316 Broad.
Moore Lemuel C., carpenter, h 129 Howard.
Morgan David, painter, 51 Waverly, h do.
MORGAN FREDERICK S., mason, Clark, h do.
Morgan George B., mason, h 16 Johnson.
Morgan George Mrs., milliner, 16 Johnson, h do.
MORGAN JOHN W., mason contractor, h 112 Lincoln.
Morley Dwight, saloon and billiards, 6 Waverly, h do.
Morris Charles, emp. Novelty Works, bds. 16 Providence.
Mosier Hiram W., carpenter, h Pine.
Moore Lemuel C., carpenter, h 22 Maple.
Moore William E., farmer, h 105 Park ave.
Mott Amasa S., tailor over 222 Broad, h 28 Park ave.
Mott William N., tailor over 222 Broad, h 28 Park ave.
Mullock Albert, (Mullock Bros.) h Elm.
Mullock Bros., (Corwin & Albert) drugs and medicines, 229 Broad.
Mullock Corwin, (Mullock Bros.) h 131 Waverly.
Mullock Gabriel L., (Ornamental Sign Company) h 135 Waverly.
MULOCK LEWIS W., retired, h 135 Waverly.
Muncey Adolph, emp. L. V. R. R., bds. Loder.
Muncey Alfred, carpenter, h Loder.
Munn Frank E., (Sager & Munn) h 106 Waverly.
Murdoch Charles, foreman Erie transfer, rooms Campbell Block, Broad.
Murdoch Eliza N., (E. N. Murdoch & Co.) h 123 Waverly.
Murdoch E. N. & Co., (J. K. Murdoch) fancy goods, 222 Broad.
Murdoch John K., (E. N. Murdoch & Co.) also agent U. S. Ex. Co., h 123 Waverly.
Murray George S., clerk, bds. Pine.
Murray Harriet E., widow Thomas J., resident, h Pine.
Murray Hattie C., dressmaker, bds. Pine.
Murray Isaac C., baker, h Pine.
Murray Jacob, retired, h Chemung.
Murray Mary L., dressmaker, Pine, bds do.
Murry George S., clerk, h 114 Pine.
Myer John M., retired, h 16 Elm.
Myer Samuel S., laborer, bds. 16 Elm.
Myers Charles K., tobacconist and gunsmith, 201 Broad, h 168 Clark.
Myers David W., carpenter, h 196 Clark.
Myers Edward D., clerk, bds. 115 Clark.
Myers George L., baker, bds. 115 Clark.

Myers Leonard D., constable and deputy sheriff, h 115 Clark.
Nelson Elmer, dentist, over 251 Broad, h Bradford.
Nelson James, mason, h 146 Waverly.
Nelson Myron H., conductor, h 123 Fulton.
Nelson Phineas, harness and trunks, 127 Broad, h Clark.
Nevins James P., clerk, bds. 37 Clark.
Newland Charles, clerk, bds. Clark.
Newland Edward H., traveling salesman, h Clark.
Newell Frank M., (Newell Mfg. Co.) h Clark.
Newell Stephen H., traveling salesman, h 30 Fulton.
Nichols Eben, carpenter, h 11 Pine.
NICHOLS HURLEY L., tobacco and cigars, 213 Broad, h Pine.
Nichols Leonard H., bartender, bds. over 209 Broad.
NOBLE ALBERT C., (Noble & Noble) h Elizabeth.
*NOBLE & NOBLE, (W. H. & A. C.) publishers *Weekly Tribune*, Elizabeth.
Noble Mary B., widow Dr. Carlton M., bds. Elizabeth.
NOBLE WILLIAM H., (Noble & Noble) h Elizabeth.
Nolan James, blacksmith, h 12 Providence.
Noonan Mortice, laborer, h 220 Erie.
North W. Edward, carpenter, h 140 Clark.
Northup Emery H., clerk, h Pitney.
O'Brian Edward, brakeman, bds. 12 Providence.
O'Brian James, retired, bds. 36 Fulton.
O'BRIAN MICHAEL D., (Mills & O'Brian) h 36 Fulton.
O'Brien Thomas, brakeman, h 27 Park Place.
O'Farrell Edward J., clerk, h Fulton.
Olney Caleb B., retired, h 16 Broad.
Orange Emily H., widow George W., h 206 Chemung.
Ornamental Sign Company, (G. L. Mullock & S. C. Smith) Broad.
Osterhout Katie, dressmaker, 23 Broad, bds do.
Owen Hannah, widow William P., resident, h 40 Fulton.
Owen Ithiel P., painter, h 343 Broad.
Palmer Kate, widow Luman, h 24 Lincoln.
Parks Albert E., painter, h 29 Providence.
Parks James R., retired, h 11 Lincoln.
Parks Ned L., emp. pipe foundry, h Erie cor. Pennsylvania ave.
Parshall Luther, real estate, h 464 Chemung.
Parshall Ransom, retired, h 12 Elm.
Parsons & Freestone, (James F. P. & George S. F.) groceries and provisions,
    207 Broad.
Parsons Fred K., fireman, h 31 Orange.
Parsons James F., (Parsons & Freestone) h Loder.
Paul James M., emp. M. Lyman and farmer 54, h Moore.
Payne Frederick Y., traveling salesman, h 6 Park Place.
Payne Sarah, widow Hiram, h 204 Chemung.
Pearman Julia M., resident, h 140 Clark.
Pease David, marble cutter, h 120 Chemung.
Peironnet Emma V., widow John S., resident, h 26 Waverly.
Pendell Charles D., emp. Toy Shop, bds. 143 Lincoln.
Pendell John Lyman, emp. Toy Shop, bds. 143 Lincoln.
Pendell John R. Rev., (Bap.) h 144 Lincoln.
Pendell Mary E. O., music teacher, bds. 143 Lincoln.
Pendleton Charles E., ex-cashier Home Savings Bank, bds. 106 Penn. ave.

Penney Eleanor, widow Nelson F., resident, h 308 Pennsylvania ave.
Pepper Frank, laborer, h 49 Orange.
Perkins Edward F., clerk, h Broad.
Perkins Frank A., clerk, bds. Broad cor. Chemung.
PERKINS FRED C., clothing, hats, caps and gents' furnishing goods, 208
    Main, h 70 Fulton.
Perkins La Fayette, traveling salesman, 1 Broad.
Perry Hanson, emp. Sniffen & Scott, h Clark.
Personius Daniel V., (Barnum & Personius) 12 Clinton ave.
Persons E. Delos, groceries, crockery and provisions, 206 Broad, h 38 Clark.
Phillips Frank W., plumber, h Chemung.
Phillips Harry E., clerk 251 Broad, h at Sayre.
Phillips John W., painter and paper-hanger, bds Chemung.
Phillips Thomas J., (Phillips & Curtis) h 45 Waverly.
Piatt Susan, widow John, bds. 443 Chemung.
Pierce Alonzo E., emp. Erie R. R., h 108 Chemung.
Pierce Amelia M., widow John H., resident, bds. 126 Waverly.
Pierce Henry G., commercial traveler, h 323 Broad.
Pierce Josiah, retired, h 106 Chemung.
Pike George, clerk, bds. 36 Pine.
Pike Grove N., meat market, 109 Broad, h 36 Pine.
PILGRIM FREDERICK, bakery and confectionery, 241 Broad, h do.
Polleys Ellen D., widow William, h 112 Waverly.
Polleys Harriet, compositor, bds. 112 Waverly.
Poole Eva M., milliner, bds. 6 Tioga.
Post Henry W., butcher, h Providence.
Post John C., laborer, h 70 Fulton.
Powers Frank, brakeman, h 111 Erie.
Powers John, shoemaker, h 130 Lincoln.
Powell Levi J., saloon and restaurant, h 115 Howard.
Price George, brakeman, h Broad n Pennsylvania ave.
Price Nathaniel W., retired, h 5 Pine.
Price N. W. Mrs., carpet weaver. 5 Pine h do.
Price Willis H., carpenter, h Blizard.
PUFF & WILLIAMS, (M. F. P. & A. D. W.) meat market, Fulton.
PUFF MYRON F., (Puff & Williams) h Pleasant.
Purdy Charles E., saloon, 125 Broad, h do.
Quick Adeline L., resident, bds. 113 Fulton.
Quick Alvin, emp. L. V. R. R., bds. 16 Providence.
Quick Fannie C., emp. Toy Factory, bds. 113 Fulton.
Quick Mary, widow Stephen C., resident, h 113 Fulton.
Quick Minnie Mrs., private school, 3 Athens, h do.
Quick Susan A., emp. Toy Factory, bds. 113 Fulton.
Quigley Michael, groceries and provisions, 263 Broad, h Loder.
Quimby Elmer, blacksmith, Broad, bds. 34 do.
Race Jabez W., resident, h Waverly.
Racklyeft John, boots and shoes, 267 Broad, h 36 Broad.
Ralyea William H., (Clark & Ralyea) h Fulton.
Randolph Byron F., conductor, h 132 Clark.
Reckhow Sarah A., widow Isaac, resident, h 21 Pennsylvania ave.
Reese Elias, night watchman, h Fulton.
Reeve James I., retired, h 27 Park avenue.
Reigeluth Conrad, drug clerk, bds. 164 Clark.

Reigeluth John J., tinsmith, h Clinton ave.
Reigeluth Louisa, dressmaker, bds. 164 Clark.
Reigeluth Mary, widow Jacob, h 164 Clark.
Rew Samuel, barber, bds. Warford House.
Reynolds James, blacksmith, bds. Broad.
Reynolds Johanna, widow John, h Broad.
Rezeau Harry G., saloon 209 Broad, h do.
Rezeau Joseph O., saloon 209 Broad, h do.
Richardson Isaac, barkeeper, h Waverly.
Riggs George W., carpenter, h 9 Pine.
RIKER JAMES, author and librarian, h 23 Park ave.
Ritz Joseph, shoemaker, bds. Christie House.
Robbins Harry E., jeweler, h 36 Broad.
Robinson Jesse, painter, h 9 Orange.
Rodhlof John, saloon, 273 Broad, h do.
ROGERS CHARLES H., contractor and builder, 413 Chemung, h do.
Rogers Edwin E., clerk L. V. R. R. Ft. office, h 125 Chemung.
Rogers Irvin H., clerk L. V. R. R. Ft. office, h Pleasant.
Rogers William T., retired, h 28 Lincoln.
Rolfe Cornelius J., brakeman, bds. 15 Providence.
Rolfe Peter B., teamster, h 15 Providence.
Rolfe Willet W., butcher, bds. 15 Providence.
Rood Horace W., brakeman, h 125 Erie.
Root Hubert A., emp. R. R. shops Sayre, h 133 Lincoln.
Rose David A., pattern maker, h 7 Loder.
Rosecrants Abram, laborer, bds. 39 Broad.
Ross Frank, carpenter and builder, 10 Pine, h do.
Rowland Bert K., clerk, bds. 13 Waverly.
Rowland John R., wines and liquors, also carriages and wagons, also Burle's
    patent egg preserver, 242 Broad, h 13 Waverly.
Rowland Kate A., teacher, bds. Pennsylvania ave. n Broad.
Rowland William A., carpenter and builder, h Pennsylvania ave. n Broad.
Ruher Louis, machinist, h over 271 Broad.
Ryan Bridget, widow Michael, h Broad.
Ryan Conrad, laborer, h Erie cor. Pennsylvania ave.
Ryan Dennis, telegraph lineman, h Erie cor. Pennsylvania ave.
Ryan Jeremiah, town collector, bds. 10 Broad.
Ryan John, railroad emp., rooms over 265 Broad.
Ryan Thomas B., ass't yard master Erie R. R., h 7 Pennsylvania ave.
Sager & Munn, (T. A. S. and F. E. Munn) groceries, crockery and provi-
    sions, 234 Broad.
Sager Alvin D., clerk, h 104 Waverly.
Sager Thaddeus A., (Sager & Munn) h 119 Fulton.
Salisbury Thomas L., painter, 130 Waverly, h do.
Salonsky Isaac, clothing and gents' furnishings, 224 Broad, h do.
SANDERS CHARLES H., (Farley & Sanders) h Fulton.
Sanders Hiram E., policeman, h 103 Howard.
Sargeant James C., emp. freight house, h 28 Orange.
Sargeant J. C. Mrs., dressmaker, 28 Orange, h do.
Sawyer Charles H., farmer 280, h 474 Chemung.
Sawyer Fannie, widow Moses, h 109 Waverly.
Sawyer Frederick A., cashier Citizens Bank, h 474 Chemung.
Sawyer Fred H., emp. Novelty Company, h 2 Orchard.

Sawyer Hugh T., clerk L. V. R. R. freight office, h 109 Waverly.
SAWYER J. THEODORE, president Citizens Bank, h 451 Chemung.
Sawyer Julina, widow John L., h 451 Chemung.
Sawyer Mary, widow James M., resident, h 25 Park Place.
SAYRE BUTTER PACKAGE CO., (R. D. and H. C. Van Deuzer, and T. F. Page) Factoryville, Main.
Scanlan Bartholomew, emp. L. V. freight house, h 9 Loder.
Scanlon Martin, telegraph operator, bds. Pennsylvania ave. n Broad.
Schutt William H., clerk, h 10 Orange.
Schutte Magdalena, widow Rudolph, h 115 Howard.
Schutte Rudolph, Jr., clerk, bds. 115 Howard.
Scott Charles E., Loyal Sock coal, 256 Broad, h 7 Athens.
Scott Robert, clerk, bds. Pennsylvania ave.
Scott Robert H., (Sniffen & Scott) h 20 Park ave.
Seacord John, contractor and builder, 27 Lincoln, h do.
Sedgwick William, retired jeweler, h 127 Clark.
Seely Charles, saloon and restaurant, 129 Broad.
Seely Edmund, boarding, 12 Park ave.
Seely Frederick, bartender, bds. 129 Broad.
SEELY WILLIAM F., groceries, crockery and provisions, 257 Broad, h 107 Pennsylvania ave.
Shaehan Michael, saloon, also prop. Tioga Bottling Works, Broad cor. Loder.
Shannessy Patrick, emp. Erie R. R., h 127 Erie.
Sharpe Arminda, widow William, h 11 Broad.
Shaw Hulda J., dress and cloak maker, 9 Waverly, h do.
Shaw Robert R., poor-master, h 11 Johnson.
SHEAR JOHN C., prop. Waverly Steam Flouring Mill, 300 Broad, h 101 Park ave.
Sheeler Edward P., night clerk U. S. Ex. Co., h Fulton.
Shehan Patrick, resident, h 375 Broad.
Sheldon Mary B., widow Charles H., resident, h 20 Park ave.
Shelp Charles F., lumber, h 131 Lincoln.
Shepard William Mrs., resident, bds. Warford House.
SHERMAN CHARLES W., mason, 428 Chemung, h do.
Sherry Hiram I., horse dealer, h 6 Pine.
Sherry J. Robert, veterinary surgeon, bds. 6 Pine.
Sherwood William, emp. pipe foundry, h 343 Broad.
Shipman Charles H., conductor, h 43 Waverly.
Shoemaker Jabez H., (B. Gerould & Co.) h Broad.
SHOEMAKER JUDGE F., att'y at law, over 214 Broad, h 505 Chemung.
Shoemaker Samuel O., emp. U. S. express company, h 156 Clark.
Shook William, commercial traveler, h 18 Pennsylvania ave.
Shriver Christina, widow Henry, h 9 Elm.
Shulenburg Sarah, dress and cloak maker, 304 Chemung.
Simmers E. Louisa, widow John W., resident, 116 Chemung.
Simmons Edward W., clerk, h 11 Johnson.
Simmons Frederick C., clerk, bds. 71 Fulton.
Simmons John H., cabinet maker, h 27 Providence.
Simmons Silas W., retired, h 71 Fulton.
Simmons William R., groceries and provisions, 269 Broad, h Howard.
Simpson Elliot B., blacksmith, bds. 437 Chemung.
Simpson Isaac D., blacksmith, cor. Penn. ave. and Broad, h 437 Chemung.
SIMPSON WILLIAM H., blacksmith, 301 Broad, h 439 Chemung.

Simcoe Eli, contractor and builder, Orange, h 15 do.

Skellenger Charles, meat cutter, bds. 36 Pine.

SLAUGHTER & VAN ATTA, (S. W. S. and J. C. Van A.) drugs, medicines and wall paper, 233 Broad.

SLAUGHTER S. W., (Slaughter & Van Atta) also vice-prest. Citizens Bank, h 408 Chemung.

Slawson Andrew A., postmaster, undertaking and furniture, 223 Broad, h 443 Chemung.

Slawson Jeremiah M., musical merchandise and sewing machines, 202 Broad, h 32 Waverly.

Sligh Susan Mrs., resident, bds. 10 Athens.

Sliney Charles, laborer, rooms 33 Waverly.

Sliney Charles H., book-keeper Erie R. R. Co., associate press correspondent, bds. Warford House.

Sliney William H., yard master Erie R. R., bds. Warford House.

Slocum Olney, clerk, bds. Orange.

Smead Edward, baker, bds. 34 Broad.

Smeaton Mary A., teacher, bds. 152 Clark.

SMEATON THOMAS, mason contractor, 152 Clark.

Smith Augustus W., emp. Novelty Works, h 28 Orange.

Smith Bros. & Co., (W. J., M. O. and H. G. S.) picture mouldings, frames, etc., over 207 Broad.

Smith Charles O., (Smith Bros.) 19 Chemung.

Smith Clayton A., foreman *Free Press* office, bds. 17 Fulton.

Smith Daniel S., baker, h 21 Fulton.

Smith D. S. Mrs., dressmaker, 21 Fulton, h do.

Smith Edwin S., resident, h 37 Waverly.

Smith Floyd, emp. Erie R. R., bds. 141 Waverly.

Smith Fred E., clerk L. V. R. R. freight office, h 70 Broad.

Smith Fred F., tinsmith, bds. 184 Clark.

Smith Henry G., (Smith Bros. & Co.) h in Candor.

Smith John L., laborer, h 184 Clark.

Smith Mary K., widow Hanford, h 37 Waverly.

Smith Merritt W., blacksmith, h 40 Broad.

Smith Minor O., (Smith Bros. & Co.) h 15 Chemung.

Smith Olin A., emp. livery, and farmer 50, h 157 Clark.

Smith S. Charles, sign writing, Broad cor. Pine, h 9 Orange.

Smith Willis J., (Smith Bros. & Co.) bds. Fulton.

Smith W. M. Adelbert, laborer, bds. 37 Waverly.

Smitt Antoni B., merchant tailor, 10 Fulton, h 125 do.

Snell Patrick, laborer, h Erie.

Sniffen & Scott, (H. H. S. and R. H. S.) grain, coal, seeds, wool, wagons and farm implements, Broad n Loder.

Sniffen Henry H., (Sniffen & Scott) bds. Tioga House.

Snook Frederick M., dentist, over 231 Broad, h 13 Pennsylvania ave.

Snyder De LaFayette, resident, h 119 Clark.

Somers Maurice, laborer, h 204 Howard.

Space Henry, traveling salesman, bds. over 267 Broad.

Space Jennie L., widow John A., dressmaker, over 267 Broad, h do.

Spaulding William H., police justice, h 113 Clark.

Speh Charles Prof., teacher of music, French and German.

Spencer Charles F., boots and shoes, 226 Broad, h 445 Chemung.

Spencer C. I. Mrs., resident, 104 Lincoln.

Spencer George M., emp. Swift's ice-house, h Broad n Pennsylvania ave.
Sproul Andrew, railroad conductor, h 5 Spaulding.
Sproul Herbert L., clerk, bds. 5 Spaulding.
Stalker Albert, emp. Novelty Works, h Broad.
Stanley Belle, art teacher, 101 Pennsylvania ave., bds. Broad.
Stanley Clark M., dentist, h Cadwell.
Stark Somers J., railroad conductor, h 203 Howard.
Steele Edward J., telegraph operator, bds. Warford House.
Stevenson William, clerk, h 244 Broad.
Stevenson William R., locomotive engineer, h 21 Providence.
Steward Malvina, widow Loren G., bds. 2 Ithaca.
Stewart William H., retired, h 13 Park Place.
Stone George P., machinist, bds. 12 Pennsylvania ave.
Stone James R., retired, h 105 Park ave.
Stone William P., resident, h 12 Pennsylvania ave.
Stout Ernest A., book-keeper, 235 Broad, h over do.
STOWELL HOLLIS L., dry goods, 237 Broad, h 405 Chemung.
Strange Matthew, laborer, h 4 Broad.
Strouse Huldah, widow Neal, dressmaker over 218 Broad, h do.
Suiter Sophia, widow Robert, bds. 28 Loder.
Sullivan Anna, dressmaker, 105 Chemung, bds. do.
Sullivan Etta, dressmaker, 315 Broad, h do.
Sullivan Hannah, dressmaker, 315 Broad, h do.
Sullivan Mary, dressmaker, 315 Broad, h do.
Sullivan Michael, emp. Erie R. R., h 26 Providence.
Sullivan Michael, track foreman, bds. 9 Loder.
Sutton Augustus, barber, bds. Warford House.
Sutton Clarence M., emp. Novelty Works, bds. 466 Chemung.
Sutton Ernest, emp. Toy works, h 101 Pennsylvania ave.
Sutton Frank M., cabinet maker, h 466 Chemung.
Swaig Henry, porter Tioga Hotel, bds. do.
SWAIN LESTER, groceries, provisions and restaurant, Fulton, h do.
Swain William H., book-keeper, 251 Broad, h 117 Howard.
SWEET WESLEY, furniture and undertaking, 243 Broad, h 10 Park ave.
Taladay Frederick, carpenter, bds. 5 Providence.
Tannery Harriet, widow James B., resident, 423 Chemung.
TANNERY IDA Miss, millinery, over 233 Broad, h 243 Chemung.
Tannery Mary, widow, h 17 Clark.
Taylor John L., pastor 1st Presbyterian church, h 11 Park Place.
Teachman Isaac P., (Carr & Teachman) h 30 Chemung.
Telephone Exchange, (F. E. Smith, of Elmira, Mgr.) over First Nat. Bank.
Terry Edward H., mason, h 5 Pennsylvania ave.
Terry Edward H., Jr., shipping clerk, 275 Broad, bds. 5 Pennsylvania ave.
Terry Edward H. Mrs., dressmaker, 5 Pennsylvania ave., h do.
Terry Fred S., city baggage express, bds. 160 Clark.
Terry Ira M., carpenter, h Broad.
Terry John, retired, h Hickory.
Terry Orrin T., clerk, bds. 5 Pennsylvania ave.
Terry T. Jefferson, car inspector, h 160 Clark.
Terry Walter T., car inspector, h 160 Clark.
Tew William E., real estate and insurance, over 214 Broad, h do.
Thatcher Harris C., manager The W. S. Thatcher Co., h 12 Park Place.
Thatcher Helen, widow Walter S., woven wire mattresses, h 12 Park Place.

Thayer Roma B.. emp. Novelty Works, h 313 Broad.

THE CITIZENS BANK, (J. T. Sawyer, pres't, S. W. Slaughter, vice-pres't, F. A. Sawyer, cashier) 214 Broad.

*THE WAVERLY ADVOCATE, (Edgar L. Vincent, pub., and George D. Genung, editor, weekly) 4 Elizabeth.

The W S. Thatcher Co., (Harry C. Thatcher, Mgr.) manuf. woven wire mattresses, Fulton.

THOMAS HOLLY W., (Fairchild & Thomas) h 14 S. Main.

Thompson Abner, brakeman, bds. Commercial Hotel.

Thompson Abram J., clerk, h 144 Waverly.

Thompson Guy M., emp. Novelty Works, bds. 144 Waverly.

Thompson Sadie, teacher, bds. 3 Providence.

Thompson William E., butcher, h 8 Pine.

Thrall Emery, R. R. conductor, h. 348 Broad.

Tillman David B., book-keeper, bds. over 253 Broad.

Tillman Moses, carpenter, h over 253 Broad.

Tilton Edson A., clerk, bds. 111 Howard.

Tilton Ira, clerk, bds. 111 Broad.

Tilton Isaac S., clerk, bds. 111 Howard.

Tioga Bottling Works, Michael Shaehan, prop., Broad cor. Loder.

TIOGA HOTEL, Ackley & Bailey, proprs., Fulton Cor. Elizabeth.

Tioga Laundry, George B. Witter, prop., 113 Broad.

Tobin James, section foreman, Erie R. R., h. 119 Erie.

Toppen Henry, painter, 114 Waverly, h do.

Towner Jane, tailoress, h 9 Waverly.

Tozer John F., livery stable, Fulton, opp. Opera House, h 30 Waverly.

Tozer Lavina, widow Charles P., h 129 Waverly.

Tracy Edward G., drugs, and wall paper, 228 Broad, h Fulton cor. Chemung.

Tracy John L., books, stationery and newsroom, 204 Broad, h 3 Orange.

Travis Landes L., locomotive engineer, h 10 Spalding.

Travis Littleton, coachman, h 401 Chemung.

Troutman Jacob, brakeman, h 30 Broad.

Tucker John T., physician and surgeon, over 224 Broad, h do.

Turner Amelia, widow Joseph, h 144 Howard.

Turner Edward, locomotive engineer, h 20 Park Place.

Turney William E, confectioner, 239 Broad, h 130 Clark.

Tuthill Caroline A., teacher, bds. Waverly.

Tuthill Charles E., clerk, h 124 Waverly.

Tuthill Elvira, widow Jacob G., h Waverly.

Twist Michael, mason, bds. 381 Broad.

Tyrrell Augustus, physician, over 222 Broad, h do.

United States Ex. Co., J. K. Murdoch, agt., 8 Fulton.

Unger Solomon, clothing and gents' furnishings, 230 Broad, h in Elmira.

Unger Adolph, clothing and merchant tailor, 221 Broad, h Fulton.

Updike Archibald, market gardener, h 85 Clark.

Updike Frank A., carpenter, h Clinton ave.

Utter John, architect, h 120 Howard.

Vail Alonzo V. C., lumber dealer, h 128 Waverly.

Vail Daniel, resident, h 121 Howard.

Vail Merton W., painter, h 309 Pennsylvania ave.

Vail Michael, brakeman, bds. Warford House.

Vail Michael, switchman, bds. over 263 Broad.

VanAmburgh Abdial B., wagon shop 304 Broad, h 133 Howard.

VanAtta Azariah, contractor and builder, 111 Pennsylvania ave., h do.
VanAtta Clarence, clerk, h 109 Fulton.
VanAtta E. Clair, clerk, h 9 Tioga.
VanAtta Edwin H., drug clerk, bds. 5 Park ave.
VAN ATTA JOHN C., (Slaughter & VanAtta) h 5 Park ave.
VanCleft Mary J., dressmaker, bds. 139 Waverly.
VanCleft Sarah A., widow Benjamin O., h 139 Waverly.
VanCleft Wells, laborer, h Hickory.
VAN DERLIP CHARLES T., D. D. S., dentist, preservation of the
    natural teeth a specialty, over 201 Broad, h Cadwell.
VanDerlip Sisters, (Mary and Elizabeth) dressmakers, h 24 Park ave.
VanDermark Edward, porter, Tioga Hotel, bds. do.
VanDermark Mrs., widow Albert, bds. 14 Pennsylvania ave.
VanDeuzer Annie, teacher, bds. 468 Chemung.
VanDeuzer Dell, emp. pipe foundry, h over 263 Broad.
VAN DEUZER HOWARD C., (Sayre Butter Package Co.) bds. Tioga
    Hotel.
VanDeuzer Richard, mechanic, bds. over 263 Broad.
VanDeuzer Richard D., (Sayre Butter Package Co.) h 468 Chemung.
Van Gaasbeck, clerk, Christie House, bds. do.
VanGaasbeck Josephine, widow John, h 132 Chemung.
VanGorden Harry M., sexton of cemetery, h 38 Pine.
VanGorden Mary E., dressmaker, bds. 38 Pine.
VanVelsor & Co., (Alexander Zoltowski) merchant tailors, 212 Broad.
VanVelsor George B., (VanVelsor & Co.) h 117 Waverly.
VanVelsor Jane, widow Benjamin, bds. 117 Waverly.
Vaughn William, retired, h 16 Park ave.
Vibbert Charles M., contractor and builder, h 148 Waverly.
VINCENT EDGAR L., publisher *The Waverly Advocate*, h Clark.
Voorheirs Barbara, widow Sherman, h Blizard.
Voorheirs Stephen, cigar maker, bds. Blizard.
Vreeland Isaac S., M. D., physician and surgeon, over 229 Broad, h Penn-
    sylvania ave.
WADSWORTH SAMUEL H., (Wadsworth & Kelsey) Hotel Warford.
WADSWORTH & KELSEY, props. Hotel Warford, Broad cor. Fulton.
Waldo George F., retired, h 101 Pennsylvania ave.
WALKER EDWARD E., (T. S. Walker & Son) h 306 Pennsylvania ave.
Walker Eliza, resident, bds. 6 Elm.
WALKER HOWARD S., clerk, bds. Waverly.
WALKER LEANDER, groceries and provisions, 253 Broad, h Waverly.
Walker N. Dell, widow George H., resident, h. 102 Lincoln.
WALKER T. S. & SON, (Edward E.) groceries and provisions, 250 and
    252 Broad.
WALKER THADDEUS S., (T. S. Walker & Son) h r 60.
WALLACE ALFRED H., carpenter, h 150 Waverly.
Wallace Grandsville, porter, Tioga Hotel, bds. do.
Wallace William A., emp. Novelty Works, bds. 150 Waverly.
Walsh Maggie, milliner, bds. over 232 Broad.
Walton S. Lincoln, tanner, h 73 Fulton.
Ward Amrose, emp. planing mill, h 37 Orange.
Ward John E., resident.
Ward Mary, widow Hugh, h Loder.
Ware Walter, inventor, h 27 Park ave.

Warner Anna P., resident, bds. 11 Park ave.
WARNER WILLIAM F., lawyer, also pres't Waverly Gas Light Co., Waverly, h 11 Providence.
Warren James, emp. wheel foundry, h Erie.
Waters Edward T., marble cutter, h Erie.
WATROUS BROS., (William L., and estate of Addison) dry goods, cloaks, and carpets, 227 Broad.
WATROUS WILLIAM L., (Watrous Bros.) h 14 Park Place.
Watson John, mason, h 102 Waverly.
WAVERLY CASH STORE., (Barnes & Miller, props.) groceries and provisions, 277 Broad.
Waverly Opera House, C. Mullock, manager. Fulton.
Waverly Steam Flouring Mills, John C. Shear, prop., 300 Broad.
*WAVERLY TRIBUNE, (weekly) Noble & Noble, publishers, Elizabeth.
Weatherly Leonora, widow Perry, h 44 Waverly.
WEBB HENRY A., prop. Webb's Dining Hall, 216 Broad, h do.
WEBB'S DINING HALL, Henry A. Webb, prop., 216 Broad.
Welch John, laborer, h Erie.
Weller Charles M., baggageman, h 105 Howard.
WELLER G. FRED, resident, h 188 Clark.
Wells Elizabeth S., widow Rev. Daniel, bds. 414 Chemung.
Welsh John, moulder, h Loder.
Welsh Julia, widow James, h Loder.
Welton Anna E., widow Lyman, h Chemung.
Welton Warner, laborer, h Pine.
West George P., retired, h 21 Orange.
Westbrook Calvin T., drayman, h 7 Broad.
Wheat Mark M., laborer, h Pine.
Whitaker Henry, engineer, h 19 Lincoln.
Whitaker Horace, street commissioner, h 435 Chemung.
Whitaker Richard, mechanic and green-house, h 102 Howard.
Whitaker William D., railroad conductor, h Providence n Pennsylvania ave.
White Horton, emp. pipe works, h 10 Tioga.
White James, bar-keeper, h Broad.
White Jerome, laborer, h 430 Chemung.
White Mary, widow Patrick h 354 Broad.
Wickham Joseph D., invalid, h 105 Howard.
Wiesmer Sarah, widow George, resident, h 101 Broad.
WILCOX & BARROWS, (W. W. W. and A. H. B.) meat market, 271 Broad.
Wilcox George S., retired, h 40 Park ave.
Wilcox H. M. & Co., (L. S. Bush) dry goods, 218 Broad.
Wilcox Howard M., (H. M. Wilcox & Co.) h 25 Waverly.
Wilcox Silas E., resident, h over 269 Broad.
WILCOX WYATT W., (Wilcox & Barrows) h 40 Park ave.
Wilkinson Margaret, widow George D., resident, h 19 Broad.
WILLIAMS ADELBERT D., (Puff & Williams) h Loder.
Williams Addie, dressmaker, 20 Clark, h do.
Williams Ann, resident, h 3 Tioga.
Williams Daniel, painter, bds. 20 Clark.
Williams John F., laborer, h 18 Chemung.
Williams Mary E., widow Gabriel, h 20 Clark.

Williams Mastin L., retired, h 129 Clark.
Wilson Alosco H., expressman, 24 Waverly.
Wilson George W., locomotive engineer, h 349 Broad.
Winnie William U., laborer, h 23 Clark.
Witter George B., prop. Tioga Laundry, 113 Broad, h do.
Woodburn James L., barber, Fulton, h do.
Wolcott Ira M., resident, bds. over 259 Broad.
Wolcott Maria, widow Silas, h 444 Chemung
Wolcott Park, clerk, h Chemung.
Wolcott Raymond, clerk, h 444 Chemung.
Wolcott Tompkins S., bartender, h over 259 Broad.
Wood Hiram C., R. R. signal tender, h 110 Chemung.
Woodruff Emma C., widow Dr. Jacob D., resident, 7 Tioga.
Woodruff James O. Rev., pastor M. E. church, h 53 Waverly.
Woodworth William H., laborer, h 26 Providence.
Wright Daniel, lumberman, h 24 Clark.
Wright Festus A., emp. J. T. Sawyer, h 451 Chemung.
Young Henry H., tanner, h 196 Clark.
Young John F., (Kinsman & Young) h 6 Providence.
Ziegler Benjamin F., cigar maker and tobacconist, Johnson, h 141 Fulton.
Zeigler William R., conductor, h Hickory.
Zoltowski Alexander, (VanVelsor & Co.) h 7 Chemung.
Zoltowski Anthony, tailor, bds. 7 Chemung.

BARTON

OUTSIDE WAVERLY VILLAGE.

(*For explanations, etc., see page 3, part second.*)

(Postoffice address is Barton, unless otherwise designated in parenthesis.)

Ackley Alexander W., (Lockwood) r 2, prop. saw-mill and farmer 1,400.
Ackley Charles E., (Lockwood) r 16, sawyer and farmer.
Ackley Francis, (Factoryville) r 47, laborer.
Ackley Samuel, (Lockwood) farm laborer.
Adell Fayette G., laborer.
Akins J. Frank, (Lockwood) r 48, farmer 58.
Akins Rebecca, (Lockwood) r 47, widow George, resident.
Albright Adam, (North Barton) r 34, prop. threshing machine and farmer 76.
Albright Hiram C., r 40, resident.
Albright Isaac D., r 40, prop. steam thresher and farmer 120.
Albright Joseph, r 27, farmer.
Albright Joseph A., (North Barton) r 34. farmer.
Albright Sarah, (Factoryville) r 42, widow Josiah, farm 50.
Allen David, (Factoryville) r 65, farmer.
ALLEN JOHN, (Waverly) r 60, prop. Cayuta Dairy milk route and farmer.
ANDRE ABRAM T., (Lockwood) lumber dealer and contractor, h Main.
Andre Isaac J., (Factoryville) laborer.
Andre John, (Lockwood) r 29, apiarist 16 swarms.
Andrew George, (Factoryville) laborer. h Owego.

STARKEY & WINTERS, Druggists, Owego. Close Prices to Dealers.

Andrus Mary D., (Lockwood) r 1, widow Thomas, farm 44.
Andrus Richard, (Lockwood) commissioner of highways and farmer 60.
Arhart Henry, (Factoryville) brakeman, bds. Jackson House.
Armstrong Joseph, retired, h Spencer.
Atchison Thomas, r 38, farmer.
Averil Miles D., (Waverly) r 65, farmer, leases of Horace Taylor 5.
Baker Alonzo, (Lockwood) r 28, farmer 50.
Ball Isaac, (Factoryville) laborer, h 533, Chemung.
Ball William N., (Factoryville) resident, h 521 Chemung.
Bandfield Ira, (Waverly) off r 65, farmer 90.
Bandfield Ira E., (Waverly) off r 65, farmer with his father Ira.
Barden Charles, (Halsey Valley) r 25, farmer.
Barden Edward, (Halsey Valley) r 25, farmer.
Barden Ira, (Halsey Valley) r 9, laborer.
Barden Simon, (Halsey Valley) r 23, farmer.
Barden Zalmon, r 39, farmer 45.
Barker Abigail, (Factoryville) widow John, resident, Main.
Barnes Christopher, (North Barton) r 17, farmer.
BARNUM ELI, (North Barton) r 4, farmer 114.
Barr John C., Jr., (Waverly) carpenter, h Chemung.
Barton Tip, r 53, laborer.
Bartron Albin, r 53, watchman.
Bartron Frank, r 54, farmer with his father Joseph.
BARTRON JACOB, r 54, farmer with his father Joseph.
Bartron Pernando, r 53, laborer.
Bartron Joseph, r 54, farmer 80.
Beams Marvin, r 41, farmer.
Beers Lyman, (Factoryville) laborer, h Charles.
Bellis William, (Factoryville) emp. Thatcher's mattress shop, h Orchard.
Bellis Marietta, (North Barton) r 35, widow Charles, resident.
Bellis Philip, (North Barton) r 35, farmer.
Bennett Emma, (Factoryville) widow David, resident, h Owego.
Bennett Lou, (Factoryville) cook, bds. Owego.
Bensley DeWitt C., justice of the peace and pension attorney, Spencer, h do.
BENSLEY ELLIOTT L., off r 55, farmer 200.
Bensley John H., teacher, bds. Spencer.
Bensley Lucina P., r 55, widow Daniel, resident.
Bensley William, poormaster, h Spencer.
Bensley William H., R. R. section hand, bds. Spencer.
Bentley George, off r 39, peddler.
BESEMER DANIEL V., (North Barton) r 18, apiarist 60 swarms and
    farmer 310.
Besemer George D., (North Barton) r 18, farmer.
Besemer James, (Lockwood) r 32, farmer 50.
BINGHAM BROTHERS, (Lockwood) (G. W. & E. J. B.) flour and feed,
    saw, lath and planing-mill, and general merchandise.
BINGHAM EDMUND J., (Lockwood) (Bingham Bros.) h Main.
BINGHAM GEORGE W., (Bingham Bros.) (Lockwood) h Main.
Bingham John, (Lockwood) r 1, farmer 27.
BOGART GEORGE W., r 40, farmer 80.
Bogart G. Fred, r 40, farmer with his father George W.
Bogart James, (Waverly) r 60, farmer 47.
Bogart John S., (Waverly) prop. saw-mill and farmer 40.

Bogart Joseph V., (Reniff) r 1, farmer 124.
Bogart Lawrence, (Factoryville) r 60, farmer.
Bogart Nathaniel V., (Waverly) r 47, farmer 130.
BOGART PETER V., (Lockwood) lumbering and farmer 65, h Main.
Bogart William, r 41, farmer.
Bowman Catharine, (Waverly) r 62, widow Absalom, resident.
Bowman Emmet, (Waverly) r 62, farmer 65, and leases of Catharine Bowman 60, and on shares with Mrs. La Mont 15.
Boyce Frank, (Factoryville) conductor, h Ithaca.
Boyce Genevieve, (Factoryville) boarding-house, Ithaca.
Boyce Lyman, (Halsey Valley) r 8, blacksmith.
Brant Mary B., (Waverly) widow Luke S., resident, h Orchard.
Brewster Harvey E., (Factoryville) r 69, farm laborer.
Brewster Henry C., (Factoryville) r 69, farm laborer.
Brewster John E., (North Barton) r 19, farmer 200.
Brink Albert J., (Factoryville) r 64, farmer.
Brink Charles, (Waverly) r 59, farmer, leases of Jacob Brink 80.
BROCK GEORGE D., (Lockwood) (A. V. C. Vail & Co.) postmaster, h Main.
BROOKS AUGUSTUS, (Lockwood) prop. turning, scroll-sawing and wagon shop, contractor and builder, and manuf. church seats.
Brown Avery, (North Barton) r 11, farmer.
Brown Charles, (Lockwood) r 2, farmer 50.
Brown Ezra, (Waverly) r 47, farmer 150.
Brown Francis, (North Barton) r 19, farmer 120.
Brown George, (Halsey Valley) r 23, farmer.
Brown Marshall, (North Barton) r 19, farmer, with his father Francis.
Brown Shubel C., (North Barton) r 4, farmer 100.
Bruster Ainslee, (Lockwood) off r 2, farmer 175.
Bruster Daniel, (North Barton) r 19, farmer 100.
Bruster Elwood, (North Barton) r 17, farmer.
Bruster Nathaniel M., (North Barton) r 17, farmer, on shares with O. M. Bruster 150.
Bruster Oliver M., (Waverly) r 49, farmer 25.
BUCK LYMAN, (Waverly) r 65, school-trustee, prop. Buck's farm, dairy milk route, and farmer 100.
Bunce Louisa, (Factoryville) widow John, resident, bds. Main.
Bunnell Henry, (Waverly) r 48½, farmer 145.
BURKE OSCAR F., (Waverly) r 60, carpenter, and farmer 6.
Burt Israel, (Waverly) retired, bds. Orchard.
Callahan Fanny, (Factoryville) widow John, resident.
Campbell Emerson, (Waverly) r 62½, farmer, leases of John Murray 100.
Canfield Amos, (Waverly) r 62, farmer 150.
CANFIELD EZRA, (Lockwood) r 46, physician and surgeon.
Carey Benjamin, (Waverly) teamster, h Main, E. Waverly.
Carey Clarissa J., widow David N., resident.
Carey Irving R., (Factoryville) laborer, h Chemung.
Carey John, R. R. section foreman, h Spencer.
Carey Samuel, r 36 farmer.
Carlisle John, (Halsey Valley) r 22, laborer.
Cary Ezra, r 66, farmer 145.
Cary Leonard, (Halsey Valley) r 25, farmer.
Cary William E., (Wright & Cary) h Spencer.

Case Isaac, (Factoryville) resident, h Owego.
Cashaday Horace, (Halsey Valley) r 12, farmer.
Casterline Coe, (Factoryville) carpenter, h Owego.
Cater William, (Waverly) laborer, h Owego.
CAYUTA CREAMERY, (Factoryville) (Schuyler & Harding, props.) near
    depot.
Central House, (Factoryville) F. D. Tooker, prop., Main cor. Ithaca.
Cheney Armenia, (Waverly) r 59, widow John, resident.
Church Franklin L., (Lockwood) r 46, apiarist 23 swarms, and farmer, leases
    of J. C. Lyons 500.
Church Walsteen A., (Lockwood) farmer with his father Franklin L.
Clark Mary, (Lockwood) r 2, farm 50.
Clarke Harmon, r 54½, school trustee, and farmer 75.
Clawson Harmon, r 40, farmer, leases of Jeremiah Bogart 80.
Clearwater Amanda, (Factoryville) r 60, widow Stephen, resident.
Clock Clarence E., (Factoryville) postmaster and station agent, h Ithaca.
COLEMAN CHARLES H., (Lockwood) r 1, prop. turning, scroll-sawing,
    wagon and blacksmith shop, also dealer in wagons, sleighs and agri-
    cultural implements.
Coleman Eliza J., widow William D., resident.
Coleman George, (Waverly) r 43, farmer 50.
Coleman Jedediah D., live stock dealer, h Main.
Coleman John B., postmaster and bridge carpenter, Main, h do.
Coleman Joshua, r 54½, farmer 45.
Coleman Sadie L., deputy postmaster, bds. Main.
Collins Cornelius, (Lockwood) r 31, farmer 100.
Collins Emeline, (Factoryville) r 60, widow Samuel, resident.
Combs Clarence, (Factoryville) r 68, farm laborer.
Combs George, (Factoryville) farm laborer, h Chemung.
Conklin Emmet, (Factoryville) r 67, laborer.
Conklin Julia, (Waverly) widow Timothy, laundress, h Main.
Cook Daniel, r 55, physician and surgeon.
Cooley Fred L., (North Barton) r 17, farmer.
Cooley Harvey L., (Factoryville) retired, h Main.
Cooley Hattie J., (North Barton) r 17, dressmaker.
Cooley Robert, (Lockwood) r 32, farmer.
Cooley Robert R., (North Barton) r 17, farmer 50.
Corey Leonel C., (Factoryville) telegraph operator, h Ithaca.
Corey William, (Factoryville) resident, h Ithaca.
Cornell Alanson, stationery engineer, h Spencer.
Cornell Daniel B., clerk, bds. Main.
Cornell William, general merchant, and prop. of feed and saw-mill, Main, h do.
Cornish Marvin J., (Factoryville) laborer, h Ithaca.
Cortright Abram, (North Barton) r 11, farmer.
Courtwright David J., (Factoryvllle) r 42, farmer on shares with M. Sawyer.
Courtwright Martin V. B., carpenter and joiner, h Spencer.
Cowles Adelbert C., (Waverly) r 60, small fruit grower.
Cowles Caleb, (Waverly) r 60, orchard 150 trees and small fruit grower.
Crandall Alfonzo, (Halsey Valley) r 5, farmer.
Crans Ard F., (Factoryville) r 60, blacksmith.
Crans Eliza, (Lockwood) r 1, resident.
CRANS FRANK, (Lockwood) r 1, apiarist 56 swarms, and farmer.
Crisfield Ellsworth E., (North Barton) r 4, farmer with his father John.

Crisfield George B., (North Barton) r 15, farmer, on shares with C. C. Hedges 145.

Crisfield John, (North Barton) r 4, farmer 180.

Cronin Bartholomew, (Lockwood) R. R. section foreman, bds. Gilbert House.

Cronin Michael, (Factoryville) R. R. section foreman, h Charles.

Crotsley George, r 41, farmer, with his father Lewis.

Crotsley Lewis. r 41, farmer 200.

Cumber Solomon, r 41, farmer.

Curran David, (Waverly) r 49½, farmer.

Curran Floyd, (Waverly) r 62, clerk.

Curran Horace H.. (Waverly) r 60, mason.

Curran John J., (Waverly) r 60, mason.

Curtis Samuel, (Factoryville) conductor, h near depot.

Dalton James, laborer, h Spencer.

Damon Edward F., (Waverly) r 62½, farmer.

Daniels Mary E., (Waverly) widow Javan, tailoress, h Main, E. Waverly.

Davenport Albert, (North Barton) r 18, farmer.

Davenport Alonzo, farm laborer, h Main.

Davenport Andrew, laborer, h Railroad.

Davenport Charles A., laborer, h Railroad.

Davenport David, r 39, retired.

Davenport George, r 39, farmer 73.

Davenport Leslie, (Factoryville) emp. Sayre Butter Package Co., bds. Chemung.

Davenport Miles, r 39, carpenter.

DAVIS MARY M. Miss, (Lockwood) r 46, resident.

DECKER TANNERY, Abram I. Decker, prop., Main, E. Waverly.

Dewandler Henry, (Waverly) r 60, farm laborer.

Dewey George, (Lockwood) r 31, farm laborer.

DeWitt William M., (Factoryville) r 60, teaming.

Deyo Isaac, Jr., (Factoryville) r 60, farm laborer.

Dickerson Orson, r 34, farmer 80.

Dillon Martin, (Reniff) foreman Reniff mills.

Dingman William E., (Waverly) laborer, h Chemung.

Doane William B., (Waverly) r 62½, farmer, on shares with J. Murray 100.

Dollason Frances H., (Factoryville) widow Austin A., dressmaker, Main.

Doney Abner, (Lockwood) carpenter, h Church.

Doty Asa, (Factoryville) r 18, farmer 55.

Doud Augustus, (Waverly) retired, h Main.

Doyle Jacob, r 40, farmer 102.

Doyle John, r 40, farmer 8.

Drake Andrew J., off r 66, farmer 200.

Drake Betsey, (Halsey Valley) r 23, farm 100.

Drake Ezra, (Halsey Valley) r 22, farmer.

Drake George C., (Waverly) r 62, carpenter.

Drake James H., (Halsey Valley) r 23, farmer.

Drake Jedediah, r 37, farmer.

Drake Nathaniel, (Lockwood) laborer.

Drake Susan, off r 66, widow Elsworth, resident.

Draper Spencer J., (Factoryville) laborer, h Owego.

Drogan John, (Factoryville) emp. Sayre freight house, h Charles.

Dunn John, (Factoryville) laborer, h Main.

Dunn John, Jr., ,Factoryville) laborer, bds. Main.

3

Dunn Kate, (Factoryville) r 65, house-keeper.
EATON AMBROSE C., (Factoryville) (D. H. E. & SON) h Main.
EATON DAVID H., (Factoryville) (D. H. E. & Son) h Main.
EATON D. H. & SON, (Factoryville) tin and hardware, manufrs. of Eaton's refrigerator butter packages.
Edgarton Willis, (Lockwood) r 46, blacksmith.
Edgcomb George G., (Factoryville) r 47, apiarist 30 swarms, and farmer 155.
Edgcomb Gilbert, (Factoryville) r 60, farmer with his mother Lucinda.
Edgcomb Lucinda, (Factoryville) r 60, widow Hobart, farm 140.
Edgcomb Lucy, (Waverly) r 60, widow Gilbert, resident.
Edwards Aaron, (Halsey Valley) r 9, farmer 45.
Edwards George F., (Halsey Valley) r 9, farmer.
Ellas A. Clark, wagon-maker, Main, h do.
Ellas Orrin, retired, h Main.
Ellas Sarah Ann, resident, h Main.
Elliott William B., (Factoryville) retired, h Chemung.
Ellis Charles B., (Waverly) off r 49, farmer 100.
ELLIS GILBERT S., (Waverly) r 64, commissioner of highways, auctioneer and farmer 35.
Ellis Ira D., (Factoryville) r 64, farmer 44.
Ellis Jesse, (Factoryville) r 59, farmer 87.
Ellis John, (Factoryville) r 65, farmer.
Ellis John, (Factoryville) painter, bds. Ithaca.
Ellis Lewis B., (Waverly) r 49, farmer 77.
Ellis Sela, (Factoryville) r 60, farmer 135.
Ellis Thaddeus W., (Factoryville) r 64, farmer 170.
Ellis William T., (Factoryville) r 65, farmer.
Ellison John, (Lockwood) r 28, farmer 50.
Ellison Samuel W., (Lockwood) r 29, farmer 118.
Ellison Susan, (Lockwood) r 29, widow Samuel, resident.
Ellison William B., (North Barton) r 16, farmer 62.
Elson Julius, r 40, farmer.
Elwell Orlando, (Reniff) r 1, sawyer and carpenter.
Evans Ziba, Rev., (Lockwood) pastor M. E. church, h Main cor. Church.
Evarts Andrew J., (Factoryville) general merchant, Main, h do.
Evelin Henry, (North Barton) r 4, farmer, leases of Dr. Vosburgh.
Evelyn Christopher, (North Barton) r 11, farmer 36.
Evenden Eliza, (North Barton) r 2, widow Robert, farm 50.
Evenden William, (North Barton) r 2, farmer.
Evens Richard E., (Waverly) laborer, h Orchard.
Fiester Jacob, retired farmer, h Main.
Filkins Cornelius, (Factoryville) carpenter, h near depot.
Finch Amasa, (Factoryville) wagon and sleigh manuf., Main, h do.
Finch Cynthia, (Factoryville) resident, bds. Main.
Finch Wilbur F., (Factoryville) postal clerk, h Main.
Fisher Douglass T., (Halsey Valley) r 21, farmer.
Fisk Willis J., (Lockwood) r 1, watch repairer and miller.
FLECKENSTINE JACOB W., (Waverly) r 60, prop. Iron Bridge stone quarry.
Fleming Oscar, (Lockwood) r 45, farmer, leases of Mrs. S. Davis 96.
Follett Harriet, (Lockwood) r 45, widow Cyrus, farm 120.
Foote Gilbert E., (Waverly) off r 46, assessor and farmer 150.
Forbes Henry S., (Waverly) r 64, farmer on shares with G. B. Pennell 100.

Forbes Hester, (Waverly) r 64, widow Archibald, resident.
Forman Edward M., r 55, farmer 100.
Forman Miles, prop. Temperance Hotel, Main.
Forsyth Edward, (Halsey Valley) r 8, farmer.
Forsyth Frederick, (Halsey Valley) r 8, farmer.
Foster Eli, (Waverly) r 47, farmer 50.
Foster Katie, (Halsey Valley) r 9, widow Daniel, resident.
Foster Shalor S., (Waverly) r 47, farmer with his father Eli.
Frisbie Charles F., (North Barton) r 14, farmer.
Frisbie Frederick, (Halsey Valley) r 8, farmer.
Frisbie William R., (North Barton) r 14, farmer 250.
Fuller Celinda, (Factoryville) widow Richard, resident, h Charles.
Fuller F. Adelbert, (Factoryville) laborer, h Charles.
Furman William A., (Reniff) r 1, farmer 35.
Garrison William R., (Factoryville) brakeman, h Charles.
Gee William, (Halsey Valley) r 21, farmer.
Genung Alva E., (Waverly) r 18, farmer 70.
Genung Harvey, (North Barton) r 27, farmer.
Genung Lydia L., (Waverly) r 18, widow Nathaniel, farm 80.
Genung William W., (Waverly) r 18, farmer.
Georgia George, (Lockwood) r 29, farmer.
Gilbert House, (Lockwood) Mrs. Eva J. Gilbert, prop., Main, opp. depot.
Gilbert Laton, (Lockwood) Gilbert House, Main.
Giles Joseph W., (Halsey Valley) r 22, farmer.
Gillan Benjamin R., (Factoryville) blacksmith, h Main.
Gillan William, (Factoryville) fireman, h Main.
Gillett Albert, (Reniff) r 1, emp. Reniff mills.
GILLETT & DECKER CREAMERY CO., (Reniff) W. E. Gillett, and
     A. I. Decker, props., near R. R.
Gillett Morris H., (Reniff) r 1, head sawyer Reniff mills.
Gillett Nathan R., (Reniff) retired.
GILLETT WILLIS E., (Reniff) (Gillett & Decker Co.) postmaster, gen-
     eral merchant, prop. Reniff Mills, and farmer 147, and in Chemung
     county 372, and in Tennessee 150.
Giltner Dexter E., (Waverly) carpenter, h Ithaca.
Giltner Ezra A., r 39, farmer 175.
Giltner Francis, r 39, farmer.
Giltner Wesley, r 54½, farmer 30.
Giltner William, off r 38, farmer.
Golden George M., (Lockwood) r 31, farmer 180.
Golden Isaac, (North Barton) r 33, farmer.
Goodwin Mrs., (Halsey Valley) r 9, widow Floyd, resident.
Gorton George, (North Barton) r 19, farmer 30.
Gorton Nathan, r 54, farmer 10.
Gould John, (Halsey Valley) r 23, farmer.
Grafft George H., (Waverly) justice of the peace, h Main, E. Waverly.
Gregory Franklin, (Lockwood) r 2, farmer, on shares with Dr. Hollenback 175.
Green Edward L., (Factoryville) express messenger, h Charles.
Green William H., r 54, farmer, on shares with H. A. Hollenback 224.
Greer Jane A., (Factoryville) widow Thomas, resident, h Ithaca.
Gridley Charles E., (Factoryville) (T. E. Gridley & Son) h Main.
Gridley T. E. & Son, (C. E. G.) (Factoryville) general store, Main.
Gridley Thomas E., (Factoryville) (T. E. Gridley & Son) h Main.

HAGADORN DE WITT C., (Lockwood) station and express agent, and telegraph operator, also dealer in coal, lime and cement, fence posts and R. R. ties.

Haley Michael, (Factoryville) off r 60, laborer.

Hallett John, (Waverly) r 62, painter.

Hallett William, (Waverly) off r 62, retired.

Hamilton Simeon, (Waverly) off r 60, carpenter.

Hammond Gordon S., (Waverly) r 49, farmer, on shares with J. C. Lyons 160.

Hanford Clark, (Factoryville) apiarist and shoemaker.

Hanford Julia A., (Factoryville) widow Noah, resident, bds. Main.

HANFORD MAURICE F., (Waverly) (Hanford & Lord) h Main, E. Waverly.

HANNA CHARLES F., (Factoryville) r 66, prop. saw-mill, and farmer 60.

Hanna George E., (Factoryville) brakeman, bds. Main.

Hanna George I., (Waverly) farmer 130.

Hanna G. Quigg, (Factoryville) resident, h Main.

Hanna Ira, r 55, farmer 100.

Hanna Lorentes J., (Factoryville) butcher, h Main.

Hanna Selah S., (Factoryville) farmer.

Hardenstine John L., (Waverly) painter.

Harding Amos, (Waverly) r 49, painter.

Harding Benjamin J., (Factoryville) r 59, farmer 54.

HARDING CHARLES E., (Factoryville) carpenter, h Ithaca.

Harding Charles H., (Waverly) r 59, farmer, leases of Ira Harding estate 80.

Harding Cornelius, (Waverly) r 48, farmer.

Harding Cynthia S., (Waverly) r 59, widow Ira, resident.

Harding Elliot, (Waverly) r 59, farmer.

HARDING FRANK W., r 52, farmer 90.

HARDING HORACE T., (Factoryville) (Schuyler & Harding) r 60, farmer $23\frac{1}{2}$, and in Chemung county 150.

Harding James B., (Waverly) r 59, teacher, and farmer 54.

Harding James N., (Factoryville) retired, bds. Ithaca.

Harding James O., (Factoryville) emp. Sayre Butter Package Company, bds. Ithaca.

Harding Nancy H., r 52, widow John, resident.

Harding Samuel T., teacher, bds. Spencer.

Harding William, (Factoryville) (Schuyler & Harding) h Owego.

Harford A. Jackson, (Reniff) off r 1, farmer.

Harford George B., (Factoryville) teaming, h Main.

Harford Lewis, (Reniff) off r 1, farmer.

HARFORD TUNIS I., (Reniff) r 1, school trustee and farmer 60, a member of the 161st Regt., N. Y. Vols.

Harris George V., (Factoryville) carpenter, h Main.

Hart Edward C., (Waverly) r 60, emp. Novelty Works.

Hazen Fred, r 41, farm laborer.

Hedges Charles C., (North Barton) r 15, farmer 145.

Hedges Christopher, (VanEttenville, Chem. Co.) r 1, lumberman and farmer.

Hedges Laura M., (Lockwood) widow John B., resident.

Hess Adelbert, (Halsey Valley) r 12, farmer.

Hess Fred, (Halsey Valley) r 20, farmer.

Hess George, (Halsey Valley) r 7, farmer.

Hess Jacob, (Halsey Valley) r 20, farmer 60.

Hess Sylvester N., (North Barton) r 11, farmer.

Hill Ira G., (Factoryville) r 60, retired.
HILL JOHN G., (Factoryville) r 68, farmer 78.
Hill Albert L.. (Factoryville) laborer, bds. Ithaca.
Hills Charles M., (Factoryville) book-agent, bds. Ithaca.
Hollenback Harry A., r 54, farmer 224.
Hollenback John W., traveling salesman, h Spencer.
Hollenback M. Hunter, retired, h Spencer.
Holt Charles B., r 53, apiarist 40 swarms, and farmer 500.
Holt Herbert, (Halsey Valley) r 5, farmer 100.
Holt Herman B., r 53, farmer.
Hooker Nelson, (North Barton) r 27, farmer, leases of George Besemer.
Hoover Martin, (Factoryville) r 65, laborer.
Hoover William, r 41, prop. steam thresher, and farmer.
Hopkins Henry, school trustee, and farmer 48.
Hopkins John Q., r 68, farmer, on shares with S. Hanna 100.
Hopkins Stephen, (Waverly) r 62, retired.
Hopkins Stephen, Jr., (Waverly) r 62, manager Electric Light Co.
Horton Beverly P., farmer 25.
Howe John W.. (Waverly) off r 49, farmer, on shares with C. B. Ellis 100.
Hoyt Edmund H., (North Barton) r 14, postmaster, and farmer 60.
Hoyt Joseph N., (Waverly) r 60, milk dealer.
Hoyt Sylvanus H., (North Barton) r 11 cor. 14, farmer 50.
Hubbell Cassius M., (North Barton) r 17, farmer, with his father Volney.
Hubbell Melissa H., widow David C., resident, bds. Charles.
Hubbell Volney, (North Barton) r 17, peach orchard 1,100 trees, and farmer 105.
Hulett John, (Factoryville) r 59, farmer 97.
Hulett Milo, (Halsey Valley) r 9, retired.
Hulett N. Tallmadge, (Factoryville) r 59, farmer with his father John.
Hulett Theophilus, r 11, district clerk, and farmer 35.
Hyatt Alanson (Lockwood) broom-maker, h Church.
Ilette Lewis, (Factoryville) retired, h Main.
Jackson Amos, (Factoryville) prop. Jackson House, Main.
Jackson House, (Factoryville) A. Jackson, prop., Main.
Jarvis Stephen, (Waverly) off r 65, farmer.
Jennings Daniel, (Waverly) r 68, teaming.
Jewell Levi, (Halsey Valley) r 9, farmer.
Johnson Arthur A., r 40, farmer on shares with C. B. Holt 200.
Johnson Cyrus, (Factoryville) r 60, farmer 53.
Johnson Edmund J., prop. Johnson House, Main.
JOHNSON HERBERT L., (Factoryville) r 67, farmer, leases of T. W. Ellis 183.
Johnson House, (E. J. Johnson, prop.) Main.
Johnson Lucinda, (Factoryville) r 60, widow Thomas F., resident.
Johnson Philetus B., (Waverly) r 62½, farmer 50.
Jones Benjamin S., (Waverly) r 65, farmer for Mrs. Sophia Howard.
Jones Edward, (Factoryville) laborer, h Main,
Jones Eugene C., (Factoryville) laborer.
Jones George, (Factoryville) off r 60, mason.
Jones William N., (Factoryville) brakeman, h Main.
Joyce F. Delphine, (Factoryville) r 60, widow Michael, resident.
Kain Edward M., station agent, express agent and telegraph operator, also coal dealer, bds. Spencer cor. Main.

Kane James F., blacksmith, bds. Main.
Kaulback John H., (Waverly) leather finisher, bds. Main, E. Waverly.
Kaulback John J., (Waverly) supt. Decker Tannery, h Main, E. Waverly.
Keeler Thomas, (Waverly) r 49, farm laborer.
Kelley Fred L., (Reniff) r 1, farmer with his father Lutheran.
Kelley Lutheran, (Reniff) r 1, apiarist 14 swarms, and farmer 130.
Kellogg Joseph, (Lockwood) off r 47, resident.
Kelsey Horace, Rev., r 37, (Bapt.) retired.
Ketcham Avery, (Lockwood) r 33, farmer.
Ketchem Ida, widow Lewis, resident.
King Clayton G., (Waverly) r 47, farmer.
King Henry, (Halsey Valley) r 21, farmer.
King John W., r 52, farmer on shares with A. J. Van Atta 103.
King Le Grand, (Lockwood) r 45, farmer 300.
King Salmon D., r 38, farmer 200.
King Sarah M., (Waverly) r 47, widow George, resident.
King Sheffield, (Lockwood) r 15, farmer.
King Warren J., (Lockwood) r 16, farmer 80.
Kingsworth Leonard, (North Barton) r 32, farmer 150.
Kinney John, off r 39, farmer 8.
Kirk Frederick H., (Factoryville) r 60, quarryman.
Kishpaugh George, (North Barton) r 16, farm laborer.
Kishpaugh Jonas, (Halsey Valley) r 26, farmer 100.
Kline Mazie A., (Waverly) r 62½ teacher.
Kline Wesley B., (Waverly) r 62½, farmer, leases of J. Beuly 170.
Knapp Azel, (Waverly) r 59, farmer 150.
Knapp Jerome B., (Waverly) r 59, farmer.
Kreamer Lot S., (Waverly) conductor, h Main, E. Waverly.
Lambert John L., (North Barton) r. 4, farmer.
LA MONT MARY C., (Factoryville) widow Allen, farm 95.
Lauderback George, r 39, farmer 30.
Lauderback Henry, r 39, farmer 30.
Laughlin Theodore, (Waverly) r 44, farmer on shares with C. Sawyer.
Lawheed Joseph S., (Factoryville) r 47 tanner.
Lawrence James C., (Factoryville) brakeman, h Charles.
Lee Henry B., (Factoryville) r 49, farm laborer.
Lee Ira H., (Factoryville) r 48½, district clerk and farmer 131.
Lee James, (North Barton) r 3, farmer.
Leonard Charles, r 55, blacksmith.
Lewis Harrison, (Waverly) r 59, farmer 53.
Liddle Richard, (Factoryville) retired farmer, h Owego.
LORD LOUIS F., (Hanford & Lord, Waverly) h Main, E. Waverly.
Lott George W., (Van Ettenville, Chem. Co.) prop. saw-mill and farmer 500.
Lott Live Oak, (Van Ettenville, Chem. Co.) r 1, lumberman and farmer.
Lubars Theodore H., (Waverly) stationary engineer, h Main, E. Waverly.
Luce Chauncey, (North Barton) r 11, farmer.
Luce John, (Waverly) resident, h Main, E. Waverly.
Lynch Uriah, (Halsey Valley) r 6, farmer.
Lyon Alonzo, (Waverly) painter and paper-hanger, h Chemung.
Lyons Henry, (Lockwood) r 46 retired farmer.
Lyons John, (Lockwood) r 1, farmer 300.
Lyons Jonathan C., (Factoryville) retired farmer, h Ithaca.
Lyons Nelson H., (Factoryville) farmer 35, h Ithaca.

Maloy I. Shepard, (Waverly) janitor High school, h Orchard.
Manderville Benjamin F., (Waverly) r 60, emp. Sayre shops and farmer 28.
Manning Betsey, (Waverly) widow Job, resident, bds. Main.
MANNING ELI D., (Halsey Valley) r 9, apiarist and farmer 46.
Manning Fred B., (Halsey Valley) r 9, feed and cidar-mill, and turning shop.
Manning John, (Halsey Valley) r 9, farmer 50.
Manning John, r 39, farmer 145.
Manning Judson, (Halsey Valley) r 9 cooper.
Manning Reuben C., (Waverly) farmer, h Main.
Mansfield Charles S., r 40, farmer on shares with J. Doyle.
Mapes Milton C., (Factoryville) blacksmith, Main, h do.
Masterton Samuel, r 41, farmer.
Masterson Urial, (Halsey Valley) r 19, farmer 15.
McCarthy Florence, (Factoryville) conductor, h Ithaca.
Mead Elizabeth, (Factoryville) r 60, widow Jacob W., resident.
Mead George H., (Factoryville) r 60, farm laborer.
Mead Judson, (Factoryville) r 60, farm laborer.
Mead Wallace, (Waverly) r 60, laborer.
Merrill A. Jackson, (Factoryville) r 59, farmer 40.
Merrill Sutherland T., (Factoryville) r 59, farmer with his father A. Jackson.
Metzker John W., (Factoryville) student, bds. Spring.
Millage Jacob A., (Factoryville) laborer, h Ball.
Millard Royal J., (Lockwood) teamster, h Main.
Millen Alonzo P., r 55, farmer on shares with C. Sawyer 96.
Miller Catharine E., (Lockwood) widow Gilbert M. L , resident, h Main.
Miller Henry, R. R. section hand, bds. Johnson House.
Miller James, (Factoryville) emp. Novelty Works, h Main.
Miller John, (Factoryville) brakeman, bds. Main.
Mills Adolphus, (Waverly) r 59, farmer.
Mills William G., (Waverly) r 59, farmer 120.
Monroe Charles, r 55, farmer.
Morse Asa, (Lockwood) off r 1, laborer.
Murray William W., (Factoryville) blacksmith, h Main.
Myers Peter, (Lockwood) r 32, farmer, leases of M. L. Williams.
New John T., (Factoryville) farm laborer, h Charles.
Newkirk Diantha (Factoryville) widow Ezra, resident, h Owego.
Nichols Charles H., (Lockwood) farm laborer.
Nichols Chauncey S., (North Barton) r 18, farmer 83.
Nichols Harriet A., (North Barton) r 18, widow Robert T., resident.
Nichols Harvey L., (Waverly) r 49, farm laborer.
Northrup Isaac D., (Waverly) r 62, farmer, leases of J. Kennedy 160.
Northrup William C., (Waverly) r 62, farmer with his father Isaac D.
Osborn John, (Factoryville) stationary engineer, h Ithaca.
Park Alvira, r 55, widow John, resident.
Park Daniel, r 55, farmer 100.
Park John J., r 55, farmer 65.
Parker Charles P., (Factoryville) r 48½, carpenter, and farmer 30.
Parks Joel, painter, h Spencer.
Parry Chauncey, r 39, farmer 15.
Partridge Sarah, (Factoryville) widow Abram, bds. Main.
Peck Luther Rev., pastor M. E. church, h Spencer.
Pembleton Charles, (Factoryville) r 69, farmer 124.
Pennell Gershem B., (Factoryville) retired farmer.

Peters Frederick J., (Waverly) clerk, h Main, E. Waverly.
Peterson Charles, (Waverly) r 62½, farm laborer.
Petty Nathan D., laborer, h Main.
Phillips Nellie S., (Factoryville) widow Addison B., resident, h Main.
Piatt Charles, (Factoryville) r 60, laborer.
Pierce Mary A., (Factoryville) resident, bds. Main.
Poole Frank, (Halsey Valley) r 9, blacksmith, and farmer 100.
Poole George, (Halsey Valley) r 6, farmer.
Porter Zeal W., (Factoryville) r 48¼, farmer.
Primrose James, r 55, laborer.
Quick Jay, (Halsey Valley) off r 12, farmer 50.
Raymond Augusta, (Factoryville) r 67, resident.
Raymond Isaac L., (Factoryville) r 67, farmer 500.
Raymond Rebecca, (Factoryville) r 67, resident.
Reed Eugene N., (North Barton) r 11, farmer.
Rezeau Henry G., (Waverly) r 62½, horse trainer and farmer.
Rezeau Joseph O., (Waverly) r 62½, farmer 60.
Rhodes Isaac, (Factoryville) carpenter, h 517 Chemung.
Richards Horace, (Waverly) r 57, school trustee, and farmer 100.
Rinker Frank, (Lockwood) r 29, farm laborer.
Robinson Frederick, (Factoryville) emp. Novelty Works, bds. Owego.
Robinson Leroy E., (Factoryville) teaming, h Owego.
Rockwell Charles M., (Factoryville) laborer, h Chemung.
Rolls Hosea H., (Waverly) r 64, farmer.
Root Frank L., (Halsey Valley) r 5, farmer 31.
Root Lester, (Halsey Valley) r 9, prop. bowling alley and pool-room.
Root Ransom R., shoemaker, Main, h North.
Ross Horace, (Lockwood) sawyer, bds. Main.
Ross John B., (Lockwood) lumberman.
Sabins Luther, (Factoryville) laborer, h Main.
Sager James, (Waverly) r 43, farmer 37.
Sager Marcus B., (Waverly) r 43, farmer 50.
Sager Philander A., (Halsey Valley) r 21, farmer.
Sager Simon, (Halsey Valley) r 25, farmer.
Salmon Franklin J., Rev., pastor Baptist church.
Saunders Charlotte, (Factoryville) r 69, widow Nathan, farm 50.
Saunders Mary W., (Factoryville) r 65, farm 83.
Saunders Nancy J., (Factoryville) r 65, resident.
Sawyer Moses E., (Factoryville) farmer, h Main.
Sawyer William A., (Factoryville) emp. Sayre shops, h Main.
SCHUYLER & HARDING, (Factoryville) props. Cayuta creamery, near
    depot.
Schuyler Ann, (Waverly) r 34, widow Philip C., farm.
Schuyler Arminda, (Lockwood) off r 47, resident.
SCHUYLER FORT A., (Factoryville) (Schuyler & Harding) highway com-
    missioner, and farmer 300, h Main.
Schuyler John, (Lockwood) r 48, farmer, leases of J. Bogart 40.
Schuyler Norman, (Waverly) r 27½, farmer.
Schuyler Speer, (Halsey Valley) r 19, farmer.
Scott Mary, (Factoryville) r 65, widow Levi, house-keeper.
Scutt Horace, (Halsey Valley) r 21, farmer.
Seaman George, (Reniff) r 1, laborer.
Searles Cornelius, (Waverly) r 57, farmer 57.

Searles J. Nicholas, (Factoryville) r 68, sawyer.
Searles Truman, (Lockwood) farm laborer.
Searles Emanuel, (Factoryville) r 18, farmer 60.
Severn Lemuel, (North Barton) r 14, farmer 50.
Shackelton John, farmer 350, and in Illinois 200.
Shadrick Henry, (Halsey Valley) r 9, farmer.
Shahan Patrick, (Waverly) R. R. section foreman, h Broad.
Shahan Patrick, Jr., (Waverly) machinist, bds. Broad, E. Waverly.
Sharp Frederick, retired, h Railroad.
Shelp Mahala, (Factoryville) r 60, widow Freeman, farm 25.
Shepard Joseph, (Factoryville) resident, bds. Main.
Sherman James, (Waverly) r 64, mason.
Sherman J. Gideon, (Factoryville) r 52, farmer on shares with James Swart-
    wood 72.
Sherman John H., (Waverly) r 64, mason.
Sherman John S., (Factoryville) r 65, farmer, leases 160.
Sherman S. Melinda, (Waverly) r 64, widow James W., resident.
Sherman Stephen, (Factoryville) r 52, retired.
Shipman Harvey D., (Waverly) r 18, school trustee, and farmer 100.
SHIPMAN PERLIE E., (Waverly) r 4, dressmaker.
Shipman Philip H., r 54, farmer 30.
SHIPMAN RUFUS T., (Waverly) r 43, apiarist 20 swarms and farmer 50.
Shipman Shaler B., (North Barton) r 34, farmer 130.
Shoemaker Aaron, r 41, farmer.
Shoemaker Henry, r 35, farmer 60.
Shoemaker Peggy A., (Factoryville) widow Daniel, resident, bds. Main.
Shores Elizabeth Mrs., (Waverly) resident, bds. Orchard.
Shorter Harriet, (Halsey Valley) r 22, widow Albert, resident.
Simons Charlotte W., (Waverly) r 47, widow Thomas, resident.
Skillings Giles, (Halsey Valley) r 9, carpenter.
Skillings James, L., (Halsey Valley) r 9, laborer.
SLITER JAMES M., (Waverly) r 49, farmer 128.   Farm for sale.
Sliter J. Watson, (Factoryville) laborer, h Orchard.
Sliter Nicholas, (Factoryville) retired, bds. Orchard.
Sliter Phoebe, Mrs. (Factoryville) resident, bds. Orchard.
Sliter Warren, (Factoryville) painter, h Orchard.
Slutzer Louis, (Factoryville) track hand, bds. Jackson House.
Sly Jeffrey A., (Waverly) r 49, farmer 75.
Smith Asa M., (Factoryville) brakeman, h Spring.
Smith Charles B., (Waverly) r 64, retired.
Smith Charles G., (Waverly) r 49½, farmer.
Smith Daniel, (Waverly) r 44, farmer.
Smith Deborah A., (Factoryville) widow Joseph, resident, h Main.
Smith Emily, (Halsey Valley) r 9, widow David.
Smith Emmet W., (Waverly) r 60, emp. Novelty Works.
Smith Freeman D., (Waverly) r 50, farmer 15.
Smith George J., (Waverly) r 49½, resident.
Smith Hannah, (Factoryville) r 47, widow Jesse, resident.
Smith Hester, (Lockwood) r 28. widow Charles, farm 50.
SMITH JAMES H., (Factoryville) telegraph operator, bds. Spring.
Smith John, Jr., (North Barton) r 17, farmer 82.
Smith Lorenzo, (Waverly) r 49, farmer, leases of Mrs. Mary C. La Mont 120.
Smith Phoebe, (Waverly) r 50, widow Benjamin, resident.

SMITH RUSHTON, (Waverly) r 64, civil engineer and farmer 50.
Smith William E., (Waverly) r 49½, farmer on shares with G. Graff 130.
Solomon George, (Waverly) r 49, farmer 90.
SOLOMON JOHN V., (Waverly) r 69, carpenter and farmer 15.
Soper Will, (Lockwood) off r 48, farmer.
Southwick Warren, (Halsey Valley) r 20, farmer.
Spear Barney B., (Lockwood) r 46, farmer on shares with J. T. Sawyer 130.
Spear Samuel (North Barton) r 14, farmer on shares with Shubel Brown 100.
Squires Frederick S., (Factoryville) emp. Novelty Works, h Orchard.
Squires James P., (Factoryville) r 60, farmer 50.
Squires Miles E., (Factoryville) resident, h Orchard.
Squires Molbrow H., (Waverly) farmer.
Stalker Albert, (Factoryville) clerk h Main.
Stanton Mary E., (Factoryville) widow Simon, laundress, h Main.
Stebbins O. Harrison, (North Barton) r 17, farmer 50.
Stebbins William H., (Factoryville) driver, h 545 Chemung.
Stevens Allen, (Factoryville) blacksmith, h Main.
Stevens Samuel, (Lockwood) r 46, groceries and meat-market.
Stever James H., (Waverly) r 62, carpenter.
Stever Jeremiah A., (Lockwood) r 46, head sawyer Bingham's mills.
Steward Adam, (Lockwood) r 45, farmer 9,
Steward Catharine, r 39, widow William, resident.
Steward Horace A., (Waverly) r 69, farmer.
Stewart Augustus, (Halsey Valley) r 21, farmer.
Stewart Edgar S., (Factoryville) r 69, emp. Novelty Works.
Stewart Harriet, (Factoryville) widow George H., resident, bds. Main.
Stewart Jane A., (Waverly) r 18, resident.
Stewart Thomas E., (Factoryville) r 60, farm laborer.
Struble John, (Waverly) r 48½, farmer.
Stuart Cornelius C., (Lockwood) laborer.
Stuart Will E., painter, Main, h do.
Sutherland Edward J., (Factoryville) tinsmith, bds. Ithaca.
Sutherland Thomas, (Factoryville) stationary engineer, h Ithaca.
Swain Mary J., (Factoryville) r 60, widow Jacob, resident.
Swarthout Charles B., (Factoryville) carpenter, h Chemung.
Swartwood Darius E., r 41, emp. Sayre shops, and farmer 61.
Swartwood Ezekiel, r 53, farmer 6.
Swartwood James, r 53, retired.
Swartwood John P., r 67, farmer 120
Swartwood Mary Miss, r 53, resident.
Swartwood Parthema Miss, r 53, resident.
Swartwood William, r 41, retired.
Talcott Oscar, (Halsey Valley) r 25, farmer.
Taylor Chester, (Halsey Valley) r 9, laborer.
Taylor Daniel, (Halsey Valley) r 6 farmer.
Taylor Edwin, (Halsey Valley) r 6, farmer.
Taylor Elizabeth, (Halsey Valley) r 5, widow Eli, farm 100.
Taylor George, (Halsey Valley) r 9, farmer 24.
Taylor Orin, (Halsey Valley) r 6, farmer.
Temperance Hotel, (M. Forman, prop.) Main.
Terry William R., (Waverly) r 64, book agent.
Thayer Mary E. Mrs., (Factoryville) r 59, resident.
Thayer William, (Factoryville) r 65 farmer.

Thomas Aaron, (Lockwood) r 46, emp. Bingham's mills.
Thomas Charles, (Factoryville) emp. Pipe Works, bds. Jackson House.
Thomas George D., (Lockwood) r 46, fireman.
THOMAS HALLOWAY W., (Waverly) insurance, h Main, E. Waverly.
Thomas Lucy, (Factoryville) widow James, h Orchard.
Thrall C. Adelbert, (Lockwood) r 2, school trustee and farmer 100.
Thrall Sarah, (Waverly) r 49, widow Charles, resident.
Tilbery Edgar, r 39, farmer 72.
Tompkins Mary A., (Factoryville) widow Charles, dressmaker, h Ithaca.
Tompkins Samuel W., r 54½, farmer on shares with Elizabeth Coleman's estate 160.
Tooker Frederick D., (Factoryville) prop. Central House.
Tozer Almerin, (Factoryville) resident, h Ithaca.
Tozer Alonzo, (Waverly) r 60, farmer.
Tozer Edward A., (Waverly) r 60. farmer 47.
Tozer Harry H., (Waverly) r 60, farm laborer.
Tozer Henry, (Waverly) r 60, farmer 100.
Tozer James, (Lockwood) r 16, farmer.
Tozer Mary A., (Lockwood) r 16, widow William, farm 40.
Tubbs Irving D., (Lockwood) r 29, farmer on shares with A. Ackley 100.
Turnbull James, (Factoryville) moulder, bds. Central House.
Tuthill James N., (Factoryville) r 69, farmer.
Tuthill William L., (Waverly) r 62, farmer 150.
VAIL A. V. C. & CO., (G. D. Brock) (Lockwood) saw and planing mill and general merchandise, Main.
Vail A. V. C., (Lockwood) (A. V. C. Vail & Co.) farmer 350, residence in Waverly.
VanAtta ——, (Factoryville) r 60, gardener.
VanAtta Benjamin, farm laborer, h Spencer.
VanAtta Fanny J., r 52, widow Peter, resident.
VAN ATTA OSCAR H., r 52, master Tioga County Pomona Grange, district clerk, and farmer 75.
VAN BUREN EUGENE L., (Lockwood) r 46, farmer 75.
VanBuren Lorenzo, (Lockwood) r 1, farm laborer.
VanCleft Wells W., (Waverly) r 62, laborer.
VanDermark Frederick, (Factoryville) r 60, farmer on shares with William Shepard estate.
VanEtten Alfred, (North Barton) r 4, farmer.
VanEtten Elisha, (Halsey Valley) r 25, farmer.
VanEtten Richard, (Halsey Valley) r 26, farmer.
VanHorn Charles, (Waverly) r 57, farm laborer.
VanLuvin Alison, (Halsey Valley) r 5, farmer 46.
VanMarter F. Wesley, (Halsey Valley) r 12, farmer 65.
VanRiper ——, (Factoryville) r 65, farmer on shares with Mary Saunders 80.
VanTyle Arthur, (Lockwood) retired, bds. Main.
VanVleet Theodore, (Halsey Valley) r 5, farmer.
Varner John H., (Waverly) emp. freight yard, h Main, E. Waverly.
Vasbinder Harrison, (Halsey Valley) r 10, farmer.
Vasbinder James H., (Halsey Valley) r 9, resident.
Vastbinder Lewis, (Halsey Valley) r 8, farmer.
Vosburgh Everett, (Halsey Valley) r 9, farmer.
Vosburgh Henry P., (Halsey Valley) r 9, physician and surgeon.
Wakefield Martha M., (Factoryville) resident, bds. Ithaca.

Walden John N., (Halsey Valley) r 12, farmer 50.
Walden Leander, (Waverly) emp. Steam mill, h Orchard.
Walden Theodore, (Factoryville) r 69, farmer on shares with S. Ellis 135.
Walden Thomas, (Waverly) r 49, farmer 25.
Walker Edward H., (Waverly) farmer.
Walker Emmet, (Waverly) r 62, farmer 170.
WALKER LEANDER, (Waverly) r 62, grocery, Broad.
Walker Loren A., (Waverly) r 60, apiarist 40 swarms, and farmer 33.
Walker Richard, (Factoryville) off r 60, laborer.
WALKER THADDEUS S., (Waverly) (T. S. Walker & Son) r 60.
Warner John A., (Waverly) r 65, milk dealer.
WASHBURN GEORGE H., (Factoryville) r 65, farmer.
Watson John F., (Factoryville) resident, h Main.
Weed Cornelius E., (Lockwood) r 32, farmer 72.
Weed William F., (Lockwood) farmer with his father Cornelius E.
Weller Erastus, (Factoryville) r 42, farmer.
Weller William S., (Factoryville) r 60, brakeman.
Wells O. Eugene, (Reniff) foreman creamery.
Welton Eugene E., (Waverly) fireman, h Orchard.
West Samuel, (Lockwood) r 45, retired.
West Wilson, (Reniff) off r 1, farmer 126.
Westbrook Henry, (North Barton) r 17, farmer.
Westfall Harry, (Factoryville) carpenter, h Main.
Westfall John V., r 55, farmer 100.
Wheeler Grant, r 34, farmer.
Wheeler H. Samuel, retired, h Main.
Wheeler Isaac R., r 66, farmer.
Wheeler Nirum, (Factoryville) r 66, farm laborer.
Wheeler Philip H., (North Barton) r 32, farmer 63.
WHITAKER LEWIS, (Factoryville) r 59, farmer 102.
Whitaker William H., (Waverly) resident, h Orchard.
Whitmarsh Ira, Jr., r 39, R. R. section hand.
Wilbur Dennison, (Halsey Valley) r 7, farmer.
Wilbur Hiram, (Halsey Valley) r 6, farmer.
Wilcox Lyman, (Factoryville) retired, h Ithaca.
Wilkinson Charles S., (Waverly) r 65, school clerk, and farmer 175.
Wilkinson C. Raymond, (Waverly) r 65, commercial traveler.
Wilkinson Joseph G., (Waverly) r 68, retired.
Williams Alanson C. (Reniff) r 1, farmer 60.
Williams Justus A., (North Barton) r 28, farmer 10.
Williams Lucinda, (North Barton) r 17, widow Sylvester H., farm 46.
Williams Mastin, (Lockwood) r 28, farmer 40.
Williams Moses S., (Reniff) r 1, farmer on shares with Joseph Bogart.
Williams Winton T., (Waverly) r 47, farmer 70.
Willis Frank, (Lockwood) r 16, farm laborer.
Willis William, r 39, farmer 150.
Wood Eunice A., (Factoryville) widow Oliver P., resident, h Main.
WOOD JAMES C., (Factoryville) general merchant, also deputy post-master, Main, h do.
Woodard Henry, (Waverly) off r 62, farmer, leases of James Benley 100.
Worrick David A., (North Barton) r 17, farmer 50.
Worster Simon, (Factoryville) emp. Novelty Works, h Owego.

Wright & Cary, (C. E. W. and W. E. C.) general merchants, Main.
Wright Charles E., (Wright & Cary) h Main.
Wright Miama, (Factoryville) r 59, widow Sylvenus, farm 40.
Yaple Amos S., r 39, carpenter.
Yaple Peter, r 57, farm laborer.
Yates Emily, (Factoryville) widow Thomas, resident.
Yates Jerome N., (Factoryville) mail carrier, bds. Main.
Yates Thomas P., (Factoryville) lumberman and farmer.

BERKSHIRE.

(For explanations, etc., see page 3, part second.)

(Postoffice address is Berkshire, unless otherwise designated in parenthesis.)

Akins Caroline P., r 21, widow Stephen, farm 140.
Akins Henry S., (Speedville, Tomp. Co.) r 18, saw and planing-mill, cheese-box factory, cider-mill, wood turner and manuf. potato crates.
Akins John P., r 21, farmer, works for Caroline P., 140.
Andrews Asa, r 3, farmer, leases of Walter Jewett 190.
Bailey Isaac B., r 28, sawyer.
Baker Clarence A., r 5, farmer, leases of Talcott Leonard 154.
Baker George W., r 11½, farmer.
Ball Asa, r 24, farmer 150.
Ball Caroline, widow of Anson, h Main.
Ball George P., produce buyer.
Ball Hannah E., widow of Alvah M., resident, h Main.
Ball John, prop. saw-mill and farmer 40.
Ball Robert H., farmer 140, h Main.
Ball Stephen L., farmer 88.
Ballard James O., (Ketchumville) r 28, farmer 39.
Ballou Alden, off r 23, farmer.
Ballou Nelson A., r 36, farmer 71.
Ballou Reuben, off r 23, farmer 97.
Bancroft William H., (Ketchumville) r 32, farmer 59.
Barr George A., farmer 50, h Glen.
Bates Otis L., r 10, farmer 75.
Bates Spencer, r 10, farmer.
Beebe Herman P., r 9, laborer.
Beebe Philo E., r 9, farmer 75.
Bennett Lucius M., laborer, h Glen.
Benton Charles W., r 17, manuf. of axe-helves, and farmer 45.
Benton Thomas J., r 17, painter and farmer.
BERKSHIRE FLOURING MILLS, Leet & Hollenbeck, proprs.
BERKSHIRE HOUSE, (Ira Crawford, prop.) livery connected.
Bidwell Elizabeth M., widow Hiram H., resident, h Main.
Bidwell Roxey A., widow Samuel C., resident, h Main.

BLACKMAN ABRAM, dealer in live stock, and farmer 160, h Main.
Borthwick Joseph, (Jenksville) r 19, farmer 81.
Boyer Stephen H., (Speedsville, Tomp. Co.) r 18, farmer 400.
BRAINARD CHARLES E., r 27 cor. 26, dealer in the Deering mower, reaper and binder, wheel rakes, spring tooth harrows, sulky and land plows, wagons and carriages, also agent for arctic creamery, and farmer 220.
Briggs Thomas, r 38, laborer.
Brookins Charles E., (Ketchumville) r 33, laborer.
Brown Abraham, carpenter, and farmer with James Cumming 50, h Main.
Brown Edwin B., r 38, farmer.
Brown Frances C., r 38, farm 80.
Brown Myron, r 38, carpenter, and farmer 12.
Brown Robert C , r 38, breeder of horses, and farmer 130.
Brown Romeo W., r 38, laborer.
BUFFINGTON CALVIN A., general blacksmith, manuf. of carriages, beam knives, mill-stone picks, etc., Railroad h Main.
Bunnell Eddie E., r 9, farmer 60.
Bunnell Henry J., (Center Lisle) r 29, resident.
Bunnell John G., (Center Lisle) r 29, farmer 125.
Bunnell Nancy A., r 9, widow Charles A., farmer 63.
Burgess Joseph, r 23, painter, and farmer 6.
Bush Marcene, r 38, farmer 80, and leases of F. C. Brown 40.
Bushnell William, (Wilson Creek) r 34, laborer.
Bushnell William B., flour, feed, coal, salt, and fertilizers, Depot, and in Newark Valley, farm 50.
Cady Gershom, (Ketchumville) r 31, laborer.
Carmer Charles, off r 29, farmer 25.
Chappins Mark, Jr., r 21, farmer, leases of Mark Chappins, of Sheldrake, N. Y., 130.
Church Elijah C., r 30, farmer 48.
CHURCH ORRIS, r 29, stone mason, carpenter, and farmer 9, served in Co. E 76th Regt., N. Y. Vols.
Christler William, (Wilson Creek) r 35, farmer.
Clark Gershom W., (Ketchumville) r 28, farmer 125.
Clark Horatio, general merchant, and deputy post-master, Main, cor. Depot, h do.
Clark Sanford H., r 36, apiarist, and farmer 70.
Clark Silas H., r 36, laborer.
Coats Charles, r 27, farmer 105.
Coats Joseph, r 27, farmer 3.
Cole James E., (Jenksville) r 19, farmer, leases of L. Maria Keeny, of Dryden, 227.
Cole Leslie, r 11½, laborer.
Collins Ambrose H., farmer 15, h Main.
COLLINS JUNIUS, wool and produce dealer, real estate agent for lands in Nebraska, also associate justice and justice of peace, h Main.
Comstock George S., (Speedsville, Tomp. Co.) r 18, teacher.
Cortright Henry, r 28, farmer 30.
CORTRIGHT JOHN, (Maine, Broome Co.) farmer, leases of Henry Van-Tyle, of Maine, 66.
Cortright William, r 14, laborer.
Costillo John, r 6, leather roller.

Courtright Darius, (Wilson Creek) r 28, farmer 95.

Crapo Richard, (Ketchumville) r 28, laborer.

Crawford Eugene, farmer, leases of Ira Crawford, h Main.

CRAWFORD IRA, prop. of Berkshire Hotel and livery, also farmer 370, and in Harford, Cortland Co., 50.

Crawford Ira O., sawyer and carpenter, h Main.

Crawford James H., carpenter, h East.

Croft Harry, emp. hub factory, bds. Glen.

Cross James O., merchant tailor, Main.

CROSS LOUIS J., house and carriage painter, paper-hanging and decorating, also breeder of Clay horses ; breaking colts a speciaity, h Mechanic.

CROSS SARAH B., (wife of Louis J.) all kinds of upholstering, h Mechanic.

Cullen Miles, r 6, emp. tannery.

Cummings James, retired farmer, h Glen.

Curtis A. V., widow Mark, h Main.

DALE JOHN, r 38, farmer 38.

Darbonnier Stephen, (Dewey & Darbonnier) h Elm.

DAVIDGE, HORTON & CO., (Mrs. E. Davidge, Lucien Horton and James Davidge) r 6, props. Berkshire tannery, and manufrs. of hemlock sole leather, also farmers 150.

DAVIDGE JAMES, r 6, (Davidge, Horton & Co., and Davidge, Landfield & Co., of Newark Valley).

Decker Gideon, r 11, resident.

Dermody Michael, emp. tannery, h Main.

DEWEY & DARBONNIER, (Chas. J. D., and Stephen D.) dealers in dry-goods, groceries, hardware, boots and shoes, clothing, &c., also farmers 12, Main.

DEWEY CHARLES J., (Dewey & Darbonnier) also justice of peace, h Main.

Dewey Dwight W., teacher, bds. Main.

Doney John J., r 30, laborer.

Doney William H., r 30, farmer 48.

Dorwin Charles H., r 6, book-keeper, and farmer 4.

Eastman Charles, r 13, farmer.

Eastman Leonard O., county school commissioner, and medical student, office in Court House, Owego, and at residence in Berkshire.

Eastman Nancy W., widow George W., resident, h Main.

EASTMAN RALPH D., physician and surgeon, farm 132, h Main.

Edwards Charles M., (Ketchumville) r 28, laborer.

Edwards Merritt P., (Ketchumville) r 28, farmer 50.

Eldred M. F., r 6, laborer.

ELDRIDGE EDWARD O., (E. O. E. & Co.) notary public, h Main.

ELDRIDGE E. O. & CO., (Edward O. Eldridge and Mrs. Caroline Johnson) dealers in dry goods, groceries, and general merchandise, Main.

Eldridge Mary S., widow of Edward H., resident.

Ellis William, teamster, h Railroad.

Ellis William, (Speedsville, Tomp. Co.) r 18, laborer.

Eston Elmer, (Ketchumville) r 31, farmer, leases of R. T. Gates, of North Lancing, 107.

Evans Irving W., r 28, farmer 83.

Evans John J., (Ketchumville) r 33, farmer, leases of Marion Rich, of Newark Valley, 60.

Evans Mary H., (Jenksville) r 19 cor. 41, widow of Joel, farm 7.

Evans William S., (Jenksville) r 19 cor. 41, farmer.
Everett Henry C., r 9, farmer 145.
Fitch Arthur, (Wilson Creek) off r 28, laborer.
FORD ARTHUR J., r 15 cor. 17, farmer 104.
FORD GEORGE, r 22, carpenter, and farmer 55.
FORD JOHN R., postmaster and farmer 171, h Elm.
FORD MARCUS J., r 16, farmer 119 and leases of James Baird of Speedsville 200.
Ford Sarah W., r 3, widow Lebbeus, resident.
FORD WILLIAM W., r 3, dairy 10 cows, farmer 117.
Foster Amos, r 11, farmer.
Foster John L., r 11, farmer, leases of Ira Crawford 165.
Freeland Lewis A., (Newark Valley) r 40, farmer 115.
Gay Isaac W., physician and surgeon, farmer 90, h Main.
Gilbert Marvin C., r 14, laborer.
Gilbert Marvin C., Jr., r 14, farmer 14.
Goldstein Brothers, (Jacob & Samuel) clothing and gents' furnishing goods.
Gould Joel, (Ketchumville) r 28, farmer 137.
Griner John N., restaurant, Depot.
HAIGHT EDITH J., art teacher, h Glen.
Haight Mary, widow Samuel F., farm 25, h Glen.
Hamilton Elliott, r 6, boarding-house.
Hamilton Susanna, r 8, widow Charles, resident.
Hart Arthur L., (Speedsville, Tomp. Co.) r 18, carpenter and farmer.
Hart Colden N., (Wilson Creek) r 34, postmaster, also dealer in cigars and tobacco.
Hart Samuel L., (Speedsville, Tomp. Co.) r 18, prop. grist-mill, also carpenter and farmer 7.
HART SARAH E., (Speedsville, Tomp. Co.) r 18, wife of Samuel L., cloth and carpet weaving.
Hart Selim M., (Speedsville, Tomp. Co.) r 18, carpenter and cabinet maker.
Hartwell Levi, r 29, farmer 50.
Hartwell Willard R., (Ketchumville) r 28, farmer 105.
Harvey Andrew J., (Wilson Creek) r 36, farmer 47.
Harvey Martin V., (Wilson Creek) farmer 140.
HAY HENRY L., painter, h Railroad.
Hay Van Rensselaer, r 11, farmer.
Hayden John, (Speedsville, Tomp. Co.) r 17, farmer 78.
HAYDEN PATSEY W., carpenter and builder, h Glen.
Higgins & Rounsevell, (Speedsville, Tomp. Co.) (John H. & George B. R.) r 18, props. Speedsville creamery and cheese factory.
Higgins John, (Speedsville, Tomp. Co.) (Higgins & Rounsevell) r 18, agricultural implements and farmer 75.
Hill T. James, emp. Berkshire Hotel, Main.
Hillsinger Charles, r 26, farmer 50.
Hillsinger William, r 26, laborer.
Hinds Robert, emp. tannery, h Main.
Hitchcock Caroline, resident, Elm.
HOLCOMB J. WALLACE, dealer in drugs, patent medicine, groceries, paints and oils, etc.
Holland Frank, r 9, farmer 30.
Holland James J., (Wilson Creek) r 11, farmer 21.
HOLLENBECK J. ERVING, (Leet & Hollenbeck).

HORTON LUCIEN, (Davidge, Horton & Co., and Davidge, Landfield & Co., of Newark Valley, also Sherwood & Horton) r 6.

Hough Rev. Joel J., pastor of Congregational Church.

Houghtaling Burt, carriage maker, millwright and wood turner, Mechanic bds. Main.

HOUGHTALING WILLIAM M., wagon-maker and repairing, h Main.

Houk Daniel, (Wilson Creek) r 35, shoemaker, apiarist and farmer 8.

Howland Fred E., r 24, laborer.

Howland George E., r 24, laborer.

Howland Harper, resident, Main.

Hubbard Howard M., r 20, carpenter and farmer, leases of J. R. Ford 112, Served in Co. B, 109th N. Y. State Vol.

Humphrey Erastus E., (Speedsville, Tomp. Co.) r 19 cor. 17, wagon maker and farmer 10.

HUTCHINSON ORRIN, (Wilson Creek) r 34, dairy 25 cows, farmer 190.

Japhet Elijah, r 28, farmer 31.

Japhet George W., r 9, dairy 7 cows, and farmer 95.

Japhet Gilbert L., r 9, farmer.

JAPHET MILO G., prop. saw-mill and novelty works, also dealer in lumber, lath, shingles, etc., Railroad.

JENKS NATHANIEL J., (Jenksville) r 42, dairy 20 cows, and farmer 157.

Jewett Asahel, r 3, dairy 15 cows, and farmer 220.

JEWETT WALTER, (Speedsville, Tomp. Co.) r 3 cor. 1, supervisor 12th term, dairy 20 cows, and farmer 420.

JOHNSON CAROLINE, (E. O. Eldridge & Co.) widow Carlisle P., h Main.

Johnson Edward, r 6, leather roller.

Johnson Eugene F., r 6, fire, life and accident insurance, sugar orchard 300 trees, and farmer 220.

Johnson Frank H., retired, bds. Main.

Johnson Frederick C., r 6, clerk.

Johnson William C., (Ketchumville) r 28, laborer.

Judd John N., r 6, dealer in harnesses, carriages, sleighs and agricultural imp., also farmer 107.

Keeny Willoughby L., (Speedsville, Tomp. Co.) r 17, farmer 120.

Kenyon William H., (Wilson Creek) r 34, farmer 50 in Maine, Broome Co.

Keyes Benjamin I., r 6, farmer, leases of George Royce.

Keyser Henry, r 15, farmer 100.

Kimball & Stannard, (Connecticut) (John F. K. and Lorenzo J. S.) r 35, stationary steam threshing machine, horse breeders, and farmers 197, and in Newark 110.

Kingsbery Henry, r 14, farmer 20.

Lacy Thomas, r 11, farmer 62½.

Lamb Lewis W., r 14, laborer.

Lee Frank L., r 27, farmer.

LEET & HOLLENBECK, (T. E. L. and J. E. H.) props. Berkshire Flouring mills, and dealers in flour, meal, feed and bran, near Depot.

LEET FRANK E. (Leet & Hollenbeck.)

LEGG ERASMUS D., (Speedsville, Tomp. Co.) r 18, breeder of English hurdle race horses, and coach horses, Holstein cattle and Hampshire sheep, dairy 15 cows, and farmer 220, sugar orchard 1,000 trees.

Legg George W., (Speedsville, Tomp. Co.) r 18, farmer.

Legg Layton J., (Jenksville) off r 41, farmer 110.

Legg Louis P., retired farmer, h Main.

4

Legg Reuben T., (Speedsville, Tomp. Co.) r 18, carp. and cabinet maker.
Leonard Charles Talcott, r 6, dairy 15 cows, and farmer 260.
Leonard Eunice C., r 14, widow George F., resident, farm with Ransom 168.
Leonard Henry G., retired tanner, h Elm.
LEONARD J. WALDO, farmer 180, h Elm.
Leonard Ransom, r 14, farmer with Eunice C. 168.
Lynch Albert C., farmer, h Main.
Lynch Charles O., r 24, deputy sheriff.
Lynch Eugene F., dealer in produce, and farmer 200.
Lynch George W., clerk, h Main.
Lynch Theodore, dealer in beef and live stock, also farmer 165, h Main.
Manning Alexander D., dealer in butter and eggs, h Main.
Manning Arthur B., r 24, farmer 10.
Manning Charles S., r 24, farmer 140.
Marshall George, r 3, laborer.
Maynard George, (Speedsville, Tomp. Co.) r 18, farmer, leases of John Cross
    of Speedsville 90.
MAYOR CHARLES, (Theodore & Son) r 38 cor. 39.
MAYOR THEODORE & SON, (Theo & Charles) r 38 cor. 39, breeders
    and dealers in Holstein cattle, dairy 16 cows, and farmers 136, sugar or-
    chard 300.
McCoy Oliver A., (Speedsville, Tomp. Co.) r 18, carpenter.
McMahon James, r 5, farmer 41.
McMahon Patrick, r 5, jarmer 40.
Meeks Edmund, (Speedsville, Tomp. Co.) r 18, farmer 105.
Merithew Edgar A.,(Connecticut) r 35,farmer, leases of Norman A. Prentice 68.
Myre Frank, r 6, laborer.
Nicholson Charles, r 36, farmer, leases of Robert E. Waldo 106.
Noiton Benjamin, (Ketchumville) r 28, farmer 50.
Northrup Frank L., (Speedsville, Tomp. Co.) r 18, carpenter and painter.
Northrup George W., (Speedsville, Tomp. Co.) r 18, retired physician.
Oaks Jerome, (Ketchumville) r 28, agt. mowers and reapers, and farmer 136.
Oliver Peter, (Speedsville, Tomp. Co.) r 19, farmer.
Olney Marvin M., emp. hub factory, served in Co. E. 76th N. Y. Vols., and
    Co. F. 5th N. Y. Cavalry, h Main.
Owen Jay, (Speedsville, Tomp. Co.) (M. A. & Bros.) r 18.
Owen M. A. & Brothers, (Speedsville, Tomp. Co.) (Mc A. and Jay) r 18,
    manuf. tubs, firkins and barrels.
Owen Mc A., (Speedsville, Tomp. Co.) (M. A. & Bro.) r 18.
Orton James, r 30, farmer 38.
Overacker John M., r 3, laborer.
Parke Anson, (Jenksville) r 42, laborer.
Palmer Robert, r 6, laborer.
Parsons George, r 26, dairy 50 cows, and farmer 750.
Parsons Jemima, widow Chauncey, resident, h Glen.
Parsons William C., (Ketchumville) r 33, farmer, leases of W. H. Jackson of
    Newark Valley 140.
PATCH EVELINE L., r 39, widow William J., administratrix of estate of
    William J., farm 230, and in Richford 210.
PATCH HENRY W., r 39, dealer in horses, and farmer, works the estate
    of William J. Patch 230, dairy 14 cows, sugar orchard 200, wool grower
    35 head.

Patch Robert C., telegraph operator, bds. Main.
Payne Charles H., laborer, h Railroad.
Payne Frederick H., r 24, postal clerk, and farmer 100.
Payne Henry A., carpenter, and farmer 250, h Main.
Phillips Elias M., r 38, farmer, leases of J. Watrous, of Cortland, 140.
Phillips Sophia L., (Speedsville, Tomp. Co.) r 18, widow of Asa E., resident.
Pierce John, (Ketchumville) r 28, farmer 30.
Pierce Sylvester, (Ketchumville) r 28, farmer 80.
Pittsley Clarence A., r 14, laborer.
Pittsley Oscar, r 26, laborer.
Pittsley Sewel, r 14, laborer.
POLLEY HIRAM, manuf. and dealer in harnesses, whips, robes and blankets, Main, h do.
PRATT MARSHALL D., carriage-maker, veterinary surgeon, and constable, h West.
Prentice Austin H., (Connecticut) r 32, dairy 14 cows, and farmer 47 in Newark Valley, and leases of George Walter 92.
Prentice Irving B., (Newark Valley) r 40, farmer 97.
PRENTICE NORMAN A., dealer in fresh and salt meats, fish, oysters, clams, poultry and veal calves, also farmer 68, Main, h do.
Prentice Will E., (Newark Valley) r 40, farmer 112.
Preston Jay R., (Jenksville) r 41, farmer, leases of Abram Blackman.
Quinliran Edward, r 6, emp. tannery.
Rightmire Elizabeth, widow William H., farm 30, h Glen.
Rightmire Nathan, r 3, farmer 140.
Rightmire Squire, retired carpenter, h Glen.
Rightmire William P., r 6, foreman tannery.
Roberts William D., r 7, farmer, leases of E. R. Adams, of Nanticoke, 200.
Robinson Frank G., r 3, farmer with Newell 180, dairy 19 cows.
Robinson Newell, r 3, farmer with Frank G. 180, dairy 19 cows.
ROCKEFELLER CHARLES H., barber and hair-dresser, livery stable and constable, Main.
Rockwell Frank, r 15, farmer, leases of H. A. Payne 209.
ROCKWELL PETER, r 36, farmer 130.
Rockwood James W., r 38, farmer 10.
Rounsevell George B., (Speedsville, Tomp. Co.) (Higgins & R.) r 18.
ROYCE AMELIA B., wife of George C., farmer 120, h Main.
Royce Frederick B., r 6, dairy 10 cows, farmer 141.
ROYCE GEORGE C., breeder and dealer in Clay horses, prop. stock horse Good Luck Clay, and farmer 120, h Main.
Royce John B., r 6, retired farmer 60, aged 92.
Sargent Orrin, (Wilson Creek) r 33, farmer 45.
Sargent Silas, (Wilson Creek) r 33, farmer.
Scott Charles & Edmund F., r 22 cor. 41, apiarists, 65 to 100 colonies, egg and poultry raising, dairy 15 cows, 70 sheep, sugar orchard 300 trees, and farmers 247.
Scudder George D., teamster, Main.
Seamans Samuel M., general blacksmith, Main.
Sears Quincy A., r 38, farmer 25.
Shaff James H., r 30, farmer 90.
Shaff John D., r 9, dairy 16 cows, farmer 125.
Shaff Joseph, r 9, farmer 5.

Shaff William H., r 11, farmer 100.

Shaw William F., r 5, farmer, son of William T.

SHAW WILLIAM T., r 5, breeder of short-horn cattle, dairy 30 cows, 20 head young stock and farmer 265.

Shepard C. Burton, r 28, farmer 50.

Shepard James, r 3, apiarist, breeder of horses and farmer 100.

Shepard John, r 29 1-2, farmer 140.

Sherman Edward A., (Ketchumville) r 33, farmer 105.

Sherman James W., (Wilson Creek) r 27, carpenter, dairy 10 cows, sugar orchard 200 trees and farmer 72.

SHERWOOD & HORTON, (H. G. S. & C. S. H. of English Center, Pa.) manuf. of wagon hubs, opp. Depot.

SIMMONDS ALPHEUS, r 3, dairy 12 cows, farmer 135.

Simmonds Charilla, r 3, wife of Alpheus, farm 55.

Simmonds George A., r 3, farmer.

SIMMONS SYLVESTER, (Jenksville) r 41, farmer.

SIMMONS WILLIAM E., (Jenksville) r 41, dairy 12 cows, breeder of horses and farmer 133.

Skellinger Daniel J., (Speedsville, Tomp. Co.) r 3 cor. 18, cooper.

SMITH ARTHUR E., r 4, sugar orchard 200 trees, farmer 93.

Smith Edwin, farmer 50, h Elm.

Smith Emory J., stone and plaster mason, h Railroad.

Smith George M., r 3, threshing and farmer 100.

Smith Ira J., r 3, tanner.

Smith John, engineer hub factory, bds. Elm.

Smith Mary J., r 4, widow Ezekiel D., resident.

Snedaker George, r 38, tool-maker.

Snedaker John, r 38, manuf. of tanners' beam knives, mill-stone picks and edge tools, also farmer 19.

Snedaker William V., r 38, laborer.

Sparrow Frank, emp. hub factory, h Glen.

Spencer Charles D., r 11 1-2, farmer 105.

Stanton Elisha W., (Speedsville, Tomp. Co.) r 18, tin pedlar.

Stephens Andrew, r 13, farmer 30.

Summerville Grant, r 6, night watch, tannery.

Sykes George D., r 39, teacher and farmer.

Sykes Horatio W., r 39, dairy 10 cows, sugar orchard 100 trees, farmer 114.

Taylor John H., farmer, leases J. W. Leonard.

Thompson Charles, r 28, laborer.

Thompson Samuel, farm in Richford 80, h Depot.

Thorn Charles F., (Wilson Creek) r 35, farmer.

Thorn Susan M., (Wilson Creek) r 35, widow Henry M., farm 63.

Thuillard Hyppolite, r 21, dairy 11 cows, farmer 110.

Torrey Betsey B., resident, h Main.

Torrey Charles S., r 40, farmer.

Torrey John, r 40, dairy 10 cows, farmer 117.

Torrey Lewis S., r 41, farmer, leases of Lyman Baker, of Candor, 143.

Towslee Delos, r 38, farmer, leases of R. Brown 13.

Turner Luther M., (Wilson Creek) r 29, road commissioner, farmer 50.

Turner William J., r 38, laborer.

Tyler Sherman B., r 14, laborer.

WALDO ELIJAH B., (Williams & Waldo) station and express agent, also dealer in butter, eggs and poultry, h Williams.

Waldo Hannah B., widow Dr. Joseph T., resident, h Main.
Waldo Juliette, widow Dwight, h Elm.
WALDO ROBERT EMMET, r 36, dairy 12 cows, farmer 106.
Walker Erastus T., r 3, farmer 68.
Walter Joseph S., r 27 cor. 11, physician and surgeon, and farmer 200.
Watkins John F., r 9, laborer.
Wauvle James A., r 9, farmer 72.
Wavle Peter, r 29½, wool grower 47 head, dairy 18 cows, and farmer with
   J. Shepard 30.
Whitaker Charles E., (Wilson Creek) r 34, dairy 7 cows, sugar orchard 400
   trees, farmer 40; served in Co. F, 144th N. Y. Vols.
Whiting Caroline, (Speedsville, Tomp. Co.) r 18, widow Samuel, farm 80.
Whiting Frank S., (Speedsville, Tomp. Co.) r 18, blacksmith and farmer.
WILLIAMS & WALDO, (M. A. W., E. B. W. and A. B. W.) apiarists, and
   dealers in honey and bee-keepers' supplies.
Williams Eugene L., (Wilson Creek) r 27, farmer, leases of Lewis Williams 100.
Williams George, apiarist, prop. saw-mill, and farmer 190.
Williams Harvey J., r 9, farmer 50.
Williams Lewis, farmer 98, h Railroad.
WILLIAMS MORRIS A., (Williams & Waldo) dealer in potatoes, h Depot.
WINSHIP EDGAR., r 9, dairy 12 cows, farmer 100.
Winship William, r 9, farmer.
Wiswell Jerome B., (Ketchumville) r 31, farmer 60.
WITTER F. A. & CO., (Fred W. Witter) dealers in hardware, cutlery and
   household furniture, agricultural implements, also horse blankets, whips,
   shingles, etc., Main, h do.
WITTER FRANK A., (F. A. W. & Co.) h Main.
WITTER FRED W., (F. A. W. & Co.) h Main.
Wooster Asher B., r 6, stationary engineer.
Wright William F., r 8, sawyer, and farmer 94.
VanDyke Egbert, blacksmith and mechanic.
VAN GORDER CHARLES B., engineer in hub factory.
VAN GORDER GEORGE, r 38, farmer.
VanNorman Don R., bridge carpenter, h Elm.
VanNorman Fred, brakeman, h Elm.
VanSusan Clause, r 13, farmer 54.
VanSusan Diedrick, r 8, laborer.
VanSusten Diedrick, r 6, laborer.
Young Edward W., carpenter, h Main.
Young David H., (Jenksville) r 44 cor. 43, farmer.
Youngs Morris, r 29, farmer 25.
Youngs Orson R., r 27, laborer.
YOUNGS PETER, r 29, farrier, dairy 6 cows, farmer 82.

CANDOR.

(For explanations, etc., see page 3, part second.)

(Postoffice address is Candor, unless otherwise designated in parenthesis.)

Abbey William, r 112, carpenter.
Adams Gaylord W., resident, bds. Spencer.
Adkin Arcelius, r 111, laborer.
Ahart George, emp. Woolen Mills, h Preston.
Ahlers Dederick G., cooper, h Gould.
Aignor William, farmer, h Kinney.
Allen Ben, farmer, h Kinney.
Allen Ben, Jr., laborer, h Main.
Allen Frank, (West Candor) r 109, farmer 54.
Allen Frank, laborer, h off Kinney.
Allen Frank G., r 57, farmer 130.
Allen Hiram, r 57, resident.
ALLEN HOUSE, Iddo Vergason, proprietor, Main.
Allen Increase, lumberman, h Kinney.
Allen James M., r 29, carpenter and farmer 32.
Allen John J., r 99, farmer 16.
Allen Judson K., farmer 100, h Owego.
Allen Matthew K., farmer 50, h Owego.
Allen William D., r 29, carpenter and farmer 10.
ANDERSON EDWIN S., (Owego) r 126, farmer 151.
Anderson Ezra L., r 46, farmer.
Anderson George M., (Owego) r 123, farmer.
Anderson Joel, (Owego) r 123, apiarist and farmer 111.
Anderson Leroy, r 46, farmer 75.
Anderson Myron, (Catatonk) r 116, farmer 100.
ANDERSON PHILANDER, (Owego) r 123, farmer 250.
Anderson Stephen, (Catatonk) r 116, farmer 139.
Anderson Sylvenus, (Owego) r 131, farmer 75.
Anderson Truman, (Catatonk) r 115, farmer 100.
Anderson Willis, (Owego) r 124, farmer 85, and leases of Philander Anderson, 200.
Andrews Charles H., (Owego) r 117, leases of D. W. Andrews, 100.
Andrews Dana H., (Owego) r 123, farmer 25, and leases of Philetus Andrews, 212.
Andrews David W., (Owego) r 118, farmer 200.
Andrews Elmer E., (Owego) r 118, school teacher and farmer.
Andrews Frank, (Flemingville) farmer with Charles Crane, leases of John M. Grimes, 120.
ANDREWS LEVI, (Owego) r 131, farmer 175.
Andrews Thomas, (Owego) r 131, farmer 103.
Andrews William H., general merchant, Front, h do.
Andrews William R., clerk, bds. Front.
Armitage Ann E., widow Alfred, h Owego.

Armitage Claude, clerk, h Owego.
ASHLAND HOUSE, Frank J. Norton, prop., Main.
Ayers Willis, (Willseyville) r 30, carpenter.
BACON GEORGE G., r 65. music teacher, agent for mnsical instruments
fruit grower, and manuf. vinegar.
Bacon Harvey, r 116 cor. 99, farmer 10.
Bacon John G., r 65, farmer 100.
Bailey Charity M., widow William, resident, bds. Main.
Baird James L., (Speedsville, Tomp. Co.) r 18, farmer 100.
Bakeman Isaac, r 54, farmer 15.
Baker Aaron, (Caroline Center, Tomp. Co.) r 12, with William L., lumberman
and farmer 180.
Baker Jesse, r 71, farmer 30.
Baker Lyman, (Caroline Center, Tomp. Co.) r 12, farmer in Berkshire 145.
Baker William L., (Caroline Center, Tomp. Co.) r 12, with Aaron Baker
lumberman and farmer 180.
Bangs Charles E., r 90, teacher, and farmer 4.
Bangs William L., r 90, farmer 100.
Banks Alanson, (Willseyville) r 31, farmer 90.
Banks Nathan J., (Willseyville) r 31, farmer.
BARAGER CHARLES F., senator 26th district, prop. Candor Woolen
Mills, also lumber business in Chenango Co., h Main.
Barber Hiram, r 139, cooper.
Barber John J., (Willseyville) r 1, leases of John Foote 37.
Barber Washington, r 57, laborer.
Barden Robert S., r 24, carpenter, and farmer 97.
Barden William, (Strait's Corners) r 112, farmer, leases of B. Coursen 108.
Barker George, r 63, laborer.
Barnes Charles W., farmer with his father James D.
Barnes Hugh S., (Catatonk) r 130, farmer 95.
Barnes James D., lumberman, and farmer 100.
Barnes Thomas, (Catatonk) r 130, farmer 70.
Barnes William, r 104, farmer 100.
Barrett Elliott, (West Newark) r 49, farmer 250.
Barrett Justus, (Weltonville) r 82, farmer, leases of Theodore Cortright, of
Owego, 40.
Barrett Sidney A., (Strait's Corners) r 139, farmer 35.
BARRETT VAN NESS, (Jenksville) r 50, farmer 225.
BARROTT AMMIEL W., (Weltonville) r 120, dealer in live stock and farm
produce, breeder of Hambletonian and Messenger horses, farmer 120,
and leases of Abel Galpin 60.
BARROTT SAMUEL R., (Weltonville) r 82, prop. of saw and grist-mill,
and dealer in lumber, lath, meal and feed, farmer 500, also lumber yard,
and two tenements at Athens, Pa.
Barrott Simeon W., (Weltonville) r 84, farmer 190.
BARROTT VAN NESS W., (Weltonville) r 84, carpenter, and farmer, leases
of Simeon W. Barrott 75.
Barto William, (Weltonville) r 83, sawyer, and farmer 50.
Bateman Joseph, (Weltonville) r 120, laborer.
Bates James D., r 99, farmer 94.
Baylor Charles F., blacksmith, Main, h Bank.
Baylor Daniel H., blacksmith, h Kinney.

Beadle Jared J., farmer.
Beebe Abram, prop. Candor grist-mill, Main, h do.
Beebe Clark, emp. Candor grist-mill, h Ithaca.
Beeley John, (Strait's Corners) r 136, farmer, leases of J. Dougherty 52.
Beers George H., (Catatonk) r 129, farmer 52.
Belden James P., r 38, farmer 220.
Benedict Archibald W., (Willseyville) r 30, farmer.
Benton James F., (Speedville, Tomp. Co.) r 13, farmer 55.
Best David, (Catatonk) r 115, farmer 186.
Best George, (Strait's Corners) r 142, farmer 100.
Best John J., (Catatonk) r 115, farmer 22.
Best Richard, r 112, laborer.
Bishop Charles E., (Jenksville) r 49, farmer, leases of I. W. Gay, of Berkshire 90.
Bishop James, fire and life insurance, Main, h do.
Blewer Fred A., (Weltonville) r 120, farmer 50.
Blewer Levi, (Weltonville) r 84, laborer.
Blewer M. Lamont, (Weltonville) r 85, farmer 45.
Blinn Burdette, (Wilseyville) r 20, laborer.
Blinn Charles, r 56, section hand.
Blinn Eli R., (Jenksville) r 24, farmer 85.
Blinn Elmer, r 44, farmer.
Blinn Lewis, r 44, farmer 94.
Blinn Samuel E., farmer 122.
Blinn Sherman P., r 29 farmer 100.
Blinn Thomas P., r 29, farmer 60.
Blodgett Charles O., (Weltonville) r 84, farmer, leases of S. R. Barrott 230.
Blow Minard, (Weltonville) r 85, farmer, leases of Jasper Galpin, 50.
Bogardus George M., (Willseyville) r 30, farmer.
Bogert Peter, farmer 84, h Owego.
Boget William, (Strait's Corners) r 137, farmer 112.
Bolton Clarence S., blacksmith and horseshoer, Main, h do.
Bolton Lewis, emp. L. A. Hart, h Main.
Booth & Williams, (E. A. B. & E. S. W.) general merchants, Front.
Booth Brothers, (J. F. & T. S.) r 56, manufs. and dealers in lumber, and
    farmers 300.
Booth Catharine, r 37, widow of Abel H., farmer with George D., 218.
Booth Dennis, r 37, retired farmer.
Booth Edwin A., (Booth & Williams) also prest. First Nat. Bank, h Main.
BOOTH FREEMAN, r 37, farmer 206.
Booth George D., r 37, farmer with Catharine 218.
BOOTH HORACE F., fire insurance, prest. board of Education, and prop.
    Candor Iron Works, Main, h do.
Booth Jesse F., (Booth Bros.) r 56.
Booth Mary, widow Horace, h Main.
Booth Orange, r 37 cor. 57, lumberman, and farmer 250.
Booth Theron S., (Booth Bros.) r 56.
Booth Wakefield, r 37, resident.
Borthwick Alexander, (Jenksville) r 50, farmer, leases of Isaac D. Van Scoy 128.
Bortle Lawrence R., r 45, laborer.
Boyd Andrew, r 69, farmer 30.
Boyd Benjamin, r 69, farmer 30.
Braman Jesse H., stone mason, h Bank.
Braman Norton M., farmer, works for Mrs. Terwilligar 200, h Owego.

Briggs Mary L., resident, bds. Foundry.

Brink Homer A., (Weltonville) r 85, farmer 81.

Brink James S., r 70, thresher, and farmer 40.

Brink Joseph, r 54, farmer 25.

Brink Laverne, emp. W. J. Milks, bds. Spencer.

Brink Marland, (Weltonville) r 84, farmer.

Brink Philemon, (Weltonville) r 81, farmer, leases of W. B. Thomas 40.

Brink Stephen I., off r 116, laborer.

Brooks George T., contractor and builder, h Owego.

Brown Frank J., (Willseyville) r 30, farmer, leases of Wakeman Smith 215.

BROWN FRANK W., (West Candor) r 61, station and Natl. express agt., and telegraph operator.

Brown Sarah J., widow Jeremiah F., dressmaker.

Brundage Lydia, widow Emmet, h Main.

Burch L. H. Rev. rector St. Mark's Church, h Main.

Burchard Dana D., (Owego) r 131, farmer 52.

Burchard Elias, (Flemingville) r 122, farmer.

Burchard Franklin, (Flemingville) r 122, farmer.

Burchard Jason, (Flemingville) r 122, farmer.

Burchard Nelson, (Owego) r 122, farmer 100.

Burleigh Alfred, r 56, laborer.

Burleigh Eben, r 39, carpenter.

Burleigh Hezekiah, r 39, farmer 44.

Burleigh Millard F., r 39, farmer 50.

Burrows James, foreman woolen mills, h Church.

Burt George, (Catatonk) r 133, farmer 138.

Burt Lincoln C., (Catatonk) r 133, farmer with George.

Bush Abram R., (Willseyville) r 30, dealer in groceries.

Bush Elizabeth B., widow Isaac L., resident, h Owego.

Butler Orrin, (Strait's Corners) r 108, farmer 100.

Candor Humboldt Tannery, (E. S. Estey & Sons, props.) Front.

CANDOR IRON WORKS, (H. F. Booth, prop.) Foundry.

CANDOR WOOLEN MILLS, (Charles F. Barager, prop.) manuf. horse blankets, Main.

Caple Adam, r 104, teacher of vocal music, farmer 172.

Capel Edward, (Owego) off r 131, laborer.

Capel George, (Owego) r 117, laborer.

Capel John, (Owego) off r 131, farmer 50.

Caple Elgin P., r 104, farmer.

Caple Philip, (Catatonk) r 129, farmer 52.

Caple Philip J., (Catatonk) r 129, farmer 50.

Card George, (Strait's Corners) r 136, farmer.

Card Timothy, r 104, laborer.

Carl Peter, carpenter, h Owego.

Carlan William, (Catatonk) r 114, farmer 100.

Carlin James, emp. Frank L. Heath, bds. Main.

Carpenter Eliza A., r 63, widow Norman L., farm 150.

Carpenter Harry L., (Weltonville) r 84, house painting and graining.

Carpenter Orby V., blacksmith, machinist, etc., R. R. ave., h do.

CARPENTER WILLIAM L., blacksmith, machinist and wagon maker, R. R. ave., h do.

Carroll Thomas, r 95, farmer, works for Eliza Carroll 57.

Cass Frank, (Strait's Corners) r 108, farmer 48, and with William 152.

Cass Samuel, (Strait's Corners) r 108, farmer 107.
Cass William, (Strait's Corners) r 108, farmer 75, and with Frank Cass 152.
Casterline Romeo W., (Strait's Corners) r 138, general blacksmithing.
Chandler William, (Catatonk) r 127, farmer 46.
Chapman Amos C., farmer, h Owego.
Chapman Foster, (Catatonk) laborer.
Chapman George, emp. woolen mill, bds. Mountain ave.
Chapman John D., farm laborer, h Mountain ave.
Chapman Milford, emp. woolen mill, h Railroad.
Chidester Chauncey W., (Weltonville) r 120, physician and surgeon. ·
CHIDSEY GEORGE C., liveryman, h Main.
CHIDSEY JOHN R., postmaster, also dealer in hardware, stoves and peddlers' supplies, Front, h do.
Chidsey Leonard, butcher, h Owego.
Clark Alexander H., (Catatonk) r 114, farmer 126.
Clark Herbert, r 54, farmer 10.
Clarke Leroy, r 44, farmer, works for Hiram J. Clark 180.
Cleveland Charles. r 29, laborer.
Cleveland George M., (Willseyville) r 1, millwright and farmer 7.
Cleveland Joseph. r 5, laborer.
Coggin Loama I., r 139, farmer, works for Mrs. L. T. Coggin 10.
Cogswell Mary J., widow Joel, resident, h Owego.
Cole Jennie Mrs., resident, h Academy.
Cole William J., retired, h Main.
Compton Amos, (Catatonk) r 127, laborer.
COMSTOCK WILLIAM I., (Jenksville) r 20, farmer 175.
Coney Stephen, (West Candor) r 107, farmer 10.
Conklin Catherine B., widow Ephraim, resident, h Church.
Conklin Christopher, farmer, h Church.
Conklin Levi, (Speedsville, Tomp. Co.) r 21, farmer 120.
Conklin Norman, farmer, h Church.
CONNELL THOMAS J., clerk Allen House, bds. do.
Conrad George, r 7, farmer 41.
Cook Ezra S., (Weltonville) r 82, laborer.
Cook John W., (Strait's Corners) r 142, farmer 70.
Cook Joseph, r 93, laborer.
Coon Alonzo H., (Strait's Corners) r 143, threshing and farmer with William I. 112.
Coon William I., (Strait's Corners) r 143, threshing and farmer with Alonzo H. 112.
Cooper & Thornton, (West Candor) (J. H. C. & G. H. T.) r 62, cider-mill and threshing machine.
Cooper Caroline J., widow Arnold N., resident, h Kinney.
Cooper Fred B., (Strait's Corners) r 128, general store.
COOPER JOHN H., (West Candor) r 62, market gardening, 5 1-2 acres.
Cornick William, r 136, laborer.
Cornish Albert A., r 95, boot and shoemaker, farmer 27.
Cortright Amos J., (Weltonville) r 120, farmer 70.
Cortright Charles H., (Weltonville) r 86, farmer 80.
Cortright Collins, (Weltonville) r 84, farmer 75.
Cortright Franklin, (Weltonville) r 84, stone mason, farmer 65.
Cortright George, (Weltonville) r 85, farmer 100.
Cortright James, r 40, resident.

Cortright James, (Weltonville) r 84, retired.
Cortright James F., (Weltonville) r 120, retired farmer.
CORTRIGHT JOSEPH J., (Weltonville) r 86, carpenter and joiner, farmer 40.
Cortright Marion A., (Weltonville) r 84, laborer.
Cortright Samuel, (Weltonville) r 120, retired farmer 30.
Cortright William C., (Weltonville) r 85, farmer 40.
Coursen Bartley, (Strait's Corners) r 139, farmer 350.
Coursen John M., (Strait's Corners) r 139, farmer 72.
Coursen Thomas H., r 95, farmer 30.
Courtright Henry A., (West Newark) r 82, dealer in agricultural implements, and farmer 100.
COWLES JAMES C., r 91, building moving, mason and farmer 65.
Cowles J. Harvey, r 116, farmer 54.
Crance DeWitt C., resident, h Railroad.
Crance Mary, widow Abram, resident, h Railroad.
Crane Charles, (Flemingville) r 122, shoemaker.
Cranmer I. J., resident, h Pond.
Crine Llewellyn, r 12, student.
Crine Perkins S., r 12, farmer.
Crine Stephen D., r 12, dairy farmer 260.
Cronk Byron E. Rev., (Bapt.) commissioner of highways; also, contractor and builder.
Cronk William D., r 90, manufacturer of birch and sarsaparilla beer, and agt. for the Grand Union Tea Co.
Crum Lafayette, (West Candor) r 108, farmer 240.
Crum McDonough, farmer, h Spencer.
Cummings William W., r 58, farmer, leases of J. Tompkins, of Spencer, 200, and of Ezra Bostwick, of Cortland, 96.
Curtis Fred, farmer.
Curtis William, r 5, wagonmaker.
Custard Anson, (Weltonville) r 84, farmer 71.
Cutchee Ambrose, (Catatonk) r 133, tanner.
Daggett William, (Jenksville) r 51, farmer, leases of Elizabeth Fuller. 73.
Dames Joseph O., retired, h Preston.
Darmody Thomas, laborer, h Railroad ave.
Davis Frank, fireman.
Dean Josie, r 57, station and express agt.
Decker Oliver H. P., resident, bds. Owego.
Decker Samuel, r 98, teaming and farmer 90.
Decker William, r 119, laborer.
DeGraw John, tin and hardware, Main, h Ann cor. McCarty.
DENNIS ALFRED, r 53, farmer 264.
Dennis Fred M., r 53, laborer.
Dennis Lorena Mrs., resident, h Owego.
Dennis Marvin, r 54, farmer with Wesley 167.
Dennis Wesley, r 54, teacher and farmer with Marvin 167.
Dewey Daniel, (Strait's Corners) r 142, laborer.
Dewey Frank E., r 111, farmer 92.
Deyo Jacob, (Weltonville) r 86, farmer 67.
Dixon Henry S., silversmith, h Church.
DIXON JOHN C., physician and surgeon, Main, h do.
Dohs George, (Catatonk) r 133, night watchman in tannery.

Dohs Jacob, (Catatonk) r 133, farmer 12½.
Doty Delos A., r 28, farmer, leases of James Doty 78.
Doty Edward J., clerk, h Thompson.
Doty George L., farmer 25.
Doty James, r 26, farmer 275.
Doty John J., r 73, farmer, leases of Samuel Decker 90.
Doty John Mrs., resident, h Kinney.
Doughty Andrew J., (Speedsville, Tomp. Co.) r 19, farmer 11.
Doughty Epenetus, (Speedsville, Tomp. Co.) r 19, farmer 140 and in Caroline 110.
Douglass George, (Strait's Corners) r 139, farmer 132.
Douglass John, farmer, 148, h Owego.
Douglass Otis A., (Strait's Corners) r 139, farmer.
Douglass William, (Strait's Corners) r 141, farmer 105.
Downing Jay S., r 87, fruit grower and farmer 39.
Downing Kay M., r 70, farmer.
Downing Lincoln L., r 70, farmer.
DOWNING STOUGHTON S., r 70, fruit grower, and farmer 120.
Draper Cynthia P., (Catatonk) r 133, widow Ira, resident.
DRAPER MENZ V., (Catatonk) r 130, blacksmith, and farmer 70.
Drew George, (Catatonk) r 114, laborer.
Duel Smith, r 36, farmer 50.
Duff Alexander B., (Strait's Corners) r 139, farmer 94.
DU MOND DAVID, cider-mill, and grain thresher, Ashland, h Main.
Dykeman Orrin, r 57, refused to give information.
Dykeman Solonas, r 56, farmer 45.
Dykeman William H., farm laborer, h Owego.
Eastham Nathan, (Strait's Corners) r 142, lumberman, and farmer 231.
Eastham Thomas, (Strait's Corners) r 142, lumberman, and farmer.
Eastman Amos, (Willseyville) r 2, farmer 75, and works for his wife Rachael 150.
Eastman John N., (Willseyville) r 1, farmer 85, and leases of Barlow Sanford 130.
Eastman Morgan, (Willseyville) r 1, farmer.
Easton Zenas R., r 98, watchman, h and lot.
Eccleston David, painter, h R. R. ave.
EDMUNDS CALEB W., r 98, sawyer, and farmer 15.
Edwards Caroline Mrs., laundress, h Owego.
Eichenburgh George, r 56, sawyer.
Eiklor George I., r 8, carpenter and builder, blacksmithing, farmer 50.
Ellison John T., r 28, farmer, leases of Joel Starkweather 84.
Ellsworth Ervin A., salesman, h Owego.
Ellsworth Frederick, r 28, farmer 50.
Eimendorf Clarence, carpenter, bds. Main.
ELMENDORF CYRENUS, contractor and builder, h Main.
Elmendorf George E., (Strait's Corners) r 141, farmer 112, and leases of Abram White 70.
Elmendorf Jonathan, (Strait's Corners) r 141, resident.
Embody Jacob, wagon-maker, Spencer, h do.
Embody Jacob C., cartman, h Gould.
Emerson Charity, (Strait's Corners) r 128, widow James, carpet-weaving.
Emerson Chester, (Strait's Corners) r 137, farmer 56.
Emerson Frederick A., (Strait's Corners) r 137, farmer 50.
Emery Sarah, (Strait's Corners) r 109, widow Isaac, farm 75.

Ervay Charles, (Willseyville) r 3, farmer, leases of Ira Hoose.
Evans Richard, (Strait's Corners) r 143, farmer 50.
Evans Stephen C., salesman, h Main.
Farley Daniel, (Speedsville, Tomp. Co.) r 13, farmer 83.
Farley Eli J., (Speedsville, Tomp. Co.) r 14, carpenter, and farmer 9.
Farley Ellyn, (Speedsville, Tomp. Co.) r 13, farmer 20.
Farley Martin, (Speedsville, Tomp. Co.) r 13, farmer 30.
Faurot Mary Mrs., emp. blanket factory, h Owego.
Fellows James, (Strait's Corners) r 143, farmer 82.
Ferris Elihu, r 35, farmer 60.
Ferris George, (West Candor) r 107, farmer 30.
Ferris James, (West Candor) r 107, farmer.
Ferris Oliver, (West Candor) r 107, farmer 40.
Ferris Richard R., r 35, farmer 61.
Ferris Sarah, (West Candor) r 107, widow Stephen, farm 25.
Ferris Theron W., r 35, farmer 50.
FESSENDEN DAVID S., (William L. & Son) cabinet-maker.
FESSENDEN WILLIAM L., (W. L. & Son) pastor Wesleyan Methodist
    church, Candor, and South Beecher hill and Spaulding hill.
FESSENDEN W. L. & SON, (William L. & David S.) manufs. and dealers
    in furniture, undertaking goods, etc., Owego, h do.
Fiebig Charles F., carriage painter, Main, h Owego.
Fiebig Frances Mrs., resident, bds. Owego.
Fiebig John P., traveling salesman, bds. Main.
FIELD RICHARD, mason, h Mountain ave.
Filcinger Gabriel, (Willseyville) r 1, resident.
FIRST NATIONAL BANK OF CANDOR, (E. A. Booth, prest., J. W.
    McCarty, vice-prest., J Thompson, cash.) Main.
Fisher John W., groceries and provisions, Main, h do.
Fitch Chancy S., r 46, farmer 114.
Fitch Frank E., r 46, farmer.
Flack Thomas W., (Catatonk) r 133, carpenter.
Fogarty John J., r 41, laborer.
Foot Sheldon W., r 103, resident.
Foot William, r 103, farmer 50.
Ford Nelson, laborer, h Owego.
Forsyth George, retired, h Humeston.
Foster Charles, (Jenksville) r 20, farmer 128.
Foster Charles H., laborer.
Foster Cyrus A., cooper, h Main.
FOSTER JONAS S., (Jenksville) r 20, farmer 178.
Foster Richard, (Jenksville) r 20, farmer.
Fredenburg Henry, (Catatonk) r 115, farmer, leases of Frank Whitmarsh,
    of Owego, 30.
Fronk Fred, (Catatonk) r 134 cor. 115, carpenter and farmer 30.
Frost John O., furniture dealer and undertaker, Main, h do.
Fuller Alvah, teamster, h Main.
Fuller Elizabeth, (Jenksville) r 51, widow Robert, farm 73.
Fuller George B., resident, bds. Kinney.
Fuller Gritman E., (Weltonville) r 78, farmer.
Fuller Jacob C., r 29, farmer 112.
Fuller Marvin, laborer, h Kinney.
Fuller Radaker, r 52, lumberman and farmer 96.

FULLER SAMUEL G., r 52, teacher and farmer 27.
Fuller Willard, r 54, farmer 25.
Gaige Henry, r 116, farmer 20.
Gaige James E., (Owego) r 118, farmer 50.
Gaige Thomas, (Owego) r 132, farmer 90.
Galpin Abel F., (Weltonville) r 84, farmer 60.
Galpin Catharine W., (Weltonville) r 85, widow Samuel, resident.
Galpin Edward, (Weltonville) r 85, carpenter and farmer 87.
Galpin George F., (Weltonville) r 74, with W. A. Mead and S. F. Galpin,
     steam threshing, hay pressing and sawing.
Galpin James T., (Weltonville) r 85, farmer 80.
Galpin Jasper, (Weltonville) r 85, farmer 95.
GALPIN JERUSHA, (Weltonville) r 53, widow Elisha, farm 58.
Galpin Luzern, (Weltonville) r 85, farmer 60.
Galpin Mary J., (Weltonville) r 53, wife of Taylor L., farm 52.
Galpin Myron E., (Weltonville) r 53, farmer.
Galpin Nelson, (Weltonville) r 78, farmer 91.
Galpin Robert C., (Weltonville) r 84, farmer 76.
Galpin Sidney F., (Weltonville) r 73, with W. A. Mead and G. F. Galpin,
     steam threshing, and farmer, leases ot Jasper Galpin 51.
Galpin Taylor L., (Weltonville) r 53, farmer.
Galpin Wayland, (Weltonville) r 85, farmer 60.
Gardner Charles, r 99, farmer 146.
Gates Eugene O., farmer, Owego.
Gay Nathaniel, (Jenksville) r 24, laborer.
German Cyrus B., contractor and builder, h Young.
German Edward C., telegraph operator, bds. Young.
German Frederick E., carpenter, bds. Young.
Gibbons Frank, mason, h Bank.
GILLMAN ROBERT C., r 30, farmer, leases of T. VanVleet 170.
Gould Franklin, (Catatonk) r 131, resident.
Graham Andrew J., (Weltonville) shoemaker.
Gransbury Edward, r 102, carpenter.
Grant James M., r 46, canvasser and farmer 58.
GRIDLEY CHARLES F., (West Candor) r 62, postmaster and farmer 250.
Gridley Charles L., (West Candor) r 60, farmer.
Gridley Charles N., r 36, farmer, leases of Newton S. Gridley 120.
Gridley Demorn, r 63, carpenter.
Gridley Newton S., r 36, farmer 120.
GRIDLEY S. EGBERT, prop. planing mill, and farmer 250, h Owego.
Gridley William C., (West Candor) r 60, lime and plaster, and farmer 115.
GRIFFIN FRED G., (N. W. Griffin & Son) bds. Main.
Griffin Lewis, r 56, farmer 295.
GRIFFIN NEHEMIAH W., (N. W. Griffin & Son) h Main.
GRIFFIN N. W. & SON., (Fred G.) livery, draymen and express, Main.
Griffin Walter, laborer.
GRIMES JOHN M., (Flemingsville) r 121, retired M. E. clergyman and
     farmer 152.
Guiles Andrew, (Strait's Corners) r 142, laborer.
Hadden Stephen, r 139, farmer.
Haddock Eugene B., (Speedsville, Tomp. Co.) r 18, farmer, leases of S.
     Blackman 100.
Haddock John V., (Speedsville, Tomp. Co.) r 18, farmer.

Hale Dorcas, widow John, h Kinney.
Hale Lester B., r 103, farmer 100.
Hale Samuel, r 103, farmer.
Hall Edward R., principal Candor Academy, bds. Allen House.
Hall Emeline, r 58, widow Lewis, resident.
Hall LaFayette, (Willseyville) r 1, farmer 2.
Hallett Charles, (Willseyville) r 1, farmer 25.
Hammond Burt, (Weltonville) r 120, farmer 58.
Hammond Seth, (Strait's Corners) r 139, farmer 91.
Hand Harold N., r 64, laborer.
Handy Fernando D., weaver, h Foundry.
Handy Hannah C., widow James, h Foundry.
Hanes Erastus, r 63, well drilling.
Harding Charles O., painter, h Kinney.
Harding Odell, painter, bds. Kinney.
Harding Sherman, carpenter, h Bank.
HARRIS ALGERNON J., physician and surgeon, Main, h do.
HARRIS CYNTHIA E., widow Dr. John J.; resident, Main.
Hart Edward D , r 29, farmer 25.
Hart George H., farmer 120, h Main.
Hart Janette, off r 36, widow William, farm 75.
Hart John N., r 88, farmer, leases of Charles Mead 76.
Hart Jonathan B., r 63 cor. 64, retired cabinet maker, and farmer 33.
HART LEWIS A., dealer in produce, agricultural implements and phosphates; also, farmer 370, Main, h do.
Hart Louisa, widow Abel, resident, h Owego.
Hart Norman, apiarist, and farmer 140, and leases of his brother Horace 50.
Hart Reuben, r 88, farmer with John N.
Hart Selah, retired farmer, h Main.
Hartwell Warren T., jeweler, Main, h do.
Hasbrouck Josephus, (Willseyville) (Hoose & Hasbrouck) r 30, farmer 200.
Haskell Theodore A., (Jenksville) r 49, farmer 50.
Haskins George, r 69, laborer.
Haskins James, laborer, h Mountain ave.
Hatch Malinda. widow Russell, resident, h Railroad.
Hatch Parker, (Weltonville) r 85, carpenter, and farmer 50.
Haynard Frink, r 97, farmer.
Hazen Daniel, (Strait's Corners) r 140, farmer 84.
Hazen Orlando L., (Strait's Corners) r 140, farmer 39, and works for Daniel Hazen 84.
Hazen William, laborer, h Pond.
Head Emmet, (Willseyville) r 32, farmer 100.
Head Isaac, (Willseyville) r 4. farmer 76.
Head Lewis, (Willseyville) r 1, laborer.
Head Thomas, r 29, laborer.
HEATH FRANK L., coal dealer, and station and express agent, h Main.
HEATH HENRY D., tin and hardware, stoves and agricultural implements, Main, h do.
Heath James H., (Willseyville) r 30, veterinary surgeon, and notary public, and farmer 6.
Hedges Daniel A., r 29, farmer 102.
Hedges Frank M., r 29, farmer.
Henderson Hiram, r 54, farmer 52.

HENDERSON JESSE W., foreman Hulmboldt tannery.
Henderson Theodore, (Johnson & Henderson) r 78, farmer 65.
Hendrickson Burton, r 99, farmer 18.
Herdic Peter, (Strait's Corners) r 139, carpenter, and farmer 47.
Herrick Alfred W., (Catatonk) r 116, refused to give information.
Herrick Burt., (Weltonville) r 120, farmer.
Herrick Stephen H., off r 116, farmer 100.
Herrick Walter, (Weltonville) r 120, farmer 116.
Hevland James, molder, h Owego.
HEWITT JASPER W. REV., r 95, retired M. E. clergyman.
Hill Charles F., Jr., (Weltonville) r 86, laborer.
Hills Charles S., (Weltonville) r 77, farmer 150.
Hills H. George, (Weltonville) r 77, farmer.
Hines Eddie G., r 54, laborer.
Hines Jesse A., r 54, farmer 18.
Hoff Lewis R., grist and flouring-mill, Main, h Owego.
Holden Dallas, (Weltonville) r 120, wagon-maker and blacksmith, and
    farmer 30.
Hollenback Eugene B., farm laborer, h Academy.
Holenback David J., (Strait's Corners) r 136, farmer 147.
Holenback James, r 99, retired.
Holenback John J., (Strait's Corners) r 136, farmer, leases of D. J. H., 67.
Hollenback Michael D., r 119, laborer.
Holenback Willard D., (Strait's Corners) r 136, farmer, leases of D. J. H., 80.
Hollister Elsie, r 36, farm 18.
Hollister George H., (Willseyville) r 30, laborer.
Hollister Harvey A., r 36, farmer 73.
HOLLISTER WARREN L., livery, Main, h Railroad.
Holmes Frank, tinsmith, bds. Owego.
Holmes John, dealer in cattle and horses, and farmer 200, h Owego.
Holmes John, farmer for L. A. Hart, h Main.
Holmes Robert B., clerk, h Main.
Holmes Samuel, retired, h Bank.
Hoose & Hasbrouck, (Willseyville) (Ira & Josephus H.) proprietors steam
    saw-mill, and lumber dealers, opp. depot.
Hoose C. Frank, (Willseyville) r 3, farmer.
Hoose Charles W., (Willseyville) r 3, farmer 150, and in Caroline 60.
Hoose Ira, (Willseyville) (Hoose & Hasbrook) farmer 150.
Houck Israel, r 95, apiarist 50 colonies, market gardening, and farmer 29.
Houk George E , r 95, blacksmith and farmer 30.
House Willard E , D.D. S., dentist, Main, h do.
Hover Adelbert D., (Weltonville) r 77, farmer 41.
Hover Benjamin, (West Newark) r 49, farmer, 122.
Hover Charles F., (Weltonville) laborer.
Hover Court L., (Jenksville) r 52, farmer, leases of James Newman.
Hover George, r 73, farmer, leases of Henry Hover 30.
Hover George F., tanner, h Foundry.
Hover Henry, (Speedsville, Tomp. Co.) r 22, farmer 100.
Hover Henry, (Weltonville) r 84, resident, aged 96.
Hover Leander, r 88, blacksmith, and farmer, leases of Henry Hover 30.
Hover Lettie, widow Alonzo, resident, h Owego.
Hover L. Frederick, (Weltonville) r 77, laborer.
Hover Merritt L., (Weltonville) r 85, farmer, leases of Henry Hover, 2d, 55.

HOVER ROBERT E., farmer.
Hover Silas. (Weltonville) r 81, laborer.
Hover Solomon, farmer 160.
Hover William P., r 73, farmer 20.
Hover Wilman S., r 43, farmer.
Howard Alvah, (West Candor) r 106, farmer.
Howard Alvin, (West Candor) r 62, farmer.
Howard Edward L., (South Danby, Tomp. Co.) r 34, farmer 184.
Howard Darius P., r 118, farmer.
HOWARD HIRAM O., r 118, breeder of horses, and farmer 128, and
  leases of Loring P. Howard, of Spencer 115.
HOWARD HIRAM O., r 118, horse breeder, and farmer 128, and leases
  of L. P. Howard, of Spencer 115.
Howard Martha, widow Samuel, resident, h Railroad.
Howard Rhoda R., (Catatonk) off r 126, widow Charles C., farm 118.
Howard Truman F., r 38, farmer 65.
HOWE EPENETUS, farmer, h Main cor. Mill.
Howell William, (Willseyville) r 1, farmer 30.
Howes Oscar, carpenter, and farmer 30, h Owego.
Howland Dana, r 5, farmer, leases of C. R. Chidsey 40.
Howland Frederick, farmer 140, h Main.
Howland Wilber F., r 38, iron and brass moulder, and farmer 97.
Hoyt Adoniram, r 28, farmer 5.
Hoyt Cordelia, widow Emanuel, h Main.
Hoyt George T., r 88, farmer 50.
Hoyt S. Judson, r 28, farmer 88.
HUBBARD ALBERT C., farmer, h Owego.
Hubbard Frank E., salesman, bds. Owego.
Hubbard George N., r 116, dealer in hop-poles, farmer 10.
HUBBARD GEORGE W., r 98, clerk.
HUBBARD WILLIAM H., r 98, with John F., of Denver, Col., prop. saw and
  grist-mill, dealer in lumber, lath, and farmer 400.
Hubbard William J., (Willseyville) r 30, saloon.
HUFTALING JOHN, apiarist, and emp. Hulmboldt tannery, a member
  Co. C., 86th Regt, N. Y. Vols.
Hughes Frank, (West Candor) r 62, laborer.
Hull Daniel O., r 65, farmer, leases of N. T. Hull 95.
Hull Frederick E., farm laborer, bds. Owego.
Hull Justin, retired, h Owego.
Hull Lebbeus, r 63, resident.
HULL LEONARD, farmer, h Owego.
Hull Nathan T., r 65, farmer 95.
Hull Warren, r 63, laborer.
Hulslander Asa, (West Candor) r 105, farmer 90.
Hulslander Henry J., r 37, farmer 110.
Hulslander Sylvester, r 101, threshing machine and stump pulling, farmer 60.
Hulslander William S., r 102, threshing and farming.
Humiston John H., music teacher, bds. Main.
Humiston Morris, harness-maker, Railroad, h Main.
Humphrey James F., (Weltonville) r 85, farmer 30, and leases of C. L.
  Deyo 65.
Hunsinger John, (Strait's Corners) r 136, farmer 83.
Hunt Henry, (Strait's Corners) r 136, farmer 50.

5

Hunt Willis S., r 94, farmer 45.
Hunt William W., retired physician, h Owego.
Hurd Edgar D., (Willseyville) r 1, farmer 35.
Hurd John, (Willseyville) r 1, farmer 75.
Hyatt Clark, (Catatonk) r 115, laborer.
Hyde Persis E., (Strait's Corners) r 109, wife of William B., farm 60.
Hyde Silas, (Strait's Corners) r 104, laborer.
Hyde William B., (Strait's Corners) r 109, farmer.
JACKSON DWIGHT P., baker, grocer and confectioner, Main, h do.
Jackson John E., emp. Dwight P. Jackson, bds. Main.
Jackson Laura, widow John, resident, h Main.
Jacobs Fred, r 28, farmer 12.
Jacobs Hiram C., (Weltonville) r 75, Baptist clergyman and farmer 50.
Jacobs James, r 25, farmer 140.
Jacobs John W., r 41, farmer 156.
Jennings Benjamin, (Willseyville) r 31, farmer 110.
Jennings Edwin, retired, h Owego.
Jennings James H., druggist, Front, h do.
Johnson Abram, (West Candor) r 62, laborer.
Johnson Albert L., printer, h Owego.
Johnson & Henderson, (Leonard A. J. & Theodore H.) manufs. whip,
    broom and pen-holders, clothes-dryers, ladies' novelty work-baskets and
    wire goods in general, Church.
Johnson Charles F., artist penman, h Church.
JOHNSON EUGENE, r 102, farmer.
Johnson George L., resident, bds. Church.
Johnson George W., r 102, carpenter and farmer, leases Daniel Johnson 200.
Johnson Harmon, (Strait's Corners) r 140, farmer 60.
Johnson Harrison T., r 119, farmer 37.
Johnson Irving L., r 101, farmer 36.
Johnson John, (Strait's Corners) r 140, farmer 60.
Johnson Leonard A., cabinet-maker, Church, h do.
Johnson Leroy N., r 102, pension agent and farmer.
JOHNSON MYRON M., clerk, h Bank.
Johnson Philo, emp. Hulmboldt tannery, h Bank.
Johnson Rhoda, widow Chester, farm 36.
JOHNSON SILAS W., r 88, dealer in fruit and berries of all kinds and
    farmer 62.
Johnson Ulysses S., medical student, bds. Owego.
Johnson Orange, r 45, farmer 44.
Jones Charles T., (Strait's Corners) r 137 cor. 134, farmer 130.
Jones Sidney W., (Strait's Corners) r 137 cor 134, farmer 25.
Jordan Elbert, laborer, h Railroad.
Jordan Milo, r 38, farmer, leases of James P. Belden 220.
Jordan Frank, r 5, farmer, leases of William Perry, of Spencer, 75.
Judd Philecta, widow William, farm 53.
Judd Henry A., resident, bds. Bank.
Kattell Harmon, r 90, farmer.
Kattell Marshall R., r 90, carpenter and farmer 150.
Keeler Ethelbert B., r 94, carpenter and mason.
Keeler Hiram, r 94, farmer 23.
KELSEY DORA G., r 95, farm with Laura A. and Sarah A. 160.

KELSEY LAURA A., r 95, farm with Dora G. and Sarah A. 160.
KELSEY SERAH A., r 95, farm with Laura A. and Dora G. 160.
Kelsey Woodbridge, r 95, farmer 112.
Kenyon John H.. r 25, farmer 53 and leases of Spaulding Bros., of Cortland, 72, and of George Truman, of Owego, 60.
KETCHUM WILLIAM P., insurance, pension attorney and notary public, Kinney, h do.
Kies Chauncey, r 7, farmer 22½.
Kirk John, r 28, farmer 70.
Kirk Richard, r 63, blacksmith.
Knapp Burr D., (Weltonville) general merchant.
Knapp Ezekiel W., r 24, farmer 104.
Knapp Harmon, r 24, farmer.
Kortright Susan, widow Abram, h Main.
Krofft George W., r 98, laborer.
Krofft William, (Catatonk) laborer.
KROM ABRAM H., r 64, farmer 200.
Kyle Daniel Y., (Speedsville, Tomp. Co.) r 22, farmer 117 and at Willseyville 54.
Kyle Enos J., (Speedsville, Tomp. Co.) r 22, blacksmith and farmer.
Kyle Samuel F., (Catatonk) (S. F. Kyle & Co.) r 27, farmer 127 and leases of James A. Kyle, of Shenandoah, Iowa, 40.
Kyle S. F. & Co., (Catatonk) (Samuel F., K. and W. H. Bailey), r 127, baled hay, straw and potatoes.
Kyle Theron D., (Owego) r 117, fruit grower and farmer 92½, and leases of J. A. Kyle 92½.
Kyle Thomas, retired, h Church.
La Barre George, blacksmith, h Bank.
LaGrange Elijah, laborer, h Owego.
Lake Augustus, (Weltonville) r 85, retired.
Lake Ebin, r 53, resident.
Lake George H., (Weltonville) r 85, farmer 101.
Lamb John, (Catatonk) r 133, retired.
Lane Bert, r 28, farmer, leases of Howard Mead 196.
Lane George A., (Weltonville) r 74 cor. 70, farmer 50, and leases of Nancy Snow, of Caroline, 29.
Lane Ceorge W., (West Candor) farmer.
Lane Harmon S., (West Candor) r 63, laborer.
Lane James, r 58, laborer.
Lane James A., r 52, farmer 87, and leases of Julia Hull, of Brookton, 135.
Lane Lamont, (Flemingville) r 121, laborer.
Lane Levi, (Weltonville) r 74 cor 70, farmer.
Lane Stephen, (Strait's Corners) r 140, farmer 53.
Lane Walter, r 116, farmer 64.
Lanphier David H., r 37, lumberman and farmer 20.
Lanphier William H., (Weltonville) r 85, farmer 112.
LARCOM ADELBERT D., r 54, farmer 53.
Larcom Julian C., r 54, farmer.
Larkin Hugh, (Catatonk) off r 114, farmer 210.
Leach William S., (Weltonville) r 84, farmer 74.
Legg Bert E., (Jenksville), r 46, farmer 30.
Legg David J., (Jenksville), r 49, farmer 30.

STARKEY & WINTERS, promptly fill Mail and Telephone Orders.

Legg George W., (Speedsville, Tomp. Co.) r 13 cor. 14, farmer 107.
Legg Leonard C., (Speedsville, Tomp. Co.) r 22, farmer 180.
Legg Otto L., (Speedsville, Tomp. Co.) r 13 cor. 14, farmer.
Legg Stillman J., shoemaker, Main, h Kinney.
Leet Julius C., (Speedsville, Tomp. Co.) r 22, carpenter.
Leet Samuel, (Speedsville, Tomp. Co.) carpenter and leader of Leets' orchestra, farmer 50.
Leonard Richard, (Slaterville, Tomp. Co.) r 5½, farmer 50.
Lewis John A., r 95, sewing machine agt.
Lewis Theodore H., carpenter and farmer 56, h Owego.
Lewis Thomas N., r 63 cor. 64, farmer 88.
Lisk William P., laborer, h R. R. ave.
Little Charles E., r 116, farmer 82.
Little Mary E., dressmaker, h Preston.
Little Mattie, teacher, h Preston.
Little Nettie, teacher, h Preston.
Little Thomas B., r 116, farmer 70.
Little William L., lumber and bark, Main, h do.
Locey Charles E., music teacher, bds. Owego.
Locey Isaac B., retired merchanic, h Main.
Logan Thomas, r 102, engineer and farmer 70.
Loring Horace W., r 56, farmer 10.
LOUNSBURY DANIEL, r 111, farmer 193.
Lovejoy Aaron, farm laborer, h Owego.
Lovejoy George W., r 45, farmer 130.
Lovejoy Jerome, r 38½, farmer 65.
Lovejoy Lucy A., widow Josiah, seamstress, h Foundry.
LOVEJOY LYMAN B., laborer, h Main.
LOVEJOY WILLARD A., tanner, h Royal.
Lyme Henry, r 58, farmer, leases of Mrs. N. Gridley 151.
Lynch Fred, farm laborer, bds. R. R. ave.
Lynch Ira, contractor and builder, h Royal.
Lynch Nathaniel, farmer, h Main.
Lynch Sylvester D., resident, h R. R. ave.
Manley Joseph N., (Strait's Corners) r 141, farmer, works for John Manley of Danby 100.
Manning Charles F., (South Danby, Tomp. Co.) r 31, farmer 50.
Manning Robert P., (South Danby, Tomp. Co.) r 31, carpenter, and farmer 72.
Markle David, r 91, brick and plaster mason, and farmer, works for Lucy Chidsey 22.
Markle Fred C., r 91, brick layer.
MASTEN GEORGE W., apiarist 80 colonies, and farmer 50.
Masten G. Wallace, farmer, leases of Simon Van Luven 116.
Masten J. Willis, r 119, farmer 50.
Mayo Charles H., (Willseyville) r 30, section hand.
Mayo Hanford, r 56, laborer.
Mayo Hiram, r 29, saw and shingle-mill, and farmer 50.
McCARTY & THOMPSON, (J. W. McC. & J. T.) general merchants, Main cor. Mill.
McCARTY JOHN W., (McCarty & Thompson) h Main.
McCoy Edwin, (Jenksville) r 49, dealer in live stock, and farmer 115.
McCully George, r 29, laborer.

McIntire Charles F., (Catatonk) r 134, farmer, leases of S. Sacket of Towanda Pa., 36.
McIntyre Frank, r 91, well-boring, and farmer 50.
McIntyre John J., 116, farmer 30.
McIntyre William, (Catatonk) r 115, farmer 25.
McPhalan John, (Speedsville, Tomp. Co.) r 13, farmer 50.
Mead Alanson, (Weltonville) r 85, farmer 75.
Mead Amzi, (Weltonville) laborer.
MEAD ASA E., r 70, fruit grower, and farmer 100.
MEAD CHARLES, (Weltonville) r 75, dry goods, groceries, boots and shoes, tobacco, patent medicines, and farmer 80.
Mead David P., retired wagon-maker, h Spencer.
Mead Ebin H., (Jenksville) r 78, farmer 62.
Mead Edward, (Flemingville) r 119, farmer 100.
Mead Ezekiel, (Flemingville) r 119, farmer 160.
Mead Fayette, (Weltonville) r 76, farmer.
Mead John G., emp. W. J. Milks, h Bank.
Mead Josephus, farmer, h Owego.
Mead Joshua E., (Flemingville) r 119, retired.
Mead Mileden, (West Newark) r 81, farmer 113.
Mead Milton, (West Newark) r 81, laborer.
Mead Nathan, (Catatonk) off r 126, farmer, leases of Roba R. Howard 118.
Mead Newton T., (Weltonville) r 45, farmer 55.
Mead Russel B., (Jenksville) r 49, farmer.
Mead Russel J., (Weltonville) r 76, carpenter, and farmer 120.
MEAD WILLIS A., r 70, with Sidney and G. F. Galpin, steam threshing machine, hay pressing and sawing.
Meddaugh Preston, (Speedsville, Tomp. Co.) r 22, farmer, leases of L. C. Leonard 180.
Meier Frederick, r 42, farmer 45.
Merchant Gideon, r 37, sawyer, and overseer of George B. Pumpelly steam saw-mill.
Merchant Gideon, (Willseyville) r 32, carpenter.
Mericle Henry, farmer 91, h Main.
Merrick Abner, (Speedsville, Tomp. Co.) r 13, mason, and farmer 90.
Merrill Ann E., (Willseyville) widow M. Nelson, station and express agent.
Merrill Nellie, (Willseyville) telegraph operator.
Merritt Abram, r 69, farmer 23.
Middaugh Asa, (Strait's Corners) r 105, farmer 60.
Milks George, clerk Ashland House, bds. do.
MILKS WILLIAM J., veterinary surgeon, and meat market, Spencer, h do.
MILLER AUGUSTINE, (Weltonville) r 120, farmer 90.
Miller Fred, (Weltonville) r 120, dealer in live stock, and farmer.
Miller Daniel S., physician and surgeon, Main, h do.
Minor Christopher C., (Willseyville) r 30, general store.
Mix Emory C., (Willseyville) r 30, postmaster, and blacksmith.
Mix John C., (Willseyville) r 1, prop. threshing-machine, and farmer 74.
Mix Miles C., (Willseyville) r 30, blacksmith, and farmer 9.
Monell Samuel, (Willseyville) r 1, farmer 14.
Mooney Burt, tanner, h Church.
Mooney Esther, widow Thomas, h Church.
Moore Betsey D., widow John R., resident, h Church.
Moore Oscar, (Speedsville, Tomp. Co.) r 14, farmer 62.

MOREY ARCHIE E., 71, apiarist 90 colonies, and carpenter.
Morey Benjamin S., saloon and restaurant, and farmer 50, Main, h do.
MOREY EDWARD A., r 71, farmer 66.
Morrison James, r 88, farmer 32.
Morrison Wesley, r 116, farmer 25.
Munroe Henry, r 63, farmer 170.
Munroe James, r 63, farmer 140.
Munroe John H., (Willseyville) r 1, laborer.
Munroe Joshua, r 63, farmer.
Mustoe Martin, r 69, farmer 46.
Nelson Asa, (Catatonk) r 115, farmer 50.
Nelson Elmore, (West Candor) r 59, farmer.
Nelson Nathaniel, (Strait's Corners) off r 139, farmer.
Nelson Orville, r 24, farmer 120.
Newman Alonzo M., (Jenksville) r 78, farmer 130.
Newman James, (Jenksville) r 50, farmer 133.
Newman William T., (Flemingville) r 123, farmer in Owego 22.
Neuse James W., laborer, h Church.
Nickerson Lucy E., widow Amos, seamstress, h R. R. ave.
North James E., manuf. washing-machines and clothes wringers, h Main.
NORTON FRANK J., prop. Ashland House, Main.
O'Brien Thomas, (Willseyville) r 30, saloon and groceries.
O'Connell Daniel, (Catatonk) fireman for National Transit Co.
Oldfield Joel, r 102, farmer.
Oliver Allen D., r 40, fireman, and farmer 5.
Oltz Deborah, widow Henry, resident, h Pond.
Oltz Frances A., resident, bds. Pond.
Orcutt David, r 95, carpenter, and farmer 12.
Orcutt Elizabeth, (Catatonk) r 115, widow James E., farm 55.
Orcutt William C., gunsmith, clock and watch repairer and general jobbing,
    Owego, h do.
Ormsby Robert L., farm laborer, h Foundry.
Osborn Arthur, r 116, physician, M. E. clergyman and farmer 50.
Osburn William V., (Speedsville, Tomp. Co.) r 18, apiarist 100 colonies,
    carpenter, wagon repairing and farmer 25.
Ott George, (Catatonk) r 135, farmer 100.
OWEN ABEL C., (Strait's Corners) r 109, carpenter and farmer 95.
Owen Christopher, (Catatonk) r 130, farmer 76.
Owen George B., (Strait's Corners) r 108, farmer 50.
Owen Jerome D., r 114, farmer 108.
Owen William, r 29, general merchant and farmer 32.
Palmatier Charles W., emp. Hulmboldt tannery, h Humiston.
PARMELE FREDERICK, retired, h Main.
Parmele John C., justice of the peace, Main, h Owego.
Palmer George W., (Jenksville) r 20, farmer with J. D. 180.
Palmer Jasper, laborer.
Palmer John D., (Jenksville) r 20, farmer with G. W. 180.
Parsons M. Eva, teacher, bds. Owego.
Parsons Minnie R., teacher, bds. Owego.
Parsons William A., traveling salesman, h Owego.
Pass Peter, (Strait's Corners) r 108, farmer with Thomas W. 160.
Pass Thomas W., (Strait's Corners) r 108, farmer with Peter 160.
Patterson John, (Willseyville) r 1, section hand.

Payne William J., clerk.
Pealing Lanis F., farm laborer, h Owego.
Pearse Charles, r 29, farmer 5.
Perham Harlow C., wagon maker, h Church.
Perrine Daniel H., (Catatonk) r 134, brick and plaster mason and farmer 183.
Perrine Henry, (Catatonk) r 134, farmer, leases of P. Caple 100.
Perrine Joseph, (Strait's Corners) r 136, farmer 50.
Perry Elizabeth, widow Solomon, h Main.
Perry Emmet J., (Willseyville) r 1, farmer, leases of H. Durfee 40.
Personeus Chester, (Willseyville) r 1, farmer 80.
Personeus Cornelius B., r 116, tin peddler.
Personeus Erwin, r 28, farmer 62.
Personeus Ezra C., r 58, farmer, works for Charles Hill, of Danby, 180.
Personeus Ira, r 28, farmer 155.
Pesoneus Lucy, widow Chauncey, laundress, h Main.
PETERS CHARLES G., r 65, dealer in live stock and breeder of fine road
    horses and Jersey cattle, farmer 200.
Peters Richard, carpenter.
Phelps Asa, (Flemingville) r 121, farmer 97.
Phelps Herrick J., (Flemingville) r 121, farmer, leases of Jesse Phelps 100.
Phelps Sheldon, (Flemingville) r 121, farmer.
Phelps Samuel, (Weltonville) r 120, farmer, leases of Eliza Brink 100.
Pierce Albert, (Slaterville, Tomp. Co.) r 5½, farmer 70.
Palmatier John, emp. Woolen mills, h Mountain ave.
Pompelly George, prop. of saw-mill at Gridleyville, h Main.
Potter Henry P., farmer 100, h Spencer.
Potter Mary, widow Harvey, resident, Spencer.
Pultz Luther, (Owego) r 131, farmer 128.
Quick Fremont, (Speedsville, Tomp. Co.) r 13, farmer 25.
Quick Henry, (Catatonk) r 127, dairy 15 cows, farmer 112½.
Quick Philip E., (Catatonk) r 127, farmer.
QUIMBY ELMER E., blacksmith ; special attention given to horse-shoe-
    ing, Owego, h do.
Quinn James, (Catatonk) r 133, tanner.
Quinn James, Jr., (Catatonk) r 133, leather finisher.
Quinn John, (Catatonk) r 133, tanner.
Quinn Thomas, (Catatonk) r 133, leather finisher.
Reasor James B., r 44, cooper and farmer 30.
Reese Henry E., (Weltonville) r 120, farmer.
Reynolds Franklin H., r 96, tin peddler.
Rice Heman, r 29, farmer 6.
Rice Lorenzo, r 29, farmer 79.
Rice Lorenzo A., (Catatonk) r 114, farmer, leases of J. M. Anderson 100.
Richardson Charles, (West Newark) r 80, farmer, works for Horace 150.
Richardson Henry H., (West Newark) r 49, farmer 90.
RICHARDSON HORACE, (West Newark) r 80, farmer 150.
Richardson Jerome, restaurant and farmer 63, Main, h Owego.
Riggs Oliver P., retired, h Owego.
Rightmire Cornelius S., (West Candor) r 59, laborer.
Roach Benny, laborer, h Humiston.
Robberts James E., laborer, h Young.
ROBBINS JOHN E., r 42, farmer 82.
ROBINSON ALDICE A., fire and life insurance, Main, h do.

Robinson Charles, (West Candor) r 59, farmer 30.
Robinson Edward J., (West Candor) r 59, farmer 50.
Robinson Harrison, (West Candor) r 59, farmer.
Robinson Luther B., painter and farmer.
Robinson Maria, r 116, widow Semour, h and lot.
Robinson Murtillow A., carpenter, h Foundry.
Robinson Philander, retired, h Main.
Rockwell Rufus, (Speedsville, Tomp. Co.) r 22, farmer 120.
Roe Emory D., r 63, farmer, leases of Irving Hart, of Waverly, 100.
ROE EUGENE F., r 5, apiarist and manuf. and dealer in apiarist supplies.
Roe Gamaliel, r 5, steam feed-mill and threshing machine, and farmer 140.
Roe George F., farm laborer, bds. Pond.
Roe Horace M., r 5, farmer.
Roe William F., r 25, apiarist, 115 colonies, and manuf. and dealer in api-
    arist supplies, carpenter and farmer 109.
Rolfe James K., r 88, farmer 50.
ROPER WILLIAM E., physician and surgeon, h Owego.
Rose Jacob P., laborer, h Main.
Rose Rodney S. Rev., retired M. E. Clergyman.
ROSS EDGAR D., r 58, farmer 100.
Ross Edmund, (Strait's Corners) r 141, farmer 44.
Ross Frank, (M. L. Ross & Son) h Spencer.
Ross Harry, (Willseyville) r 3, farmer 230.
Ross Lester Z., r 58, farmer 163.
Ross Milton L., (M. L. Ross & Son) also commercial traveler, also farmer
    54. h Spencer.
Ross M. L. & Son, (Frank) druggists, Main.
Rowe Henry R , (Catatonk) r 133, telegraph operator for National Transit Co.
Royal Morris B., insurance and farmer 30, h Owego.
Ryan John, (Catatonk) r 133, laborer.
RYAN JOHN, lumber and hides, Mill, h Main.
Sabin Edgar D., r 65, farmer with M. E. Cowles, of Spencer, 125.
Sackett Lucy, widow Nathaniel L., resident, h Owego.
Sackett Mary, dressmaker, h Owego.
Sackett Nathaniel O., retired, h Main.
Sanford Harmon, (Willseyville) r 1 cor. 31, farmer, leases of Lewis Grif-
    fin 107.
Sarson John, (Willseyville) r 3, farmer 137.
Sarson John C. F., (Willseyville) r 3, house-painter.
Sarson Samuel T., (Willseyville) r 3, carpenter.
Sarson Thomas E., (Willseyville) r 3, works for John Sarson 137.
Sawyer Frank, (West Candor) r 61, deputy-postmaster, and farmer 46.
Sawyer Fred W., emp. D. L. & W. R. R., h Railroad.
Sawyer Ira, (West Candor) r 62, farmer 123.
Sawyer Luther, (West Candor) r 62, general merchant.
Scharf George W., tinsmith, h Preston.
Scofield Clarence H., r 63, well drilling.
Scofield Truman, (West Candor) r 62, dealer in live stock, and farmer 82.
Schooley Edmund, r 6, farmer 100.
Scott Elbert O., att'y and counselor at law, Main, bds. Allen House.
Seaman Joel, r 116, dealer in sheep and cattle, farmer 60.
SEAMAN LE GRAND, r 89, dealer in live stock, and farmer 75, and works
    for Amanda Gosen 80.

Searles George M., carriage and sleigh manufactory, Main, h Railroad.
Sewell John, (Weltonville) r 78, carpenter, and farmer 55, and saw-mill with
    R. Fuller and Julia Hull.
Shaffer Joseph, (Catatonk) r 133, farmer with Wesley 50.
Shaffer Wesley, (Catatonk) r 133, farmer with Joseph 50.
Shaler Frederick, r 95, laborer.
Shaw James, (Flemingville) r 123, laborer.
Sheerer John D., peddler, h Church.
Sherman Elisha J., r 114, farmer 37.
Sherman James, laborer, h Mountain ave.
Shipman Charles, (Strait's Corners) r 109, farmer 70.
Shulenburg Alvin, r 113, farmer 30.
Shulenburg Fred J., (West Candor) r 105, dairy 18 cows, farmer 57, and
    leases of S. E. Gridley 250.
Shulenburg Horace, (West Candor) r 105, farmer.
Shulenburg James, r 56, farmer 100.
Silvernail Hiram, (Strait's Corners) r 139, resident.
Silvernail John, (Strait's Corners) r 139, farmer 79.
Simmons Edward, laborer, h Humiston.
Simpson Franklin, (Willseyville) r 4, farmer 50.
Slate Alfonzo, (West Candor) r 59, farmer.
Slate Francis, r 58, laborer.
Slate Nelson, (Jenksville) r 49, farmer, works estate of Arnold Blanchard 90.
Slater Bartholomew G., farmer on shares with Peter Carr 85, h Owego.
Slater Harry, clerk, h Owego.
Slawson James G., blacksmith, Foundry, h do.
Smith Alanson J., r 53, farmer 100.
Smith Angeline C., widow Jesse A., resident, bds. Owego.
Smith Charles S., saloon, Main, bds. Railroad.
Smith Clarissa Mrs., resident, h Mountain ave.
Smith Edgar M., farmer 50.
Smith Fred W., ass't cashier First Nat. Bank, h Main.
Smith H. Alanson, (Catatonk) r 133, postmaster, station agent, and general
    merchant.
Smith Hannah M., (Catatonk) r 127, widow Alanson Smith, farm 27.
Smith Henry, school director, lumberman, and farmer 160, h Owego.
Smith James, (Willseyville) r 1, farmer 15.
Smith James J., (Catatonk) r 115, farmer, works for Emma Smith 13.
SMITH J. LEWIS, deputy postmaster and town clerk, h Owego.
Smith John J., carpenter and farmer 17, and with Lucius H. 35.
Smith Judson, r 37, laborer.
Smith Lewis W., (Catatonk) r 127, laborer.
Smith L. Everett, r 95, brakeman.
Smith Lavelle, r 37, carpenter.
Smith Lucius H., r 95, carpenter and builder.
Smith Mantlebert H., farmer with his father Edgar M., 50.
Smith Nelson, (Willseyville) r 1, laborer.
Smith Wakeman B., farmer 218, h Main.
Smith William, farm laborer, h Owego.
Smith William B., druggist, bds. Main.
Smith William R., r 37, carpenter.
Smullen George B., (Weltonville) r 20, blacksmith.
Smullen Patrick, (Weltonville) r 120, blacksmith.

Snover John F., r 64, farmer 90.

Snow Roswell, (Caroline Center, Tomp. Co.) r 10, farmer.

Snow Walstein, (Caroline Center, Tomp. Co.) r 10, farmer 161.

Snow William H., r 39, farmer 60.

Snyder Benjamin C., r 13, farmer 141.

Snyder Dewitt M., (Willseyville) r 1, saw and cider-mill and farmer 126.

Snyder Lewis H., laborer, h Mountain ave.

Snyder Samuel, r 56, resident.

Snyder William H., r 56, foreman E. C. & N. R. R.

Spaulding Alonzo, r 9, farmer 90.

SPAULDING URBON P., fire and life insurance, and loan and investment and real estate, Main, h Kinney.

Speers Joel W., (Willseyville) r 30, farmer 8 and leases of Amanda Willsey 175.

Spellman Michael, (Catatonk) r 115, farmer 36.

Southwick Aaron B., (Strait's Corners) r 140, farmer 104.

Stafford Horace G., (Owego) r 131, farmer 52.

Stafford Randolph, (Strait's Corners) r 137, farmer, leases of Arba Campbell, of Owego, 160.

Starks James O., off r 6, farmer with John 65.

Starks John, off r 6, farmer with J. O. 65.

Starkweather Charles, r 28, farmer 67.

Starkweather Joel, millwright and carpenter, h Pond.

Starkweather Lewis S , resident, bds. Pond.

Stevens Andrew T., (Willseyville) r 3, painter and farmer 26.

Stevens David, r 29, farmer 25.

Stevens Della, r 32, wife of John, farm with Mary J. Southwick, of Halsey Valley, 163.

Stevens George, (Willseyville) r 1, farmer, leases of David Stevens 30.

Stevens James M., (Willseyville) r 1, basket-maker and farmer 25.

Stevens John, r 32, farmer, works for Della Stevens 81½, and leases of Mary J. Southwick, of Halsey Valley, 81 1-2.

Stevens Lafayette, r 29, laborer.

Stevens Loren, (Willseyville) r 1, fireman.

Stevens Wilber, off r 36, farmer 25.

Stever Frank, (Jenksville) r 49, laborer.

Stewart Adelbert, r 70, farmer 20.

Stewart Augustus, barber, bds. Railroad.

Stewart Charles, barber, Main, h Railroad.

Stewart Henry B., tin-peddler, h Hulmboldt.

Stinard Abigail D., widow Oglesbary, resident, h Pond.

STINARD ALANSON K., (Jenksville) r 49, farmer 26.

Stinard Andrew, laborer, h off Owego.

Stinard Sylvester, (Jenksville) r 50, breeder and trainer of horses, proprietor of stock horse Prince, and farmer, leases of J. W. McCarty 244.

Stone Charles E., r 41, farmer.

Stone Eli, (Willseyville) laborer.

Stone Nelson, r 95, leases of the heirs of Geo. Andrews 143.

STOWELL ALMOND F., contractor and builder, Railroad, h do.

Strait Adelbert, (Willseyville) farmer, leases of Lewis Griffin 185.

Strait Henry, r 73, farmer 26.

Strait Sylvester, (Strait's Corners) off r 139, farmer, leases of Wm. Harlan 130

STRONG ANSON B., r 45, farmer 13, works for Hebron Strong 50 and for Orange Johnson 44.

Strong Charles S., r 24, farmer 133.

Strong Eugene B., (Willseyville) r 3, assessor, manuftr. of tubs, firkins, etc., and farmer 75.

Strong Hebron, r 45, farmer 50.

Strong Joel H., r 98, dealer in wool, hides, pelts and produce.

Strong Josiah C., r 41, farmer 40.

Strong Manley, (Jenksville) r 50, laborer.

Strong Raymond, r 98, lumberman.

Sturdevant Judson, r 119, farmer 5.

Swartwood Edmund, (Strait's Corners) r 143, farmer, leases of Alfred Evelien, of Tioga, 82.

Sweetman Joanna, widow David, resident, h Owego.

Tacey Alexander, carpenter, h Church.

Tacey Melvin, laborer, h Church.

Taylor Abram, (West Newark) r 81, farmer 437.

Taylor Eugene C., (Weltonville) r 86, farmer 33.

Taylor Martin W., (West Candor) r 109, farmer 82.

Taylor Merton L., (Weltonville) r 86, farmer 50.

Taylor Samuel E., (Weltonville) r 86, farmer 84.

Taylor Walter, r 12, farmer, leases of J. S. Whitney 239.

Taylor William J., (West Newark) r 81, farmer.

Taylor William J., (Weltonville) r 86, teacher, apiarist 50 colonies, farmer, leases of Samuel Taylor 84.

Templeton Albert J., tinsmith, h Foundry.

Terwilliar Abigail J., (Owego) r 118, widow of Nathan, leases of Franklin W. Truman, of Owego, 200.

Terwilliger Andrew J., (Strait's Corners) r 111, prop. English coach stock horse, Tim Valons, farmer 136.

Terwilliger Levi G., (Catatonk) r 133, musician and sawyer.

Terwilligar Solomon E., (Catatonk) r 133, blacksmith.

Terwilliger Stephen E., (Strait's Corners) r 109, farmer.

Thayer John B., (South Danby, Tomp. Co.) r 34, farmer with William H.

Thayer William H., (South Danby, Tomp. Co.) r 34, farmer, leases of Marvin Reed, of Ithaca, 140, and of Eleanor Dewitt, of Danby, 62.

Thomas George H., (Weltonville) r 81, farmer 80.

Thompson Anthony H., r 38, farmer 41.

THOMPSON JEROME, (McCarty & Thompson) cashier, First Nat. Bank, also farmer in Spencer 420, h Main.

Thornton James J., r 93, basket-maker.

Throop William, r 35, farmer 33.

Tidd Francis T., farm laborer, h Foundry.

Tidd Mary E., laundress, h Foundry.

Toft George, (Catatonk) r 114, farmer 4, works for Elizabeth Orcutt 55.

Townley Mary J., widow James L., resident, h Owego.

Townley Reid W., farmer, h Owego.

Tracy Maria E., (Catatonk) r 133, widow James, resident.

Truman Lyman R., (Owego) r 132, farmer 130.

Tubbs Charles N., r 41, carpenter and with Ebenezer, farmer $25\frac{1}{2}$.

Tubbs Ebenezer, r 41, carpenter, and farmer with Charles N., $25\frac{1}{2}$.

Tubbs Isaac, r 41, tin-peddlar, and farmer 61.

Tubbs J. Thomas, tin-peddler, h Main.

Tubbs Orlando, r 69, farmer 20.

Tucker Charles E., r 29, farmer.

Tucker Frank, (Willseyville) r 30, laborer.
Tucker Matthew, (Willseyville) r 30, laborer.
Tucker William, r 29, farmer 108.
Turk John, retired, h Owego.
Turk Levi, carpenter, h R. R. ave.
TURNER GEORGE, (Strait's Corners) r 143, carpenter, and farmer 103.
Tuttle Warren H., 104, farmer 75.
Tyler Charles, off r 88, farmer 37.
Tyler Edward, r 119, laborer.
Tyler James, off r 88, farmer.
Ulrick Henry W., r 25, farmer, leases of John Ulrick, of Tioga, 161.
VanDebogart Francis, retired, h Church.
VanDebogart Frank L., general merchant, Main, h do.
Van Debogart Lawrence, (Willseyville) r 30, carpenter, and farmer 100.
Van Debogart Peter, dealer in agl. implements, Main, h do.
Van Deerveer Warren C., (Strait's Corners) r 142, farmer 110.
Van Dermark Joseph, r 65, farmer.
Van Dermark Peter, laborer, h Main.
Van Dermark Wayland L., r 65, farmer 37.
Van Dermark Wilson, r 23, farmer, leases of Morgan White 156.
VAN DEUSER H. & M., (Catatonk) r 133, proprietors saw-mill, also dealers in lumber and potatoes, and farmer 47.
VAN DEUSER HENRY, (Catatonk) (H. & M. Van D.) r 133.
VAN DEUSER JERRY, (Catatonk) (H. & M. Van D.) farmer 5.
VAN DEUSER MARTIN, (Catatonk) (H. & M. Van D.) r 133.
VanEtten George, r 5, refused to give information.
VanEtten George F., r 29, farmer 60.
Vanglone Schuyler, (Jenksville) r 13, farmer.
VanGorder Charles E., peddler, h R. R. ave.
VanGorder Elias, (Weltonville) r 82, laborer.
VanKleeck James, retired, h Owego.
VanKleeck Jane, r 36, wife of Charles H., farm 106.
VanKleeck John M., r 36, farmer.
VanLuven Simon, justice of the peace, Main, h Owego.
VanLuven Robert, (Strait's Corners) r 137, farmer 48.
VanPelt Sarah, widow Garrett, resident, h Owego.
VanScoy Augusta, r 40, widow Knowlton, farm 130.
VAN SCOY BURT R., r 70, fruit grower, and farmer 108.
VAN SCOY ISAAC D., (Jenksville) r 50, farmer 108.
VanScoy Simeon, r 40, farmer, works for Augusta VanScoy 130.
VanVleet Theodore, lumber dealer, Main, h do.
VanWoert Lebbeus, r 56, laborer.
VanWoert Levi, (West Candor) r 59, farmer 90.
VanWoert R. Smith, farmer, h Main.
VanZyle Stephen, r 69, farmer 10.
Vergason George, (Strait's Corners) r 140, wool buyer, and farmer 93.
VERGASON IDDO. prop. Allen House, Main.
VERGASON SOLOMON, r 112 cor. 114, manuf. and dealer in lumber, dairy 18 cows, and farmer 620.
Vergason Stephen, (Strait's Corners) r 142, farmer 125.
VOSE ENOCH, (West Candor) r 108, contractor and builder, also farmer.
Vorce Volney, (Weltonville) farmer 72.
Wake James, r 67, farmer.

Walker John, laborer, h Owego.
Walts Conrad, (Strait's Corners) r 109, farmer 80.
Ward and VanVleet Misses, (Elmira A Ward and Eva D. VanVleet) dealers in millinery and fancy goods.
WARD HARVEY H., farmer 75, h Owego.
Ward Hiram, farmer 75.
Ward Oscar, farmer.
Ward Oswald J., live stock dealer, h Owego.
Wardwell & Cooper, (West Candor) (William C. and J. H.) r 62, groceries.
Wardwell William R., drug clerk, bds. Main.
Warner John C., r 93, farmer, works for Minda Warner 45.
Warner Richard E., r 44, farmer with Shelden P., leases of R. P. Warner 254.
Warner Richard P., r 44, farmer 254.
Warner Shelden P., r 44, farmer with Richard E., leases of R. P. Warner 254.
Watkins Ephraim C., (Flemigville) laborer.
Watrous Sherman, farm laborer, h Foundry.
Watson James, resident, h Owego.
Webster Edwin, (Owego) r 132, dealer in live stock, and farmer 275.
Wentnorth John W., farm laborer, h Church.
Wentworth Noyes D., painter, h Church.
Wheeler Abram T., cider-mill and farmer 33.
Wheeler Charles T., (Owego) r 124, farmer 86.
Wheeler Frank G., (Owego) r 124, farmer.
Wheeler Ira E., r 63, farmer.
Wheeler John H., farmer, h Railroad ave.
Wheeler Mary, r 41, widow Lewis, farm 59.
Wheeler Myron F., r 41, farmer.
Whipple Marietta R., widow Solomon, resident, h Owego.
White Abram, (Strait's Corners), r 141, farmer 70.
WHITE A. FRANK, (Willseyville) (White Bros.)
WHITE BROS., (Willseyville) (A. Frank, Charles O. and Edward M.) r 30, manufacturers of White's patent bent chairs and patent folding tables.
White Charles B., (Willseyville) r 1, farmer 300.
WHITE CHARLES O., (Willseyville) (White Bros.) r 30, commercial traveler.
WHITE EDWARD M., (Willseyville) (White Bros.) r 1.
White Jacob N., (Strait's Corners), r 141, farmer 50.
White John B., (Strait's Corners) r 110, farmer 83.
WHITE MARY A., widow Leonard, resident, h Owego.
White Morgan A., (Willseyville) groceries and manuftr. and dealer in lumber, and farmer 1,065.
Whitley Andrew J., r 7, farmer 90.
Whitley Demoma, (Willseyville) r 30, laborer.
WHITLEY FLORILLA S., r 65, widow John, Jr.
Whitley George M., r 29, farmer 28.
Whitley Ira, r 29, farmer.
Whitley Newton D., r 7, farmer.
Whitley Sarah, r 28, wife of Joseph, h and lot.
Whitley Philip A., r 29, farmer 27.
Whitley Warren, r 29, farmer 133.
Whitmarsh Ambrose, (Catatonk) r 115, farmer 60.
Whitmarsh Andrew J., r 95, laborer.
Whitmarsh Charles, laborer.

Whitmarsh Eben, r 116, dairy 11 cows, and farmer 96.
Whitmarsh Edward, (Catatonk) r 129, farmer 200.
Whitmarsh Edwin, (Catatonk) r 129, farmer 59.
Whitmarsh James, r 116, resident, age 87.
Whitmarsh John, (Catatonk) r 115, farmer.
Whitmarsh Luther, (Catatonk) r 129, farmer.
Whitmarsh Robert L., (Catatonk) r 134, farmer 100.
Whitmarsh Simon, (Catatonk) r 129, farmer.
Whitney George, r 71, laborer.
Whitney Joseph S., live stock dealer and farmer 230, h Railroad.
Whitney Martin D., r 88, agt. for Auburn Art Union Co.
Whitney Perry B., r 56, farmer 50.
Wiest George A., (West Newark) r 77, farmer, leases of Abram Taylor 270.
Wilber William H., (Speedsville, Tomp. Co.) r 18, farmer 100.
Willard Lewis D., speculator, and farmer 40.
Williston Horace, Rev., pastor M. E. church, h Owego.
Williams Enoch S., (Booth & Williams) h Main.
Williams Ezra O., teamster, h Owego.
Williams George F. (Catatonk) r 126, farmer 50.
Williams George R., r 40, farmer, leases of Henry Merikle 97.
Williams LaFayette, (Catatonk) r 126, farmer 90.
Williams William I., (Catatonk) r 116, farmer 93.
Willsey Gaylord, retired, h Spencer.
Willsey Harriet A., (Willseyville) r 30, widow of William W., farm 175.
Willsey Margerite M., widow Warren, resident, h Spencer.
Willsey Martin E., farmer, h Bank.
Wilson Ephraim J., farmer 5.
Wilson William H., laborer.
Winfield Simon, (Strait's Corners) r 139, farmer.
Woodard Elias H., (Weltonville) r 82, blacksmith.
Woodard Mary G , (Weltonville) r 82, wife of E. H., dealer in groceries and provisions.
WOODFORD ALBERT H., r 63, farmer 160.
Woodford Asel H., (West Candor) r 62, farmer 10, and with Charles Woodford 58.
Woodford Chauncey C., farmer 97, h Owego.
Woodford Edwin F., r 63, farmer.
Woodford Edward G., (West Candor) r 63, farmer.
Woodford E. Jerome, (West Candor) r 62, agriculural implements, and farmer with Elbert C. 150.
Woodford Elbert C., (West Candor) r 62, carpenter, farmer, E. Jerome, 150.
Woodford Frank S., r 56, farmer with Sylvester 100.
WOODFORD GEORGE, (West Candor) r 62, farmer 220.
Woodford Myron L., (West Candor) r 63, farmer 156.
Woodford Rhoda, r 56, widow Luther, farm 125.
WOODFORD SYLVSTER, r 56, farmer with F. S. Woodford 100.
Wool Joseph D., (Willseyville) r 3, justice of the peace, and farmer 12.
Wolverton Charles A., (Owego) r 131, cooper.
Wright Calvin, (West Candor) r 109, farmer 57.
Wright Charles H., r 111, farmer 135.
Wright Edwin J., r 111, farmer.
Wright John, retired, h Kinney.

Wright Leroy, (Strait's Corners) r 109, farmer 10.
Wright William A., r 37, farmer 60, and works for the heirs of Sterling J. Barber 97.
Young David, (Jenksville) farmer 85.
Zimmer Alvah, (West Candor) r 61, laborer.
Zimmer Ira, (Jenksville) r 47, farmer 125.

NEWARK VALLEY.

(For explanations, etc., see page 3, part second.)

(Postoffice address is Newark Valley, unless otherwise designated in parenthesis.)

Abbey Reuben, r 16, carpenter.
Abbott George, (Howlan & Abbott) h Mill.
Ackerman Cornelius R., (Jenksville) contractor and builder, and farmer 40.
ACKERMAN JOSEPH, r 21, district collector and farmer 125.
Allen Charles W., (Jenksville) off r 1, retired.
Allen James, r 16, retired.
ALLEN JAMES H., Jenksville) r 2, farmer on shares with F. W. Richardson, 200.
Ames Henry W., r 16, farm laborer.
Ames Stephen W., r 18, farmer 100.
Ames William, r 6, carpenter.
Andrews Charles F., r 9, farmer 100.
Andrews Deborah, r 55, widow Chester, resident.
Andrews Ezra J., r 42, farmer 52.
Andrews Frank, r 42, teacher.
Andrews Heman N., r 42, farmer 48.
Andrews Jane, r 9, widow Luther, farm 200.
Andrews Jesse, r 42, farmer, on shares with W. Elwell, 40.
Andrews Judson, r 42, farmer 43.
Andrews Lucinda, r 42, widow Daniel, resident.
Andrews Sarah, r 9, resident.
Angell Elworth J., contractor and builder, also small fruit grower, h Whig.
Angell Thomas, (Ketchumville) r 9, retired Methodist preacher and farmer 40.
Arnold Frederick C., harness-maker, bds. Elm.
Arnold Harley, r 25, farm laborer.
Arnold James, r 25, farmer 89.
Ashley Frank D., clerk, h Whig.
Avery Samuel M., (Jenksville) r 1, postmaster.
Ayres Charles H., laborer, bds. Maple ave.
Ayers James, cooper, h Maple ave.
Ayers John S., tinsmith, h Maple.
Bailey Charles, (Maine, Broome Co.) r 26, farmer for his mother Mrs. M. Bailey.

STARKEY & WINTERS, promptly fill Mail and Telephone Orders.

Bailey Henry, (Maine, Broome Co.) r 26, farmer for his mother Mrs. M. Bailey.
Bailey Hiram C., (Maine, Broome Co.) r 26, farmer 125.
Bailey Margaret, (Maine, Broome Co.) r 26, widow Amos, farmer 70.
Baldwin Charles, r 38, farmer.
Baldwin Royal C., r 38, farmer 10.
Baldwin William, farmer, leases of E. Barber 22.
Ball A. Rodney, r 5, farmer, with his son William H., 60.
Ball Fred, emp. N. K. Waring, h Elm.
BALL HENRY W., (Jayne & Ball) h Maple.
Ball Margaret, widow Frank, resident, h Elm.
Ball William H., r 5, farmer 60 on shares with his father A. Rodney.
Ballard Addison L., laborer, h East ave.
Ballard Andrew M., emp. tannery, h Whig.
Ballard Ann, (Ketchumville) r 10, resident.
Ballard George W., deputy sheriff, h Maple.
Ballard George W. Mrs., laundress and general work, h Maple.
Ballard Horatio, r 25$\frac{1}{2}$, farmer 62.
Ballard John, r 26$\frac{1}{2}$, farmer 50.
Ballard Lewis, r 26$\frac{1}{2}$, farmer 50.
Barber Frederick W., emp. Donley Marble Works, h Whig.
Barber George, r 38$\frac{1}{2}$, farmer 100.
Barber Virgil C., carpenter, h Rewey ave.
Barclay Mitchell, emp. tannery, h off East ave.
Barnes Charles H., r 16, farmer 52.
Barnes Lewis W., r 16, farmer.
Barrett Holmes, retired, bds. Main.
Barrett Monroe, (West Newark) r 22, farmer 200.
BARROTT JOSEPHAS, (Weltonville) r 40, farmer 175.
Barton James H., r 6, farmer 85.
Barber William C., painter, h Maple.
Bean Fred C., (Maine, Broome Co.) r 47, farmer 100.
Becker Charles, retired, h Elm.
Beecher Lambert, harness-maker, h Maple.
Belcher J. Waldo, painter and paper-hanger, h Brook.
BELCHER SIDNEY, r 40$\frac{1}{2}$, lumberman, and farmer 150.
Belden Uriah L., blacksmith, off Water, h Whig.
Belden William H., (West Newark) r 22, blacksmith.
Bement Celia, resident, bds. Whig.
Bement Egbert, milk dealer, and farmer 75, h Whig.
BENHAM CHARLES M., r 35, farmer for his father Martinus L.
Benham Martinus L., r 35, book-keeper in Utica, also farm 75.
Benton Lyman C., (Jenksville) r 1, shoemaker.
BENTON WILLIS S., (Jenksville) r 1, groceries, also reporter for Owego *Gazette* and Newark Valley *Herald*.
Benton Wilson, (Jenksville) r 1, farmer.
BERKLEY CHARLES E., r 53, carpenter, and farmer 43.
Berkley Egbert D., r 53, farmer 60.
Berkley Elizabeth, r 53, widow Charles, resident.
Berlin David, laborer, h Dam lane.
Bevier Daniel, farmer, bds. Whig.
Bevier Elizabeth, widow Ralph, resident, h Whig.
Bieber Allie V., r 42, dressmaker.

Bieber Catherine, widow Henry, resident, bds. Whig.

Bieber Philip, r 42, live stock dealer, and farmer 73.

BIEBER ROMAINE F., lawyer, Water, h Whig.

Billings William, farmer, bds. Main.

BISHOP FRANCIS M., physician and surgeon, Water, h Elm.

Bishop Lamont, carpenter, h Water.

Bishop Lewis D., carpenter, h Water.

Blewer Adelaide, r 40, widow Henry, resident.

Blewer J. Frank, r 40, farmer 200.

Blewer Jesse, r 40, farmer, with his mother Mary.

Blewer Mary E., r 40, widow Charles, farm 95.

Blewer Sarah J., r 60, widow Charles, resident.

Borthwick Delphine, (Jenksville) r 1, resident.

BORTHWICK D JAMES, (Jenksville), r 1, farmer.

Borthwick George H., (Jenksville) r 22, assessor and farmer 50, and leases of D. J. Borthwick 112.

Bowen Eugene, r 15½, farmer 50.

Boyce J. Edgar, painter, h Maple ave.

Boyce Henry W., retired, h Main.

Bradley Elmina, widow Lambert, resident, bds. Main.

Bradley Mary A., widow Lambert, h Main.

Brick Thomas, laborer, h Moore.

Briggs Sally, r 16, widow Salem, resident.

Brink John J., (West Newark) r 22, farmer 90.

Brink Peter G., (West Newark) r 22, justice of the peace, and farmer 110.

Brockway Joseph B., r 6, farmer 74½.

Brockway Lewellyn, r 6, farmer with his father Joseph B.

Brougham (Helen and Sarah), milliners, Water, h do.

Brougham William, r 53, farmer 50.

Brown Elmina, widow Amos P., resident, h Main.

Brown Mary A., dressmaker, Main, bds. do.

Brown Orpha Mrs., laundress, bds. Bridge.

Buckley Patrick, night watchman, h Maple.

Buffington Chauncey L., (Ketchumville) r 11, blacksmith, and farmer 25.

BURCH & WELLS (L. S. B. and L. E. W.) saw, planing and grain threshing mills, Main.

BURCH LEVI S., (Burch & Wells) h Maple.

Burch Mary A., resident, h Main.

Burchard Harvey J., (Ketchumville) r 9, justice of the peace and apiasist.

Burr William H., veterinary surgeon, bds. Whig.

BURR WILLIAM J., physician and surgeon, office Whig, h do.

Burroughs Cornelius S., (Clinton & Burroughs) r 9, h do.

Bushnell Calvin, r 15, farmer 64.

Bushnell Edwin G., (Ketchumville) r 9, farmer 101.

Bushnell Frank G., r 15, commissioner of highways, dairy 9 cows, farmer 93.

Bushnell Philo C., farmer for his father Calvin 64.

Bushnell Theron H., telegraph line repairer, h Whig.

Bushnell Zina H., retired, h John.

Butler John, farmer 200, h Main.

Buttles William R., retired, bds. Bridge.

Byington Alphonso, general merchant, Main, bds. do.

Byington Clayton, speculator, h Main.

Byington Savilla, widow Lawyer, resident, h Main.

6

BYINGTON SHERMAN W., postmaster and meat-market, Main, h do.
Cady Gershom, (Ketchumville) r 9, farmer 16.
Cady Luther, (Ketchumville) r 14, farmer 125.
Caldwell William J., deputy postmaster, h Main.
Cameron Eugene, (Ketchumville) r 9, farmer 202.
Cameron Harry A., farmer on shares with E. Saddlemire, h Main.
Cameron John, r 41, farmer on shares with G. B. Sutton 100.
Campbell Harrison, (West Newark) r 22, farm laborer.
Cargill Heman, retired, bds. Main.
Cargill Julius C., resident, bds. Bridge.
CARGILL WILLIAM, furniture and undertaking, Main, h do.
Carpenter Anna C., widow Joshua L., resident, h Main.
Carty Henry J., laborer, h Main.
Cary Thomas A., farmer 82, h Main.
Castline Moses P., (Weltonville) r 40, farmer 35.
Chamberlain Daniel, r 16, retired.
CHAMBERLAIN THEODORE F., r 16, assessor and farmer 84.
Chambers Charles, wagon-maker, Water, h do.
Chapman Canfield, contractor and builder.
CHAPMAN EDGAR E., hardware, Water, h Main.
Chapman George M., contractor and builder, h Main.
Chapman Lyman F., groceries and provisions, Water, h Main.
Chapman Noyce P., retired, h Silk.
Chittenden Lester, r 40½, school collector and farmer 175.
Christensen Peter, laborer, h Whig.
Clark Edgar, (Ketchumville) r 14, farmer 100.
Clark Elizabeth, r 15, invalid, resides with G. M. Dickinson.
CLARK ENOS M., r 25, bridge builder and farmer 50, and leases of L. B.
    West 180.
Cleveland John, r 56, farm laborer.
Clifford John M., r 29, farmer 120.
CLINTON & BURROUGHS, (R. W. C. & C. S. B.) r 9, steam saw-mill.
Clinton Alice E., clerk, bds. Elm.
Clinton Edwin V., farmer 22, h Main.
Clinton Emma, widow Stephen P., h Elm.
Clinton George L., laborer, h Elm.
CLINTON JULIAN S., r 35, farm 120.
Clinton Henry W., retired, h Main.
Clinton Lydia B., r 42, widow George, resident.
Clinton Morris D., r 42 farmer 111.
CLINTON ROYAL W., lumber dealer and farmer, h Main.
Clizbe Jay, clergyman, (Cong.) retired.
Cole Edward, (Ketchumville) r 12, farmer.
Coney Alfred T., emp. tannery, h Main.
Coney Lewis J., laborer, h Main.
Cook Eugene D., farm laborer, bds. Bridge.
Cook Henry H., r 24, farmer.
Cook Lovisa F., laundress, h Bridge.
Cook Orson L., farm laborer, bds Bridge.
COOLEY BENJAMIN F., boarding-house and farmer 25.
Cooley Charles H., bridge-builder, h Silk.
Cooley John, (Ketchumville) r 10, farmer 155.
Cortright Angeline A., (Weltonville) r 40, resident.

Cortright Josephus M., (Weltonville) r 40, farmer 65.
Cortright L. Elton, (West Newark) r 22, farmer 147.
Cortright Willie N., (West Newark) r 22, farmer with his father Elton.
Councilman Edwin W., r 35, apiarist, 60 swarms, poultry raiser and farmer 40.
COUNCILMAN JIRA F., r 19, farmer with his father Timothy S.
Councilman Timothy S., farmer, h Whig.
CRONCE JOHN H., r 15, farmer 70.
Crounse Charles G., r 24, farmer 50.
Culver Frank, resident, h East ave.
Curtis Isaac, farmer 6, h Main.
Custard William, r 40, farmer 50.
DAGGETT BARNEY, (West Newark) r 22, farmer 86.
Dalton William, r 15½, farmer 30.
Davern William. r 25, farmer 55.
DAVIDGE EUNICE, (Davidge, Landfield & Co.) widow John, h Whig.
Davidge John, resident, bds. Whig.
DAVIDGE, LANDFIELD & CO., (S. B. D., J. B. L. and Eunice D.) sole-
    leather mnfrs.; also, lumber in Pa. and W. Va., Main.
DAVIDGE SHERWOOD B., (Davidge, Lanfield & Co.) h Whig.
DAVIS FRANKLIN, prop. saw-mill and farm 100 on r 25, h Whig.
Davis John T., engineer and farmer with his father, Franklin, bds. Whig.
Davison D. Henry, (West Newark) r 22, carpenter.
Dean Charles E., (Ketchumville) r 10, farmer.
Dean Charles H., (Ketchumville) r 9, farmer 32.
Dean Franklin G., r 39, farmer 175.
Decker Abram D. W., cartman, h Whig.
Decker Abram L., laborer, h East ave.
Decker Ira, emp. William's saw-mill, h Elm.
Decker Joseph, stage express to Owego, h East ave.
DeGARAMO JAMES, r 15, farmer 51.
DeGaramo Peter, r 15, farmer 120.
De Garamo William, r 35, farmer 58.
DeGROAT JAMES F., r 40½, lumberman.
Delaney James, off r 25, farm laborer.
Delaney John, off r 25, farmer 96.
De Laney Michael, emp. tannery, h off East ave.
Delaney William, off r 25, farm laborer.
Dennison Joseph H., r 5, farmer 24.
Dickerson Austin, farmer 25, h John.
Dickinson Lyman, r 42, farmer 60.
Dickinson Orville, r 42, resident.
Dickson George M., (Connecticut) r 15, farmer 52.
DIMMICK & YOUNG, (O. D. & H.Y.) props. Dimmick House, also dealers
    in coal, lime, brick and cement, and produce shippers, opp. Depot.
DIMMICK HOUSE, Dimmick & Young, props., opp. Depot.
DIMMICK OSSIAN, (Dimmick & Young) bds. Dimmick House.
Dimmick Simeon L., (Ketchumville) r 11, retired Methodist minister, and
    farmer 60.
Dingman Andrew, r 53, farm laborer.
Dingman Ostrom, r 53, farm laborer.
Doan Daniel, r 25, school trustee, and farmer 65.
Dohs Daniel, retired builder, h Main.
Dohs George, furnace builder, and farmer 11.

Doney Catherine M., r 58, teacher.
Doney John A., r 58, farmer with his mother Saloma.
Doney Randall, (Connecticut) r 9, emp. lumber mill.
Doney Saloma C. Mrs. r 58, farmer 114.
DONLEY BROS., (James G. & Robert) all kinds of granite and marble
    work, Maple, also branch at Greene, N. Y.
DONLEY ROBERT, (Donley Bros.) h Watson.
Dooley Catherine, widow John, resident, h East ave.
Downey Robert, emp. tannery, h East ave.
Duran Mrs., resident, h Ward.
Durfee Samantha, widow Amasa, resident, h Rewey ave.
Duygan James, (Connecticut) r 15, farmer 50.
Duygan John, r 15, farmer for his father James.
Edwards Albert, stage express, Newark Valley to Whitney's Point, h East ave.
Elwell Catharine, widow Rev. King, h Main.
Elwell Morris, resident, h Main.
ELWELL WILLIAM, general merchant, Main, h do.
Fairchild Salley A., r 24, widow Hiram Z., resident.
Fellows Russell S. dentist, Main, h do.
Fellows William A., carpenter, h Whig.
Finch Charles, (Ketchumville) postmaster, and general merchant.
Fisk James, r 51, farm laborer.
Fivaz Jules B., farmer 40, h Whig.
Flanagan John H., retired, h Elm.
Flanagan Susie, dressmaker, Elm, bds. do.
FLANAGAN WILLIAM J., foreman Donley Bros. marble works, also
    prop. orange grove in Hernando, Fla., h Elm.
Fogle Elias E., 52, farmer.
Fogle George F., r 51, farmer.
Fogle Jacob, r 51, farmer 80.
FORD ALBERT N., general merchant, Water, h Elm.
Ford Herbert, clerk, bds. Elm.
Ford Ichabod A., farmer 83, h Main.
FRANK CHARLES, jeweler, Water, h Whig.
Freeland Lyman, r 21, farmer 110.
French Charles, r 25, farmer 31.
French Jerry, r 25, farmer for his father Charles.
Gage Rilla, r 60 farmer 44.
GAGER ULYSSES S., r 45, farmer for Peter Settle, also dealer in Cham-
    pion drills.
Gale Hiram, (Ketchumville) r 9, reformed Methodist minister, and farmer 12.
Gaskill Levi C., r 41, carpenter, and farmer 60.
Gates Norton S., farm laborer, h Bridge.
Gleason George, r 39, farmer.
Gleazen Julia, resident, h Rewey ave.
Gleazen Sabrina, resident, h Rewey ave.
Golden Augustus H., (West Newark) r 22, cooper.
Golden Prentis E., (West Newark) r 22, school trustee, and cooper.
GOODFELLOW HEZEKIAH, r 40½, mason, and farmer 50.
Gould Arthur J., r 15½, farmer 50.
GOULD MELVIN J., r 4, farmer, leases of D. Sturtevant.
Gould Thaddeus, stationary engineer, h Silk.
Gould Warren Mrs., resident, bds. Brook.

Grenell Sherman, r 25, farmer 100.
Griffin Hiram, r 39, farmer 105.
Griffin Irving D., r 39, farmer with his father Hiram.
Griner George Mrs., resident, h Elm.
Griswold Eben, r 41, farmer 25, and 275 in Pennsylvania.
Grummons Truman, sawyer, h Moore.
GUYON CHARLES S., r 23, farmer 70.
Hale Adelbert, (Maine, Broome Co. 127, farm laborer.
Hale Jerome H., (Connecticut) r 15, farmer, leases of Frank Ashley 100.
Hale Simeon, r 15, farmer with his son Jerome H.
Hall Abner G., r 19, farmer 90.
Hall Polley B., resident, bds. Whig.
Hall Sheridan G., (Jenksville) r 22, constable, also shoemaker, and farmer 35.
HAMMOND ADELBERT C., r 16, carpenter and joiner, also farmer 37.
Hammond Levi B., r 16, farmer 56.
Hammond Melville F., r 6, carpenter and joiner, and farmer 90.
Hancy William B., r 23, farmer on shares with M. Mead 160.
Hand Delmer C., laborer, h Maple ave.
Hardendorf George M., (Ketchumville) r 13, farmer 100.
Hardendorf Henry D., (Ketchumville) r 13, farmer 30.
Harris Emma, r 16, widow John, resident.
Harris Isaac, tailor, h Bridge.
Harris Luther C., r 5, farmer 46.
Harris William H., (Connecticut) r 15, farmer 50.
Harvey Catharine, widow Abel, resident, h East ave.
Harvey Jed, laborer, h East ave.
Harvey Mark, laborer, h Maple.
HAVENS GEORGE, shoemaker, Water, h do.
Henderson Alexander, r 24, farmer 170.
Henderson Irving, r 24, farmer with his father Alexander.
Henry George, emp. tannery, h Main.
Herrick Perlee, r 40, farmer 175.
Hess David, resident, h Maple.
Higbe Charles, retired farmer, h Main.
Hill Chauncey, (Ketchumville) r 11, resident.
Hilligas Charles, (Maine, Broome Co.) r 26, farmer 57.
HILLIGAS LORENZO D., mason and builder, h Maple.
Hinsdale Frank, r 23, farmer 160.
HINSDALE FRANK W., r 23, farmer 130.
Hinsdale James E., r 21, farm laborer.
HOFF ERASTUS, r 19, farmer 165.
Hoff George, retired, h Whig.
Holden Ermina, r 41, teacher.
Holden Harlan P., farm laborer, h Main.
Holden Hiram, r 41, farmer 110.
Holden Laura E., r 5, widow Walter, resident.
Holdrege Ira J., (Ketchumville) r 11, shoemaker.
Holes John, farm laborer, h Moore.
Holladay Anna M., milliner, Water, h do.
Holladay Eli J., egg buyer, h Water.
Holladay Herbert, farmer, h Water.
Holland Vienna, widow Abram, resident, h Main.
Hollenbeck Chester, (Maine, Broome Co.) r 48, farmer 200.

Hollenbeck Harrison, (Maine, Broome Co.) r 48, farmer 60.
Hollenbeck Whitfield, (Maine, Broome Co.) r 29, farmer 100.
Hollister Herbert, r 15½, farmer 56.
Holmes Jerome D., dealer in horses, h Main.
Holmes Rufus, dealer in horses, h Main.
Hooker Charles B., painter and paper-hanger, Whig, h do.
Hooker Frederick, r 15, farmer for Frank G. Bushnell.
Hooker John J., bridge builder, h Maple.
Hooker Mary E., teacher, bds. Whig.
Hopkins George, emp. N. K. Waring, h Whig.
Hooper Peter Q., farm laborer, h Silk.
Hotchkin Mary E., widow Marshal, resident, h Main.
Hover Albert, (West Newark) r 22, farmer 85.
Hover Albertus C., (West Newark) r 22, farmer 25, and leases of W. Watkins 125.
Hover Cornelius, (West Newark) retired.
Hover Hannah, r 20, widow Gilbert, resident.
Hover James, r 20, farm laborer.
Hover Lucinda A., r 38, widow Charles, carpet-weaver.
Hover Marvin L., (West Newark) r 22, carpenter.
Hover Willis E., (West Newark) r 22, postmaster, and farmer 66.
Howard Anderson, marble and granite polisher, h Maple.
Howard Barzillia S., laborer, h Maple ave.
Howard Uriel A., painter, John, h do.
Howard William R., r 21, farmer.
Howland Henry H., (Howland & Hill, Auburn) creamery, h Elm.
Howland Jane E., resident, h Main.
Hulslander John H., r 24, small beer manuf.
Humphrey Cyrus, r 24, farmer, leases of W. Tappan.
Humphrey Edward G., (Jenksville) off r 1, farm laborer.
Humphrey Jacob V., r 24, milk dealer.
HUNT LEWIS, fire and life insurance, Water, h Bridge.
HUTCHINSON HORACE W., hardware, Water, h Whig.
Hyden Charles, (Ketchumville) r 9, farmer 72.
Hyden John, laborer, h Main.
Hyden Henry, retired, h East ave.
Jackson Nelson E., r 16, farmer 50.
Jackson O. Lester, carpenter, h Whig.
Jackson Robert, r 25, farmer, leases of Alfred Roulet 140.
Jackson William H., (Byington & Jackson) h Whig.
Japhet Levi, r 15½, farmer 55.
Japhet Mrs., resident, h Ward.
JAYNE & BALL, (G. F., J. and H. W. B.) meat market and produce dealers, Water.
JAYNE ANNA M., teacher, bds. Whig.
JAYNE GEORGE F., (Jayne & Ball) h Whig.
Jayne Henry F., produce dealer and farmer, h Whig.
Jennings Mary, widow David, resident, bds. Whig.
Johnson Clark H., r 41, farmer 350.
Johnson Jefferson, r 16, farmer 80.
Joslin Almond, (Flemingville) r 61½, lumberman and farmer.
Joslin Daniel, (Flemingville) r 61½, lumberman and farmer 97.

Joslin Edward A., r 41, farmer.
Joslin Joseph D., r 41, telegraph operator.
Kaley Ira, laborer, h John.
Kattell Erskine, r 35, farm laborer.
Keith Frank R., (Jenksville) r 1, farm laborer.
Keith Lucius A., (Jenksville) r 1, carpenter.
Kelleher Timothy, laborer, h Dam lane.
Kelleher Thomas, hostler, bds. Dam lane.
Kellogg Alva D., r 41, farmer 40.
Kellum Bradford, (Maine, Broome Co.) r 47, farmer 20.
Kellum Frederick, (Main, Broome Co.) r 47, farmer, leases of Freeman
    Madison 100.
Kennedy Charles, r 25, farmer 90.
Kennedy J. Arthur, laborer, h Watson.
KENNEDY JOSEPH L., r 25, farmer with his father Charles.
Kennedy LaMont, r 25, farmer with his father Charles.
KENYON CHARLES E., r 53, dealer in Wiard plows, farmer 50 and in
    Owego 100.
Kenyon Edwin, r 23, farmer 18.
Kenyon Frank, r 53, farmer.
Kenyon Lorenzo, r 23, farmer 42.
Kenyon Lydia, r 23, widow Howland, resident.
Kenyon Raymond, r 53, farmer.
Kershaw C. Benjamin, r 41, farmer 73.
Ketchum Seneca, (Ketchumville) r 12, prop. hotel and farmer 80.
Kinney Edward G., school trustee, h Whig.
Knapp Frank J., r 40½, farmer.
Knapp George, off r 41, farmer with his father Gaylord.
Knapp M. Gaylord, off r 41, farmer.
Knapp William T., r 58, farmer 95.
Kniskern E. Ann, widow George, resident, h Moore.
Lainhart Abram, r 46, farmer 96.
Lainhart Arthur, (Maine, Broome Co.) r 50, farmer for his father Aaron 140.
LAINHART ELIAS, r 51, farmer 135.
Lainhart Ephraim, farmer 30, and leases of W. Elwell 150, h Whig.
Lainhart John, (Ketchumville) r 14, farmer 300.
Lamb J. Bruce, (Maine, Broome Co.) r 14, farmer 90.
Lane Jacob, r 15½, farmer 50.
LANDFIELD JEROME B., (Davidge, Landfield & Co.) h Main.
LAWRENCE HORACE F., r 61, farmer 30.
Lawrence Melton, r 15, farmer for W. H. Harris.
LAWRENCE MILES A., r 16, school trustee, also farmer 20.
Lawrence Sarah A., r 61, widow Joel, carpet-weaver.
Lawrence William J., r 15, farmer 100.
Leach Daniel F. Rev., pastor Baptist church, h Whig.
Leach R. Jennette, widow John, resident, h Main.
Legg Melville M., carpenter, h Spring.
Leonard Arthur, farm laborer, bds. Franklin.
Leonard Augustus N., retired, bds. Franklin.
Leonard Grace A., dressmaker, bds. Franklin.
Leonard Herbert, marble-cutter, h Franklin.
Lipe Albert, r 55, farmer, leases of Romaine Bieber 50.

Lipe Austin, r 57, farmer with his father Jacob.
Lipe David, r 58, farmer 45.
Lipe George F., r 57, farmer with his father John W.
LIPE GILBERT, r 57, farmer with his father Jacob.
Lipe Jacob, r 57, farmer 125.
Lipe John W., r 57, farmer 165.
Lipe Lyman, r 42, farm laborer.
Livermore Bert J., clerk, h Main.
Livermore James M., retired farmer, h Main.
Livingston Eugene, r 45, farmer 55.
LOCKWOOD DANIEL, (Ketchumville) r 9, farmer 117.
Loomis Anson, (Maine, Broome Co.) r 50, farmer 79.
LOOMIS GEORGE W., resident, h Bridge.
Loomis Myron L., (Maine, Broome Co.) r 49, farmer, works on shares for
    his father 50.
Lord John, farm laborer, h East ave.
Loveland Elizabeth H., teacher, bds. Whig.
Loveland Henry B., sugar orchard 500 trees, farmer 115, h Whig.
Loveland William, farmer with his father Henry B., bds. Whig.
Luck Ozias F., r 35, carpenter.
Lull Charlotte Mrs., resident, h Maple.
Lull George T., farm laborer, h Maple ave.
Lynch J. Henry, r 25, farm laborer.
Madan R. Jennie, (Jenksville) r 1, widow Benjamin C., seamstress.
Mahar John, r 25, farmer 150.
Marean Alson J., r 61, farmer 25.
Marean Lucien B., off r 60, resident.
Marinus David, r 21, farmer 82 1-2.
Marshall John, r 26, farm laborer.
Matile Mary L., widow G. August, h Elm.
McCabe William, laborer, h East ave.
McCrady William H., r 25, farmer 78.
McCullough Catharine, r 45, widow William, farm 38.
McCullough Lorenzo D., r 53, farmer 150.
McMahan Patrick, laborer, h Whig.
McPherson George B., r 5, farmer with his father John.
McPherson John, r 5, farmer 225.
McPherson Robert, r 5, retired farmer.
McVean Charles U., (Ketchumville) r 13, farmer 120.
Mead Clyde V., (Jenksville) r 1, farmer with his father Rogers D.
Mead Levi, (Weltonville) r 40, farmer 45.
Mead Lewis J., r 40 1-2, farmer.
Mead Martin, farmer 15, h Moore.
Mead Marvin, r 25, farm laborer.
Mead Nelson C., r 24, farmer 116.
MEAD ROGERS D., (Jenksville) r 1, orchard 400 trees and farmer 400.
Mead William R., r 40, farmer 85.
Meara Margarite, resident, h Elm.
MERRILL LUCINDA B., widow Abel, resident.
Millen Arthur L., (Jenksville) r 1, farmer with his father Elisha.
Millen Elisha, (Jenksville) r 1, farmer 114.
Millen Myron L., (Jenksville) r 1, farmer with his father Elisha.
Miller Daniel H., r 5, carpenter, also farmer 24.

Miller Sarah, widow Robert B., resident, h Main.
Minard Theodore, farmer on shares with Thomas Cary 70, h Main.
Minturn A. Mary, dressmaker, bds Main.
Minturn Amelia F. Mrs., teacher, h Main.
Mix Eugene P., blacksmith, Main, h Franklin.
Monell Wilford, (Ketchumville) r 9, farm laborer.
Monell William F., r 41, farmer 187.
Monigan Barney, emp. tannery, h East ave.
Monigan Patrick C., emp. tannery, bds. East ave.
Moon Levi B., cooper, Spring, h do.
Moon W. Adelbert, stationary engineer, h Elm.
Mooney Kernen, emp. tannery, h East ave.
Moore Frank, r 25½, farmer 100.
Moore Lucy M., r 41, widow David R., resident.
Moore Mary, r 41, resident.
Moore Winnie, (Ketchumville) r 9, farmer 300.
More Cornelia, r 35, resident.
Moseman Naomi J., widow William, h Silk.
Moses Frederick E., miller, bds. Main.
Moses Philander P., prop. Newark Valley custom mill, Main, h do.
Mott William H., r 60, farmer 25.
Munson Nathan J., r 15½, farmer 81.
Murray Thomas D., section foreman S. C. R. R., h Elm.
Muzzy Charles, r 24, farmer 50.
Muzzy Emily, resident, bds. Main.
Muzzy Frank H., r 6, farmer 100.
MUZZY GEORGE B., r 6, surveyor, and farmer 100.
Mynard Benajah, r 18, farmer.
Neal Amy, teacher, bds. Brook.
Neal Harvey, stone mason, h Brook.
Neal Mary, teacher, bds. Brook.
Neal Nettie, teacher, bds. Brook.
Neal Orlie Mrs., dressmaker, h Brook.
Nearing Ira, (Maine, Broome Co.) r 49, farmer 250.
Neff Asel, basket-maker, h East ave.
Neff Stephen, laborer, h Main.
Nicholson Colonel H., (Connecticut) r 15, farmer 40.
Nicholson Grant, r 15, farmer for his father C. H.
Niefer George P., r 46, farmer with his brother John 160.
Niefer John, r 46, farmer with his brother George P. 160.
NIXON CHARLES D., prop. Jenksville steam mills, residence in Owego.
Nixon Ephraim, r 40½, retired.
NIXON GEORGE H., (Jenksville) r 1, sup't Jenksville steam mills.
Nixon Isabella, (Jenksville) r 1, widow William, resident.
Nixon Jane F., (Jenksville) r 1, widow George G., resident.
Nixon John G., (Jenksville) r 1, general store.
*NOBLE & PURPLE, (C. L. N. and G. E. P.) props. Tioga County *Herald*, Water.
NOBLE CHARLES L., (Noble & Purple) h Main.
Noble C. S. Miss, farm, h Main.
Noble David W., farmer 75, h Main.
Noble E. George, farmer 30, h Main.
Noble James T., farmer, h Main.

NOBLE LYMAN B., dealer in eggs and poultry, bds. Main.
Noble Mary L., resident, bds. Main.
Noble Washington A., farmer, h Main.
Nolan Mary, widow John, general housework, h Main.
Nolan Patrick, emp. tannery, h East ave.
Nolton Byron, r 55, farmer 51.
Nolton William, carpenter, h Maple.
North Sarah A., r 24, widow Samuel D., resident.
Nowlan & Abbott, (E. G. N. & G. A.) blacksmiths, Main.
Nowlan Edward G., (Nowlan & Abbott) h Main.
Owen James K., (Ketchumville) r 11, farmer 30.
Owen Wesley, (Ketchumville) r 11, watch and clock repairer.
Pangburn Stephen, r 15 1-2, farmer 56.
Partridge John B., (West Newark) r 22, farmer.
Patrick Leroy, (Maine, Broome Co.) r 49, farmer, leases of Turner estate 150.
Patterson Alfred, off r 39, farmer 100.
PATTERSON D. WILLIAMS, genealogist, h Main.
Payne Ellis, (Maine, Broome Co.) r 47, farmer 50.
Pearl Albertine Mrs., housekeeper, h Main.
Pease George W., (Ketchumville) r 9, farmer, leases of Fred North 20.
Pease Henry F., (Ketchumville) r 12, carpenter.
Pease Morris, (Ketchumville) r 12, farmer.
Pellett George, r 21, farmer 30.
Pellett William M., r 21, farmer 132.
Perry Cephas, (Ketchumville) r 13, farmer 30.
Perry George, stone mason, h Ward.
Phelps Diana, widow Jason, resident, h Main.
Phillips Harriet, widow William, resident, h Moore.
Phillips John M., painter, h Moore.
Phipps George, (Ketchumville) r 12, peddler.
Pier Bradford S., r 46, farm laborer.
Pierce Hiram C., r 16, farmer 25.
PIERSON CHARLES O., harness-maker, Water, h Elm.
Pierson William, r 6, retired farmer.
Pinney Egbert B., traveling salesman, h Silk.
Pitcher Adelbert, (Maine, Broome Co.) r 28, farm laborer.
Pitcher Alfred, r 30, farmer 50.
Pitcher Allie De F., r 35, farmer for his father, Harrison.
Pitcher Eli (Maine, Broome Co.) r 28, farmer 80.
Pitcher Harrison, r 35, farmer 111.
Pitcher James, (Maine, Broome Co.) r 29, farmer, leases of Frank Lewis 50.
Pitcher Nathan, (Maine, Broome Co.) r 29, farm laborer.
Pitcher Silas, (Maine, Broome Co.) r 29, farmer 90.
Pitcher Wesley, off r 35, farmer, leases of David J. Shear 50.
Pollard Ira J., (Ketchumville) r 9, teamster.
PRENTICE ELMER E., r 20, farmer.
PRENTICE ULYSSES G. Jr., r 4, farmer with his father William F.
Prentice William F., r 4, farmer 110.
Prentice William G., emp., William's saw-mill, h Franklin.
PURPLE GILBERT E., (Noble & Purple) h Main.
Quail William, r 8, farm laborer.
Quick Frederick, r 52, farmer.
Race Lucy A., resident, bds. Whig.

Raleigh Orrin, emp. N. K. Waring, h Maple.
RANDALL OSCAR S., general merchant, Water, h do.
Recordon Theodore, r 60, farmer 50.
Reeves William J., r 20, excise commissioner, and farmer 145.
Rewey Emeline, widow Oliver, resident, h Main.
Rice James, laborer, h Main.
Rice John, retired, h Silk.
Rich Marion F., (Connecticut) r 15, farmer, works on shores for William
   Bushnell 50.
RICHARDSON FRED W., traveling salesman, and farmer 200, h Whig.
Riley Andrew, clerk, h Maple.
Riley Andrew B., carpenter, also dealer in wagons, h Maple.
Riley Kate, widow Michael, laundress, h off East ave.
Riley Maggie, clerk, h Water.
Riley William, (Ketchumville) r 13, blacksmith and farmer 25.
Robbins Clark M., (West Newark) r 22, farm laborer.
Robbins George, traveling hair-dresser, h Maple.
Robbins George E. Mrs., dressmaker, h Maple.
ROBERTS JOHN O., groceries and provisions, and wholesale dealer in
butter and eggs, Water, h Elm.
Rockwood Lorenzo F., station agt. S. C. R. R., also agt. U. S. express, and
   telegraph operator, h East ave.
ROGERS CORNELIUS R., physician and surgeon, Main, h do.
Rogers Edward, (Maine, Broom Co.) r 47, farmer 16.
Ross John, (Maine, Broome Co.) r 27, farmer 50.
Roulet Alfred, farmer 140.
Roulet Felix, traveling salesman, h Elm.
ROYS ALPHEUS D., (Roys & Todd) h Main.
ROYS & TODD, (A. D. R. & Mrs. P. E. T.) general merchants, Main.
Russell Henry, (Main, Broome Co.) r 14, farmer 93.
Ryan Mary, widow Michael, bds. Brook.
Ryan William, principal school, h Main.
Saddlemire Alexander, r 26, farmer 80.
Saddlemire Anna E., r 30, widow David, resident.
Saddlemire Daniel J., r 31, carpenter, and farmer 25.
Saddlemire Elias, r 41, farmer.
Saddlemire Emily Mrs., r 26, farm 40.
Saddlemire Ephraim, (Main, Broome Co.) r 29, farmer 61,
Saddlemire Fenton R., r 31, farmer with his father, Noyes P.
Saddlemire Frank, r 57, farmer 60.
Saddlemire Jacob H., r 25, egg buyer, and farmer 78.
Saddlemire Jerome, r 43, farmer 111.
Saddlemire Manfred, r 26, farmer for his mother, Mrs. Emily Saddlemire.
Saddlemire Noyes P., r 31, farmer 188.
Salisbury William H., (Weltonville) r 40, farmer on shares with J. W. Barrett.
SANDWICK JOHN K., barber, water, h Whig.
Schnapp Jacob, Jr., r 53, farmer 25.
Schoolcraft Hattie E., r 42, widow Lucius, resident.
Schoolcraft John, laborer, h East ave.
Schoolcraft John D., r 35, farmer 19.
Schoolcraft Minor, r 42, farm laborer.
Schoolcraft Paul, r 35, resident.
Schoolcroft Abagail, r 45, widow David, resident.

Schoolcroft Adam, (Maine, Broome Co.) r 29, farmer 102.
Schoolcroft Earnest, r 26, farmer, leases of D. Pitcher estate 200.
Schoolcroft Henry, r 34, farmer 40.
Searles Ezra, r 61, mason and farmer 50.
Searles Jack E., r 41, painter.
Sears Lizzie M., dressmaker, Elm, bds. do.
Sears Sophronia M. Mrs., resident, h Elm.
Sebastian Christina, r 53, widow G. O., resident.
Settel Deidamia, r 46, widow John, resident.
Settel Oscar, r 46, farmer 300.
Settell David, retired, h White.
Settell Elmer E., r 32, farmer with his father, Ira D.
Settell George, r 51, farmer 90.
Settell Ira D., r 32, farmer 177.
SETTLE PETER, r 45, farmer 105.
Shafer Egbert, r 41, farm laborer.
Shaffer Charles E., r 25, farmer 50.
Sharp Osmer, (Ketchumville) r 9, farm laborer.
Sharp Robert B., (Ketchumville), r 11, blacksmith and farmer 152.
Shaw Laura M., widow Joel, h Main.
Shaw Philander M., farmer 62, h Main.
Shay James, laborer, h Maple ave.
Shear David J., resident, h Elm.
Shear John I., r 35, farmer 64.
Sheldon Harley G., retired farmer, h Main.
Sherman Hiram L., carpenter, h Maple.
Sherman Peter, (Ketchumville) r 13, farmer.
SHERWOOD GEORGE F., supt. Davidge & Landfield's tannery, h Maple.
Sherwood Warren D., sewing machines, h Main.
Shoultes Chauncey, r 53, farm laborer.
Shoultes Edward W., r 32, farmer with his father, William H.
Shoultes Frederick, r 53, farmer 95.
Shoultes George, r 53, farmer 50.
Shoultes Ira., off r 53, farmer 100.
Shoultes Ira A., r 35, farm laborer.
Shoultes William H., r 32, farmer 75.
Shulenburg Wallace H., r 41, farm laborer.
Simmons Joseph, retired, h Elm.
SLOSSON GEORGE W., justice of the peace, h Maple.
SMITH ALFRED, (Jenksville) r 51, horse-breeder and farmer 120; farm
    for sale.
Smith Benjamin F., resident, h Main.
SMITH EDWIN P., farmer, h Main.
Smith Elijah, (Maine, Broome Co.) r 27, farmer, works on shares for Frank
    Lewis 315.
Smith Harvey B., resident, h Brook.
Smith Jabez C., farmer, leases of E. P. Smith 70.
SMITH JOEL E., r 41, farmer 25.
SMITH JOHN E., r 40½, excise com. and farmer 100.
Smith John S., resident, h Bridge.
SMITH L. M. & SON, (Lewis H.) drugs and wall-paper, 5 Water.
SMITH LEWIS H., (L. M. Smith & Son) h Water.
SMITH LUCIUS M., (L. M. Smith & Son) h Water.

Smith Randolph L., r 40 1-2, farmer 58.
Smith William H., r 5, farmer 45.
Smullen Charles M., (Jenksville) r 1, blacksmith.
Snapp Edward E., r 53, farmer 106.
Snapp Emeline, r 53, widow George, resident.
SNAPP FRANK, r 53, farmer 90.
Snapp Henry O., r 15, farmer 75.
Spaulding Lucius W., r 41, farmer 160.
Spaulding Luther J., retired, h Main.
Spaulding Marcus M., retired, h Main.
Sprague Almander, retired, h Main.
Sprague Henry A., resident, h Main.
Sprague Lewis H., resident, h Main.
Stannard Aretus R., emp. Donley Brothers, h Brook.
Stannard Henry, r 26 1-2, farmer 100.
Stannard Hiram R., bakery, Water, h do.
Stannard John M., r 25, farmer 104.
Stevens Aaron C., r 41, millwright and turner.
Stevens Elvira Mrs., r 42, resident.
STEVENS HENRY W., r 42, apiarist, small fruit grower and poultry.
Stevens William W., r 41, farmer 23.
Stever Fred A., painter, h Whig.
Stinard Jane H., r 4, widow James D., resident.
Stowell Alexander D., r 16, farmer 18.
Strait Edward, r 19, farmer, leases of J. R. Johnson 63.
Strait Joseph, (Connecticut) r 8, lumberman and shingleman.
Strong Fanny C., (Jenksville) r 1, widow Isaac B., resident.
Strong Fred W., (Jenksville) r 1, farmer, leases of J. Evans 10.
Strong Orin, (Jenksville) r 1, farmer 200.
Sturtevant David M., carriage painter, Brook, h Whig.
Sutphen Horace, (Jenksville) r 1, supt. Nixon farm.
SUTTON GEORGE B., r 41, artist and farmer 100.
Sweet Charles E., (Ketchumville) r 13, blacksmith.
Sweigler Robert, r 58, farmer 45.
TAPPAN CHARLES, small fruit grower and farmer, bds. Whig.
Tappan John C., farm laborer, h Whig cor. Moore.
Tappan Rebecca A., widow Asher C., resident, Whig cor. Moore.
Tappan Revere C., physician and surgeon, Main, h do.
Tappan Riley A., farmer 150.
THORNTON C. FRANK, stone mason and prop. of quarry, East ave.
Thornton Chauncey G., resident, h Franklin.
Thornton George, r 16, farm laborer.
Thornton Mary E., laundress, h Franklin.
TIBBITTS ELI D., retired farmer, Main.
TIDD JOHN, r 41, retired.
*TIOGA COUNTY HERALD, (Noble & Purple) weekly, issued Saturday, Water.
TODD FRANK H., clerk, h Main.
TODD PHEBE E., (Roys & Todd) h Main.
Tompkins George, (Ketchumville) r 10, farmer.
Towner Lucy M., r 4, widow Milo B., resident.
Treible Wilson Rev., pastor M. E. church, h Main.
Tripp Emma, (Maine, Broome Co.) r 47, widow Frank, resident.

Turner Charles, (Maine, Broome Co.) r 49, farmer 113.
Turner Leroy, (Maine, Broome Co.) r 49, farmer 400.
VanDemark John, (Weltonville) r 40, farmer 62.
VanDemark Lucius, r 16, farm laborer.
VanGlowe Abram, (Jenksville) off r 1, farm laborer.
VanPatten Richard H., farmer 40, h East ave.
Wade Edgar O., r 41, farmer with his father William H.
Wade William H., r 41, farmer 86.
Waldo Betsey C., resident, h Main.
Waldo William D., r 6, farmer 46.
Walter Charles, off r 41, farmer 63.
Walter Clarence S., r 41, carpenter and joiner.
Walter Eugene C., r 39, farmer 30.
Walworth Clark, r 23, farmer 140.
Walworth LaVern, r 4, farmer 96.
Walworth William, r 23, farmer with his father Clark.
Waring Norman K., manuf. fly-rods, Spring, h do.
Warner Frank, (Connecticut) r 9, emp. lumber-mill.
Warner William, (Connecticut) r 9, emp. lumber-mill.
Washburn Stoddard, farm laborer, h Maple ave.
Waterman Charles H., r 5, farmer, leases of A. C. Matthews 128.
Watkins William, (West Newark) r 22, farmer.
Watrous Frank, r 15, farmer 185.
Watson Abbie J., widow Seth, bds. Whig.
Wells Henry L., book-keeper for Davidge, Landfield & Co., h Main.
Wells Jane B., widow Frederick, farm 130, h Main.
WELLS LUCIUS E., (Burch & Wells) h Main.
Wells William F., farmer with his mother Jane B., bds. Main.
Westfall E. Frank, r 55, farm laborer.
Westfall Frank, r 56, farmer 15.
Westfall Frederick W., r 16, farmer with his father Joseph F.
Westfall Joseph F., r 16, farmer 100.
White George W., (Jenksville) custom grist and saw-mill.
WHITING BROS., (J. E. and W. V. B.) wagon and carriage makers, re-pairing done with neatness and dispatch, Brook.
WHITING WARREN V. B., (Whiting Bros.) h Main.
WHITING JERRY E., (Whiting Bros.) h Main.
Whitmore Horace L., leather finisher, h Whig.
Whitmore Martha, widow Hezekiah, resident, h Whig.
Williams Edson, r 41, farmer, leases, of James Reed 100.
Williams Lucius E., saw, planing and feed-mill, and dealer in coal and lumber, off Main, h Rewey ave.
Williams Margaret, widow Almeran, bds. off Bridge.
Williams Oliver G., laborer, h Maple.
Williams Royal R., farmer 85, h off Bridge.
Williams Theodore, carpenter, h Elm.
Willis Henry, (Maine, Broome Co.) r 47, farm laborer.
Willis Horace B., (Maine, Broome Co.) r 47, farmer 43.
Wilson Elnora, widow Charles F., resident, h Main.
Winship Charles B., boarding-house, Maple.
Winship Henry, retired, h Main.
WOOD HENRY A., billiard room and shoemaker, Water. h do.

STARKEY & WINTERS, Wholesale and Retail Druggists, Owego.

Wood Joseph, retired, h Rewey ave.
Woodard Andrew J., laborer, bds. Maple.
Wright Malborn W., resident, h Main.
Wright Sarah, widow Giles, resident, h Main.
YOUNG HIRAM, (Dimmick & Young) bds. Dimmick House.
Young John, r 51, farmer 96.
Young Wilson, r 51, farmer with his father John.
Zimmer Addie Mrs., nurse, h Whig.
Zimmer Asa W., r 45, farmer with his father Elias.
Zimmer Charles, r 31, farmer.
Zimmer Charles W., r 45, farmer with his father Elias.
Zimmer Daniel, r 53, farmer 70.
Zimmer Delmar, r 43, farmer with his father Seymour E.
Zimmer Edgar, (West Newark) r 22, farm laborer.
Zimmer Edward, r 45, farmer with his father Seymour E.
Zimmer Edward, r 46, farmer 85.
Zimmer Elias, r 45, farmer 180.
Zimmer Eva M., teacher, bds. Whig.
Zimmer Henry S., r 35, farmer 65.
Zimmer Jacob, r 26, farmer 20.
Zimmer Lyman, r 26, farmer 125,
Zimmer Manier, (Maine, Broome Co.) r 29, farmer 93.
Zimmer Miner S., r 34, farmer 54.
Zimmer Nathaniel, (Maine, Broome Co.) r 47, farmer 96.
Zimmer Peter A., r 40 1-2, farmer 115.
Zimmer Peter B., r 30, farmer 200.
Zimmer Ransom J., r 30, farmer 128.
Zimmer Seymour E., r 45, farmer 112.
Zimmer Sherman, r 45, farmer with his father Seymour E.
Zimmer Wesley, r 45, farmer with his father Elias.

NICHOLS.

(*For explanations, etc., see page 3, part second.*)

(Postoffice address is Nichols, unless otherwise designated in parenthesis.)

Adams Eliza S., (Hooper's Valley) r 5, resident.
Adams Maria, widow Absalom, resident.
ADAMS STEPHEN B.(Hooper's Valley) r 5, McCormick Harvesting
    Machine Company's agt. for Tioga County, and farmer 140.
Alen Clarence B., (Owego) r 20, farm laborer.
Allen John, (Owego) r 10, farm laborer.
Allen Robert A., laborer, h Main.
Allington Emily J., (Hooper's Valley) r 1, resident.
Allington Sarah A., (Hooper's Valley) r 3, widow Rev. Jacob, farm 34.
Ames Lloyd H , (Owego) r 21, stationary engineer.

Ames Orley L. Mrs., laundress, h River.
Anderson H. Beecher, hostler, bds. Main.
Angell Benjamin P., retired, h Main.
Angell Charles D., (Hooper's Valley) r 1, farmer, leases of Pearsall & Gray 250.
Annable Lovisa, r 40, widow, resident.
ANTHONY FLOYD H., groceries and provisions and livery, Main, h do.
Atwood Harrison, r 10, farm laborer.
BABCOCK WILLARD, farmer, h Railroad.
Babcock William, laborer, h Main.
Baird Frances C., resident, bds. River.
BAKER BROTHERS, (W. W. and R. B.) props. Nichols creamery.
Baker Frank B., emp. creamery, bds. Cady ave.
BAKER ROBERT B., (Baker Bros.) h Cady ave.
BAKER WILLIAM W., (Baker Bros.) h Cady ave.
Barnes George W., (Hooper's Valley) off r 5, farm laborer.
Barr George, r 30, farm laborer.
Barr John, r, 30, farmer 150.
Barr John, Jr., r 2, farmer.
Barr Lawrence, r 30, farm laborer.
BARSTOW MARY L., resident, bds. River.
Barstow Oliver A., (Hooper's Valley) r 5, retired.
BAXTER FREDERICK H., r 26, farmer.
Baxter George T., off r 26, farmer, leases 200.
Beach Ernest C., miller, bds. Main.
Bennett Abraham, (Hooper's Valley) r 5, resident.
Bennett Elizabeth, r 26, widow Elijah, farm 25.
Bensley Fred, (Hooper's Valley) r 1, farmer.
BENSLEY JOHN, (Hooper's Valley) r 1, school trustee and farmer 200.
Bensley John C., (Hooper's Valley) r 1, farmer.
Bixby Charles R., carpenter and builder, h Cady ave.
Bixby Chester, carpenter, h Main.
Bixby George W., r 37, farmer.
Bixby Schuyler, r 37, farmer on shares with Jos. Reynolds 130.
BIXBY SMITH R., contractor and builder, h River.
Blair Linus, r 23, farm laborer.
Bliven Cranston, member of school board; also, dealer in produce and general merchandise, Main, h River.
Bliven Cranston V. S., retired, bds. River.
Boardman Elizabeth P., r 10, widow Edward, resident.
Bonham Jonas, retired, h Cady ave.
Booth Franklin, (Hooper's Valley) off r 5, farmer.
Boyce David M., laborer, h River.
Bradley Hiram, (Tioga Centre) r 10, farmer on shares with C. Lounsberry.
Bradley Marcus, farmer on shares with Warren A. Smith 60, h River.
Briggs Ebenezer, (E. Nichols) r 39, farmer 56.
Briggs Edward W., (E. Nichols) r 22, farmer 91½.
Briggs Elihu, (E. Nichols) r 22, farmer 94.
Brigg Herman I., off r 9, stock dealer and farmer 87½.
Briggs Ira, r 39, farmer 75.
Briggs Julius, (E. Nichols), r 46, farmer.
Briggs Melvin, (E. Nichols) r 40, apiarist and farmer.
Brott David, (Owego) r 21, farmer.
Brougham John W., emp. Harris, DeGroat & Co., h Main.

Brown Elizabeth, off r 2, widow Peter, resident.
Brown Fanny, widow, h Main.
Brown George, retired, h Oxford.
Brown James M., r 8, carpenter.
Brown John W., r 1, farmer 6.
BROWN S. OTIS, off r 2, farmer 114.
Burrell Isaac, farm laborer, h River.
Burrell Lott S., laborer, bds. River.
Butolph Frank E., r 9, farmer 76.
Butolph Leroy, r 37, farmer 115.
Butolph Sybil, r 48, farm 35.
Cady George M., (Latham & Cady) also physician and surgeon, bds. River.
CADY GEORGE P., physician and surgeon, River, h do.
Cady William, retired, bds. Cady ave. (Died July 2, 1887.)
Campbell Amos B., (Owego) r 42, cooper and farmer on shares with Charles
    Dunham 80.
Campbell George W., (Hooper's Valley) r 5, laborer.
Campbell Smith, r 9, farmer 31.
Campion Frank, r 12, teacher and farmer.
Carpenter Allen O., farm laborer, h Cady ave.
Carter Alexander, (East Nichols) r 47, farm laborer.
Childs Marcus W., principal of the Union School.
Chubbuck Francis Rev., (Hooper's Valley) r 1, retired M. E. clergyman and
    small fruit grower.
CLAIR HIRAM, (Hooper's Valley) r 3, farmer 253.
Clair William H., (Hooper's Valley) r 3, farmer with his father Hiram.
CLAPP SAMUEL, lumber dealer and farmer 60, bds. River.
Clarke Howard W., traveling salesman, h Cady ave.
Cogswell Henry S., (East Nichols) r 47, farmer, leases of G. Newman 50.
COLE HORACE, r 3, farmer.
Cole Truman, 27, farmer 114.
Coleman & Horton, (E. C. & G. H. H.) hardware, stoves and tinware, Main.
Coleman Emmet, (Coleman & Horton) also postmaster, bds. Nichols House.
Conant Edward H., painter, h River.
Conant Luther, boots and shoes, Main, h River.
Cortright Charles F., r 37, laborer.
Cortright Elijah, r 24, cooper.
Cortright John, (Tioga Center) r 10, laborer.
Coryell Arthur, (Hooper's Valley) r 4, farm laborer.
Coryell Augusta, widow Henry P., resident, h Cady Block.
Coryell Emanuel, (Hooper's Valley) r 4, farmer 65.
Coryell Emanuel, Jr., (Hooper's Valley) r 4, farm laborer.
Coryell Mary, teacher, bds. Cady Block.
CORYELL ROBERT P., r 1, school trustee and farmer 250.
Crandall Charles, r 10, farmer on shares with I. Dunham.
CRANDALL GEORGE E., (Tioga Center) r 10, farmer.
Crandall William, r 10, basket-maker.
Cure Andrew J., r 10, farmer.
Curkendoll William, r 10, carpenter and small fruit grower.
Davenport Abraham, r 30, farm laborer.
Davenport Amelia Mrs., (Hooper's Valley) r 2, farm 30.
Davenport Charlotte D., r 30, farm 25.
Davenport Ellen, (Hooper's Valley) farm 30.

7

Davenport Ira, (Hooper's Valley) r 2, farmer.
Davenport Joseph, r 2, farmer.
DEAN JULIA A., (Hooper's Valley) r 3, farm 34.
DEAN NATHAN S., r 1, apiarist 30 swarms, fruit grower, and farmer 60.
De Bolder Lawrence, r 24, farmer 42.
De Bolder William E., stationary engineer, h Walnut.
De Groat J. Fields, (Harris, De Groat & Co.) h Main.
De Groat William, (Owego) r 16, blacksmith.
Derring Herman, r 9, laborer.
Doty Charles H., laborer, bds. Cady ave.
Doty George W., retired, h Cady ave.
Drake C. Sidney, clerk, bds. Nichols Hotel.
Duncan James (E. Nicholas), r 40, farm laborer.
Dunham Benjamin, (Owego) r 36, carpener, and farmer 74.
Dunham Charles, (Owego) r 32, farmer 100.
Dunham Charles, r 49½ , farmer with his father Samuel.
Dunham Charles L., r 10, farmer.
DUNHAM EBENEZER, produce dealer, Main, h do.
Dunham Elemer E., (Owego), r 35, farm laborer.
Dunham Frances J., (Owego), r 36, teacher.
Dunham Harriet P., (Owego) r 33, widow Anson, resident.
Dunham Harvey W., r 10, farmer 135.
Dunham Isaac, r 10, farmer 300, and in Penn. 100.
Dunham James, (Owego) r 17, farmer, leases of John Smith 100.
Dunham Joseph M. r 10, farmer.
Dunham Mary E., resident, h Main.
Dunham Melissa S. Miss, (Owego) r 16, resident.
Dunham Nehemiah, (Owego) r 35, farmer 50.
Dunham Platt, (Owego) r 32, farmer 50.
Dunham Platt Jr., (Owego), r 42, farmer 114.
Dunham Samuel, (Owego) r 32, farmer.
Dunham Samuel, r 49 1-2, farmer 71.
Dunham Sands, r 23, farmer.
Dunham Stephen H., r 10, farmer 135.
Edsall Benjamin F., carpenter, h Howell.
Edsall Brice P., retired, h Walnut.
Edsall Ida O., widow David, resident, bds. River.
EDSALL JOHN R., town clerk, also general merchant and dealer in agri-
    cultural implements, Main, bds. Walnut.
Edwards Ann E., (Hooper's Valley) r 5, widow Albertus, resident.
Edwards Cyrus, (Hooper's Valley) r 5, farm laborer.
Ellis George, r 29, farmer.
Ellis George, Jr., (Hooper's Valley) r 5, carpenter and ferryman.
Ellis Hiram, (Hooper's Valley) r 28, farmer on shares with S. Kirby estate 67.
Ellis John, (Waverly) r 30, farmer 15.
Ellsworth Aurelia, widow Francis H., resident, h River.
Ellsworth Elwin F., painter and paper-hanger, bds. River.
Ellsworth Henry N., carpenter, also farmer 31, h Cole.
Elsbree Emily C., widow Manning, resident, h head of Main.
Evans Amanda C., (Tioga Centre) r 22, widow Cyrus G., farm 52.
Evans Cyrus, (Tiga Center) r 13, farmer 50.
Evans Edward E., well driver, also agt. for wind-mils, h Walnut.
Evans Elijah K., r 8, contractor and builder, and farmer 20.

Everitt Elmore, r 8, supervisor, and farmer 38.
Everitt Frederick M., tinsmith, h Main.
Everitt George E., farmer, h Main.
Everitt Harvey C., farmer 50, h Main.
Everitt Hovey E., drug clerk, bds. r 8.
Everson George T., (Owego) r 17, farm laborer.
Everson Oliver C., (Owego) r 17, farm laborer.
FARNHAM OSCAR E., r 49½, patentee egg preserving rack, also prop. wood turning shop, and cidar-mill, and farmer 4½.
FENDERSON JOHN, prop. Nichols steam flour, saw and planing-mills, h River.
Ferris Horace, (Owego) r 17, farmer 50.
Field Lucas T., (Hooper's Valley) r 5, postmaster.
Ford George, r 9, farmer.
FORMAN JOHN, r 10, member of school board, excise commissioner, small fruit grower, and farmer 200.
Forman Miles, resident, h Main.
Forman Smith, r 10, farmer with his father John.
Fox Alfred J., farmer.
Fox Harry, r 26, retired.
Fox Isaac D., farmer 25, on shares with F. C. Lowman.
Goetchins Maurice L., r 1, farmer.
Goodenough Delos, boots and shoes, Main, h do.
Goodsell William S., (Athens, Pa.) r 1, farmer 50, and leases of H. Kiff 70.
Goodsell Zina, r 26, farmer 50.
Granger Daniel, (Owego) r 20, farmer 36.
Granger George M., (Owego) r 17, farmer 25.
Greene Joseph G., (Owego) r 19, farmer on shares with S. Evans.
Griswold Martha, (Waverly) r 1, widow Henry, farmer 25.
Griswold Thoms, (Waverly) r 1, farmer 50.
Hamel Charles E., (Owego) r 18, watch repairer.
Hamel Clark, (Owego) r 18, gardener.
Harden Ida Mrs., dressmaker, off Main.
Harden Samuel W., farmer 26, h off Main.
Harris, DeGroat & Co., (O. P. H., J. F. DeG. and R. C. H.) wholesale dealers and shippers of hay, grain, potatoes and general farm products, Main.
Harris Elizabeth D., widow Nathaniel B., resident, h Main.
Harris Oliver P., (Harris, DeGroat & Co.) Main.
Harris R. Corsa, (Harris, DeGroat & Co.) h Main.
HAUVER GEORGE L., (Owego) r 16, farmer, leases of J. Hunt estate 90.
Hazard Lois, r 10, widow Dwight, resident.
Hazard Willis W., r 8, farm laborer.
Herrick Henry B., (Waverly) r 30, farmer 6¼.
HERRICK WILLIAM, r 1, apiariast 11 swarms, assessor, and farmer on shares with Julia A. Dean 31.
Hill Abner, r 10, farm laborer.
Hill Morris M., (Hooper's Valley) r 3, farmer.
Hilligass David, (Hooper's Valley) r 4, district collector, and farmer 27.
Hilligass Jacob, r 49, farmer.
Hoover William, (Hooper's Valley) r 5, retired.
Horton Betsey, widow Stephen S., h River.
Horton G. Henry, (Coleman & Horton) also farmer 300, h River.
Howell Arthur M., r 49½, farmer.

Howell John J., r 8, resident.
Howell John L., retired, h Main.
HOWELL ROBERT, r 49½, geologist, mineralogist, and farmer 127, and in Pennsylvania 20.
HUNT ADONIJAH, (Owego) r 37, prop. saw and grist-mill, and farmer 140.
Hunt Brothers, (Enos and Seth) r 10, farmers 60.
Hunt Charles E., clerk, bds. Main.
Hunt Ebenezer, r 10, farmer 53.
HUNT ELIZABETH, (Owego) r 36, farm 194.
HUNT EZRA C., (Owego) r 21, farmer 110.
Hunt George B., (Owego) r 17, farmer with his father Thomas J.
Hunt John W., (Waverly) r 1, farmer 160.
Hunt Julia S., (Owego) r 17, widow Jonathan, 2d, farm 40.
HUNT MARCELLA, (Owego) r 36, farm 194.
HUNT SAMUEL, (Waverly) r 1, farmer 155.
HUNT SISTERS, (Owego) (E. and M. Hunt) r 36, farmer 194.
Hunt Thomas J., (Owego) r 17, farmer 188.
Hunt Timothy, (Owego) r 13, farmer.
HUNT WILLISTON, r 10, farmer 115.
Hyres Frances, widow Jerry W., resident, h Main.
INGERSOLL GEORGE A., r 10, member of school board, also stock breeder, and farmer 103.
Jansen Abram, (Owego) r 33, retired.
Johnson Charles H., r 23, farmer 47.
Johnson Eliza J., r 10, widow Parley, resident.
Johnson John A., r 23, farmer.
Johnson John E., r 10, farmer 40.
Jones Charles M., laborer, h Railroad.
Jones Eveline, r 49, resident.
Jones Lewis, r 39, road commissioner and farmer 100.
JOSLIN EDWARD, dry and fancy goods, millinery and wall-paper, Main, h do.
Joslyn Louisa, (Owego) r 21, widow Peter, resident.
Kane Michael, laborer, h Cady ave.
Keech Miles W., r 46, mason, carpenter and farmer.
KEECH T. WILBER, r 39, farmer, leases of his mother Laura 50.
Kelso Harry, r 38, cigar-maker.
Kennedy John M., telegraph operator, bds. Main.
Kent Pulaski P., (Owego) r 17, farm laborer.
KETCHAM ELI G., (Owego) r 35, justice of the peace, school trustee and farmer 226.
Ketcham William, butcher, Main, h Walnut.
KIRBY ALLEN B., agent D. L. & W. R. R., also, U. S. express agent, Main cor. Life.
Lane David J., (Owego) r 17, apairist and farmer.
Lane Fred H., (Owego) r 17, teacher.
Lane George S., (Tioga Centre) r 13, farmer 127.
Lane Harvey P., (Tioga Centre) r 13, farmer.
Lane Lucinda, (Owego) r 16, widow Amos, farm 46.
Lane Warren A., (Owego) r 17, school trustee and farmer 47.
Laning Charles P., carpenter, h Howell.
LaRue Isaac L., prop. hotel, Main.

STARKEY & WINTERS, Wholesale and Retail Druggists, Owego.

Latham & Cady (S. H. L. and G. M. C.) druggists, toilet articles and confectionary, Main cor. River.

Latham Sidney H., (Latham & Cady) h Main.

Lisenby Charles F., r 8, farmer on shares with E. Dunham 240.

Lisenby John, r 1, farm laborer.

Lollis William, r 16, nurse.

Losaw Daniel, r 25, farmer.

Lounsberry Benjamin, (Owego) r 17, farmer 138.

Lounsberry Frederick, (Owego) r 21, farmer.

Lounsberry George, (Tioga Centre) r 11, farmer 100.

Lounsberry George F., (Tioga Centre) r 11, farmer 62.

LOUNSBERRY HARRIET E., (Tioga Centre) r 10, farm 50.

Lounsberry Harriet E., (Tioga Centre) r 10, widow James, farm 60.

Lounsberry Horace, (Tioga Centre) r 13, farmer 241.

Lounsberry Horace, Second, (Owego) r 21, farmer 70, and with Horace Lounsberry, First 241.

Lounsberry James, (Tioga Centre) r 22, farmer 113.

Lounsberry John, (Owego) r 21, saw-mill and farmer 159.

Lounsberry Platt, (Tioga Centre) r 10, retired farmer 28.

LOUNSBURY WILLIAM R., r 12, excise commissioner and farmer 64.

Loveland Mary A., widow Lewis, laundress, h Main.

Loveland Seth H., (Waverly) r 1, saw-mill and carpenter.

LOWMAN FREDERIC C., r 3, breeder of thoroughbred short-horn cattle and farmer 525 ; stock for sale at all times.

Lunn William H., r 8, farm laborer.

Lurcock Adelbert, r 3, farm laborer.

Lurcock Frederick, (Tioga Centre) r 12, farmer.

Lurcock William, emp. De Groat, Harris & Co., h Main.

Lynch William, r 9, laborer.

Mallory Frederick O., (Owego) r 32, farmer, leases of J. Smith, Jr., 50.

Mallory John L., (Owego), r 23, local preacher, carpenter, and farmer 35.

Mallory Susan, widow Harrison, resident, bds. Cady ave.

Mallory William W., barber, Main, h Cady ave.

MARSHALL TIMOTHY B., r 49, town collector, and farmer 50.

Mason Fritz, gardener, h Main.

Matthews Hiram P., r 38, apiarist 25 swarms, small fruit grower, and farmer 113.

MATTHEWS ISAIAH, r 38, cigar manufacturer, and prop. cider-mill.

MATTHEWS STEPHEN P., (Owego) off r 32, retired physician, and farmer 40.

Matthews Susie, widow Ephraim, art teacher, h Cady Block.

McNeil George K., constable and collector, h Main.

Measer Ernest H., r 30, farmer 70.

Merrill Albert S., carpenter and builder, h Howell.

Mettler James L., (Waterman & Mettler) h Cady ave.

Mikels George H., laborer, h Howell.

Mikels J. Henry, r 12, farm laborer.

Miller Edmund S., blacksmith, Main, h Oxford.

Miller James, off r 23, farmer.

Miller William, off r 23, farmer.

Mills Delavan, r 39, farmer 90.

Mills Francis, r 37, school trustee, and farmer 140.

MITCHELL IDA A., art teacher, h Cady ave.
MITCHELL MARY J., art teacher, h Cady ave.
Mitchell Sally C., widow Nathan, resident, h Cady ave.
Mollet Betsey, (Owego) r 19, widow Peter, farm 70.
Moody George, r 26, farm laborer.
Moody George H., r 26, farmer 45.
Moore Edwin T., (Owego) r 22, building mover, and farmer 114.
Moore Frank H., (Owego) r 36, farmer.
Moore George, r 37, farmer 260.
Moore Ruth A., (Owego) r 36, widow Hezelton N., resident.
Morey Robert, off r 9, farmer.
Morse Frank J., R. R. section hand, bds. Main.
Mosher Edwin, carpenter, h Main.
Moulton Morris B., farmer 12, and 160 in Penn., h Main.
Neal Henry C., off r 2, farmer 52.
Neal Linus, r 23, farmer.
Neal Nehemiah E., furniture dealer and carriage painter, Cady ave., h do.
Newland Samuel, (Owego) r 18, carpenter.
Newman George, (East Nichols) r 47, farmer 200.
NICHOLS HOTEL, J. Platt, prop., River.
Nichols James, (East Nichols) r 44, farmer.
Nichols John E., (East Nichols) prop. threshing machine and farm laborer.
Northrop Charles T., (East Nichols) r 44, farmer 25.
Olmstead Joseph, ferryman, h Ferry.
Orsburn Charles, (Hooper's Valley) r 1, farmer.
Orsburn Miers, (Hooper's Valley) r 1, farmer 240.
Orsburn Miles, (Hooper's Valley) r 1, farmer.
Osburn William, retired, h Cady ave.
Paris Peter, r 10, farmer on shares with Ebenezer Hunt 53.
PARK JOSEPH, (Waverly) r 1, farmer 162.
Pearl Eunice, (East Nichols) r 35, widow Daniel, farm 103.
Pearl Fred G., (Owego) r 35, farmer 50.
Pearl Walter H., (Owego) r 17, farmer 25.
PEARSALL L. BURR, (Hooper's Valley) r 5, prop. steam saw-mill and
    farmer 386, and in Penn. 300.
Peck William C. Rev., (Hooper's Valley) r 3, Free Baptist, retired.
Peet Henry, (Owego) r 19, farm laborer.
Pendleton Caleb F., foreman Nichols creamery, bds. Cady ave.
PETTY FOSTER, (Hooper's Valley) r 1, farmer.
Pitcher Eliza, widow John, resident, h River.
Pitcher Elvira, (Owego) r 18, widow Heman, farm 125.
Pitcher John, (Hooper's Valley) r 5, farm laborer.
Pitcher William A., emp. creamery, bds. River.
Platt Frank, clerk Nichols Hotel, River.
PLATT JOHN, prop. Nichols Hotel, Main.
Presher Benjamin, (Tioga Center) r 21, farm laborer.
Quilty Michael, r 8, farmer 50.
Ratchford John, miller, bds. Main.
Reed Adeline, (Owego) r 17, widow Ezra, farm 70.
Reeves Ella, widow George, dressmaker, h River.
Reynolds Albert S., r 39, farmer 50.
Reynolds Amanda, r 9, widow Vincent, resident.
Reynolds Enoch J., r 8, farmer on shares with A. Waterman 80.

REYNOLDS ISUM I., r 48, farmer 80, and leases of Miss S. Butolph 35.

Reynolds John E., r 9, farmer 170.

REYNOLDS JOHN S., r 8, member of school board, and farmer 160.

Reynolds Joseph, r 37, retired farmer.

Reynolds Lester, farm laborer, h Main.

Richardson Ester A. Mrs., (Owego) r 32, resident.

Robertson Albert, (Owego) r 13, farmer 72.

Robertson Charles T., (Owego) r 13, farmer.

Robinson William O., traveling salesman, h Main.

Rogers John H., (Hooper's Valley) r 2, farmer.

Rogers Lorenzo, drayman, h River.

Roper Frank H., (Owego) r 18, milk dealer, and farmer 54, and 25 in Owego.

Ross Leonard B., cabinet-maker, and undertaker, Main, h River.

Russell Frederick W., (E. Nichols) r 44, farmer.

Russell Horace G., r 8, farmer with Ulysses G., leases of J. H. Morey 304.

Russell Justin A., (E. Nichols) r 44, farmer 75.

Russell Ulysses G., r 8, farmer with his brother Horace, leases of J. H, Morey 304.

Ryan Johanna, widow William, resident, bds. River.

Sanford Jay, (Owego) r 17, farmer 100.

Scott Alonzo J., laborer, bds. Cady ave.

Scott David C., farm laborer, h Cady ave.

Scott Ella F., dressmaker, Cady ave., bds. do.

Scott George B., emp. DeGroat, Harris & Co., h Main.

Scott Libbie M., dressmaker, bds. Cady ave.

Scott Perry L., laborer, bds. Cady ave.

Searles Aaron P., (E. Nichols) r 44, farmer.

Sears Charles, (Owego) r 21, farmer on shares with L. H. Pitcher 105.

Sears David, (Owego) r 21, farmer on shares with Ezra Hunt 110.

Sears Spencer, (Owego) r 36, farmer.

Seymour Herrick H., (Owego) r 16, farmer 170.

Sharp Charles, laborer, h Railroad.

Sharp Rufus G., r 8, miller.

Sherwood Casper I., general merchant, Main, h River.

Sherwood Silas, r 7, poor-master, and farmer 68½.

Sherwood Thomas B., (Tioga Center) r 22, farmer on shares with Mrs. Amanda Evans 52.

Sherwood Wesley W., (Tioga Center) r 10, apiarist, and blacksmith.

Shipman Edmund, r 24, farmer 6.

Shipman Selem, r 24, laborer.

SHOEMAKER EDGAR, r 1, farmer 97.

SHOEMAKER HORACE A., r 23, farmer.

Shoemaker Lyman H., harnessmaker, Main, h do.

Shoemaker William R., r 1, farmer 180.

Sibley Herbert L., (Owego) r 35, farmer, leases of S. Sibley 125.

Sibley John G., (E. Nichols) r 43, farmer 150.

Sibley Samuel, (Owego) r 35, retired farmer.

Sibley William H., (E. Nichols) r 43, farmer with his father John.

Sisk Harriet, r 49½, widow John, resident.

Sisson Wheeler, (Hooper's Valley) r 4, farm laborer.

Smith Charles H., (Owego) r 16, farmer 80.

Smith Charles O., (Owego) r 23, farmer 90.

SMITH HARVEY R., (Owego) r 10, farmer 100.

Smith Jane B., (Hooper's Valley) r 1, widow Washington, farm 120.
Smith Jay L., (Owego) r 32, farmer.
Smith John, (Owego) r 16, retired.
SMITH JOHN., Jr., (Owego) r 18, milk dealer, and farmer 230.
Smith Oliver P., (Hooper's Valley) r 5, blacksmith.
Smith Samuel B., r 16, retired.
SMITH SISTERS, (Catherine E. and Phebe A.) farm 120.
SMITH WARREN A., justice of the peace, deputy postmaster, and farmer.
Stanton Eben, r 27, farmer on shares with Z. Goodsell 100.
Stanton Frank E., r 27, farmer with his father Eben.
Stauff Elizabeth, (Hooper's Valley) r 28, farm 50.
Stauff Frederick, (Hooper's Valley) r 28, farm laborer.
Stauff George C., (Hooper's Valley) r 29, farmer.
Stauff Henry, (Hooper's Valley) r 28, farm laborer.
Steen Benjamin, (Owego) r 43, farm laborer.
Steward Charles B., (Hooper's Valley) off r 1, farmer with his father Jacob.
Steward Franklin P., (Hooper's Valley) off r 1, farmer.
Steward Jacob, (Hooper's Valley) off r 1, farmer 145.
Steward Thaddeus, (Hooper's Valley) r 3, small fruit grower, and farmer 97.
Steward Thaddeus J., (Hooper's Valley) off r 1, farmer.
Strong Sadie, clerk, bds. Main.
Sullivan Dennis O., mason, h Cady ave.
Sullivan Fred J., farm laborer, bds. River.
Sullivan John, farm laborer, h River.
Sullivan J. Whitmore, emp. E. Dunham, bds. River.
Taylor Lucretia, widow Stephen R., resident, h Howell.
Thorn Warren, (Owego) r 21, farmer on shares with James Nelson, Jr. 75.
Townsend James, (Owego) r 16, farm laborer.
Tripp Seymour C., watch repairer and jeweler, Main, h at Smithboro.
Turner G. M. Dallas, carpenter and joiner, h Cole.
Turner Harvey, wagon-maker, off Main, h Walnut.
Turner Jacob, mail carrier, bds. Walnut.
Van Demark Charles, farmer, h River.
Van Demark Emma Mrs., milliner, bds. Main.
Van Dermark Beniah, r 9, farm laborer.
Van Dermark Josiah, (Hooper's Valley) r 4, farmer 9.
Van Deusen Ella G., teacher, bds. Main.
Van Deusen H. Newton Rev., pastor M. E. church, h. Main.
Van Gorder Aaron, (Hooper's Valley) r 2, farmer 30.
Van Gorder Allen, (Hooper's Valley) r 28, farmer 126.
Van Gorder Edward S., r 16, sawyer.
Van Gorder Esther, r 16, widow Enos, resident.
Van Gorder George, r 1, farmer.
Van Gorder John, (Waverly) r 1, farm laborer.
Vannatta William, (Owego) r 18, farm laborer.
Van Ness Belle H. Mrs., groceries and provisions, Main, h Cady ave.
Van Ness Elias, manager of store for Mrs. B. H. Van Ness, h Cady ave.
Van Ness John H., r 48, farmer, leases of Jos. Olmstead 150.
Van Ness Myron, (Hooper's Valley) r 3, farmer 150.
Van Ness William W., shoemaker, Main, h River.
Van Norstran Andrew L., traveling salesman, h River.
Van Norstran Dora, teacher, bds. River.
Verguson Israel, (Owego) r 17, farmer.

Verguson Phoebe M., (Owego) r 17, widow L. Nelson, resident.
Vincent Oliver L., r 16, laborer.
Wait Austin D., (Owego) r 33, farmer 86.
WAIT GEORGE A., (Owego) r 50, farmer 75, and leases in Penn. 50.
Wait Jefferson, (E. Nichols) r 44, farmer.
Wait Joseph, (E. Nichols) r 44, farmer 25.
Walker Aaron, (Owego) r 12, farm laborer.
Walker Eliot, (Owego) r 32, farm laborer.
Ward Mahala, (E. Nichols) r 41, widow Abraham B., farmer 42.
Warner Jane, (Hooper's Valley) r 4, widow Frederick, resident.
Warner Sarah, widow Oscar T., h Walnut.
Warwick Laura D., widow William, h Cady ave.
Washburn Henry H., r 30, retired farmer.
WASHBURN JOHN H., (Hooper's Valley) off r 29, farmer 50.
Washburn Joshua, r 28, farmer 40.
WATERMAN & METLER, blacksmiths, Main.
Waterman Abraham, (Hooper's Valley) r 5, farm laborer.
WATERMAN ALONZO C., r 8, apiarist 20 swarms, and farmer 80.
WATERMAN BENJAMIN M., (Waterman & Mettler) h Main.
Waterman Charles, (Hooper's Valley) off r 5, farm laborer.
Waterman Charles H., r 8, blacksmith.
Waterman James H., r 8, carpenter.
WATERMAN JOHN G., r 8, blacksmith.
Waterman Thomas, (Hooper's Valley) farmer on shares with M. Van Ness 160.
Waterman Walter S., meat-market, Main, h do.
Webb Vestus R. (Waverly) r 1, laborer.
Webber Andrewson A., (Hooper's Valley) r 3, farm laborer.
Welch John F., R. R. section foreman, h River.
Wells Charles S., painter, bds. River.
Westbrook Levi, cigars and fruit, Main, h River.
Wheeler Charles J., r 10, laborer.
WHIPPLE ANDREW G., (Owego) r 33, school trustee and farmer 179.
White Anson, (East Nichols) r 51, farmer 50.
White Carrie H., (East Nichols) r 40, teacher.
White Charles L., (East Nichols) r 40, farmer with his father Henry.
WHITE DANIEL, (East Nichols) r 46, farmer 100.
White Elizabeth A., (East Nichols) widow Enoch, postmistress, and farm 30.
White Frank P., r 7, farmer with his father Platt White.
White George, (East Nichols) r 40, school trustee and farmer 60.
White Harriet, r 23, widow Lyman, resident.
White Hattie C., (East Nichols) r 43, teacher.
White Henry, (East Nichols) r 40, farmer 185.
White J. Lawrence, (Owego) r 22, overseer of the poor and farmer 128.
WHITE JOSEPH W., (East Nichols) r 45, assessor and farmer 168.
White Leonard, r 46, farmer 71.
White Myron P., (East Nichols) farmer 50.
White Perry F., (Owego) r 21, farmer on shares with Rachel Newland 40.
White Perry H., (East Nichols) r 43, farmer 100.
WHITE PLATT, r 7, farmer 80.
White Samuel H., (East Nichols) r 45, school trustee and farmer.
White Wellington, r 46, farmer 125.
White William, (East Nichols) r 43, farmer 140.

WHITE WILLIAM W., (Owego) r 21, assessor, apiarist 32 swarms and farmer 175.

Whiting Edward I., (Owego) r 17, farmer 26.

WICKHAM ALBERT, (Owego) r 16, farmer on shares with H. H. Seymour 170.

Wiggins Absalom J., emp. DeGroat & Harris, h Cady ave.

WIGGINS CLOID B., r 8, contractor and builder.

Wiggins George, r 8, carpenter and millwright.

Wiggins Silas, gardener, h Cole.

Wilber David, (Owego) r 32, farmer 25.

Wilber Horace, (Owego) r 32, farmer.

Wilbur Spencer, (Owego) r 18, farmer on shares with Mrs. E. Pitcher 125.

Williams George, laborer, bds. Main.

Williams George F., barber, Main, h do.

Williams Harry G., barber, bds. Main.

Williams Squire L., r 8, laborer.

Williams Stephen, r 8, stone-mason.

Wilson James M., M.D., Rev., pastor Presbyterian church, h Cady ave.

Wilson James P., medical student, bds. Cady ave.

Wilson John, r 49, farm laborer.

Wilson Louisa, widow George, laundress, h Main.

Wiswell Leon O., teacher, h Cady ave.

Witty Kate, (Owego) r 19, widow Thomas, resident.

Wood Allen, (Owego) r 42, farmer 50.

Wood Charles O., r 7, farmer 16.

Woodard Thaddeus, (Waverly) r 1, farm laborer.

Woodruff Joseph J., (East Nichols) r 43, farmer, leases of W. White 93.

Wright Caleb, r 8, prop. Dunham's mill.

Wright James, (Owego) r 17, farm laborer.

Wright Nancy W., r 8, carpet-weaver.

Yarrington James, (Owego) r 20, farm laborer.

Young O. Warren, (Owego) r 16, school trustee and farmer 90.

OWEGO.

INSIDE CORPORATION.

(For explanations, etc., see page 3, part second.)

(Postoffice address is Owego, unless otherwise designated in parenthesis.)

Abel Alonzo, carpenter, h 84, McMaster.

Abel Frank W., clerk, bds., McMaster, cor. Temple.

Aberhart Peter, baker, h over 56 North ave.

ADAMS HORACE B., tinwork, stoves and plumbing, 40 Lake, h 18 Ross.

Adams Joseph, retired, bds. Forsyth Block, North ave.

Adams Newton W., printer, h Forsyth Block, North ave.
Adams Ray, baker, h 100 Talcott.
AH-WA-GA HALL, G. W. Fay, agent, 203 Front.
AH-WA-GA HOUSE, B. J. Davis prop., Front, cor. Church.
Allen Alexander P., traveling salesman, h 26 George.
Allen Charles, farmer, h n Dean's Tannery.
Allen Edward, tanner, h n Dean's Tannery.
Allen Eugene, emp. Dean's Tannery, h n tannery, North ave.
Allen Guerdon L., collector for U. S. Express Co., h George.
Allen James, laborer, bds. 93 Erie.
Allen John, laborer, h 45 Erie.
Allen Lucius H., physician and surgeon, 140 Main, h do.
ALLEN LUCIUS H., 2nd, meat cutter, h 56 George.
Allen Matthew, laborer, h 47 Erie.
Allen Matthew J., laborer, bds. 93 Erie.
Allen Patrick, laborer, h 93 Erie.
Anderson Johnson M., (J. W. Jansen & Co.,) and with W. H. Bailey produce, h over 60 Main.
ANDREWS GEORGE F., attorney and counselor at law, 214 Front, h 117 Liberty.
Andrews Philetus, farmer, h 566 Fifth ave.
Andross & Groo, (W. W. A. and L. G.) wholesale commission fruit dealers, 136 North ave.
Andross Keziah, widow Stebbins, 46 Temple.
Andross William W., (Andross & Groo) 136 North ave, h 46 Temple.
Anthofer Anna, teacher German, bds. 54 Liberty.
Archibald Almon W., resident, h 35 Front.
Archibald Charles, farmer with his father, South Side.
Archibald Samuel, farmer 50, leases of A. N. Potter, South Side.
Arnold Charles E., painter, bds. 240 Temple.
Arnold George M., brakeman, bds. 240 Temple.
Atchison William J., clerk, bds. over 54 North ave.
Atkins Galen H., shoemaker, h 40 Lake.
Auffhammer Eugene, teacher of languages, h 215 Prospect.
Augusta Lucinda, tailoress, bds. 524 Main.
AYER WARREN L., physician and surgeon, 207 E. Main, h 203 do.
Ayers Elmer, porter Park hotel, bds. do.
Ayers Julia, widow Capt. Henry, bds. 51 Front.
BABCOCK JOHN B., machinest, h 240 E. Temple.
Babcock Zachary T., clerk, h over 69 North ave.
Bailey Deborah, widow Alexander, h 620 Fifth ave.
Bailey Mary Mrs., tailoress, h 194 East Temple.
BAILEY W. H. & CO. (W. J. Mawhiney) hay, grain and potatoes, 164 North ave.
BAILEY WILLIAM H., (W. H. Bailey & Co. and J. W. Jansen & Co.) overseer of the poor, h 80 East ave.
BAIRD LEWIS J., fireman, h 10 Adaline.
Baird Sabrina, widow John, h 10 Adaline.
Baker Charles, brakeman, h 222 North ave.
Baker Edwin T., clerk, h South Side.
Baker Frank M., supt. Addison & Northern Pennsylvania R. R., h Main.
Baker James R., farmer, h 173 North ave.

BAKER JULIA A., widow John D., h Spencer block, Lake.
BALL JOHN P., general variety and auction, 170 Front, h 27 Front.
Ball Mariette, widow George, bds. 5 Spruce.
Ball William W., clerk, bds. Front.
BANDLER ROBERT, clothing, hats, caps and gent's furnishing goods, 19 and 21 Lake, h 13 Park.
Banta Alonzo H., harness-maker, h 204 Bell.
Barber Edbert, farmer, bds. 405 Front.
Barden Ezra D., traveling salesman, h 234 North ave.
Barnes Clarissa Mrs., resident, bds. 313 Main.
Barnes Eliza, widow William, resident, h 123 Liberty.
Barnes Katie, telegraph operator, bds. 73 Liberty.
Barnes Theodore, farmer, h 103 Liberty.
Barnett John W., plumber, h 157 Erie.
BARRETT JAMES M., physician and coroner, Main cor. North ave., h 63 Liberty.
Barstow Oliver A., retired, bds. McMaster.
Bartholomew Phoebe A., resident, bds. rear 18 Adaline.
Bartlett Oscar J., blacksmith, h 94 Talcott.
Barton Eugene F., (G. W. Barton & Son) h over 59 North ave.
Barton George W., cigar manuf., 191 Main, h 166 Temple.
BARTON ISAAC, (Isaac W. Barton & Co.) produce, h 71 Liberty.
BARTON ISAAC W. & CO., (Frank H. Catlin) produce.
Barton Maggie E., widow Festus L., bds. 473 Front.
Barton Walton A., town clerk and book-keeper, h 202 East Temple.
Basford Albert, laborer, h 76 South Depot.
Basford Henry, harness-maker, h near tannery, North ave.
Basford Hiram, laborer, bds. 24 Temple.
Basford James, shoemaker, 150 River, South Side, h do.
Bassett James A., teller Owego Nat. Bank, h 41 Paige cor. Main.
Battersby Joseph, retired, h 359 Main.
Batterson Helen, clerk, bds. 38 Spencer ave.
Bauer Caroline Mrs., dressmaker, h 26 Adaline.
Bauer Elizabeth, dressmaker, 26 Adaline, h do.
Baxter Daniel M., laborer, h 489 Front.
BEACH & PARMELEE, (O. S. B. and A. W. P.) druggists, Main cor. North ave.
Beach D. & Co., (G. W. Derrickson) manufs. cordage, and dealers in sporting goods, 197 Main.
Beach Darius, (D. Beach & Co.) h over 197 Main.
BEACH OTIS S., (Beach & Parmelee) h McMaster.
Beach William, emp. planing-mill, h 60 McMaster.
Beard David O., barber, bds. Lake.
Beard James C., retired farmer, bds. 380 Main.
Beard James C., Jr., sup't Beard Manuf. Company, h 380 Main.
Beard Manuf. Co., (W. A. and G. A. King) manufs. of saddlery, 24, 26 and 28 Lake.
Beardsley Nathaniel A., harness-maker, 291 Prospect.
Beaumont John H., botanic drug store, 135 North ave., h do.
Beck Charles, laborer, h 208 North ave.
Beck Edward, medical student, bds. 115 West ave.
Beck Edward S., teacher, h 115 West ave.
Beck Frank, law clerk, bds. 115 West ave.

Beck George P., resident, bds. 115 West ave.
Beck Louie A.. clerk, bds. 115 West ave.
Becker Delevan, conductor Erie R. R., h Spencer Block, Lake.
Becker Fayette A., carpenter, h Fifth ave.
Beebe Hiram A., retired, h 345 E. Main.
Beecher Frederick, baggageman, h 115 North ave.
Beecher Lambert, emp. King & Co., bds. 118 Temple, h at Newark Valley.
Beeman Harman S., cartman, h 117 North ave.
Beers Charles, farmer 150, h 221 Main.
Beers Edwin W., carpenter, h South Side.
Beers Frank J., baker, confectioner, and oyster dealer, 55 North ave., h do.
Belden Martha M., widow Henry A., h Temple.
Bell James, laborer, bds. 225 Erie.
Bell Mary A., widow Charles T., h 394 Main.
Bell William, laborer, h 225 Erie.
Bennett Caroline, widow William, h 80 Temple.
Bennett Dana, engineer, h 264 North ave.
Bennett Harry A., clerk, bds. Temple cor. Church.
Bennett Hattie A., dressmaker, bds. 80 Temple.
Bennett Nathaniel, shoemaker, Fox, h do.
Bennett Nelson R., engineer, h 102 Temple.
Bennett William, hostler, h Main.
Benson Hattie A., artist, bds. 112 Fox.
Benson Mary A., cook and laundress, h 112 Fox.
Benson Robert F., laborer, bds. 112 Fox.
Benson W. Henry, gardener and sexton, h 112 Fox.
Bergen Bridget, widow James, saloon and confectionary, 80 So. Depot, h do.
Bergen Timothy, laborer, h 94 Spencer ave.
Berger Andrew F. F., clothing and gents.' furnishing goods, Lake, h 72 Talcott.
BERRY JOSEPH, (Sporer, Carlson & Berry) h 373 Front.
Besler C. William, prop. Excelsior Soap Factory, cor. Temple and Liberty, h 95 Main.
Bicknell Hiram D., locomotive engineer, h Spencer, cor. George.
Bignall Juliet C., widow Burnett B., resident, h 90 Spencer.
Bikely Frederick, employee Gas Company, h 440 Main.
Billings Georgie Miss, clerk, h 61 Forsyth.
BILLINGS HENRY, pres. Owego village, h 109 Main.
Billings John A., magr. W. U. Tel. office, 30 Lake, h 73 Liberty.
Billings Mary E. Mrs., boarding-house, 73 Liberty.
Billings Mary E., widow William, h 61 Forsyth.
Billings Nancy, widow Henry, h 198 E. Temple.
Billings Richard, resident, bds. 198 E. Temple.
Billings Will, printer, bds. 73 Liberty.
Bing Wah, Chinese laundry, 71 North ave., h do.
Bird Henry, laborer, h 109 Paige.
Bird Lawrence, laborer, h 113 Paige.
Birdsall Benjamin, bartender, bds. 154 North ave.
Blair Parmelia, widow Stephen O., resident, bds. 92 Adaline.
Bliss Francis A., (Bliss, Thompson & Co.) h 30 William.
Bliss, Thompson & Co., (F. A. B., A. C. T. and George Truman, Jr.) wool dealers, 174 Front.
BLOODGOOD DARWIN H., clerk U. S. Ex. Co., h 33 Park.

BLOODGOOD FRANK S., manager Telephone Exchange, h 33 Park.
Bly Benjamin F., laborer, h Constine's lane.
Boardman Edward W., fireman, h over 130 North ave.
Bodle Sarah A., widow James, bds. 66 Church.
Bonham Emma, widow John S., bakery 3 Park, h do.
Booth Fred E., telegraph operator, bds. Delphine.
Booth Celestia, widow of Ransom, h 92 Liberty.
Bostwick Lewis W., farmer 100, h 61 Talcott.
Boughton William H., painter, h 45 Adeline.
Bourke John, laborer, 289 Front.
Bouquet Albert, saloon and restaurant, 13 Lake, h do.
Bouquet Frank, emp. Drill Works, h n Dean's Tannery.
Bouquet George, tanner, h n Dean's Tannery.
Bowen Abbey A., dressmaker, over Owego Nat. Bank, h do.
Bowen Franklin L., resident, h 236 North ave.
Bowen Timothy, laborer, h West ave.
Boyd Mary, widow Andrew, bds. 134 Talcott.
Boylen Frank F., clerk, h over 72 North ave.
Bradbury Amanda L., widow Charles, h 89 William.
BRADLEY CHAUNCEY A., market gardener, h South Side.
Brady John, laborer, h 36 John.
Brady Thomas F., recording clerk county clerk's office, h 162 West ave.
Brainard Burnette E., clerk, bds. 249 Prospect.
Brainard Henry C., printer, h 249 Prospect.
Brant F. Lester, clerk, bds. 195 Main.
Brant Hiram H., liquor dealer, 169 Main, h 70 Liberty.
Brant Julia, dressmaker, 122 River, South Side, h do.
Brant Nelson, saloon, 195 Main, h do.
Bravo Eugene J., clerk, bds. over 23 Lake.
Bridgman Alfred T., traveling auditor D. L. & W. R. R., h Main.
Briggs Belle M., widow George N., h 359 Front.
Briggs Diana G., M. D., widow Isaac S., resident, h 5 Park.
Briggs Mary L., M. D., physician, 5 Park, h do.
Briggs N. Smith, farmer, bds. 5 Park.
Briggs William F., brakeman, h 204 East Temple.
Brink Edward T., well-driver, h 448 Front.
Brink Eliza D., widow Nelson, market garden, fruit nursery, etc., h 577 Main.
Brink John, laborer, h Canal.
Britenbaker Jennie, widow George, saloon and restaurant, Delphine, h do.
Brobasco Westbrook G., farm laborer, h South Side.
Brockway Francis E., deputy county treas., teller First Nat. Bank, h 24 Paige.
BROCKWAY LEON L., prop. parlor job printing house, 34 Lake, bds. 24 Paige.
Brooke James W., tailor, h 29 Temple.
Brooks Chester P., traveling salesman, bds. 153 Temple.
Brooks Chloe M., deputy county clerk, Court House, h 153 Temple.
Brooks David, locomotive engineer, h over 72 North ave.
Brooks Edward P., clerk, bds. North ave.
BROOKS HORACE A., justice of the peace and conveyancer, over 191 Main, h 153 Temple.
Brooks James L., mason, h Gere.

Brooks Lucy G., widow Benjamin, h 153 Temple.
Brooks Martha, resident, bds. 153 Temple.
Brooks M. Mandane, resident, bds. 153 Temple.
Brott Anna, widow John W., nurse, 162 West ave.
Brott Anthony P., farmer 15 and leases of Peter Brott 36, h 82 Temple.
Brott Joseph, porter Ahwaga House, h 121 Franklin.
Broughman R. Frank, book-keeper, h 67 West ave.
Brown Abram, laborer, h 73 Fox.
Brown Charlotte M., widow Frederick, h 18 Front.
Brown Della, widow James, millinery, 67 North ave., h do.
Brown Ebenezer S., traveling salesman, h 122 West ave.
Brown Edward, farmer, h 273 North ave.
BROWN GEORGE, (L. & G. Brown) h off North ave. near S. C. R. R. round house.
BROWN H. CORYDON, book-keeper Owego Mutual Benefit Association, Lake, h 78 Chestnut.
Brown John, hotel and restaurant, and liquor dealer, 171 Main, h do.
Brown John J., butcher, h over 82 North ave.
BROWN L. & G., (Lyman & George) farmers 50, apiarists 135 swarms, and manufs. of apiarist's supplies, off North ave. n S. C. R. R. round house.
BROWN LYMAN, (L & G. Brown) h off North ave. n S. C. R. R. round house.
Brown Lyman, farmer, bds. 273 North ave.
Brown Mary E. Mrs., h 111 Paige.
Brown M. J., clerk Central House, bds. do.
BROWN PATRICK, tel. operator D. L. & W. depot, h 182 River, S. Side.
Brundage Daniel, blacksmith, h John R.
Bruneman August, laborer, h 268 North ave.
Bryan Esther C., widow George H., dressmaking, Spencer block, Lake, h do.
Buckbee Frances, widow Ezra, h 364, Front.
BUCKBEE, PETERSON, WOOD & CO., (P. C. Peterson, C. L. Wood, C. E. Schoonmaker, and F. J. Burgess) dry goods, carpets and millinery, 190 and 192 Front.
Buffum Charles, drug clerk, h Paige.
Buffum Edward, bar-tender, h over 167 Main.
Buffum Ellen E., widow George W., h 20 Paige.
Bulloch Lewis, barber, bds. 63 Spencer ave.
Bunzey Adelbert T., clerk, bds. 36 William.
BUNZEY JOHN H., salesman, h 36 William.
Bunzey Nelson P., farmer, h Pumpelly, So. Side.
Burbank Horace J., apprentice, bds. 70 Spencer.
Burbank Joseph T., baker, h 70 Spencer ave.
Burdick Edgar L., harnessmaker, h r 38 Temple.
Burdick Lewis C., cleaning and dying, 67 Fox, h do.
BURGESS FRANK J., (Buckbee, Peterson, Wood & Co.) h Fox cor. Liberty.
BURNETTE CHARLES R., printer, *Gazette* office, h 62 Liberty.
Burns Nellie T., saleslady, bds. 530 Main.
Burrows James, restaurant and saloon, 218 Front, h do.
Burt Martha, widow James M., h 359 Front.
Burton Nathaniel T., bakery, 61 North ave. h do.
Burton Reuben E. Rev., pastor First Bapt. church, h 19 Ross.
Bush James L., peddler, h Constine's Lane.

Butler James, barber, 65 North ave., h 89 Fox.
Cable Edmund, baggagemaster, bds. 289 Main.
CABLE FREDERIC O., postmaster, h 289 Main.
Cafferty Edward, gardener, h Water.
Cafferty Margarett, widow William J., bds. Water.
Cain Patrick, laborer, h John R.
Caley Charles, farm laborer, h 18 Adaline.
Calkins Benjamin S., emp. D. L. & W. R. R, bds. Dugan House.
Cameron Charles, painter, h 98 Spencer ave.
Cameron Charles A., resident, bds. 208 E. Temple.
Cameron Delray A , clerk, h 61 Liberty.
Cameron Frederick H., law clerk, bds. 208 E. Temple.
Cameron John, clerk, 208 E. Temple.
Cameron Larne J., resident, h over 170 Front.
Cameron Robert, retired, h over 170 Front.
CAMP GEORGE SIDNEY, atty. at law and farm 132, h Front near Park.
Camp Hermon H., (H. H. Camp & Co.) h 24 Front.
Camp H. H. & Co. (Lucy A. Camp) foundry, 136 Front.
CAMP JOHN, baggageman, h 447 Main.
Camp John, shoemaker, bds. 52 Fox.
Camp Lucy A., (H. H. Camp & Co.) widow Henry W., h 24 Front.
CAMP MARY L. MRS., art teacher, h 259 Erie.
Camp William, brakeman N. Y. & Erie R. R., h 368 Main.
CAMP W. HARRISON, postal clerk, h 259 Erie.
CAMPBELL ARBA, tanner, dealer in phosphates and other fertilizers ; farm in Tiogo 300, Candor 250, in Rome, Pa., 200, h 289 Front.
CAMPBELL'S TANNERY, A. Campbell prop., Talcott.
Campion Edward, tinsmith, h Fulton.
Campion Michael, tinsmith, h 68 McMaster.
Campion William, emp. gas company, h 495 Main.
CARD ALBERT A., foreman contract work, h over 7 Adaline.
Card George, farmer in Candor 40, h 7 Adaline.
Card Irving, farm laborer, bds. 7 Adaline.
Carleton Edward D., gardener, h 161 Talcott.
Carleton Fanny A., dressmaker, bds. 161 Talcott.
Carlson John M., piano tuner, h 63 Paige.
CARLSON OTTO M., (Sporer, Carlson & Berry) h Paige cor. Bell.
Carmichael Charles S., manuf., h 194 East Temple.
Carpenter Charles B., book-keeper 200 Front, bds. at Ah-wa-ga House.
Carpenter Collins A., salesman, h 38 George.
Carrigan Henry K., tanner, h near Dean's tannery.
Carrigg Michael, machinist, bds. 118 Paige.
Carrigg Patrick, yardmaster Erie R. R., h 118 Paige.
Carter Charles, stationary engineer, h 120 River, South Side.
Carter Frances F., hair-worker, h 89 Fox.
Carter Sarah Mrs., resident, h over 109 North ave.
Cartledge Elizabeth, widow John, bds. 499 Front.
Cartwright Estes, clerk, bds. Front.
Case Ellis L., carpenter and painter, h 216 East Temple.
Case Nancy, widow Chauncy F., bds. 216 East Temple.
Casey Margarett, widow John, h 64 Paige.
Casey Thomas F., laundry 210 Front, h do.
Casterline Evi E., carpenter Erie R. R., h 108 Chestnut.

Catlin Calvin H., clerk Ah-wa-ga House, bds. do.
Catlin Charles A., wind-mills, bds. 75 Talcott.
Catlin Charles M., supt. saw-mill, h 75 Talcott.
CATLIN FRANK H., (I. W. Barton & Co.) bds. 337 Front.
Catlin John, clerk, bds. North ave.
Catlin Mary E., dressmaker 75 Talcott, bds. do.
Catlin Sarah E., dressmaker 75 Talcott, bds. do.
Catlin Thomas, laborer, h 228 North ave.
Caughlin Catherine, widow Patrick, h 31, Erie.
*CAULDWELL & GRAY, (J. A. C. and J. C. G.,) engines, boilers, cast-
   ings, mill-work, and boiler-iron jails, McMaster cor. Delphine.
CAULDWELL JAMES A., (Cauldwell & Gray) h 56 Spencer ave.
Cauldwell James A., Jr., clerk, bds. 56 Spencer ave.
CENTRAL HOUSE, W. G. Gardener, manager, cor. Main and Lake,
   Free buss to all trains.
Chaffee Caleb J., resident, h 122 Main.
Chaffee Catherine, widow Barney, h off Water.
Chaffee Martha, dressmaker, bds. off Water.
Chamberlain Lee N. & Son, (Stephen) boots and shoes, Chamberlain block,
   Lake.
Chamberlain Lee N., (L. N. Chamberlain & Son) wholesale boots and shoes,
   Lake, h 317 Front.
Chamberlain Stephen, (L. N. Chamberlain & Son) wholesale boots and shoes,
   Lake, h 37 Paige.
Chambers George, bartender, bds. 161 North ave.
Chappel Frederick, emp. King & Co., bds. 14 West ave.
Chappel Hattie, tailoress, bds. 14 West ave.
Chappel Lyman, retired, h 14 West ave.
Chappell Matilda, widow William, laundress, 100 Talcott.
Chatfield George S., (Storrs, Chatfield & Co.) h 149 Front.
Chatfield John R., (Storrs, Chatfield & Co.) h 44 Front.
Chatfield Lucy B., widow of Thomas I., h 337 Front.
Cheeks Abraham, tinsmith, h 240 Prospect.
Cheeks Ellen, resident, h 238 Prospect.
Cheeks Enoch J., laborer, h 263 Prospect.
Cheeks Moulton, carpenter, h 508 Main.
Cheeks Samuel L., laborer, h 240 Prospect.
Chillson Hope Miss, resident, h 15 Temple.
Chitry Charles E., postal clerk, h 318 Front.
Chitry Francis, silversmith, h 374 Main.
Chitry William F., traveling salesman, bds. 374 Main.
Chittenden Josie M., widow W. Gus, bds. 147 Main.
Church Lewis W., clerk, h Fifth ave.
CITY STEAM LAUNDRY, (J. B. Keeler and J. A. Mabee) 83 North ave.
CLARK C. A. & H. A., attys. and counselors at law, Academy Bldg., Court.
CLARK CHARLES A., (C. A. & H. A. Clark) h Main.
Clark Fred, painter, h 16 Paige.
CLARK H. AUSTIN, (C. A. & H. A. Clark) h Main.
CLARK HERMAN C., confectionary and tobacco, 68 North ave., h do.
Clarke Eliza B., widow Timothy, h 53 Liberty.
Clarke Lizzie A., teacher, bds., 53 Liberty.
Clem Anton, tailor, h over 76 North ave..
CLEVELAND ALBERT P., supt. Cruciform Casket Co., h 26 W. Fox.

8

Coakley James, telegraph repairer, h 92 Paige.
Cobb Alanson L., emp. Casket Co., h 37 Delphine.
Cobleigh Harrison, blacksmith, h 249 Erie.
Cobleigh Ida J., dressmaker, bds. 249 Erie.
Coburn Andrew, resident, h 135 Main.
COBURN & STRAIT, (E. D. C. & E. E. S.) books, stationery and wall-
    paper, 17 Lake.
Coburn Ebenezer. resident, h 135 Main.
COBURN EDWARD D., (Coburn & Strait) h 67 Liberty.
COBWEB BOTTLING WORKS, Pat. Maloney prop., cor. Paige and Fox.
Coe Jesse W., lumber, h River, South Side.
Coe Jesse W., Jr., lumberman with his father, bds. River, South Side.
Cole Ida M., dressmaker, 261 Erie, bds. do.
Cole Ira J., blacksmith, h 261 Erie.
Cole Russell S., painter, h 84 Temple.
Cole Smith B., carpenter, h 40 Adaline.
COLEMAN JULIET, clothing, 9 and 11 Lake, h 212 Main.
Coleman Louisa, widow James, laundress, h 121 Green.
Coleman Morris, mgr. for J. Coleman, h 212 Main.
Coleman William, bookkeeper, 9 and 11 Lake, bds. Main, cor. Church.
Colgan Christopher, cigarmaker, bds. 92 South Depot.
Colgan Edward, drug clerk, h 7 Fox.
Colgan Mary, widow Thomas, h 92 South Depot.
Collins Daniel, mechanic, h 98 Paige.
Collins Dennis, harness-maker, h 18 Paige.
Collins Ellen, dressmaker. bds. Delphine.
Collins John, laborer, h Delphine.
Collins Joseph J., emp. Cobweb Bottling Works, bds. Green.
Collins Timothy, brakeman, h 109 Green.
Collins Timothy, Jr., emp. Cobweb Bottling Works, bds. Green.
Collins William, shoemaker, Lake, h 108 Spencer ave.
COMFORT MELVILLE L., jeweler and optician, 25 Lake, bds. Ah-wa-ga
    House.
Conant Frank L., carpenter, h 122 Franklin.
Conant James C., (Corchran & Conant) h Prospect.
Cone Cynthia C., widow Charles, h 82 Temple.
Congdon Daniel O., (Congdon & Robinson) h 188 Temple.
Congdon Nettie A., widow George E., seamstress, h 102 Fox.
Conklin Ira, teamster, h River, South Side.
Conklin Larne H., under sheriff, Main cor. Court, h do.
Conklyn Michael, retired, h 223 E. Temple.
Conley Emma M., widow John, laundress, h 448 Front.
Conlon Bridget, widow Timothy. laundress, h 112 Green.
Conlon John T., engineer, h 116 Green.
Connell John, laborer, h 109 Spencer ave.
Connell Patrick, track-walker Erie R. R., h 23 Fox.
Connell Thomas, laborer, h 250 East Temple.
Connell Timothy, tanner, h Canal.
Connelly Bridget, widow David, h 68 Paige.
Constine Michael, resident, h 123 Green.
Cook Allen E., switchman, h Constine's Lane.
Cook John, emp. casket shop, h 31 Fox.
Cook John, emp. livery, h 35 Talcott.

Cook Nelson C., locomotive engineer, h 41 Fox.
Cook William, brakeman, h 195 East Temple.
Cooley La Forest B., tanner, h 30 West Main.
Cooper Byron, farmer, h 147 Talcott.
Cooper Frank E., clerk, h 195 East Temple.
Coppins Amelia E., milliner, bds. 152 Central ave.
Coppins James H., engineer, h 152 Central ave.
Corchran & Conant, (J. T. C. & J. C.) contractors and builders, 62 Temple.
Corchran John T., (Corchran & Conant) h 51 George.
Corchran Nathan E., cabinet-maker, h 61 Adaline.
Corey William H., station agent D. L. & W. R. R., h 268 Main.
Cornell Charles, emp. foundry, h Adaline.
Cornell Edward, laborer, h off Water.
Cornell Edwin W., (H. W. Cornell & Son) h 18 John.
Cornell Elizabeth, widow David, bds. 29 Talcott.
Cornell Harmon W., (H. W. Cornell & Son) h 112 Chestnut.
Cornell H. W. & Son, groceries and provisions, 405 Main.
Corrigan John, Jr., traveling salesman, bds. 117 Chestnut.
Corrigan John, clerk, h Chestnut.
Corseni F., fruit dealer, 10 Lake.
Cortright Albert, grocery, North ave., h 22 Fox.
Cortright Charles E., brakeman, bds 237 Erie.
Cortright Dorcas, widow Nicholas, h 44 West Main.
CORTRIGHT HOUSE. J. A. Cortright & Son, props. 157 North ave.
CORTRIGHT J. A. & SON, (Mahlon A.) props. Cortright House.
CORTRIGHT JAMES A., (J. A. Cortright & Son) h 157 North ave.
Cortright John, clerk, h 201 East Temple.
Cortright John Mrs., dressmaker. 201 East Temple, h do.
CORTRIGHT MAHLON A., (J. A. Cortright & Son) h 157 North ave.
CORTRIGHT REUBEN W., brakeman, h 237 Erie.
Cortright Richard W., emp. foundry, bds. 44 W. Main.
Cortright Theodore, groceries and provisions, 64 North ave, h 62 Liberty.
Corwin Estelle H., clerk, h Church.
Corwin Harriet E., saleswoman, bds. East Main.
Courtright Charles, emp. foundry, h 100 Franklin.
Couton Adolph R., resident, bds. 265 Main.
Couton Charles E., retired, h 265 Main.
Covert Mary A., widow William H., h 232 North ave.
COYLE WILLIAM, livery, 73 North ave., h do.
Crabb Alice, widow Robert, h 150 Central ave.
Crabb Daniel, emp. foundry, h 50 W. Main.
Crabb George, hostler, bds. 150 Central ave.
CRABB ISAAC, market gardener, and wholesale dealer in vegetables, h Water.
Crabb Robert, h 212 North ave.
Crandall Ellis, jeweler, bds. 63 Paige.
Crandall Morris, painter, h 265 Erie.
Cramer Jennie W., widow Wallace E., bds. 99 Franklin.
CRANS ABRAM F., physician and surgeon, 126 North ave., h do.
Crans Egbert, carpenter, h 67 Central ave.
Crater Marinda, resident, h 91 Franklin.
Croak Thomas, liveryman, 73 North ave., bds. do.
Croff Isaac, cartman, h 146 River, South Side.

Croft Charles, hostler, bds. 56 Front.
Crowel Margaret, widow John, resident, h 50 W. Main.
Crowley Charles, laborer, h 90, S. Depot.
Crumley Thomas F., laborer, h 124 Paige.
Cuddeback William A., retired, h 38 William.
Cummings William, currier, h near Dean's tannery.
Cuneo Pietro, confectionery, 181 Front, h 8 Main.
Curtis Alson, conductor, h 29 Talcott.
Curtis A. Maria, widow Oliver D., h 101 Franklin.
Curtis Mary, widow, h 567 Front.
Cushman Eliza, resident, h 67 Forsyth.
Cusick John, laborer, h 129 Chestnut.
Cutler Thomas, gardner, h Canal.
Daggett Charles W., manager Postal Telegraph & Cable Co., bds. 34 Fox.
DANA CHARLES, custom boot and shoe maker, 65 North ave., h 322 Front.
Dana Lena J., saleswoman, bds. 322 Front.
Danforth Fred, emp. King & Co., bds. 118 Temple.
Danforth Joseph A., drayman, h Commerce.
Daniels Emily M., widow Dr. Ezekiel, h 217 Main.
Darrow Asa A., retired, h South Side.
DARROW FRANK A., (Mead & Darrow) h South Side.
Darrow Hill, mechanic, h 105 North ave.
DAVIS BURR J., prop. Ah-wa-ga House, Main cor. Church.
Davis William, steward Ah-wa-ga House, bds. do.
Dawes Etta, tailoress, bds. 229 Prospect.
Dawes Joseph M., locksmith, 69 North ave., h 229 Prospect.
Day Marvin, resident, bds. 313 Main.
Day Warren, farm laborer, bds. 596 Fifth ave.
Day William, farm laborer, h 596 Fifth ave.
Dean Alanson P., retired, h 63 Paige.
DEAN CALVIN B., livery, hack and sale stable, Church, h 30 do.
DEAN CAMERON B., ticket agent N. Y. L. E. & W. R. R., rooms Main.
Dean Charles R., (Shaw & Dean) h 274 Main.
DEAN H. N. & SON, (Ransom B.) props. tannery, North ave.
Dean James A., contractor and builder, Spencer ave., h do.
Dean John E., produce, h 122 River, South Side.
Dean Mary, widow H. Nelson, 255 Front.
Dean Mortimer C., yard-master S. C. R. R., h 248 North ave.
DEAN RANSOM B., (H. N. Dean & Son) vice-prest. Owego Nat. Bank, h in Adams, Mass.
Dean Sumner R., bar-keeper Ah-wa-ga House, bds. do.
Dearstine Charles, brakeman, bds. 124 Chestnut.
Dearstine Elias, brakeman, bds. 124 Chestnut.
Dearstine Jane A., widow John, h 124 Chestnut.
Decker Abram C., laborer, h South Side.
Decker Alexander, market gardener, h Fifth ave.
Decker Andrew J., laborer, h Canal Front.
Decker Frederick, emp. King & Co., bds. Canal Front.
Decker John, soda and mineral waters, Fifth ave., h do.
Decker John, laborer, h 220 North ave.
Decker Morgan, night-watchman, h 553 Front.
Decker Phoebe, widow Anson, books, stationery and wall-paper, 186 Main, h 472 do.

Decker Samuel H., laborer, h 24 Temple.
Decker Silas, emp. foundry, h North ave. cor. Temple.
Decker William, brakeman, h 36 W. Main.
Decker Victor, resident, h Main.
Decker Ward, manager of store for Mrs. A. Decker, bds. 472 Main.
Dee James, telegraph operator, bds. 313 Main.
Degarmo Alonzo, billiards, South Depot, h 178 River, South Side.
Delevan Irving J., produce and live stock, Front, h 233 do.
DeLong John Mrs., h 105 Talcott.
DeLong Pertilla, widow George, h 125 Talcott.
DEMUN CLINTON L., Singer sewing machines, 155 North ave, bds. European House.
Denison Alonzo H., laborer, h 146 River, South Side.
Dennis Catharine, widow Charles, h 111 Paige.
Dennis Mary, resident, h 223 North ave.
Densmore Anson, farmer, h South Side.
Densmore Eliza, widow John, bds. Delphine.
Densmore Franklin J., laborer, h 215 Prospect.
Densmore John J., emp. casket company, h Delphine.
Densmore William H., laborer, h over 168 Front.
DEPOT D. L. & W. R. R., River, South Side.
DEPOT N. Y., L. E. & W. R. R., North ave.
Derrickson George W., (D. Beach & Co.) h over 197 Main.
Deremer Theresa A. Mrs., resident, h over 177 Main.
De VALLIERE ERNEST, baggageman, h 55 Spencer ave.
De Valliere Nina A., sales-lady, bds. 55 Spencer ave.
Devine Mary, tailoress, bds. South Depot.
DeWitt Catharine, widow Joseph, resident, h 58 Liberty.
DeWitt Elizabeth, widow Thomas, resident, h 25 George.
DEWITT HENRY B., saloon, 76 North ave, bds. Central House.
Dewitt Margaret, resident, bds. 25 George.
Deyo Jay, cartman, bds. West ave., n Creek.
Diamond Irvin, carpenter, h 126 McMaster.
Dibble Clement, laborer, h Division.
Dickerson Fountain F., bartender, h Liberty.
Dildine Albert, fireman, h 73 East ave.
Dildine William J., cigarmaker, bds. 73 East ave.
Dingman Henry B., painter, h Decker Block, Main.
Dodd Thomas, railroad conductor, bds. 113 North ave.
Dodge Alfred, retired farmer, h 387 Front.
Dodge Edmund, upholster and furniture repairer, h 479 Front.
Dodge Emily Mrs., h 88 Paige.
Dodge Joseph A., clerk, h over 69 North ave.
Dollaway Frank L. Miss, resident, h 65 Central ave.
Donovan James H., R. R. section foreman, h 18 W. Main.
Donovan Mary A., dressmaker, 102 Paige, bds. do.
Donovan Michael, laborer, h 102 Paige.
Doody John, laborer, h 112 Spencer ave.
Doody Patrick, laborer, h 112 Spencer ave.
Dooley Alice, widow James, h 117 Erie.
Dooley James F., cigarmaker, bds. 117 Erie.
Dorcas Hannah, widow Moses, h 110 Paige.
Dorsey Alma J., dressmaker, 207 E. Temple, bds. do.

Dorsey James, painter, h 123 Chestnut.
Dorsey Sarah E., widow Allen R., h 207 E. Temple.
Dorsey William, tinsmith, bds. 123 Chestnut.
DORWIN, RICH & STONE (W. E. D., G. E. R. and J. F. S.) millers office 177 Front, mills foot of Main.
DORWIN WILLIAM E., (Dorwin, Rich & Stone) h Glen Mary.
Dotson Matthew, chimney sweep, h John R.
Doty Elijah, tailoring, cleaning and repairing, rear 63 North ave., h 69 Adaline.
Douglas Charles, traveling salesman, h over 80 North ave.
Dowd Anna E., dressmaker, 5 Park, h do.
Dowd Charles H., blacksmith, h 574 Main.
Dowd Mary A., bds. 574 Main.
DOWNS EDWIN D., D. D. S., dentist, 192 Front, h 239 do.
Doyle Bridget, widow Patrick, h 93 Spencer ave.
Doyle Mary, housekeeper, Pumpelly, South Side.
Doyle Mary, widow Dennis, saloon 121 Franklin, h do.
Doyle Peter, J., (Richards & Doyle) bds. Ah-wa-ga House.
Drake Dolly, emp. King & Co., bds. 118 Temple.
Drake Eli B., farmer and cooper, 74 Temple, h 95 Liberty.
Driscoll Cornelius, blacksmith, h 279 E. Temple.
Druckenmiller Charles, prof. music, bds. 73 Liberty.
Duel Betsey, widow Samuel L., h 193 North ave.
DUGAN CHARLES B., prop. Dugan House, 139-145 Front.
DUGAN HOUSE, Charles B. Dugan, prop., 139–145 Front.
Dugan Jeanette, widow Hugh, h Dugan House.
DUGAN JOHN, grocer 173 Front, h 64 North ave.
Duncan Agnes, clerk, bds. Paige.
Duncan Stephen, carpenter, h 85 Paige.
Dundon John, laborer, h 141 Erie.
Dundon John, Jr., laborer, bds. 141 Erie.
Dunham Frederick, clerk, h 191 E. Temple.
Dunham Hannah, boarding-house, 118 Temple.
Dunham Mahlon G., bartender, h 88 Page.
Dunn Dennis, book-keeper, Dean's tannery, bds. Decker blk., Main.
Dunn Jeremiah, tanner, h n Dean's tannery.
Dunn Michael J., laborer, h 530 Main.
Dunn Paul, currier, bds. n Dean's tannery.
Dunn Thomas W., express messenger, bds. 530 Main.
Dunning Catharine, widow Horace, h 322 Front.
Duren Loren D., foreman casket company, h 3 Adaline.
Duren W. Warren, laundryman, bds. 109 Fox.
Durfee Edgar S., carpenter, h 137 North ave.
DURFEE FRANK G., cutter, also correspondent Elmira *Advertiser*, h 99 Liberty.
Durkee Charles R., carpenter, h 32 Main.
Durphy Lyman D., retired lumber dealer, h Durphy block, Lake.
DURUSSEL & SON, (L. F. & G. A.) jewelers, 35 Lake.
DURUSSEL GEORGE A., (Duressel & Son) h 275 Main.
DURUSSEL LEWIS F., (Durussel & Son) h 191 E. Temple.
DUTCHER MERRITT T., physician and surgeon, over 15 Lake, h do.
Dwelle & Link, (J. C. Dwelle and C. A. Link) Clothing, Front.
Dwelle Clinton W., clerk, bds. 249 Front.

Dwelle Jefferson C., (Dwelle & Link) h 249 Front.
Earsley Belle Mrs., dressmaker, Commerce, h do.
Earsley Harriet, resident, h 259 McMaster.
EARSLEY JOHN F., drayman, h Commerce.
Easton John M., resident, bds., Main.
EASTON DAVID T., lawyer, over 168 Front, h 571 E. Main.
Eastwood Charles K., clerk, bds. Ah-wa-ga House.
Eberhart George D., Lockwood Mail and express, 43 Talcott, h do.
Eckert A. F., conductor, h over 58 North ave.
Eckter Frank, drayman, bds. 188 West ave.
Eckter Fred, resident, 188 West ave.
Eckter Louis, stone mason, h 188 West ave.
Eckter Marvin, well driver, bds. 188 West ave.
Eddie Ester A., widow David S., cook, h 102 Fox.
Eddy Wilber H., laborer, h 206, North ave.
Edson George, carpenter, h over 107 North ave.
Eldridge Mrs., widow James, h Front.
Ellis Alexander D., manuf. shirts, and agent for John Wanemaker, h Church.
Ellis A. H. Mrs., milliner, h Front.
Ellis Lydia J., widow Virgil, 34 Paige.
Ellis Stella A., clerk, h 34 Paige.
ELLIS WILLIAM H., (Goodrich & Co.) bds. 271 Front.
Elston George, laborer, h over 86 North ave.
Ely Alfred G., (Ely Brothers) h Front.
Ely Brothers, (Alfred G., Charles C. and Frederick) Ely's cream balm,
    235 Greenwich street, New York.
Ely Charles C., (Ely Brothers) h Front.
Ely Frederick, (Ely Brothers) h Front.
Embody Abram, resident, bds. 7 Adaline.
EMERY DAVID H., (Raymond & Emery) h 56 West ave.
Emery Paul, h 52 Fox.
EMPIRE SOAP WORKS, (James B. Keeler, prop.) 191 McMaster, office
    83 North ave.
Engelbreckt Peter, pianos, h rear 182 River, South Side.
Erie Express Co., Foster N. Mabee, agent, 18 Lake.
EUROPEAN HOUSE, John Hayes, prop., 151 North ave.
Evans Andrew, butcher, h 160 McMaster.
Evans Charles W., baggage-master, h 53 Paige.
Evans Josiah R., carpenter, h 4 William.
Everhart Peter, baker, h over 56 North ave.
Every William B., 62 North ave., wholesale liquors, h over do.
Ewalt —, tailor, bds. 73 Liberty.
Excelsior Soap Factory, C. W. Beseler prop., 37 Temple.
Fahey Michael, laborer, h 133 Erie.
Fairchild Samuel F., Agent, hats, caps and gents.' furnishings, 27 Lake, h 55
    Central ave.
Fancher Herman P., wood-turner, h 55 Talcott.
Farnham Albert S., teamster, bds. 235 E. Temple.
Farnham Melissa, widow Edwin, h 235 E. Temple.
FAY GEORGE W., excise commissioner and insurance, 203 Front, h 334
    Main.
Ferguson Frederick, emp. foundry, bds. 151 Talcott.
Ferguson Irving, emp. foundry, bds. Talcott.

Ferguson Laura, widow John, resident, h 113 Liberty.
Ferguson Royal B., foreman Gere, Truman, Platt & Co., h 7 George.
FERGUSON T. JEFFERSON, carpenter, h 151 Talcott.
Ferris Samuel W., pattern maker, h 110 McMaster.
Fiddis Emeline Mrs., bds. 104 West ave.
Fiddis Lucy A., teacher, bds. 93 Franklin.
Fiddis Lucy G., widow Robert, resident, h 93 Franklin.
Field John H., conductor, h 13 George.
Finch Smith, carpenter, h 170 West ave.
FIRST NATIONAL BANK OF OWEGO, (George Truman, Sr., prest.,
    W. S. Truman, cash., F. E. Brockway, teller) 179 Front.
Fisher George, sewing machine repairer, North ave., h South Erie.
Fisher James, molder, h 113 Liberty.
Fitzgerald Catherine, widow, Morris, resident, 120 Fox.
Fitzgerald Deborah, cleaning and dying, 105 Fox, h do.
Fitzgerald Edward, emp. Drill Works, h 43 Temple.
Fitzgerald Thomas, painter, bds. 120 Fox.
Fitzgibbons John, watchman, h Bell.
Flamer Isaiah, barber, 154 Front, h 184 River, South Side.
Flamer Julia, widow Jeremiah, h 184 River, South Side.
Flanigan James P., laborer, h 21 Adaline.
Flanigan Mary, dressmaker, bds. 21 Adaline.
Flanigan Patrick, laborer, h 106 South Depot.
Flanigan Thomas F., machinist, bds. 21 Adaline.
Foley James, laborer, h 113 Spencer ave.
Foot Frederick, bridge builder, bds. Lackawanna House, South Side.
Foot Sarah M. Mrs., dressmaker, bds. River, South Side.
Ford George, resident. bds. over 17 Lake.
Ford Lewis, livery, 132 North ave., h do.
Ford Lucius, carpenter, h 607 Main.
Forgason Charles, carpenter, bds. over 19 Lake.
FORGASON THADDEUS C., V. S., veterinary surgeon, stable Central
    ave. rear Park Hotel, h over 19 Lake.
Forsyth Charles E., clerk, bds. 245 Erie.
FORSYTH ELDRIDGE, retired, h 67 Forsyth.
Forsyth Eleazur V., emp. Erie R. R., h 11 Adaline.
Forsyth Eva B., dressmaker, bds. 11 Adaline.
Forsyth George F., painter, bds. 245 Erie.
FORSYTH GILBERT T., decorative painter, h 435 Main.
FORSYTH HUBBARD T., house and decorative painter and paper-hanger,
    h 245 Erie.
FORSYTH JAMES, resident, h 113 Front.
Forsyth Rachel, widow George, bds. 60 Forsyth.
FORSYTH WILLIAM S., landscape, frescoe and decorative painter, h 60
    Forsyth.
Foster & Hampton, (J. F. & J. W. H.) barbers, 129 North ave.
Foster Joseph, (Foster & Hampton) h 129 North ave.
FOSTER LEONARD, r 27, prop. saw and feed-mill. all kinds of pine and
    oak lumber on sale at lowest market prices, farmer 135, h McMaster.
Foster William C., clerk, h Fulton.
Fowley Michael, laborer, h 216 North ave.
Fox Lydia N., widow Edward, carpet-weaver, h 142 Central ave.
Fox Stuart E., emp. foundry, h 115 Chestnut.

Fralley Robert, baggageman, h 144 Central ave.
France Francis, emp. casket shop, bds. 142 Central ave.
FRANK JOHN, physician, 115 Main, h do.
Franz Conrad, tailor, h Gere.
Fraser Daniel, traveling salesman, bds. 143 Temple.
Fraser Reuben, farmer 140, h 143 Temple.
Fredenburg Catharine, widow Virgil, h 265 North ave.
Fredenburg Edward E., law student, bds. 215 North ave.
Fredenburg Fred J., laborer, h 215 North ave.
Freehill Maria, widow Patrick, boarding-house and lodging, 64 South Depot.
Freight-house and Office Erie R. R., South Depot, head Spencer ave.
French Charles O., farm laborer, h Constine's Lane.
French Orrin, laborer, h 460 Main.
Frisbie Sarah Mrs., laundress, h 5 Adaline.
Fritcher George, retired, bds. 128 Temple.
Frutchey Erastus, teamster, h Temple.
Fulton Market., (P. Hyde and G. Saltsman) general store, 32 Fulton.
Gaher Henry, tailor, bds. 73 Liberty.
Gale William E., station agent S. C. R. R., h 47 George.
Gallagher Dryden, widow William, bds. 41 Paige.
GARDNER WILLIAM G., manager Central House, Main cor. Lake.
Garey Henry J., brakeman, h 236 E. Temple.
Garvey Michael, laborer, h 111 Erie.
Garvey Patrick, emp. Erie R. R., h Delphine.
Gates Anna, widow Simon, bds. 229 Main.
Gavell Edward, cigar manuf., over 169 Main, h do.
Gavin Catherine, resident, bds. 125 Chestnnt.
Gavin Mary, widow Patrick, h 125 Chestnut.
Geary Patrick, laborer, h 22 Temple.
Genung Abram C., carpenter, h 118 Franklin.
Gere Adaline, widow Bradford, 192 North ave.
GERE EUGENE B., attorney at law, 112 Front.
GERE THEODORE D., (Gere, Truman, Platt & Co.) h 118 Main.
GERE, TRUMAN, PLATT & CO., (T. D. G., F. W. T., T. C. P. and C.
    F. Johnson) manufs., "Champion" wagons, grain and fertilizer drills,
    harrows, etc., Central ave.
Gibbons John H., laborer, bds. Constine's lane.
Gibson Charlotte, widow Stephen D., h 205 North ave.
Gibson Donald, bridge builder, h 205 North ave.
Gibson Frank, laborer, h 205 North ave.
Gibson Sarah, widow Edward G., resident, h 127 North ave.
Gilbert Charity, widow John H., h 115 Temple.
Gilday Edward, clerk, bds. 54 Delphine.
Gilday John, emp. foundry, bds. 54 Delphine.
Gilday Michael, laborer, h 54 Delphine.
Gilday William, emp. foundry, bds. 54, Delphine.
Giles Chester, emp. foundry, bds. Canal.
Gill Ellen, widow Christopher, h 16 Paige.
Gillett Luther W., (Riley & Gillett) Front, h 114 McMaster.
Gillett J. Fred, clerk, bds. 114 McMaster.
GILLSON WILLIAM H., bridge carpenter, h 116 West ave.
Gilman Herbert, stage driver, bds. Lackawanna House, South Side.
Gilman Milton H., prop. mill-yard, lumberland in Sullivan Co., Pa., h Front

Gilman N. M. Mrs., millinery, 204 Front, h do.
Ginnane Joseph, emp. foundry, h 161 West ave.
Ginnane Mary, widow Edward, h 135 West ave.
Ginnane Mary A., teacher, bds. 161 West ave.
Ginnane Thomas, laborer, h 448 Front.
Glaseo Thomas, gardner, h 112 Paige.
GLEZEN OSCAR B., att'y at law, and justice of the peace, Academy Bldg., Court, h 9 Front.
Goodnough William, expressman, h 268 North ave.
GOODRICH & CO., (J. W. Goodrich and W. H. Ellis) drygoods, 196 Front.
Goodrich David L., surveyor, h 388 Front.
Goodrich Frank, sewing-machine agent, h over 80 North ave.
GOODRICH JAMES W., (Goodrich & Co.) h 27 Front.
Goodrich Lyman T., traveling agent, h 425 Front.
Goodrich Samuel, yard-master Erie R. R., h 123 Liberty.
Goodspeed Eliza A., widow Joel J., h 57 Paige.
Goodspeed Elizabeth, teacher, bds. 57 Paige.
Goodwill Burdett D., laborer, h 22 Temple.
Goodwill Martha M., widow James G., h 22 Temple.
Gordon Martha N., widow William C., resident, h 229 Main.
Gordon Samuel, laborer, h off North ave. near S. C. R. R. round-house.
Gorman Dorinda M., widow Capt. John, h 383 Front.
Gorman James, switchman, bds. 64 South Depot.
Gorman Orrin T., shipping-clerk, Gere, Truman, Platt & Co., h 339 Main.
Goss Seward, retired, h 25 Ross.
Gotleiber Victor, policeman, bds. 88 Chestnut.
Gould Adam C., blacksmith, Temple, h 16 do.
Gould Appleton H., leather-cutter, h 290 Prospect.
Gould Ephraim, retired, h Talcott.
Gould Ephraim C., drayman, bds. 112 West ave.
Gould Frederick, emp. Drill Works, h 87 Liberty.
Gould Jane, widow Wilber D., h 234 Main.
Gould Joel S., retired, h 146 Talcott.
Gould Joseph, laborer, h Canal Front.
Gould Marion D., emp. foundry, bds. 16 Temple.
Gould Morris P., emp. foundry, h 8 Temple.
GOULD WILLIAM L., blacksmith, h 112 West ave.
GRAND ARMY HALL, over 76 North ave.
GRAND UNION TEA COMPANY, Milton T. Knight, agt., 42 Lake.
Granger Cora A., teacher, bds. 135 Main.
Grant Simon, produce, bds. 264 Main.
Graves Henry A., news, cigars and confectionary, 49 Lake, h 62 Church.
Gray George, painter, h Delphine.
GRAY JOHN C., (Cauldwell & Gray) h McMaster opp. Academy.
Gray John H., clerk, h North ave.
Green James W., miller, h 119 Liberty.
Greenleaf Emeline, widow John M., bds. 105 Main.
GREENLEAF JOHN T., physician and surgeon, 101 Main, h 105 do.
Greenwood Frank A., printer, bds. 80 William.
Greenwood James, custom boot and shoemaker, 188 Front, h 80 William.
Greenwood James W., emp. foundry, bds. 80 William.
Greenwood John E., emp. U. S. Express Co., bds. 80 William.
Greenwood Lizzie M., dressmaker, 80 William, bds. do.

Griffin Emma, laundress, 138 Talcott.
Griffin Margaret Mrs., h 148 Fox.
GRIFFING SAMUEL B., village alderman and salesman, h 226 E. Temple.
Grimes James, brakeman, h 27 Adaline.
Grimes Sarah, widow James, Jr., bds. 36 William.
Groat Abram W., confectionery and cigars, 115 North, h do.
Groo Lines, (Andross & Groo) residence in New Jersey.
GROSS JERRY S., lawyer, 178 Main, h do.
Hall George H., dry goods, h 122 Main.
Hall Granville W., carpenter, bds. Cortright House.
Hall James D., apprentice, bds. 105 Franklin.
Hall Mary, widow Edward, h 105 Franklin.
Hall Michael, confectionery, h 59 Church.
Hall William, laborer, h Water.
Hallock Andrew J., brakeman, h 61 Forsyth.
Hamilton Joel A., contractor and builder, h 3 Front.
Hammond ——, laborer, h 136 Main.
HAMMOND EDGAR, baker, h over 69 North ave.
Hammond Edwin, printer, h Buckbee Block.
Hampton James W., (Foster & Hampton) h 129 North ave.
Handlon Jerry, saloon-keeper, bds. 133 North ave.
Haner John, tanner, h 274 North ave.
Hannon John, laborer, h 107 Fox.
Hannon Patrick, laborer, 88 South Depot.
Hannon Thomas, local mail agent, h South Depot.
Hansell George I., book-keeper, Storrs, Chatfield & Co., h River, So. Side.
Hanvey Eliza, resident, h 2 W. Main.
Hanvey Hugh, retired, h 2 W. Main.
Hanvey John, retired, bds, 2 W. Main.
Hanvey Rosanna, resident, 2 W. Main.
Hard Horace, miller, h W. Main.
HARDER EMMOTT, boots and shoes, 23 Lake, h 279 Main.
Harding George A., farm laborer, h Pumpelly, South Side.
Harding Grant, laborer, h 222 North ave.
Harding Hannah T., widow Robert, h 143 Temple.
Harding Osee, widow John, h 222 North ave.
Harding Ward, baggageman, bds. 222 North ave.
*HARGRAVE WILLIAM G., artist and photographer, 38 and 40 Record
block, Lake, h do.

Harold Edward, R. R. section foreman, h 149 Fox.
Harold James J., foreman Owego *Blade*, h 149 Fox.
Harrington Thomas, track foreman D. L. & W. R. R., h 122 Fox.
Harris Scott, cashier Erie express office, h 68 Liberty.
Harris William M., book-keeper, 180 Front, bds. 12 Liberty.
Harris William S., resident, h 377 Main.
Harrison James, laborer, h 24 Temple.
Harrison John B., R. R. signal tender, h 11 East ave.
Harrison Lewis, clerk, bds. 115 North ave.
Harrison Samuel, teamster, h 36 W. Main.
Harrison S. M. Mrs., resident, h 115 North.
Harrison William L., harness-maker, 127 North, h do.
Harros Daniel, cartman, h 153 Erie.
Hart Alfred, laborer, bds. 256 Prospect.
Hart Daniel, machinist, h 483 Front.
Hart Horace, miller, h 12 Temple.
Hart Lewis, laborer, h 104 South Depot.
Hartnett Maria, resident, h John R.
Hartnett Michael, emp. Haywood's Marble Works, h 100 South Depot.
Haskins Edward T., engineer, h 34 George.
HASTINGS & STRATTON, (J. M. H. & E. S.) dry and fancy goods, 186 Front.
HASTINGS JAMES M., (Hastings & Stratton) school commissioner, h 351 Main.
Hastings Rebecca, widow William, bds. 351 Main.
Haughy Robert, laborer, h 108 Green.
Haupt Frank, emp. King & Co., bds. 118 Temple.
Havland Harriet, widow George, h 254 North ave.
Havland Ruth, widow Frederick, housekeeper, Spruce.
Hawes Judson, harness-maker, bds. 133 North ave.
Hawkins Philander, tanner, h n Dean's Tannery.
Hayden James J., emp. King & Co., bds. 31 Delphine.
Hayden Maggie, tailoress, bds. 87 Paige.
Hayden Mary Mrs., resident, h 87 Paige.
Hayden William P., retired, h 31 Delphine.
Hayden William P., Jr., foreman King & Co., bds. 31 Delphine.
HAYES JOHN, prop. European House, 151 North ave.
Hayes Michael J., peddler, h 185 E. Temple.
Hayes Richard J., bartender, bds. European House.
Haynes George L., painter, h 42 William.
Hays Richard, laborer, bds. Water.
HAYWOOD CHARLES M., marble and granite work, 80 North ave., h 42 Temple cor. Liberty.
Haywood Harry C., marble-cutter, bds. 42 Temple.
Hazzard Ella, clerk, bds. 118 Temple.
HEAD KATE Mrs., nurse, 104 West ave.
HEAD MELINDA, widow John M., resident, h 152 Talcott.
HEATON CARLTON R., physician and surgeon, treas. Cruciform Casket Company, and medical director O. M. B. Association, Park cor. Main, h do.
Hemstrought Abram V., carpenter, h 198 E. Temple.
Herrick John J., market gardner, 577 Main, bds. do.
Herrick Laura A., teacher, bds. 577 Main.

Hevland George W., emp. Grain Drill Works, h 242 North ave.
HEWITT FREDERICK C., retired, h 223 Front.
HEWITT GURDON, retired, h 223 Front.
HIBBARD GEORGE R., crockery, 84 Front, h Spencer ave.
Hibbard Jemima, widow Ralph, bds. 101 Franklin.
Hibbard Ralph W., cabinet-maker, h 112 Franklin.
Hickey James, cigarmaker, bds. 301 Prospect.
Hickey John, laborer, h 301 Prospect.
Hickey John, clerk, bds. 68 South Depot.
Hickey Lizzie C., dressmaker, 399 Main, bds. do.
Hickey Mame, tailoress, bds. 68 South Depot.
Hickey Mary, widow Patrick h 68 South Depot.
Hickey Thomas, shoemaker, h 399 Main.
Hicks Horace H., blacksmith, h 52 Fox.
Hierstiner Moses, resident, h 88 Chestnut.
Hill Alfred, janitor, h William.
HILL BROTHERS, (H. H. and C. C.) dentists, Front.
HILL CHARLES C., Dr., (Hill Brothers) h Binghamton, N. Y.
Hill Charles F., special claim agt. for pensions, h 354 Front.
Hill Charles O., manuf. and dealer in lumber and shingles (estate of James
    Hill,) 89 Central ave., 99 do.
Hill Edward, coachman, bds. William.
Hill Fred C., atty. at law and clerk Surrogate's court, Court House, h Main.
HILL HARRIET, widow James, h 84 North ave.
HILL HOMER H., (Hill Brothers) bds. Dugan House.
Hill James, (Estate) manuf. and dealer in lumber and shingles, 89 Central ave.
HILL LUCY, widow Chauncey, bds. 254 E. Temple.
Hinckley Alphonso J., restaurant and saloon, 189 Main, h do.
Hines Belle, widow Rufus W., h 447 Main.
Hines Louise, clerk, h 447 Main.
Hitchcock Eugene, cartman, h Canal.
Hoagland Alexander D., commercial traveler, h Buckbee block, Lake.
Hoagland Emma D., dressmaking, Buckbee block, h do.
Hoagland James R., laborer, h John R.
Hobler George, telephone operator, McMaster.
Hobler Philip, engineer, h 255 McMaster.
Hodge Caroline A., widow Henry J., resident, h 86 Temple.
Hodge Ella A., dressmaker, 86 Temple, bds. do.
Hodge Frederick S., painter, h 41 Temple.
Hodge Henry J., painter, h Water.
Hodge Joseph, laborer, h Constine's Lane.
Hogan Catharine, widow Philip, h 38 W. Main.
Hogan Catharine M., dressmaker, 60 Delphine, bds. do.
Hogan James, laborer, h 60 Delphine.
Hogan James J., fireman, bds. 60 Delphine.
Hogan John F., second hand store, 57 North ave., h do.
Hogan Roger P., reporter, h 38 W. Main.
Hoghey Sarah, widow James, h 118 Fox.
Holes George, carpenter and saw filing, 7 Park, h do.
Hollenback David J., farmer, h 117 North ave.
Hollenback Sisters, (Mary and Alice) farm 200, h 412 Front.
Hollensworth Jeremiah M., barber 22 Lake, h 158 Temple.

Hooper Warren, tanner, h 62 George.
Hopkins John, cigar-maker, bds. Park Hotel.
Horgan Jerry, retired, h 56 Delphine.
Horgan Katie, dressmaker, 56 Delphine, bds. do.
Horgan Mary, widow John, h 56 Delphine.
Horigan Daniel J., prop. Erie House, 70 South Depot.
Horn Eva, widow Matthias, bds. Gere.
Hornbeck Cornelius F., machinest, h 273 Erie.
Horrigan Margaret, widow Michael, tailoress, h 152 Green.
Horrigan William, barber, 152 North ave., h Green.
Hortnet Andrew, emp. foundry, bds. 109 Spencer ave.
Hortnet Mary, laundress, h 109 Spencer ave.
Horton John J., resident, h 105 North ave.
Hoskins Franklin F., machinest, h 8 Temple.
Hoskins James B., delivery clerk freight depot, h 65 Spencer ave.
Hoskins Mary M., widow Fayette F., bds. 223 East Temple.
HOSKINS WATSON L., insurance and jeweler, 185 Front, h 311 Main.
Houk Cora B., book-keeper, 184 Main, bds. 122 Temple.
Houk Frederick G., clerk, bds. 122 Temple.
Houk Harry, clerk, bds. 131 Talcott.
Houk Jennie M., book-keeper, 184 Main, bds. 122 Temple.
HOUK JONATHAN S., hardware, 184 Main, h 122 Temple.
Houk Lewis C., tinsmith and plumber, h 131 Talcott.
*HOUSE EPHRAIM H., coal, wood and lumber dealer, and farmer 75, office 229 McMaster, h 220 Main.
House Oakley, clerk, h 57 Church.
House Oakley A., horse farrier, h 76 South Depot.
Hover Robert, produce buyer, h 274 North ave.
Howard Orville, carpenter, h 7 Spruce.
Howe Olin R., pastor Park Cong. church, bds. 290 Main.
Howe Rufus, farmer, h 45 West Main.
Howe Ransom, cartman, h 115 Temple.
HUBBARD & KING, (I. M. H. & O. G. K.) furniture and undertaking, 29 Lake.
Hubbard Charles, emp. foundry, h rear 59 Church.
Hubbard Emeline M., widow Henry N., resident, h 275 Main.
Hubbard Henry D., clerk, 210 Front, h 160 Temple.
Hubbard Thomas, barber, Lake, h 60 Spencer ave.
HUBBARD TRUMAN M., (Hubbard & King) h Lake.
Hubbard Willis, emp. foundry, bds. rear 59 Church.
Huber Albert D., (Nichols & Huber) h 161 Main.
Hugaboone Matthias, laborer, h 460 Main.
Hughs Almira Mrs., laundress, h 32 Adaline.
Hughs George, stationary engineer, h John R.
HULL ALFRED H., resident, h 120 Chestnut.
Hull Byron O., resident, bds. 120 Chestnut.
Hull Frederick K., retired, h over 17 Lake.
Hull Hattie R., teacher, bds. 340 Main.
Hull Margaret S., teacher, bds. 340 Main.
Hull Mary A., h 340 Main.
Hulslander Levi T., dry and fancy goods, 59 North ave., bds. Central House.
HUMISTON FRANK M., (White & Humiston) h over 194 Front.
Hunt Arthur E., wind-mills and pumps, 134 Front, bds. Dugan House.

Hollister Charles J., silversmith and sewing machine agent, Fox cor. Central ave., h do.

Hollister George W., clerk, bds. 283, Prospect.

Hollister Joseph D., painter, Canal, h do.

Hollister Julius, silversmith, and sewing machine agt., Fox cor. Central ave., h do.

Hollister Mercy, widow Horace J., h Canal.

Hollister Myron E., printer, h 283 Prospect.

Hollister William S., painter, h Canal.

Holmes Oscar H., coachman, h 104 Paige.

Holmes Thomas H., clerk, bds. 358 Front.

Holt Mary, widow Edwin H., resident, h 94 Fox.

Home Rufus C., mason, Main, h do.

Hooker Archie S., carpenter, h 113 Franklin.

Hooker Warren, bridge carpenter, h George.

Hunt Emily J., widow William, h 14 Lake.

Hurlburt E. Burritt, flour, h 211 Main.

Hutchins Frank F., United States express agent, h 314 Main.

Hutchinson Alice M., teacher, bds. 232 E. Temple.

Hutchinson James, carpenter, 232 E. Temple, h do.

Hutchinson William, watch-maker, bds. 243 Main.

Hyde & Winters, (C. H. H. and J. B. W.) groceries and provisions, Front cor. Court.

Hyde Charles H., (Hyde & Winters) h 358 Front.

Hyde Earl, telephone operator, h Main.

Hyde Earl Mrs., dry goods and notions, Main.

Hyde Francis Mrs., bds. 67 Erie.

Hyde Merritt, emp. U. S. Express Co., h 91 Talcott.

Hyde Nelson H., wood-worker, 135 Talcott, h do.

Hyde Otis B., sup't cemetery, h 243 Main.

Hyde Perry, book-keeper, Hyde & Winters, also prop. Fulton Market, h Main cor. Fulton.

Hymes Edgar W., miller, h W. Main near Mill.

Ingersoll Charles A., teamster, h 18 Lake.

Isenburg William, cartman, h 190 River, South Side.

Jackson John, dentist, 12 Lake, h do.

Jackson John T., photographer, 12 Lake, bds. do.

Jackson Lois M., widow George W., dressmaker, 63 Liberty, h do.

Jackson Sarah, widow James, h Commerce.

Jackson W. Mianda, widow Harvey, h West ave., near creek.

Jansen Jesse W., (J. W. Jasen & Co.) also physician and surgeon, 60 North ave., h do.

JANSEN J. W. & CO., (W. H. Bailey and J. M. Anderson) drugs, medicines, and paints, 60 North ave.

JENKS ELIZA J., widow Sabin M., resident, h 15 Front.

JEWETT HARRY, retired, h 108 Liberty.

JOHNSON ABIGAIL M., caterer, widow Joshua C., h 459 Main.

Johnson Calvin, laborer, h 225 Prospect.

Johnson Caroline, widow David, resident, h 45 Front.

Johnson Charles W., retired, bds. 32 William.

Johnson Cyrene Mrs., resident, h 81 Liberty.

Johnson Edward J., groceries and provisions, 100 North ave., h North ave., cor. Chestnut.

Johnson Edward S., emp. agricultural works, h over 100 North ave.
JOHNSON FRANCES M., music teacher, also caterer for weddings, parties
    and private teas, Saratoga potatoes furnished to dealers, h 459 Main.
Johnson Frank H. Mrs., resident, h 85 North ave.
Johnson Harlen F., resident, h 275 E. Temple.
Johnson Henry, horse-trainer, h 98 Spencer ave.
Johnson Hiram R., resident, h 12 Talcott.
JOHNSON HORACE A., painter and paper-hanger, and decorative
    work, 52 George, h do.
Johnson James H., postal clerk, h 358 Main.
Johnson Lottie G., teacher, bds. 358 Main.
Johnson Thomas D. Rev., pastor St. Patrick's church, h Main.
Johnson Winfield, drug clerk, h 358 Main cor. Ross.
Jones Albert, laborer, h 493 Front.
Jones George W., mason, h 517 Front.
JONES JAMES E., carpenter, pattern and general job shop, 191 McMaster,
    h 116 Franklin.
Jones John, lumber at Nanticoke, Pa., h 41 Front.
Jones John B., moulder, h 254 E. Temple.
Jones Moses C., laborer, bds. 69 Fox.
Jones Peter, coachman, h 96 Spencer ave.
Jones Pierson, laborer, h 69 Fox.
Joslyn H. B., cabinet-maker, h 118 Temple.
Joslyn Hulda Mrs., resident, h over 57 North ave.
JOSLYN JUDSON, bridge carpenter, h 7 Hill.
Kaley Charles, laborer, h 11 Fox.
Kaley John W., emp. King & Co., h 90 Talcott.
Kaley William H., carpenter and stone mason, h over 177 Main.
Kanane Frank, gardener, bds. 43 Delphine.
Kanane Mary, tailoress, bds. 43 Delphine.
Kanane Patrick, laborer, h 43 Delphine.
Keefe Owen, blacksmith, h 283 E. Temple.
KEELER ALBERT H., contractor and builder, and dealer in lime, cement
    and fertilizers, h Temple cor. Central ave.
Keeler Charles P., mason and contractor, h rear 68 Paige.
KEELER JAMES B., (City Steam Laundry) prop. Empire Soap Works,
    Temple cor. Central ave.
KEITH GEORGE W., brakeman, h 15 East ave.
KEITH MARY B., widow Luther T., bds. 15 East ave.
Kellogg Charles T., contractor and builder, h 262 Prospect.
Kellogg Julia, widow Charles, h 73 Forsyth.
Kellogg Ulysses P., carpenter, h 22 Fulton.
Kelly Julia F., widow Frederick P., dressmaker, 246 E. Temple, bds. do.
Kelly Matthew, laborer, h 112 Green.
Kempson Emily P., widow Peter T., h 80 McMaster.
Kendall Frank B., traveling salesman, h 96 Franklin.
Kennedy Lee, insurance, h 73 West ave.
Kennedy Peter G., barber, h 106 Paige.
KENYON ALBERT J., chief engineer, U. S. Navy, h 163 Temple.
KENYON JAMES, retired, h 163 Temple.
Kenyon Joel C., druggist, 5 Lake, h do.
Kershner Eugene K., clerk Dugan House, bds. do.
Ketchum John, hack driver, h Main.

Ketchum La Fayette F. Rev., Reformed Methodist, h 92 Franklin.
Kettle John, porter Dugan House, bds. do.
Kidder James H. Rev., rector St. Paul's Church, h 100 Main.
Kidder Phœbe Mrs., resident, h 195 North ave.
Kiernan Margaret, dressmaker, bds. Canal.
Kiernan Patrick, laborer, h Canal.
Kile Lowell E., laborer, h over 67 North ave.
Kimball Ebenezer, bridge builder, h 126 McMaster.
Kimball Helen, widow Calvin S., artist, bds 425 Main.
King & Co., (W. A. and G. A. K.) manufs. of and wholesale dealers in har-
    nesses, 24, 26 and 28 Lake.
King Charles H., barber, Ah-wa-ga House, bds. 112 Fox.
King George A., (King & Co.) h 58 Paige.
KING ORLANDO, (Hubbard & King) county supervisor, bds. Ah-wa-ga
    House.
King Seth L., machinist, h 234 Main.
King William A., (King & Co.) h 250 Front.
King William H. Rev., retired Bapt., h 369 Front.
Kingcade Charles, shoemaker, h 90 Paige.
Kingcade Charles Mrs., dressmaker, 90 Paige, h do.
Kingfield Ellen Mrs., mailing clerk, postoffice, h 184 E. Temple.
Kingfield Fanny B., book-keeper, 196 Front, h 184 E. Temple.
KINGMAN LEROY W., editor and pub. Owego *Gazette,* h 2 Academy.
Kingman Lyman R., bartender, h North ave.
Kingman Maria L., widow Leroy W., h 260 Main.
Kinney Susan J., widow J. Alphonso, h 18 Fulton.
Kinney Willis D., printer, bds. 18 Fulton.
Kipp George, butcher, h 111 North ave.
Kline Orion, carriage-maker, h 144 Temple.
Knapp Maria R., widow Dr. Jerome, bds. Front.
Knight Catharine, widow Cornelius, h 56 Forsyth.
KNIGHT ELIZABETH, dressmaker, bds. 59 Church.
Knight Mary J., widow Moses, h 59 Church.
KNIGHT MILTON T., agt. G. U. Tea Co., bds. Dugan House.
Knight Milton W., carpenter, bds. 56 Forsyth.
Korbmann Rosa, widow Christian, h over 13 Lake.
Labarron Sarah A., widow Edson, h 234 North ave.
Lackawanna House, Ira J. VanDemark, prop., 176 River, South Side.
LaGrange Abram, carpenter, bds. 52 West ave.
LaGrange Charles, carriage-painter, h 52 West ave.
Lainhart George, variety store, 212 Front, h 132 Main.
Lake Martha D. Mrs., resident, h 58 Spencer ave.
Lake Thomas B., meat-market and grocery, 119 North ave., h 65 Talcott.
Lake William A., butcher, h over 119 Lake.
Lamb Charles B., brakeman, h 174 North ave.
LAMEREAUX NATHAN, saloon, 76 North ave., bds. 57 Church.
LaMonte Fred S., (LaMonte & Rodman) produce, h 442 Front.
LaMonte Samuel M., retired, h 105 Liberty.
Lane Bert J., clerk, bds. 12 Adaline.
Lane Leonard, clerk, bds. near Dean's tannery.
Laning John, retired, h 143 Main.
Larkin Thomas, laborer, h 62 Talcott.
Lawheed Joseph W., boarding-house, 118 Temple.

9

Lawrence Laura, widow William, bds. 69 Church.
Lawrence Oscar S., emp. Erie Express Co., h 69 Church.
Lawrence William A., jeweler, h McMaster.
Lawrence William D., express messenger, h 58 Church.
Layton Daniel, laborer, h 238 E. Temple.
Layton James F., laborer, bds. 238 E. Temple.
Layton John J., printer, bds. 239 E. Temple.
Leach Benjamin C., grocery and music, North ave., h do.
Leach John J., locomotive engineer, h 158 McMaster.
Leach Tillie C.. music teacher, bds. North ave.
Leahy James J., (P. Leahy & Son) bds. 310 Main.
Leahy Patrick & Son, (James J.) groceries, provisions, and meats, Main cor. North ave.
Leahy Patrick, (P. Leahy & Son) h 310 Main.
Lee Albert S., barber, 109 North ave., h do.
Lee William, farm laborer, h 534 Main.
Legg Dolphus, emp. D., L. & W. R. R. freight depot, h 198 North ave.
Legg Louis H., law clerk, bds. 69 Church.
Lenon John, clerk, bds. European House.
Leonard Allen, carpenter, h Water.
Leonard Emily C., resident, h 313 Main.
Leonard Frank, laborer, h W. Main, near Mill.
LEONARD GEORGE S., loan, investment and insurance, 209 Front, h Main.
Leonard John, saloon, 135 North ave., h do.
Leonard Laura A., resident, h 313 East Main.
Leonard Lewis S., clerk. h over 195 Main.
LEONARD NATHANIEL, laborer, h Canal.
LEONARD WILLIAM B., retired, h Front.
Leonard Willis B., tobacco grower, h Pumpelly, South Side.
Leroy Peter H., laborer, h Prospect, cor. Green.
Letts Armena, widow John D., resident, h rear 18 Adaline.
Levene Abram, tailor, h 42 Temple.
Lewis Fred W., machinist, h 109 Fox.
LEWIS GEORGE B., M. D., physician and surgeon, Lake, cor. Main, rooms do.
Lewis Milo, contractor, Owego Casket Company, h 95 West ave.
Lewis Robert, laborer, h 93 Paige.
Lillie George W., retired, h 103 River, South Side.
Lillie Jared, saloon, 104 North ave., h do.
Lincoln & Co., (C. K. Lincoln) coal and wood, 59 Central ave.
Lincoln Charles K., (Lincoln & Co.) h 294 Main.
Link Charles A., (Dwelle & Link) h 348 Front.
Livermore Cyrus E., clerk, h 20 Ross.
Livermore Otis W., general repair shop, rear 117 North ave., h 84 Chestnut.
Livingston Amos, groceries and provisions, 56 North ave, h do.
Loader Richard, painter, h 64 Forsyth.
Locke Mary E., carpet weaver, h 91 Fox.
LOCKE REUBEN B., carpenter, h 241 Erie.
Long Jeremiah, resident, h 25 Temple.
Loring Benjamin W., retired lieut. U. S. revenue marine service, h 351 Front.

Loring Benjamin W., Jr., law student, bds. Front.
Lounsbury William H., boot and shoemaker, 63 North ave., h 37 Main.
Lovejoy Charles L., photographer, Front cor. Court, h 313 Main.
Lynch Daniel, bartender, bds. 7 Fulton.
Lynch Martin S., atty. at law, Lake, cor. Main h 495 Main.
Lynch Michael, mason, h 7 Fulton.
Lynch Michael, (Wall & Lynch) h Chestnut.
Lynde Marion, widow James G., resident, bds. 51 Front.
Lynn Luzern, laborer, h 65 Adaline.
LYON & RIPLEY, (F. D. L. & H. C. R.) boots and shoes, 188 Front.
Lyon & Robinson, (J. R. L. & G. R.) liquor dealers, 187 Main.
LYON FRANCIS D., (Lyon & Ripley) h 7 Park.
Lyon John R., (Lyon & Robinson) h 60 Paige.
Mabee Foster N., agent Erie Express Co., h 333 Main.
MABEE JOHN A., (City Steam Laundry) h Temple cor. Central ave.
Mabee William, emp. Owego Casket Company, bds. 73 Liberty.
Macbeth Margaret, resident, h 22 William.
MADAN ANDREW J., emp. James Hill estate, h 111 Talcott.
Male William, carpenter, h 22 William.
Maloney Ann, resident, h 121 Erie.
Maloney Bridget, resident, h 121 Erie.
Maloney Catherine, widow Michael C., h 98 Temple.
Maloney Catherine A., clerk, bds. 98 Temple.
Maloney Julia, resident, h 121 Erie.
Maloney Minnie, dressmaker, bds. 73 Liberty.
Maloney Owen T., bookbinder, h 98 Temple.
MALONEY PATRICK, prop. Cobweb Bottling Works, Paige cor. Fox, also
  general grocery and liquors, 122 Paige, h do.
Maloney William P., clerk, bds. 122 Paige.
Manas Julia, dressmaker, bds. 7 East ave.
Manas Patrick, R. R. signal tender, h 7 East ave.
Manning Caroline M. Mrs., millinery, 206 Front, h do.
Manning Ellen, dressmaker, bds. Division.
Manning James, foreman Owego *Times*, h over 193 Main.
Manning Josephine, tailoress, bds. Division.
Manning Lewis, printer, bds. 133 North ave.
Manning Margaret, widow John, h Division.
MANNING MARION L., shoemaker, h 206 Front.
Manning Mary, widow James, bds. 57 Church.
Manning Michael J., laborer, bds. Division.
Manning William H., carpenter, 113 Main, h do.
Mareane James, engineer, bds. 150 Central ave.
Maroney Daniel, laborer, h 245 E. Temple.
Maroney John F., groceries, 56 North ave, h over do.
Marquart Gideon, farmer, bds. 139 North ave.
Marquart Levi, retired, h 17 West ave.
Marquart Levier, bds. Commerce.
Marquart Simeon, farmer, h 139 North ave.
Marquett John M., shoemaker, h 473 Front.
Marquett Larenzo, clerk, bds. 473 E. Front.
Marquette Alanson A., resident, h 230 Prospect.
Marquette Jerome N., clerk, 14 W. Main.

Marshall Mrs., resident, h 167 North ave.
Martin Benjamin B., carriage-trimmer, bds. 73 Liberty.
Marvin Harrison, orderly at State Capitol, h 94 Liberty.
Mason Allen J., painter, bds. 113 Chestnut.
Mason Harriet Mrs., widow Roswell A., laundress, h 113 Chestnut.
Matson Cynthia E. Miss, resident, h 14 Front.
Matson John L., furniture and undertaking, 183 Front, h 27 Park.
Mawhiney Edward, bookkeeper, 164 North ave., bds. 5 Spruce.
MAWHINEY WILLIAM J., (W. H. Bailey & Co.) h 5 Spruce.
May William, laborer, h 209 Prospect.
Maynard William, shoemaker, h 64 Spencer ave.
MAYOR EDWARD A., D. D. S., dentist, over 173 Front, h Academy.
Mayor William E., D. D. S., dentist, over 173 Front, bds. Academy.
McArthur John, confectionery, 107 North ave., h do.
McCofferty Anthony C., horse-dealer, bds. European House.
McColly Thomas, resident, bds. United States Hotel.
McCARTHY FLORENCE, laborer, h 604 Fifth ave.
McCarthy John, laborer, h 119 Fox.
McCarthy John P., clerk, bds. 604 Fifth ave.
McCaslin John H., (Smith & McCaslin) blacksmith, h 190 River, So. Side.
McCullock ——, h 107, Chestnut.
McCormick Daniel, brakeman, h 99 Fox.
McDonald John, mason, bds. 18 West Main.
McDowell Fayette, cabinet-maker, h Canal.
McDowell Betty, widow Augustus, bds. Ah-wa-ga House.
McGiffin John L., emp. grist-mill, h 102 Chestnut.
McGratch Patrick, laborer, h 115 Paige.
McKee Robert, retired, h 387 Main.
McKenzie Alexander C. Rev., pastor First Pres. church, h 321 Front.
McLean Ezra, carpenter and builder, h 172 Talcott.
McManus Rose, widow Patrick, laundress, h 91 Fox.
McMaster Frank, liquor store, 70 North ave., h do.
McNulty Barney, tanner, bds. 133 North ave.
McNulty James, baggageman, h 107 River, South Side.
McNulty Thomas, emp. Dean's tannery, bds. near tannery, North ave.
MEACHAM CHARLES D., carpenter, h 99 Talcott.
Meacham Erastus, blacksmith, 221 North ave., h do.
MEAD & DARROW, (H. J. M. & F. A. D.) attorneys at law, Main cor. North ave.
MEAD HOWARD J., (Mead & Darrow) h Main, cor. Spencer ave.
Mericle Alfred, baggageman, h 200 North ave.
Mericle Charles D., clerk, h 439 Main.
Merritt Ephraim J., brakeman, h 167 North ave.
Merrick John, salesman, h 57 Main.
Metcalf Charles, miller, h 114 Central ave.
Metcalf Hannah M., widow Dr. A. E., h 207 East Main.
Middaugh Augustus B., carpenter, h 32 Adaline.
Middaugh Elijah, retired, h off Water.
Middaugh James E., laborer, h Canal Front.
Miller Edith L., tailoress, bds. 88 Adaline.
Miller Lorenzo, clerk, h Central ave.
Miller Mrs., widow Abram, h 405 Front.

MILLREA BROTHERS, (W. A., J. F. & T.) meat-market and grocery, 178 Front.

MILLREA J. FRED, (Millrea Bros.) h 377 Main.

MILLREA THOMAS, (Millrea Bros.) bds. Dugan House.

MILLREA WILLIAM A., (Millrea Bros.) h 55 Paige.

Mills Robert, cooper, h 102 McMaster.

Minehan John, tanner, h 64 Temple.

Minehan William, miller, bds. 14 W. Main.

Miner William D., book-keeper 174 Front, bds. Dugan House.

Mitchell Bartlett, tanner, h 107 River, South Side.

Mitchell Eliza A. B., widow Henry A., bds. 153 Temple.

Mitchell William J., emp. King & Co., bds. 107 River, South Side.

Moak Robert T., retired carpenter, h 130 North ave.

Moffitt James R., laborer, h 117 Green.

Moffitt Robert J., laborer, h 117 Green.

Moloney Agnes K., clerk, bds. 98 Temple.

Moneypenny Elizabeth, widow Robert L., resident, h 388 Main.

Monyhan George, hostler, bds. United States Hotel.

Moody Winfield S., harness-maker, h 59 Main.

Moon Reuben, cooper, h John R.

Moore & Ross, (T. F. M. & J. S. R.) carriage and wagon manufs., 146 North ave.

Moore Charles, wagon-maker, h 134 North ave.

Moore Helen E. B., widow Dr. Robert, resident, h 227 Front.

Moore Theodore F., (Moore & Ross) h 82 Chestnut.

Moran James, well driver, bds. 89 William.

Morann Thomas, blacksmith, h 105 Fox.

MOREHOUSE ALLIE, art teacher, h Spencer ave.

Morehouse Charles H., printer, h Spencer ave.

Morehouse John, carpenter, h off Water.

Morgan Delos, carpenter, h 18 Paige.

Morgan William B., horse-trainer, h 607 Main.

Morris Anna, widow John, bds. 104 Paige.

Morris Frank, clerk, bds. 110 Spencer ave.

Morris Patrick, laborer, h 110 Spencer ave.

Morris Thomas, resident, bds. 110 Spencer ave.

Morse Charles, printer, h 31 Temple.

Morse Henry H., butcher and farmer, h Pumpelly, South Side, h do.

Morse Mrs., resident, h 100 East ave.

Morse Newell, coal, wood and shingles, 133 Temple, h do.

Morton Durwent, laborer, h 169 North ave.

Morton Edward, laborer, h 215 North ave.

Morton Ida E., widow G. A., h 84 North ave.

Morton John, constable and tanner, h South Side.

Moulton Michael A., sewing machine repairer 10 Lake, bds. do.

Mulks Frank H., emp. foundry, h 130 Chestnut.

Munger Cynthia L., widow Alanson, h 285 Main.

Munn Sarah E. Mrs., resident, bds. 7 George.

Murray Ida Mrs., laundress, h 26 Talcott.

Muzzy Cornelius, clerk, bds. 279 Main.

Myers Andrew, butcher, h 6 West ave.

Myers Jessie, teacher, bds. 6 West ave.

Myers Philip, emp. casket works, bds. 6 West ave.

Neally Sarah F., teacher, bds. 560 Fifth ave.
Neaves Edmund J., clerk, bds. Front.
Nelson Bert E., drug clerk, bds. North ave. extension.
Nelson James, retired, bds. 48 West Main.
Nelson James, Jr., notions, 48 West Main, h do.
Nelson Willa M., dressmaker, bds 21 George.
Nelson William, engineer, h 21 George.
Newell Frank, carpenter, h 117 Central ave.
Newell Friend G., cabinet-maker, rear 17 Lake, h 57 Liberty.
Newell Gilbert, resident, h 34 Fox.
Newell Gilbert C., emp. foundry, bds. 77 West ave.
Newell Orvin L., emp. foundry, h 77 West ave.
*NEWGEON MARY F., physician, 295 Main, h do.
Newiand James D., laborer, h 248 North ave.
Newman Adolphus, (Newman Bros.) h 47 Temple.
Newman Brothers, (A. & G.) dry goods and millinery, 31 and 33 Lake.
Newman George, (Newman Bros.) h 47 Temple.
NEWMAN SIMON, optician, h 54 Temple.
Newton Charles D., printer, h 43 Talcott.
Newton Frank, laborer, h 152 River, South Side.
Newton George, emp. Chamberlain's boot and shoe factory, h 125 Main.
Nichols George A., (Nichols & Huber) h 161 Main.
Nichols Susan B., widow Thomas M., h 55 Front.
Nichols Susan B. Miss, resident, bds. 55 Front.
Nichols Washington, resident, h 55 Front.
NIXON CHARLES D., loan and investment, real estate and lawyer ; also
    prop. Jenksville steam mills, Front cor. Court, bds. Ah-wa-ga House.
Nixon Walter, harness-maker, h over 168 Front.
N. Y., L. E. & W. R. R. Depot, Cameron B. Dean, agent, North ave., cor.
    Depot.
Noble Asa S., carpenter, h 12 Adaline.
Noonan David E., carpenter, h 96 Franklin.
Noonnan Daniel, mason, h Paige.
Norris Charles P., carriage-smith, h 266 Prospect.
Norris George E., lamp-lighter, h 521 Front.
Norris Hampton M., barber, bds. 266 Prospect.
Norris Theodore, teamster, bds., Decker Block, Main.
Northrop Tilly, book-canvasser, bds. 113 Chestnut.
Northrop William T., painter, h 113 Chestnut.
Norton Harriet A., widow Colden O., h 164 Temple.
Norwood Erastus, retired, bds. 7 Hill.
Nugent Mary, pastry-cook Ah-wa-ga House, bds. do.
Nutt Hamer, emp. King & Co., bds. 118 Temple.
N. Y. & PA. TELEPHONE AND TELEGRAPH CO., Frank S. Blood-
    good, manager, 178 Main.
NYE ARTHUR E., (Nye Brothers) h Fox.
NYE BROTHERS, (M. G. & A. E.) bakers and confectioners, 44 Lake.
NYE MELVIN G., (Nye Brothers) bds. Fox.
Oakley Timothy B., counselor at law, 214 Front, h River Road.
ODD FELLOWS' HALL, W. Stewart, janitor, over 80 North ave.
Odell Hiram A., engineer, h 36 George.
Ogden Aaron, tobacconist, 7 Lake, h Front.
Ogden Frederic L., traveling salesman, bds. Front.

Ogden Harriet A., widow Walter, h 229 Main.
Ogden Priscilla C., widow Isaac, h 194 River, South Side.
Ogden S. Jane, widow Jehiel, resident, h 125 Main.
OHART S. JAY, att'y and counselor at law, Academy Bld'g, Court, h at Tioga Center.
Ohern Bartholomew, track foreman S. C. R. R., h near tannery, North ave.
Ohmar Patrick, gardener, bds. Front.
Olmstead Franklin H., machinist, bds. 227 Erie.
Olmstead Freeborn W., machinist, h 227 Erie.
O'Neil Maggie, clerk, 61 East ave.
O'Neil Michael, laborer, h 61 East ave.
Orcutt J. Allan, carpenter, h 126 Chestnut.
Orcutt Isaac D., bridge carpenter, h 45 Fox.
O'ROURKE MICHAEL F., keeper Auburn prison, h Lake.
Ostrander Edward, emp. King & Co., bds. 14 West ave.
*OWEGO CRUCIFORM CASKET CO., (John Jones, pres't; J. J. Van-Kleeck, sec'y; and C. R. Heaton, treas.) burial caskets and undertakers' supplies, lumber, sash, doors, and blinds, 42, 44 and 46 Delphine.
*OWEGO DAILY AND WEEKLY RECORD, (Scott & Watros) 172 Front.
Owego Gas Light Co., A. P. Storrs, Jr., pres't, office Front cor. Lake.
*OWEGO GAZETTE, (weekly) Leroy W. Kingman, editor and publisher, 28 Lake.
*OWEGO IRON WORKS, Cauldwell & Gray. props., McMaster cor. Dalton.

OWEGO IRON WORKS

CAULDWELL & GRAY, Proprietors.

FOUNDRY AND MACHINE SHOPS.

WE MANUFACTURE NEARLY ALL KINDS OF CASTINGS.

Engines and Boilers Repaired

ALSO MACHINE WORK DONE ON SHORT NOTICE.

We Manufacture Patent Cast Iron Standards and Lasts for Shoemakers' use.

OWEGO NATIONAL BANK, (Charles E. Parker, pres't; R. B. Dean, vice-pres't; C. A. Thompson, cashier; J. A. Bassett, teller) 6 Lake.
OWEGO POSTOFFICE, F. O. Cable, postmaster, Lake.
*OWEGO TIMES, (Weekly) W. Smyth & Son, props., 193 Main.
OWEGO TIMES BINDERY AND BLANK-BOOK MANUF., W. Smyth & Son, props., 193 Main.
OWEGO WATER WORKS, George Y. Robertson, sup't, 69 North ave.
Owen Elias H. Mrs., h 314 Front.
Padgett Gurdon E., emp. Canawanna mills, bds. Canal.
Padgett William S., laborer, h off Water.
Paine Thomas, saloon and restaurant, 229 North ave., h do.

Park George W., carpenter, h 74 Fox.

Park Hotel, (Nichols & Huber, props.) 161 Main.

PARKER CHARLES E., county judge, surrogate, and att'y at law, pres't Owego National Bank, Court House, h 108 Main.

PARKER STELLA, widow John M., h 113 Front.

Parmelee Alburn S., manager Western Union and Erie telegraph offices, Erie Depot, h 77 Liberty.

PARMELEE ALBURN W., (Beach & Parmelee) h Main.

Parmeter Edward, lumber, h 3 Spruce.

Parris Stephen, billiards, h 206 Front.

Partridge Frank J., soapmaker, h George.

Partridge John F., resident, h 48 George.

Partridge John F., Jr., soapmaker, bds. 48 George.

Partridge Walter B., clerk, bds. 48 George.

Partridge William J., baggageman S. C. R. R. depot, h 91 Talcott.

Patghard Gordon, laborer, h Canal.

Patrick George W., resident, bds. Park Hotel.

Payne Frank A., hack driver, bds. Central ave.

PAYNE FRANK F., printer, bds. Main.

Payne John, gardener, h 256 Prospect.

Payne William A., porter Ah-wa-ga House, bds. do.

Peabody Oliver A., harness-maker, h 19 John.

PEARSALL ANDREW T., physician and surgeon, Taylor Block, h Main cor. Spencer ave.

Pearsall Dwight, engineer, h 192, North ave.

Pearsall Gilbert, medical student, bds. Main cor. Spencer ave.

PEARSALL RANSOM S., justice of the peace, over 168 Front, h in Apalachin.

Pease George, shoemaker, 160 North ave., h do.

Pease Johanna, widow David, bds. 56 George.

Peck Ezra J., principal of academy and supt. of schools, h 104 Main.

Peck Nancy M., widow Rev. Philetus B., h 347 Main.

Peck Sarah N., resident, bds. 347 Main.

Peck William A., resident, h 105 Talcott.

Pelham John W., cooper, h 39 Temple.

Pelham William, cooper, bds. 133 North ave.

PELLUM MARGARET MRS., shampooer of ladies' hair, also hair worker, h 459 Main.

Penney Ella G., book-keeper, bds. 59 Spencer ave.

Penney Joseph H., cutter, h 59 Spencer ave.

PENNY CORNELIUS S., bridge carpenter, h 16 Adaline.

Penny Frederick C., clerk, h 31 Church.

Perkins Frederick, carpenter, h 21 Fulton.

Perrine Joanna, widow John K., h Buckbee Block.

Perry Harley, emp. foundry, bds. 118 Temple.

Perry John M., blacksmith, h 30 Temple.

Perry Lottie A., teacher, South Side, bds. do.

Perry William H., carpenter, h South Side.

Pert Thomas, express messenger, h 31 Front.

Pert William, tel. op., bds. 31 Front.

Peters William, resident, h 162 McMaster.

PETERSON PETER C., (Buckbee, Peterson, Wood & Co.) h 16 Ross.

Phelps E. B., retired physician and surgeon, Front cor. Paige.

Phillips Augustus H., retired, bds. 113 Franklin.
Phillips Betie, clerk, bds. 68 Adaline.
Phililps Carrie, clerk, bds. 228 Front.
Phillips James H., bridge carpenter, h 68 Adaline.
Phillips William H., gardener, bds. 68 Adaline.
Pike Augusta, widow Horace, h 8 W. Main.
Pinney Hammon D., books, stationery and wall-paper, 45 Lake, h 437 Front.
Pippett Mary, widow James, laundress, h 101 Fox.
PITCHER DANIEL M., wool, hides and pelts, 175 Front, h 325 Main.
Pitcher Lena, resident, h over Lake cor. Main.
Plakenpol John, farmer, h n Dean's Tannery.
PLATT FREDERICK E., cashier Tioga Nat. Bank, h 256 Main.
Platt George, resident, h 33 Church.
Platt George Mrs., cancer specialist, h 33 Church.
Platt Henry B., (Gere, Truman, Platt & Co.) rooms 33 Park.
Platt Harry P., supt. for Gere, Truman, Platt & Co., bds. Court.
Poltzen Peter, piano-maker, h n Dean's Tannery.
Porter Frances S., widow Rev. George P., bds. 322 Main.
Postal Telegraph and Cable Co., (C. W. Daggett, mgr.) 40 Lake.
Potter Asa N., retired, h 87 Main.
Potter Isaac L., carpenter, h 100 Chestnut.
Powell William, gardener, h Front.
Powell William H., jeweler, bds. Front.
Prendergast John, pattern-maker, h 78 Paige.
Prendergast John, Jr., resident, bds. 78 Paige.
Pride Eliza, widow William, h Water.
Prime Aaron P., gardener, h Constine's lane.
Pritchard Albert J., clerk, h Spencer Block, Lake.
Probert Daniel, laborer, bds. Canal.
Probert Emma, dressmaker, bds. Canal.
Pultz Frank, photographer, bds. 38 Lake.
Pultz Griffin, locomotive engineer, h 51 Fox.
Pultz Griffin, Jr., music teacher, bds. 51 Fox.
Pumpelly Caroline A., resident, bds. 113 Front.
Pumpelly Gurdon H., wholesale leaf tobacco dealer, and farmer 250, h Pumpelly, South Side.
Pumpelly James F., real estate dealer and farmer, h Pumpelly, South Side.
Purdy Emma D., music teacher, bds. 147 Main.
Purple George B., expressman, h 102 Liberty.
Purple Jasper L., contractor, h 99 Franklin.
Putnam Archibald, painter, h 425 Main.
Putnam Frederick, (Leverson & Putnam) h Main.
Putnam Frederick J., painter, h 427 Main.
Putnam Jennie C., milliner, bds. 425 Main.
Putnam Louis H., house-painter and music teacher, bds. 425 Main.
Putney Cyrus, shoemaker, h 97 Paige.
Quetschenbach Anna, widow Walter, h 269 Erie.
Quetschenbach Grace, dressmaker, 269 Erie, bds. do.
Quetschenbach Joseph, cigarmaker, bds. 269 Erie.
Quinn Ann, resident, h 88 South Depot.
Quinn Frank, laborer, bds. 18 West Main.
Quinn Julia, dressmaker, bds. 18 West Main.
Quinn Richard, brakeman, h 5 Fox.

Rader Lawrence W., plumber, h South Side.
Rady Kate E., widow Hugh, dressmaker, h 124 Paige.
Randall Frank, carpenter, h 607 Main.
Randall Samuel, carpenter, h 607 Main.
Ransom John, laborer, h 111 Paige.
Ransom Margaret, widow Robert, h 115 Fox.
Rapp Charles F., salesman, bds. Dugan House.
RAYMOND & EMERY (F. L. R. and D. H. E.) carriage and wagon manufrs., Central ave. cor. Temple.
Raymond Chauncey L., mgr. of store for Mary F. Raymond, h 199 Main.
RAYMOND FRANK L., (Raymond & Emery) h 29 Fox.
Raymond George C., carriage-maker, h 72 McMaster.
Raymond Mary F., groceries and meats, 199 Main, h do.
Raymond Mrs., resident, h 64 Spencer ave.
Raymond William B., clerk, bds. Ah-wa-ga House.
Raymond William B., farmer 75, h 228 Main.
Raymond William W., clerk, bds. over 199 Main.
Ready James, laborer, h 149 Erie.
Redding Hugh, dyeing and cleaning, 65 Central ave., h McMaster.
REED SARAH, widow Timothy C., resident, h 26 Ross.
Regan Edward, bartender, bds. 16 Lake.
Regan Jane, widow Thomas, resident, h 109 Paige.
Regan Jerry, cigarmaker, h 99 Erie.
Regan John, saloon and restaurant 16 Lake, h do.
Relyea Andrew, carpenter, h 26 Fulton.
RENWICK WILLIAM C., (Battelle & Renwick of New York city) h 79 Front.
Reynolds Peter, carpenter, h 270 North ave.
Reynolds Smith, peddler, bds. 133 North ave.
Rhinevault Myron, blacksmith rear 81 North ave., h 53 Talcott.
Rice Catherine, resident, h 65 Adaline.
Rich George E., (Dorwin, Stone & Rich) h 40 Front.
Richards & Doyle (W. N. R. & P. J. D.) wholesale and retail liquors, 168 Front.
Richards William N., (Richards & Doyle) bds. Ah-wa-ga House.
Richardson Wesley L., carpenter, 557 Front.
Rightmire Charles H., carpenter, h 17 George.
Rigney Thomas, harness-maker, bds. 64 South depot.
Riley & Gillett, (M. R. & L. W. G.) blacksmiths, 140 Front.
Riley George, blacksmith. h 140 Central ave.
Riley James, laborer, h Constine's lane.
Riley James, blacksmith 81 North, h 34 Main.
Riley Martin, (Riley & Gillett) h 27 Fox.
Ringrose Ellen, widow Patrick, h 117 Franklin.
Ringrose John, clerk, bds. 117 Franklin.
Ringrose Thomas J., printer, bds. 117 Franklin.
Ringrose William E., (Shaw & Ringrose) bds. 117 Franklin.
RIPLEY HENRY C., (Lyon & Ripley) h 359 Main.
Ripley Sarah P., resident, h 53 Paige.
Roach David, blacksmith, h 113 Spencer ave.
Roach Ellen, widow David, h 100 Spencer ave.
Roache David, laborer, h 231 Temple.
Roak Alvin P., salesman 198 Front, bds. Main.

Roberts J., traveling salesman, bds. 67 Central ave.
Roberts Lincoln, emp. drill shop, bds. 67 Central ave.
Robertson Frank W., bds. 123 North ave.
ROBERTSON GEORGE Y., supt. water works, h 489 Main.
Robertson Jason J., street commissioner, h 79 Talcott.
Robertson A. Jerry, chief of police, h 123 North ave.
Robertson Peter, gardener, h 489 Main.
Robertson Peter J., emp. Erie freight-house, h 26 John.
Robertson Ralph H., clerk, h 9 Spruce.
Robertson Will P., emp. foundry, bds. 79 Talcott.
Robinson Alexander, laborer, h 98 Fox.
Robinson Alvin T., carpenter, h Adaline.
Robinson Bert E., emp. casket company, bds. Adaline.
Robinson Charles, harness-maker, bds. 177 Main.
Robinson Edwin, moulder, bds. 115 Temple.
Robinson Elvira, widow J. Owen, bds. Adaline.
Robinson George, laborer, h 121 Green.
Robinson George, carpenter, h 115 Temple.
Robinson George, (Lyon & Robinson) h over 187 Main.
Robinson Jacob H., blacksmith and farmer 61, h 552 Main.
Robinson James V., bar-tender, h North ave. cor. Fox.
Robinson Martin V., clerk, bds. Adaline.
Robinson Matthew, saloon, 20 Lake, bds. Dugan House.
Robinson William, constable, h 109 North ave.
Rockwell Marvin, emp. foundry, h 116 Chestnut.
RODMAN CHARLES, county sheriff and produce, Front, and Main cor.
    Court, h do.
Rodman Edward D., deputy sheriff and produce dealer, Main cor. Court,
    h do.
Rogers Arthur L., saloon, 152 Front, h do.
Rogers Elias H., emp. drill works, h Fox cor. Central ave.
Rogers James T., assistant postmaster, bds. Ah-wa-ga House.
Roland John, laborer, bds. near tannery, North ave.
Roll Joseph, cigar-maker, bds. 269 Erie.
ROMINE CHARLES F., house, sign, fresco and decorative painter and
    paper-hanger, 121 Erie, h do.
Romine Clarence W., painter and paper-hanger, 119 Chestnut, h do.
ROMINE DEMOSTHENES, piano-varnisher, h 279 Prospect.
ROMINE EDWIN B., house-painting and decorating, Opera House Block,
    h 95 Fox.
Romine Joseph, painter, bds. 119 Chestnut.
ROMINE PERCIVAL H., scenic, fresco, ornamental and house-painting,
    paper-hanging, etc., 81 Fox, h do.
Romine Samuel L., painter, h 104 Fox.
Rose Jane, widow Albin, h 164 Temple.
Ross Allie M., dressmaker, 42 William, bds. do.
Ross Delia, widow Horatio, h 42 William.
Ross Ed. L., machinest, bds. 93 West ave.
Ross John S., (Moore & Ross) bds. Ah-wa-ga House.
Ross Oliver L., salesman, h 492 Main.
Ross William E., laborer, h 15 Fox.
Rounsville Caroline E., widow Charles J., resident, bds. 15 Front.
Rowe Henry W., clerk, h over 19 Main.

Rowe Joseph, blacksmith, h 100 Liberty.
Rowe Louise, clerk, bds. Front.
Rowe M. & G., (Mary & Gussie) dressmakers, 192 Front, h do.
Rubert Charles B., jeweler, bds. Dugan House.
Rumph David, lather, h 217 North ave.
Russell Howard A., emp. Erie R. R., h 54 Fox.
Russell Van Ness, retired, h 91 Talcott.
Ryan Annis, widow Thomas, h Canal.
Ryan Charlotte, widow Joseph, resident, h near Dean's tannery.
Ryan Michael, laborer, h 17 Park.
Ryan Patrick, laborer, h 19 West ave.
Ryan Thomas E., moulder, h 65 George.
Ryan William, machinist, bds. Canal.
Sackett Hattie, teacher, bds. 100 Front.
Sackett Mary T., widow Charles, resident, h 100 Front.
Sackett Richard G., express messenger, bds. 45 Front.
Saltsman George, clerk, bds. 488 Main.
Sample Arche, laborer, h 493 Front.
Samuels Yetta, widow Jacob, h 60 Spencer ave.
Sanford Dayton M., clerk, h 108 Liberty.
Sanford William Rev., African M. E. Zion church, bds. 106 Paige.
Saxton Edward, carpenter, h 96 Liberty.
SCHNEPPER JACOB, supt. Canawanna mill, h Water.
SCHOONMAKER CHRISTOPHER E., (Buckbee, Peterson, Wood & Co.)
    bds. 313 Main.
Schoonmaker John, cooper, h Railroad.
Schoonmaker John, cooper, h 112 Liberty.
Schopp Francis A., mason, bds. Pumpelly, South Side.
Schopp John P., gardener, bds. Pumpelly, South Side.
Schopp Peter, mason and farmer, h Pumpelly, South Side.
Schopp Stephen M., farmer, bds. Pumpelly, South Side.
Schopp William T., farmer, bds. Pumpelly, South Side.
SCOTT & WATROS, (C. S. Scott and O. J. Watros) publishers *Owego
    Record*, 172 Front.
Scott Charles, farmer with his brother Edmund 250, h 6 Adaline.
SCOTT CLAYTON S., (Scott & Watros) h William.
Scott George, cartman, h 206 North ave.
Scott Lee, laborer, h 531 Front.
Scott Lizzie, teacher, bds. 6 Adeline.
Scott Harriet, resident, h Fox cor. Central ave.
Scrafford Robert, janitor, h 226 North ave.
Searles John T., (J. T. Searls & Son) h over 136 North ave.
Searles J. T. & Son, (Louie F.) groceries and provisions, 136 North ave.
Searles Lot, carpenter, h 97 Central ave.
Searles Louie F., (J. T. Searles & Son) h 119 West ave.
SEARS JOHN G., district attorney, Lake cor. Main, h 56 Front.
Seely Lewis, boarding, 133 North ave.
SETTEL LYMAN L., atty. at law, Postoffice Bldg., bds. Ah-wa-ga House.
Severn Franklin L., bridge builder, h 318 Front.
Severson & Putnam, (G. R. S. and F. P.) saloon and pool-room, 78 North ave.
Severson & Williamson, (G. S. & C. W.) saloon 53 North ave.
Severson Edward, steward Ah-wa-ga House, bds. do.
Severson George, (Severson & Williamson) h Main cor. Forsyth.

Severson George R., (Severson & Putnam) h 417 Main.
Severson Mary, dressmaker, bds. 417 Main.
SEYMOUR LOUISA L., widow Dr. Elias W., 113 North ave., h do.
Shanahan Patrick H., clerk, h 87 Liberty.
Shaughnessy Luke, marble-worker, h 100 McMaster.
Shaw & Dean, (C. E. S. and C. R. D.) merchant millers, 110 Central ave.
Shaw & Ringrose (E. J. S. and W. E. R.) wholesale and retail grocers, Lake cor. Main.
Shaw Charles E., (Shaw & Dean) h 276 Main.
Shaw Elmer J., (Shaw & Ringrose) h Church.
Shaw William, farmer, h South Side.
SHAW WILLIAM H., saloon, 156 Front, h do.
Shay Bridget, widow Henry, h 89 Paige.
Shay James, laborer, bds. 113 Erie.
Shay John, clerk, bds. 44 Fox.
Shay John, laborer, h 113 Erie.
Shay Maggie, tailoress, bds. 44 Fox.
Shay Mary A., dressmaker, bds. 113 Erie.
Shay Nellie, tailoress, bds. 44 Fox.
Shay Owen, railroad car inspector, h 44 Fox.
Shays George, meat market, 82 North ave., also fish market 84½ do., h 60 West ave.
Shays Jonas, groceries and provisions, 72 North ave, h 63 McMaster.
Shays Lucinda, widow Hiram, h 60 West ave.
Shays Rilla, bookkeeper, bds. 60 West ave.
Shea John, laborer, h 505 Front.
Shea William, emp. Cobweb Bottling Works, bds. Chestnut.
Shehan Timothy, mason, h 105 Paige.
Sheldon & Yates, (W. H. S. and A. Y.) groceries and provisions, 131 North ave.
Sheldon Erastus, sawfiler, h over 131 North ave.
Sheldon William H., (Sheldon & Yates) h 117 Central ave.
Shepard W. Henry, carpenter, h Main.
Sheridan Robert E., moulder, h 395 Main.
Sherlock Robert J., tailor, h 524 Main.
Sherman Frederick S., farmer, h South Side.
Sherman Harriet, widow Reuben, h South Side.
Shields James, section foreman Erie R. R., h 566 Fifth ave.
Shipman Ernest R., clerk, bds. Adaline.
Shipman Prosper, emp. Gere, Truman, Platt & Co., h Adaline.
Shipman Rufus, emp. Gere, Truman, Platt & Co., h 131 Talcott.
Shuler Andrew, clerk, bds. 147 Talcott.
Shupp Lawrence, shoemaker, 18 Lake, h do.
SIBLEY OLIVER P., (Stiles & Sibley) also produce dealer, and farmer 100, h 96 Chestnut.
SIGNOR ALBERT, pianos, organs and spring-beds, 207 Front, h Fifth ave.
Signor Loreta, saleswoman, bds. Fifth ave.
Simmons George, stationary engineer, bds. off North ave. n S. C. R. R. round-house.
Simmons John, emp. Casket Factory, bds. off North ave. n S. C. R. R. round-house.
Sinon Patrick, laborer, bds. 103 Erie.
Sinon Robert, laborer, h 103 Erie.

Sinon Susan, widow John, h 67 Erie.
Sisson Cornelia, widow, h over 102 North ave.
Sisson Sarah, teacher, h over 102 North ave.
Sisson William D., carpenter, h 18 Fulton.
Skeels Frederick, resident, h over 64 North ave.
Skeels Irving D., postal clerk, h over 17 Lake.
Skellenger Emma E., dressmaker, 51 Forsyth, h do.
Skellenger James C., moulder, bds. 73 George.
Skellenger Martin E., conductor, h 73 George.
Skellinger William H , brakeman, h 51 Forsyth.
Skillman David, mason, h 219 North ave.
Skinner Emily, widow Charles P., resident, h 80 Main.
SLATER FRANK B., variety store and job printing, 75 Paige cor. Temple, h do.
Slater Phœbe A., widow David, bds. 75 Paige.
Slocum Ethan A., emp. drill works, h W. Main near Mill.
Smead David J., harness-maker 150 Front, h 49 Temple.
Smith Catherine, widow Silas J., laundress, h Gere.
SMITH CHARLES F., groceries, bds. Central House.
Smith Charles W. H., book-keeper Lake, h 99 Green.
Smith Chauncey G., tailor, h 443 Main.
Smith Edward, moulder, bds 79 George.
Smith Enos, resident, bds. 229 Main.
SMITH FRED W., milk products and farm produce, 38 Lake, h Fifth ave.
Smith George W., laborer, h 79 George.
Smith George W., laborer, h 208 North ave.
Smith Hannah, widow Philip, resident, h 32 Temple.
SMITH HATTIE A., art teacher, bds. 443 Main.
Smith Herbert, clerk, bds. 73 Liberty.
Smith James L., hats, caps, robes, &c., 8 Lake, also book-keeper 190 Front, h 15 John.
Smith John, laborer, h 94 Fox.
Smith John, laborer, h 220 North ave.
Smith Jonathan M , clerk, h Main.
Smith Joseph W., (Smith & McCaslin) h River, South Side.
Smith Julius. baggageman, h 21 Fox.
SMITH LEWIS, blacksmith 168 North ave., h 96 Temple.
Smith Patty A., widow Milo, h 18 William.
Smith Philip, emp. foundry, bds. 32 Temple.
Smith Samuel H., freight agent Erie R. R., h 30 Paige.
Smith Samuel L., hatter, h 23 John.
Smith William, blacksmith, bds. 96 Temple.
Smith William E., ice peddler, bds. 117 North ave.
Smith William H., engineer, h 59 West ave.
Smith William L., blacksmith, bds. 96 Temple.
Smullen Edward, laborer, h 26 W. Main.
SMYTH WILLIAM & SON, (William A.) props. *Owego Times*, and bindery and blank-book mnfy., 193 Main.
SMYTH WILLIAM, (William Smyth & Son) h 110 Temple cor. Church.
SMYTH WILLIAM A , (William Smyth & Son) h 70 Church.
Snyder George, life insurance, h over 63 North ave.
Solomon Eleanor P., widow William C., h 32 William.
Solomon Cecil, emp. casket company, bds. 32 William.

Somers Daniel T., carpenter, h 130 Talcott.
Soper Frances, wid. Frederick, h 123 Green.
Southerland Washington R., resident, h 134 Talcott.
SOUTHERN CENTRAL RAILROAD DEPOT, Delphine.
Spaulding Enoch R., barber. 47 Lake, h 63 Spencer ave.
Spaulding Francis, barber, bds. 63 Spencer ave.
Spaulding Harriet S., widow John, h 65 East ave.
Spaulding Harry B., apprentice, bds. 65 East ave.
SPEERS WILLIAM S., hay and general produce, 207 North ave., h 52 Church.
Spelecy Thomas, R. R. track foreman, h 96 South Depot.
Spelecy William, laborer, bds. 96 South Depot.
SPENCER WILLIAM H., pianos, organs and sewing machines, h 220 East Temple.
SPORER, CARLSON & BERRY, (F. S., O. M. C. & J. B.) piano manufs. and dealers in musical merchandise, 58 North ave.
SPORER FRANCIS M , (Sporer, Carlson & Berry) h 97 Main.
Sprague Rowland, 'bus-driver, bds. Ah-wa-ga House.
Spring Liba G., resident, h 65 East ave.
Sprong Eugene, resident, h 254 North ave.
Sprong Hannah J., widow John V., h 12 Talcott.
STANBROUGH JOHN B., hardware and stoves, 180 Front, h do.
Stanbrough Lyman T., lawyer, bds. Front.
*STARKEY & WINTERS, (J. C. S. & E. W.) drugs and medicines, cor. Front and Lake.

STARKEY & WINTERS,

Druggists and Chemists

The Prescription Department is in charge of a graduate of the College of Pharmacy, of the City of New York, and who was formerly with Caswell. Hazard & Co., of that city.

Since taking the Ely Drug Store, they have established a reputation for skillfulness and accuracy in selecting, manufacturing and dispensing Drugs and Medicines, which has gained for them the entire confidence of the public.

COR. FRONT AND LAKE STS.,   -   OWEGO, N. Y.

Persons out of town can order by mail or telephone.

STARKEY EMMA A., (Starkey & Winters) widow Dr. John E., bds. 3 Park.
Starr A. Lorena, book-keeper, 15 Lake, bds. 290 Main.
STARR CHARLES P., jeweler, 15 Lake, h 290 Main.
STEARNS PHINEAS S., physician, bds. Park Hotel.
Stebbins Ann E., widow Charles, h 560 Fifth ave.
STEBBINS BARNEY M., insurance and real estate, 34 Lake, h 33 Paige.
Stebbins Charles L., traveling salesman, bds. 560 Fifth ave.
Stebbins Fanny, teacher, bds. 560 Fifth ave.
Stebbins George M., book-keeper, 34 Lake, bds. South Side.
Stebbins John E., resident, bds. South Side.
Stebbins William M., resident, h South Side.
Steele Don, book-keeper Owego Nat. Bk., h over Cole's clothing store, Lake.

Steele G. Odell, groceries and provisions, 177 Front, h 30 Ross.
Steele John F., harness-maker, h 164 Temple.
Steen Bert, coachman, bds. Canal.
Steen Stogdill S., farmer, h near Dean's tannery.
STEEVENS NORTON A., foreman Champion Wagon Works, h 90 Chestnut.
STEPHENS W. HENRY, mechanic, h 577 Front.
Stevens Alexander, laborer, h 63 North ave.
Stevens Charles J., emp. grain drill works, h near tannery, North ave.
Stevens Frank Mrs., resident, h 105 North ave.
Stevens John, piano-maker, h Canal.
Stevens Romeo, shoemaker, h 32 John.
Stever Alvin C., resident, h over 167 Main.
Stever Amanda E. Mrs., dressmaker, over 78 North ave., h do.
STEVER PETER, butcher, 74 North ave., h over do.
Stewart James W., minstrel performer, Constine's Lane.
Stewart Wilmot L., soap-maker, h 28 Temple.
STILES & SIBLEY, (F. H. S. & O. P. S.) agricultural implements, North ave.
Stiles Charles L., physician and surgeon, 228 Front, h do.
Stiles George, clerk, bds. 67 Central ave.
Stiles Mary, resident, bds. 206 Front.
Stillman Phineas, harness-maker, bds. Decker Block, Main.
Stockwell R., harness-maker, bds. Decker Block, Main.
Stone Eli W., teller Tioga Nat. Bank, h Front.
Stone James T., (Dorwin, Rich & Stone) h Front.
Stone William P., retired merchant, h Front.
Storm Cora, teacher, bds. 36 Adaline.
Storm Elias P., farmer, leases of E. Brown 25, h 36 Adaline.
Storm Elizabeth, widow Jonn C., resident, h 42 George.
Storm John C., carpenter, bds. 42 George.
Storms George, cartman, h 25 Adaline.
STORRS AARON P., (Storrs, Chatfield & Co.) h River, South Side.
STORRS AARON P., Jr., (Storrs, Chatfield & Co.) h River, South Side.
STORRS, CHATFIELD & CO., (A. P. S., J. R. C., A. P. S., Jr., and G. S. C.) hardware, Front cor. Lake.
Stout Richard S., resident, h 212 E. Temple.
STRAIT EDWARD E., (Coburn & Strait) h King Block, Lake.
Strait Julia A., widow William, bds. 48 Talcott.
Strait Seeley P., resident, h 190 E. Temple.
Strang Anna L., widow Charles R., resident, h 83 Paige.
Strang Benjamin H., teamster, h 20 Talcott.
STRANG GEORGE H., teaming, h 47 Talcott.
STRATTON EDWIN, (Hastings & Stratton), h 383 Front.
Straus Alfred M., clerk, bds. 147 Main.
Straus Julius L., prop. "New York Bazaar," ladies' furnishing goods, 43 Lake, h 147 Main.
Strong Lewis, carpenter, h 258 North ave.
Sullivan Ellen, widow John, resident, h Temple.
Sullivan Frank, resident, bds. 1 Temple.
Sullivan Hannah, widow Nathaniel, cook, h 87 Fox.
Sullivan James, contractor and builder, 58 Liberty, h do.
Sullivan William, salesman, bds. 1 Temple.

Swartout Abram, emp. foundry, h 159 Temple.
Swartout Caroline, teacher, bds. 159 Temple.
Swartout Helen, teacher, bds. 159 Temple.
Swartwout George W., laborer, h 70 Fox.
Sweeney Dennis J., painter, bds. 137 Erie.
Sweeney Edward F., fireman, h 50 Delphine.
Sweeney James, book-keeper, h 126 Fox.
Sweeney John, brakeman, bds. 180 North ave.
Sweeney John E., saloon, 88 North ave., bds. 126 Fox.
Sweeney Kate, widow Edward, h 180 North ave.
Sweeney Maggie G., tailoress, bds. 137 Erie.
Sweeney Margaret, widow Thomas, h 101 Erie.
Sweeney Margaret L., widow Dennis, h 137 Erie.
Sweeney Matie L., book-keeper, Lake, bds. 137 Erie.
Sweeney Michael, laborer, bds. 101 Erie.
Sweeney Michael, engineer, h 180 North ave.
Sweeney Thomas, laborer, bds. 101 Erie.
SWEET BROS. (J. R. and est. of G. W.), boots and shoes, 54 North ave.
SWEET JOHN R., (Sweet Bros.) h over 54 North ave.
Sweet Rose E., widow George W., livery, rear 64 and 68 North ave., h over 64 do.
Sweig Saul, tailor, bds. 93 Liberty.
Sykes Maria B., widow Edward, boarding-house, 313 Main.
SYKES THEODORE P., carpenter, h 52 Liberty.
Talcott Francis B., harness-maker, h 67 Paige.
Talcott George, farmer 70, h North ave. cor. Talcott.
Talcott Harriet, widow William C., h 363 Front.
Tate Emma, teacher, bds. 51 Front.
Taylor Alonzo A., gardener, h John R.
Taylor Annie M., widow James E., h 194 River, South Side.
Taylor Daniel G., retired, h 317 Front.
Taylor Ellen, tailoress, bds. 73 Liberty.
Taylor James H., book-keeper Campbell's Tannery, bds. Front cor. Paige.
Taylor James R., blacksmith, bds. South Side.
TAYLOR JOHN J., lawyer, Front cor. Court, h Front.
TAYLOR JOHN L., resident, h 377 Front.
Taylor Julia, widow William C., h over 100 North ave.
Taylor Susan, widow James, resident, h 41 Fox.
Taylor Robert J., fancy goods and notions, bds. 377 Front.
Temple M. D. Mrs., widow Austin J., h 125 Main.
Tench Richard, emp. Dean's tannery, h near tannery, North ave.
Terrill L. Fontenell, contractor, h 100, Franklin.
TERWILLIGER BENJAMIN D., mason and bricklayer, h 120 North ave.
Terwilliger Jesse E., brick-mason, h 305 Prospect.
Thatcher Sumner, locomotive engineer, h 137 North ave.
Thayer Arthur P., emp. Gere, Truman, Platt & Co., h 44 Adaline.
Thayer William, harness-maker, h Main.
*THE OWEGO MUTUAL BENEFIT ASSOCIATION, J. J. Van Kleeck, sec'y, 30 Lake.
THOMAS ALEXANDER J., florist and green-house, Main h do.
THOMAS CHARLES C., retired, h 322 Main.
Thomas Ida C., teacher, bds. 44 Talcott.
Thomas Lewis, mail-carrier, h over 59 North ave.

THOMAS MOSES H., dealer in the "Bradley" reapers, mowers and horse-rakes, full line of Syracuse chilled plows, cultivaters, and sulky plows, the "clipper" chilled, reversible and sulky plows, of Elmira, and a general line of agricultural implements, 64 Temple, h 112 Liberty.

Thomas Samuel H., hotel and restaurant 54 South Depot, h do.

Thomas William H., saloon and restaurant, 154 North ave., h do.

Thomas William W., farmer 60, h 44 Talcott.

Thomas Wilnettie, teacher. bds. 44 Talcott.

Thompson A. Chase, (G. T. Sons & Co.) h 101 Front.

Thompson Ambrose B., machine shop 62 Temple, h 93 West ave.

THOMPSON ANTHONY D., excise commissioner,and Erie R. R. conductor, h 382 Main.

THOMPSON CLARENCE A., cashier Owego Nat. Bank, h 18 Front.

Thompson George H., book-keeper Gere, Truman, Platt & Co., bds. 311 Main.

Thompson George W., laborer, h 105 Green.

Thompson Harry G., clerk Owego Nat. Bank, bds. E. Main.

Thompson John M., sewing machines and organs, 107 North ave., bds. do.

Thorington Levi, gardener, h 178 River, South Side.

Thorn Warren, teamster, bds. 8 W. Main.

Thornton Jeremiah, basket-maker, h 32 W. Main.

THURSTON CHESTER P., grocery, 176 Front, and village clerk, h 145 Temple.

Thurston George, farmer, h 105 North ave.

Thurston Frederick G., groceries and fish, 130 North ave., h over 111 do.

Thurston George S. clerk, bds. over 63 North ave.

Thurston William C., clerk, h over 63 North ave.

Tickner Byron J., harness-maker, bds. Dugan House.

Tierney Charles, harness-maker, h over 17 Lake.

Tilbury Edgar E., clerk, h Temple.

Tilbury Edward, emp. L. Matson, h North ave.

Tillotson James E., confectionery and cigars, 86 North ave., h Temple cor. Spencer ave.

TINKHAM HARRIET, widow David P., h 127 North ave.

Tinkham Lois, widow Standish S., h 120 North ave.

TIOGA NATIONAL BANK OF OWEGO, (T. C. Platt, prest., F. E. Platt, cashier) 199 Front.

Tomkins Eber L., postal clerk, bds. Ah-wa-ga House.

Towsand Alva, emp. Erie freight house, h 102 Spencer ave.

Towsand Jeremiah, brakeman, h 67 McMaster.

Tracy Ellen P., widow George W., resident, h 57 Central ave.

Treat Betsey, widow Sylvester, h Decker Block, Main.

Trimnell John, laborer, h 100 Spencer ave.

Tripp Daniel, watch repairer 10 Lake, h do.

Tripp Frank, painter, h 204 North ave.

Truax Anna E , widow Isaac R , h 91 Liberty.

Truesdell Lewis W., tinsmith, plumber, &c., h 64 McMaster.

Truman Benjamin L., groceries 182 Front, h 329 Main.

Truman Emily M., widow Lyman, h Front.

TRUMAN FRANCIS W., (Gere, Truman, Platt & Co) h Front.

TRUMAN G. SONS & CO., (G. & G. Truman, Jr., and A. Chase Thompson) produce, 174 Front.

TRUMAN GEORGE (Truman, Sons & Co.) also prest. First Nat. Bank, h 374 Front.

TRUMAN GEORGE, Jr., (Truman, Sons & Co.) bds. 374 Front.

Truman Gilbert T., county supt. of the poor, h 391 Front.

Truman, Stephen S., clerk., bds. Main.

TRUMAN WILLIAM S., cashier First Nat. Bank, h 347 Front.

Trutchey Erastus, express driver, h 45 Temple.

Tuch Isaac, dry and fancy goods, 198 Front, h 54 Temple.

Tuch Louis, retired, bds. 60 Spencer ave.

Tuch Meyer H., variety store, 202 Front, h 317 E. Main.

Tuch Morris R., salesman, bds. 54 Temple.

Tuck George, manager Whiteson's clothing store, Front, h 264 Main.

Tucker Oren, drayman, h 57 Adaline.

Turner Edwin B., retired Congregational clergyman, h 371 Main,

Tuthill Demon C., retired, h 121 Temple.

Tuttle Joel A., produce, h 21 Fulton.

Tuttle Minnie, milliner, bds. 92 Adaline.

Tuttle Wilbert, emp. foundry, h 92 Adaline.

Tuttle William H., emp, foundry, h 92 Adaline.

Tyler Isaiah, laborer, h South Side.

United States Express Co., F. F. Hutchins, agent, 34 Lake.

Upham Macus K., carpenter, h 5 Temple.

UPTON ALBERT H., sup't Dean's tannery, bds. 279 Main.

VanAuken Alvin, hack-driver, h 22 John.

VanAuken Benjamin, hackman, h 72 Central ave.

VanAuken Russell, porter Central House, bds. do.

VanBrunt Henry, carpenter, h 20 Temple.

VanBrunt Margaret, widow William, h 20 Temple.

VanBuren Elmer L., stage-driver, h 23 Temple.

VanDemark Rebecca, widow James, bds. 27 Adaline.

VanDerlip Wesley W., brakeman, h 168 Temple.

VanFleet James, mason, h Blade building.

VanGorder Elizabeth, widow Charles E., h 118 Paige.

VanGorder Fred C., machinist, h 118 Paige.

*VAN KLEECK JOHN J., county clerk, fire and life insurance, sec'y Cruci-
form Casket Co., western loans and investments, Court House, h 228 Main.

Vanover David, ice-peddler, h 138 Central ave.
Vanover Frank W., clerk, bds. River, South Side.
Vanover Jacob, carpenter, h River, South Side.
Vanover James H., carpenter, h River, South Side.
VANOVER WESLEY, emp. Chamberlain's boot and shoe factory, h 54
     Liberty.
VanPatten Abram, resident, bds. 582 Main.
VanPatten Frederick, farm laborer, h 582 Main.
Vargason Welton W., emp. Gere, Truman, Platt & Co., h Gere.
Vermilyea Abram, carpenter, h 39 West ave.
Vetter John G., tanner, h near tannery, North ave.
Vickery Almira B., widow John, h 84 Paige.
VICKERY CHARLES S., piano tuner, h 84 Paige.
Vincelett John, mason, h 79 Forsyth.
Vose Charles E., resident, bds. 240 E. Temple.
Vose Nancy B., widow J. Parker, h 240 E. Temple.
Vroman Peter, farmer, bds. 32 Temple.
Wade Charles M., carpenter, h 119 West ave.
Wade George N., groceries and provisions, 1 West ave., h do.
Wade Lewis N., cartman, h 175 North ave.
Wade L. N. Mrs., dressmaking, 175 North ave., h do.
Waggoner John, laborer, h off Water.
Wagner Clarence L., upholster, h near Dean's tannery.
Walbridge Charles M., fireman, h 40 Talcott.
Walker Amos, carpenter, h Adaline.
Walker Henry L., conductor, h Erie near Main.
Walker Jesse, harnessmaker, bds. over 177 Main.
Walker Lydia C., widow William, h 136 Temple.
Walker Ransom, D. D. S., dentist, over 200 and 202 Front, h do.
Walker Rial H., carpenter, h Buckbee Block.
WALL & CO., (Mrs. Charles and C. T. Wall) boots, shoes and rubbers,
     200 Front.
WALL ABIGAIL F., (Wall & Co.,) widow Charles, h Front.
WALL CLARENCE T., (Wall & Co.) h Front.
Wallace Harry, clerk, bds. 67 Central ave.
Wallace Lewis, laborer, h rear 123 North ave.
Wallis Stephen S., law student, h in Tioga.
Walsh Lewis A., clerk, bds. 122 Paige.
Walsh William M., tailor, h 502 Main.
Walts John, bridge carpenter, bds. 43 Talcott.
Walter Ralph H., farmer, leases of Mrs. Julia Kellogg 70, h 73 Forsyth.
Wand James, laborer, bds. 63 Spencer ave.
Ward Anna E., widow Willard W., h 499 Front.
Ward Daniel, laborer, h 109 Franklin.
Ward Edward, emp. foundry, bds. 109 Franklin.
Ward Ezra, mason, h South Side.
Ward Frances L., dressmaker, bds. South Side.
Ward Kate M., book-keeper, 229 McMaster, h 48 West ave.
Ward John F., clerk Ah-wa-ga House, bds. do.
Ward Laura F., teacher, bds. South Side.
Ward Michael, laborer, bds. 109 Franklin.
Ward Patrick, drayman, h 47 West ave.
Ward Polly R., widow William, h 51 West ave.

Ward Thomas J., drayman, h 48 West ave.
WARNER FRANK H., contractor and builder, Fox, h 122 Franklin.
Warner Montgomery, saloon and restaurant, 203 Front, h do.
Warner William M., baker, h Buckbee Block.
Warren Lamira, widow Charles W., h 102 Chestnut.
Warrick Lillie J., teacher, bds. 363 Front.
Watkins Annie, clerk, bds. Main.
Watkins Charles D., lawyer, over 168 Front, h 57½ East Main.
Watkins Frederick, blacksmith, bds. 142 Central ave.
Wrtkins Hollis, stationary engineer, 212 North ave.
Watkins Miner D., clerk, bds. Ah-wa-ga House.
Watkins William, traveling salesman, h 391 Main.
WATROS ODELL J., (Scott & Watros) h 234 North ave.
Watson Harmon S., drover, h Canal Front.
Watson James, painter, h 89 Franklin.
Watson Wallace, emp. casket shop, h 61 George.
Way William E., carpenter and saw-filer, 174 North ave., h do.
Webb James, carriage-painter, 72 Temple, h 97 Forsyth.
WEBSTER GEORGE H., painter and paper-hanger; decorative work a
    specialty, 242 East Temple, h do.
WEBSTER GILBERT E., meat-market, 133 North ave., h over 131 do.
Webster James, resident, h 25 John.
Webster Mason, painter, h 4 Fox.
Webster Rachel E., widow Charles, h 350 Main.
Webster William H., painter, bds. 88 Adaline.
Wedon Herbert, harness-maker, bds. Decker Block, Main.
Weed & Co., (J. D. & G. W. Weed) custom saw, grist and planing-mill,
    River, South Side.
Weed George W., (J. D. & G. W. Weed) h River, South Side.
Weed John D., (J. D. & G. W. Weed) h River, South Side.
Weed Joseph H., emp. Weed & Co.'s mill, bds. River, South Side.
Welch Charles, carpenter, h Adaline.
WELCH DAVID A., contractor and builder, cane-chairs reseated and
    general repairing, 243 Prospect, h do.
WELCH GEORGE H., clerk, bds. 243 Prospect.
Welch Harriet, widow Hiram, bds. 243 Prospect.
Welch William H., contractor and builder, 267 Prospect, h do.
Wentz Sarah, widow Rev. William, h 101 Franklin.
Whipple Daniel A., farmer, h 139 Main.
Whipple Sisters, (Martha A., Addie and Emma) dressmakers, 139 Main, h do.
Whipple William, hostler, bds. Ah-wa-ga House.
Whitaker A. B. Mrs., widow, bds. 41 Front.
WHITE & HUMISTON, (P. H. W. and F. M. H.) drugs and medicines,
    194 Front.
White Charles, meat market, 36 Lake, h 64 Liberty.
White Darius, mason, h over 154 Front.
White Delia, widow Perry, milliner, h 51 Fox.
White Frederick, bartender, bds. 187 McMaster.
White Henry O., emp. King & Co., bds. 64 Liberty.
White John, carpenter, h 26 William.
WHITE PAUL H., (White & Humiston) bds., Ah-wa-ga House.
White Roderick, laborer, h 187 McMaster.
White Tryphena P., dressmaker, bds. 58 Spencer ave.

Whiteson Isidor, (George Tuck, manager) clothing, 201 Front, h at Cortland.
Whitfield Samuel, laborer, h 239 Prospect.
Whitfield Samuel Mrs., laundress, 239 Prospect.
Whitmarsh Polly, widow Daniel, bds. 18 Fulton.
Whitney Nathan R., engineer, h 128 Temple.
Whitton Fred, meat-cutter, h 103 Paige.
Wicks L. Emmet, bookkeeper, 19 and 21 Lake, bds. 239 Main.
Wiggins Maria, widow John, h John R.
Wilbur Lebbeus, traveling salesman, h 496 Main.
Wilbur William E., boots, shoes and restaurant. 182 Main, h do.
Wilcox Sarah A. Mrs., resident, h 67 Paige.
WILCOX JOHN A., repair foreman Erie R. R. car shop, h 239 Main.
Williams Abram, gunsmith, h 132 Main.
WILLIAMS ALBERT S., bridge inspector, h 106 Chestnut.
Williams Burton, emp. C. M. Haywood, h 147 Temple.
Williams Charles D., laborer, h 99 Paige.
Williams Chester D., bridge carpenter, h 59 West ave.
Williams Daniel, gardener, h John R.
Williams Edward W., carpenter, h 119 Main.
Williams Fred D., drug clerk, bds. Park Hotel.
Williams George, porter, bds. 115 Fox.
Williams Henry F., produce, h 32 William.
Williams Laura M., widow Thomas, h George.
Williams Maria A., widow Thomas, h 115 Fox.
Williams Marshall G., salesman, h 27 Ross.
Williams Morgan, teamster, h Water.
Williams Nathan L., emp. Campbell's tannery, bds. George.
Williams William B., farm laborer, h George.
Williamson Charles, (Leverson & Williamson) h Erie.
Williamson Loesa, resident, bds. 241 Erie.
Willis William, laborer, h 257 Prospect.
*WILSON JAMES, physician and surgeon, 295 Main, h do.
WILSON OPERA HOUSE, S. F. Fairchild, manager, Lake.
Winans Edwin W., clerk, h 58 Spencer ave
Winions William, laborer, h 149 Erie.
Winne Catharine, widow Peter, h 11 Fox.
Winnie Franklin, farmer h 11 Fox.
Winner James, cartman, h Division.
Winow Simon P., barber, bds. Fox.
Wilsey Kelsey, painter, h over 62 North ave.
Wilson Samuel, tanner, bds. 187 McMaster.
Wilts Portis L., emp. drill works, h 140 Central ave.
Wiltse Kelsey, painter, h 104 Spencer ave.
Wiltse William, saloon, 65 North ave.
WINTERS EDGAR, (Starkey & Winters) h John.
Winters Judson B., (Hyde & Winters) h Main cor. Spencer ave.
Witters Ralph C., retired, h 94 Chestnut.
Woeppel Alvis, gardener for A. J. Thomas, bds. Main.
WOOD CHARLES L., (Buckbee, Peterson, Wood & Co.) bds. 364 Front.
Wood George H., blacksmith, North ave., h 104 Franklin.
Wood Hester, widow William, h 76 Talcott.
Wood Lydia, dressmaker, 76 Talcott, bds. do.

STARKEY & WINTERS, Wholesale and Retail Druggists, Owego.

Woodard Lucretia, widow Joseph, h 4 West ave.
Woodburn David M., laborer, h 43 Talcott.
Woodford Bissell, farmer 200, h 417 Front.
Woodford Charles G., teller First Nat. Bank, bds 374 Main.
Woodford George R., clerk, bds. 417 Front.
Works Frederick, emp. casket factory, h over 161 Main.
Works Russell S., shoe-cutter, h Park cor. Main.
Worthington Jennie, widow Robert, resident, h 51 Front.
Woughter Adelaide, widow Lysander G., bds. 15 Adaline.
Woughter Charles, emp. Lincoln coal yard, h 104 Spencer ave.
Woughter Eugene F., emp. foundry, h 15 Adaline.
Wright Albert G., retired, h 222 E. Temple.
Wright Frank N., moulder, h 89 Paige.
Wright Frederick, painter, h 222 E Temple.
Wright Joseph A., tinsmith, bds. 467 Front.
Wright Patrick, laborer, h 121 Paige.
Writer Gabriel M., conductor N. Y. L. E. & W. R. R., h 381 Main.
Writer Lena M., teacher, bds. 381 Main.
Wyckoff Abram, type-writer and stenographer, bds. Dugan House.
Wyman William, harness-maker, 112 North ave., bds. Central ave.
Wyman William, tailor, h 78 Paige.
Yates Alanson, (Sheldon & Yates) h 114 Liberty.
Yates Mary L. Mrs., teacher, h 194 River, South Side.
Yerks Catherine, resident, bds. 31 Adaline.
Yerks Clarissa, carpet-weaver, h 31 Adaline.
Yerks Emmet, farm laborer, h 40 Adaline.
Yerks William A., carpenter, h 246 E. Temple.
Yost Mary E. Mrs., hair-worker, h over Owego Nat. Bank.
Yothers Charles D., book-keeper First Nat. Bank, h 433 Front.
Yothers Horace, telegraph operator, D. L. & W. depot, bds. 433 Front.
Young H. Earl, clerk, bds. 455 Main.
Zimmer Al, carpenter, h 66 Adaline.
Zweig Samuel, clerk, bds. Central House.

OWEGO

OUTSIDE CORPORATION.

(For explanations, etc., see page 3, part second.)

(Postoffice address is Owego, unless otherwise designated in parenthesis.)

Ahern Daniel, (Apalachin) r 69, book-keeper.
Akerly Charles, (Campville) r 54, laborer.
Akerly Jerry, (Campville) r 54, laborer.
Aldrich Aaron, (Apalachin) r 81, farmer.
Aldrich Charles, (Apalachin) off r 81, farm laborer.
Aldrich Charles E., r 95, farmer with his mother Minerva H.
Aldrich Frederick, (Apalachin) retired, h Main.
Aldrich Heman B., (Apalachin) resident, bds. Main.

Aldrich Melvin O., r 95, farmer 20.
Aldrich Minerva H., r 96, widow Olney, farm 50.
Alger Phineas, r 56½, cooper.
Allen John, (Gaskill's Corners) r 35, farm laborer.
Allen Reuben, (Flemingville) r 4, retired farmer.
Ames Lydia, (Apalachin) r 80, resident.
AMES PHINEAS N., r 65, farmer 6.
Anaville Charles, r 117, farmer, leases of Mr. Thomas 130.
Andrews Romeo, r 40, butcher and cattle dealer.
Annable Jarvis B., r 95, farmer 50.
Anson Mary, (Apalachin) widow Amos, resident, h Main.
Appleby Francis, (Union Broome Co.) r 30, farm laborer.
Arnold George, (Apalachin) r 70, farm laborer.
Ayer Mary A., (Apalachin) widow Isaac, resident, h Main.
Ayer Warren, (Apalachin) r 83, farmer 125.
Ayers Charles, r 94, physician.
Ayers Loren F., r 94, farmer.
Bailey James, r 42, farmer 82.
Bailey Thomas, r 42, farmer.
Bakeman David, (Gaskill's Corners) r 25, farmer 3.
Bakeman Philip, (Gaskill's Corners) r 12, farmer 95.
Baker Albert E., r 54, farmer for C. LaMonte.
Baker Charles, (Apalachin) carpenter, h Ferry.
Baker E. Vandaber, (Flemingville) r 6, farmer 54, and in Newark Valley 25.
Baker William, (Flemingville) r 6, farm laborer.
Ballard James, (Campville) r 54, peddler.
Ballou Hartwell M., r 12, wagon-maker, carpenter and farmer 25.
Ballou Wendell D., r 56½, music teacher.
Banney John F., (Apalachin) r 103, farmer with his father Ransom.
Barker Chauncey, (Apalachin) r 113, farmer 30.
Barker Chauncey, Jr., r 113, farmer 36.
Barker Simeon, (Apalachin) r 113, farmer.
Barnes Newton W. Rev., (Apalachin) pastor M. E. Church, h Church.
Barnes Reed A., r 67, farmer 75.
Barney E. Allen, (Apalachin) resident, h Church.
Barney Ransom (Apalachin) r 103, farmer 55.
Barnhart Alanson D., r 69, farm laborer.
BARRETT EUGENE, (Gaskill's Corners) r 25, farmer 117.
Barrett Simeon L., (Flemingville) r 40, farmer 80.
Barton Albert, (Apalachin) r 87, farmer.
Barton Andrew J., (Flemingville) r 5, farmer 100.
Barton Charles, (Apalachin) r 108, farmer with his mother Jane.
Barton Charles L., (Apalachin) r 87, butcher.
Barton Effy A. Mrs., off r 54, prop. LaMonte ferry.
Barton George H., (Apalachin) off r 108, farmer 40.
Barton Jane, (Apalachin) r 108, widow Isaac, farmer 107.
Barton Lester, (Union, Broome Co.) r 28, farmer 40.
Barton Louis A., r 94, carpenter and farmer 47.
Barton Rebecca W., r 101½, widow Morris W., resident.
Barton Renselaer, off r 54, blacksmith and farmer.
Barton Smith, Jr., (Apalachin) r 108, farmer 80.
Barton Thomas, (Apalachin) r 86, farmer.
Barton Thomas, r 87, carpenter and farmer.

Barton Virgil P., (Flemingville) r 5, farmer 80.
Barton William, (Apalachin) r 89½, farmer 45.
Barton William, (Apalachin) produce, h William.
Barto Charles, (Apalachin) laborer, h Church.
Bateman Isaac, (Campville) r 48, farmer 40.
Bates German A., (Apalachin) r 113, farmer with his father Gilford.
Bates Gilford, (Apalachin) r 113, farmer 40.
Beach George W., (Apalachin) physician and surgeon, Main, h Ferry.
Beach Olive, r 56, widow Nathan, farmer 33.
Beardslee William L., (South Owego) r 128, farmer 114.
Becker Fayette, r 54, retired farmer.
Beebe Orin, (South Apalachin) r 110, postal clerk and farmer.
Beebe Reuben (South Apalachin) r 110, farmer 119.
Beecher Edgar R., r 39, farmer with his father, Isaac S.
Beecher Isaac S., r 39, farmer 71.
BEEMAN HORACE W., r 116, wood-sawing and feed-mill, and farmer 40.
Beers Charles M., r 32, farmer 47.
Beers Julia M., r 40, widow James, farmer 65.
Belknap John J., (Campville) r 71, farmer 120.
Belknap Parmelia Miss, (Campville) r 71, resident.
Bell John, (Apalachin) trackman, bds. Exchange Hotel.
Benjamin Albert, r 95, farmer 55.
Benjamin J. Allan, r 95, farmer with his father Albert.
Benjamin James, r 95, retired.
Benjamin James U., r 117, farmer 165.
Benner Louise E., (Apalachin) music teacher, bds. Main.
Benner Ordelia, (Apalachin) widow Philip R., resident, h Main.
Bennett William (Campville) r 49, farmer.
Berdine Laramie, (South Apalachin) r 10, widow William, resident.
Berdine William P., (South Apalachin) r 110, farmer 186.
Billings Charles, (Little Meadows, Pa.) r 110, farmer 28.
Billings Norman, (Apalachin) r 110, farmer 55.
Billings Ransom, (Apalachin) r 102, farmer on shares with Almon Hotchkiss.
Bills Alonzo, (South Apalachin) r 111, deputy postmaster.
Bills Amari, (Apalachin) off r 107, farmer 30.
Bills James H., r 98, school trustee and farmer 100.
Bills Maria, (Apalachin) r 110, widow Warren, farm 125.
Bills Nehemiah, (Apalachin) laborer.
Bills Paul, (Apalachin) r 101½, farmer 6.
Bills Ulysses, r 99, farmer 25.
Bishop Gilbert, (Apalachin) carpenter, h Main.
Blair Asa, (Flemingville)) r 40, farmer.
Blair Ezra, r 39, farm laborer.
BLOW AMANDA, r 120, widow Francis, farm 50.
Blow Arthur, r 116½, farmer on shares with H. Codner 90.
BLOW FRANK L., r 59, prop. threshing-machine and farmer 25.
Blow George, r 96, farmer with his father Henry.
Blow Henry, r 96, farmer 80.
Blow William, r 120, farmer 18, and on shares with his mother Amanda 50.
Bodle Arthur, r 59, farmer.
Bornt Anna Mrs., r 54, farm 35.
Bornt Frederick, (Campville) r 48, farmer 80.
Bornt Levi, (Union, Broome Co.) r 73, farmer 91.

Bornt Peter, (Campville) r 50, farmer 10.

Bornt Samuel, (Campville) r 48, farmer 40.

Bornt William H., (Union, Broome Co.) r 73, farmer with his father Levi.

Bostwick Curtis, r 95, farmer 52.

Bostwick Fred, r 116½, farmer 138.

Bostwick Melvin F., r 40. farmer 105.

Bostwick Oliver, r 120½, farmer 50.

Bostwick Spencer, r 117, farmer 70.

Bostwick Thomas, r 117, farmer 85.

Bostwick Willis, r 117, farmer 40.

Bourst Menzo, r 61, farm laborer.

Bowen Isaac A., r 96, law student.

Bowen Jonathan P., r 96, farmer 50.

Bowen William J., r 94, farmer, leases of J. F. Holmes 55.

Boyce John R., (Apalachin) clerk for Sleeper & Whitaker, bds. Main.

Bradley Otis, r 56½, farmer 33.

Bradt Anthony, r 37, farmer 15.

Bradt Frank, r 43, farmer, works on shares for his father John 108.

Bradt John, r 38, farmer 108.

Bradt Peter, r 43, farmer 40.

Brainard Polly, (South Owego) r 99, widow Albert, resident.

Branch Andrew, (Campville) r 54, shoemaker.

Branch Charles, (Campville) r 54, brakeman.

Brewster John, (Apalachin) off r 102, farmer 50.

Briggs Anson, r 14, farmer 60.

Briggs Charles, r 54, farmer, leases of Mrs. George Smith 83.

Brink Jefferson H., r 58, farm laborer.

Brink Mulford, (Union, Broome Co.) r 71, farmer for his father John 60.

Brink William, (Apalachin) r 69, farm laborer.

Brooks Henry G., (Campville) r 53, farmer 69.

Brooks John, (Campville) r 53, retired farmer.

Brooks John G., r 95, farmer 19.

Brougham Henry A., r 94, farmer 10.

Brougham Joseph, (Union Center, Broome Co.) r 28, farmer, leases of William Conell 200.

Brougham Peter, (Union Center, Broome Co.) r 11, farmer 50.

Brown Asel, (Little Meadows, Pa.) r 110, farmer 50.

Brown Edgar, (Apalachin) r 81, farmer.

Brown Frank, (Litte Meadows, Pa.) r 110, farmer, 98.

Brown Frank L., (Apalachin) painter, h Cross.

Brown George, (Union, Broome Co.) r 80, school trustee, and farmer 125.

Brown Royal S., (Apalachin) butcher, h Main.

Brown Simeon, (Apalachin) r 83, farmer 27.

Brown William H., (Apalachin) farm laborer.

Brownell Benjamin W,, r 40, farmer 50 and wood lot 36.

Brownell George, r 40, farmer with his father Benjamin W.

Brownell John C., (Flemingville) r 22, farmer 84 and wood lot 86.

Brumage Ann, (Flemingville) r 5, widow William, resident.

Brumage David, (Flemingville) r 5, farmer 20.

Buck Alonzo D., r 54, farmer 46½.

Buck Charles W., r 54, carpenter and farmer.

Buck George H., r 54, carpenter.

BUNZEY CHARLES H., r 63, farmer, works on shares 150.

Bunzey Sophia, r 63, widow Jacob, resident.
Burgett Robert, r 20, farmer 80.
Burton Amelia, (South Owego) r 128, widow Obadiah, farm 100.
Burton Ann, (Apalachin) r 83, widow Benjamin.
Burton Oliver, (South Owego) r 128, farmer 50.
Cafferty Asa, (Campville) r 71, farmer 120.
Cafferty Fayette, (Campville) r 48, farmer 55.
Cafferty Frank B., r 54, farmer 50.
Cafferty James, (Union, Broome Co.) r 74, farmer 200.
Cafferty James, Jr., (Union, Broome Co.) r 74, farmer 50.
Cafferty Myron, r 93, farmer, leases of James Armstrong 105.
CAMP GURDON H., (Apalachin) horse dealer, h Main.
Camp Nathan, (Campville) r 71, farmer 129.
Camp Orin, r 54, threshing machine and farm laborer.
CAMPBELL & LAMPHERE, (Apalachin) (I. W. C. & G. U. L.) saw and
    planning-mill, depot.
Campbell David S., r 94, farmer 85.
CAMPBELL ISAAC W., (Apalachin) (Campbell & Lamphere) h depot.
Campbell John A., r 94, farmer with his father.
Campbell Joseph, r 93, farmer, leases of Elin Gould 160.
Campbell Joseph, Jr., r 93, emp. Coe's saw-mill.
Campbell Ralph, r 94, fireman Coe's mill.
Cane Ezra, r 65, farmer on shares with Mrs. Steele 105.
Cane Peter, r 65, farmer with his father Ezra.
Card Abel, (Apalachin) r 108, farmer 27.
Card Albert, (Apalachin) r 108, farmer with his mother Eliza 24.
Card Charles, (Apalachin) r 108, farmer 24.
Card David, (Apalachin) r 108, farmer 32.
Card Eliza, (Apalachin) r 108, widow Harrison, farm 24.
Card Henry, (Apalachin) r 108, farmer with his mother Eliza 24.
Card Isaac, (Flemingville) r 4, engineer.
Card John, (Apalachin) r 108, farmer with his father David 32.
Carleton M. Dwight, r 69, farm laborer.
Carman Charles, (Apalachin) r 80, farm laborer.
Carpenter Albert J., r 97, farmer 54.
Carpenter Ann M., r 40, widow Joseph S., resident.
Carrier A. B., (Apalachin) laborer, h River.
Carrier Hartley, (Apalachin) r 113, farmer, leases of Simeon Barker 50.
Carte Louise, r 54, widow Eli, farmer 50.
Case Daniel, (Campville) r 71, farmer 50.
Case Hiram, (Campville) r 48, farmer 50.
Case Marilla D., (Campville) widow Zenos, resident.
Case Peter, (Union, Broome Co.) r 71, farmer 50.
Castle Albert, r 4, laborer.
Catlin George L., (Apalachin) r 96, supt. Marshland stock farm.
Catlin Jacob, (Apalachin) farmer 40, h Main.
Central House, (Apalachin) Alanson Goodenow, prop., h do.
Chaffee Elizabeth, r 96, widow Oliver P., resident.
Chandler Harrison, r 120½, farmer.
Chapman Horace, r 96, resident.
Chidester John, (Little Meadows, Pa.) r 133, farmer.
Childs Mark W., (Campville) r 54, school teacher.

Clapham Harry J., (Flemingville) r 2, manager and prop. Globe Theatre Co., and farmer 160.
Clark David L., (Apalachin) r 68, farmer 75.
Clark James, r 93, farmer 100.
Clanson Albert, (Apalachin) r 70, farmer on shares with W. Hilton 50.
Codner Charles N., r 116, farmer with his father Nelson.
Codner Hiram, r 116, farmer 90.
Codner John, (East Nichols) off r 118, farmer 100.
Codner Nelson, r 116, farmer 100.
Coffin Frank, (South Apalachin) r 128, farmer with his father.
Coffin Harvey, farm laborer.
Coffin Lucy, (South Owego) r 128, widow Henry, resident.
Coffin William H., (South Apalachin) r 128, farmer 75, and on shares with F. D. Coffin 130.
Cole Abram, r 40, farmer 75.
Cole Helen, r 40, matron County Alms House.
Cole William T., off r 65, farmer 25.
Coleman Peter, (Campville) r 54, trackman.
Conant Emery, (Little Meadows, Pa.) r 110, farmer.
Congdon Amos, (East Nichols) r 119, farmer 100.
Conklin Alfred, r 39, farmer 100.
Conklin Charles H., r 54, farmer, leases of Mrs. Anson Decker 60.
Conklin David, (Apalachin) farm laborer, h River.
Conklin Lewis D., r 60, mason.
Conklin Marcus A., (Apalachin) bds. River.
Conklin Matthew H., (Apalachin) laborer, bds. River.
Conklin William, r 40, carriage-maker.
Connant Simeon, r 117, blacksmith.
Connell Edward, r 60, farmer 20.
Connell Joseph, r 60, resident.
Connor Martin, (Campville) r 54, trackman.
Cooper Charles, (Union, Broome Co.) r 30, farmer 70.
Cooper George P., (Apalachin) r 80, farmer on shares with F. Aldrich 40.
Cooper Hiram, (Apalachin) r 84, farmer.
Coots Henry D., r 42, milk dealer and farmer, works on shares for Reuben Fraser 140.
Corbin Arthur L., (South Owego) r 122, farmer 30, and on shares with Myron Prince 100.
Corbin George, r 69, farm laborer.
Corbin Neweil, (South Apalachin) r 110, farmer 50.
Cornell Daniel, (Union Center, Broome Co.) r 28, farmer 150.
Cornell Eli, (Union Center, Broome Co.) r 28, farmer 150.
Cornell Eugene, (Union, Broome Co.) r 29, farmer 64.
Cornell Henry, r 56, blacksmith.
Cornell Thomas, (Union, Broome Co.) r 47½, farmer 70.
Courtright Herbert N., (Apalachin) r 106, shoemaker.
Cragan John, (Apalachin) mason, h William.
Crandall Amos J., r 98, farmer on shares with Asa Stanton 135.
Crater Samuel, r 97, farmer 50.
Crawford Arthur, r 27, farmer 100.
Crawford Merrills J., (South Owego) r 122, farmer 100.
Creemon Aaron, (Apalachin) off r 80, farmer.
Crounse Henry E., (Gaskill's Corners) r 45, farmer 175.

Crum James, r 99, farmer 20.
Curtis Bertie D., (Gaskill's Corners), r 35 invalid.
CURTIS HARMON, (Gaskill's Corners) r 35, postmaster and prop. saw and feed-mill and grocery.
Curtis Harvey, r 56½, nurseryman 2.
Daniels Darwin H., (Union Center, Broome Co.) r 11, farmer 50.
Daniels Douglas, (Union Center, Broome Co.) r 11, farmer 60.
Daniels George F., r 56, farmer 20.
Daniels Gustavas, (Union Center, Broome Co.) r 11, farmer 70.
Darling Albert, (Little Meadows, Pa.) r 110, farmer 70.
Davidson John, (South Apalachin) r 111, farmer 107.
Davis Leslie R., r 95, farmer with his mother Mary A.
Davis Mary A., r 95, widow James, farm 19.
Davis Walter J.. r 95, farm laborer.
Davis William, r 40, farm laborer.
Davison Lucius, (Apalachin) r 107, farmer 70.
Decker Albert L., r 59, farm laborer.
Decker Emanuel, (Union, Broome Co.) r 47, farmer.
Decker Gideon, r 42, farm laborer.
Decker John S., (Apalachin) carpenter.
Decker John W.. r 41, farmer 85.
Decker Jonathan, r 46, laborer.
Decker Marvin W., r 65, farm laborer.
Decker Narcis Mrs., r 27, resident.
Decker Wayne, r 31, farmer.
GeGroat J. DeWitt, r 67, musical instruments, and milk dealer.
DeGroat Lorenzo, r 67, farmer 99.
Delaney Richard, (Apalachin) trackman, bds. Exchange Hotel.
Dennison Cerene, r 99, widow Henry, farm 25.
Dennison George, r 99, farmer with his mother Cerene.
Dennison Joseph, r 116, farm laborer.
Deuel Augustus S., r 93, farmer 59.
Dexter Adelia, r 54, widow Frank B., farmer 40.
Dexter Edwin J., (Campville) r 54, carpenter and farmer.
Deyo William, r 37, farmer, works for Michael Lynch 100.
Dickinson Ira W., (Campville) r 73, Methodist clergyman, and farmer 44.
Dickinson McKenzie, (Campville) r 54, postmaster and grocery.
Dingman Abraham, (Apalachin), retired, h William.
Dingman John, (South Owego) r 128, farmer 160.
Dodge Asa J., r 93, farmer 70.
Dodge Benjamin F., r 93, farmer.
Dodge Daniel S., r 93, farmer 120.
Dodge John G., r 56, expressman.
Donnelly Joanna, 93, widow John, resident.
Donnelly Matthew, r 93, farmer 141.
Donnovan John, off r 54, track-hand.
Doty James, r 20, farm laborer.
Dougherty James R., r 20, farmer.
Dowd James, (Little Meadows, Pa.) r 135, farmer.
Downs William, (Apalachin) blacksmith, h Main.
Doyle Bernard, (Apalachin) laborer, h Main.
Drake Charles, (Apalachin) off r 102, farmer 40.
Drake Tamar, (Apalachin) r 87, widow Jerome.

Duane Burr, r 99, farmer 100.
Duane John, r 99, farmer 100.
Dunham Asa, r 99, farmer 131.
Dunham Burdett N., (South Apalachin) r 108, farmer.
Dunham Chauncey R., r 43, dairy 35 cows and farmer for G. S. Camp 130.
Dunham Dudley J., (South Apalachin) r 108, farmer.
Dunham Jennie, (South Apalachin) r 108, teacher.
Dunham Nathan Y., r 99, farmer.
Dunham Sylman, (South Apalachin) r 108, farmer 95.
Dunham Willard F., r 99, farmer.
Dutton Mortimer E., (Apalachin) r 69, boarding-house.
Easton Mary, (Apalachin) r 83, widow Julien G., resident.
Edward Edward, (Campville) r 54, blacksmith.
Edwards Edson, (Apalachin) r 110, resident.
Edwards Fred, (Apalachin) r 83, farmer with his father Ira.
Edwards Ira, 1st, (Apalachin) r 83, farmer 65.
Edwards Ira, (Apalachin) butcher and farmer, h Main.
Edwards Nelson, (Apalachin) r 107, resident.
Edwards Susie, (Apalachin) r 83, dressmaker.
Eldred Nelson, r 27, farmer 60.
Eldridge Chester, off r 27, farm laborer.
Eldridge Simeon, (Union, Broome Co.) r 29, laborer.
Elliott Francis H., (Apalachin) painter, h Main.
Ellis Airy Mrs., r 39, resident.
Ellis Nathan H., r 40, prop. grist and flouring-mill.
Evans Truman (Campville) r 54, carpenter.
EXCHANGE HOTEL, (Apalachin) John S. Ryan, prop., Main.
Fairbanks Benjamin R., (Apalachin) hostler Exchange Hotel, bds. do.
Fairbanks Benjamin R., (Apalachin) r 110, laborer.
Fairbanks Harriet E., (Apalachin) r 110, farm 47½.
Terbush Lancelott B , (Flemingville) r 16, blacksmith, wagon-maker and feed-mill, h r 4.
Ferguson David, (South Owego) r 123, farmer with Mrs. Slawson 160.
Ferguson Eugene B., (Flemingville) r 15, farmer 100.
Fessenden Adelbert N., (Apalachin) resident, h Cross.
Fessenden Nelson Rev., (Apalachin) Wesleyan Methodist, h Cross.
Finch Jehial S., r 22, farmer 79.
Finch Russell, r 22, farmer 25.
Fish Frank E., (Apalachin) r 113, farm laborer.
Fisk Darwin, (Gaskill's Corners) r 35, farm laborer.
Fleming John, (Flemingville) r 40, farmer 120.
Fleming Luke, (Flemingville) r 4, farmer 54.
Folker Frank, (Apalachin) r 69, farm laborer.
Ford Charles H., (Gaskill's Corners) r 35, carpenter.
Ford George L., (Gaskill's Corners) r 25, farmer 350.
Foster David, (Apalachin) farm laborer.
Foster Electa, r 27, widow Daniel R., resident.
Foster Phileman A., (Apalachin) r 101½, farmer 6.
Fox Alanson, off r 95, farmer 75.
Fox Albert, (Apalachin) off r 113, retired.
Fox Allen, r 95, farmer 50.
Fox Charles, off r 91, apiarist, and farmer 32.
Fox Fred, r 67, farmer 51.

Fox Fred E., (Apalachin) r 84, farmer with E. Jones 31.
Fox George, (Apalachin) off r 108, farmer.
Fox Ira, (East Nichols) r 118, farmer 50.
Fox James, (Apalachin) r 113, farm laborer.
FOX JEROME, (Gaskill's Corners) r 25, farmer, works on shares for Charles. Becker 120
Fox John, (Gaskill's Corners) r 35, laborer.
Fox Julia A., (Apalachin) widow Charles T., resident, bds. Cross.
Fox Lewis L., (Apalachin) telegraph operator, h William.
Fox Oliza, r 60, resident.
Fox Russell, (Apalachin) r 113, farmer 53.
Fox Thomas, (Campville) r 53, farm laborer.
Fox William, r 120½, farmer 100.
Fox William S., (Apalachin) contractor and builder, h William.
Frear Elias, (Apalachin) r 113, farmer.
Frear Hannah, r 54, widow John, farmer 40.
French William, r 91, farmer 75.
Fuller Benjamin F., (Apalachin) carriage-maker, Main, h William.
Fulmer Charles, r 27, farmer 112.
Fulmer Peter, (Gaskill's Corners) r 34, farmer 80.
Fulmer Philip, r 22, farmer 45.
Gage Ellen, r 54, widow Jeremiah, resident.
Gage Ezra M., r 14, farmer 50.
Gage Mary A. Mrs., (Apalachin) teacher, bds. Cross.
Gage Miner, r 37, apiarist 50 swarms, and farmer 75.
Gage Walter, r 37, apiarist 38 swarms, and farmer 37.
Garrison Chester, (Apalachin) r 108, farmer 35.
Garrison James, (Apalachin) r 70, farm laborer.
Gaskill David W., r 32, farmer 40.
Gaskill Frank, r 54, milk peddler.
Gaskill Paul, (Gaskill's Corners) r 45, farmer 110.
Gaskill Stephen H., (Gaskill's Corners) r 45, farmer for his father Paul.
Gaskill Wilder J., (Apalachin) retired merchant, h Main.
Gaskill William C., (Apalachin) farmer 13, h Main.
Gibson David W., (South Apalachin) r 111, farmer on shares with Orin Bebee 100.
Gibson Frank, (Little Meadows, Pa.) r 135, farmer.
Gibson George, (Apalachin) off r 108, farmer.
Gibson William, (Apalachin) laborer, h Ferry.
Gifford Albert R., (South Owego) r 122, farmer with his mother Sophia H.
Gifford David S., (South Owego) r 122, farmer 100.
Gifford Sophia H., (South Owego) r 122, widow Russell D., farm 85
Gile Orton, r 60, gardener.
Giles Alexander, (South Owego) r 126, farmer.
Giles Ebenezer, (South Owego) r 126, farmer 50.
GILES JOHN S., (Apalachin) r 87, pres't School Board, small fruit and hop grower, apiarist 200 swarms, and farmer 115.
Glann George W., (Apalachin) r 80, farmer.
Glann James H., (Apalachin) r 83, farmer 160.
Glann Martin, (Apalachin) r 85, farmer 50.
Glann William (Apalachin) r 83, farmer 140.
Glover Anson, (Apalachin) r 110, farmer.
Glover George (Apalachin) r 110 farmer.

Glover Stephen B., (Apalachin) r 110 farmer.
Goodenow Abram (Apalachin) r 102, farmer 42.
Goodenow Alanson, (Apalachin) prop. Central House, and farmer 26.
Goodenow Chauncey B., (Apalachin) clerk Central House, bds. do.
Goodenow Henry, (Apalachin) r 87, farmer 38.
Goodenow Isaac, (Apalachin) farmer 5.
Goodenow John W., (Apalachin) hostler Central House, bds. do.
Goodenow Peter, (Apalachin) r 87, resident.
Goodenow Ransom B., (Apalachin) r 114, farmer on shares with his father Abram, 140.
Goodrich Edwin, r 69 farmer.
Goodrich Matthew, r 95, farmer 87.
Goodsel A. Ford, r 56, farmer 61.
Goodspeed Alden, r 118½, farmer 100, and leases of Abner Goodspeed 50.
Goodspeed James, (East Nichols) off r 118, farmer 100.
Gould Andrew C., r 94, farm laborer.
Gould Charles P., r 94, farm laborer.
Gould Elin, (Apalachin) r 87, resident.
Gould George W., r 114, farmer with George Sandford.
Gould Smith, (South Owego) r 123, farmer 160.
Gould Stanley H., r 101½, farmer, leases of Joel Tuttle, 60.
Gower Charles, (Union Center, Broome Co.) r 9, farmer.
Gower Thomas, (Union Center, Broome Co.) r 9, farmer.
Graves Chester W., (South Owego) r 115, farmer 260.
Graves E. Talmage, (South Owego) r 115, teacher.
Graves Horace, (Little Meadows, Pa.) r 131, farmer 100.
Gray John H., (Apalachin) (Kinney & Gray) h Main.
GREEN A. L. & R. D., (Gaskill's Corners) r 25, groceries and provisions.
GREEN ALLEN L., (A. L. & R. D. Green) (Gaskill's Corners) r 25, h r 35.
Green Mary A., (Apalachin) widow Nathan, resident.
GREEN R. DEVERE (A. L. & R. D. Green) (Gaskill's Corners) r 25.
Green Will M., (Apalachin) r 102, farmer.
Griffin Alfred, r 56½, retired carpenter.
Griffin Alvah, (Campville) r 48, farm laborer.
Griffin Edward E., r 56, farmer, leases of Mrs. B. W. Spencer 65.
Griffin Emily, r 56½, widow Seth.
Griffin Fanny, (Gaskill's Corners) r 25, widow Alvah, resident.
Griswold George M., r 93, school trustee and farmer 92.
Griswold Jacob, (Apalachin) laborer, h Ferry.
Groesbeck Betsey, r 68, widow Cornelius, farm 70.
Groesbeck Charles H., r 67, farmer, leases of his father Isaac 50.
Groesbeck Frank P., r 68, farmer on shares with Mrs. Betsey Groesbeck.
Groesbeck George B., (South Owego) r 99, farmer on shares with Elin Gould.
Groesbeck George S., r 61, contractor and builder.
Groesbeck Isaac W., r 68, farmer 170.
Groesbeck Theodore P., r 68, farmer with his father Isaac W.
Groesbeck William, (Apalachin) r 88, farmer, leases of I. W. Groesbeck 50.
HAGADORN FRANK E., r 95, farmer with his father William A.
Hagadorn William A., r 95, farmer 108.
HALL EUNICE E. Mrs., (Flemingville) r 40, prop. Flemingville Hotel, special attractions for summer boarders.
HALL GEORGE W., (Flemingville) r 40 hotel.

Hall Peter, (Apalachin) r 87, laborer.
Hall Temperance (Apalachin) r 87, widow John, resident.
Hall William, (Little Meadows, Pa.) r 131, farmer 50.
Halsted Thomas D., (Gaskill's Corners) r 25½, farmer 52.
Hammond Frederick, r 17, farmer 50.
Haner Addison L., r 96, carpenter and farmer 64.
Haner Irving J., r 96, farmer with his father Levi J.
Haner Levi J., r 96, farmer 45.
Haradon Julius S., r 54, gardener.
Harden Ford, (Flemingville) r 4, laborer.
Harrington George W., (South Owego) r 123, farmer 34.
Harrington Lyman D., r 96, farmer 41.
Harrington Russell, r 96, farmer 41.
Harris David, (South Owego) r 123, farmer 168.
Harris Levi (Apalachin) r 107, resident.
Harris Linus, (South Apalachin) r 111, farmer 100.
Hart Daniel, off r 46, farmer 37.
Harvey Charles, (Apalachin) off r 80, farmer, works for Charles Gland 50.
Hatfield Harry, (Apalachin) laborer, h Main.
HAUVER FRANK M., r 64, farmer 35, and leases of James Archibald 160.
Hayes Henry (Apalachin) r 68, lumberman.
Hayes Ira P., (Apalachin) r 89½, farmer 36.
Hayner David H., (Campville) r 52, farmer 340.
Hemstrought Charles, (Campville) r 50, farmer 20.
Hemstrought Harvey, (Campville) r 54, farmer 24.
Hemstrought Jacob, (Campville) r 54, brakeman and farmer 45.
Hemstrought James, (Campville) r 54, wagon-maker and farmer 30.
Hemstrought Jesse, (Campville) r 54, laborer.
Hemstrought Joseph, (Campville) r 51, farmer 50.
Hemstrought Lovejoy, (Campville) r 54, laborer.
Hendershott Adelbert, r 40, emp. grist-mill.
Herrick Bert, r 40, farm-hand county alms-house.
Herrick Edward P., (Flemingville) r 40, retired farmer.
Herzig Julius, r 37, farmer, works for Mrs. Shannon 37.
Hiawatha House, on Hiawatha Island, estate of E. G. Brown, of N. Y. city,
    Eugene F. Baton, lesee.
Hickein John, r 69, farm laborer.
Hickey John, (Apalachin) r 106, farmer 112.
Hickey Patrick J., (Apalachin) r 106, farmer with his father John.
Hickok Gideon F., (South Owego) r 122, farmer 25.
Hicks Eber, (Apalachin) off r 108, farmer 40.
Higbee George, r 46, farmer 135.
Higbee Orson, r 46, farmer with his father George.
Higbee Sidney C., r 46, farmer with his father George.
Hills George H., (Apalachin) r 113, farmer 130.
Hills John F., (Apalachin) r 113, resident.
Hills Marvin L., (Apalachin) r 113, farmer with his father George H.
Hills Phoebe, (Apalachin) widow Abner.
Hiller Levi G., (Apalachin) r 110, lawyer.
Hilton George, (Apalachin) r 89½, farmsr 50.
Hilton William, (Apalachin) farmer 45, h Main.
Hoagland Fred, r 56, farmer with his father William.
Hoagland William, r 56, farmer 60.

11

Hoary Edward, (Campville) r 54, trackman.
Hodge William, r 39, laborer.
Holbrook Albert, r 94, lumberman.
Holbrook Frank r 94, lumberman.
Holbrook George, r 94, lumberman.
Holbrook Herman, r 94, lumberman.
Holden Edward P., r 22, farmer 100.
Holden Fred, (Flemingville) r 3, farm laborer.
Holden John F., r 22, farmer with his father Edward P.
Holden Jonathan P., (Apalachin) r 102, farmer with I. W. Barton, 200.
Holden Melvin, (Flemingville) r 3, farm laborer.
Holden Oliver, (Flemingville) r 3, farmer 120.
Hollenbeck William, r 43, farmer 110
Hollister Edwin S., (Gaskill's Corners) r 24, farmer 75.
Hollister Eliakim H., (Gaskill's Corners) r 24, farmer 73.
Hollister Watson P., (Gaskill's Corners) r 24, farmer 143
Holmes Anson C., r 91, farmer with his father Elston.
Holmes Asher, (Apalachin) retired, h Main.
HOLMES BROS., (Apalachin) (James & Gilbert) dealers in horses, Depot.
Holmes Elston, r 91, farmer 200.
HOLMES GILBERT, (Apalachin) (Holmes Bros.) also potato dealer and
    farmer 200, h Main.
HOLMES JAMES, (Apalachin) (Holmes Bros.) also commissioner high-
    ways, insurance agent and farmer 16.
Holmes John, (Apalachin) r 70, notary public, lumberman, and farmer 200.
Holmes John, Jr., clerk for Kinney & Gray, h William.
Holmes Ransom S., (Apalachin) farmer, leases of John Thurber 40, h Main.
Holmes Susan W., (Apalachin) widow Stephen, resident, bds. Main.
Hopkins Clark, (Union, Broome Co.) r 47, farmer.
HOPKINS LANCY N., (Apalachin) drugs and medicines, Main, h do.
Hopler Peter Q., (Flemingville) r 4, laborer.
Hotchkiss Almond, (Apalachin) farmer 40, h Main.
Hotchkiss Edward, off r 27, farmer 90.
Howe Peter R., (Apalachin) r 102, farmer 40.
Howe Ralph, r 40, farmer 36.
Howell & Tracy, (Apalachin) (G. W. H. & P. T.) blacksmiths and horse-
    shoers, Main.
Howell Charles W., (Apalachin) blacksmith.
Howell George W., (Apalachin) (Howell & Tracy) h Main.
Howes Joshua F., r 94, farmer.
Hoxie Raymond J., (Apalachin) r 101, farmer 50.
Hullett Oney, r 27, teamster.
Hull Catharine, r 25, widow Clark, resident.
Hull Dwight, (Gaskill's Corners) r 25½, farmer 23.
Hull George W., (Gaskill's Corners) r 25, farmer 60.
Hull Wellington G., r 25, farmer 78.
Hunt Bros. & Co. (John, Charles, Samuel and Susan) r 43, farmer 224.
Hunt Charles, (Hunt Bros. & Co.) r 43, farmer.
Hunt Charles H., (Apalachin) r 70, farmer for Mrs. Mersereau.
Hunt Ellen, r 43, widow John, resident.
Hunt John, (Hunt Bros. & Co.) r 43, farmer.
Hunt Harriet L., (Apalachin) r 70, widow Thomas H., resident.
Hunt Samuel, (Hunt Bros. Co.) r 43, farmer.

Hunt Susan, (Hunt Bros. & Co.) r 43, farm.
Hyde William, r 20, cooper.
Ingersoll Eugene F., r 46, cooper.
Ingersoll Guy, r 27, farmer for his father James H.
Ingersoll Irving, r 46, farmer 97.
Ingersoll James E., (Union, Broome Co.) r 72, farmer, works on shares for John Wenn 112.
Ingersoll James H., r 27, farmer 100.
Jakway Fred D., r 66 farmer, leases of Rev. Mr. King 68.
Jaycox Alvin, (Gaskill's Corners) r 25, farm laborer.
Jenks Byron J., r 93, farmer 211.
Jennings Ransom, (Little Meadows, Pa.) farmer, leases of A. Jennings 70.
Jewett Charles, (Apalachin) r 104, produce.
Jewett George, (Apalachin) r 88, farmer 43.
Jewett Maurice W., (Apalachin) r 69, retired.
Jewett John, (Union, Broome Co.) r 71, farmer 40.
Jewett John W., (Union, Broome Co.) r 71, farmer 112.
Johnson Albert, r 40, attendant County Insane Asylum.
Johnson Andrew J., (Apalachin) r 104, contractor and builder.
JOHNSON DANIEL, r 40, sup't County Alms House and Asylum, and in Candor farm 208.
Johnson Horace, r 43, farm laborer.
Johnson John, r 22, farm laborer.
Johnson Nathan A., r 28, farmer, leases of Mrs. Hauver 20.
Johnson Stillman, r 40, blacksmith.
Johnson Taylor, r 21, farmer 50.
Jones Edward, (Apalachin) r 84, carpenter, and farmer 31.
Jones George, (Apalachin) r 87, farm laborer.
Jones Pardon, (Apalachin) carpenter.
Joslin Daniel F., (Flemingville) r 3, farmer 18.
Judge Thomas L., r 120½, farmer 8.
Judge Thomas, Jr., r 120, farmer 72.
Judge William, (Little Meadows, Pa) r 132, farmer.
Judge William H., r 120, farmer 36.
Kaley Adam I., (Flemingville) r 4, carpenter, and works farm 53.
Kaley John, (Gaskill's Corners) r 25½, farmer 25.
Kattell Willard, (Flemingville) r 3, farm laborer.
Keeler James, (Union, Broome Co.) r 30, farmer 8.
Kellum Ambrose, (Apalachin) wagon-maker, Main, h do.
Keltz Henry, (Union Center, Broome Co.) r 28, farmer.
Kent Fred, r 91, farm laborer.
Kent Gibson, (Apalachin) r 113, farmer 10.
Kent Mary A., r 91, widow Amos. resident.
Kenyon Egbert, (Union Center, Broome Co.) r 11, farmer 40.
Ketchum Charles H., r 97, butcher, and farmer 42.
Ketchum Dell, r 97, farmer 15.
Ketchum Frederick, r 97, farmer with his father Charles H.
Keth Jackson, (Campville) r 48, farmer 75.
Kettell George, (Gaskill's Corners) r 35, farmer, works for John Scrofford 75.
Kile George O., r 95, prop. feed and shingle-mill, and farmer 130.
King Andrew, (South Owego) r 126, farmer 70.
Kinney & Gray, (Apalachin) (J. D. K. and J. H. G.) general merchants, Main cor. Depot.

Kinney John D., (Warren Center, Pa.) (Kinney & Gray) also store at Warren Center, and at Burchardville, Pa., h at Warren Center, Pa.
Kinney Thomas, (Apalachin) r 69, farm laborer.
Kipp Clinton, r 46, farmer 51.
Kipp Wallace, r 46, butcher, and farmer 20.
Knapp Amos, (Apalachin) r 87 farmer.
Knapp Charles R., (Apalachin) hardware, flour and feed, boots and shoes, Main, h do.
KNAPP FRANK J., (Apalachin) postmaster and tinsmith, h Main.
Knapp Henry, (Apalachin) r 110, farmer.
Knapp Ira, (Apalachin) 108, farmer 80.
Knapp James, (Apalachin) r 110, farmer.
Knapp Joel. (Apalachin) r 110, farmer 7.
KNAPP WILBUR F., (Apalachin) groceries and provisions, Main, h do.
Knapp William (Apalachin) r 110, farmer.
Knickerbocker Harvey, r 56½, laborer.
Knight Ambrose, (Apalachin) off r 80, farmer.
Knight Irvin, (Apalachin) off r 80, farmer.
Kyle Thomas, r 56½, farmer 130.
Ladd Isabella, r 91, widow Cyrus, resident.
Lainhart Addison, r 35, farmer 135.
Lainhart Simeon, (Gaskill's Corners) r 34, farmer 60.
Lainhart Thomas, (Union, Broome Co.) r 30, carpenter.
Laird George H., (Apalachin) insurance, h Church.
Laird George H. Mrs., (Apalachin), dressmaker, h Church.
LA MONTE CYRENE M., r 54, farmer 115, and prop. Hiawatha Island and picnic grounds.
La Monte David M., r 68, breeder fine horses, and farmer 75.
La Monte Hannah, r 54, widow Marcus, resident.
LAMPHERE GRANT U., (Apalachin) (Campbell & Lamphere) h Depot.
Lampman Jared, (Little Meadows, Pa.) r 130, resident.
LANE A. LINDSLEY (Apalachin) r 69, farmer 80.
Lane Don C., (Apalachin) r 83 farmer.
Lane Edgar S., (Apalachin) r 69, farmer with his father A. Lindsley.
Lataurette Androette, (Campville), r 49, farmer 88.
Leasure George, (South Owego) r 123, carpenter, and farmer 10.
Leonard Leonard, (Apalachin) r 108, farmer 80.
Letts Matthew, (Gaskill's Corners) r 45, farmer.
Lewis Edgar, (Apalachin) r 69, farmer 50.
Lewis Hiram, (Apalachin) r 69 farmer.
LEWIS ISAAC W., (Apalachin) physician and surgeon, and farmer 314, and in Kansas 160, and in Iowa 80, h Main.
Lewis Maria, r 56. widow of James, carpet-weaver.
Like George W., (Apalachin) r 106, agricultural implements, and farmer 56.
Like William, (Apalachin) r 106, farm laborer.
Lillie Charles T., (Apalachin) r 108, farmer on shares with John Decker.
Lillie George M., (Apalachin) r 108, farmer 35.
Lillie Lucina, (Apalachin) r 108, widow Jared, resident.
Lillie Merritt F. (Apalachin) r 108, farmer 66.
Lillie William, (Apalachin) r 108, mason, and farmer 63.
Lindsly Hiram, r 40, carpenter.
Livingston Amos, r 54, gardener 7½.

Livingston Christiana, widow Peter, r 67 resident.
Livingston John, (Campville) r 71, lawyer in New York city and farmer 83.
Livingston Marcus, (Campville) r 51, farmer 66.
Livingston Peter, (Campville) r 48, farmer 160.
Lory Joseph (Apalachin) r 83, bartender.
Lory Kaziah, (Apalachin) r 83, widow David, resident.
Lown Catherine, (South Owego) r 122, widow Jacob, resident.
Lown William P., (South Owego) r 122, horse-dealer and farmer 47.
Lucas Daniel T., r 99, farmer, works on shares with Mr. Drake 80.
Lyke Peter (Campville) r 54 farmer 120.
Lyke Rufus F., r 91, farmer 30.
Mabee Robert, (Apalachin) r 87, farmer.
Mack Thomas, off r 54, track-hand.
McGee Griffin, r 43, farm laborer.
Mahar Michael, r 41, farmer 72.
Maloney Jeremiah, (Apalachin) r 103, farmer 92.
Marean Duane, (Flemingville) r 6, farmer 42.
Marean George, (Union, Broome Co.) r 31, farmer 113.
Mason Albert G., r. 27, farmer 60.
Mason Albert G., Jr., r 27, farmer 12.
Mason Samuel, r 22, locomotive engineer.
Mason Samuel, r 22, farmer 42.
Mason Thomas, r 22, farmer with his father Samuel 77.
Mason William (Apalachin) off r 108, farmer.
Maston Charles, r 120½, farmer 10.
Maston John, r 120½, farmer 40.
Mayhew Charles, (Little Meadows, Pa.) r 110, painter.
Mayhew George W., (Apalachin) resident, h Main.
McCann George E., (Campville) r 54, upholsterer.
McCann J. William, (Campville) r 54, farmer 44.
McCaslin Alexander (Apalachin) blacksmith Main, h do.
McClain Charles, (Gaskill's Corners) r 35, farm laborer.
McClain Polly, r 20, widow Charles, farm 20.
McClary Rexford, (Union, Broome Co.) r 71, farmer 46.
McCoy Stiles, r 56½, retired farmer.
McDonald Cameron, r 40, painter.
McHenry Francis B., (Apalachin) farmer, h Church.
McHenry James (Apalachin) r 103, farmer with his mother Sally J.
McHenry Sally J., (Apalachin) r 103, farmer 92.
McMahon Thomas, off r 54, track-hand.
McNeil Roswell C., (Campville) r 54, farmer.
McNeil Sarah, (Campville) r 54, widow Roswell C., resident.
Mead George, off r 22, farmer 175.
Mead Holloway, (Flemingville) r 2, farmer 90.
Mead John, (East Nichols) r 119, farmer 50.
Mead Ransom H., (Gaskill's Corners) r 12, farm laborer.
Mead William E., (Gaskill's Corners) r 35, farmer 150.
Meade Fayette E., r 20, farmer 83.
Meade Maria, r 20, widow Isaac, resident.
Meads Peter, (Little Meadows, Pa.) r 135, farmer.
Mericle Jacob, r 118½ farmer 112.
Mericle James H., r 116, farmer 52.

Meircle John, r 116½, farmer 110.
Mericle William H., r 116½ farmer 110.
Merrick Austin B., off r 65, farm laborer.
Merrick John B., r 65, farmer for L. H. Pitcher.
Mersereau Adeline, r 69,widow George, farm 100.
Mersereau Frank, r 68, farmer 150.
Mersereau Grant, r 68, farmer 150.
Millage Brinton, (Campville) r 52, farmer 64.
Miller Augustus, (Apalachin) farm laborer, h Church.
Miller Cornelia, (Gaskill's Corners) r 11, widow Alexander, farm 40.
Miller Emanuel, (Apalachin) cooper.
Miller John, (South Apalachin) r 128, farmer 50.
Miller John, Mrs., r 56, residen.
Miller Jonas, (Gaskill's Corners) r 11, farmer for his mother Cornelia.
Millrea Edward, r 39, farmer for his father, Thomas.
Millrea Thomas, r 39, farmer 110.
Mills Gurdon T., (Union, Broome Co.) r 31, farmer 5.
Moe Ezra, (South Apalachin) r 112 farmer 56.
Moe Sherman, (Little Meadows, Pa.) r 110, farmer 40.
Montanyea Buffum D., (Campville) r 54 farmer 65.
Moot Peter, r 20, farmer 60.
Morgan Alexander, (Union, Broome Co.) r 29, farmer 50.
Morgan William, off r 27, farmer 100.
Morton David, (South Apalachin) off r 108, farmer 70.
MORTON LEVI, (Apalachin) boot and shoe dealer, also custom work, Main, h do.
Moss Samuel, r 99, farmer, leases of James Clark 50.
Mott Frank C., (Apalachin) r 80, farm laborer.
Mott Israel D., r 54, stone-mason.
Mott Lorenzo, r 90, resident.
Murphy Edward, (Apalachin) retired, h Church.
Myers John, off r 54, emp. Mrs. E. A. Barton.
Myers Joseph H., r 91, farmer 23.
Narsh Frederick, r 32, farmer, leases of Leonard Foster.
Narsh Marvin A., r 56½, farmer 6.
Nash Allen, (Gaskill's Corners) r 25, painter.
Newman Maria, (Apalachin) r 84, widow Nelson S., resident.
Newman Warren A., (Apalachin) r 84, farmer 34.
Newman William, (Flemingville) r 16½, farmer 24.
Nichols Betsey, (Apalachin) widow William, h Main.
Nichols Charles, r 68, farmer 112.
Nichols Charles H., r 67, farmer with his father Justus.
Nichols George, r 60, farmer 160.
Nichols George S., r 60 farm laborer.
Nichols Justus, r 67, farmer 145.
Nichols Robert, r 60, farmer with his father George.
Nichols Washington, (Apalachin) r 102½, apiarist, and farmer 35.
Nichols Will F., (Apalachin) hostler.
Noteware Frederick H., (South Apalachin) r 110, farmer 90.
Noteware Wallace R., (South Apalachin) r 110, apiarist, and farmer 170.
Noteware Walter R., (Apalachin) r 89½, farmer 35.
Northrop Arthur T., r 23, farmer, leases of Lainhart estate 300.
Ogden Catherine E., (Apalachin) widow Isaac, resident, h Main.

Ogden Frank C., (Apalachin) teacher, bds. Main.

Olmstead Augustus, r 80, farmer 120.

Olmstead Daniel B., (Apalachin) r 80, farmer 71.

Olmstead Maria S., (Apalachin) r 80, widow Avery, farm 200.

Olmstead Luman, r 40, farmer.

Olmstead Robert, r 80, farmer with his father Augustus, 120.

Olmstead Seth, r 40, grocery, and farmer 28.

Olmstead Whiting W., r 40, farm laborer.

O'Neill James M., r 22, farmer 89.

Orford Charles F., (Apalachin) carpenter, h Church.

Orford David (Apalachin) shoemaker, h Church.

Padgett Allen W., r 40, farm laborer.

Pangburn Jacob, (Union, Broome Co.) r 28, farmer 50.

Pearl Charles E., r 95, farmer, leases of his father Loring C.

Pearl Frederick J., r 95, farmer, leases of his father Loring C.

Pearl Diana B., r 95, widow Austin, resident.

PEARL LORING C., r 95, farmer 240.

PEARL MYRAM W., off r 65, farmer, leases of J. F. DeGroat 123.

Pearsall Grace L., (Apalachin) teacher, bds. William.

PEARSALL RANSOM S., (Apalachin) justice of the peace and farmer, h William.

Pease Joseph N., r 39, farmer 130.

Pendleton Jenks, (Little Meadows, Pa.) r 132, farmer.

Pendleton Loren, (Little Meadows, Pa.) r 132, farmer.

Pendleton Monroe, (Little Meadows, Pa.) r 133, farmer.

Perkins Barney, (Apalachin) r 89 1-2, peddler, and farmer 5.

Perkins Maggie, r 40, matron County Insane Asylum.

Perry Charles F., (South Owego) r 122, farmer on shares with L. B. Truman, 250.

Perry George H., (South Owego) r 122, farmer with his father Charles F.

Pettigrove Laura J., r 40, farm 47.

Pettigrove Sewell, r 40, miller, and farmer 6.

Phalen Patrick, r 14, farmer, works on shares for William P. Stone, 110.

Phelps George, (Gaskill's Corners) r 25, farm laborer.

Phelps Jesse, (Flemingville) r 40, farmer 11, and in Candor 100.

Phelps Philip, (Gaskill's Corners) r 25, farmer 50.

Phelps William, r 56, farmer 16.

Phillips James, (Apalachin) r 90, farmer 101.

Phinleyson Richard, (Apalachin) off r 108, farmer.

Pitcher Harvey, r 65 resident.

Pitcher Leroy H., r 65, agricultural implements, and farmer 100.

Potter John, (Flemingville) r 16, farmer for Frank Scott.

Potter Wendall, farmer 78.

Powell John H., (Union, Broome Co.) r 47, farmer.

Powers Angeline, (Apalachin) r 110, widow John J., resident.

Powers Francis J., (Apalachin) r 110, farm laborer.

Powers Frederick A., (Apalachin) r 110, farm laborer.

Post Gardner, (Apalachin) r 85, farmer 75.

Pray Ephraim, (Apalachin) r 83, resident.

PRITCHARD ASA., (Flemingville) r 3, farmer 37, and wood lot 14.

Pritchard James, (Flemingville) r 4, farmer with his brother Truman 30.

Pritchard Herbert E., (Flemingville) r 3, farmer with his father Sylvester.

Pritchard Sylvester H., (Flemingville) r 3, farmer 126.

Pritchard Truman, (Flemingville) r 4, farmer with his brother James 30.
Pritchard William H., (Flemingville) r 2, farm laborer.
Probasco Elmer, r 68, farm laborer.
Probasco Frank M., r 67, farmer 75.
Probasco Gurdon, r 68, farm laborer.
Pultz Henry, r 17, farmer.
Pultz Henry, Jr., r 17, farmer.
Pultz Putnam, r 17, farmer 40.
Pultz Ransom, r 17, farmer 50.
Queeman West, (Apalachin) r 83, resident.
Quimby Adelbert H., (Apalachin) laborer, h William.
Quimby John W., (Apalachin) r 87, farmer.
Randall Henry, r 26, farmer 80.
Rauch George F., (Flemingville) r 3, farmer, leases of the Allen estate 38.
Recorden Charles, (Flemingville) r 5, farmer 87.
Reed James L., (Flemingville) r 4, blacksmith, and farmer in Newark 100.
Redding John, r 120, farmer 50.
Reynolds Albert L., r 94, farm laborer.
Richardson Austin, r 31, farmer for his father Cephas.
Richardson Cephas, r 31, farmer 90.
Richardson Harry, r 31, farmer for his father Cephas.
Richardson Jerome B., r 99, farmer 35.
Rinevault Amanda, r 40, widow Alfred.
Rising James H., (Gaskill's Corners) r 25, farmer 108.
Rising Jeanette, (Gaskill's Corners) r 25, widow John, farm 100.
Rising William H., (Gaskill's Corners) r 25, farmer 57.
Robbins Ephraim, (Union, Broome Co.) r 47, farmer.
Robinson Benjamin, r 56, farmer 25.
Robinson Bridget, r 22, widow Matthew, farm 118.
Robinson Henry, (Union, Broome Co.) r 74, farmer 64.
Robinson Howard, r 46, farmer 123.
Robinson Jacob, r 27, farmer 61.
Robinson John, r 22, farmer 118.
Robinson John L., r 94, farmer, leases of Frank Bliss 47.
Rockwood Charles, r 40, farm laborer.
Rodman Benjamin, (Union, Broome Co.) r 47, farmer 60.
Rodman Calvin, (Union, Broome Co.) r 47, farmer.
Rodman Nicholas, (Apalachin) r 68, farmer.
Romain Benjamin, r 27, farm laborer.
Romain Charles, (Campville) r 54, farmer 15.
Romain George, (Campville) r 54, laborer.
Romain Jesse, (South Owego) r 123, farmer on shares with D. Gifford.
Rounds Simeon, (Apalachin) r 83, cider and shingle-mill, and farmer 25.
Rowe Edward, r 54, gardener 17.
Rowley James, (Apalachin) r 87, resident.
Rulison George P., (Apalachin) mason, h Main.
Rundle James A., r 95, farmer on shares with Mrs. G. Van Bunschoten 76.
Russell Daniel, r 20, farmer.
Russell Elbridge, r 20, farmer 75.
Russell Minor, (South Apalachin) r 108, carpenter and wagon-maker.
Ryan Michael, (Apalachin) r 89½, farmer 56.
Ryan James, (Apalachin) r 70, farmer 35.
RYAN JOHN S., (Apalachin) prop. Exchange Hotel, h do.

Ryan Thomas, (Apalachin) laborer.
Ryan Walter, (Union Center, Broome Co.) r 11, farmer 100.
Sandford George, (South Owego) r 114, farmer 160.
Sandford Lewis C., r 98, farmer with his father Oliver B.
Sandford Oliver B., r 98, farmer 80.
Savey Edmund G., (Apalachin) carpenter, h Main.
Savey Seth, (Apalachin) r 87, carpenter.
Savey William, (Apalachin) carpenter and builder, h Main.
Sawyer George, r 56½, farmer with his father Nathan.
Sawyer Nancy M., r 54, widow William, farm 60.
Sawyer Nathan, r 54, farmer 50.
Sawyer Oscar W., r 54, farmer for his mother, Mrs. Nancy M.
Schoolcroft Peter, r 14, farmer 200.
Schoolcroft Philip, r 14, farmer 60.
Scott Abram, (Campville) r 69, cartman and mail-carrier.
Scott Clinton, r 40, farmer 50.
Scott Elizabeth, (Flemingville) r 16, widow Frederick, resident.
Scott Emery, (Flemingville) r 16, farmer with his father Frank.
Scott Frank, (Flemingville) r 16, farmer 92.
Scott Phoebe, r 40, widow Alonzo, farm 10.
Scrafford James, (Gaskill's Corners) r 25½, farmer 75.
Scrafford John, (Gaskill's Corners) r 35, farmer 75.
Scutt Dell, r 54, farm laborer.
Scutt George, r 54, farm laborer.
Scutt Isaac, r 54, farmer 4.
Searl Edward, r 37, farmer 86.
Searl Edward F., r 56, farmer 75.
Searles Amos, (Flemingville) farmer 14.
Searles Asahel, (Flemingville) r 4, farmer 50.
Searles Esther, (Flemigville) widow Chester, farmer 15.
Searles George, (Flemingville) r 4, Mason.
Searles Homer, (Flemingville) r 16½, prop. steam saw-mill and farmer 10.
Searles Lot, (Flemingville) r 16½, farmer 13.
Searles Luke E., (Flemingville) r 15, farmer, leases of G. Pultz 100.
Searles Nathan P., (Flemingville) r 16½, mason and farmer 90.
Severson George, (Campville) r 51, blacksmith.
Shaffer Abram, r 17, farmer 50.
Shaffer Abram, Jr., r 17, farmer.
Shannon Elizabeth, r 37, widow Cornelius, farm 37.
Shaw Hiram D., (South Owego) r 123, farmer 130.
Shay John, (Apalachin) section foreman D. L. & W. R. R., bds. Exchange Hotel.
Shay Wesley W., r 58, milk dealer and farmer, leases of B Woodford 160.
Shellman Chauncey, (Campville) r 51, cobbler and ferryman.
Shepard Charles D. Rev., (Flemingville) r 40, pastor M. E. Church.
Sherwood Charles, r 56½, farmer, works on shares for George Young 128.
Sherwood Elsworth, (South Apalachin) r 128, farmer 150.
Sherwood George J., (Apalachin) r 106, stock-breeder and farmer 55.
Sherwood John, (Apalachin) r 70, farmer 25.
Sherwood Nathaniel, (Apalachin) r 88, farmer 50.
SHERWOOD VAN NESS (Apalachin) r 88, farmer with his father Nathaniel.
SHERWOOD WILLIAM H., (Apalachin) r 162, farmer 145.

Shirley Jonathan, r 38, farmer 13.
Shirley John, r 36, farmer 20.
Shirley Nathaniel, r 38, farm laborer.
Shirley Rial, r 36, farmer 30.
Shirley Samuel, r 37, farmer 40.
Shopp John, (Union, Broome Co.) r 28, farmer.
Short Frank (Apalachin) r 88, farmer with his father Uriah.
Short Fred, (Apalachin) r 88, farmer, leases of Uriah Short, Sr., 35.
Short G. Ransom, (Apalachin) r 89½, farmer 15.
Short Lorenzo, (Apalachin) r 88, farmer, leases of Uriah Short, Sr., 35.
Short Uriah, Sr., (Apalachin) r 88, farmer 152.
Short Uriah, (Apalachin) r 87, laborer.
Shultz John, (South Apalachin) off r 110, farmer.
Sibley Charles V., off r 97, farmer 65.
Sibley Elvira S., r 98, resident.
Sibley George D., (Flemingville) r 15, farmer, works on shares for S. Marquit 70.
Slawson George, (South Owego) r 126, farmer 75.
Slawson Schuyler M., r 99, farmer 35.
Slawson Milton, (South Owego) r 123, farmer 160.
SLEEPER THOMAS J., (Apalachin) (Sleeper & Whittaker) h Main.
SLEEPER & WHITTAKER, (Apalachin) (T. J. S. & W. W.) produce and general merchants, Main.
Slocum Humphrey C., r 54, farmer 25.
Smith Albert, (Apalachin) r 86, farmer.
Smith Aurelia, (Gaskill's Corners) r 25, widow James, resident.
Smith Charles F., r 14, farmer 200.
Smith Elizabeth, r 54, widow George, farm 83.
Smith Franklin E., (Apalachin) laborer, bds. Cross.
SMITH FRED W., r 54, milk dealer and farmer 323.
Smith George W., r 41, bridge builder.
Smith Henry W., r 65, deputy sheriff and farmer 32.
Smith Ira A., r 22, farmer 108.
Smith Jerome, (Campville) r 54, farmer, leases of Dr. Allen 100.
Smith Orville, (Campville) r 54, prop. cider-mill and farmer 100.
Smith Phoebe, r 54, widow Stephen W., resident.
Smith Robert C., (Gaskill's Corners) r 25, farmer 140.
Smith Robert E., (Gaskill's Corners) r 35, farm laborer.
Smith Royal Y., (Apalachin) r 86, farmer.
Snell Robert, r 98, farmer 10.
Snell Samuel B., r 98, emp. Coe's saw-mill.
Snooks Halsey, (Apalachin) r 113, chair-seating.
Snooks William D., (Apalachin) r 114, farm laborer.
Snyder Nett, r 61, widow Edward D., resident.
Southwick William, (Flemingville) r 5, sugar orchard 76 trees, and farmer 100.
Spencer A. Judson, farmer 180.
Spencer Arminda, r 59, widow Brinton W., farm 65.
Spencer George, (Campville) r 54, trackman.
Spencer Hiram, r 96, farm laborer.
Sprong Christopher C., r 20, farmer 75.
Sprong George, r 20, farmer.
Stage Clarence, (Flemingville) r 2, farmer, leases of Harry I. Clapham 125.
Stalker Charles, farm laborer.
Stalker George, r 31, emp. Leonard Foster.

STANTON ASA, r 96, surveyor and farmer 195.
Stanton Mary, (Union, Broome Co.) r 47, widow Edward, resident.
Stedman Lyman, (Flemingville) r 3, farmer 58.
STEDMAN WHEELER,(Flemingville) r 40, hay, coal, lumber, produce, and farmer 170.
STEELE AARON, (Apalachin) express and station agt. D. L. & W. R. R., and farmer 400, h Main.
Steele Aurelia, r 93, widow William, farm 105.
Steele E. Jennie, r 93, teacher.
Steele George, r 56, farmer 26.
Steele James, (Apalachin) farmer 42, h Main.
Steele Maria, (Apalachin) widow Lucius, h Main.
Steele Marinda, r 66, widow Aaron W., resident.
Steele Philetus, r 66, farmer, leases of Aaron W. Steele 160.
Steenburg Fred, (Apalachin) r 102½, farmer 70.
Steenburg Isaac, (Apalachin) r 107, farmer 30.
Steenburg Nicholas, (Apalachin) off r 108, farmer.
Stein Jacob, r 39, laborer.
Stephens Bert. (South Apalachin) r 110, farmer 100.
Stephens Henry, (South Apalachin) r 110, farmer 125.
Stephens Samuel J., r 116, farmer 52.
Stevens Charles, r 56, farm laborer.
Stockwell Frank, (Gaskill's Corners) r 45, farm laborer.
Stone Charles M., r 116, farmer 28.
Stratton James H., r 20, farmer, leases of Hiram Johnson 40.
Stratton John, (Union, Broome Co.) farmer.
Stratton Richard, r 20, wagon-maker, and farmer 35.
Strong Beri, (Flemingville) r 4, farm laborer.
Strong Charles, r 39, farmer, leases of Mrs. Caroline Allen 90.
Strong Clayton B., r 66, farmer.
Strong Susan A., r 66, widow Levi, leases of Dr. Phelps 100.
Sturtevant Harrison C., r 20, farm laborer.
Stilson Eugene, (Apalachin) r 69, farm laborer.
Stilson Sarah E., (Apalachin) r 69, widow Hiram, farm 6.
Stinard Joseph, r 63, miller.
Stinard R. Charles, r 63 farmer.
Surdam P. Smith, (Union, Broome Co.) r 31, farmer 127.
Swartwood Joseph A., (Apalachin) gardener, h Cross.
Swart J. Walter, (Campville) r 51, farmer 42.
TALCOTT CHARLES, r 40, apiarist 35 swarms, and farmer 75.
Talcott Frederick, r 40, farmer.
Talcott Eunice B., r 40, widow Joel, resident.
Talcott George B., r 40, apiarist 70 swarms, 90 head sheep, and farmer 207.
Talcott William H., r 20, farmer 75.
TALLMADGE EZRA W., r 99, fruit grower, 600 apple trees, and farmer 116.
Taylor Frank, r 95, resident.
Teater Philip, (Union, Broome Co.) r 28, farmer 80.
Terbush Clark, (South Owego) off r 90, farmer 188.
Terbush Hiram, (Apalachin) r 106, farmer 46.
Thomas Jane E. Mrs., r 95, resident.
Thomas William, off r 56 1-2,, farmer 44.
Thompson John A., (Apalachin) r 69, farm laborer.
Thompson William, (Apalachin) shoemaker, Main, h William.

Thornton Abram, r 31, emp. Foster's saw-mill.
Thornton Thomas, r 27, basket and shoemaker.
Throop John G., (Apalachin) r 106, farmer 25.
Tilbury Charles F., (Campville) r 71, farmer 50.
Tilbury Frederick, (Union, Broome Co.) r 71, farmer 100.
Tilbury Herman M., (Campville) r 71, potato dealer, and farmer 40.
Tilbury Isaac, r 53, farmer 96.
Tilbury James, (Campville) r 71, farmer 100.
Tobey James D., (Apalachin) r 83, saw-mill, and farmer 30.
Tobey Ruel L., (Apalachin) r 83, farm laborer.
Toburn Richard, (Campville) r 54, trackman.
Tousley Silas G., r 54, farmer 50.
Towsand Frederick, off r 120, farmer 91.
Towsand Joel, r 120, farmer 100.
Towsand John, r 120 1-2, farmer 110.
Towser John, r 41, farm laborer.
TRACY BENJAMIN F., (Apalachin) (B. F. Tracy & Son) r 69.
TRACY B. F. & SON, (Apalachin) (Frank B.) r 69, props. Marshland stock
    farms.
TRACY FRANK B., (Apalachin) (B. F. Tracy & Son) r 69.
Tracy Frank Y., (Apalachin) (Howell & Tracy) h Cross.
Tracy Harrison (Apalachin) off r 110, farmer 110.
Tracy Harvey J., (Apalachin) r 83, stock raising and farmer 105.
Tracy Pardon, (Apalachin) (Howell & Tracy) h Church.
Travis Charles J., r 68, farmer with his father James.
Travis James, r 68, farmer 50.
Travis Samuel, (Apalachin) off r 102, farmer 50.
Travis William, (Apalachin) r 69, hostler.
Truman Aaron B., (Gaskill's Corners) r 35, farmer 203.
Truman Charles E., (Flemingville) r 40, postmaster, justice of the peace
    and farmer 70.
Truman Charles F., (Flemingville) r 40, farmer 150.
Truman Elias, r 120 1-2, farmer 160.
Truman Elias W., (Apalachin) r 87, farmer.
Truman Lyman B., (South Owego) r 123, postmaster and farmer 250.
Trusdell Morris, (Campville) r 71, farmer, leases of Michael Livingston 80.
Tucker Nelson, (Apalachin) off r 113, resident.
Tullock James A., (Flemingville) r 4, farmer 40.
Tuttle Jason, (Campville) r 51, laborer.
Tyrrell Henry I., r 116, farmer 33.
Tyrrell Walter D., farmer, leases of W. Fox estate 100.
Van Brunschoten George W., (Apalachin) r 110, farmer 6.
Van Dermark, r 69, farm laborer.
Van Gorder Ezra, (Apalachin) r 85, farmer.
Van Gorder James, (Apalachin) off r 110, farmer.
Van Gorder Jonathan, r 93, retired.
Vanorder Frederick, (Gaskill's Corners) r 45, farm laborer.
Van Riper Fred, (Apalachin) r 102, farmer.
Van Riper Morris, (Apalachin) r 90, farmer 27.
Verguson Edward, (Gaskill's Corners) r 25, farmer for F. W. Smith 240.
Verry Russell, (Little Meadows, Pa.) r 132, farmer.
Viele John N., off r 96, farmer 25.
Vincent Dexter C., r 46, cooper.

Vosburgh Stephen H., r 40, saw-filer.
Wade John, (Flemingville) r 5, farm laborer.
Wade Ozias D., (Flemingville) r 5, farmer 41, and in Newark 65.
Wait Charles B., (East Nichols) off r 119, farmer 90.
Wait Frederick C., (East Nichols) r 120, farmer 200.
Wait Henry, (East Nichols) r 119, farmer 112.
Wait Horace, (East Nichols) off r 119, farmer with his father Charles.
Wait John, r 54, farmer 50.
Wait John H., (East Nichols) r 119, farmer with his father William 225.
Wait William, (East Nichols) r 119, farmer 225.
Wait William H., r 54, farmer with his father John 50.
Walker Abram, (Campville) r 54, laborer.
Walker Frank, r 27, carpenter.
Walker George D., (Union, Broome Co.) r 30, farmer 128.
Walker Judson R., r 59, farmer, with his father Rial.
Walker Rial, r 59, farmer 36.
WALTER ARTEMAS, (Gaskill's Corners) r 35, farmer 250.
Walter Franklin A., (Gaskill's Corners) r 25, carpenter.
Walter Lester, (Gaskill's Corners) r 35, farmer for his father Artemas.
Walter Lyman, (Gaskill's Corners) r 35, farm laborer.
Walters Herman, (Gaskill's Corners) r 45, student.
Walters Margaret, (Gaskill's Corners) r 45, widow William, farm 300.
Walters Orin, (Gaskill's Corners) r 45, farmer, leases of Mrs. M. Walters 300.
Ward Charles, off r 113, farmer, leases of Ira Edwards.
Ward Daniel, off r 46, farmer with his father Richard 55.
Ward Richard, off r 46, farmer with his son Daniel 55.
Warrick Peter, r 32, retired farmer.
Warrick Samuel, (Union, Broome Co.) off r 47, farmer.
Welch Charles, r 43, farmer, works on shares for the Misses. Hollenback 275.
Welch James, (Gaskill's Corners) r 11, farmer 80.
Welch Herbert, r 37, farmer 40.
Wells Maria K., r 32, resident.
Wemple Isaac S., (Union, Broome Co.) r 30, farmer 84.
Wenn John, (Union, Broome Co.) r 71, farmer 100.
Wheeler Charles, (Apalachin) r 86, farmer.
Wheeler Fred S., (Campville) r 54, clerk.
Wheeler John, (Campville) r 54, groceries and provisions.
White Andrew, (Apalachin) r 101 1-2, farmer 110.
Whitmarsh Andrew, on Hiawatha Island, works on shares for C. M. La-
    Monte 100.
Whitney David H., (Campville) r 54, farmer 23.
Whitney Nathan S., (Campville) r 54, farmer.
WHITTAKER WELLINGTON,(Apalachin) (Sleeper & Whittaker) h Main
WHITTEMORE ALVIN, (Union, Broome Co.) r 28, farmer 85.
Whittemore Charles, r 27, farmer 80.
Whittemore Egbert, (Union, Broome Co.) r 29, farmer 17.
Whittemore Fred, (Union, Broome Co.) r 46, farmer, works on shares for
    Charles J. Stanton 162.
Whittemore George, (Union, Broome Co.) r 30, farmer 120.
Whittemore John, r 27, carpenter and farmer 40.
Whittemore Marcus, (Campville) r 48, laborer.
Whittemore Virgil, r 26, farmer 200.
Whittemore William, (Gaskill's Corners) r 43, farmer 140.

Wicks Lucius M., r 54, ice-dealer.
Wilcox Elizabeth Mrs., (Apalachin) resident, h Main.
Williams Emeline, r 117, widow James H., resident.
Williams George E., r 99, farmer 110.
Williams Isaac F., r 95, farmer 41.
Williams Jacob, r 99, retired.
Williams John E., (Apalachin) harness-maker, Main, h Church.
Williams Lucy, r 95, widow Reuben, resident.
Williams Stephen L., r 95, farmer, and leases of Mrs. Lucy Williams 100,
WILLIAMS WRIGHT B., r 115, fruit-grower and farmer 100.
Williamson Ezra M., r 22, farmer 80.
Williamson George D., agt. for the "Sprague" farm wagon, and farmer, leases
    of Mrs. M. McLean 30.
Williamson Isaac, r 17, farmer.
Wilsey Otis, (South Owego) r 113, farmer 150.
Winans Ernest, r 117, farmer with his father Orlando.
Winans Orlando, r 117, farmer 110.
Winchell John J., (Flemingville) r 4, farmer 71.
Winne Ajelica, (Gaskill's Corners) r 35, widow Walter V., resident.
Winne Eugene, (Gaskill's Corners) r 35, farmer with his brother James 183.
Winne Jacob, r 14, farmer 30.
Winne James, (Gaskill's Corners) r 35, farmer with his brother Eugene 183.
Winship Frank, (Flemingville) r 4, farm laborer.
Witter Lyman, r 94, farmer 70.
Witter William, off r 96, shingle-maker and farmer.
Wolcott Aaron, (South Owego) r 128, farmer 50.
Wood Alva, (Apalachin) off r 108, farmer 37.
Wood Andrew J., off r 96, farmer 41.
Wood Catherine E., (Apalachin) r 114, widow Luman B., farmer 75.
Wood Charles E., (Flemingville) r 30, dealer in agricultural implements and
    well-driver.
Wood Charles H., r 60, cabinet-maker.
Wood Clarence, r 40, farmer.
Wood C. Leonard, r 60, emp. King & Co.
WOOD EDWARD B., (Apalachin) r 114, farmer with his mother Catherine.
Wood Frank T., (Gaskill's Corners) r 25, farmer 75.
Wood J. Henry, off r 96, farm laborer.
Wood Nelson, (Flemingville) r 5, farm laborer.
Wood Royal, (Apalachin) r 104, farm laborer.
Wood Royal P., r 40, farmer 85.
Wood Samuel H., off r 96, farmer with his father Andrew J.
Worrick Charles T., r 101½, farmer 70, and leases of Anna M. Boyce 110.
Worrick Freeman, (Apalachin) r 101½, farmer.
Worrick Nathaniel S., r 32, farmer 130.
Woughter Andrew C., (Union, Broom Co.) r 73, farmer 113.
Woughter Avery, (Union, Broome Co.) r 71, farmer 70.
Woughter Chester, (Union, Broom Co.) r 73, farmer 50.
Woughter Cornelius, (Union, Broome Co.) r 72, farmer 85.
Woughter Vol, r 54, farmer 57½.
Wright Adam, r 16, farmer, works on shares for Joseph Young 100.
Wright Elson, r 20, farm laborer.
Yarrington Sylvia, (Apalachin) widow Washington, bds. Main.

Yates Daniel, (Campville) r 54, farmer 36.
Yates Frank, (Apalachin) r 85, farmer.
Yates George L., r 91, farmer with his father John.
Yates John, r 91, farmer 70.
Yates John S., (Apalachin) r 70, farmer 85.
Yates Mary A., r 91, resident.
Yearsley Aaron, (Apalachin) r 69, horseman.
Yearsley William, (Apalachin) emp. Marshland stock farm, h Main.
York Abram, (Apalachin) r 104, farm laborer.
Young Charles, r 20, farmer 50.
Young George, r 54, farmer 265.
Young Joseph, r 21, farmer 200.

———

RICHFORD.

(*For explanations, etc., see page 3, part second.*)

(Postoffice address is Richford, unless otherwise designated in parenthesis.)

Abbey Edward B., r 25, carpenter. and farmer 52.
Allen Carlton E., (Caroline, Tomp. Co.) r 26, farmer with H. C. Allen 134.
Allen Elmer, r 42, carpenter.
Allen George W., farmer 35, h Main.
Allen Henry C., (Caroline, Tomp. Co.) r 26, farmer 77, and with C. E. A.
134.
Allen James, physician and surgeon, h Main. ~
ALLEN J. W., (Finch & Allen) r 18, prop. saw-mill, lumber dealer, and farmer
330.
Allen Sidney B., (Caroline, Tomp. Co.) r 23, farmer 102.
Allen William B., commercial traveler, h Main.
Avery Ebeneazer, (Caroline, Tomp. Co.) r 26, farmer 12.
Ayers Elias, r 49, farmer 110.
AYERS FREDERICK A., r 37, farmer 110. ~
AYERS JAMES W., shoemaker, h Mill.
Ayers Jeptha L., r 46, laborer.
Ayers Job, r 28, farmer 230.
Ayers John L., r 46, farmer, leases of W. F. Wright, of Berkshire, 92.
Ayers Marietta, r 41, widow of Albert, farm 11½.
Ayers Rudolph, r 27, farmer 219.
AYERS WAYLAND B., r 28, farmer.
Barden Charles F., off r 26, farmer, leases of W. S. Goodrich 167.
Barden Edmund, r 18, carpenter.
Barden Ezra S., farmer 30, h Main.
Barden Frank, r 18, farmer 117.
Barnes Arba P., harness-maker, h Front.
Barnes George S., (Caroline, Tomp. Co.) r 22, farmer, leases of C. A. Fellows 100.

BARNES GRANT W., manuf. and dealer in harnesses, saddles, whips, nets, robes, and dusters, also county superintendent of poor, h Aurora.

Barney George E., r 18, farmer 30.

Beam Charles, (Caroline, Tomp. Co.) r 23, farmer 34.

Belden Edgar F., clerk for W. C. Smith & Co., and farmer with William F. Belden 156.

Belden Frederick C., r 39, farmer 160.

Belden George R., r 39, farmer.

BELDEN WILLIAM F., r 39, farmer 144.

Bell Augustus E., shoemaker, Main.

Benjamin Frank E., (Caroline, Tomp. Co.) r 23, farmer, leases of Sarah A. Benjamin, of McGrawville, 60.

Benjamin Luther U., (Harford, Cort. Co.) r 8, laborer, h and lot.

Berry Benjamin, (Harford Mills, Cort. Co.) r 12.

Blakeman Allen, (Harford Mills, Cort. Co.) r 14, farmer 161.

Blakeman Asahel, r 11, farmer 155.

Blakeman William, (Harford Mills, Cort. Co.) r 14.

Bliss Bert, laborer.

Bliss Franklin, prop. grist-mill, and farmer 30, opp. depot.

Boice William J., (Harford Mills, Cort. Co.) farmer 30.

Boyce Charles, (Harford Mills, Cort. Co.) r 10, laborer, h and lot.

Brace Francis, resident, h Aurora, served in Co. D, 76th N. Y. Vols.

BRIGHAM BOSTWICK, r 27, farmer 130.

Brink Theodore, r 45 1-2, farmer.

Brookins George W., r 33, farmer 25.

Brumage John, (Speedsville, Tomp. Co.) r 44, farmer 4.

Brusie Granville, (Harford Mills, Cort. Co.) off r 14, farmer, leases of Allen Blakeman.

BUNCE HARVEY A., r 49, farmer with William A., 65.

Bunce William A., r 49, farmer with Harvey A., 65.

Chaffee Varnum, r 37 cor. 50, farmer 72.

Chambers Samuel, (Slaterville, Tomp. Co.) r 3, farmer 90.

Chapman Amos E., r 35, farmer.

Clark Birdsell, (Berkshire) r 47, farmer, leases of Abram Clark, of Owego, 180

Clark Charles A., postmaster, and farmer 188 1-2.

Clark Erastus W., r 19, farmer 8.

Clark George, off r 18, laborer.

Clark John D., laborer, h Aurora.

Cleveland Ezekiel, off r 10, farmer 140.

Cleveland Justus, r 42, farmer 110.

Colby Lewis I., r 41, farmer 144.

Cole John, (Berkshire) r 48, farmer 28.

Coney William, (Harford Mills, Cort. Co.) r 14, laborer.

Congdon Peter, r 39, farmer 122.

CONRAD CHARLES H., r 37, farmer 28.

Cooper Ephraim A., (Slaterville, Tomp. Co.) r 3, prop. saw-mill and farm 12.

Cortright Charles, r 42, laborer.

Cortright James, sawyer, h Main.

Cox Sarah, r 31 1-2.

Crain Marvin, (Harford Mills) r 9, laborer.

Crandall Ira, (Caroline, Tomp. Co.) r 23, farmer 15.

Culver John L., (Harford Mills, Cort. Co.) r 11, farmer, leases of A. Boyce of Harford 47.

FINCH CHARLES R., farmer, and breeder of Clydesdale horses.
FINCH CLARENCE W., (H. S. & C. W.) (W. C. Smith & Co.) h Main.
Finch Elam, emp. H. S. & C. W. Finch.
FINCH H. S. & C. W., (Hotchkiss S. and Clarence W.) props. steam saw-
    mill, and manufs. of lath, flooring, ceiling, etc., also woven wire mat-
    tress frames, corn knife, grass hook, and hay-knife handles, sythe boxes,
    extension table slides, bed slats, etc.
FINCH HOTCHKISS S., manuf. and dealer in soft and hard wood lumber,
    lath, posts and shingles, farmer 1,200, 12 houses and 20 vacant lots in
    Auburn.   Fish property, West ave. cor. King st., and with J. W. Allen,
    block cor. State, Perry and Mill sts., Rochester.
Finch Philander W., justice of the peace, and dealer in live stock and pro-
    duce, h Aurora.
Foote George M., farmer 50 in Candor, h Main.
Foster Brewster, r 35, farmer 60.
Foster Miles, r 42, farmer, leases of R. Holmes, of Newark, 74.

CURTIS CHARLES F., r 39, justice of the peace, breeder and dealer in horses, dairy 16 cows and farmer 200.

Curtis Loren H., r 39, resident.

Dalrymple Lydo H., (Harford Mills, Cort. Co.) farmer.

Dalrymple Samuel A. (Harford Mills, Cort. Co.) r 8, farmer 100.

Daniels H. & S. H., r 10 cor. 19, dairy 15 cows and farmers 180.

Daniels Heman, (H. & S. H.) r 10 cor. 19.

Daniels Samuel H., (H. & S. H.,) r 10 cor. 19, also civil engineer and surveyor.

Darlin Preston, (Slaterville, Tomp. Co.) r 3, farmer 4.

Davis Charles P., (Harford Mills) r 10, farmer, leases of Alfred Davis of Harford, 80.

Davis John M., r 33, teacher and farmer 188.

Decker Peter N., (Harford Mills, Cort. Co.) r 14, farmer 102.

Decker Rensselaer, (Harford Mills, Cort. Co.) r 13, farmer 40.

Decker Stephen, (Harford Mills, Cort. Co.) r 11, farmer 60.

Dennis Frank, r 16, farmer 50.

Dennis Franklin J., r 16, farmer 50.

Deuel Oliver, (Harford Mills) r 10, farmer 100.

Dimon John, (Harford, Cort. Co.) r 6, farmer 136.

Dodge Charles, r 35, farmer 73.

Donley David, cigar-maker, bds. Main.

Dow Dewitt C., (Slaterville, Tomp. Co.) r 3, farmer, leases of Mrs. Sumner, of Ithaca 230.

Dye Ansel M., r 17 cor. 11, blacksmith.

Dye Milton R., r 17 cor. 11, farmer 81.

Earsley Frederick L., r 26, farmer.

Earsley Richard, r 26, farmer 148.

Ellis Anson, r 17, laborer.

Ellis John, r 33, laborer.

Ellis Pison, r 31, farmer 34.

Ellis William, (Speedsville, Tomp. Co.) r 48, laborer.

Fellows Catherine A., (Caroline, Tomp.Co.) r 22, widow of Edward, farm 100.

Fellows Egbert M., (Harford Mills, Cort. Co.) r 8, farmer 131.

Fellows Gardner, (Harford Mills, Cort. Co.) r 21, farmer 116.

Fellows Lucius, (Harford Mills, Cort. Co.) r 9, farmer 120.

Fenner Alfred, r 18, laborer.

Fenner Arthur, (Harford Mills, Cort. Co.) r 15, laborer.

Freeland Eugene L., (Speedsville, Tomp. Co.) r 43, farmer, leases of S. Freeland 150.

Fries James M., (Harford Mills, Cort. Co.) r 14, farmer 25.

Friss Philip, r 35, farmer 50.

Fundis John, off r 30, dairy farmer 335.

Fundis John, Jr., off r 18, farmer, leases of John Fundis 54.

Gee Charles, farmer 25, h Main.

Gee Moses L., farmer 107, h Aurora.

Gee Noah, r 17, farmer 25.

Geer Calphernia, widow Henry, resident, h Main.

Geer George M., r 31 1-2, supervisor, and farmer 200.

Geer Ichabod H., r 31 1-2, resident.

Genung Edward, r 34, farmer, leases 80.

Genung Orrin L., r 45 1-2, wagon-maker and carpenter, also farmer 6.

Gilbert Milo, (Center Lisle, Broome Co.) r 51, farmer 58.

12

Gilbert William, (Center Lisle, Broome Co.) r 36, laborer.

Glezen Charles A., (Center Lisle, Broome Co.) r 35, farmer 246.

GOODRICH WILLIAM S., dealer in cattle, sheep, calves and swine, and farmer 167, h Main.

Gostley Peter, off r 17, farmer 30.

GRANGER EDMUND R., (Harford Mills, Cort. Co.) (Francis & Son) r 10.

GRANGER FRANCIS & SON (Harford Mills, Cort. Co.) (Edmund R.) r 10, prop. of saw and grist mill, and manuf. of yard-sticks, bee-hives, honey sections, shipping crates, potato crates, mouldings, brackets and novelty goods.

Gray Dennis, live stock and farm produce, also farmer 44, h Main.

Greaves Susan D., widow George, resident.

Griswold Lavina, (Harford Mills, Cort. Co.) r 14, widow William, farm 180.

Griswold William, (Harford Mills, Cort. Co.) r 14, laborer.

HALE SAMUEL B., r 37, farmer 60., served in Co. B 104th N. Y. Vols.

Hall Leonard, (Harford Mills, Cort. Co.) r 10, laborer.

Hamilton Alexander, r 33, farmer 20.

Hamilton Luther B., (Harford Mills, Cort. Co.) r 11, farmer 138.

Haynes Charles A., r 17, farmer.

Haynes Sylvester C., r 17, farmer 100.

Heath Ambrose B., r 40, farmer 37 1-2, leases of Nathaniel 28 1-2.

HEATH NATHANIEL, r 40, carpenter, and farmer 28 1-2, served in Co. H 146th N. Y. Vols.

Heath Seymour, r 40, resident.

Hefron Leroy, (Slaterville, Tomp. Co.) r 3, portable saw-mill.

Herrick Amos, r 37, farmer 80.

Hill Charles H., r 26, laborer.

Hill Ignatius, r 30, resident.

Hill Wilson I., r 30, farmer 93.

Hoaglin Edward, r 43, farmer.

HOAGLIN MARVIN A., r 43, dealer in organs and sewing machines, and farmer 42.

Holcomb Adelbert, r 35, farmer 50.

Holcomb Timothy M., r 35, farmer.

Hopkins Daniel H., house, sign and carriage painting and paper-hanging, kalsomining, etc., h Main.

Horton Bros., (Orlando and Stephen L.) r 46, farmers 140.

Horton Horace, section hand.

HOUK GEORGE, r 21, farmer 40, and leases of Lydia Houk 130.

Houk Lydia, r 21, widow Benjamin, farm 100.

HOWLAND HARRISON, (Center Lisle, Broome Co.) r 36, carpenter, and farmer 174.

Howland Wilber, (Center Lisle, Broome Co.)r 48, farmer 68.

HUBBARD LINDERMAN M., r 51, farmer 11 1-2.

Hulsander George, emp. H. S. & C. W. Finch, h Mill.

Hulslander Jacob, r 17, farmer, leases of M. L. Gee 107.

Hunt Daniel E., r 43, miller, and farmer 37.

Hutchinson Alzina, widow John, resident, h Railroad.

Hutchinson Edward, r 31 1-2, farmer, leases of George M. Geer 200.

Hutchinson Frank, resident, h Aurora.

Hutchinson Wesley J., carpenter, h Railroad.

Japhet George, r 35, laborer.

Jayne Amzi L., r 30,farmer 115.
Jayne Charles F., r 30, farmer.
Jayne Samuel A., r 30, farmer 150.
Jennings George, r 40, laborer.
Jennings Henry A.. r 35, breeder and dealer in horses, and farmer 170.
Jennings William H., off r 41, farmer 175.
Jewett Caroline, r 45, widow Richard, farm 96.
Jewett Charles F., (Berkshire) r 95, dairy 14 cows, farmer 125.
Jewett Lyman, r 45, farmer, leases of James Smith estate of Caroline 147.
Jewett Oliver, r 43, retired farmer.
Jewett Orrin, r 45, farmer, works for Caroline Jewett 96.
Johnson James B., r 40, farmer 100.
Johnson William, (Center Lisle, Broome Co.) r 36, farmer, leases of Gama-
    liel H. Tubbs 115.
Johnson William R., r 40, strawberry culturist, and farmer 50.
Jones Lucius A., farmer 16, h Main.
Jordan Franklin, (Berkshire) r 36, farmer.
Kent Isman, off r 18, farmer 10.
Keyes Thomas S., r 46, farmer 58.
King William W., (Harford Mills, Cort. Co.) r 10, carpenter, and farmer 30.
Krum Charles G., r 41 cor. 42, dairy 15 cows, farmer 240.
Lacey Charles, laborer, h Main.
Lacey George, r 42, laborer.
Lacey Louis V., telegraph operator.
Lacey Philip, laborer, h Main.
Lacey Rufus, laborer, h Railroad.
Lacy James, r 28 cor. 29, farmer 160.
Leach Daniel, r 44, farmer 45.
Leebody Henry, laborer, h Aurora.
Leebody Robert, r 40, laborer.
Leonard John B., 35, millwright, and farmer 25.
Lewis William, r 18, laborer.
Livermore Walton, sawyer, h Aurora.
Locke Benjamin, (Slaterville, Tomp. Co.) r 3, laborer.
Locke Henry D., (Slaterville, Tomp. Co.) farmer, leases of Mrs. S. A.
    White 250.
Marsh Aaron, r 46, dairy 12 cows, farmer 120.
Marsh Burr, (Center Lisle, Broome Co.) r 36, farmer 134.
Marsh Washington, r 35, farmer 70, served in Co. E., 76th N. Y. Vols., and
    Co. F., 1st Ver. Cavalry.
Marshall Charles, laborer.
Marshall Charles, r 31, blacksmith.
Marshall William, laborer, h Main.
Marshall Wilson, off r 18, farmer 13.
Matson Frank,(Harford, Cort.'Co.) r 7, farmer, works for Orrin Matson 90.
Matson Lucy A., (Caroline, Tomp. Co.) r 24, widow Isaac, farm 17, and
    with Seth Matson 200.
Matson Ormal, (Harford, Cort. Co.) r 7, laborer.
Matson Orrin, (Harford, Cort. Co.) r 7, farmer 90.
Matson Seth, (Caroline, Tomp. Co.) r 24, farmer with Lucy A. 200.
Mayo William W., r 46, farmer.
McIntyre John, (Harford Mills, Cort. Co.) r 19, farmer.

Meacham George W., r 37, farmer.

MEACHAM JAMES W., r 37, brick and plaster mason.

MEACHAM ORRIN N., r 37, carpenter, also mason, and farmer 32.

Meloy Charles T., r 33, farmer 50.

Meloy Frank P., r 33, lumberman, breeder and dealer in horses, and farmer 96½.

MILLER WILLIAM F., dealer in groceries and provision, and farm produce, Read & Co.'s fertilizers and champion mowers and reapers, and Perry spring tooth harrow, Main.

Mills George F., r 33, laborer.

Moore Charles H., justice of the peace and produce dealer, h Main, served in Co. G., 137, N. Y. Vols.

Moore Dana A., r 46, farmer 28.

Moore Emily A., r 46, widow Elijah, farm 112.

Moore Enoch N., r 33, laborer.

Moore Helen A., r 46, farm with Diadama Walker 71.

Moreland George D., general blacksmith, served in Co. G, 109th N. Y. Vols., h Main.

Morenus Chancey, r 33, farmer 100.

Morenus William H., r 33, farmer.

Morton Agnes, r 18, widow Spencer, resident.

Morton Edward, r 18, laborer.

Morton John, off r 10, farmer.

Morton Lewis, r 10, sawyer and farmer 20.

Morton William, r 10, mason, carpenter and farmer 18.

Myers Fred, (Harford Mills, Cort. Co.) r 11, lumberman and farmer.

Myres John S., (Harford Mills, Cort. Co.) r 11, farmer 53, served in Co. E, 157th N. Y. Vols.

Nash David, laborer, h Mill.

Neff Alexander, r 34, laborer, served in 109th Artillery, N. Y. Vols.

Neff Harrison, r 15, farmer 67.

Neff Jerome, r 34, farmer 60.

Newton Delay, r 31½, farmer 38.

Nigus Judson, (Harford, Cort. Co.) r 7, stone-mason.

Nixon Albert, r 31, laborer.

Norton Cyrus, (Caroline, Tomp. Co.) r 24, laborer.

O'Brien Dennis, farmer 50, h Main.

O'Brien James, r 26, farmer 130.

Ostrander Lorenzo, r 35, farmer 127.

Owens Levi, r 31 cor. 18, blacksmith, and farmer 20.

Owens Phineas, laborer.

Owens William, r 31, well-drilling.

Packard George, r 18, farmer 26.

Packard John, r 18, farmer 30.

Palmerton Fred H., r 49, laborer.

Palmerton George, r 37, farmer 40.

Parker William W., (Harford Mills) r 9, dairy 28 cows, farm 260.

Patch Edward H., (Berkshire) r 45½, farmer, works for Mrs. E. L. Patch, of Berkshire 222.

Perry Ebenezer, (Caroline, Tomp. Co.) r 5, farmer 20.

PERRY EDWIN A., r 43, steam-threshing and grist-mill, wagon maker, and farmer 110.

Perry Frank, r 44, music teacher, and farmer 25.

Perry Lewis, (Caroline, Tomp. Co.) r 5, laborer.
Perry Richard H., (Caroline, Tomp. Co.) r 51, resident.
Personius John J., (Slaterville, Tomp. Co.) r 3, farmer 8.
Phelan Patrick, section boss.
Phillips C. Martin, (Center Lisle, Broome Co.) r 48, farmer.
Phillips Franklin, (Center Lisle, Broome Co.) r 48, farmer 66.
Phillips W. Ardell, (Berkshire) r 47, leases of C. Arnold of Geneva 90.
Pierce Benjamin, (Harford, Cort Co.) r 6, dealer in charcoal, and farmer 60.
Pierce George H., (Harford, Cort. Co.) r 6, resident.
Pierce John, (Harford, Cort. Co.) r 21, laborer.
PIERCE WALLACE C., dealer in furniture and household goods, also un-
    dertaker and dealer in breech-loading shotguns and rifles, agent for
    the Ithaca breech-loading shotguns.
Polley Amos, r 31, farmer 275.
Polley Lemuel, r 31, farmer 68.
Polley Solomon, r 32, farmer 62.
Quail Fred, (Caroline, Tomp. Co.) r 4, laborer.
Rawley Daniel T., retired farmer.
Rawley George W., dentist and jeweler, Main.
Rawley Hiram B., general store.
Rice William, laborer, h Railroad.
RICH CHAUNCEY L., retired treasurer Southern Central R. R.
Rich Henry L., book-keeper, bds Main.
Rich Lucian D. station and express agent.
RICHFORD HOTEL, H. W. Theleman, prop.
Root Reuben, (Berkshire) r 46, farmer 43.
Robinson Asher, (Caroline, Tomp. Co.) farmer, leases of M. Robinson 90.
ROBINSON CALVIN J., att'y and counselor at law, notary public, and
    pension agent, h Main.
Robinson Fred J., telegraph operator, bds. Main.
Robinson Hiland, mechanic, h Main.
Robinson Isaac N., r 21, carpenter, and wagon repairer, also farmer 60.
Robinson James, telegraph operator, h Main.
Robinson Martin, r 42, farmer 290.
Rockefeller Egbert, (Harford Mills, Cort. Co.) r 11, farmer 135.
Rockefeller Henry, (Harford Mills, Cort. Co.) off r 14, farmer 30.
Rockefeller Jacob, (Caroline, Tomp. Co.) r 22.
Rockefeller John, (Caroline, Tomp. Co.) r 22, farmer 82.
Rockefeller Simeon W., (Harford Mills, Cort. Co.) r 12, farmer 100.
Rogers Mary Powell, resident, h Aurora.
Royce Dewitt, (Harford, Cort. Co.) r 5, farmer with Herman 63.
Royce Herman, (Harford, Cort. Co.) farmer with Dewitt 63.
Rusher William, (Harford, Cort. Co.) r 8, farmer, leases of Jane Sheldon, of
    Newark, 144.
Satterly Charles, r 17, farmer 5.
Satterly Ira, r 33, farmer 15.
Satterly Lyman J., r 17, farmer 18.
Satterly Willard, r 17, lumberman, and farmer 62.
Satterly William B., (Center Lisle, Broome Co.) r 36, farmer 41.
Sears Dioclesian, r 16, retired farmer.
Sears James M., r 16, stock breeder and dealer, and farmer 237.
Sexton Ransom, (Harford Mills, Cort. Co.) r 18, dairy 17 cows, farmer 160.
Sherwood Isaac, (Berkshire) r 47, dairy 15 cows, farmer 150.

Slater George, emp. H. S. & C. W. Finch, h Aurora.

Slater Joseph, r 16, farmer 22.

Slater Timothy, off r 18, farmer 15.

Smith Eliza, r 45, widow James, farm 147.

Smith Jerome, r 11, laborer.

Smith Julius C., millwright, and wagon-maker, h Aurora.

Smith Nicholas, (Harford Mills, Cort. Co.) r 14, farmer 80.

SMITH RALPH P., r 35, breeder and dealer in Clay and Hambletonian horses, dairy 30 cows, farmer 200.

Smith W. C. & Co., (H. S. and C. W. Finch) general store.

Smith William R., r 18, laborer.

STANLEY ANSON, (Center Lisle, Broome Co.) r 51, farmer 56.

Steele Andrew, (Caroline, Tomp. Co.) r 4, farmer 160.

Stephens Hector, teamster.

Stewart Lewis, r 31, laborer.

SWIFT CHARLES H., dealer in hardware, tinware, stoves and ranges, hanging lamps, Rogers Bros.' plated-ware, cutlery, alarm clocks. agate ware, churns and churn-powers, bird cages. horse-blankets, syrup cans, sap-buckets, tin-roofing, eave-troughs, tobacco and cigars, etc., Main, h Main.

Talbot Selah, r 11, farmer 32.

Talcott Horace B., r 17, farmer 25.

Talcott Jessie F., r 17, farmer 25.

Talcott Willard, r 17, farmer 27.

Tarbox Benjamin, r 10, farmer 40.

Theleman Frank, porter Richford Hotel.

THELEMAN HIRAM W., prop. Richford Hotel, and livery, also dealer in wagons, mowing-machines, horse-rakes, etc., and farmer 50.

Thomas Theodore F., r 42, farmer 6.

THOMPSON ALEXANDER, (Harford Mills, Cort. Co.) r 11, farmer 85½.

Thompson Benjamin, r 44, cooper, and farmer 2¼.

Thompson Charles, r 16, farmer 40.

Thompson Charles H., r 44, farmer.

Thompson William H., (Harford Mills, Cort. Co.) r 11, farmer 22, leases of Mrs. E. N. VanDyke 80.

Tobey Josiah G., (Caroline, Tomp. Co.) r 26, prop. saw-mill, and farmer 118.

Tryon Daniel, (Harford Mills, Cort. Co.) r 11, farmer 64.

Tubbs Elbert, r 49, laborer.

Tubbs Freedom U., r. 34, widow Robert, farmer 35.

TUBBS GAMALIEL C., (Center Lisle, Broome Co.) r 36, prop. steam saw-mill, dealer in lumber and farmer 300.

TUBBS GAMALIEL H., (Whitney's Point, Broome Co.) farmer 100 and at Whitney's Point steam saw-mill, and mnfr. and dealer in lumber, doors, blinds, sash, mouldings and butter packages.

Turk George H., r 32, farmer, leases of Amos Polley.

Tyler Edward, (Harford Mills, Cort. Co.) r 10, clergyman (Chris.) and farmer 10.

Tyler Laura, widow Ezra, resident, h Main.

Vandemark Samuel, r 17, farmer 72 1-2.

Van Gorder Charles H., r 49, farmer 25.

Vincent Delia, (Harford Mills, Cort. Co.) r 10, widow Peter, farmer 142.

Vincent Henry, (Harford Mills, Cort. Co.) farmer, leases of James Foster 52.

Vincent Henry G., (Harford Mills, Cort. Co.) r 10, farmer, leases of Delia Vincent 142.

Vunk J. Frank, carpenter, h Main.

Walker Albert, (Berkshire) r 45, farmer 86.

Walker Lyman M., r 43, farmer 130.

Walker Orrin, r 40, farmer 196.

WATKINS AMOS G., justice of the peace and dealer in horses, cattle, sheep and swine, also farmer 400, and with James L. Watson estate 195, h Main.

Watkins Eugene, (Harford, Cort. Co.) r 23, farmer 31.

Welch Luther H., (Caroline, Tomp. Co.) off r 23, farmer 84.

Welch Rufus H., (Caroline, Tomp. Co.) off r 23, carpenter and farmer 130.

Westcott Matthew, conductor Southern Central R. R., h Main.

Wheaton Mason S., (Harford, Cort. Co.) r. 29, farmer 67.

Wightman George W., r 43, farmer.

Wilbur James F., prop. grist mill at Harford and dealer in flour, meal and feed.

Wilcox Frederick, off r 18, laborer.

Wilcox Gardner, (Harford Mills, Cort. Co.) r 9, farmer 160.

Wilcox John, (Harford Mills, Cort. Co.) r 8 cor. 21, farmer 95.

Wilcox Justin, (Harford Mills, Cort. Co.) r 9, farmer.

Wilcox Smith, r 10, farmer 10, and leases of Ransom Sexton 160.

Williams Cyrel, (Harford Mills, Cortland Co.) r 12, farmer 52.

Williamson James, r 50, farmer 43.

Wilson Josiah, r 50, farmer 44.

Witter Daniel P., r 44, dairy 14 cows, farmer 143.

Woodard Edgar, r 10, laborer.

Woodard Elijah, r 10, laborer.

Woodard John, r 33, farmer 54.

Woodard John P., r 33, farmer 50.

Woods Elisha B., r 40, contractor and builder, and dealer in apples and all kinds of furs and hides.

YAPLE DELOSS, teaming, h Main.

YAPLE O. A., wife of Deloss, dealer in millinery and fancy goods Main.

Yaple Philip H., r 25 cor. 26, farmer 100.

Zee Franklin, r 33, farmer 28.

Zee Horner, r 50, farmer.

Zimmer Hiram, r 17, laborer.

SPENCER.

(For explanations, etc., see page 3, part second.)

(Postoffice address is Spencer, unless otherwise designated in parenthesis.)

Abbey Lizzie, millinery, Main, h do.

Abbott Andrew, (North Spencer) r 1, farmer 100.

Abbott Reuben, cartman, h Brooklyn.

Abbott Solomon, drug clerk, h Academy.

STARKEY & WINTERS, promptly fill Mail and Telephone Orders.

Ackerman Riley, farm laborer, h Main.
Ackerman Roscoe E., r 34, farmer, leases of Samuel Eastham 40.
Ackles Lewis, (North Spencer) r 22, laborer.
Ackles Truman, r 29, farmer.
Adams Frank W., (North Spencer) r 19, justice of the peace, and farmer 120.
Adams William, r 48, farmer.
Aldred Cynthia, widow Robert B., resident, h Park.
Allen Jerome, r 8, laborer.
Allen Olive, widow Joel, resident, bds. Main.
Ammerman Daniel, r 43, retired farmer.
Armstrong Dennison B., laborer, h Liberty.
Armstrong William H., emp. Seely's Mill, h Van Etten.
Bacorn Darius, r 27, farmer, leases of Dr. Davis 40.
Bailey Oliver P., r 48, farmer 50.
Baker Emily, widow Epaphras, resident, h Van Etten.
BAKER L. E., prop. Spencer Marble Works, h Academy.
Barber Adeline, off r 41, widow of Stockholm, farmer 50.
Barber Charles, r 61, laborer.
Barber Fred C., off r 41, farmer.
Bartley Larow, farmer, h Mill.
Bartrom John P., (Halsey Valley), r 54, farmer 50.
Batz Jacob, retired, h North ave.
Beadle Edward G., laborer, bds. Liberty.
Beadle George, resident, h Liberty.
Bell Alfred F., r 17, farmer.
Bellis Elizabeth Miss, laundress, h Academy.
Benedict William H., emp. Seely's Mill, h Liberty.
Benton Harry, r 13, farmer.
Benton James, r 14, farmer 103.
Benton William, r 13, farmer 10.
Berry Nathaniel, (North Spencer) r 19, farmer 8.
Besley Reuben D., emp. Seely's Mill, h Laurel.
Bidlack Ranson, r 54, farmer 177.
BINGHAM I. AUGUSTUS, r 10, farmer 250.
Bingham Seth H., r 10, farmer.
Blanch Maria, widow David, resident, h Brooklyn.
Bliven Charles, resident, h Main.
Bliven Luther, r 33, farmer 92.
Bliven Samuel G., retired, h Van Etten.
Boda Charles, r 11, farmer 150.
Boda Frederick C., breeder and dealer in horses and cattle, and farmer 50.
Boda George, r 10½, farmer 50.
Bogart John J., r 42, laborer.
Bogert Clarence, r 53, laborer.
Bogert Franklin, r 33, laborer.
Bogert Orlando W., r 33, laborer.
Bogert William W., r 49, farmer 50, and leases of Jane Williams 128.
Bosley Asa, r 27, dairy 30 cows, farmer, leases of Seymour Seeley 360.
Bowen James G., r 28, laborer.
Bower Brothers, (Philip and Levi) furniture and undertaking, Main.
Bower Philip A., (Bower Bros.) h Main.
Bower Levi, (Bower Bros.) bds. at Van Ettenville.
Bowen Samuel, r 24, laborer.
Bowen Seth, groceries, Academy, bds. do.

Bradley Calvin W., retired, h Main.
Bradley Charles E., merchant, Main, h do.
Brearley Arthur J., r 43, brickmaker.
Brearley Willie J., r 43, laborer.
Breese Frank, r 42, farmer, leases of L. Emmons 80.
Breese Fred P., r 43, emp. brickyard.
Brock Clinton, r 18, farmer 50.
Brock Estella, teacher, bds. Academy.
Brock Ethel, farmer, h Academy.
BROCK JOHN, r 42, dealer in cattle and breeder of sheep and lambs, also wool-buyer, and farmer 280.
Brock John A., r 34, farmer, leases of Ethel Brock 150.
Brooks Daniel, r 26, farmer 85.
Brooks Daniel C., agricultural implements, and farmer 145, h Maple ave.
BROOKS GEORGE, r 45, justice of the peace, and farmer 55.
Brooks Leonard, r 15, clerk.
Brooks Victor W., r 45, farmer 47.
Brown Frederick R., r 33, farmer 50 in Candor, and leases of J. Thompson, of Candor, 250.
Brown Lee A., r 43, laborer.
Brown William, r 18, cooper.
BRUNDAGE DeWITT C., carriage, wagon, and sleigh manuf., VanEtten, h. do.
Brundage Jay C., wagon-maker, bds. VanEtten.
Buckley Frank A., r 43, laborer.
Bunnell Charles, r 37, farmer 53.
Burchard Stephen, r 34, farmer 16.
Burdick Peter, r 42, stone mason.
Burhyte Andrew, r 43, farmer 147.
Burtless James, (North Spencer) r 2, basket-maker.
Buttles Morden U., (VanEttenville, Chemung Co.) r 43, farmer 75.
Butts Andrew P., retired tanner, h Main.
Butts Celestia, widow Hyatt, resident.
Butts Charles E., justice of the peace, and farmer 127, h Main.
Butts Charles E., Jr., carpenter, bds. Main.
Butts Fred G., farmer with his father Charles E., bds. Main.
Butts Harvey, laborer, bds. Main.
Canfield Edgar E., teamster, h VanEtten.
Canfield Fred U., miller, h Liberty.
Card Albert J., street commissioner, and farmer 52, h VanEtten.
CARD ALVIN D., r 43, farmer 94.
Card Charles B., r 43, cider-mill.
Carter Frank E., barber, Main, h Water.
Cashady Guy, meat-market, Main, h Brooklyn.
Cashady John, (Halsey Valley) r 54, farmer 133.
Cashman William H., r 37, farmer.
Cavanaugh Edwin, (North Spencer) r 21, farmer 50.
Chadrick Lewis, r 41, farmer 97.
Chapman Samuel, lumberman, h Main.
Chapman Willard E., (North Spencer) r 2, laborer.
Clapp John W., miller, h VanEtten.
Clapp Walker G., photographer, VanEtten, h do.
Clarey Dennis, emp. L. V. R. R., h Liberty.

Clark Howard, carpenter, h Brooklyn.

Clark John S., upholsterer, bds. Brooklyn.

Clark Lewis, r 34, blacksmith, and farmer 90, and leases of James Bishop, of Candor, 100.

Clark Samuel, (Halsey Valley) r 59.

Clark Shepard B., medical student, bds. Brooklyn.

Clark Sylvenus B., r 38, blacksmith and farmer, works for Lewis Clark 90.

Clark Theodore A., r 9, farmer 215.

Clark William A., (Halsey Valley) r 59, farmer 12.

Clay John, r 26, farmer 85.

Coggin George E., r 15, farmer 100.

COMPTON SILAS, (West Candor) r 37, general blacksmith and wagon-maker, horse-shoeing a specialty, served in Co. F, 76th N. Y. Vols.

Coney Frank G., emp. Seely's mill, h Liberty.

Coney Irving M., r 28, lumberman.

Congdon V. B., r 51, farmer 56.

Converse Lottie, r 41, widow Theodore, farmer 160.

Cook Almon, (North Spencer) r 1, resident.

Cook Anderson B., (North Spencer) station agent and telegraph operator, also machinist.

Cornell Charles S., r 43, grain threshing, and farmer 100.

Cortright Albert, r 48, farmer 8, and leases of A. S. Emmons 120.

Cortright Ayres D., (Halsey Valley) r 54, mason and farmer.

Cortright David, (Halsey Valley) r 54, farmer 16.

Cowell Alvah, (North Spencer) r 19, farmer.

Cowell Betsey, (North Spencer) r 1, widow Lewis, farm 45.

Cowell Charles, (North Spencer) r 1, farmer 150.

Cowell Edward, (North Spencer) r 19, farmer 150.

Cowell Eliza, (North Spencer) r 19, widow James, resident.

Cowell Eva S., teacher, bds. Maple ave.

Cowell Mariette, (North Spencer) r 1, widow John A., farm 19.

Cowell Mary A., widow John, resident, h Main.

Cowles Aaron, (North Spencer) r 1, farmer, leases of A. Abbott 100.

Cowles Almiron, (North Spencer) r 1, farmer 50, and leases of D. Randall of Etna 50.

Cowles Ebenezer, emp. Seely's Mill, h Liberty.

Cowles Jason, r 24, farmer 50.

Cowles John S., (North Spencer) r 2, farmer, leases of Almiron Cowles 50.

Cowles Marcus E., (North Spencer) r 2, lumberman, and farmer 127.

Cowles Mary L., (North Spencer) r 2, owns with Edgar D. Sabin of Candor 107.

Cowles Sylvester, (North Spencer) r 2, carpenter.

Crafts Calvin B., student, bds. Main.

Crane John, r 27, farmer 22.

Crum Peter, r 48, farmer 50.

Cummings Albert, r 40, lumberman and farmer, leases of Jerome Thompson of Candor 180.

Cummings Andrew, r 61, laborer.

Cummings Jacob W., r 42½, farmer 12.

Cummings Williams P., (Van Ettenville) r 43, musician and farmer.

Daughty Robert, laborer, bds. Liberty.

Davenport Arthur V., r 66, farmer.

Davenport John S., clerk, bds. Main.

DAVENPORT SHERMAN, r 66, farmer 50.

Davis Cornelius W., farmer, h Academy.

DAVIS GEORGE W., physician and surgeon, Main, h do.

Davis Isaac S., r 38, laborer.

DAVIS JEROME S., manuf. of all kinds mowing machine knives, and Buckeye hand cornplanters, also all kinds of machine job work, Cedar, bds. do.

Dawson Chester, r 32, farmer 173.

Dawson John, peddler, h Liberty.

Dawson Mary E., widow Myron, resident, bds. Main.

Dawson Nelson, retired, h Main.

Dawson Seth W., r 32, farmer, leases of Chester 173.

Dawson Sidney A., r 32, threshing, and farmer 65.

DAY CYRENUS N., general merchant, h North ave.

DAY JOHN & SON, (Cyrenus N.) hardware, stoves and tinware, groceries and provisions, boots and shoes, and agricultural implements, Main.

DAY JOHN, general merchant, h Maple.

Day William S., r 28, blacksmith, and farmer 78.

DEAN EDWARD E·, atty. at law, Main, h do.

Dean Mary, r 47, widow Casper, farm 16.

Dean Orrin F., farmer 54, h Main.

Decker Andrew, r 61, laborer.

Decker William, emp. Bower Bros., h at Van Ettenville.

Deming Augustus C., r 61, farmer 192.

Deming Joseph B., r 61, farmer.

Deming William H., r 63, stump-pulling and farmer 36.

Denniston Chester B., asst. station agt. G. I. & S. R. R. and telegraph opp. h Liberty.

De Remer Enos, (West Candor) r 36, carpenter.

De Remer Olan, (West Candor) r 36, farmer 75.

Devereaux Seymour, r 61, laborer.

Dewey Charles, r 11, farmer.

Deyo Chauncey, r 33, mason.

Deyo Harry, r 33, mason.

Dickens Robert E., emp. Seely's mill, h off Liberty.

Dikeman George, r 59, farmer 103.

Dodge Alvin, retired, h Myrtle.

Dodge Anthony, r 49, lumberman.

Dodge Sarah A., r 18, widow Edwin, saw-mill and farm 190.

Dorn Abram, r 32, farmer 60, and leases of Nelson Dawson 107.

Doty Asa T., r 26, farmer 109.

Douglass James, r 26, farmer, leases of Edward Cowell 100.

Downey Frank, laborer, h Academy.

Downey Robert L., sawyer, h Academy.

Drake Charles W., farmer 35, h Van Etten.

Dresser Jacob S., clerk for S. A. Seely, h Railroad ave.

Dumond Harry, watchmaker and jeweler Main, h Center.

Dutton James, r 45, laborer.

Eastham John, (West Candor) farmer 40.

Eastham Lucy A., (West Candor) r 39, widow of Edmund, farm 59.

Eastham Peter, farmer 50.

EASTHAM SAMUEL, (West Candor) r 37, prop. saw-mill and manf. and dealer in hemlock lumber, lath and wood, also shipper of baled hay and straw, and farmer 165, and works for Maggie Eastham 100.

Eastham Thomas, (West Candor) r 39, farmer 106.

Eastham Thomas J., farmer 80.

Eaton Harris, (North Spencer) r 22, farmer 2.

Edwards Clarissa, widow Philo, resident, h Liberty.

Edwards George, r 28, laborer.

Elbrooks Charles, clerk, bds. Main.

Elbrooks Elmore L., clerk, h Main.

Ellis Edwin R., lumberman, h Van Etten.

Embody Isaac, laborer, h Main.

Emery David, r 32, farmer 90.

Emery James C., r 13, prop. saw-mill and farmer 33.

EMMONS ALFRED S., general merchant and farmer 260, Van Et ten, h do.

EMMONS LUCIUS E., drugs, books and stationery, Main, h do.

English Minor W., (Van Ettenville, Chemung Co.) r 64, farmer 150.

Ennis Aldis F., farmer, h Academy.

Ennis Samuel, farmer, h Academy.

Esmay Claude H., drug clerk, bds. Main.

Eveland Samuel, r 53, laborer.

Fanning Andrew J., r 41, laborer.

FARMERS' AND MERCHANTS' BANK OF SPENCER, (Thomas Brock, pres't; O. P. Dimon, vice-pres't; M. D. Fisher, cashier; M. B. Ferris, ass't cashier, Main.

Farnsworth Edgar, farmer, h Main.

Farnsworth George, laborer, h Cedar.

Farnsworth James, r 45, farmer 26.

Farnsworth Marcellus, r 24, laborer.

Ferguson George N., shoemaker, Main, h do.

Ferris Andrew P., laborer, h Laurel.

Ferris S. Arthur, r 49, farmer.

Ferris Charles, (Halsey Valley) r 53, farmer 50.

Ferris Cornelia, widow George H., resident, h Main.

Ferris Cyrus B., r 49, farmer 82.

Ferris Daniel, (Halsey Valley) r 53, farmer 63.

Ferris David A., r 63, carpenter and farmer, works for Electa A. Ferris 30.

Ferris Edmund r 53, farmer 127.

Ferris Gabriel, off r 41, farmer.

FERRIS GEORGE C., (West Candor) r 35, apiarist 50 colonies, and far- mer 100.

Ferris James, off r 41, farmer 50.

Ferris John, r 40, farmer 90.

Ferris Harvey, r 53, farmer.

Ferris Louisa, widow Joshua H., resident, Main.

Ferris Moses, r 49, farmer 50.

Ferris Myron, (West Candor) r 36, laborer.

FERRIS MYRON B., ass't cashier Farmers' and Merchants' Bank, also fire and life insurance, h Main.

Ferris Willis C., r 57, farmer, leases of D. B. Hadorn 120.

Field Henry E., farmer, h Main.

Fields Noah, farmer 50, h Main.

FISHER BERT F., (Fisher Bros.) r 19, musician.

FISHER BROTHERS, (B. F. and S. J. F.) r 19, dairy 20 cows, farmers, lease of J. P. Fisher 190.

Fisher Charles, (Halsey Valley) r 59, farmer 25.

Fisher Charles A., r 28, farmer, leases of Harriet L. Fisher 80.
Fisher Charles J., drugs and medicines, Main, h do.
Fisher Clarence, (Halsey Valley) r 59, laborer.
Fisher Fred M., laborer, h Main.
Fisher Joseph T., r 17, farmer.
Fisher Leonard, farmer, h Liberty.
FISHER MARVIN D., postmaster, and general merchant, Main, h do.
Fisher Philip J., farmer, h Main.
Fisher Robert H., r 17, dairy 30 cows, farmer 375.
FISHER STEPHEN J., (Fisher Bros.) r 19.
Fisher Susan, widow Thomas, resident, h Main.
Fisher William H., physician and surgeon, Main, h do.
Fleming William H., farmer 280, h Academy.
Forsyth Augustus, r 33, laborer.
Forsyth Henry, r 37, farmer 77.
Forsyth Henry B., (Halsey Valley) r 59, farmer 60.
Forsyth Hettie, resident, bds. North ave.
Forsyth Nelson A., r 40, apiarist, and dealer in bee-keeper's supplies, also
    farmer 25.
Forsyth Perry, r 13, laborer.
Forsyth Rumsey, (Halsey Valley) r 59, farmer 50.
Forsyth Wallace, r 40, laborer.
Fox John, (North Spencer) r 2, leases of Bethaney Hill 50.
Frisbie Lucinda, widow Charles, resident, h Academy.
Fulton Frederic, r 66, farmer 50.
Fulton Maria, r 47, wife of Frederic, farm 45.
Furman Horace, (North Spencer) off r 19, farmer 80.
Gallagher Patrick, emp. Seeley's mill, h off Liberty.
Galpin George R., r 34, farmer.
Galpin James, r 34, farmer 60.
Galpin Orrin B., r 34, farmer.
Garatt Elmore, r 38, farmer with Harriet 218.
Garatt Harriet, r 38, widow Corinth, farmer with Elmore 218.
Garatt S. C., widow Amasa, milliner, Van Etten, h do.
Garey Abram L., wagon-maker, h Brooklyn.
Garey Daniel, (North Spencer) r 2, shoemaker.
Gay Patrick, (West Candor) r 37, farmer 150.
GEORGIA D. LAMONT, supt. Spencer creamery, h Liberty.
Georgia Mary M., widow Nathan S., resident, h Liberty.
Georgia William W., emp. Spencer creamery, h Liberty.
Gilbert Burdett, r 42, laborer.
Gilbert Norman A., barber, Brooklyn cor. Main, h Creek.
Giles Mary, r 41, farm 75.
Gilkie Riley, r 61, farmer 3.
GOEHNER LOUIS G., r 54, cigar manuf. and farmer.
Goodrich Austin L., foreman Seeley's mill, h Liberty.
Goodrich Calvin E., r 61, farmer 30.
Goodrich Calvin J., r 61, stone mason, h Myrtle.
Goodsell Rebecca A., widow Jared H., resident, bds. Liberty.
Green Anson, (North Spencer) r 2, farmer.
Green John B., resident, h Park.
Green Wheeler C., (Halsey Valley) r 54, farmer 105.
Greer Charlotte, r 61, farm 24.

Griffin James A., carpenter and builder, Park, h do.
Griffith Absalom, r 14, blacksmith and farmer 60.
Griffith Frederick D., clerk, h Center.
Grinnell Daniel P., r 13, laborer.
GROVE HOTEL, C. J. Rice, manager, opp. G. I. & S. depot.
GUINNIP DEMPSTER N., painter, paper-hanger, Brooklyn, h North ave.
GUINNIP GEORGE, painter and paper-hanger, Brooklyn, h North ave.
HAGADORN DAVID B., r 57, feed-mill, and farmer 193.
Hall Cornelia L., r 38 cor. 41, wife of H. S., farm in Ulysses, Tomp. Co. 95.
Hall Harvey Smith, r 38 cor. 41, manuf. and dealer in lumber and shingles, and farmer 600.
Hall Leonard F., r 38, wagon-maker.
Hallock Emily, widow John, resident, h Main.
Hallock William M., farmer 138, h Main.
Hanson Charles, tinsmith, h Main.
Harding Ella Mrs., resident, h Main.
Hart Morris, r 8, farmer 50.
Haskins Charles, laborer, h Brooklyn.
Hawkins Albert, r 49, farmer.
Hawley Edward, laborer, h Myrtle.
Hawley Edward, r 18, farmer.
Head Bradford, r 47, laborer.
Head Theron, r 47, tobacco-grower and farmer, leases of A. J. Card 21.
Hedges Frank L., emp. Seely's mill, h Academy.
Hedges Laton N., resident, h Aurora.
Hess John. (Halsey Valley) r 53, farmer, leases of Daniel Ferris 63.
Hevland William H., r 45, laborer.
Hiers Theodore, laborer, h Main.
Hike W. Harvey, mason, h Academy.
Hill Bethaney, (North Spencer) r 2, widow Luther, farm 50.
Hilligas Joshua, life insurance, h Tompkins ave.
Hinds James H., (Halsey Valley) r 54, laborer.
Hinds William H.,(Halsey Valley) r 54, farmer leases of Joshua Tompkins 110.
Holdridge Amos, r 41, with William A., farmer 217.
HOLDRIDGE WILLIAM A., r 41, apiarist, and with Amos farmer 217.
Hollister Warren L., (West Candor) off r 39, farmer 90.
Homiston Ezra W., physician and surgeon, Main, h do.
Hover Elisha, (West Candor) r 39, farmer.
House George W.,(North Spencer) r 1, farmer 107.
House John P., mason, h Academy.
House Lewis M., (North Spencer) r 22, farmer 175.
Howard Alvin, (West Candor) laborer.
Howard Henry, off r 66, laborer.
Howard Loring P. Rev., pastor M. E. church, h Van Etten.
Howell Charles, r 47, laborer.
Howell Frank C., book-keeper Bachelor's endowment association, h Main.
Howell Henry H., r 61, farmer 50.
Howell Ira M., farmer 45, h Van Etten.
Howell James K., r 47, farmer 5.
Howell John, r 47, farmer 27.
Howell Myron P., station agt. G. I. & S. R. R., h Park.
Howell Norman J., r 61, brickmaker.

Hubbell Ira, r 27, laborer.
Hugg Horace A., carpenter, h Liberty.
Hugg Luman H., r 28, farmer 119,
Hulburt Luther J., (North Spencer) r 20, farmer 130.
Hulet George, r 26, farmer.
Hull Eben, blacksmith, Cedar, h Main.
Hull James B., r 30 cor. 54, farmer 125.
Hull Loring W., farmer 100, h Main.
Hunt Isaiah, retired, h Main.
Hunt James O., off r 51, farmer, leases of Isaiah Hunt 87.
Hutchings Eli M., carpenter, h Laurel.
Hyatt William, farmer 14, h Main.
Johnson Allen, off r 66, laborer.
Johnston Chauncey, (North Spencer) r 2, farmer.
Johnston David, (North Spencer) r 2, farmer 140.
Johnston Ira, (North Spencer) r 2, farmer.
Joy Abel, off r 13, farmer.
Joy Alvah, r 10, farmer 50.
Joy Daniel, r 42½, tobacco grower, and farmer 70.
Joyce Joseph, resident, h Academy.
Kellogg Mahlon A., (North Spencer) postmaster, and general merchant.
Kelsey Charles, r 23, farmer 100.
Kelsey Lewis, off r 24, farmer 50.
Kelsey Walter, r 61, farmer.
Kelsh John G., laborer, h Brooklyn.
Ketcham Henry, r 33, laborer.
Keyes Nathan, r 23, resident.
King Duane C., clerk, h North ave.
Kinner Asa, emp. Seely's mill, h Van Etten.
Kirk Charles, (Halsey Valley) r 59, carpenter, and farmer 33.
Kirk Charles N., (Halsey Valley) r 59, blacksmith, and farmer 40.
Kirk Fred G., (Halsey Valley) r 59, farmer.
Kirk Henry P., (West Candor) off r 39, farmer 75.
Kirk Stephen, (Halsey Valley) r 59, farmer 64.
Knapp Elias, r 53, farmer, leases of Franklin Poole of Barton 75.
Knapp Isaac, (Halsey Valley) r 53, farmer 30.
Knupenburg Frank, r 28, laborer.
Knupenburg Myron, (North Spencer) r 2, laborer.
Lake Fred W., (North Spencer) r 2, farmer 99.
Lake George W., (North Spencer), r 19, farmer 150.
Lake Harvey, (North Spencer) r 19, farmer 10.
Lake Orlando, (North Spencer) r 19, farmer 15.
Lane Oscar, (West Candor) r 39, farmer 40.
Lang Charles F., blacksmith Brooklyn, h Maple.
Lange Frederick W., r 10½, farmer 175.
Lange Parker P., r 10½, farmer.
Lange William H., blacksmith and horse-shoer, h Water.
Larne James C., r 8, farmer 75.
Lawrence Ernest, butcher, h Van Etten.
Lawrence Sevellan F., off r 17, laborer.
Leonard John, r 31, farmer.
Leonard Michael, r 31, farmer 94.

Leonard Sarah J., teacher, bds. Main.
Leonard William J., butcher, h Main.
Lewis Benjamin F., r 28, farmer 300.
Lewis Fred, r 28, farmer.
Livermore Albert Rev., pastor Presbyterian Church, h Aurora.
Loomis Herman, r 56, farmer 80.
Lotz Hartman, (North Spencer) r 2, farmer 56.
Lyke Stanley, r 3, farmer.
Lott Benjamin, carpenter, h Laurel.
Lott Isaac M., clerk, h Water.
LOUSHAY ADELBERT E., fireman N. Y. L. E. & W. R. R., bds. Liberty.
Loushay Julia A., widow Henry, h Liberty.
Mabee Clarence, r 11, farmer.
Mabee Daniel, blacksmith Van Etten, h do.
Mabee Franklin H., (Halsey Valley) r 54, farmer 103.
Mabee John B., r 43, farmer 40.
Mabee Theodore, r 11, farmer 258.
Maine Ira L., r 42½, farmer 57.
Maine William F., painter and paper-hanger, h North ave.
Manning Frank D., (Halsey Valley) r 53, farmer 100.
Manning Robert, (Halsey Valley) r 53, farmer.
Manning William H., r 13, farmer 170.
Marsh William, r 61, laborer.
Martin Charles, laborer, h Main.
Martin Frank A., r 17, farmer, leases 105.
Martin Jane B., r 17, widow Ira, farm 85.
Martin Olive C., r 17, farm 50.
Matteson George E., dentist, Main, h Center.
McFall Dorus H., farmer, h Tompkins ave.
McKee George R., carpenter, h Van Etten.
McKoon Patrick, (West Candor) r 34, laborer.
McMaster James O., manf. and dealer in lumber, lath and wood, with
    Jeremiah T.
McMaster Jeremiah T., r 53, prop. saw-mill, dealer in lumber, lath and
    wood, also farmer 550.
McMaster Susan Mrs., bds. Van Etten.
Mead John, (North Spencer) r 2, farmer 50.
Mead Lewis, (North Spencer) r 2, laborer.
Messenger Chauncey P., emp. Seely's mill, h off Liberty.
Middaugh John, r 61, farmer.
Miller Edmund, emp. A. Seely, h Liberty.
Miller Sherman, laborer, h Main.
Mills Henry C., station agent E. C. & N. R. R., also National Express agent,
    h Brooklyn.
Montgomery George, expressman, bds. Academy.
Montgomery John, expressman, h Academy.
Montgomery William, shoemaker, Brooklyn, h Maple.
Moody Charles E., r 42, milk dealer, market gardener and farmer, leases of
    Charles Moody 95.
Morse Dana, peddler, h Van Etten.
Morse Mary M., resident, h Van Etten.
Mosher Stephen G., stationary engineer, h Park.
Mosher William G., emp. Seely's mill, h Liberty.

Mosier Bartley L., r 13, farmer 32.

Mowers Jacob Henry, (North Spencer) r 20½, prop. saw-mill, and farmer 60.

Nelson William B., emp. Seely's mill, h Academy.

Newman Daniel, mason, h Main.

Newman Henry, r 48, farmer 50.

Newman William H., r 48, cabinet-maker and farmer, leases of Henry Newman 50.

News Gabriel P., off r 41, farmer 97.

News Jane, resident, h Cedar.

Nichols Charles, porter Grove Hotel, bds. do.

Nichols David A., groceries and provisions, Main, h Liberty.

Nichols Jane, widow John A., resident, h Academy.

NORRIS ALONZO, M. D., physician and surgeon, also farm 550.

O'Connor Jerry, R. R. section foreman, h North ave.

Odell Marcellus C., billiards, pool-room and restaurant Main, h do.

Odell William H., r 40, farmer 83.

Osborn John, meat market, h Van Etten.

Osborn John C., r 43, carpenter.

Ostrander Jerome, retired, bds. Aurora.

Ostrander Mary J., widow William, h Aurora.

Owen Fidelia, widow Elijah, resident, h Liberty.

PALMER HEMAN L., (J. H. Palmer & Son), also telegraph opp. h Main.

PALMER J. H. & SON, (Heman L.) undertakers, Main.

PALMER JOHN H., (J. H. Palmer & Son) also farmer 45.

Parks Anthony, farm laborer, h Main.

Parlett Robert, Jr., bakery Academy, h Railroad.

Patrick Alva T., clerk, h Liberty.

Patty Jasper, r 66, farmer 105.

Pelan James, r 18, laborer.

Perrin Alexander, r 31, farmer 60.

Perrin Daniel, r 31, farmer.

Perrin William, r 13, blacksmith, and farmer 73.

Personius Ester, widow Jacob, housekeeper, Maple ave.

Personius Myron C., (North Spencer) off r 19, section hand, and farmer 50.

PERT ELLEN P., widow Rev. Luther B., resident, h Liberty.

Pierson George, carpenter and builder, h Academy.

Post Catherine, widow Thomas L., resident, h Main.

Post Thomas, r 3, farmer 280.

Post William, resident, h Van Etten.

Pritchard Pratt A., blacksmith, h Academy.

Puff Charles H., buyer for S. A. Seely, h Park.

Quick Elmer, (West Candor) r 37, farmer 50.

Radeline Sarah A., r 6, farmer 40.

RANSOM WILLIAM, r 41, farmer 124.

Raub Henry S., r 50, farmer 150, and in Tomp. Co., 18.

Raub Robert J., r 50, farmer.

Reeve Aaron D., carpenter, h Liberty.

RICE CHARLES J., manager Grove Hotel, bds. do.

Richardson & Campbell, r 43, contractors and builders, also manuf. of Spencer brick, residence in Ithaca.

Richardson Sherman, r 32, farmer, works for Milton Dawson estate 100.

Riker Captain L., r 34, carpenter, and farmer, works for Mrs. C. L. Riker 48.

Riker Charles F., r 38, farmer 50.

13

Riker Eugene, r 38, farmer, works for Anthony Riker estate.
Riker James L. Rev., (local M. E.) retired, h Main.
Riker Oliver P., r 38, farmer 50.
Riker William H., r 38, carpenter.
Ritchie George, r 24, farmer.
Ritter Charles W., emp. Seely's mill, bds. Academy.
Ritzler Charles C., r 48, photographer, and farmer 22.
Robinson Clarissa, widow Dana, resident, bds. North ave.
Robinson Fletcher O., carpenter and builder, h Maple ave.
Roe William W., r 38, carpenter.
Rogers Benjamin F., emp. Seely's mill, h Liberty.
Rogers John F., resident, h VanEtten.
Rolfe Leonard, r 40, farmer 50.
Rumsey Johnson, (Halsey Valley) r 58, farmer 73.
Rumsey Nelson, laborer, h Maple ave.
Ryant Daniel J., (North Spencer) r 20, blacksmith.
RYANT JAMES P., (North Spencer) r 20, with Ransom steam threshing,
    and farmer 100.
RYANT RANSOM, (North Spencer) r 20, with James P., steam threshing,
    and farmer 100.
Ryder Thena J., widow James, resident, h Laurel.
Sabin Otis L., r 42½, with William P., farmer 160.
Sabin Seth O., r 42½, blacksmith.
Sabin William P., r 42½, farmer with Otis L., 160.
Sager Cornelius, (Halsey Valley) off r 58, farmer 52.
Sager Douglass C., (Halsey Valley) off r 58, farmer 80.
Sager Willard J., jeweler, Main, h Creek.
Sammons Matthew, (West Candor) r 37, farmer.
Sandford James, traveling salesman, h Brooklyn.
Sawyer Carrie C., teacher, bds. Academy.
Sawyer Ezra O., contractor and builder, Academy, h do.
Sawyer Viola M., teacher, bds. Academy.
Sayles Charles E., (North Spencer) r 1, farmer 56.
Schutt Charles, (Halsey Valley) r 58, farmer 78.
Schutt Lemuel H., (Halsey Valley) r 58, farmer 25.
Scofield Albert L., r 32, farmer.
Scofield Horace, r 32, farmer 111.
SCOFIELD WALLACE L., r 15, farmer 115.
Seely David N., book-keeper for S. A. Seely, h Railroad ave.
SEELY FRANCIS S., miller, h Mill.
Seely Fred, emp. Seely's mill, h Mill.
Seely Myron, off r 45, farmer 70.
SEELY S. ALFRED, general merchant, saw and grist-mill, creamery,
    blacksmith shop, and farmer 140, h head of Academy.
Seely Seymour, farmer, h Mill.
Seely Seymour A., resident, bds. Maple ave.
SHAW GEORGE E., r 40, apiarist 70 swarms, and farmer 25.
Shaw Henry C., r 56, farmer 90.
Shaw Henry W., r 57, farmer 71.
Shaw John W., (West Candor) r 39, carpenter and farmer 54.
SHAW JOSEPH B., (West Candor) r 39, farmer 100, served in Co. G, 1st
    N. Y. Veteran Cavalry.
Shaw Silas H., r 40, farmer 60.

Shaw William, r 54, mason and farmer 87.
Shepard George T., r 28 cor. 30, live stock dealer and farmer with J. Q.
  Shepard.
Shepard Goodrich C., r 33, farmer 107.
Shepard Hattie F., teacher, bds. Liberty.
Shepard Heth H., r 43, laborer.
Shepard John Q., r 28 cor. 30, dealer in cattle and sheep, and farmer 255.
Shepard La Grange S., r 6, farmer 106.
Shepard Lewis A., clerk, bds. Main.
Shepard Myra A., widow Sylvester, resident, h Liberty.
SHEPARD SYLVENUS, general merchant, Van Etten, h do.
Signer Adonijah, (North Spencer) r 2, lumberman and farmer.
Signer Albert, (North Spencer) r 2, prop. saw-mill and farmer 519.
Signer Edward, r 28, farmer 4.
Silke Louisa, clerk, h Railroad ave.
SILKE JAMES, supt. Seely's mill, h Railroad.
Simms John C., (Van Ettenville, Chemung Co.) r 43, carpenter, farmer 50.
Simms William R., (Van Ettenville, Chemung Co.) farmer.
Sincepaugh William, farm laborer, h Main.
Sipley Sidney W., r 49, traveling salesman and farmer 50.
Skinner Oliver, farmer, h Main.
Smith Edmund, off r 47, farmer 140.
Smith Leroy, (North Spencer) r 22, farmer.
Smith Schuyler F., (Halsey Valley) r 59, farmer 40.
Smith William H., (North Spencer) r 1, leases of F. B. Clark 46.
Sniffin William A., general merchant, Main, h Liberty.
SNOOK DAVID L., apiarist 75 swarms, and harness-maker, Main, h do.
Snook Esther, widow Peter, resident, bds. Main.
Snyder Sely, r 40, farmer 130.
Southern Tier Bachelors' Endowment Association, (W. H. Fisher, M. D.,
  prest.; W. R. Swartout, secy.; M. P. Howell, treas.) Academy.
Spaulding Adelbert, r 47, laborer.
Spaulding Frances, r 43, wife of G. S., farm 100.
Spaulding John J., r 47, farmer 128.
Spaulding John P., r 47, laborer.
Spaulding John S., r 43, farmer, works 100.
Spaulding Maria, widow Joseph, resident, h Main.
Spaulding Phineas E., traveling salesman, h Liberty.
SPENCER CREAMERY, (S. A. Seely, prop., D. La M. Georgia, supt.)
  Liberty.
*SPENCER HERALD, (Van Gelder & Son, publishers) Main.
Spencer Hezekiah, r 65, farmer 55.
SPENCER MARBLE WORKS, L. E. Baker, prop., Academy.
Stage Eliab, clerk, bds. Main.
Stage Philip A., (North Spencer) r 21, farmer 92.
Stanclift Elizabeth, teacher, bds. Main.
Stanclift Isaac S., general merchant, Van Etten, h do.
Starkes Charles, laborer.
Stebbins Frederick, farm laborer, h Liberty.
STEENBURG ALBION L., r 13, with Francis E., prop. Spencer Springs
  farm 119.
Steenburg Asa H., r 13, farmer.

STEENBURG FRANCIS E., r 13, with Albion L., prop. Spencer Springs farm 119.

Stevens Charles N., (North Spencer) r 1, farmer 64.

Stevens David, r 11, farmer 75.

Stevens Harmon, r 13 cor. 10½, farmer 158.

Stevens Jacob, r 33, farmer 59, and in Candor 75.

Stevens John, (West Candor) r 36, laborer.

Stevens Seneca, r 65, carpenter and farmer 30.

Stevens Thomas J., (North Spencer) r 1, farmer 50.

Stevens William H.. r 41, basket-maker.

Stewart Ira, (North Spencer) r 20½, farmer 80.

Stilson Dianna, (West Candor) widow of James L., farm 37, and with N. T. Stilson 60.

Stilson James L., (West Candor) off r 39, farmer 97.

STILSON NELSON T., (West Candor) off r 39, farmer 100, and with Diana 60.

Stone Silas, (West Candor) r 37, farmer, leases of Patrick Gay 150.

Stow John M., turning and sawing, North ave., h do.

Strait David, r 37, laborer.

Stubbs William A., r 43, farmer 42, served in Co. C, 76th N. Y. Vols.

Sutton Charles A., emp. Seely's mill, h off Liberty.

Sutton William W., emp. Seely's mill, h Liberty.

Swartout James, (North Spencer) r 22, farmer.

Swartout Lewis, (North Spencer) r 22, farmer 28.

SWARTOUT MARCUS L., (M. L. Swartout & Son) h Ithaca.

SWARTOUT M. L. & SON, (William R.) produce dealers, Academy.

SWARTOUT WILLIAM R., (M. L. Swartout & Son) also secretary Southern Tier Bachelors Endowment Association, h Academy.

Tanner J. Henry, laborer, bds. Centre.

Tanner John H., physician and surgeon, h Centre.

Taylor Simeon, r 43, engineer.

Thornton Fred V., emp. Seely's mill, bds. Van Etten.

Thornton George, (West Candor) r 37, carpenter.

Thornton John J., emp. Seely's mill, h Van Etten.

Thornton Mary, (North Spencer) r 19, widow of Charles, resident.

Tollman Ansel B., r 27, farmer 20.

Tompkins James, r 37, farmer 217.

Tompkins James B., r 37, farmer, leases of James Tompkins 217.

TOMPKINS JOSHUA, farmer, h Tompkins ave.

Tucker William, r 42, farmer 53.

Tuckerman Hector, laborer.

Turk Charles M., resident, bds. Maple ave.

Turk Charles, blacksmith, h Myrtle.

Turk David, blacksmith, Academy, h Main.

Turk Stephen D., blacksmith and constable, Academy, h Main.

Tuttle Benjamin F., emp. Seely's mill, h Liberty.

Tyler George, r 51, farmer 56.

Tyler Henry E., r 59, farmer 101.

Tyler James, off r 66, laborer.

Valentine Adrian A., r 54, farmer.

Valentine Electa J., r 54, widow William, farm 104.

Valentine Elvin, (West Candor) r 35, farmer 30.

Valentine Fred, (West Candor) r 35, farmer 50.

Valentine Jacob E., r 54, teacher.
Vallentine William O., r 54, teacher.
Van Duyn William C., emp. Seely's Mill, h Liberty.
VAN GELDER & SON, (Phineas C. and Charles J.) publishers of Spencer *Herald*, Main.
VAN GELDER CHARLES J. (Van Gelder & Son) h Park.
VAN GELDER PHINEAS C., (Van Gelder & Son) h Park.
Van Gelder William, emp. A. Seely, h Railroad.
Van Gorder Lafayette, r 50, farmer 28.
Van Marter Aaron, resident, h North ave.
Van Marter Amos, r 41, apiarist 42 colonies, farmer 58, and leases of Silas Shaw 60.
Van Marter Enos T., (West Candor) r 35, dealer in groceries, and farmer 5.
VAN MARTER HOUSE, Jacob Van Kuren, prop., Main.
Van Marter Jared, (Halsey Valley) r 54, saw-mill.
Van Marter Nelson, (West Candor) farmer.
Van Natta Edwin, r 66, farmer 85, and leases of W. H. Fleming 275.
Van Natta Fred, r 47, carpenter, and farmer 111.
Van Natta John, r 52, farmer 107.
Vankleek Jesse B., r 63, carpenter, and farmer 16.
VAN KUREN BEN S., clerk Van Marter House, bds. do.
VAN KUREN JACOB, prop. Van Marter House, Main.
Van Natta John D., r 47, butcher.
Van Norman Cassius M., emp. Seely's mill, h Railroad.
Van Norton John, r 65, laborer.
Van Norton Warren, r 65, laborer.
Van Ostrand Peter, off r 47, farmer 30.
Van Ostrand Truman, off r 47, laborer.
VAN WOERT LEWIS J., r 7, assessor, and farmer 175.
Van Woert Maria E., r 13, wife of Samuel, farm 25.
VAN WOERT WILLIAM G., r 15, auctioneer, and farmer 65.
Vorhis A. Louisa, widow Rev. Stephen, resident, h Aurora.
Vorhis James W., mason, h Brooklyn.
Vorhis John W., retired, bds. North ave.
Vorhis J. Wallace, mason, h North ave.
Vorhis Mary H., teacher, bds. Aurora.
Vorhis Mead, cartman, h Main.
Vorhis Rebecca, (North Spencer) r 19, widow Jacob, farm 50.
Vorhis Truman, (North Spencer) r 19, manuf. washing machines, and farmer 43.
Vose Ephriam, r 38, carpenter and manuf. of lumber.
Vose George H., r 66, farmer, leases of George Pierson 95.
Vose Lavina, (West Candor) r 37, widow Alfred.
Vose O. Sumner, r 11, farmer 75.
Vose Othniel J., r 11, farmer.
Vose Samuel, r 10½, farmer 50.
Vose Sylvenus, r 15, farmer 85, and leases of E. S. Willet, 75.
Vose Sylvester S., r 6, farmer 82.
Wait George, r 13, farmer 104.
Waggett John, r 13, miner.
Walden Charles, r 17, laborer.
Warner William W., r 48, farmer 100.
Washburn Charles, (West Candor) r 36, laborer.

Watkins David, r 13, farmer 113.
WEEKS JOSHUA P., livery, Water, bds. Van Marter House.
Weeks Stephen M., r 41, farmer 100.
Weeks William W., r 38, carpenter.
Wells Josiah, blacksmith, Main, h do.
West Marshall C., contractor and builder, h Railroad.
Westbrook Arthur, carpenter, bds. Main.
Westervelt Leslie, r 65, farmer.
Wetzel Elmer, marble-cutter, bds. Academy.
Whalen Edmund, (West Candor) r 36, laborer.
Wheeler Frank E., emp. Spencer Creamery, bds. Liberty.
Wheeler Frank R., laborer, h Maple ave.
Wheeler Jesse, r 31, farmer 103.
Wheeler William C., r 31, farmer.
White George G., r 13, farmer 70.
White Squire, r 49, laborer.
Whitlock Ramer, r 42½, laborer.
Wild Joseph, laborer.
Willett Edward S., dealer in hides, and farmer 75, h Maple.
Williams Ziba, laborer, h Main.
Wilson Peter, r 41, laborer.
Winchell James N., (Halsey Valley) r 59, farmer 56.
Witherall Henry, r 47, farmer 40.
Wood William H., wagon and sleigh manuf., Brooklyn, h Maple.
Woodford Harriet, r 33, farmer 185.
Woodruff George, r 61, farmer 31.
Woodruff S. Delevan, r 28, farmer.
WOODRUFF THOMAS, r 28, farmer 80.

TIOGA.

(For explanations, etc., see page 3, part second.)

Ackley Nathan G., (Smithboro) prop. pool-room.
Ahart Albert, (Strait's Corners) r 6, farmer with his father George.
Ahart George, Strait's Corners) r 66, farmer 45.
Allen George, (Smithboro) r 58, farmer 50.
Anderson Ezra F., (Owego) r 12, farmer 125.
ANDERSON JAMES M., (Owego) r 10, farmer 200, and in Candor 100.
Anderson John J., (Owego) r 10, dentist.
Anderson Willis D., (Owego) r 12, farmer, works on shares for his brother
    James M. 74.
Andrus Peter J., (Smithboro) off r 61, farmer 77.
Armstrong James R., (Smithboro) r 73, resident.
Armstrong William, (Owego) r 12, farmer, works for his brother Fred 50.
Ayers Angelo, (Owego) r 12, farmer.

Badger Celia, (Owego) r 18, widow Lucius, farm 100.
Badger Luke, (Tioga Center) farmer.
Badger Noah, (Tioga Center) r 40, farmer 50.
Bailey Eugene, (Smithboro) trackman.
Bailey Lucy, (Smithboro) widow, resident.
Ballou Charles, (Owego) r 28, laborer.
Banfield Elmer, (Tioga Center) r 57, farm laborer.
Barber Ami W., (Halsey Valley) general merchant.
Barden A. E., (Smithboro) carpenter.
Barnes Charles E., (Owego) r 34. farmer 20, and in Pa. 80.
Bartron Alonzo, (Smithboro) r 58, farmer with his father Moses.
Bartron Moses, (Smithboro) r 58. farmer 75.
Bates William, (Halsey Valley) r 21, prop. blacksmith shop.
Bauer Adam, (Strait's Corners) r 5, farmer 100.
Bauer Christian, (Strait's Corners) r 17, farmer 130.
Bauer George W., (Strait's Corners) r 5, farmer.
Bauer Martin, (Strait's Corners) r 5, tanner.
BAUER MARTIN L., (Strait's Corners) (Ford & Bauer) r 5.
Bauer Simon, (Strait's Corners) r 5, farmer.
Beddell Mary G., (Smithboro) widow Bently F., farm 100.
Bedell Charles M., (Smithboro) r 40, farmer 50.
Bedell William H., (Smithboro) r 40, farmer 100.
Beilis William L., (Smithboro) station agt. Erie R. R.
Bennett Sabrina, (Tioga Center) r 51, widow Chester, resident.
Bentley Webster, (Halsey Valley) r 22, farmer.
Best Charles, (Tioga Center) r 36, farmer 60.
Best Jay, (Tioga Center) r 36, farmer.
Best Jay C., (Tioga Center) r 36, farmer 100.
Best William H., (Tioga Center) r 58, farmer 55.
Blake John, (Tioga Center) currier, h Main.
BLAKE WILLIAM, (Tioga Center) drugs and medicines, Main, h do.
Bogart Almon, (Owego) r 33. farmer 35, and works for Oliver P. Ford 60.
Bogart David R., (Halsey Valley) farmer.
BOGART EUGENE D., (Owego) r 14, farmer with his father Henry.
BOGART HENRY, (Owego) r 14, farmer 51.
Bogart Peter V., (Smithboro) r 66, farmer 150.
Bogart William, (Strait's Corners) r 3. farmer.
BONHAM CHARLES H., (Tioga Center) general merchant, Main, h do.
Bonham Morris, (Tioga Center) retired merchant, h Main.
Booth Ann E., (Owego) r 48, resident.
Bowman Ann, (Smithboro) r 73. widow Zebulon, resident.
Bowman Charles, (Smithboro) r 73, teamster.
Bowman Isaac, (Smithboro) resident.
Bowman John A., (Smithboro) rector of Emanuel Church.
Bradley Andrew, (Smithboro) farm laborer.
Bradley Edward (Tioga Center) farm laborer.
Bradley Mariette Miss, (Smithboro) resident.
Brearley John W., (Tioga Center) r 57, farmer 100.
Briggs David, (Smithboro) r 69, farmer, works for George Eckert 60.
Brink Amos, (Owego) r 25, farmer.
Brink Edward, (Tioga Center) r 43, laborer.
Brink Frederick, (Strait's Corners) r 19, farm laborer.

Brink George, (Halsey Valley) r 37, farmer 20.
Brink Joseph, (Owego) r 33, farmer 90.
Brink William, (Tioga Center) laborer.
Brooks Benjamin J., (Tioga Center) r 52, farmer.
Brooks Charles, (Tioga Center) off r 40, farmer 50.
Brooks Cornelius, (Tioga Center) r 43, farmer 40.
Brooks Frank, (Smithboro) off r 58, farmer for his father William.
Brooks George H., (Tioga Center) r 52, farm laborer.
Brooks Lot M., (Tioga Center) r 51, bridge carpenter.
Brooks Nicholas, (Tioga Center) r 36, farmer 100.
Brooks William, (Tioga Center) farmer 100.
Brown Alvah S., (Halsey Valley) shoemaker.
Brown David L., (Tioga Center) drug clerk, bds. Main.
Brown John B., (Owego) r 44, farmer 48.
Brown William H., (Tioga Center) r 19, farmer, works for C. D. Hoff 76.
Brundage Matthias, (Owego) off r 6, farmer 35.
Buchanan James H., (Halsey Valley) farmer 58.
Burlington Ephraim, (Owego) r 30, farmer 61.
Burlington Hugh W., (Owego) r 30, farmer 100.
BURLINGTON JOHN A., (Owego) r 8, farmer 125.
Burlington Joseph, (Owego) r 8, farmer 58.
Burnham Elizabeth Mrs., (Smithboro) resident.
Burns Robert, (Owego) r 31, farmer 60.
Burns Willie J., (Owego) r 31, farmer for his father Robert.
Butler William, (Tioga Center) trackman.
Cable Silas, (Owego) r 32, farmer, works for Mrs. John Taylor 100.
Campbell Alexander, (Owego) r 48, laborer.
Campbell Bert, (Owego) r 28, farmer.
Campbell Fred, (Halsey Valley) r 21, farmer for L. B. West.
Campbell Jacob, (Halsey Valley) r 21, farmer for L. B. West.
Campbell Orlando, (Owego) off r 12, farmer.
Canfield Alfred, (Smithboro) r 71, farmer, works for his father Amos 160.
Canfield Amos, (Smithboro) r 71. farmer 170.
Caple John, (Owego) r 7, farmer 50.
CAPLE PHILIP, (Catatonk) r 7, farmer 100.
Carlisle William, (Tioga Center) r 22, laborer.
Carmer Amasa, (Halsey Valley) off r 2, farmer 140.
Carns John A., (Owego) r 12, farm laborer.
Carpenter Charles E., (Smithboro) r 60, farmer with his father Peter R.
Carpenter Jesse C., (Tioga Center) r 53, farmer 200.
Carpenter Peter R., (Smithboro) r 60, farmer 75.
Casterline Stephen B., (Tioga Center) r 40, farmer 54.
Casterline Warren, (Smithboro) r 60, farmer 50.
Catlin Andrew R., (Tioga Center) off r 40, farmer, works for George Truman 150.
Catlin Benjamin F., (Owego) r 25, farmer 110.
Catlin Charles, (Owego) r 18, farmer 123.
Catlin Edmund S., (Tioga Center) r 43, carpenter, and farmer 51.
Catlin Emeline, (Owego) r 32, widow Jonathan, farmer 42.
CATLIN FRANK H., (Owego) r 45, produce dealer, and farmer.
Catlin Frederick H., r 33, farmer 42.
Catlin George, (Tioga Center) r 52, wagon-maker.
Catlin Jacob, (Tioga Center) r 43, farmer 55.

CATLIN JAMES H., (Tioga Center) r 43, physician, and farmer 50.
Catlin Laverne, (Owego) r 33, farm laborer.
Catlin Mary J., (Owego) r 33, widow Nathaniel, farmer 27.
Catlin Mead, (Owego) r 47, emp. foundry.
Catlin Nathan S., (Tioga Center) r 56, farmer 80.
CATLIN NATHANIEL, (Owego) r 33, farmer 38.
Catlin Sarah E. Mrs., (Owego) r 34, farm 20.
Catlin William, (Owego) r 44, farm laborer.
Catlin Willis E., (Owego) r 25, farmer with his father Benjamin F.
Chamberlain Oscar C., (Owego) r 12, farmer.
Chandler Horace, (Owego) r 12, laborer.
Chew Clark, (Owego) r 11, farmer.
Chew Guy, (Owego) r 11, farmer 167.
Clune James, (Smithboro) r 61, farmer 50.
Coburn & Van Norstran, (Tioga Center) (C. S. B. & G. Van N.) r 51, tin and
    iron roofing, and manuf. eve spouting.
Coburn C. Sidney,(Tioga Center) (Coburn & Van Norstran) r 51. also tin shop.
Coburn Eliza, (Tioga Center) r 51,widow Charles R., resident.
Coffin Milton, (Owego) r 45, farmer.
Cole Alfred, (Owego) r 31, farmer, leases of James Taylor 30.
COLE AUSTIN R., (Smithboro) r 73, farmer 50.
Cole Benjamin F., (Smithboro) r 71, farmer.
Cole Daniel H., (Tioga Center) r 51, retired farmer.
Cole Frank, (Smithboro) off r 58, farmer 100.
Cole Frank, (Smithboro) r 40, farm laborer.
Cole Horace, (Owego) r 48, farmer.
COLE SAMUEL E., (Smithboro) r 73, farmer 50.
Cole William, (Halsey Valley) r 22, farmer.
Coleman Isaac, (Tioga Center) r 52, bridge carpenter.
Coleman Jackson, (Halsey Valley) r 22, farmer 116.
Coleman James, (Tioga Center) r 52, carpenter.
Coleman John P., (Tioga Center) r 41, farmer 180.
Coleman William D., (Tioga Center) r 52, carpenter.
Congdon Harry,(Tioga Center) r 36, farmer, leases of Mrs. Mary Munnohan 12.
Conklin Elizabeth, (Owego) r 30, widow John, resident.
Conklin Sylvenas, (Owego) r 18, farmer, works on shares for Alexander
    Duncan 110.
Conway John, (Smithboro) r 55, farmer 50.
Cook DeWitt C., (Halsey Valley) r 2, farmer 53.
Cook Esther, (Strait's Corners) r 20, widow Samuel, farmer 100.
Cook Florence, (Strait's Corners) r 20, farmer for his mother Esther.
Coon Walter, (Strait's Corners) r 18, farmer 104.
Coons Arthur, (Tioga Center) r 22, farmer with his father Johnson.
Coons Daniel, (Strait's Corners) r 4, farmer 100.
Coons George B., (Tioga Center) r 58, farmer, works for Mrs. Perry Ward 75.
Coons Hiram, (Strait's Corners) r 4, farmer.
Coons John, (Tioga Center) r 22, farmer with his father Johnson.
Coons Johnson, (Tioga Center) r 22, farmer 200.
Coons Lemuel, (Tioga Center) r 22, farmer 50.
Cooper Frank A., (Halsey Valley) r 2, farmer 50.
Corsin William, (Owego) r 47, farm laborer.
Cortright Alfred, (Tioga Center) r 43, laborer.
Cortright Charles, (Tioga Center) farm laborer.

Cortright James, (Tioga Center) farm laborer.
Cortright John, (Tioga Center) farm laborer.
Cortright Richard, (Tioga Center) farm laborer.
Crandall Benjamin, (Tioga Center) off r 40 farmer 50.
Crandall Daniel, (Smithboro) r 66, farmer, works for Mrs. M. Richards 117.
Crawford Absalom, (Smithboro) laborer.
Crawford Abram, (Tioga Center) r 40, farmer 95.
Croft Michael, (Smithboro) trackman.
Crum Henry, (Owego) r 28, resident.
Cunningham Daniel, (Owego) r 32, farmer 33.
Curkendoll Cornelius, (Smithboro) prop. Erie Hotel.
Curkendoll Prudence Mrs., (Smithboro) resident.
DAILY DANIEL, (Barton) r 64, farmer 380.
DAILY EUGENE E., (Barton) r 64, farmer 150.
DAILY FRED C., (Barton) r 64, dealer in agricultural implements, wag-
    ons, etc., and farmer 75.
Davenport Adelbert, (Halsey Valley) r 39, farmer 50.
Davenport Alvin M., (Smithboro) r 71, works on shares for Henry Light 73.
Davenport Emmet J., (Smithboro) r 71, farmer with his father Alvin M.
Davenport George, (Smithboro) r 71, section-hand.
Davenport Henry, (Strait's Corners) r 4, farmer 70.
Davenport Jackson, (Smithboro) r 59, farmer 50.
Davenport Judson, (Barton) r 64, farmer, works for James J. Green 73.
Davis Albert J., (Tioga Center) r 40, farmer 82.
Davis Nathaniel W., (Owego) r 45, farmer 117.
DAY GEORGE H., (Owego) r 12, farmer, works for Herbert Farnham 65.
Day Marvin G., (Owego) r 29, farmer.
Dean Franklin S., (Smithboro) resident.
Decker Alexander D., (Tioga Center) Methodist minister, h Main.
DeCaytor Ralph, (Owego) r 16, farm laborer.
DeHart Sanda, (Tioga Center) laborer, h Main.
DeHart Thomas, (Owego) r 45, laborer.
Delano Charles, (Owego) r 28, mason.
Delano Sarah, (Owego) r 28, widow Reuben, resident.
Densmore Samuel, (Owego) r 26, farmer, works on shares for A. J. Good-
    rich 240.
Deyo Charles, (Tioga Center) r 53, farmer, works for Joseph DuBois 220.
Deyo Chauncey (Owego) r 47, farmer.
Deyo Elijah W., (Tioga Center) r 41, miller.
Dinehart John, (Tioga Center) r 41, farm laborer.
Dinehart Robert, (Smithboro) farm laborer.
Doane Jane Mrs., (Smithboro) resident.
Doane Leroy, (Smithboro) laborer.
Doane Timothy, (Strait's Corners) r 3, prop. saw-mill and farmer.
Doane William H., (Smithboro) r 59, farmer 50.
Dorn David, (Halsey Valley) r 20, farmer 160.
Dorn Willis, (Halsey Valley) r 20, farmer for his father David.
Dorwin Asa F., (Owego) r 46, farmer.
DORWIN WILLIAM E., (Owego) (Dorwin, Rich & Stone) r 46, also rail-
    road contractor and farmer 235.
DRAKE C. SIDNEY, (Smithboro) (W. J. Drake & Son) h Main.
Drake Ezra P., (Halsey Valley) r 39, farmer 100.
Drake George P., (Smithboro) tinsmith.

DRAKE WILLIAM J., (Smithboro) (W. J. Drake & Son) postmaster, h Main.

DRAKE W. J. & SON, (Smithboro) (C. S. Drake) general merchants, hardware and tinshop and dealers in agt. imp., coal, lime, plaster and cement, Main.

DuBois John E., (Tioga Center) lumberman, h in DuBois, Pa.

DuBois Lucy, (Tioga Center) resident, h Main.

DuBois William, (Tioga Center) r 53, farmer, works for Charles Poole 234.

Duff Alexander, (Strait's Corners) r 19, farmer 150.

Duff Andrew, (Strait's Corners) r 19, farmer.

Duff Harry, (Strait's Corners) r 19, farmer with his father Alexander.

Duff James, (Owego) r 25, farmer 90.

Duff Millie, (Tioga Center) r 36, widow Moses, resident.

Duff Robert H., (Tioga Center) r 36, farmer 206.

Duff Thomas, (Strait's Corners) r 2, farmer 75.

DUNCAN ALEXANDER, (Owego) r 29, farmer 150.

Duncan James, (Owego) r 30, farmer 30.

Earll David, (Tioga Center) r 49, retired physician and farmer 28.

Easton Frances M., (Catatonk) r 9, resident.

EATON AMBROSE P., lawyer, office at Waverly.

Eaton Daniel B., (Smithboro) cooper.

Eckert George F., (Smithboro) r 71, manf. eave-spouts.

Eckert Maria J., (Smithboro) r 71, widow Alexander B., resident.

Edwards Christopher, (Halsey Valley) laborer.

Edwards Samuel, (Owego) r 9, meat and grocery peddler.

Ehle George, (Strait's Corners) r 3, laborer.

Elliot Sarah A., (Smithboro) widow, resident.

EVELIEN ALFRED, (Tioga Center) hay and potato dealer, and farmer in Candor 97, h Main.

Evelien Christopher, (Tioga Center) farmer 100.

Evlin John, (Strait's Corners) r 3, farmer.

Emerson Charles, (Strait's Corners) r 4, farmer 160, and in Candor 40.

Emerson David B.,(Strait's Corners) r 24, farmer 96.

Emerson Frank, (Strait's Corners) r 4, farmer 108.

Emerson George, (Strait's Corners) off r 34, farmer 50.

Emerson Lot S., (Strait's Corners) r 5, farmer for his father William.

Emerson Luther, (Halsey Valley) r 37, farmer.

Emerson Mary, (Owego) r 18, widow Jonathan, resident.

Emerson Robert H., (Strait's Corners) r 4, farmer.

EMERSON SAMUEL H., (Owego) r 24, farmer 200.

Emerson Walter, (Strait's Corners) r 4, farmer.

Emerson William, (Strait's Corners) r 5, farmer 70.

Erie Hotel, (Smithboro) Cornelius Curkendoll, prop.

Estep Jacob, (Tioga Center) r 58, farmer 45.

Estep Loren, (Tioga Center) r 51, blacksmith and wagon-maker, h do.

FARNHAM AGNES L., (Owego) off r 12, widow Frederick A., resident.

FARNHAM ENOS S., (Owego) r 13, commercial traveler and farmer 80.

FARNHAM GEORGE A., (Owego) r 12, farmer 65.

FARNHAM HERBERT A., (Owego) off r 12, wool-carding, wood-turning, cider-mill and farmer 250.

FARNHAM JOEL S., (Owego) off r 12, farmer 40.

Farnham Orin, (Smithboro) blacksmith.

Farnham Roland B., (Owego) r 12, farmer with his father George A.

Farnham Sylvester J., (Owego) off r 12, farmer 7.
Fassett Alonzo, (Tioga Center) r 22, farmer 25.
Fenderson Althier, (Tioga Center) r 41, widow Isaiah, resident.
Fenderson Ely, (Tioga Center) r 41, carpenter.
Finch Herbert, (Owego) r 48, farm laborer.
Finn William H., (Owego) r 8, sup't Campbell farm 230.
Finnegan Barney, (Owego) r 27, farmer 30.
Fisher Frank, (Strait's Corners) r 5, laborer.
FOOTE JARED A., (Owego) r 13, farmer 13.
Foote Jared H., (Owego) r 28, traveling salesman.
Foote Lyman C., (Owego) r 28, farmer 12.
FORD & BAUER, (Strait's Corners) (L. F. and M. L. B.) r 5, contractors
    and builders.
Ford Lucius, (Strait's Corners) (Ford & Bauer,) r 5.
Ford Zera T., (Tioga Center) r 52, farm laborer.
Forsyth W. Henry, (Halsey Valley) r 21, cooper.
Franklin Burton B., (Tioga Center) r 52, prop. grist-mill.
Franklin Ransom J., (Tioga Center) r 52, miller.
French Jeremiah, (Tioga Center) shoemaker, and farmer 13.
Fox Henry, (Owego) r 47, carpenter.
Frister Noah, (Smithboro) r 70, farmer.
Garber John, (Tioga Center) r 40, resident.
Gardner Frederick, (Tioga Center) nurseryman, h Main.
Gasier William H., (Tioga Center) r 19, laborer.
Gavin Michael, (Tioga Center) trackman.
Geer Rezin J., (Strait's Corners) r 19, farmer 83.
Genung Adam S., (Smithboro) wagon-maker.
Gile Adelbert, (Tioga Center) r 24, farm laborer.
Gile George, (Tioga Center) r 24, farmer for his father Leonard.
Gile Joseph, (Halsey Valley) r 39, farmer for his father William W.
Gile Leonard, (Tioga Center) r 24, farmer 63.
Gile Samuel, (Tioga Center) r 23, farmer 25.
Gile William W., (Halsey Valley) r 39, farmer 100.
Gile Willis, (Tioga Center) r 24, farm laborer.
Giles Cyrus, (Halsey Valley) r 22, farmer.
Giles Daniel, (Strait's Corners) r 3, farmer.
Giles George, (Tioga Center) r 22, laborer.
Giles George, (Strait's Corners) r 3, invalid.
Giles Rufus, (Strait's Corners) r 3, laborer.
Giles Rufus D., (Strait's Corners) r 3, farmer 60.
Giles Sophia Mrs., (Smithboro) resident.
Giles Waterman, (Halsey Valley) r 22, farmer 100.
Gilkey Martha M., (Halsey Valley) r 1, widow Peter P., farm 60.
Gilkey Samuel G., (Halsey Valley) off r 2, farmer 102.
Gillson Nathan S., (Owego) r 34, farmer 38.
Giltner William, (Barton) r 63, farmer 100.
GOODENOUGH CHANCEY J., (Tioga Center) shoe-shop, and grape
    grower, Main, h do.
GOODRICH ANDREW J., (Owego) r 48, farmer 1,150.
GOODRICH CHARLES P., (Owego) r 12, farmer 44.
Goodrich Charles T., (Owego) r 48, farmer 100.
GOODRICH EPHRAIM, r 48, farmer 160.
Goodrich George L., (Owego) r 45, farmer 170.

GOODRICH HIRAM E., (Owego) r 47, farmer 85.

Goodrich Jairus T., (Owego) r 45, farmer 27.

Goodrich Louisa, (Owego) r 45, resident.

GOODRICH NOAH, (Owego) r 48, justice of the peace, and farmer 25.

Goodrich Sarah, (Owego) r 48, widow Herman, resident.

Goodrich Sarah, (Owego) r 46, farm 12.

GOODRICH STEPHEN S., (Owego) r 46, apiarist 15 swarms, poultry raiser, and farmer 60.

Goodwin William H., (Halsey Valley) r 1, farmer.

Gould Charles, (Halsey Valley) r 21, farm laborer.

Gould William, (Halsey Valley) r 39, farmer 50.

Green James J., (Barton) r 64, farmer 73.

Green James L., (Halsey Valley) r 39, farmer 50.

Groat Ira, (Owego) r 25, farmer 70.

Gulden Henry J., (Owego) r 30, works for A. J. Goodrich 230.

Gulden John, (Owego) r 31, farmer.

Guyles Charles P., (Strait's Corners) r 32, farmer, works for James Taylor 50.

Haddock Andrew J., (Tioga Center) r 41, farmer 96.

Haddock Lamont, (Tioga Center) r 41, farmer with his father Andrew J.

Halsey Valley House, (Halsey Valley) Mrs. Jane P. Higgins, prop.

Hamilton Charles, (Tioga Center) r 22, carpenter.

Hamilton George, (Halsey Valley) harness-maker.

Hamilton Henry, (Halsey Valley) teamster.

Hamilton Sarah Miss, (Smithboro) school teacher.

Hamilton Thomas A., (Halsey Valley), farmer.

Hanbury Adam, Jr., (Owego) r 6, farmer 105.

Hanbury Ezra, (Strait's Corners) r 17, farmer 58.

Hanmer George W., (Catatonk) r 9, telegrah operator.

Hanna John, (Smithboro) trackman.

Harding Adna, (Owego) r 13, farm laborer.

Harding Alonzo, (Owego) r 9, farm laborer.

Hardman John, (Owego) r 47, retired tanner.

Hardman John, (Owego) r 16, farm laborer.

Hardman John F., (Owego) r 47, drug clerk.

Hardman Patrick, (Owego) r 16, farmer 100.

Hardy Lizzie, (Smithboro) r 68, widow John, farmer 60.

Harford Edward, (Smithboro) r 54, farmer 70.

Harlin Lott, (Strait's Corners) r 4, farmer.

Harlin William, (Strait's Corners) r 4, farmer 120.

Heath Rebecca, (Halsey Valley) widow.

Hermberger Adam, (Strait's Corners) r 5, farmer 42.

Hess William, (Strait's Corners) r 3, laborer.

Hevland Douglass (Owego) r 28, cooper.

Higbee Augusta, (Tioga Center) r 51, widow Forman S., resident.

Higby James, (Tioga Center) laborer.

Higgins Jane P. Mrs., (Halsey Valley) prop. Halsey Valley House.

HILL ABNER G., (Tioga Center) r 51, justice of the peace and sawyer.

Hill Ward, (Smithboro) r 71, trackman.

Hoaglin Peter, (Owego) r 45 laborer.

Hobler Peter, (Owego) r 18, farmer 50.

Hodge Adelia, (Owego) r 29, widow Andrew C., resident.

Hoff Cornelius, (Strait's Corners) r 19, farmer 75.

Hoff Hiram, (Tioga Center) r 19, farmer 100.

HOLLENBECK CHARLES E., (Halsey Valley) r 21, physician and surgeon, and farmer 90.
Hollister William H., (Halsey Valley) r 22, farmer 95.
Holloway John, (Tioga Center) r 52, farm laborer.
Holmes John C., (Tioga Center) r 36, farmer 23.
Holt C. Edgar, (Tioga Center) r 52, farmer 96.
Holt William, (Smithboro) r 73, farmer 70.
Hoover Benjamin, (Smithboro) r66, farmer with his father Smith F.
Hoover Smith F., (Smithboro) r 66, farmer 73.
HORTON ABRAM, (Owego) r 48, farmer 220.
Horton Ada F., (Owego) r 28, farm 25.
Horton Charles, (Owego) r 32, farmer 90.
Horton George M., (Smithboro) r 70, carpenter, and farmer 12.
Horton Gurdon, (Owego) r 48, farmer 100.
Horton Hannah, (Owego) r 48, widow George C., resident.
Horton Isaac S., (Owego) r 48, farmer 100.
HORTON JOHN, (Owego) r 28, farmer 105.
Horton Julia A., (Owego) r 28, widow Daniel B., farmer 25.
HORTON THEODORE, (Owego) r 49, agricultural implements, and farmer 100.
Houghtaling William, (Owego) r 8, farmer 14.
Housten George, (Owego) r 6, farmer 5.
Howard Bishop, (Owego) r 6, farmer 25.
Hoyt Fred D., (Halsey Valley) general merchant.
HOYT IRA, (Halsey Valley) r 21, prop. cooper shop, and farmer 95.
Hoyt LaGrange, (Tioga Center) r 43, laborer.
Hunt Theodore, (Catatnnk) r 9, farmer 34.
Hurlburt Henry, (Owego) r 9, farm laborer.
Hurlburt Perrine, (Owego) r 13, farmer.
Hyatt John D., (Owego) r 14, retired farmer.
Hyatt John M., (Owego) r 14, farmer 121.
Hyde Gordon, (Owego) r 12, cooper.
Hyres Charles, (Halsey Valley) cooper.
Ide Irwin N., (Smithboro) r 70, small fruits, and farmer 52.
Ide Jacob A., (Smithboro) r 69, berry raiser, and farmer 25.
Ingersoll Susan, (Tioga Center) widow Ebenezer, resident.
JEWETT CHARLES F., (Catatonk) r 9, lumberman, and farmer 120.
Jewett Harris, (Catatonk) r 9, farmer 110.
Jewett Henry, (Catatonk) r 9, farmer 87.
Johnson Abigail Mrs., (Smithsboro) resident.
Johnson Jay, (Halsey Valley) r 22, farmer 100.
Johnson J. Edward, (Smithboro) undertaker and carpenter.
Johnson Julius, (Barton) r 63, farmer 100.
Johnson Peter M., (Tioga Center) r 53, carpenter, and farmer 18.
Johnson Thomas, (Tioga Center) r 52, farmer, works for William Ransom 96.
Johnson Warren, (Smithboro) r 55, carpenter.
Johnson William H., (Smithboro) r 58, farmer 100.
Johnson William W., (Tioga Center) farmer.
Jones Anna, (Owego) r 28, widow Horton, resident.
Jones Horace, (Owego) r 28, farmer 60.
Jones Levi J., (Owego) r 29, farmer, works for Mrs. Beers 60.

JONES STEPHEN W., (Owego) r 9, saw and grist-mill, turning shop, plaining-mill, etc., and farmer 10.

Kane John, (Smithboro) trackman.

KEELER EGBERT, (Owego) r 29, miller for Shaw & Dean, h 2½.

Kelly Johanna Mrs. (Smithboro) resident.

Kelly John, (Tioga Center) watchman.

Ketchum Ruth M., (Barton) r 63, widow Seymour, resident.

Ketchum Seymour C., (Barton) r 63, farmer 50, and works for Daniel Daily 50.

King Adam, (Owego) r 6, farmer 185.

King Charles C., (Barton) r 64, farmer 45.

King Ezra, (Owego) r 7, farmer, works for his father Adam 53.

King Frank, (Owego) r 17, farmer 50.

King George, (Owego) farmer with his father Adam.

Kinney Amzi, (Smithboro) resident.

Kline Philip, (Tioga Center) r 51, tanner.

KIRK CHARLES N., (Halsey Valley) blacksmith, and farmer 52.

KNAPP FREDERICK J., (Smithboro) boots & shoes, barber, Main, h do.

Knapp Sylvester, (Smithboro) physician.

Knowlton William, (Tioga Center) farm laborer.

Krum Dillen, (Owego) r 14, farmer 25.

KURKENDALL SAMUEL, (Tioga Center) r 53, farmer 37.

Lamberson Jedusen, (Halsey Valley) r 39, farmer 100.

La Monte Allen D., (Tioga Center) r 36, farmer with his father Seth D.

LA MONTE SETH D., (Tioga Center) r 36, horse farrier and farmer 60.

Landers William, (Owego) r 25, farmer 100.

Lane Charles, (Owego) r 31, farmer, works for Thomas Dundon 50.

LATIMER JONATHAN C., (Tioga Center) assemblyman for Tioga Co., lumberman and farmer 1,300.

Lawler John, (Owego) r 25, farmer with his brother Patrick 110.

Lawler Patrick, (Owego) r 25, farmer with his brother John 110.

Leach Stephen W., (Owego) r 28, prop. "Leach's Mills" grist-mill.

Leach William H., (Owego) r 28, farmer 30.

Leonard Elbridge, (Tioga Center) r 40, farmer 42.

Leonard George, (Tioga Center) r 51, mason and farmer 50.

Levett Edward, (Tioga Center) laborer.

Lewis David, (Owego) r 45, farmer 15 and works for Gilbert Truman 126.

Lewis Martin V., (Owego) r 30, farmer 75.

Light Mary, (Smithboro) r 71, widow Ely S., farm 160.

Link Joseph, (Tioga Center) r 51. laborer.

Lockwood Charles, (Tioga Center) peddler.

Lollis Mercy Mrs., (Smithboro) resident.

Lollis Samuel C., (Smithboro) general merchant, Main, h do.

Longley James F., (Owego) resident.

Lounsberry Amos L., (Smithboro) r 71, farmer 100.

Lounsberry Benjamin, 2d, (Smithboro) r 71, farmer 109, and in Nichols 52.

Lounsberry Robert L., (Smithboro) r 71, medical student.

Lounsbury Amy F., (Tioga Center) r 36, school teacher.

LOUNSBURY ANSON B., (Tioga Center) r 36, farmer with his mother Mary.

LOUNSBURY CLARK, (Tioga Center) r 36, farmer 32.

LOUNSBURY CORNELIA H., (Tioga Center) r 36, school teacher.

LOUNSBURY HARRIET A., (Tioga Center) r 36, school teacher.

LOUNSBURY JOHN L., (Tioga Center) r 36, farmer with his mother Mary.

LOUNSBURY MARY, (Tioga Center) r 36, widow Lewis, farm 150.
Lounsbury Sheldon, (Smithboro) r 61, apiarist 52 swarms and farmer 129.
Loveless James J., (Smithboro) r 40, farmer 25.
Lovell House, (Smithboro) O. E. Lovell, prop.
Lovell Oliver E., (Smithboro) prop. Lovell House.
Luce Parmelia P., (Smithboro) r 40, widow Lot, farmer 75.
Luddington James A., (Smithboro) r 58, farmer 85.
Luddington Joseph, (Smithboro) r 58, farmer.
Lunger Alvin, (Owego) r 49, laborer.
Lyons Marvin, (Tioga Center) r 52, laborer.
Mack Anthony, (Smithboro) section boss.
Madden John, (Smithboro) trackwalker.
Madden Martin, (Smithboro) retired.
Mallery George, (Smithboro) mason.
Mallery Henry, (Smithboro) mason.
Manchester Henry H., (Owego) r 47, life insurance.
Manley Frank N., (Halsey Valley) farmer.
Manley George S., (Halsey Valley) farmer 50.
Mapes Lewis, (Owego) r 28, blacksmith, bds. do.
Martin Fred, (Tioga Center) general merchant, Main, h do.
Martin Jay H., (Tioga Center) r 51, retired merchant, and farmer 113.
Mastin Julia Mrs., (Smithboro) resident.
MATTESON FAYETTE A., (Smithboro) r 71, Baptist clergyman.
Matteson Frank, (Smithboro) r 71, divinity student.
Matteson George M., (Tioga Center) r 53, laborer.
McBride John, (Tioga Center) tanner, Main.
McCormick Elias, (Smithboro) laborer.
McDermott Michael, (Catatonk) r 9, fireman N. T. Co.
McDonald Charles H., (Smithboro) r 68, physician and surgeon.
McDonald Edward, (Tioga Center) trackman.
McDuffee Nathaniel J., (Smithboro) r 68, farmer.
McNeal Jane, (Smithboro) r 70, widow George, resident.
McNeil ——, (Smithboro) r 70, works for L. B. Pearsall 160.
McWhorter DeForest, (Tioga Center) clerk, bds. 1 Main.
MEAD JAMES R., (Owego) r 25, farmer 100.
Meder Paul, (Owego) r 7, farmer 25.
Meeker Jane, (Smithboro) r 53, resident.
Merritt John, (Tioga Center) r 52, laborer.
Mespell Joshua, (Owego) r 6, farmer 40.
Mespell Willis, (Owego) r 6, farmer.
Middaugh Jacob, (Owego) r 13, resident.
Middaugh Lorenzo T., (Smithboro) r 73, carpenter, and farmer.
Miller C. Henry, (Smithboro) r 53, farmer 400.
Miller George, (Tioga Center) tanner.
Miller Julia A., (Smithboro) r 53, widow Henry, resident.
Morris Caroline D., (Tioga Center) widow Almon, h Main.
Mortz George, (Tioga Center) tanner, bds. Main.
Mortz William, (Tioga Center) tanner, bds. Main.
Mulligan Thomas, (Owego) r 11, farmer 42.
Mulock Chancy, (Smithboro) farmer.
Mulock David, (Smithboro) farmer.
Mulock Edwin, (Smithboro) r 71, carpenter.
Munnahun Charles, (Tioga Center) r 52, farm laborer.

Munnahun Mary, (Tioga Center) r 36, widow Martin, farm 12.
Munson Frederick, (Owego) r 28, farmer.
Munson Heman, (Owego) r 28, farmer.
Myers Alford, (Owego) r 33, farmer, leases of Charles Catlin 40.
Nelson George, (Owego) r 32, farmer.
Nelson James J., (Owego) r 12, farmer 20.
Nelson Winslow, (Owego) r 26, farmer 50.
Nichols Addie R. Mrs., (Smithboro) r 58, resident.
Northrop James B., (Tioga Center) r 57, farmer, works for Dr. J. Wilson 200.
Oakley Joshua, (Smithboro) r 59, farmer 50.
O'Connor James, (Owego) r 30, invalid.
O'Connor John, (Owego) r 30, farmer.
O'Connor Joseph, (Owego) r 30, gardener.
O'Hara John, (Smithboro) trackman.
Ohart Moses, (Tioga Center) prop. Tioga Center Hotel, Main.
O'Hern William, (Smithboro) trackman.
Osborn Joseph, (Strait's Corners) r 3, farmer 50.
Ott Frank U., (Owego) r 14, farmer for his father Nicholas.
Ott George D., (Owego) r 14, farmer for his father Nicholas.
Ott Nicholas, (Owego) r 14, farmer 159.
Ott Sophia, (Owego), r 14, widow Nicholas, Sr., resident.
Pace John, (Tioga Center) r 43, trackman.
Park Dunham, (Barton) r 65, farmer 200.
Parmentier Franklin M., (Owego) r 28, butcher.
Pearsall John C., (Smithboro) r 71, carpenter.
Pease William (Owego) r 14, farmer, leases Mrs. Sisson 20.
Pelham Charles (Owego) r 44, carpenter and farmer.
PEMBLETON JOHN E, (Tioga Center) lumberman, farmer 350 and wild land 318.
Pepper Jackson S., (Smithboro) r 60, farmer 50.
Pepper John F., (Smithboro) r 68, grain and potato dealer, and farmer 100.
PERRY ALBERT A., (Smithboro) carpenter and joiner.
Perry Leonard, (Smithboro) farmer 45, h Main.
Perry Milo M., (Smithboro) hostler.
Piche Gasper Mrs., (Tioga Center) r 51, resident.
Pickering Joseph, (Smithboro) resident.
Pilkington Charles (Catatonk) r 9, telegraph operator.
Platt Houston, (Smithboro) r 71, farmer 10.
Poole Charles F., (Tioga Center) r 53, farmer 234.
Poole Edward V., (Smithboro) retired merchant.
Poole Murray, (Smithboro) lawyer.
Post Albert W., (Tioga Center) r 51, physician and surgeon, and farmer 160.
Pressure George, (Tioga Center) laborer.
Preston Frederick, (Owego) r 48, farm laborer.
Preston Louis, (Owego) r 48, farmer, works for A. J. Goodrich 100.
Preston Silas, (Owego) r 48, farmer.
Price John, (Owego) r 26, farm laborer.
Pudbuagh John, (Tioga Center) r 23, farm laborer.
Quirin Charles M., (J. G. Quirin & Co.) (Tioga Center) h Main.
Quirin Edward, (Tioga Center) r 49. tanner.
Quirin Emil J. F., (Tioga Center) tanner, h Main.
Quirin Emil F., (J. G. Quirin & Co.) (Tioga Center) h Main.
Quirin George L. A., (Tioga Center) tanner, Main.
14

Quirin J. G. & Co., (W. C. A., E. P. and C. H. N. Quirin) (Tioga Center)
    tanners, Main.
Quirin John G., (J. G. Quirin & Co.) (Tioga Center) also farmer 137, h Main.
Quirin William, (Tioga Center) tanner, h Main.
Quirin William C. A., (J. G. Quirin & Co.) (Tioga Center) h Main.
Ragan Daniel, (Owego) r 9, laborer.
Randall Walter C., (Smithboro) justice of the peace and farmer.
Ransom Warren W., (Tioga Center) r 49, farmer 130.
RAUCH GEORGE, (Strait's Corners) r 5, farmer, 117.
Rauch Henry E., (Strait's Corners) r 5, farmer.
Rauch John M., (Strait's Corners) r 5, farmer.
Rauch Peter A., (Strait's Corners) r 5, farmer.
Rauch Wesley, (Owego) r 16, farmer, works for Rev. S. Evans 115.
Reed Maria, (Catatonk) r 9, widow George, house-keeper.
Rice Chauncey, (Owego) r 18, farmer, leases of James Anderson 125.
Rice Rachel, (Owego) r 9, widow Merrick, resident.
Richards Benjamin, (Smithboro) r 68, farmer 168.
Richards Eugene, (Tioga Center) clerk, bds. Main.
Rider Amos L., (Strait's Corners) r 4, farmer 96.
Rider Dana B., (Halsey Valley) r 22, farmer 90.
Rider David, (Strait's Corners) r 24, farmer 100.
Rider Elethere, (Strait's Corners) r 19, resident.
Rider George T., (Halsey Valley), bartender Halsey Valley House.
Rider Isaac, (Halsey Valley) r 22, farmer 80.
Rider Jacob S., (Tioga Center) r 23, thresher and farmer 105.
Rider Seymour, (Halsey Valley) 22, farmer with his father Dana B.
Rider Stephen J., (Strait's Corners) r 19, farmer 98.
Rider William, (Halsey Valley) mason.
Ring Jesse B., (Owego) off r 12, resident.
Ring Theron S., (Owego) off r 12, farmer.
Roberts James A., (Smithboro) painter.
Robinson Duncan, (Owego) r 26, farm laborer.
Robinson Joel, (Owego) r 45, farmer, works for Henry Young 150.
Romine Hannah, (Owego) r 47, widow Samuel, resident.
Romine William, (Owego) r 47, tailor.
Root Oris L., (Halsey Valley) billiard and pool room and farmer in Barton 36.
Ross John W., (Smithboro) r 58, farmer 300.
Rousier Charles, (Owego) r 8, farmer 30.
Rumsey James, (Halsey Valley) r 1, farmer, works for Fred Taylor 150.
Russell Holmes W., (Owego) r 14, farmer 160.
Sanderson P. W. N., (Tioga Center) station and express agt. and telegraph
    op. Erie R. R., h Main.
Sargent Alvin, (Smithboro) carpenter.
Schoonover Ambrose L., (Barton) r 73, farmer 117.
Schoonover Eliza, (Tioga Center) r 53, widow Smith, farm 16.
Schoonover Eugene S., (Tioga Center) r 53, farmer with his father Nicholas.
Schoonover Jackson J. F., (Tioga Center) 35, farmer 63.
Schoonover James M., (Tioga Center) r 35, lumberman.
Schoonover Jerome J., (Tioga Center) r 53, farmer with his father Nicholas.
Schoonover Nicholas, (Tioga Center) r 53, farmer 200.
Schoonover Nicholas M., (Barton) r 73, resident.
Schoonover Simeon L., (Barton) r 73, farmer 170.
Scott Wilson, (Owego) r 48, gardener.

Searles Martha, (Owego) r 28, widow John, farmer 80.
Severn George W., (Smithboro) resident.
Sexsmith Thomas, (Tioga Center) section foreman.
Sharp Samuel, (Tioga Center) r 41, farm laborer.
Sharp William, (Smithboro) r 73, farmer 65.
SHAW W. HULSE, (Owego) r 28, prest. Tioga Co. Agr'l Society, breeder of Holstein cattle and fine horses, and farmer 133.
Sherman John, (Owego) r 14, farmer 5.
Sherwood William, (Tioga Center) laborer, h Main.
SHIFFER GEORGE B., (Owego) r 13, farmer.
Shipman George, (Halsey Valley) laborer.
Signor Charles, (Tioga Center) r 36, prop. saw mill and farmer with his son George H. 100.
Signor George H., (Tioga Center) r 36, wagon-maker and farmer 10, and with his father Charles 100.
Sly John M., (Smithboro) resident.
Smith & Truesdail, (Owego) (H. K. Smith & George Truesdail) r 44, props. of hay press and threshing machine.
Smith Cornelius D., (Tioga Center) r 51, farmer 100.
Smith David T., (Tioga Center) r 50, farmer 100.
Smith Frank, (Tioga Center) r 51, farmer 87.
Smith George, (Tioga Center) r 36, farmer 240.
Smith George A., (Owego) r 12, farm laborer.
Smith Harry J., (Tioga Center) r 36, farmer with his father George.
Smith Horace K., (Tioga Center) r 36, agrl. implements and farmer 50.
Smith James E., (Smithboro) r 40, steam thresher and farmer 150.
Smith John E., (Smithboro) r 40, farmer 125.
Smith John J., (Tioga Center) r 36, farmer with his father Horace K.
Smith John Y., (Smithboro) r 40, resident.
Smith Losey M., (Smithboro) r 68, farmer 100.
Smith Michael, (Smithboro) farmer 125.
Smith Spencer E., (Owego) r 34, farmer 35.
Snyder Adam, (Strait's Corners) r 17, farmer 113.
Snyder Charles, (Owego) r 6, carpenter.
Snyder Frank, (Strait's Corners) r 5, laborer.
Snyder George, (Strait's Corners) r 4, farm laborer.
Snyder Henry A., (Strait's Corners) r 5, prop. saw-mill, and farmer 57.
Snyder Nicholas, (Owego) r 6, farmer 100.
Snyder Nicholas N., (Strait's Corners) r 4, carpenter.
Snyder Peter, (Owego) r 14, laborer.
Snyder Samuel, (Owego) r 6, farmer with his father Nicholas.
Southwick Mary J. Mrs., (Halsey Valley) general merchant.
Speer Irwin L., (Strait's Corners) r 24, farm laborer.
Speer Tunis, (Strait's Corners) r 24, farmer 32.
Spencer Albert O., (Tioga Center) r 36, laborer.
Spencer Alvah, (Owego) off r 34, farmer 122.
Spencer Ambrose G., (Owego) r 31, farmer.
Spencer Charles (Owego) r 34, farmer 76.
Spencer Charles, (Owego) r 25, farmer 50.
Spencer Elijah C., (Tioga Center) mail messenger.
Spencer John, (Owego) off r 34, farmer.
Spendley Araminta, (Nichols) r 53 widow Anderson.
Spendley Robert H., (Nichols) r 53, farmer 100.

Spicer Harry, (Halsey Valley) r 22, laborer.
Springstead Alfred, (Halsey Valley), r 37, farmer for J. C. Latimer.
Springstead Daniel P., (Tioga Center) r 51, farm laborer.
Starks James, (Strait's Corners) r 4, farmer 260.
Starks William, (Strait's Corners) r 4, farmer for his father James.
STEELE FRED C., (Owego) farmer 65.
Steele James, (Owego) r 31, farmer 212.
STEELE JANE Miss, (Smithboro) resident.
Sterling John, (Smithboro) laborer.
Stetler Charles J., (Tioga Center) r 35, farmer 126.
Stetler Irving F., (Tioga Center) r 35, school teacher.
Stetler Stokes, (Tioga Center) r 35, farmer.
Stetler William, (Tioga Center) r 35, farmer with his father Stokes.
Steward John, (Smithboro) off r 66, farmer 100.
Stewart Delos, (Owego) off r 12, mason.
STEWART EDWARD, (Owego) off r 12, mason and farmer.
STEWART EMILY A., (Owego) off r 12, dressmaker.
STILES FRED H., (Stiles & Sibley) (Owego) r 47, farmer.
STILES GEORGE B., (Owego) r 46, farmer.
STILES RHODA, (Owego) r 46, widow Benjamin C., farmer 15.
Stimpson Charles, (Smithboro) cooper.
Stimson Henry (Smithboro) station agent Southern Central R. R.
Stone Edward F., (Tioga Center) drug clerk.
Stone William, (Owego) r 28, laborer.
STOWELL CORNELL S., (Smithboro) r 73, lumberman, and farmer 236.
Strait Alvinza, (Strait's Corners) r 4, postmaster and farmer.
Strait Aretus A., (Strait's Corners) r 4, hay-dealer and farmer 66.
Streibel Peter, (Tioga Center) tanner.
Stutler Andrew, (Tioga Center) r 36, laborer.
Sullivan Thomas, (Smithboro) section boss.
Swartwood Charles, (Halsey Valley) r 37, farmer.
Swartwood Edwin, (Owego) r 30, farmer 100.
Swartwood Eugene, (Owego) r 30, farmer.
Swartwood Frank, (Strait's Corners) r 3, farm laborer.
Taylor Addison J., (Owego) r 44, farmer 50.
Taylor Charles D., (Owego) r 29, fatmer.
Taylor Cynthia. (Owego) r 32, widow John T., farmer 113.
Taylor Frank E., (Owego) r 32, farmer with his mother Cynthia.
Taylor John E., (Owego) r 26, farmer, leases of Abram Vermilyea 50.
Taylor John H., (Owego) r 47, painter.
Taylor John M., (Owego) r 28, farmer 22.
Taylor John T., (Owego) farmer, works for Abram Vermilyea 50.
Taylor Norman, (Owego) r 32, farmer 50.
Taylor Rodney, (Smithboro) r 58, farmer 50.
Tewilleger Jay, (Strait's Corners) r 4, farm laborer.
Thomas David B., (Owego) r 13, farmer 53.
Thomas Delos H., (Owego) r 13, farmer with his father David B.
Thomas Frank, (Owego) r 13, keeper at Binghamton asylum.
Thomas George, (Halsey Valley) r 2, farmer 27.
Thomas John D., (Smithboro) r 71, millwright, and farmer 4.
Thorn Warren, (Owego) r 31, farmer.
Tiffany Austin, (Owego) r 28. farmer 6½.
Tilden Alanson Rev., (Tioga Center) pastor Baptist church.

Tioga Center Hotel, (Tioga Center) Moses Ohart, prop., Main.

Toff William, (Tioga Center) r 35, laborer.

TOFT ISAAC, (Owego) r 18, farmer 153.

Towner Andrew J., (Smithboro) r 60, farmer 50.

Traynor Mary, (Owego) r 48, widow Edward.

TRIBE CHARLES H., (Tioga Center) carpenter and joiner, and prop. saw and plaining-mill, Railroad cor. Alden.

Tribe Frank B., (Tioga Center) r 52, farmer 50.

Tribe James P., (Halsey Valley) r 38, farmer 104.

Tribe John, (Halsey Valley) off r 2, farmer 56.

Tripp Seymour, (Smithboro) jeweler at Nichols.

Trowbridge E. Owen, (Smithboro) school teacher.

Truesdail David S., (Owego) r 44, farmer 57.

Truesdail Frank J., (Owego) r 44, farmer.

Truesdail George, (Owego) (Smith & Truesdail) r 44, thresher.

Truesdail Jeremiah, (Owego) r 44, farmer 60.

Truesdail John, (Tioga Center) r 43, laborer.

Truesdail William, (Owego) r 44, carpenter, and farmer 36.

Truesdell Alvin, (Owego) r 47, laborer.

Tuff Sarah, (Tioga Center) r 41, widow Thomas, resident.

Turner Cornelius, (Tioga Center) trackman.

Turner Peter, (Strait's Corners) r 3, justice of the peace, and farmer 200.

Tuthill Joseph M., (Smithboro) groceries, provisions and drugs, Main.

Tyler Luzerne, (Halsey Valley) invalid.

Ulrick George, (Owego) r 7, farmer for Adam King.

Ulrick John, (Owego) r 6, farmer 150.

Ulrick John, Jr., (Owego) r 15, farmer 7.

Valentine Louisa, (Strait's Corners) r 8, resident.

Van Dermark John, (Smithboro) r 40, farmer 50.

Van Dermark Mary, (Smithboro) r 40, widow Henry, resident.

Van Dermark Selinda, (Smithboro) r 73, widow George, farmer 50.

Van Duser Frank, (Catatonk) r 9, farm laborer.

VAN DUSER GILBERT, (Catatonk) r 9, laborer.

Van Duser Henry, (Catatonk) r 9, laborer.

Van Etten Alonzo, (Smithboro) r 58, farm laborer.

Van Etten Lorenzo, (Halsey Valley), r 37, farmer 50.

Van Leven Elias, (Strait's Corners) r 4, butcher and farmer 32, and in Candor 52.

Van Luven John B., (Halsey Valley) stock-buyer and farmer.

Van Norstran Arthur G., (Smithboro) r 55, farmer for his father James.

Van Norstran Charles C., (Tioga Center) r 53, farmer 125.

Van Norstran George, (Tioga Center) (Coburn & Van Norstran) r 51, also farmer 16.

Van Norstran James, (Tioga Center) r 58, farmer 30.

Van Norstran James, (Smithboro) r 55, farmer 30.

Van Riper George W., (Halsey Valley) r 38, farmer 90.

Van Tyl Anthony W., (Tioga Center) r 36, farmer, works for Henry Wiggins 40.

Vincent Colvin, (Barton) r 65, farmer 50.

Vosburgh Henry P., (Halsey Valley) physician and surgeon, and farmer 285.

Vroman Moses, (Owego) r 30, farm laborer.

Walden Joseph, (Halsey Valley) r 21, laborer.

Wallace David B., (Owego) r 48, farmer for his mother Rachel.

Wallace Rachel, (Owego) r 48, widow David, farm 140.

Wallace William, (Tioga Center) r 40, farmer 100.

Wallis Harry C., (Owego) r 48, farmer.

Walworth Seymour E., (Owego) M. E. clergyman and farmer 17.

Ward Lewis J., (Smithboro) r 70, farmer, works for Judson Winters 260.

Ward Perry C., (Tioga Center) r 41, carpenter and farmer 40.

Waterman Oren, (Owego) r 48, farmer, works on shares for Lottie A. Horton 100.

WATERMAN WILLIAM P., (Tioga Center) r 54, farmer, works for C. H. Van Norstran 50.

Watkins Charles H., (Catatonk) r 9, engineer N. T. Co.

Watkins Elizabeth Mrs., (Tioga Center) r 53, resident.

Watkins John, (Smithboro) stone mason.

Watkins Thomas, (Smithboro) r 54, farmer 50.

Watkins William H., (Tioga Center) meat market in Binghamton.

Weber George, (Owego) r 7, farmer 63.

Weber Philip, (Owego) r 7, farmer.

Weber Philip, Jr., (Owego) r 7, carpenter and farmer 55.

Weiss Sebastian, (Owego) r 16, farmer 100.

West Andrew L., (Halsey Valley) r 1, farmer 140.

West Charles, (Halsey Valley) r 22, farmer.

West Grant M., (Halsey Valley) r 21, postmaster and assistant to his father Luther B.

WEST LUTHER B., (Halsey Valley) r 21, retired merchant, lumberman, dairyman and farmer 530, and in Newark Valley 181.

Wheeler John N., (Strait's Corners) r 4, general merchant.

Whitcomb Benjamin R., (Smithboro) r 68, farmer 55.

Whitcomb John M., (Smithboro) r 59, farmer 50.

White Dudley, (Owego) farmer 35.

White Jerome, (Smithboro) r 54, farmer, works on shares for Henry Miller 50.

White Leon, (Halsey Valley) physician and surgeon.

White Lewis, (Smithboro) r 73, farmer 95.

White Lorenzo, (Catatonk) r 9, laboror.

Whipple Fernando, (Tioga Center) r 50, farmer 50.

Whitley Emily, (Owego) r 13, widow Joel S., farm 141.

Whitmarsh Abram, (Owego) r 28, farmer 74.

WHITMARSH AVERY, (Owego) r 9, sawyer and farmer 5.

Whitmarsh Harvey, (Owego) r 28, sawyer.

Whitmarsh Herrick, (Tioga Center) r 52, farmer.

Whitmarsh Sidney D., (Tioga Center) r 52, farm laborer.

Whitney Isaac N., (Owego) r 33, farm laborer.

Wiggins Eliza, (Tioga Center) widow George.

Wiggins Henry, (Tioga Center) r 36, farmer 40.

Wiggins Silas, (Tioga Center) r 36, blacksmith, h do.

Wilbur Frederick, (Halsey Valley) laborer.

Williams Charles, (Tioga Center) off r 57, farm laborer.

Willis Sylvester, (Halsey Valley) r 22, farmer 75.

Willmott George W., (Owego) r 14, farmer 133.

WILLMOTT JAMES R., (Owego) r 28, prop. saw and plaster-mill, and ice-dealer.

Wilson William, (Owego) r 34, resident.

Winfield James, (Owego) r 28, retired farmer.

Winner James F., (Owego) r 47, cartman.

Winter Byron L., (Tioga Center) law student, bds. Main.

Winters Harry B., (Tioga Center) clerk, bds. Main.

Winters Joseph, (Tioga Center) postmaster and grocery, and farmer 159, h Main.

Winters Thomas, (Tioga Center) laborer.

Wolcott George B., (Smithboro) r 58, farmer 60.

Wood Edward, (Tioga Center) r 53, laborer.

Wood Elmer, (Tioga Center) r 53, farm laborer.

Wood George, (Strait's Corners) r 3, farmer 50.

Wood James, (Strait's Corners) farmer 50.

Wood Joseph, (Strait's Corners) r 3, farmer 100.

Wood Spencer (Halsey Valley) r 39, farmer 90.

Woodburn Clarence, (Tioga Center) r 36, laborer.

Woodburn David P., (Tioga Center) farmer.

Woodburn Henry Q., (Tioga Center) laborer.

Woodcox Richard, (Tioga Center) trackman, h Main.

Wright William, (Tioga Center) stone mason and carpenter.

Yaples Charles, (Owego) r 31, carpenter.

Yearsley Frank, (Smithboro) r 54, farmer with his father John.

Yearsley John, (Smithboro) r 54, farmer, works for Henry Miller 250.

Yontz Chloe, (Smithboro) r 71, widow John, resident.

Young Franklin H., (Owego) r 48, farmer with his father Henry.

Young Henry, (Owego), r 48, speculator, dairy 14 cows and farmer 200.

Zorn Charles, (Owego) r 14, farmer 27.

Zorn Christopher, (Owego) r 17, farmer 15.

Zorn George, (Owego) r 17, farmer 39.

Zorn Jacob, (Owego) r 14, farmer 27.

THE

OWEGO ✦ GAZETTE.

ESTABLISHED NOVEMBER 23, 1800.

The ❋ Only ❋ Democratic ❋ Paper

PUBLISHED IN TIOGA COUNTY.

A GOOD ADVERTISING MEDIUM.

Sample · Copies · Sent · on · Application.

THE FINEST JOB PRINTING

Neatly and Promptly Done, and at Low Prices.

TIOGA COUNTY

CLASSIFIED BUSINESS DIRECTORY

EXPLANATION.

The towns are alphabetically arranged at the end of the line, under the business classifications. The postoffice address of each individual or firm follows after the name, except in cases where the name of the postoffice and the township is the same. In the villages the name of the street is generally given, and precedes that of the postoffice. The classification of farmers is omitted in this list, as they can readily be found in the general list, by noting the figures at the end of the line, which indicate the number of acres owned or leased by each. Road numbers signify the same as in the general list.

Agents Railroad.
See Railroad Agents.

Agents Ticket.
See Railroad Agents.

Agricultural Implements.
(See also Hardware, also General Merchants.)

COLEMAN CHARLES H., (dealer) Lockwood, Barton
Guyer H. E., Broad cor. Clark st., Waverly, "
Sneffin & Scott, Broad st., Waverly, "
BRAINARD CHARLES E., Berkshire
Higgins John, r 18, Speedsville, Tomp. Co., "
Judd John N., r 6, "
WITTER F. A. & CO., "
Courtright Henry A., (dealer) West Newark, Candor
HART LEWIS A., (dealer) Main st., "
HEATH HENRY D., (dealer) Main st., "
Van Debogart Peter, Main st., "
Woodford E. Jerome, (dealer) r 62, "
GAGER ULYSSES S., r 45, (Champion drills) Newark Valley
Kenyon Charles E., r 53, "
ADAMS S. B., r 5, (harvesters) Hoopers' Valley, Nichols
EDSALL JOHN R., (dealer) Main st., "
GERE, TRUMAN, PLATT & CO., (manuf.) Central ave., Owego
Like George W., r 106, Apalachin, "

Pitcher Leroy H., r 65, Owego
THOMAS MOSES H., (dealer) 64 Temple st., "
Wood Charles E., r 40, Flemingville. "
MILLER WILLIAM F., Main st., Richford
THELEMAN HIRAM W., "
Brooks Daniel C., Maple ave., Spencer
DAVIS JEROME S., Cedar st., "
DAY JOHN & SON, Main st., "
HORTON THEODORE, r 49, Owego st., Tioga
Smith Horace K., r 36, Tioga Center, "

Apiarists.

Andre John, Lockwood, Barton
BESEMER DANIEL V., North Barton, "
Church Franklin L., r 46, Lockwood, "
CRANS FRANK, Lockwood, "
Edgcomb George G., Factoryville, "
Hanford Clark, Factoryville, "
Holt Charles B., r 53, "
Lent W. Nelson, Lincoln st., Waverly, "
MANNING ELI D., Halsey Valley, "
SHIPMAN RUFUS T., r 43, Waverly, "
Walker Loren A., Waverly, "
Clark Sanford H., r 36, Berkshire
Houk Daniel, Wilson Creek, r 35, "
Scott Charles & Edward F., r 22 cor. 41, "
Shepard James, r 3, "
WILLIAMS & WALDO, "
Williams George, "
Anderson Joel, r 125, Owego, Candor
Houck Israel, r 95, "

STARKEY & WINTERS, promptly fill Mail and Telephone Orders.

ESTABLISHED IN 1835.

THE FARMERS' FAVORITE!

THE OWEGO TIMES

The largest and best weekly paper published in Tioga county, and contains more reading matter. The TIMES is the paper for the Farmer, Mechanic, Merchant, Laboring Man, in fact, for all classes to take. Correspondence from every Town in the County. The TIMES has the largest circulation by many hundreds of any paper published in Tioga county, consequently it is the BEST ADVERTISING MEDIUM.

SEND FOR A SAMPLE COPY.

FOR

FINE JOB WORK

Of all kinds, from the smallest Visiting Card to the Mammoth Poster, go to the Times Office.   Our Jobbing Facilities are unequaled in the Southern Tier.

BOOK-BINDING.

Book-binding, in all its branches, neatly, cheaply and promptly done. Paper Ruling in every conceivable style and form.   Especial attention given to, and best facilities for, manufacturing Blank Books, Ledgers, Hotel Registers, &c.   Pamphlets, Magazines and Old Books skillfully and neatly rebound.   Persons wishing anything pertaining to this business will do well to call at the Owego Times Bindery.

WM. SMYTH & SON, Propietors.

193 Main St., opposite Lake St.,   -   Owego, Tioga Co., N. Y

HOFTALING JOHN, R. R. ave.   Candor
MASTEN GEORGE W.,   "
MOREY ARCHIE E., r 71,   "
Osburn William, r 18, Speedsville,   "
ROE EUGENE F., r 5,   "
Roe William F., r 25,   "
Taylor William J., r 86, Weltonville,   "
Burchard Harvey J., r 9, Ketchumville,
    Newark Valley
Councilman Edwin W., r 35,   "
STEVENS HENRY W., r 42,   "
DEAN NATHAN S., r 1,   Nichols
HERRICK WILLIAM, r 1,   "
Lane David J., r 17,   "
Matthews Hiram P., r 38,   "
Sherwood Wesley W., r 10,   "
WATERMAN ALONZO C., r 8,   "
WHITE WILLIAM W., r 21,   "
BROWN L. & G., off North ave., (near S.
    C. R. R. Round house,   Owego
Fox Charles, off r 91,   "
Gage Miner, r 37,   "
Gage Walter, r 37,   "
GILES JOHN S., r 87, Apalachin,   "
Nichols Washington, r 102½, Apalachin,   "
Noteware Wallace R., r 110, South Apa-
    lachin,   "
TALCOTT CHARLES, r 40,   "
Talcott George B., r 40,   "
Ferris George C., r 35, West Candor,   Spencer
Forsyth Nelson A., r 40,   "
Holdridge William A., r 41,   "
SHAW GEORGE E., r 30,   "
SNOOK DAVID L., Main st.,   "
Van Marter, r 41,   "
GOODRICH STEPHEN S., r 46, Owego, Tioga

Apothecaries.

See Drugs and Medicines.

Architects and Builders.

(See also Carpenters and Builders, and Masons and Builders.)

Utter John, 120 Howard st., Waverly,   Barton

Artists, Portrait, Landscape, etc:

(See also Photographers.)

Comstock A. B. Mrs., 126 Waverly st.,
    Waverly,   Barton
Stanley Belle, (teacher) 101 Penn. ave.,
    Waverly,   "
HAIGHT EDITH J., (teacher) Glen st.,
    Berkshire
SUTTON GEORGE B., r 41,   Newark Valley
MITCHELL IDA A., Cady ave.,   Nichols
MITCHELL MARY J., Cady ave.,   "
CAMP MARY L., Mrs., 259 Erie st.,   Owego
*HARGRAVE, W. G., 38 and 40 Lake st.,   "
Kimball Helen Mrs., 425 Main st.,   "
MOREHOUSE ALLIE, Spencer ave.,   "
SMITH HATTIE A., 443 Main st.,   "

Bakers and Confectioners.

(See also Confectionery, Fruits, etc.)

Clark Charles H., 121 Broad st., Waver-
    ly,   Barton
HANFORD & LORD, 222, Broad st.,
    Waverly,   "
PILGRIM FREDERIC, 241 Broad st.,
    Waverly,   "
JACKSON DWIGHT P., Main st.,   Candor
Stannard Hiram R.,   Newark Valley
Bonham Emma, 3 Park st.,   Owego
Burton Nathaniel T., 61 North ave.   "

NYE BROTHERS, 44 Lake st.,   Owego
PARLETT ROBERT JR., Academy st.,
    Spencer

Bands.

(In Societies, See Contents.)

Banks.

FIRST NATIONAL, Broad cor. Fulton st.,
    Waverly,   Barton
THE CITIZENS' BANK, 214 Broad st.,
    Waverly,   "
FIRST NAT. BANK, Main st.,   Candor
FIRST NATIONAL BANK, 179 Front st.,
    Owego
OWEGO NATIONAL BANK, 6 Lake st.,   "
TIOGA NATIONAL BANK OF OWEGO,
    199 Front st.,   "
FARMERS' & MERCHANTS', Main st.,
    Spencer

Barbers and Hair-Dressers.

Gibson Robert W., 213 Broad st., Wa-
    verly,   Barton
Hancock Irving, 225 Broad st., Waverly,   "
Henry Edward, 209 Broad st. Waverly,   "
Lockerby Wallace H., 12 Fulton st., Wa-
    verly,   "
Woodburn James L., Fulton st., Waverly,   "
ROCKEFELLER CHARLES H., Main
    st.,   Berkshire
Stewart Charles, Main st.,   Candor
SANDWICK JOHN R.,   Newark Valley
Mallory William W., Main st.,   Nichols
Williams George F., Main st.,   "
Butler James, 65 North ave.,   Owego
Flamer Isaiah, 154 Front st.,   "
Foster & Hampton, 129 North ave.,   "
Hollensworth Jeremiah M., 22 Lake st.,   "
Horrigan William, 152 North ave.,   "
Hubbard Thomas, Lake st.,   "
King Charles H., Ah-wa-ga House,   "
Lee Albert S., 109 North ave.,   "
Spaulding Enoch R., 47 Lake st.,   "
Carter Frank E., Main st.,   Spencer
Gilbert Norman A.,   "

Basket Makers.

Stevens James M., Willseyville, r 1,   Candor
Thornton James J., r 93,   "
Neff Asel,   Newark Valley
Crandall William, r 10,   Nichols
Thornton Jeremiah, 32 W. Main st.,   Owego
Thornton Thomas, r 27,   "
Burtless James, r 2, North Spencer,   Spencer
Stevens William H., r 1,   "

Bee Keepers.

See Apiarists.

Blacksmiths and Horseshoers.

Boyce Lyman, Halsey Valley,   Barton
COLEMAN CHAS. H., Lockwood,   "
Crans Ard F., Factoryville,   "
Edgarton Willis, Lockwood,   "
Gillan Ben. R., Main st., Factoryville,   "
Kinsman & Young, 3 Penn. ave., Waverly,   "
Leonard Charles, r 55,   "
Mapes Milton C., Factoryville,   "
McArdle Bernard, 302 Broad st., Waverly,   "
Murray William, W. Factoryville,   "
Poole Frank, Halsey Valley,   "
Quinly Elmer, Broad st., Waverly,   "
Simpson Elliot, Elizabeth st., Waverly,   "
Simpson Isaac, Broad st., Waverly,   "
SIMPSON WILLIAM H., 301 Broad st.,
    Waverly,   "

BUFFINGTON CALVIN A. Railroad st., Berkshire
Whiting Frank S., Speedsville, Tomp. Co., "
Baylor Charles T., Main st., Candor
Bolton Clarence S., Main st., "
CARPENTER WILLIAM L., Railroad ave., "
Casterline Romeo W., Strait's Corners, "
DRAPER MENZ V., Catatonk, "
Eiklor George I., r 8, "
Holden Dallas, r 120, Weltonville, "
Houck George E., r 95, "
Hover Leander, r 88, "
Kirk Richard, r 63, "
Kyle Enos J., r 22, Speedsville, Tomp. Co., "
Mix Emory C., Willseyville, r 30, "
QUIMLY ELMINA E.. Owego st., "
Slawson James G., Foundry st., "
Smullen George B., Weltonville, r 120, "
Smullen Patrick, r 120, Weltonville, "
Tetwilliger Solomou E., r 133, Catatonk, "
Woodard Elias H., r 82, Weltonville, "
Belden Uriah L., Newark Valley
Belden William H., r 22, West Newark, "
Buffington Chancey L., r 11, Ketchumville, "
Mix Eugene P., "
Nowlan & Abbott, "
Sharp Robert B., r 11, Ketchumville, "
Smullen Charles M., r 1, Jenksville, "
Sweet Charles E., r 13, Ketchumville, "
Riley William. r 13, Ketchumville, "
DeGroat William, r 16, Owego, Nichols
Miller Edmund S., Main st., "
Smith Oliver P., Hooper's Valley, "
WATERMAN & METTLER, Main st., "
WATERMAN JOHN G., r 8, "
Dye Ansel M., r 17 cor. 11, Richford
Marshall Charles, r 31, "
Moreland George D., "
Owens Levi, r 31 cor. 18, "
Connant Simeon, r 117, Owego
Cornell Henry, r 56, "
Edward Edward, r 54, Campville, "
Gould Adam C., 16 Temple st., "
Howell & Tracy, Apalachin, "
Johnson Stillman, r 40, "
McCaslin Alexander, Apalachin, "
Meachan Erastus, 221 North ave., "
Reed James, L., r 4, Flemingville, "
Rhinevault Myron, 81 North ave., "
Riley & Gillett, 140 Front st., "
Riley James, 81 North ave., "
Severson George, r 51, Campville, "
SMITH LEWIS, 168 North ave., "
Terbush Lancelott B., r 16, Flemingville, "
Wood George H., North ave., "
Clark Lewis, r 34, Spencer
Clark Sylvenus B., r 38, "
COMPTON SILAS, r 37, West Candor, "
Day William S , r 28, "
Griffith Absalom, r 14, "
Hull Eben, "
Kirk Charles N., r 59, Halsey Valley, "
Lang Charles F., "
Lange William H., "
Mabee Daniel, "
Perrin William, r 13, "
Pritchard Pratt A., "
Ryant Daniel J., r 20, North Spencer "
Sabin Seth O., r 42½, "
SEELY S. ALFRED, (prop.) "
Turk David, Academy st., "

Turk Stephen D., Spencer
Wells Josiah, Main st., "
Bates William, Halsey Valley, r 21, Tioga
Estep Loren, r 51 Tioga Center, "
Farnham Orin, Smithboro, "
KIRK CHARLES N., Halsey Valley, "
Mapes Lewis, r 28, Owego, "
Wiggins Silas, r 36 Tioga Center, "

Boarding Houses.

Boyce Genevieve, Factoryville, Barton
Hinman Eliza A., 114 Chemung st., Waverly, "
Seely Edmund, 12 Park ave., Waverly, "
Hamilton Elliott, r 6, Berkshire
COOLEY BENJAMIN F., Newark Valley
Winship Charles B., "
Dunham Hannah, 118 Temple st., Owego
Dutton Mortimer E., r 69, Apalachin, "
Freehill Maria, 64 South Depot st., "
Lawheed Joseph W., 118 Temple st., "
Seely Lewis, 133 North ave., "
Sykes Maria B., 313 Main st., "

Book Binderies.

OWEGO TIMES, W. Smyth & Son, props., 193 Main, "

Books and Stationery.

Tracy John L., 204 Broad st., Waverly, Barton
COBURN & STRAIT, 17 Lake st., Owego
Decker Phoebe Mrs., 186 Main st., "
Pinney Hammon D., 45 Lake st., "
EMMONS LUCIUS E., Main st., Spencer

Boots and Shoes, Dealers and Shoe-makers.

(See also General Merchants.)

Baldwin Albert B., 6 Fulton st., Waverly, Barton
BUNN ALBERT R., 73 Broad st., Waverly, "
Demorest Clarence L., 247 Broad st., Waverly, "
Hildebrand Andrew, 225 Broad st., Waverly, "
Racklyeft John, 267 Broad st., Waverly, "
Spencer Charles F., 226 Broad st., Waverly, "
Conant Luther, Main st., Nichols
Goodenough Delos, Main st., "
DANA CHARLES, (custom) 65 North ave., Owego
Greenwood James (custom) 188 Front st., "
HARDER EMMOTT, 23 Lake st., "
Chamberlain L. N. & Son, Lake st., "
Lounsbury William H., 63 North ave., "
Lyon & Ripley, 188 Front st., "
MORTON LEVI, Apalachin, "
SWEET BROTHERS, 54 North ave., "
WALL & CO., 200 Front st., "
Wilbur William E., 182 Main st., "
DAY JOHN & SON, Main st., Spencer
KNAPP FREDERICK J., Main st., Smithboro, Tioga

Bottling Works.

MILLS & O'BRIEN, Elizabeth st., Waverly, Barton
Sheahan Michael, Broad cor. Loder st., Waverly, "
Cronk W. D., r 90. Candor
Hulslander John H., r 24, Newark Valley

STARKEY & WINTERS, Wholesale and Retail Druggists, Owego.

COBWEB BOTTLING WORKS, P. Maloney, prop., Fox st.,   Owego

Cabinet Makers.

(See also Furniture Dealers and Manufacturers.)

Barr John C., Elizabeth st , Waverly,   Barton
Hart Selem M., (Speedsville, Tomp. Co.)
   r 18,   Berkshire
FESSENDEN W. L. & SON,   Candor
Johnson Leonard A., Church st.,   "
Ross Leonard B., Main st.,   Nichols
Corchran John T., 51, George st.,   Owego
Hibbard Ralph W., 112 Franklin st.,   "
Newell Friend G., 17 Lake st.,   "
Wood Charles H., r 60,   "
Newman William H., r 48,   Spencer

Carpenters and Builders.

(See also Architects and Builders, Masons and Builders, Contractors and Builders.)

BALDWIN HUGH, Broad n Penn. ave.,
   Waverly,   Barton
Barr John C., Jr., Waverly,   "
BURKE OSCAR F., Waverly,   "
Casterline Coe, Factoryville,   "
Courtwright M. V. B.,   "
Davenport Miles, r 39,   "
Drake George C., Waverly,   "
Filkins Cornelius, Factoryville,   "
Hamilton Simeon, off r 60, Waverly,   "
HARDING CHARLES E., Ithaca st.,
   Factoryville,   "
Harris George V., Factoryville,   "
Giltner Dexter E., Waverly,   "
Parker Charles P., Factoryville,   "
Rhodes Isaac, Factoryville,   "
Ross Frank, 10 Pine st., Waverly,   "
Rowland William A., Waverly,   "
Skillings Giles, r 9, Hals.y Valley,   "
SOLOMON JOHN V., Waverly,   "
Swarthout Charles B., Factoryville,   "
Westfall Harry, Factoryville,   "
Yaple Amos S., r 39,   "
Brown Abraham, Main st.,   Berkshire
Brown Myron, r 38,   "
Church Orris, r 29,   "
Crawford James H.,   "
Hart Arthur L., r 18, Speedsville, Tomp.
   Co.,   "
Hart Samuel L., r 18, Speedsville, Tomp.
   Co.,   "
Hart Selem, r 18, Speedsville, Tomp. Co., "
Hayden Patsey W., Glen st.,   "
Hubbard Howard M., r 20,   "
Legg Reuben T., r 18, Speedsville, Tomp.
   Co.,   "
McCoy Oliver A., r18, Speedsville, Tomp.
   Co.,   "
Northrup Frank L., r 18, Speedsville, Tomp.
   Co.,   "
Payne Henry A.,   "
Sherman James W., r 27,   "
Young Edward W.,   "
Abbey William, r 112,   Candor
Allen James M., r 29,   "
Allen William D., r 29,   "
Ayers Willis, Wilseyville,   "
Barden Robert S., r 24,   "
BARROTT VAN NESS W., r 84, Welton-
   ville,   "
Burleigh Eben, r 39,   "
Carl Peter, Owego st.,   "
CORTRIGHT JOSEPH J., Weltonville,   "

Eiklor George I., r 8,   Candor
Elmendorf Clarence,   "
Farley Eli J., r 14, Speedsville, Tomp. Co., "
Frank Fred, r 134, Catatonk,   "
Flack Thomas W., r 133, Catatonk,   "
Galpin Edward, r 85, Weltonville,   "
German Frederick E.,   "
Gransbury Edward, r 102,   "
Gridley Demorn, r 63,   "
Harding Sherman,   "
Hatch Parker, r 85, Weltonville,   "
Herdic Peter, r 139, Strait's Corners,   "
Howes Oscar,   "
Katell Marshall R., r 90,   "
Keeler Ethelbert B., r 94,   "
Leet Julius C., r 22, Speedsville,   "
Leet Samuel, Speedsville,   "
Lewis Theodore H., Owego st.,   "
Lynch Ira, Royal st.,   "
Manning Robert P., r 31, South Danby,   "
Mead Russel J., Weltonville,   "
Merchant Gideon, r 32, Willseyville,   "
Orcott David, r 95,   "
OWEN ABEL, C., r 109,   "
Robinson Murtillow A.,   "
Sarson Samuel T., r 3,   "
Sewell John, r 78, Weltonville,   "
Smith John J.,   "
Smith Davelle, r 37,   "
Smith Lucius, r 95,   "
Smith William R., r 37,   "
Starkweather Joel, Pond st.,   "
Tacey Alexander,   "
Tubbs Charles N., r 41,   "
Tubbs Ebenezer, r 41,   "
Turk Levi,   "
TURNER GEORGE C., r 143, Strait's
   Corners,   "
Van Debogart Lawrence, r 30, Willsey-
   ville,   "
Woodford Elbert C., r 62, West Candor,   "
Abbey Reuben, r 16,   Newark Valley
Barber Virgil C.,   "
BERKLEY CHARLES E., r 53,   "
Bishop La Mont,   "
Davison D. Henry, r 22, West Newark,   "
Fellows William A.,   "
Gaskill Levi C., r 41,   "
HAMMOND ADELBERT C., r 16,   "
Hammond Melville F., r 6,   "
Hover Marvin L., r 22, West Newark,   "
Jackson O. Lester,   "
Keith Lucius A., r 1, Jenksville,   "
Legg Melville M.,   "
Luck Ozias F., r 35,   "
Miller Daniel H., r 5,   "
Nolton William,   "
Pease Henry F., r 12, Ketchumville,   "
Riley Andrew B.,   "
Saddlemire Alexander, r 31.   "
Sherman Hiram L.,   "
Walter Clarence S., r 41,   "
Williams Theodore,   "
Bixby Charles R.,   Nichols
Bixby Chester,   "
Curkendoll William, r 10,   "
Dunham Benjamin, r 36, Owego,   "
Edsall Benjamin F.,   "
Ellis George, Jr., Hooper's Valley,   "
Ellsworth Henry N.,   "
Laning Charles P.,   "
Loveland Seth H., Waverly,   "
Mallery John L., r 23, Owego,   "
Merrill Albert S.,   "

Mosher Edwin, Nichols
Newland Samuel, r 18, Owego, "
Turner G. M. Dallas, "
Waterman James H., r 8, "
Wiggins George, r 8, "
Abel Alonzo, 84 McMaster st., Owego
Becker Fayette A., Fifth ave., "
Beers Edwin W., South Side, "
Case Ellis L., 216 East Temple st., "
Cheeks Moulton, 508 Main st., "
Cole Smith B., 40 Adaline st., "
Conant Frank L., 122 Franklin st. "
Crans Egbert, 67 Central ave., "
Decker John S., Apalachin, "
Dexter Edwin J., r 54, Campville, "
Diamond Irving, 126 McMaster st., "
Duncan Stephen, 85 Paige st., "
Durfee Edgar S., 137 North ave., "
Durkee Charles R., 32 Main st., "
Edson George, over 107 North ave., "
Evans Josiah R., 4 William st., "
Evans Truman, r 54 Campville, "
FERGUSON T. JEFFERSON, 151 Talcott st.
Finch Smith, 170 West ave., "
Ford Charles H., r 35 Gaskills Corners, "
Ford Lucius, 607 Main st., "
Forgason Charles, 19 Lake st., "
Frank Walker, r 27, "
Genung Abram C., 118 Franklin st., "
GILLSON WILLIAM H., 116 West ave., "
Hall Granville W., Cortright House, "
Haner Addison L., r 96, "
Hemstrought Abram V., 198 E. Temple st., "
Holes George, 7 Park st., "
Hooker Archie S., 113 Franklin st., "
Hooker Warren, George st., "
Howard Orville, 7 Spruce st., "
Hutchinson James, 232 E. Temple st., "
Jones Edward, r 84, Apalachin, "
JONES JAMES E., 191 McMaster st., "
Jones Pardon, Apalachin, "
Kaley Adam I., r 4, "
Kaley William H., 177 Main st., "
Kellogg Ulysses P., 22 Fulton st., "
Knight Milton W., 56 Forsyth st., "
Lainhart Thomas, r 30 Union, Broome Co., "
Leasure George, r 123 South Owego, "
Leonard Allen, Water st., "
Lindsley Hiram, r 40, "
LOCKE REUBEN B., 241 Erie st., "
Male William, 22 William st., "
Manning William H., 113 Main st., "
McLean Ezra, 172 Talcott st., "
MEACHAM CHARLES D., 99 Talcott st., "
Middaugh Augustus B., 32 Adaline st., "
Newell Frank, 117 Central ave., "
Noble Asa S., 12 Adaline st., "
Noonan David E., 96 Franklin st., "
Orford Charles F., Apalachin, "
Park George W., 74 Fox st., "
Perkins Frederick, 21 Fulton st., "
Perry William H., South Side, "
Potter Isaac L., 100 Chestnut st., "
Randall Frank, 607 Main st., "
Relyea Andrew, 26 Fulton st., "
Reynolds Peter, 27 North ave., "
Richardson Wesley L., 557 Front st., "
Rightmier Charles H., 17 George st., "
Robinson Alvin T., Adaline st., "
Robinson George, 115 Temple st., "
Russell Minor, r 108 South Apalachin, "
Savey Edmund G., Apalachin, "
Savey William, Apalachin, "

Saxton Edward, 96 Liberty st., Owego
Searles Lot, 97 Central ave., "
Shepard W. Henry, Main st. "
Sisson William D., 18 Fulton st., "
Somers Daniel T., 130 Talcott st., "
Storm John C., 42 George st., "
Strong Lewis, 258 North ave., "
SYKES THEODORE P., 52 Liberty st., "
Upham Marcus K., 5 Temple st., "
VanBrunt Henry, 20 Temple st., "
VanOver Jacob, River st., "
Vermilyea Abram, 39 West ave., "
Wade Charles M., 119 West ave., "
Walker Amos, Adaline st., "
Walker Rial H., Buckbee Block, "
Walter Franklin A., r 25, Gaskill's Corners, "
Way William E., 174 North ave., "
Welch Charles, Adaline st., "
White John, 26 William st., "
Whittemore John, r 27, "
Williams Chester D., 59 West ave., "
Williams Edward W., 119 Main st., "
Yerks William A., 246 E. Temple st., "
Zimmer Albert, 66 Adaline st., "
Abbey Edward B., r 25, Richford
Allen Elmer, r 42, "
Barden Edward, r 18, "
Genung Orrin L., r 45½, "
HEATH NATHANIEL, r 40, "
HOWLAND HARRISON r 36, Center Lisle, Broome Co., "
Hutchinson Wesley J., Railroad st., "
King William W., r 10, Harford Mills, "
MEACHAM ORRIN N., r 37, "
Morton William, r 10, "
Robinson Isaac N., r 21, "
Vunk J. Frank, Main st., "
Welch Rufus H., Caroline, Tomp. Co., off r 23, "
Butts Charles E., Jr., Spencer
Clark Howard, "
Cowles Sylvester, r 2, North Spencer, "
De Remer Enos, r 36, West Candor, "
Ferris David A., r 63, "
Griffin James A., "
Hugg Horace A., "
Hutchings Eli M., "
Kirk Charles, r 59, Halsey Valley, "
Lott Benjamin, "
McKee George R., "
Osborn John C., r 43, "
Pierson George, "
Reeve Aaron D., "
Riker C. L., r 34, "
Riker William H., r 38, "
Robinson Fletcher O., "
Roe William W., r 38, "
Shaw John W., r 39, West Candor, "
Simms John C., r 43, Van Etten st., "
Stevens Seneca, r 65, "
Thornton George, r 37, West Candor, "
Van Kleek Jesse B., r 63, "
Van Natta Fred, r 47, "
VOSE EPHRAIM, r 38, "
Westbrook Arthur, "
Weeks William W., r 38, "
Barden A. E., Smithboro, Tioga
Bogart David R., Halsey Valley, "
Coleman James, r 52, Tioga Center, "
Coleman William D., r 52, Tioga Center, "
Fenderson Ely, r 41, Tioga Center, "
Fox Henry, r 47, Owego, "
Hamilton Charles, r 22, Tioga Center, "
Horton George M., r 70, Smithboro, "

Johnson J. Edward, Smithboro, Tioga
Johnson Peter M., r 53, Tioga Center, "
Johnson Warren, r 55, Smithboro, "
Middaugh Lorenzo T., r 73, Smithboro, "
Mulock Edwin, r 71, Smithboro, "
Pearsall John C., r 71, Smithboro, "
Pelham Charles, r 44, Owego, "
PERRY ALBERT A., Smithboro, "
Sargent Alvin. Smithboro, "
Snyder Charles, r 6, Owego, "
Snyder Nicholas N., r 4, Strait's Corners, "
TRIBE CHARLES H., Tioga Center, "
Truesdail William, r 44, Owego, "
Ward Perry C., r 41, Tioga Center, "
Weber Philip, jr., r 7, Owego, "
Wright William, Tioga Center, "
Yaples Charles, r 31, Owego, "

Carpet Weavers.

Price N. W. Mrs., 5 Pine st., Waverly, Barton
HART SARAH E., Speedsville, Tomp.
  Co., r 18, Berkshire
Emerson Charity, r 128, Strait's Corners,
  Candor
Hover Lucinda A., r 38, Newark Valley
LAWRENCE SARAH A., r 61, "
Wright Nancy W., r 8. Nichols
Lewis Maria Mrs., r 56, Owego
Locke Mary E., 91 Fox st., "
Yerks Clarissa, 31 Adaline st., "

Carriage, Wagon and Sleigh Manufacturers, and Wheelwrights.

COLEMAN CHARLES H., Lockwood, Barton
Dunham James J., Broad st., Waverly, "
Ellas A. Clark, Main st., "
Finch Amasa. Factoryville, "
Guyer H. E.. Broad c. Clark st , Waverly, "
Rowland John R., 242 Broad st., Waverly, "
VanAmburgh Abdial B., 304 Broad st.,
  Waverly, "
BRAINARD CHARLES E., Berkshire
BUFFINGTON CALVIN A., Railroad st., "
Houghtaling Burt, "
HOUGHTALING WILLIAM M., Main st., "
Humphreys Erastus E., Speedsville,
  Tomp. Co., r 19 cor. 17, "
Judd John N., r 6. "
PRATT MARSHALL D., "
CARPENTER WILLIAM L., Candor
Curtis William, r 5, "
Embody Jacob, "
Holden Dallas, r 120, Weltonville, "
PARMELE FREDERICK,(dealer)Main st., "
Searles George M., Main st., "
Chambers Charles, Newark Valley
Riley Andrew B., (dealer) "
WHITING BROS., "
Turner Harvey, off Main st., Nichols
Ballou Hartwell M., r 12, Owego
Hemstrought James, r 54, Campville, "
Hill Charles O., 89 Central ave., "
Kellum Ambrose, Apalachin, "
Moore & Ross, 146 North ave., "
Raymond & Emery, Central ave., cor.
  Temple st. "
Russell Minor, r 108, South Apalachin, "
Stratton Richard, r 20, "
Terbush Lancelott B., r 16, Flemingville, "
Genung Orrin L., r 45½, Richford
PERRY EDWIN A., r 43, "
Smith Julius C., "
BRUNDAGE DeWITT C., VanEtten st.,
  Spencer
CAMPTON SILAS, r 37, West Candor, "

Garey Abram L., Spencer
Hall Leonard F., r 28, "
Wood William H., "
Catlin George, r 52, Tioga Center, Tioga
Genung Adam S., Smithboro, "
Signor George H., r 36, Tioga Center, "

Cider Mills.

Manning Fred B., Halsey Valley, Barton
Mercereau & Co., Broad st., Waverly, "
Akins Henry S., r 18, Speedsville, Tomp.
  Co., Berkshire
Cooper & Thornton, r 62, West Candor, Candor
DU MOND DAVID, "
Snyder DeWitt M., r 1, Willseyville, "
Wheeler Abram T., "
FARNHAM OSCAR E., r 49½, Nichols
MATTHEWS ISAIAH, r 38, "
Rounds Simeon, r 83, Apalachin, Owego
Smith Orville, r 54, Campville, "
Card Charles P., r 43, Spencer
FARNHAM HERBERT, off r 12, Owego, Tioga

Clergymen.

Bowen George N., (Episcopal) Waverly, Barton
Cooper David H., (Baptist) Waverly, "
Evans Ziba, (M. E.) Lockwood, "
McShane Edward, (R. C.) 103 Clark st.,
  Waverly, "
Peck Luther, (M. E.) "
Pendell John R., (Bapt.) Waverly, "
Salmon Franklin J,, (Bapt.) "
Taylor John L., (Pres.) Waverly, "
Woodruff James O., (M. E.) Waverly, "
Hough Joel J., (Cong.) Berkshire
Cronk Byron E., (Bapt.) Candor
Jacobs Hiram C., (Bapt.) r 75, "
Osburn Arthur, (M. E.) r 116, "
Williston Horace, (M. E.) Owego st., "
Angell Thomas, (retired M. E.)
  Ketchumville. Newark Valley
Gale Hiram, (reform Meth.)
  Ketchumville, "
Leach Daniel F., (Bapt.) "
Treible Wilson, (M. E.) "
Van Deusen H. Newton, (M. E.) Nichols
Wilson James M., M. D. (Pres.) "
Barnes Newton W., (M. E.) Apalachin, Owego
Burton Reuben E., (Bapt.) 19 Ross st., "
Dickinson Ira W., (M. E.) r 73, Camp-
  ville, "
Fessenden Nelson, (W. Meth.) Apalachin, "
Howe Olin R., (Cong.) 290 Main st., "
Johnson Thomas D. (R. C.) Main st., "
Ketchum La Fayette F., (reform Meth.)
  92 Franklin st., "
Kidder James H., (P. E.) 100 Main st., "
McKenzie Alexander, (Pres.) 321 Front, "
Sandford William, (African M. E.) bds.
  106 Paige st.. "
Shepard Charles D., (M. E.) r 40 Flem-
  ingville, "
Tyler Edward, (Christian) Harford Mills,
  Richford
Howard Loring P., (M. E.) Spencer
Livermore Albert, (Pres.) "
Matteson Fayette A., (Bapt.) r 71,
  Smithboro, Tioga
Tilden Alanson, Tioga Center, "

Clothiers, Merchant Tailors, and Tailors.

(See also General Merchants.)

Betowski W. Leon, 123 Broad st.,
  Waverly, Barton

Mott Amasa S., 222 Broad st., Waverly, Barton
PERKINS FRED. C., 208 Main st.,
  Waverly,   "
Salousky Isaac, 224 Broad st., Waverly,   "
Smitt Antoni B., 10 Fulton st., Waverly,   "
Unger Adolph, Waverly,   "
Unger Solomon, 230 Broad st., Waverly,   "
Van Velsor & Co., 212 Broad st., Waverly,   "
Cross James O.,   Berkshire
Goldstein Bros ,   "
BANDLER ROBERT, 19 and 21 Lake st.,
            Owego
Berger Andrew F. F., Lake st.,   "
Coleman Juliette, 9 and 11 Lake st.,   "
Dwelle & Link, Front st.,   "
Whitson Isidor, 201 Front st.,   "

Coal and Wood Dealers, also Lime and Cement.

Gray DeWitt C., Erie st.. Waverly,   Barton
Guyer H. E., Broad cor. Clark st., Wa-
  verly,   "
HAGADORN DeWITT C., Lockwood,   "
Kane Edward M.,   "
Scott Charles, 256 Broad st., Waverly,   "
Sneffin & Scott, Broad st., Waverly,   "
Gridley William C., West Candor,   Candor
HEATH FRANK L., Main st.,   "
DIMMICK & YOUNG,   Newark Valley,
Williams Lucius E.,   "
*HOUSE EPHRAIM H., cor. West ave.
  and McMaster,   Owego
KEELER ALBERT H., Temple cor. Cen-
  tral ave,   "
Morse Newell, 133 Temple,   "
STEDMAN WHEELER, r 40, Flemingville, "
Smith W. C. & Co.,   Richford

Confectioners, Fruits, Ice Cream, Etc.

(See also Bakers and Confectioners, also Grocers)

Frauenthal Isedore E., 244 Broad st.,
  Waverly,   Barton
Horton Emma E. Mrs., 210 Broad st.,   "
Larnard Asolph S., 3 Elizabeth st.,   "
Turney William E., 239 Broad st., Waverly, "
JACKSON DWIGHT P., Main st.,   Candor
Johnson Silas W., r 88,   "
Westbrook Levi, Main st.,   Nichols
Beers Frank J., 55 North ave.,   Owego
CLARK HERMAN C., 68 North ave.,   "
Cuneo Pietro, 181 Front st.,   "
Graves Henry A., 49 Lake st.,   "
Groat Abram W., 115 North ave.,   "
McArthur John, 107 North ave.,   "
Tillotson James E., 86 North ave.,   "

Contractors and Builders.

(See also Architects and Builders, Carpenters
and Builders, and Masons and Builders.)

Blossom Jason B., 16 Chemung st., Wa-
  verly,   Barton
BROOKS AUGUSTUS. Lockwood,   "
Doane Gabriel P., 138 Chemung st., Wa-
  verly,   "
GENUNG SHERMAN A., Fulton st., Wa-
  verly,   "
Hess Nirum J., Fulton st., Waverly,   "
LARNARD A. WARREN, Lyman ave.,
  Waverly.   "
LENT CLARENCE A., Lincoln cor.
  Spring st., Waverly,   "
ROGERS CHARLES H., 413 Chemung
  st., Waverly,   "

Seacord John, 27 Lincoln st., Waverly, Barton
Simcoe Eli, Waverly,   "
VanAtta Azariah, 111 Penn. ave.. Waverly "
Vibbert Charles M., 148 Waverly st.,   Waverly
WALLACE ALFRED H., 150 Waverly
  st., Waverly,   Barton
Brooks George T., Owego st.,   Candor
Cronk Byron E.,   "
ELMENDORF CYRENUS, Main st.,   "
German Cyrus B.,   "
STOWELL ALMOND F., Railroad st.,   "
VOSE ENOCH, West Candor, r 108,   "
Ackerman Cornelius R., Jenksville,
         Newark Valley
Angell Elworth J.,   "
Chapman Canfield,   "
Chapman George M.,   "
BIXBY SMITH R., River st.,   Nichols
Evans Elijah K., r 8,   "
WIGGINS CLOYD B., r 8,   "
Woods Elisha B., r 40,   Richford
Corchrane & Conant, 62 Temple st.,   Owego
Dean James A., Spencer ave.,   "
Fox William S., Apalachin,   "
Groesbeck George S., r 61,   "
Hamilton Joel A., 3 Front st.,   "
Johnson Andrew J., r 104, Apalachin,   "
KEELER ALBERT H., Temple cor.
  Central ave.,   "
Kellogg Charles T., 262 Prospect st.,   "
Sullivan James, 58 Liberty st.,   "
Terrill L. Fontenell, 100 Franklin st.,   "
WARNER FRANK H., Fox st.,   "
WELCH DAVID A., 243 Prospect st.,   "
Welch William H., 267 Prospect st.,   "
Richardson & Campbell, r 43,   Spencer
Sawyer Ezra O.,   "
West Marshall C.,   "
FORD & BAUER, Strait's Corners,   Tioga

Coopers.

Manning Judson, r 9, Halsey Valley,   Barton
Skellenger Daniel J., Speedsville, Tomp.
  Co.,   Berkshire
Ahlers Dedrick G., Gould st.,   Candor
Barber Hiram, r 139,   "
Reasor James B., r 44,   "
Strong Eugene B., Willseyville, r 3,   "
Wolverton Charles A., r 131,   "
Golden Augustus H., r 22, West Newark,
         Newark Valley
Golden Prentis E., r 22, West Newark,   "
Moon Levi B.,   "
Campbell Amos B.. Owego,   Nichols
Hyde William, r 20,   Owego
Ingersoll Eugene F., r 46,   "
Vincent Dexter C., r 46,   "
Thompson Benjamin, r 44,   Richford
Brown William, r 18,   Spencer
Eaton Daniel B., Smithboro.   Tioga
Forsyth W. Henry, r 21, Halsey Valley,   "
Hevland Douglass, r 28, Owego,   "
HOYT IRA, r 21, Halsey Valley,   "
Hyde Gordon, r 12, Owego,   "
Hynes Charles, Halsey Valley,   "
Stimpson Charles, Smithboro,   "

Country Stores.
(See General Merchants.)

Creameries.

CAYUTA CREAMERY, Schuyler & Hard-
  ing, props.. Factoryville,   Barton
GILLETT & DECKER CREAMERY, W.
  E. Gillett and A. I. Decker, props.,
  Reniff,   "

Higgins & Rounsevell, Speedsville, Tomp.
Co., Berkshire
BAKER BROS., Nichols
SPENCER CREAMERY, S. A. Seely,
prop.; D. La M. Georgia, sup't; Liberty st., Spencer

Crockery and Glassware.

FARLEY & SANDERS, 231 Broad st.,
Waverly, Barton
HIBBARD GEORGE R., 84 Front st., Owego

Dentists.

Nelson Elmer, 251 Broad st., Waverly, Barton
Snook Frederick M., 231 Broad st., Waverly, "
VanDERLIP CHARLES T., 201 Broad
st., Waverly, "
House Willard E., Main st., Candor
Fellows Russell S., Newark Valley
DOWNS EDWIN D., 192 Front st., Owego
HILL BROTHERS, Front st., "
Jackson John, 12 Lake st., "
MAYOR WILLIAM E., over 173 Front st., "
Walker Ransom, over 200 and 202 Front st., "
Rawley George W., Main st., Richford
Matteson George E., Main st., Spencer
Anderson John J., r 12, Tioga

Dressmakers.

Aikins Jane, 118 Clark st., Waverly, Barton
Beardslee Mary Mrs., 2 Ithaca st., Waverly, "
Beekman Emma, 127 Chemung st., Waverly, "
Brooks Lizzie D., 12 Waverly st., Waverly, "
Cooley Hattie J., North Barton, "
Dollason Frances H., "
Falsey Sarah A., Clark st., Waverly, "
French Carrie, 314 Broad st., Waverly, "
Miller Cassandra B., 482 Chemung st.,
Waverly, "
Minnick J. H. Mrs., 28 Loder st., Waverly, "
Murray Mary L., Pine st., Waverly, "
Osterhout Katie, 23 Broad st., Waverly, "
Sargeant J. C. Mrs., 28 Orange st.,
Waverly, "
Shaw Hulda J., 9 Waverly st., Waverly, "
SHIPMAN PERLIE E., r 34, Waverly, "
Shulenburg Sarah, 304 Cherry st.,
Waverly. "
Smith D. S. Mrs., 21 Fulton st., Waverly, "
Strause Huldah, 218 Broad st., Waverly, "
Sullivan Anna. 105 Chemung st., Waverly, "
Sullivan Etta, 315 Broad st., Waverly, "
Terry E. H. Mrs., 5 Penn. ave., Waverly, "
Tompkins Mary A., Factoryville, "
VanDerlip Sisters, 24 Park ave., Waverly, "
Williams Addie, 20 Clark st., Waverly, "
Brown Sarah J., Candor
Brown Mary A., Newark Valley
Flannigan Susie, "
Sears Lizzie M., "
Reeves Ella, River st., Nichols
Scott Sisters, Cady ave. "
Bauer Elizabeth, 26 Adaline st., Owego
Bowen Abby A., over Owego Nat. Bank, "
Bryan Esther C., Spencer Blk. Lake st., "
Catlin Sarah E., 75 Talcott st., "
Catlin Mary E., 75 Talcott st., "
Cortright John Mrs., 201 E. Temple st., "
Cole Ida M., 261 Erie st., "
Donovan Mary A., 102 Paige st., "
Dorsey Alma J., 207 E. Temple st., "
Dowd Anna E., 5 Park st., "
Earsley Belle Mrs., Commerce st., "

Edwards Susie, r 83, Apalachin, Owego
Greenwood Lizzie M., 80 William st., "
Hickey Lizzie C., 399 Main st. "
Hoagland Emma D., Buckbee Blk., "
Hodge Ella A., 86 Temple st., "
Hogan Catherine M., 60 Delphine st., "
Horgan Katie, 56 Delphine st., "
Kelly Julia F., 246 E. Temple st., "
Kincade Charles Mrs., 90 Paige st., "
Laird George H. Mrs., Apalachin, "
Ross Allie M., 42 William st., "
Rowe M. & G., 192 Front st., "
Skellenger Emma E., 51 Forsyth st., "
Stever Amanda E. Mrs., over 78 North
ave., "
Wade L. N. Mrs., 175 North ave., "
Whipple Sisters, 139 Main st., "
Wood Lydia, 76 Talcott st., "
STEWART EMILY A , off r 12, Owego, Tioga

Drugs and Medicines.

Bennet Stephen, Broad st., Waverly, Barton
Hayes H. H. & Son, 236 Broad st.,
Waverly, "
Mullock Bros., 229 Broad st., Waverly, "
SLAUGHTER & VAN ATTA, 233 Broad
st., Waverly, "
Tracy Edward G., 228 Broad st., Waverly "
HOLCOMB WALLACE, Berkshire
Jennings James H., Front st., Candor
Ross M. L. & Son, Main st., "
Smith William B., Main st., "
SMITH L. M. & SON, Newark Valley
Latham & Cady. Main st., Nichols
BEACH & PARMELEE, Main cor. North
ave., Owego
Beaumont John H., 135 North ave., "
HOPKINS LANCY N., Apalachin, "
JANSEN J. W. & Co., 60 North ave., "
Kenyon Joel C., 5 Lake st., "
*STARKEY & WINTERS, cor. Front and
Lake sts.. "
WHITE & HUMISTON, 194 Front st., "
Rawley Hiram B., Richford
Fisher Charles J., Main st., Spencer
EMMONS LUCIUS E., Main st., "
Blake William, Tioga Center, Tioga

Dry Goods.

KNAPP JOSEPH W., 203 Broad st.,
Waverly, Barton
Murdoch E. N. & Co., 222 Broad st.,
Waverly, "
STOWELL HOLLIS R., 237 Broad st.,
Waverly, "
WATROS BROS., 227 Broad st., Waverly, "
Wilcox H. M. & Co., 218 Broad st.,
Waverly, "
JOSLYN EDWARD, Main st., Nichols
BUCKBEE, PETERSON, WOOD & CO.,
190 and 192 Front st.. Owego
GOODRICH & CO., 196 Front st., "
Hall George H., 122 Main st., "
HASTINGS & STRATTON, 186 Front st., "
Hulslander Levi S., 59 North ave. "
Hyde Earl Mrs., Main st., "
Newman Bros., 31 and 33 Lake st., "
Tuck Isaac, 198 Front st., "
Taylor Robert J., 377 Front st., "

Eggs and Poultry.

(See also Fancy Fowls, etc., Poultry Dealers.)

ROBERTS JOHN O., (wholesale) Newark Valley

Express Agents.

HAGADORN DeWITT C., Lockwood,   Barton
Kane Edward M.,   "
Murdoch John K., (U. S.) Waverly, "
BROWN FRANK W., West Candor,   Candor
HEATH FRANK L., Main st.,   "
Rockwood Lorenzo F., (U. S.) Newark Valley
KIRBY ALLEN B.,   Nichols
Hutchins Frank F., (U. S. Ex.) 34 Lake st.,
                                Owego
Mabee Foster N., (Erie Ex. Co.) 18 Lake st. "
STEELE AARON, Apalachin,   "
Rich Lucien D.,   Richford
Mills Henry C.,   Spencer
Sanderson P. W. N., Tioga Center,   Tioga

Fertilizers.

Bushnell William B.,   Berkshire
HART LEWIS A., Main st.,   Candor
CAMPBELL ARBA, Talcott st.,   Owego
KEELER ALBERT H., Temple cor. Cen-
tral ave.,   "

Florists and Seedsmen.

(See also Seedsmen.)

Angell Mary L., 472 Chemung st., Wa-
verly,   Barton
Dingee John T., 116 Lincoln st., Waverly, "
THOMAS ALEXANDER J., Main st.,   Owego

Furniture Dealers.

HALL & LYON, 356 Broad st., Waverly,
                                 Barton
Slawson Andrew A., Waverly,   "
Sweet C. W., Broad st., Waverly,   "
WITTER F. A. & CO.,   Berkshire
Frost John O., Main st.,   Candor
CARGILL WILLIAM,   Newark Valley
Neal N. E., Cady ave.,   Nichols
HUBBARD & KING, 29 Lake st.,   Owego
Matson John L., 183 Front st.,   "
PIERCE WALLACE C.,   Richford
Bower Bros.,   Spencer

Gents' Furnishing Goods.

(See also Clothing, also Dry Goods, also General Merchants.)

McDONALD SARAH A. Mrs., 265 Broad
st., Waverly,   Barton
PERKINS FRED C., 208 Main st., Wa-
verly,   "
Salonsky Isaac, 224 Broad st., Waverly, "
Goldstein Bros.,   Berkshire
BANDLER ROBERT, 19 and 21 Lake st.,
                                Owego
Berger Andrew F. F., Lake st.,   "
Fairchild Samuel F., 27 Lake st., "

General Merchants.

(Who keep a general assortment of Dry
Goods, Groceries, Hardware, etc. See also
Dry Goods, also Groceries.)

BINGHAM BROS., Lockwood,   Barton
Cornell William,   "
Evarts Andrew J., Factoryville,   "
GILLETT WILLIS E., Reniff,   "
Gridley T. E. & Son, Main st., Factory-
ville,   "
VAIL A. V. C. & CO., Lockwood,   "
WOOD JAMES C., Main st., Factoryville, "
Wright & Cary, Main st.,   "
Clark Horatio, Main cor. Depot sts., Berkshire
DEWEY & DARBONNIE,   "
Eldrige E. O. & Co., Main st.   "

Andrews William H., Front st.,   Candor
Booth & Williams, Front st.,   "
Cooper Fred B., Strait's Corners, "
Knapp Burr D., Weltonville,   "
McCARTHY & THOMPSON, Main st.,   "
MEAD CHARLES, r 75, Weltonville,   "
Minor Christopher, r 30, Willseyville, "
Orcutt William C., Owego st.,   "
Owen William, r 29,   "
Sawyer Luther, r 62, West Candor, "
Smith H. A., Catatonk, r 133,   "
VanDebogart Frank L., Main st.,   "
Byington Alphonso,   Newark Valley
ELWELL WILLIAM,   "
Finch Charles, Ketchumville,   "
FORD ALBERT N.,   "
Nixon John G., r 1, Jenksville,   "
RANDALL OSCAR S.,   "
ROYS & TODD,   "
Bliven Cranston, Main st.,   Nichols
EDSALL JOHN R., Main st.,   "
Sherwood Casper I.. Main st.,   "
Kinney & Gray, Apalachin,   Owego
KNAPP CHARLES R., Apalachin,   "
SLEEPER & WHITTAKER, Apalachin,   "
Rawley Hiram B.,   Richford
Smith W. C. & Co.,   "
Bradley Chas. E., Main st.,   Spencer
DAY JOHN & SON, Main st.,   "
EMMONS ALFRED S.. Van Etten st.,   "
FISHER MARVIN D., Main st.,   "
Kellogg Mahlon A., North Spencer, "
SEELY S. ALFRED, Academy st.,   "
SHEPARD SYLVENES, Van Etten st.,   "
Sniffin William A., Main st.,   "
Stanclift Isaac S., Van Etten st., "
Barber Ami W., Halsey Valley,   Tioga
Bonham Charles H., Main st.,   "
Drake W. J. & Son, Main st., Smithboro, "
Hoyt Fred. D., Halsey Valley,   "
Lollis Samuel C., Smithboro,   "
Martin Fred, Main st., Tioga Center, "
Southwick Mary J. Mrs., Halsey Valley, "
Wheeler John N., Strait's Corners, "

Grain Threshers.

Albright Adam, North Barton,   "
Hoover William, r 41,   Barton
Cooper & Thornton, r 62 West Candor, Candor
Coon A. H. & W. I., Strait's Corners, "
DU MOND DAVID,   "
Hulslander Sylvester, r 101,   "
MEAD WILLIS A., r 70,   "
Mix John C.. Willseyville, r 1,   "
BURCH & WELLS,   Newark Valley
Nichols John E., East Nichols, Nichols
BLOW FRANK L., r 95,   Owego
Camp Orin, r 54,   "
RYANT R. & J. P., r 20. North Spen-
cer,   Spencer
Smith & Truesdail, r 44, Owego,   Tioga

Grist and Flouring Mills and Dealers.

BINGHAM BRO'S, Lockwood,   Barton
Manning Fred. B., Halsey Valley,   "
Waverly Steam Flouring Mills, (J. C.
Shear prop.) 300 Broad st., Waverly, "
BERKSHIRE FLOURING MILLS, Berkshire
Bushnell William B.,   "
Hart Samuel L., (grist) Speedsville
Tomp. Co., r 18,   "
BARROTT SAMUEL R., r 82, Welton-
ville,   Candor
Candor Mill, A. Beebe prop. Main st. "

Hoff Lewis R., Main st.,   Candor
HUBBARD WILLIAM H., r 98,   "
JENKSVILLE STEAM MILL, C. D. Nixon, prop., Jenksville,   Newark Valley
Moses Philander P., (custom)   "
White George W., (custom) Jenksville,   "
Williams Lucius E., (feed)   "
Dunham's Mills, Caleb Wright, prop., r 8,   Nichols
HUNT ADONIJAH. r 37, Owego,   "
NICHOLS STEAM FLOUR MILLS, John Fenderson, prop..
Beeman Horace W., (feed) r 116,   Owego
Curtis Harmon, r 35, Gaskill Corners,   "
DORWIN, RICH & STONE, office 177 Front st.,   "
Ellis Nathan H., r 40,   "
FOSTER LEONARD, (feed) r 27,   "
Kile George O., (feed) r 95,   "
Terbush Lancelott B., (feed) r 16, Flemingville,   "
Weed J. D. & G. W., (Custom)   "
Bliss Franklin,   Richford
HARFORD MILLS, Granger Francis & Son, props.,   "
PERRY EDWIN A., r 43,   "
Wilbur James F.,   "
HAGADORN DAVID B., r 57,   Spencer
SEELY S. ALFRED,   "
Franklin Burton B., r 52, Tioga Center, Tioga
JONES STEPHEN W., r 9, Owego,   "
Leach Stephen W., Owego,   "
Tuthill Joseph M., Smithboro.   "

Groceries and Provisions.

(See also General Merchants.
BARNES & MILLER, 227 Broad st., Waverly,   Barton
FARLEY & SANDERS, 231 Broad st., Waverly,   "
Gerould B. & Co., 111 Broad st., Waverly, "
Gibbons James S., 246 Broad st., Waverly, "
Hallet & Son, 245 Broad st., Waverly, "
HANFORD & LORD, 222 Broad st., Waverly,   "
Hart Brothers, 205 Broad st., Waverly, "
Hern John, 117 Broad st., Waverly, "
Parsons & Freestone, 207 Broad st., Waverly,   "
Persons E. Delos, 206 Broad st., Waverly, "
Quigley Michael, 263 Broad st., Waverly, "
Sager & Munn, 234 Broad st., Waverly. "
SEELY WILLIAM F., 257 Broad st., Waverly,   "
SWAIN LESTER, Fulton st., Waverly, "
Stevens Samuel, r 46, Lockwood, "
WALKER LEANDER, 253 Broad st., "
WALKER T. S. & Son, 250 and 252 Broad st., Waverly,   "
WAVERLY CASH STORE, 227 Broad st., Waverly,   "
HOLCOMB WALLACE,   Berkshire
Bush Abram R. Willseyville,   Candor
Fister John W., Main st.,   "
JACKSON DWIGHT P., Main st.   "
O'Brien Thomas, r 30, Willseyville,   "
Wardwell & Cooper, r 62, West Candor.   "
White Morgan A., Willseyville.   "
Woodard Mary G., r 82, Weltonville,   "
BENTON WILLIS S., r 1, Jenksville,   Newark Valley
Chapman Lyman F.,   "
ROBERTS JOHN O.,   "
ANTHONY FLOYD H., Main st.,   Nichols

Van Ness Belle H. Mrs., Main st.,   Nichols
Cornell H. W. & Son, 405 Main st.,   Owego
Cortright Albert, North ave.   "
Cortright Theodore, 64 North ave.   "
Curtis Harmon, r 35, Gaskell's Corners,   "
Dickinson McKenzie, r 54, Campville,   "
DUGAN JOHN, 173 Front st.,   "
GREEN A. L. & R. D. r 25, Gaskell's Corners,   "
Hyde & Winters, Front cor. Court sts.,   "
Johnson Edward J., 100 North ave.   "
KNAPP WILBUR F., Apalachin,   "
Lake Thomas B., 119 North ave.,   "
Leach Benjamin C., North ave.,   "
Leahy Patrick & Son, Main cor North ave.,   "
Maroney John F., 56 North ave.   "
MILLREA BROTHERS, 178 Front st.,   "
Olmstead Seth, r 40,   "
Raymond Mary F., 199 Main st.,   "
Searles J. F. & Son, 136 North ave.,   "
Shays Jonas, 72 North ave.,   "
Shaw & Ringrose, Lake cor. Main sts.,   "
Sheldon & Yates, 131 North ave.,   "
SMITH CHARLES F., 172 Front st.,   "
Steele G. Odell, 177 Front st.,   "
Thurston Chester P., 176 Front st.,   "
Thurston Frederick G., 130 North ave.,   "
Truman Benjamin L., 182 Front st.,   "
Wade George N., West ave.,   "
Wheeler John, r 54, Campville,   "
MILLER WILLIAM F., Main st.,   Richford
Bowen Seth,   Spencer
DAY JOHN & SON, Main st.,   "
Nichols David A., Main st.,   "
Van Marter Enos T., r 35,   "

Hair Goods.

PELLUM MARGARET H., 459 Main st.,   Owego
Yost Mary E. Mrs., over Owego National Bank,   "

Hardware, Stoves and Tinware.

(See also General Merchants.)
CLARK JAMES A., 217 Broad st., Waverly,   Barton
EATON D. H. & SONS, Factoryville,   "
MERRIAM BROS., 235 Broad st., Waverly, "
WITTER F. A. & CO.,   Berkshire
CHIDSEY JOHN R.,   Candor
DeGraw John, Main st.,   "
HEATH HENRY D., Main st.,   "
CHAPMAN EDGAR E.,   Newark Valley
HUTCHINSON HORACE W.,   "
Coleman & Horton, Main st.,   Nichols
Everitt Fred M.,   "
HOUK JONATHAN S., 184 Main st.,   Owego
KNAPP FRANK J., Apalachin,   "
STANBROUGH JOHN B., 180 Front st.,   "
STORRS, CHATFIELD & CO., Front cor. Lake st.,   "
Swift Charles H., Main st.,   Richford
DAY JOHN & SON, Main st.,   Spencer

Harness, Trunks, etc.

Deuel Amos E., 250 Broad st., Waverly, Barton
Nelson Phineas, 127 Broad st., Waverly,   "
ROLLEY HIRAM,   Berkshire
Humiston Morris, Railroad st.,   Candor
PIERSON CHARLES O.   Newark Valley
Smead David J., 150 Front st.,   Owego
Williams John E., Apalachin,   "
Wyman William, 112 North ave.,   "
BARNES GRANT W.,   Richford

SNOOK DAVID L., Main st.,   Spencer
Hamilton George, Halsey Valley,   Tioga

Hats, Caps and Furs.

(See Clothiers, also General Merchants.)
PERKINS FRED C., 208 Main st., Waverly,   Barton
BANDLER ROBERT, 19 and 21 Lake st.,   Owego
Fairchild Samuel F., 27 Lake st.,   "
Smith James L., 8 Lake st.,   "

Hay and Grain.

Barnum & Personius, 264 Broad st., Waverly,   Barton
BAILEY W. H. & CO., 164 North ave., Owego
SPEERS WILLIAM S., 207 North ave.,   "
STEDMAN WHEELER, r 40, Flemingville,   "

Hotels.

American House, A. P. Head, prop., 260 Broad st., Waverly,   Barton
Central House, F. D. Tooker, prop., Factoryville,   "
Christie House, W. H. Goldsmith, prop., Fulton st., Waverly,   "
Commercial Hotel, D. S. Kennedy, prop., Fulton cor. Elizabeth sts., Waverly,   "
Gilbert House, Mrs. Eva J. Gilbert, prop., Lockwood,   "
HOTEL WARFORD, Wadsworth & Kelsey, props., Broad cor. Fulton, Waverly,   "
Jackson House, A. Jackson, prop., Factoryville,   "
Johnson House, E. J. Johnson, prop., Main st.,   "
Temperance Hotel, Miles Forman, prop.,   "
TIOGA HOTEL, Ackley & Bailey, props., Fulton Cor. Elizabeth, Waverly,   "
BERKSHIRE HOUSE, Ira Crawford, prop.,   Berkshire
ALLEN HOUSE, Iddo Vergason, prop., Main st.,   "
ASHLAND HOUSE, Frank J. Norton, prop., Main st.,   Candor
DIMMICK HOUSE, Dimmick & Young, props.,   Newark Valley
Ketchum's Hotel, Seneca Ketchum, prop., r 12, Ketchumville,   Newark Valley
NICHOLS HOTEL, J. Platt, prop., River st.,   Nichols
AH-WA-GA HOUSE, B. J. Davis, prop., Front cor. Church sts.,   Owego
Central House, Alanson Goodenow, prop., Apalachin,   "
CENTRAL HOUSE, W. G. Gardner, mgr., Main cor. Lake sts.,   "
CORTRIGHT HOUSE, J. A. Cortright & Son, props., 157 North ave.,   "
DUGAN HOUSE, Charles B. Dugan, prop., 139-145 Front st.,   "
EUROPEAN HOUSE, John Hayes, prop., 151 North ave.,   "
EXCHANGE HOTEL, John S. Ryan, prop., Apalachin,   "
FLEMINGVILLE HOTEL, Mrs. Eunice E. Hall, prop., r 40, Flemingville,   "
Hiawatha House, (summer) Hiawatha Island.   "
Lackawanna House, Ira J. VanDemark, prop., 176 River, South Side,   "
Park Hotel, Nichols & Huber, props.; 161 Main st.,   "
Thomas Samuel H., 54 South Depot st.,   "

RICHFORD HOTEL, H. W. Theleman, prop.,   Richford
GROVE HOTEL, C. J. Rice, manager, opp. G. I. & S. depot,   Spencer
VAN MARTER HOUSE, J. VanKeuren, prop., Main st.,   "
Erie Hotel, Cornelius Curkendoll, prop., Smithboro,   Tioga
Halsey Valley House, Mrs. Jane P. Higgins, prop., Halsey Valley,   "
Lovell House, Smithboro,   "
Tioga Center Hotel, Moses Ohart, prop., Main st., Tioga Center,   "

Insurance Agents.

BROOKS CHARLES C., 201 Broad st., Waverly.   Barton
Excelsior Mutual Benefit Association, 201 Broad st., Waverly,   "
FAIRCHILD & THOMAS, First Nat. Bank Bld'g, Waverly,   "
Hallett Joseph E., 409 Chemung st., Waverly,   "
Lemon Israel G., (fire and life) 245 Broad st., Waverly,   "
LUM DANIEL J., Waverly st., Waverly,   "
Tew William E., 214 Broad st., Waverly,   "
Johnson Eugene F., agt. r 6,   Berkshire
Bishop James (fire and life) Main st.,   Candor
BOOTH HORACE F., Main st.,   "
KETCHUM WILLIAM P., Kinney st.,   "
ROBINSON ALDICE A., (fire and life) Main st.,   "
Royal Morris B., Owego st.,   "
SPAULDING U. P., (fire and life) Main st.,   "
HUNT LEWIS,   Newark Valley
FAY GEORGE W., 203 Front st.,   Owego
HOSKINS WATSON L., 185 Front st.,   "
Laird George H., Apalachin,   "
LEONARD GEORGE S., 209 Front st.,   "
Snyder George, (life) over 63 North ave.,   "
STEBBINS BARNEY M., 34 Lake st.,   "
VAN KLEECK JOHN J., Court House,   "
Hilligas Joshua, (life) Tompkins ave., Spencer
Manchester Henry H., (life) r 47, Owego,   Tioga

Iron Founders and Machinists.

LEMON JAMES, Broad st., Waverly,   Barton
CANDOR IRON WORKS, H. F. Booth prop.   Candor
*CAULDWELL & GRAY, (engines, boilers, castings, &c.,) McMaster cor. Delphine,   Owego

Jewelry, Watches, Etc.

Harris George L., 2 Fulton st., Waverly,   Barton
Knapp David D., 211 Broad st., Waverly,   "
Mandeville Mahlon H., 228 Broad st., Waverly,   "
Hartwell Warren T., Main st.,   Candor
FRANK CHARLES,   Newark Valley
Tripp Seymour C., Main st.,   Nichols
COMFORT MELVILLE L., 25 Lake st', Owego
DURUSSEL & SON, 35 Lake st.,   "
HOSKINS WATSON L., 185 Front st.,   "
STARR CHARLES P., 15 Lake st.,   "
Rawley George W., Main st.,   Richford
Dumond Harry, Main st.,   Spencer
Sagar Willard J., Main st.,   "

Laundries.

Tioga Laundry, Geo. B. Witter prop.
113 Broad st., Waverly,   Barton
Bing Wah, (Chinese Laundry) 71 North
ave.,   Owego
Casey Thomas F., 210 Front st.,   "
CITY STEAM LAUNDRY, 83 North ave.,   "

Lawyers.

ALLEN ADOLPHUS G., 203 Broad st.,
Waverly,   Barton
Allen D. Wellington, Waverly,   "
EATON AMBROSE P., Exchange Blk.,
Main st., Waverly,   "
Floyd Jacob B., Broad st., Waverly,   "
SHOEMAKER JUDGE F., 214 Broad st.,
Waverly,   "
WARNER WILLIAM F., Waverly,   "
Scott Elbert O., Main st.,   Candor
BIEBER ROMAINE F.,   Newark Valley
ANDREWS GEORGE F., 214 Front st., Owego
CAMP GEORGE SIDNEY, 132 Front st.,   "
CLARK C. A. & H. A., Academy Bldg.,
Court st.,   "
EASTON DAVID T., over 168 Front st.,   "
GLEZEN OSCAR B., Academy Bldg.,
Court, st.,   "
GROSS JERRY S., 178 Main st.,   "
Hill Fred C., Court House,   "
Lynch Martin T., Lake cor. Main st.,   "
MEAD & DARROW, Main cor. North ave.,   "
NIXON CHARLES D., Front cor. Court st.   "
Oakley Timothy B., 214 Front st.,   "
OHART S. JAY, Academy Bldg., Court,   "
PARKER CHARLES E., Court House,   "
SEARS JOHN G., Lake cor. Main st.,   "
SETTEL LYMAN L., Post-Office Bldg.,   "
TAYLOR JOHN J., Front cor. Court st.,   "
Watkins Charles D., over 168 Front st.,   "
ROBINSON CALVIN J.,   Richford
DEAN EDWARD E., Main st.,   Spencer
Poole Murray, Smithboro,   Tioga

Livery Stables.

Atwater DeWitt C., Clark st., Waverly, Barton
Bentley Abram W., Broad st., Waverly,   "
Hagadorn Henry, 2 Broad st., Waverly,   "
LASSLY ELIJAH M., Clark cor. Broad
st., Waverly,   "
Tozer John F., Fulton st., Waverly,   "
ROCKFELLER CHARLES H., Main st.,
Berkshire
CHIDSEY GEORGE C., Main st.,   Candor
GRIFFIN N. W., Main st.,   "
HOLLISTER WARREN L., Main st.,   "
ANTHONY FLOYD H., Main st.,   Nichols
DEAN CALVIN B., Church st.,   Owego
COYLE WILLIAM, 73 North ave.,   "
FORGASON THADDEUS, Central ave.,   "
Ford Lewis, 132 North ave.,   "
WEEKS JOSHUA P., Water st.,   Spencer

Live Stock Breeders and Dealers.

Coleman Jedediah D., (dealer)   Barton
BLACKMAN ABRAM, (dealer)   Berkshire
Brown Robert C., (breeder) r 38,   "
CROSS LOUIS J., (horse breeder)   "
Kimball & Stannard, (horse breeders) r 35, "
LEGG ERASMUS D., Speedsville, Tomp.
Co., (breeder)   "
Lynch Theodore, (dealer)   "
MAYOR THEODORE & SONS, (dealers
and breeders) r 38,   "
PATCH HENRY W., (dealer in horses) r 39,   "

ROYCE GEORGE C., (breeder of horses)
Main st.,   Berkshire
SHAW WILLIAM T., (breeder) r 5,   "
Shepard James, r 3, (breeder of horses)   "
SIMMONS WILLIAM E., (breeder of
horses) Jenksville, r 41,   "
BARROTT AMMIEL W., (breeder and
dealer) r 120,   Candor
Holmes John, (dealer)   "
HOWARD HIRAM O., (horse breeder) r
118,   "
McCay Edwin C., Jenksville, r 49, (dealer) "
Miller Fred, Weltonville, (dealer) r 120,   "
PETERS CHARLES G., (breeder and
dealer) r 65,   "
Schofield Truman, West Candor, (dealer)
r 62,   "
SEAMAN LeGRAND, (dealer) r 89,   "
Stinard Sylvester, Jenksville, r 50,
(breeder)   "
Ward Oswald J., (dealer)   "
Webster Edwin, (breeder and dealer) r
132, Owego,   "
Whitney Joseph S., (dealer)   "
Bieber Philip, (dealer) r 42,   Newark Valley
Holmes Jerome D., (horse dealer)   "
SMITH ALFRED, (horse breeder) r 51,
Jenksville,   "
Briggs Herman I., (dealer) off r 9,   Nichols
INGERSOLL GEORGE A., r 10, (breeder)   "
LOWMAN FREDERIC C., (breeder) r 3,   "
CAMP GURDON H., (horse) Apalachin, Owego
Delavan Irving J., (dealer) Front st.,   "
HOLMES BROS., (horses) Apalachin,   "
LaMonte David M., (horse breeder) r 68,   "
MARSHLAND STOCK FARMS, B. F.
Tracy & Son, prop., (breeders) r 69,
Apalachin,   "
McCofferty Anthony C., (horses) Euro-
pean House,   "
Sherwood George J., (breeder) r 106,
Apalachin,   "
Town William P., (horses) r 122, South
Owego,   "
Tracy Harvey J., (breeder) r 83, Apa-
lachin,   "
Clark Charles A., (horses)   Richford
Curtis Charles F., (breeder and dealer)
r 39,   "
FINCH CHARLES R., (breeder) horses,   "
Finch Philander W., (dealer)   "
GOODRICH WILLIAM S.,   "
Jennings Henry A., (breeder and dealer)
r 35,   "
Meloy Frank P., (breeder and dealer) r 33, "
Sears James M., (breeder and dealer) r 16, "
Smith Ralph P., (breeder and dealer) r 35, "
WATKINS AMOS G., (dealer)   "
Roda Frederick C., r 9,   Spencer
BROCK JOHN, r 42,   "
Shepard J. Q. & G. T., r 28,   "
SHAW W. HULSE, (breeder Holstein)
r 28, Owego,   Tioga

Lumber Manufacturers and Dealers.

(See also Saw Mills.)

ANDRE ABRAM T., (contractor) Lock-
wood,   Barton
BALDWIN HUGH, Broad n Penn. ave.,
Waverly,   "
Dodge Ira G., Waverly,   "
HAGADORN DeWITT C., (fence-posts
and R. R. ties) Lockwood,   "

Ball John,   Berkshire
JAPHET MILO G.,   "
Williams George,   "
Booth Brothers, (manufrs. and dealers)
  r 56.   Candor
Little William L., Main st.,   "
RYAN JOHN, Mill st.,   "
VAN DEUSER H. & M., r 133, Catatonk, "
Van Vleet Theodore, (dealer) Main st., "
VERGASON SOLOMAN, (dealer) r 112,   "
CLINTON ROYAL W.,   Newark Valley
Williams Lucius E.,   "
CLAPP SAMUEL, River st.,   Nichols
Hill Charles O., 89, Central ave.,   Owego
*HOUSE E. H., 299, McMaster st.,   "
*OWEGO CRUCIFORM CASKET CO.,
  42, 44 and 46 Delphine st.,   "
STEDMAN WHEELER, r 40, Flemingville, "
ALLEN J. W., r 18,   Richford
FINCH H. S. & C. W.,   "
EASTHAM SAMUEL, r 37, West Candor,
                                     Spencer
Hall H. S., r 38,   "
McMaster J. O. & J. T.,   "

Marble and Granite Workers and Dealers.

DONLEY BROS.,   Newark Valley
HAYWOOD CHARLES M., 80 North
  ave., Owego, and 107 Broad st.,
  Waverly,   Barton
SPENCER MARBLE WORKS, L. E.
  Baker, prop., Academy st.,   Spencer

Masons and Builders.

(See also Architects and Builders, also Car-
  penters and Builders, and Contractors
  and Builders.)
Curran Horace H., Waverly,   Barton
Curran John J., Waverly,   "
DAILEY WILLIAM E., Spring st.,
  Waverly,   .‘
ISLEY & SONS, 36 Waverly st., Waverly, "
Jones George, off r 60, Factoryville,   "
McINTYRE ALBERT J., Lincoln st.,
  Waverly,   "
MORGAN FRED S., Clark st., Waverly,   "
MORGAN JOHN W., 112 Lincoln st.,
  Waverly,   .‘
SHERMAN CHARLES W., 428 Chemung
  st., Waverly,   "
Sherman James, r 64, Waverly,   "
Sherman John H., r 64, Waverly,   "
SMEATON THOMAS, 152 Clark st.,
  Waverly,   "
CHURCH ORRIS, r 29,   Berkshire
Smith Emory J., Railroad st.,   "
Braman Jesse H.,   Candor
Cortright Franklin, Weltonville,   "
COWLES JAMES C., r 91,   "
FIELD RICHARD, Mountain ave.,   "
Gibbons Frank,   "
Keeler Ethelbert B., r 94,   "
Markle David, r 91,   "
Merrick Abner, r 13, Speedsville, Tomp.Co., "
Perrine Daniel H., r 134,   "
GOODFELLOW HEZEKIAH, r 40½,
                               Newark Valley
HILLIGAS LORENZO D.,   "
Neal Harvey, (stone)   "
Perry George, (stone)   "
Searles Ezra, r 61,   "
THORNTON C. FRANK, (stone)   "
Keech Miles W., r 46,   Nichols
Sullivan Dennis O.,   "

Williams Stephen, r 8,   Nichols
Conklin Lewis D., r 60,   Owego
Cragan John, Apalachin,   "
Eckler Marvin, (stone) 188 West ave.,   "
Howe Rufus C., Main st.,   "
Kaley William H., 177 Main st.,   "
Keeler Charles P., 68 Paige st.,   "
Lillie William, r 108, Apalachin,   "
Lynch Michael, 7 Fulton st.,   "
McDonald John, 18 W. Main st.,   "
Mott Israel D., r 54,   "
Noonan Daniel, Paige st.,   "
Rulison George P., Apalachin,   "
Schopp Francis A., River Road, South
  Side,   "
Schopp Peter, River Road, South Side,   "
Searles George, r 4, Flemingville,   "
Searles Nathan P., r 16½, Flemingville, "
Shehan Timothy, 105 Paige st.,   "
Skillman David, 219 North ave.,   "
Van Fleet James,   "
Vincelett John, 79 Forsyth st.,   "
Ward Ezra, South Side,   "
White Davis, 154 Front st.,   "
Nigus Judson, (stone) r 7,   Richford
Morton William, r 10,   "
MEACHAM JAMES W., (brick) r 37,   "
MEACHAM ORRIN W., r 37,   "
Burdick Peter, r 42,   Spencer
Cortright Ayres D., r 54, Halsey Valley, "
Deyo Chauncey, r 33,   "
Goodrich Calvin J.,   "
Hike W. Harvey,   "
House John P.,   "
Newman Daniel,   "
Shaw William, r 54,   "
Vorhis J. Wallace,   "
Delano Charles, r 28, Owego,   Tioga
Leonard George, r 51, Tioga Center,   "
Mallery George, Smithboro,   "
Mallery Henry, Smithboro.   "
Stewart Delos, off r 12, Owego,   "
STEWART EDWARD, off r 12, Owego,   "
Watkins John, Smithboro,   "
Wright William, Tioga Center,   "

Meat Markets and Butchers.

Boda & Dimmick, 231 Broad st., Waverly,
                                     Barton
Carr & Teachman, 119 Broad st., Waverly, "
Dorsett & Faulkner, 215 Broad st., Waverly, "
Hanna Lorentes J., Main st., Factoryville, "
Miller Samuel W., 248 Broad st., Waverly, "
Pike Grove N., 109 Broad st., Waverly, "
PUFF & WILLIAMS, Fulton st., Waverly,   "
Stevens Samuel, r 46, Lockwood,   "
WILCOX & BARROWS, 271 Broad st.,
  Waverly,   "
PRENTICE NORMAN A., (fish) Main st.,
                                   Berkshire
MILKS WILLIAM J., Spencer st.,   Candor
BYINGTON SHERMAN W.,   Newark Valley
JAYNE & BALL,   "
Waterman Walter S., Main st.,   Nichols
Lake Thomas B., 119 North ave.,   Owego
MILLREA BROTHERS, 178 Front st.,   "
Shays George, 82 North ave..   "
STEVER PETER, 74 North ave.,   "
WEBSTER GILBERT E., 133 North ave.,   "
White Charles, 36 Lake st.,   "
Cashaday Guy, Main st.,   Spencer
Osborn John,   "
Watkins William H., Tioga Center,   Tioga

TIOGA COUNTY HERALD

PUBLISHED WEEKLY AT

NEWARK VALLEY, N. Y.

CHARLES L. NOBLE ————— AND ————— **G. E. PURPLE,**

PUBLISHERS AND PROPRIETORS.

AN INDEPENDENT FAMILY NEWSPAPER, DEVOTED
TO HOME INTERESTS AND GENERAL NEWS.

SUBSCRIPTION PRICE,   -   - $1.25 PER YEAR

IF PAID IN ADVANCE.

JOB * PRINTING

Of all kinds done in the Best Style and at the Lowest Prices.

Milk Dealers.

ALLEN JOHN, Waverly, Barton
BUCK LYMAN, Waverly, "
Hoyt Joseph N., Waverly, "
Warner John A., r 65, Waverly, Barton
Roper Frank H., r 18, Owego, Nichols
SMITH JOHN JR., r 18, Owego, "
Moody Chas. E., r 42, Spencer

Milliners, Millinery and Fancy Goods.

Delaney Josie E., 211 Broad st., Waverly, Barton
Manning E. W. Mrs., 249 Broad st., Waverly, "
Morgan George Mrs., 16 Johnson st., Waverly, "
TANNERY IDA, 233 Broad st., Waverly, "
Walsh Maggie, 232 Broad st., Waverly, "
Ward & Van Vleet Misses, Candor
Brougham (Helen & Sarah) Newark Valley
Holladay Anna M., "
JOSLYN EDWARD, Main st., Nichols
Van Demark Emma Mrs., Main st., "
Brown Della, 67 North ave., Owego
BUCKBEE, PETERSON, WOOD & CO., 190 & 192 Front st., "
Gilman N. M. Mrs., 204 Front st., "
Manning Caroline M., 206 Front st., "
Newman Brothers, 31 and 33 Lake st., "
YAPLE O. A. MRS., Main st., Richford
Abbey Lizzie, Main st., Spencer
Garatt S. C., Van Etten st., "

Millwrights.

Houghtaling Burt, Berkshire
Cleveland George M., r 1, Willseyville, Candor
Starkweather Joel, Pond st., "
Stevens Aaron C., r 41, Newark Valley
Wiggins George, r 8, Nichols
Leonard John B., r 35, Richford
Smith Julius C., "
Thomas John D., r 71, Smithboro, Tioga

Music and Musical Instruments.

BROWN CHARLES E., 267 Broad st., Waverly, Barton
Slawson Jeremiah M., 202 Broad st., Waverly, "
BACON GEORGE G., dealer, r 65, Candor
DeGroat J. DeWitt, (pianos) r 67, Owego
Leach Benjamin C., North ave., "
SIGNOR ALBERT, 207 Front st., "
SPENCER WILLIAM H., 220 E. Temple st., "
Thompson John M., 107 North ave., "
HOAGLIN MARVIN A., r 43, Richford

Music Teachers.

Speh Charles Prof., Waverly, Barton
Pendell Mary E. O., Waverly, "
BACON GEORGE G., r 65, Candor
Caple Adam, r 104, "
Humiston John H., Main st., "
Locey Charles E., "
Ballou Wendell D.. r 56 1-2, Owego
Benner Louise E., Apalachin, "
Druckenmiller Charles Prof., 73 Liberty, "
JOHNSON FRANCES M., 459 Main st., "
Leach Tillie C., North ave., "
Pultz Griffin, jr, 51 Fox st., "
Purdy Emma D., 147 Main st., "
Putman Louis H., 425 Main st., "
Perry Frank, r 44, Richford

Painters and Paper Hangers.

(See also Artists.)
Bostwick Silas W.,Waverly st.,Waverly, Barton
Keeler Thomas, Broad st., Waverly, "
Lyon Alonzo, Waverly, "
Salisbury Thomas L., 130 Waverly st., Waverly, "
Sliter Warren, Factoryville, "
Smith S. Charles, Broad c. Pine, Waverly, "
Stuart Will E., Main st., "
Toppen Henry, 114 Waverly st., Waverly, "
CROSS LEWIS J., Berkshire
HAY HENRY L., "
Carpenter Harry L., (house) Weltonville, Candor
Sarson John C. F., (house) r 3, "
Stevens Andrew T., r 3, "
Hooker Charles B., Newark Valley
Howard Urial A., "
Sturtevant David M., (carriage) "
Ellsworth Elwin T., Nichols
JOHNSON HORACE A., 52 George st., Owego
ROMINE CHARLES F., 121 Erie st., "
Romine Clarence W., 119 Chestnut st., "
ROMINE EDWIN B., (house and decorative) Opera House Block, "
ROMINE PERCIVAL H., (house and ornamental) 81 Fox st., "
WEBSTER GEORGE H., 242 E. Temple st., "
Hopkins Daniel H., Main st., Richford
GUINNIP DEMPSTER N., Brooklyn st., Spencer
GUINNIP GEORGE, Brooklyn st., "
Maine William F., "
Roberts James A., Smithboro, Tioga

Patent Medicine Manufacturers.

Butts Henry S., 204 Penn ave., Waverly, Barton
Carey Daniel G., Broad st., Waverly, "

Peddlers.

Bently George, off r 39, Barton
Stanton Elisha W., Speedsville. Tomp. Co., r 18, Berkshire
Phipps George, r 12, Ketchumville, Newark Valley
Bush James L., Constines Lane, Owego
Hayes Michael J., 185 E. Temple st., "
Perkins Barney, r 89½, Apalachin, "
Reynolds Smith, 133 North ave., "
Damson John, Liberty st., Spencer
Morse Dana, "
Edwards Samuel, r 9, Owego, Tioga
Lockwood Charles, Tioga Center, "

Photographers.

Comstock A. B., 208 Broad st., Waverly, Barton
Mead Tabatha J. Mrs., 204 Broad st,, Waverly, ..
*HARGRAVE WILLIAM G., 38 and 40 Lake st., Owego
Jackson John T., 12 Lake st., "
Lovejoy Charles L., Front cor. Court sts., "
Clapp Walker G., Van Etten st., Spencer
Ritzler Charles C., r 48, "

Piano Manufactures.

SPORER, CARLSON & BERRY, 58 North ave., Owego

Piano Tuners.

Carlson John M., 63 Paige st., Owego
VICKERY CHARLES S., 84 Paige st., "

Physicians and Surgeons.

Beach Eliza J., 208 Penn. ave., Waverly, Barton
CANFIELD EZRA, Lockwood, "
Cook Daniel, r 55, "
Harnden Daniel D., 7 Waverly st., Waverly, "
Harnden Rufus S., 31 Fulton st., Waverly, "
Johnson Parmeous A., 14 Pennsylvania ave., Waverly, "
JOHNSON WILLIAM E., Waverly st., Waverly, "
Tucker John T., Waverly, "
Tyrrell Augustus, 222 Broad st., Waverly, "
Vosburgh Henry P., Halsey Valley, "
Vreeland Isaac S., 229 Broad st., Waverly, "
EASTMAN RALPH D., Main st., Berkshire
Gay Isaac W., Main st., "
Walter Joseph S., r 27 cor. 11, "
Chidester Chauncey W., Weltonville, Candor
DIXON JOHN C., Main st., "
HARRIS ALGERNON J., Main st. "
Miller Daniel S., Main st., "
Osburn Arthur, r 116, "
ROPER WILLIAM E., Owego st., "
BISHOP FRANCIS M., Newark Valley
BURR WILLIAM J., "
ROGERS CORNELIUS R., "
Tappan Revere C., "
Cady George M., River st., Nichols
CADY GEORGE P., River st., "
Allen Lucius H., 140 Main st., Owego
AYER WARREN L., 207 E. Main st., "
Ayers Charles, r 94, "
BARRETT JAMES M., Main c. North ave., "
Beach George W., Apalachin, "
Briggs Mary L., 5 Park st., "
CRANS ABRAM F., 126 North ave., "
DUTCHER MERRITT T., over 15 Lake st., "
FRANK JOHN, 115 Main, "
GREENLEAF JOHN T., 101 Main st., "
HEATON CARLTON R., Park cor. Main, "
Jansen Jesse W., 60 North ave., "
LEWIS GEORGE B., Lake cor. Main, "
LEWIS ISAAC W., r 314, Apalachin, "
*NEWGEON MARY F., 295 Main st., "
PEARSALL ANDREW T., Taylor Blk., Main cor. Spencer ave., "
STEARNS PHINEHAS S., "
*WILSON JAMES, 295 Main st., "
Allen James, Main st., Richford
DAVIS GEORGE W., Main st., Spencer
Fisher William H., Main st., "
Homiston Ezra W., Main st. "
NORRIS ALONZO, "
Tanner John H., Center st., "
CATLIN JAMES H., r 43, Tioga Center, Tioga
HOLLENBACK CHARLES E., r 21, Halsey Valley, "
Knapp Sylvester, Smithboro, "
McDonald Charles H., r 68, Smithboro, "
Post Albert W., r 51, Tioga Center, "
White Leon, Halsey Valley, "

Planing Mills.

BINGHAM BROS., Lockwood, Barton
GILLETT W. E., Reniff. "
VAIL A. V. C. & CO., Lockwood, "
GRIDLEY S. EGBERT, Candor
BURCH & WELLS, Newark Valley
FENDERSON JOHN, Nichols
CAMPBELL & LAMPHERE, Apalachin, Owego
Weed J. D. & G. W., "

JONES STEPHEN W., r 9, Owego, Tioga
TRIBE CHARLES H., Tioga Center, "

Poultry Dealers and Raisers.

(See also Produce Dealers.)
Councilman Edwin W., r 35, (breeder)
NOBLE LYMAN B., (dealer) "
STEVENS HENRY W., r 42, (raiser) "
GOODRICH STEPHEN S., r 46, Owego, "

Printing Offices.

*FREE PRESS, James B. Bray, prop., 15 Fulton st., Waverly, Barton
*THE WAVERLY ADVOCATE, E. L. Vincent, prop., 4 Elizabeth, Waverly, "
*WAVERLY TRIBUNE, Noble & Noble, props., Elizabeth st., Waverly, "
*TIOGA COUNTY HERALD, Noble & Purple, props., Newark Valley
BROCKWAY LEON L., 34 Lake st., Owego
*OWEGO GAZETTE, L. W., Kingman, prop., 28 Lake st., "
*OWEGO RECORD, Scott & Watros, props., 172 Front st., "
*OWEGO TIMES, W. Smyth & Son, props., 193 Main st., "
SLATER FRANK B., 75 Paige cor. Temple sts., "
*SPENCER HERALD, VanGelder & Son, props., Main st., Spencer

Produce (Country) Dealers.

(See also General Merchants.)
Jones John R., 268 Broad st., Waverly, Barton
Ball George P., (buyer) Berkshire
COLLINS JUNIUS, (dealer) "
Lynch Eugene F., "
Manning Alexander D., (buyer) "
Waldo Elijah B., William st., "
WILLIAMS MORRIS, A., (potatoes) "
BARROTT AMMIEL W., Weltonville, Candor
HART LEWIS A., Main st., "
Kyle S. F. & Co., Catatonk, "
Strong Joel H., r 98, "
DIMMICK & YOUNG, (shippers) Newark Valley
JAYNE & BALL, "
Bliven Cranston, Main st., Nichols
DUNHAM EBENEZER, Main st., "
Harris, DeGroat & Co., Main st., "
BARTON ISAAC W & CO., 114 Front st., Owego
Barton William, Apalachin, "
Delavan Irving J., Front st., "
Hover Robert, (buyer) 274 North ave., "
Jewett Charles, r 104, Apalachin, "
RODMAN CHARLES, Front st., "
Rodman Edward D., Main cor. Court st., "
SLEEPER & WHITTAKER, Apalachin, "
SPEERS WILLIAM S., 207 North ave., "
SMITH FRED W., 38 Lake st., "
Stedman Wheeler, r 40, Flemingville, "
STILES & SIBLEY, "
TRUMAN G., SONS & CO., 174 Front st., "
Finch Philander W., Richford
MILLER WILLIAM F., Main st., "
Moore Charles H., (butter and eggs) "
SWARTOUT M. L & SON, Academy st., Spencer
EVELIEN ALFRED, Tioga Center, Tioga
Pepper Jackson S., r 60, Smithboro, "

Real Estate.

Parshall Luther, Waverly,   Barton
Tew William E., 214 Broad st., Waverly,   "
SPAULDING U. P., Main st.,   Candor
NIXON CHARLES D., Front cor. Court,
        Owego
Pumpelly James F., South Side,   "
Stebbins Barney M., 34 Lake st..

Restaurants.

(See also Hotels.)

Head Richard, 252 Broad st., Wa-
  verly,   Barton
SWAIN LESTER, Fulton st., Waverly,   "
WEBBS DINING HALL, (Henry A.
  Webb, prop.) 216 Broad st., Wa-
  verly.   "
Griner John N., Depot st.,   Berkshire
Wilbur William E., 182 Main st.,   Owego

Saw Mills.

(See also Lumber Manufacturers and Dealers.)

Ackley Alex. W., Lockwood,   Barton
BINGHAM BROS., Lockwood,   "
Bogart John, Waverly,   "
Cornell William,   "
GILLETT W. E., Reniff,   "
HANNA CHARLES F., off r 66, Factory-
  ville,   "
Lott George W., r 1, Van Ettenville,
  Chem. Co.,   "
VAIL A. V. C. & CO., Lockwood,   "
Akins Henry S., r 18, Speedsville, Tomp.
  Co.,   Berkshire
Ball John,   "
JAPHET MILO G.,   "
Williams George,   "
BARROTT SAMUEL R., r 82, Welton-
  ville,   Candor
Hoose & Hasbrouck, Willseyville,   "
HUBBARD WILLIAM H., r 98,   "
Snyder Dewitt M., Willseyville, r 1,   "
Mayo Hiram, r 29,   "
VAN DEUSER H & M., Catatonk, r 133,   "
White Morgan A., Willseyville,   "
BURCH & WELLS,   Newark Valley
CLINTON & BURROUGHS, r 9,   "
Davis Franklin, r 25,   "
White George W.,   "
Williams Lucius E.,   "
HUNT ADONIJAH, r 37, Owego,   Nichols
Lounsberry John, r 21,   "
Loveland Seth H., Waverly,   "
NICHOLS STEAM SAW MILL, John
  Fenderson, prop.,   "
PEARSALL L. BURR, r 5, Hooper's Val-
  ley,   "
CAMPBELL & LAMPHERE, Apalachin,
        Owego
Curtis Harmon, r 35, Gaskill's Corners,   "
FOSTER LEONARD, r 27,   "
Kile George O., r 95,   "
Rounds Simeon, r 83 Apalachin,   "
Searles Homer, r 16½, Flemingville,   "
Tobey James D., r 83, Apalachin,   "
Weed J. D. & G. W.,   "
ALLEN J. W., r 18,   Richford
Cooper Ephraim A., r 3, Slaterville,
  Tomp. Co.,   "
FINCH H. S. & C. W.,   "
HARFORD MILLS, Francis Granger &
  Son, prop.,   "
Tobey Josiah G., r 26,   "

TUBBS GAMALIEL C., Center Lisle,
  Broome Co., r 36,   Richford
EASTHAM SAMUEL, r 37, W. Candor,
        Spencer
Emery James C., r 13,   "
Mowers Jacob H., r 20 1-2, North Spencer, "
SEELY S. ALFRED,   "
Signer Albert, r 2, North Spencer,   "
Doane Timothy, r 3, Strait's Corners,   Tioga
JONES STEPHEN W.. r 9, Owego,   "
Signor Charles, r 36, Tioga Center,   "
Snyder Henry A., r 5, Strait's Corners,   "
TRIBE CHARLES H., Tioga Center,   "
WILLMOT JAMES R., r 28, Owego,   "

Seedsmen.

(See also General Merchants, also Hardware.)

Barnum & Personius, 264 Broad st.,
  Waverly,   Barton
Corwin Oliver B., 270 Broad st., Waverly, "
Sneffin & Scott, Broad st., Waverly,   "

Sewing Machines.

Slawson Jeremiah M., 202 Broad st.,
  Waverly,   "
Sherwood Warren D.,   Newark Valley
Lewis John A., r 95,   Candor

Shoemakers.

(See also Boots and Shoes.)

Corwin Lewis, Broad st., Waverly,   Barton
Donnelly Owen, 218 Erie st., Waverly,   "
Hanford Clark, Factoryville,   "
Hill George W., 127 Broad st., Waverly,   "
Mahoney John, Broad st., Waverly,   "
Root Ransom R., Main st.,   "
Houk Daniel, r 35, Wilson Creek,   Berkshire
Cornish Albert A., r 95,   Candor
Graham Andrew J., Weltonville,   "
Legg Stillman J., Main st.,   "
Benton Lyman C., r 1, Jenksville,
      Newark Valley
Hall Sheridan G., r 22, Jenksville,   "
HAVENS GEORGE,   "
Holdridge Ira J., r 11, Ketchumville,   "
WOOD HENRY A.,   "
VanNess William W., Main st.,   Nichols
Basford James, 150 River st., South Side,
        Owego
Bennett Nathaniel, Fox st.,   "
Branch Andrew, r 54, Campville,   "
Collins William, Lake st.,   "
Courtright Herbert N., r 106, Apalachin,   "
MORTON LEVI, Apalachin,   "
Pease George, 160 North ave.,   "
Shupp Lawrence, 18 Lake st.,   "
Thornton Thomas, r 27,   "
AYERS JAMES W.,   Richford
Bell Augustus E., Main st.,   "
Garey Daniel, r 2, North Spencer,   Spencer
Montgomery Wm.,   "
Brown Alvah S., Halsey Valley,   Tioga
French Jeremiah, Tioga Center,   "
Goodenough Chauncey J., Main st.,
  Tioga Center,   "

Soap Manufactories.

Beseler C. William, cor. Temple and
  Liberty sts.,   Owego
Excelsior Soap Factory, 37 Temple st.,   "
EMPIRE SOAP WORKS, office 83 North
  ave.,   "

P. C. VanGelder.   C. J. VanGelder.

THE

SPENCER HERALD

A Five Column Quarto Weekly Newspaper,
Eight Pages, Forty Columns.

VAN GELDER & SON,   P. C. VAN GELDER,
Publishers.   Editor and Proprietor.

SPENCER, TIOGA COUNTY, N. Y.

It has a large and growing circulation, is an outspoken
independent journal, and has a liberal local advertising
patronage.

The office is located in the extreme northwest corner
of Tioga County, N. Y., and adjoining Tompkins and
Chemung Counties. Two railroads run through the
place—the E. C. & N. and the G. I. & S.—which make
it invaluable to local advertisers.

Sporting Goods.

Bennet Stephen, Broad st., Waverly, Barton
Waring Norman K., (fly rod manuf.)
Newark Valley
Beach D. & Co., 197 Main st., Owego
PIERCE WALLACE C., Richford

Station Agents.

Atwood Wm. W., (D. L. & W.,) Waverly, Barton
Clock C. E., (G. I. & S.,) Factoryville, "
Hubbell Nelson, (Erie R. R.,) Waverly, "
Kane Edward M., "
HAGADORN DEWITT C., Lockwood, "
Waldo Elijah B., William st., Berkshire
BROWN FRANK W., West Candor, Candor
HEATH FRANK L., Main st., "
Smith H. A., r 133, Catatonk, "
Rockwood Lorenzo F., (S. C. R. R.)
Newark Valley
KIRBY ALLEN B., (D. L. & W. R. R.) Nichols
DEAN CAMERON B., (N. Y. L. E. & W.)
Owego
Corey William H., (D. L. & W.) "
Gale William E., (S. C. R. R.) "
STEELE AARON, (D. L. & W.) Apala-
chin, "
Rich Lucien D., Richford
Cook Anderson B., North Spencer, Spencer
Howell Myron P., (G. I. & S.) "
Mills Henry C., (E. C. & N.) "
Bellis William L., (Erie R. R.) Smith-
boro, Tioga
Sanderson P. W. N., Tioga Center, "
Stimpson Henry, (S. C. R. R.) Smithboro, "

Tanners.

DECKER TANNERY, A. I. Decker, prop.,
Factoryville, Barton
DAVIDGE, HORTON & CO., Berkshire
Hulmboldt Tannery. Candor
DAVIDGE, LANDFIELD & CO., Newark Valley
CAMPBELL ARBA, Talcott st., Owego
DEAN H. N. & SON, North ave., "
Quirin J. G. & Co., Tioga Center, Tioga

Telegraph Operators.

Beach Arthur N., Waverly, Barton
Bixby Fred, Waverly, "
Corey Leonel C., Factoryville, "
HAGADORN DeWITT C., Lockwood, "
Kane Edward M., "
Kinney F. Eloise, Waverly, "
Scanlon Martin, Waverly, "
SMITH JAMES H., Factoryville, "
Steele Edward J., Waverly, "
Patch Robert C., Main st., Berkshire
BROWN FRANK W., West Candor, Candor
German Edward C., "
Merrill Nellie, Willseyville, "
Joslin Joseph D., r 41, Newark Valley
Rockwood Lorenzo F., "
Kennedy John M., Nichols
Barnes Katie, 73 Liberty st., Owego
Billings John, 73 Liberty st., "
BROWN PATRICK, 182 River, South Side, "
Dee James, 313 Main st., "
Fox Lewis L., Apalachin, "
Gale William E., (S. C. R. R.) "
Pert William, 31 Front st., "
Yothers Horace, "
Lacy Louis V., Richford

Robinson James, Richford
Robinson Fred J., "
Cook Anderson B., North Spencer Spencer
Denniston Chester B., "
PALMER HEMAN L., "
Hanmer George W., r 9, Catatonk, Tioga
Pilkington Charles, r 9, Catatonk, "

Tobacco and Cigars.

Clark & Ralyea, 275 Broad st., Waverly,
Barton
Ferguson Hartwell M. & Co., 200 Broad
st., Waverly, "
Myers Charles K., 201 Broad st., Wa-
verly, "
NICHOLS HURLEY L., 213, Broad st.,
Waverly, "
Ziegler Benjamin F., Johnson st., Wa-
verly, "
Hart Colden H., r 34, Wilson Creek, Berkshire
MATTHEWS ISAIAH, r 38, (manuf.) Nichols
Barton George W., 191, Main st., Owego
Gavell Edward, 169, Main st., "
Ogden Aaron, 7 Lake st., "

Toy Manufacturers.

Crandall Charles M., Broad st., Waverly, Barton

Undertakers.

Fessenden Harvey G., Waverly, "
Slawson Andrew A., Waverly, "
Sweet C. W., 243 Broad st., Waverly, "
CARGILL WILLIAM, Newark Valley
HUBBARD & KING, 23 Lake, st., Owego
Matson John L., 183 Front st., "
PIERCE WALLACE C., Richford
PALMER J. H. & SON, Main st., Spencer

Variety Stores.

Brewster Curtis, Broad st., Waverly, Barton
ENGLEMAN GUS, 131 Broad st., Waverly, "
McDONALD DUNCAN J., 247, Broad st.,
Waverly, "
BALL JOHN P., 170 Front st., Owego
Lainhart George, 212 Front st., "
SLATER FRANK B., 75 Paige cor. Tem-
ple sts., "
Straus Julius L., 43 Lake st., "

Veterinary Surgeons.

Sherry J. Robert, 6 Pine st., Waverly, Barton
PRATT MARSHALL D., Berkshire
Heath James H., r 30, Wilseyville, Candor
MILKS WILLIAM J., Spencer st., "
Burr William H., Newark Valley
FORGASON THADDEUS, Central ave., Owege

Wood Turning.

BROOKS AUGUSTUS, Lockwood, Barton
COLEMAN CHARLES H., Lockwood, "
FARNHAM OSCAR E., r 49½, Nichols
FARNHAM HERBERT, off r 12, Owego, Tioga
JONES STEPHEN W., r 9, Owego. "

Wool Carding.

FARNHAM HERBERT, off r 12, Owego, Tioga

Wool Dealers.

COLLINS JUNIUS, Berkshire
Bliss, Thompson & Co., 174 Front st., Owego
PITCHER DANIEL M., 175 Front st., "

Woolen Mill.

BARAGER CHARLES F., Candor

THE

Waverly

Tribune

A LIVE LOCAL NEWSPAPER.

GIVES ALL THE LOCAL, COUNTY AND NEAR-BY HAPPENINGS.

FIRST IN THE WEEK,

IS ALWAYS FREE FROM VULGARITY.

IS A GOOD FAMILY NEWSPAPER THAT WE SHOULD GET $2.00 A YEAR FOR, BUT WE LET YOU HAVE IT FOR $1.50, ON ACCOUNT OF LOCAL CUSTOM.

ADVERTISERS LIKE IT,

BECAUSE THE READER HAS CONFIDENCE IN IT, AND BEING EIGHT-PAGE THERE ARE MORE CHOICE LOCATIONS FOR THEM.

ADVERTISEMENTS—RATES GIVEN ON APPLICATION.

SOCIETIES.

Masonic Fraternity.

BARTON.—Waverly Lodge, No. 407, F. & A. M., meets first, third and fifth Monday evenings of each month, in Masonic Hall.

Cayuga Chapter, No. 245, R. A. M., Waverly, meets second and fourth Monday evenings of each month.

NEWARK VALLEY.—Newark Valley Lodge, No. 614, F. & A. M., meets in Davidge, Landfield & Co.'s Hall, second and fourth Monday evenings of each month; E. G. Nowlan, W. M.

NICHOLS.—Westbrook Lodge, No. 333, F. & A. M., meets the Wednesday evening on or after the full moon in each month; Samuel Clapp, W. M.; E. Coleman, S. W.; Dr. George P. Cady, Sec.

OWEGO.—Friendship Lodge, No. 153, F. & A. M., meets on the first Wednesday evening after the first Monday in each month; B. J. Davis, W. M.; C. S. Carmichael, Sec.

New Jerusalem Chapter, No. 47, R. A. M., meets at Masonic Hall, first and third Mondays of each month; F. M. Mabee, H.P.; M. B. Watkins, Sec.

Owego Chapter, No. 510, R. M. R., meets at Masonic Hall, monthly, C. M. Haywood, M. W.; N. A. Steevens, Sec.

Ahwaga Lodge, No. 587, F. & A. M., meets at Masonic Hall, first and third Tuesdays after the first Monday in each month; N. A. Steevens, W. M.; George H. Thompson, Sec.

Evening Star Lodge, No. 19, F. & A. M., meets first and third Monday evenings of each month, opposite Ahwaga House; J. W. Barrett, W. M.; A. Sample, Sec.

SPENCER.—Spencer Lodge, No. 290, F. & A. M., meets first and third Tuesday evenings of each month; Charles Riker, W. M.; I. S. Stancliff, Sec.

TIOGA.—Tioga Lodge, No. 534, F. & A. M., was organized at Smithboro, 1863; William J. Drake, W. M.; John P. Swartwood, Sec.

Temperance Societies.

NEWARK VALLEY.—North Star Lodge, No. 21, P. of T., Jenksville, meets every Saturday evening; Monroe Barrett, W.S., Frank Keith, Sec.

OWEGO.—Apalachin Lodge, No. 564, I. O. G. T., Apalachin; S. M. Rulison, C.T., Carrie Rulison, Sec.

Union Council, No. 47, R. T. of T., meets at Odd Fellows' Hall, the second Wednesday evening of each month; F. S. Hodge, S.C., H. C. Brainard, Sec.

SPENCER.—Spencer Council, No. 181, R. T. of T., meets second and fourth Tuesday evenings of each month; William Swartout, S.C., David Seely, Sec.

Grand Army of the Republic.

BARTON.—Stebbins Post, G. A. R., No. 361, Lockwood, meets first and third Thursday evenings of each month; Richard Andrus, Com., G. W. Brink, Adj.

CANDOR.—Candor Post, No. 383, meets at Grand Army Hall, first and third Tuesday evenings of each month; B. E. Cronk, Com., S. J. Legg, Adj.

NEWARK VALLEY.—Williams Post, No. 245, G. A. R., meets second and fourth Saturday evenings of each month, in Roys Block Hall; Harvey Neal, Com., B. S. Harvard, Adj.

NICHOLS.—Warwick Post, No. 259, G. A. R., meets second and fourth Tuesday evenings of each month; William Herrick, Com., L. B. Ross, Adj.

OWEGO.—Babcock Post, No. 59, G. A. R., meets every Wednesday evening, at Grand Army Hall; D. S. Legg, Com., O. L. Newell, Adj.

Tracy Post, No. 613, G. A. R., Apalachin; J. S. Giles, Com., H. J. Cooper, Adj.

RICHFORD.—Belden Post, No. 342, G. A. R., meets every Saturday evening; F. Hutchinson, Com., N. Heath, Adj.

SPENCER.—Dawson Post, No. 464, G. A. R., meets second and fourth Saturday evenings of each month; W. A. Stubbs, Com., L. Brooks, Adj.

Patrons of Husbandry.

BARTON.—North Barton Grange, No. 45, P. of H., meets every Saturday evening; C. S. Nichols, W. M., John F. Hoyt, Sec.

Sullivan Grange, No. 217, P. of H., meets every Saturday evening at Grange Hall, Shepard's Creek; H. Bunnell, W. M., T. Hulett, Sec.

Acme Grange, P. of H., meets weekly; R. R. Cooley, W. M., H. Stebbins, Sec.

16

CANDOR.—Candor Grange, No. 203, P. of H., meets at Grange Hall, first and third Fridays of each month; Epenetus Howe, W. M., G. H. Hart, Sec.

Weltonville Grange, P. of H., meets every Thursday evening; W. R. Mead, W. M., H. E. Reese, Sec.

Strait's Corners Grange, No. 453, P. of H., meets on the first and third Saturdays of each month; A. L. Rider, W. M., S. Hammond, Sec.

NEWARK VALLEY.—Newark Valley Grange, No. 476, P. of H., meets Friday evening of each week; W. F. Prentice, W. M., Mrs. C. S. Shaffer, Sec.

NICHOLS.—Wappasening Grange, No. 522, P. of H., meets on the first and third Saturday evenings of each month; F. C. Lowman, W. M., Robert P. Coryell, Sec.

OWEGO.—Pomona Grange, a county organization, made up of members of subordinate Granges, meets regularly at Owego every three months; O. H. Van Atta of Barton, W. M., Mrs. B. J. Brooks of Barton, Sec.

Gaskill Corners Grange, No. 403, P. of H., meets every Saturday evening; George W. Hull, W. M., Mrs. G. W. Hull, Sec.

RICHFORD.—Eureka Grange, No. 345, P. of H., meets every Friday evening; Mrs. Emma Jayne, Sec.

Knights of Honor.

BARTON.—Waverly Lodge, No. 293, K. of H., meets every Friday evening in K. of H. Hall.

CANDOR.—Candor Lodge, No. 542, K. of H., meets first and third Tuesdays of each month; Richard Fields, Dic., J. O. Frost, Rep.

NICHOLS.—Susquehanna Lodge, K. & L. of H., meets on the first and third Wednesday evenings of each month; Rev. H. N. Van Deusen, Prot., Sarah A. Ketcham, Sec.

OWEGO.—Owego Lodge, No. 54, K. of H., meets at Odd Fellows' Hall, second and fourth Tuesday evenings of each month; G. Strang, Dic., F. A. Darrow, Rep.

Diamond Lodge, No. 76, K. and L. of H., meets at Odd Fellows' Hall the first and third Tuesday of each month; S. Goodrich, Prot., M. H. Tuch, Rep.

TIOGA.—Tioga Lodge, No. 263, K. of H., organized at Tioga Center in 1880.

Emerald Lodge, No. 384, K. & L. of H., organized at Tioga Center in 1881.

Independent Order of Odd Fellows.

BARTON.—Manoca Lodge, No. 219, I. O. of O. F., Waverly, meets every Tuesday evening, in Odd Fellows' Hall.

Spanish Hill Encampment, No. 52, I. O. of O. F., Waverly, meets first, third and fifth Friday evenings of each month, in Odd Fellows' Hall.

Cayuta Lodge, I. O. of O. F., No. 159, Lockwood, meets every Friday evening; G. W. Bingham, N. G., D. C. Hagadorn, Sec.

OWEGO.—Tioga Lodge, No. 335, I. O. of O. F., meets every Friday evening; W. L. Stewart, N. G., W. H. Thomas, Sec.

Order of the Iron Hall.

BARTON.—Local Branch, No. 23, O. of I. H., Waverly, meets Monday evenings at K. of H. Hall·

NEWARK VALLEY.—Local Branch, No. 281, O. of I. H., meets the first and third Monday evening of each month; Robert Donley, C. J., D. C. Hand, Acct.

OWEGO.—Branch No. 256, meets first and third Saturday evenings of each month; E. Kimball, C. J., A. S. Hooker, Acct.

Branch No. 306, Apalachin, J. S. Giles, C. J., C. L. Barton, Acct.

Improved Order of Red Men.

BARTON.—Iroquois Tribe, No. 42, I. O. of R. M., Waverly, meets every Thursday sleep at eight run.

NEWARK VALLEY.—Council fire the first and third Tuesday's sleep, each moon, in Masonic Hall; M. A. Howard, Sachem, H. Leonard, C. of R.

OWEGO.—Ahwaga Tribe, No. 40, I. O. of R. M., meets at the Wigwam, every Friday's sleep; James T. Rogers, Sachem, C. H. Keeler, C. of R.

SPENCER.—Mascawa Tribe, No. 88, I. O. of R. M., meets on the second and fourth Friday's sleep of each moon; J. M. Stowe, Sachem, E. L. Brooks, C. of R.

Miscellaneous Societies.

BARTON.—Cayuga Lodge, No. 35, A. O. U. W., Waverly, meets every Wednesday evening, in Select Knights' Hall.

Schoeffeld Legion, No. 19, Select Knights of A. O. U. W., Waverly, meets every Friday evening in Select Knights' Hall.

Tioga Lodge, No. 101, K. of P., Waverly, meets at Mott's Hall every Wednesday evening.

Equitable Aid Union, No. 417, Factoryville, meets every Thursday evening; J. C. Wood, Dis. Dep. Supreme Pres., F. A. Squires, Pres., Fred Brewster, Sec.

CANDOR.—Candor Council, Royal Arcanum, No. 928; H. P. Potter, Reg., F. S. Woodford, Sec.

OWEGO.—Progressive Assembly, No. 3147, K. of L., meets every Tuesday evening; M. J. Murrey, M. W., J. A. Dodge, R. S.

Star Lodge, No. 91, A. O. U. W., meets on the second and fourth Monday evenings of each month; E. Fitzgerald, M. W., C. Dana, Rec.

SPENCER.— The Tioga County Patron's Fire Relief Association; S. Alfred Seely, Pres., L. W. Hull, Sec.

Markell & Butts orchestra, four pieces.

Robinson Cornet Band, twelve pieces, F. O. Robinson, leader.

TIOGA.—Lodge No. 106, A. O. U. W., meets on the second and third Mondays of each month; Edward M. Forman, M. W., Robert H. Spendley, Recorder.

THE RATES OF POSTAGE.

Postal cards one cent each, to all parts of the United States and Canada.

FIRST-CLASS MATTER—TWO CENTS PER OUNCE OR FRACTION THEREOF.

Letters and all other mailable matter of other classes subject to letter postage by reason of a violation of the postal laws, two cents per ounce to all parts of the United States and Canada.

REGISTRATION, DROP LETTERS, ETC.

On registered domestic letters and third and fourth-class matter an additional fee of ten cents is required.

Local, or "Drop" letters, that is for the city or town where deposited, two cents if delivered by carriers, and one cent if there is no carrier system, per ounce.

Manuscript for publication in books, (except when accompanied by proof-sheets), newspapers and magazines chargeable as letters.

FREE.

Newspapers, to each actual subscriber in the county, where published, free of charge.

SECOND-CLASS MATTER—ONE CENT PER POUND.

Newspapers and periodicals, transient excepted, to be prepaid, at the office of publication at one cent per pound, or fraction thereof.

THIRD-CLASS MATTER—ONE CENT FOR TWO OUNCES.

(Must not be sealed.)

Mail matter of the third-class embraces printed books, (except transient newspapers, four ounces for one cent,) and periodicals, circulars, proof-sheets and corrected proof-sheets, manuscript copy accompanying the same, and all matter of the same general character, as above enumerated, the printing upon which is designed to instruct, amuse, cultivate the mind or taste, or impart general information, and postage shall be paid thereon at the rate of one cent for each two ounces or fractional part thereof.

FOURTH-CLASS MATTER—ONE CENT FOR EACH OUNCE.

Mail matter of the fourth-class embraces labels, patterns, photographs, playing cards, visiting cards, address tags, paper sacks, wrapping paper and blotting pads with or without printed address thereon, ornamented paper, and all other matter of the same general character, the printing upon which is not designed to instruct, amuse, cultivate the mind or taste, or impart general information. This class also includes merchandise, and samples of merchandise, models, samples of ores, metals, minerals, seeds, &c., and any other matter not included in the first, second or third-class, and which is not in its form or nature liable to destroy, deface or otherwise damage the contents of the mail-bag, or harm the person of any one engaged in the postal service. Postage rate thereon, one cent for each ounce or fractional part thereof.

Packages of mail-matter must not exceed four pounds each in weight, except in cases of single volumes of books.

Undelivered letters and postal cards can be re-sent to a new address without additional charge.

Senders may write their names on transient newspapers, books or any package in either class, preceded by the word "from."

Stamps cut from the stamped envelopes are rejected by the postoffice.

Stamped envelopes and wrappers, postal cards, and stamps of different denominations for sale at the postoffices.

Stamped envelopes accidentally spoiled redeemed at the postoffice where bought.

POSTOFFICES AND POSTMASTERS.

POSTOFFICES.	TOWNS.	POSTMASTERS.
Apalachin,	Owego,	Frank J. Knapp.
Barton,	Barton,	John B. Coleman.
Berkshire,	Berkshire,	John R. Ford.
Campville,	Owego,	McKenzie Dickinson.
*Candor,	Candor,	John R. Chidsey.
Catatonk,	Candor,	Alanson H. Smith.
Connecticut,	Newark Valley,	James DeGaramo.
East Nichols,	Nichols,	Elizabeth A. White.
Factoryville,	Barton,	Clarence E. Clock.
Flemingsville,	Owego,	Charles E. Truman.
Gaskill's Corners,	Owego,	Harmon Curtis.
Halsey Valley,	Tioga,	Grant M. West.
Hooper's Valley,	Nichols,	Lucas T. Field.
Jenksville,	Newark Valley,	Samuel M. Avery.
Ketchumville,	Newark Valley,	Charles Finch.
Lockwood,	Barton,	George D. Brock.
*Newark Valley,	Newark Valley,	Sherman W. Byington.
Nichols,	Nichols,	Emmet Coleman.
North Barton,	Barton,	Edmund H. Hoyt.
North Spencer,	Spencer,	Mahlon A. Kellogg.
*Owego,	Owego,	Frederick O. Cable.
Reniff,	Barton,	Willis E. Gillett.
Richford,	Richford,	Charles A. Clark.
Smithsboro.	Tioga,	William J. Drake.
South Apalachin,	Owego,	Alonzo Bills.
South Owego,	Owego,	Lyman B. Truman.
*Spencer,	Spencer,	Marvin D. Fisher.
Strait's Corners,	Tioga,	Alvinza Strait.
Tioga Center,	Tioga,	Joseph Winters.
*Waverly,	Barton,	Andrew A. Slawson.
Weltonville,	Candor,	Andrew J. Graham.
West Candor,	Candor,	Charles F. Gridley.
West Newark,	Newark Valley,	Willis E. Hover.
Willseyville,	Candor,	Emory C. Mix.
Wilson Creek,	Berkshire.	Colden N. Hart.

Rate of Commission Charged for Money Orders.

On orders not exceeding $10, eight cents ; over $10, and not exceeding $15, ten cents ; over $15, and not exceeding $30, fifteen cents : over $30, and not exceeding $40, twenty cents ; over $40, and not exceeding $50, twenty-five cents ; over $50, and not exceeding $60, thirty cents ; over $60, and not exceeding $70, thirty-five cents ; over $70, and not exceeding $80, forty cents ; over $80, and not exceeding $100, forty-five cents. No single order issued for a greater sum than $100.

---

*Money order offices.

INDEX.

—OF—

Tioga County, New York,

1785–1888.

- 8 -

GOODSELL
  Jane J., 293
  Joshua, 293
  Laura A., 282, 293
  Lorraine, 381
  Lydia (Slawson), 293
  Sarah A., 293
  William, 293
  Zina, 282, 293
GOODSPEED
  Nathaniel, 459
GOODWIN
  Nancy A.. 280
GORBET
  Peter, 200
  Sarah, 200
GORDAN
  Augusta, 374
  George, 374
GORDON
  Dr., 291
  Jane, 373
  Susan (White), 291
GORSE
  Hannah, 360
GORSLINE
  Charlotte (Lawrence),
    213
  James L., 213
  Pomeroy, 213
  Susan (Lawrence), 213
GOSHEN
  N. Y., 377
GOSS
  Peter, 291
  Ruth (Hale), Rogers),
    291
GOULD
  Adam, 371
  Amanda, 192
  Ephraim C., 192
  Jane (Clark(, 192
  John, 242, 151
  John, Rev., 200, 269
  Judith (Coffin), 371
  Laura, 475
  Sarah, 192
  Tabitha, 446
  William, 192
  Zilpha, 372
GRAGG
  Francis, 465
  Margaret, 465
  Sally, 465
GRAHAM
  Aleck, 170
GRAND RAPIDS
  Mich., 326, 366
GRANGER
  Mr., 434
  Abigail (Bement), 209
  Almira, 286
  Daniel, 285
  Henry S., 209
  Joel, 213
  Joseph, 286
  Lucina, 212, 213
  Mary (White), 285
  Sally (Roach), 286
GRANT
  Gen., 173, 335

GRANT continued
  Pres., 351
GRANVILLE
  Mass., 342
  Wash. Co., N.Y., 340,
    445
GRAVES
  Rev. Mr., 437
  Adaline A., 262
  Gideon, 292
  Nancy, 292
GRAY
  Ann (VanNanre), 144
  Arthur, 144
  Hattie (Hill), 473
  John, 473
  John C., 360, 492
  Maria, 81
  Mary Jane, 144
  Samuel, 81
GREAT BARRINGTON
  Mass., 349, 352
GREELEY
  --- 359
GREEN
  Gen., 172
  Rev. Mr., 438
  Clark, 401
  Harriet Eliza (Dwight),
    230
  Mary, 223
  Mary P., 179
  Warren, 230
GREENBUSH
  N. Y., 191
GREENLEAF
  & Hewitt, 340
  Hattie (Meeker), 393
  John M., 340
  John T. (Dr.), 343,
    393
GREENLY
  & Shapley, 350
GREENVILLE
  N. Y., 445, 449
GREENWICH
  Wash. Co., 287
GREGG
  William H. (Dr.), 453
GREGORY
  Abigail (Huntington),
    139
  Alvah, 230
  Electa, 139
  Eli Benedict, 139
  Eliza Ann, 139
  Henry, 139
  John III, 138, 139, 147
  Lucy, 139
  Lydia Dewey (Dwight),
    230
  Rachel (Benedict), 138
GRIDLEY
  Russel, 168, 169
  S. E., 197
  Selah, 168, 194
  Thomas, 169, 193
  William C., 168
GRIFFIN
  Amanda Leonard, 135
  Anna (Leonard), 121,

GRIFFIN continued
  Anna (Leonard) continued, 135
  Franklin, 135
  George Henry, 135
  Henry (Capt.), 121, 123, 134,
    135
  Jemima (Vail), 134
  John, 135, 199
  Julia Ann Colt, 135
  Lewis, 199
  Lydia (Redfield), 135
  Mary (Butler), 135
  Osmyn, 135
  Semantha (Slosson), 206
  Simeon Rich, 206
GRIFFING
  Mrs., 133
  Artemesia, 364
  Augusta J. (Goodrich), 468
  Beriah R., 364
  Daniel S., 364
  David T., 364
  Helena D., 364
  Henry, 364
  Hiram, 210
  James S., 364, 468
  John, 364
  John (Rev.), 312, 364, 404
  Lydia, 364
  Lydia Permelia, 364
  Lydia (Redfield), 364
  Lucy M. (Taylor), 364
  Mary M., 364
  Osymn, 364
  Permelia, 364
  Samuel B., 364
  Sarah (Stedman), 425
  Simeon Rich, 425
GRIMES
  Carrie, 368
  Frederick, 368
  George, 368
  James A., 368
  Margaret (Whitney), 368
  Moses, 367
  Sarah (Dennis), 368
GRISWOLD
  Eben, Dea., 232
  Sarah, 142
GROTON
  Ct., 338
GROUT
  Margaret, 474
GROW
  Platt F., 430
GUILFORD
  Center, N. Y., 355
GUENON
  Jean, 101
GUYON
  Charles, 266
  Charles S., 266
  Dorcas (Borthwick),
    266
  Esther, 266
  Henry B., 266, 267
  Henry T., 266
  James, 266
  John W., 266
  Josiah J., 266
  Mahala, 266

HART continued
  Theodore, 131
  William, 184
HASTINGS
  Joel, 409
  Lucia, 409
  Marcia, 428
HATCH
  Asahel, 123
  Elizabeth, 183
  Elsie B., 184
  Hannah, 157
  Josiah, 184
  Parker, 184
HAUVER
  Charles, 378
  Delmar G., 378
  E. Jane, 378
  F. Earl, 378
  Frank, 378
  George, 378
  Lora (Buttles), 378
  Lucy, 378
  Margaret, 378
  Martha (Smith), 378
  Mary (Maine), 378
  Samuel, 378
HAVANNA
  ---, 444
HAWLEY
  Climena Ann, 131
HAYDEN
  Sidney, 185
HAYES
  Henry, 360
  Mary J. (Rodman),
    360
HAYNES
  George Landers, 156
HAYWARD
  S. O., 181
HAYWOOD
  C. M., 380
  Charles M., 379, 380
  Hannah (Kneeland),
    380
HEACOCK
  Mary, 467
HEAD
  Anna M., 367
  Cora, 362
  Eddie B., 367
  Frank L., 367
  Frederick L., 367
  Ida M., 367
  John J., 367
  John M., 367
  Kate (Fiddis), 362
  Linnie B., 367
  Lottie A., 367
  Melinda (Meacham),
    367
  Sarah, 367
  William, 362
HEATH
  Alzina, 137
  Mr., 230, 231
HEATON
  C. R. (Dr.), 394
HEBRON
  Ct., 340

HECKWELDER
  ---, 319
HEDGES
  Catharine, 225, 226
  Daniel, 225
  Esther, 225, 226
  Jason, 225, 242
  Jonathan, 223, 225, 226,
    242, 254
  John, 218, 225, 226
  Lyon C., 78
  Phebe, 222, 223
HEFFORD
  ---, 226, 227
HEGGIE
  John Harper, 156
HEIGHTS
  of Abraham, 328
HEMINGWAY
  ---, 425
  C. B., 164
HENDERSON
  ---, 190, 191, 250
  Alexander, 175
  Charles, 177, 179
  Celestia, 179
  Fred D., 191
  Hiram, 182
  J. W., 190, 197
  Nellie E., 191
HERKIMER
  Co., N. Y., 350
HERRICK
  Celestia, 179
  Charlotte M., 383
  Edward, 131, 179
  Edward P., 383
  Edward W., 383
  Eliza, 179
  Ellen A. (Miller), 187
  Harriet, 179
  Jennie, 383
  Maria, 179
  Minerva, 179
  Perlee, 383
  Stephen, 179
  Walter, 179, 187
HEWEN
  Loring, 239
HEWITT
  Frederick C., 339,
    340, 390
  Gurdon, 221, 281, 283,
    339, 340, 390
  Thomas, 199
  Thomas (Mrs.), 199
HIBBARD
  Charles, 371
  Ebenezer, 372
  Elizabeth (Sweet), 372
  Frances, 372
  George R., 372
  Jemima (Maynard) (Mrs.),
    372
  Ralph, 372
  Ralph, Jr., 372
  Ralph A., 372
HIGBE
  Anson, 242, 252, 255,
    256
  Elijah, 243, 251

HIGBE continued
  Forman S., 481
  James (Higbee), 464
  Lucretia, 243
HIGGINS
  Chloe, 467
  John, 164
  Mary A., 161
HILL
  Abial, 82
  Abner, 481
  Albert J., 375
  Amanda, 375
  Amanda M., 473
  Anna L., 375
  Augustus, 429
  Caleb, 80, 81
  Calvin F., 375
  Charles, 266
  Charles O., 380
  Chauncey, 375, 377,
    472, 473
  David B. (Hon.),
    80, 81
  Elisha, 76, 77, 78,
    80, 81
  Elisha E., 287
  Elizabeth, 80, 81, 287
  Emily, 473
  Hannah, 80, 81
  Ida E., 380
  James, 384
  James N., 380, 381
  John, 472, 473,
    479
  John G., 81
  Lesbia, 375
  Lucy, 473
  Lydia L., 380
  Maryann S., 473
  Philomina, 80, 81
  Polly, 80, 81
  Sabrina, 377
  Sarah, 80, 81
  Sarah E., 380
  Susan, 473
  Tabitha, 80, 81
HILLER
  W. M. (Rev.), 403
HILLS
  Chauncey, 380
  Harriet Emily
    (Madan), 380
  James N., 380
  Leonard Mariner, 260,
    261
  Lucy (Sexton), 380
  Mary Eliza, 260,
    261
HILLYER
  James (Capt), 471
HILTON
  Daniel, 323
HINCHMAN
  Lesbia, 333
HINES
  William A., 409
HINMAN
  Stanley Sheffield,
    158
HINSDALE

-23-

HINSDALE continued
  Mrs., 248
  R. W. (Mrs.), 363
HITCHCOCK
  Charlotte, 153
  Chauncey B., 152
  Horatio, 152
  Isaac, 121, 146,
    152, 153
  Juliet, 152
HIXON
  Amos, 168
  Foxter, 197
HOAG
  Fred, 191
  Sarah L. (Carpenter),
    191
HOAGLAND
  Abraham, 402
  Hannah, 372
HOBART COLLEGE
  Geneva, N. Y., 345
HOBART
  Edmond, 441
  Edward, 446
HO-DE-NO-SAU-NEE
  ---, 319
HODGES
  Eleazer, 148
  Evelyn Amelia, 356
HOFF
  Alice M., 265
  Carrie E., 265
  Cornelius D., 481
  Erastus, 265, 481
  George, 265
  Jennie, 265
  John H., 265
  Lewis, 197
  Lewis R., 197
  Stella E., 265
HOFFMAN
  Gov., 344
  Miss, 475
  Peter, 79
HOGAN
  Frances, 401
HOKE
  & Seely, 455
HOLBROOK
  Lucy, 144
  Reuben, 323
HOLCOMB
  Julia A., 281
  Milton, 434
  Timothy, 423
HOLDRIDGE
  Amos, 446
  Elisha, 446
HOLLAND
  ---, 281
HOLLENBACK
  Charles E., 374
  George, 373
  George F., 374
  George Frederick, 374
  Jane (Gordon), 373
  John, 327, 328,
    373, 374, 386
  John G., 328, 374
  John Gordon, 374

HOLLENBACK continued
  Mary McLain, 374
  William Henry, 328,
    374
HOLLENBECK
  ---, 163
  Mrs., 488
  Augusta (Gordon), 374
  Charles E. (Dr.),
    487, 488
  Charles Edward, 375
  Eugene (Mrs.), 188
  Frederick, 328
  George F., 374
  George Frederick, 374
  George W., 328, 373
  John, 327, 328,
    386
  Richard, 488
  & Nixon, 375
HOLLEY
  Morris W., 195
  William, 207
HOLLISTER
  Thomas, 167, 168,
    175
HOLMAN
  Gideon P., 284
  Maude, 284
HOLMES
  Augustus, 188
  Caroline, 188
  Cinerella, 188
  Dr., 442
  Ebenezer, 188
  Eliza, 187
  Job, 188
  John, 371
  John T., 188
  Oliver Wendell, 347
  Rufus, 188
  Samuel, 188
  Susan, 188
  Waty (Tanner), 188
HOMISTON
  Ezra W. (Dr.), 447
HOOKER
  Mary, 223
HOOPER
  Elisha (Capt.), 244
  Lucinda, 138
  Malvina (Jackson), 190
  Robert L. (Col.),
    271, 272
  Robert Lettice, 281
HOOPERS
  Patent, 270
  Valley, 274, 290, 295,
    305, 308, 398
HOOVER
  Betsey, 281
  John, 281
  Mercy, 290
HOPKINS
  Minerva, 179
  Stephen (Dr.), 179
HORTON
  ---, 163, 164
  D. B., 27
  George C., 467
  Gurdon, 468

HORTON continued
  Hannah B., 467
  John Hicks, 399
  Theodore, 464
  Willis D., 130
HOSFORD
  Abigail, 214, 215
  Charles, 214, 215
  E., 391
  Electa, 214, 215
  Joseph, 214, 215
  Franklin, 214, 215
  Eunice Williams,
    214, 215
  Joseph, 214, 215
  Mary, 214, 215
HOSKINS
  W. L., 388
HOTCHKIN
  Miss, 158
  Abby Lavina, 230,
    231
  Abraham, 147, 158,
    209, 256
  Marshal, 217, 229
  Mary E. (Mrs.),
    237
HOUGH
  J. J. (Rev.), 164
HOUSE
  Catharine, 143
  John P., 212
  Sarah, 212
HOVER
  Abram, 265
  Benjamin, 181
  Cornelius, 243, 409
  Eleanor, 181
  Elijah, 181
  Frederick, 189
  Gilbert, 181
  Henry, 181
  Jemima, 264, 265
  Joseph, 181
  Katy, 181
  Lodowick, 181, 247
  Margaret, 383
  Margaret Barrett, 383
  Martha, 264, 265
  Sait, 409
  Sally, 181
  Solomon, 181
HOVEY
  Mother, 221
HOVER
  Abigail, 123, 129,
    130
HOVEY
  Azel, 123, 221,
    232, 233
  Azel, Jr., 123, 124
  Calvin, 123, 124
  Charlotte, 232, 233
  Chester, 232, 233
  Clarinda, 123, 124
  David, 123, 232,
    233, 242
  David, Jr., 232, 233
  Eliza, 123, 124
  Eunice, 123
  Hannah, 123, 124

JENKS continued
  215, 216, 224
  Eliza (Armstrong),
    382
  Isaac, 149, 215
  Laban, 149, 156,
    215, 216, 324
  Laban M., 381, 382
  Mary E., 381, 382
  Mary J., 146, 149,
    162
  Michael, 149, 215,
    216, 220, 221,
    257, 258
  Otis, 215, 216
  Polly, 146, 156
  Robert B., 382
  Susan, 224
  Susan A., 264
  Theodore, 246, 247
  William W., 382
JENKSVILLE
  ---, 215, 257
JENNINGS
  Benjamin, 442
JEWETT
  Andrew, 475
  Asa, 368, 399
  Asahel, 144
  Bathsheba (Woodin),
    368
  Charles F., 183, 475
  Emily, 183, 475
  Esther (Finley), 381
  Ezekiel, 224
  Frederick G., 381
  Hannah (Livingston),
    369
  Harris, 129, 475,
    480
  Harry, 368, 381,
    399
  Henry, 475
  Henry L., 381
  Henry M., 177
  John, 368, 399
  John, Jr., 399
  Lorraine (Goodsell),
    381
  Lyman, 124, 421
  Matilda, 368
  Maurice, 368
  Olive, 234
  Platt, 369
  Walter, 475
  William A., 475
JOHNSON
  Abigail, 138
  Abraham, 242
  Abraham W., 207, 209,
    210, 221
  Abram, 82, 83, 88
  Almira, 376
  Amyette, 82, 83,
    88
  C. F., 477
  C. P. (Hon.), 164
  Carlisle P., 116
  Cassandra, 118, 138
  Charles, 82, 83, 88
  Charles F., 490

JOHNSON continued
  Chester, 258
  Cinderella, 138
  Cynthia, 82, 83, 88
  Daniel, 402
  David, 81
  Eber, 411
  Elijah, 138, 241,
    242
  Elisha, 169
  Eloise (Lane), 369
  Elvira, 82, 83, 88
  Eunice, 138
  George W., 83, 83,
    88
  Harriet, 82, 83,
    88
  Herbert, 369
  Israel, 180
  James, 82, 83, 88
  Jane, 82, 83, 88
  John, 82, 83
  John S., 473
  Joshua (Rev.), 403
  Joshua, 82, 83,
    88
  Julius, 82, 83, 88
  Laura E., 177
  Lucinda, 210
  Lucy, 134, 410,
    414, 415
  Lyman, 210
  Mary, 473, 474
  Matilda, 82, 83,
    88
  Nancy, 138, 218
  Nathan, 413
  Nathanial, 407, 414,
    418, 429
  Norman, 411
  Orton, 177
  Peter, 470, 473
  Polly, 464
  Pres., 351
  Rachael, 411
  Rhoda Ann, 117
  ---, 411
  Sally, 138, 140
  Salmon, 81
  Samuel, 137, 138,
    218, 233, 241,
    242, 268
  Smith, 410
  Thomas, 473, 474
  Thomas D. (Rev. Father),
    404
  Thomas Floyd, 78, 81
  Washington, 82, 83,
    88
  William E. (Dr.),
    94
  William H., 473
  Zilpha, 411
JOHNSTOWN
  Montgomery Co., 339
JONES
  ---, 271
  Baskia, 76, 78
  Carrie, 474
  Charles E., 474
  Clara M., 473

JONES continued
  Ephraim, 182
  Flora A., 372
  Frances (Hibbard),
    372
  Frank L., 349
  George E., 474
  Grace, 474
  Horace, 242, 251,
    474
  James, 372
  James E., 372
  John, 442
  John B., 473
  Leonard, 442
  Minnie, 474
  Miss, 234
  Sarah, 244, 474
  Solomon, 138, 402,
    403, 481
  Stephen P., 474
  Stephen, Sr., 474
  Susanna, 244
JORDAN
  Phoebe A., 189
  Thomas, 323
JOSLIN
  P. H., 304
  Peter (Capt), 314
  Edward, 232, 236,
    307
JOSLYN
  Polly, 383
JOYCE
  Joseph, 81
JUDD
  Charles S. (Rev.),
    176, 177
  Gaylord (Rev.),
    177, 200
  Isaac, 167, 176
  Job, 193, 198
  Job, Sr., 167
  Marie, 177
  Sophronia, 176
JUDSON
  Elbert, 180
  John, 133

KANE
  Colonel, 396
KARSCADDEN
  Lydia, 425
KEELER
  A. H., 381
  Caroline, 238
  James B., 381
  Julia A., 381
  Minnie, 381
  Sarah E., 381, 382
  Sarah (Hill), 381
KEENY
  Miss, 150
  Thomas, 146, 150,
    151, 423
KEITH
  Ann (Court), 370
  Deborah, 223
  Eleazer, 223
  Eunice, 223, 224
  George W., 370

LaMONT continued
  Ruth (McNeil), 372
  Susan J., 372
  W. C. (Hon.), 188
LaMONTE
  Phoebe, 360
LAMPHERE
  (Campbell & Lamphere's
    Saw & Planing mill),
    402
LAMPMAN
  Betsey (Bogart),
    81
  Casper, 81
LAMSON
  (Sherwood & Lamson),
    165
LANDFIELD
  Clark, 261
  Elizabeth (Canouse),
    261
  Grace H., 262
  Hannah (Thomas),
    261
  Helen (Rogers), 262
  Jerome B. (Hon.),
    261, 262
  Jerome B., Jr., 262
LANDON
  Ezra, 147, 157,
    158
  Ruby (Chapin), 158
LANE
  A. Lindsley, 368,
    369
  Alice, 369
  Amos, 286
  Annie, 369
  Bethia, 227
  Catherine, 369
  Charles, 369
  Charlotte, 369
  Charlotte R., 467
  Don Carlos, 369
  Edgar S., 369
  Egbert, 369
  Eliza, 369
  Eloise, 369
  Esther, 175
  Fannie, 369
  Floyd L., 369
  Frances E. (Pearl),
    371
  Frank, 369
  Frederica (Olmstead),
    369
  Frederick, 369
  George, 179, 200,
    241, 243
  James, Jr., 369
  James, Sr., 369
  Jane (Taylor), 369
  Lewis, 369
  Libbie, 369
  Lucinda (Smith), 286
  Mary, 179
  Mary (Brownell), 369
  Mary J. (Nutt),
    368, 369
  Nancy, 369
  Samuel (Rev.), 369

LANE continued
  Sarah, 200
  W. A., 91
  Warren A., 371
  Winnie, 369
LANESBORO
  Pa., 283
LANESBOROUGH
  Mass., 145
LANG
  William, 446
LANGDON
  Benjamin, 158
  Eliza, 158
  Eveline (Perry), 158
  Maria (Lawrence),
    120, 158
  Thomas, 120, 147,
    158
  Wealthy, 158
LANGFORD
  Joseph, 78
  Sarah (Swartwood),
    78
LANING
  Amelia, 288
  Augustus C., 347
  Ellen H., 347
  Emily, 347
  Harriet (Lounsberry),
    284
  John (Gen.), 326,
    333, 386
  John C., 326, 347
  John W., 284
  Judd, 292
  Mary, 284
  Mary Anne, 347
  Matthias H., 347
  Robert, 288, 292
  Robert F., 292
  Sarah, 284
  Willett S., 292
LaROW
  Family, 450
LATHAM
  & Cady, Druggists,
    293
LATHROP
  Edward, 473
  Susan (Hill), 473
LATIMER
  Angie D. (Ransom),
    469
  Clara, 469
  Jonathan, 468
  Jonathan (Col.), 468
  Jonathan C., 468,
    469, 470, 480,
    483
  Sally, 469
LAWRENCE
  Abel, 212, 213,
    219, 221, 241,
    365
  Abigail, 213
  Abigail (Rockwell),
    212, 213
  Abigail Salome, 213
  Amy, 143
  Bersheba Lucina, 213

LAWRENCE continued
  Betsey, 120, 212
  Catharine (Cole), 120
  Charlotte, 212,
    213, 424
  Consider, 120,
    147, 221
  Cyrus, 212
  Erastus, 212
  Esther (Dutton), 212
  Experience, 212, 227
  Isaac Peck, 120
  Jowl Granger, 213
  Jonas, 212, 213,
    424
  Josiah, 120
  Laura (Woodruff),
    120
  Lucinda Granger, 213
  Maria, 120, 158
  Martha (Baird),
    120
  Miles Lewis, 120
  Milla (Richardson),
    247, 266
  Milla M., 212, 219,
    266
  Orange, 212
  Rebecca, 212
  Sarah (House), 212
  Sophia, 212
  Susan, 213
  Sylvia C. (Foote),
    120
  Tryphena (Lawrence),
    212, 213, 424
  Wealthy (Peck),
    120
  Wealthy L., 213, 365
  William, 120
  William S., 212, 266
  William Solomon,
    212, 213, 219,
    236, 247
LEACH
  Caleb, 402, 490,
    491
  D. T. (Rev.), 269
  Daniel, 421, 427
  Ephraim, 477, 480,
    491
  Ruby (Miss), 204
  Stephen W., 477,
    480, 481, 491
LEACH'S
  Grist Mill, 490
  Mills, 318
LEAGUE
  of Iroquois, 319
LEATHE
  Achsah, 423
LEAVETT
  (see also Fellows),
    219
LEBANON
  Madison Co., N. Y.,
    350
LEE
  Lavina, 361
  Mass., 378
LEET

LYMAN continued
  Eleazer, 142, 146,
    155
  Eleazer, Jr., 150
  George, 134
  Henry, 134
  James Wellman, 151
  Laura (Thurston),
    134
  Lavina, 134
  Lucy, 132, 133,
    234
  Lucy (Bishop), 132
  Mary, 156
  Nancy, 156
  Nancy Bishop, 133
  Noah, 132, 145
  Obias, 156
  Ozias, Maj., 155
  Persis, 156
  Raymond, 155
  Ruth Bartlett, 133
  Sally (Clark), 150
  Sally (Parker), 155
  Sally (Payne), 155
  Sarah, 156
  Sarah Jane (Blair),
    156
  Vincent Page, 151
LYNCH
  William, 421
LYON
  Mr., 489
LYONS
  Caleb, 481
  David C., 77
  Justice, 78
  Sally (Hanna), 77

McCALLUM
  D. C., 490
McCAPES
  Spencer, 199
McCARTY
  John W., 195, 196
  Margaret, 280
McCORMICK
  Henry (Col.), 338
McCULLOCH
  Margaret, 76, 77
McDANIEL
  Alexander, 241, 243
  Elihu, 241, 243
McDONALD
  Clarissa (Primrose),
    474
  Edward, 474
McDONEL
  ---, 243
McEWEN
  Rev., 438
McGILL
  A. A., 189
  Adaline (Ward), 189
McGRAW-FISKE
  Case, 332
McGREGOR
  John, 223
  Lydia (Williams), 223
McINTYRE
  Betsey (Williams), 182

McINTYRE continued
  John J., 182, 183
  Samuel, 182
McKEE
  Sarah, 370
McKENZIE
  Alexander C. (Rev.),
    403
McKERLIE
  Mary, 285
  William, 285
McKINNEY
  John, 238
  Mary (Edwards), 238
McLAIN
  Mary, 374
McLEAN
  Mary, 370
McMASTER
  David, 163
  James, 193, 317, 320,
    322, 323, 384, 386,
    388, 391, 466
  Lucinda (Williams),
    246
  Luke, 241, 246
  Miriam, 246
  Robert, 32 , 387
  J. T. McMasters
    Steam Saw Mill,
    455
McMASTER'S
  Half Township, 387
McNEIL
  Catharine, 373
  Charles, 369
  Fannie (Lane), 369
  John, 373
  Ruth, 372
McQUIGG
  David, 328
  Harriet (Pumpelly),
    328
  Jesse, 365
  John, 322, 323,
    324, 388
  Mary, 365
MABEE
  J. A., 381
  John A., 381
  Minnie (Keeler), 381
MACADAM
  Isabel, 272, 278
MACK
  Horace, 326
  Stephen, 324, 326,
    329, 384
  Stephen (Judge), 329
  Widow, 326
MACKAY
  Daniel Stewart, 352,
    353
  Martha, 353
MADAN
  Andrew, 381
  Anna Eliza, 381
  Benjamin C., 381
  Carolina A., 381
  Charity (Odell), 381
  Edward S., 381
  Frances M., 381

MADAN continued
  Harriet E., 381
  Harriet Emily, 381
  Lydia (Curry), 381
  Mary L., 381
  Phoebe (Sears), 381
  Sarah J., 381
  Sarah (Searls), 381
  Thomas D., 381
MAINE
  Charlotte A., 187
  Collins, 187
  James S., 378
  Mary, 378
MALTA
  N. Y., 372
MANDEVILLE
  David, Sr., 91
MANHART
  John, 78
MANLEY
  Abigail, 161
MANLIUS
  N. Y., 318
MANNING
  Andrew, 144
  Barnabas, 124, 144,
    147
  Betsey (Cobb),
    159
  Catharine Lincoln,
    144
  Charles S., 115,
    159
  Charles Seabury, 144
  D. O., 176
  Eliza, 144
  Esther (Belcher),
    144
  Esther Maria, 116,
    144
  Gurdon G., 159
  Jane, 144
  Maria (Adams), 292
  Maria (Archiball),
    159
  Mary Jane (Gray),
    144
  Phebe (Lincoln), 144
  Ralph, 147, 159
  Sophia, 159
  William H., 292
MANSFIELD
  Ct., 340
MANUFACTURING
  Industries, Banks, &
    Businesses, 106,
    163, 194, 257,
    311, 383, 430,
    433, 454
MAPLES
  Alexander, 131
  Lydia (Carpenter),
    131
MAREAN
  Lydia, 211
MARIETTA
  Pa., 80, 364
MARKELL
  Capt., 173
  Charles F., 174

-32-

MARKELL continued
  Henry, 174
  Jacob, 174
  John, 174
  Mary, 173
  Ruhamah Sears, 174
  Samuel Frank, 174
  Vida Mary, 174
MARKRAM
  Samuel, 237
MARKS
  Abijah, 459
MARSH
  Benjamin, 323
MARSHALL
  Harvey, 242, 250,
    251
MARTIN
  Amos (Col.), 339,
    390
  Angeline, 461
  Jay H., 339
  John H., 339
MARTINSBURG
  Va., 373
MASON
  Margaret, 382,
    383
MASONIC
  Lodge, 390
  Relief Assoc., 380
MASSACHUSETTS
  --- 326
MASTEN
  Amanda, 131
MATHEWS
  Joseph, 170, 171,
    180
  Loisa (Woodford),
    180
  Olive L., 263
  Vincent (Hon.), 278
MATILE
  Prof., 261
MATSON
  George, 480
  Sypha, 116
MATTESON'S
  Mill, 479
MAUGHANTOWANO
  Flats, 274, 280
MAXWELL
  Guy, 384
  (Ranson, Maxwell &
    Co.), 482
MAYNARD
  Jemima, 372
  Zebadiah, 372
MAYOR
  Charles D., 161
  Charles L., 161
  E. (Dr.), 165
  Edward (Dr.), 161
  Emma (Root), 161
  Harriet (Patch), 161
  Jennie, 161
  Julia, 161
  Paul, 161
  Theodore, 161
MEACHAM
  Betsey (Lake), 367,

MEACHAM continued
  449
  Charles D., 366, 367
  Clarence L., 367
  Ella M., 367
  Erastus, 367, 449
  Fred R., 367
  Leon, 367
  Lottie (Head), 367
  Maria, 367
  Mary A., 367
  Melinda, 367
  Merle L., 367
  Milton H., 367
  Myron E., 367
  Silas, 367
MEAD
  Abel, 179
  Abigail (Owen), 178
  Alanson, 178
  Amos, 178, 323
  Arletta, 264, 265
  Asa E., 178
  Aseneth, 178, 180
  Benjamin, 178
  Charles, 179
  Clyde V., 264, 265
  Daniel, 241, 243
  David P., 179
  Edward, 179
  Elizabeth, 178
  Emma K., 179
  Ezekiel, 178, 179
  Fayette, 165
  George, 165, 178
  Hattie, 264, 265
  Holloway, 165, 179
  Howard J., 132, 179
  Isaac, 165
  Israel, 167, 194
  James R., 192
  Jane (Elliston), 178
  John, 165, 192
  John A. R., 264,
    265
  John G., 179
  Joshua, 178, 179
  Lewis, 178, 180,
    192
  Lewis J., 178
  Louis, 200
  Lovina, 200
  Lucy (Truman), 398
  Maggie J., 264, 265
  Maria, 165
  Martha (Hover), 265
  Martin, 238, 250
  Mary P. (Green),
    179
  Milden, 264, 265
  Milton, 265, 265
  Montgomery, 80, 81
  Priscilla, 264, 265
  Ransom H., 165
  Riley, 179
  Rogers, D., 264, 265
  Russell, 184, 264,
    265
  Russell B., 264, 265
  Russell J., 178
  S. Amy, 264, 265

MEAD continued
  Sally Ann (Barrott),
    264
  Sarah, 178
  Sarah J., 178
  Solomon, 195, 196,
    442
  Tabitha J. (Hill),
    81
  William, 167, 178,
    398
  William E., 165
  & Darrow, 132,
    179
MEADOWSIDE
  Farm, 286
MEAGHER
  Margaret, 117
MECKIN
  Ebenezer, 480
MEEKER
  Hattie, 393
  P. W., 393
MENOMONEE
  Wisc., 283
MERCHANT
  Sarah Jane, 154
  Sylvanus, 255
MERICLE
  Sarah (Fox), 373
  Jacob, 373
MERRIAM
  C. E., 89
  Fanny W. (White),
    98
  Grace M., 97, 98
  Harry E., 97, 98
  Henry G., 97, 98
  Ruth, 236
MERRICK
  Abner, 361
  Emma, 371
  George, 371
  Georgiana, 361
MERRILL
  Abel, 266
  Louisa S., 266
  Lucinda (Bullock),
    266
  Mary B., 266
  Mattie A., 266
  Norman L., 266
MERRITT
  J. E., 77, 78
  Lena, 77, 78
  Leonora (Hanna),
    77
  Orrin, 77, 78
  Ralph, 77, 78
  Ray, 77, 78
MERROW
  Joseph Munsell, 236
  Mindwell (Newell),
    236
MERSEREAU
  Daniel, 466
MESSENGER
  Almira, 134, 415
  Margaret (Woodruff),
    134
  Martin, 134

METHODIST
  Episcopal Church,
    269, 279
  University, Syracuse,
    279
MIDDAUGH
  Jacob, 276, 298
  Mary J., 376
MIDDLEBORO
  Mass., 382
MIDDLE HADDAM
  Mass., 350
MIDDLEBURGH
  Academy, 283
MIDDLEBURY
  College, 344
MILLEN
  Cynthia, 247
  Elisha, 247
  James, 247
  John, 241, 247
  Rachel, 247
  Sarah (Mrs.), 247
  William, 241, 247
MILLER
  Ada, 187
  Alexander, 166
  Amos, 462, 463
  Augustine, 166,
    186, 187
  Burt W., 187
  Charlotte A. (Maine),
    187
  Cornelia, 166
  Cyrus, 186, 187
  D. H., 249
  Daniel, 186, 187
  Daniel S. (Dr.),
    187
  Edwin A., 187
  Ellen A., 186, 187
  Emanuel, 166
  Emeline, 186, 187
  E. P., 179
  Eunice (Storke), 186
  Ezra, 456, 462, 463,
    480
  Francis F., 481
  Frank G., 186,
    187
  Fred, 187
  George (Rev.), 438
  Helen J. (Caruth),
    187
  Henry, 442
  Isaac, 226
  James, 459, 462,
    480
  Jerusha, 459, 462,
    480
  Jesse, 459, 462,
    480
  Jesse, Jr., 459,
    462, 480
  John, 166, 186,
    187, 362
  Jonas, 166
  Julia, 186, 187
  Lucinda, 186, 187
  Lucy, 459, 462,
    463, 465, 480

MILLER continued
  Margaret (McCarty),
    281
  Martha, 281
  Mary F. (Webster),
    187
  Mary (Ingersoll), 362
  Nancy, 186, 187
  Peter, 186, 187
  Polly, 459, 462,
    480
  Samuel, 186, 187
  Sophronia, 185
  W. F., 431
  William, 186, 187
  Ziba, 459, 462, 480
MILLREA
  William, 467
MILLS
  ---, 271
  Adolphus, 76
  Anna, 76
  Augusta, 76, 285
  B. H., 199
  Betsey (Hanna), 77
  Caroline (Reynolds),
    287
  Charles, 76, 122
  Charlotte, 76
  Elizabeth, 76
  Frances (Hanna), 287
  Francis, 287
  John, 76, 77
  Lewis, 76, 77, 78
  Miama, 76, 77
  S. Edware, 482
  Samuel, 88
  Stephen, 76, 77
  Theodore, 76
  William G., 76, 77
  Wilson, 76
MINISINK
  River, N. J., 264
MOE
  Sarah J., 476
MOHAWKS
  ---, 317
MONELL
  William Floyd, 213,
    218
MONTONTOWANGO
  ---, 274
MONTROSE
  Volunteers, 352
MONROE
  Co., Pa., 274
MOODY
  Miriam, 134
MOORE
  Alvah Churchill, 222
  Cargill & Co., 258
  Caroline (Ford), 221
  Caroline, 116
  Daniel, 222, 238
  Electa (Porter), 222
  Eliza Harper (Hyde),
    222
  Elizabeth, 221, 222
  Henry, 117, 216, 218,
    221, 222, 242, 253
  Lucy (Churchill),

MOORE continued
  216, 221
  Mary Almira (Smith)
    Copley, 222
  Nancy (White), 285,
    291
  Nathaniel, 285, 291,
    431
  Olive Leonard, 222
  Peter, 222, 232,
    255
  Richard, 409
  Sarah Judd, 117, 222
  Sophronia, 222
  Thersey, 216, 221
  William Henry, 221,
    222
  & Ross, 391
MOORE'S
  Corner, 250, 253
  Corners, 238
MOREHOUSE
  Alice, 473
  Charles H., 473
  Edward, 473
  Elijah, 473
  Etta, 473
  Hattie, 473
  James, 473
  Mary Ann (Hill),
    473
MOREY
  Frances (Howell),
    289
  James, 284
  Joseph, 289
  Maria, 291
  Mary A. (Howell),
    289
  Prudence (Lounsberry),
    284
  Rhoda, 289
  Stephen, 289
  William, 289
MORGAN
  Henry, 418, 419
  Lewis H., 319
MORMONS
  ---, 314
MORRISON
  Charlotte, 230
MORSE
  David S. (Rev.),
    437, 438
  Elias, 238
  Jane, 238
  Levina (Brown),
    292
MORTON
  Ellen, 368
  Elizabeth, 368
  Emily, 368
  G. A., 380
  Josiah, 368, 369
  Levi, 368
  Lucinda (Sholes),
    368
  Margaret (Freeland),
    368
  Maria (Smith), 369
MOSES

-34-

MOSES continued
P. P., 251
Philander P., 206,
220, 225
Samuel, 214
MOSHER
Harriet (Goodrich),
468
Sherman, 468
Thomas, 442
MOSS
Maria, 291
MOTTVILLE
---, 444
MULOCK
Albert, 86
Angeline, 86
Corwin, 86
Gabriel, 86
Lewis, 86
Mary (Corwin), 86
Mary A., 86
Rebecca (Seymolt),
86
Theodore, 86
William, 86
MUNCY
Pa., 316
MUNDY
Benajah, 79
Beriah, 489
Samuel, 79
MUNGER
Alanson, 349, 350
Charles, 350
MUNN
Alanson, 293
Lemira, 293
MURRAY
Harris, 90
MURRAY'S
Stonehouse, 90
MUZZY
Charles, 216,
217, 232
Emily, 216,
217
Gilbert, 216
Henry Moore, 216,
220
Jonas, 138, 215,
216, 217, 218,
219, 220, 221,
233, 242
Lucy, 216
Mary Edwards, 158,
216, 217
Sabrina Leonard,
216, 217
Sarah, 216
William Henry, 216,
217

NANTAQUAKS
---, 318
NANTICOKE
---, 321
Tribes, 317
NARAMORE
Anna S., 229
NAVERINO

NAVERINO continued
N. Y., 283
NEAL
Hannah, 236
Henry, 290
Ruth, 116, 208,
230, 235
NEALEY
John, 387
NEALY
John, 321, 323
& Smith, 483
NELSON
George, 176, 177
NESBITT
Mary, 461
NESCOPECK
Falls, 330
NEVIN
Andrew, 81
NE-WA-NA
Canoeush, 319
NEW
Bedford, Mass., 340
Brunswick, 280
Connecticut, 234,
256, 257
NEWELL
Dennis, 236
Hart, 212, 233,
236, 252
John, 236
Layton, 78
Mindwell, 236
NEW
England States, 325
NEWFIELD
---, 317, 439, 450
NEW
Granada, 331
NEW
Hampshire, 320,
322
NEWKIRK
Jacob, 89
NEW
Malbury, N. Y.,
449
NEWMAN
Ezekiel, 288,
489
George Kennedy, 447
Helen M. (Pert),
447
Oliver Shaw, 447
Rachel, 288
W. W., Jr. (Rev.),
447
William Whiting,
447
NEW
Marlboro, N. H.,
282
NEWPORT
---, 320
NEW
Preston, Conn., 330
NEWTON
N. J., 396
NEWTOWN
---, 326

NEW
York City, 325
NICE
J. F., 151
NICHOLS
---, 442
Caleb, 398, 399
Joseph, 378
Simeon, 398, 399
NICHOLSON
Miss, 483
Thomas, 483
NICKERSON
Amos, 70
Lucy E., 70
NINEVEH
Broome Co., N. Y.,
448
NIXON
C. D., 375
Charles, 152
Charles D., 258
Ephraim, 251
& Hollenback, 375
NOBLE
Carlton Monroe
(Dr.), 233, 234
David W., 211
Ezekiel, 192
J. T., 251
James T., 425
W. A., 251
Washington A.,
'229, 425
William T., 211
NORFOLK
Va., 355
NORRIS
Alonzo, 447
Dr., 446
John N., 447
Olive K., 447
NORTH
Anna, 320
Asa, 180, 193,
198
Deacon Asa, 169
Eunice, 183
George, 183
Glastonbury, Conn.,
330
Helen T., 217
Horace, 183
James, 180
Laura, 198
Nancy, 180
Romeo, 183
Rufus, 183
Shubael, 183
NORTHROP
Ebenezer G., 161
George W., 161
Miriam, 130
NORTHRUP
J., 176
NORTHWESTERN
Bank of Va., 330
NORTON
H., 391
Nelson, 425
NORWOOD

NORWOOD continued
Frances, 323
NUTT
David (Capt.),
368, 369, 371
Fidelia, 368
Lorenzo, 368
Maurice, 368
Mary J., 368, 369
Romanzo, 368
Sally, 368, 371
Susan (Bell), 368
NUTTING
Susanna, 240
NYCE
Elizabeth (Shoe-
maker), 282
George, 274, 281,
282
N.Y.L.E.
& W.R.R., 282
N. Y.
Medical University,
293

OAKLEY
Ada M., 182
Daniel, 182
O'BRIEN
John, 378
Sophia, 378
ODELL
Charity, 381
OGDEN
Elizabeth, 280
Isaac B. (Gen.),
332
Rhoda, 237, 238
O'HART
Moses, 481
OHIO
--- 276, 329,
481
OLIVET
Daniel, 170
OLMSTEAD
Augustus, 369
Avery, 363
Frederica, 369
Maria (Catlin), 363
OLNEY
Benjamin, 125, 419
Caroline (Burghart),
423
Franklin, 423
John, 419
Oman, 419
Sally Lovisa, 422
Samuel, 418, 419,
422, 423
Zelotes, 418, 419
ONEIDA
Conference, 456
ONEIDAS
---, 317, 318
ONEY
Benjamin, 221
Zelotes, 221
ONONDAGA
County, 279
ONONDAGAS

ONONDAGAS continued
---, 317, 318
ONTARIO
Co., N. Y., 364
ORANGE
Co., N. Y., 283,
292, 337
ORCUTT
Ella M., 473
Emily (Russell), 283,
473
John G. (Dr.), 394
John S., 473
ORTON
Demias, 164
ORVEN
Marcia Belinda,
252
ORWELL
Pa., 378
OSBORN
Betsey, 149
Chauncey, 240
Clarinda, 240
Erie, 430, 433
Hezekiah Woodruff,
239, 240
Jeremiah, 198
Jeremiah (Rev.), 127,
130, 185, 239, 240,
249, 267, 268
Josiah Olmstead, 240
Maria Elizabeth, 240
Samuel, 146, 149,
150
Sarah Alden, 240
Susanna, 240
OSBORNE
A. (Rev.), 493
OSTERHOUT
Ann, 281
OSWEGO
River, 318
OSWEGY
---, 319
OTSEGO
N. Y., 354
Co., 325, 187
Lake, 321
OTTER
Lake, 318
OWEGA
---, 319
OWEGO
---, 270, 317, 318,
325, 439
OWEGY
---, 319
OWEIGY
---, 319
OWEGO
Advertiser, 345
Cruciform Casket
Co., 391
Gas Light Co., 346
Gazette, 338
& Towanda Maile
Line, 306
Town, 162, 317,
338, 405
OWEN

OWEN continued
Abel, 184
Abel C., 184
Abigail, 178, 179
Daniel R., 184
Emeline Corson, 184
M. A., 164
Sarah M., 184

PACKARD
Fanny, 416
Oscar, 416
PACKER
Harriet W., 192
William S., Jr.,
192
PADDOCK
Bethia, 239
PAGE
Rev., 438
PAIGE
Joel S. (Dr.),
390
PAIN
Edward, 324
PAINE
Brinton, 460
Edward, 126
Selick, 146, 153
Susana, 126
Thomas, 126
PAINTED
Post, N. Y.,
281, 338
PAKE
Anson W., 149,
162
PALMER
Edmund, 274
Ezekiel, 442
family, 274, 280
Lucy, 456
Shubael, 442
Thomas, 459
Urban, 456
PALMETER
Dexter, 251
PALMETIER
Magdalena, 369
PARK
Abigail, 370
Daniel (Capt.),
168
Daniel, 77, 287
Elizabeth (Hill),
81, 287
Eunice, 137, 138
Experience, 341
Freelove, 364
Joseph, 81, 287
Martha A., 77
Moses, 137
Nancy (Ellis), 287
Nancy (Brown), 292
Oren, 292
Patty (Saunders),
287
Sarah (Brewster),
137
Settlement, 342
Thomas, 168, 287

PETTS continued
John (Dr.), 299
PHELPS
Antoinette, 235
Asa, 174
Ezekiel B. (Dr.),
340
Jemima, 123, 232,
233
Jesse, 179
Jonathan, 185
Laura O., 185
PHILADELPHIA
--- 278, 280, 281
PHILLIPS
Pearson, 169
PICKERING
Josiah, 480
PICKET
Eldah, 193
PIERCE
---, 271
Adolphus, 242, 250
Benjamin F., 347
Ebenezer (Dea.),
232
Ebenezer, 232, 241,
249, 255
George T., 416
Warren, 220
PIERSON
Indiana Louise,
416
Jerusha, 125, 133
William, 220
PINNEY
Hammon D., 199,
345
Joshua L., 345
PIONEER
(3rd steamboat),
385
PITCHER
D. M., 379
Daniel M., 359
PITTSFIELD
Mass., 293
PIXLEY
David, Jr., 387,
477, 479
David (Colonel),
324, 341, 364,
391, 463, 479
Mary, 364
Mary A., 468
Polly, 463
PLATT
(Gere, Truman,
Platt & Co.),
391
---, 287
(Smith), 284
Adell, 293
Ann, 281
Charles, 333
Edward J., 333
Edward T., 334
Elizabeth, 284
Ellen Lucy (Barstow),
334
Frank H., 334

PLATT continued
F. E., 392, 393
Frederick E., 333
Henry B., 334
Homestead, 275
Jonathan, 275, 284,
293, 334
Jonathan (Major), 275,
316, 333, 334
Jonathan, Jr., 333,
339, 340
Lesbia (Hinchman), 333
Mr., 275
Nehemiah (Hon.),
293, 314, 315,
334
Rev. Mr., 314
Susan, 293
Thomas Collier (Hon.),
333, 337, 393
William, Esq., 333
William H., 333
PLATTERKILL
Orange Co., N. Y.,
366
PLUMMER
G. W., 91
PLYMOUTH
N. H., 337
POIRS
Jonas, 459
POLLEY
Lemuel D., 428
Polly (Smith), 428
Solomon, 428
POLLEYS
William, 99, 100
POND
Enoch (Rev.), 470
Sarah, 470
POOLE
Charles F., 489,
490
Clara I., 489, 490
Daniel, 489, 490
Edward V., 489
Laura F., 489, 490
Murry E., 489, 490
POOR
General, 320
PORTER
Electa, 221, 222
George (Rev.), 438
Mary, 414
Sarah, 265, 266
POST
Eldad, 129
POTTER
Co., Pa., 349
Clarissa (Rodman),
360
Elijah, 426, 427,
429
Fear, 468
Harvey, 169
Isaac L., 360
Julia, 174
Nathaniel, 88
Rachel, 193
Rhoda, 180
Sarah, 285

POWELL
Elijah, 426, 427,
429
W. H., 431
POWERS
James, 227
Rebecca Ann, 227
PRATT
Elizabeth (Chaffee),
382
George H. (Mrs.),
382
PRENTICE
Dr., 88
Alfred Belcher, 217
Joseph, 242, 250
PRESBYTERIAN
---, 315, 327
PRESBYTERY
---, 320
PRESHER
Martha L., 485,
487
William, 485
PRESTON
Annice, 177
PRICE
Andrew, 91
George T. (Rev.),
404
Jacob, 393
Sally, 393
PRICHARD
Amzi, 177
PRIMROSE
Betsey J., 473,
474
Clarissa, 473, 474
Henry (Rev.), 85,
86
Henry, 470, 473,
474
Jacob, 473, 474
James, 473, 474
Martha, 473, 474
Martha (Runyon),
473
Mary E., 473, 474
Mary (Johnson),
473
Nellie A., 473
Orpha W., 85, 86,
473, 474
Peter J., 473
William, 473, 474
PRINCE
Charles, 378
Lucy (Hauver), 378
PRINCE
of Orange, 352
PRINDLE
Prof., 375
PRINGLE
John Hobart, 137
PRITCHARD
Asa, 383, 396
Asahel, 383, 396
Polly (Stedman),
383, 396
PROCTORSVILLE
Vt., 380

Index of Names continued

PROVIDENCE
  R. I., 346, 382
PUFFER
  Rachel, 365
PULT
  Lewis, 178
  Lucinda, 178
PULTZ
  Almira (Anderson),
    177
  Almira Clark), 192
  Lewis, 177
  Ransom (Mrs.), 192
PUMPELLY
  Catherine Ann, 344
  Charles, 328, 344,
    386, 390
  Delphine (Drake),
    366
  Frederick H., 328
  George B., 198
  George J., 328
  Harmon, 328, 329,
    366, 384, 388
  Harriet, 328
  James, 258, 328,
    385, 388, 390,
    402, 491
  John, 328, 329
  Maria, 328
  Mary H. (Welles),
    329
  Rafhael, 329
  Sarah (Tinkham),
    364
  Stella A., 344
  William, 318, 328,
    329, 364, 403, 434
PURDY
  Andrew, 442, 484
  Hester Ann, 456
PUTNAM
  Aaron (The Rev),
    (Jr.), 136,
    340, 390
  Eliza, 136, 137
  Sally, 369
  Co., N. Y., 379

QUICK
  Lewis, 91
  Peter, 91
QUIMBY
  Joseph, 427
  Maria, 427
QUINCY
  Mr., 389, 390
QUIRIN
  J., 482
  J. G. & Co., 483
  Philip, 482

RAISING
  Andrew, 290
  Esther (Washburn),
    290
RALYEA
  Derick, 209
  Mary Ann, 118
RANDALL
  Ann Eliza (Whitaker),

RANDALL continued
    135
  Chester, 135
  David Kimball, 136
  Eunice, 135
  Hannah (Smith), 135
  Nathan, 136
  Peleg, 135, 136,
    146
  W. C., 492
  Walter Crowley, 463,
    481, 488, 490, 492
  William C., 481
RANSOM
  Angeline (Martin),
    461
  Angie D., 469
  Benjamin, 461, 470
  Charles, 461, 480
  Charles E., 481
  Charlotte, 462
  David, 461
  Elisha D., 481
  Esther, 461
  Fanny (Thurston),
    462
  Harriet, 462
  Hope Maria (Talcott),
    461
  Ira, 461, 469
  John, 459
  Lucy (Frost), 461
  Mary Johnson, 461,
    462
  Mary (Nesbitt), 461
  Printice, 55, 461,
    462
  Rachel (Brooks), 461
  Samuel, 459, 460,
    461, 479
  Samuel (Capt.), 460,
    469
  Sarah (Forman), 461
  Sybil, 461
  William, 461
  William (Col.), 459,
    460, 461, 480, 481,
    482, 483, 486
  William (Maj.), 459,
    460, 461, 462, 479,
    483
  Maxwell & Co., 482
RANSTEAD
  L. (Rev.), 269
RAPPLEGREE
  Catherine, 371
RATHBONE
  Nancy, 411
RATHBUN
  Benjamin, 418
RAWSON
  Isaac, 138, 223
  Lyman, 238, 253
RAY
  Lydia, 177
RAYMOND
  Amos, 418, 420
  Betsey, 155, 156
  Daniel, 418, 420
  Green (Deac.), 423
  Isaac, 77, 299

RAYMOND continued
  Jane, 76, 77
  Mary E., 467
  Sarah, 285
  William G., 418,
    420, 429
RAYNOR
  John, 223
  Maria (Williams),
    223
RAYNSFORD
  Charlotte (Drake),
    366
  Edward, 366
READ
  Daniel, 323
  William, 323
REED
  Fitch, 269
  Frances D., 181
  Herbert B., 181
  Jane (Richardson),
    186
  Lyllis, 233
  Mary T., 181
  Moses, 323, 442
  Nancy, 398
  Sarah J., 181, 348
  Timothy, 186
  Timothy C., 181
REEL
  Jacob, 91
REES
  Andrew, 146, 153
  Caroline, 128, 129,
    422
  Louisa, 422, 423
  Lovisa, 422
REEVES
  Mr., 253
  William, 250
REMELE
  Jacob, 241, 244
  Jacob, Sr., 244
RENIFF
  Ephraim, 146, 149
  Mills, 108
  (P. O.), 105
RENSOM
  Emeline, 362
RENWICK
  W. C., 364
REWEY
  Elbridge Gerry,
    237
  Emily, 237
  Eunice, 160, 237
  Hannah, 237
  Henry, 237
  John, 230, 231,
    236, 237, 242,
    256
  John, Sr., 236
  Lewis, 230, 231,
    237
  Oliver, 237
  Phebe, 237
  Sarah, 230, 231,
    237
REYNOLDS
  Albert, 287

-39-

REYNOLDS continued
Alvy, 287
Amanda (Babcock), 287
Amos, 287
Angeline, 287
Caroline, 287
Carrie (Baker), 287
Charles Levi, 287
Curtis, 287
Deliverance A. (Boxby), 287
Eben, 287
Elizabeth, 287
Ella, 287
Enoch, 287
George, 287
Isaac S., 287
Isum I., 287
John S., 287
Joseph, 287
Joseph J., 287
Lottie, 287
Mary A., 287
Roxany (Sipperly), 287
Sara A. (Buttolph), 287
Sarah (Babcock), 287
Stephen, 276, 287
RHODES
Dey, 180
RICH
C. L., 431, 432
David, 245
(Dorwin, Rich & Stone), 391
Edward, 431
Ezekiel, 242, 251, 426, 430
George, 431
George L., 321
Josiah, 52
Laura, 426
Lucien Densmore, 424
Luther, 234
Maria Louisa, 424
Mary Ann, 424
Nancy, 206
Polly, 234, 235
Ranson, 128
Repina, 245
Simeon, 424
RICHARDS
David N. (Dr.), 137
Ira, 408
RICHARDSON
Abigail (White), 246
Elias, 186, 247
Esther (Waldo), 247
Fanny, 186, 247
Fred Waldo, 247, 253
Hannah, 186
Hannah Maria, 247
Henrietta (Brown), 247
Henry, 243

RICHARDSON continued
Herbert, 54, 247
Horace, 186, 247
Jane, 186
Josiah, 459
Melicent (Capron), 247
Milla (Capron), 247
Milla Capron, 247
Millie (Capron), 186
Nancy, 186
Nancy Capron, 247
Sarah J., 181
Sarah (Foster), 247
Sarah Jane, 247
Vinton, 246
William, 181, 186, 241, 246, 247, 256, 270
& Campbell's Brick Yard, 456
RICHFORD
N. Y., 113, 317, 405
RICHMOND
N. Y., 264
RIDDLE
Betsey (Washburn), 290
Henry, 290
RIDER
Stephen J., 481
RIGGS
Zenus (Rev.), 270
RIGHTMIRE
John, 143, 159, 415
Mary Ann, 131, 132
Nathan, 153, 415
William H., 55
RIKER
---, 442
Antoinette, 445
Eleanor (Moore), 446
O. P., 445
Tunis (Maj.), 445, 446
RIPLEY
Edwin, 314
Hannah, 137
John, 51, 337
Rev. Mr., 315, 437, 438
RISEN
Callie (Rodman), 360
James, 360
RIVER
Valley Methodist Church, 316
RIVERSIDE
Cemetery, Nichols, 316
ROACH
Sally, 286
ROADS
Jacob, 418, 419
ROBBINS
Ebenezer, 241, 248, 256
Harlow, 248
James, 144

ROBBINS continued
John E., 186
ROBERTS
Helen M., 488
James A., 472
Jerusha, 366
Joseph (Rev.), 366
ROBERTSON
Albert, 285
Timothy, 55
ROBINS
James, 430, 431, 432
Jonathan, 91
ROBINSON
Bridget, 266
C. J., 405, 410, 431
Charlotte Clark, 426
Henry, 223
Jedediah Leathe, 137, 423
Keen, 423
Millesent, 184
Newell, 149
Polly, 463
Thomas Amsdell, 137, 418, 423, 426
Zelotes, 241, 247
ROCKWELL
Abigail, 212, 213
Lucy, 123, 124
RODMAN
Calista J., 265
Callie, 360
Charles, 360
Clarissa, 360
Hannah (Gorse), 360
John, 360
Phoebe (Clark), 360
Marilla, 360
Mary J., 360
Nicholas, 360
Samuel S., 265
ROE
William, 323
ROGERS
Amelia, 81
Cornelius R. (Dr.), 263
Daniel, 81, 263
Helen, 262
Hiram, 291
James T., 263
M. Anna, 263
Mary (Leonard), 122
Melancthon, 122
Rev. Mr., 492
ROME
Pa., 294
ROMULUS
N. Y., 450
ROOT
R. B. (Dr.), 207
ROOTS
Bartley, 445
ROPER

SAWYER continued
    365
    Charles, 91
    Ellen, 97
    George, 365
    Henry M., 97
    J. Theodore, 97
    Joel, 88
    John L., 97
    Julia (Smith), 97
    Maria (Bristol),
        97
SAYBROOK
    Ct., 147, 325
SAYRE
    Butter Package
        Co., 105, 107
SCHALENGER
    Phebe, 415
SCHENICHS
    Jacobus, 453
SCHOHARIE
    Co., N. Y., 283
SCHOOLEY
    V. W., 162
SCHOOLS
    --- 295
SCHOONMAKER
    Nicholas, 484
    Sarah J. (West),
        484
SCHOONOVER
    ---, 197
    Beniah, 285
    Benjamin, 176
    Catharine (White),
        285
    Chloe, 176
    Christopher, 459
    Daniel, 176
    David, 176
    Edwin H., 481
    Elias, 176
    Elizabeth (Decker),
        176
    Eudora, 176
    Fayette, 176
    Franklin, 176
    Hannah, 161, 176
    Harriet E., 413
    Ira, 176
    J., 483
    Jacob, 176
    James, Jr., 489
    Jerome, 465
    Joseph, 176, 193
    Lola, 176
    Lydia, 176
    Mary, 176, 266
    Mary (Chittenden),
        176
    Mundy, 489
    Nicholas, 32, 484
    Nicholas, Jr., 481
    Olive, 176
    Oscar, 176
    Sarah, 176, 185
    Sarah J. (West),
        484
    Simeon, 176
SCIPIO

SCIPIO continued
    N. Y., 370
SCHUYLER
    A. H., 88
SCOFIELD
    ---, 442
    Betsy M., 445
    Horace, 445
    Mary A., 445
    Naomi (Cowell), 445
    Nathan, 445
    Nathaniel, 445
    Roxanna, 445
    Truman, 445
SCOTLAND
    Windham Co., Ct.,
        337
SCOTT
    Alexander, 193
    Charles, 150, 473
    Clara Janet (Lyman),
        151
    Elbert O., 188
    Esther, 227
    Frances, 131
    J. C., 151
    John (Rev.), 492
    Mary, 410
    Rosalia (Russell),
        473
    Sally, 474
    Susanna, 118, 119,
        132, 411
    William, 193, 460
    William (Capt.), 183
SCRANTON
    Eleanor, 427
    Ichabod, 427
SEAGER
    Clara, 378
    George, 378
SEAMAN
    Dr., 431
    Mr., 189
    Store, 431
SEARLES
    Daniel, 184, 185
    Homer, 402
    Jane, 184, 185
    Richard, 397
SEARLS
    Elizabeth (Goodrich),
        468
    John C., 468
    Sarah, 381
SEARS
    Catharine (Warren),
        171
    Daniel, 171
    Dioclesian, 428
    Helen L., 288
    James, 406
    James M., 428
    Knowles, 171
    Mary Ann, 237
    Olive, 262
    Philip, 428
    Phoebe, 381
    Richard, 171
    Ruhana, 171, 172
SEBASTION

SEBASTION continued
    Catharine, 264
SEELEY
    Israel, 75
    John D., 484
    Josiah, 125, 221
    Lydia (Ellis), 75
SEELY
    A. Seely & Bro.,
        484
    Alfred, 450
    Emily (LaRow),
        450
    S. A. Seely's Flour
        & Custom Mill, 455
    S. Alfred, 450
    Mary E. (Williams),
        450
    Polly, 450
    Seymour A., 450
SELDEN
    Benjamin, 323
SEMPRONIUS
    N. Y., 233
SETTLE
    Alma, 264
SEVERN
    Betsey, 82
SEXTON
    Benjamin, 472
    Lucy, 380, 472
    Mary (Gleazen),
        412
    Ransom, 412
SEYMOUR
    Gov., 377
    Elias W. (Dr.),
        377, 378
    John, 245
    Louisa (Dodd), 377
    Nancy, 245
    Sarah (Stoddard),
        245
    William, 377
SHAKELTOWN
    John O., 76
    Susan, 76
SHAFF
    Frederick, 160,
        161, 164
SHAPLEY
    & Greenley, 350
SHARP
    Isaac, 271
SHAW
    ---, 391
    & Dean, 391
    Betsey (Talmage),
        161
    Chloe, 266
    Elizabeth, 161
    Hannah M., 161
    Henry, 161
    Henry C., 447
    Jacob, 178
    Jacob T., 447
    Joel, 244
    Lucy M., 161
    Mary A., 178
    Rebecca (Hagadorn),
        447

-42-

SWARTWOOD continued
  Catherine (Williams),
    78
  Ebenezer, 76, 78
  Hannah (Shoemaker),
    282
  Harriet, 78
  Isaac S., 282
  Jacob, 78
  James, 76, 78
  John, 78
  John M., 78
  Katie, 78
  Lydia, 78
  Margaret A. (VanAtta),
    78
  Martha, 78
  Mary, 78
  Nancy, 78, 84
  Sarah, 78
  William, 78
SWEET
  Charles H., 340
  Elizabeth, 372
  Ezra S., 340,
    388
  John, 372
SWIFT
  C. H., 341
SWINTON
  A. A., 304
SYKES
  Ambrose B., 363
  Edward F., 363
  Electa B. (Chap-
    man), 363
  George, 240, 241,
    363
  George M., 363
  Horatio W., 363
  Increase, 363
  Jonathon, 363
  Lucy J., 363
  Phoebe, 363
  Richard, 363
  Ruth (Gaylord), 363
  Samuel, 363
  Theodore P., 363
  Victory, 363
SYRACUSE
  N. Y., 275, 277

TALCOTT
  Charles, 382
  Dolly, 239
  Dorothy (Lord),
    239, 382
  Elizur, Jr., 382,
    384
  Elizur, Sr., 239,
    382, 384
  Eunice (Benton),
    382
  Family, 330
  George B., 382
  George L., 382,
    384
  Hope Maria, 461
  Joel, 226, 382
  John, 382
  Margaret (Mason), 383

TALCOTT continued
  Sarah (VanAtta),
    383
TANE
  H., 431
TALLMADGE
  Angeline (Waite),
    373
  Ezra, 372
  Ezra W., 372
  Franklin, 80
  Fruitilla J., 373
  Gurdon, 373
  Ida M., 373
  John, 372
  Joseph, 88
  Mary P., 372, 373
  Philip Albert, 373
  Sutherland, 80
  Zilpha (Gould), 372
TALMAGE
  Betsey, 161
  Henry, 429
TANNER
  J. H. (Dr.), 448
  Waty, 188
TAPPAN
  Anna (Cook), 267
  Anthony, 267
  Asher, 267
  Asher C. (Mrs.),
    221
  Charles A., 267
  Harriet (Tyler),
    192
  Hellena, 267, 363
  Jane (Watson), 267
  John C., 267
  Nancy, 267
  Riley A., 267
  Silas, 192, 267
  Watson, 267
  William, 267
TAPPER
  Betsey, 226, 227
TAYLOR
  (a blacksmith),
    367
  Ann, 237
  Anne, 347
  Benoni, 459
  Calvin, 176
  Catherine, 176, 200,
    363
  Charles, 193, 363
  Charles (Rev.),
    369
  Cornelius, 363, 466
  David, 267, 363,
    364, 480
  David C., 363
  Ebenezer, Jr., 459
  Edgar, 481
  Emile G., 348
  Emily, 348
  Emily (Laning), 347
  Emma, 365
  Ephraim, 236
  Helena (Tappan),
    363
  James, 176

TAYLOR continued
  Jane, 175, 176,
    369
  Jared, 176
  Jasper, 176, 194,
    200
  Jeremiah, 323
  John, 323
  John J. (Hon.),
    331, 347, 348,
    349, 375
  John Laning, 347,
    348
  John L., 181, 348
  John W., 383
  Levi, 176
  Lucy, 134, 230,
    231, 236, 409
  Lucy M., 363, 364
  Luther, 176
  Maria, 176
  Mary, 176
  Mary D., 363
  Mary L., 348
  Minerva (Barrett),
    383
  Nancy A., 363
  Robert, 176
  Robert J., 348
  Samuel, 176
  Samuel E., 176
  Sarah, 348, 363
  Silas, 459
  Tappan A., 363
  William, 176, 193,
    321, 466
TEALL
  Sabrina, 182
TEFFT
  Deloss, 421
TERBUSH
  Levi, 292
  Mary P. (Whipple),
    292
TERRY
  Jerome Ward, 189
  Luella Spaulding
    (Ward), 189
  W. J., 189
THAYER
  Gideon, 323
  Phoebe (Harris),
    399
  Thomas, 217, 220,
    221
  Willard, 399
THOMAS
  Albert, 393
  Alexander J., 392
  Ann, 212, 213
  Benjamin, 428
  Catherine (Frank),
    393
  Charles C., 378
  Charles F., 378, 379
  David B., 285
  Emma A., 378, 379
  Frank A. (White),
    285
  George, 186
  Hannah, 261

-48-

Index of Names continued

Index of Names continued

WICKSOM continued
Polly, 371
WILBUR
William, 242, 252
WILCOX
Erastus, 421
Eunice, 205
Jane A., 421
Jerusha, 231
Laura, 421
Mariam, 401
Rachel, 223
Samuel C. (Rev.),
404
WILKES
-Barre, Pa., 282,
327
WILKINSON
---, 400
Catherine (Hedges),
226
Harvey, 226
John, 230
Joseph G., 77
Martha (Hanna),
77
Nancy D., 230
Polly D., 230
Rufus, 230
WILKINSONS
---, 319
WILLARD
L. D., 190
WILLEY
J. A., 181
WILLIAMS
Mr., 126
Mrs., 477
Mrs. --- (Gaskill),
175
Mrs. --- (---)
Keyes, 222
Judge, 210, 125
Abijah, 207, 228
Abigail (Ford), 175
Ada A., 265
Adalinda, 265
Adelma, 265
Alanson (Mrs.), 82
Alfred, 175
Almerin, 229, 265
Almira (Allen), 229
Angeline, 265
Anna, 175
Anna S. (Naramore),
229
Azariah, 206, 213,
214
Bennie C., 266
Betsey, 175, 182,
225, 229
Betsey (Hull), 228
Beulah (Brown),
206, 213, 214
Brothers, 251
Cammilla, 265
Carrie, 175
Catherine, 78
Charlotte (Bogart),
82
Charlotte (Ketcham),

WILLIAMS continued
292
Connie,
David, 125, 126,
131, 147, 164,
201, 406
Dency, 222
Edgar, 175
Electa, 206, 213,
424
Elias, 169, 323
Elisha, 214, 223
Eliza, 225, 265
Eliza Ann, 227
Elizabeth, 225
Elizabeth Rachel, 229
Emeline, 223, 229
Emily (Brown), 229
Emily (Royce), 214
Emily (Winship), 125
Emma L., 266
Enoch S., 143, 214,
215, 241
Enoch Slosson, 207,
228, 229
Esther (Lane), 175
Esther Miranda, 148
Eunice, 175, 223
Eunice Augusta, 229
Ezekiel, 76, 78
Frank, 175
Franklin, 229
George, 125, 209,
214, 256
George A., 266
Heman, 126
Henry, 225, 229, 242,
251, 254, 255
Hephzibah (Hart),
213
Hiram, 175, 183
Horatio Nelson, 229
Ira, 175
James, 127, 214, 474
Jane Elizabeth (Royce),
214
Jerusha (Pierson),
125
Jerusha (White), 175
Job (Mrs.), 378
Joel, 175
John, 445
John Chamberlin, 125
Jonas, 459
Josie C., 188
Joshua, 207
Juliaette, 158
Juliet, 229, 265
L. E., 262, 322
LaFayette, 292
Levi, 175
Lewis, 175
Lill (Bunzy), 378
Louisa Janette
(Barnes), 125
Lucia Ann (Legg),
229
Lucinda, 125, 246
Lucinda (Slosson),
207, 228
Lucius F., 258

WILLIAMS continued
Lucy Maria, 123
Lydia Selina, 223
Lyman F., 266
Margaret Eugenia
(Farley), 229
Margaret (Van Wormer),
229
Maria, 223
Marquis de la
Fayette, 229
Martha, 175
Mary, 175, 214
Mary (Bement), 209,
214
Mary E. (Primrose),
474
Mary Elizabeth, 209,
214
Matilda, 82
N. Adaline, 365
Nancy, 175, 214,
223
Nathan, 222
Olive (Collins), 126
Oliver, 225, 229,
236, 242, 251
Phebe (Hedges), 222
Pluma, 175
Polly, 214
Prudence, 222
Rachel (Halliday),
224
Rachel (Wilcox),
222
Rachel (Wood), 228
Ransom, 126, 132,
147
Robert, 214, 298,
365
Roxa, 225, 229
Royal R., 228, 254,
265
Sabrina, 214
Sally, 175, 183,
222, 223
Samantha (Collins),
125
Sarah, 214
Sarah Jane, 229
Selecta, 269
Selecta D., 321
Solomon, 221, 242,
244, 251
Stella, 265
Stephen, 175, 222,
223, 224, 229,
233, 321
Stephen, Jr., 242,
251, 254, 322
Stephen, Sr., 224,
225
Susan, 175
Susan Elizabeth
(Goodrich), 319
Susanna, 139
Theodore, 229
Tracy, 175
Uzal, 175
William Hart, 214
William I., 175

-55-